Plants and People of Nepal

Plants and People
of Nepal

Narayan P. Manandhar

with the assistance of Sanjay Manandhar

Timber Press
Portland, Oregon

All plant drawings are by the author. Frontispiece: *Rosa macrophylla*

Printed in Hong Kong

Published in 2002 by
Timber Press, Inc.
The Haseltine Building
133 S.W. Second Avenue, Suite 450
Portland, Oregon 97204, U.S.A.

Reasonable efforts have been made to publish reliable data on the use of plants in Nepal. However, the author and publisher make no representations and expressly disclaim any responsibility regarding the validity, efficacy, safety, or consequences of such uses, for misidentification of plants by users of this book, or for any illness, injury, or other consequence that might result from their consumption or other use.

Library of Congress Cataloging-in-Publication Data

Manandhar, N. P.
    Plants and people of Nepal / Narayan P. Manandhar with the assistance of Sanjay Manandhar.
        p.   cm.
    Includes bibliographical references (p.   ).
    ISBN 0-88192-527-6
    1. Ethnobotany—Nepal. I. Manandhar, Sanjay. II. Title.

GN635.N35 M36 2002
581.6'3—dc21

2001037538

To the sacred memory of my grandparents

Mr. Siddhi Narayan Manandhar
and
Mrs. Jagat Maya Manandhar

Contents

Color plates follow page 48

Foreword

A comprehensive and detailed work on the ethnobotany of Nepal is greatly needed by the botanists and pharmacognosists of the world. The rich complex of plants found in this small country is truly astonishing. This variety has been explained by the differences in elevation of the country together with varying climates and soils. The prospect of new and valuable medicinal discoveries among the flora is a challenge to the phytochemical and pharmacological investigators of the world.

It seems doubtful that anyone could be found who is more competent and devoted to this subject matter than Narayan Prasad Manandhar. His knowledge of the botany and materia medica of Nepal is based not so much on libraries, herbaria, and museums as on his long and persistent study, firsthand, of the plant life in many parts of this historic land, and more especially on his thorough investigations of the native peoples and their knowledge of the properties and uses of the plants among which they have lived for generations. Dr. Manandhar's dedication is truly an inspiration to anyone contemplating plant exploration of this kind. He has shown extraordinary skill in telling us about his interesting experiences and discoveries.

Dr. Manandhar's previous publications are very useful and instructive, but in *Plants and People of Nepal* he has presented in much more detail the pharmacopoeia of Nepal. With the ongoing modernization taking place all over the world, including the field of medicine, it is important that the accumulation of folk wisdom be recorded before the information is lost forever.

Efforts at giving in detail the folk medical lore are being made in many areas, and *Plants and People of Nepal* represents a valuable addition to this worldwide collection effort. Dr. Manandhar should be applauded and generously complimented on this successful undertaking.

The late George M. Hocking was Professor Emeritus of Pharmacognosy at Auburn University in Alabama.

Preface

I was born and brought up in a rural village in Nepal, where a symbiotic relationship with nature was not only beneficial but indispensable for survival. For instance, we had a family horse and after each trip the horse's back would be lacerated by the homemade bamboo saddle. My grandfather sent me and other children to climb the neem tree, *Azadirachta indica,* to collect leaves for a decoction that was applied to the horse's back. The healing was complete enough to allow the use of the horse for the next trip. My grandfather also prescribed medicinal plants for other villagers and explained how to collect, prepare, and use them. He was always keen to hear about the efficacy of his prescription from his patients. I remember collecting a total of about 50 species of plants for him—for their root, bark, leaves, flowers, fruits, or seeds. At that time, nobody thought of recording his knowledge. Today I remember only 5 species from his collection of medicinal plants.

As in our village, villagers throughout Nepal used plants out of necessity. Village women picked tender shoots of wild plants for vegetables. To construct a family house, neighbors cooperated in erecting poles, splitting bamboo, and thatching the roof. Children helped their parents in preparing twine from the bark of local plants. At the time of fairs and festivals, village folk erected a bamboo-frame *mandap* (stage) to observe religious functions, and decorated it with banana leaves and branches of other plants.

In 1966, as a young botanist working for His Majesty's Government of Nepal, I was quite surprised to find that many city folk did not have much knowledge of local plants, nor did they depend on them. The knowledge that I had thought was pervasive, I realized was local. This knowledge varied between ethnic groups and regions but remained unrecorded. This valuable heritage was passed down across Nepal from generation to generation as an oral tradition.

Plants and People of Nepal is intended to serve three purposes. First, I wish to record and disseminate the vast knowledge that the various Nepalese ethnic groups have accumulated. Much of the corpus of practical knowledge of plants has remained within a family, ethnic group, village, or region. I hope that with this book, this knowledge can be shared by many more. Second, the book can serve as a field guide for both experts and interested nonexperts. For this reason I have included my line drawings and a selection of color photographs as well as all vernacular names recorded to date. Third, the book is an attempt to catalog local knowledge in an organized way. With the advance of modernization throughout Nepal, indigenous knowledge is dying with the older generation. Unless the ethnobotanical knowledge of Nepal is published, there is real danger of much oral tradition becoming extinct.

This book is also an attempt at organizing more than 30 years of field information into a cohesive whole. Almost all collecting was done on foot during arduous treks, especially in very remote regions of mountainous Nepal. During the first 15 years, I conducted as many as four field trips per year, each lasting 10 days to 2 months. In later years, I made about two trips a year.

Most of the information was collected against many odds, some of which are worth mentioning here:

Most of the time, the budget for the field trip was so limited that it was hard to hire more than one or two porters. In remote areas we had to carry food for many days, sleeping bags, personal items, and camera as well as materials such as blotting paper and wooden frames for pressing herbarium specimens.

We rarely carried enough tents because we did not have enough porters. Hence our shelter became the homes of villagers along the trails. If we arrived late at a village, we were left to spend the night in the open. We even spent whole nights sitting under an umbrella in heavy monsoon downpours, our clothes drenched, not getting a wink of sleep.

We had to respond to the requests of villagers. On many occasions I mediated disputes between families at the end of 14- or 15-hour days because that was the only way to secure paid food or shelter from the villagers. At other times, the villagers asked for roads and irrigation facilities to be built, which were projects I could not arrange for them.

The pervasive nature of the caste system also made our lives difficult. Many villagers hesitated to give food, water, or shelter to our porters, who were sometimes considered of low caste or untouchable. Some would not even allow the porters to wait on the porch while I collected information.

Some villagers scolded us and got irritated by our collecting botanical information. Most villagers were very poor and saw little to gain for their information. Although we gave them many household articles such as plastic bottles, film canisters, used clothes, utensils, bangles, ribbons, and candies—even salt and sugar—we gave them little money for reasons I explain in the following paragraphs.

As we had to meet people in the villages, we had to walk almost everywhere, up and down many mountains with consequent hazards of altitude sickness, fast rivers, snow, and wild animals. Some of the more memorable moments included spending a night atop a glacier with the sound of the water flowing underneath, or having to scale a sheer rock face with very rudimentary ropes. Many times we were trapped as a result of landslides and could neither advance nor retreat. Detouring through forests and over ridges or rivers to bypass a landslide only a few hundred meters wide sometimes took hours and at times an entire day.

Perhaps the most difficult aspect of being a government ethnobotanist was that much of the work was carried out without cooperation from departmental superiors and, in many instances, in the face of active interference and blockage. For instance, it was very difficult to get permission to publish an article or book. My previous publications were written in secrecy and without much knowledge of my superiors. It was still more difficult to attend any seminars and conferences officially. I have no idea why the superiors did not like individual experts to publish or attend conferences. I put it down to Nepalese dynamics. Whatever the reason, valuable Nepalese assets were underexploited and unappreciated.

I adapted my field methodology to suit the Nepalese context. Typically, ethnobotanical exploration includes interviews and research in published references. Many experts in Nepal, both foreign and Nepalese, elicit information quickly by paying their informants so as to meet the researchers' own tight schedules. While this method may be useful elsewhere, I have found that quick information collection (especially using monetary incentives) is counterproductive and affects the accuracy of the findings as the paid informant feels obligated to provide a long list of plants and their uses, which are typically fabricated. Instead of cash inducements for informants, I distributed goods of everyday use. I sometimes gave cigarettes to insistent informants but rarely money.

My methodology puts a premium on building a firm rapport with villagers and informants. Only after that trust and rapport is built do I engage in information collection. Hence this method is very time-consuming and not suited for a quick trip. Typically, the information presented in this book came from communities and healers after two to seven visits. In the first visit, I collected only 10–20% of the required information. In the second visit, I asked about new plants along with verifying information for previously collected plants. I spent 2–3 hours with adult villagers and 4–5 hours with native healers. Ordinarily, I chose informants who were 60 years of age or older, as only they possessed the knowledge that was necessary to survive in the era prior to modern medicine. I stayed 1–4 days in a village, depending on the schedule of my interviewees. I accepted the medicinal value of a plant if at least five adult informants or three native healers corroborated similar uses of a plant on separate occasions.

My team consisted of the same three or four porters. Usually, we traveled to trailheads by local buses when a road was available and then walked, as that is the best method for collecting a variety of information and plants. We carried a portable herbarium and engaged in collecting plants, numbering, pressing, drying, labeling, and adding remarks when we were not talking to the villagers. My porters were able rapport builders who helped my information collection process. It must be stressed that not many outsiders asked pointed questions of the villagers; hence they were naturally suspicious of my motives. My porters were encouraged to banter and mingle with the villagers and were directed never to address me as a government official or as "Doctor Sahib" (the villagers are always frightened and suspicious of government officials and confuse Ph.D.'s with M.D.'s and demand allopathic medicine). My porters were usually briefed about our destination and objectives, and we collected as much information as possible from walkers on the trail even before we entered a village. We tried to identify the ethnic groups in the community, key members of the village, including schoolteachers, influential villagers, and local government members, and the number and practices of the local healers. In addition, we tried to establish the family background, temperament, and personality of each prospective interviewee and attempted to seek shelter at his or her house. Although we carried our own food and tents for camping in remote areas, in villages where we needed to collect information we always chose to stay with the family whose member we needed to interview. Evening and morning meals presented the best opportunities for building trust, by bantering and talking about the problems of the family and the village. Eating their food and living as they did also lessened suspicions.

As part of rapport building, I participated in village activities and mediated village disputes and family problems even before any data collection commenced. The objective was to help the villagers before seeking their help. After such activities, the ease of data collection was remarkable. Many a time, I came across problems and disputes that I solved with arbitration and disbursement of only a few rupees.

It is also important to respect village customs and traditions. For example, it is unwise to touch villagers' objects and tools of worship, or their water, or to enter their houses without permission. Similarly, touching someone's head or walking over people's extended legs or walking sticks at rest stops is very impolite. Villagers are sensitive to caste demarcation, so it is unwise to ask if someone is of a certain caste because of the danger of mistaking him or her for someone of a lower caste. In 1975, in a remote part of western Nepal, my French ethnobotanist colleague inquired if someone was a *kami* (blacksmith) as his face was quite dark. The person happened to be of the *chhetri* (warrior) caste and was extremely upset that my colleague had degraded him in the caste hierarchy. Our entire team asked for forgiveness. We pleaded, but nothing helped. To help the man regain his rightful caste, we sponsored a ritual that entailed treating the entire village to a feast. In addition, the victim had to sit inside an earthen grain silo situated on an upper floor of the house. He then had to break the bottom of the silo, make a hole through the floor, and exit from the ground floor door. Our party had to pay for the village feast, the earthen silo, the damage to the victim's first floor, and had to spend 2 extra days dealing with the faux pas.

As Nepal is rapidly changing, even the information collected over the years has changed, usually for the worse. The younger generation prefers the quick efficacy of modern allopathic medicine, so the oral tradition has stopped and the knowledge of the plants will most likely die with the current generation of healers. Even the information from established informants has changed as a result of old age, memory loss, or the loss of plant habitat. For example, when I first met a local healer in central Nepal, Mr. Sher Bahadur Tamang (then 60 years of age), he gave me a list of three plants (*Achyranthes aspera, Psidium guajava, Urena lobata*) pounded to extract their juice, which is used as a treatment for diarrhea and dysentery. I interviewed a patient and learned that the prescription was effective. After a decade I asked Mr. Tamang the same question but he gave the names of only two plants (*A. aspera, P. guajava*) for treating the same problem. When I asked him about the third plant, he said he did not remember it. On my last visit, Mr. Tamang, almost 80 years of age, talked of only *P. guajava,* and even the patient said that Mr. Tamang was too old and could not remember the ingredients. The efficacy was not as swift as when the three plants were mixed together; it is possible that the cause was the reduction in the number of plant ingredients in the admixture.

It is my hope that *Plants and People of Nepal* will help in shaping the future of indigenous knowledge in Nepal and shed light on many social and economic issues of village life. Many villagers gave me information, knowing that such information needed to be preserved for the future and also hoping that such cooperation might help their social and economic welfare. Without their support and cooperation, this book would not exist. It is their joy, their laughter, and their hope that allowed me to continue my work for more than three decades in the face of utmost difficulties.

There are about 7000 species of flowering plants and 400 species of pteridophytes native to Nepal. In 1997, I reported 800 species of plants used in ethnomedicine and 440 species of wild food plants used by villagers in Nepal. *Plants and People of Nepal* documents the various uses of 1517 taxa belonging to 858 genera and 195 families, including 1434 flowering plants, 65 pteridophytes, and 18 gymnosperms. About 80 species of cultivated plants are included. Thus the number of plants used in Nepal is equal to about 20% of the flora of the country. Many of the plants have more than one use, and 1002 medicinal plants, 651 food plants, and 696 plants used for a variety of other purposes are recorded here, an increase indicative of continued research and discovery.

ACKNOWLEDGMENTS

I would like to extend a special note of appreciation to the village people who shared their knowledge of plants with me. Their enthusiasm and smiles made it worthwhile for me to carry out the work over three decades of hardship, collecting plants and information in parts of Nepal that could easily be classified as among the most remote and dangerous parts of the world. It was also their valuable contribution that gave me the courage to remain undaunted by bureaucratic obstacles.

This book would have remained just a dream had I not received tremendous encouragement and support from my family. My wife, Narayani, not only gave me invaluable moral support and advice while I wrote this book, but more importantly helped me raise our family of three sons while I went on numerous field trips to collect data for this and previous publications. In 1991, when I visited my three sons in Boston, Massachusetts, they put me in front of a computer and suggested that I use it as a tool to start cataloging all the plants I was studying. Sanjay, my oldest son, has been instrumental in establishing my relationship with Timber Press and acting as the editor of many drafts. Uday, my middle son, has been the wizard one often needs when one's own computer capability is severely limited. Binay, through his work at a publishing house, has provided much advice and explained the publication process.

I would like to thank Prof. George M. Hocking, School of Pharmacy, Auburn University, Alabama, for writing the foreword, and Dr. G. H. Neil Towers, Department of Botany, University of British Columbia, Vancouver, for his assistance and suggestions concerning the ethnobotanical work. Roy Vickery of the Natural History Museum, London, deserves special thanks for allowing me to draw plants not found in the herbarium in Nepal. Dr. Saman Bahadur Rajbhandary of the Royal Nepal Academy of Science & Technology provided much encouragement for my professional endeavors.

I would also like to express my appreciation to Timber Press, who suggested a more extensive coverage for the book and helped in editing the manuscript. My thanks also go to Geoff Wisner and Jesuit Fathers James J. Donnelley, Everett Mibach, and Gregory Sharkey for their comments on the manuscript. Finally, I thank Siddhant Pandey of London, who carried several versions of the manuscript between London and Kathmandu.

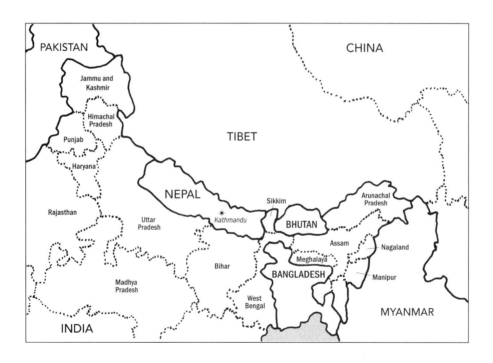

Figure 1. Nepal's place in the world

CHAPTER 1

The Land of Nepal

Nepal has enchanted travelers throughout the ages, who have appreciated the diversity of this landlocked Himalayan country. Perhaps nowhere else will one find the extreme juxtaposition of high mountains and lowlands, and luxuriant tropical or subtropical forests and barren tundra, in such a small area. Augmented by climactic conditions such as the monsoon, these extreme situations are the cause of the rich diversity of flora, fauna, and human habitation.

Nepal is tightly squeezed between the Tibetan Autonomous Region of China in the north and India in the south, east, and west. Perhaps as many as 25 million people inhabit an area of 147,181 square kilometers (Central Bureau of Statistics 2000) located in the central Himalaya (Figure 1). Since 82% of the land area is occupied by mountains, hills, rivers, and other nonarable land, more than 600 persons occupy each square kilometer of arable land, one of the highest population densities in the world. Almost 90% of Nepalese live in rural areas, most in poverty. The people of Nepal are far from a homogeneous whole. Instead, the nation was a crossroads for different people moving across Asia over the ages, some making their home in this tiny kingdom. The diversity of the different ethnic groups is accentuated by limited amount of mingling because of the difficult terrain and many natural boundaries such as high mountains, rivers, and forests.

Since its unification in the mid-eighteenth century, Nepal has remained a kingdom. However, until 1951 Nepal was almost fully closed to the outside world by the decree of an autocratic ruling family who kept the monarchy devoid of real power. In the parliamentary elections of 1991, the absolute monarchy gave way to a parliamentary system after demands by a prodemocracy movement. Despite many political changes, the social indicators of the country remain dire, even compared to its poor neighbors in South Asia. Nepal's poor economic status and lack of access to modern medicine have made the ethnobotany of the country a valuable corpus of knowledge. Sadly, much of the practice of ethnobotany recorded here has disappeared or is in the process of disappearing.

EMERGENCE OF NEPAL

It is said that Nepal has had as many kings as it has hilltops. Stark physical boundaries such as mountains, ridges, and rivers helped create many small principalities and kingdoms as the control of passes and dominant hills became a constant struggle. Political unions were established to protect the scarce land in small pockets in the V-shaped valleys in the Himalaya. Historical records of the 1600s and 1700s record the Baise Rajya (22 kingdoms) of the Karnali River basin in far western Nepal (called the Ghaghara River outside Nepal), and the Chaubise Rajya (24 kingdoms) of the Gandaki River basin. Although historians cannot fully confirm the number of these kingdoms or whether they were contemporary, it is clear that a large number of kingdoms fought constant battles over territory.

Unification of Nepal

There was a delicate balance of power among the various ministates so that none possessed dominance. Gorkha, a poor state sandwiched between the Rajputs in the west and the Mallas in Kathmandu in the center, jostled with its neighbors but was not able to improve its landholding. It was Prithvi Narayan Shah who became king of Gorkha in 1742 at 22 years of age, who marched east to conquer the Malla kingdoms, and whose control of the trade between India and Tibet helped it amass land and wealth. Since its unification, Nepal has remained a kingdom despite two wars with the Chinese and the Tibetans and one with the British and the

East India Company in 1814–1816. According to a noted historian, Ludwig Stiller (1993), "The Nepalese nation was born against improbable odds. In the most difficult terrain imaginable, the Nepalese achieved unity and then withstood the British threat to rule all South Asia."

Monarchy and Political Systems

Prithvi Narayan Shah believed in a strong administration and a fair justice system to rule a diverse collection of territories, peoples, and cultures. He understood the value of peace and stability and maintained friendly relations with China and the East India Company. However, he kept the country closed to foreign merchants for both political and trade reasons. Hinduism was the religion of the state but he was tolerant of all faiths. Above all, he considered the farmers of Nepal as important as his army. Unlike previous kings who used the state as their fiefs or kingly possessions, he attempted to keep his peasantry prosperous and did not use their tenancy as his personal revenue system (it was common for the state's demand on individual household to be 50% of the rice crop). Prithvi Narayan Shah died in 1775 after a lifetime of great contributions.

The newly formed nation of Nepal needed a strong leadership but was ruled for 40 years by successive generations of monarchs, most of them minors. Regents were appointed to run the nation in the names of the infant kings. The power struggle between regents, princes, and queen mothers split the nation into factions. Favoritism and nepotism replaced impartiality, and the elite who were so loyal to the nation in the days of Prithvi Narayan Shah were preoccupied with their own prosperity. Amazingly, the expansion of Nepal continued in successive military campaigns but the systems of administration, revenue, and justice suffered.

The noninterventionist policy of the British, Indian, and Chinese toward Nepal was a recipe for abuse of power internally. Deceit, assassinations, and power brokering became rampant, and in 1846 Jung Bahadur Rana, following a massacre of most of the country's elite, appointed himself prime minister and centralized power in the Rana prime ministers and the Rana families. The country was isolated from the rest of the world for about a century, with the monarchy remaining under the influence of the Ranas and the people of Nepal banned from education and modernization.

In 1950, King Tribhuvan led the revolution that resulted in the downfall of the Rana regime. In May 1959, the first elected government was formed, but in December 1960, King Mahendra exercised emergency powers, dissolved the parliament, and began a period of direct rule. Political parties were banned, and he introduced the partyless Panchayat system, which existed for almost 30 years. At the beginning of 1990, the banned Nepalese Congress and Communist Parties jointly initiated a popular political movement against the Panchayat system. After more than a month of uprising, the Panchayat system came to an end. King Birendra dismissed the government and announced a multiparty system. A new constitution based on democratic principles, a multiparty system, and constitutional monarchy was promulgated in November 1990, and general elections were held in 1991. Regrettably, in a decade of democracy, the government changed hands almost as many times. The frequent changes in the government have adversely affected the continuity in the management of development.

Administrative Divisions

Administratively, Nepal is divided into five development regions, 14 zones (*anchal* in Nepali), and 75 districts (Figure 2). In each district, the lowest local administrative unit is either the municipality or the village development committee (VDC). There are 36 municipalities and 3995 VDCs. There are nine wards in each VDC, but the number of wards in a municipality may be higher if population density warrants. The regional offices of the departments and ministries of the government are located in each of the five development regions. Each district also has a chief district officer (CDO) who maintains law and order in the district and also checks district-level developmental activities. A CDO wields significant power as this post is an amalgamation of both executive and judiciary powers; abuse of these powers over the years has been rampant. The local development officer coordinates district-level programs and plans. Education, health, and agricultural services are generally made available at the VDC level.

The constitution mandates creation of a parliament with elected local members. Local elections are carried out at the VDC level, and the constituency boundaries used for elections are drawn up according to population density. The VDC includes an elected governing body at the grassroots level.

Population

According to the census conducted in 1991, the population of Nepal was 18.5 million, of which 49.86% were men and 50.14% women. The annual growth rate of the population was estimated to be a staggering 2.08%. The Central Bureau of Statistics projected an even higher population growth rate of 2.66% between 1991 and 1996. According to this projection, the population of Nepal in 2000 would top 23 million, with men constituting 50.2% and women 49.8%, indicating that maternal mortality is high and life expectancy for women is lower than for men. The projection estimated the under-15 population to be 40% and the under-5 population to be 14.7% of the total population. The reason for the high rate of population growth and a population bulge in the lower age category is the high proportion of women of reproductive age. According to the 1996 projection, about 5 million women would be considered to be of reproductive age.

Nepal's population is predominantly rural. In 1996, about 89% of the population lived in rural areas. Less than half the

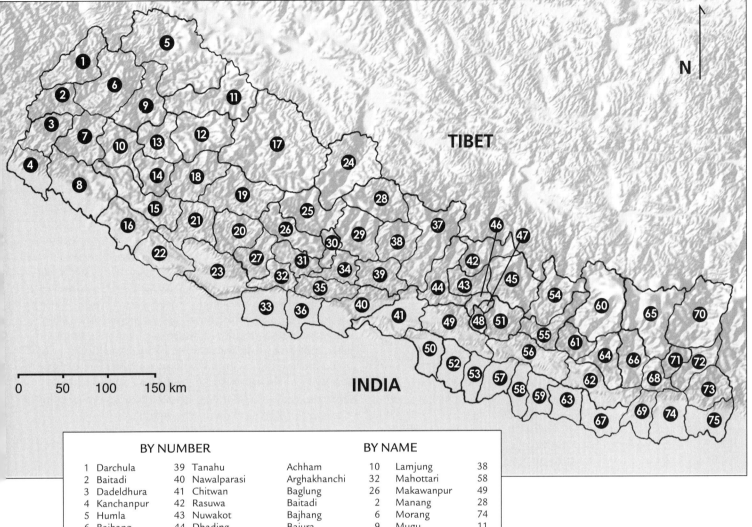

BY NUMBER

1	Darchula	39	Tanahu
2	Baitadi	40	Nawalparasi
3	Dadeldhura	41	Chitwan
4	Kanchanpur	42	Rasuwa
5	Humla	43	Nuwakot
6	Bajhang	44	Dhading
7	Doti	45	Sindhupalchok
8	Kailali	46	Kathmandu
9	Bajura	47	Bhaktapur
10	Achham	48	Lalitpur
11	Mugu	49	Makawanpur
12	Jumla	50	Parsa
13	Kalikot	51	Kabhrepalanchok
14	Dailekh	52	Bara
15	Surkhet	53	Rautahat
16	Bardiya	54	Dolkha
17	Dolpa	55	Ramechhap
18	Jajarkot	56	Sindhuli
19	Rukum	57	Sarlahi
20	Rolpa	58	Mahottari
21	Salyan	59	Dhanusha
22	Banke	60	Solukhumbu
23	Dangdeokhuri	61	Okhaldhunga
24	Mustang	62	Udaypur
25	Myagdi	63	Siraha
26	Baglung	64	Khotang
27	Pyuthan	65	Sankhuwasabha
28	Manang	66	Bhojpur
29	Kaski	67	Saptari
30	Parbat	68	Dhankuta
31	Gulmi	69	Sunsari
32	Arghakhanchi	70	Taplejung
33	Kapilbastu	71	Terhathum
34	Syanja	72	Panchathar
35	Palpa	73	Ilam
36	Rupandehi	74	Morang
37	Gorkha	75	Jhapa
38	Lamjung		

BY NAME

Achham	10	Lamjung	38
Arghakhanchi	32	Mahottari	58
Baglung	26	Makawanpur	49
Baitadi	2	Manang	28
Bajhang	6	Morang	74
Bajura	9	Mugu	11
Banke	22	Mustang	24
Bara	52	Myagdi	25
Bardiya	16	Nawalparasi	40
Bhaktapur	47	Nuwakot	43
Bhojpur	66	Okhaldhunga	61
Chitwan	41	Palpa	35
Dadeldhura	3	Panchathar	72
Dailekh	14	Parbat	30
Dangdeokhuri	23	Parsa	50
Darchula	1	Pyuthan	27
Dhading	44	Ramechhap	55
Dhankuta	68	Rasuwa	42
Dhanusha	59	Rautahat	53
Dolkha	54	Rolpa	20
Dolpa	17	Rukum	19
Doti	7	Rupandehi	36
Gorkha	37	Salyan	21
Gulmi	31	Sankhuwasabha	65
Humla	5	Saptari	67
Ilam	73	Sarlahi	57
Jajarkot	18	Sindhuli	56
Jhapa	75	Sindhupalchok	45
Jumla	12	Siraha	63
Kabhrepalanchok	51	Solukhumbu	60
Kailali	8	Sunsari	69
Kalikot	13	Surkhet	15
Kanchanpur	4	Syanja	34
Kapilbastu	33	Tanahu	39
Kaski	29	Taplejung	70
Kathmandu	46	Terhathum	71
Khotang	64	Udaypur	62
Lalitpur	48		

Figure 2. Districts of Nepal

rural population had access to safe water and less than 6% to sanitation. As agriculture is the principal means of livelihood, the growth in population has put a severe strain on other development efforts such as education and irrigation. In the face of ever-decreasing landholding sizes, many people have chosen to migrate to urban areas. The migration rate of population to urban areas between 1980 and 1993 was 7.7% annually, the highest in South Asia (World Bank 1995). Such rapid growth of metropolitan areas naturally puts tremendous strain on existing infrastructures and systems, causing havoc with limited electrical, drinking water, and sewage facilities. The quality of river water has deteriorated, and air and noise pollution have significantly increased. Population density is highest in the southern plains regions, lowest in northern mountain regions. The proportion of people living in hilly and mountainous regions, where transportation facilities are lacking, is 52.6%.

It is not surprising that the World Bank ranks Nepal as one of the poorest nations in the world, with fully 9 million people living below the international poverty level. Nepal's social indicators remain well below average for South Asia. Life expectancy at birth is 55 years (compared to 63 years in India and Pakistan, 73 years in Sri Lanka), and infant mortality is 91 per 1000 live births, the highest in the region. The general literacy rate is 27% (49% for South Asia) and is even lower, 14%, for women. Access to safe water is 48% in Nepal, 77% for neighbors in South Asia.

Economy

Agriculture permeates the life of most Nepalese. More than 80% of employment and 40% of the gross domestic product is dependent on agriculture. Of the rural and agricultural output, crop production accounts for 60%, livestock 30%, and forest products 10% of the total. It is for this reason that much of rural Nepal's life revolves around the fields, animals, and forests. Per capita income in Nepal in 2000 was $210 (versus an average of $508 for other South Asian nations), meaning that most of the population are subsistence farmers who contribute little to the cash economy. Furthermore, cash in the villages is expended on much needed food rations and other daily essentials. Little spare cash remains for other needed items such as medical facilities, education, and travel. In such circumstances, even by necessity, much of the rural population is forced to resort to local plants for medicine, food, clothing, and other uses.

Tourism accounts for 11% of exports. Many rural men are engaged as porters and guides during the peak tourist seasons, spring and fall. Manufactured exports such as carpets and garments account for 70% of exports, and the remainder comprises raw or semiprocessed materials such as jute (*Corchorus capsularis*) and tea (*Camellia sinensis*).

GEOGRAPHY

Nepal occupies the central third of the Himalaya called the Nepal Himalaya. The country lies between latitudes 26°22′ and 30°27′ north and longitudes 80°4′ and 88°12′ east (Figure 1). Nepal's east–west extent is about 885 km. The mean breadth north–south is about 193 km; the greatest north–south distance is about 230 km in the west. The rivers Mechi and Mahakali form Nepal's eastern and western borders, respectively, with India.

The geographical features of Nepal are complex. Giant mountain peaks (as high as 8848 m), deep valleys and gorges, alluvial plains (as low as 70 m), and cold deserts are found within a distance of a few kilometers. The slope of the land from the flat river plain in the south to the Himalaya in the north has a marked effect on all aspects of Nepalese life. Climate, vegetation, agricultural crops, ethnic groups, livelihoods, and culture are dictated by this topography.

The elevations of the mountains and valleys extend approximately parallel east–west. Himalayan geologists have adapted Hagen's (1960) seven topographical zones, proceeding from south to north: Terai, Siwalik Hills, Mahabharat Mountains, midlands, the Himalaya, high mountain valleys, and Tibetan marginal mountains.

Terai

The Terai is a narrow strip of fertile alluvial soil in the south of Nepal, extending east–west with an average elevation of 200 m. The width of this fertile land is 32 km, with maximum of 45 km. Most of Nepal's arable land, about 20,720 square kilometers, is in this belt, hence it is known as the granary of Nepal. The Terai opens to the northern plains of India across the open border between the two countries. This area was feared because of malaria before DDT spraying in the 1950s, but since then there has been a large-scale migration of populations from both India and the hilly regions of Nepal. The thick forests that were impenetrable have been greatly reduced through rampant lumbering and clearing for agriculture. Many of the wild animals have also disappeared, except in a few conservation areas, because of game hunting during the Rana era.

The road network built since the 1950s in the Terai is also important for transport in Nepal. The East–West Highway runs along the Terai, and numerous other highways run north–south, connecting the Nepalese interior with the markets of the Terai and India.

Siwalik Hills

The Siwalik Hills rise from the flatland of the Terai to a height of almost 1800 m (the average is about 1000 m). In comparison to the area of the south, this region is only sparsely populated. Geologically, it consists of younger sedimentary deposits from south-flowing rivers: coarsely bedded sandstones and conglomerates of sand, clay, and sandy limestones. The soil contains negligible humus and is porous. It is believed that the deposits of the Siwalik Hills were raised as a result of tectonic movements. Certain valleys (called Dun or Doon valleys by some experts) such as Chitwan, Dangdeokhuri, and Surkhet are slightly more populated than the other parts of this topographical zone. As with the Terai Hills, the Dun valleys were cleared of their primeval forest after the DDT sprayings, which made mass migration from the hills in the north possible.

Mahabharat Mountains

The Mahabharat Mountains occupy the central part of the country, where mountain ranges extend almost uninterrupted east–west, ranging up to 2750 m in elevation. The climate of this topographical zone is cool and humid. This belt is made up of metamorphosed, sedimentary, and igneous rocks of different ages (Rimal 1967). The ridges of the Mahabharat Mountains are conspicuous features of the topography, doubtless acting as a cultural and defensive barrier against violent conflicts in the Indian lowlands. It was also the fighting in these hills, with their Nepalese interlocking hill fortresses, that thwarted many British advances. Following the Anglo-Nepali war of 1814–1816, the British formed the British Gurkha regiments to recruit Nepalese men for their proven fighting abilities.

The Mahabharat Mountains display spectacular valleys and river gorges cut by the south-flowing rivers. The mountains are sparsely populated above 2000 m but the valleys, which are so deep that the floors of the valleys or riverbeds are only 200–400 m above sea level, are more densely populated. Before the modest road network of today, much of the trade and traffic flowed along these deep valleys with the goods mostly on people's backs. Towns such as Bandipur, Tansen, and Dhankuta, which have lost their trading significance today, were important market places and trading posts between the Terai and Midlands.

Midlands

Hagen (1960) called the midlands of Nepal the "heart of the country." The topographical zone lies between the Mahabharat Mountains and the high Himalaya. Hagen divided the midlands into nine natural regions, each one with wide valleys drained by one of the branches of Nepal's great river system. The valleys of Pokhara, Kathmandu, and Banepa are located in this belt, which is situated about 600–1980 m above sea level. The Pokhara Valley of central Nepal is characterized by numerous terraced fields and a congenial climate. Geologically, the midland belt consists of crystalline and metamorphic rocks (granites, gneisses, and schists).

The midlands have a characteristically Nepalese culture. Crops and fruit are also varied and support many different people. The mild climate also makes the midlands the home of the majority of the Nepalese today.

The Himalaya

The word Himalaya comes from the Sanskrit, meaning abode of the snow (*him,* snow, and *alaya,* abode). The Himalaya, in its most general definition, covers a collection of towering mountain ranges extending about 2500 km, tilting from the west-northwest to the east-southeast. Politically, it traverses two kingdoms, Nepal and Bhutan, as well as a small part of Pakistan, the Tibetan (Xizang) Autonomous Region of China, and parts of northwestern and northeastern India (Figure 1). The Himalaya extends from the Indus Trench below Nanga Parbat (8126 m) in the west to the Yarlungtsangpo-Brahmaputra Gorge below Namche Barwa (7756 m) in the east. The Himalayan topographical zone includes 612,000 square kilometers between latitudes 26°20′ and 35°40′ north and longitudes 74°50′ and 95°40′ east.

The formation of the Himalaya is generally accepted to be the result of collision of tectonic plates. The Himalaya is a system of young fold mountains. They were formed relatively recently in the earth's history, compared to mountains such as the Appalachians in the United States or the Aravalli Range in India, and extend east–west in successive series of parallel ridges or folds.

Mountain building went through phases of major upheavals over a period of about 40 million years. The initial process started 70 million years ago when the first folds of the Himalaya were formed. Paleozoology reveals that marine animals, ammonites, lived at the bottom of the Tethys Sea, which existed where the Himalaya stands today; fossils of ammonites (*shaligram* in Nepali) have been found in Mustang, western Nepal. Two land masses moved ever closer, closing the Tethys; the Indian plate moved north at about 15 cm per year. About 65 million years ago, the second phase of mountain building pushed the sea bed of the Tethys to the high mountain ranges. About 25 million years ago came another mountain building period, which created the slightly lower Siwalik Hills. The last major phase of mountain building occurred about 600,000 years ago, but the Himalaya is still in the process of adjustment. The Indian plate is thrusting north under the northern plate at about 2 cm every year, causing the Himalaya to rise about 5 mm each year.

In the late, Pleistocene epoch phase, the east–west trough accumulated alluvium brought by the south-flowing rivers, developing a fertile belt in the Gangetic Plain in southern Nepal, which is known as the Terai. The major rivers have maintained their general southward flow despite the convergence of the tectonic plates, but their courses have been deflected by the movement of the plates, resulting in right-angular changes in course. This pattern, the extreme elevations, and the limited north–south extent of the Himalaya (less than 150 km in places) reflect the enormous horizontal compression (crustal shortening) and folding, which surpasses any other mountain system both in vertical height and longitudinal extent.

The Himalaya consists of high ranges and spectacular massifs with steep slopes; most of the peaks are snowcapped year-round. The snowline occurs at elevations of 4500 to 6000 m, depending on precipitation. Settlements exist only up to 2400 m, above which only thick forests give way to alpine pasturelands and, eventually, perennial snow. Eight of the 10 highest peaks in the world are Himalayan, including Mount Everest (8848 m), the highest mountain in the world. The 15 highest peaks in the Himalaya in Nepal range in elevation from 7059 to 8848 m. In addition, the deepest river cuts in the world flow between Himalayan peaks, making for breathtakingly beautiful gorges and steep slopes but also making trails extremely challenging. For example, the distance between Annapurna (8091 m) and Dhaulagiri (8167 m) is only 35 km, yet the Kali Gandaki River between these two massifs flows only 1200 m above sea level at its middle point. Similarly, Annapurna II (7937 m) and Manaslu (8156 m) are only 35 km apart, with the Marsyangdi River (1400 m) between.

The Himalaya serves as a barrier to water and wind, nature and culture, ecology and economy between central and South Asia. It directly or indirectly supports about 50 million mountain people and probably in excess of 450 million people in the Gangetic Plain, many of whom suffer from poverty, malnutrition, and accelerating population growth. The Himalaya and the corresponding plains form one of the world's largest "highland-lowland interactive systems" (Ives and Messerli 1989).

High Mountain Valleys

The areas between the high Himalaya and the Plateau of Tibet are referred to as the inner Himalaya. These high mountain valleys are 1970–4500 m above sea level and typically run east–west. They are arid areas, lying in the rain shadow of the higher ranges. The districts of Manang, Mustang, Dolpa, Jumla, and Humla are part of this distinct topographical zone (Figure 2).

The people who inhabit these high mountain valleys have distinctly Tibetan features. Before the Chinese occupation of Tibet, the people in these valleys had very successful trading business between Tibet and the midlands of Nepal. Today, most are engaged in general trade, carpet trade with the West, or tourism.

Tibetan Marginal Mountains

The northernmost belt of Nepal, 6000–7000 m above sea level, is characterized by a series of peaks that are part of a great solid wall of snow and ice. Geologically, these mountains formed first, before the Himalaya, accounting for the age and symmetrical flow of rivers from these mountains into Nepal and Tibet. The Tibetan marginal mountains line the southern margin of the Plateau of Tibet and are the source of the Ganga (Ganges in English) and Brahmaputra (Tsangpo in Tibetan) Rivers, which flow toward India. Ironically, the south-flowing rivers breach a higher range, the Himalaya, before they drain into the Gangetic Plain.

The Tibetan marginal mountains crown the northern part of the subcontinent and act as the last barrier to monsoon rains, which is favorable for agrarian countries south of the mountains. This mountainous region doubtless acted as a protective wall against early invasion from the north, but it has also produced a marked aridity in northwestern Nepal and in the high-elevation Plateau of Tibet to the north. Reaching these mountains from the south can take several weeks of trekking because of the lack of roads in this region. The marginal mountains separate the undulating Plateau of Tibet from the geological jumble of Nepal, adding to the difficulties of transportation and development.

CLIMATE

Nowhere else in the world are such enormous differences in climate to be found within such a short distance. Nepal's "normal" climate for its latitude, the subtropical monsoon type, is strongly modified by two factors: mountain barriers and elevation. Nepal enjoys a privileged position geographically. The towering Himalaya acts as a barrier against cold fronts from central Asia, ensuring warmer winters for Nepal and northern India. The same mountains retain the water from the moist monsoon from the south, keeping the Plateau of Tibet in a rain shadow. Given the enormous range of elevation, it follows that Nepal, with its rugged terrain, has numerous small climatic differences over short horizontal distances. That elevations range from 70 to 8848 m within only 150 km explains why Nepal has no one dominant climate. Of the total land surface, about 20% has an elevation less than 300 m. Except for the Terai in the south, even the valleys, with some exceptions, are more than 1200 m above sea level.

As a result of these extreme variations in elevation, almost all types of climates are found within Nepal. A warm, humid climate prevails in the Terai, Siwalik Hills, and Dun valleys. In the midlands a temperate climate prevails, cool and humid. Subalpine and alpine climates characterize the high mountain peaks and valleys, with arctic conditions surrounding the high peaks. Above 4500 m and in the rain shadow of the mountain ranges, the climate is cold desert.

Monsoon

The monsoon is the name for the heavy rains from storms that originate in the Bay of Bengal. A wave of humid air reaches Nepal at the beginning of June and lasts till the end of September or middle of October, bringing about 80% of the country's annual rainfall. July and August are the two rainiest months, with rainfall tapering down beginning in September. The distribution of rainfall is different for each region, depending on location and elevation. Precipitation levels are generally lower in the west than in the east, because east Nepal is closer to the Bay of Bengal.

As moist monsoon air is forced to rise against each successively higher ridge, precipitation is generally much heavier to the south of the ridge. In contrast, north-facing slopes experience rain shadow effects to varying degrees. Annual rainfall totals increase with rising elevation in central Nepal to about 3000 m; thereafter, annual totals diminish with rising elevation. Above about 5500 m, all precipitation is in the form of snow. The starkest rain shadows are north of the Himalaya. For instance, two weather stations on the south and north of the Annapurna massif (Lumle at 1642 m and Jomsom at 2650 m, respectively) recorded mean annual precipitation of 5550 mm and 255 mm, respectively. A large area extending along the entire east–west range of the country in the south and in the central midlands, including valleys, experiences moderate rainfall (100–2000 mm). South of the Siwalik Hills, rainfall is high (2000–3000 mm). Climatalogical data show that the two rainiest places are Lamachaur and Lumle in central Nepal where maximum annual rainfall is about 5000 mm. To the west or east, rainfall does not exceed 3000 mm. It drops to 250–500 mm annually along the Tibetan border in western Nepal because of rain shadow and distance from the Bay of Bengal. The rain shadow is limited to small areas in the east. North of the main Himalayan range is an area of wet alpine (4000–4570 m) and dry alpine belts (4700 m upward).

Despite general climate patterns formed by distance from the Bay of Bengal and blocking of rain clouds by mountain crests, it can be misleading to generalize about regional climates as there are pockets of high precipitation and aridity, which have long been recognized in vegetation mapping (Schweinfurth 1957). But the scatter and range of climatic data can be best viewed in the context of the rhythm of the monsoon climate at large. This rhythm is well known to all Nepalese farmers: pre-monsoon (April–May), monsoon (June–September), post-monsoon (October–December), winter (January–March).

The highest temperatures, with maximums exceeding 40°C recorded at many lowland stations, occur during April and May. Many hill valleys such as Kathmandu record maximums of about 33°C and minimums in the winter of a few degrees below freezing.

The monsoon is the most important season for the Nepalese since crop growth and the harvest depend on its length and intensity. Much of the agricultural output of the country is, therefore, dependent on monsoon rains. The monsoon sometimes brings not only blessings but also hardships, however, such as flooding of rivers, wrecking of laboriously constructed terraces, and gigantic mountain slides, wiping out villages.

VEGETATION ZONES

In parallel with the extreme differences in climate in Nepal, the variety of vegetation is also vast in such a small span of area. The distribution of vegetation is governed by elevation, temperature, and rainfall. In Nepal, the Indian, Southeast Asiatic, and Sino-Japanese floristic regions merge. Also, Nepal is the meeting place of western and eastern Himalayan plants. For example, *Aesculus indica* and *Cedrus deodara* are only found in the west or in certain places in central Nepal. Trees such as *Castanopsis hystrix* and *Larix griffithiana* of eastern and central Nepal are absent in the west. Schweinfurth (1957) produced the first vegetation map of the entire Himalaya, illustrating the strong parallelism between climate and vegetation north–south and east–west. South to north, natural vegetation belts range from subtropical monsoon rain forests (*Shorea robusta* or *sal* forests) through a series of forest belts to timberline at 4000–4500 m. Above timberline, a rhododendron-shrub belt gives way to alpine meadows or extensive bare ground and scattered dwarf plants, mosses, and lichens, and finally, at 5000–5500 m, permanent ice and snow with rock outcrops.

In Dolpa and Mustang, the vegetation is different from that of the rest of Nepal. These districts are located beyond high mountain ridges and are shielded from the monsoon rains that come from the southeast. As a result, temperatures and rainfall on the leeward side are both low, effecting the vegetation difference.

About 54% of Nepal has some sort of vegetation cover. Forested area constitutes 37%, shrublands and depleted forest 5%, and grasslands 12% (Shakya and Joshi 1995). It is estimated that there are about 7000 species of flowering plants native to Nepal, about 300 of which are endemic (Lacoul 1995).

Scientists have divided Nepal in different ways to study its flora and vegetation. This is another illustration of the complexity of the plant life of Nepal. Stearn (1960) proposed three divisions, based on three important river systems: (1) Karnali, west, (2) Gandaki, central, and (3) Koshi, east. On the bases of ecology and vegetation, Dobremez (1972) recognized four vegetation belts: (1) western, (2) northwestern, (3) central, and (4) eastern. Swan and Leviton (1962) classified the vegetation of Nepal into seven vegetation zones: (1) lower monsoon, (2) middle monsoon, (3) upper monsoon, (4) deciduous and rhododendron, (5) conifer and rhododendron, (6) wet alpine, and (7) dry alpine. Stainton (1972) made further phytogeographical divisions and identified eight climatic and vegetational divisions. (1) Terai and outer foothills, including the Siwalik Hills and the valleys, (2) midlands and southern slopes of the main Himalayan ranges, (3) western midlands, (4) central midlands, (5) eastern midlands, (6) south of Annapurna and Himalchuli, (7) dry river valleys, and (8) arid zone.

These divisions are based on elevation, river systems, and other specific areas such as Annapurna. Simpler generalizations about the vegetation based on forest types are attractive alternatives. These divisions extend from east–west, though the forests do not always strictly adhere to the elevations: (1) tropical and subtropical vegetation (to 1200 m), (2) temperate vegetation (1200–2900 m), and (3) subalpine and alpine vegetation (2900–5000 m) (Figure 3).

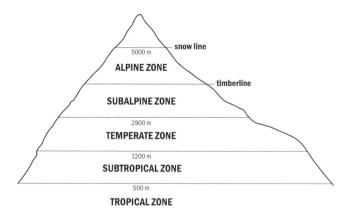

Figure 3. Vegetation zones of Nepal

Tropical and Subtropical Vegetation

From the Indian border to about 500 m, there is tropical vegetation, and above that to about 1200 m, subtropical vegetation. But some trees such as *Semecarpus anacardium, Shorea robusta, Terminalia bellirica,* and *T. chebula* are common in both belts. Until about the mid-twentieth century, the northern part of this region was covered with dense subtropical vegetation, giving rise to its name, Charkose Jhari (Nepali for 8-mile-wide brush). As a result of population pressure and political corruption, Charkose Jhari is badly deforested and most of the flatlands are under cultivation, which encroaches on the forest land. The vegetation is dominated by deciduous trees: *Adina cordifolia, Aegle marmelos, Cassia fistula, Dillenia indica, Holarrhena pubescens, Mallotus philippensis, Schleichera oleosa, Semecarpus anacardium, Shorea robusta, Terminalia bellirica,* and *T. chebula.* Near rivers, some *Acacia* and *Dalbergia* trees can be found. Toward the eastern part of this vegetation zone some plants are found that have affinity to the Southeast Asiatic flora: *Duabanga grandiflora, Gnetum montanum, Pandanus,* and *Podocarpus.* Many of them do not occur beyond the central part of Nepal. In the subtropical belt of eastern and central Nepal, *Castanopsis, Pinus,* and *Schima* are slightly more prevalent.

In contrast to the Terai, which has been largely denuded of its forest cover, some forests still remain in the flatlands of the Dun valleys in the subtropical belt. Dangdeokhuri Valley in western Nepal is an exception in that negligible forests remain because the Dangdeokhuri area came under intensive cultivation long ago. Because of growing population and unemployment of the hill people (who are attracted to the flatlands for its agriculture), it is more likely that in the future these areas will be as deforested as the Terai or other midland areas.

Temperate Vegetation

The midland belt between the Siwalik Hills and the Himalaya is heavily populated, covering many mountain slopes, river basins, and flat valleys. At lower elevations and within the 5- to 7-km periphery of village areas, forests are badly denuded. These areas are either terraced for cultivation or heavily grazed. Some dense tree patches remain, which tend to be protected religious forests.

Vegetation in the temperate region is composed of evergreen trees and appears quite lush. Toward the eastern part of Nepal, evergreen oaks (*Quercus*), maples (*Acer*), *Myrsine, Rhododendron,* and laurels (*Actinodaphne, Cinnamomum, Lindera, Litsea, Persea*) are the principal trees, whereas western temperate Nepal is dominated by conifers and mixed deciduous vegetation. Conifers are important components of higher elevation vegetation. *Abies spectabilis* and *Cedrus deodara* are common forest trees at 3000 m. *Cupressus torulosa, Picea smithiana,* and *Pinus wallichiana* are fairly widespread on mountain slopes between 2000 and 3000 m. Deciduous forest of *Aesculus indica* and *Juglans regia* var. *kamaonia* are common along the riverbanks.

Toward the central and eastern portions of the temperate belt, *Quercus lamellosa, Daphniphyllum himalense,* and *Magnolia campbellii* are some noteworthy species that provide forest cover. The purple-flowered *Daphne* and yellow-flowered *Mahonia* are conspicuous in the rhododendron and oak forests of central Nepal.

The forests in the eastern midlands are thick in comparison to those in the west as the monsoon effects are heaviest in the east. The wide, open passage of the Arun River Valley allows the monsoon to reach to the northernmost part, favoring the region's vegetation. In wet localities, tree ferns (*Cyathea*) and *Pandanus* are prominent in the forest. At lower elevations of the temperate belt, broad-leaved vegetation comprises *Lithocarpus elegans, Quercus glauca, Michelia,* and some members of the family Lauraceae.

Subalpine and Alpine Vegetation

The vegetation of the subalpine zone consists of *Abies spectabilis, Betula utilis, Rhododendron barbatum,* and *R. campanulatum* up to timberline. The elevation of timberline varies across Nepal according to the pattern of monsoon rains. According to Swan and Leviton (1962) and Bhatta (1977), timberline in eastern Nepal reaches a maximum elevation of 4110 m. In the central Himalaya, however, it varies, 3048–3962 m. In the western Himalaya the upper limit of timberline is about 3048 m. Many species of *Rhododendron* in eastern Nepal decrease progressively toward central and western Nepal. In contrast, *Quercus* is mostly seen in the forests of western Nepal. Alpine vegetation consists mainly of shrubby plants of *Berberis, Caragana, Lonicera,* and *Rhododendron,* which occur in patches at upper elevations near timberline. Many beautiful herbaceous species of *Gentiana, Meconopsis, Primula,* and *Saxifraga* are also found in open alpine meadows, used as pasture.

HISTORY OF PLANT COLLECTING IN NEPAL

Nepal, however small, is rich in plant resources; it is considered a naturalist's paradise. Until Francis Buchanan-Hamilton began collecting plants in Nepal in 1801–1802, little was known about the flora of the country. Because of its geographical features and the isolationist policy of the Rana rulers, Nepal remained inaccessible to Westerners. Nevertheless, British botanists were actively engaged in the study of the Indian flora and attempted to include the Nepalese flora to some extent. The pioneering work of Nathaniel Wallich, William Roxburgh, and Joseph Dalton Hooker resulted in the production of excellent studies of the flora such as *Tentamen Florae Napalensis Illustratae* (Wallich 1824–1826), *Flora Indica* (Roxburgh 1820–1824, 1832), and *Flora of British India* (Hooker 1872–1897).

After the downfall of the Rana regime, the country was opened to Westerners. The opportunity to explore was exploited primarily by mountaineers, who organized expeditions to scale the highest Himalayan peaks. In time, other foreign explorers, scientists, and tourists also took advantage of the opening of Nepal. However, the study of Nepalese flora and vegetation was challenging because of Nepal's topography and the lack of transportation and communication. The British Museum (Natural History) sent some teams to collect plants in 1949–1954 and 1969. Likewise, the University of Tokyo and Chiba University in Japan organized plant collecting expeditions in Nepal in 1960–1972.

CONSERVATION

Most Nepalese depend on plant resources for their livelihood. Traditionally, people of Nepal have considered forests as a source of life and a symbol of creation. Nepalese culture has always given due respect to preservation of plants and forests. More recently, scholars have pointed out the sharp depletion of the forests and the general environmental degradation and have developed the eight-point theory of Himalayan environmental degradation (THED; Ives and Messerli 1989). Some experts, however, believe that the very pessimistic view taken by the THED is not borne out by the scientific data and is, therefore, a result of more emotional perception.

As the forest is an integral part of rural life in Nepal, a Nepalese villager will not willingly destroy all the forest. Hence, the oft-repeated statement that Nepal lost half its forest cover within a 30-year period (1950–1980) and that by the year 2000 no accessible forests would remain (World Bank 1979) is unnecessarily alarmist and goes against the subsistence model of the Nepalese villagers. There is increasing evidence that the extent and quality of tree and forest cover have actually improved since 1980. Many experts believe that the rejuvenation of forests is a result of growing awareness of forest depauperization and progressive governmental decentralization rather than outside aid and development activity.

History of Deforestation in Nepal

The process of deforestation occurred over several hundred years, with a sharp acceleration following Prithvi Narayan Shah's militant unification of Nepal. Arable land provided the most important revenues to the treasury (as noted before, 50% of the crop was paid to the state or landlord). Hence, the state encouraged conversion of forest area to arable land by providing tax breaks for the first 3 years of cultivation after any forest clearing. As the claiming of half of a farmer's crop was very severe even in the best of times, the motivation for forest clearing to supplement income was strong. Although forest cover was vanishing quickly in the Mahabharat Mountains and midlands, it was actually increasing in the Terai as the Rana regime used the thick, malaria-infested forests as a strategic shield against any threats to the country from the south, especially from British expansion.

According to Stiller (1993), another important form of taxation was the requirement to supply iron to the state. Local low-grade ores were extracted and smelted to supply the armories of the rapidly expanding militant state of Gorkha. As the smelting process was inefficient and the demand for iron heavy, much charcoal was needed to turn ore into iron, which depleted forest cover at an alarming rate.

Temple and palace building in the Kathmandu Valley from the early nineteenth century to the 1930s also put severe pressures on the forest trees. Hence, Mahat et al. (1986) concluded that most of the conversion of forest land to arable land occurred in the early 1900s. Reforestation has been retarded in areas where livestock grazing has been intensive; this has been called the "nibble effect" by Moench and Bandyopadhyay (1986).

Until 1950, forestry administration was governed by the feudal system, and general management was largely in local hands. In many places in the midlands, villagers had established rules and regulations for managing the local forests. These systems consisted of locally accepted rules, which regularized the use of forest products. Such a management system was recognized by the Rana regime. After the democratic revolution of 1950, the government nationalized all forests through promulgation of the Forest Nationalization Act of 1957. No compensation was given to private forest owners for the loss of ownership. This was an attempt to prevent the feudal Rana rulers from continuing to treat the Terai forests as their own property. Later, the Forest Act of 1961 established punishments for certain offenses. It also classified the national forests into four different categories: Panchayat Forest, Panchayat Protected Forest, Religious Forest, and Leasehold Forest. Following the act of 1961, the Panchayat Forest Rule and Panchayat Protected Forest Rule of 1978 were enacted to hand over the national forest to the local village Panchayats (the smallest administrative unit under the Panchayat system) as Panchayat Forest. This rule was amended twice, in 1979 and 1987. In 1989, the Panchayat system collapsed and the term Panchayat, used in the Forest Act of 1961, was converted to "User Group." In 1993, another forest act was implemented and is in force.

Causes of Forest Depletion

The degradation of forests is a global problem caused by excessive exploitation of forests by industry for monetary gain, expanding area under subsistence farming, increase in livestock numbers and overgrazing, demands on wood for fuel, and rapidly increasing population. The relationship between the forest cover and climate, as well as the loss of gene pool and loss of wildlife habitat, are very emotionally charged topics. Sadly, the rate of forest depletion is higher in developing countries, including Nepal.

One of the main factors responsible for forest depletion in Nepal was the Forest Nationalization Act of 1957, which was so wrong-footed in its policy that it encouraged people to destroy rather than protect the forest. Forest experts agree that the act broke the traditional relationship between the community and the forest (J. B. S. Karki 1992). The most comprehensive air photography and satellite imagery suggest that little deforestation has occurred in the Mahabharat Mountains and midlands in more recent times but that deforestation has been significant in the Terai and the Siwalik Hills. The Nepal Water and Energy Commission Study (Yatri 1983) presented photographic analysis of cover from 1964 to 1977. The loss was calculated to be 47,200 hectares (1.5% of the original cover) in the Mahabharat Mountains, representing an annual loss of 0.11%, not significant. In the Terai and Siwalik Hills, however, losses of 250,000 and 148,500 hectares, respectively, constitute 2.1% and 0.8% annual loss, very significant. Hence, there is no question that massive deforestation has occurred since the 1950s in the Terai and the Siwalik Hills.

Of the population of Nepal, 90% reside in remote rural areas, where agricultural yields are so low that the crops cannot meet food requirements. As a result, people have to rely on plant-based forest products. According to the *Gorkhapatra News* (1992), about 21% of the total land area of the forest remains, and Pudasaini (1992) noted that forest depletion is at the rate of 2.1% per year.

Infrastructure building activities such as construction of roads, hydroelectric power stations, dams, and canals also disturb plants and forests as the projects are often implemented without due attention to the natural habitat and ecology. Especially when the projects provide employment opportunities for the local people, the needs of forest protection fall low on the list of priorities of project implementers. In addition, forest land often becomes an excavation site for marble, slate, and other quarry stones and soils for both rural and urban use. Similarly, about 86% of total timber production in Nepal comes from the forests (K. Poudel 1992), which accelerates the degradation of forest habitat.

The dire economy of Nepal affects the circumstances of the common people. With such a large population living below subsistence level, encroachment on forest lands for the expansion of agriculture and habitation is understandable. Yet such activities have a marked effect on the deterioration of plant species and their habitats.

Forest fires are an important factor in degradation. Knowingly or unknowingly, villagers cause them. Some fires start when villagers passing along forest trails throw cigarette butts and unintentionally start them. Others are started intentionally with the view that luxuriant growth of grasses will follow, increasing the amount of fodder.

The poor economic climate of Nepal provides few alternatives for fuel. Officially, it is prohibited to cut trees for fuelwood, but because there are few alternatives, all collection of fuelwood is done illegally. In such circumstances, haphazard cutting for fuelwood is rampant and people do not care about disturbing other plants. The traditional sources of energy constitute 94.5% of all energy consumed in Nepal; fuelwoods constitute 83.7% (Plate 1), agricultural residues 9.2%, and animal dung 1.6% (Pudasaini 1992).

Increasing population pressures and decreasing forest resources have given rise to hoarding or misuse of plants. Most villagers collect larger quantities or a greater number of species than they actually need. For example, people may cut a whole plant for about 100 g of bark (Plate 2). In the collection of medicinal plants, the main intention would be to earn money from the sale of the medicinal plant species, so the collectors care less about the preservation of other species in the surrounding area. The situation is exacerbated by the smuggling of forest products.

Local methods of plant collection are rough and unsystematic, causing the habitat of many species of plants to be disturbed, threatening some with extinction. Typically, the collection of plants is centered around an area or species. If some medicinal plants are abundant in an area, people collect these plants continuously until the supply is exhausted.

The grazing of animals on hills and mountains, particularly those on open pasturelands, poses a serious threat to the biodiversity of the area. It is estimated that Nepal loses 240 million cubic meters of soil annually as a result of grazing alone (World Health Organization 1993). About 14 million livestock graze in the forests and pastures of Nepal, putting excessive stress on the delicate ecosystem of the forests (Pudasaini 1992). Moreover, these livestock are low-yielding traditional breeds that require more fodder per unit of milk or meat; experts believe that 70% of their fodder needs come from the forest (Uprety 1985).

Threatened and Endangered Plants

Depletion of the forest and loss of plant habitat has pushed many plants to extinction. Others are on the brink of extinction, balancing precariously in the category of endangered plants. Many species of trees are threatened, including *Shorea robusta,* which takes about half a century to attain maturity (Plate 3). Examples of endangered medicinal plants are *Dac-*

Threatened or Endangered Plants of Nepal

Plant	Part Used	Threat or Endangerment
Acacia catechu	wood	collected commercially to prepare catechu
Aconitum ferox	root	trade
Aconitum heterophyllum	root	trade
Aeginetia indica	root	limited natural distribution
Aesculus indica	fruit	trade, limited natural distribution
Alstonia scholaris	bark	trade
Asparagus racemosus	root	trade, habitat disturbance
Bauhinia vahlii	bark, leaf	overcollection
Bergenia ciliata	rhizome	domestic and international trade
Bombax ceiba	wood, flower, seed	collected commercially for matches (wood), gathered for domestic sale and use (wood for fuel and other uses, seed fiber, flowers) or trade (seed fiber)
Brachycorythis obcordata	root, pseudobulb	endangered; trade
Cedrus deodara	wood	gathered for fuel and other domestic uses, limited natural distribution
Cinnamomum glaucescens	seed	trade
Cinnamomum tamala	bark, leaf	domestic and international trade
Curculigo orchioides	root	trade
Dactylorhiza hatagirea	root, leaf	endangered; trade though collection of roots is banned, and roots and leaves gathered for local consumption before plants have chance to flower and set seed
Dioscorea deltoidea	root	trade and local consumption
Diplokenma butyracea	wood, fruit	timber, fuel (wood), trade (fruit)
Elaeocarpus sphaericus	fruit	trade, limited natural distribution
Juglans regia var. *kamaonia*	bark	limited natural distribution
Madhuca longifolia	wood, flower	endangered; forest depletion
Manglietia insignis	wood	endangered; gathered for fuel, limited natural distribution, forest depletion
Nardostachys grandiflora	rhizome	trade
Paeonia emodi	root	endangered; extensive use, forest depletion
Paris polyphylla	root	endangered; trade
Picrorhiza scrophulariiflora	rhizome	endangered; trade
Podophyllum hexandrum	rhizome	endangered; trade
Rauvolfia serpentina	root	endangered; trade
Rheum australe	rhizome, leaf	endangered; trade (rhizome), local consumption (leaf stalk)
Rhododendron arboreum	wood	timber, fuel
Shorea robusta	wood, leaf	timber, fuel, fodder
Swertia chirayita	plant	trade
Talauma hodgsonii	wood	endangered; gathered for fuel, limited natural distribution, habitat destruction
Taxus baccata subsp. *wallichiana*	leaf	trade
Terminalia bellirica	wood, leaf, fruit	timber, fuel, trade (fruit)
Terminalia chebula	wood, leaf, fruit	timber, fuel, trade (fruit)
Valeriana jatamansii	rhizome	trade
Woodfordia fruticosa	flower	trade, habitat destruction
Zanthoxylum armatum	fruit	trade, habitat destruction

tylorhiza hatagirea, Nardostachys grandiflora, and *Podophyllum hexandrum,* whose roots or rhizomes are exported; haphazard collection practices have allowed little opportunity for the regeneration of these plants. Threatened plants are those that are likely to become endangered throughout all or a significant part of their ranges.

Forest Management

In 1912, the Rana prime minister Chandra Shamsher started efforts toward proper forest management. He assigned Lieutenant Basu Dev Sharma, trained at Dehra Dun Forest College, India, to demarcate forest areas of the western Terai. Although the prime minister had assigned a trained man to begin scientific forest management, not much else changed. The Rana regime's plundering of the Terai forest as an inexhaustible source of revenue continued (Stiller 1993). Even after independence from the Rana regime, Nepal was slow to adopt new developments in forest management, extraction, research, and planning. Some programs were launched, but because of the bureaucratic machinery, little success was achieved.

In 1976, the government realized that management of forests by the villagers, who used them sustainably in the past, was the only way to ensure protection and a sustainable supply of forest products for subsistence needs. As a result, a project of forestry management at the village level was implemented through the local political body (then the Panchayat). After a decade, it was recognized as ineffective. The local political body was too large to develop genuine interest in supervision and management of the forest. In 1989, the new Forestry Master Plan recognized the community forestry program as the best program. In this plan, establishing community forests is seen as a way to meet local demand for firewood, leaf fodder, and other forest products. It relies on user groups for protection, management, and utilization of the forests. According to the Forestry Master Plan, six types of forests are recognized: community forest, government-managed forest, leasehold forest, private forest, religious forest, and conserved forest.

Community Forest. The process of handing over forest to a community requires the formation of a user group, which in turn is supposed to prepare an operational plan concerning the patch of forest. In the beginning, the formation of user groups and handing over was very slow as the field-level preparation was inadequate. Now the focus of the community forestry program is on natural forests because villagers prefer to take over existing forests rather than establish new ones. Villagers handle all the management aspects, including establishment of nurseries and plantations, for which they receive a cash subsidy, which is gradually withdrawn to make the program sustainable. Actual ownership of the forest land is not transferred to the user groups; rather, it remains with the government.

Government-Managed Forest. Government forest in each district is managed by the local forest bureaucracy, which is headed by the district forest officer. Government-managed forest is divided into ranges, and each range into units. The district forest office deals with all procedures concerning the forest, such as issuing permits for collection of forest products, management, and supervision.

Leasehold Forest. The rules concerning leasehold forest have stemmed depletion of the forests. If a deforested area is found to be suitable for leasing, the users living around the area have to be informed of the government's intention, enabling them to decide if they wish to take up that forest area as a community forest. The lessees can be communities, corporate bodies, or industrial groups. If more parties apply for the same forest as a leasehold forest, priority is given to the community and forest-based industries are given second priority. Forest products from leasehold forests can be consumed or sold only in quantities as specified in the operational plan. Additionally, the lessee has to inform the district forest officer about the species of plants and numbers planted in the leasehold forest. Ownership of the trees existing in the leasehold forest at the time of its handing over is vested to the government. The lessee must elaborate the management and protection of the forest in the operational plan. Trees located in leasehold forest are valued, and a deposit or bank guarantee of not more than 10% of the total value may be demanded from the lessee. A leasehold forest may be handed over for a period not exceeding 40 years. If the performance of a lessee is satisfactory, the period of license may be exceeded another 40 years.

Private Forest. Although private forests were more prevalent many decades ago, with nationalization of the forests, people in the hills of Nepal started converting their private forest into farmland, either by cutting or by burning the area to prevent the government from classifying it as forest and claiming it. Now the laws of the land identify private forest as trees planted on private land; such forest is to be registered in the Revenue Office, which is indicative of governmental centralization even after the realization that nationalization of forests was a huge blunder. The government subsidy for private forest is in the form of reduced land taxes if individuals manage their own forests.

Religious Forest. The religious and cultural beliefs of the people of Nepal have also contributed to the protection of plants and their habitat. Some plant species are closely associated with social customs and religious rituals. In addition, temples are surrounded by sacred groves. No study has been done to identify the number of religious forests, but they exist throughout Nepal. For example, the forest around the Pashupati Nath temple in Kathmandu, the forest of Suryabinayak in Bhaktapur district, the forest of Bajrabarahi in Lalitpur district, and the forest of Bhumithan in Nuwakot dis-

Protected Areas of Nepal

Protected Area	Zone	District	Area (km^2)	Established
Annapurna Conservation Area	Dhaulagiri, Gandaki	Kaski, Lamjung, Manang, Mustang, Myagdi	7629	1986
Shey-Phoksundo National Park	Karnali	Dolpa, Mugu	3555	1984
Langtang National Park	Bagmati	Nuwakot, Rasuwa, Sindhupalchok	1710	1976
Makalu-Barun National Park	Koshi, Sagarmatha	Sankhuwasabha, Solukhumbu	1500	1991
Dhorpatan Hunting Reserve	Dhaulagiri, Rapti	Baglung, Myagdi, Rukum	1325	1987
Sagarmatha National Park	Sagarmatha	Solukhumbu	1148	1976
Royal Bardiya National Park	Bheri	Bardiya	968	1988
Royal Chitwan National Park	Lumbini, Narayani	Chitwan, Makawanpur, Nawalparasi, Parsa	932	1973
Makalu-Barun Conservation Area	Koshi, Sagarmatha	Sankhuwasabha, Solukhumbu	830	1991
Parsa Wildlife Reserve	Narayani	Bara, Chitwan, Parsa, Makawanpur	499	1984
Khaptad National Park	Seti	Achham, Bajhang, Bajura, Doti	225	1984
Koshi Tappu Wildlife Reserve	Koshi	Saptari, Sunsari	175	1976
Royal Suklaphanta Wildlife Reserve	Mahakali	Kanchanpur	155	1976
Shivapuri Watershed and Wildlife Reserve	Bagmati	Kathmandu, Nuwakot, Sindhupalchok	144	1984
Rara National Park	Karnali	Jumla, Mugu	106	1976

trict are well protected. People are very conscious of the need to protect plants at religious locations.

Conserved Forest. Various programs have been formulated to conserve biodiversity in Nepal. Conservation efforts are mostly concentrated in protected areas such as national parks, wildlife reserves, conservation areas, and hunting reserves. Protected areas constitute about 20,902 square kilometers, about 14% of the land area of Nepal.

Local Management of Plant Resources

Needless to say, it is difficult to meet the demand for forest products only from natural resources. It would be beneficial to encourage cultivation of plants used for food, fodder, medicine, timber, and fuel. The importance of forest resources in the lives of the Nepalese people should be addressed in a way similar to that of governmental agricultural policy. For instance, cultivation programs should be eligible for government grants and interest-free or low-interest loans. The government should be involved either by holding a share of capital in private enterprise or by assuming responsibility for smooth operation of the program. Villagers should be provided with seeds and seedlings and the technical knowhow for growing food, fodder, timber, and fuel plants on their private land. For efficiency, it would be better to encourage their indigenous knowledge instead of imposing sophisticated modern technology.

The conservation of biodiversity can be achieved only if local people participate in local development programs that are based on an understanding of local needs. Some kinds of local management of plant resources have been practiced for generations. During planting and harvest, and traditional rituals and festivals, for instance, villagers do not have time to collect fodder from the forest. So fodder trees were planted on farmland or around the kitchen garden. Some local practitioners of herbal medicine make sure that resources are easily available by planting important medicinal plants in their kitchen gardens.

Preservation of plants and trees around sources of drinking water (*panero* in Nepali) in the villages is also common. Villagers believe that the source of drinking water can dry out if they destroy the plants around the *panero*; hence, any tree or plant around the *panero* gets very good protection. Similarly, it is customary to plant evergreen trees along trails for shelter, or at rest stops (*chautara*) for walkers. Nobody disturbs plants created for the *chautara*; furthermore, people feel that maintaining plants of the *chautara* is a pious deed. Such local management makes a positive contribution to overall conservation.

Some plants have great religious significance. People worship them as icons of gods and goddesses so they are grown or protected with special care. Sacred trees are mentioned in ancient Hindu literature, including the vedas, the puranas, the *Ramayana,* and the *Mahabharata.* The *pipal* (*Ficus religiosa*) is one of the most sacred trees. It is considered the king of the trees and plants because it is believed that the three most important Hindu gods—Brahma, Vishnu, and Mahesh—keep their abodes in it. In Buddhism, this tree is worshiped because it is said that Siddhartha Gautama, the Buddha, sat under this tree for 7 consecutive days and obtained the knowledge of enlightenment (Nirvana). Hindu women worship it each Monday falling on the fifteenth day of the new-moon half of any lunar month. This special day is known as Somavati Amavashya, which is symbolic of conjugal love, fertility, and happiness. Hence, the *pipal* tree is worshipped to ward off widowhood. So strong are the religious connotations of the *pipal* tree that it is not used as firewood, and no one cuts or damages this tree.

The banyan tree (*Ficus benghalensis*) is equally important religiously; its religious virtues are mentioned in ancient Hindu and Buddhist epics. Therefore, the tree is worshiped by both Hindus and Buddhists. Married Hindu women worship this tree on the fifteenth day of the new-moon half of the month of Jeshtha (May–June), wishing long life for their husbands. It is believed that many good spirits and gods and goddesses rest in this tree, and Vishnu is said to have been born under this tree. Hence, the legends grant eternal power to it. A common belief is that anybody who damages this tree will never be blessed with a son. People plant it along with the *pipal* tree for its luxuriant shade as well as religious significance (as discussed in Chapter 3 under Nepalese Plant Folklore). Many people grow *rudraksha* (Nepali for *Elaeocarpus sphaericus*) for its fruits, as *rudraksha* seeds are considered Shiva's tears of joy. The seeds have medicinal value for blood pressure and heart ailments. Thus the planting and protecting of religious plants by the local people are good examples of conservation.

Regulations. Local management, however, needs careful coordination by governmental as well as nongovernmental organizations, which have a role in making people aware of the importance of plant resources. But lack of coordination and duplication of programs are confusing to local people. Rural handicrafts should be encouraged as income-generating businesses; they can provide employment for rural people and concentrate people's attention on conservation. Simply postulating lofty ideological or moral imperatives for conservation, especially by city folks or foreign development entities, has a very small chance of success when immediate local needs and benefits are overlooked.

Administrative procedures for marketing plants should be simple and practical. Cumbersome administrative procedures for obtaining permits for plant collection, trading forest products, and so on discourage villagers. Bureaucracy can subvert well-meaning policies.

Control of the overexploitation and misuse of plants is essential. A permit system helps minimize the haphazard collection of forest resources but will only operate satisfactorily if there is adequate knowledge of the distribution, conservation status, and ecology of the species. A permit should con-

tain the amount or number of plants to be collected, and the area and duration of collection. Such systematic implementation requires adequate staff and appropriate penalties for violation of permits; mere cancellation of permits and prohibition to apply for new ones should not be regarded as an adequate deterrent. Regular or surprise inspection in the field would deter collectors from misconduct.

Restrictions on export of certain forest products may be essential, particularly as short-term measures. There is a lack of reliable data on supply and demand of forest products, and data collection on a regular basis would help in the formulation of developmental programs at the village level.

Royalty fees for wild plant products are very haphazard. Practicality calls for fees to be proportional to the quantity and the value of the plants. For example, *Shorea robusta* is the best timber tree, also used for firewood, with bark used for tanning, leaves for packing and for making plates and bowls, and seeds for oil. Yet the governmental fee per cubic foot is 250 rupees (about 3.50 U.S. dollars) whereas its market price is 900 rupees. The rhizome of *Nardostachys grandiflora,* a medicinal plant, is one of the more important export commodities. It is collected by digging the whole plant, and the royalty fee for its root is 15 rupees per kilogram but the market price is 100 rupees.

Plants regenerate well if collected on a rotational basis. Current collection methods and governmental oversight do not provide any relief to plants for regeneration. There are some limits on the time allowed for exploitation of forest resources, but in practice they are not followed. For instance, woodcutters and shepherds collect medicinal plants in small quantities throughout the year and store them in their houses. When the actual collection season starts, they sell their products to middlemen who sell them to wholesalers or other businessmen who have export licenses. The plants get little chance to attain maturity, resulting in less chance for seed dispersal, hence the rationale for an appropriate collection season is thwarted.

Conservation awareness would do much for successful management of plant resources. For example, *Ephedra gerardiana* is useful in treating asthma and hay fever; unfortunately, it is used extensively for fuel. Moreover, the local people collect plants in excess of their immediate need and throw away whatever is not used. Such negligence results from lack of education and from the perception that forest products are free and will continue to be freely available. Another hazard to plants during collection is disturbance of the habitat of other plants. When the collector digs one plant, he disturbs the habitat of all plants nearby. During collection season, when the appropriate permit is obtained, collectors have free access to the entire forest and are under no supervision. Their main intention is to earn money, so they care little about the existence of other plants or other parts of the collected plants. Plants collected for their roots and bark are especially threatened because of poor collection procedures.

CHAPTER 2

The People of Nepal

A first-time visitor to Nepal is usually amazed how different Nepalese look and that a "typical" Nepalese physiognomy does not exist. Nepal has been a crossroads for north-, south-, east-, and west-moving people in Asia. There are people in Nepal who look like Caucasians, Mongols of northern Asia, or Chinese with a slightly darker pigmentation. Nepal is itself a microcosm of dynamics in South Asia. Texts such as the *Rigveda* mention a southern Asian people called Dasyu, said to have been short and dark skinned. Between 2000 and 1500 B.C., groups speaking Indo-Germanic languages invaded from the northwest, displacing the original inhabitants. Infiltration from the north across the Himalaya is the reason for presence of Mongoloid groups.

The topography of Nepal, marked by very high mountains and deep valleys and accentuated by wide variations in climate and vegetation, resulted in settlers from different areas picking localities most suitable to each. Hence, the distribution of the various ethnic groups in Nepal follow contour lines, paralleling preferred climates and crops. It is, therefore, not unusual to find several different ethnic communities stacked on top of each other from the river valley to an elevation of about 2500 m.

There are two major groups in Nepal based on origin: Tibeto-Nepali and Indo-Nepali. There are also ethnic subgroups that still lead a life of hunting and living in temporary dwellings. Some trading communities such as the Thakalis (of Tibetan stock) and Newars (whose language is of Tibeto-Burman origin) inhabit areas where trade is most feasible. In all, there are about 60 ethnic groups in Nepal within the two broad categories.

Information in *Plants and People of Nepal* was gathered in the course of studying many areas, at many elevations. Fast rivers and high mountains have played a part in isolating various ethnic groups with their distinctive languages, cultures, and other traits, including ethnobotanical knowledge. About a quarter of the 60 or so ethnic communities with significant or newly available ethnobotanical data are included: Chepang, Danuwar, Gurung, Lepcha, Limbu, Magar, Mooshar, Newar, Rai (including Khaling), Raute, Satar, Sherpa, Tamang, and Tharu. The customs of these communities are described in this chapter. In addition, information on plant use by the Majhi (similar to Magar), Sunwar (similar to Rai), and Tibetan (similar to Gurung and Sherpa) is provided. Most other ethnic groups use plants similarly or make only limited use of plants in their lives. Nepali is the official language of Nepal, understood by nearly everyone, but only about half of the Nepalese speak Nepali as their mother tongue. Bhojpuri, one of the languages in which vernacular names are also listed, is spoken by various ethnic groups, including the Danuwar and Mooshar, in the Terai.

The Terai in the south of Nepal is inhabited by the Indo-Nepali Danuwar, Mooshar, and Tharu communities. The Indo-Nepali communities also include the Bhojpuri-speaking ones; the Majhi and Sunwar speak their own native languages. There are Tibeto-Nepali ethnic groups in the midlands, including the Chepang, Gurung, Limbu, Magar, Rai, Raute, and Tamang communities. The Lepcha are also Tibeto-Nepali. Traditionally, the Kathmandu Valley has been inhabited by the Newar community. In the upper reaches of Nepal such as the high mountain valleys, Tibeto-Nepali groups (with strong tilt toward the Tibetan stock) such as the Sherpa make their home. Generally, the people living near the border area with Tibet are called Bhotia, a collective term for communities including the Gurung, Sherpa, Tibetan, and so on, whose customs and traditions are similar. In some Indian books there is the occasional mention of plant names in Bhotia, but the names used by the different communities are distinguished here.

Within ethnic communities, those engaged in nonagricultural occupations have their own occupational communities. The main occupational communities include priests, goldsmiths, silversmiths, blacksmiths, tailors, cobblers, cleaners, traders, and healers. Many caste demarcations are based on occupational distinctions. Except for some high Himalayan regions, occupational communities exist throughout Nepal. In the Kathmandu Valley, during the 300-year-long golden age of Nepal's culture that began in the late fourteenth century, King Jayasthithi Malla categorized society according to Hindu caste laws. Instead of the four varnas of the typical caste system, the Malla kings grouped the Hindus and Buddhists of Kathmandu into 64 occupational castes to ease social intercourse. Although most of the caste system has died away, among Newars some of the 64 divisions remain.

ETHNIC COMMUNITIES

Chepang

In 1989, I met a boy who was sitting with bundles of leaves and the bark of *Bauhinia vahlii*, ready to carry them to the small market of Lothar, a town in the subtropical belt of southern Nepal. He described the uses of many plants in his area. In the course of the conversation it became clear that he was a Chepang from the village of Kamle (1000 m). I was then curious to meet Chepangs, and after a month managed a visit to a Chepang village.

Chepangs, whose population is estimated to be 32,000, are considered one of the most primitive communities of Nepal. They inhabit central Nepal, in districts mainly along the border of northern Chitwan, in northwestern Makawanpur, and southern Dhading. There are different views about the origin of the name Chepang. One view maintains that Chepangs are traditionally hunters who use bows and arrows and hunting dogs. As hunting is an important element of their livelihood, two words are central in their language: *che,* dog, and *pang,* arrow. The word Siyowang (from which the word Chepang probably evolved) in their native language means dwellers living on difficult slopes and pinnacles of the hills. They themselves like to be called *praja,* citizens of the country.

Chepangs typically have a medium build with Mongoloid features and are considered simple, honest, and obedient. Traditional garments for male Chepangs are the *dhoti* (loincloth), *kachhar* (short tunic), and *bhoto* (top garment), and for females, the *gunyu* (long skirt), *cholo* (blouse with long sleeves), and *patuka* (a very long cloth belt wrapped several times around the waist).

Chepangs usually build their houses in the middle of the forest. They have small, narrow houses with a small entrance, a low roof thatched with grass, and typically no ventilation. Walls are made of tree branches, and the house contains only one room on the ground floor, on one side of which they sleep and use the other side as a kitchen. The attic space is used for storage. Chepangs sleep outside in summer, inside around a fire in winter.

Most Chepangs have limited landholdings, which tend to be forest land of poor quality found around their houses. Moreover, the hilly slopes of their fields lessen the yield from crops such as millet (*Eleusine coracana*) and maize (*Zea mays*). Agricultural output supports Chepangs at most about 7 months a year, and for the rest of the year they depend on wild plants. Family members who do not hunt dig up roots of yam (*Dioscorea deltoidea*) and wild yam (*D. pentaphylla*) in April–May and they are the main source of food. The method of preparing the roots is slicing followed by simple boiling (Plate 4).

Chepangs are fond of hunting. They like monkeys and trap them skillfully in nets, which they make from the bark fiber of Himalayan nettle (*Girardinia diversifolia*). They also trap birds in a bow trap. The main source of their edible oil is seeds of the Indian butter tree (*Diplokenma butyracea*).

Chepangs do not celebrate many festivals, considering them very extravagant. During festivals, Chepangs eat plain rice. The main festivals observed by Chepangs include Maghe Sankranti (January–February), Chait Dasain (February–March), and Saune Sankranti (July), Dasain (September–October), and Tihar (October–November). They believe that misfortune and ill health are caused by the evil wishes of spirits or the wrath of gods and goddesses (Plate 5). Chepangs worship three deities: Namrung, the god of hunting, which is central to Chepang survival; Bhuin, the earth deity, worshipped for good agricultural production; Gaidu, the god who protects the health and security of their domestic animals. Both arranged and love marriages are prevalent, and there is an entrenched system for the men to marry their cousins or sisters-in-law. The dead are either buried or cremated. The *pande,* religious priest, performs the ritual ceremonies for this community.

Danuwar

Danuwars, a community of 48,110, are scattered in the southern part of the Dhanusha, Sindhuli, and Makawanpur districts in the Terai. The word Danuwar is derived from *dalwar,* fighter. There are different views about the origin of this community, but according to a legend, King Hari Singhdev of Karnatak in India entered the territory of Nepal with some Danuwar people who later settled in the southern part of the country.

Danuwars are thin, tall, and dark skinned. They are shy and do not like to harm others in any way. They speak Maithili, one of the regional languages, as well as Nepali. Men wear short tunics and, sometimes, shirts, but most of the time they wear nothing on the upper part of the body. Women wear a sari and *cholo,* a blouse with long sleeves. Women also tattoo their hands and legs.

Danuwars prefer to settle in larger groups, although their lifestyle is very simple. Their traditional house is made of mud walls and thatched with straw, and is one story high with a small porch leading to the front entrance. Bamboo and small tree branches are used as supporting poles for the structure. Except for a small smoke outlet near the kitchen, there is no real ventilation. In each Danuwar house there is a *kothi,* a clay container for storing food grains. Typically, they use earthen containers for daily use.

Marriage at an early age is common among Danuwars. Often, the girl is older than the boy; typical ages would be 12–15 for the girl, 8–10 for the boy. The reason for the older bride is that she can look after the household chores. Couples may also marry between the age of 15 and 20, and widows are permitted to remarry.

The main festivals celebrated by Danuwars are Maghe Sankranti (January–February), Jurshital (March–April), Dasain (September–October), and Tihar (October–November). Danuwars are Hindus and pantheists with Kali, Kamla, Bhimsen, and Rajdhami as their lineage gods. In addition, each family contributes to the worship of the village god, Dihabar, once a year. Favorite Danuwar dances are *gomna mela, brijabhanu, sheet basant, rani saranga, salhes, gopichandra, alha rudal,* and *karikha nach.* Their dances feature very ornate movements of the hands, legs, heads, and eyes. Most dances have both religious and social significance and are performed on occasions such as weddings and festivals. Songs and dances recount the good deeds of ancient kings and queens, such as how they dug wells and constructed shelter for travelers.

Agriculture is their main livelihood, but Danuwars are also fond of fishing, which provides an important contribution to their diet. They do not sell their catch but prefer to dry the fish for future use. They have their own traditional system of health care, catered for and practiced by *dhami* and *jhankri* (local physicians). Danuwars wrap their dead with fishnet, then a piece of white cloth; after this preparation the corpse is cremated on the bank of a river or stream.

Gurung

The community of about 424,700 Gurungs is principally concentrated in central Nepal in Syanja, Kaski, Manang, Lamjung, and Gorkha districts. There are many different views about the origin of this community and the name Gurung. In their language, they refer to themselves as Tamu, from *ta,* horse, and *mu,* man, signifying trader of horses.

Gurungs are short, stocky, and have slanted eyes and broad faces with flat noses. They are Mongoloid in appearance. Male Gurungs wear a sleeveless jacket, *dhoti* (loincloth), *patuka* (a sash wrapped around the waist), cap, and turban. Women wear a bodice, *phariya* (a type of long skirt) and *patuka.* Women's ornaments include a nose pendant, earrings, amulets, colored glass and silver coin bracelets, and necklaces of gold, silver coins, or colorful beads.

Gurungs live in large villages, probably the largest settlements in the midlands. They prefer to live on the upper elevations of steep hills and tend to have fields in terraces on the hill or on the valley floor (Plate 6). Gurungs build two-story houses with a narrow entrance and small windows for ventilation. On the ground floor, there is a kitchen and a storeroom; the upper floor is used for sleeping. The house is neatly painted with red or white clay; window frames are painted black with a paint obtained from the bark of *Alnus nepalensis* and *Juglans regia.* Some Gurungs west of Pokhara also construct unique, elliptical or oblong houses with conical roofs. Gurungs keep some open space in front of the house for drying grains and keeping various household goods. This front yard is also important as a place for festivals and other ceremonies.

Agriculture and animal husbandry are the main sources of income for Gurungs. However, service in the Indian army and Gurkha regiments of the British army is also an important source of income. Nowadays, they also engage in business and trade.

Their language has a close affinity to the Tibeto-Burmese language groups. Gurungs are Buddhists, and their religious activities are performed by the *lama, klehepre,* and *pachyu,* their priests, who use written documents to guide them in their religious practices. In many aspects, Gurung customs and traditions resemble Tibetan ones. The main festival of Gurungs is Lhosar, the festival of the new year, similar to that of the Tibetans (and Sherpas) except that Gurungs observe it in December, 45 days before the Tibetans. Buddha Jayanti or the birthday of Gautama Buddha (April–May) is also observed with enthusiasm; during Buddha Jayanti they prepare fine dishes and gather together to wish each other a happy life. Dances include *ghantu, sorathi, maruni, churka,* and *jhora,* which provide important means of entertainment. Another form of relaxation is the *rodhi* (*ro,* to sleep, *dhi,* house), the house for sleeping and relaxation. This is like a club where unmarried boys and girls gather to sing and dance after a hard day's work in the fields. The *rodhi* is under the supervision of a woman, the *rodhin* mother.

Marriage is arranged and settled by the parents. The boy and girl are introduced to each other, and if they like each other, marriage is agreed. Traditional rites such as funerals are performed by the *lama* or *pachyu;* for instance, funeral processions are led by a *lama* blowing a conch shell. Immediately in front of the dead body, female members carry a white cloth called *kyankui* (the cloth to lead the way) and sprinkle parched rice on the path ahead. The body is buried a short distance from the village.

Lepcha

Long ago, Lepchas were cave dwellers. Over time, they built small huts of bamboo, straw, and mud at the bases of hills and mountains. It is believed that about the year 1800, 800 Lepcha families entered the area of the district of Ilam in eastern Nepal from Darjeeling, Kalimpong, and Sikkim in India during the reign of the seventh ruler of Sikkim. The Lepcha population in eastern Nepal numbers about 4826.

Generally, Lepchas resemble Rais and Limbus in appearance as well as in rituals. Lepchas have five subtribes: Sauden Yu, Lingsing Yu, Hi Yu, Karthak Yu, and Thikung Salanka. But some Lepcha subtribes differ according to location; in the district of Ilam the subtribes are Sangen Yu, Pheng Yu, and Namchhamu, and in the vicinity of the small town of Namche, Solukhumbu district, the subtribe is Namchi Yu.

Lepchas worship most of the gods and goddesses of Rais and Limbus. In addition, Lepchas consider that gods and goddesses reside on the tops of mountains, so they worship hills and mountains. The priest of Lepchas is called *bung-thing*, who performs all the sacred performances of the tribe. They use ginger, *Zingiber officinale* (*aduwa* in Nepali) in all their religious performances. *Ashtachyo* and *Namthar* are the religious books of the Lepchas. Lepchas worship the Himalayan mountain Kanchenjunga (8586 m) on a full-moon night in March, considering it the day of creation of the Lepchas. On this occasion, all family members assemble to sing and dance. According to Lepcha religion, there is no distinction among humans: all are equal and all the children of the same creator. They consider themselves specialists in magico-religious performances and herbal treatment.

When someone dies, the *bung-thing* comes to the family of the deceased. The priest chants hymns, addressing the corpse, chanting that there is no relation between the dead body and the living family members. After that, the clothes and ornaments are removed from the dead body, the body is bathed with lukewarm water, and it is clothed with a new set of garments. The head is wrapped in a white cloth, a 1-rupee coin is put on the forehead, and a packet of about 200 g of rice is placed beside the head. The body is taken out of the house through the window or by breaking the wall of the house instead of removing it through the main door. Generally, the body is buried, but today, in some cases, it is cremated. The *bung-thing* writes on the cremated ground words that say no living soul comes there. From the funeral ground, the funeral party returns to the house, where the priest purifies the house as well as the funeral party, sprinkling water with nine twigs from different species of plants. On the third day after the death, the local beer, an egg, and some food items are placed on the cremation area, symbolizing the dead's share. On the seventh day, the ritual performances (*kriya karma*) are complete.

Limbu

Limbus inhabit an area from the Arun River (east of Mount Everest) to the eastern border of Nepal, an area popularly known as Limbuwan and including the districts of Taplejung, Sankhuwasabha, Dhankuta, Panchathar, Ilam, and Jhapa. Many Limbus have migrated to neighboring districts such as Morang, Dhankuta, and Sunsari, south of their original area. There are no reliable government statistics relating to the Limbu population, but according to the 1991 census their numbers are estimated to be 283,000.

Limbus are of Mongoloid appearance, and it is believed that they came to Nepal from Lhasa in Tibet. Limbus, along with the Rais and Lepchas of eastern Nepal, are together called Kirants. The traditions of these three ethnic communities speak of Kirants living in a large, fertile valley in central Nepal. It is possible that the Kirants of eastern Nepal are related to Newars, the original people of the Kathmandu Valley.

The Limbus have their own language, which has been identified as a Tibeto-Burman Himalayan dialect. It has its own script, the *sirijonga*, which is not typical of the many local languages of Nepal. They worship their own god but have rites influenced by Buddhism from Tibet, and Hindu-Tantric rites from the south. Limbus build two-story houses on hillsides or on terraced ground. With some exceptions, the houses are thatched with grass and painted with white and red clay paint; window frames are painted black. Those who have some money attach a veranda to the house.

Limbus are said to be honest and simple, but with tempers that may lead them to kill. They work hard on their farmland and produce crops such as rice (*Oryza sativa*), wheat (*Triticum aestivum*), maize (*Zea mays*), millet (*Eleusine coracana*), potatoes (*Solanum tuberosum*), and mustard (*Brassica napus*). They also grow temperate climate fruits and tobacco for their own use. Most of them keep some cattle for milk, manure, and tilling the land. They keep goats, pigs, and chickens, mostly for meat. They do not work in the field during *aunsi* (new moon), *purnima* (full moon), and festival days. They are fond of liquor and beer and generally drink *jand,* a local beer prepared from millet. Limbus have also served in the military and the police for numerous generations and earn reasonable amounts of money from these jobs.

Limbus have two main types of marriage: arranged (*niks-ingma mekkhim*) and free choice (*nanumna khemma mekkhim*). In arranged marriages, the bridegroom's family initiates negotiations via a team of matchmakers. Otherwise, marriage may take place in one of two ways: elopement without prior consent of the parents (*nanumna khemma mekkhim*) or the boy making his choice of the girl and forcing her to elope (*khumna mekkhim*), with the latter practice slowly decreasing. Courting by young people is done during communal events such as the rice dance (*yarakma*), which is the main place to bring boys and girls of varied interests together for singing, dancing, and getting to know each other.

Rituals for children are numerous among the Limbus. It is believed that the fate of a child is decided by a god, Hang, within 4 days of the child's birth, during which time the Limbus keep their house neat and clean to please Hang. The newborn's naming ceremony (*nwaran*) is performed by a priest, the *phedangma*. This ceremony is performed on the third day for a girl, the fourth for a boy; the child's real name and nickname are decided by the *phedangma*. In odd-numbered months for a girl child, even-numbered for a boy, the senior member of the family feeds rice to the child; the event is also celebrated with dances and feasts.

The haircutting ceremony (*chudakarm*) is performed for boys between 3 and 5 months of age. The maternal uncle cuts his hair, and the maternal aunt collects it in a *tapari* (a bowl made of the leaves of broad-leaved plants) and throws it into a stream or river that is considered holy.

When someone dies in a Limbu family, the family fires a gun to inform relatives and neighbors. They bury the dead and build a triangular wall around the grave if the deceased is female, rectangular if male. The *phedangma* announces the *jutho chokhyaune* (purification of the impure), a ceremony performed with feast and alcoholic beverages. The spouse and sons mourn a whole year, other family members 10 days, by wearing white clothes and abstaining from any religious functions. After the *phedangma* performs the rituals, the house and family of the dead are considered pure.

Magar

It is estimated that the Magars entered Nepal around 1100 B.C. The main districts where they live are Jajarkot, Rukum, Myagdi, Baglung, Pyuthan, Parbat, Gorkha, and Tanahu in western and central Nepal, and Sindhuli and Udaypur toward eastern Nepal. The Magars have subsequently migrated to most parts of Nepal. On the basis of language, customs, and geographical distribution, the Magars are divided into Barha Magarat Magar, Atha Magarat Magar, high-mountain Magars, Chhantyal, and other Magars. On the whole, these four groups do not differ in their original traditions and other social affairs. Within the various Magar communities, there are also different clans: Aale, Benglasi, Budhathoki, Dharti, Thapa, Pun, Rana, Gurungachan, and Thumsing. The Magar population is estimated to be 1,320,900.

Magars are short and stocky, and considered very honest and loyal. Male Magars wear a short tunic, shirt, and vest. Female Magars wear a *cholo* (blouse with long sleeves), a short wrap instead of a full-length *sari* (skirt), and a *patuka* (sash wrapped around the waist) as a belt. The women are fond of wearing a lot of ornaments, especially during festivals.

Magars prefer to marry within their own caste. Generally, the members of the groom's family propose marriage to the bride's family. This type of arrangement is known as *magi bibaha,* or proposed marriage. In *magi bibaha,* members of the boy's side, including the matchmaker, go to the house of the girl with a wooden pot (*theki*) full of yogurt. If the parents of the girl accept the yogurt, it means they agree to give her daughter in marriage. After that, the father of the groom along with the matchmaker go to the house of the bride to fix the date of the wedding. Love marriage and elopement are also prevalent. The system of marriage among Magars is mostly similar to that in other communities yet there are some very interesting alternatives. In a system of marriage called *jari,* a married woman is taken away for marriage by another person. The second husband has to reimburse all expenses of the first wedding to the first husband, then the second marriage is considered legitimate. But the *jari* system of marriage is becoming less common. Another system of marriage is *keti chhopne* (to capture the girl). A girl of 17–18 who shows some affection or closeness to a boy is forcibly taken away for marriage, and this is considered a valid marriage. Other traditions and customs of Magars resemble those of the Gurungs.

Magars living in western Nepal build small egg-shaped houses thatched with grass. They also build two-story houses roofed with grass thatching, wooden planks, or slates. Materials used for house building depend on what is available locally and the Magar family's investment. Houses are painted white or red, depending on the availability of natural paint in the surrounding area.

Mooshar

Mooshars are probably the most traditional of the communities of the Terai of southern Nepal. They are concentrated in the Morang, Saptari, Siraha, Dhanusha, and Mahottari districts. Their population is estimated to be 135,170.

Mooshars are dark skinned. Their traditional huts are made of mud walls, straw, bamboo, and reeds. Socially and economically they lag far behind other ethnic groups. Their literacy rate is almost nil. They do not have their own agricultural land and often only own a small hut surrounded by a small garden. As a result, they depend on wage earnings and buy daily necessities like food grains from their wages. When they do not get work, they go hungry for a day or two. Unlike other ethnic groups that have some metal kitchenware, Mooshars mostly use earthen containers in the house.

Mooshars clothe themselves very meagerly. Men wear a small *langauti* (loincloth) and sometimes a small turban. Women cover their body with a short *sari* (skirt). Men and women wear shirts and blouses only during festivals and other important occasions.

Mooshars are fully dependent on local therapy for their health care. Whenever they have any ailments, they worship their gods and goddesses, and the local healer for their community prescribes plant-based medicine (Plate 7).

Mooshars follow the Hindu religion. Their favorite deities are Dinabhadri and Dihabar, and they observe festivals such as Fagu (February–March), Jursital (March–April), Chaurchan (July–August), and Dasain (September–October). During these festivals, Mooshars celebrate by throwing muddy water at each other, which signifies the forgetting of any enmity. They prepare a sweet drink by mixing molasses with water. They speak Maithili, a regional language. Like the Danuwars, Mooshars marry early, but unlike the Danuwars the bride is not usually older than the groom.

Newar

Newars are the indigenous people of the Kathmandu Valley. Over time, and as a result of persecution during Rana times, many Newars have been scattered outside the valley and continue mostly in the trading profession. According to the 1991 census the population of Newars is 1 million.

Newars are well known for their arts and cultural traditions. They have created a distinct architectural tradition in and around the Kathmandu Valley and in the locations of their diaspora. The traditional arts and architecture of the Newars received international recognition when the Newar artist Arniko introduced the pagoda style of architecture into China in the fourteenth century. Although there are many variations in today's Newar dwellings, traditional Newar dwellings in the Kathmandu Valley are built in small areas along the narrow streets, and courtyards or quadrangles (*bahal*). The houses are three or four stories high. The ground floor (*chhyali*) is generally used for storage space and for keeping animals, as it is the coldest part of the house. The first floor (*matan*) consists of small bedrooms and rooms for visitors. The *matan* rooms have small windows for privacy and safety. On the second floor (*chota*) the living room is larger and the windows are also larger. There are, typically, larger bedrooms, a storeroom (*dhukuti*), and rooms for knitting, weaving, and other work. This floor has better light and ventilation. The attic floor (*baiga*) accommodates the kitchen, dining room, and shrine room (*puja kotha*). The kitchen is more hygienic as shoes are not allowed on this floor. The *puja kotha* is located on this top floor because gods are never placed below humans.

The main occupations of Newars are agriculture and trade. In addition, they engage in business and in pottery, metal, stone, and wood crafts. Most Newars are followers of the Buddhist religion, but there is a splendid blend of Buddhism and Hinduism in all Newar families.

From birth to death, Newars have rich rites and rituals. The *didi aji*, the traditional midwife, takes care of the birth of a child and serves the mother and child for a month. After the birth, the parents and *didi aji* become ritually impure and are not supposed to do any auspicious tasks. On the sixth day, purifying religious activities known as *macha bu bynakegu* are performed. *Namakaran,* the naming rite, takes place when the family astrologer, using astrological data, gives the name of a child. The maternal uncle of a child arranges for a feast on this occasion. At the age of 5–7 months, *ja nakegu,* the rice feeding ceremony, is performed.

Other rituals in a child's life include the haircutting ceremony, *busakha,* at 3–7 years, and the fixing of the loincloth, *kaita puja,* at about 11 years, for a male child. The roles of the maternal uncles and the paternal aunts are important in *busakha*. In *kaita puja* a loincloth is tied onto the child by the chief of the clan, and later by the maternal uncle; *kaita puja* signifies advancement into self-guidance and self-control.

At 5–11 years a Newar girl undergoes *ihi,* the symbolic marriage of a virgin girl to Vishnu. It is believed that a girl will never be a widow after undergoing this ritual since she has been married to a god who never dies. *Ihi* symbolizes the deep respect for feminine chastity and guarantees the girl's freedom to choose a groom as her life partner. During *ihi,* the girl's body is measured with a cotton thread known as *kumbha-ka* (*kumbha,* human body, and *ka,* thread), which she subsequently wears to signify that she will remain chaste until her actual wedding to a human husband. *Barha* takes place when a girl has her first menstruation. A girl is kept in complete isolation from all males and away from the light of the sun for 12 days. Before the dawn of the twelfth day, the purification rite takes place. The girl, dressed in a gala outfit that is mostly red, pays homage to the sun. The *nakin* (wife of the head of the family, the *nayo*) adorns the *barha* girl with

vermilion powder, combs her hair, offers *sagun* (fried geese eggs, fish, meat, yogurt) and fine clothing. *Purna kalash* (the holy water jar) adorned with *dapswan* (*Jasminum multiflorum*) is symbolically worshipped by the girl with the hope that her life will be like the flower-wreathed *purna kalash.*

Newar marriages are generally arranged by negotiation through a mediator, the *lami*. Relatives also extend a helping hand in this negotiation. When the families of the bride and the groom agree to marriage, the groom confirms the betrothal by offering betel nuts (*Areca catechu*), sweets, fruits, ornaments, and clothes to the bride. This process is known as *gwe bigu*. The most auspicious date and time of the wedding is settled by the astrologer, and a procession goes to the bride's house to bring her to the groom. At the groom's house, the *nakin* receives the bride at the main entrance and performs a rite known as *honke,* which symbolizes their unity for life. *Honke* is followed by *chipa thike,* tasting of 84 dishes by the bride and groom, as a symbol of conjugal union. *Sapa pyaye* is another feature of the wedding: dressing, decoration, and ornamentation of the bride by the groom. *Khwa swey* (monitoring the bride's physical being) and *didi chyayeke* (reception of the new groom) are two rites performed in the groom's house on the fourth evening of the marriage. The bride's relatives visit the groom's house to see how the new bride is doing at her new home. The two families exchange betel nuts, signifying deepening kinship, followed by a final feast.

Later rites of the Newars include *janko,* the old age ceremony. It is celebrated in three stages. The first is *bhim rath arohan,* accession to the superior caravan, celebrated at the age of 77 years, 7 months, 7 days, 7 *ghadis* (hours), and 7 *pals* (minutes). The second and third *janko* are performed a few years later. The *janko* man or woman is seated in a wooden *khat,* a box-like chariot, and pulled by relatives around a religious location in honor of his or her long life. Newars cremate the body of the deceased by the bank of a river. A series of rites are performed until the thirteenth day after death. Monthly, bimonthly, and yearly *shraddha,* homage to the departed soul, continue for a year, often longer.

Rai

The term Rai refers to 10–18 major tribes or subtribes, including the Athapahariya, Bantawa, Chamling, Khaling, Kulung, and Thulung. Each tribe has its own language, culture, and rituals, but the tribes treat themselves as a single group, collectively known as Rai (Kirat Rai). According to the census of 1991, the Rai population is 501,800. Over time, Rais became more populous in a number of eastern hill districts such as Solukhumbu, Okhaldhunga, Khotang, Udaypur, Sankhuwasabha, Bhojpur, Terhathum, and Dhankuta. According to the religious epic, the *Rigveda,* they came to Nepal from Kangra (India) in 1200 B.C. when they were chased by the Aryans. It is now agreed that Rais are the earliest settlers of ancient Nepal (Baral 1997).

Rais are considered brave, hardworking, and warrior-like. They engage in agriculture, business, industry, and the armed forces such as the Gurkha regiments of the British army. Male Rais wear a tunic, trousers, cap, turban, and jacket with a handkerchief in the upper pocket. They carry the Nepalese curved knife, *khukuri,* in a wooden sheath hanging from the waist. Female Rais wear a *cholo* (blouse with long sleeves), handwoven black *sari* (skirt), *patuka* (sash wrapped around the waist), and *odhane* (shawl). Ornaments include a bangle on the wrist, a necklace of precious coins, and different types of ornaments on the nose, ears, and head. *Phuli* and *bulaki* are jewelry for the nose, *dhungri* are earring and studs for the ear, and anklets and one or two rings may be worn on the toes. Rai and Limbu women also wear hair clips and a large, round, golden ornamental flower on the head.

Rais are devoted to their traditions and customs. The *bijuwa* is the religious priest who performs all the religious activities in a Rai community. Khamang is their lineage god, an idol of whom they keep in a corner of the house in an earthen pot. Preparation of any food in the house is first offered to this god. *Cannabis sativa* is worshipped for protection from boils and pimples and to prevent the birth of a handicapped child. They worship the serpent god, Nagi, to increase the fertility of the soil; in addition, they worship the land god, Niwa Bhuma. Fish, meat, locally brewed liquor, and beer are essential for social and religious activities and for feasts of the Rai people. Rais are fond of alcoholic beverages.

Among Rais, there are four types of marriage systems, similar to those of some of the other ethnic communities. Rais are very fond of songs, dances, and feasts. Most Rai youth play musical instruments such as the *binayo,* made of a bamboo strip and blown with the mouth like a reed instrument, and *murchanga,* a triangular wind instrument made of iron. *Chandi nach* is the original Rai dance.

Death in a Rai family is announced to relatives and neighbors by firing a gun. The body is either buried or cremated; each Rai community maintains its own cemetery on a hilltop near the village for those wishing to be buried. Rituals of preparing a body for burial include pouring some water on the body and placing essentials by its side. These essentials include a *khukuri* (the curved knife), *chulesi* (kitchen knife), bow and arrow, hookah, *chilim* (pipe for smoking tobacco), and a pot of local beer. When the mourners return from the funeral, they erect a tree branch peeled of its bark in front of the house to symbolize death in the family. After funeral duties, the *bijuwa* observes death rituals after 3, 5, 7, or 10 days, according to the custom of the family. On this occasion, the *bijuwa* slaughters a chicken and sprinkles beer in and around the house to purify the house and family members.

Raute

I had heard much about the Raute ethnic group from anthropologists who described them as hunters and plant gatherers. However, all my attempts to meet Rautes were in vain. One day, during a plant collecting trek, I happened to meet two local villagers while I was climbing up from the base of a mountain to spend the night in a small village on top. The two villagers were descending and coming out of a dense forest. I told them that there were no villages in the valley below; they stopped and just asked for cigarettes. One of them uttered the word Raute and pointed down toward the valley where they said they would sleep the night. Thus in a chance meeting I ran into a pair of Rautes and was even shown their village. The next morning I went down to meet the pair; they were talking inside a temporary hut and revealed a wealth of information on plants among this elusive community.

Historical evidence is meager on the origin of the Rautes. They themselves claim to be of Thakuri (Indo-Nepali group) ancestry, however, and say they are Ban ko Raja, king of the forest. On the basis of language, culture, and history, Reinhard (1976) and Yatri (1983) relate these communities to the Raji, a tribe of the Kumaon people in Uttar Pradesh, India. Rautes are nomadic and roam the forested area of western Nepal, living by hunting and gathering useful plants. Their population is estimated to be 400–600. Rautes have their own language, Khamchi, which is different from other languages of the Himalayan communities. It has not been corrupted much by influence from the dominant languages of the region.

Rautes are short, stocky, and dark skinned. Their eyes are beady and deeply inset; their teeth are small and closely set in two thin rows. Their other features in common are straight shoulders, square flat chest, short neck, short arms and legs, and very little facial hair. These shy, amiable people do not like intruders and do not permit visitors in their encampments. They select campsites secretively and move as soon as they think outsiders have come to know where their encampment is. They never stop in a village for the night and always carry a sickle, which is passed through a wooden holder. The sickle holder, which is fastened to a belt, rattles rhythmically when the Rautes walk.

Rautes live in temporary huts made of leaves and branches of trees to provide protection from the sun and heavy downpours. These huts or shacks are roundish, crudely formed, and barely 1.5–2 m high. They do not sleep inside the huts but lie down outside them. Tools, utensils, and foodstuffs are stored inside the shacks, which outsiders are not allowed to enter. The monsoon is a very cruel season for the Rautes as cooking with wet firewood is difficult. Rautes do not stay long in any one location; they move from place to place with the change of seasons and the duration of their trade with rural communities. Their mobility also depends on the availability of wild food plants and monkeys, their favorite meat. Another inducement for the Rautes to stay in one place is the availability of smooth, relatively soft-wooded trees such as *Alnus nepalensis, Boehmeria rugulosa, Bombax ceiba, Pinus roxburghii, Rhododendron arboreum,* and *Toona ciliata* because from these plants they craft wooden articles and utensils that they trade with other tribes. When they move, the huts are left intact or burned.

Rautes have very simple marriage systems. When the wedding date is fixed, the ceremony is simple and short; it is celebrated with a simple preparation of homemade liquor and monkey meat. Generally, Rautes marry between 15 and 18 years of age and there is no restriction of kith and kin. A Raute widow is not allowed to marry again, and she is expected to live in a hut apart from the other huts. Rautes believe that it is a bad omen to see a widow when setting out for a journey or hunting.

Satar

The Santhals of the Chota Nagpur district, Bihar, India, are considered to have migrated to the Terai of Nepal about the year 1800. After arriving in Nepal, they were known as the Satars. The scholars consider them to be descended from the Dravidian people. At first, they arrived in very small numbers in far eastern Nepal in the Jhapa district. Afterward, they moved to neighboring Morang. The Satar population is estimated to be 26,000.

Satars have black skin pigmentation and sparse body and facial hair. Their eyes are dark brown to black and slightly oblique. The nose is depressed at the base, broad and fleshy at the tip. A large mouth can also be characteristic.

Satar houses are wattle and mud structures approximately square in shape. Their villages are clustered together but scattered over an area consisting of Satar houses only.

Satars follow the Hindu religion. They are animists, however, worshipping elements such as the sun (Thakuriya), mountain (Mrang Badu) and fire (Mode Ko). Manas is their lineage god. They also worship other goddesses, including Kali Mai and Durga Mai among others. Worship is done as a community, mostly with sacrifices of fowls, pigeons, hens, ducks, and goats. The Hinduistic way of worshipping god by bathing and burning incense for the deity is followed by Satars in their rituals.

Satars have their own social organization; all members of this organization are elected. The Majhi Ildam, chairman, is the decision maker. The Pranik, secretary, and Jog Pranik, joint secretary, judge criminal cases. Community-related work such as marriage is dealt with by the Jag Majhi, and the Gudit acts as assistant, guard, and caretaker. There are ten types of marriage among Satars: (1) *kirin vhu vapla,* in which the bride is purchased, (2) *tunki dipil vapla,* poor man's marriage in which the expense is nominal, (3) *hirom chetan vapla,* the man marries polygamously because the previous wife or wives did not bear any children, (4) *sanya vapla,* marriage of a widow, (5) *ghardi jvai vapla,* the potential husband is forced to sleep at the woman's house, (6) *golat vapla,* the man's parents have to give one of their daughters in a sort of exchange to get a wife for their son, (7) *jvai kirinok vapla,* the man has to be bought to cover an unmarried girl's pregnancy, (8) *nirvolok vapla,* a woman who likes a man enters his house forcibly, (9) *itut vapla,* the man expresses his liking for a girl, and when the girl indicates her agreement the man smears vermilion powder (*sindur*) on her head, and (10) *apangir vapla,* marriage occurs after elopement. Child marriage is also common among Satars. Divorce is decided by the social organization.

Family members stop worshipping gods and goddesses when a Satar woman enters her eighth month of pregnancy. They consider the family polluted after that period till the birth of the child. The naming ceremony, Chatier, is performed on second, third, or fifth day after the birth. The name of a deceased grandfather or grandmother is given to the child. The mother cooks food and serves all present at the ceremony, after which she is considered purified. Satars believe in rebirth and the cyclic order of the universe. The dead are buried.

Sherpa

Sherpas are the main inhabitants of the northeastern part of Nepal. The word Sherpa is derived from the Tibetan words *shar,* east, and *va,* settler, thus denoting an inhabitant of the east. Sherpas moved from Tibet and first settled in the Khumbu area of the Solukhumbu district at the base of Mount Everest. According to the 1991 census, Sherpas number about 110,000.

The Sherpa dwelling is generally a two-story house with stone walls. Livestock, firewood, and potatoes are kept on the ground floor. The upper floor has a fire pit and living rooms. The front wall has several windows for ventilation. On the side and back walls, shelves and cupboards are used for storage; shelves are filled with shining pots. The rooms of rich families are painted colorfully and have gold-plated or bronze Buddhist images.

Agriculture is the mainstay of the Sherpa community, with potatoes (*Solanum tuberosum*), maize (*Zea mays*), barley (*Hordeum vulgare*), buckwheat (*Fagopyrum esculentum*), and millet (*Eleusine coracana*) the principal crops. Sherpas also keep herds of yak, sheep, and other domestic animals, which are sources of income. Sherpas travel widely, reaching as far south as Kathmandu or the plains of the Terai. They cross the northern border through Nangpa La (5486 m) into Tibet to trade salt, wool, food grains, and other household commodities. Mountaineering has spurred the Sherpa economy; many Sherpas are employed as guides and porters in trekking. Mountaineering has brought the Sherpas into close contact with non-Tibetan-speaking people of Nepal and with foreigners.

Sherpas observe a number of colorful festivals. Lhosar is celebrated on the occasion of their new year, which begins around the end of February. They celebrate it with feasting, drinking, dancing, and singing. Most Sherpas who are away from their villages return to join their families for Lhosar. Dumdze is observed in the village *gompa* (monastery) for a week during July. This festival signifies prosperity, good health, and the welfare of the entire nation, not only the village. The *lamas* worship the deities while the villagers gather in the *gompa* in the evening and have their share of food and drink; the young people dance and sing merrily. Mani-Rimdu is a dance drama with origins in the Tibetan theatrical genre and lasts for a week. It is performed by the monks of the Tenboche and Chiwong monasteries in November or early December and at the Thami monastery in May. This colorful display is enjoyed by people from the surrounding villages and by foreigners who trek or climb in the region. Yardzang (November–December) is observed on the pasturelands when the people are tending their cattle. All these festivals include the worship of deities and merry dancing, singing, and drinking.

According to Bista (1980), marriage among Sherpas follows the tradition of polyandry. Two brothers may take a woman as their joint wife; more than two brothers are not allowed to marry a woman. Sometimes two brothers marry two wives together, whom they share. The brothers go together in the wedding procession and take part in the wedding activities, establishing equal right over each wife. Marriage between cousins, prevalent in some ethnic groups, is not allowed among Sherpas.

Boys and girls usually choose their partners themselves, but sometimes the parents arrange partners for their sons and daughters. An arranged marriage is completed in four stages. First, the relatives of the boy go to the girl's house with some *chhang*, rice beer. If the girl's parents accept the *chhang*, it indicates the acceptance of the proposal. Second, the girl's parents arrange a party, serving *chhang*, meat, and rice. The men and women in their beautiful dresses and ornaments attend the party. Third, the boy's parents send some relatives to the girl's house to fix the date of marriage. Finally, a procession from the boy's side goes to bring the bride back to the boy's house; they spend a day and a night at the bride's house, and the next day the groom and the procession leave with the bride. The bride's parents, other relatives, and friends give a dowry and gifts to the bride. After marriage, the groom's juniors and colleagues attach "father" after the groom's regular name, which means that the groom should have a child before the wife comes to visit the house of a junior. Having a child greatly raises the social status of a groom's family.

Tamang

The important districts of Tamang settlement are Kabhre-palanchok, Dhading, Sindhupalchok, and Lalitpur in central Nepal. The estimated population of the community is 989,820. Tamangs are amiable, stout, and strong, with brown or light complexions and slanted eyes. Tamangs generally settle in groups but some families live in isolated places, primarily because scarce land and agriculturally difficult hillsides limit the number of inhabitants in an area. Most settlements are found at elevations of 1400–2500 m, and it is not uncommon for a single family to own plots on the valley floor for rice (*Oryza sativa*) and near timberline for other crops such as potatoes (*Solanum tuberosum*) and millet (*Eleusine coracana*).

Tamangs build two-story houses, using stones, mud, bamboo, and branches of trees (Plate 8). The roof is thatched with grass but Tamangs of the Rasuwa district thatch the roof with planks of *Abies spectabilis* wood. The ground floor is used for sleeping and the kitchen, and the upper floor is used for storage. A separate hut houses domestic animals. The clothes resemble those of Magars; Tamang women wear ornaments whenever they go out of the house. As in other communities, males and females divide the agricultural labor. Men do the plowing and spading; women help in the planting of rice seedlings and weeding (Plate 9). Tamangs use composted fertilizer in the fields. During the peak of the agricultural season, children take care of domestic animals and women carry small babies with them when they go to work in the field, returning home with the baby, fodder for the animals, and fuelwood for cooking. In addition, the women husk and winnow the grains, getting little help from the men (Plates 10, 11), indicative of the inequality of labor between the men and women in almost all ethnic communities in Nepal.

The purest Tamang groups still follow the pre-Buddhist religion, Bon, which has a remote Tibetan heritage. At the lower elevations, some Tamangs have adopted Indo-Nepali traditions and mingle Hindu rituals with their own. Most Tamangs follow the Buddhist religion and perform religious activities at the village *gompa* (monastery). Lha is their lineage god. They sing their own folk songs (*hwai, tamb keitan, deita,* and *phawar*) during festive occasions. *Dora, damphu,* and *saraswati* are some of their favorite dances. Marrying the son or daughter of a maternal uncle is common among Tamangs. From early on, the son of a sister is called *jwain* (son-in-law), and the son or daughter of *mama* (maternal uncle) is called *sala* (for a son-in-law) or *sali* (for a daughter-in-law). The son of an aunt is called *bhena*, and the daughter, *solteni*. Thus there is a traditional custom for establishing nuptial relations among *sala, bhena, sali,* and *solteni*.

In Tamang culture, the body of the deceased is kept for a day and a *lama* performs the religious activities. The corpse is then cremated and a *mane* (prayer wheel) erected over the cremation ground. Favorite articles of the deceased are kept inside the *mane*, in the belief that they are used by the dead in the afterlife. On the forty-fifth day after death, the *lama* performs religious dances for the peace of the dead soul; the dances continue 1–9 days.

Tharu

There are differing views about the origin of the Tharus. According to one school of thought, they are the descendants of the Shakyas, the clansmen of Gautama Buddha, who was born in Nepal. Others believe that the Tharus came to Nepal in the thirteenth century from the Thar Desert in India as refugees fleeing from the Muslim invaders (Lal 1983). Hagen (1960) believed that Tharus belong to the ancient Nepalese population, which came from the original, autochthonous people of the subcontinent.

Over time, Tharus have moved on when the yield from their land deteriorated or when they lost their land to other people for commercial or other reasons. Thus they have spread out from their traditional habitat and can be found throughout the Terai. It is important to note that even when the Terai was avoided because of its deadly malaria, only the Tharus managed to eke out a living there.

Tharus are simple, honest, gentle, and industrious people, but as a result of their rigid religious and social structure, they labor under myths and superstitions. A Tharu wears little clothing: a meter or two of thin cotton fabric is worn as a wrap by the women, and the men use even less of the same material. Women love to cover their arms and legs with tattoo marks and also have ornate hairdressing.

Tharu villages are found in open spaces with few tall trees and consist of a dozen or more houses built close together. The houses are made of rough-hewn logs and bamboo, secured with ropes and vines, and thatched with grass. Wattle plastered with mud make the wall. The houses are always oblong and one-story high. Small holes serve as windows and there is only one doorway. One corner of the house is dedicated to the kitchen and another to sleeping quarters. Household goods, farming implements, and food are kept in the middle of the house. The floor is swept two or three times a day, so the house is always neat and clean. Pigeons fly in and out of dovecotes, and chickens and ducks wander about the courtyard. Domestic animals are kept in separate shacks.

Agriculture is the main livelihood of the Tharus but it is usually not enough to support the families. Therefore, Tharus also work as land tenants, for which they share the crop half-and-half with the landlord. They work as wage laborers for very low pay. Both male and female Tharus are very good at fishing and hunting; their hunting and fishing implements and traps are derived from bamboo and other plant fibers. Tharus go fishing whenever they have some leisure time (Plate 12).

Tharus are fond of festivities. Women dance the *zamda*, a swaying, hand-clapping dance accompanied by singing in a falsetto voice. The male dance is vigorous, colorful, and accompanied by drums. There are also many dances in which both men and women participate. The religion of the Tharus is mostly Hindu but includes belief in spirits and devils. The traditional marriage system is followed, including a payment by the groom to the bride's family called the *jhanga*. The custom of *sattapatta* (tit for tat) also prevails, in which a daughter is given in marriage to the household that has given one of their daughters in marriage. A Tharu landlord keeps Tharu servants who work in the house and live there as family members, and it is not unusual for one of them to marry into the master's family. Health care among the Tharus is the responsibility of the local *gurewa* (medicine man), who performs ancient rites of protection, blessing, and healing with the help of herbal remedies.

LANGUAGES

Nepal is a multilinguistic country and is the meeting place of Caucasoid (from the southwest), Mongoloid (from the northeast), Indo-Aryan, and Tibeto-Burman language groups. There are more than 50 varieties of languages and their dialects spoken in Nepal. Scholars of regional languages call Nepal one of the world's most linguistically rich countries.

About a dozen languages have their own scripts. About half the people speak Nepali, the official language of the country, as their mother tongue. Almost all the Nepalese understand and speak Nepali; hence it is an essential medium for bringing people into the mainstream of national affairs and allowing interethnic contact despite differences in customs, religions, and local languages.

Sanskrit has influenced the languages of Nepal. There is much diversity in the languages of the Terai, where Maithili, Bhojpuri, Hindi, and Urdu are widely spoken. The Kathmandu Valley is traditionally inhabited by Newars who speak their own language, Newari, which belongs to the Tibeto-Burman linguistic group. Maithili has a script like that of Hindi or Nepali. Languages such as Limbu and Newari have their traditional scripts but now follow Devnagari, the script used for Nepali, Sanskrit, and other languages of South Asia.

Devnagari is a phonetic script, which means that what is written is pronounced only one way and what is pronounced is written only one way, unlike English, in which a combination of letters can be pronounced in different ways (for example, "ough" in tough, through, thorough). For the vernacular names in *Plants and People of Nepal*, Devnagari has been used (except for English names) to transcribe sounds, especially for ethnic words that do not have a script of their own. The Devnagari transcriptions were then transliterated into roman text.

Devnagari has a set of 11 vowels and 33 consonants as well as a number of two or more consonants that act as single consonants. The way a sound is produced can be aspirated (with strong expulsion of a breath of air), dental (with the tongue touching the upper teeth), retroflex (produced at the roof of the mouth by curled tongue), velar or guttural (produced in the throat), or labial (produced by the lips). The panoply of sounds means that Devnagari becomes a very important tool for transcribing sounds in many different languages for future reference. Devnagari has the same punctuation as English, except that the period is denoted as a vertical line, not a dot. Devnagari has no capital letters.

In Chapter 4, vernacular names have been transcribed so that their pronunciation is as close to the real pronunciation as possible. Although there are very technical notations for re-creating non-English sounds, they tend to be approximate at best. Hence, for simplicity, such special notation has not been used. The following, however, should be noted:

Where a hyphen appears between letters (especially for Tibetan words), it denotes a break between syllables that is almost as long as the break between words.

Where *an* appears, nasalization is denoted and the pronunciation is *on* as in the French word *bon* (as in bon vivant).

Where *h* appears after a consonant, it denotes the aspirated version of the consonant. For example, *dh* is the aspirated version of *d, gh* the aspirated version of *g*, and *kh* the aspirated version of *k*.

Where *i* appears, the sound is always *ee* as in feet, not *i* as in kite. For the *i* sound in kite the combination of letters would be *ai*.

Where *u* appears, the sound is always *oo* as in choose, not *u* as in but.

RELIGIONS

Religion is an important aspect of Nepalese life, yet unlike in most other countries, religious demarcation is not very strict and most Nepalese tolerate and follow many different religions, all as one great religion. Visitors find symbols of other religions in famous religious temples and stupas and may find it very confusing and contradictory, but that is indicative of the Western "count, contrast, and measure" culture versus the collectivism and pantheism practiced in most parts of Nepal. In general, there are two main types of religion, Buddhism and Hinduism, with very few people following a very pure form of either; the majority of the population follows a mixture of the two. Hinduism dominates among the Indo-Aryans in the Terai. Followers of Buddhism are found among the Tibeto-Mongoloid groups living in the northern regions near Tibet. Minority religious communities include Muslims, who are concentrated in western Nepal, the Terai, and Kathmandu Valley. Christians are found mostly in eastern Nepal. Chepangs, Rautes, and Tharus have their own distinct religious beliefs and practices.

Historically, Nepal (especially Kathmandu) has had many different religious influences. Legend has it that Kathmandu Valley was a lake (confirmed by geological evidence) in which there was an island that had a lotus growing on it. Hearing the divine apparition of the island, Bodhisattva Manjushree arrived from Tibet and found the island inaccessible because of the water around it. Hence, it is said that he cut the limestone ridge at present-day Chobhar in the south of Kathmandu Valley to drain the water and make the lakebed habitable. The island (now a hill in the west of Kathmandu Valley) was consecrated to the Adi Buddha (the original Buddha) by Manjushree; the spot came to be known as Swayambhunath, with its large Buddhist stupa, one of the oldest relics in all of South Asia. The stupa also has the Buddha's eyes, visible from around the valley. It is said that since Buddha did not want people to be cruel to animals, Kathmandu's famed farmers never used animal plows but instead used an old-fashioned spade that made for very strenuous manual tilling.

It is believed that the Kirants (Tibeto-Burman), considered to be ancestors of Limbus and Rais, and most likely also of the Newars of Kathmandu, ruled Kathmandu Valley (known as Nepal Valley until the 1950s) from around 700 B.C. It is the Kirants who may have brought Buddhism to the central Himalaya around 100 B.C. Gautama Buddha was born in 563 B.C. in Lumbini in the central Terai of Nepal, yet Lumbini was not rediscovered until 1896. The rediscovery came about because the British in India went on to discover many sites of religious significance in Buddhism but were unable to locate the birthplace, Lumbini, described by ancient Chinese travelers, Fa-hsein and Hsuan Tsang. In 1896, upon hearing about a stone pillar buried in the forest in Rummindei (local name for the area), the governor of the district started an excavation and uncovered a memorial inscription on a pillar erected around 250 B.C. by the Indian emperor Ashoka to commemorate his pilgrimage to the birthplace of Gautama Buddha. The authenticity of the pillar was confirmed by the German archaeologist Alois Anton Führer. Buddhism spread through Nepal to Tibet and beyond to the East.

Kathmandu Valley itself was dominated by Hinduism, though with the spread of Buddhism the two religions coexisted along with worship of animist spirits. Although no documentary account of Kathmandu is available before the fifth century A.D., the Licchavi dynasty ruled Kathmandu Valley from the fifth to the ninth centuries and left many inscriptions and temples, proving their rule. The Licchavis were Vaishnavite (followers of Vishnu, a Hindu god) and were responsible for one of the oldest temples, Changunarayan, situated northwest of Bhaktapur, and the seventh-century statue of a reclining Vishnu in Budhanilkantha, crafted from a stone 5 m long. Over time, Hindu orthodoxy penetrated and affected many ancient religious practices, but Buddhism itself was well entrenched. Nevertheless, following the split of Buddhism, Nepal was affected more by Vajrayana (thunderbolt doctrine), which had more magic formulas and initiation cults and adjusted well to preexisting local customs.

Although the orthodoxy of Brahmanism swept most of India, it had little effect on Nepal's existing Tantric magic doctrines. Even though the rulers of Kathmandu, the Mallas, were devout Hindus, Kathmandu's unique flavor of Buddhism remained entrenched and the two faiths coexist harmoniously.

Festivals and Religious Ceremonies

"There are as many festivals as there are days in the year" is a common Nepalese saying, and given the number of ethnic groups, religious rites and rituals, gods and goddesses, it is very possible that the saying is true. Each ethnic group has its own festivals; in fact, each locality, village, and family in Nepal typically has its own unique festivities. What follows is a list of the more common festivals. Almost all the festivals have religious connotations but have been intermingled with the practicalities of an essentially agrarian society. Because festivals are typically based on the lunar calendar, the dates given are approximate.

Maghe Sankranti (January–February). Maghe Sankranti is a major winter festival. It starts on the first day of the Nepali month of Magh (January–February) and is considered an important day for Hindus. On this day, the sun leaves its southernmost position for its northward (*uttarayan*) journey, so it is similar to many solstice celebrations in Western civilizations. It is considered a celebration of the victory of warmth over cold. Hindus believe that a person who dies when the sun is on its way north is fortunate, for he will enjoy bright sunny days in his life after death. Hence, this day is an auspicious time for death. If possible, people take holy baths at the junction of holy rivers such as the *triveni* (confluence of three rivers) early in the morning. On this day, people give the Brahmin or hermit the *sidha* (a gift of a meal), which includes about 1 kg of rice (*Oryza sativa*), a handful of *daal* (lentils, *Lens culinaris*), a small bundle of spinach (*Spinacia oleracea*), a small quantity of clarified butter, molasses, a small bundle of firewood, a little salt and turmeric powder, and some money. Some people also give an earthen firepot with some hot charcoal along with the *sidha*. There are special food items for the day as well: sesame seeds (*Sesamum orientale*) are roasted until they pop like popcorn, then mixed in syrupy *jaggar* (juice from sugarcane) to form small balls known as *tilwa*. Likewise, the roots of yams (*Dioscorea bulbifera* and *D. pentaphylla*), sweet potato (*Ipomoea batatas*), and christophine (*Sechium edule*) are boiled and eaten.

Maghe Sankranti is also the day when the mother of the house wishes good health for all family members. First, offerings are made to Vishnu, the preserver god, then to Agni, the fire goddess, then to the four directions, the ghosts, and spirits. Then, mustard oil (*Brassica napus*) with seeds of fenugreek (*Trigonella foenum-graecum*) boiled in it is applied on a family member's head by the mother with wishes for good health. She distributes *tilwa*, boiled yam, a lump of clarified butter, molasses, a fried fish, and *chyura* (beaten rice). The family members sit around, basking in the sun, and enjoy their special food items. The next day the family gives a feast to their married daughters and their husbands and children.

Maha Shivaratri (February). This festival is consecrated in honor of Shiva. *Damaru*, a two-sided hourglass-like small drum; *trishul*, a trident; *bhashma*, ashes; a garland of *rudraksha*, the utrasum bead tree (*Elaeocarpus sphaericus*); and *bel patra* (leaf of *Aegle marmelos*) are the most popular symbols of Shiva, leaving aside, of course, the coiling serpents and the Shiva Linga, the phallic symbol of Shiva. The *rudraksha* beads are considered Shiva's tears of joy. These beads have medicinal value as a remedy for blood pressure; they have a varying number of longitudinal scars on the surface (the fewer lines, the more valuable the bead). Likewise, the fruit and leaves of *bel* are favorites of Shiva. The *bel* fruit also has medicinal value and continues to be used to cure various ailments, including heart ailments.

In addition, Maha Shivaratri is observed with a bath in a holy river and a fast for the day. People worship Shiva by offering flowers, garlands, *bel* fruit, sweets, and coins and by chanting prayers and hymns. On this day, the temples of Shiva are crowded with devotees. People, especially the hermits, smoke *ganja* (*Cannabis sativa*). The seeds of *dhatura*, the thorn apple (*Datura metel*), mixed with sweets are also consumed as these are favorites of Shiva.

Rato Machhendranath (late April or early May). The chariot festival of Rato Machhendranath is one of the important festivals in the Kathmandu Valley. Machhendranath is a deity of rain and good harvest, and the patron deity of the people of Kathmandu. It is said that this god was brought to Kathmandu from Kamrup in the eastern Himalaya in mythical times when there was a great drought in the country. Most of the year the deity resides in a temple in Bungmati, on the south side of Kathmandu. The ritual procession and the festival (*jatra*) take place in Patan, one of the three towns in the valley. If the chariot lands on its side, as it sometimes does, people say a national calamity is in the making for the coming year.

The festival starts on the first day of the new moon. The god's image is first bathed in holy water and repainted. It is then placed in a small ornate temple, which is mounted on an enormous chariot with four large pinewood wheels, each about 3 m in diameter. The four big wheels represent four furious Bhairab gods. The chariot has a characteristic steeple-like crown because of the many 15-m oak poles that extend from the chariot platform; these oak poles are covered with evergreen boughs of *Juniperus* and *Quercus*, which give the upper part of the chariot a green appearance. The horizontal central beam, made of pinewood, is the prow of the chariot. The prow extends about 6 m and is emblazoned on the front with a brass mask of Karkot, the mythical king of the Nags, the snake deities.

The astrologers decide the date of the god's excursion. On the chosen day, the chariot is slowly pulled through the streets of Patan by scores of men using strong ropes as long as 10 m. The chariot trundles along, stopping frequently at places where the townspeople make offerings and entertain the god with music and dances. The surrounding households indulge in feasting, drinking, and celebrating. The chariot may travel only a few hundred meters in a day. Attention is given to every detail of the god's journey because it is through his blessing that the farmers receive adequate rain in the coming monsoon season. During the journey, the main deity is followed by a smaller chariot, that of Minnath, Machhendranath's child. Finally, the chariots are parked in the open field of Jawalakhel, where (on a day fixed by the astrologers) people witness the display of the *bhoto,* the sacred, jewel-encrusted vest of Machhendranath. The precious *bhoto* is said to be the unclaimed item to which two poor farmers laid claim but were asked to assert their rightful ownership with Machhendranath as their witness; the one who was lying would die on the spot. Given the harsh punishment, neither had the courage to lay claim; hence, the *bhoto* is shown to the crowds in all four directions from the platform of the chariot, in essence, continuing the tradition of looking for the rightful owner. The showing of the *bhoto* concludes the festival of Machhendranath, and the throngs go home hoping for a good rainy season.

Gathan-Muga (early August). Gathan-Muga, also known as Ghantakarna, represents the banishment of evil spirits from a city. Effigies of the evil demons are erected at street intersections and a man painted in black (representing the demon) asks passersby for money. The painted man is made to sit on the effigy at the end of the day, when local children pull the effigy to the river or the outskirts of the city. In the ancient town of Bhaktapur, the effigy is burned in a display in public squares. In addition, households leave cooked rice on their doorsteps and nail the doors shut with iron nails; iron is meant to scare the demons away.

Gunla (mid-August). Gunla means the end of the ninth month (and beginning of the tenth) of the Newari calendar, which is a sacred month dedicated to Gautama Buddha. The festival commemorates the retreat of the rains and the teaching of the principles of the Buddha to his disciples through solitary meditation. Buddhists spend the month in prayer, fasting, and visiting shrines to the Buddha (Swayambhu, for example) with traditional musical instruments known as Gunla *bajan* (music). Monasteries are open to visitors for worshiping special images of Buddha displayed only during Gunla. The Gunla *lakhé* (masked dancer) also dances energetically on the streets, lifting sprits.

Janai Purnima (late August). On the day of this full moon (*purnima*), Hindus change their *janai,* the sacred thread worn by men. Brahmins (Hindu priests) take a holy dip in rivers and offer ablution to the gods. They then change their *janai* and proceed around town, offering their service in tying the sacred yellow thread to the populace. The Newars of Kathmandu Valley call this festival Gunhi Punhi and it is the day to have *kwati* soup, made from nine different beans. In Patan, a richly decorated *lingam,* a phallic symbol of Shiva, is raised in the middle of Kumbheswor (Kwonti) Pond. The pond is said to be filled with holy water from Gosainkunda, a lake in a high Himalayan valley of central Nepal. In Bhaktapur, a colorful procession known as Jujuya Ghintang-Gishi (king's carnival) goes around town in the evening.

Gai Jatra (late August). On Gai Jatra or Saparu (cow festival), families with members who died in the past year parade a garishly decorated cow through the city. Some also dress children as cows or ascetics to represent the family of the deceased in the procession, which goes on for the major part of the day. It is said that the sacred cow helps the departed soul cross the cosmic chasm in the afterworld. In Kathmandu, the bereaved families follow in the procession; in Patan, the participants gather in Durbar Square (an old palace square), then fall into a procession; in Bhaktapur, tall bamboo poles wrapped in cloth and topped with horns fashioned from straw are carried around the city in memory of the dead. It is also a time for gaiety, so humor is an important aspect of the day, when newspapers put out special "mad" editions, and comic dramas and street shows depict farce and satire (especially politically).

Teej (early September). Teej is a Hindu festival celebrating womanhood. It commemorates the success of Parvati, the daughter of Himalaya, in winning the hand of Shiva after intense meditation and fasting. On the first day, mothers send gifts of food and *saris* (skirts) to their daughters, and groups of women gather to feast, dance, and sing. It is common to see throngs of girls and women, wearing red *saris* and gold jewelry, going to these feasts. At midnight, women emulate the hardship of Parvati by fasting, and the second day is devoted fully to worship and meditation. The women typically start with an early bath and brush their teeth with 365 twigs of *Achyranthes aspera* (in the Terai, where it is plentiful) or *A. bidentata* (in the midlands). It is believed that that each twig represents a day of the coming year and that brushing the teeth with these plants is good for the teeth. On the third day (Rishi Panchami), women wearing red *saris* throng Shiva's temples around Nepal (the most popular is the temple of Pashupatinath in Kathmandu), singing loudly and dancing along the way. Married women ask for a happy marriage and long life for their husbands, and the unmarried girls ask for a good husband.

Indra Jatra (late September). Indra Jatra honors Indra as a god of rain and grains and is observed for 8 days in September. On the first day, an ornately decorated pine pole (locally known as *lingo*) 15 m long is erected in a colorful religious function. This ceremonial pole is divided into several *puras* (segments); each *puras* signifies a city-state. The Vedic name for Indra is Purandara, which means the great destroyer of city-states. It is said that Indra had 99 hands, which he used in destroying several enemy states. This victory was achieved only after receiving a great victory banner from Vishnu. The Nepalese have much respect for this banner, the Indra Dhwaj, which is believed to symbolize unity, strength, and peace.

There are many references in the *Rigveda* to Indra as giver of rain and grains. The festival appears to be very old and closely associated with agricultural life. According to a legend, the mother of Indra wanted the flower of *parijat* (*Nyctanthes arbor-tritis*) for Teej, a festival commemorating womanhood. As Teej was nearing, she was saddened that this flower was not available in the gardens of heaven. The dutiful son, Indra, set out to fulfill his mother's wish; he ascertained that *parijat* could be found in abundance in Kantipur (the old name for Kathmandu). Thus he assumed a normal human form and descended on Kantipur to steal the *parijat* flower. Fortune was not on his side, however, and he was caught red-handed by the local people. He was released when his mother came down to investigate. In return for his release, she gave the valley dew and fog to ripen the crops. On her return to heaven, she was followed by a long procession of departed souls. Even today, families of the recently deceased place butter lamps behind the procession of Indra Jatra around Kathmandu, symbolizing the illumination of the path toward heaven.

On the last 3 days, chariots with human representatives of the goddess Kumari (the living goddess), Bhairab, and Ganesh are pulled through the streets of old Kathmandu.

The chariot festival begins at Basantpur Square (an old palace square), across from the temple of Kumari in the heart of Kathmandu. In addition, wild street dances of masked gods and goddesses entertain the residents in various parts of town. The enraged dance of the Lakhé (a demon) and that of the two-person mask-and-frame model of Pulu-Kishi (the elephant god) are very energetic street dances, making Indra Jatra a hearty and spectacular Kathmandu Valley festival.

Dasain (September–October). Dasain celebrates the victory of virtue over evil and includes the token of a blessing by senior members of the family as well. This festival needs lots of advance preparation, including the stocking of necessary foodstuffs. Sacrificial animals such as buffalo, sheep, and goats, and fowls such as chickens, ducks, and pigeons, are bought. On the first day of the festival (Ghatasthapana), a sacred vessel (usually made of clay) is filled with river sand. Seeds of barley (*Hordeum vulgare*) and maize (*Zea mays*) are sown and allowed to grow 9 days. For the 9 days, people go to different holy places situated on riverbanks for their morning bath. On the ninth day, the mother goddess, Durga, is bathed in sacrificial blood of various animals and fowls, as seen in most Durga temples around Nepal. (For the first-time visitor, this is a very gory sight, indeed, but the Nepalese are quite accustomed to the slaughter of animals at temples.) On the tenth day, after the final ritual worship, family members dress in new clothes and are anointed with the holy water. Probably the highlight of the day is when the senior members of the family put *tika,* rice mixed with vermilion and yogurt, on the foreheads of family members and give each other bunches of the sprouted barley and maize seedlings. Unlike Indra Jatra and Rato Machhendranath, which have many street activities, Dasain is more a family affair, and family members who are away make a point of rejoining the family at least once a year during this festival. Like most Nepali festivals, Dasain ends with a large feast.

Tihar (October–November). Tihar is the festival of lights in honor of Laxmi, the goddess of wealth. The festival lasts 5 days and is marked by the worship of birds and other animals. The first day is Kag Tihar, meaning worship of the crow. The crow is offered good food early in the morning before anyone else has had a morsel to eat. The crow is significant as the representative of Yama, the god of death. The second day is Kukur Tihar, when dogs are decorated with marigold garlands (*Tagetes erecta*) and *tika,* rice mixed with vermilion and yogurt. Throughout the 5 days, the cow is worshipped in the morning and evening, as it is considered an incarnation of Laxmi. Some communities offer a few twigs of *jaita* (*Sesbania sesban*), which is considered a favorite of Laxmi. A myriad of oil lamps are also burned to welcome the goddess. On the last day, sisters show their affection toward their brothers by observing Bhai Puja. A symmetrical circular pattern of marigolds, soybeans, roasted rice, and vermilion powder known as a *mandala* is created on the ground in front of each brother. The sister worships the brother and garlands him with bachelor's buttons (*Gomphrena globosa*) and *dub* grass (*Cynodon dactylon*), wishing him a long life. In addition, sweets, including chestnuts (*Castanopsis indica*) and walnuts (*Juglans regia* var. *kamaonia*), are offered to the brother. Most of these rituals signify the love of the sister for her brother and her wish that the brother's fame will spread and that he is kept safe from Yama Raj, the god of death.

CHAPTER 3

The Ethnobotany of Nepal

The word ethnobotany was coined by an American botanist, John W. Harshberger, in 1895, originally for the study of "plants used by primitive and aboriginal people." The word is derived from two Greek words: *ethnos,* referring to the human aspects in biological relationships, and *botanikos,* denoting the study of plants. Ethnobotany is a multidisciplinary science, embracing botany, ecology, and anthropology. Ethnobotanical knowledge can be divided into two parts: that gained in schools and universities, that acquired from local knowledge or folklore, which is usually communicated verbally. In Nepal, it is the traditional knowledge acquired by experience and observation, which is communicated mainly by word of mouth, that has formed the basis of Nepalese ethnobotany.

HISTORY OF ETHNOBOTANICAL RESEARCH IN NEPAL

Ethnobotany is a relatively new field of study in Nepal, as it is in many other developing countries. It has taken its own way of development, depending on local traditions and other differences. Because about 73% of Nepalese are illiterate, superstitions and various cultural taboos hinder systematic ethnobotanical research. Yet people residing in rural areas (about 90%) have a close association with the natural resources of their surroundings and possess hands-on knowledge about the various uses of plants that they need. Nevertheless, this knowledge is scattered, communicated orally, and confined to certain key village members. Therefore, this body of knowledge has not reached all who would benefit from it. Even in their own circles, villagers are unaware of the uses of some plants. Similarly, gaps in knowledge exist between different communities and different parts of the country. Consequently, over the years, some of this traditional knowledge has been permanently lost or modified.

In Nepal, ethnobotanical study started when Banerji (1955) published a paper on medicinal and food plants of eastern Nepal. In it, he mentioned 13 species, of which 9 were of medicinal value and 4 were noted for their food value. Five years later, S. C. Singh (1960) recorded some 20 species of food plants, mainly ones sold by villagers in Kathmandu markets. These first steps engendered further development of ethnobotanical study; although it advanced at a slow pace, study continued. B. D. Pandey (1964) presented a paper on Nepalese medicinal plants at a symposium in China, where he mentioned some drug plants used by local people in Nepal. Bhatta (1970) wrote a book, mentioning more than 60 species of medicinal plants and a few species of wild food plants. The first study of a particular community was conducted by Sacherer (1979), on plants used by the Sherpa community of Rolwaling near the northern border with Tibet. Coburn (1984) reported about 100 species of herbal drugs from the Gurung community, of which about 50% were named scientifically and the rest in Nepali or Gurung.

In 1980, I published a book on 50 species of medicinal plants that are export commodities from Nepal (Manandhar 1980a). Ethnobotanical information on 102 species was included in a book (Manandhar 1989), with studies continued to other areas of the country. The documentation of plant uses was continued in Rasuwa, Nuwakot, and Jumla districts (Manandhar 1980b, 1982, 1986a), areas mostly covered with alpine vegetation, and as a result the information is mostly on alpine plants. I recorded 43 drug plants used by the Tharus of western Nepal (Manandhar 1985), 58 species of medicinal plants used by the Mooshars of the Terai (Manandhar 1986b), 60 species used by the Danuwars of the Siwalik Hills (Manandhar 1990), and 95 species used by the Tamangs of the midlands (Manandhar 1991). Ethnobotanical notes on *Bauhinia vahlii* and *Millettia pinnata* (the latter as *Pongamia pinnata*) were published by me (Manandhar 1994) and K. Shrestha and Nobuo (1995–1996), respectively. Finally, prior to publication of the present book, I recorded 47 species used by the Rautes of far western Nepal (Manandhar 1998). Additional details on ethnobotanical research in Nepal are given under Medicinal Plants, History, in this chapter.

PLANTS IN ANIMAL HUSBANDRY AND AGRICULTURE

Fodder Plants

Nepal is an agrarian country where agricultural produce is supplemented by animal husbandry and livestock farming. People also domesticate animals for their meat, milk, hide, manure, tillage, and cultural values. Culturally, cows and oxen are sacred and worshiped during Tihar as they are considered incarnations of Laxmi, the god of wealth. The midlands of Nepal lack the infrastructure needed for agriculture, and the yield of farmlands is low because of the hilly and mountainous terrain. Except in the better valleys, the difficult terrain adversely affects crop production. Therefore, raising livestock is a household occupation in the midlands, an area that accounts for 62% of the livestock population. The cattle population in Nepal is estimated to be 20 million (Basnyat 1995).

Keeping livestock is not only beneficial but indispensable for wholesome agricultural practice. Villagers are small landholding farmers, the majority of whom live below the poverty line. Hence, they cannot afford chemical fertilizers and depend on animal manure. Moreover, male cattle and buffalo make their greatest contribution to farming as the source of draft power as mechanized machinery is unaffordable.

The success of animal husbandry in rural Nepal is dependent on fodder plants as animal feeds are not only unaffordable but unheard of. The main sources of fodder are agricultural by-products, grass from terraced fields, hills, and highland pastures, and forest foliage. Generally, the villagers collectively pay a shepherd, in cash or crop, who takes the animals to the forest or pastures. Animals used for milk and plowing are not taken to graze but instead are given fodder in the form of stall feed. The tree fodder is a blessing to the poor farmers because it provides a badly needed supplement to the agricultural by-products and grass. Fodder, therefore, is one of the major components of livestock development and agricultural productivity. Fodder resources are of two types: private and public. Agricultural residues such as straw, weeds, and fodder from privately owned trees are private (Plate 13); fodder from government forest and pastures is considered public. Forest fodder is an important source of livestock food in the hill areas (Plate 14). It has been estimated that about 60% of the fodder consumed in rural Nepal comes from the forests (Uprety 1985).

There is an imbalance between supply and demand of fodder as the livestock population is on the increase and fodder production in the forest is on the decline. Trees on public lands are mercilessly lopped because they are considered nobody's property (Plate 3). Private pasturelands have also been turned into farmland because of growing population pressures. Like all trees, fodder trees are important in checking soil erosion, restoring nutrients, and retaining moisture. The imbalance in fodder supply and demand has jeopardized equilibrium in the ecosystem.

Declining yields of fodder from the forest and private lands adversely affect the local economy. The agricultural value of fodder is well known to the farmers. Crop yield is dependent on the amount of manure produced by livestock, and the success of livestock farming is dependent on the availability of fodder. As a result, it is clear that agriculture and livestock farming are inseparably interrelated, and fodder has a vital role to play in livestock development.

Meat and Dairy Products. Livestock provide nourishment in the form of milk and meat. The greatest contribution of livestock is manure and milk production. After fulfilling family needs, any surplus of milk and butter (*ghee*) can be sold for cash to help the rural people buy nonagricultural requirements.

Despite the value of livestock for dairy production, most Nepalese livestock are low-yielding. For instance, a cow in Nepal averages 170 kg of milk annually whereas in New Zealand the average is 3902 kg, in the United Kingdom 3950 kg, and in the United States 4154 kg (R. S. Pandey 1982). It is important to introduce high-yielding animals to get the most benefit from livestock farming. There are many governmental programs to improve livestock by importing higher-yielding breeds.

Fodder Tree Agroforestry. Agroforestry is a system of land use that integrates trees, agricultural crops, and animals in a way that is scientifically sound, ecologically desirable, practical, and socially acceptable to the farmers. Agroforestry has been put forward as a good method to increase agricultural output, forest resources, and livestock products so that villagers can generate extra income. Furthermore, agroforestry is of value in environmental conservation. An important aspect of agroforestry consists of intercropping a forest plantation with agricultural crops. Intercropping is not new to the rural people in Nepal. Unknowingly, some communities, since long ago, have been planting and protecting some wild and cultivated plants in home plots, for fodder and fruit, for example. Because of population pressure and decreasing acreage of forest, agroforestry is becoming indispensable to get maximum benefit from limited land.

The depletion of forests forces villagers to travel farther to collect fodder, which is time-consuming. Villagers are also aware that it is illegal to steal from the forest and fear penalty, insult, and abuse from the forest guards. Hence, increasingly, villagers plant some important trees on their private land and find it convenient and time-saving to use them for fodder, fuel, medicine, or food, especially during the peak season of their agricultural activity. Villagers prefer to plant trees that have multiple uses and look for seven qualities in deciding which fodder trees to plant: (1) fast-growing and quickly regenerating, (2) available year-round, (3) able to be lopped more than once a year, (4) contains large amounts of moisture, (5) suitable for mixing with all grades of fodder, (6) suitable for animal bedding, and (7) limited canopy spread.

Only a few families keep nurseries of their preferred species. Most protect self-sown seedlings and transplant them during the rainy season (July–August), when according to the villagers the survival rate of the seedlings is higher. This folklore is supported by the experiments of L. Joshi and Sherpa (1992), who planted seedlings of four fodder trees (*Alnus nepalensis, Ficus auriculata, F. semicordata,* and *Saurauia napaulensis*) in different months from April to November and found that seedlings planted during July–August had 100% survivability. Villagers also grow some plants such as *F. sarmentosa* and *Schefflera venulosa* by cutting branches and rooting them. Some plants pose special problems. For example, seedlings of *Artocarpus lakoocha* and *Bauhinia purpurea* grow during March. To get the seeds of these trees, villagers leave some fruit-bearing twigs at the tops of trees so that children cannot reach them.

Villagers generally transplant trees along the border of a terraced field in a sequence of big tree followed by a smaller one, or wide-canopied tree followed one with a smaller canopy. The space between trees depends on the species and topography. On the basis of my observation, the spacing is 8–12 m for trees higher than 7 m, and 3–5 m for trees 3–7 m high. Spacing between smaller plants is about 2–3 m. But this spacing is not uniform. There are gaps in places; sometimes a whole terraced plot is left treeless to provide sunlight and air to the crops. To replace old, worn-out plants, young seedlings are planted near the old plants. Such management promotes rhythmic production, maturation of trees, and the ecological requirements of each species.

Fodder trees planted in the spirit of agroforestry have some adverse effects on the production of agricultural crops, especially if the trees have healthy canopies. The main problems posed to the crops are delayed ripening, susceptibility to disease, longer stalks that bend before harvest, and thinning of the crop plant population.

Lopping and Grading. Villagers have practical experience in stretching the supply of fodder the longest time. When lopping, they consider the canopy of the tree and the agricultural crop underneath. To allow sunlight to reach the crop, they try to lop from the bottom to the top of the tree. If the canopy is wide, they try to thin it from the top. Since tree fodder is generally available through January, when the dry season sets in and it becomes more difficult to find fodder, farmers reserve some top branches for the dry season. For example, the top branches of *Artocarpus lakoocha, Bauhinia malabarica,* and *Litsea monopetala* are reserved for supplying fodder starting in February when other tree fodder is hard to come by. When villagers select trees for their fodder value, fodder supply during the flush as well as the dry season is carefully considered.

Villagers also have their own way of grading fodder, which becomes the basis for feeding animals maintained for different uses. Fodder is divided into three grades: (A) very good, (B) good, and (C) normal. Grading takes into account the fodder's nutritional value, tastiness to the animals, and amount of milk produced when fed to livestock. The A fodder is generally supplied to milking animals; other animals are given a mixture of A with B or C to maintain a longer supply of fodder.

Other Uses of Fodder Trees. Dried branches of fodder trees can serve as fuel for rural people. Traditional sources of fuel in rural Nepal are agricultural by-products, livestock waste, and forest products. Fuelwood from the forest has an important role in the energy supply of the country. About 76% of all energy consumed comes from fuelwood, of which household consumption is 96% and industrial use 4% (S. Shrestha 1992). The shortfall of fuelwood is met by the substitution of agricultural residues such as rice and rice husks, corncobs, wheat, millet, maize, soybean straw, bamboo, and cow dung. Agricultural residues provide 11% of the energy consumed; 1 kg of agricultural residue is equivalent to the energy output of 0.7 kg of fuelwood (Shrestha 1992). It is estimated that annual fuelwood consumption per capita in Nepal is 725 kg. Animal dung provides 8.5% of the energy consumed; 1 kg of dung is equivalent to 0.9 kg of fuelwood.

Many fodder trees have other uses as well. Among forest trees, oak (*Quercus*) is preferred for fodder because its leaves are available in the hot, dry season when other tree fodder is scarce. Fodder trees whose fruits are edible include *Antidesma acidum, Artocarpus lakoocha, Bridelia retusa, Diplokenma butyracea, Ficus auriculata, F. hispida, F. semicordata, Prunus cerasoides,* and *Saurauia napaulensis.* Tender leaves of *Crateva unilocularis,* fruits of *Bauhinia purpurea,* and flowers of *B. variegata* are cooked as a vegetable or pickled. Fiber from the bark of *F. semicordata, Grewia disperma,* and *Sterculia villosa* is used to make rope and other household goods.

Different parts of fodder trees are used medicinally. Latex of *Ficus auriculata* and bark juice of *Artocarpus lakoocha* are used to treat cuts and wounds. Leaves of *A. lakoocha, Bauhinia vahlii,* and *F. auriculata* are used as plates and to wrap goods.

Agriculture

Agriculture contributes the largest share of national output; the livelihood of 90% of the population of Nepal is agricultural. Agriculture in the hilly regions is mainly for home consumption, yet there are many short of food. On the other hand, some of the agricultural products of the Terai are sold commercially as there is usually some surplus. Much effort has been put into developing the agricultural sector through high-yielding cultivars and technology transfer. There are extension agents and land reform officers in most of the 75 districts of the country, but the nature of the work of the agents varies as farming is not the same in each district.

The agrarian system that existed at the end of the Rana regime (1846–1950) encouraged a social and economic differentiation of land ownership. It failed to protect the rights and interests of the farmers who worked on the land. Before 1950, land constituted a basis for governmental power; ownership was concentrated in the hands of few. Agriculture was dominated by subsistence farming within a tenure system, and tenants who paid rent but were sometimes subjected to unpaid and forced labor. According to M. M. Poudel (1986) the percentages of land in the different classes of ownership were 50% *raikar,* ownership by state landlords; 36.3% *birta,* ownership by individuals as a result of currying the favor of *raikar* owners; 4% *kipad,* communal ownership; 7.7% combined for *rajya,* ownership by a member of the royal family, and *jagir,* ownership of land as a benefit of employment service; and 2% *guthi,* apportionment of land for temples, monasteries, and for religious and charitable purposes.

After the Rana regime, the government made various land reforms between 1951 and 1963, bringing changes in land ownership, abolishing the tenure system, and improving the security of tenancy through rent control and limitation of landholding. The limitation of land ownership was important for equalizing the distribution of land and income.

Land Use. Cultivated land in Nepal amounts to 2,641,000 hectares, 18% of the area of the country. Most farmers have small landholdings with a farm size of less than 0.6 hectare in the hills and about 1.48 hectares in the Terai (Anonymous 1998). The high peaks, steep slopes, and narrow valleys of the mountainous regions are not well suited for crop farming. Hence, much of the people's livelihood is livestock oriented. The cultivated area in the mountainous regions is 227,000 hectares, only 8.6% of the cultivated land area.

The soil in the midlands is of low to medium grade with respect to nitrogen and organic matter. The cultivated area of this belt is 1,055,000 hectares, 39.9% of the cultivated land area.

The 15- to 20-km-wide strip of the Terai running east–west the length of Nepal is an extension of Indo-Gangetic Plain. This belt comprises 23% of the area of the country but 51.5% of the cultivated land. The Terai is composed of alluvial soil very suitable for agriculture.

Cropping System. In Nepal, agricultural activities are complex because of the diversity of environments. Mountain ranges, deep valleys, and slopes of different exposures give rise to a number of microclimatic belts within a short distance south–north. In addition to climate, the cropping system chosen by farmers is based on availability of irrigation, labor, markets, and the ethnic communities in a particular area. Cropping patterns may range from three crops per year in subtropical areas with irrigation, to two crops in some temperate hilly regions, to one crop, often confined to potato production, at high elevation.

Farmers try to adopt diversified cropping patterns to maintain soil fertility and to gain maximum advantage from their limited landholdings. Thus mixed cropping, relay cropping, and intercropping systems are common in all ecological regions of Nepal.

There are two distinct cropping seasons: the wet season (April–October) and dry season (November–March). The main wet season crops are rice (*Oryza sativa*), maize (*Zea mays*), millet (*Eleusine coracana*), soybeans (*Glycine max*), and chickpeas (*Cicer arietinum*). Wheat (*Triticum aestivum*; Plate 15), mustard, (*Brassica napus*) lentils (*Lens culinaris*), potatoes (*Solanum tuberosum*), also chickpeas, are crops for the dry season. Areas with irrigation, river basins, and valley bottoms in the Siwalik Hills and midlands have a common cropping pattern of wet season rice followed by a dry season winter crop such as wheat. In mountainous regions, the cropping is predominantly maize followed by buckwheat (*Fagopyrum esculentum*) or barley (*Hordeum vulgare*). In some places, maize is grown mixed with potatoes, sweet potatoes (*Ipomoea batatas*), and cowpeas (*Vigna unguiculata*).

Yields. The three major crops, rice (*Oryza sativa*), maize (*Zea mays*), and wheat (*Triticum aestivum*), account for 51.5%, 25.8%, and 16.4%, respectively, of the agricultural production of Nepal. Millet (*Eleusine coracana*), barley (*Hordeum vulgare*), and potatoes (*Solanum tuberosum*) are also important in the middle and higher hills of the midlands. The return on investment in crop production is higher in the Terai than in other regions; production in the hills and mountains is mainly subsistence agriculture. Most crops have no satisfactory production above 2700 m in the midlands and high mountain valleys because of low solar radiation and aridity (Carson 1985).

The cultivation of rice occupies 60% of the cultivated area of the country. Rice growing is concentrated in the subtropical climatic region of the Terai, the Dun valleys of the Siwalik Hills, and equivalent climatic regions of the inner basins and valleys up to 900 m. These regions contribute 88% of the rice production. About 23.75% and 2.5% of the area of rice production is located in the warm temperate regions of the midlands and mountains to 1000–1400 m, respectively, but the midlands and mountains account for only 12% and 0.5% of the rice production, respectively. The highest-elevation rice production area (2780 m) is located in Jumla district where the local variety of rice, Jumli marsi, is grown (D. N. Manandhar and Shakya 1996).

Maize cultivation occupies about 28% of the cultivated land area. Nearly two-thirds of maize production comes from the hills. It is cultivated as an inter crop with a variety of beans, including soybeans. The summer maize in the hills is grown as a monsoon crop whereas in the Terai regions it is grown as a winter crop.

Wheat occupies 25% of the cultivated land area. With the introduction of high-yielding cultivars in late 1960s, wheat production has increased in the Terai. It is grown on terraced land in hilly regions, where its production has also increased. Wheat was not a traditional crop in Nepal prior to 1960.

Potatoes are an important crop and grow well up to 4400 m. They are grown as an irrigated winter crop in the Terai and as a summer crop in the Siwalik Hills and midlands and mountainous regions.

The production of sugarcane (*Saccharum officinarum*) and tobacco (*Nicotiana tabacum*) is confined mainly to the Terai. Jute (*Corchorus capsularis*) is produced in the eastern Terai very close to Bangladesh, one of the main jute growing countries. Oilseeds are grown in Terai and valleys of the Siwalik Hills and midlands. The hilly districts of Dhankuta, Terhathum, Panchathar, and Ilam, are noted for the cultivation of tea (*Camellia sinensis*). These districts have geographical features similar to those of Darjeeling, India, which is famous for tea. There are ample possibilities for the extension of tea cultivation in these areas. In addition to tea, cardamom (*Amomum subulatum*) is another cash crop of eastern Nepal. The hilly regions of western Nepal offer opportunities for growing ginger (*Zingiber officinale*). The cultivation of cotton (*Gossypium*) is feasible in Banke and Bardiya districts, western Nepal.

FOOD AND BEVERAGE PLANTS

Many crops are the result of improvement of wild plants through cultivation and eventually domestication by humans. Many more wild plants, even today, serve as food and drink for different ethnic communities in Nepal.

Roots and Tubers. Roots and tubers are important in the human diet. Even in ancient books we find references to *kandamul* (roots and tubers), which the hermits used to dig up in the forests during their meditations. Some of these tubers are considered important in religious festivals. For example, during Maghe Sankranti, different species of yam (*Dioscorea*), sweet potatoes (*Ipomoea batatas*), and christophine (*Sechium edule*) are indispensable and consumed as sacred diet. Generally, they are baked and boiled, but people also consume them as a vegetable curry, fried, or roasted. Roots and tubers are a staple food for the poor when food supplies run low as they are cheap and provide ample energy. Villagers consider them easy to cultivate, so they grow yams and sweet potatoes at their homesteads and on private lands.

The food value of underground parts of plants cannot be ignored but some species of aroids and yams are poisonous. People attempt to neutralize the poisonous effects by boiling the tubers with wood ash or immersing cut pieces of the tubers in flowing water for a long time. Underground parts of *Asparagus racemosus, Fritillaria cirrhosa, Lilium nepalense, Platanthera clavigera,* and *Satyrium nepalense* are boiled and eaten, but the fresh roots or tubers of *Eriosema himalaicum, Gonostegia hirta,* and *Nephrolepis cordifolia* are consumed raw, especially by children.

Potherbs. Plants with tender stems and leaves possessing little or no wood are categorized as herbs. The Nepalese consume herbs, often cooked, as they are easy to prepare, nutritious, and tasty. *Hariyo pariyo ramro ra swadilo hunchha,* greens are tasty and good for you, is a common Nepali saying. Rural people eat them less for health than out of necessity because they are cheap and readily available. In fact, herbs contain ample amounts of vitamins A and C, but these vitamins are destroyed when plants are boiled a long time, which is how most greens are prepared in Nepal. When the plants are washed, the villagers squeeze them tightly until the green chlorophyll of the plants is washed out. These destructive methods of preparation are often used for mustard (*Brassica juncea* var. *cuneifolia, B. napus*), turnip (*B. rapa*), radish leaves (*Raphanus sativus*), and the common gourd (*Cucurbita maxima*). Villagers eat the young leaves of radish and fenugreek (*Trigonella foenum-graecum*) raw.

Herbs are collected from the wild or from crop fields, where they grow as weeds. common weeds such as khaki weed (*Alternanthera sessilis*), pigweeds (*Amaranthus viridis, Chenopodium album*), shepherd's purse (*Capsella bursa-pastoris*), false daisy (*Eclipta prostrata*), purslane (*Portulaca oleracea*), and horse purslane (*Trianthema portulacastrum*) are collected for salads and vegetables. Tender leaves, shoots, or other parts of *Arisaema utile* (Plates 16, 22), Turk's turban (*Clerodendrum* spp.), Himalayan nettle (*Girardinia diversifolia*), *Remusatia vivipara,* and stinging nettle (*Urtica dioica*) are collected for curries and soups. Tender fronds of many species of ferns are collected from the forest to prepare as vegetables. The fresh petioles of rhubarb (*Rheum australe*) are consumed as a pickle, but mostly the petioles are dried and pickled in the off-season; it is slightly sour in taste.

Flowers. The flowers of wild plants are important food ingredients in rural foods. Villagers collect some flowers from the forest and sell them in the market; with the money earned, they buy other food items such as salt, spices, and vegetables. For instance, the flowers of *Indigofera pulchella* are eaten as a pickle or vegetable; these flowers are eaten fresh or dried. In many places, villagers suck the sweet nectar of the flower and thus enjoy the sweet taste.

Fruits. Fruits are important for a balanced diet. In urban areas of Nepal, people purchase cultivated fruits according to their taste, but most rural people cannot afford to fulfill their fruit requirements from the market. Hence, they have to depend on natural and personal sources such as fruit trees grown in their own backyards. Most of the tasty fruits are also sold in the market (Plate 17), and those that are not tasty or cannot be sold in the market usually become the base for making liquor. The ripe fruit of *Berberis aristata, B. asiatica, Cornus capitata,* and *Gaultheria fragrantissima* are generally used to prepare local liquor but are also eaten fresh because they are abundantly available. Fruits of *Diplokenma butyracea, Myrica esculenta, Rhus javanica, Rubus* spp., and *Syzygium cumini* have a different taste and are eaten raw rather than used for liquor.

Villagers do not generally preserve fruits, primarily because they do not know the methods of preservation. Increasingly, some plants such as *Choerospondias axillaris* are used to prepare marmalades or jams using modern methods; some of these products are sold in the urban markets and exported, as candy or dried fruit pulp, to countries such as Japan.

Because food from farming in the villages of Nepal is scarce and valued, quite sophisticated methods for storing and milling of grains have been perfected over the years. Danuwars, Mooshars, and Tharus make earthen vessels for storage by mixing rice husks and clay. The mouth of the vessel is big, to facilitate the transfer of large amounts of grain. There is also a small opening at the bottom of the vessel through which everyday needs are removed. The vessel has an earthen lid, which is tightly plastered using clay. Thus the grain is protected from humidity and vermin but allows easy access. Among Gurungs, Magars, and Tamangs, dried corn on the cob (*Zea mays*) is stored atop a platform in the front yard to save space inside the house (Plate 18). The four legs of the platform are protected from mice and wild animals by tying pine needles facing downward.

Grains are ground in a water mill (*ghatta* in Nepali). In a *ghatta*, a log passes through center holes in two circular stone blocks, the grinding stones. One end of the log is fixed to the upper stone (which rests on the other stone), and the other end has a wooden turbine attached to it that makes contact with the water flowing below the mill house. Thus the upper grinder rotates and grain is fed from a conical hopper above the grinders. Since the wooden turbine can only withstand a certain water volume and speed, during times of flooding the miller makes sure that most of the water is directed to a bypass above the mill.

There are other kinds of grinding and pressing equipment and techniques. A *janto* is a round, manually operated, two-stone grinder with a wooden handle on the top for the user to crank. The user feeds grain into the central opening, and flour is expelled to the outside by the circular motion. A *dhiki*, a manual wooden thresher, is a common sight in rural Nepal. It consists of a 2-m-long piece of wood with a fulcrum toward one end and a metal hammer at the other. Village women or children are usually the ones who rhythmically press the end closer to the fulcrum like a seesaw. The grains or vegetables under the hammer are ground. Use of the *janto* and *dhiki* is common among Gurungs, Limbus, Magars, Rais, Tamang, and in most hill communities. In the Kathmandu Valley, Newars use a wooden mortar about 1 m high with a hole about 20 cm wide. Often, two women each use a wooden hammer about 1.5 m long and rhythmically hammer the grain in the mortar.

Seeds. Most commonly, seeds are roasted and pickled, which is the method of preparation for the seeds of *Abelmoschus moschatus*, *Cannabis sativa*, and *Meconopsis grandis*. The nutlets of *Elsholtzia flava* and *E. stachyodes* are treated similarly. Roasted seeds of *Bauhinia vahlii* and *Sterculia foetida* are eaten unpickled; the taste is very similar to that of cashew nut. Oil extracted from the seeds of *Diplokenma butyracea*, *Symplocos ramosissima*, and *Viburnum cylindricum* is used for cooking.

Spices. Spices add flavor and aroma to foods that are bland or that become unappetizing after repetitive preparation. Spices are valued in cookery, confectionery, alcoholic and nonalcoholic beverages, including tea, and perfumery. Villagers of Nepal chiefly use spices for flavoring. *Jimbu*, a popular flavoring agent for soups (*daal*), is made by drying *Allium hypsistum*. Likewise, *tejpat* consists of dried leaves of *Cinnamomum tamala*. The villagers sell these spices in the village or urban markets (Plate 19). Spices also have their place in medicine, where they act to disguise the unpleasant taste of other drugs. Some spices are burned as incense in certain social and religious customs. For example, *Micromeria biflora* and *Thymus linearis* are dried, powdered, and burned over hot coals at religious activities.

Most farmers in Nepal have very small landholdings, so the spices obtained from their own land are insufficient. To supplement homegrown spices such as onion (*Allium cepa*), garlic (*A. sativum*), chili (*Capsicum annuum*), coriander (*Coriandrum sativum*), turmeric (*Curcuma domestica*), and ginger (*Zingiber officinale*), people use spices obtained from wild plants. It is prohibitively expensive for villagers to buy spices in the market. In the course of my ethnobotanical study in different parts of Nepal, I asked informants about the spices they used. They readily listed the spices with which they were familiar, even showing me samples and displaying the use of these spices in food preparation. These spices were used to add flavor and taste to curries, vegetables, *daal*, salads, teas, and pickles. Spices may be derived from bark, leaf, flower, fruit, or seed and may be used as a powder or paste. Villagers sometimes fry spices in mustard oil and add the spiced oil to foods.

Fermented Vegetables

Fresh vegetables are often scarce in rural areas of Nepal because people do not own large fields to grow vegetables year-round, and they cannot afford to buy them in the market. To counter the scarcity of fresh vegetables, villagers either dry or ferment green vegetables for future use. *Tama* is a fermented, preserved vegetable used as a flavoring, made from *Bambusa nepalensis*, *Dendrocalamus hamiltonii*, and *Drepanostachyum falcatum*, for example. *Gundruk* is a preparation of fermented leafy vegetables that has long been part of rural Nepalese diet (Plate 20). Green and overly matured leaves of cultivated species not normally used fresh are used for *gundruk* preparation in order to minimize waste: *Brassica campestris* var. *sarson*, *B. juncea* var. *cuneifolia*, *B. napus*, *B. nigra*, *B. oleracea* vars. *botrytis* (Plate 23), *capitata*, and *caulorapa*, *B. rapa*, and *Raphanus sativus*. Some wild plants are also used to prepare *gundruk*: *Arisaema jacquemontii*, *A. utile* (Plates 16, 22), *Ranunculus diffusus*, *R. scleratus*, and *Rumex nepalensis* (Plate 21). The process of preparing *gundruk* differs slightly between Chepangs, Danuwars, Gurungs, Tamangs and Tharus, but

Plate 1. Fuelwood stored on rooftops in the district of Mustang, the author in the foreground

Plate 2. An entire plant (here, *Maesa macrophylla*) may be cut down for a few strips of bark for medicine

Plate 3. *Shorea robusta* forest trees lopped for fodder

Plate 4. *Dioscorea deltoidea* roots sliced into pieces prior to boiling for food

Plate 8. Tamang house in the district of Makawanpur, the wall decorated using bark juice of *Betula alnoides*

Plate 9. Tamang women planting rice in terraced fields flooded by monsoon rains in the district of Nuwakot, using the seedlings in the foreground

Plate 4. *Dioscorea deltoidea* roots sliced into pieces prior to boiling for food

Plate 5. Chepang healer who prescribes herbal medicines and over-
sees religious rituals

Plate 6. Gurung village surrounded by terraced fields in the district of Gorkha

Plate 7. Mooshar midwives in the district of Dhanusha with
medicinal plants used after delivery

Plate 8. Tamang house in the district of Makawanpur, the wall decorated using bark juice of *Betula alnoides*

Plate 9. Tamang women planting rice in terraced fields flooded by monsoon rains in the district of Nuwakot, using the seedlings in the foreground

Plate 10. Tamang woman winnowing maize

Plate 11. Tamang woman making a cushion from the husks of maize
in the district of Ramechhap

Plate 12. Tharu women trapping fish in their leisure time, using conical bamboo traps

Plate 13. *Ficus semicordata* lopped for fodder on private land in the district of Rasuwa

Plate 14. Fodder carried from the forest

Plate 15. Wheat carried home from the field

Plate 16. Spathes of *Arisaema utile* gathered for cooking in the district of Surkhet

Plate 17. Village woman selling wild fruits, including *Phyllanthus emblica* and *Rhus parviflora*, in Kathmandu

Plate 18. Outdoor maize storage in the district of Ramechhap, with needles of *Pinus roxburghii* attached to the poles to deter rats or other animals from climbing up

Plate 19. Leaves of *Cinnamomum tamala* for sale in a village market in the district of Dhanusha

Plate 20. Village women making thread and weaving rugs, with drying *gundruk* in the foreground

Plate 21. Magar woman in the district of Myagdi picking tender leaves of *Rumex nepalensis* for *gundruk*

Plate 22. Magar woman in the district of Myagdi crushing leaves of
Arisaema utile for *gundruk*

Plate 23. Newar woman in Kathmandu stuffing squeezed leaves of
Brassica oleracea var. *botrytis* in an earthen vessel to prepare *gundruk*

Plate 24. Village woman in the district of Dhading displaying cakes of
marcha yeast and the plants used to make them

Plate 25. Woman in the district of Kabhrepalanchok mixing *nidar* vigorously to prepare *jand*, the local beer

Plate 26. Tamang woman in the district of Nuwakot changing cooling water in the course of distilling *raksi*, the local liquor

Plate 27. Gurung healer in the district of Lamjung with plants collected for the treatment of his patient

Plate 28. Tibetan healer digging the root of a medicinal plant

Plate 29. Villager in the district of Kaski pounding bark of *Schima wallichii* with a *hansiya,* sickle, to make a paste to apply to the wound on the author's left shin; photographed by another villager, using the author's camera

Plate 30. Village woman selling flowers of *Woodfordia fruticosa* in Kathmandu

Plate 31. Drying crude drugs collected from the forest to sell in the market

Plate 32. Magar man smoking with a bamboo pipe

Plate 33. Rough strips of bamboo woven into mats for fences

Plate 34. Thin strips of bamboo prepared by splitting culms lengthwise

Plate 35. Weaving a bamboo basket

Plate 36. Magar man in the district of Rolpa peeling bark from *Cannabis sativa* for use in spinning thread

Plate 37. Spinning thread from the fiber of *Girardinia diversifolia* using
a *katuwa,* wooden top, in the district of Dolkha

Plate 38. Tamang woman weaving rough cloth from the thread of *Cannabis sativa*

Plate 39. Chepang man making a container from the leaves of
Bauhinia vahlii

Plate 40. Tharu man in the district of Banke with cups he made from the leaves of *Bauhinia vahlii*

Plate 41. Hats made by Chepangs from the leaves of *Bauhinia vahlii*

Plate 42. Rai family hammering bark of *Bauhinia vahlii* to produce soft
fibers

Plate 43. Making twine from the bark of *Bauhinia vahlii*

Plate 44. Bark fibers mixed with water to prepare a homogeneous pulp used for making Nepalese handmade paper; note the rectangular frame at the right, with the cloth mesh onto which the pulp is poured, then left to dry into paper

Plate 45. Nepalese handmade paper ready for transport to the market

Plate 46. Combs being made from the wood of *Euonymus hamiltoni-anus* in the district of Doti

Plate 47. Newar woman making a mat from rice straw and wearing
shoes she made from the straw

Plate 48. Fruits of *Sapindus mukorossi* being broken for use as soap to wash clothes at a river in the district of Dailekh

the taste is similar, usually slightly sour. Like *sinki,* a similar fermented vegetable preparation from Sikkim, but unlike *kimchi* of Korea, *gundruk* is dried after preparation for future use. There are several different methods for preparing *gundruk*:

Wilted Leaf Method. This method is used by most ethnic groups. Leaves are cleaned, washed, left in mild sun or shade for a day, then beaten with a mallet or log, or threshed in a *dhiki,* a manually operated wooden thresher, to squeeze out the green juice. The metal hammer of the *dhiki* (described previously under Fruits) pounds the leaves in a wooden mortar as the other end of the *dhiki* is operated by pressing with the leg and foot. The residue is stuffed in an earthen vessel with little air inside. The mouth of the vessel is tightly closed with straw and left for a week in the sun. During this time, leaves start to ferment and the mouth of the vessel becomes frothy, after which a brown liquid seeps out. The squeezed leaves in the vessel give off an odor. The fermented *gundruk* is then removed from the vessel and spread out on a straw or bamboo mat or a piece of cloth for drying. The dried *gundruk* is then stored in a dry place and cooked as a vegetable when needed.

Boiled Leaf Method. The people of central Nepal, especially Gurungs and Tamangs, adopt this method. The leaf of *Arisaema utile* is half boiled, squeezed, and tightly stuffed in a *doko* or *thunse,* a conical bamboo basket. The upper part of the basket is covered with straw and kept in the dark 3–6 days, depending on the ambient temperature, before being taken out for drying. Some Gurung families hammer the wilted leaves into smaller pieces. Leaves are then pressed in a *doko* to remove the green juice, and boiling water is added. The entire apparatus is left near the hearth 4–5 days until some reddishness is seen in the water. At this point, the leafy pieces develop a sour taste. Leaves are then squeezed to remove water and dried in the sun.

Fresh Leaf Method. Fresh leaves are beaten with a wooden hammer or log (Plate 22), squeezed, and the residue is stuffed in an earthen vessel or bamboo basket (Plate 23). The container is then placed in a sunny place until it imparts a pungent odor. This method is generally used by Chepangs, Danuwars, and Tharus in southern Nepal.

Drying Method. Fresh leaves are either boiled or simply dried in the sun in this method, common in all communities. Since it is simply dehydration, there is little fermentation and no sour taste.

Gundruk can be eaten cooked as a vegetable or pickled. The taste depends on the plants used, the method of preparation, and the ingredients and spices used in the final preparation. Whatever quantity of *gundruk* is needed is taken from the family's storage container and soaked in water about 5–10 minutes to make it soft. Recipes and preparation differ according to taste. Soaked *gundruk* is lightly beaten with a pestle and mixed with salt and chili to prepare a pickle. For curried vegetables, it is mixed with potatoes, tomatoes, soybeans, onions, or other vegetables and boiled, mixing in chili, salt, and spices according to taste. Some Tamang and Gurung families in the villages have also introduced *gundruk* powder into their diet.

Gundruk has touched the palette of the urban and tourist population. Hence, the traditional free offering or bartering of *gundruk* in rural communities, especially at times of vegetable scarcity, has given way to commercial trade. Outsiders such as our expedition team were given *gundruk* freely to prepare meals, a mark of rural goodwill that used to be quite prevalent throughout Nepal. Increasingly, the urban populace as well as many Western tourists have been attracted to the taste of *gundruk* and enjoy it as a soup. As a result, villagers have started businesses, selling *gundruk* in urban markets, which provide a good source of rural income. As a result, villagers seem to be aware of the need to protect the wild plants used for *gundruk.*

According to T. Karki et al. (1986), the quality of *gundruk* is judged primarily on the basis of its acidic taste and characteristic flavor. Hence, Karki et al. selected lactic strains for improvement of *gundruk* processing that would help in the development this useful rural technology. It would be beneficial if attention is paid to the rural way of preparation and storage of *gundruk* so that *gundruk* of good quality can be produced to satisfy the increasing demand and thus help upgrade the standard of living in the villages. A better organized, small-scale *gundruk* industry, complete with training and quality-control facilities in rural areas, would not only benefit local employment but also focus villagers' awareness and resources on the conservation of wild plant resources.

Alcoholic Beverages

Jand, the local beer, and *raksi,* the local liquor, are enhancements in the lives of most Nepalese. Moreover, *jand* and *raksi* are obligatory in the festivals and other ceremonial activities of the Chepang, Danuwar, Gurung, Newar, Tamang, and Tharu communities. Villagers generally prepare these beverages for their own consumption, but some families also trade in them for their livelihood. Although it is illegal to prepare liquor at home without permission from the authorities, villagers do so quietly.

Marcha. The fermenting cake, *marcha,* has an important role in the preparation of *jand* and *raksi. Marcha* is prepared by the villagers by mixing powdered plant or plant parts into rice (*Oryza sativa*) or millet (*Eleusine coracana*) flour to bring out a sweet, bitter, or strong taste in the liquor, as shown in the accompanying table. Different communities use different plants in the preparation of *marcha,* depending on the availability of plants in the vicinity.

Dried plants or parts of three to seven species are powdered together in the mortar of a *dhiki* (described previously under Fruits, and Fermented Vegetables) or *okhal* (manual

Plants Used to Make *Marcha*

Plant	Part Used	Taste of *Jand* and *Raksi*		
		Sweet	Bitter	Strong
Aerva sanguinolenta	plant	+	+	−
Artocarpus heterophyllus	leaf	+	−	−
Blumea lacera	plant	−	+	−
Blumeopsis flava	plant	−	+	+
Capsicum annuum	fruit	−	−	+
Clematis buchananiana	plant	+	−	+
Conyza japonica	flower head	−	+	−
Drymaria diandra	plant	+	+	−
Elephantopus scaber	plant	+	+	+
Emilia sonchifolia	plant	−	+	−
Eupatorium chinense	plant	−	+	−
Inula cappa	plant	+	+	+
Natsiatum herpeticum	plant	+	+	+
Polygala persicariifolia	plant	−	+	+
Psidium guajava	bark	+	−	−
Rungia parviflora	plant	+	+	−
Schima wallichii	flower	+	−	−
Senecio cappa	plant	−	+	+
Senecio diversifolius	plant	−	+	+
Solanum torvum	leaf, fruit	+	−	+
Tridax procumbens	plant	−	+	+
Vernonia cinerea	plant	+	+	+
Vernonia squarrosa	plant	+	+	+

wooden thresher). For every kilogram of flour, 200–300 g of plant powder is mixed in. Warm or cold water is added, and the mixture is worked into dough. From this dough, small patties 4–7 cm in diameter are formed and spread on dried straw or matting inside the house. Some powder of fermented cake is spread over these cakes as a starter. The cakes are covered with dried straw and left 5–8 days, depending on the ambient temperature. During summer, cakes ferment within 5 days; they become white like the starter *marcha*, exuding its characteristic smell of liquor (Plate 24). These fermented cakes are then dried in mild sun; in some communities, shade is preferred for drying.

***Jand* and *Raksi*.** Once *marcha* is at hand it is quite easy to produce *jand* and *raksi*. The process begins by boiling 5 pathi (1 pathi = 3.7 kg) of wheat (*Triticum aestivum*), which is then spread out on a mat. When it cools, 500 g of *marcha* powder is added and mixed well. The mixture is packed in a sack about 24 hours, after which it is known as *nidar* and gives off a characteristic liquor smell. To produce *jand*, water is vigorously mixed into the *nidar*, forming a drink with a heavy stock of fermented wheat (Plate 25). Some prefer to drink just the liquid *jand* without the stock, which requires straining of the stock, typically with a bamboo strainer. On the other hand, if the final beverage is to be *raksi*, water is added to the *nidar* in a big vessel, which is left inside the house 4–5 days; then the stock is distilled to produce *raksi* (Plate 26). In the accompanying table, a + sign means that the plant used to make the *marcha* imparts the indicated taste or character to the *jand* or *raksi* whereas a − sign means that it does not.

MEDICINAL PLANTS

Most Nepalese live in very remote rural areas, at least 4–8 hours' walk from the nearest health post (rudimentary clinic) or hospital. There is a shortage of medicines and health professionals, even those with very basic training. As a result, the rural people of Nepal continue to depend on local therapy for their health care, which is cheap, convenient, and readily available. Furthermore, the villagers are acquainted with or related to the local healer. The healer's fee can be paid either in cash (which is very scarce in rural areas) or crops, and villagers may pay whenever they have the cash or crop. My survey shows that more than 900 species of medicinal plants have been recorded in Nepal, and about 70 are exported.

History

The use of medicinal plants in Hindu culture was first mentioned in the *Rigveda* (4500–1600 B.C.). The *Ayurveda* (2500–600 B.C.), is considered the earliest source on medicinal plants in which the properties of drugs and their uses are given in detail (Chopra et al. 1958). *Ayurveda* is derived from two Sanskrit words: *ayur,* life, and *veda,* the science. This ancient system of medicine has eight divisions dealing with different aspects of the science of life and the art of healing. Ayurvedic medicine is based on plants, animal products, and minerals. The *Ayurveda* was followed by the *Charaka* and the *Susruta;* the dates of these works are debated by scholars but they could not have been written later than 1000 B.C. These treatises are the nuclei for the development of the ancient medical science of South Asia.

It is estimated that Ayurvedic medicine came into Kathmandu as early as A.D. 879. It was not formally organized until the Malla regime (about 1500), however, when a *vaidyakhana* (Ayurvedic pharmacy) was started at Hanuman Dhoka palace square in Kathmandu to prepare medicine (T. B. Shrestha 1979). Although there was a lack of adequate facilities to refine plants and a shortage of skilled labor, preventing large-scale operation, some medicines were prepared on a limited scale. The *vaidyas* (traditional drug practitioners) of Kathmandu followed the Ayurvedic system, but their skill in preparing medicines from plants and their art of diagnosis were handed down from their ancestors.

During the Rana autocracy, the role of the *vaidya* or *kabiraj* was important in the palaces. The *vaidyakhana* of Hanuman Dhoka was moved, and Ayurvedic medicines were made available only to Rana rulers and their families, ending the tradition of a public dispensary. Prime Minister Jung Bahadur had a personal physician, Kabiraj Chakrapani Vaidya, who accompanied him during his visit to England in 1850. The new location of the *vaidyakhana* was in the enormous and newly built personal palace of Prime Minister Chandra Shamsher, called Singha Durbar, which was completed in 1904. Since then, this pharmacy has been known as Singha Durbar Vaidyakhana and has served as the national center for the development of herbal medicines. At the time of Chandra Shamsher, physicians were given opportunities to train in their respective areas of interest. He sent Ayurvedic physician Kabiraj Shiv Nath Rimal to India for training (T. B. Shrestha 1979), which is evidence that Chandra Shamsher tried to develop trained Ayurvedic practitioners as well as medicine.

After the dawn of democracy, King Tribhuvan declared the availability of Ayurvedic medicines for the general public. Hence, the responsibility and significance of the *vaidyakhana* intensified. In 1961, it began distributing Ayurvedic medicines free of charge to people through centers located in each district of Nepal.

The history of homeopathic health care in Nepal dates back to about 1930. In 1950, a homeopathic dispensary was established in Kathmandu and still serves many patients.

Likewise, unani health care is used in some parts of the country. These systems of treatment use fewer drug plants but their role in public healthcare has been important. Increasingly, allopathic medicine and growing numbers of hospitals and physicians means that, in Nepal, traditional medicine, homeopathy, and unani are used less and less.

Later Developments. Medicinal plants collected by the rural people of Nepal had long been in great demand in neighboring countries. But the business of export was limited to private traders only. In the 1930s, a chemist, Prof. Khadananda Sharma, identified the potential for the development of Nepalese medicinal herbs, writing a report on the subject for the government of Nepal. As a result, the Vanaspati Goswara (botany section) was established at Tebahal, Kathmandu, where trading of crude herbal drugs used to be a prime activity. In 1937, this office was moved to Pakanajol, Kathmandu, and named Vanaspati Phant (botany department), with Prof. Sharma as its head. Later, an herbal farm was created with about 25 ropanies (1 ropani = 0.05 hectare) of land at the foot of the Shivapuri Hills north of Kathmandu. Some important exotic herbs such as *Digitalis purpurea* and *Saussurea lappa,* and indigenous plants such as *Aconitum laciniatum,* were cultivated there. There was a record of the introduction in Kathmandu of the camphor tree, *Cinnamomum camphora,* from China in 1890, for both medicinal and aromatic purposes, but the cultivation of these plants did not flourish. Commercial cultivation of medicinal plants is discussed subsequently under Collection, Trade, and Cultivation.

In 1960, the Vanaspati Phant was converted into a department under the Ministry of Forests. This department was responsible for the formulation and implementation of government policies on research, collection, cultivation, and sale of Nepalese medicinal plants. To achieve these objectives, five sections were set up: the Royal Botanical Garden, Royal Drug Research Laboratory, Botanical Survey and Herbarium, Herbal Farms, and Herbal Trading Center.

The Royal Botanical Garden was established in 1960, 16 km southeast of Kathmandu at Godawari, for various species of plants, including medicinal plants. The Royal Drug Research Laboratory, started in 1964, was concerned with research on the utilization of herbal plants, development of technology, testing, standardization, and quality control of the drugs. The Herbal Farms were located in different ecological zones to develop the technology for cultivation, utilization, and processing of medicinal plants. Vegetation surveys and taxonomic research in different parts of Nepal were conducted by the Botanical Survey and Herbarium. At the same time, the first ethnobotanical information about useful plants, including medicinal ones, was being recorded. Statistical data on exported herbs started to be recorded by the Herbal Trading Center, where prevailing procedures for trading medicinal plants were also studied, providing useful information for business people and the collectors.

In 1971, the Production Unit of the Royal Drug Research Laboratory was converted into a commercial organization,

Royal Drugs Limited, which started commercial production of drugs. However, the new organization could utilize only a small fraction of plant-based crude drugs in its products. Later, it was felt that in order to safeguard the interest of the general public, a regulatory climate for drugs and pharmaceuticals had to be created to control their import, manufacture, storage, distribution, and use. In 1979, a draft of Drug Act 2035 was passed by the National Assembly (then the National Panchayat), creating the Department of Drug Administration.

Local Therapy

About 90% of Nepalese reside in rural areas where modern health care facilities are lacking. It is estimated that there is one physician for 30,000 people whereas there is one healer for fewer than 100 people (Gillam 1989). Moreover, modern medicines are expensive and difficult to find when needed. As a result, villagers in Nepal have to depend on local therapy, which caters to the masses in the traditional way. This therapy is based on plants that are readily available locally (Plate 27). The local healers have no instruments to detect disease; it is their experienced observations that help detect ailments. They observe the eyes, nose, mouth, urine, and feces and feel the pulse of a patient. Healers also advise the patient to worship gods and goddesses, sacrificing birds and other animals in the process.

The healers generally examine their patients in the morning or evening; daytime is allocated for domestic work such as farming and caring for the animals. Generally, three to seven patients a day visit a healer at his or her house. Healers visit the house of the patient for treatment and stay at patient's house if necessary.

In collecting herbal medicines, there are some requisites listed by the healers. Depending on the nature of the disease and plant species, the drug should be collected before sunrise, after sunrise, midday, or before sunset (Plate 28). Generally, the healers do not collect plants on rainy days. Drying and storage are performed with special care; the healers try to dry leafy parts in shade, and roots in sun. The healers then pack small and leafy drugs in a piece of cloth to hang them from the ceiling. Similarly, larger drug materials such as bark are kept in dry places.

Medicinal plants or their parts may be administered as a juice, paste, infusion, decoction, powder, or by smoking powder. To get juice and paste, a stone mortar and pestle is used. Paste is mostly used externally (Plate 29), and for internal use, the juice, a decoction, or an infusion is used. The dose is estimated and varies by healer and community. For medicinal uses, according to the villagers the color of parts of the plant may indicate usefulness in the treatment of disease. For example, juice of the yellow dodder, *Cuscuta reflexa,* which is a parasitic plant, is used to treat jaundice. Juice of the red flowers of *Rhododendron arboreum* and *Woodfordia fruticosa* is used to stop profuse bleeding during menstruation and to treat bloody dysentery (Plate 30).

The method of payment by the patient to the healer is very flexible and suited to the rural setting of Nepal. Food grains, clothes, vegetables, chickens, and locally brewed alcoholic beverages can be used to pay the healer. If the patient does not have any of these items, he can make the payment in the future; money is paid by only a few patients.

When I interviewed patients about the efficacy of local treatment, more than 65% of the patients were satisfied with their treatments, 15% replied that they had no alternative or could not afford modern treatment, and 5–10% of the patients were not satisfied. Most rural patients go to hospitals and health care centers only on the recommendation of the local healer.

Collection, Trade, and Cultivation

The business of herbal drugs is important for the rural economy and the country as well. The export of herbal drugs to neighboring countries is an age-old tradition. Villagers collect the crude drugs from wild stocks (Plate 31) during various collection seasons. Much of the collection for trade is quite haphazard and tends to disturb the habitat, as discussed in Chapter 1 under Conservation (Threatened and Endangered Plants). For most villagers the collection of herbs is a leisure-time activity, not a profession. Hence, most villagers get a minimal price from middlemen who transfer the products to urban centers, where they often command many times the price paid to the villagers.

Commercial cultivation and trade of drug plants was initiated by the Herbs Production and Processing Company Limited, established in 1981. The company has its own herbal farms in several areas of the Terai. Some of the medicinal plants cultivated there are *Cymbopogon flexuosus, C. martinii, C. winterianus, Matricaria chamomilla,* and *Ocimum basilicum* (which also grows wild). The company also has its own processing units.

According to government rules, some wild herbs can be exported only after processing, including *Acorus calamus, Gaultheria fragrantissima, Justicia adhatoda, Pinus roxburghii, Rhododendron anthopogon,* and some species of lichens. Also regulated are a number of plants that are threatened or endangered, as explained in Chapter 1 under Conservation, including *Cinnamomum glaucescens, Dioscorea deltoidea, Nardostachys grandiflora, Picrorhiza scrophulariiflora, Swertia chirayita, Taxus baccata* subsp. *wallichiana, Valeriana jatamansii,* and *Zanthoxylum armatum.* The export of processed and semi-processed extracts of these plants is encouraging economically. The Herbs Production and Processing Company also supplies extracts to Royal Drugs Limited and other manufacturers in Nepal.

BAMBOO AND OTHER FIBER PLANTS

Bamboo is an important forest plant from which many of the rural population of the world make innumerable uses. The beauty and durability of bamboo has long been known in other Asian countries. Traditional uses of these plants have become part of Nepalese culture. There is hardly any other kind of plant that has so many uses. Bamboo is essential literally from the cradle to the grave as it is used to make a cradle after the birth of a child and a stretcher to carry a corpse to its cremation or burial. The fiber obtained from different parts of bamboo has tremendous contributions to fulfill basic requirements.

Bamboo species are found in different ecological zones of Nepal. The distribution and abundance of bamboo seem to be directly linked to the amount of rainfall. Hence, the eastern half of the country is more abundant in bamboo distribution and also has more species. Bamboo in the villages is cultivated, usually in gullies, on steep slopes, and in rocky areas unfit for agriculture. Forest bamboo is owned by the government, but the wild stands of bamboo face uncontrolled exploitation, chiefly because of the lack of proper management or plantation development programs.

The use of bamboo in Nepalese villages awaits systematic study. Morphologically, forest bamboo is thinner walled compared to the species cultivated around villages. Moreover, many species of wild bamboo are known only by their local names. There are two main forms of bamboo: tree bamboo and shrubby bamboo. Bamboo in tree form, more than 8 m high, is important commercially. Locally, it is used in construction to create scaffolding or poles and beams. This type of bamboo has a wide distribution, especially in the deciduous forest belts. Examples include *Bambusa balcooa, B. nutans* subsp. *cupulata, B. tulda, Dendrocalamus hamiltonii, D. hookeri,* and *D. strictus.* Shrubby bamboo grows by streams and on the margins of evergreen forests. Examples include *Drepanostachyum falcatum, D. intermedium, Sinarundinaria maling,* and *Thamnocalamus aristatus.*

Bamboo is characteristically fast-growing. Because bamboo is good at soil binding, it is considered ideal for afforestation. The traditional method for producing planting material for bamboo is by vegetative propagation. Many techniques have been developed such as rhizome planting, culm and branch cutting, and layering. The conventional method for propagating bamboo in the rural communities of Nepal is the rhizome method: people take some rhizomes from the mother plant, trim the culms above a few branching nodes, and transplant them, especially during the rainy season as this obviates the need for watering. New culms start growing within a few months after transplanting. Propagation from seed is not practiced as it takes a long time.

Uses of Bamboo

Bamboo has long been considered a source of wealth in Nepal, and it remains important in the life of the rural people. Bamboo is used for food, fodder, medicine, fiber, and construction among many other purposes. Tender shoots of *Bambusa tulda, Dendrocalamus hamiltonii* and *D. strictus* are used as a vegetable or pickle. Tamangs and Gurungs ferment small slices of young shoots, which are later cooked with vegetables; these fermented shoots are popular throughout Nepal. Chepangs, Danuwars, and Tharus consume bamboo seeds when food is scarce.

Bamboo has an important role in construction. It is used in the construction of dams, canals, and bridges. Bamboo sometimes provides the framing, including windows, and gates for houses. Bamboo is put up for fences and forms good support for bean vines and other climbers in the garden.

Bamboo is also used to manufacture a variety of everyday articles. Whole culms can be used for various purposes, depending on the length and diameter of the culm. Chepangs, Danuwars, Tharus, and sometimes Gurung and Tamangs, use large hollow culms for storing salt, spices, oil, and valuable documents. Some also use culms as water containers. Culms are used to make furniture such as cots and chairs, and household goods such as ladders, dustpans, pen holders, walking sticks, umbrella handles, and brooms. The springiness of bamboo is vital in building fishing rods, and traps for fish, birds, and other animals. Smaller culms can be fashioned into tobacco pipes (Plate 32), blowpipes, musical flutes, palettes for carrying loads, handles of agricultural tools, birdcages, and stands.

Strips from bamboo culms also serve various purposes and are categorized as "rough strip" or "thin strip," according to use. To get rough strips, the culms are beaten with a log. The rough fibers are then woven into mats (Plate 33). These mats serve as walls, fences, and roofs for temporary huts. Thin strips of bamboo are prepared by splitting the culms lengthwise (Plate 34). From these strips are made bangles, baskets (Plate 35), strainers, grain storage bins (*bhakari*), backpacks (*doko*), head straps for carrying loads (*namlo*), hats, mats, winnowing trays (*nanglo*), fans, rings, ropes, screens, toys, Nepalese poncho frames, and cradles for carrying babies. Kitchenware and other household goods are also made from thin bamboo strips.

The medical use of bamboo is also varied. Villagers apply herbal medicines to dislocated bones and bind limbs with strips of bamboo as splints. The siliceous secretion found in the culms of some species is used as a cooling tonic and aphrodisiac, and to relieve asthma and cough. The leaves of bamboo are a good substitute fodder, especially in winter when green fodder is scarce. They are considered nutritious.

Bamboo fulfills many functions for which the villagers would otherwise have to buy expensive manufactured goods. In addition, most bamboo articles made by the villagers on a small scale are sold in the market. To some extent, bamboo provides an employment opportunity for rural people, at the same time generating income, helping families buy other essentials.

Other Fiber Plants

The first human technical invention was probably a knot, tied with a vegetable fiber. Later, vegetable fibers, such as those from bamboo, were used for various purposes, in handicrafts and industrially. Cotton (*Gossypium*) is in great demand for various uses, so in rural communities other plant fibers are used for nets, twine, binding, and thatching among other purposes, as done by Chepangs, Danuwars, and Tharus. The use of vegetable fibers introduced changes in clothing, for which animal hides had been used. Many rural people in Nepal use handwoven rough clothes, which are prepared from the fibers of wild plants. One may see Tamangs in Bharkhu, Rasuwa district, and Gurungs in Saindu, Kaski district, weaving clothes from plant fibers. Fibers are obtained from different parts of different species of plants, thus the qualities and uses of fibers differ. Plant fibers used by Nepalese villagers are of three kinds: seed fiber, leaf fiber, and bast fiber.

Seed fibers are obtained from the seed hairs of the silk cotton tree (*Bombax ceiba*), for example. This deciduous tree of the subtropical belt bears oblong fruits with abundant hairy seeds inside. The fiber is generally used for stuffing; silk cotton is also traded in urban markets. The shrub, swallow wort (*Calotropis gigantea*), grows on open, dry land and bears conical, curved fruits with numerous seeds. At the top of each seed there are silky white fibers, used as pillow stuffing by Danuwars and Tharus. The pillows are given to children or sick persons as the stuffing is meant to be cool and soothing. *Cryptolepis buchananii*, a climber, also produces seed fibers that Gurungs present as a garland whenever anyone sets out on a journey, as a wish for a successful journey.

Leaf fiber is obtained from *Agave cantala* and *Yucca gloriosa*, for example. Fibrous vascular bundles and other sheathing cells are found scattered in the pithy matrix of the leaves. The vascular bundles are separated by crushing leaves between wooden blocks, by beating them with a mallet, or by retting. The fibers are used to prepare ropes, mats, carpets, and head straps (*namlo*).

Bast fiber obtained from *Boehmeria macrophylla, Girardinia diversifolia,* and *Maoutia puya* is especially suitable for weaving clothes, sacks, and fishnets. Some extra work has to be done to get refined fiber. First, bark is peeled off from the stem and boiled with wood ash about 3 hours, the time depending on the amount of fiber. The ash makes the bark soft and easy to separate into individual strands. The bark is then washed in water, shaking vigorously. The cleaned fibers are immersed in water mixed with talc, then dried in the sun. After drying, the talc powder is shaken off and the fiber is ready for use.

The straight branches and stalks of *Grewia optiva* and *Sterculia villosa* are also a source of bast fiber. They are cut and left in the sun to dry for a whole day, then immersed in fresh water. The stems are pressed underwater with stones or heavy objects and left 3 weeks to a month. After retting, fiber is stripped from the stems by hand, then beaten on the water surface, washed, and dried. They furnish a rough white fiber, used mostly for ropes, sacks, bags, cots, and head straps (*namlo*). Fiber of the elephant rope tree (*S. villosa*) looks brownish when washed. Similarly, dried stems of *Cannabis sativa* are immersed in water about a week, then dried in the sun.

After drying, the bark is removed (Plate 36) and used for spinning thread. A *katuwa* (wooden top) is used for spinning

thread (Plate 37), but the traditional *charkha* (spinning wheel) is also popular for this purpose. The thread is suitable for making cloth, sacks, bags, head straps, and rope (Plate 38).

Camel's Foot Climber. A versatile fiber plant is camel's foot climber (*Bauhinia vahlii*), which has numerous uses in rural Nepal. It is a giant climber with an irregular stem about 60–50 cm in diameter. Its branches generally terminate in a pair of revolute tendrils, and the leaves are stalked variable in size, and deeply cordate. Flowers are white but on exposure turn yellow. The fruit is a long, flat woody pod clothed with dense brown hairs.

Many parts of the camel's foot climber are edible. Its tender pods and leaves are cooked as vegetables. Mature pods are placed over hot ashes to roast; they burst open with a loud pop and the seeds inside are eaten like cashew nuts. In some places, villagers soak dried seeds in water about 2 hours, then fry and eat them. According to Watt (1889–1896), seeds contain appreciable quantities of protein.

Most parts of camel's foot climber are used in folk medicine, as described in Chapter 4. Everyday uses of the climber are numerous. Leaves are used as a tobacco wrapper for smoking. A mat made from the leaves is warm and comfortable in the cold winter season. Leaves are used to construct containers for storing foodstuffs; it is believed that food stored in such a container is not susceptible to attack by insects or worms (Plate 39). The leaves can also be made into plates, cups, and hats (Plates 40, 41). Moreover, the leaves, which are water resistant, are placed on a bamboo frame to fashion an umbrella. In some places, leaves are used to thatch roofs and also serve as a good animal fodder.

Peeled bark is soaked in water, hammered with a wooden mallet (Plate 42), and washed to produce a soft bast fiber used for twine, nets, ropes, sacks, mats, shoes, head straps (*namlo*), and rings for the bottoms of round-bottomed vessels and pots (Plate 43). String made of the fiber is used to tie splints. A suitable stem may serve as a walking stick.

Handmade Paper. The technology for making paper was introduced into Nepal from China in the fourteenth century. Since then, it has been passed on as a tradition. Bark fibers of *Daphne bholua, D. papyracea, Edgeworthia gardneri,* and *Wikstroemia canescens* are used to prepare Nepalese paper. The Tamangs of Bharkhu, Rasuwa district, about 115 km northwest of Kathmandu, used to prepare Nepalese paper but have stopped since the establishment of the Langtang National Park in 1976. However, Tamangs have continued papermaking at Manthali, Dolkha district, about 200 km east of Kathmandu, and surrounding areas.

The process is simple. Bark of the plant is peeled off and dried. It is then soaked in water to remove the epidermis, any hard knots, and other imperfections. It is then boiled 2–3 hours, depending on the amount of raw material, with wood ash to soften the bark, then washed. The substance thus obtained is beaten with a hard object to convert it into refined fibers, which are mixed with water to create a homogeneous pulp (Plate 44). This pulp is uniformly spread on a cloth mesh bordered by a wooden frame, which is immersed in water; the amount of pulp determines the thickness of the paper. The frame is lifted from the water and left to dry in the sun. After drying, the paper is removed from the mesh, yielding Nepalese handmade paper (Plate 45).

Nettle Fiber. Plants of the nettle family (*sisnu* in Nepali), the Urticaceae, have long been used for fiber. Villagers also use various species for food, fodder, and medicine. It is important to revive the extensive use of nettle fiber. With adequate planning, it could meet local demand and be exported as well, helping upgrade the rural economy.

The plants generally grow in moist and neglected areas, attaining a height of 1.5–3.5 m. They are available throughout the country in mountain forests 1200–3500 m in elevation. No attempt has been made to cultivate them. Some, *Girardinia diversifolia* and *Urtica dioica* in particular, are covered with stinging hairs with hooked protrusions that cause irritation to human skin. *Boehmeria macrophylla, B. platyphylla, Girardinia diversifolia, Maoutia puya,* and *Urtica dioica* yield fine, soft fiber used to make sacks, bags, coarse clothes, and fishnets. These products are bartered for food or other necessary items among the rural communities, and increasingly are sold in urban markets for cash. Various items made from nettle fiber are exported from Nepal as handicrafts. Some enterprises have also started to mix nettle fiber with wool to make carpets and other semiwoolen products. *Boehmeria polystachya, B. rugulosa, Debregeasia longifolia, D. salicifolia,* and *Oreocnide frutescens* are used to make rope, twine, and head straps (*namlo*).

The process of fiber extraction is similar to that used for other plants. The fibrous bark of the stem is separated with the help of a sickle. In some places, villagers cut a small section of the bark (about 5 cm) from the bottom, then peel off the intact bark by hand. Villagers of the Pyuthan district in western Nepal cut the stem and remove the spines and leaves with a piece of cloth. The bark is removed from the green stem and dried. Fibers are teased out.

Treatment of the fiber differs according to place and the plants used. Bark is used directly to make ropes and twine, but to make clothes, bags, and sacks, some extra treatment is necessary. In the district of Rolpa in western Nepal, dried bark is boiled with wood ash 3–4 hours and allowed to cool. It is then beaten on a flat stone or wooden plank, washed, and dried in the sun to make clothing and so on. In the district of Dolkha in central Nepal, dried bark is boiled in water with wood ash, washed, mixed with talc (*kamero* in Nepali), and dried in shade or mild sun. After complete drying, the talc is removed by shaking. Some people of Dolkha use rice husks instead of talc. This process adds luster and softness to the fiber, which is used for weaving clothes and fishnets. To spin fiber into yarn, a *katuwa* (wooden top) is typically used, but the *charkha* (spinning wheel) is also employed, depending on the locale and ethnic community. The fineness of the yarn largely depends on the skill of the spinner and the quality of the fiber.

OTHER USES OF PLANTS

The villagers of Nepal have developed their own plant-based technologies to meet their basic requirements. In rural Nepal, people are very dependent on plants because access to machinery or processed material is extremely limited.

House Building

Unlike urban people, villagers do not require large trees to construct multistoried houses. They use clay, bamboo, timber, plant fiber, and grass thatching, which are locally available. Most dwellings are one- or two-story houses that have flat, two-sloped, or four-sloped roofs. At upper elevations or in the high mountain valleys, where trees and other plants are scarce, stones and boulders form the frames, walls, and roofs. In the rest of the country, however, very spacious dwellings with one or two floors are constructed entirely using plants. Generally, Chepangs, Danuwars, Mooshars, and Tharus have one-story dwellings with few or no windows. Gurungs, Limbus, Magars, Rais, and Tamangs install windows in their two-story dwellings.

The species of plants used for house building differ from one vegetation zone to the next, depending on local availability. For pole and beam construction, people in the Terai generally use saffron (*Adina cordifolia*), *sisso* (*Dalbergia sisso*), *sal* (*Shorea robusta*), and Indian laurel (*Terminalia alata*). In the midlands, Nepalese alder (*Alnus nepalensis*), Indian chestnut (*Castanopsis indica*), walnut (*Juglans regia* var. *kamaonia*), Persian lilac (*Melia azedarach*), and needle wood (*Schima wallichii*) are used. Toward subalpine regions, Himalayan silver birch (*Betula utilis*), *Rhododendron,* and yew (*Taxus baccata* subsp. *wallichiana*) are used. The outer structure of the house is constructed using bamboo and small branches of plants, and walls are plastered by mixing clay and husks of plants such as rice (*Oryza sativa*), mustards (*Brassica campestris* var. *sarson, B. napus*), and wheat (*Triticum aestivum*). Roofing is typically in the form of grass thatching. To tie bunches of thatch together, villagers use camel's foot climber (*Bauhinia vahlii*), jute (*Corchorus capsularis*), *babi* grass (*Eulaliopsis binata*), *Grewia,* and bark of the elephant rope tree (*Sterculia villosa*) among other plants.

Implements

The design of agricultural implements in Nepal varies according to topography and ethnic community. For example, wooden plows used in the plains of the Terai and in hilly regions differ slightly in design and shape because in hilly regions, fields are terraced. Likewise, the shape and size of spades and sickles differ. Often, hilly terraces are too small to use a plow, which means that most hill terraces are tilled using a spade. In the high mountain valleys, yaks are sometimes used for plowing. The Kathmandu Valley is an exception, where a spade is used to till the land even though a plow could be used.

Villages turn the wood of *Boehmeria rugulosa, Mangifera indica, Rhododendron arboreum*, and other soft-wooded trees to make household containers and utensils. Some families run a larger-scale operation and sell these items for cash or crops. Gurungs, Magars, Rais, Tamangs, and Limbus make combs out of soft wood (Plate 46). Danuwars, Mooshars, and Tharus make *thakari*, a hairbrush, out of the midveins of coconut leaves or leaves of other palms.

Except during very busy planting and harvesting seasons for various crops, leisure time in the village is a time to engage oneself in weaving, building, or making implements. Women, in particular, apply themselves to gainful activities within the house to fulfill the family's requirements. For example, they prepare mats and shoes of straw whenever they are free of other household chores (Plate 47).

Entertainment

Many radios have found their way into the interior of rural Nepal, but televisions and video tape recorders are rarer. Increasingly, Hindi or Nepali movies are shown in many urban areas, but there are no cinemas in rural Nepal. Hence, most rural entertainment is limited to songs and dances during festivals and rituals such as weddings. Occasionally, village children take turns on a *ping* (swing), built with four tall bamboo poles joined in a pyramidal structure, with two thick ropes made from plant fibers hung from the top. A form of Ferris wheel (*rote ping*) made of wood was very common in rural Nepal, but it is becoming very rare. Around October, however, when the harvests are done and the Dasain festivities approach, many villages have *ping* and *rote ping* built.

Dyes and Paints

The use of dyes from natural resources has a long history. These natural dyes are of vegetable, animal, or mineral origin. Production of dyestuff from plants involves collecting parts of plants, and the dye-making process is time-consuming. In contrast, chemical dyes can be produced in large quantities and need no further processing by the user, which makes them popular. Chemical dyes have disadvantages for the poor in rural communities, however, because chemical dyes are often prohibitively expensive. Also, most natural dyes are not toxic and do not pollute the water or air. To this day, hand spinning and dyeing with vegetable dye are practiced in rural Nepal.

Malla (1993) identified 182 species of dye plants available in Nepal. Besides price, vegetable dyes are more desirable than synthetic dyes because the colors they produce. Vegetable dyes are derived from roots, wood, bark, flowers, fruits, and seeds. It is important to know the best collection period and storage method to retain properties such as brilliance and colorfastness. It is best to collect roots in the fall, and leaves when they are in full growth. Bark is also collected in the fall, except for bark with resinous substances, which is collected in spring. Fruits and seeds give good results if collected when they are ripe. Lichens should be collected in winter or after the rainy season, when they are easy to scrape off the substrate. Fresh parts of plants produce better color, and flowers lose brilliance if boiled too long. Lichens, fruits, and seeds for dyes can be dried but should be stored in dry places.

Vegetable dyestuffs yield a wide range of shades useful in garments, carpets, and everyday objects. In the mountain villages, a popular color for dyeing is red, which is derived from *majitho* (*Rubia manjith*). It releases its color when boiled in water. The popular shades used in carpet making are derived cheaply from plants and are readily available. Carpets dyed with natural dyestuffs are renowned and praised by Western carpet importers and tourists. The bark of *Lagerstroemia parviflora* and *Shorea robusta* yields a black color, and that of *Juglans regia* var. *kamaonia*, brown. Bark of *Berberis aristata* and *Terminalia bellirica* give a yellow color. Flower petals of *Hibiscus rosa-sinensis* are used for purple, and the corolla tube of *Nyctanthes arbor-tritis* for orange.

The art of painting in Nepal has a long history, especially for religious paintings such as *thanka* and *pauva*. In rural areas, people used to portray trees, flowers, animals, and other symbolic objects in their paintings; these paintings still hang in many village houses. Increasingly, old *thanka* and *pauva* paintings are in great demand in foreign countries. The quantity of paint needed for the number of new paintings requires increasing use of synthetic paints, but in older times these paints were derived exclusively from different parts of plants, usually by boiling.

Decoration and Ornament

Villagers like to decorate their houses with flowers from their kitchen garden or from the wild, especially during feasts and festivals. First, they paint the floor and wall with locally available white or red soil and paint the windows and doorways black. They prepare the black color by boiling the bark of walnut (*Juglans regia* var. *kamaonia*) or other plants, as described under Dyes and Paints. Then they attach a bunch of flowers above the main door and the windows. They also put bunches of flowers in holes in the wall, as the use of vases is not common.

In urban areas of Nepal, imported cosmetics are in vogue and women decorate themselves in Western style. However, the desire of women in rural areas to ornament themselves is not any less. Especially during festivals and other ceremonies, women and girls in the village use plant sources for ornament. A Tamang woman once showed me red liquid in a small flat bottle that she used on her cheeks and lips as a cosmetic during festival (*jatra*). The liquid was prepared from the fruit of *chugo*, the sea buckthorn (*Hippophae tibetana*), prepared by squeezing ripe fruit, straining in a clean cloth, and boiling the juice till the liquid was syrupy. The liquid was cooled and put in the bottle.

Danuwars and Tharus, among others, use the leaves of the henna plant (*Lawsonia inermis*) to decorate their palms, as do many women throughout South Asia. They pick fresh leaves, mix them with some old straw and old cow dung, and pound them together, adding some water. The resulting paste is then applied to the palms in artistic patterns, left to dry about 4–6 hours, then washed, leaving the characteristic crimson of henna.

Other methods are also used to beautify teeth, hands, wrists, and feet. Village women chew the black seeds of *Neohymenopogon parasiticus* about 5–10 minutes, spit them out, and wash their mouths. This leaves black marks between the teeth, which are said to look beautiful when the women smile. Women also rub their palms and soles with the corolla tube of the tree of sorrow (*Nyctanthes arbor-tritis*), which leaves orange marks. Red powder from ripe fruit of *Mallotus philippensis* is collected and used by women of the Terai as a substitute for vermilion powder on their foreheads; this powder is also used for coloring the palms, especially by Danuwar and Tharu women. Tamang women of Bharkhu, Rasuwa district, use bangles made from of the vine, *Smilax aspera*. They heat the stem and shape it into a bangle.

Bathing and Washing

In Nepal, where soap made from industrial chemicals is scarce, plants substitute for soap and detergents. Different parts of plants are used, but whatever parts is used, it is first squeezed before adding to the water. Some plants are used for bathing, some for washing clothes, and a few species are used for both.

Bark of *Albizia lucidior* is used for bathing as are seeds of *Diplocyclos palmatus* and roots of *Gonostegia hirta*. The root of *Silene stracheyi* is also used for soap. Whole plants of *Persicaria lapathifolia* var. *lanata* and the fruit of *Catunaregam spinosa* are also used for bathing and washing. Plants used for bathing are squeezed and pounded finely for even mixing in the water. Chepangs, Danuwars, Tamangs, and Tharus bathe and wash the head with the entire mixture, but Gurungs let the plant residue settle to the bottom and use only the water for bathing.

When washing laundry with plant parts, it is important to mix the squeezed plant parts in water before washing starts. After that, if the laundry is not very dirty, it is simply immersed in hot water about an hour, then washed, beating it with a log. Dirtier laundry is boiled in water 1–2 hours, depending on the amount of clothes, then beaten with a log on a hard surface and washed. Whole plants of *Euphorbia parviflora* and *Persicaria nepalensis*, roots of *Asparagus racemosus* and *Cyathula tomentosa*, and fruit of *Sapindus mukorossi*, *Solanum aculeatissimum*, and *S. anguivi* are used for washing clothes (Plate 48).

There is another traditional process used for washing laundry. Gurungs and Tamangs add ash of rice straw to boiling water, put the laundry in, boil it again a few hours, then wash as usual at a water source such as a pond or river. Danuwars and Tharus burn mustard (*Brassica napus*), make a cake of the ash, and use it whenever they need to do washing. Danuwars, Gurungs, Tamangs, and Tharus also use wood ash for washing clothes.

Fish Poisons

Among the different uses of plants, the piscicidal one is very creative and versatile. Freshwater fish in Nepal are found in rivers, streams, ponds, and rice fields. Fish are considered auspicious, especially for religious activities. For instance, the fish is a sign of bon voyage at the start of a journey. Fish dishes are enjoyed by all Nepalese, but Danuwars and Tharus are especially fond of fish in their diet. They devote much time to catching fish; it is very common to see Danuwars and Tharus fishing near their villages. Fish may be caught by netting, trapping, or using poison plants.

Netting and trapping fish requires making the net. Danuwars and Tharus weave nets from imported thread whereas Chepangs make them from the fibers of *Maoutia puya*. Danuwars and Tharus are experienced in making fish traps using bamboo sticks. Much skill is needed to weave nets or design traps, whereas using plants to poison fish is easy and convenient. Many villagers have some knowledge of piscicidal plants and collect and use them as needed. Danuwars and Tharus know the piscicidal plants in the subtropical Terai, whereas Gurungs and Tamangs know the poisonous plants in the temperate midlands. Chepangs live at the margin between these two zones and thus have some knowledge of the plants in both.

Fish are commonly poisoned by simply dispersing an appropriate amount of poison in the water. Before spreading the poison, the villagers try to ascertain that the water is shallow, still, or slow-flowing so the poison will not be dispersed before affecting the fish. The duration and the amount of poison differ according to the plants and the amount of water. The poison is extracted by pounding the plant with a stone or log. The resultant mass is then spread on the water. Or poison may introduced by squeezing the plant in the water. Some people put squeezed plant in the water, then rub it with their legs. Fishermen disturb the water in all directions to spread the poison.

The affected fish remain motionless or float to the surface and are retrieved easily. Villagers say that the poison stings the fish's gills, disturbs their eyesight, or renders them senseless. According to P. Joshi (1986), the toxicity of various piscicidal plants has been attributed to the presence of saponins, alkaloids, glycosides, tannins, resins, and essential oils. These substances disturb different systems of the fish body. For example, the poison may enter the bloodstream, disturbing the respiratory or nervous system, or prevent oxygen intake by lowering surface tension between the water and the gills. Poisoned fish do not require special treatment when preparing them for cooking. No side effects were noted by the villagers when eating plant-poisoned fish.

Different plants and parts are used for fish poison; most are common in the wild. Hence, fresh plants are used because they are available most of the time. Latex from cut pieces of *Euphorbia royleana* constitutes one fish poison. The whole plant of *Anagallis arvensis* is pounded before introducing it into the water. Bark of *Catunaregam spinosa*, *Millettia extensa*, and *Plumeria rubra* are crushed, and the leaves of *Agave cantala, Annona squamata, Buddleja asiatica,* and *B. paniculata* are squeezed to spread the poison. Oil cake of *Diplokenma butyracea* and *Madhuca longifolia* is soaked in water 5–7 hours to prepare a liquid poison. Chepangs, Danuwars, and Tharus put plants of *Persicaria barbata, P. hydropiper,* and *P. pubescens* in the water and crush them with their legs; they also use fruit of *Acacia pennata.* Gurungs and Tamangs use plants of *Hedyotis scandens, Hydrocotyle himalaica,* and *Spilanthes paniculata.* Roots of *Cyathula tomentosa* and *Dioscorea deltoidea,* leaves of *Engelhardia spicata, Maesa macrophylla,* and *Rhododendron arboreum,* and immature fruit of *Juglans regia* var. *kamaonia* are crushed in the water to introduce the poison. Both bark and leaves of *Sapium insigne, Schima wallichii, Ulmus wallichiana,* and *Zanthoxylum armatum* are commonly used to stupefy fish.

NEPALESE PLANT FOLKLORE

Many folk stories, proverbs, or word puzzles in Nepal refer to characteristic features of plants. Likewise, local names for plants reflect the characteristics of the plants, birds, or other animals. Besides color and taste, for example, the names may refer to the plant's use in the treatment of disease.

Stories

Some stories concern the habitat or habit of plants. For example, once rhododendron (*R. arboreum*), the female, went to the Nepalese alder (*Alnus nepalensis*), the male, with a proposal of marriage. She expressed her desire to alder and proclaimed that he was handsome and tall, with straight, smooth stems. The soft-wooded alder listened to her adulation but refused her proposal in anger. He insulted her for daring to come to his place with a marriage proposal and said she was ugly and had no manners. Alder said rhododendron had straggly stems and branches, which were truly unsightly. The encounter with alder disappointed rhododendron but still she did not despair, and during the month of April–May she bloomed with beautiful red flowers that covered the mountain slope where she grew. When alder saw the mountain slopes covered with flowers, he began to regret rejecting the marriage offer from rhododendron. He visited rhododendron and asked for forgiveness. She replied by saying she did not want to marry him because he was proud and had no manners. He pleaded many times but she refused. Alder became disappointed and decided to commit suicide. He went to the steep slopes and jumped. For this reason, it is said that alder grows around river gorges and other steep areas.

Or a story may refer to a plant's role in disease, including disease of plants. For example, *kanda daraune,* to burn spiny and thorny plants, is a common practice in the hilly regions of Nepal, where villagers burn the bushes of *Berberis* after harvesting the wheat crop (*Triticum aestivum*). The reason given is that the barberry is simply not good for the crop, but there is a scientific reason as well. There is a fungal disease of wheat

caused by *Puccinia graminis,* which has a detrimental effect on the production of wheat. This disease completes half its life cycle on the wheat, but when the wheat is mature and harvested, the fungus attacks the barberry, where it remains until the new wheat crop grows, when it again attacks the wheat plant. Although the fruit of the barberry is edible and plants are used for fencing crop fields, villagers burn the barberries around wheat fields, thus indirectly helping control the fungal disease of wheat.

A legend explains why *pipal* (*Ficus religiosa*) and *bar* (*F. benghalensis*) are planted at *chautara* (a trailside rest stop built by a family as a gift for tired travelers in memory of departed elders) and in cemeteries. Once there was a Limbu couple living in a place in eastern Nepal (Thakkekmalung in Limbu). They had five sons: the first son was a tiger, the second a bear, the third a leopard, the fourth a man, and the last one a dog. The eldest son, the tiger, always tried to attack the man. Once the man trapped the tiger and was about to kill it when their mother arrived and told the man to free the tiger, because he was the man's elder brother. After the incident, the tiger requested his parents' permission to leave the area and went into the forest. Two brothers, the bear and leopard, also followed the tiger into the forest. The youngest, the dog, told his brother the man that he would stay with him and serve him well. When the parents got old, the mother told the man that he should make a *chautara* (trailside rest stop) after his parents' death and that they would grow as *pipal* and *bar* trees under which travelers could rest during their journeys. The man did as his mother wished. Hence, Limbus plant *pipal* and *bar* in cemeteries. They believe that the tiger, bear, and leopard live in the forest, and the dog lives with man.

Proverbs

Rukh ma bel pakyo, kag lai harsh na bismat. Literally, for a crow it is of no importance if *bel* fruit (*Aegle marmelos*) is ripe on the tree; figuratively, that which is of no use has no value.

Kankro lai thankro diyo, thankrai dhani. Literally, cucumber (*kankro, Cucumis sativus*) gets support (*thankro*) for climbing but later dies, yet the support prospers; figuratively, he who supports others in adverse circumstances becomes better off in the long run.

Besar bhanna jane pachhi kotyai rahanu pardaina. Literally, those who can identify turmeric (*Curcuma domestica*) need not scratch the rhizome with their nail to know it; figuratively, for those who know, profuse explanation is not necessary.

Push ko kera sauta ko chhora lai. The banana (*Musa paradisiaca*) that ripens in winter (November–December) is not tasty, so it is given to the stepson (who is generally neglected among family members).

Janne lai shrikhand, na janne lai khurpa ko bind. Literally, *shrikhand* (sandalwood, *Santalum album,* imported into Nepal from India and used extensively in religious ceremonies) is highly valued by one who knows its uses, but to one who does not, it is as mundane as the handle of a sickle; figuratively, only those know the value of something can appreciate it.

Aduwa khai sabha basnu, mula khai ban pasnu. Ginger (*aduwa, Zingiber officinale*) gives a refreshing smell to the mouth of one who eats it, so it is good to talk with people and attend gatherings after eating it, but radish (*mula, Raphanus sativus*) gives a bad smell, so it is better to go to lonely places (such as the forest) if one eats that.

Gulab ko phul ma pani kanda hunchha. Literally, even a flower as pretty as the rose comes with spines; figuratively, it is natural to find bad things among the good.

Phul ko basna waripari manis ko basna danda pari. The fragrance of a flower is limited to its vicinity, but the fame of a person will spread far and wide.

Jahan phal pakchha tyahin chari nachchha. Literally, birds gather to eat where fruit is ripe; figuratively, when one has nothing, people stay away, but when one has wealth, people come.

Phale ko rukh nihuranchha. Literally, the tree with fruit bends down; figuratively, people with wisdom are modest and amiable.

Word Puzzles

Jiu bhari kandai kanda, chhaina khali thaun. Pake pachhi tyahi chij ko, andra bhuri khaun. Spines all over without leaving any room. When ripe, eat the inside. Answer: *rukha katahar* (jackfruit, *Artocarpus heterophyllus*), denoting the spiny fruit with its sweet inside when ripe.

Sun phulne, tama phalne. Flowers gold, fruits copper. Answer: *chutro* (barberry, *Berberis aristata*), a spiny shrub with yellow flowers and coppery fruit.

Dharti muni jaunla chhata odhunla. I'll go underground and wear an umbrella. Answer: *pindalu* (taro, *Colocasia esculenta*), denoting the tuberous root of taro, which after planting bears a long-stalked leaf with a round blade.

Rup usko jamin muni, jamin mahti kan. Tarkari, achar khan, kan samati tan. The body is below ground, the ear above. To make vegetable and pickle, grab by the ear. Answer: *mula* (radish, *Raphanus sativus*), denoting the underground root of radish with whorls of leaves above, which are pulled to bring up the root, which is eaten.

Chandi phulne, sun phalne. Grows silver, fruits gold. Answer: *ainselu* (yellow bramble, *Rubus ellipticus*), the yellow bramble being a straggling shrub bearing beautiful white flowers and golden fruit.

Tanlai khanchhan, tanlai thukchhan. They eat you, they spit you out. Answer: *ukhu* (sugarcane, *Saccharum officinarum*), denoting the stem of sugarcane, which is peeled, cut into pieces, the juice sucked, and the remains spit out.

Aama bhand chhori kupri. The daughter is more hunchbacked than her mother. Answer: *nyuro* (fern), because a young fern

has a curled frond whereas a mature fern has a spreading frond.

Ek khutte aglo dai ko rup hunchha chamro. Mathi pugda jhuknu parne shiksha dincha ramro. One-legged older brother has a fine appearance. As he grows, he bends and gives good tutelage. Answer: *bans* (bamboo), denoting the straightness of bamboo, with strong culms but bending as it grows tall.

Sano chhanda dherai luga, thulo hunda nango, jasto paryo ustai hune, sojho ani bango. Many clothes while young, naked when older, becomes whatever you make it, straight then bent. Answer: *bans* (bamboo), describing the young, tender shoots of bamboo, covered with scales but the scales disappearing with age. The bamboo can be bent to any form according to need.

Origins of Local Names for Plants

Many common names for plants reflect a broad spectrum of local knowledge about their habitats (including their roles in the habitat), forms, similarities to other plants, resemblances to animals (including humans, birds, and insects), and their uses or other attributes. This is only natural, for many in rural Nepal interact with the plant life around them.

Many places in Nepal are named after plants. In the district of Gorkha there is a place named Chilaune (*Schima wallichii*) because of the abundance of those plants (discussed under Names Based on Use). Guranse in the district of Dhankuta in eastern Nepal is named after the *gurans* tree (*Rhododendron arboreum*). In the same district there is a place called Tin Pipale after three *pipal* trees (*Ficus religiosa*) that grew in the large rhododendron forest. Some places are named Bans Ghari, from *bans* (bamboo), or Salla Ghari, *salla* referring to *Pinus roxburghii* (*ghari* is grove). An abundance of timur (*Zanthoxylum armatum*) resulted in the place name Timure. If a locality has one prominent tree, people have often named that place after that tree, for example, Labsi Phedi (*Choerospondias axillaris*), Kabhro (*Ficus lacor*), and Bar Gachhi (*F. benghalensis*; *gachhi* is tree).

Sometimes the vernacular name for the plant differs from the word or words from which the name is derived. For example, *jhule* and *talche* are colloquialisms for *jhulne* and *talcha*, respectively.

Names Based on Habitat

Aakash beli, Chepang and Nepali for *Cuscuta reflexa, aakash* meaning sky or air, *beli*, vine, denoting its parasitic nature.

Aule sag, Nepali for *Boerhavia diffusa, aul* meaning hot lowland, *sag*, vegetable or herb, referring to its lowland subtropical habitat.

Bagarni, Danuwar for *Calotropis gigantea, bagar* meaning dry sandy ground, especially riverbanks, where it grows in abundance.

Dhape jhar, Nepali for *Monochoria vaginalis, dhap* meaning a boggy place, *jhar*, herb, referring to the aquatic herb's habitat.

Ghar tyaur, Raute for *Dioscorea bulbifera, ghar* meaning house, *tyaur,* yam, since it is grown around the homestead.

Jhinga jale, Nepali for *Drosera peltata, jhinga* meaning fly, *jali,* net, since flies are trapped when they come in contact with the sticky hairs of the plant, which is carnivorous.

Khole jhar, Nepali for *Lecanthus peduncularis, khola* meaning stream or rivulet, *jhar* herb, since it grows on moist banks.

Pani sag, Nepali for *Rorippa nasturtium-aquaticum, pani* meaning water, *sag,* vegetable or herb, since it grows on moist ground.

Sim jhar and *sim sag,* Nepali for *Cardamine impatiens, Rorippa nasturtium-aquaticum,* and *Rotala rotundifolia, sim* meaning moist or boggy places, *jhar* and *sag,* herb or vegetable, since the plants grows in moist or boggy places.

Names Based on Form

Aek patiya, Tharu for *Ophioglossum nudicaule, aek* meaning one, *patiya,* leaf bearing, since it bears only one leaf.

Ajamari jhar, Nepali for *Kalanchoe spathulata, ajamari* meaning immortal, *jhar,* herb, because it never dies since it can grow from even a leaf.

Ban kapas, Nepali for *Abelmoschus manihot* and *A. moschatus,* and Nepali and Magar for *Thespesia lampas, ban* meaning wild, *kapas,* cotton, since the seeds bear cottony fiber.

Bulake jhar, Nepali for *Tridax procumbens, bulake* meaning nose pendant, *jhar,* herb, since its inflorescence is shaped like a nose pendant.

Chyau phul, Nepali for *Bistorta amplexicaulis* and *B. macrophylla, chyau* meaning mushroom, *phul,* flower, since the round inflorescence is the shape of a mushroom.

Ghanti phul, Nepali for *Hibiscus rosa-sinensis, ghanti* meaning bell, *phul,* flower, since its flower has the shape of a bell.

Ghortapre, Bhojpuri, Magar, Nepali, Sunwar, Tamang, and Tharu for *Centella asiatica, ghora* meaning horse, *tap,* horseshoe, since its leaf is shaped like a horseshoe.

Jali swan, Newari for *Sambucus adnata, jali* meaning net, *swan,* flower, since the arrangement of flowers in the inflorescence resembles a net.

Jhule jhar, Nepali for *Crassocephalum crepidioides, jhulne* meaning to hang, *jhar,* herb, since its inflorescence hangs.

Kangiyo phul, Nepali for *Grevillea robusta, kangiyo* meaning comb, *phul,* flower, since the arrangement of flowers in the inflorescence is like that of the teeth in a comb.

Lal geri, Lepcha and Nepali for *Abrus precatorius, lal* meaning red, *geri,* seed, since its seed is red.

Lalpatta, Bhojpuri, and *Lalupate,* Nepali, for *Euphorbia pulcherrima, lal* and *lalu* meaning red, *patta* and *pat,* leaf, since the floral bract is red and looks like a leaf.

Moti phul, Nepali for *Sambucus adnata, moti* meaning pearl, *phul,* flower, since the arrangement of the small flowers in the inflorescence looks like a string of pearls.

Talche jhar, Nepali for *Equisetum diffusum, talcha* meaning lock, *jhar,* herb, since the stem joints can be pulled apart and rejoined.

Tarwar sima, Newari for *Oroxylum indicum, tarwar* meaning sword, *sima,* tree, since it bears a sword-shaped fruit.

Udho munto jhar, Nepali for *Crassocephalum crepidioides, udho* meaning down, *munto,* head, *jhar,* herb, since the flower head is nodding.

Yarling jhar, Nepali for *Dicentra scandens,* yarling meaning earring, *jhar,* herb, since the flowers hang like earrings.

Names Based on Similarity

Anare phul, Nepali for *Woodfordia fruticosa, anar* meaning pomegranate, *phul,* flower, since its red flower looks like the red seed of a pomegranate (*Punica granatum*).

Ban besar, Nepali for *Cautleya spicata, ban* meaning wild, *besar,* turmeric, since the rhizome resembles that of turmeric (*Curcuma domestica*).

Ban lasun, Nepali for *Allium wallichii, ban* meaning wild, *lasun,* garlic, since the odor of the wild plant is similar to that of cultivated garlic (*A. sativum*).

Ban tori, Danuwar for *Blumeopsis flava, ban* meaning wild, *tori,* mustard, since the wild plant has an inflorescence and flowers resembling those of cultivated mustard (*Brassica*).

Gahun jhar, Nepali for *Plantago erosa, gahun* meaning wheat, *jhar,* herb, since its inflorescence is like that of wheat (*Triticum aestivum*).

Gwe swan, Newari, and *supari phul,* Nepali, for *Gomphrena globosa, gwe* and *supari* meaning areca nut, *swan* and *phul,* flower, since the globose flower head resembles the areca nut (*Areca catechu*).

Jangali jira, Nepali for *Carum carvi, jangali* meaning wild, *jira,* cumin seed, since the seed resembles that of cumin seed (*Cuminum cyminum*).

Kodo ghans, Nepali for *Eleusine indica, kodo* meaning millet, *ghans,* grass or herb, since the inflorescence resembles that of millet (*Eleusine coracana*).

Lwange jhar, Majhi for *Ludwigia perennis, lwang* meaning cloves, *jhar,* herb, since the flowers resembles cloves (*Syzygium aromaticum;* imported into Nepal).

Mas gera, Nepali for *Cipadessa baccifera, mas* meaning black gram, *gera,* seed, since the ripe fruit resembles the seed of black gram (*Vigna mungo*).

Mula pate, Chepang and Nepali for *Elephantopus scaber, mula* meaning radish, *pat,* leaf, since the leaves resemble those of radish (*Raphanus sativus*).

Names Based on Animals

Bakhra kane, Nepali for *Inula cappa* and *Oxyspora paniculata, bakhra* meaning goat, *kan,* ear, since the leaf is shaped like a goat's ear.

Bandar puchhare, Nepali for *Verbascum thapsus, bandar* meaning monkey, *puchhar,* tail, since the inflorescence is shaped like a monkey's tail.

Bhalu paile, Nepali for *Alangium chinense, bhalu* meaning bear, *paila,* foot, since the leaf is shaped like a bear's foot.

Bhere kuro, Nepali for *Cyathula tomentosa* and *Cynoglossum zeylanicum, bhera* meaning sheep, *kuro,* spine, since the spiny fruits stick to the hairs of sheep and other animals.

Buhari jhar, Nepali for *Mimosa pudica, buhari* meaning bride, *jhar,* herb, because when the plant is touched, its leaflets fold, recalling the shyness of a new bride who covers her face in her *sari* (dress). Similarly, *lajauni,* Danuwar and Mooshar, *lajjawati,* Nepali, and *lajuwa,* Rai, are names also given to *M. pudica* and mean shy.

Chara ko khutta, Nepali for *Gentiana pedicellata, chara* meaning bird, *ko,* of, and *khutta,* leg, since the inflorescence resembles the leg of a small bird.

Chhatare, Nepali for *Heracleum nepalense* and *Pleurospermum hookeri, chhata* meaning umbrella, since the inflorescence is shaped like an umbrella.

Dudhilo, Nepali for *Ficus neriifolia* var. *nemoralis, dudhilo* meaning with milk, since the plant is fed to cows or buffalo to increase milk production.

Goru singe, Nepali for *Martynia annua, goru* meaning ox or cow, *sing,* horn, since the fruit is shaped like the horn of those animals.

Hathi tauke, Nepali for *Pleione humilis, hathi* meaning elephant, *tauko,* head, since the flower is shaped like an elephant's head.

Hati paila, Nepali for *Brassaiopsis hainla, hati* meaning elephant, *paila,* foot, since the leaf is shaped like an elephant's foot.

Jibre sag, Nepali for *Ophioglossum nudicaule* and *O. reticulatum, jibro* meaning tongue, *sag,* vegetable or herb, since the single leaf resembles a human tongue.

Kag chuchche, Nepali for *Thunbergia grandiflora, kag* meaning crow, *chuchcho,* beak, since the fruit is shaped like a crow's beak.

Kukur paile, Nepali for *Hydrocotyle nepalensis, kukur* meaning dog, *paila,* foot, since the leaf is shaped like a dog's foot.

Panch aunle, Nepali for *Gymnadenia orchidis, panch* meaning five, *aunla,* finger, since the root is shaped like a hand.

Ranabhyang, Tamang for *Inula cappa, rana* meaning ear, *bhyang,* sheep, since the leaf is shaped like a sheep's ear.

Tauke jhar, Nepali for *Leucas cephalotes, tauko* meaning head, *jhar,* herb, since the round inflorescence is shaped like a person's head.

Names Based on Use

Amil, Tharu, and *amilo,* Nepali, for *Rhus javanica, amil* and *amilo* meaning sour, since the fruit tastes sour.

Bajra danti, Nepali for *Potentilla fulgens* and *P. supina, bajra,* meaning strong, *dant,* teeth, since the roots are used to treat toothaches and make teeth strong.

Bikh, Nepali and Tamang for *Aconitum ferox, bikh,* meaning poison, and the root is poisonous. Similarly, *bish,* Nepali, is a name given to *A. gammiei, A. heterophyllum,* and *Delphinium denudatum* and means poison.

Chhyun jhar and *hachhyun jhar,* Nepali for *Centipeda minima* and *Dichrocephala integrifolia, chhyun* and *hachhyun* meaning sneezing, *jhar,* herb, because when flower heads are squeezed and the aroma is inhaled, it causes sneezing.

Chilaune, Nepali for *Schima wallichii, chilaune* meaning itchy, since if dried inner bark of the tree comes in contact with skin, it causes itching.

Chini jhar, Nepali for *Scoparia dulcis, chini,* meaning sugar, *jhar,* herb, since the plant is used to treat diabetes.

Chiple ghans and *chiple jhar,* Nepali for *Oreocnide frutescens* and *Pouzolzia zeylanica,* respectively, *chiplo* meaning slippery, *ghans* and *jhar,* grass or herb, since the plant, when rubbed, produces a slippery, viscous substance.

Chulthi amilo, Nepali for *Rheum australe* and *R. nobile, chulthi* meaning plaited hair, *amilo,* sour, since dried leaf stalks are bundled like plaited hair, taste sour, and are eaten pickled.

Dhun swan, Newari for *Artemisia indica, dhun* meaning incense, *swan,* flower, since the plant is used as incense.

Dudhe lahara, Nepali, and *dudh latti,* Mooshar, for *Ichnocarpus frutescens, dudha* meaning milk, *lahara* and *latti,* vine, since the plant exudes milky latex.

Duru kan, Newari for *Euphorbia royleana, duru* meaning milk, *kan,* prick or spine, since the spiny plant exudes milky latex.

Laxmi swan, Newari for *Sesbania sesban,* Laxmi, the goddess of wealth, *swan,* flower, since the flower or leaf is offered to Laxmi during Tihar.

Sabune jhar, Nepali for *Anagallis arvensis, sabun* meaning soap, *jhar,* herb, since the plant, when rubbed, produces a foam that lathers like soap.

Tita pati, Chepang, and *titepati,* Nepali, for *Artemisia indica, tito* meaning bitter, *pat,* leaf, since leaves taste bitter.

Plants on Postage Stamps

Most countries of the world have issued postage stamps featuring plants, including wild or cultivated plants that have economic, religious, or other importance. In Nepal, postage stamps were first issued in 1881. The first stamps with plants on them were issued in September 1969 as a set of four, each depicting flowers: *Euphorbia pulcherrima* (*lalupate*), *Narcissus* (*gunkeshar*), *Rhododendron arboreum* (*laliguras*), and *Tagetes erecta* (*sayapatri*). Of these, *R. arboreum* is the national flower of Nepal and has many folk uses. The other three plants are valued for ornamental or religious purposes even though *Narcissus,* for example, is an exotic, not native to Nepal.

In September 1976, a stamp depicting *Lilium nepalense* was issued, a plant valued for its edible bulbs and its epithet commemorating its home in Nepal. In November, another three stamps were issued featuring *Cardiocrinum giganteum, Meconopsis grandis,* and *Megacodon stylophorus,* which have medicinal or other uses. (The names on two of the stamps are switched: *C. giganteum* for *Megacodon stylophorus* and vice versa.)

In October 1978, the fruit series was issued: *Castanopsis indica, Choerospondias axillaris,* and *Elaeocarpus sphaericus,* all with edible fruits. The fruit of *E. sphaericus* is also valued for religious rituals.

In March 1980, the herb series was issued: *Ocimum tenuiflorum,* with religious as well as medicinal uses, and *Rheum australe, Valeriana jatamansii,* and *Zanthoxylum armatum,* all with medicinal uses.

In November 1994, the orchid series was issued: *Coelogyne corymbosa, C. flaccida, Cymbidium devonianum,* and *Dendrobium densiflorum,* of ornamental value.

In December 1997, the Postal Services Department issued a flower series: *Callistephus chinensis, Jasminum gracile,* and *Luculia gratissima,* of ornamental value (and *L. gratissima* with religious significance), and *Manglietia insignis,* an endangered tree.

Another endangered tree, *Talauma hodgsonii,* was depicted on a postage stamp issued December 2000. On the same day two more stamps with *Dactylorhiza hatagirea* and *Mahonia napaulensis* were also issued. The Nepalese government has banned collection and export of the rare *D. hatagirea* from the wild.

CHAPTER 4

The Useful Plants of Nepal

This chapter is a catalog of the more than 1500 kinds of plants used by people in the rural communities of Nepal. Most of the information is based on field data collected over three decades from firsthand observations made in each of the 75 districts of Nepal. Care has been taken to avoid technical terms as much as possible, but they cannot be avoided entirely so a Glossary is provided. The plants have been arranged alphabetically by their accepted scientific names for ready reference, but an Index of Common Names and an Index of Scientific Names (with cross-references from families to genera, and from synonyms to accepted names) have been provided to facilitate use. Also, genera are listed according to use and ethnic community in Appendix 1 and Appendix 2, respectively.

Each entry begins with the accepted scientific name of the plant, followed by synonyms (if any), followed by vernacular names. The family to which the plant belongs begins its description (including habitat and distribution), which is followed by its uses, divided into uses for food, medicine, and other uses. Communities or geographic names, such as the districts of Nepal, are mentioned where usage is specific. Otherwise, it can be assumed that all the ethnic communities covered here use the plants. Together with the many illustrations, the information presented here enables *Plants and People of Nepal* to serve as a field guide, helpful for the rural people of Nepal, and especially as a record of the ethnobotanical knowledge passed down over many generations in the ethnic communities of Nepal. It should, however, be added that there remain many species whose ethnobotany still awaits scientific confirmation, so the number of plants known to be used as well as the number and kinds of their uses can only increase with further study.

Vernacular names have been provided even when pronunciations differ slightly from one community to another or from one geographic locale to another (see Chapter 2 under Languages). For example, the Nepali name for *Berberis aristata* and *B. asiatica* is *chutro,* but in the districts of Jajarkot and Jumla, people call these barberries *chotra* or *chotro,* and those names are also recorded here.

Where dosage of medicine is mentioned, I have used a teaspoon (about 5 milliliters) to normalize the measurement as different villagers speak of different measures. Scale bars in the drawings represent 2 cm.

A

Abelmoschus esculentus (Linnaeus) Moench

CHEPANG *bheri* ENGLISH *lady's finger, okra* NEPALI *ramtoria* NEWARI *ramtoriya*

Malvaceae. Erect, coarsely hairy shrub about 1.5 m high. Leaves stalked, alternate, cordate, three- or five-lobed, margin notched or dentate, hairy. Flowers large, yellow with a crimson center. Fruit a capsule, ribbed. Flowers and fruits June–October. Propagated by seeds. Distributed throughout Nepal to about 2000 m, cultivated.

FOOD. Tender fruits are prepared as a vegetable.

MEDICINE. Juice of the plant is applied to cuts, wounds, and boils.

Abelmoschus manihot (Linnaeus) Medikus

Hibiscus manihot Linnaeus

NEPALI *ban kapas, ban lasun* TAMANG *somjaja*

Malvaceae. Erect perennial herb about 3 m high, densely covered with long, yellow, bristly hairs. Leaves stalked, 8–

13 cm long, suborbiculate to cordate, deeply five- or seven-lobed, lobes crenate or serrate. Flowers solitary, axillary, yellow. Fruit a capsule, ovoid to ellipsoidal, hispid. Flowers August–October. Propagated by seeds. Distributed throughout Nepal at 700–1700 m in rocky places with shrubs; also in northern India, Myanmar, China, and Malaysia.

MEDICINE. Root juice is warmed and applied to sprains. A paste of the bark is applied to cuts and wounds. New paste is applied every 2–3 days and is continued about 3 weeks. Juice of the flower is used to treat chronic bronchitis and toothache.

Abelmoschus moschatus Medikus

Hibiscus abelmoschus Linnaeus, *Bamia abelmoschus* (Linnaeus) R. Brown ex Wallich
CHEPANG *aampruk* ENGLISH *musk mallow* NEPALI *ban bheri, ban kapas, kasturi*

Malvaceae. Annual shrub about 2 m high. Leaves stalked, cordate, three- to seven-lobed, hairy on both surfaces. Flowers yellow, axillary in few-flowered racemes. Fruit a capsule, ovate, hispid. Seeds reniform, black. Flowers and fruits October–November. Propagated by seeds. Distributed throughout Nepal at 600–1100 m in open places; also in most parts of the world.

FOOD. Tender leaves, shoots, and fruits are cooked as a vegetable. Seeds are roasted and pickled for future consumption. I had known about the use as a vegetable but did not know about the food value of its seeds. In 1974, in the village of Orbang, Dhading district, a Tamang man collected and fried some seeds in front of me to taste; they tasted like seeds of fried sesame (*Sesamum orientale*).

MEDICINE. A paste of the bark is applied to cuts, wounds, and sprains.

OTHER USES. Fiber from the bark of the stem is used to make ropes.

Abies spectabilis (D. Don) Mirbel

Pinus spectabilis D. Don
Pinus tinctoria Wallich ex D. Don
Pinus webbiana Lindley
ENGLISH *Himalayan silver fir* NEPALI *bunga salla, gobre salla, talispatra, thingo, thingre salla* SHERPA *tashing* TAMANG *kalta, kel*

Pinaceae. Evergreen coniferous tree about 50 m high. Leaves nearly sessile, linear, flattened, notched at the top. Male cones usually clustered, yellowish, female cones solitary, situated a little below the tips of shoots. Cones April–May. Propagated by seeds. Distributed in western and central Nepal at 2400–4200 m in moist, open areas; also in India and Bhutan.

MEDICINE. Leaves are carminative and expectorant. Juice of the leaves is taken for asthma and bronchitis. Essential oil from the needles is used for colds, rheumatism, and nasal congestion.

OTHER USES. Wood is used for thatching roofs and for other construction. It is also used for fuelwood. Dried needles mixed with other ingredients are used in the preparation of incense.

Abelmoschus moschatus

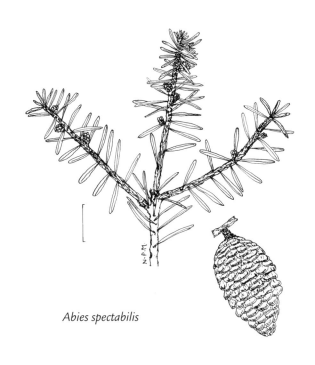

Abies spectabilis

Abroma angusta (Linnaeus) Linnaeus fil.

Theobroma angusta Linnaeus
ENGLISH *cotton abroma, devil's cotton* NEPALI *chinne, sanu kapase, shringraj, twari*

Sterculiaceae. Shrub about 2 m high with irritating hairs. Leaves stalked, 10–21 cm long, 5.5–13 cm wide, margin weakly sinuate, denticulate. Flowers purple, each with a stalk. Fruit a capsule, glabrous. Flowers July–August, fruits August–October. Propagated by seeds. Distributed in eastern and central Nepal at 300–1100 m in open, dry places; also in northern India, Micronesia, Malaysia, and Africa.

MEDICINE. Juice of the bark is given in cases of irregularity of menstruation.

OTHER USES. Fiber from the bark is soft and glossy and is used to make ropes and cordage. Bark is first retted in water, and it takes about a week before the fibers can be removed.

Abrus precatorius Linnaeus

CHEPANG *rati* DANUWAR *rato geri* ENGLISH *bead vine, crab's eye, jequirith bean, licorice bean, rosary pea* GURUNG *janai lahara* LEPCHA *lal geri* MAGAR *rati geri* MAJHI *rato geri* MOOSHAR *karjani* NEPALI *lal geri, rati geri* NEWARI *rati* RAI *maru* THARU *chilahariyak thond*

Leguminosae. Perennial climber. Leaves short-stalked, even-pinnate, leaflets in 10–20 pairs, opposite, 0.8–2.3 cm

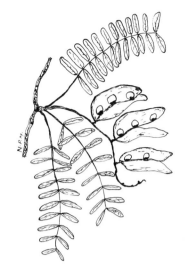

Abrus precatorius

long, 0.5–0.8 cm wide, oblong, minutely apiculate, margin entire, underside glabrous or silky. Flowers red, pinkish, or white in many-flowered racemes. Fruit a pod, stout, rigid. Seeds subglobose, polished, usually scarlet with a black eye, sometimes white with a black spot. Flowers May–September, fruits November–December. Propagated by seeds. Distributed throughout Nepal to about 1000 m, common in open or shady places, trailing over thickets and hedges; also in the tropics and subtropics of Asia and Africa, to Australia and the islands of the Pacific Ocean.

FOOD. Chepangs and Mooshars cook the tender leaves when other food is scarce.

MEDICINE. A paste of the root is applied to boils. It is also applied to the forehead, temple, and throat to treat cough, sore throat, headache, and rheumatic pains. The fresh leaf, when chewed with sugar, relieves cough and hoarseness of voice. Leaf paste is applied for leukoderma, swellings, boils, rheumatism, asthma, tubercular glands, dental caries, and is also a cure for baldness. Leaf juice is given for dry cough and fever, and is considered a blood purifier. The seed is antiperiodic, bitter, toxic, aphrodisiac, diaphoretic, emetic, expectorant, and purgative. It is used for biliousness, eye diseases, leukoderma, and itching. Seed paste is used to treat sciatica, fever, headache, malaria, paralysis, skin diseases, and nervous diseases.

OTHER USES. Thin stems or branches are used for temporary binding. Seeds are used as beads in rosaries and necklaces. The seed is also used as a measure of weight for minute amounts of gold and precious metals and stones.

Abutilon indicum (Linnaeus) Sweet

Sida indica Linnaeus
Sida populifera Lamarck, *Abutilon populifera* (Lamarck) Sweet
ENGLISH *country mallow* MAJHI *poti* NEPALI *kangiyo*

Malvaceae. Shrub about 2 m high. Leaves stalked, 2.5–10 cm long, 2–7.5 cm wide, ovate or orbiculate to cordate, irregularly crenate or dentate, acuminate, minutely hoary

Abroma angusta

tomentose on both surfaces. Flowers orange-yellow, solitary, axillary. Flowers and fruits May–December. Propagated by seeds. Distributed throughout Nepal to about 700 m in open areas and on uncultivated land; also in India, Sri Lanka, Myanmar, Thailand, Malaysia, southern China, Taiwan, southern Japan, and Australia.

FOOD. Roasted seeds are eaten.

MEDICINE. An infusion of the root is employed as a remedy for leprosy and is also taken internally as a cooling medicine for fever. According to Sarin and Kapoor (1962), the root is used to treat cough and fever. Juice of the leaves is demulcent. A paste of the leaves or seeds is applied to wounds and is also used for boils. Seeds are laxative and also useful in cases of hemorrhoids and cough.

OTHER USES. Bark of the stem yields fiber that is suitable for cordage, twine, and rope.

Abutilon indicum

Acacia catechu (Linnaeus fil.) Willdenow

Mimosa catechu Linnaeus fil.
Mimosa catechoides Roxburgh

CHEPANG *khayar* DANUWAR *khaira* ENGLISH *black cutch, black catechu, catechu tree, cutch tree, Jerusalem thorn* LEPCHA *khayer* LIMBU *khonri, khuri* MAGAR *khayar* MAJHI *khayar* NEPALI *khayar* NEWARI *khaya sima* RAI *rakhokwa* SUNWAR *khayar* TAMANG *khayar* THARU *khayar*

Leguminosae. Deciduous tree about 15 m high. Leaves stalked, bipinnate, pinnae in 10–30 pairs, pinnules in 30–

50 pairs, linear. Flowers creamy white in axillary pedunculate spikes. Fruit a pod, flat. Flowers March–September, fruits October–November. Propagated by seeds. Distributed throughout Nepal to about 1200 m, generally in open places, but commercial collection of wood for catechu is a cause of conservation concern; also in India, Myanmar, Thailand, and southern China.

MEDICINE. A decoction of the root is applied to swellings caused by pain or injury. Catechu, obtained from the heartwood, is astringent and is used for diarrhea, dysentery, hemorrhoids, leukorrhea, and uterine hemorrhage. Wood is collected commercially for the preparation of catechu. An infusion of catechu is valued in treating nosebleeds, skin eruptions, and sore nipples. The heartwood is boiled in water about 15 minutes, strained, and the liquid applied to relieve backache and other pains caused by arduous work. The liquid is also given in cases of cough and colds. Catechu powder is applied to relieve toothache. The bark is astringent.

OTHER USES. Wood is strong and water resistant and is used for poles, timber, and other household purposes. It is also used for fuelwood and is ideal for making charcoal. Catechu is used as a masticatory and is also good for dyeing.

Acacia farnesiana (Linnaeus) Willdenow

Mimosa farnesiana Linnaeus

ENGLISH *cassie flower, sweet acacia, huisache* NEPALI *jait*

Leguminosae. Thorny shrub about 5 m high, branches gray-dotted, armed with stipular spines. Leaves stalked, pinnate, leaflets small, elliptic, rigid. Flowers yellow in globose heads, fragrant. Fruit a pod, cylindrical, dark brown, with a double row of seeds. Flowers January–March, fruits June–July. Propagated by seeds. Distributed throughout Nepal to about 1100 m in open, dry places; also in India, Sri Lanka, and Myanmar.

MEDICINE. Juice of the bark is applied to treat muscular swellings.

OTHER USES. Plants are useful for checking soil erosion. The plant yields a low-quality gum that is used to prepare sweets. Bark is good for tanning and contains 2% tannin. Leaves and pods are used for fodder.

Acacia intsia (Linnaeus) Willdenow

Mimosa intsia Linnaeus
Mimosa caesia Linnaeus, *Acacia caesia* (Linnaeus) Wight & Arnott

CHEPANG *chekru* MAGAR *arkhu* NEPALI *arkhu, kayensi*

Leguminosae. Spiny shrub about 5 m high. Leaves stalked, opposite, pinnate, leaflets sessile, 0.8–1 cm long, 0.1–0.2 cm wide, linear, margin entire, tip spinous. Flowers yellowish. Fruit a pod. Flowers August–September, fruits October–December. Propagated by seeds. Distributed throughout Nepal to about 1100 m in open places; also in India, Bhutan, and Myanmar.

OTHER USES. Plants are lopped for fodder. Bark is squeezed and spread in water to poison fish.

Acacia nilotica (Linnaeus) Willdenow ex Delile

Mimosa nilotica Linnaeus
Mimosa arabica Lamarck, *Acacia arabica* (Lamarck) Willdenow
ENGLISH *Australian wattle* NEPALI *babul*

Leguminosae. Evergreen tree armed with spines, bark dark brown, fissured. Leaves stalked, bipinnate, pinnae in three to six pairs, 1.5–5 cm long, pinnules in 10–20 pairs, linear oblong. Flowers yellowish, fragrant, in axillary fascicled heads. Fruit a pod, white tomentose. Flowers July–December, fruits January–April. Propagated by seeds. Distributed throughout Nepal to about 500 m, common along streams, riverbanks, and on uncultivated land; also in India and Sri Lanka.

MEDICINE. Bark, leaf, and gum are used for medicinal purposes.

OTHER USES. Wood is used for agricultural implements. Bark is a source of tannin.

Acacia pennata (Linnaeus) Willdenow

Mimosa pennata Linnaeus
Acacia arrophula D. Don
Acacia megaladena Desvaux

CHEPANG *kekru, moro* ENGLISH *wattle plant* GURUNG *agalai*
NEPALI *agela, areri, arkhu, arphu, madise syuri, sikakai*

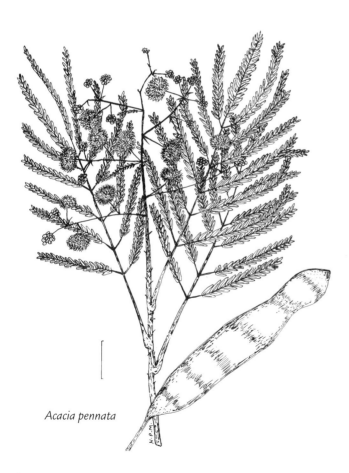

Acacia pennata

Leguminosae. Prickly climber. Leaves stalked, alternate, bipinnate, pinnules in 30–60 pairs on each pinna, linear oblong, acute. Flowers yellowish in panicles. Fruit a pod. Flowers May–August, fruits November–February. Propagated by seeds. Distributed throughout Nepal to about 1100 m in open places; also in India, Bhutan, Sri Lanka, Southeast Asia, China, and tropical Africa.

MEDICINE. A paste of the bark is applied to treat scabies, cuts, and wounds. Juice of the bark is fed to domestic animals with muscular swellings and sprains. Fresh leaves are chewed to control bleeding from the gums. Juice of the leaves, about 1 teaspoon twice a day, is given with milk to children for indigestion. Jain (1965) reported from India that a decoction of the leaves is taken to relieve body pain, fever, and headache. A poultice of fresh seeds is applied for burns.

OTHER USES. Bark contains tannin. Branches are lopped for fodder. Leaves are used for green manure. Fruit is used to poison fish. Juice of the seeds is used for washing clothes.

Acacia rugata (Lamarck) Voigt

Mimosa rugata Lamarck
Mimosa concinna Willdenow, *Acacia concinna* (Willdenow) de Candolle

CHEPANG *rangso* MAGAR *ramapa* NEPALI *arali, rasula, sikakai*

Leguminosae. Scrambling shrub about 5 m high. Leaves stalked, pinnate, leaflets sessile, linear. Flowers yellow. Fruit a pod. Flowers March–September, fruits November–January. Propagated by seeds. Distributed in western and central Nepal at 400–800 m in *Shorea robusta* forest along riverbanks; also in India, Southeast Asia, and southern China.

MEDICINE. Juice of the leaves is applied to boils.

OTHER USES. Fruit is used for washing hair and clothes.

Acer acuminatum Wallich ex D. Don

Acer caudatum Wallich
MAGAR *lampate pangro* NEPALI *kanchiro, tilyal*

Aceraceae. Deciduous tree to 15 m high. Leaves stalked, 5–12 cm long, 3–9.5 cm wide, five-lobed, lobes caudate-acuminate. Flowers stalked in lateral and terminal racemes, white. Fruit a samara, globose, irregularly grooved. Flowers March–April, fruits July–September. Propagated by seeds. Distributed throughout Nepal at 2000–3500 m in open ravines in shady places; also in India.

OTHER USES. Leaves are lopped for fodder.

Acer caesium Wallich ex Brandis

NEPALI *kanchiro*

Aceraceae. Deciduous tree about 20 m high, bark pale gray with silvery patches, exfoliating in irregular, thin, small scales. Leaves stalked, 10–20 cm long, 11.5–25 cm wide, five-lobed, cordate, serrate, acuminate, dull green above, pale and glaucous beneath. Flowers yellowish green in terminal corymbs. Fruit a samara, the wings divergent, erect, or sometimes overlapping, the beak slightly curved. Flowers March–April, fruits October–November. Propagated by seeds. Distributed in western and central Nepal at 2200–3000 m, common in oak forests and sometimes gregarious; also in northern India.

MEDICINE. Juice of the bark is applied to treat muscular swellings, boils, and pimples.

Acer campbellii Hooker fil. & Thomson ex Hiern

Acer campbellii var. *serratifolia* Banerji
ENGLISH *Campbell's maple*   NEPALI *phirphire*

Aceraceae. Deciduous tree about 17 m high. Leaves stalked, cordate, palmate, five- or seven-lobed, lobes serrate, acuminate. Flowers yellowish. Fruit a samara, red. Flowers May–April, fruits July–October. Propagated by seeds. Distributed throughout Nepal at 2100–3400 m on open, moist hillsides; also in northern India and Myanmar.

OTHER USES. The plant is lopped for fodder.

Acer oblongum Wallich ex de Candolle

Acer buzimpala Buchanan-Hamilton ex D. Don
Acer laurifolium D. Don
ENGLISH *Himalayan maple*   NEPALI *phirphire, putali phul*

Aceraceae. Deciduous tree to 15 m high. Leaves stalked, 6–16 cm long, 2–5 cm wide, ovate or oblong, long-pointed, entire, glaucous beneath. Flowers stalked in terminal corymbose panicles, white. Fruit a samara, more or less angular, the wings narrowed toward the base, widely divergent or parallel to each other. Flowers February–April, fruits May–October. Propagated by seeds. Distributed throughout Nepal at 1200–2400 m in ravines in moist places; also in Pakistan, northeastern India, Bhutan, southwestern China, and Southeast Asia.

OTHER USES. Plants are lopped for fodder. Wood is generally used to make agricultural implements and for minor construction. It is also turned to make drinking cups.

Acer pectinatum Wallich

NEPALI *thusi pangri*

Aceraceae. Tree about 6 m high. Leaves stalked, 6–15 cm long, 3–15 cm wide, unequally three- or five-lobed, lobes acuminate, serrate, lower surface hairy with pink hairs. Flowers yellowish. Fruit a samara. Flowers May–June, fruits July–November. Propagated by seeds. Distributed throughout Nepal at 2700–3800 m on open, moist hillsides; also in northern India, southern Tibet, and northern Myanmar.

OTHER USES. Wood is used for framing in house construction. It is also used as fuelwood.

Acer oblongum

Achyranthes aspera Linnaeus

Achyranthes aspera var. *indica* Linnaeus
CHEPANG *churut jhar, datil, jatengu*   DANUWAR *ulta chirchiri*
ENGLISH *prickly chaff flower*   GURUNG *tine, ulte puju*   MAGAR *jamjite*
MAJHI *bipyu kanda, chorato*   MOOSHAR *chirchiri*   NEPALI *akamaro, jamdi, kali jhar, kuro, ulte kuro*   RAI *ultokuruva*   TAMANG *hyurpuju*
THARU *gorsava, serangomen, ultakur*

Amaranthaceae. Erect herb about 1 m high. Leaves stalked, 2–13 cm long, 1.5–7 cm wide, variable in size, opposite, elliptic to ovate, entire, abruptly acuminate, pubescent, silky tomentose beneath. Flowers greenish white in long terminal spikes. Fruit a utricle, oblong, enclosed in the hardened perianth. Flowers June–October, fruits July–December. Propagated by seeds. Distributed throughout Nepal to about 2000 m, common in open, dry places; also in Afghanistan, Pakistan, India, Sri Lanka, northern Myanmar, China, Australia, Africa, and the Americas.

MEDICINE. The root is mixed with that of *Urena lobata* and bark of *Psidium guajava,* pounded, and the extracted juice, 4 teaspoons three times a day, is given to treat diarrhea and dysentery. An infusion of the root is astringent, and paste or juice of the root is valued in treating stomach troubles, cholera, skin diseases, and rheumatic problems. The juice is used to treat postnatal pain and to accelerate expulsion of the placenta, and about 6 teaspoons twice a day is given in cases of indigestion, colic, and food poisoning. Powdered root is given for diarrhea and dysentery, and an infusion for indigestion.

Chepangs use a decoction of the plant to relieve fever. Ash of the burned plant is used as a tooth powder for brushing teeth and is believed to relieve pyorrhea and toothache. My grandfather used to brush his teeth with the powder, mixing with mustard oil and a pinch of salt. He had no dental problems up to 80 years of age.

The plant is digestive, diuretic, purgative, laxative, stomachic, and astringent. Juice of the plant is a remedy for boils, diarrhea, dysentery, hemorrhoids, rheumatic pains, itches, and skin eruptions. The leaf is emetic, and a decoction is given for diarrhea and dysentery. A paste is applied in cases of rabies, hysteria, nervous disorder, insect bite, and snakebite. Seeds are emetic and are also used for rabies. There are interesting reports about the uses of seeds from the Himalayan regions of India. Majumdar et al. (1978) reported that seeds are taken with milk to check hunger without loss of body weight. Tharus and Mooshars use paste of the seeds for snakebites.

OTHER USES. Ash of the burned plant contains a large quantity of potash and is used for washing clothes. Twigs are used as a toothbrush in the festival of Teej.

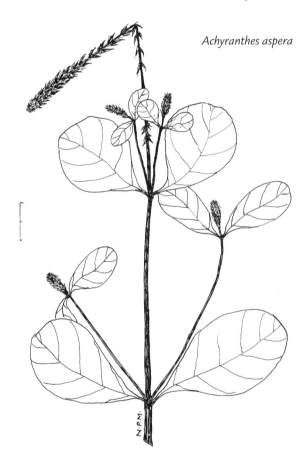

Achyranthes aspera

Achyranthes bidentata Blume

MAGAR *datiwan* NEPALI *datiwan* TAMANG *datiwan, phrekphrek* TIBETAN *lel-mo-ses*

Amaranthaceae. Erect herb about 1 m high, branches pubescent, more or less quadrangular. Leaves stalked, 3.5–18.5 cm long, 1.5–9 cm wide, elliptic, entire, acuminate, pubescent, base obtuse or acute. Flowers greenish in axillary and terminal spikes. Fruit a urticle, oblong, enclosed in the hardened perianth. Flowers June–October, fruits

July–December. Propagated by seeds. Distributed in central and eastern Nepal at 1200–3000 m in moist, shady places; also in India eastward to China, and Malaysia and tropical Africa.

MEDICINE. A decoction of the plant is diuretic. Juice of the root is applied to treat toothaches. About 6 teaspoons of this juice three times a day is prescribed for indigestion and is also considered good for asthma. The stem is used as a toothbrush and is considered good for teeth and said to counter pyorrhea.

OTHER USES. Twigs are used as a toothbrush in the festival of Teej.

Aconitum ferox Wallich ex Seringe

Aconitum virosum D. Don
ENGLISH *aconite* NEPALI *bikh, nilo bikh* TAMANG *bikh*

Ranunculaceae. Herb to 1 m high. Leaves stalked, alternate, nearly round, palmately lobed. Flowers blue or violet in racemes. Fruit a follicle, sometimes densely villous. Flowers July–September, fruits October–December. Propagated by seeds. Distributed in eastern and central Nepal at 2100–3800 m in shady places or on hillsides but collection of roots for sale in the trade is a cause of conservation concern; also in India and Bhutan.

MEDICINE. A paste of the roots is applied in cases of neuralgia, leprosy, cholera, and rheumatism. Roots are col-

Aconitum ferox

lected for sale in the trade. It is also considered diuretic and diaphoretic.

OTHER USES. The root is used to poison arrows for hunting.

Aconitum gammiei Stapf

Aconitum dissectum D. Don
Aconitum napellus Linnaeus
Aconitum wallichianum Lauener
NEPALI *bish*

Ranunculaceae. Herb about 75 cm high. Lower leaves deeply divided into narrow acute segments, upper leaves smaller, less divided. Flowers pale blue or yellowish, August–September. Propagated by seeds. Distributed in eastern and central Nepal at 3300–4300 m on open, moist slopes; also in northeastern India, Bhutan, and southeastern Tibet.

MEDICINE. Juice of the roots is used for stomachaches.

Aconitum heterophyllum Wallich ex Royle

Aconitum atees Royle
Aconitum cordatum Royle
Aconitum ovatum Lindley
NEPALI *bish*

Ranunculaceae. Herb about 2 m high. Lower leaves long-stalked, ovate, deeply lobed, upper leaves sessile, clasping the stem, coarsely dentate. Flowers greenish purple with dark-veined petals. Fruit a follicle, slightly hairy. Flowers July–August, fruits September–October. Propagated by seeds. Distributed in central Nepal at 3200–3700 m in moist, open places but collection of roots for sale in the trade is a cause of conservation concern; also in Pakistan and northeastern India.

MEDICINE. Roots are used as a tonic.

OTHER USES. The plant is poisonous to livestock and humans.

Aconitum laciniatum (Brühl) Stapf

Aconitum ferox var. *laciniata* Brühl
NEPALI *kalo bikh*

Ranunculaceae. Herb about 50 cm high. Leaves stalked, five-lobed, margin finely pubescent. Flowers blue in a loose panicle, September–October. Propagated by seeds. Distributed in central and eastern Nepal at 2800–4600 m in moist, shady places; also in India, Bhutan, and southeastern Tibet.

OTHER USES. Roots are poisonous; villagers use them to poison animals. Roots are exported.

Aconitum spicatum (Brühl) Stapf

ENGLISH *Nepal aconite* GURUNG *glantu*
NEPALI *atibish, aikh, ailo bikh*

Ranunculaceae. Erect herb about 1 m high. Leaves stalked, broadly ovate, digitate, three- or five-parted. Flowers purple in racemes, August–September. Propa-

gated by seeds. Distributed throughout Nepal at 1800–4200 m on moist, steep slopes; also in northern India, Bhutan, and southern Tibet.

OTHER USES. The root is used to poison the hunting spikes used to kill musk deer in western Nepal. In 1982 in Chakhure Lekh, Jumla district, I saw a patch in the forest covered with plants in flower. As I entered the bush to collect some good flowering specimens for the herbarium, a shepherd came running and screaming, motioning to me not to enter the area covered by this plant. He said the root is very poisonous and that the odor of this flower is also poisonous, and that animals do not feed on the leaves. Then, with a pale face, he told me that its root is used to poison the arrows used to hunt musk deer. The root is dried in mild sun about 4 hours, pounded into a paste. The pointed iron of the arrow is smeared with the paste, dried, then used for hunting. The animals hunted in this manner are not fit for eating but instead are used for their skin, hair, bones, and other parts.

Acorus calamus Linnaeus

CHEPANG *bodi* DANUWAR *bojho* ENGLISH *sweet flag, sweet sage* GURUNG *bojho* LEPCHA *rakalop* LIMBU *luplak* MAGAR *bojho* NEPALI *bojho, sripadi* NEWARI *bach* RAI *bachinampa* SUNWAR *bojho* TAMANG *sete, syede*

Acoraceae. Herb about 1 m high with aromatic rhizome. Leaves basal, flat, linear, midrib distinct, margin

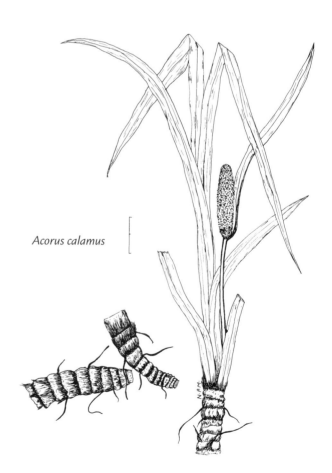

Acorus calamus

wavy. Spathe elongated, similar in shape to the leaves. Flowers small, bisexual, yellowish, condensed on a cylindrical spadix. Fruit a berry with few seeds. Flowers April–June. Propagated by splitting the rhizome. Distributed throughout Nepal at 200–2300 m, common in wet, marshy places; also in temperate and subtropical regions of Asia, Europe, and North America.

FOOD. A pinch of rhizome powder is put in a cup of tea for flavor.

MEDICINE. The rhizome is carminative, stimulant, aphrodisiac, and is also used as a tonic. An infusion is given to treat asthma, cough, colds, and bronchial and chest pains. About 6 teaspoons of juice of fresh rhizome is taken once a day to treat diarrhea and dysentery. A paste of the rhizome is applied for rheumatism. Powdered rhizome, mixed with mustard oil, is applied to treat scabies and other fungal skin diseases.

OTHER USES. An essential oil is obtained from the rhizome, and the rhizome has insecticidal properties.

Acrocephalus indicus (Burman fil.) Kuntze

Prunella indica Burman fil.
Acrocephalus blumei Bentham
Acrocephalus capitatus (Roth) Bentham
Acrocephalus scariosus Bentham
NEPALI *kambari jhar*

Labiatae. Annual herb about 30 cm high. Leaves stalked, 2–4 cm long, ovate to lanceolate, serrate, glabrous. Flowers purplish in cylindrical spikes. Fruit a nutlet, compressed. Flowers and fruits August–October. Propagated by seeds. Distributed throughout Nepal at 600–900 m in moist,

Acrocephalus indicus

open places; also in India, Bhutan, southern China, and Southeast Asia.

MEDICINE. A paste of the leaf is applied to cuts and wounds.

Actinidia callosa Lindley

NEPALI *theki phal*

Actinidiaceae. Large climber. Leaves stalked, 8–15 cm long, elliptic, pointed. Flowers white in lax axillary clusters. Fruit a berry, ovoid. Flowers May–July. Propagated by seeds. Distributed in western and central Nepal at 1300–3000 m in open places; also in northern India, Bhutan, western and central China, and Southeast Asia.

FOOD. Ripe fruits are eaten fresh.

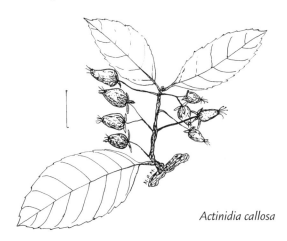

Actinidia callosa

Actinodaphne angustifolia Nees

NEPALI *lampate, penpe*

Lauraceae. Tree with grayish bark with white patches. Leaves stalked, 10–18 cm long, 5–7 cm wide, oblanceolate, entire. Flowers yellow. Fruit a berry, globose, red when ripe, seated on a cup-shaped perianth tube. Flowers September–October, fruits December–January. Propagated by seeds. Distributed in eastern and central Nepal at 450–1000 m in subtropical forest; also in India and Myanmar.

OTHER USES. Wood is used for construction (p. 72).

Adenocaulon himalaicum Edgeworth

Adenocaulon bicolor Hooker
TIBETAN *gnalep*

Compositae. Herb. Lower leaves long-stalked, alternate, orbiculate to cordate, undulate or dentate, glabrous above, white tomentose beneath, upper leaves sessile, smaller. Flower heads white. Fruit an achene. Flowers July–August. Propagated by seeds. Distributed throughout Nepal at 2000–4000 m in moist, shady places; also in India, Bhutan, southern China, and Japan.

MEDICINE. A paste of the plant is applied to wounds (p. 72).

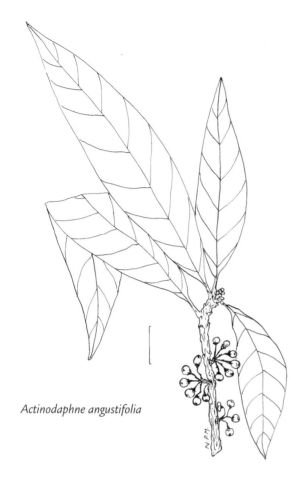

Actinodaphne angustifolia

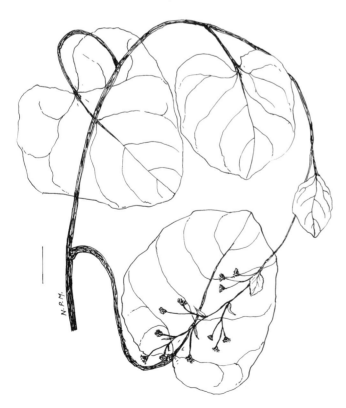

Adenocaulon himalaicum

Adiantum capillus-veneris Linnaeus

CHEPANG *nesinka jhar* ENGLISH *black maidenhair, Venus hair*
NEPALI *pakhale unyu*

Pteridaceae. Fern with a long rhizome, creeping. Stipe and rachis thin, shiny blackish, fronds 10–25 cm long, 1.5–11 cm wide, bi- or tripinnate. Sori oblong, at the margins of lobes. Propagated by spores or fragments of rhizomes. Distributed throughout Nepal at 300–2700 m in rock crevices in shady areas; also in tropical and temperate regions of the world.

MEDICINE. A paste of the plant is applied to the forehead to relieve headache, and to the chest to relieve chest pain. Chepangs apply it to boils. Juice of the frond mixed with honey is taken in cases of cough. It is also used for irregular menstruation.

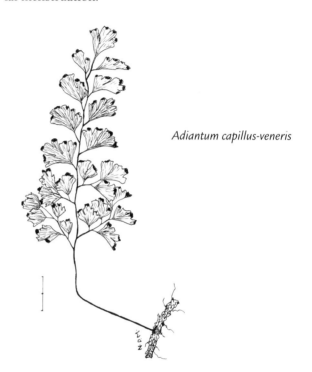

Adiantum capillus-veneris

Adiantum caudatum Linnaeus

NEPALI *daluko, dan sinki, seto sinki* TAMANG *twasilwa*

Pteridaceae. Epiphytic or terrestrial fern. Rhizome short, slender, covered with woolly brown hairs. Fronds simple, 5–35 cm long, 4–7 cm wide, pinnate, pinnae wedge shaped, hairy. Sori round or oblong at the edges of lobes. Spores June–July. Propagated by spores or fragments of rhizomes. Distributed in central and western Nepal at 200–3000 m in rock crevices in shady places; also in India, Sri Lanka, southern and central China, Southeast Asia, the Philippines, Taiwan, New Guinea, Africa, and Arabia.

MEDICINE. A decoction of plant, about 4 teaspoons twice a day, is given for gastric trouble. Juice of the rhizome, about 4 teaspoons three times a day, is given in cases of fever. It is also used to treat indigestion.

Adiantum philippense Linnaeus

Adiantum lunulatum Burman fil.

NEPALI *kani unyun* THARU *ratamur*

Pteridaceae. Tufted fern. Fronds 8–25 cm long, 3–5.5 cm wide, pinnate, pinnae alternate, lunate. Sori brown, along the edge of the frond, protected by the reflexed margin. Spores June–July. Propagated by spores or fragments of rhizomes. Distributed throughout Nepal to about 2000 m in rock crevices, on moist walls, and along stream banks; also in India, Sri Lanka, and Myanmar.

MEDICINE. Juice of the rhizome is given in cases of fever, dysentery, and glandular swelling.

Adiantum venustum D. Don

NEPALI *daluko*

Pteridaceae. Terrestrial fern. Fronds light green, 15–30 cm long, 5–10 cm wide, triangular, decompound, with glossy purple stipes. Sori on the upper part of the margin. Spores June–July. Propagated by spores or fragments of rhizomes. Distributed in western and central Nepal at 300–3600 m in moist, shady, rocky places; also in Afghanistan, northern India, and western China.

MEDICINE. A paste of the rhizome is applied to cuts and wounds.

Adina cordifolia (Willdenow ex Roxburgh) Bentham & Hooker fil. ex Brandis

Nauclela cordifolia Willdenow ex Roxburgh

CHEPANG *kalama, kalambo* DANUWAR *karam* ENGLISH *saffron, yellow teak* MOOSHAR *karama* NEPALI *chinne, haledu, karam* TAMANG *karam*

Rubiaceae. Deciduous tree to 30 m high. Leaves stalked, orbiculate to cordate, abruptly acuminate, pubescent beneath. Flowers yellow. Fruit a capsule, cuneate, with six seeds. Flowers June–July, fruits September–November. Propagated by seeds. Distributed throughout Nepal to about 800 m, common in forested areas of tropical and subtropical regions; also in India, Sri Lanka, and Indo-China.

MEDICINE. Juice of the plant is applied to cuts and wounds. It is considered effective in killing germs in wounds. The bark is considered to have febrifuge properties. Leaves are ground and snuffed to relieve headache. Juice of the leaves is applied to wounds between the toes caused by prolonged walking barefooted in muddy water during the rainy season.

OTHER USES. Wood is highly prized by wood-carvers and is also used to make furniture and agricultural implements. It is also used for house building. Young leaves are poisonous to cattle.

Aechmanthera gossypina (Wallich) Nees

Ruellia gossypina Wallich
Aechmanthera wallichii Nees

CHEPANG *bhuling* NEPALI *kangaraito phul, nune, sundal* TAMANG *magamanda, pingman*

Acanthaceae. Erect shrub about 2 m high, branches pubescent or clothed with dense, white, woolly tomentum. Leaves stalked, 2.5–9 cm long, 1–9 cm wide, oblanceolate, crenulate, entire or subentire, pubescent on both surfaces, base rounded or cordate. Flowers violet in four- to eight-flowered clusters. Fruit a capsule, oblong. Flowers and fruits September–December. Propagated by seeds. Distributed throughout Nepal at 300–2500 m, common on open hillsides and uncultivated land; also in northern India and Bhutan.

Adina cordifolia

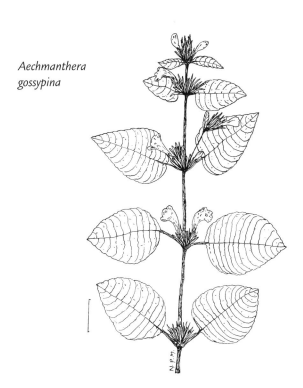

Aechmanthera gossypina

MEDICINE. Juice of the root, about 4 teaspoons three times a day, is given in cases of diarrhea and colic.

OTHER USES. The plant is gathered for fodder. According to Raizada and Saxena (1978), in India the white woolly hairs that cover the stem and leaves are used in making a kind of cloth. In Nepal, such a use has not been reported.

Aeginetia indica Linnaeus

Orobanche aeginetia Linnaeus

ENGLISH *broomrape*   NEPALI *aankuri bankuri, gaibyai, nila jhar, puksur*

Orobanchaceae. Leafless herb about 20 cm high. Rootstock slender, root fleshy. Scape purplish, with or without a few scales at the base. Flowers crimson, solitary, terminal. Fruit a capsule, ovoid, beaked, enclosed in a persistent calyx. Flowers May–October, fruits October–November. Propagated by seeds. Distributed throughout Nepal at 600–2000 m on hillsides, often under shrubs, but the plant's limited natural distribution is a cause of conservation concern; also in India, Sri Lanka, Myanmar, China, the Philippines, Malaysia, and Japan.

MEDICINE. Juice of the root is taken to treat fever.

Aeginetia indica

Aegle marmelos (Linnaeus) Corrêa

Crateva marmelos Linnaeus

CHEPANG *belasi*   DANUWAR *bel*   ENGLISH *bail fruit tree*   LEPCHA *belpit*   LIMBU *anajamse*   MAJHI *bel*   MOOSHAR *bel*   NEPALI *bel*   NEWARI *bya*   RAI *bel*   SATAR *asare*   SUNWAR *bel*   TAMANG *bel*   THARU *bel*

Rutaceae. Deciduous, thorny tree about 15 m high. Leaves stalked, alternate, trifoliolate, leaflets ovate to lanceolate, crenate, gland-dotted. Flowers white in subterminal panicles. Fruit yellowish, globose, with woody rind and sweet pulp. Flowers March–May, fruits March–June the following year. Propagated by seeds or root offshoots.

Distributed throughout Nepal to about 1100 m, apparently wild in open, dry places, and planted around villages; also in India, Bhutan, Myanmar, Malaysia, and Indo-China.

FOOD. Pulp of ripe fruit is eaten fresh or mixed with cold water to prepare a juice, *sarbat* in Nepali, during the hot summer season. In some places marmalade is made from ripe pulp.

MEDICINE. Juice of the root, about 3 teaspoons twice a day, is given for fever. Wood ash, mixed with some water, is spread over swollen parts of the body, especially when someone has a fever. A paste of wood ash, water, and turmeric powder (*Curcuma domestica*) is applied to aching parts of the body, especially for those suffering from fever. Juice of the bark is pounded into paste with some mustard seeds and is given to treat diarrhea and dysentery. Leaves are astringent, digestive, febrifuge, and laxative. Juice of fresh leaves, which is bitter, is diluted with water and given to treat catarrh and feverishness. A poultice of the leaves is used by the villagers for eye diseases. Unripe fruit is astringent, digestive, and stomachic. Pulp of unripe fruit, about 6 teaspoons three times a day, is given for diarrhea and dysentery. A paste of the gum is mixed with double the amount of water, and about 3 teaspoons of the liquid is given four times a day for amebic dysentery.

OTHER USES. Wood is burned for sacrificial fires, especially in the Hindu religion. Leaves are offered to Shiva in religious functions. Leaves are also used as fodder, espe-

Aegle marmelos

cially for goats. Dried fruits freed of pulp are used as cups, also for storing snuff. The gummy substance around the seed is used as an adhesive.

Aerva sanguinolenta (Linnaeus) Blume

Achyranthes sanguinolenta Linnaeus
Achyranthes scandens Roxburgh, *Aerva scandens* (Roxburgh) Wallich

NEPALI *mansi ghans*

Amaranthaceae. Deciduous shrub, stems weak, straggling. Leaves stalked, alternate, 2.5–10 cm long, 1–5 cm wide, elliptic to lanceolate, acute at both ends, gray pubescent on both surfaces. Flowers whitish in axillary and terminal spikes, October–February. Propagated by seeds. Distributed throughout Nepal to about 1400 m in open, dry places on forest floors or uncultivated land; also in India, Myanmar, China, Taiwan, and Malaysia.

OTHER USES. The plant is used to make *marcha,* a fermenting cake from which liquor is distilled.

Aerva sanguinolenta

Aeschynanthus parviflorus (D. Don) Sprengel

Trichosporum parviflorum D. Don
Aeschynanthus ramosissima Wallich

NEPALI *thirjo*   TAMANG *syabal*

Gesneriaceae. Epiphytic herb. Leaves stalked, 3.5–12 cm long, 0.8–3.8 cm wide, ovate to lanceolate, entire, tip pointed, narrowed toward the base, fleshy, midvein distinct. Flowers red. Fruit linear, about 22 cm long. Flowers May–September, fruits March–April. Propagated by seeds or root offshoots. Distributed in central and western Nepal at 1200–1600 m, hanging on trees; also in northern India and southern and eastern Tibet.

MEDICINE. Juice of the plant, about 4 teaspoons twice a day, is given for a month to sterile women to help them conceive. Powdered leaf, along with rice flour, is baked and taken to provide relief from backache.

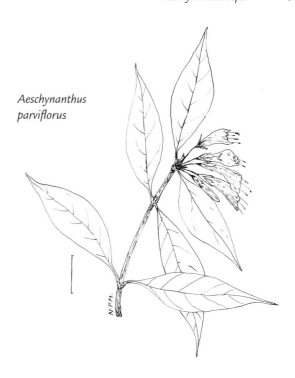

Aeschynanthus parviflorus

Aeschynomene asper Linnaeus

ENGLISH *sola plant*   NEPALI *dhondia*

Leguminosae. Shrub about 2 m high. Leaves stalked, odd-pinnate, leaflets numerous, small, linear, obtuse. Flowers pale yellow in axillary racemes. Fruit a pod, jointed. Flowers and fruits July–December. Propagated by seeds. Distributed throughout Nepal to about 1300 m in swampy places; also in India, Sri Lanka, Myanmar, China, the Philippines, Malaysia, and Japan.

OTHER USES. Pith is used as floats for fishing. It is also used to make various types of articles such as flowers and

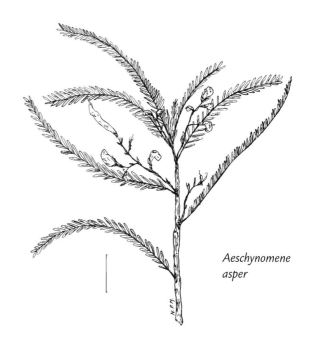

Aeschynomene asper

other decorations to offer to gods and goddesses during festivals.

Aesculus indica (Colebrooke ex Cambessèdes) Hooker

Pavia indica Colebrooke ex Cambessèdes

ENGLISH *horse chestnut* NEPALI *bankhor, kandar, karu, lampate, lekh pangro, pangra*

Hippocastanaceae. Deciduous tree to 20 m high. Leaves stalked, opposite, digitate, leaflets five to nine, 10–20 cm long, 2.5–6 cm wide, oblanceolate, long-pointed, serrate, central leaflet bigger than other leaflets. Flowers white, tinged with pink, in terminal panicles. Fruit a capsule, brown, ovoid, with one to three cells. Seeds globose. Flowers April–July, fruits September–November. Propagated by seeds. Distributed in western and central Nepal at 1900–2400 m in moist, shaded valleys, often on open, rocky hillsides but the plant's limited natural distribution and collection of fruits for sale in the trade are cause of conservation concern; also in Afghanistan and northern India.

FOOD. Roasted cotyledons are edible. Ground seeds are mixed with flour to develop the taste of baked bread. The embryo is eaten as a vegetable.

MEDICINE. Juice of the bark or seed oil is applied in cases of rheumatism. The cotyledon is fed to animals as an anthelmintic. Seeds are astringent, acrid, and narcotic. Oil from the seed is applied to treat skin disease. A paste of the oil cake is applied to the forehead to relieve headache.

OTHER USES. Twigs and leaves are lopped for fodder.

Agapetes serpens (Wight) Sleumer

Vaccinium serpens Wight, *Pentapterygium serpens* (Wight) Klotzsch

NEPALI *khursani* LEPCHA *kimbutan*

Ericaceae. Epiphytic shrub, branches drooping. Leaves short-stalked, 0.8–2 cm long, 0.4–0.8 cm wide, ovate, thick, edge curved. Flowers tubular, red. Fruit a berry, five-winged. Flowers April–June, fruits July–August. Propagated by seeds or branch cuttings. Distributed in eastern Nepal at 1200–3000 m in shady places; also in northern India.

FOOD. Ripe fruits are eaten fresh.

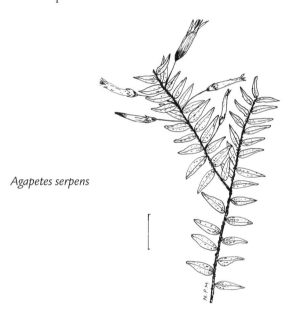

Agapetes serpens

Agave cantala Roxburgh ex Salm-Dyck

ENGLISH *maguey* MAGAR *kituki* NEPALI *ketuki*

Agavaceae. Tufted shrub. Leaves about 1.5 m long, narrow, pointed, margin spiny. Flowers white, December–March. Fruits most of the year. Propagated by seeds or root offshoots. Distributed throughout Nepal to about 2000 m, generally in open, dry places; also in tropical Asia.

MEDICINE. The root is diuretic. Leaves have a laxative property.

OTHER USES. Plants are cultivated as hedges and are useful in checking soil erosion. Leaves provide fibers used to make ropes, cordage, and twine. Squeezed leaf is spread in water to poison fish.

Ageratum conyzoides Linnaeus

CHEPANG *raunde, raunja, sang jhar* DANUWAR *ganhiya jhar*
ENGLISH *appa grass, bastard agrimony, goat weed* GURUNG *angale no, dalidare, gande, tirino* MAGAR *gande, namche jhar, ponge jhar*

Aesculus indica

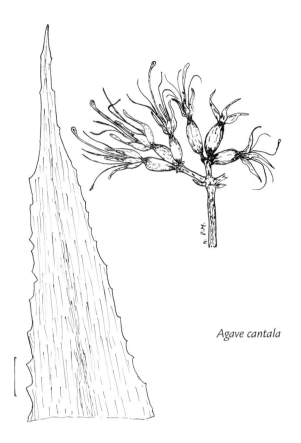

Agave cantala

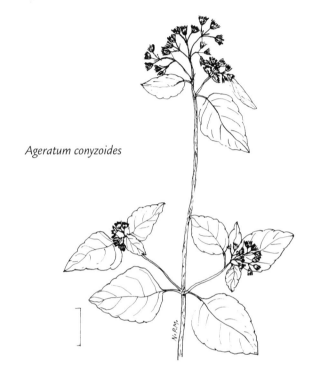

Ageratum conyzoides

minor, *Drymaria cordata, Galinsoga parviflora,* and rhizome of *Zingiber officinale,* and the resultant paste is applied to snakebites. A paste of warmed leaves is applied to boils. Squeezed leaves are rubbed on the head to rid it of lice. Juice of the flower heads is applied to treat scabies, and a paste of them is applied to treat rheumatism. Flower heads are mixed with half the amount of *Ocimum tenuiflorum,* boiled about 10 minutes, and the strained liquid, about 6 teaspoons four times a day, is given in cases of cough and colds.

MOOSHAR *ganki* NEPALI *bhera jhar, boke, ganamane, ganaune jhar, gande, ganne jhar, hanuman, raunne, seto raunne* NEWARI *kegucha ghyan* RAUTE *gyaine* TAMANG *bratar, manthani mran, thang mran, thangawinowa*

Compositae. Annual herb about 80 cm high. Leaves stalked, 2–6 cm long, 1–3.5 cm wide, opposite, ovate, crenate, slightly hairy on both surfaces, apex obtuse, base rounded or truncate. Flower heads bluish in terminal corymbs. Fruit an achene, angled, black. Flowers November–March. Propagated by seeds. Distributed throughout Nepal to about 2200 m, usually in damp places; also pantropical.

MEDICINE. Powder of the dried plant is applied to wounds and on ruptures caused by leprosy. This powder absorbs the moisture of the disease and forms a layer that is removed after 1–2 days. In Budha Gaun, Rolpa district, in western Nepal and a few other places, I saw that the wounds were healed, but in cases of leprosy powdered plant ameliorated skin ruptures but did not effect a complete cure.

A paste of the root, mixed with bark of *Schima wallichii,* is applied to set dislocated bones. After application of the paste, the affected part is usually covered with a piece of cloth and three or four bamboo strips are attached with some string to fashion a splint. Juice of the plant is applied to cuts, wounds, and bruises. A paste of the leaves is applied to remove thorns lodged in the feet. Paste of the leaves is pounded with equal amounts of *Bidens pilosa* var.

Ageratum houstonianum Miller

NEPALI *gandhe jhar, nilo gandhe*

Compositae. Annual herb about 1.2 m high. Leaves stalked, 4–9 cm long, 1.5–4 cm wide, ovate, serrate, hairy, acute, base almost cordate or truncate. Flower heads blue or purple in dense terminal corymbs. Fruit an achene, black or brown, sparsely hairy. Flowers and fruits most of the year. Propagated by seeds. Distributed in eastern and central Nepal to about 1300 m; also pantropical.

MEDICINE. Juice of the plant is applied to cuts and wounds.

Aglaomorpha coronans (Wallich ex Mettenius) Copeland

NEPALI *harchur*

Polypodiaceae. Epiphytic or terrestrial fern. Fronds bright green, 40–70 cm long, 20–30 cm wide, stout, lamina deeply divided. Sori brown, conspicuous, on either side of the main vein. Propagated by spores or fragments of rhizomes. Distributed in western and central Nepal at 600–

Aglaomorpha coronans

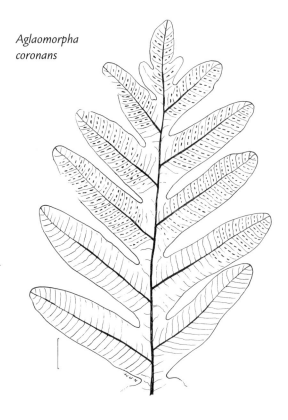

Agrimonia pilosa

1200 m, often on tree trunks and thick branches; also in northern India, southern China, and eastern Taiwan.

MEDICINE. A paste of the rhizome is applied to treat backache.

Agrimonia pilosa Ledebour

Agrimonia eupatorium Linnaeus
Agrimonia lanata Wallich ex Wallroth
Agrimonia nepalensis D. Don
CHEPANG *thaklange* ENGLISH *agrimony, cocklebur, common agrimony, stickwort* NEPALI *bherakuro, ganthe jhar, kable, shila jhar* TAMANG *bokro mran, dapchhe, nambu, tinai, urman*

Rosaceae. Herb to 1 m high. Leaves pinnate, leaflets elliptic to lanceolate, acute, coarsely dentate, hairy on both surfaces, upper leaves sessile, elliptic or orbiculate. Flowers yellow in terminal spike-like racemes. Fruit an achene enclosed in the hardened bristly calyx. Flowers July–October, fruits November–December. Propagated by seeds. Distributed throughout Nepal at 1000–3000 m, common along the wayside in shady places or in forest undergrowth; also in northern India, Bhutan, southern Tibet, eastward to China, and Myanmar.

MEDICINE. A decoction of the plant is given for abdominal pain, diarrhea, dysentery, hemorrhoids, bloody and white discharges, sore throat, tuberculosis, hematuria, and a paste of the plant is applied to the temples to relieve headache. It is also used on snakebites. Ash of the plant is applied to wounds to provide relief. The root is considered a tonic, astringent, and diuretic and is used for treatment of tuberculosis; a decoction is used for cough, colds,

and diarrhea. About 4 teaspoons of root juice three times a day is given for peptic ulcer. A paste of the root is given for stomachache.

Agrostemma sarmentosum Wallich

Sonerila squarrosa Wallich
NEPALI *satuwa ghans*

Caryophyllaceae. Small herb. Leaves sessile, opposite, elliptic, acute, sparingly pubescent. Flowers white in terminal umbels, June–July. Propagated by seeds. Distributed throughout Nepal at 300–2100 m; also in India, Bhutan, southeastern China, and Indo-China.

MEDICINE. Juice of the plant is applied to cuts and wounds.

Ajuga bracteosa Wallich ex Bentham

Ajuga integrifolia Buchanan-Hamilton ex D. Don
Ajuga remota Wallich
NEPALI *nil pate* TAMANG *lungememen*

Labiatae. Herb about 30 cm high, villous. Lower leaves short-stalked, 2.5–8 cm long, 1–3 cm wide, oblanceolate, margin dentate, cuneate at the base, woolly, upper leaves sessile. Flowers bluish, crowded in axillary whorls or in short dense spikes. Flowers March–July, fruits August–September. Propagated by seeds or root offshoots. Distributed throughout Nepal at 700–4000 m, often along trails on moist ground or on open slopes; also in Afghanistan, northern India, Tibet, Bhutan, China, the Philippines, southern Japan, and Malaysia.

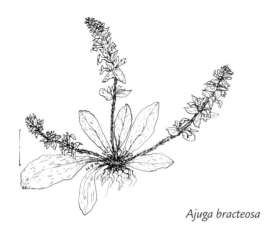

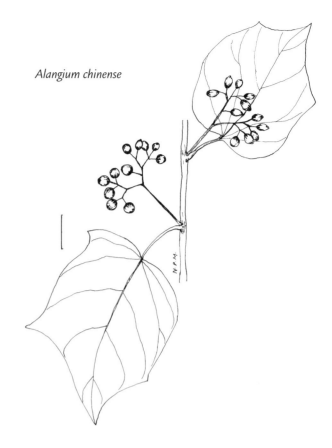

Alangium chinense

Ajuga bracteosa

MEDICINE. Juice of the root is given to treat diarrhea and dysentery. About 2 teaspoons of juice of the plant is given three times a day to treat cough and colds. This juice, about 3 teaspoons twice a day, is given to treat problems of the bile duct.

Ajuga lupulina Maximowicz

TIBETAN *jhyasuk*

Labiatae. Perennial herb about 25 cm high, densely covered with hairs. Leaves stalked, 4.5–10 cm long, 1.5–3.5 cm wide, obovate, coarsely dentate. Flowers pale blue in dense ovoid spikes, June–July. Propagated by seeds or root offshoots. Distributed in western and central Nepal at 2200–4500 m on open slopes; also in northern India and China.

MEDICINE. A paste of the plant is applied to muscular swellings.

Ajuga macrosperma Wallich ex Bentham

Ajuga repens Roxburgh
NEPALI *ghoke ghans*

Labiatae. Prostrate herb. Leaves stalked, 3–12.5 cm long, 1.5–7 cm wide, ovate to oblong, sinuate to crenate, sparsely hairy on both surfaces, base decurrent. Flowers blue. Fruit a nutlet, deeply pitted. Flowers and fruits March–October. Propagated by seeds. Distributed throughout Nepal at 750–1500 m in moist, rocky places; also in India, Myanmar, southwestern China, and Indo-China.

MEDICINE. Tamangs apply juice of the root to boils and pimples.

Alangium chinense (Loureiro) Harms

Stylidium chinense Loureiro, *Marlea chinense* (Loureiro) Druce
Marlea affinis Decaisne
Marlea begoniaefolia Roxburgh, *Alangium begoniaefolium* (Roxburgh) Baillon
NEPALI *bhalu paile, phir phire*

Alangiaceae. Evergreen tree about 5 m high. Leaves stalked, alternate, oblong to elliptic, acuminate, glabrous.

Flowers white, solitary or fascicled in axillary cymes. Fruit a berry, black outside when ripe, ovoid, succulent. Flowers February–April, fruits May–October. Propagated by seeds. Distributed throughout Nepal at 300–2400 m in open places around villages; also in northern India, Bhutan, eastern China, Myanmar, Malaysia, and tropical Africa.

MEDICINE. A paste of the root is applied around the area of dislocated bone to help its setting, and this paste is also fed to animals with dislocated bones.

OTHER USES. Oil extracted from the seeds is used for lighting lamps.

Albizia chinensis (Osbeck) Merrill

Mimosa chinensis Osbeck
Mimosa stipulata Roxburgh, *Albizia stipulata* (Roxburgh) Boivin
NEPALI *kulo siris, sirun, siris* SHERPA *thomsing*

Leguminosae. Deciduous tree. Leaves stalked, bipin-nate, leaflets in 20–45 pairs, oblong, slightly falcate. Flowers cream in axillary and terminal panicles. Fruit a pod, light brown, remaining a long time on the tree. Flowers April–May, fruits September–November. Propagated by seeds. Distributed throughout Nepal at 200–1500 m in swampy places; also in India, Sri Lanka, southern and eastern Asia including China, and Malaysia.

MEDICINE. Juice of the bark is applied to cuts and wounds, and a paste is applied to treat scabies.

OTHER USES. Leaves provide fodder.

Albizia julibrissin Durazzini

Acacia julibrissin (Durazzini) Willdenow
Acacia mollis Wallich, *Albizia mollis* (Wallich) Boivin
ENGLISH *mimosa tree, Persian acacia, pink siris, silk siris*
NEPALI *seto siris, siris*

Leguminosae. Deciduous tree to 10 m high. Leaves stalked, pinnate, leaflets sessile, obliquely oblong. Flowers stalked in globose heads, pink. Flowers April–June, fruits September–November. Propagated by seeds. Distributed throughout Nepal at 1000–2000 m, generally in open places; also in northern India, western China, and Myanmar.

MEDICINE. Bark of the stem is stimulant, vermifuge, sedative, and tranquilizing.

OTHER USES. Trees are planted to provide shade in tea estates. Wood is used for furniture and fuelwood.

Albizia lebbeck (Linnaeus) Bentham

Mimosa lebbeck Linnaeus, *Acacia lebbeck* (Linnaeus) Willdenow
Mimosa sirissa Roxburgh
CHEPANG *siris* ENGLISH *black siris, lebbeck tree, kokko*
NEPALI *kalo siris, siris, tate*

Leguminosae. Deciduous tree about 25 m high. Leaves stalked, pinnate, leaflets in four to nine pairs, short-stalked, oblong, oblique, glabrous, lateral veins not very prominent. Flowers greenish white, fragrant. Fruit a pod, flat, thin, straw colored, with 6–10 seeds. Flowers April–May, fruits October–November. Propagated by seeds and

Albizia lebbeck

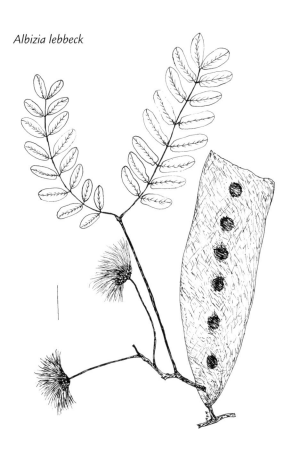

cuttings. Distributed throughout Nepal to about 1000 m in open places, generally along the stream banks; also in India, Sri Lanka, and southern and eastern Asia including southern China.

MEDICINE. Bark of dried root is put in the mouth about an hour to strengthen gums and prevent bleeding. A paste of the bark is applied to treat hemorrhoids. Juice of the leaf has use externally in cases of night blindness.

OTHER USES. Generally cultivated as an avenue tree, the plant also fixes atmospheric nitrogen, making it available in the soil. Leaves make a good manure. Wood is used for furniture.

Albizia lucidior (Steudel) I. Nielson ex Hara

Inga lucidior Steudel
Albizia gamblei Prain
Mimosa lucida Roxburgh, *Albizia lucida* (Roxburgh) Bentham
CHEPANG *musi* ENGLISH *Burmese siris* MAGAR *padake*
NEPALI *padake, tapri siris*

Leguminosae. Tree about 10 m high. Leaves stalked, pinnate, leaflets short-stalked, 2–15 cm long, 1–6 cm wide, elliptic, pointed, entire. Flowers yellowish. Fruit a pod. Flowers April–August, fruits September–January. Propagated by seeds. Distributed in central and eastern Nepal to about 1000 m along stream banks on rocky ground; also in northeastern India, China, and Southeast Asia.

MEDICINE. Bark is boiled in water about 10 minutes and the liquid strained and given in doses of about 3 teaspoons as an anthelmintic. About 3 teaspoons of this juice is given three times a day to treat diarrhea and dysentery.

OTHER USES. Trees are planted as ornamentals along roadsides. Bark is used for fish poison, and for bathing.

Albizia procera (Roxburgh) Bentham

Mimosa procera Roxburgh, *Acacia procera* (Roxburgh) Willdenow
NEPALI *seto siris*

Leguminosae. Deciduous tree about 35 m, bark smooth, exfoliating in thin woody plates. Leaves stalked, 13–50 cm long, pinnate, leaflets in 6–16 pairs, short-stalked, 2.5–5 cm long, 1.5–2 cm wide, ovate to oblong, oblique, obtuse, pubescent on both surfaces. Flowers yellowish white in large, lax, terminal panicles. Fruit a pod, brown, glabrous. Flowers June–August. Propagated by seeds. Distributed in eastern and central Nepal at 300–1100 m in open places; also in India and Myanmar.

OTHER USES. Wood is excellent for making charcoal and is also used as fuelwood.

Aletris pauciflora (Klotzsch) Handel-Mazzetti

Stachyopogon pauciflorus Klotzsch
Tofieldia nepalensis Wallich, *Aletris nepalensis* (Wallich) Hooker fil.
TAMANG *pang*

Melanthiaceae. Small herb. Leaves sessile, linear, woolly haired or glandular. Flowers pinkish or whitish in few- or many-flowered spikes, June–August. Propagated by seeds or tubers. Distributed throughout Nepal at 2500–4900 m on alpine slopes; also in India, Bhutan, southeastern Tibet, and western China.

MEDICINE. The tuber is chewed in cases of cough and colds.

Aletris pauciflora

Allium ascalonicum Linnaeus

BHOJPURI *chhyapi* DANUWAR *chhyapi* ENGLISH *shallot* LEPCHA *dung dungbi* LIMBU *ankkhen* MAGAR *chhyapim* NEPALI *chhyapi* NEWARI *chha* SUNWAR *chhyapi* TAMANG *chhyapi*

Alliaceae. Herb about 25 cm high. Leaves linear, flat, entire. Flowers violet in a terminal corymb. Propagated by seeds or bulbs. Distributed throughout Nepal at 500–2000 m, cultivated.

FOOD. Bulbs are eaten, and leaves are used as a vegetable.

Allium cepa Linnaeus

BHOJPURI *pyaj* CHEPANG *pyaj* DANUWAR *pyaj* ENGLISH *onion* GURUNG *pyaj* LEPCHA *ochong* LIMBU *makkhang* MAGAR *pyaj* MOOSHAR *pyaj* NEPALI *pyaj* NEWARI *pyaj* SUNWAR *pyaj* TAMANG *pyaj* THARU *pyaj* TIBETAN *btsong, ri-sgog*

Alliaceae. Bulbous herb. Leaves all basal, hollow, linear, opposite surfaces alike. Flowers many, white, in dense umbels, November–February. Propagated by seeds or bulbs. Distributed throughout Nepal to about 3000 m, cultivated.

FOOD. The bulb and green leaves are consumed as a vegetable and used as a flavoring for curries and other vegetables. Bulbs of mature plants are eaten raw. Raw onion contains about 2% protein.

Allium hypsistum Stearn

BHOJPURI *jimbu* DANUWAR *jimbu* GURUNG *jimbu* LEPCHA *jimbu* LIMBU *sambhakhu* MAGAR *jyammu* NEPALI *jimbu* NEWARI *jhingucha* RAI *dundunge* SUNWAR *jimbu* TAMANG *jimbu* THARU *jimbu*

Alliaceae. Herb about 25 cm high. Leaves linear, round in cross section, with an onion-like odor. Flowers pinkish when young, white at maturity, clustered at the end of a scape. Flowers July–August, fruits October–November. Propagated by seeds or bulbs. Distributed in western and central Nepal at 2000–4500 m in open, moist, rocky places; endemic.

FOOD. Dried leaves are used for flavoring curry, meat, and lentil soup (*daal* in Nepali) and are also sold in markets.

MEDICINE. Juice of boiled leaves is taken to treat cough and colds.

Allium sativum Linnaeus

BHOJPURI *lahasun* CHEPANG *bin* DANUWAR *lasun* ENGLISH *garlic* MOOSHAR *lasun* NEPALI *lasun* NEWARI *lava* RAI *manmuk* SHERPA *gogpa* SUNWAR *lasun* TAMANG *noh* THARU *lasun* TIBETAN *lha-ming-khrag*

Alliaceae. Bulbous herb, bulblets enclosed in a white or purple envelope. Leaves all basal, flat. Flowers white or pink in lax umbels on a long, terete scape exceeding the leaves. Propagated by seeds or bulbs. Distributed throughout Nepal to about 3000 m, cultivated; also in most parts of the world.

FOOD. Cloves of the bulb are used as a condiment. Garlic powder is extensively used as a spice.

MEDICINE. The cloves are carminative and stimulating. The bulb possesses antiseptic, antibacterial properties.

Allium wallichii Kunth

Allium coeruleum Wallich
Allium violaceum Wallich ex Regel

DANUWAR *dunda* ENGLISH *wild garlic* GURUNG *nota* LIMBU *khong* MAGAR *dond* NEPALI *ban lasun, dable sag, dundu, jimbu jhar* NEWARI *dhoh* RAI *wathatwa* SHERPA *gokpa, oksa* SUNWAR *joi chaiba damphu* TAMANG *dundudhap* THARU *dhonr* TIBETAN *yang*

Alliaceae. Bulbous herb about 65 cm high, bulbs small, clustered, stem base covered with leaf sheath. Leaves linear, flat, longer than the main flower stalk, having a garlic-like odor when squeezed. Flowers purple, stalked, in terminal clusters of cymes. Flowers August–September, fruits September–October. Propagated by bulbs or by seeds. Distributed throughout Nepal at 2400–4500 m in moist, rocky places; also in India, Bangladesh, Sri Lanka, southeastern Tibet, and western China.

FOOD. Young leaves are eaten as a vegetable. Dried leaves are used as a spice in curry, meat, and pickle. The cloves are used as a substitute for garlic (*Allium sativum*).

MEDICINE. Bulbs are boiled, fried in clarified butter, then eaten in cases of cholera and diarrhea. They are simply

Allium wallichii

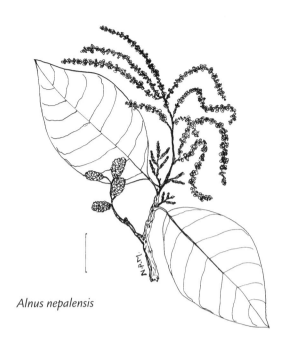

Alnus nepalensis

chewed to treat cough and colds. According to Dobremez (1976), bulbs are eaten to alleviate altitude sickness in Nepal.

Alnus nepalensis D. Don

CHEPANG *harshi* ENGLISH *Nepalese alder* GURUNG *dhunsi, myunsi, tesang* LIMBU *wadsoma* NEPALI *utis* RAI *wakuma* SHERPA *ramsyang* TAMANG *bomsin, dengsin, ghozel, gyansin*

Betulaceae. Tree about 9 m high, bark silver-gray. Leaves stalked, 4–17 cm long, 2–9 cm wide, elliptic to lanceolate, entire, acute, glabrous above, slightly glaucous beneath. Male flower spikes long, slender, drooping, in terminal panicles, yellowish; female spikes cone-like, shorter than the male. Fruit a nut, cylindrical, with membranous wing. Flowers October–December, fruits January–February. Propagated by seeds. Distributed in eastern and central Nepal at 1000–2200 m on moist slopes, especially the banks of rivers and streams; also in northern India, Tibet, and Indo-China.

MEDICINE. Juice of the bark is boiled and the gelatinous liquid is applied to burns.

OTHER USES. Plants are established rapidly on landslides, making them ideal for erosion control. Wood is used for furniture and other construction purposes, and it is also used for fuel. Bark is valued for dyeing and tanning. Leaves are used as cattle fodder.

Alnus nitida (Spach) Endlicher

Clethropsis nitida Spach
ENGLISH *Himalayan black cedar* NEPALI *utis*

Betulaceae. Tree about 7 m high, bark dark brown, deeply furrowed. Leaves stalked, 6.5–12.5 cm long, 1.5–6.5 cm wide, elliptic to ovate, acuminate, entire, glabrous. Male flower spikes long, in terminal racemes, yellowish; female spikes shorter than the male. Fruit a nut, ovoid, with thickened margin. Flowers and fruits July–August. Propagated by seeds. Distributed in western Nepal at 1800–2800 m on the fringes of rivers and streams; also in the rest of the Himalaya.

MEDICINE. A decoction of the bark is applied to treat swelling and body pain.

OTHER USES. Wood is used for construction and furniture. Bark yields a dye and tannin.

Aloe vera (Linnaeus) Burman fil.

Aloe perfolia var. *vera* Linnaeus
Aloe barbadensis Miller
Aloe indica Royle
Aloe vulgaris Lamarck
DANUWAR *ghyukumari* ENGLISH *aloe, Barbados aloe* GURUNG *chhigu*
LEPCHA *miplayutamon* LIMBU *mithiksida* MAGAR *ghyukumari*
NEPALI *ghyukumari* NEWARI *kunhu* RAI *chaklebtutwa*
SUNWAR *ghyukumari* TAMANG *ghyukumari* THARU *ghyukuwanr*

Asphodelaceae. Stoloniferous herb to 1 m high. Leaves forming a rosette immediately above the ground, fleshy, long, convex below, tapering to a blunt point, smooth, pale green, irregularly white blotched, margin with thorny prickles. Flowers yellow or orange, cylindrical, in a raceme. Fruit a capsule with angular seeds. Propagated by root offshoots. Distributed throughout Nepal to about 1400 m, common on open, rocky ground, also planted as an orna-

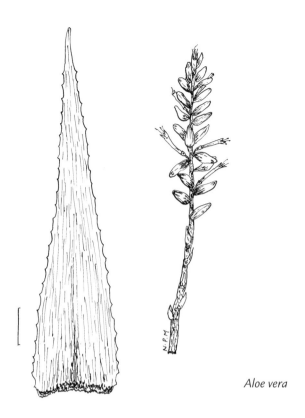

Aloe vera

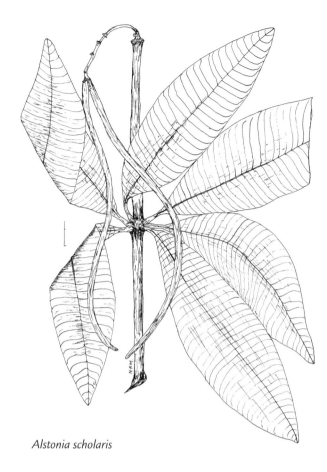

Alstonia scholaris

mental; also in Asia, southern Africa, the Canary Islands, Central America, and the West Indies.

MEDICINE. Juice of the leaf is astringent, laxative, and purgative and is applied to treat burns, rheumatic pains, and skin irritations. This juice is also taken for fever, constipation, jaundice, menstrual suppression, gonorrhea, and kidney pains. The juice is slightly warmed and given in cases of indigestion, hemorrhoids, peptic ulcer, cough, and colds. Boiled juice is considered useful in retarding hair loss. A paste of the plant is given for dropsy and enlargement of the liver.

Alstonia scholaris (Linnaeus) R. Brown

Echites scholaris Linnaeus

CHEPANG *chhataun* DANUWAR *chhatiwan* ENGLISH *devil's tree, dita bark tree* LEPCHA *purbo* MOOSHAR *chhatamain* NEPALI *chhatiwan, palimara* RAI *wallun*

Apocynaceae. Evergreen tree to 20 m high with abundant, bitter, milky sap, bark rough, dark gray. Leaves short-stalked, 10–24 cm long, 4–7.5 cm wide, in whorls of four to seven, oblong to ovate, leathery, entire, tip rounded. Flowers greenish white, crowded on terminal cymes. Fruit a double follicle. Seeds brown with ciliate hairs at the end. Flowers December–February, fruits March–June. Propagated by seeds. Distributed throughout Nepal to about 1200 m, generally in drier parts of subtropical regions, but collection of bark for sale in the trade is a cause of conservation concern; also in tropical Asia, and Africa.

MEDICINE. A decoction of the bark is tonic, alterative, antiperiodic, febrifuge, vermifuge, and anticholeric. About

4 teaspoons of juice of the bark is given three times a day to treat diarrhea and dysentery; for fever the dose varies from 3 to 5 teaspoons two or three times a day. This juice, mixed with double the amount of milk, is considered useful for leprosy. Mooshar mothers take this fluid after childbirth to improve lactation. A poultice of dried leaf is used for skin ulcers. The latex, mixed with mustard oil, is applied on boils and areas with rheumatic pain, and a few drops are put in the ear to relieve earache. Latex is also given to increase lactation.

OTHER USES. Powdered seeds, mixed with corn flour, are given to livestock to improve strength and vigor.

Alternanthera sessilis (Linnaeus) de Candolle

Gomphrena sessilis Linnaeus
Achyranthes triandra Roxburgh
Alternanthera prostrata D. Don

CHEPANG *mambolan* DANUWAR *saranchi sag* ENGLISH *khaki weed* MOOSHAR *saranchi sag* NEPALI *aankhle jhar, bhale bhringaraj, bhiringi jhar, bisaune jhar, dube jhar, jibre pate* TAMANG *mambolan, tawang* THARU *gantha phula, garri*

Amaranthaceae. Prostrate herb. Leaves sessile, opposite, 0.5–6.5 cm long, 0.2–3 cm wide, oblong to lanceolate, entire, smooth, base acute. Flowers sessile, minute, white, condensed in an axillary spike, May–October. Propagated by division of underground stems or by nodal rooting.

Alternanthera sessilis

Alysicarpus vaginalis (Linnaeus) de Candolle

Hedysarum vaginale Linnaeus
Hedysarum nummularifolium Linnaeus, *Alysicarpus
   nummularifolius* (Linnaeus) de Candolle
NEPALI *jhar*

Leguminosae. Much branched shrub about 40 cm high.
Leaves stalked, 0.5–4.5 cm long, 0.4–2 cm wide, ovate
acute, parallel veined, unifoliolate, leaflets variable in size
and shape, suborbiculate. Flowers yellowish, tinged with
pink or purple, in lax racemes. Fruit a pod. Flowers and
fruits September–December. Propagated by seeds. Distributed throughout Nepal at 200–1200 m, common on
lawns and in open pastures; also in the tropics of the eastern hemisphere and America.

MEDICINE. Roots are chewed in cases of fever.

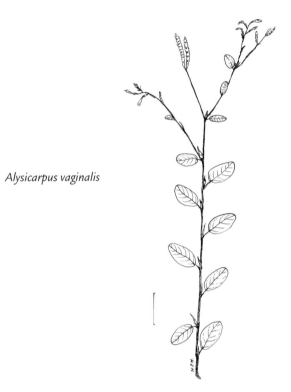

Alysicarpus vaginalis

Distributed throughout Nepal to about 2400 m in moist,
shady places; also in Pakistan, India, Bhutan, Bangladesh,
and Sri Lanka.

FOOD. Tender leaves and shoots are eaten as a vegetable.
When I was about 6 years old, I used to go with the local
Danuwar villagers to pick the tender shoots. My grandfather, who instructed the villagers to collect this plant in
exchange for beaten rice (*chyura* in Nepali), told us that
the shoots are good for health and give "some flavor of
the soil."

MEDICINE. Juice of the plant is given in doses of about 2
teaspoons twice a day to treat white discharge in urine.
This juice is considered good for scabies and is also applied to cuts and wounds. A paste of the plant is applied to
wounds and to treat venereal diseases. A paste of the plant
is mixed with corn flour, baked, and eaten to treat menstrual disorder. About 2 teaspoons of juice of the root is
given three times a day to treat fever and dysuria. This
juice is also given to treat bloody dysentery.

Amaranthus lividus Linnaeus

Amaranthus blitum Linnaeus
NEPALI *ban lunde*

Amaranthaceae. Prostrate annual herb. Leaves stalked,
0.5–1.5 cm long, 0.5–1.2 cm wide, elliptic to ovate, deeply
emarginate, usually purple blotched, base cuneate. Flowers greenish. Flowers and fruits April–July. Propagated by
seeds. Distributed in western and central Nepal at 1500–
2300 m in open places; also in the tropics and temperate
regions of the world.

FOOD. Tender leaves and shoots are cooked as a vegetable.

MEDICINE. Juice of the root is applied to relieve headaches.

Amaranthus spinosus Linnaeus

CHEPANG *rangalo, rangan*   DANUWAR *katageni*
ENGLISH *prickly amaranth*   GURUNG *chikli, lode, lungedha*
LEPCHA *phakurikabi*   LIMBU *tingenodi*   MAGAR *lunde*   MAJHI *gandri*
MOOSHAR *katar*   NEPALI *bandani, banlunde, dhalya, dhutighans,
kande, kanre mate, lunde kanda*   NEWARI *bakan*   RAI *kande, maruwa*
RAUTE *mayaso*   SATAR *lude*   SUNWAR *syolbakhaia*
TAMANG *bagani dhap*   THARU *kantiya, makhan*

Amaranthaceae. Annual herb about 75 m high, armed with slender axillary spines. Leaves long-stalked, alternate, 1–5.5 cm long, 0.3–2.5 cm wide, ovate to lanceolate, entire, smooth, spine-tipped, tapering toward the base. Flowers small, many, clustered in densely flowered spikes, greenish. Flowers and fruits most of the year. Propagated by seeds. Distributed throughout Nepal to about 1500 m, common on uncultivated land and as a weed in harvested fields; also common in warm, temperate, and tropical regions of the world.

FOOD. Tender shoots and leaves are cooked as a vegetable.

MEDICINE. Juice of the root is recommended for fever and urinary trouble, and 3 teaspoons is given twice a day to treat diarrhea and dysentery. Rautes use this juice in cases of indigestion and vomiting, following the consumption of abnormal foods. About 2 teaspoons of juice of the root, mixed with root juice of *Dichrocephala integrifolia* and *Rubus ellipticus,* is given twice a day to treat stomach disorders. A paste of the root is applied to treat gonorrhea and menorrhagia, and is also diuretic. The paste is applied to remove pus from boils and is considered an antidote for snakebites. The plant is cooling, diuretic, febrifuge, expectorant, and galactagogue. Squeezed leaf is used for boils, burns, pimples, and eczema, and it is also considered a good emollient. About 4 teaspoons of a paste of the seeds is given four times a day to treat fever.

Amaranthus viridis Linnaeus

Amaranthus fasciatus Roxburgh

CHEPANG *longe sag, rangan, ranghya*   DANUWAR *ganheri, katageni,
morche sag*   ENGLISH *pigweed*   GURUNG *chikli*   MAJHI *gandri*
NEPALI *latte, lunde, mate, seto lunde*   SATAR *lude*
TAMANG *bagani dhap*   THARU *kantiya, matiya sag*

Amaranthaceae. Herb to 30 cm tall. Leaves stalked, alternate, 2–9.5 cm long, 1.5–4.5 cm wide, ovate to lanceolate, entire, acuminate, smooth, base rounded or cuneate. Flowers sessile, unisexual, greenish, condensed in a long inflorescence. Flowers and fruits most of the year. Propagated by seeds. Distributed throughout Nepal to about 1400 m, common on open land and uncultivated land; also pantropical.

FOOD. Tender shoots and leaves are cooked as a vegetable.

MEDICINE. Gurungs take about 4 teaspoons of juice of the root three times a day to relieve inflammation during urination. Chepangs take this juice to treat constipation.

Ammannia auriculata Weddell

Ammannia senegalensis Lamarck

NEPALI *jarayu*

Lythraceae. Annual herb about 50 cm high. Leaves sessile, opposite, 0.5–4 cm long, lanceolate, entire. Flowers pinkish in trichotomous cymes. Fruit a capsule. Flowers and fruits September–December. Propagated by seeds. Distributed in western and central Nepal at 700–1400 m; also in India, central Asia including China, Malaysia, Australia, tropical Africa, and North and South America.

MEDICINE. A paste of the leaf is applied to boils and pimples.

Ammannia baccifera Linnaeus

Ammannia versicaroria Roxburgh

NEPALI *ambar*

Lythraceae. Annual herb about 40 cm high. Leaves stalked, about 7 cm long, oblong to lanceolate, narrowed toward both ends. Flowers greenish in dense axillary cymes. Fruit a capsule, depressed globose. Flowers and fruits August–December. Propagated by seeds. Distributed throughout Nepal to about 1200 m; also in India, central Asia including China, Malaysia, Japan, Australia, southern Europe, and tropical Africa.

MEDICINE. Juice of the root is given in cases of fever among Danuwars, Mooshars, and Tharus, who refer to the plant simply as *jhar,* herb.

*Amaranthus
spinosus*

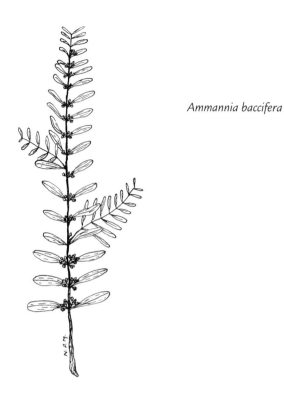

Ammannia baccifera

tral and eastern Nepal at 1000–2000 m in moist places, cultivated; also in northeastern India.

FOOD. Seeds are used as a condiment, in the preparation of sweets, and for flavoring beverages.

OTHER USES. The fruit contains 1.5% essential oils.

Amorphophallus campanulatus Blume

ENGLISH *elephant foot yam, Stanley's washtub*   NEPALI *ol*   SATAR *ol*

Araceae. Herb with a tuberous root. Leaves stalked, dark green with pale patches, smooth, three-lobed, lobes sessile, oblong, short-pointed. Male and female flowers on the same plant, enclosed in a spathe 20–25 cm broad, mottled dark and light green. Fruit a berry with two or three seeds. Flowers May–June. Propagated by corms. Distributed throughout Nepal to about 1000 m, generally in moist, shady locations, also planted in kitchen gardens; also in India, Bhutan, and Myanmar.

FOOD. Corms are boiled and are eaten as a vegetable and pickled.

MEDICINE. The corm is stomachic and carminative, and is used as a remedy for hemorrhoids and dysentery.

Amorphophallus campanulatus

Amomum subulatum Roxburgh

ENGLISH *greater cardamom, Nepalese cardamom*
NEPALI *thulo elainchi*   NEWARI *yela*   TIBETAN *su-kshme-la*

Zingiberaceae. Herb about 1 m high. Leaves 30–60 cm long, 7.5–10.5 cm wide, oblong to lanceolate, green, glabrous beneath. Flowers yellowish. Fruit a capsule, globose. Propagated by splitting the rhizome. Distributed in cen-

Amomum subulatum

Ampelocissus divaricata (Wallich ex Lawson)
Planchon

Vitis divaricata Wallich ex Lawson

CHEPANG *rejom srok, sokro*   MAGAR *ghangol*   NEPALI *pureni*

Vitaceae. Trailing herb. Leaves stalked, digitately three-parted, sometimes five-parted, leaflets ovate, lateral leaflets oblique, cuspidate, serrate, tomentose beneath. Flowers purple in cymes. Fruit black, globose. Flowers June–September, fruits September–November. Propagated by seeds. Distributed throughout Nepal at 300–1700 m in open, moist places; also in northeastern India and Indo-China.

FOOD. Ripe fruits are eaten fresh.

MEDICINE. Juice of the root is used for snake or scorpion bites.

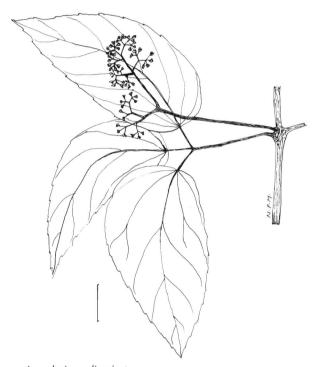

Ampelocissus divaricata

Ampelocissus latifolia (Roxburgh) Planchon
Vitis latifolia Roxburgh, *Ampelopsis latifolia* (Roxburgh) Tausch
Vitis montana Lawson
NEPALI *pureni* SATAR *chimbers*

Vitaceae. Large climber. Leaves stalked, 10–20 cm long, 3–5 cm wide, angled or lobed. Flowers reddish. Fruit a berry, black when ripe, sweet. Flowers June–July, fruits August–October. Propagated by seeds. Distributed in eastern and central Nepal at 300–1600 m in open places; also in northern India.

MEDICINE. A paste of the root is applied to cuts and wounds.

Ampelocissus rugosa (Wallich) Planchon
Vitis rugosa Wallich, *V. lanata* var. *rugosa* (Wallich) Lawson
NEPALI *airi lahara*

Vitaceae. Climber, usually trailing on the ground, young shoots covered with rusty wool. Leaves stalked, orbiculate or sometimes broader than long, five- or seven-parted, lower leaflets sometimes obscure, margin sinuate,

shortly dentate, pubescent above, densely felted beneath with rusty tomentum. Flowers small, reddish, in cymes. Fruit a berry, black when ripe. Flowers June–July, fruits September–November. Propagated by seeds. Distributed throughout Nepal at 1000–2400 m in open places; also in northern India and Myanmar.

MEDICINE. A paste of the stem is applied for muscular swellings and sprains. It is also used to set dislocated bone.

Ampelocissus sikkimensis (Lawson) Planchon
Vitis sikkimensis Lawson
NEPALI *pureni*

Vitaceae. Trailing herb, young parts often glaucous. Leaves stalked, 12–19 cm long, 10–18 cm wide, orbiculate to ovate, base deeply rounded to cordate, denticulate, abruptly acuminate. Flowers pinkish in umbellate cymes. Fruit a berry, obovoid. Flowers July–August, fruits September–October. Propagated by seeds. Distributed throughout Nepal at 700–2000 m, mostly in moist rock crevices; also in northeastern India and Bhutan.

FOOD. Ripe fruits are eaten fresh.

Anagallis arvensis Linnaeus
ENGLISH *pimpernel, shepherd's weather grass* MOOSHAR *aamrora*
NEPALI *armale, kalo gojale, pitamari, sabune jhar*

Primulaceae. Annual herb about 20 cm high. Leaves sessile, opposite, 1.5–2.5 cm long, 0.5–1.5 cm wide, ovate, acute, entire, glabrous, gland-dotted. Flowers solitary, axillary, stalked, blue. Fruit a capsule, globose. Flowers and fruits January–April. Propagated by seeds. Distributed throughout Nepal to about 2000 m as a weed in moist places; also in western Asia, Pakistan, India, Sri Lanka, and Europe.

FOOD. Tender shoots are cooked as a vegetable.

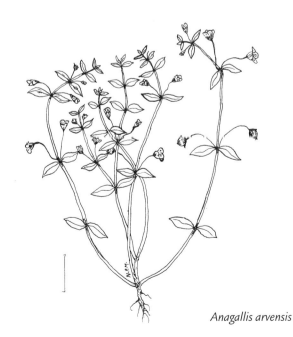

Anagallis arvensis

MEDICINE. The plant is used to treat dropsy, epilepsy, and rabies. About 2 teaspoons of juice of the plant is given three times a day to treat bile problems. The juice is also given in cases of fever.

OTHER USES. Squeezed plant is used for washing and bathing. It is also used to intoxicate fish.

Ananas comosus (Linnaeus) Merrill

Bromelia comosa Linnaeus
Ananassa sativa Lindley, *Ananas sativus* (Lindley) Schultes & Schultes fil.
Bromelia ananas Linnaeus
DANUWAR *bhuin katahar* ENGLISH *pineapple* MAJHI *kauli katahar*
NEPALI *bhuin kathar* TAMANG *sa katahar*

Bromeliaceae. Perennial herb. Leaves sessile, rigid, linear, spiny serrate, concave on the upper side. Flowers sessile, small, reddish purple, thickly crowded on the axis. Fruit a fleshy elongated body, the pineapple. Propagated by offshoot buds. Distributed throughout Nepal to 1800 m, cultivated; also in Pakistan, India, Myanmar, China, Thailand, the Philippines, Africa, and Central and South America.

FOOD. Ripe fruit is eaten fresh; it is a good source of vitamins A and B and is rich in vitamin C.

MEDICINE. Juice of the plant is applied to burns, itches, and boils. Juice of the leaf is anthelmintic and purgative.

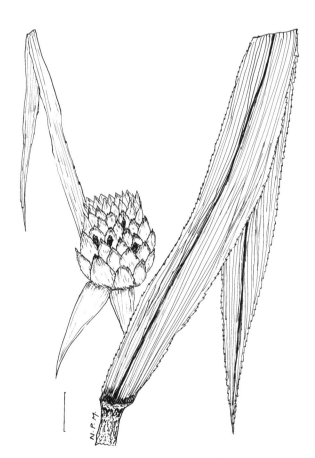

Ananas comosus

Juice of unripe fruit is anthelmintic, expectorant, and abortifacient.

Anaphalis adnata (Wallich) de Candolle

Gnaphalium adnatum Wallich
NEPALI *buki phul*

Compositae. Hairy herb. Leaves alternate, 3–6 cm long, 0.5–1 cm wide, lanceolate, acute, white woolly on both surfaces, half-clasping the stem at their base. Flower heads white, subglobose. Fruit an achene, oblong. Flowers and fruits January–October. Propagated by seeds. Distributed throughout Nepal at 800–3200 m in open grassland; also in India, Bhutan, China, Taiwan, Indo-China, and the Philippines.

MEDICINE. Juice of the leaves is applied to fresh cuts and wounds, which are then covered with woolly hairs of the leaves.

Anaphalis busua (Buchanan-Hamilton ex D. Don) Wallich ex de Candolle

Gnaphalium busua Buchanan-Hamilton ex D. Don
Anaphalis araneosa de Candolle
Gnaphalium semidecurrens Wallich ex de Candolle, *Anaphalis semidecurrens* (Wallich ex de Candolle) de Candolle
TAMANG *taptap mhendo*

Compositae. Erect herb about 60 cm high. Leaves sessile, crowded, 2–9 cm long, 0.2–0.8 cm wide, linear, one-veined, cottony beneath, margin recurved, base decurrent. Flower heads white, numerous in terminal corymbs. Fruit an achene. Flowers August–September. Propagated by seeds. Distributed throughout Nepal at 1500–2900 m in open areas; also in northern India, Bhutan, and Myanmar.

MEDICINE. Juice of the plant is applied to cuts and wounds.

OTHER USES. The flower head is offered to gods and goddesses.

Anaphalis contorta (D. Don) Hooker fil.

Antennaria contorta D. Don, *Gnaphalium contortum* Buchanan-Hamilton ex Sprengel
Anaphalis hondae Kitamura
GURUNG *taptap, napta* NEPALI *bhuko, buki phul* TIBETAN *sukhar*

Compositae. Herb about 30 cm high. Leaves sessile, crowded, linear or oblong, acute, one-veined, cottony, recurved margin. Flower heads white in a terminal corymb. Fruit an achene. Flowers and fruits December–February. Propagated by seeds. Distributed throughout Nepal at 1400–4000 m in open spaces; also in Afghanistan, India, Bhutan, and southwestern China.

MEDICINE. A paste of the plant is taken in cases of cough and colds. A paste of the root is applied to wounds and boils.

OTHER USES. The plant is hung from the ceiling of a house as a cockroach repellent.

Anaphalis triplinervis (Sims) C. B. Clarke

Antennaria triplinervis Sims
Helichrysum stoloniferum D. Don
TAMANG *taptap*

Compositae. Erect herb about 50 cm high. Leaves 3–11 cm long, 0.6–3.5 cm wide, ovate, oblong, or elliptic, acute, clasping the stem at their base, three- or five-veined, tipped with a small black point. Flower heads white in terminal corymbs. Fruit an achene. Flowers August–December. Propagated by seeds. Distributed throughout Nepal at 1800–3300 m in open spaces; also in Afghanistan, northwestern Pakistan, India, Bhutan, southern Tibet, southern China, and Taiwan.

MEDICINE. A paste of flower heads is applied to wounds.

OTHER USES. Flower heads are offered to gods and goddesses.

Andropogon munroi

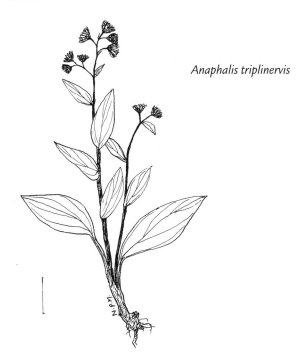

Anaphalis triplinervis

Androsace strigillosa

Andropogon munroi C. B. Clarke

Andropogon tritis Nees ex Hackel
NEPALI *dhalke khar*

Gramineae. Large grass. Leaves linear lanceolate, acuminate, sheaths hairy. Inflorescence greenish. Propagated by splitting the rhizomes. Distributed throughout Nepal at 2100–4000 m in rocky, open places; also in northern India.

OTHER USES. The plant is used as fodder.

Androsace strigillosa Franchet

Androsace sarmentosa var. *grandiflora* Hooker fil.
TIBETAN *khalyu*

Primulaceae. Erect, tufted herb about 30 cm high, rootstocks branched. Leaves stalked, 1.5–6 cm long, 0.5–2.5 cm wide, elliptic, entire. Flowers pink in lax umbels, May–July. Propagated by seeds. Distributed in western and central Nepal at 2400–4700 m in open, forested areas; also in India, Bhutan, and southeastern Tibet.

MEDICINE. The root is chewed to treat boils on the tongue.

Anemone elongata D. Don

Anemonastrum elongatum (D. Don) Holub
NEPALI *dhanero, seto bikh*

Ranunculaceae. Herb about 3 m high. Lower leaves orbiculate, cordate, or three-lobed, lobes divided into two or three segments, dentate, sparingly hairy, upper leaves sessile. Flowers white in few-flowered compound cymes. Fruit an achene. Flowers and fruits June–August. Propagated by seeds. Distributed throughout Nepal at 2600–3600 m in open, moist places; also in northern India and northern Myanmar.

OTHER USES. Juice of the plant is applied to rid sheep of lice and other ectoparasites. It is also employed as an insecticide.

Anemone obtusiloba D. Don

Anemone govaniana Wallich
Anemone discolor Royle
NEPALI *ratan jot* SHERPA *khisakimba, sitini*

Ranunculaceae. Herb with a thick, densely white woolly rootstock. Leaves basal, three-lobed, deeply cordate, densely silky pubescent. Flowers stalked, from blue to white. Fruit an achene. Flowers and fruits June–August. Propagated by seeds. Distributed throughout Nepal at 2300–4000 m in open, moist places; also in India, southern Tibet, and Myanmar.

MEDICINE. Juice of the root is an ophthalmic medicine.

Anemone rivularis Buchanan-Hamilton ex de Candolle

Anemone dubia Wallich
Anemone geraniifolia Wallich
Anemone hispida Wallich
Anemone wightiana Wallich
ENGLISH *common wild anemone* NEPALI *bagh paile, bhattemla, kagarete, kangarata, moramal, seto bikh* SHERPA *patidhuk* TAMANG *nashar, praba* TIBETAN *rheuka*

Ranunculaceae. Herb about 1 m high, rootstock silky pubescent, stout, sheathed with fibers. Lower leaves long-stalked, palmately three-lobed, serrate, silky pubescent beneath, upper leaves sessile, rounded, silky haired on both sides. Flowers white or bluish outside, in many-flowered compound cymes. Fruit an achene, oblong, glabrous. Flowers May–June. Propagated by seeds. Distributed throughout Nepal at 1600–4000 m in open, moist places, also on grazing grounds; also in northern India, Bhutan, Sri Lanka, southern Tibet, southwestern China, and Myanmar.

FOOD. Roasted seeds are pickled.

MEDICINE. A paste of the plant is given to treat cough and fever. A decoction of the root is applied to cuts and wounds. Juice of the leaf is mixed with some water and inhaled through each nostril to relieve sinusitis.

Anemone trullifolia Hooker fil. & Thomson

Anemone trullifolia var. *luxurians* Tamura
NEPALI *jhare jara*

Ranunculaceae. Herb about 30 cm high. Leaves short-stalked, deeply three-lobed, lobes cut into segments, hairy beneath. Flowers white, purplish under the petal, June–October. Fruit an achene. Propagated by seeds. Distributed in eastern Nepal at 3500–4100 m in moist, shady places; also in India, Bhutan, southern Tibet, and western China.

MEDICINE. An infusion of the root is mixed with water and taken to relieve body pain.

Anemone vitifolia Buchanan-Hamilton ex de Candolle

CHEPANG *yasik* ENGLISH *grape-leaved anemone* GURUNG *panta* MAGAR *bhaisya marelo* NEPALI *dhanero, kapase, madilo, mauro mulo* TAMANG *mankapi, phoksarpa, praba, rikabe* TIBETAN *zulo*

Ranunculaceae. Perennial herb about 50 cm high. Lower leaves long-stalked, five-lobed, orbiculate, serrate, white tomentose beneath, upper leaves short-stalked. Flowers white with pink markings under the petals. Fruit an achene. Flowers August–September, fruits October–November. Propagated by seeds. Distributed throughout Nepal at 1600–3000 m, common along waysides in open, moist places; also in Afghanistan, northern India, western China, and northern Myanmar.

Anemone vitifolia

MEDICINE. A paste of the root is applied to treat scabies. Juice of the root is used in cases of toothache and is also vermifuge. It is also applied to the forehead to relieve headaches. About 3 teaspoons of this juice is given twice a day for dysentery. Powdered leaves are applied to kill head lice.

OTHER USES. The plant is used to intoxicate fish. Woolly hairs of the achenes are kept on a stone that when rubbed with a piece of iron lights a small flame, thus these hairs serve as tinder.

Anisomeles indica (Linnaeus) Kuntze

Nepeta indica Linnaeus
Anisomeles glabrata Bentham
Anisomeles ovata R. Brown
NEPALI *rato charpate*

Labiatae. Erect herb about 1.5 cm high, stems quadrangular. Leaves stalked, 3–10 cm long, broadly ovate, crenate to serrate. Flowers white in axillary whorls of spikes. Propagated by seeds. Distributed throughout Nepal at 200–2400 m in open places; also in India, Sri Lanka, China, and Malaysia.

MEDICINE. The plant is carminative, astringent, and tonic. Oil from the plant is used for uterine infections.

Annona reticulata Linnaeus

DANUWAR *aanta*   ENGLISH *bullock's heart, custard apple, sugar apple*
MOOSHAR *aanta*   NEPALI *aanti, sita phal*

Annonaceae. Tree about 10 m high. Leaves stalked, oblong to lanceolate, acuminate, entire, glabrous. Flowers yellowish, fragrant. Fruit subglobose, large, fleshy, with pentagonal areoles (open spaces defined by veins) on the outside. Propagated by seeds or by grafting. Distributed throughout Nepal to about 900 m, cultivated; also in India and the West Indies.

FOOD. Ripe fruits are edible.

MEDICINE. The bark is astringent in cases of diarrhea and dysentery. Fresh leaves and seeds are anthelmintic.

OTHER USES. Seed oil has an insecticidal property.

Annona squamata Linnaeus

DANUWAR *sharipha*   ENGLISH *custard apple, sugar apple, sweetsop*
MAJHI *aant*   MOOSHAR *saripha*   NEPALI *banjhi, saripha*
NEWARI *maka ya gala*   TAMANG *aant*

Annonaceae. Tree to 5 m high. Leaves short-stalked, 2–11 cm long, 1.5–4 cm wide, elliptic to oblong, entire, tip acute, somewhat hairy. Flowers pendulous, three-angled, greenish white or yellowish, solitary, axillary. Fruit somewhat cordate, the outside marked by polygonal tubercles, the inside fleshy, white, soft, juicy, sweet with a mild, agreeable flavor. Flowers and fruits May–December. Propagated by seeds or by grafting. Distributed throughout Nepal to about 900 m, planted on private lands; also in India and the Philippines.

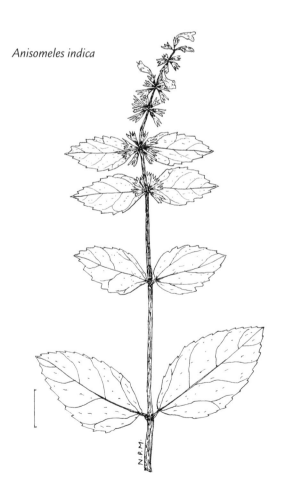

Anisomeles indica

Annona squamata

FOOD. Ripe fruits are eaten fresh.

MEDICINE. A decoction of the root is purgative. A paste of the root is applied to the forehead to relieve headaches. A paste of the leaves, mixed with mustard oil, is used to treat baldness. A paste of unripe fruit, about 6 teaspoons twice a day, is given in cases of diarrhea and dysentery.

OTHER USES. The leaf is used to poison fish. Unripe fruits, seeds, and young leaves have insecticidal properties.

Anogeissus latifolius (Roxburgh ex de Candolle) Beddome

Conocarpus latifolius Roxburgh ex de Candolle
DANUWAR *dhawa* ENGLISH *axle wood, button tree, gum ghatti*
NEPALI *dhauti, hade*

Combretaceae. Deciduous tree about 40 m high, bark smooth, greenish white. Leaves stalked, alternate, 3–12 cm long, 2–7 cm wide, ovate, elliptic, or lanceolate, acute or obtuse, glabrous. Flowers small in globose heads, greenish. Fruit a dry drupe, compressed, narrowly two-winged. Flowers May–August, fruits September–December. Propagated by seeds. Distributed throughout Nepal to about 1200 m in forest openings; also in India and Sri Lanka.

FOOD. Fried gum is powdered and eaten with salt and chili (*Capsicum annuum*).

MEDICINE. Juice of bark, mixed with turmeric powder (*Curcuma domestica*), is applied to the throat and chest to treat cough.

OTHER USES. Wood is used for construction, including support posts for houses, and agricultural implements. Leaves are valued for tanning.

Antidesma acidum Retzius

Stilago diandra Roxburgh, *Antidesma diandrum* (Roxburgh) Roth
NEPALI *amali, archal, himal churi* TAMANG *nakadansing*

Euphorbiaceae. Tree about 5 m high. Leaves stalked, alternate, 3.5–8 cm long, 2–3 cm wide, ovate or elliptic, en-

Anogeissus latifolius

tire, acuminate. Flowers stalked, yellow. Fruit small, purplish when ripe. Flowers September–December, fruits June–July. Propagated by seeds. Distributed in central and eastern Nepal at 150–1300 m in open places; also in India, Myanmar, southern China, Indo-China, and Java.

FOOD. Ripe fruits are eaten fresh or pickled. Children also eat the tender acidic leaves.

MEDICINE. A paste of the bark is applied to treat mumps.
OTHER USES. The tree provides fodder.

Antidesma acidum

Apluda mutica Linnaeus

Apluda aristata Linnaeus
Apluda varia Hackel
CHEPANG *phokro no* NEPALI *dhalke khar*

Gramineae. Tufted grass. Leaves stalked, linear lanceolate, caudate-acuminate. Inflorescence brown. Flowers and fruits September–January. Propagated by seeds. Distributed throughout Nepal at 500–2500 m in open places; also in India, Southeast Asia, and Australia.

OTHER USES. Plants are used for fodder and for thatching roofs.

Arachis hypogaea Linnaeus

CHEPANG *badam* DANUWAR *badam* ENGLISH *ground nut, peanut*
LEPCHA *badam* LIMBU *khamse* MAGAR *badam* NEPALI *badam*
NEWARI *baranha* RAI *domchhedama* SUNWAR *badam*
TAMANG *badam* THARU *mumphali*

Leguminosae. Annual herb about 60 cm high. Leaves stalked, bipinnate, leaflets short-stalked, 3.5–5 cm long, 2–2.5 cm wide, obovate, entire. Flowers yellow. Fruit a pod constricted between the seeds. Flowers and fruits August–November. Propagated by seeds. Distributed throughout

Apluda mutica

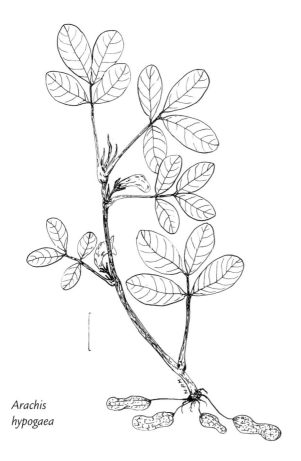

Arachis hypogaea

Nepal at 800–1000 m, cultivated; probably native to South America, also found throughout the world.

FOOD. Seeds are edible, and the oil is used for cooking.

OTHER USES. Herbage is used for fodder.

Araucaria bidwillii Hooker

ENGLISH *monkey puzzle*   NEPALI *kanre salla*

Araucariaceae. Coniferous tree about 25 m high. Leaves sessile, 0.8–6.5 cm long, 0.5–1.5 cm wide, ovate, leathery, ending at a spiny tip. Cones March–May. Propagated by seeds. Distributed in central Nepal at 1200–1300 m, planted on private lands; also in Australia.

FOOD. Roasted seeds are edible.

OTHER USES. Branches are used for fences and fuel.

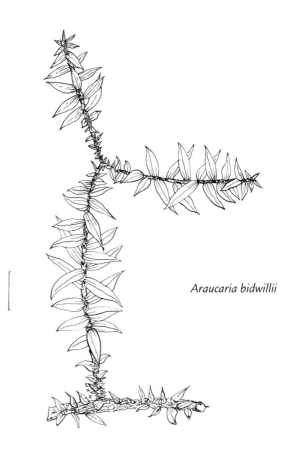

Araucaria bidwillii

Arctium lappa Linnaeus

ENGLISH *beggar's button, burdock, thorny bur*   NEPALI *kurya*
TAMANG *melpang*   TIBETAN *byi-bzung, byid-zung*

Compositae. Herb about 2 m high. Leaves stalked, 5–21 cm long, 3–14 cm wide, ovate to cordate, serrate, hairy on both surfaces. Flower heads purple. Fruit an achene. Flowers and fruits April–October. Propagated by seeds. Distributed in central and western Nepal at 2000–3600 m in open, moist places; also in Eurasia.

MEDICINE. Juice of the plant is applied to boils. The root is diuretic, diaphoretic, and alterative.

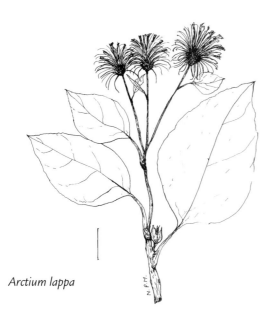

Arctium lappa

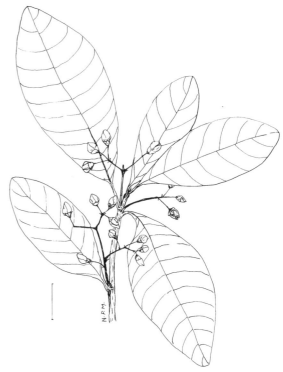

Ardisia solanacea

Ardisia macrocarpa Wallich

NEPALI *damai phal*

Myrsinaceae. Shrub about 1.5 m high. Leaves stalked, 4.5–15.5 cm long, 1.8–3.5 cm wide, narrowly lanceolate, crenulate with a marginal row of dots, acute at both ends. Flowers pinkish. Fruit a berry, globose, bright red, January–February. Propagated by seeds. Distributed in central and eastern Nepal at 1300–2200 m in moist, shady places; also in northern India.

FOOD. Ripe fruits are edible.

Ardisia solanacea Roxburgh

Ardisia humilis Vahl

NEPALI *damai phal, hala lunde, khali kaphal, maya, seti kath*
RAUTE *halyune*

Myrsinaceae. Shrub about 2 m high. Leaves stalked, 6.5–22 cm long, 2.5–9.5 cm wide, ovate to oblong, acute, leathery, entire, base cuneate. Flowers pinkish in axillary corymbose racemes. Fruit globose, black when ripe. Flowers March–April, fruits November–December. Propagated by seeds. Distributed throughout Nepal at 200–1000 m in moist, shady places; also in northern India, Sri Lanka, Myanmar, western China, and Malaysia.

FOOD. Ripe fruits are eaten fresh.

MEDICINE. Juice of the root, about 2 teaspoons three times a day, is given to relieve indigestion.

Areca catechu Linnaeus

DANUWAR *supari* ENGLISH *areca nut tree, betel nut palm, catechu palm* GURUNG *supari* LEPCHA *supri* LIMBU *kuwase* MAGAR *supari* MOOSHAR *kasaili* NEPALI *supari* NEWARI *gwaye* RAI *waklonwaphrun* SUNWAR *supari* TAMANG *ghuyu, supari* THARU *supari* TIBETAN *go-yu, gu-yu*

Palmae. Palm about 25 m high, trunk marked with annular scars. Leaves with sheathing stalk, about 4 m long,

pinnate, leaflets many, linear, tips pointed. Inflorescence much branched, compressed, bearing numerous distichous, yellowish male flowers, the female flowers at the base of the branch and in the axils. Fruit ovoid, smooth, orange, the pericarp somewhat fleshy, the mesocarp fibrous. Propagated by seeds. Distributed throughout Nepal to about 400 m, cultivated.

MEDICINE. A decoction of fruit has an abortifacient property. The mature nut is purgative whereas the immature one is vermifuge and good for urinary disorders. The fresh nut is intoxicating to some people. Paste of the nut is applied to remove scars on the skin caused by burns. Powdered nut is anthelmintic and antiseptic.

OTHER USES. The seed is used as a masticatory. Betel nuts are used in Newari wedding ceremonies.

Argemone mexicana Linnaeus

DANUWAR *katara* ENGLISH *Mexican poppy, prickly poppy* MAJHI *sungure kanto* MOOSHAR *palanti kanta* NEPALI *kande, satyanashi, sungure kanda, thakal* THARU *barbanda*

Papaveraceae. Prickly herb about 1.5 m high. Leaves sessile, sinuately pinnatifid, variegated green and white. Flowers subsessile, yellow, in a terminal stalk. Fruit a capsule, elliptic or oblong, prickly. Flowers April–July, fruits June–November. Propagated by seeds. Distributed throughout Nepal to about 1400 m in open areas and on uncultivated land; also pantropical.

MEDICINE. Roots are alterative. Latex is used for dropsy, jaundice, and eye troubles. A paste of the green fruit is ap-

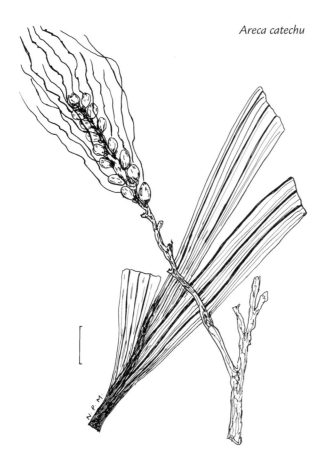

Areca catechu

clusters. Fruit globose. Flowers and fruits July–September. Propagated by seeds. Distributed in eastern and central Nepal at 800–2300 m, rambling along stream banks; also in India and Bhutan.

OTHER USES. The plant is browsed by goats and sheep.

Argyreia hookeri

plied to treat burns. Seeds are laxative and demulcent. Pounded seeds, mixed with mustard oil, are applied to treat itching of the skin.

OTHER USES. Seed oil is used for lamps.

Argyreia hookeri C. B. Clarke

NEPALI *suntiki*

Convolvulaceae. Large climber. Leaves stalked, 10–20 cm long, ovate to cordate, acute. Flowers pink in axillary

Argemone mexicana

Arisaema consanguineum Schott

Arisaema vituperatum Schott

CHEPANG *banku* NEPALI *kal, raksya banko*

Araceae. Perennial herb about 1 m high. Leaf solitary, leaflets many, whorled, linear lanceolate with a long filiform tail. Spathe pink, the tube cylindrical, the apex prolonged into a filiform tail. Flowers June–July. Propagated by corms. Distributed throughout Nepal at 1600–2800 m; also in northern India, southeastern Tibet, western and central China, Myanmar, and Thailand.

FOOD. Leaves are boiled and eaten as vegetables.

Arisaema flavum (Forsskål) Schott

Arum flavum Forsskål, *Dochafa flava* (Forsskål) Schott

NEPALI *banko, timchu*

Araceae. Herb about 35 cm high. Leaves stalked, digitate, leaflets sessile, varying in size, glabrous, entire, acuminate. Spathe yellowish outside and purplish inside, covering the flowers inside. Flowers sessile, yellow, June–July. Propagated by corms. Distributed in western and central Nepal at 2000–3600 m in open, moist places; also in Afghanistan, Kashmir, Bhutan, southeastern Tibet, and western China.

FOOD. Tender leaves are eaten as vegetables.

Arisaema flavum

Arisaema jacquemontii Blume

Arisaema cornutum Schott
Arisaema exile Schott
SHERPA *tuklom*   TAMANG *aaltano*

Araceae. Herb about 70 cm high. Leaves usually one, palmately five- to nine-lobed, lobes narrow elliptic, long-pointed. Spathe green with fine white stripes, the tip tail-like, curved upward. Flowers June–August. Propagated by corms. Distributed throughout Nepal at 2700–4000 m in moist places; also in Afghanistan, northern India, Bhutan, and southeastern Tibet.

FOOD. Corms are eaten like potatoes, and leaves are fermented for making *gundruk*.

Arisaema nepenthoides (Wallich) Martius

Arum nepenthoides Wallich
Arisaema ochraceum Schott
ENGLISH *cobra plant*   NEPALI *tuwa*

Araceae. Herb, stem with greenish or reddish brown spots. Leaves generally two, palmate, lobes thick, glossy, narrow elliptic. Spathe greenish brown with white stripes on the back, triangular ovate, curved forward. Spadix scarcely longer than the spathe tube. Flowers May–June, fruits August–November. Propagated by corms. Distributed in central and eastern Nepal at 2100–2900 m in moist, shady places in shrubby areas in forests; also in northern India, Bhutan, western China, and northern Myanmar.

OTHER USES. The plant is poisonous but corms are eaten by bears.

Arisaema tortuosum (Wallich) Schott

Arum tortuosum Wallich
Arisaema helleborifolium Schott
ENGLISH *jack-in-the-pulpit*   GURUNG *puri makhan*   NEPALI *banko, barkaunle, bir banko, chari banko, galeni, sarpa maka*

Araceae. Tuberous herb. Leaves one or two, leaflets 11–13, linear or lanceolate. Spathe greenish, the tube long, the mouth contracted, ending in a long, pointed tip. Fruit a berry. Seeds four or five, angular, yellowish brown. Flowers May–June, fruits August–October. Propagated by corms. Distributed in western and central Nepal at 1500–2200 m in moist, shady places; also in northern India, western China, and northern Myanmar.

FOOD. The corm is boiled and eaten, mixed with some lime juice (*Citrus aurantifolia*) or other sour substance.

MEDICINE. Juice of the corm is applied to remove worms from the wounds of animals, and the powder is applied to snakebites. Seeds are given with salt to treat sheep with colic.

OTHER USES. The corms have an insecticidal property.

Arisaema utile Hooker fil. ex Schott

GURUNG *ghyani, glinji*   MAGAR *dhokai*   NEPALI *dhokaya, tinpate*

Araceae. Herb. Leaves stalked, three-parted, leaflets rhombic ovate, reddish near the margin, leaf stalk dark-spotted. Spathe dark purple with whitish stripes, the blade broadly ovate, the apex rounded or notched with a short tail-like tip. Flowers May–July, fruits August–October. Propagated by corms. Distributed throughout Nepal at 1800–3700 m in forest openings; also in Pakistan, northern India, and Bhutan.

FOOD. Leaves, including spathes, are used as a potherb and fermented to prepare *gundruk* (Plates 16, 22).

Artemisia caruifolia Buchanan-Hamilton

NEPALI *titepati*

Compositae. Herb about 1 m high. Leaves sessile, alternate, pinnate, segments linear, pointed. Flower heads yellowish. Fruit an achene. Flowers and fruits July–August. Propagated by seeds. Distributed in western and central Nepal at 3900–4600 m in moist places; also in India, China, and Myanmar.

MEDICINE. About 10 g of the root is boiled with a cup of water about 5 minutes, and the filtered liquid given in cases of asthma.

OTHER USES. Pieces of the plant are mixed with horse feed to keep the horse warm during winter.

Artemisia dubia Wallich ex Besser

Artemisia lavandulaefolia de Candolle
Artemisia umbrosa Turczaninow ex de Candolle
NEPALI *titepati*

Compositae. Robust herb about 2 m high. Leaves short-stalked, laciniate or pinnatisect, hoary on both surfaces, lobes acute. Flower heads greenish, globose, in leafy panicled racemes. Fruit an achene. Flowers and fruits most of the year. Propagated by seeds. Distributed throughout Nepal at 1200–3400 m in open areas and on uncultivated land; also in India, Bhutan, China, Korea, and Japan.

MEDICINE. Juice of the plant is applied to boils. This juice is also applied to the forehead to treat headaches. Juice of the leaves is given in doses of about 3 teaspoons twice a day in cases of fever and gastric trouble. It is also considered useful for cough and colds.

Artemisia indica Willdenow

Artemisia grata Wallich
Artemisia vulgaris Linnaeus
CHEPANG *patek, tita pati* DANUWAR *titepati* ENGLISH *fleabane, mugwort* GURUNG *chyonre, chyonthe, pacha* MAGAR *pati* NEPALI *titepati* NEWARI *dhun swan* SHERPA *kemba girbu* SUNWAR *lhospan* TAMANG *chandre, chenji, chenti, chyandhen* THARU *pati* TIBETAN *chhaphung*

Compositae. Gregarious shrub about 2 m high. Lower leaves stalked, alternate, one- to three-pinnatisect, pubescent above, white tomentose beneath, upper leaves sessile, trifid. Flower heads yellowish in spicate panicled racemes. Fruit an achene, minute. Flowers and fruits August–October. Propagated by splitting the root or by seeds. Distributed throughout Nepal at 300–2500 m, common along waysides and in the margins of cleared forest; also in India, Sri Lanka, Myanmar, Thailand, Indonesia, the Philippines, southern China, and Japan.

Artemisia indica

MEDICINE. The plant is valued as an anthelmintic, expectorant, stomachic, antiseptic, and emmenagogue. It is also used for dyspepsia, hemorrhage, and menorrhagia. About 4 teaspoons of juice of the plant is given three times a day for diarrhea, dysentery, and abdominal pains. It is also applied to prevent convulsions and to alleviate the burning sensation in conjunctivitis. A paste of the plant is applied to wounds. The root has a tonic and antispasmodic property.

An infusion of leaves is applied for asthma, headaches, cuts, and wounds. This infusion is taken in an amount of about 6 teaspoons twice a day to treat profuse menstruation. It is considered useful for increasing appetite. For quick relief from diarrhea and dysentery, the patient is seated over the heated plant. A decoction of leaves is carminative, diuretic, expectorant, stimulant, and abortifacient. Juice of the leaves is given in doses of about 2 teaspoons as an anthelmintic and is also considered efficacious in cases of cough. This juice is applied to treat ringworm.

OTHER USES. Dried leaves and flowers are used as incense. The essential oil of the leaves has an insecticidal property.

Artemisia japonica Thunberg

Artemisia glabra de Candolle
Artemisia parviflora Roxburgh ex D. Don
TAMANG *chyenti*

Compositae. Erect herb about 75 cm high. Leaves sessile, 1–3.5 cm long, 0.2–1.3 cm wide, wedge shaped, entire or incised near the top, narrowing toward the base. Flower heads greenish white. Fruit an achene. Flowers and fruits August–November. Propagated by seeds. Distributed in eastern and central Nepal at 1900–2900 m on south-facing slopes of dry meadows; also in Afghanistan, Pakistan, India, Bhutan, China, and Japan.

MEDICINE. Juice of the leaves is applied to treat skin diseases.

OTHER USES. Powder of dried plant is used for incense.

Artemisia sieversiana Willdenow

NEPALI *guhyapati* TIBETAN *khan-kra, tshar-bong, yog-mo*

Compositae. Erect annual or perennial herb about 75 cm high, stems grooved. Lower leaves stalked, broadly ovate, bipinnatifid, segments hoary gray on both sides, upper leaves lanceolate, entire. Flower heads yellowish. Fruit an achene. Flowers and fruits July–September. Propagated by seeds. Distributed in central and western Nepal at 2000–4200 m in rocky, dry places; also in southern Russia and Korea.

MEDICINE. The plant, along with *Ajuga lupulina* and *Ephedra gerardiana,* is immersed in boiling water about 15 minutes, and a patient suffering from joint pains sits in the water about an hour to relieve the pain. A paste of the root is applied to boils.

Arthromeris wallichiana (Sprengel) Ching

MAJHI *nigro* NEPALI *chhepare unyu, harchur*

Polypodiaceae. Fern. Fronds bright green, 40–60 cm long, 15–25 cm wide, pinnate, pinnae lanceolate. Sori round, conspicuous, in a single row on either side of the midrib. Propagated by spores or by splitting the rhizomes. Distributed throughout Nepal at 1300–2800 m on mossy tree trunks, thick branches, or rocks; also in northern India, western China, and Myanmar.

FOOD. Tender fronds are cooked as a vegetable.

MEDICINE. A paste of the rhizome is applied to boils and wounds as an antiseptic.

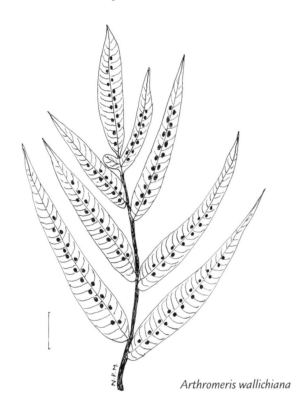

Arthromeris wallichiana

Artocarpus heterophyllus Lamarck

Artocarpus philippinensis Lamarck

DANUWAR *katahar* ENGLISH *jackfruit* LEPCHA *rabhasepot*
LIMBU *phenars* MAGAR *katahar* MAJHI *katar* NEPALI *katahar*
NEWARI *phonsi* SUNWAR *kathar* TAMANG *sing katahar*
THARU *katahar*

Moraceae. Evergreen tree about 15 m high. Leaves stalked, alternate, 5.5–14 cm long, 3.5–8 cm wide, elliptic to oblong to ovate, narrowed toward the base, entire, glabrous. Female flower heads embraced in spathaceous, deciduous, stipular sheaths. Fruits hanging on short stalks, yellowish when ripe, oblong, 25–60 cm long. Flowers February–April. Propagated by seeds. Distributed throughout Nepal to about 800 m, planted on private lands around villages; also in India, Bhutan, Sri Lanka, Myanmar, and the Philippines.

FOOD. Unripe fruit is peeled and cooked as a vegetable or pickled. Ripe fruits are delicious, and the pulp eaten raw. Seeds are either roasted or prepared as curry.

MEDICINE. A decoction of the root, about 4 teaspoons three times a day, is given for diarrhea and dysentery. The milky latex is applied for glandular swellings and promotes suppuration. Ripe fruit is nutritive, demulcent, and laxative. Roasted seeds have an aphrodisiac property.

OTHER USES. Bark of the stem contains tannin and yields a yellow dye. Leaves are used to make *marcha*, a fermenting cake from which liquor is distilled.

Artocarpus lakoocha Wallich ex Roxburgh

Artocarpus mollis Wallich

CHEPANG *badar, dhausi* DANUWAR *barahar* ENGLISH *monkey jack*
GURUNG *baral, batal* LIMBU *muchhe* MOOSHAR *barahar*
NEPALI *barahar*

Moraceae. Deciduous tree 10–50 m high. Leaves stalked, 3–27 cm long, 2–16 cm wide, dark green, tomentose beneath, entire. Male flower head receptacle yellow. Fruit velvety, yellow when ripe. Flowers March–May, fruits July–August. Propagated by seeds. Distributed throughout Nepal to about 900 m, generally planted on private land around villages; also in India, Bhutan, Sri Lanka, Myanmar, and Malaysia.

FOOD. Ripe fruits are eaten fresh, and immature ones are cooked as curry. The male receptacles are pickled.

MEDICINE. Sap and juice of the bark are applied to boils and pimples; bark juice is applied to cuts and wounds. The bark and that of *Psidium guajava* are squeezed to extract a liquid that is given in doses of about 4 teaspoons twice a day in cases of bloody dysentery.

OTHER USES. The plant is important as fodder. Wood, resistant to termites, is used for timber.

Artocarpus lakoocha

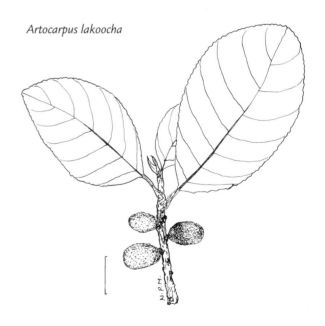

Arundinella hookeri Munro ex Keng

Arundinella villosa var. *himalaica* Hooker fil.
NEPALI *phurke khar*

Gramineae. Tufted bamboo about 6 m high, culms glaucous green, culm sheaths papery, striate, broad at the base. Leaves 15–30 cm long, oblong to lanceolate, base attenuate into a short stalk, glaucous green when young, ending at the top in a rough, bristly point, pale and glabrous beneath. Inflorescence greenish. Fruit a grain, ellipsoidal, smooth. Propagated by splitting the rhizomes. Distributed throughout Nepal at 2400–3500 m in open, rocky places; also in northern India, Bhutan, and Myanmar.

OTHER USES. The plant is used for thatching and also serves as fodder.

Arundinella nepalensis Trinius

Arundinella brasiliensis Raddi
CHEPANG *les, pukya, saiphing* NEPALI *phurke khar* THARU *dhohalni*

Gramineae. Perennial grass about 2 m high, culms slender, smooth, nodes usually glabrous. Leaves 15–30 cm long, 0.4–1.8 cm wide, flat, often involute, surface villous with long, soft hairs on tubercles. Inflorescence yellowish. Propagated by splitting the rhizomes. Distributed throughout Nepal at 300–2500 m in open places; also in northeastern India, China, and Southeast Asia.

OTHER USES. Culms are used for thatching and fences.

Arundinella nepalensis

Arundo donax Linnaeus

BHOJPURI *narkat* CHEPANG *bhok* DANUWAR *narkat*
ENGLISH *bamboo reed, Danubian reed, donax cane, giant reed, great reed, Italian reed, Provence cane* GURUNG *narkat*
LEPCHA *manglong* LIMBU *baktusing* NEPALI *narkat, thagal*
NEWARI *nhyapan kathi* RAI *honrkandma* SUNWAR *narkat*
TAMANG *narkat* THARU *lenrakut*

Gramineae. Tall reedy grass, culm hollow. Leaves tapering from the base, which clasps the stem. Inflorescence light brown on an elongated axis. Propagated by splitting the rhizomes or by root offshoots. Distributed in central and western Nepal at 1500–2400 m in open, moist places; also in tropical Asia and the Mediterranean region.

MEDICINE. A paste of the root is applied to the forehead to relieve headaches. The rhizome is diuretic, and its juice is taken to stimulate menstrual flow.

OTHER USES. The bamboo is planted as a barrier or marker in fields. The hollow culms are used in making musical pipes such as flutes for children. Villagers use culms to construct walls and the roofing of huts.

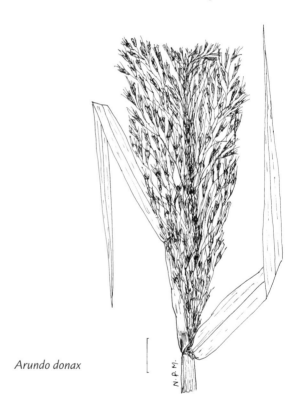

Arundo donax

Asclepias curassavica Linnaeus

ENGLISH *blood flower, curassavian swallow wort, false ipecac, silk weed* GURUNG *dori phul* MAGAR *sima* NEPALI *hiralal, machha phul, madane, shanikhar* NEWARI *nyacha swan*

Asclepiadaceae. Erect shrub about 1 m high. Leaves stalked, opposite, 9–15 cm long, 1–3.5 cm wide, lanceolate, narrowed toward the stem, entire, acute. Flowers orange-yellow in terminal umbels. Flowers June–July, fruits October–November. Propagated by seeds. Distributed throughout Nepal at 700–1900 m, generally in open places along watercourses; also in India and tropical America.

MEDICINE. Juice of the leaves has an anthelmintic property and is also applied to boils. Latex is applied to treat warts.

Asclepias curassavica

Asparagus filicinus Buchanan-Hamilton ex D. Don

NEPALI *kurilo*

Asparagaceae. Erect perennial shrub about 1.75 m high, stems and branches without spines. Cladodes flat, curved, clustered. Flowers greenish or reddish green, solitary or paired on stalks. Fruit globose, black. Flowers June–August, fruits October–November. Propagated by seeds or by splitting the roots. Distributed in western and central Nepal at 2000–2400 m in rocky, shady places; also in Pakistan, India, Bhutan, southwestern China, and Southeast Asia.

FOOD. Tender shoots are cooked as a vegetable.

Asparagus racemosus Willdenow

Asparagus volubilis Buchanan-Hamilton

CHEPANG *gaidung, jodung, jorbhok* DANUWAR *kurilo* ENGLISH *wild asparagus* GURUNG *lahaitu, pajothor, pujutoro, pustu* LEPCHA *takolkrim, khikkithuk* MOOSHAR *satawari* NEPALI *kuril, satawari* NEWARI *kuril* RAI *bongsalim* SHERPA *kopi* SUNWAR *chyabra* TAMANG *kobi, koibet, pororo* THARU *kurela* TIBETAN *ibarara, rtsa-ba-brgya*

Asparagaceae. Straggling, much branched, slender shrub about 1.5 m high, shoots covered with reflexed spines. Cladodes needle shaped, somewhat curved, triquetrous, channeled beneath. Flowers small, stalked, white, fragrant, in racemes. Fruit a berry, globose. Flowers August–November, fruits June–July. Propagated by seeds

or by splitting the roots. Distributed throughout Nepal at 300–2200 m, generally in dry places in subtropical regions, moist places in temperate regions but disturbance of the plant's habitat and collection of roots for sale in the trade are causes of conservation concern; also in Pakistan, India, Southeast Asia, Australia, and Africa.

FOOD. Tender shoots are cooked as a vegetable.

MEDICINE. Roots are one of the important commodities of export from Nepal. The root is much valued in herbal medicine as diuretic, demulcent, aphrodisiac, laxative, refrigerant, tonic, expectorant, galactagogue, refrigerant, astringent, antiseptic, alterative, appetite inducing, antidysenteric, antispasmodic, stomachic, and as a demulcent in veterinary medicine. The root is considered efficacious in preventing flatulence and to be good for bile. It is roasted over an open fire and left outside overnight. It is then pounded, mixed with water, and taken to relieve the burning sensation during urination. Powdered root is given as a tonic. Juice of the root is used for worms in the hoofs or stomachs of animals. It is also helpful in expelling the placenta of animals after delivery. The tubers are fed to cattle with mulching disorders. They are also used to treat amenorrhea, diarrhea, dysentery, biliousness, kidney and liver troubles, throat complaints, epilepsy, rheumatism, dyspepsia, gonorrhea, and are considered beneficial in treatment of impotency. Leaves are fried in clarified butter and given to relieve night blindness. Fruits are chewed to treat pimples.

OTHER USES. Squeezed root is used for washing clothes.

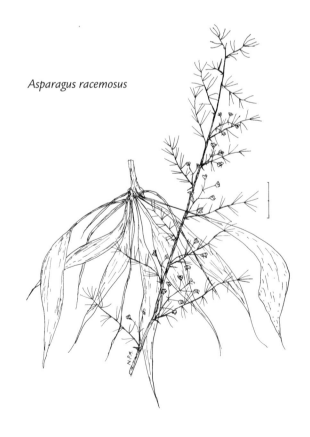

Asparagus racemosus

Aster barbellatus Grierson

TAMANG *mhendo*

Compositae. Hairy herb. Basal leaves stalked, spatulate, ovate, cauline leaves lanceolate, puberulent. Flower heads solitary, pinkish. Fruit an achene. Propagated by seeds. Distributed in central Nepal at 2500–4300 m in open places; also in northern India, Bhutan, and Tibet.

MEDICINE. A paste of the root is applied to cuts and wounds.

OTHER USES. Flower heads are offered to the gods and goddesses.

Aster falconeri (C. B. Clarke) Hutchinson

NEPALI *tare phul*

Compositae. Erect herb about 25 cm high. Lower leaves spatulate, broadly oblong to ovate, narrowed to a short stalk, pubescent, upper leaves sessile. Flower heads violet. Fruit an achene. Flowers July–August. Propagated by seeds. Distributed in central and western Nepal at 3300–4300 m on open alpine slopes; also in northern India and Bhutan.

MEDICINE. Juice of the root is applied to fresh cuts and wounds.

Aster trinervius Roxburgh ex D. Don

Aster asperrimus Wallich
Aster scabridus C. B. Clarke
Galatella asperrima Nees, *Diplopappus asperrimus* (Nees) de Candolle

CHEPANG *bhulingaro*

Compositae. Erect perennial herb about 1 m high. Leaves stalked, 2.5–10 cm long, lanceolate to elliptic, irregularly dentate. Flower heads white. Fruit an achene with reddish pappus. Flowers and fruits July–October. Propagated by seeds. Distributed throughout Nepal at 1500–2600 m in moist areas of shrubby land, forests, and cultivated areas; also in India, Myanmar, and southwestern China.

MEDICINE. Juice of the root is given for indigestion and is also applied to boils.

Astilbe rivularis Buchanan-Hamilton ex D. Don

Spiraea barbata Wallich ex Cambessèdes

NEPALI *bedango, budho aushadhi, gane gurjo, thulo aushadhi*
TAMANG *ganchhyung mran, pabale*

Saxifragaceae. Shrub. Leaves stalked, pinnate, leaflets elliptic to ovate, acuminate, base rounded or cordate, margin doubly serrate, petiolules with long brown hairs, especially at the points of attachment of the leaflets. Flowers yellowish. Fruit a capsule, ovoid. Seeds ellipsoidal, tapering at either end into a tail as much as twice as long as the seed. Flowers July–October, fruits October–November. Propagated by rootstocks. Distributed throughout Nepal at 2000–3600 m on moist, rocky hillsides; also in northern India, southern Tibet, Myanmar, Thailand, Laos, and the Philippines.

MEDICINE. Juice of the plant is applied to sprains and muscular swellings. The root is valued in curing diarrhea, dysentery, prolapse of the uterus, and hemorrhage. Juice

Aster falconeri

Astilbe rivularis

of the root or its powder, mixed with honey, is given after delivery to regain strength and stop excessive bleeding during menstruation. This juice, about 6 teaspoons three times a day, is given in cases of peptic ulcer and also for diarrhea and dysentery.

Astragalus leucocephalus Graham ex Bentham

TIBETAN *pataka*

Leguminosae. Shrub, stems densely tufted, spreading. Leaves stalked, 0.2–2.5 cm long, 0.1–1 cm wide, pinnate, leaflets oblong, densely gray woolly. Flowers pinkish, in dense silky haired clusters. Fruit a pod, finely hairy. Flowers August–September, fruits November–January. Propagated by seeds. Distributed in western and central Nepal at 1500–3700 m in open pastureland; also in Afghanistan, Pakistan, and India.

OTHER USES. The plant is poisonous to cattle and humans.

Avena fatua Linnaeus

ENGLISH *wild oat* NEPALI *jangali jau*

Gramineae. Annual grass about 60 cm high. Leaves 10–15 cm long, linear, spatulate, hairy. Inflorescence yellowish. Flowers and fruits July–November. Propagated by seeds. Distributed in western and central Nepal at 2100–3700 m on moist ground; also in India, Tibet, central Asia, and Europe.

OTHER USES. The plant is used for fodder.

Avena fatua

Avena sativa Linnaeus

CHEPANG *jau* DANUWAR *jau* ENGLISH *oat* GURUNG *jau* LEPCHA *kachyer* LIMBU *hongma summ* MAGAR *jau* NEPALI *jau* NEWARI *tachhi* RAI *chhong* SUNWAR *kyo* TAMANG *jau* THARU *jau*

Gramineae. Erect annual grass, culms moderately stout, hollow. Leaves linear lanceolate. Inflorescence yellowish in terminal open panicles. Fruit a grain, tightly enclosed by the glume and palea, free, silky. Flowers and fruits January–March. Propagated by seeds. Distributed throughout Nepal to about 1300 m, cultivated.

FOOD. The plant is consumed.

OTHER USES. The plant is used for cattle fodder.

Averrhoa carambola Linnaeus

ENGLISH *carambola* NEPALI *kamarakh, madhane phal*

Oxalidaceae. Tree about 6 m high. Leaves stalked, pinnate, leaflets in about five pairs, ovate to lanceolate, entire, acuminate, glabrous. Flowers pale purple, often margined with white. Fruit greenish yellow, with five longitudinal, sharp, angular lobes, fleshy, the juice acidic. Seeds arillate. Flowers June–September, fruits September–October. Propagated by seeds or by budding. Distributed throughout Nepal to about 300 m, cultivated.

FOOD. Fruits are eaten fresh or are pickled; fresh fruit is rich in vitamin C. Unripe fruit is mixed in curries.

MEDICINE. Pounded leaves are applied for chicken pox, ringworm, and headache. The fruit is laxative, refrigerant, stimulant, and febrifuge. Juice of the fruit is prescribed in cases of fever. A decoction of crushed seeds is emmenagogue, galactagogue, and abortifacient. Powdered seed is a good anodyne for asthma, colic, and jaundice.

OTHER USES. Juice of unripe fruits is astringent and used to remove iron, mold, and other stains from linen. Wood is used for construction and making furniture.

Azadirachta indica A. Jussieu

Melia azadirachta Linnaeus, not *M. azedarach* Linnaeus

BHOJPURI *nim* CHEPANG *nim* DANUWAR *nim* ENGLISH *margosa tree, neem tree* GURUNG *nim* LIMBU *khiksing* MAGAR *nim* MOOSHAR *nim* NEPALI *nim* NEWARI *nim* RAI *khaksan* SUNWAR *nim* TAMANG *nim* THARU *nim* TIBETAN *nim-pa, pa-ru-ru*

Meliaceae. Evergreen tree about 15 m high. Leaves crowded near the ends of branches, stalked, odd-pinnate, leaflets subsessile, subopposite, 3–10 cm long, 1–2.5 cm wide, lanceolate, unequally sided, serrate, acuminate, shiny bright green above. Flowers white, fragrant, in numerous axillary panicles. Fruit a drupe, oblong, greenish yellow. Flowers March–May, fruits June–August. Propagated by seeds. Distributed throughout Nepal to about 900 m, fairly common in open places around villages; also in Pakistan, India, Bangladesh, Myanmar, Thailand, and Indonesia.

MEDICINE. The bark is febrifuge. Juice of the bark is used for fever, thirst, cough, urinary complaints, and blood discharges. The juice or a paste is applied to treat swelling or bleeding from the gums. A paste of the leaves is applied to wounds on the backs of animals, especially horses. The juice, about 2 teaspoons once a day, is given to relieve fever. Fruit is purgative, and the juice is used for urinary discharges, skin diseases, hemorrhoids, and headaches. Seed oil is applied to burns. This oil, about 4 teaspoons, is given as an anthelmintic. It is also applied to burns and has antiseptic value. A paste of the seeds, mixed with mustard oil and turmeric powder (*Curcuma domestica*), is applied in cases of leprosy. A paste of the gum is given to treat dysentery.

OTHER USES. Slender twigs are used as toothbrushes. Leaves are used to protect clothes from moths. The seed contains 40–45% nonvolatile oil of deep yellow color. Seed oil has an insecticidal property. Oil cake is used as fertilizer.

Azadirachta indica

B

Bacopa monnieri (Linnaeus) Pennell

Lysimachia monnieri Linnaeus, *Bramia monnieri* (Linnaeus) Pennell
Bramia indica Lamarck
Gratiola monnieria Linnaeus, *Bacopa monnieria* (Linnaeus) Wettstein, *Herpestis monnieria* (Linnaeus) Kunth
ENGLISH *water hyssop* NEPALI *medha giri*

Scrophulariaceae. Succulent perennial herb, stems creeping, rooting at nodes. Leaves stalked, 0.8–2 cm long, 0.2–0.7 cm wide, obovate to lanceolate, obtuse, entire, base narrowed. Flowers white or pale blue. Fruit a capsule, ovoid, enclosed in the calyx. Flowers April–July. Propagated by seeds. Distributed in western and central Nepal at 700–900 m in moist, rocky areas; also in India, Sri Lanka, western and southern China, and Taiwan.

MEDICINE. Juice of the plant is applied to treat burns.

Bacopa monnieri

Bambusa balcooa Roxburgh

Dendrocalamus balcooa (Roxburgh) Voigt
NEPALI *ban bans, bhalu bans, dhanu bans*

Gramineae. Thick-walled bamboo about 20 m high, branches large, nodes swollen, with whitish ring above, hairy below, internodes 20–45 cm long, 8–15 cm wide, lower culm sheath short, broad, hairy on the upper surface, ciliate on the edges, tip rounded, auricles fringed, upper culm sheath nearly glabrous, truncate, closely hairy below. Leaves stalked, lanceolate, attenuate at the base, sometimes long ciliate at the base, broad, slightly hairy below, leaf sheath striate, white hairy, truncate above with a narrow callus, few stiff bristles. Inflorescence a compound panicle. Propagated by culm cuttings. Distributed throughout Nepal to about 1600 m in open places; also India, Bangladesh, introduced into Australia, cultivated in South Africa.

MEDICINE. The siliceous secretion of the culm is considered aphrodisiac and tonic.

OTHER USES. Culms are used for poles, scaffolding, house walls, and roofing.

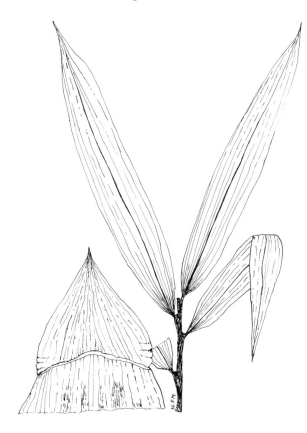

Bambusa balcooa

Bambusa multiplex (Loureiro) Räuschel ex Schultes & Schultes fil.

Arundo multiplex Loureiro
Bambusa glaucescens (Willdenow) Merrill
Bambusa nana Roxburgh
NEPALI *thulo nigalo*

Gramineae. Bamboo about 10 m high, internodes to 4 cm in diameter, shiny dark green, glossy, smooth, culm sheath small, narrow, triangular, leathery, stiff, gradually tapering toward the apex. Leaves linear, glabrous, leaf sheath smooth, auricles bristly. Propagated by splitting the rhizome. Distributed throughout Nepal at 200–1500 m in open places, cultivated; also in India and China.

OTHER USES. Culms are used for weaving mats, baskets, and other household goods.

Bambusa nepalensis Stapleton

NEPALI *choya bans, phusre bans, tama bans*

Gramineae. Bamboo about 20 m high, culm large, densely covered with brownish fur, culm sheath broad, hairy on outer surface, margin hairy, flattened, giving a smooth, furry appearance, pointed at the tip, nodes are not raised. Leaves lanceolate, leaf sheath white hairy. Inflorescence a panicle. Propagated by culm cuttings. Distributed in eastern and central Nepal at 500–1300 m, common in open places, cultivated; also in India, Bhutan, and China.

FOOD. Tender shoots are cooked as a vegetable; they are also preserved (*tama* in Nepali) and used as an off-season vegetable.

OTHER USES. Culms are used for construction and weaving mats, baskets, and other household goods.

Bambusa nutans Wallich ex Munro subsp. cupulata Stapleton

Bambusa macala Wallich
NEPALI *mala bans, taru bans*

Gramineae. Bamboo about 23 m high, culm green, smooth, shiny, internodes 36–45 cm long, 4–8 cm wide, nodes not raised, culm sheath ovate, pointed at the apex, 15–30 cm long, with fringed, bristly auricles, black hairs scattered on the outside. Leaves short-stalked, 15–30 cm long, 2.5–3.5 cm wide, linear lanceolate, margin rough, base rounded. Propagated by culm cuttings. Distributed in eastern Nepal to about 1500 m, cultivated; also in India and Bangladesh.

OTHER USES. Culms are strong and highly prized for construction. They can also be used for rough baskets and mats. Leaves are widely used for fodder.

Bambusa tulda Roxburgh

Dendrocalamus tulda (Roxburgh) Voigt
NEPALI *taru bans*

Gramineae. Thick-walled bamboo about 20 m high, almost unbranched below but heavily branched above, nodes slightly thickened, lower ones with fibrous roots, internodes 40–65 cm long, 5–10 cm wide, with a white ring below the node, glabrous, gray-green at maturity, culm sheath 10–20 cm long. Leaves stalked, 15–25 cm long, 2–4 cm wide, linear lanceolate, glabrous above, pubescent beneath, apex acuminate, base obliquely rounded, leaf sheath auricled, striate, glabrous. Propagated by branch or culm cuttings. Distributed in central Nepal at 200–1200 m, often occurring in moist alluvial land along watercourses; also in India, Myanmar, and Thailand.

FOOD. Tender shoots are cooked as a vegetable.

MEDICINE. The siliceous secretion of the culm is considered aphrodisiac and tonic.

OTHER USES. Strips from the culm are used for making house walls and roofing. They are also used for weaving mats, baskets, and other containers and for scaffolding. Leaves are fed to animals after delivery to hasten removal of the placenta and also to help increase the amount of milk.

Barbarea intermedia Boreau

Campe intermedia (Boreau) Rauschert
Barbarea vulgaris var. *sicula* Hooker fil. & Anderson
NEPALI *khole sag*

Cruciferae. Erect perennial herb about 60 cm high. Lower leaves five- or seven-lobed, terminal lobe ovate. Flowers yellow. Fruit long, linear, terete. Flowers May–June. Propagated by seeds. Distributed in western and central Nepal at 3000–3500 m in moist, rocky areas; also in India, Tibet, central Asia, southern and central Europe, and North Africa.

FOOD. Tender leaves and shoots are eaten as a green vegetable.

Barleria cristata

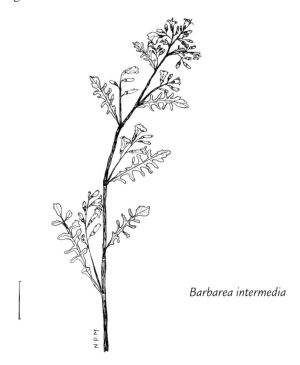

Barbarea intermedia

Barleria cristata Linnaeus

Barleria ciliata Roxburgh
Barleria dichotoma Roxburgh
Barleria nepalensis Nees
NEPALI *bande kuro, lari phul, nilamani*

Acanthaceae. Erect herb about 1.5 m high, stem pale brown, slightly rough. Leaves stalked, 2.5–12 cm long, 1–3.5 cm wide, elliptic to oblong, acute, hairy on both surfaces, base narrowed. Flowers purplish in axillary and terminal spikes. Fruit a capsule, ellipsoidal, glabrous. Flowers October–November, fruits December–February. Propagated by seeds. Distributed throughout Nepal at 200–2000 m, common in open, dry places; also in India, southern China, Indo-China, and the Philippines.

MEDICINE. Juice of the root, about 4 teaspoons three times a day, is given in cases of indigestion. Juice of the leaves, about 2 teaspoons three times a day, is given for bronchitis. A paste of the leaf is applied to boils and pimples.

Basella alba Linnaeus

Basella rubra Linnaeus
ENGLISH *Ceylon spinach, Malabar nightshade*   NEPALI *poi sag*

Basellaceae. Succulent, twining herb. Leaves stalked, alternate, 4–9.5 cm long, 2–5 cm wide, broadly ovate, acuminate, often cordate at the base. Flowers sessile, white or pinkish. Fruit ovoid or globose, red or black, enclosed in the fleshy perianth. Flowers and fruits November–June. Propagated by seeds or stem cuttings. Distributed throughout Nepal to about 500 m, generally in moist places in hedges; also in India, Pakistan, Bhutan, Myanmar, and the Philippines.

FOOD. Young leaves and shoots are cooked as a vegetable or used for salad.

MEDICINE. A paste of the root is applied to swellings and also employed as a rubefacient. Local healers prescribe juice of the leaves to treat catarrh, and leaf paste to treat boils.

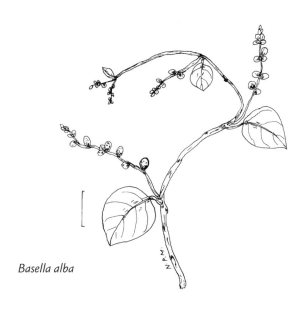

Basella alba

Bauhinia malabarica Roxburgh

Piliostigma malabaricum (Roxburgh) Bentham

CHEPANG *gochhchhi* DANUWAR *mahuli* ENGLISH *Malabar ebony, mountain ebony* GURUNG *aamba* MAGAR *kurgan* NEPALI *tanki* TAMANG *aambu*

Leguminosae. Deciduous tree about 10 m high. Leaves stalked, alternate, smooth, base slightly cordate, tip notched. Flowers stalked, pinkish. Fruit a pod, flat, many-seeded, more or less straight, gradually tapering toward the tip, marked with irregular reticulate veins. Flowers August–September, fruits December–April. Propagated by seeds. Distributed throughout Nepal at 200–1200 m in open areas on hillsides; also in India, Southeast Asia.

FOOD. Young leaves are cooked as a vegetable.

OTHER USES. Bark yields tannin. Mature leaves are lopped for cattle fodder.

Bauhinia purpurea Linnaeus

Bauhinia triandra Roxburgh

CHEPANG *gotsai sag* GURUNG *tanki* MAGAR *tanki gan, tate koiralo* NEPALI *tanki* TAMANG *kanur, kontap*

Leguminosae. Tree about 6 m high. Leaves stalked, alternate, widely cleft about halfway to the base, ovate, nearly cordate. Flowers stalked, purple, in panicled or corymbose racemes. Fruit a pod, stout, thick, pointed, slightly falcate, greenish purple. Flowers September–November, fruits January–March. Propagated by seeds. Distributed throughout Nepal at 300–3000 m, generally planted in moist places on private farmland; also in India, Bhutan, southern and western China, and Southeast Asia.

FOOD. Flower buds and young fruits are cooked as a vegetable; they are also pickled. Seeds are fried and eaten.

OTHER USES. Wood is used for agricultural implements and in construction. Bark is used for dyeing and tanning. Strong woody fiber from the bark is used for cordage. Leaves provide fodder.

Bauhinia vahlii Wight & Arnott

Phanera vahlii (Wight & Arnott) Bentham
Bauhinia racemosa Vahl

CHEPANG *maklo* DANUWAR *madhan* ENGLISH *camel's foot climber* GURUNG *malu, peli* MAJHI *bhorla* MOOSHAR *malhan* NEPALI *bhorla, malu* NEWARI *kusa lapte ma* RAI *bharla* THARU *moharain*

Leguminosae. Gigantic climber, branches terminating in a pair of revolute tendrils. Leaves stalked, as broad as long and varying in size, cleft through about a third of their length, more or less densely tomentose beneath. Flowers white, fading to yellow, in corymbs. Fruit a woody flat pod, rusty velvety. Flowers April–June, fruits November–January. Propagated by seeds. Distributed throughout Nepal at 200–1500 m, especially in *Shorea robusta* forest, but overcollection for bark and leaves is a cause of conservation concern; also in India and Bhutan.

FOOD. Tender pods and leaves are cooked as vegetables. Seeds are eaten raw, roasted, or dried and fried.

MEDICINE. Juice of the root, about 4 teaspoons twice a day, is given to treat amebic dysentery. Small pieces of bark are boiled in water, the liquid is strained and boiled again, reducing it to a gelatinous mass that is applied to boils, taking care to leave a small opening for the flow of pus. A decoction of the leaf is given to treat diarrhea and dysentery. Seeds have aphrodisiac properties and are considered tonic, too. A paste of the seeds is applied to boils and given to children suffering from indigestion.

OTHER USES. The plant is considered a great enemy of forest trees; it is such a large, woody climber and when it climbs through the supporting tree, it surrounds it, resulting in disturbance to the host tree's development and eventually killing it. Stems are used as walking sticks. The bark is a source of strong, coarse fiber used to make ropes and a variety of other things (Plates 42, 43), as described in Chapter 3 under Other Fiber Plants. Bark also yields tannin. Leaves are used for fodder, to make mats and containers for foodstuffs, sometimes for thatching, also for tobacco (*Nicotiana tabacum*) wrappers for smoking. They are sewn together with thin bamboo sticks to serve as plates, cups, umbrellas, and rain caps (Plates 39–41).

Bauhinia vahlii

Bauhinia variegata Linnaeus

Bauhinia candida Aiton

BHOJPURI *kachanar* CHEPANG *rimsi* DANUWAR *koilar*
ENGLISH *mountain ebony, orchid tree, variegated bauhinia*
LEPCHA *rakung* LIMBU *aajising* MAGAR *byahagan, kurugan*
MAJHI *koirali* NEPALI *koiralo, puwangma* NEWARI *konabu, kunhabu*
RAI *chibung, puvanma* TAMANG *aanbu* THARU *koilar*

Leguminosae. Deciduous tree about 10 m high. Leaves stalked, sometimes broader than long, cordate, pubescent beneath when young. Flowers large, white or purplish, fragrant, on leafless branches in few-flowered racemes. Fruit a pod, flat, glabrous. Flowers February–April, fruits May–June. Propagated by seeds. Distributed throughout Nepal at 150–1800 m in open valleys with good loamy soil but generally planted on private land for fodder and as a fuelwood substitute; also in India, Bhutan, China, and Myanmar.

FOOD. Young leaves, flowers, and fruits are boiled and cooked as a vegetable or are pickled.

MEDICINE. The bark is astringent and alterative. Juice of the bark, about 2 teaspoons three times a day, is given to treat amebic dysentery. It is also given as an anthelmintic. The juice is also taken to treat dysentery, diarrhea, and other stomach disorders and is valued as a tonic. A paste of the bark is applied to cuts and wounds. Juice of the flower is taken to treat dysentery, diarrhea, and other stomach disorders.

OTHER USES. Wood is used for house construction and to make household implements. Bark is used for dyeing and tanning. Leaves are cut for fodder.

Begonia picta Smith

Begonia erosa Wallich
Begonia rex Putzeys

GURUNG *kyubro, kyumru, namkimro* MAGAR *magarkanchuli*
NEPALI *magarkanche* TAMANG *braju, nakhru kyamba, pragyum*

Begoniaceae. Herb with reddish stem. Leaves stalked, alternate, 8–10 cm long, 6–9 cm wide, broadly ovate to cordate, pointed, margin irregularly serrate, hairy, variegated with pink patches. Flowers stalked, bracteate, pink. Fruit winged, one wing much longer than the other. Flowers April–September, fruits October–December. Propagated by seeds or rhizomes. Distributed throughout Nepal at 1000 2500 m in moist, shady places, generally in rock crevices; also in northern India and Bhutan.

FOOD. The leaf stalk and stem are sour in taste and are pickled.

MEDICINE. Juice of the plant, about 4 teaspoons three times a day, is given to relieve headaches. Leaves are crushed and applied to sore nipples. The plant is fed to sterile animals to help them conceive. Juice of the root is applied to treat conjunctivitis. This juice, about 6 teaspoons three times a day, is given in cases of peptic ulcer.

OTHER USES. The plant is squeezed and mixed with vegetable colors to make the hue colorfast.

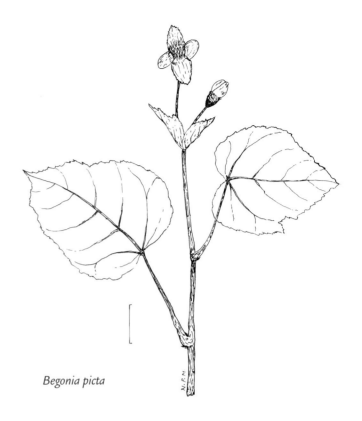

Begonia picta

Begonia rubella Buchanan-Hamilton ex D. Don

Begonia scutata Wallich ex A. de Candolle
NEPALI *magar kanche* TAMANG *bregal*

Begoniaceae. Herb about 30 cm high. Leaves stalked, alternate, 8–10 cm long, 3.5–7.5 cm wide, ovate, base cordate with subequal lobes, serrate, glabrous. Flowers stalked, pink. Fruit flat with unequal wings. Flowers and fruits June–September. Propagated by seeds or root offshoots. Distributed throughout Nepal at 1200–2600 m in moist, shady places, especially on rocky ground; also in northern India and Bhutan.

FOOD. The leaf stalk and stem taste sour and are generally pickled.

Belamcanda chinensis (Linnaeus) Redouté

Ixia chinensis Linnaeus, *Moraea chinensis* (Linnaeus) Willdenow, *Pardanthus chinensis* (Linnaeus) Ker-Gawler
ENGLISH *blackberry lily, leopard lily* NEPALI *tarbare*

Iridaceae. Tufted glabrous herb about 1.5 m high. Leaves imbricated at base, crowded, ascending, narrowly lanceolate, acuminate, leathery. Inflorescence terminal, dichotomously branched. Flowers yellowish outside, reddish yellow with darker spots inside, June–July. Propagated by roots or seeds. Distributed in western and central Nepal at 1200–2300 m in open, moist places; also in India, Bhutan, Southeast Asia, China, and Japan.

MEDICINE. Juice of the root is given as an expectorant and carminative. About half a teaspoon of this juice is

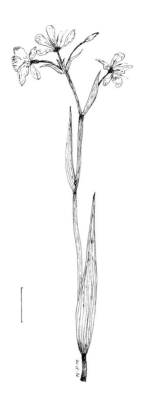

Belamcanda chinensis

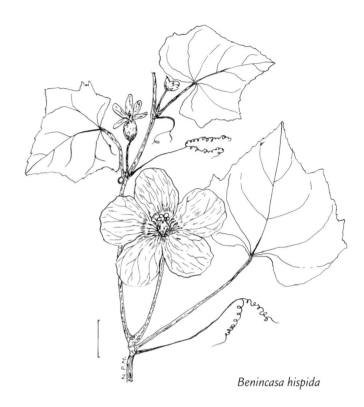

Benincasa hispida

taken to abort 2- or 3-month pregnancies. It is also given for liver complaints and has an appetizing property as well.

OTHER USES. The root contains tannin.

Benincasa hispida (Thunberg) Cogniaux

BHOJPURI *madhuwa* CHEPANG *kubhindo* DANUWAR *kumdha* ENGLISH *ash pumpkin, white gourd, white pumpkin* GURUNG *unsye* LEPCHA *tangjong tangat* LIMBU *phutra* MAGAR *bomosyo* MOOSHAR *kumhara* NEPALI *kubhindo* NEWARI *bhuyu phasi* RAI *chhomlokasi* SUNWAR *kupindo* TAMANG *kubhindo* THARU *bhunru* TIBETAN *kush-man-da-k*

Cucurbitaceae. Large annual climber, tendrils bifid. Leaves stalked, 10–15 cm in diameter, five- or seven-lobed, hispid beneath, base cordate. Flowers yellow, solitary. Fruit large, with waxy bloom. Flowers and fruits August–November. Propagated by seeds. Distributed throughout Nepal to about 1400 m on sandy soils, cultivated; native to tropical Asia.

FOOD. Fruits are used as a vegetable and also in various food preparations.

Berberis aristata de Candolle

ENGLISH *barberry* GURUNG *chutro, gome, kobe, komme, tisy* NEPALI *ban chutro, barhamase chutro, chotra, chutro, masleri* NEWARI *marpesi* TAMANG *kerba, kerpa, pichar, pichyar* TIBETAN *puchu, syker-pa*

Berberidaceae. Spiny shrub about 3 m high. Leaves subsessile, clustered, 2–7 cm long, 0.5–2 cm wide, ovate, with trifid spines, entire or spinous dentate, smooth, base tapering. Flowers stalked, yellow, in drooping racemes.

Fruit ovoid, blue-black when ripe. Flowers March–June, fruits July–November. Propagated by seeds. Distributed throughout Nepal at 1800–3000 m on open hillsides; also in India.

FOOD. Ripe fruit is eaten fresh and also pickled. Alcohol is distilled from ripe fruit.

MEDICINE. An extract from the stem and root is used in ophthalmic medicine. This extract is also used for jaundice, malarial fever, and diarrhea.

OTHER USES. Root and stem bark are a source of yellow dye. Branches are used for fencing fields around villages.

Berberis asiatica Roxburgh ex de Candolle

ENGLISH *barberry* GURUNG *chotr* MAGAR *chutra, chutro* NEPALI *aul chotra, chotro, chutro, muse chutro* SHERPA *namli* TAMANG *chaturo, chhulumase, chyungba, ghyudangdi, kerpa, tigari* TIBETAN *kyumsa, skyer-pai-me-tong*

Berberidaceae. Spiny shrub about 3 m high. Leaves short-stalked, clustered, 1.5–9 cm long, 0.5–2 cm wide, ovate, leathery, margin coarsely spinous, venation netted. Flowers stalked, yellow. Fruit fleshy or pulpy, blue-black when ripe. Flowers March–May, fruits June–July. Propagated by seeds. Distributed throughout Nepal at 600–2500 m on exposed, rocky hillsides; also in Bhutan, Assam in northeastern India, and southwestern China.

FOOD. Ripe fruits are eaten fresh or pickled. Alcohol is distilled from ripe fruit.

MEDICINE. Bark and wood are crushed, boiled in water, strained, and evaporated until a viscous mass is obtained. This mass is given to treat fever and is applied to the eyes to treat conjunctivitis and inflammation of the eyes. In

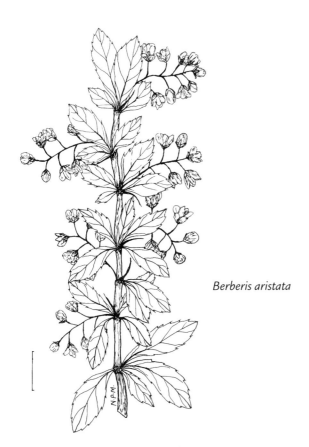

Berberis aristata

addition, it is also a mild laxative and tonic. Squeezed bark is fed to animals with stomach trouble. Tender leaf buds are chewed and kept in the mouth, touching the teeth about 15 minutes, to treat dental caries. The fruit has cooling and laxative properties.

OTHER USES. Root and stem are a source of yellow dye. Branches are used for fencing fields around villages.

Berberis chitria Lindley

NEPALI *choto, chutro, juga chutro, lekh chutro* SHERPA *kernapa, kerpa ko therma* TAMANG *choto pichar* TIBETAN *kerpa, puchu balcha*

Berberidaceae. Straggling shrub about 5 m high, branches usually red. Leaves sessile, clustered, 2–7.5 cm long, 0.5–3 cm wide, elliptic, acute, with trifid spines, spinous serrate, sometimes entire. Flowers yellow in corymbose branched panicles. Fruit a berry, red. Flowers May–June, fruits July–September. Propagated by seeds. Distributed throughout Nepal at 2000–3000 m, generally in moist places; also in northern India and Bhutan.

FOOD. Ripe fruits are eaten fresh. Roasted seeds are pickled.

MEDICINE. Juice of the bark, about 4 teaspoons three times a day, is given to treat peptic ulcer. This juice is boiled and filtered for use as drops in cases of inflammation of the eye.

OTHER USES. Root and stem yield a yellow dye. Goats and sheep browse the leaves.

Berberis erythroclada Ahrendt

NEPALI *lekh chutro*

Berberidaceae. Much branched spiny shrub about 1 m high, branches grooved, shiny dark red. Leaves stalked, 1–2 cm long, ovate, margin dentate. Flowers yellow, solitary, on a slender stalk. Fruit red. Flowers June–July. Propagated by seeds. Distributed in eastern and central Nepal at 3000–3600 m, forming thickets in open places; also in northern India and southeastern Tibet.

FOOD. Ripe fruits are eaten fresh.

Berberis everstiana Ahrendt

NEPALI *kanike chutro*

Berberidaceae. Spiny, much branched shrub about 1.5 m high, branches slightly grooved. Leaves sessile, clustered, 0.5–2.5 cm long, 0.2–1 cm wide, spatulate, tip rounded, narrowed toward the base, with trifid spines, spinous serrate toward the tip. Flowers yellow, May–June. Fruits June–August. Propagated by seeds. Distributed in western and central Nepal at 3000–4000 m in open, rocky places; also in northern India and Tibet.

FOOD. Ripe fruits are eaten fresh.

Berberis ulcina Hooker fil. & Thomson

TIBETAN *puchu*

Berberidaceae. Spiny shrub about 60 cm high. Leaves sessile or short-stalked, 0.7–2 cm long, 0.2–0.8 cm wide, elliptic, entire, tip spiny. Flowers orange, May–June. Fruits July–October. Propagated by seeds. Distributed in western and central Nepal at 2500–3500 m on open, windy slopes; also in northern India and Tibet.

FOOD. Ripe fruits are eaten fresh.

Berberis wallichiana de Candolle

Berberis asiatica Griffith, not Roxburgh ex de Candolle
Berberis wallichiana var. *atroviridis* Hooker fil. & Thomson
NEPALI *barhamase chutro*

Berberidaceae. Spiny shrub about 3 m high. Leaves stalked, generally in fascicles of three or four, oblong to lanceolate, serrulate, with sharp spines, acute at both ends. Flowers yellow on an axillary stalk. Fruit a berry, oblong ellipsoidal, deep purple when ripe. Flowers July–September, fruits October–November. Propagated by seeds. Distributed in central and eastern Nepal at 2000–3400 m on open ground; also in India, Bhutan, and China.

FOOD. Ripe fruits are eaten fresh.

Berchemia edgeworthii Lawson

Berchemia axilliflora Cheng
Berchemia lineata de Candolle
Berchemia nana W. W. Smith
NEPALI *muse lari*

Rhamnaceae. Straggling shrub about 3 m high. Leaves stalked, 0.5–3 cm long, 0.3–1.8 cm wide, oblong to ovate, acuminate, entire, glabrous. Flowers minute, greenish, in axillary or terminal clusters. Fruit a berry, blue when ripe. Flowers July–September, fruits May–June. Propagated by seeds. Distributed in western and central Nepal at 2400–4000 m, frequent in scrub thickets in dry places; also in northwestern India, Bhutan, southern Tibet, and western China.

FOOD. Ripe fruit is edible.

Berchemia edgeworthii

Berchemia flavescens (Wallich ex Roxburgh) Brongniart

Ziziphus flavescens Wallich ex Roxburgh
SHERPA *ghugi*

Rhamnaceae. Shrub about 3 m high. Leaves stalked, alternate, 2.3–7.5 cm long, 1–4 cm wide, elliptic, acute, mucronate, entire, parallel veined. Flowers cream. Flowers and fruits April–July. Propagated by seeds. Distributed throughout Nepal at 2000–3400 m in wet, shady places in forested areas; endemic.

FOOD. Ripe fruit is edible.

Bergenia ciliata (Haworth) Sternberg

Megasea ciliata Haworth, *Saxifraga ciliata* (Haworth) Royle, *S. ligulata* var. *cililata* (Haworth) Hooker fil. & Thomson
ENGLISH *rockfoil* GURUNG *padambet, pakhanbed*
NEPALI *dhungri ko jara, pakhanbed, silparo, silpu, simpate*
SHERPA *chyucha, chyurpu* TAMANG *bregyal* TIBETAN *a-ama-bhe-da*

Saxifragaceae. Herb with thick rootstocks. Leaves stalked, 3.5–16.5 cm long, 3–12 cm wide, suborbiculate, entire, fringed with short, stiff hairs. Flowers pink, March–July. Propagated by root offshoots or by rhizomes. Distributed throughout Nepal at 1300–3000 m in moist, rocky places but collection of rhizomes are collected for sale in the domestic and international trade is a cause of conservation concern; also in Afghanistan, northern

India, Bhutan, northern Tibet, western China, and northern Myanmar.

FOOD. Flowers are boiled and pickled.

MEDICINE. Juice or powder of the whole plant is taken to treat urinary trouble. Juice of the rhizome is taken in cases of hemorrhoids, asthma, and urinary trouble. This juice is given, about 6 teaspoon three times a day, for cough and colds. Squeezed rhizome is boiled and the filtered water taken for gout by Gurungs, and for indigestion generally. A paste of the rhizome is applied to boils and is also considered good for backache. Powdered rhizome is used to treat fever, colic, and diarrhea. This powder is given in doses of about 3 teaspoons with warm water as an anthelmintic. Juice of the leaves is used as drops to relieve earaches.

OTHER USES. The root contains 14–16% tannin.

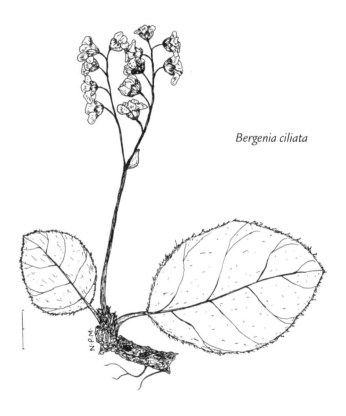

Bergenia ciliata

Betula alnoides Buchanan-Hamilton ex D. Don

Betula acuminata Lindley, *B. alnoides* var. *acuminata* (Lindley) Winkler
Betula cylindrostachya Lindley
ENGLISH *birch* GURUNG *chyarbi* NEPALI *paiyun, saur* TAMANG *takpa*

Betulaceae. Tree about 23 m high, shoot pubescent when young. Leaves stalked, 3–11.5 cm long, 1.3–6.5 cm wide, ovate to lanceolate, acuminate, irregularly and doubly serrate, pubescent beneath when young, gland-dotted when old. Inflorescence yellowish in the axil of each leaf, fascicled with long slender spikes. Fruit a nut. Flowers March–May, fruits July–August. Propagated by seeds. Distributed throughout Nepal at 1200–2600 m on hillsides near stream banks; also in India, Bhutan, southern Tibet, and western and central China.

MEDICINE. Bark is boiled with water about 15 minutes and the liquid mass thus obtained is applied in cases of dislocated bone.

OTHER USES. Bark juice is used for decorating wood (Plate 8). Wood is used for minor construction. Leaves are lopped for fodder.

Betula utilis D. Don

Betula bhojpattra Wallich

ENGLISH *Himalayan silver birch* GURUNG *bhuspat, kella* NEPALI *bhojapatra, bhuj* SHERPA *takpa* TAMANG *tangru* TIBETAN *khel, sla*

Betulaceae. Tree about 30 m high. Leaves stalked, 3–12 cm long, 2–7 cm wide, ovate, acute, irregularly serrate, base broadly cuneate or rounded, sticky when young because of yellow resinous scales. Inflorescences yellowish, the male catkins at the top of long shoots, female catkin solitary. Flowers June–September. Propagated by seeds. Distributed throughout Nepal at 2000–4000 m on moist hillsides; also in Afghanistan, India, Bhutan, Tibet, and western China.

MEDICINE. The bark has carminative and antiseptic properties, and an infusion of it is given for hysteria. A paste of the bark is applied to cuts, wounds, and burns. Water boiled with bark is taken in cases of jaundice and is also used as drops to relieve earache. A paste of the resin is applied to boils, but people in the Kumaon region of Uttar

Pradesh, India, west of Nepal, use the resin for contraceptive purposes (N. C. Shah and Joshi 1971).

OTHER USES. The plant is lopped for fodder. Wood is moderately hard and is used for construction. The papery bark is used for lining the roofs of houses in Jumla and Dolpa districts. It is also used for incense.

Bidens pilosa Linnaeus var. *minor* (Blume) Sherff

Bidens sundaica var. *minor* Blume

CHEPANG *jhyapmuja, nir* ENGLISH *beggar's stick, hairy beggar's-ticks* GURUNG *borso tene, lunge pucha, nange arthunge* MAJHI *lwange jhar* NEPALI *arthunge, kalo kuro, katare, kuro, sinke kuro* TAMANG *happa myan, mangdhap, tinet*

Compositae. Herb about 1 m high. Leaves stalked, 3.5–10.5 cm long, trifoliolate, leaflets lanceolate, acute, serrate, glabrous or hairy. Flower heads yellow or white. Fruit an achene, black. Flowers April–November, fruits October–February. Propagated by seeds. Distributed throughout Nepal at 700–2000 m in moist, open, neglected places; a pantropical weed.

FOOD. Tender leaves are cooked as a vegetable by poor people. They are a good source of iodine.

MEDICINE. Juice of the plant is applied to fresh cuts and wounds.

Bidens pilosa var. *minor*

Betula utilis

Biophytum sensitivum (Linnaeus) de Candolle

Oxalis sensitiva Linnaeus

NEPALI *lajabati*

Oxalidaceae. Erect annual herb about 20 cm high. Leaves stalked, 5–14 cm long, pinnate, leaflets in 6–15 pairs, 0.5–1 cm long, 0.4–0.7 cm wide, oblong, entire. Flowers orange in short umbels. Fruit a capsule, ellipsoidal, grooved, apiculate. Flowers and fruits July–December. Propagated by seeds. Distributed in eastern and central Nepal at 300–900 m in moist, shady places; also in

India, Sri Lanka, Thailand, Malaysia, China, Taiwan, and tropical Africa.

MEDICINE. Juice of the plant, about 4 teaspoons three times a day, is given in cases of fever.

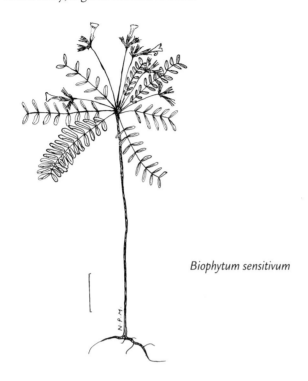

Biophytum sensitivum

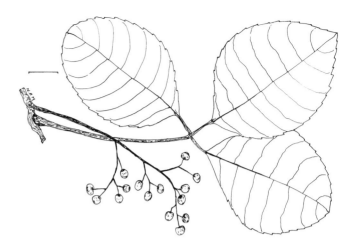

Bischofia javanica

Bischofia javanica Blume

ENGLISH *bishop wood, Java cedar* NEPALI *kainjalo*

Euphorbiaceae. Deciduous tree. Leaves stalked, alternate, variable in size, trifoliolate, leaflets ovate to oblong, acuminate, crenate. Flowers greenish. Fruit a globose berry, brown when fully ripe. Flowers April–May, fruits November–December. Propagated by seeds or cuttings. Distributed throughout Nepal to about 1000 m in moist, open places; also in India, eastern and western China, Taiwan, Malaysia, and Polynesia.

FOOD. Ripe fruit is eaten fresh and is sweet.

MEDICINE. The root is used for controlling bedwetting.

OTHER USES. Wood is used for furniture. A red dye is obtained from the bark.

Bistorta amplexicaulis (D. Don) Greene

Polygonum amplexicaule D. Don
Polygonum ambiguum Meissner
Polygonum oxyphyllum Wallich
Polygonum petiolatum D. Don
Polygonum speciosum Meissner
NEPALI *chyau phul*

Polygonaceae. Erect perennial herb about 60 cm high. Leaves long-stalked, alternate, ovate, acuminate, crenulate, base cordate. Flowers pink in long-peduncled racemes. Fruit a nut, three-angled. Flowers and fruits June–November. Propagated by seeds. Distributed throughout

Nepal at 2100–4800 m in moist places; also in Afghanistan, India, Bhutan, and western and central China.

MEDICINE. A paste of the plant is applied to cuts and wounds.

Bistorta macrophylla (D. Don) Soják

Polygonum macrophyllum D. Don
Polygonum affine D. Don
Polygonum sphaerostachyum Meissner, *Bistorta sphaerostachya* (Meissner) Greene
Polygonum tenue D. Don
NEPALI *chyau phul* TIBETAN *tambur*

Polygonaceae. Herb about 30 cm high with fibrous rootstocks. Basal leaves stalked, ovate to lanceolate, acuminate, margin often strongly rolled in, marginal veins prominent, pubescent beneath, base rounded or cordate, upper leaves sessile, linear or lanceolate, acuminate, entire. Flowers pink in racemes. Fruit an achene, brown. Flowers May–September. Propagated by seeds. Distributed throughout Nepal at 2600–4500 m on damp ground and in alpine meadows; also in northern India, Bhutan, and western and central China.

MEDICINE. Juice of the root is given in cases of diarrhea and dysentery.

Bistorta milletii Léveillé

Polygonum milletii Léveillé
NEPALI *mhyakure* TIBETAN *rambu*

Polygonaceae. Herb about 30 cm with fibrous rootstocks. Basal leaves lanceolate, gradually acuminate, abruptly narrowed toward the base, margin flat, veins scarcely prominent, upper leaves sessile. Flowers red in racemes. Flowers and fruits July–August. Propagated by seeds. Distributed in western and central Nepal at 2900–4000 m on shady banks of rivers and streams; also in Bhutan and western China.

FOOD. Roasted seeds are pickled.

Bistorta vaccinifolia (Wallich ex Meissner) Greene

Polygonum vaccinifolium Wallich ex Meissner, *Persicaria vaccinifolia* (Wallich ex Meissner) Ronse Decraene
NEPALI *pulunge jhar*

Polygonaceae. Herb about 40 cm high, branches slender, trailing over rocks and scree slopes. Leaves short-stalked, elliptic or suborbiculate, acute at both ends, entire, glabrous on both surfaces. Flowers deep pink in terminal racemes, July–October. Propagated by seeds. Distributed throughout Nepal at 3000–4500 m on rocky ground; also in northern India, Bhutan, and western Tibet.

MEDICINE. Juice of the root, about 4 teaspoons three times a day, is given to treat fever.

Bistorta vivipara (Linnaeus) S. F. Gray

Polygonum viviparum Linnaeus, *Persicaria vivipara* (Linnaeus) Ronse Decraene
NEPALI *khalti* TIBETAN *na-ram*

Polygonaceae. Herb about 40 cm high. Leaves stalked, 4–10 cm long, 1.3–2.5 cm wide, linear oblong, acute, glabrous, margin recurved. Flowers pink in slender terminal spikes. Flowers and fruits June–September. Propagated by seeds. Distributed in central and eastern Nepal at 3000–4500 m in alpine meadows; also in Tibet, western and central Asia, Siberia, China, Japan, Europe, Greenland, and North America.

FOOD. Seeds are pickled.

Bistorta vivipara

Bixa orellana Linnaeus

ENGLISH *annatto* NEPALI *sindure*

Bixaceae. Evergreen tree about 5 m high, bark brown, fairly smooth. Leaves stalked, 7.5–20 cm long, 5–12.5 cm wide, broadly ovate, acuminate, margin entire or sinuate, glabrous and shiny above, with minute scurfy dots beneath. Flowers white or pinkish in short terminal panicles. Fruit a capsule, ovoid, densely echinate. Flowers July–October, fruits October–December. Propagated by seeds. Distributed in eastern and central Nepal to about 300 m in open places around villages; also in India and tropical America.

OTHER USES. The inner bark is used to make ropes. The red powder surrounding the seed is used on the forehead of a woman, signifying her status as married, just as the vermilion powder (*sindur* in Nepali) does for other Hindu women. Pulp of the seed is also used to color oil and butter, and to dye clothes. Women in the villages use this pulp for cosmetic dyeing of their hands.

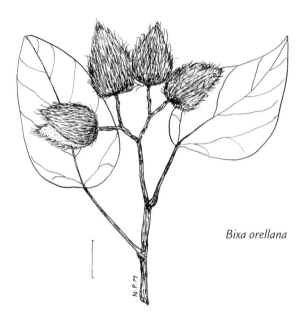

Bixa orellana

Blumea hieraciifolia (D. Don) de Candolle

Erigeron hieraciifolia D. Don
Blumea macrostachya de Candolle, *Conyza macrostachya* Wallich
Blumea sericans Hooker fil.
NEPALI *sahasrabuti*

Compositae. Woolly herb. Lower leaves stalked, upper leaves sessile, oblong, serrate. Flower heads yellow. Fruit an achene, hairy, ribbed. Flowers and fruits April–June. Propagated by seeds. Distributed in eastern and central Nepal at 900–1800 m in moist, open places; also in Pakistan, India, China, Taiwan, the Philippines, Indo-China, and New Guinea.

MEDICINE. A decoction of the root, about 1 teaspoon twice a day, is given in cases of indigestion.

Blumea lacera (Burman fil.) de Candolle

Conyza lacera Burman fil.
Blumea cinerascens de Candolle
Blumea subcapitata de Candolle, *Conyza subcapitata* Wallich
Conyza runcinata Wallich

DANUWAR *badaki ganhuwa*   NEPALI *bugi, kopile jhar*

Compositae. Erect herb about 75 cm high. Leaves sub-sessile, 3–15 cm long, 1–5.5 cm wide, elliptic to oblong, entire or serrate, velvety tomentose above, woolly tomentose beneath. Flower heads yellowish in axillary and terminal panicles. Fruit an achene, oblong, brown. Flowers and fruits February–June. Propagated by seeds. Distributed throughout Nepal to about 800 m; also in India, Pakistan, Sri Lanka, China, Southeast Asia, Indonesia, New Guinea, the Philippines, Japan, Australia, and Africa.

MEDICINE. Juice of the root, about 6 teaspoons three times a day, is taken in cases of fever.

OTHER USES. The plant is used to prepare *marcha,* a fermenting cake from which liquor is distilled.

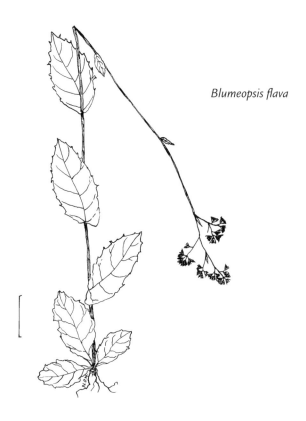

Blumeopsis flava

Blumea lacera

Blumeopsis flava (de Candolle) Gagnepain

Blumea flava de Candolle, *Laggera flava* (de Candolle)
C. B. Clarke
Blumeopsis falcata (D. Don) Merrill

DANUWAR *ban tori*

Compositae. Erect herb about 70 cm high. Lower leaves stalked, elliptic to oblong, sharply dentate, upper leaves sessile, alternate, half-clasping the stem at their base, 1.5–7.5 cm long, oblong to ovate, irregularly dentate. Flower heads yellow. Fruit an achene. Flowers and fruits October–December. Propagated by seeds. Distributed throughout Nepal to about 1000 m; also in India, China, and Southeast Asia.

MEDICINE. Juice of the plant is applied to cuts and wounds.

OTHER USES. The plant is used to make *marcha,* a fermenting cake from which liquor is distilled.

Blyxa aubertii L. C. Richard

Blyxa griffithii Planchon ex Hooker fil.
Diplosiphon oryzetorum Decaisne, *Blyxa oryzetorum* (Decaisne)
Hooker fil.

NEPALI *lasune*

Hydrocharitaceae. Aquatic herb about 20 cm high. Leaves sessile, 2–18 cm long, 0.5–1 cm wide, linear. Fruits November–December. Propagated by seeds or by splitting the roots. Distributed in eastern and central Nepal at 700–1200 m in boggy areas; also in India, Japan, Korea, Malaysia, New Guinea, northern Australia, and Madagascar.

FOOD. Tender parts are cooked as a green vegetable.

Boehmeria macrophylla D. Don

Boehmeria penduliflora Weddell, *Urtica penduliflora* Wallich
Urtica angustifolia Buchanan-Hamilton ex D. Don
Urtica pulcherrima Wallich

NEPALI *bhraun*

Urticaceae. Large shrub, bark dark brown. Leaves stalked, opposite, 12–15 cm long, 4–6 cm wide, lanceolate, acute or rounded, serrate, three-veined at the base. Flowers yellowish in long, drooping, axillary spikes. Fruit ovate, compressed, ciliate. Flowers August–September, fruits November–January. Propagated by seeds or root offshoots. Distributed in eastern and central Nepal at 500–1400 m on slopes; also in India, Bhutan, western China, and Indo-China.

OTHER USES. Fiber from the bark of the stem is used to make sacks, bags, rough clothes, and fishnets.

Blyxa aubertii

Boehmeria platyphylla

Boehmeria platyphylla D. Don

Boehmeria rotundifolia Buchanan-Hamilton ex D. Don
Boehmeria scabrella Gaudichaud
Urtica macrostachya Wallich ex D. Don, *Boehmeria macrostachya*
    (Wallich ex D. Don) Weddell, *Splitgerbera macrostachya*
    (Wallich ex D. Don) Wight
Urtica scabrella Roxburgh, *Boehmeria platyphylla* var. *scabrella*
    (Roxburgh) Weddell

CHEPANG *ammarak, cheklo, tikromsi* ENGLISH *China grass*
GURUNG *pleta, pomla, pondo, sabonla* MAGAR *kamle, kharchauti,
rani ghyeb* NEPALI *chalnesisnu, gargalo, jhilleri, kalo bharaun,
kharseti, langduma* NEWARI *kisi nhyakan* SHERPA *sotero*
TAMANG *aasyangpolo, balba pungi, chhyal, chyongapolo, dobapongi,
phese, mampolo, nikipolo* THARU *khasreti*

Urticaceae. Shrub about 5 m high. Leaves, stalked, usually opposite, 6–19 cm long, 5.5–15.5 cm wide, broadly ovate, acuminate, closely dentate, base cordate or rounded. Flowers subsessile, purple. Fruit compressed or angled. Flowers April–August, fruits October–December. Propagated by seeds or root offshoots. Distributed throughout Nepal at 500–2500 m on moist hillsides; also in northern India, Sri Lanka, Myanmar, and eastern and western China.

MEDICINE. A decoction of the plant is given to cattle for diarrhea and dysentery. A paste of the root is given to treat diarrhea in cattle and is also applied to relieve the pain of their wounds. Juice of the root, about 4 teaspoons twice a day, is given to treat bloody dysentery. A paste of the bark is applied to boils. Juice of the leaves is applied to cuts and wounds.

OTHER USES. Bark yields a shiny, white, strong fiber, good for making fishnets, sacks, and rough clothes. Leaves are nutritious cattle fodder.

Boehmeria polystachya Weddell

Urtica polystachya Wallich
NEPALI *bharaun*

Urticaceae. Robust shrub. Leaves stalked, opposite, 12–23 cm long, 6–13 cm wide, oblong to ovate, acuminate, serrate, nearly glabrous, base rounded. Flowers reddish green in axillary panicles. Flowers and fruits July–Octo-ber. Propagated by seeds or root offshoots. Distributed throughout Nepal at 2200–3000 m in shady or open places; also in India, Bhutan, and Myanmar.

OTHER USES. Fiber from the bark of the stem is used to make fishnets.

Boehmeria rugulosa Weddell

Boehmeria nervosa Madden
Urtica rugulosa Wallich

CHEPANG *syans* GURUNG *dar* MAGAR *dar* NEPALI *dar, githa*
RAUTE *gethi* TAMANG *bhlan chhing, dar, syom sing*

Urticaceae. Medium-sized tree. Leaves stalked, alternate, 5.5–18 cm long, 2–4.5 cm wide, elliptic to lanceolate, acuminate, crenulate, glabrous and dark green above, strongly three-veined. Flowers sessile, greenish, in a simple spike. Fruit an achene, acute at both ends. Flowers August–September, fruits October–November. Propagated by seeds or branch cuttings. Distributed throughout Nepal at 300–1700 m, common on open hillsides; also in northern India and Bhutan.

FOOD. Powdered bark is mixed with flour to make baked foodstuffs soft and tasty.

MEDICINE. Juice of the bark is applied to treat fresh cuts and also helps coagulate blood. Gurungs apply the juice to relieve body pains caused by wounds. Rautes apply a paste of the bark to muscular swellings caused by some injuries.

OTHER USES. The plant is lopped for fodder. Wood is used for making bowls and various household utensils. Inner bark of the stem is used for temporary binding.

Boehmeria ternifolia D. Don

Urtica caudigera Wallich

GURUNG *pokrono, sabonla, sapalan* NEPALI *dhadale, kamle*
TAMANG *dalwa bungi, sanbolo*

Urticaceae. Shrub about 3 m high. Leaves stalked, 5.5–16 cm long, 3.5–15 cm wide, orbiculate or suborbiculate, margin coarsely crenate to serrate or dentate, densely appressed pubescent, apex rounded and abruptly cuspidate, base rounded. Flowers yellowish. Fruit an achene. Flowers and fruits April–July. Propagated by seeds or root offshoots. Distributed throughout Nepal at 900–2300 m on open hillsides; also in Pakistan, northern India, and Bhutan.

FOOD. Tender leaves and shoots are cooked as a vegetable.

MEDICINE. Juice of the leaves is applied to boils.

OTHER USES. The plant is lopped for fodder.

Boenninghausenia albiflora (Hooker) Reichenbach ex Meissner

Ruta albiflora Hooker

CHEPANG *gane jhar* ENGLISH *flea plant, white rue*
GURUNG *kopyanchhi, makhamar, min* NEPALI *dampate, gwame jhar, jhinga jhar, jumalo, jumarijhar, jwane jhar, karna, kire jhar, mauro malo, uruse jhar, upiyan jhar* TAMANG *chhotang nau, laimran, merere, min, nagpadong, saman, serangomen, tagling sibaman*

Rutaceae. Herb about 1 cm high. Leaves stalked, pinnate, leaflets 0.5–2.5 cm long, 0.3–2 cm wide, ovate, with broad tip, entire, smooth, gland-dotted. Flowers stalked, white, in terminal cymes. Flowers August–September, fruits October–November. Propagated by seeds or root offshoots. Distributed throughout Nepal at 500–3000 m, generally in moist places; also in northern India, Bhutan, China, Taiwan, and Malaysia.

MEDICINE. Juice of the plant is applied to fresh cuts to stop bleeding and is believed to help healing. This juice is also applied to treat scabies. The plant is kept under the pillow while sleeping, in the belief that it relieves headaches. An infusion of the plant is mixed with water for bathing, in cases of fever. Juice of the leaves is dropped into wounds to kill germs, and the juice is applied to treat headaches. A paste is mixed with water to wash the face of an ill person, in the belief that it provides relief from fever. Squeezed leaf is pressed against the teeth for toothache.

OTHER USES. The plant is poisonous to cattle. It contains 0.2–0.4% essential oils. A squeezed leaf is rubbed on the body of cattle to remove lice or other parasitic insects. Dried leaves, which emit a strong fetid odor, are crushed to make antiflea powder as well as a retardant for some body worms of ducks and poultry.

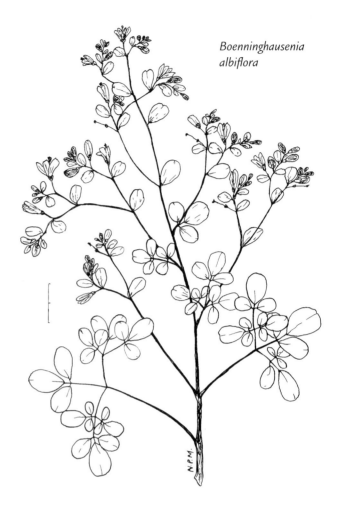

Boenninghausenia albiflora

Boerhavia diffusa Linnaeus

Boerhavia repens Linnaeus

CHEPANG *kharkane, tambrat* DANUWAR *gadapurena*
ENGLISH *hog weed* MAGAR *putali* MAJHI *lelbadri* NEPALI *aule sag, punarnava* RAI *ratanaulo* SHERPA *kharkane* THARU *chuchuriya*

Nyctaginaceae. Diffuse herb with stout rootstocks. Leaves stalked, opposite, in an unequal pair at each node, 1.5–4 cm long, 1–3 cm wide, ovate to oblong, margin undulate. Flowers pink on long-stalked axillary and terminal panicles. Flowers and fruits May–October. Propagated by seeds or root offshoots. Distributed throughout Nepal to about 2300 m; also in Afghanistan, Pakistan, India, Bhutan, Sri Lanka, Thailand, Malaysia, Africa, and North and South America.

FOOD. Tender leaves and shoots are cooked as vegetables.

MEDICINE. The plant is stomachic and carminative. It is useful for asthma, inflammation during urination, blood impurities, biliousness, and leukorrhea. A paste of the plant is applied to the forehead to relieve headaches. Juice of the plant is applied to wounds and to treat backaches. Water boiled with squeezed root and leaf is given to treat fever and is also recommended for jaundice and stomach troubles.

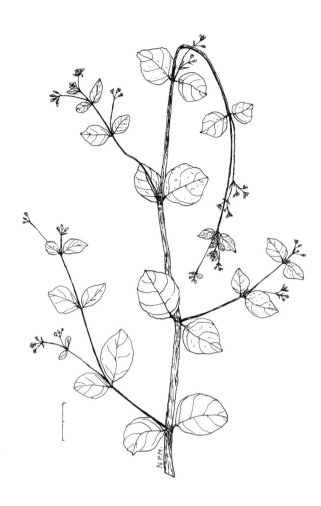

Boerhavia diffusa

cough, indigestion, and stomachaches. The root and gum are used in cases of impotency, diarrhea, and dysentery. The root is sweet, cooling, slightly diuretic, and its powder is taken as a tonic. Juice of the root is valued for gonorrhea. A paste of the root is given to treat abdominal pain caused by severe dysentery. Root juice of the young plant is given to treat difficulty in discharge of urine. A decoction of the bark, about 6 teaspoons three times a day, is given for fever. A paste of the gum is applied to wounds. The floss surrounding the seeds, mixed with mustard oil, is pounded and applied on wounds of animals. Powdered seeds, mixed with yogurt, are given twice a day to treat amebic dysentery.

OTHER USES. The soft wood is used for planking. The floss surrounding the seeds is commonly used for stuffing pillows, cushions, quilts, and mattresses.

Bombax ceiba

Bombax ceiba Linnaeus

Bombax malabaricum de Candolle, *Salmalia malabarica* (de Candolle) Schott & Endlicher

CHEPANG *glausi* DANUWAR *simal* ENGLISH *silk cotton tree* GURUNG *chongonchhi, simaltun* LIMBU *teaggo* KHALING *ghruksu* MAGAR *simal* MAJHI *simal* MOOSHAR *simar* NEPALI *simal* NEWARI *sinbasi* RAI *gayongma* TAMANG *kagdhong, simal* THARU *semara* TIBETAN *ge-ser, so-chhas*

Bombacaceae. Deciduous tree about 40 m high. Leaves long-stalked, digitate, leaflets five to seven, stalked, 5–20 cm long, 2–6 cm wide, lanceolate, cuspidate, entire, smooth, base tapering. Flowers red, fascicled at or near the ends of the branches. Fruit a capsule, five-valved, lined inside with white silky hairs. Flowers December–March, fruits April–May. Propagated by seeds. Distributed in the subtropical belt of Nepal to about 1200 m in open places but commercial collection of wood and other parts of the plant is a cause of conservation concern; also in India, Bhutan, western China, Myanmar, Malaysia, Sumatra, and Australia.

FOOD. Flowers are cooked as a vegetable or are pickled.

MEDICINE. Juice of the plant is applied to treat headaches, cuts, and wounds. Juice of the bark is given for

Borreria alata (Aublet) de Candolle

Spermacoce alata Aublet
Spermacoce latifolia Aublet, *Borreria latifolia* (Aublet) K. Schumann

DANUWAR *dulphi* TAMANG *ursing* THARU *paundhi*

Rubiaceae. Prostrate herb. Leaves short-stalked, 0.8–5 cm long, 0.5–3 cm wide, ovate, acute, entire, hairy on both surfaces, narrowed toward the base. Flowers faint violet. Flowers and fruits July–November. Propagated by seeds.

Distributed throughout Nepal to about 1800 m in moist, shady places; also in tropical Asia and America.

MEDICINE. Juice of the plant is applied to treat fractured bones. This juice, about 2 teaspoons three times a day, is given in cases of fever.

Borreria articularis (Linnaeus fil.) F. N. Williams

Spermacoce articularis Linnaeus fil.
Spermacoce hispida Linnaeus, *Borreria hispida* (Linnaeus) K. Schumacher
NEPALI *ganele jhar*

Rubiaceae. Annual herb about 40 cm high. Leaves stalked, 1–2 cm long, 0.5–1 cm wide, oblong to lanceolate, acute, margin undulate, somewhat rough in texture, base narrowed. Flowers whitish or purplish in axillary clusters. Fruit a capsule, obovoid. Flowers and fruits July–November. Propagated by seeds. Distributed throughout Nepal to about 1100 m in open, dry places; also in India, Sri Lanka, eastward to China, and Malaysia.

MEDICINE. Juice of the plant is given in cases of fever.

Boschniakia himalaica Hooker & Thomson ex Hooker fil.

Xylanche himalaica (Hooker & Thomson ex Hooker fil.) G. Beck
TIBETAN *jhomasin*

Orobanchaceae. Herb about 50 cm high. Flowers pale brown, streaked with red-brown. Fruit a capsule, ovoid oblong. Flowers and fruits June–August. Propagated by seeds. Distributed in eastern and central Nepal at 2900–4300 m in moist, open places; also in India, China, and Taiwan.

MEDICINE. A paste of the plant is taken in cases of constipation.

Botrychium lanuginosum Wallich ex Hooker & Greville

Japonobotrychium langinosum (Wallich ex Hooker & Greville) Nishida ex Tagawa
ENGLISH *grape fern* NEPALI *jaluko* SHERPA *dha* TAMANG *degani, tamjha*

Ophioglossaceae. Terrestrial fern. Rhizome stout, covered with hair-like scales. Stipes about 30 cm long, fiber-like. Fertile branch arising from the middle of the sterile portion, tripinnate. Sporangia sessile, yellowish, in two rows. Propagated by spores or fragments of rhizomes. Distributed throughout Nepal at 1500–3000 m in exposed, wet places.

FOOD. Tender fronds are cooked as a green vegetable.

MEDICINE. Pounded root is applied to boils on the tongue. Juice of the root is applied to the forehead to relieve headaches.

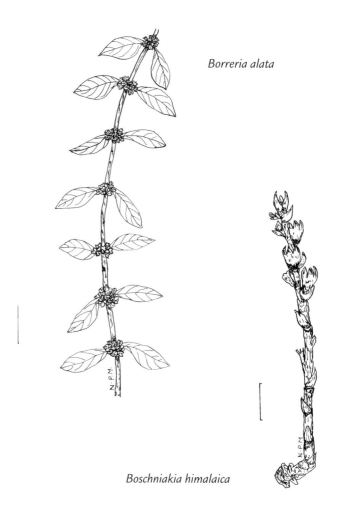

Borreria alata

Boschniakia himalaica

Botrychium multifidum (Gmelin) Ruprecht

Sceptridium multifidum (Gmelin) Nishida ex Tagawa
NEPALI *bayakhra* TAMANG *tana*

Ophioglossaceae. Terrestrial fern. Fronds deep green, 30–40 cm long, 15–25 cm wide, fleshy, decompound. Fertile fronds arising from the base of sterile fronds. Propagated by spores or fragments of rhizomes. Distributed throughout Nepal at 1400–2800 m, often in shady places; also in India, Japan, Australia, Tasmania, New Zealand, and the Americas.

MEDICINE. A paste of the root is applied on the forehead to treat headaches. It is also used for blemishes on the tongue. Juice of the frond is given in cases of stomach disorder.

Brachiaria ramosa (Linnaeus) Stapf

Panicum ramosum Linnaeus
Panicum supervacuum C. B. Clarke
ENGLISH *signal grass* NEPALI *banspate, likhe banso*

Gramineae. Annual grass about 60 cm high, culms rooting from the lower nodes. Leaves 5–12.5 cm long, 0.6–1.5 cm wide, lanceolate to cordate, soft, flaccid, margin sharp, somewhat roughly textured, glabrous or finely pubescent. Inflorescences greenish in long racemes. Flowers and fruits July–November. Propagated by seeds or by splitting the rhizomes. Distributed in eastern and central Nepal to about 1800 m in open, rocky places; also in the tropics of the eastern hemisphere.

OTHER USES. The plant is used for fodder.

Brachycorythis obcordata (Lindley) Summerhayes

Platanthera obcordata Lindley, *Gymnadenia obcordata* (Lindley) Reichenbach, *Habenaria obcordata* (Lindley) Fyson, *Orchis obcordata* Buchanan-Hamilton ex D. Don, *Phyllomphax obcordata* (Lindley) Schlechter
Habenaria galendra Reichenbach fil.

NEPALI *gangdol*

Orchidaceae. Orchid about 20 cm high, pseudobulbs small, globose or oblong. Leaves sessile, 2–4 cm long, 0.8–1.8 cm wide, oblong to lanceolate, subacute, base narrowed, clasping the stem. Flowers pale purple, July–September. Propagated by seeds or pseudobulbs. Distributed throughout Nepal at 900–2000 m on open, rocky hillsides but the gathering of its roots and pseudobulbs for sale in

Brachycorythis obcordata

Botrychium multifidum

Brachiaria ramosa

the trade endangers plant populations; also in northern India, Bhutan, China, and Myanmar.

FOOD. Pseudobulbs are boiled and eaten. Tender leaves and shoots are cooked as a vegetable.

MEDICINE. The root is astringent, expectorant, and is also used as a tonic.

Brassaiopsis hainla (Buchanan-Hamilton ex D. Don) Seemann

Hedera hainla Buchanan-Hamilton ex D. Don

GURUNG *pudichhi, pata*   NEPALI *hati paila, putho, seto chuletro*
RAI *chhechhedungma*   TAMANG *lumasin, pota, pudachhe*

Araliaceae. Tree about 10 m high, young parts stellately hairy. Leaves stalked, alternate, palmately three- or five-lobed, spinous dentate. Flowers yellowish in large compound panicles, March–May. Fruits June–August. Propagated by seeds or cuttings. Distributed throughout Nepal at 1000–1800 m in open places around villages, also in northeastern India, Bhutan, and southwestern China.

OTHER USES. The plant is lopped for fodder (p. 120).

Brassaiopsis polyacantha (Wallich) Banerjee

Hedera polycantha Wallich
Panax palmatum Roxburgh, *Brassaiopsis palmata* (Roxburgh) Kurz

NEPALI *dangdinge*   TAMANG *lumsign*

Araliaceae. Deciduous tree with thorny stems. Leaves stalked, palmately divided about halfway toward the center of the leaf, segments oblong, acute. Flowers yellowish.

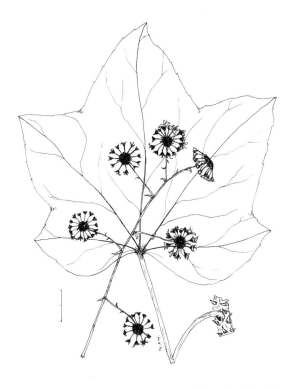

Brassaiopsis hainla

Fruit a pod 5–6 cm long including the beak. Seeds about 40 in a pod. Flowers April–May. Propagated by seeds. Distributed throughout Nepal to about 1800 m, cultivated.

FOOD. Tender leaves and shoots are cooked as a vegetable or fermented for making *gundruk*.

Brassica napus Linnaeus

BHOJPURI *tori* CHEPANG *tori* DANUWAR *tori* ENGLISH *Indian rape, mustard, rape seed* GURUNG *nun, tur* LEPCHA *kunhang* LIMBU *ningebung* MAGAR *tori* MOOSHAR *tori* NEPALI *tori* NEWARI *tu* RAI *aakwabob* SUNWAR *tori* TAMANG *nam nam* THARU *lahi*

Cruciferae. Herb. Leaves clasping the stem, glabrous, glaucous beneath. Flowers stalked, yellow. Fruit a pod 5–6 cm long including the beak. Seeds about 20 in a pod. Propagated by seeds. Distributed throughout Nepal to about 2500 m, cultivated.

FOOD. Tender green leaves are cooked as a vegetable. Mature leaves are fermented to prepare *gundruk*. Seeds are important for making cooking oil.

MEDICINE. Seed oil is put in the ear to relieve earaches. Seeds of fenugreek (*Trigonella foenum-graecum*) are rubbed on a brass plate with the oil, and the mass thus obtained is put in the eye to relieve inflammation of the eye.

OTHER USES. Husks are used in plastering house walls.

Fruit elliptic or turbinate. Propagated by seeds or cuttings. Distributed in central Nepal at 1800–2100 m in open places around villages; also in India and Myanmar.

OTHER USES. The plant is lopped for fodder.

Brassica campestris Linnaeus var. *sarson* Prain

ENGLISH *Indian colza, yellow sarson* NEPALI *sarson* NEWARI *ika*

Cruciferae. Annual herb. Leaves clasping the stem, glabrous. Flowers yellow. Fruit a pod 5–8 cm long. Seeds 30–80 in a pod. Flowers February–March. Propagated by seeds. Distributed throughout Nepal to about 1800 m, cultivated.

FOOD. Tender leaves and shoots are consumed as a green vegetable; it is also fermented to make *gundruk*. Seed oil is much used for cooking and lighting. Oil cake is an important item of cattle feed.

OTHER USES. Husks are used in plastering house walls.

Brassica juncea (Linnaeus) Czerniakowska & Cosson var. *cuneifolia* (Roxburgh) Kitamura

Sinapis cuneifolia Roxburgh, *Brassica rugosa* var. *cuneifolia* (Roxburgh) Prain

BHOJPURI *rai* DANUWAR *rayo* ENGLISH *Indian mustard, leaf mustard* GURUNG *paski taha* LEPCHA *pachyebi* LIMBU *yachenodi* MAGAR *bhaji* MOOSHAR *rai sag* NEPALI *rayo* NEWARI *pachhai* RAI *yasaibagwa* SHERPA *chhermang* TAMANG *nam nam, rayol dhap* THARU *rai sag* TIBETAN *yungs-dkar*

Cruciferae. Erect herb. Leaves sessile or stalked, lyrate, lower leaves larger, upper leaves smaller. Flowers yellow.

Brassica napus

Brassica nigra (Linnaeus) W. D. J. Koch

Sinapis nigra Linnaeus
ENGLISH *black mustard* NEPALI *kalo tori* TIBETAN *yungs-nag*

Cruciferae. Annual herb about 1 m high. Leaves stalked, clasping the stem, 10–20 cm long, glabrous. Flowers yellow. Fruit a pod, three- to five-seeded. Flowers February–March, fruits April–May. Propagated by seeds. Distributed throughout Nepal to about 2000 m, cultivated; also in western Asia, Europe, and North Africa.

FOOD. Tender leaves and shoots are cooked as a green vegetable or fermented for making *gundruk*. Seed oil is used for cooking.

Brassica oleracea Linnaeus var. *botrytis* Linnaeus

BHOJPURI *kobhi* DANUWAR *kauli* ENGLISH *cauliflower* LEPCHA *kopibur* LIMBU *kapiphung* MAGAR *kauli* MOOSHAR *kobi* NEPALI *kaule* NEWARI *bunga, kaule* RAI *bunbobhu* SUNWAR *kopi* TAMANG *kauli* THARU *phul gobi*

Cruciferae. Herb. Leaves all basal, clasping the stem, ovate or oblong, fleshy. Flowers yellowish, condensed. Available for use October–April. Propagated by seeds. Distributed throughout Nepal to about 1800 m, cultivated; also in most parts of the world.

FOOD. The condensed inflorescence is cooked as a vegetable; leaves are fermented for making *gundruk* (Plate 23).

Brassica oleracea Linnaeus var. *capitata* Linnaeus

BHOJPURI *banda kobi* DANUWAR *banda kobi* ENGLISH *cabbage* GURUNG *banda gobi* MAGAR *banda kobhi* NEPALI *banda, banda kaule, banda kobi* NEWARI *banda* RAI *bakarphawa khangn* SUNWAR *banada kopi* TAMANG *banda gobi*

Cruciferae. Herb with thick stem. Leaves closely packed into a large head or bud, thick, fleshy. Flowers yellowish. Available for use October–April. Propagated by seeds. Distributed throughout Nepal to about 1800 m, cultivated; also in most parts of the world.

FOOD. The plant is eaten raw or cooked as a vegetable; mature leaves are fermented for making *gundruk*.

Brassica oleracea Linnaeus var. *caulorapa* de Candolle

ENGLISH *kohlrabi* NEPALI *gyanth kobi* NEWARI *gyanth kauli*

Cruciferae. Herb. Leaves stalked, margin undulating, glabrous. Flowers yellow. Propagated by seeds. Distributed throughout Nepal to about 1400 m, cultivated.

FOOD. The bulbous stem is eaten as a vegetable; mature leaves are fermented for making *gundruk*.

Brassica oleracea Linnaeus var. *gemmifera* Zenk

ENGLISH *Brussels sprouts, bud-bearing cabbage* NEPALI *aanda kaule, batan gobi*

Cruciferae. Erect herb. Leaves stalked, ovate, slightly lobed. Flowers yellowish. Propagated by seeds. Distributed throughout Nepal to about 1800 m, cultivated.

FOOD. Axillary buds are eaten as a vegetable.

Brassica rapa Linnaeus

BHOJPURI *shalgam* DANUWAR *gantemula* ENGLISH *turnip* LEPCHA *kanyong* LIMBU *tanglabank* MAGAR *gante mula* NEPALI *gantemula, shalgam* NEWARI *pwatyacha* RAI *puntaluk, boba* SUNWAR *labu* TAMANG *gantemula* TIBETAN *nyung-kar, nyung-ma*

Cruciferae. Erect annual herb, stem often tinged reddish purple. Leaves lyrate or evenly pinnatifid, upper leaves decreasing in size. Flowers white or yellowish. Fruit a pod, slender. Propagated by seeds. Distributed throughout Nepal to about 2500 m, cultivated.

FOOD. The tuberous roots and tender leaves are cooked as a vegetable; mature leaves are fermented for making *gundruk*.

Breynia retusa (Dennstaedt) Alston

Phyllanthus retusus Dennstaedt
Melanthesa turbinata Wight
Phyllanthus patens Roxburgh, *Breynia patens* (Roxburgh) Bentham
NEPALI *sano nundhiki*

Euphorbiaceae. Shrub about 2 m high. Leaves short-stalked, elliptic to oblong, obtuse, entire. Flowers yellowish in axillary fascicles, April–May. Propagated by seeds. Distributed in eastern and central Nepal at 1100–1800 m on open slopes; also in India, Sri Lanka, and Myanmar.

MEDICINE. Juice of the bark is given in cases of indigestion. A paste of the leaves is applied to cuts and wounds.

Breynia retusa

Bridelia retusa (Linnaeus) Sprengel

Clutia retusa Linnaeus

CHEPANG *ranbo, ropsi* DANUWAR *gaiyo, kanjhi*
ENGLISH *Gamble's man* MAGAR *gayo* MOOSHAR *kanjhi* NEPALI *gayo, gudi, kaja* RAI *hasung* TAMANG *gramsachhe*

Euphorbiaceae. Deciduous tree about 6 m high. Leaves stalked, alternate, 6–15 cm long, 3.5–8 cm wide, ovate to elliptic, leathery, entire, tip tapering, base rounded or slightly tapering, lateral veins numerous, parallel, distinct. Flowers subsessile, yellowish, clustered in axillary or terminal panicles. Fruit a drupe, globose, purplish black when ripe, seated on a persistent calyx. Flowers May–July, fruits October–December. Propagated by seeds or cuttings. Distributed throughout Nepal to about 1200 m in open places; also in India, Sri Lanka, Indo-China, Malaysia, and Indonesia.

FOOD. Ripe fruits are edible.

MEDICINE. Juice of the bark, about 6 teaspoons three times a day, is prescribed for peptic ulcer.

OTHER USES. Bark yields tannin. Leaves are lopped for fodder.

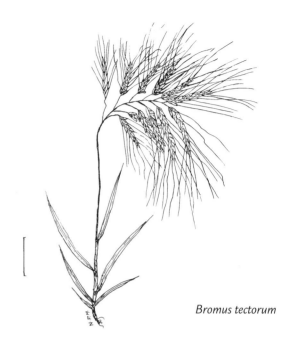

Bromus tectorum

Bridelia retusa

Bromus tectorum Linnaeus

TIBETAN *juku*

Gramineae. Annual grass about 50 cm high. Leaves 7.5 cm long, 0.3 cm wide, linear, acute, flaccid hairy. Inflorescences greenish in nodding panicles. Fruit a grain, linear oblong, dorsally compressed. Propagated by seeds. Distributed in western and central Nepal at 2000–4100 m; also in northwestern Asia, Europe, and North Africa.

MEDICINE. A paste of the grains is applied to the chest to relieve chest pain.

OTHER USES. The plant is used for fodder.

Buchanania latifolia Roxburgh

DANUWAR *pyari* ENGLISH *Calumpang nut tree, Cuddapah almond*
NEPALI *pyar* TAMANG *tilari*

Anacardiaceae. Tree about 12 m high. Leaves stalked, alternate, 7–20 cm long, 4–9 cm wide, oblong to elliptic, obtuse at both ends, leathery, entire, pubescent beneath. Flowers sessile, yellowish, in axillary and terminal pyramidal panicles. Fruit a drupe, oblong ovoid, black when ripe. Flowers February–March, fruits May–June. Propagated by seeds. Distributed in western and central Nepal to about 1500 m, common in *Shorea robusta* forest; also in India, Myanmar, and Thailand.

FOOD. Ripe fruit is eaten raw and is sweet.

OTHER USES. Wood is used to make boxes, doors, and furniture and is employed for various construction purposes. Bark contains tannin. Leaves are used as a substitute for plates. Seed oil is used in the manufacture of candies.

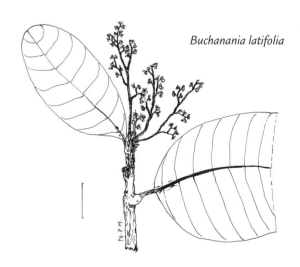

Buchanania latifolia

Buddleja asiatica Loureiro

Buddleja neemda Buchanan-Hamilton ex Roxburgh
Buddleja subserrata Buchanan-Hamilton ex D. Don
BHOJPURI *bhimsenpati* CHEPANG *goihamro, kaski lang*
DANUWAR *bhimsenpati* ENGLISH *butterfly bush* GURUNG *randaur sar*
LEPCHA *pandam* LIMBU *limtelasing* MAGAR *bhimsenpati, phultit*
NEPALI *bhimsenpati, sano phultis* NEWARI *sina swan* RAI *khakunma,
sayuba* SUNWAR *barno* TAMANG *besya, bhisa, lamhendo,
phawar singo, tar mhendo* THARU *bhimpati* TIBETAN *bhisa*

Buddlejaceae. Evergreen shrub about 4 m high. Leaves stalked, 11.5–14.5 cm long, 1.5–5 cm wide, lanceolate, serrulate, glabrous, dark green above, densely gray or white tomentose beneath. Flowers sessile in dense bracteate spikes in terminal panicles, white. Fruit a capsule, ellipsoidal, two-valved. Flowers March–June, fruits September–November. Propagated by seeds, branch cuttings, or root offshoots. Distributed throughout Nepal at 300–2000 m, common in open places and often planted in gardens for ornamental; also in India, central and southern China, Taiwan, and Southeast Asia.

MEDICINE. Juice of the plant is applied to treat skin diseases.

OTHER USES. The leaf and flower are used as a religious offering to gods and goddesses. Squeezed leaves are used as fish poison.

Buddleja asiatica

Buddleja paniculata Wallich

CHEPANG *bhimsen pati* GURUNG *jinchhi* NEPALI *narayan pati,
phultis, phursedo, simtaro* TAMANG *kosyang, phawar, singo*

Buddlejaceae. Evergreen shrub about 5 m high. Leaves stalked, 3–14.5 cm long, 0.8–4.5 cm wide, lanceolate to triangular ovate, dentate or crenate. Flowers subsessile, white or pinkish, condensed on irregular panicle. Fruit ellipsoidal. Flowers March–June, fruits September–No-

vember. Propagated by seeds, branch cuttings, or root offshoots. Distributed in central and western Nepal at 800–2400 m, common on exposed sunny slopes; also in Bhutan, Assam in northeastern India, Myanmar, and China.

MEDICINE. The leaf, mixed with the leaf of *Crotalaria alata*, is boiled 10 minutes, and the filtered water, about 6 teaspoons twice a day, is given to treat fever. A decoction is given in cases of diarrhea and dysentery.

OTHER USES. The plant is a good substitute for other fodder plants when those are scarce, especially during winter. Young leaves are used to poison fish.

Bulbostylis densa (Wallich) Handel-Mazzetti

Scripus densus Wallich, *Isolepis densa* (Wallich) Schultes
Isolepis tenuissima D. Don
Isolepis trifida Nees
NEPALI *jhuse jhar*

Cyperaceae. Annual herb about 20 cm high. Leaves lanceolate, shorter than the stem. Inflorescence brownish. Fruit a nut, obovoid, triquetrous. Flowers and fruits May–November Propagated by seeds or tubers. Distributed throughout Nepal at 1500–3500 m on dry, sandy soil; also in India, Bhutan, China, Japan, and Africa.

OTHER USES. The plant is used for fodder.

Bulbostylis densa

Bupleurum candollii Wallich ex de Candolle

NEPALI *chadu* SHERPA *choto*

Umbelliferae. Erect perennial herb about 1 m high. Leaves stalked, 2.5–13 cm long, 0.5–2.5 cm wide, oblong to ovate, upper leaves clasping the stem, acute, glabrous. Flowers white. Fruit elliptic, ribbed. Flowers June–July, fruits August–September. Propagated by seeds. Distributed throughout Nepal at 2400–4000 m on open slopes and in shrubby areas; also in northern India, Bhutan, Tibet, and northern Myanmar.

OTHER USES. Tender leaves are poisonous to cattle.

Bupleurum candollii

Bupleurum falcatum Linnaeus

Bupleurum gracillimum Klotzsch

TIBETAN *tangu nhapu*

Umbelliferae. Herb about 40 cm high. Leaves sessile, clasping the stem at their base, linear, mucronate. Flowers small, pinkish, in terminal compound umbels. Flowers and fruits July–October. Propagated by seeds. Distributed in western and central Nepal at 2700–4200 m in moist, shady places; also in northern Pakistan, northern India, Bhutan, and China.

MEDICINE. A paste of the plant is applied to boils. Juice of the root mixed with the juice of *Centella asiatica* is given in cases of liver trouble.

Bupleurum hamiltonii Balakrishnan

Bupleurum tenue Buchanan-Hamilton ex D. Don

MAGAR *murba* NEPALI *ban sampu, jembir, mariche ghans* SHERPA *chatu* TAMANG *chadu* TIBETAN *chhiple*

Umbelliferae. Annual herb about 75 cm high. Leaves sessile, 0.8–4.5 cm long, 0.2–0.5 cm wide, lanceolate, mucronate, membranous. Flowers yellowish. Flowers and fruits July–September. Propagated by seeds. Distributed throughout Nepal at 1300–3000 m on grassy slopes and mossy rocks; also in northern India and Bhutan.

OTHER USES. The plant is poisonous to animals.

Butea buteiformis (Voigt) Mabberley

Meizotropis buteiformis Voigt

Butea minor (Buchanan-Hamilton ex Wallich) Baker

CHEPANG *dibhar* GURUNG *pipli, plume ro ro* MAGAR *bhuje bho lha, dharpat* NEPALI *bhujetro, bhuletro* TAMANG *chhargu lhapti, panga lhapti, ringamala* TIBETAN *papa lhapti*

Leguminosae. Shrub about 2 m high. Leaves stalked, trifoliolate, leaflets 15–38 cm long, broadly ovate, terminal leaflets long-stalked, lateral two asymmetrical, silky hairs beneath. Flowers red in axillary and terminal spike-like clusters. Fruit a pod, densely hairy. Flowers April–May. Propagated by seeds. Distributed throughout Nepal at 300–2000 m in rocky, open places; also in Bhutan, and Assam in northeastern India.

MEDICINE. The seed has anthelmintic value.

OTHER USES. Fiber from the bark is used for cordage. The leaf is used as a plate.

Butea monosperma (Lamarck) Kuntze

Erythrina monosperma Lamarck

Butea frondosa Koenig ex Roxburgh

DANUWAR *palans* ENGLISH *bastard teak, Bengal kino, flame of the forest* LEPCHA *riphikung* NEPALI *palans* NEWARI *palwi* RAI *hoyobama* SUNWAR *palans* TAMANG *palans* THARU *palans* TIBETAN *ma-ru-tse, tshos-shing*

Leguminosae. Deciduous tree about 25 m high. Leaves stalked, trifoliolate, leaflets obliquely ovate or broadly el-

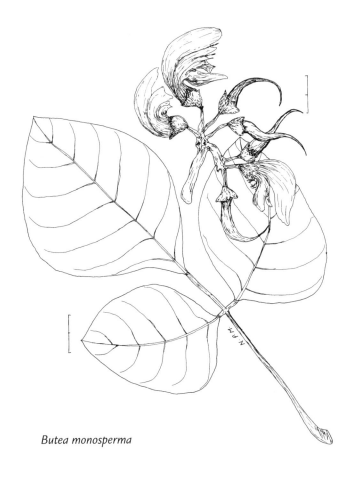

Butea monosperma

liptic, leathery, glabrescent above, silky tomentose beneath. Flowers orange-red, fascicled in rigid axillary and terminal racemes. Fruit a pod, silky tomentose, abruptly narrowed to a stalk. Flowers April–May, fruits June–July. Propagated by seeds. Distributed throughout Nepal to about 1100 m in open places; also in India, Sri Lanka, and Southeast Asia.

MEDICINE. Juice of the bark is given in cases of fever. Powdered seed, about 1 teaspoon, is given as an anthelmintic.

OTHER USES. Bark of the root yields coarse fiber used for rough cordage. The leaf is used as a plate for serving and wrapping food. Flowers yield a yellow dye.

Butomopsis latifolia (D. Don) Kunth

Butomus latifolius D. Don, *Tenagocharis latifolia* (D. Don) Buchenau
Butomus lanceolatus Roxburgh, *Butomopsis lanceolata* (Roxburgh) Kunth, *Tenagocharis lanceolata* (Roxburgh) Thieret
ENGLISH *bladderwort* NEPALI *karkale jhar*

Alismataceae. Annual herb about 45 cm high. Leaves stalked, 5–15 cm long, 2–6 cm wide, oblanceolate, entire. Flowers white in terminal umbels. Fruit an achene, shortly beaked. Flowers and fruits September–November. Propagated by seeds. Distributed throughout Nepal to about 600 m in marshy or waterlogged places; also in India, western China, Southeast Asia, western Australia, and Africa.

MEDICINE. A paste of the plant is applied to boils.

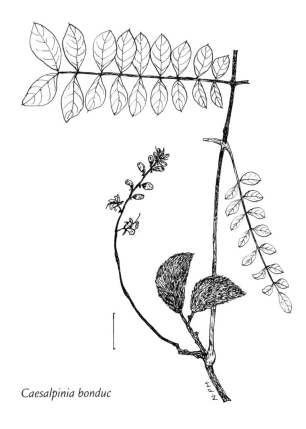

Caesalpinia bonduc

C

Caesalpinia bonduc (Linnaeus) Roxburgh

Guilandina bonduc Linnaeus
Caesalpinia crista Linnaeus
Guilandina bonducella Linnaeus, *Caesalpinia bonducella* (Linnaeus) Fleming
ENGLISH *fever nut* NEPALI *boksi kanda, ganegeri, kanja, karkera* TAMANG *melkar*

Leguminosae. Prickly shrub. Leaves stalked, stipulate, pinnate, rachis and its branches armed with recurved prickles, pinnae in 6–10 pairs, short-stalked, oblong or elliptic, mucronate, membranous, downy beneath. Flowers yellow in racemes. Fruit a pod, leathery, dehiscent, thickly beset with sharp wiry prickles. Seeds globose or ovoid, shiny, lead colored. Flowers July–September, fruits November–February. Propagated by seeds. Distributed throughout Nepal to about 900 m in open, dry places; also in India and Pakistan.

MEDICINE. Juice of tender shoots and seeds is given in cases of fever. Powdered seed, about 2 teaspoons three times a day, is given to treat gastric troubles and is also taken as an anthelmintic.

Caesalpinia decapetala (Roth) Alston

Reichardia decapetala Roth
Caesalpinia sepiaria Roxburgh
NEPALI *arile kanda, ulte kanda*

Leguminosae. Large, prickly, scandent shrub armed with short, brown, recurved prickles. Leaves abruptly bipinnate, pinnae in 6–10 pairs, pinnules opposite, 1.2–2 cm long, oblong or ovate, rounded at both ends, glabrous above, glaucous beneath. Flowers golden in axillary or terminal racemes. Fruit a pod, smooth, beaked. Flowers December–May, fruits April–September. Propagated by seeds. Distributed throughout Nepal at 1000–2200 m in open places among bushes; also in India, Sri Lanka, Southeast Asia, China, Japan, Africa, and the Americas.

MEDICINE. Juice of the root is applied to sprains and muscular swellings of animals.

OTHER USES. Plants are often cultivated to serve as fences. Bark yields tannin.

Caesalpinia pulcherrima (Linnaeus) Swartz

Poinciana pulcherrima Linnaeus
ENGLISH *paradise flower, peacock flower* NEPALI *bas phul*

Leguminosae. Erect shrub about 6 m high. Leaves stalked, bipinnate, pinnae in 4–8 pairs, pinnules in 7–11 pairs, sessile, elliptic, obtuse, entire. Flowers red and yellow in a terminal lax raceme. Fruit a pod. Flowers and fruits July–December. Propagated by seeds. Distributed in eastern and central Nepal to about 1000 m in open places; also in tropical parts of the world.

MEDICINE. Juice of the root, about 3 teaspoons four times a day, is taken in cases of intermittent fever. Juice of the bark is given for colds and skin diseases. A decoction of leaves is used as a wash to treat ulcers of the mouth and throat. An infusion of the flower is used for inflammation of the eyes. Fruits are astringent and their juice is taken to treat diarrhea and dysentery. The seeds have an abortifacient property.

Caesulia axillaris Roxburgh

Meyera orientalis D. Don

DANUWAR *phalewa, thukaha* ENGLISH *chicory weed, spittle weed* MAJHI *kanthamale* NEPALI *galphule, thuk jhar*

Compositae. Erect herb about 50 cm high. Leaves short-stalked, 5–15 cm long, 1–1.8 cm wide, lanceolate, acute, serrate, glabrous, narrowed at the base. Flower heads axillary, pinkish. Fruit an achene, flat, with one rib on each side. Flowers and fruits October–May. Propagated by seeds or by nodal rooting. Distributed throughout Nepal to about 1500 m, in marshy places near streams or in rice fields; also in India, Bhutan, and Myanmar.

MEDICINE. Juice of the plant is applied to cuts and wounds. It is also given to animals as tonic.

Caesulia axillaris

Cajanus cajan (Linnaeus) Huth

Cytisus cajan Linnaeus
Cajanus indicus Sprengel

CHEPANG *lahari* ENGLISH *pigeon pea, red gram* MAJHI *rahar* NEPALI *rahar* TAMANG *radal* TIBETAN *a-bi-sa, nim-pa*

Leguminosae. Shrub about 3 m high. Leaves stalked, trifoliolate, leaflets ovate to oblong, glabrescent, gland-dotted beneath. Flowers yellow in loose corymbose racemes. Fruit a pod, brown tomentose. Flowers and fruits November–April. Propagated by seeds. Distributed throughout Nepal to about 2000 m, cultivated in tropical and subtropical regions.

FOOD. Seeds are mainly used for soup (*daal* in Nepali).

MEDICINE. Roots have anthelmintic, sedative, expectorant, and vulnerary properties. Young leaves are chewed to treat boils on the tongue. Juice of the leaves, about 4 teaspoons three times a day, is used for cough and diarrhea. The pulp is applied to wounds.

OTHER USES. Plants provide thatching materials and are often used as brooms. Leaves serve as a good fodder.

Cajanus scarabaeoides (Linnaeus) Thouars

Dolichos scarabaeoides Linnaeus, *Atylosia scarabaeoides* (Linnaeus) Bentham, *Cantharospermum scarabaeoides* (Linnaeus) Baillon

CHEPANG *ban bori, gahate* DANUWAR *ban kurthi* MAJHI *gahate jhar* NEPALI *ban gahate, mas lahari* TAMANG *kolte mran* THARU *ban bhart*

Leguminosae. Slender, trailing herb. Leaves stalked, trifoliolate, leaflets elliptic to ovate, densely gray pubescent. Flowers yellow on a short axillary stalk. Fruit a pod clothed with fine silky hairs, transversely grooved between

Cajanus cajan

the seeds. Flowers August–September, fruits October–November. Propagated by seeds. Distributed throughout Nepal to about 1000 m, occasional in *Shorea robusta* forest; also in India, Sri Lanka, Southeast Asia, China, the Ryukyu Islands, Malaysia, Australia, and Africa.

FOOD. Young fruits are cooked as a vegetable.

MEDICINE. Juice of plant, about 4 teaspoons twice a day, is given to treat diarrhea and dysentery.

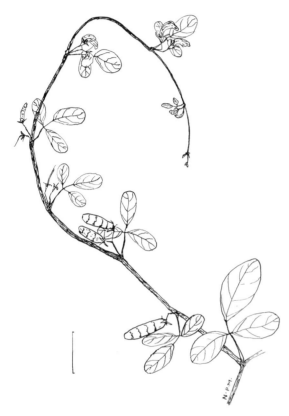

Cajanus scarabaeoides

Calamus tenuis Roxburgh

NEPALI *pani bet*

Palmae. Climbing palm, stem smooth, bright green, more or less covered by the persistent leaf sheaths. Leaves about 1.25 m long, pinnate, rachis covered with a row of recurved prickles, leaflets many, stalked, 14.5–30 cm long, 1–1.7 cm wide, smaller toward the top, linear lanceolate, acuminate, three-veined, margins with scattered bristles or prickles, dark glossy green on both surfaces. Flowers small, the male flowers in three or four series, female flowers distichous in spikelets. Fruit ellipsoidal, clothed with closely imbricate pale scales with dark margins. Flowers June–July. Propagated by seeds. Distributed throughout Nepal to about 600 m in swampy areas.

OTHER USES. Stems are used to make baskets, furniture, and other household goods.

Calanthe masuca (D. Don) Lindley

Bletia masuca D. Don, *Zoduba masuca* Buchanan-Hamilton ex D. Don

NEPALI *pakha phul*

Orchidaceae. Terrestrial orchid. Leaves stalked, elliptic to lanceolate, glabrous, acute. Flowers pink in many-flowered racemes, March–April. Propagated by seeds or root offshoots. Distributed throughout Nepal at 2000–2800 m in shady places; also in India.

MEDICINE. A paste of the stem is applied to treat dislocated bones.

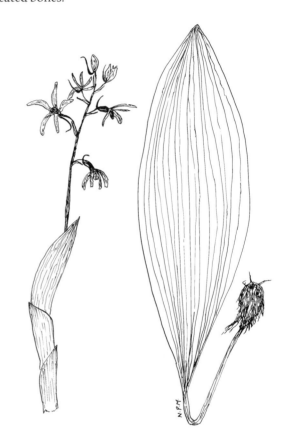

Calanthe masuca

Callicarpa arborea Roxburgh

CHEPANG *chyangsi* GURUNG *chhimnva, danamusi, guren* MAGAR *guyela* NEPALI *ghunyalo, guren, masgedi, phultusm, thulo guyenlo* TAMANG *golbho, goldar*

Labiatae. Tree about 20 m high, bark brown, rough, thinly corky. Leaves stalked, opposite, 9–30 cm long, 4–14 cm wide, elliptic to lanceolate, acuminate, entire, densely stellate tomentose on both surfaces when young, glossy above when mature, clothed with gray pubescence beneath, base rounded or cuneate. Flowers light purple, fragrant, in axillary dichotomous corymbose cymes. Fruit a drupe, purplish black when ripe. Flowers April–July, fruits August–December. Propagated by seeds. Distributed throughout Nepal to about 1500 m in the margins of forestland; also in northern India, southern China, and Southeast Asia.

FOOD. Ripe fruits are eaten fresh.

MEDICINE. The root is chewed to treat boils on the tongue. Bark is carminative and tonic. A decoction is applied for cutaneous diseases. Juice of the bark, mixed with bark juice of *Cordia dichotoma* and *Psidium guajava,* is given in doses of about 2 teaspoons three times a day to treat indigestion. Powdered bark, mixed with a pinch of turmeric powder (*Curcuma domestica*), is given to relieve fever. Ash of the leaves is applied to boils.

OTHER USES. Wood is used to make utensils. The plant is lopped for fodder.

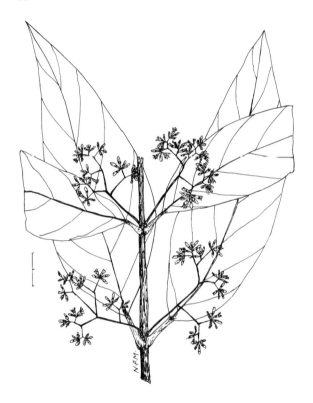

Callicarpa arborea

Callicarpa macrophylla Vahl

Callicarpa incana Roxburgh

CHEPANG *tichangs* ENGLISH *beauty berry, urn fruit*
GURUNG *danamusi, guren, kurli* MAGAR *malaburu, pulikhaja*
NEPALI *dahijalo, dahikaula, daindali, goldar, guyenlo, kamla, sumali*
TIBETAN *pri-yung-ku*

Labiatae. Shrub about 3 m high with straggling branches. Leaves stalked, 10–25 cm long, 3.5–10 cm wide, oblong to lanceolate, acuminate, crenate, soft pubescent above, thickly cottony tomentose beneath. Flowers small, pinkish, in a dense compound cyme. Fruit a drupe, white, spongy, succulent when fully ripe. Flowers May–Novem-

ber, fruits November–January. Propagated by seeds. Distributed throughout Nepal to about 1500 m in moist places; also in northern India, Bhutan, southern China, and Indo-China.

FOOD. Ripe fruits are eaten fresh and are sweet.

MEDICINE. Roots are chewed to treat rashes on the tongue. A paste of the root is taken to treat fever. Juice of the root, about 4 teaspoons three times a day, is given for indigestion. The inner bark is pounded and applied to cuts and wounds. A heated leaf is pressed on affected areas of the body to relieve rheumatic pain. A decoction of the leaves is given in cases of diarrhea and dysentery. Tender leaves, mixed with *Drymaria diandra* and *Oxalis corniculata* plants in equal parts, is pounded and the juice, about 6 teaspoons three times a day, is given to treat gastric trouble. Fruits are chewed to treat boils on the tongue. Juice of ripe fruits, about 2 teaspoons three times a day, is given for indigestion. It is also given to treat fever.

OTHER USES. Wood serves as fuel. Leaves are gathered for fodder. If the plant is given as fodder to animals during winter, it causes diarrhea.

Callistemon citrinus (Curtis) Skeels

Metrosideros citrina Curtis
Metrosideros lanceolata Smith, *Callistemon lanceolatus* (Smith) Sweet

ENGLISH *bottlebrush* NEPALI *kalki phul* NEWARI *kalki swan*

Myrtaceae. Evergreen tree. Leaves short-stalked, crowded, alternate, linear lanceolate, pointed, gland-dotted. Flowers crimson in terminal drooping spikes, May–August. Fruits September–December. Propagated by seeds. Distributed in central Nepal at 700–1300 m, cultivated; also in eastern Australia.

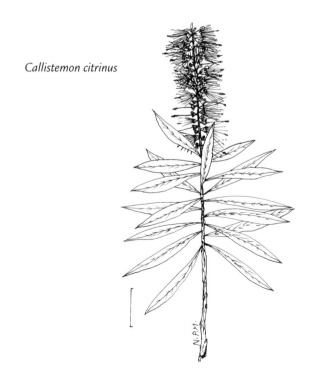

Callistemon citrinus

OTHER USES. The plant is grown as an avenue tree and also used as fuelwood. Flowers are used as religious offerings to gods and goddesses.

Callistephus chinensis (Linnaeus) Nees

Aster chinensis Linnaeus
Callistephus hortensis Cassini
ENGLISH *China aster* NEWARI *gyantaka swan*

Compositae. Annual herb about 1 m high. Leaves stalked, 3–6 cm long, 2.5–3 cm wide, alternate, broadly ovate, margin toothed. Flower heads 0.2–1 cm wide, purple, pink, or violet. Fruit an achene. Flowers July–September. Propagated by seeds. Distributed throughout Nepal to about 1400 m, cultivated; also in India, China, and Southeast Asia.

MEDICINE. Juice of the flower head is given for bloody dysentery.

Calotropis gigantea (Linnaeus) Dryander

Asclepias gigantea Linnaeus
CHEPANG *bhakmat* DANUWAR *akon, bagarni* ENGLISH *swallow wort* MOOSHAR *akon* NEPALI *aank* RAUTE *anket* THARU *madar* TIBETAN *a-rga, shing-a-rka-pa-rna*

Asclepiadaceae. Much branched shrub about 3 m high, young parts white tomentose. Leaves subsessile, 6–18.5 cm long, 2.3–11.5 cm wide, obovate or oblong, acuminate, leathery, cottony beneath. Flowers light purple in axillary umbels. Fruit a follicle. Flowers and fruits most of the year. Propagated by seeds. Distributed throughout Nepal to about 1000 m in open, dry, sandy places; also in India, western and central China, Malaysia, and the Philippines.

MEDICINE. Milky juice of the plant is applied as a remedy for sprains, body pains, boils, and pimples. The same juice is also applied on wounds or affected areas caused by leprosy because it provides temporary relief from itching, inflammation of the wound. A paste of the root is applied to boils, pimples, and other skin diseases. Juice of the bark or root is given in cases of diarrhea and dysentery. Leaves are warmed are applied to the abdomen to relieve pain and are also useful on muscular swellings caused by pain. Dried leaves are smoked like tobacco (*Nicotiana tabacum*), and the smoke is exhaled through the nose to relieve sinusitis. Juice of the leaf is given to treat intermittent fever. Juice of young buds is dropped in the ear to relieve earache. Powdered flower is valued in treating cough, colds, and asthma.

OTHER USES. Wood is burned to make charcoal for gunpowder. Fiber obtained from the bark is made into twine and thread. Seed hairs are used for stuffing pillows.

Caltha palustris Linnaeus

Caltha himalensis D. Don
Caltha paniculata Wallich
ENGLISH *marsh marigold* NEPALI *eka aankhle phul*

Ranunculaceae. Erect herb about 50 cm high. Leaves stalked, 2–10 cm long, 2.5–9 cm wide, reniform or deltoid, margin wavy or dentate. Flowers solitary, axillary or terminal, yellow. Fruit a follicle, ovoid. Flowers May–August. Propagated by seeds. Distributed throughout Nepal at 2400–4200 m, common in moist places; also in the rest of the Himalayan region.

MEDICINE. The root is considered poisonous.

Caltha palustris

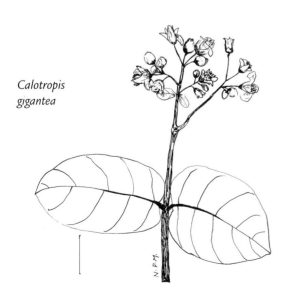

Calotropis gigantea

Camellia kissi Wallich

Camellia drupifera Loureiro
Camellia keina Buchanan-Hamilton ex D. Don
ENGLISH *wild tea* NEPALI *ban chiya, chiya pate, gulaure, hinguwa*
TAMANG *kasing, tepsing, syosing*

Theaceae. Shrub about 2 m high. Leaves subsessile, 3–10 cm long, 1.5–4.5 cm wide, elliptic, acuminate, serrate, glabrous. Flowers usually solitary, axillary, white, fragrant. Fruit a capsule, globose, reddish. Flowers October–November. Propagated by seeds or cuttings. Distributed throughout Nepal at 900–2100 m on moist ground of hill forest; also in Assam in northeastern India, western and southern China, and Indo-China.

FOOD. Leaves are steamed, dried, and used as a substitute for tea. Flowers are boiled and pickled. Seed oil is used for cooking.

Camellia kissi

Camellia sinensis (Linnaeus) Kuntze

Thea sinensis Linnaeus
Thea bohea Linnaeus

BHOJPURI *chay* DANUWAR *chiya* ENGLISH *tea* GURUNG *chad*
LEPCHA *chhyo* LIMBU *chhapa* MAGAR *chiya* NEPALI *chiya*
NEWARI *chya* RAI *mukuwa* SUNWAR *hoshadawaku* TAMANG *chya*
THARU *chah* TIBETAN *rdo-rta*

Theaceae. Shrub about 75 cm high. Leaves stalked, 2.5–10 cm long, 1–3.5 cm wide, oblanceolate, acute, glabrous. Flowers white, fragrant. Propagated by seeds or cuttings. Distributed in central and eastern Nepal at 450–1200 m, cultivated; also in eastern India, Myanmar, Thailand, Vietnam, southern China, and Taiwan.

FOOD. Leaves are used to make a beverage, tea.

Campanula pallida Wallich

Campanula colorata Wallich
Campanula himalayensis Klotzsch
Campanula hoffmeisteri Klotzsch
Campanula moorcroftiana Wallich
Campanula nervosa Royle
Campanula ramulosa Wallich

GURUNG *kati* NEPALI *ganobuti, majari*, NEPALI *bikh*
TIBETAN *ki-sin men toq*

Campanulaceae. Hispid herb about 50 cm high. Leaves short-stalked, alternate, oblong to elliptic, acute, serrate.

Flowers bluish or purplish, solitary, axillary, in terminal panicles. Fruit a capsule, hemispheric, hairy. Flowers March–July, fruits July–November. Propagated by seeds. Distributed throughout Nepal at 700–4500 m, generally in moist rock crevices or on walls; also in Afghanistan, southern Tibet, India, western China, and Indo-China.

MEDICINE. Juice of the root is used for diarrhea and dysentery.

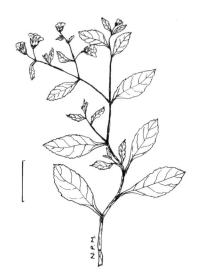

Campanula pallida

Campylotropis speciosa (Royle ex Schindler) Schindler

Lespedeza speciosa Royle ex Schindler
Lespedeza eriocarpa de Candolle, *Campylotropis eriocarpa* (de Candolle) Schindler
NEPALI *sakhino*

Leguminosae. Much branched shrub about 1 m high. Leaves stalked, trifoliolate, leaflets sessile or the middle one stalked, 1–2 cm long, ovate, densely white hairy beneath. Flowers pink or purple in axillary or terminal spikes. Fruit a pod, ovate with persistent beak, densely hairy. Flowers September–October. Propagated by seeds. Distributed throughout Nepal at 2000–3100 m on open slopes; also in northern India and Bhutan.

FOOD. Flowers are boiled and pickled.

Canavalia cathartica Thouars

ENGLISH *jack bean, horse bean, sword bean* NEPALI *tarwar simi*
TAMANG *ganja*

Leguminosae. Climber. Leaves stalked, trifoliolate, veins prominent on upper surface, stalk grooved. Flowers white or lilac in axillary racemes. Fruit a pod, often curved. Propagated by seeds. Distributed in eastern and central Nepal at 1000–1400 m, cultivated; also in India and other Asian regions.

FOOD. Tender fruits are cooked as a vegetable. Mature ones are poisonous so must be boiled with several changes of water.

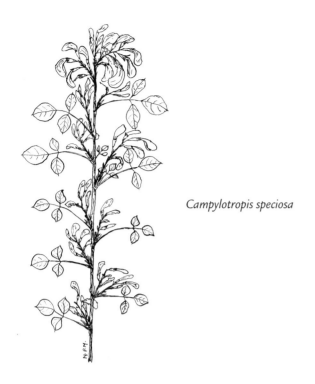

Campylotropis speciosa

Canna chinensis Willdenow

Canna nepalensis Wallich ex Bouché, *C. indica* var. *nepalensis* (Wallich ex Bouché) Baker
NEPALI *bhuinchapo*

Cannaceae. Herb about 1 m high with stout rootstock. Leaves elliptic to oblong, caudate-acuminate, glabrous. Flowers yellow or scarlet. Fruit subglobose, obscurely three-lobed. Flowers and fruits most of the year. Propagated by rhizomes. Distributed in western and central Nepal at 600–1500 m in moist places; also in India and China.

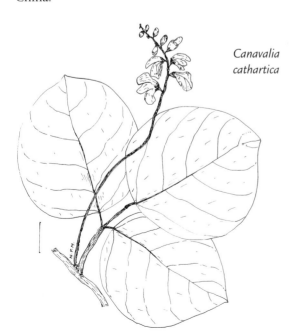

Canavalia cathartica

MEDICINE. A paste of the root is applied to muscular swellings and sprains.

Cannabis sativa Linnaeus

Cannabis indica Lamarck
Cannabis indica var. *kafiristanica* Vavilov

BHOJPURI *ganja* CHEPANG *ganja* DANUWAR *ganja* ENGLISH *hemp, marijuana, soft hemp* GURUNG *ganja* LEPCHA *shwingmuk* LIMBU *mobasung* MAGAR *bhango* NEPALI *bhang, bhango, charas, ganja* NEWARI *gnaji* RAI *harandupunwa* RAUTE *bhanga* SUNWAR *ganja* TAMANG *ganja* THARU *ganja* TIBETAN *chhima, sima, so-ma ra-dza, tarch*

Cannabaceae. Shrub about 2 m high. Leaves stalked, alternate, digitately three- to seven-foliolate, leaflets lanceolate, long-pointed, coarsely dentate, rough in texture. Flowers stalked or sessile, yellowish, male and female flowers on separate plants, the male flowers clustered in axillary panicles, female flowers sessile, axillary, the perianth a single leafy structure enclosing the ovary. Fruit an achene enclosed in the persistent perianth. Flowers and fruits May–December. Propagated by seeds. Distributed throughout Nepal to about 2700 m on open and neglected land; also in most temperate and tropical areas of the world.

FOOD. Seeds are roasted and pickled. People of western Nepal chew roasted seeds.

MEDICINE. Juice of the leaf, about 6 teaspoons twice a day, is given in cases of diarrhea and dysentery. For diar-

Canna chinensis

rhea and dysentery in animals, powdered leaves are mixed with feed. A paste of the leaves is applied to cuts and wounds. A powder of dried leaves is fed to animals with cough and colds. Powdered seeds in doses of about 4 teaspoons are given as an anthelmintic.

OTHER USES. Stem bark gives a good fiber for cordage, sacks, and rough clothes (Plates 36, 38). Leaves, resin, buds, and seeds are used as an intoxicant. *Ganja* and *bhang* are smoked like tobacco. *Bhang* is also eaten, mixing it with sweets or desserts. *Charas* is mixed with tobacco (*Nicotiana tabacum*) or other smoking materials. The plant is a figure of worship among Rais.

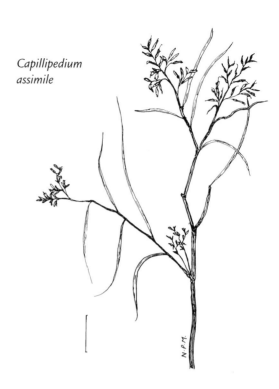

Capillipedium assimile

Cannabis sativa

Capillipedium assimile (Steudel) A. Camus

Andropogon assimilis Steudel
Andropogon glaucosis Steudel, *Capillipedium glaucopsis* (Steudel) Stapf
CHEPANG *kharo, prat, prongsai* GURUNG *masen* NEPALI *kharu, kharusi* TAMANG *pang, sangsa chhe*

Gramineae. Perennial grass, culms decumbent, rooting at the base, culm sheath somewhat compressed. Leaves 6–15 cm long, 3–6 cm wide, linear lanceolate, much narrowed at the base, margin spinous dentate. Inflorescence greenish. Flowers November–December. Propagated by rhizomes. Distributed throughout Nepal at 600–2100 m in open places; also in India, Tibet, China, and Southeast Asia.

OTHER USES. Plants are gathered for fodder. They are also used for fences.

Capparis spinosa Linnaeus

Capparis himalatensis Jafri
Capparis napaulensis de Candolle
ENGLISH *caper* NEPALI *bagh mukhe* SATAR *asaria*

Capparaceae. Trailing shrub, young parts covered with white tomentum, thorns straight, rarely absent. Leaves stalked, stipulate, 1.5–7 cm long, 1–4 cm wide, broadly ovate, mucronate, entire, nearly glabrous. Flowers axillary, stalked, mostly solitary, white, fading to purple. Fruit oblong, many-seeded. Flowers January–June, fruits November–December. Propagated by seeds. Distributed throughout Nepal to about 2000 m in dry, open places; also in India.

FOOD. Buds and unripe fruits are either cooked as a vegetable or pickled. Ripe fruits are eaten fresh.

MEDICINE. The root is valued as a tonic and expectorant. A paste of the root is applied for rheumatism, and the juice is given as an anthelmintic.

Capsella bursa-pastoris (Linnaeus) Medikus

Thlaspi bursa-pastoris Linnaeus
ENGLISH *shepherd's purse* MAGAR *nimale, pojagan* NEPALI *chalne, masu ko sag, swanle jhar, tori ghans, tori sag* TAMANG *syaudhap* TIBETAN *par-pa-ta, sog-ka-pa*

Cruciferae. Erect herb about 60 cm high. Basal leaves variable in size, pinnatifid, lanceolate, broadly triangular at the tip, upper leaves pinnatifid, clasping the stem. Flowers white. Fruit a pod, flat, triangular. Flowers and fruits January–November. Propagated by seeds. Distributed throughout Nepal to about 4000 m in open places; also in India, Pakistan, Bhutan, Myanmar, and Thailand.

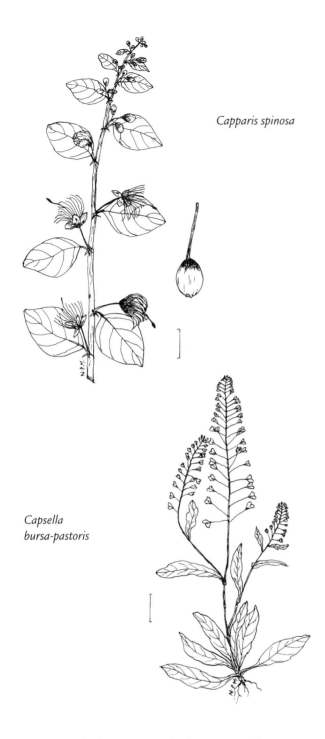

Capparis spinosa

Capsella bursa-pastoris

ing. Flowers and fruits June–October. Propagated by seeds. Distributed throughout Nepal to about 2000 m, cultivated; also in most parts of the world.

FOOD. Green pods are pickled or eaten fresh. Dried fruits are used as a spice for curries and other food preparations.

MEDICINE. Powdered fruit is taken with food in cases of dyspepsia. It is considered rubefacient, stimulant, and stomachic.

OTHER USES. The stem contains tannin. Fruit is used to make *marcha*, a fermenting cake from which liquor is distilled.

Capsicum annuum

FOOD. Tender leaves are cooked as a vegetable.

MEDICINE. The plant is used as an astringent for treating diarrhea and as a diuretic for dropsy.

Capsicum annuum Linnaeus

BHOJPURI *mirch* CHEPANG *khursya* DANUWAR *khursani*
ENGLISH *chile, chili, red pepper* GURUNG *khorsani* LEPCHA *saghakar*
LIMBU *marchi* MAGAR *khursani* MAJHI *khursani* MOOSHAR *mirchai*
NEPALI *khursani* NEWARI *malta* RAI *birosi* SUNWAR *du*
TAMANG *marcha* THARU *mircha* TIBETAN *tsi-tra-ka*

Solanaceae. Annual shrub. Leaves stalked, elliptic to ovate, acuminate, entire, glabrous. Flowers white, droop-

Caragana brevispina Royle

Caragana bicolor Komarov
Caragana williamsii Vassiljeva
NEPALI *bebali kanda, jhyaure kanda, sabalo* SHERPA *puchu*
TAMANG *khor puju* TIBETAN *jomosing*

Leguminosae. Spiny shrub about 2 m high. Leaves stalked, even-pinnate, leaflets obovate, pubescent beneath. Flowers stalked, yellow. Fruit a pod, straight, cylindrical, glabrous outside, woolly inside. Flowers April–June, fruits August–October. Propagated by seeds. Distributed in western and central Nepal at 2400–3500 m in open, sandy places; also in northern India.

FOOD. Young buds are cooked as a green vegetable.

MEDICINE. A decoction of the plant is taken in cases of joint ache.

OTHER USES. The plant provides fodder. It is an important fuelwood for people at high elevations.

Caragana brevispina

Caragana sukiensis C. K. Schneider

Caragana hoplites Dunn
Caragana nepalensis Kitamura
TIBETAN *pakchar*

Leguminosae. Shrub about 2.5 m high. Leaves stalked, pinnate, leaflets more than 12, about 4–7 mm long, elliptic, entire. Flowers yellow. Fruit a pod, hairless at maturity. Flowers June–July. Propagated by seeds. Distributed in western and central Nepal at 3000–3700 m; also in India and Bhutan.

MEDICINE. A paste of the root is applied in cases of dislocated bone.

Cardamine impatiens Linnaeus

NEPALI *sim sag*

Cruciferae. Herb about 40 cm high. Leaves stalked, 3–7 cm long, pinnately lobed, lobes short-stalked or sessile, elliptic or ovate, acute, slightly dentate or entire. Flowers white. Fruit a pod. Flowers and fruits March–April. Propagated by seeds. Distributed throughout Nepal at 1500–4000 m on moist, open ground; also in Eurasia and Japan.

FOOD. Tender shoots and leaves are cooked as a vegetable.

Cardamine loxostemonoides O. E. Schulz

Cardamine pratensis Linnaeus
ENGLISH *cuckoo flower* NEPALI *chamsure ghans*

Cruciferae. Annual herb about 30 cm high. Leaves stalked, pinnate, leaflets sessile, elliptic, entire or three-lobed. Flowers white in racemes. Fruit a pod, linear. Flowers and fruits May–August. Propagated by seeds. Distributed throughout Nepal at 2900–5500 m in open places; also in India, Bhutan, Tibet, and southern China.

FOOD. Tender shoots and leaves are cooked as a vegetable.

Cardamine scutata Thunberg subsp. *flexuosa* (Withering) Hara

Cardamine flexuosa Withering
Cardamine deblis D. Don, *C. flexuosa* subsp. *deblis* (D. Don) O. E. Schulz
Cardamine hirsuta var. *sylvatica* Link
NEPALI *chamsure ghans* TAMANG *chom*

Cruciferae. Annual herb about 30 cm high. Leaves stalked, pinnate, leaflets short-stalked, ovate, acute, coarsely dentate. Flowers white in terminal racemes. Fruit a pod, slender. Flowers and fruits March–November. Propagated by seeds. Distributed throughout Nepal at 1000–4000 m in moist, open places; also in temperate Asia, Europe, and North America.

OTHER USES. The plant is a nutritious fodder.

Cardamine violacea (D. Don) Wallich

Erysimum violaceum D. Don
NEPALI *tuki jhar*

Cruciferae. Herb. Lower leaves stalked, broad, upper leaves sessile, clasping the stem, lanceolate, tapering to the apex, dentate, base arrow shaped. Flowers large, purple, in terminal stalk-like clusters, April–June. Propagated by seeds. Distributed throughout Nepal at 2500–3600 m in

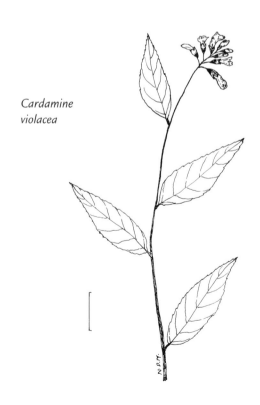

Cardamine violacea

moist places in forested areas; also in northern India and Bhutan.

FOOD. Tender shoots and leaves are cooked as a vegetable.

Cardiocrinum giganteum (Wallich) Makino

Lilium giganteum Wallich
Lilium cordifolium Thunberg
GURUNG *bhogati*

Liliaceae. Herb about 2 m high. Leaves stalked, 8–34 cm long, 5–28 cm wide, broadly ovate, leathery, shiny above. Flowers white with pinkish stripes, fragrant, in many-flowered racemes, June–July. Propagated by seeds or bulbs. Distributed throughout Nepal at 1800–3000 m in moist, shady places; also in northern India, southern Tibet, and northern Myanmar.

MEDICINE. A paste of the root is applied to treat dislocated bones.

OTHER USES. A kind of flute is made from the hollow stem.

Cardiospermum halicacabum Linnaeus

CHEPANG *ban chichinda* ENGLISH *balloon vine, love-in-a-puff, smooth-leaved heart pea* NEPALI *kesh lahara*

Sapindaceae. Herbaceous vine about 3 m long, stem slender, grooved. Leaves stalked, alternate, bipinnate, pinnae divided into three pinnules, pinnules lanceolate, long-pointed. Flowers white with a pair of tendrils at the base of the clusters, in axillary racemes. Fruit a capsule, three-celled, winged at the angles. Seeds globose, smooth, black. Flowers and fruits July–December. Propagated by seeds. Distributed throughout Nepal to about 1500 m in thickets and on uncultivated land; also in India and Bhutan.

FOOD. Tender leaves and shoots are eaten as a leafy vegetable by Chepangs.

MEDICINE. Juice of the plant is used as a remedy for dropsy, gonorrhea, fever, nerve complaints, muscular swellings, and sprains. This juice is also considered useful for rheumatic pains, hemorrhoids, and asthma. The root is emetic, laxative, demulcent, stomachic, and rubefacient. An infusion of the leaves is given to treat diarrhea and dysentery. Seeds are tonic in cases of fever and diaphoretic in rheumatism.

Carex filicina Nees

Cyperus caricinus D. Don
Carex meiogyna Nees
TAMANG *sindurpang*

Cyperaceae. Herb about 70 cm high. Leaves long, flat, midrib distinct. Inflorescences brown in pyramidal compound panicles. Flowers and fruits April–October. Propagated by seeds or bulbs. Distributed throughout Nepal at 1200–4000 m in forest openings; also in India, Sri Lanka, China, Indo-China, Malaysia, and Java.

OTHER USES. Plant are gathered for fodder.

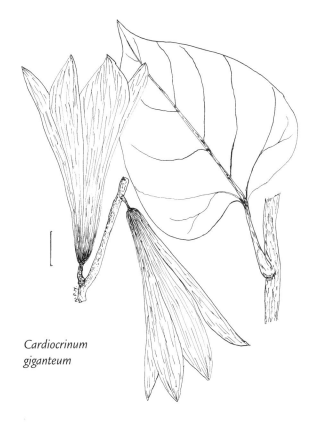

Cardiocrinum giganteum

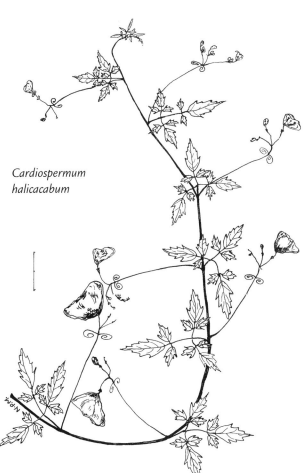

Cardiospermum halicacabum

Carex filicina

Careya arborea

Carex nivalis Boott

NEPALI *gauri dhan*

Cyperaceae. Herbaceous vine about 3 m long, stem slender, grooved. Leaves stalked, alternate, bipinnate, leaflets divided into three, deeply cut. Inflorescence brown. Propagated by seeds or bulbs. Distributed in western and central Nepal at 3500–4500 m in open, moist places; also in Afghanistan, Pakistan, India, western Tibet, and central China.

OTHER USES. The plant is offered to gods and goddesses by people in western Nepal.

Careya arborea Roxburgh

CHEPANG *khumbu*   DANUWAR *kumbhi*   ENGLISH *Patana oak*
NEPALI *bhorle, kumbhi*

Lecythidaceae. Deciduous tree about 20 m high, bark dark gray, exfoliating in thin, narrow strips. Leaves short-stalked, alternate, ovate or oblong, obtuse or shortly acuminate, denticulate, glabrous, narrowed toward the base. Flowers sessile, white or pink, few in a terminal spike, odor unpleasant. Fruit globose. Flowers March–May, fruits July–August. Propagated by seeds. Distributed throughout Nepal to about 900 m, usually in shady places; also in Afghanistan, Pakistan, India, Bhutan, Bangladesh, Sri Lanka, Myanmar, Thailand, Malaysia, and Australia.

MEDICINE. An infusion or paste of the plant is applied for vaginal ruptures caused by childbirth. Juice of the bark is astringent and is given in doses of about 4 teaspoons three times a day for cough and colds. From India, G. L. Shah and Gopal (1982) reported that a decoction of the fruit is useful for indigestion, but such a use has not been reported in Nepal.

OTHER USES. Wood is light gray and light, making it useful for furniture and agricultural implements. It also yields tannin. Bark and leaves are used to poison fish. Fiber from the bark is valued in preparing coarse cordage.

Carica papaya Linnaeus

BHOJPURI *papita*   DANUWAR *mewa*   ENGLISH *papaw, papaya*
GURUNG *mewa*   LEPCHA *santong*   LIMBU *phengse*   MAGAR *mewa*
MAJHI *mewa*   MOOSHAR *arnema*   NEPALI *mewa*   NEWARI *mewa*
RAI *chomchhadersi*   SUNWAR *mewa*   TAMANG *mewa*   THARU *mewa*

Caricaceae. Soft-wooded, fast-growing tree about 6 m high, stem grayish, marked with large petiole scars. Leaves stalked, nearly rounded, palmately seven- or nine-lobed, each lobe pinnately incised or lobed. Inflorescences axillary, pendulous panicules, the male flowers yellowish, fragrant, in short axillary spikes or racemes. Fruit obovoid or oblong cylindrical, shades of yellow when mature, fleshy. Seeds numerous, black. Flowers and fruits most of the year. Propagated easily by seeds. Distributed throughout Nepal to about 1500 m; also in Afghanistan, Pakistan, India, Bhutan, Myanmar, Thailand, Malaysia, Indonesia, the Philippines, and tropical America.

FOOD. Plants are cultivated in kitchen gardens or on private land. Ripe fruits are edible. Immature fruits are cooked as a vegetable.

MEDICINE. Latex of the plant is taken as an anthelmintic and applied to treat scorpion bites. It is also applied externally to get rid of freckles and to treat other skin diseases. Juice of the root is digestive. A decoction of the leaf is used for asthma, and a poultice for rheumatism.

Carica papaya

Carissa carandas

Carissa carandas Linnaeus

DANUWAR *karona* ENGLISH *karanda* MOOSHAR *karona*
NEPALI *karaunte, karonda* THARU *karonda*

Apocynaceae. Spiny shrub about 4 m high. Leaves sub-sessile, opposite, 1–7 cm long, 1–3 cm wide, elliptic to oblong, obtuse, entire, leathery. Flowers short-stalked, white, fragrant. Fruit an ovoid berry, purple when ripe. Flowers February–May, fruits June–October. Propagated by seeds. Distributed in western and central Nepal to about 1000 m in dry, sunny places; also in India, Sri Lanka, Myanmar, and Malaysia.

FOOD. Ripe fruits are eaten fresh and are also pickled.

MEDICINE. The root is stomachic. A decoction of the root is given to cattle and other animals with bloody dysentery. The root is boiled in water for 5 minutes and the filtered liquid given as an anthelmintic in doses of about 4 teaspoons. Juice of the root is dripped in the wounds of animals to destroy any worms or germs, hastening healing. Juice of the leaves, about 4 teaspoons three times a day, is given to treat fever. Ripe fruits are eaten to combat diarrhea.

OTHER USES. The plant makes an excellent fence.

Carpesium nepalense Lessing

Carpesium cernuum var. *nepalense* (Lessing) C. B. Clarke
Carpesium cernuum Linnaeus
Carpesium pubescens Wallich

NEPALI *gobarya, padake ghans*

Compositae. Profusely branched herb about 40 cm high. Leaves stalked, alternate, elliptic to lanceolate, acute, serrulate, pubescent on both surfaces. Flower heads yellowish. Fruit an achene. Flowers July–August. Propagated

Carpesium nepalense

by seeds. Distributed throughout Nepal at 1400–3500 m in open places; also in China and Taiwan.

MEDICINE. Juice of the plant is applied to wounds between the toes caused by prolonged walking barefooted in muddy water during the rainy season.

Carum carvi Linnaeus

ENGLISH *caraway* NEPALI *jangali jira* SHERPA *goyne*
TIBETAN *go-snyod, konyo*

Umbelliferae. Erect herb about 40 cm high. Leaves stalked, bipinnate, finely dissected, upper leaves smaller, less divided. Flowers white. Fruit linear oblong, usually with distinct ribs. Flowers June–July, fruits August–October. Propagated by seeds. Distributed in western and central Nepal at 2500–4500 m in moist, open places; also in Afghanistan, Pakistan, India, Tibet, and Bhutan.

FOOD. Tender leaves and shoots are cooked as a vegetable. Fruitlets are used as a condiment in flavoring curries, meats, lentil soup (*daal* in Nepali), and vegetables. They are also used as a substitute for cumin (*Cuminum cyminum*).

MEDICINE. Juice of the plant is taken as a tonic. Fruits are stomachic and carminative and are also used for dyspepsia and spasmodic problems of the bowels. Powdered fruits are appetite inducing. Fruits are boiled with water, strained, and the liquid thus obtained is taken to treat cough and colds. Koelz (1979) reported that the plant is used for gonorrhea in Lahul, India. Kirtikar and Basu (1935) mentioned that a caraway bath is good for painful swelling of the womb. In some places in Nepal, caraway

fruits are boiled in water with some rhizome of turmeric (*Curcuma domestica*), and the water is used in a hot compress for muscular swellings.

Caryopteris bicolor (Roxburgh ex Hardwicke) Mabberley

Volkameria bicolor Roxburgh ex Hardwicke
Caryopteris wallichiana Schauer
Clerodendrum odoratum D. Don, *Caryopteris odorata* (D. Don) B. L. Robinson, *Volkameria odorata* Roxburgh
NEPALI *dhyapinu, mhyuni, munge pati, nilo ghusure, thyaule* TAMANG *siman*

Labiatae. Shrub about 4 m high. Leaves stalked, 1.5–14 cm long, 0.5–5 cm wide, elliptic to lanceolate, acuminate, serrate. Flowers purplish, fragrant, in dense axillary cymes. Fruit globose, densely pubescent. Flowers and fruits most of the year. Propagated by seeds. Distributed throughout Nepal at 400–2200 m, common in open or shady places.

OTHER USES. The plant provides fodder.

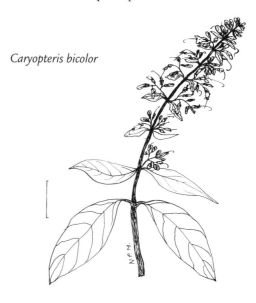

Caryopteris bicolor

Caryopteris foetida (D. Don) Thellung

Clerodendrum foetidum D. Don
Volkameria buchanani Roxburgh
Clerodendrum gratum Wallich ex Walpers, *Caryopteris grata* (Wallich ex Walpers) Bentham ex C. B. Clarke
Vitex sex-dentata Wallich ex Schauer
TAMANG *mohini*

Labiatae. Rambling shrub about 1.5 m high. Leaves stalked, 4–15 cm long, 1.5–5.5 cm wide, oblong to lanceolate, acute, crenate to serrate. Flowers purplish or white in axillary cymes. Fruit a capsule, red, globose. Flowers and fruits March–July. Propagated by seeds. Distributed throughout Nepal at 1200–2200 m, in open or shady places; also in India and Pakistan.

MEDICINE. Juice of the root is given in cases of diarrhea and dysentery.

OTHER USES. The plant provides fodder.

Carum carvi

Casearia elliptica Willdenow

NEPALI *thulo dedri*

Flacourtiaceae. Tree about 12 m high. Leaves stalked, 10–18 cm long, 4–7 cm wide, slightly dentate, with a few hairs on both sides. Flowers greenish, April–May. Fruits August–September. Propagated by seeds. Distributed throughout Nepal to about 500 m in open places; also in India, Sri Lanka, and Myanmar.

OTHER USES. The fruit is used to poison fish.

Casearia graveolens Dalzell

NEPALI *sano dedri*

Flacourtiaceae. Small deciduous tree, bark dark gray with white specks and a few longitudinal wrinkles. Leaves stalked, elliptic, short acuminate, nearly crenate, glabrous, base rounded or sometimes acute. Flowers clustered, axillary. Fruit ellipsoidal, three-valved, glabrous. Flowers May–June, fruits July–August. Propagated by seeds. Distributed throughout Nepal to about 500 m on open hillsides; also in India, Bhutan, and Myanmar.

OTHER USES. Bark, leaf, and fruit are used to poison fish.

Cassia fistula Linnaeus

Cassia rhombifolia Roxburgh

CHEPANG *briksha* DANUWAR *argho, banarsota* ENGLISH *drumstick, golden shower, Indian laburnum, pudding pipe tree, purging cassia* MAGAR *rajbriksha* MAJHI *rajbriksha* NEPALI *amaltas, rajbriksha* RAI *rajbriksha* RAUTE *rajbrik* TAMANG *gle mhendo* THARU *ashok* TIBETAN *dong-ga*

Leguminosae. Deciduous tree about 10 m high. Leaves stalked, even-pinnate, leaflets short-stalked, opposite in three to eight pairs, 7–15 cm long, 3–9.5 cm wide, ovate to oblong, acuminate, entire. Flowers bright yellow in drooping axillary racemes. Fruit a pod 20–30 cm long, brownish black when ripe. Flowers May–July, fruits October–January. Propagated by seeds. Distributed throughout Nepal to about 1500 m in open, dry places or with other trees in the forest; also in India, southern, eastern, and western Asia including China, Malaysia, and Polynesia.

FOOD. Young leaves and fruits are cooked as a vegetable.

MEDICINE. Juice of the root is applied to treat skin diseases and syphilis. Bark of the stem is boiled in water to which some salt has been added for about 15 minutes, strained, and the liquid is used in gargling to relieve sore throat. Fruit pulp is purgative, tonic, and appetite inducing. It is also useful for asthma, diabetes, and eczema. This pulp, about 4 teaspoons three times a day, is given in cases of hematuria and is also taken for diarrhea and dysentery. Rautes soak the pulp in water to make a paste that is taken in doses of about 6 teaspoons four times a day to treat giddiness; alternatively, the paste is applied to the forehead. The Tharus of Dangdeokhuri district apply the paste to snake or scorpion bites. The seed is laxative and a decoction is used as a gargle to treat toothache and sore throat.

OTHER USES. The wood makes excellent charcoal. Bark contains 10–12% tannin. Twigs are lopped for fodder.

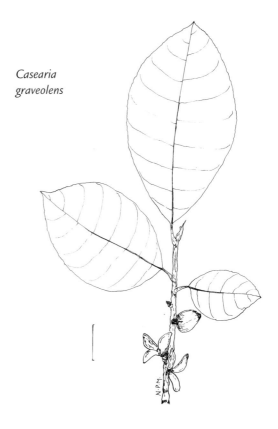

Casearia graveolens

Cassia fistula

Cassia floribunda Cavanilles

Cassia laevigata Willdenow

NEPALI *bhatte, chhinchhie, chhirlinge, kodari phul, tapre*

Leguminosae. Shrub about 3 m high. Leaves stalked, pinnate, leaflets elliptic to lanceolate, acuminate, entire, with glabrous glands on rachis between the leaflets. Flowers yellow in axillary racemes. Fruit a pod, cylindrical. Flowers June–July, fruits August–November. Propagated by seeds. Distributed throughout Nepal at 700–2200 m on moist ground, especially along the margins of cultivated fields; also on subtropical plains of the rest of the Himalaya, and tropical America.

FOOD. Tender fruits are cooked as a vegetable.

MEDICINE. A paste of the seeds is applied to treat scabies. Roasted seeds are chewed in cases of cough.

Cassia mimosoides Linnaeus

Cassia angustissima Lamarck
Cassia dimidiata Buchanan-Hamilton ex D. Don
Cassia myriophylla Wallich
Cassia telfairiana Wallich
Cassia wallichiana de Candolle
Senna sensitiva Roxburgh
Senna tenella Roxburgh

ENGLISH *dwarf cassia, tea senna* NEPALI *amala jhar*

Leguminosae. Herb about 50 cm high. Leaves stalked, even-pinnate, leaflets many, linear, mucronate, base oblique, margin ciliate. Flowers yellow, axillary. Fruit a pod, linear, flat. Flowers and fruits July–September. Propagated by seeds. Distributed throughout Nepal at 500–2500 m in open grassland; also pantropical.

FOOD. Young leaves are used as a substitute for tea.

MEDICINE. A paste of the plant is applied to treat leprosy.

Cassia occidentalis Linnaeus

Senna occidentalis (Linnaeus) Roxburgh

DANUWAR *barkichakor, chilmile, gahat* ENGLISH *coffee senna, Negro coffee, wild coffee* MAGAR *kwnar, tapre* NEPALI *chhinchhine, kodari phul, panwar, sani, syang syange, thulo tapre* RAI *tapre*

Leguminosae. Erect shrub about 1 m high. Leaves, stalked, alternate, even-pinnate, leaflets in three to five pairs, short-stalked, 2–9.5 cm long, 1–3.5 cm wide, ovate to oblong, acuminate, entire. Flowers stalked, yellow, in few-flowered axillary and terminal corymbs. Fruit a pod 10–12 cm long, distinctly constricted at regular intervals. Flowers and fruits June–January. Propagated by seeds. Distributed throughout Nepal to about 1500 m in open areas and on uncultivated land; also in Pakistan, India, Bhutan, Sri Lanka, Myanmar, Thailand, Malaysia, the Philippines, Arabia, Africa, and tropical America.

FOOD. Seeds are roasted and used as a substitute for coffee.

MEDICINE. The plant is considered to be diuretic, stomachic, and to possess febrifuge properties. A paste of the plant is applied for dropsy, rheumatism, venereal diseases, and snakebites. It is mixed with hot water for gargling in cases of sore throat. Juice of the root, about 6 teaspoons, is taken at bedtime as an anthelmintic. This juice is also given in cases of fever. A paste is applied to snakebites. The root and seeds are purgative and are useful for whooping cough. Juice of the leaf is applied to treat ringworm, eczema, and other skin diseases. An infusion of the leaf is purgative. Seeds are purgative and antiperiodic and are considered useful for indigestion, gastric troubles, and asthma. They also have anthelmintic properties. Roasted seeds are eaten for cough and headache. A paste of the seeds is applied to the forehead to treat headaches.

Cassia tora Linnaeus

Senna tora (Linnaeus) Roxburgh

CHEPANG *tapre* DANUWAR *chakor* ENGLISH *fever weed, fetid cassia, ringworm plant, sickle senna* MAGAR *tapre* MAJHI *tapre* MOOSHAR *chakor* NEPALI *chakramandi, chhinchhine, methighans, sanotapre, tapre* RAI *tapre* RAUTE *tinkose* TAMANG *sasa lingling* THARU *chakon, chilbile* TIBETAN *thal kar rdo rje*

Leguminosae. Gregarious shrub about 2 m high. Leaves stalked, alternate, pinnate, leaflets six, in three pairs, short-stalked, 1–5.5 cm long, 0.8–2.5 cm wide, ovate, entire, tip rounded. Flowers orange-yellow, usually in pairs, axillary. Fruit a pod, linear. Flowers and fruits March–November. Propagated by seeds. Distributed throughout Nepal to about 1400 m in open areas, grasslands, and on uncultivated land; also in Pakistan, India, Bhutan, Sri Lanka, Myanmar, Thailand, the Philippines, Arabia, Africa, and South America.

FOOD. Young leaves are cooked as a vegetable. Roasted seeds are used as a substitute for coffee.

MEDICINE. A paste of the root, mixed with lemon juice (*Citrus limon*), is applied to treat ringworm. A decoction of the leaves is purgative and is also applied to treat skin diseases. Powdered leaves are given in cases of indigestion and stomach pain. A decoction of the fruit is taken to treat fever. Seeds are anthelmintic and a paste of them is applied for leukoderma, leprosy, and itches. V. Singh (1976) reported that in India the seeds are used to treat earaches but this use has not been reported in Nepal. Rautes mix a paste of the seeds with paste of *Curcuma domestica,* and the resultant paste is applied with a light massage around dislocated bones.

Castanopsis hystrix Miquel

ENGLISH *chestnut* NEPALI *patale katus*

Fagaceae. Tree about 20 m high. Leaves stalked, 2.5–15 cm long, 1.5–5 cm wide, ovate to lanceolate, acuminate, more or less entire, glabrous above, finely reddish tomentose beneath. Flowers yellowish in drooping spikes, April–June. Fruits July–November. Propagated by seeds. Distributed in central and eastern Nepal at 1000–2500 m in broad-leaved forests; also in northern India, Bhutan, southern China, Taiwan, and Indo-China.

FOOD. Cotyledons are edible.

OTHER USES. The plant is lopped for fodder. Wood is used as fuel.

Castanopsis indica (Roxburgh) Miquel

Castanea indica Roxburgh
Quercus serrata Thunberg

BHOJPURI *katus* CHEPANG *bhasin, chakyal, katus* DANUWAR *katus* ENGLISH *Indian chestnut* GURUNG *kasintu, khansi* LEPCHA *kashyopot* LIMBU *khochchhinse* MAGAR *jhiru* NEPALI *berkap, dhale katus, dharni, kastus* NEWARI *khasin, syanguli ma* RAI *baisi, chikap* TAMANG *berkap, katus, kyakar polo, singarala dong, singring, thangra* THARU *katus*

Fagaceae. Evergreen tree about 15 m high. Leaves stalked, alternate, 7–18 cm long, 3.5–8 cm wide, oblanceolate, serrate, clothed underneath with soft hairs. Flowers sessile, yellowish, covered with brown, dense, soft hairs. Fruit a nut enclosed in an involucre covered with dense, thick spines. Flowers October–November, fruits August–September. Propagated by seeds. Distributed in central and eastern Nepal at 1000–2500 m in open places; also in northeastern India, western China, and Indo-China.

FOOD. Cotyledons are edible.

MEDICINE. Juice of the bark, about 6 teaspoons twice a day, is given in cases of indigestion. Juice of young leaves, about 2 teaspoons twice a day, is given for stomach disorder. Resin of the plant and water are pounded into a paste and given in doses of about 2 teaspoons three times a day to treat diarrhea.

OTHER USES. Wood is used for fuel and construction. Leaves are used as fodder. Villagers use the leaves to wrap tobacco (*Nicotiana tabacum*) to smoke like a cigarette.

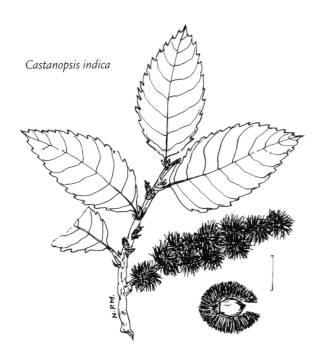

Castanopsis indica

Castanopsis tribuloides (Smith) A. de Candolle

Quercus tribuloides Smith, *Castanea tribuloides* (Smith) Lindley
Quercus armata D. Don

ENGLISH *hill chestnut* NEPALI *katus, musure katus* RAI *wahi* TAMANG *toi sing*

Fagaceae. Evergreen tree about 20 m high. Leaves stalked, 4.5–19 cm long, 1.5–7 cm wide, lanceolate, long acuminate, entire, smooth. Flowers sessile, white. Fruit a nut enclosed in a spiny top-shaped involucre. Flowers March–August, fruits September–November. Propagated by seeds. Distributed throughout Nepal at 700–2200 m in association with other forest plant species; also in northern India, Myanmar, southwestern China, and Indo-China.

FOOD. Seeds are eaten raw or roasted.

OTHER USES. The plant is lopped for fodder. Wood is moderately hard and used for planks.

Catharanthus roseus (Linnaeus) G. Don

Lochnera rosea (Linnaeus) Spach

ENGLISH *periwinkle* NEPALI *barhamase phul* NEWARI *ukhaji swan*

Apocynaceae. Smooth shrub about 50 cm high. Leaves stalked, 4–7 cm long, oblong, entire, glabrous, tapering toward the base, tip rounded. Flowers axillary, pinkish or white. Fruit a follicle. Propagated by seeds. Distributed throughout Nepal at 100–1500 m, cultivated in gardens; also in India, Pakistan, Southeast Asia, tropical America, and widely naturalized in the tropics.

MEDICINE. A decoction of the root is valued as a remedy for toothache and is also considered to be purgative. An infusion of the leaf is given in cases of diarrhea.

Catharanthus roseus

Catunaregam spinosa (Thunberg) Tirvengadum

Gardenia spinosa Thunberg, *Randia spinosa* (Thunberg) Poiret, *Xeromphis spinosa* (Thunberg) Keay
Gardenia dumetorum Retzius, *Randia dumetorum* (Retzius) Lamarck

CHEPANG *madham* DANUWAR *gorer, main* ENGLISH *emetic nut* GURUNG *bhainsi kanda, malkanda, thadhu* MAGAR *main* MAJHI *goldharni, maidal* NEPALI *bhadal, maindalkanda, mainphal, mairalu* RAI *boksiambo* TAMANG *bisiri, maidalo, maingdarju* THARU *main* TIBETAN *po-son-chha*

Rubiaceae. Thorny deciduous shrub about 5 m high. Leaves stalked, 2–10 cm long, 1–3.5 cm wide, ovate, entire, cuneate at the base. Flowers white, turning yellow at maturity. Fruit yellow, globose, slightly ribbed. Flowers May–June, fruits July–December. Propagated by seeds. Distributed throughout Nepal to about 1500 m in open, dry places; also in India, southern China, and Southeast Asia.

FOOD. Unripe fruits are pickled.

MEDICINE. Juice of the bark, about 4 teaspoons three times a day, is given to treat fever, diarrhea, and dysentery. This juice is also used for rheumatic pain. Bark, mixed with roots of *Cissampelos pareira, Inula cappa, Ziziphus mauritiana,* and bark of *Psidium guajava* in equal amounts, is pounded and the juice, about 2 teaspoons three times a day, is given in cases of peptic ulcer. A paste of the bark is used to treat cuts and wounds. A paste of the stem and leaf is applied for joint aches. A paste of fresh fruit is applied over the navel region for abdominal pains. Pulp of the fruit is anthelmintic and abortifacient and is chewed to treat diarrhea and dysentery. Powder of dried fruit is emetic.

OTHER USES. Crushed bark or fruit is used to poison fish. A squeezed mass of ripe fruits is mixed with water for bathing and washing clothes.

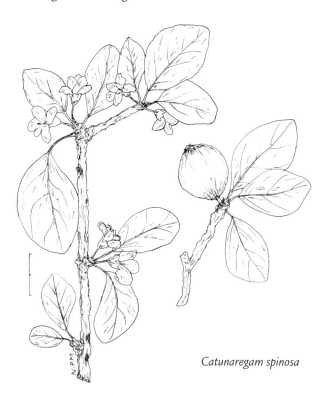

Catunaregam spinosa

Catunaregam uliginosa (Retzius) V. V. Sivarajan

Gardenia uliginosa Retzius, *Xeromphis uliginosa* (Retzius) Maheshwari
Posqueria uliginosa Roxburgh, *Randia uliginosa* de Candolle
ENGLISH *brilliant gardenia* NEPALI *pirar*

Rubiaceae. Tree about 10 m high, branches terminating in one or two pairs of strong sharp thorns. Leaves

stalked, gathered in tufts on shortened branches, 2.5–14 cm long, 1–6.5 cm wide, ovate to oblong, entire, tip rounded, narrowed toward the base. Flowers white, fragrant. Fruit ovoid or elliptic, crowded with the remains of the persistent calyx. Flowers May–July, fruits August–October. Propagated by seeds. Distributed throughout Nepal to about 300 m in open places, cultivated; also in India, Sri Lanka, and Indo-China.

FOOD. Fruits are eaten.

MEDICINE. Juice of the fruit is given in cases of diarrhea and dysentery.

OTHER USES. Foliage provides good fodder for cattle. Fruit is used as a color intensifier in dyeing. Unripe fruit is used for fish poison.

Cautleya spicata (Smith) Baker

Roscoea spicata Smith
GURUNG *onsila, tyauda* NEPALI *ban besar, gagleto, pani saro, sano saro*

Zingiberaceae. Herb about 50 cm high. Leaves short-stalked, elliptic, acuminate. Flowers yellow in short-stalked spikes, August–September. Propagated by bulbs. Distributed in central and eastern Nepal at 1000–2600 m in moist, shady places; also in northern India.

FOOD. Stem pith is eaten as a vegetable.

MEDICINE. Juice of the rhizome is used for stomach disorders.

Cautleya spicata

Cedrus deodara (Roxburgh ex D. Don) G. Don

Pinus deodara Roxburgh ex D. Don, *Cedrus libani* var. *deodara* (Roxburgh ex D. Don) Hooker fil.

ENGLISH *Himalayan cedar*   NEPALI *deudar, diyar*
TIBETAN *thang-shing*

Pinaceae. Evergreen coniferous tree about 40 m high, branches horizontally spreading. Leaves needle-like, sharply pointed, 2–5.5 cm long, glaucous green, in dense whorls. Seeds triangular or broadly crescent shaped. Cones March–July, mature July–September. Propagated by seeds. Distributed in western and central Nepal at 1100–2900 m in open places but the plant's limited natural distribution and the gathering of its wood are causes of conservation concern; also in Afghanistan and north-western India.

MEDICINE. The wood is diuretic, carminative, and expectorant. Pieces of it are boiled with water, strained, and boiled again until a gelatinous mass is formed. This mass is considered good for fever, rheumatic pains, hemorrhoids, and pulmonary problems. Wood is rubbed on a flat stone and the paste thus obtained is applied to the forehead to relieve headaches. Resin from the wood is used to treat bruises, skin diseases, and injuries to joints. Seed oil is diaphoretic and is applied to treat skin diseases.

OTHER USES. Wood is durable and resistant to termites. It is used for construction. In Jumla district, western Nepal, wood is also used as fuel though it produces a lot of smoke.

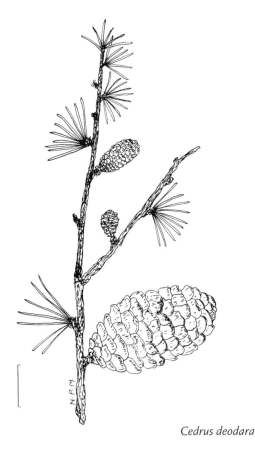

Cedrus deodara

Celastrus paniculatus Willdenow

Celastrus multiflorus Roxburgh, *C. paniculatus* var. *multiflorus* (Roxburgh) Ding
Celastrus nutans Roxburgh

LEPCHA *ruglim*   NEPALI *lhoro, malkauna*

Celastraceae. Scandent shrub, bark corky, young shoots marked with lenticels. Leaves variable in shape, generally obovate, elliptic, or oblanceolate, short acuminate, crenate, more or less leathery, glabrous. Flowers yellowish in terminal panicles. Fruit a capsule, bright yellow when ripe. Flowers April–June, fruits October December. Propagated by seeds. Distributed in central and eastern Nepal to about 300 m in open, moist places; also in India, Sri Lanka, China, Taiwan, Indo-China, Malaysia, New Caledonia, and Australia.

MEDICINE. Juice of the bark, about 6 teaspoons three times a day, is given in cases of indigestion. Seeds are used for rheumatism, leprosy, and fever.

OTHER USES. The plant is lopped for fodder. Seed oil is used for lighting lamps.

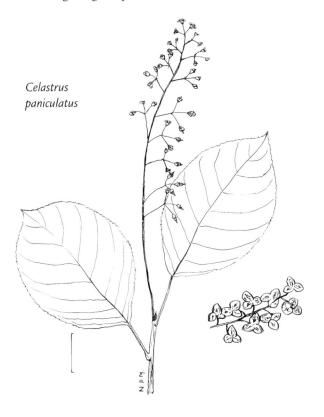

Celastrus paniculatus

Celastrus stylosus Wallich

Celastrus neglecta Wallich, *Gymnosporia neglecta* Wallich ex Lawson

RAUTE *saunr*

Celastraceae. Woody climber. Leaves stalked, alternate, 3–9.5 cm long, 1.5–4 cm wide, oblanceolate, acute, serrate, glabrous. Flowers greenish white in panicles. Flowers April–May, fruits June–November. Propagated by seeds.

Distributed in eastern and central Nepal at 1500–2600 m in open forested areas; also in India, Bhutan, southern Tibet, and western Java.

MEDICINE. Juice of the root, about 2 teaspoons three times a day, is given in cases of fever.

Celosia argentea Linnaeus

Celosia margaritacea Linnaeus
CHEPANG *siraula* ENGLISH *quail grass* NEPALI *choya phul, siraula, seto chande*

Amaranthaceae. Erect herb. Leaves stalked, 2–15 cm long, 0.3–3.5 cm wide, elliptic to ovate, acute, entire, glabrous. Flowers pinkish white in cylindrical spikes. Flowers and fruits August–November. Propagated by seeds. Distributed throughout Nepal to about 1600 m in open, moist places; also in most other parts of the world.

FOOD. Tender shoots and leaves are cooked as a vegetable.

OTHER USES. Plants are gathered for feeding animals in stalls.

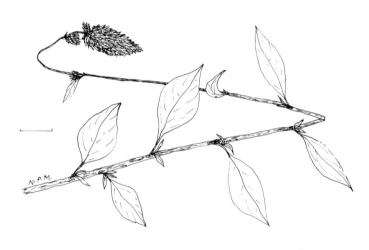

Celosia argentea

Celtis australis Linnaeus

ENGLISH *nettle tree* NEPALI *khari*

Ulmaceae. Deciduous tree. Bark bluish gray, often with whitish specks. Leaves stalked, alternate, ovate or elliptic, long acuminate, serrate, leathery and rough when matured, dark green and glabrous above, base acute or rounded, sometimes oblique, with three basal veins. Flowers yellowish green. Fruit a drupe, ellipsoidal, purplish black when ripe. Flowers March–May, fruits June–September. Propagated by seeds. Distributed in central Nepal at 1300–2200 m in open places; also in India.

OTHER USES. The plant is lopped for fodder. Wood is strong and used for handles of agricultural implements.

Celtis tetrandra Roxburgh

Celtis serotina Planchon
Celtis trinervi Roxburgh
CHEPANG *khari ko sing* ENGLISH *hackberry* LIMBU *kharising* MAGAR *khu* NEPALI *khari* NEWARI *kusi ma* SUNWAR *kharirwa* TAMANG *kusung tong* THARU *khari*

Ulmaceae. Deciduous tree. Leaves stalked, alternate, 2–12.5 cm long, 0.8–5.5 cm wide, obliquely ovate to lanceolate, caudate-acuminate, serrate above the middle. Flowers small, yellowish, in axillary or lateral cymes. Fruit a drupe, orange-red when ripe. Flowers February–March. Propagated by seeds. Distributed throughout Nepal at 700–2500 m on the edges of terraced fields; also in northern India and Southeast Asia.

MEDICINE. Juice of the seed is given in cases of indigestion.

OTHER USES. Leaves are lopped for fodder.

Celtis tetrandra

Centella asiatica (Linnaeus) Urban

Hydrocotyle asiatica Linnaeus
BHOJPURI *ghortapre* CHEPANG *bhuin jhar, ghortaprya* DANUWAR *dokni, ghortapa* ENGLISH *Indian pennywort* GURUNG *jasundo, lemsyu, topre jhar* LEPCHA *phirumuk* LIMBU *lakphesungm* MAGAR *ghortapre, tapre jhar* MOOSHAR *ghortap* NEPALI *ghortapre, golpat, tin aankhle, tobre* NEWARI *bakucha ghyan, kholcha ghyan, salakha* RAI *yuklamwasun* RAUTE *khocha* SHERPA *chhimile, ghumen* SUNWAR *ghortapre* TAMANG *ghortapre, nagasalamran, tajhawai, tilikosyo* THARU *ghortapre*

Umbelliferae. Prostrate herb with trailing stem, rooting at the nodes. Leaves stalked, 1–1.5 cm long, 1–3 cm wide, reniform or orbiculate, smooth. Flowers reddish in umbels. Fruit oblong, curved, brown. Flowers and fruits most of the year. Propagated by nodal rooting of the prostrate stem. Distributed throughout Nepal to about 2800 m in moist, open places; also in Pakistan, India, Bhutan, Bangladesh, Sri Lanka, and tropical and subtropical regions throughout the world.

FOOD. The plant is cooked as a vegetable and is also used as a potherb or salad.

MEDICINE. The plant is fed to cattle that have urinary troubles. A paste of the plant is applied to reduce muscular pain and swelling. It is also applied in cases of skin disease such as ringworm, eczema, and pimples and to treat leprosy, nerve troubles, cuts, and wounds. Rautes apply this paste to the forehead to relieve headache. Juice of the plant, about 4 teaspoons six times a day, is given to treat fever and indigestion. It is also efficacious in jaundice. This juice, mixed with cow's milk, is given for acidity. It is also used to treat various illnesses when blood is coughed up.

Leaves are diuretic and tonic. Their juice is considered a purifier of the blood, an appetite inducer, and also helpful in improving memory. The juice is taken with water for refreshment and is considered useful in treating inflammation of the urinary tract. A paste of the leaf is given for dysentery. People of Rasuwa district, central Nepal, take the juice to treat fever and throat troubles. An infusion of the leaf is used for the treatment of liver complaints and gastric troubles.

Centella asiatica

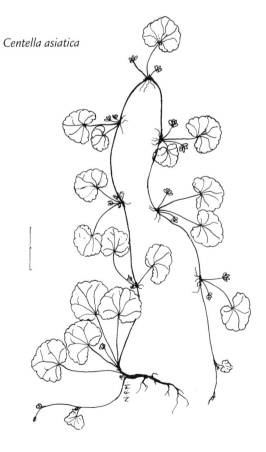

Centipeda minima (Linnaeus) A. Brown & Ascherson

Artemisia minima Linnaeus
Artemisia sternutatoria Roxburgh
Centipeda orbicularis Loureiro
GURUNG *sano* MAGAR *chhischchar jhar* MOOSHAR *nakachikini*
NEPALI *chhin jhar, chhiuke jhar, chhyun jhar, hachhyun jhar*
NEWARI *hachhyun ghyan*

Compositae. Prostrate annual herb. Leaves subsessile, alternate, 0.5–1 cm long, 0.1–0.3 cm wide, ovate, distantly dentate. Flower heads globose, solitary, axillary, yellowish. Fruit an achene, minute, without pappus. Flowers and fruits May–November. Propagated by seeds. Distributed throughout Nepal to about 1900 m; also in Afghanistan, India, Sri Lanka, tropical Asia, Australia, islands of the Pacific Ocean, and Africa.

MEDICINE. When the aroma of squeezed flower heads is inhaled, it induces sneezing and thus relieves nasal congestion, especially during coughs and colds. A paste of flower heads is applied to treat swellings and inflammation of the skin.

Centipeda minima

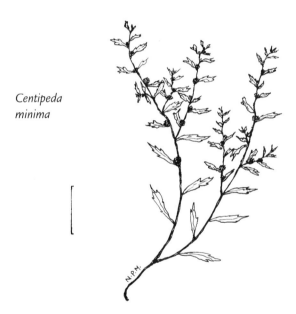

Centranthera nepalensis D. Don

Centranthera cochinchinensis Merrill
Centranthera hispida R. Brown
NEPALI *dhamura ghans*

Scrophulariaceae. Annual erect herb about 40 cm high. Leaves sessile, narrowly oblong, acute, entire, base broad. Flowers yellow in long axillary or terminal spikes. Fruit a capsule, ovoid. Flowers and fruits July–October. Propagated by seeds. Distributed throughout Nepal to about 1800 m in open, sunny places; also in India, Bhutan, Tibet, western China, and Myanmar.

MEDICINE. Juice of the plant is applied to cuts and wounds.

Centranthera nepalensis

Cerastium glomeratum Thuillier

Cerastium vulgatum var. *glomeratum* (Thuillier) Edgeworth
Cerastium viscosum Linnaeus

NEPALI *musa kane*

Caryophyllaceae. Perennial or annual herb about 30 cm high. Leaves stalked, 0.5–2 cm long, 0.3–0.8 cm wide, ovate or lanceolate, acute or obtuse, glandular pubescent, base narrowed. Flowers white. Fruit a capsule, straw colored. Flowers March–September, fruits May–December. Propagated by seeds. Distributed in western and central Nepal at 1500–3800 m; also in most other parts of the world.

MEDICINE. Juice of the plant is applied to the forehead to relieve headaches. The juice is also dropped inside the nostril in cases of nosebleed.

Cerastium glomeratum

Ceropegia pubescens Wallich

NEPALI *ban semi, mirkey laharo*

Asclepiadaceae. Climber. Leaves stalked, 3–15.5 cm long, 1.7–6.5 cm wide, lanceolate, acuminate, entire, membranous, pubescent. Flowers yellowish in axillary cymes, July–August. Propagated by seeds or root tubers. Distributed in central and eastern Nepal at 900–2700 m; also in India, Bhutan, southeastern Tibet, western China, and Myanmar.

MEDICINE. Juice of the bark is applied to boils, pimples, cuts, and wounds.

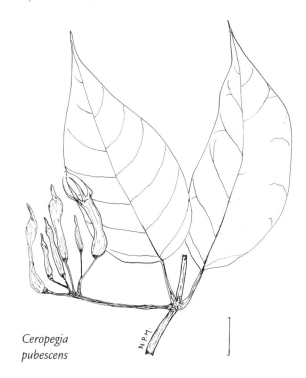

Ceropegia pubescens

Cestrum nocturnum Linnaeus

ENGLISH *lady of the night, night jessamine* NEPALI *basana, hasina*

Solanaceae. Diffuse shrub about 4 m high. Leaves short-stalked, lanceolate, acuminate, entire. Flowers greenish yellow in axillary or terminal more or less leafy panicles, fragrant at night, July–September. Propagated by stem cuttings. Distributed throughout Nepal to about 1500 m; also in India, Pakistan, the West Indies, Central America, and cultivated elsewhere for ornament.

OTHER USES. Plants are cultivated for ornament.

Chaerophyllum villosum Wallich ex de Candolle

TAMANG *chyaun*

Umbelliferae. Slender perennial herb. Leaves stalked, pinnate, leaflets lanceolate, divided into lobed segments. Flowers white or pinkish. Flowers and fruits May–August. Propagated by seeds. Distributed in western and central

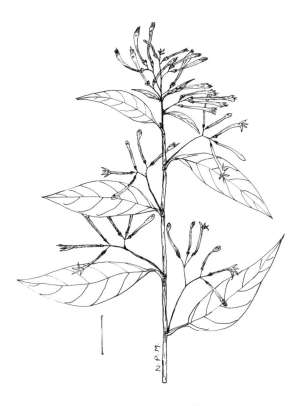

Cestrum nocturnum

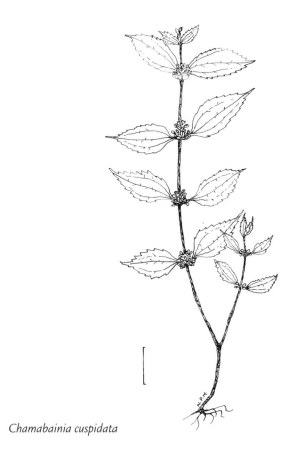

Chamabainia cuspidata

Nepal at 2100–3500 m in moist, shady places; also in northern India and Bhutan.

FOOD. Tender leaves and shoots are cooked as a vegetable.

OTHER USES. Plants supply nutritious feed for animals.

Chamabainia cuspidata Wight

Boehmeria squamigera Weddell ex Blume, *Chamabainia squamigera* (Weddell ex Blume) Weddell, *Urtica squamigera* Wallich

NEPALI *pamle*

Urticaceae. Herb. Leaves stalked, opposite, 1.5–5 cm long, ovate, acute, serrate, base rounded or cuneate. Flowers yellowish. Fruit an achene, compressed, ovate. Propagated by seeds or root offshoots. Distributed throughout Nepal at 1800–2900 m in moist places; also in India, Bhutan, Sri Lanka, eastern China, Taiwan, and Java.

MEDICINE. Juice of the root is applied to treat headaches.

Cheilanthes albomarginata C. B. Clarke

Aleuitopteris albomarginata (C. B. Clarke) Panigrahi

GURUNG *mhroghya senkha, ta* NEPALI *damini sinka, dankernu, dum kalleti, kalsinkha, rani sinka, raone, sunaule unyu* SHERPA *kalising* TAMANG *kalising* THARU *duwane sinka*

Pteridaceae. Herbaceous terrestrial fern. Stipe 6–7 cm long, purple-brown, linear lanceolate, sparsely scaly, scales brown. Fronds deltoid to lanceolate, pinnate, veins forked repeatedly. Sori yellowish brown, marginal. Propagated

Cheilanthes albomarginata

by spores or by splitting the rhizomes. Distributed throughout Nepal to about 3200 m in moist, rocky, shady places; also in India and Bhutan.

MEDICINE. Juice of the rhizome is used to treat peptic ulcer. This juice is taken as an appetizer and is given in doses of about 2 teaspoons twice a day in cases of stomach disorder. A paste is used externally to treat cuts and wounds. Juice of the frond, about 6 teaspoons three times a day, is given to treat gastric troubles.

Cheilanthes anceps C. B. Clarke

NEPALI *rani sinka*

Pteridaceae. Fern with short, erect rhizomes. Stipes covered with dark brown linear scales. Fronds bipinnate, lanceolate, lamina covered with waxy powder on the lower surface. Sori continuous along the margin. Spores June–July. Propagated by spores or by splitting the rhizomes. Distributed throughout Nepal to about 1600 m in dry, exposed places; also in India and Bhutan.

MEDICINE. Juice of the plant, mixed with juice of *Drymaria diandra*, is given in doses of about 6 teaspoons twice a day for peptic ulcer.

Cheilanthes dalhousiae Hooker

Cheilanthes farinosa var. *dalhousiae* (Hooker) C. B. Clarke
NEPALI *rani sinka*

Pteridaceae. Terrestrial fern. Rhizome tufted with ovate to lanceolate, membranous scales. Stipe with bright brown scales, rachis sparsely hairy. Fronds deltoid to lanceolate, pinnate, acuminate, pinnae without hairs, veins pinnate. Sori marginal, greenish when young. Propagated by spores or by splitting the rhizomes. Distributed throughout Nepal to about 3500 m on moist brick or rock walls; also in northern India.

MEDICINE. A paste of the rhizome is applied to boils and ruptured skin.

Cheilanthes rufa D. Don

NEPALI *bish kabre, sunauli unyu*

Pteridaceae. Terrestrial fern. Rhizome short, creeping, with linear scales. Stipes short, tufted with dull brown, fine, hair-like scales, rachis woolly. Fronds bipinnatifid, woolly throughout, veins pinnate. Sori marginal, brown. Propagated by spores or by splitting the rhizomes. Distributed in western and central Nepal at 600–3000 m in mossy rock crevices; also in northern India.

MEDICINE. Juice of the plant, about 2 teaspoons three times a day, is given to treat indigestion.

Cheilanthes tenuifolia (Burman fil.) Swartz

Trichomanes tenuifolium Burman fil.
NEPALI *kali sinka*

Pteridaceae. Fern with short, creeping rhizome. Stipes blackish purple, covered with scales. Fronds broad, ovate,

pubescent, tripinnatifid, lamina covered with waxy powder on the lower surface. Sori at the ends of veins. Spores June–August. Propagated by spores or by splitting the rhizomes. Distributed in eastern and central Nepal to about 1900 m in sunny, damp places; also in India, Sri Lanka, Malaysia, Australia, New Zealand, the Philippines, and Polynesia.

MEDICINE. Juice of the frond, about 4 teaspoons twice a day, is given in cases of peptic ulcer.

Chenopodium album Linnaeus

DANUWAR *bathuwa* ENGLISH *bacon weed, fat hen, lamb's quarter, pigweed, white goosefoot* GURUNG *bethe* MAGAR *bethe gan* MAJHI *methi jhar* MOOSHAR *bathuwa* NEPALI *bathu* NEWARI *ikancha* RAI *hubek* SATAR *bethu arak* SHERPA *nachanni* TAMANG *gugu, nana* TIBETAN *anyi-ba*

Chenopodiaceae. Erect herb covered with mealy, granular substances. Leaves stalked, variable in size, 0.4–15 cm long, 0.3–10 cm wide, elliptic to ovate, acute, dentate or lobed, fleshy. Flowers greenish in a compact panicle, January–July. Propagated by seeds. Distributed throughout Nepal to about 4000 m in moist, open places; also in India, Pakistan, Bangladesh, Sri Lanka, China, Korea, Japan, Myanmar, Thailand, Malaysia, Europe, Africa, and North America.

FOOD. Tender leaves and shoots are cooked as vegetables.

MEDICINE. The plant is laxative and anthelmintic. Juice of the plant relieves eye troubles. Juice of the root, about 6 teaspoons three times a day, is given to treat bloody dysentery. Seeds are chewed in cases of urinary trouble and are also useful to relieve the discharge of semen through the urine.

Chenopodium album

Chenopodium ambrosoides Linnaeus

ENGLISH *Mexican tea, worm grass, wormseed* NEPALI *pasare bethe, rato latte* TAMANG *betu*

Chenopodiaceae. Gregarious herb about 1 m high. Leaves short-stalked, 3–15 cm long, 1–3 cm wide, oblong to lanceolate, acute or obtuse, sinuate and dentate, upper leaves almost entire, base narrowed into a short petiole. Flowers small, greenish, some turning purplish, in axillary and terminal panicled spikes. Flowers and fruits most of the year. Propagated by seeds. Distributed throughout Nepal at 500–3000 m as a weed on uncultivated or cultivated land; found in many places in the world as a relict of cultivation.

MEDICINE. Powdered seeds, about 4 teaspoons for 4 days, are taken at bedtime as an anthelmintic. A paste of the seeds is given in cases of peptic ulcer. The essential oil from the plant is said to possess tonic and antispasmodic properties (Watt 1889–1896).

Chenopodium murale Linnaeus

Chenopodium gandhium Buchanan-Hamilton
NEPALI *kalo bethe*

Chenopodiaceae. Erect annual herb. Leaves stalked, rhombic deltoid, acute or obtuse, irregularly serrate, glabrous, base cuneate. Flowers yellowish in clusters of cymes. Flowers and fruits June–September. Propagated by seeds. Distributed in central Nepal to about 1200 m in moist, neglected places; found in many places around the world.

FOOD. Tender leaves and shoots are cooked as a vegetable.

OTHER USES. The plant is used for fodder.

Chesneya nubigena (D. Don) Ali

Astragalus nubigenus D. Don
Astragalus crassicaulis Graham, *Caragana crassicaulis* Bentham
ex Baker
Astragalus larkyaensis Kitamura
NEPALI *chyali*

Leguminosae. Herb. Leaves stalked, 2.5–4 cm long, pinnate, leaflets many, oblong, apex notched, silvery hairy. Flowers yellow or purple, solitary. Fruit a pod, finely hairy. Flowers June–July. Propagated by seeds. Distributed throughout Nepal at 3000–4000 m in moist pastureland; also in northern India, western Tibet, China, and Myanmar.

FOOD. Seeds are eaten fresh.

Chesneya nubigena

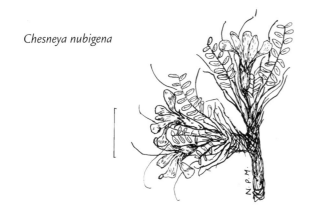

Chirita urticifolia Buchanan-Hamilton ex D. Don

Calosacme grandiflora Wallich, *Chirita grandiflora* Wallich
NEPALI *aankhle*

Gesneriaceae. Herb about 40 cm high. Leaves stalked, opposite, 2.5–16 cm long, 1.7–6.8 cm wide, elliptic, acute, serrate, hispid above, hairy on the veins beneath. Flowers purple-blue, August–September. Propagated by seeds. Distributed throughout Nepal at 1000–3400 m on moist ground under trees; also in northern India, Bhutan, western China, and northern Myanmar.

OTHER USES. The plant is gathered for fodder.

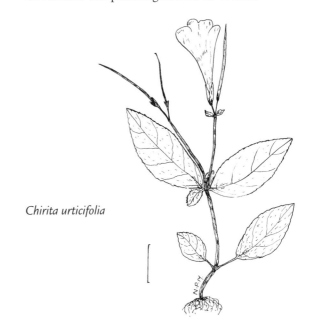

Chirita urticifolia

Chlorophytum khasianum Hooker fil.

TAMANG *chyali*

Anthericaceae. Herb about 50 cm high. Leaves all basal, 30–45 cm long, 0.5–0.8 cm wide, linear. Flowers yellowish. Flowers and fruits July–October. Propagated by seeds or bulbs. Distributed in eastern and central Nepal at 1200–3200 m on moist, rocky ground; also in northern India, Bhutan, western China, and northern Myanmar.

FOOD. Roots are boiled and eaten. Tender leaves and shoots are cooked as a vegetable.

Chlorophytum nepalense (Lindley) Baker

Phalangium nepalense Lindley, *Anthericum nepalense* (Lindley)
Sprengel
Chlorophytum undulatum Wallich ex Hooker fil.
DANUWAR *danti sag* GURUNG *kyaurino* NEPALI *ban pyaj*
TAMANG *chali dhap* THARU *tagu bhula*

Anthericaceae. Gregarious herb about 60 cm high. Leaves basal, linear, acuminate, narrowed toward the base. Flowers white in long, erect racemes, July–September. Propagated by seeds or bulbs. Distributed throughout

Nepal at 1400–2500 m in moist, shady places; also in northern India.

FOOD. Danuwars cook the tender leaves as a vegetable.

MEDICINE. A paste of the root, mixed with mustard oil, is applied in cases of gout.

Chlorophytum nepalense

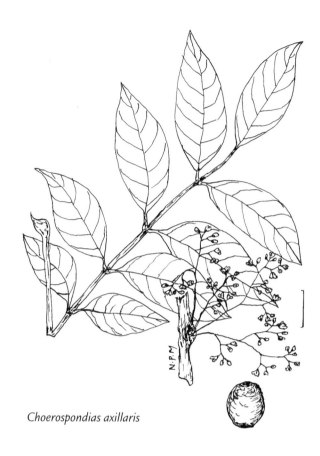

Choerospondias axillaris

Choerospondias axillaris (Roxburgh) B. L. Burtt & A. W. Hill

Sapondias axillaris Roxburgh

BHOJPURI *lapsi* CHEPANG *lapsi* DANUWAR *lapsi*
ENGLISH *Nepalese plum* GURUNG *khaiya, kalan* LEPCHA *salotapot*
LIMBU *phinnarukkwa* NEPALI *labasi* NEWARI *aamali* RAI *phintusi*
SUNWAR *lapsi* TAMANG *kalang* THARU *lapsi*

Anacardiaceae. Deciduous tree about 30 m high. Leaves stalked, odd-pinnate, leaflets subsessile, ovate to lanceolate, tapering to a sharp point. Flowers small, greenish. Fruit smooth, oblong, fleshy. Flowers April–May, fruits November–December. Propagated by seeds. Distributed in central and eastern Nepal at 1200–1500 m; also in northeastern India, central and southern China, Thailand, and southern Japan.

FOOD. Fruits are eaten fresh or pickled. Increasingly, the pulp is dried to make marmalades or jams, or candy or dried fruit pulp that is exported to Japan and other countries. Thus it is a good source of income for many rural people, who protect and grow this plant on their private land.

Chonemorpha fragrans (Moon) Alston

Echites fragrans Moon
Echites macrophylla Roxburgh, *Chonemorpha macrophylla* (Roxburgh) G. Don
GURUNG *ghibinduri* NEPALI *ghoryu, gothala phul, hammal kanda*

Apocynaceae. Robust climber. Leaves stalked, 10–33 cm long, 9.5–20 cm wide, ovate or orbiculate, entire, tip acute or rounded, glabrous above, slightly hairy beneath. Flowers white, fragrant, May–June. Fruits June–November. Propagated by seeds or cuttings. Distributed throughout Nepal at 400–1800 m in open places; also in northern India, Sri Lanka, Myanmar, Malaysia, and Indonesia.

OTHER USES. Fiber from the bark is used to make fishnets.

Chrozophora rottleri (Geiseler) A. Jussieu ex Sprengel

Croton rottleri Geiseler
THARU *chotaki hunkatath*

Euphorbiaceae. Erect herb with silvery hairs. Leaves stalked, 3.5–9.5 cm long, 2.3–8 cm wide, ovate to orbiculate, margin wavy, densely hairy on both sides. Flowers yellowish. Fruit a capsule. Flowers and fruits February–August. Propagated by seeds. Distributed throughout Nepal to about 250 m in dry places along roadsides; also in India, Sri Lanka, and Indo-China.

MEDICINE. Juice of the fruit is given in cases of cough and colds.

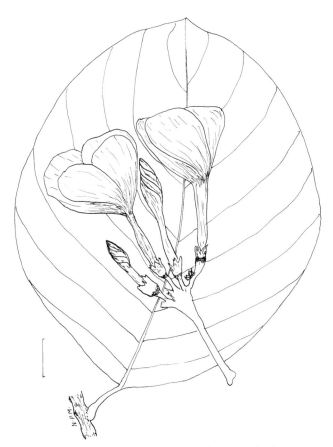

Chonemorpha fragrans

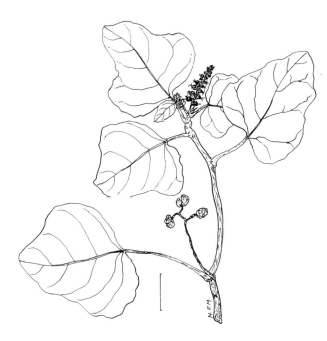

Chrozophora rottleri

Chrysopogon aciculatus (Retzius) Trinius

Andropogon aciculatus Retzius
Andropogon acicularis Retzius ex Roemer & Schultes
DANUWAR *chirchiri, nakasurka* GURUNG *chhindari*
MOOSHAR *chhimra* NEPALI *ghore dubo* THARU *sarauth*

Gramineae. Erect perennial grass with woody, creeping rhizome. Leaves densely tufted, linear, margin with small spines. Inflorescence purplish. Flowers and fruits August–October. Propagated by seeds or by splitting the roots. Distributed throughout Nepal to about 1800 m on uncultivated land and in pastures; also in India, Sri Lanka, China, Southeast Asia, Australia, and Polynesia.

MEDICINE. A paste of the root is applied to boils.

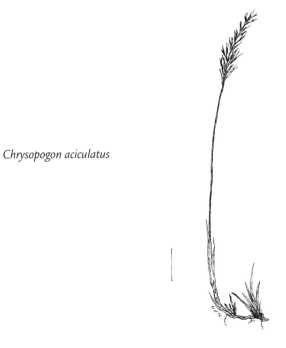

Chrysopogon aciculatus

Chrysopogon gryllus (Linnaeus) Trinius

Andropogon gryllus Linnaeus
CHEPANG *sinkauli on* NEPALI *dhaple ghans, patapate khar*
TAMANG *salima*

Gramineae. Erect grass about 1 m high. Leaves long, linear, acute. Inflorescence brown. Propagated by seeds or by splitting the roots. Distributed throughout Nepal to about 3000 m; also in northern India, southern Europe, and North Africa.

MEDICINE. A paste of the root is applied to boils and wounds.

OTHER USES. The plant is used for fodder.

Cicer arietinum Linnaeus

ENGLISH *chickpea, gram* GURUNG *chana* MOOSHAR *badam*
NEPALI *chana*

Leguminosae. Diffuse annual herb about 50 cm high. Leaves stalked, alternate, pinnate, leaflets ovate to oblong, serrate. Flowers solitary, axillary, blue, purple, or white. Fruit a pod, oblong, turgid, two- or three-seeded. Flowers September–October. Propagated by seeds. Distributed throughout Nepal to about 1300 m, cultivated; also in India, Bhutan, Australia, Europe, Africa, and the Americas.

FOOD. Dried seeds are consumed as food and are also eaten green.

OTHER USES. Dried plants are used as fodder for cattle and horses. Juice of fresh leaves is used as a hair tonic.

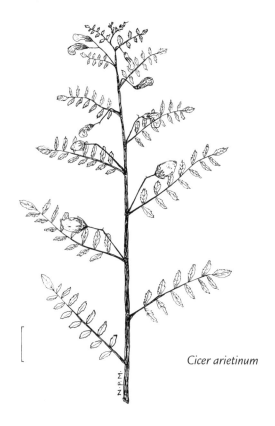

Cicer arietinum

Cicerbita macrorhiza (Royle) Palisot de Beauvois

Mulgedium macrorhizum Royle, *Lactuca macrorhiza* (Royle) Hooker fil.
Melanoseris saxatilis Edgeworth, *Lactuca laevigata* var. *saxatilis* (Edgeworth) C. B. Clarke
Lactuca hoffmeisteri Klotzsch

TIBETAN *chyate*

Compositae. Erect herb with thick woody rootstock. Leaves variable, pinnately lobed, lobes rounded, terminal lobes largest. Flower heads mauve-blue in terminal branched clusters. Flowers and fruits July–September. Propagated by seeds. Distributed throughout Nepal at 1300–4500 m on rocky slopes along the banks of streams or rivers; also in northwestern Pakistan, northern India, Bhutan, southern Tibet, southwestern China, and Myanmar.

MEDICINE. Powdered plant is mixed with powdered *Picris hieracioides,* and a pea-sized tablet is made by adding water. This tablet is taken twice a day to relieve fever.

Cicerbita macrorhiza

Cinnamomum camphora (Linnaeus) J. Presl

Laurus camphora Linnaeus

BHOJPURI *kapur* DANUWAR *kapur* ENGLISH *camphor tree*
GURUNG *kapur* LEPCHA *kapur* LIMBU *namnasing* MAGAR *kapur*
NEPALI *kapur* NEWARI *kapu ma* RAI *pungnamu* SUNWAR *kapur*
TAMANG *kapur* TIBETAN *cin-tsh, ga-bur*

Lauraceae. Evergreen tree about 10 m high. Leaves stalked, alternate, 3.5–11.5 cm long, 1.5–5.5 cm wide, ovate to lanceolate, acuminate, glabrous. Flowers yellowish in axillary and terminal panicles, March–April. Propagated by seeds. Distributed in central Nepal at 1300–1500 m in open places; native to China, Taiwan, and Japan, also found in India.

MEDICINE. Leaves are boiled with water, and the vapor is inhaled for cough and colds.

OTHER USES. The plant is a source of camphor, a white crystalline solid at room temperature, which is obtained by boiling chips of wood and root. Camphor oil is used in perfumery.

Cinnamomum glaucescens (Nees) Handel-Mazzetti

Cecidodaphne glaucescens Nees, *Tetranthera glaucescens* Wallich
NEPALI *malagiri, sugandha kokila, thulo sugandha kokila*

Lauraceae. Tree about 15 m high. Leaves stalked, 4–17 cm long, 1.5–9 cm wide, elliptic to ovate, pointed, entire. Flowers yellowish. Fruit globose, green, black when ripe.

Flowers April–May, fruits September–October. Propagated by seeds. Distributed in western and central Nepal at 1000–2500 m in *Schima* forest on hillsides along stream banks but collection of seed for sale in the trade is a cause of conservation concern; also in India and Bhutan.

MEDICINE. A paste of the seeds is applied to treat muscular swellings.

OTHER USES. Seeds are exported from Nepal for medicinal use.

Cinnamomum tamala (Buchanan-Hamilton)
Nees & Ebermaier

Laurus tamala Buchanan-Hamilton
Cinnamomum cassia Blume
Laurus albiflora Wallich

BHOJPURI *tejpatta* DANUWAR *tejpat* ENGLISH *Indian cassia lignea, Nepalese cinnamon* GURUNG *lepe* LEPCHA *sangsornyom* LIMBU *sorong tetala* NEPALI *dalchini, tejpat* NEWARI *tejpat* RAI *belakhan* SUNWAR *sijakaulisapha* TAMANG *dalchini, lepte*

Lauraceae. Evergreen tree about 15 m high, bark dark brown, wrinkled. Leaves stalked, alternate or subopposite, 7.5–20 cm long, 3.5–6.5 cm wide, ovate to oblong, long-pointed, three-veined, entire, glabrous, shiny above, pink when young. Flowers stalked, yellowish. Fruit a drupe, ovoid, succulent, supported by the thickened peduncle, black when ripe. Flowers April–May, fruits December–February. Propagated by seeds. Distributed throughout Nepal at 500–2000 m on moist slopes of forested land but collection of bark and leaves for sale in the domestic and international trade is a cause of conservation concern; also in northern India and Myanmar.

FOOD. Bark and leaves are used as spices in curries, meats, vegetables, and pickle. The ingredients are also exported from Nepal (Plate 19).

MEDICINE. Leaf and bark are extensively used to treat colic and diarrhea.

OTHER USES. Leaves contain 2% essential oil.

Cipadessa baccifera (Roth) Miquel

Melia baccifera Roth
Cipadessa fruticosa Blume

CHEPANG *asinam sai, khatrya, yukisap* GURUNG *dhanseri* MAGAR *kali kath* MAJHI *pairethi* NEPALI *asare, bugaino, kali geri, khatire, mas gera, paireti* TAMANG *bhaska, painnati*

Meliaceae. Shrub about 1 m high. Leaves stalked, odd-pinnate, leaflets subsessile, elliptic, acute or acuminate, entire, hairy on the upper surface, mainly on the veins beneath. Flowers small, greenish, in an axillary panicle. Propagated by seeds. Distributed throughout Nepal at 250–1700 m in open places; also in India, Sri Lanka, western China, and Southeast Asia.

FOOD. Leaves are used for flavoring curries and pickle. Ripe fruits are eaten fresh.

MEDICINE. Juice of the root, about 3 teaspoons three times a day, is given in cases of indigestion. It is also given to treat cough and colds. Bark is boiled 10 minutes and the filtered liquid, 2 teaspoons, is given as an anthelmintic. A paste of the bark is pressed against the teeth about 15 minutes to relieve bleeding and swelling of the gums. Juice of the bark, about 2 teaspoons twice a day, is given to treat indigestion.

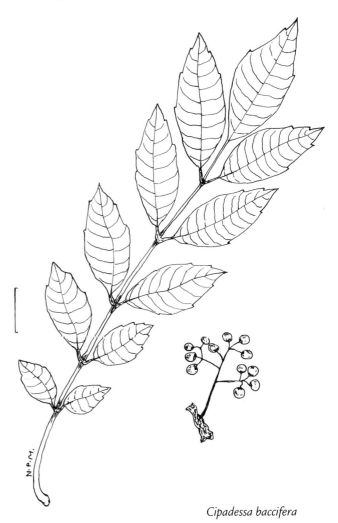

Cipadessa baccifera

Cinnamomum tamala

Cirsium arvense (Linnaeus) Scopoli

Serratula arvensis Linnaeus, *Breea arvensis* (Linnaeus) Lessing,
    Cnicus arvensis (Linnaeus) Roth
Cnicus candicans Wallich
Carduus lanatus Roxburgh
ENGLISH *Canada thistle* NEPALI *gainda kande*

Compositae. Erect herb about 70 cm high. Leaves sessile, 2–4 cm long, white above, woolly beneath. Flower heads purple, ovoid, solitary. Fruit an achene, oblong, truncate at the apex. Flowers February–June, fruits May–July. Propagated by seeds. Distributed in eastern and central Nepal to about 1200 m; also in Asia, Europe, and North America.

MEDICINE. A paste of the root, mixed with paste of the root of *Amaranthus spinosus* in equal amount, is given in cases of indigestion.

Cirsium falconeri (Hooker fil.) Petrak

Cnicus falconeri Hooker fil.
NEPALI *giddha pwankhe*

Compositae. Robust shrub about 1.5 m tall, stems villous. Leaves spiny, cauline leaves larger, broadly ovate. Flower heads cream, densely woolly. Fruit an achene. Flowers July–August. Propagated by seeds. Distributed in eastern and central Nepal at 3000–4300 m in alpine meadows; also in India, Bhutan, southern Tibet, and Myanmar.

OTHER USES. The flower head is considered poisonous to humans.

Cirsium verutum (D. Don) Sprengel

Cnicus verutus D. Don
Carduus argyracanthus Wallich
Cirsium involucratum de Candolle, *Cnicus involucratus*
    (de Candolle) Hooker fil.
Cirsium argyracanthum de Candolle, *Cnicus argyracanthus*
    (de Candolle) C. B. Clarke
NEPALI *dhode kanda, kairun, kareli, konrayo, thakal kanda,
thotane kanda* TAMANG *chokam*

Compositae. Herb about 1 m high. Basal leaves stalked, deeply lobed, teeth strongly spiny, glabrous above, cottony beneath, cauline leaves sessile, clasping the stem at their base, broader. Flower heads pinkish. Flowers and fruits July–December. Propagated by seeds. Distributed throughout Nepal at 700–3100 m; also in Afghanistan, Pakistan, India, Bhutan, and Myanmar.

FOOD. Tender roots are chewed fresh.

MEDICINE. Juice of the root, about 6 teaspoons three times a day, is taken to relieve fever. Fresh root is chewed in cases of nosebleed, especially during the dry summer. It also relieves throat aches. A paste of the root is given for stomach disorders.

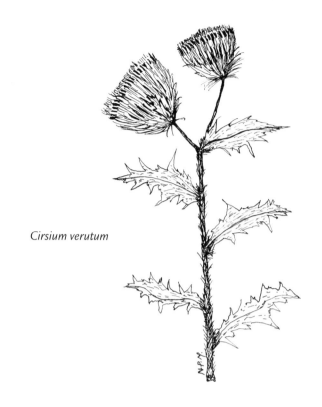

Cirsium verutum

Cirsium wallichii de Candolle

Cnicus arachnoideus Wallich
Cnicus cernuua Wallich
Cirsium nepalense de Candolle
DANUWAR *kanta* ENGLISH *Canada thistle* NEPALI *kanchuli, karai,
sungur, thakal* NEWARI *chwakan* TAMANG *wongchagalin*

Compositae. Herb about 1 m high. Leaves sessile, 3–15 cm long, sinuately pinnatifid, margin spiny, spines longer at the ends of lobes. Flower heads violet. Flowers and fruits April–September. Propagated by seeds. Distributed throughout Nepal at 1000–3500 m on moist open ground; also in Afghanistan, India, Bhutan, and China.

MEDICINE. Juice of the root is used to treat fever. This juice is also dripped into the eyes for eye troubles. A paste of the root is given to treat inflammation of the stomach. Juice of the plant, about 6 teaspoons three times a day, is given for constipation. Pith of the stem is chewed to relieve a burning sensation during urination.

Cissampelos pareira Linnaeus

Cissampelos hirsuta Buchanan-Hamilton ex de Candolle
Cissampelos nepalensis Rhodes
CHEPANG *torola* ENGLISH *ice vine, velvet leaf* GURUNG *gurubuti,
lungri* MAJHI *batulpate, dalli laharo, dhakani* NEPALI *batulpate,
chillo batulpate, jaluko, patha* RAUTE *musya belo*
TAMANG *chhelem langdu, kwartang gugai, tanga*
TIBETAN *ma-nu-pa-tra, phorgel gil*

Menispermaceae. Climbing herb with perennial rootstock. Leaves stalked, 2.5–8 cm long, 2–7.5 cm wide, orbiculate or reniform, usually peltate, mucronate, base cordate or truncate, more or less tomentose on both sides.

Flowers minute, yellowish, clustered in the axils or on long axillary stalks. Fruit a drupe, subglobose, red when ripe. Flowers April–June, fruits July–November. Propagated by seeds or root offshoots. Distributed throughout Nepal to about 3000 m, common in moist, shady places; also pantropical.

MEDICINE. Juice of the plant, about 6 teaspoons twice a day, is given after delivery to stop bleeding and to counteract the loss of blood. It is tonic and diuretic. The juice, about 3 teaspoons three times a day, is given in cases of fever and indigestion. A decoction of the leaves is applied to soothe the pain of dislocated bones. The juice is applied to treat skin diseases and is taken internally as a cooling medicine for gonorrhea.

The root is rubbed on a flat stone, adding some water, and the paste thus obtained is applied to snakebites. This paste is also given in cases of colic and is applied to treat swelling of the gums. The paste, about 4 teaspoons twice a day, is given to treat peptic ulcer. Juice of the root, about 4 teaspoons three times a day, is given to treat a burning sensation during urination and is also useful for indigestion. This juice, about 2 teaspoons three times a day, is given to treat cough and colds. The juice is also dripped into wounds to kill germs and worms. The tuberous roots are boiled and eaten to alleviate constipation. Sliced tuberous roots are fed to animals as a nutritious feed.

OTHER USES. The stem yields fiber that is used for temporary binding.

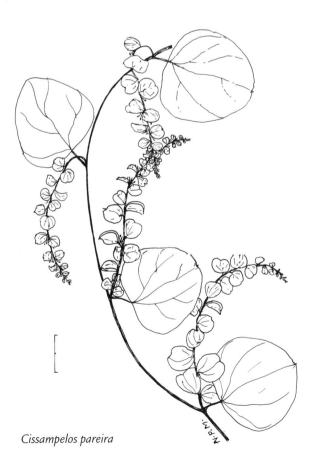

Cissampelos pareira

Cissus adnata Roxburgh

Vitis adnata (Roxburgh) Wallich
NEPALI *pureni*

Vitaceae. Climber. Leaves stalked, 4–15 cm long, 1.5–8.5 cm wide, long-pointed, serrate, glabrous, base cordate. Flowers pinkish, the lower half yellow. Fruit a drupe, black when ripe, one-seeded. Flowers and fruits June–October. Propagated by seeds. Distributed in central Nepal at 1000–1100 m in moist, open places; also in northern India, Sri Lanka, and Malaysia.

FOOD. Ripe fruits are eaten fresh.

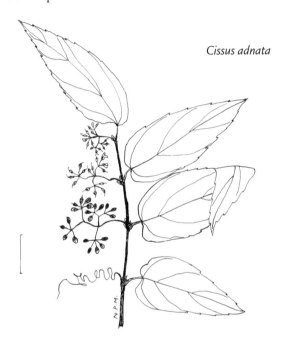

Cissus adnata

Cissus javanica de Candolle

Cissus discolor Blume, *Vitis discolor* (Blume) Dalzell
NEPALI *jogi lahara* TAMANG *gongap*

Vitaceae. Climber. Leaves stalked, alternate, 7–13 cm long, 2–9.5 cm wide, lanceolate, long-pointed, serrate, glabrous, base cordate. Flowers yellowish. Fruit deep blue when ripe. Flowers June–July, fruits September–December. Propagated by seeds. Distributed in central and eastern Nepal at 300–1200 m; also in northern India, western China, and Southeast Asia.

MEDICINE. A paste of the plant is applied to reset dislocated bones of animals.

OTHER USES. The plant is used for fodder.

Citrullus lanatus (Thunberg) Matsumura & Nakai

ENGLISH *watermelon* NEPALI *tarabuja* TIBETAN *ka-bed*

Cucurbitaceae. Hairy annual herb with rough, angular stems, tendrils branched, usually divided into two. Leaves stalked, alternate, deeply palmately lobed. Flowers solitary, axillary, pale yellow. Fruit large, rounded or oblong, with hard, smooth rind. Propagated by seeds. Distributed throughout Nepal to about 200 m, cultivated; also in tropical and warmer regions, including Africa.

FOOD. Fruit pulp is edible.

Citrullus lanatus

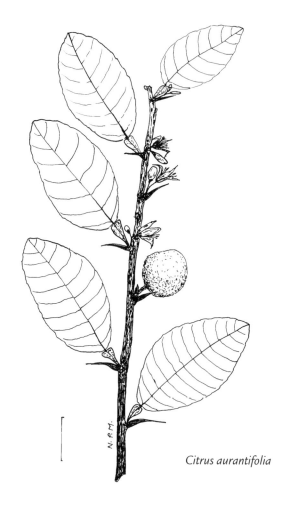

Citrus aurantifolia

Citrus aurantifolia (Christmann) Swingle

BHOJPURI *nimbu* CHEPANG *kagati* DANUWAR *kagati* ENGLISH *lime* GURUNG *kunba* LEPCHA *samabri* LIMBU *sarongse* MAGAR *kagati* NEPALI *kagati* NEWARI *kagati* RAI *chhambowsi* SUNWAR *kakati* TAMANG *kagat* THARU *kagati*

Rutaceae. Small tree, young foliage and flower buds pinkish. Leaves stalked, elliptic to ovate, obtuse, crenate, stalks winged. Flowers white. Fruit ovoid. Flowers and fruits most of the year. Propagated by seeds or by grafting. Distributed throughout Nepal to about 1800 m, cultivated.

FOOD. Juice of the fruit is eaten in curries and lentil soup (*daal* in Nepali). Fresh fruit is a good source of vitamin C; fruits are also pickled.

Citrus aurantium Linnaeus

BHOJPURI *samtola* DANUWAR *suntala* GURUNG *suntala* LEPCHA *chhalam* LIMBU *rerimse* MAGAR *suntala* MOOSHAR *samtola* NEPALI *suntala* NEWARI *santalasi* RAI *chhokawasi* SUNWAR *suntola* TAMANG *suntalo* THARU *suntala*

Rutaceae. Shrub with spiny branches. Leaves stalked, 5–8 cm long, dark green above, pale below, stalks narrowly winged. Flowers white, fragrant. Flowers white. Fruit ovate, greenish yellow when ripe. Flowers and fruits most of the year. Propagated by seeds or by grafting. Distrib-

uted in eastern and central Nepal at 1000–1400 m, cultivated; also in India, China, and Indo-China.

FOOD. Ripe fruits are edible.

MEDICINE. Juice of the outer rind of the fruit is given as a tonic, and it possesses stomachic and sedative properties.

Citrus limon (Linnaeus) Burman fil.

Citrus medica var. *limon* Linnaeus

BHOJPURI *nibo* CHEPANG *nibuwa* ENGLISH *lemon* GURUNG *mhibo* LEPCHA *samabri* LIMBU *soippa* MAGAR *bir* MOOSHAR *nebu* NEPALI *nibuwa* NEWARI *nebu* RAI *sunhanduwa* SUNWAR *nibnuwa* TAMANG *nibuwa* THARU *nimawa*

Rutaceae. Thorny tree about 5 m high, young foliage and flower buds pinkish. Leaves short-stalked, 5–10 cm long, ovate, margin of the stalk winged. Flowers white. Fruit ovoid, skin rough, yellow when ripe. Flowers and fruits most of the year. Propagated by seeds or by grafting. Distributed throughout Nepal to about 1600 m, cultivated; also in India, Bhutan, China, and Thailand, and widely cultivated throughout the subtropics.

FOOD. Fruits are pickled. Juice of the fruit is used as a flavoring for lemonade and other beverages.

OTHER USES. Juice of the fruit is used as a bleaching agent and stain remover.

Citrus margarita Loureiro

BHOJPURI *gogal* CHEPANG *dhusi* DANUWAR *bhokat*
ENGLISH *pummelo, shaddock* GURUNG *setchhi* LEPCHA *samyulop*
LIMBU *nambora* MAGAR *bhogat* NEPALI *bhogate* NEWARI *bhogatya,*
sunchakasi SUNWAR *bhokate* TAMANG *bhogate* THARU *bhogate*

Rutaceae. Tree about 4 m high. Leaves stalked, obtuse, entire, leathery. Flowers white. Propagated by seeds or by grafting. Distributed throughout Nepal at 1000–1400 m, cultivated.

FOOD. The fruit is edible.

Citrus medica Linnaeus

CHEPANG *mangsai* DANUWAR *bimiro* ENGLISH *citron*
LEPCHA *kachchhe* LIMBU *soippa* MAGAR *langkok* NEPALI *bimiro*
NEWARI *tasi* RAI *sunpekawa* TAMANG *bimara* THARU *lanagi*
TIBETAN *bil-ba*

Rutaceae. Small tree with strong axillary spines. Leaves stalked, unifoliolate, ovate to lanceolate, entire or nearly serrate, glabrous. Flowers white, fragrant. Fruit oblong, ovoid, or globose, yellow when ripe. Flowers April–May, fruits July–November. Propagated by seeds or by grafting. Distributed throughout Nepal to about 1500 m, cultivated; also in tropical and temperate regions of the world.

FOOD. Fruits are eaten fresh or pickled.

MEDICINE. Fruit is made into a preserve and used for dysentery; it also helps digestion.

Citrus sinensis (Linnaeus) Osbeck

ENGLISH *sweet orange* NEPALI *mausami*

Rutaceae. Tree about 12 m high. Leaves short-stalked, auricled, 7–10 cm long, elliptic to ovate, dark green, base rounded. Flowers white, fragrant. Fruit globose, deep yellow-orange when ripe. Propagated by seeds or by grafting. Distributed in eastern and central Nepal at 1000–1300 m, cultivated; also in India, China, Italy, Spain, the United States, Mexico, and Brazil.

FOOD. Ripe fruits are eaten fresh and are a good source of vitamin C. The juice is used to make marmalade.

Clausena excavata Burman fil.

Amyris punctata Roxburgh
Amyris sumatrana Roxburgh

CHEPANG *asanyam* DANUWAR *bhan bhaniya*

Rutaceae. Shrub about 4 m high, young parts with gray tomentum. Leaves stalked, odd-pinnate, leaflets 15–31, short-stalked, 2.5–7.5 cm long, 0.8–2.5 cm wide, obliquely oblong, acute, finely crenulate, with marginal translucent, pubescent glands, membranous, pubescent beneath. Flowers yellowish. Fruit oblong, August–October. Propagated by seeds. Distributed in central and eastern Nepal to about 500 m, on the floor of *Shorea robusta* forest; also in northern India and Southeast Asia.

FOOD. Ripe fruits are edible.

MEDICINE. Juice of the root is given to treat stomach acidity.

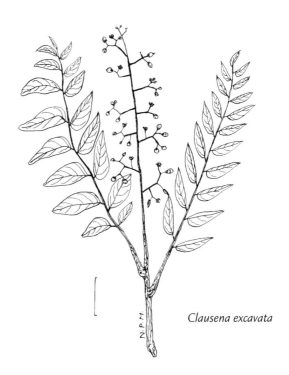

Clausena excavata

OTHER USES. The plant is kept in animal pens to rid poultry of ectoparasites.

Cleistocalyx operculatus (Roxburgh) Murray & Perry

Eugenia operculata Roxburgh, *Syzygium operculatum* (Roxburgh) Niedenzu
Eugenia cerasoides Roxburgh

DANUWAR *kemna* GURUNG *kemna* LIMBU *hekse* MAGAR *kyamuna*
NEPALI *kyamun* RAI *pitlemsi* SUNWAR *kyamuna* TAMANG *kyamuna*

Myrtaceae. Tree about 6 m high. Leaves stalked, 8.5–17 cm long, 4–9.5 cm wide, broadly elliptic, acute, entire, leathery, narrowing toward the base. Flowers white, May–June. Fruits July–August. Propagated by seeds. Distributed in central and eastern Nepal to about 1100 m in open places; also in northern India, Sri Lanka, southern China, Myanmar, Malaysia, and Australia (p. 158).

FOOD. Ripe fruits are eaten fresh.

MEDICINE. Juice of the bark is boiled to make a gelatinous liquid given to cattle to treat their muscular swellings caused by soreness. A powder of dried leaf and bark is smoked like cigarettes in cases of sinusitis and colds.

Clematis acuminata de Candolle

NEPALI *ransag*

Ranunculaceae. Climbing shrub, branches ribbed, pubescent. Leaves stalked, trifoliolate, leaflets 2–11 cm long, 1–5.4 cm wide, ovate to lanceolate, coarsely dentate, sometimes deeply three-lobed, acuminate, glabrous above, pubescent beneath, base rounded or more or less cordate. Flowers creamy white in few-flowered lax panicles. Fruit an achene, densely hairy. Flowers October–January, fruits

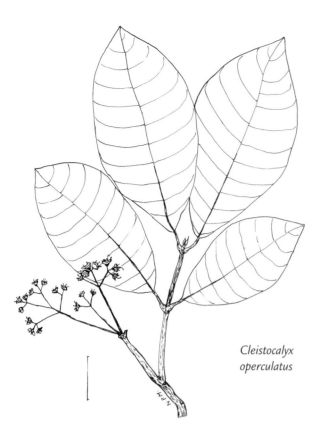

Cleistocalyx operculatus

April–May. Propagated by seeds. Distributed in central Nepal at 900–2000 m in shady, cool places; also in Pakistan and northern India.

FOOD. Tender shoots and leaves are cooked as a vegetable.

Clematis alternata Kitamura & Tamura

Archiclematis alternata (Kitamura & Tamura) Tamura
NEPALI *gurubuti*

Ranunculaceae. Trailing shrub. Leaves stalked, opposite, pinnate, leaflets stalked, 3.5–7 cm long, 3–6 cm wide, tip pointed, serrate, hairy on both surfaces. Flowers cream. Flowers and fruits June–October. Propagated by seeds. Distributed in central Nepal at 1500–3000 m in rocky places; endemic.

MEDICINE. Juice of the leaf is dripped into the eye to treat conjunctivitis but it is painful for about an hour.

Clematis barbellata Edgeworth

Clematis japonica of authors, not Thunberg
Clematis nepalensis in the sense of Royle, not de Candolle
NEPALI *junge lahara* TAMANG *khursani lahara*

Ranunculaceae. Shrubby climber. Leaves stalked, trifoliolate, leaflets 2.5–6 cm long, 0.6–3.5 cm wide, ovate to lanceolate, more or less coarsely dentate, glabrous or occasionally pubescent. Flowers large, dull purple, long-stalked in axillary fascicles. Fruit an achene, glabrous or

pubescent. Flowers May–July, fruits August–October. Propagated by seeds. Distributed in western and central Nepal at 2500–3200 m, frequent in the margin of the forest; also in northern India.

MEDICINE. The Tamangs of Dhading district take juice of the leaf, about 2 teaspoons twice a day, to relieve stomachaches, especially those from indigestion, diarrhea, and dysentery. People of Achham and Dailekh districts put the juice inside the nostril to relieve sinusitis. Some communities in the districts of Kabhrepalanchok and Sindhupalchok rub the leaves between the palms and sniff the fragrance in cases of headache.

Clematis buchananiana de Candolle

Clematis buchananiana var. *rugosa* Hooker fil. & Thomson
CHEPANG *surtilang* GURUNG *lanke chanke, shikari jhar*
MAGAR *baghjunge, chituwa nimur, sano kakchukya*
NEPALI *baghjwen, charchare, ghante phul, junge lahara, khursani lahara, pahenlo junge, selang* TAMANG *brama, chyanmangre, langdu, khondro langdu, nashar, thegor, thenr langadu*

Ranunculaceae. Trailing shrub, branches pubescent when young. Leaves stalked, pinnate, leaflets stalked, 3.5–8 cm long, 3–7 cm wide, ovate or orbiculate, coarsely lobed. Flowers large, cream, scented, in many-flowered panicles, October–December. Fruits February–March. Propagated by seeds. Distributed throughout Nepal at 1000–3300 m in open, moist places; also in northern India, western China, and Indo-China.

FOOD. Tender leaves are cooked as a vegetable.

MEDICINE. A paste of the root is applied to treat swelling caused by inflammation. A paste of stem or root bark is kept pressed against the teeth about 15 minutes to relieve toothaches. Juice of the root, about 4 teaspoons three times a day, is given in cases of peptic ulcer. This juice is

Clematis buchananiana

inhaled to get rid of cough and colds. Juice of the plant is applied to cuts and wounds. This juice, about 4 teaspoons three times a day, is given in cases of indigestion. Juice of the leaf, about 4 teaspoons four times a day, is given for cough and colds and is also applied to the forehead for the same ailment. This juice is warmed and put inside the nose to treat sinusitis.

OTHER USES. The plant is used to make *marcha,* a fermenting cake from which liquor is distilled. Leaves are used as animal feed.

Clematis connata de Candolle

Clematis amplexicaulis Edgeworth
Clematis gracilis Edgeworth
Clematis trullifera (Franchet) Finet & Gagnepain
Clematis velutina Edgeworth
Clematis venosa Royle
NEPALI *bhainse laharo*

Ranunculaceae. Deciduous climber, stems deeply ribbed, bark yellowish brown, fibrous. Leaves stalked, 15–30 cm long, pinnate, leaflets short-stalked, 5–15 cm long, 4–10 cm wide, broadly ovate to cordate, acuminate, coarsely serrate, glabrous above, hairy on the veins beneath, dull green above, glossy beneath. Flowers greenish yellow in few- or many-flowered lax axillary panicles. Fruit an achene, silky. Flowers August–September. Propagated by seeds. Distributed throughout Nepal at 2400–3300 m, common in shady forests; also in India, Bhutan, Tibet, and western China.

MEDICINE. Juice of the plant is inhaled to relieve sinusitis.

Clematis gouriana Roxburgh ex de Candolle

Clematis vitalba subsp. *gouriana* (Roxburgh) Kuntze
Clematis cana Wallich
MAGAR *kureni* NEPALI *junge lahara*

Ranunculaceae. Trailing shrub. Leaves stalked, bipinnate, leaflets 1.7–6.5 cm long, 1–3.5 cm wide, oblong to lanceolate, acuminate, entire or distantly dentate, base cordate, glabrous or rarely pubescent beneath. Flowers small, cream, in dense axillary panicles. Fruit an achene, lanceolate. Flowers August–September. Propagated by seeds. Distributed throughout Nepal at 500–1600 m in open, moist places; also in India, Sri Lanka, western and central China, and Myanmar.

MEDICINE. Juice of the leaf has an anthelmintic value.

Clematis graveolens Lindley

Clematis orientalis subsp. *graveolens* (Lindley) Kuntze
Clematis parvifolia Edgeworth
TAMANG *nashar* TIBETAN *emau phanjau*

Ranunculaceae. Climbing shrub. Leaves stalked, bi- or tripinnate, leaflets 1–2.5 cm long, lanceolate, entire. Flowers pale yellow, fragrant, in branched clusters. Fruit an achene, hairy. Flowers and fruits July–September. Propagated by seeds. Distributed in western and central Nepal at 900–3000 m in dry places and at the borders of cultivation, often on hedgerow shrubs; also in Afghanistan and India.

MEDICINE. The plant is fed to horses during the winter to keep their bodies warm. Powdered stem, mixed with powdered *Bistorta milletii,* is taken with warm water to treat cough and colds. Squeezed seeds are applied to the forehead to relieve headaches.

Clematis grewiiflora de Candolle

Clematis buchananiana subsp. *grewiiflora* (de Candolle) Kuntze
Clematis loasaefolia de Candolle
GURUNG *kyu tini* NEPALI *bhere kuro* TAMANG *bhramlaman*

Ranunculaceae. Densely pubescent twining shrub. Leaves stalked, pinnate, leaflets 1.8–9 cm long, 1.5–6.5 cm wide, ovate, serrate, acuminate, densely brown tomentose, base cordate. Flowers yellowish in many-flowered panicles, September–December. Fruits February–March. Propagated by seeds. Distributed throughout Nepal at 900–1800 m in open, rocky places; also in northern India and northern Myanmar.

MEDICINE. A paste of the fruit is given in cases of diarrhea and dysentery.

Cleome gynandra Linnaeus

Cleome pentaphylla Linnaeus, *Gynandropsis pentaphylla* (Linnaeus) de Candolle
NEPALI *tori jhar* SATAR *seta kanta arak, seta kata arak*

Capparaceae. Annual herb about 1.5 m high. Leaves stalked, three- or five-foliolate, leaflets subsessile, 2–10 cm long, elliptic to ovate, obtuse to acuminate, entire. Flowers pinkish in terminal subcorymbose racemes. Fruit a capsule. Flowers and fruits July–November. Propagated by seeds. Distributed throughout Nepal to about 300 m in open areas and on uncultivated land; also in India, Sri Lanka, eastern China, and Malaysia.

MEDICINE. Juice of the root is given to treat fever. It is also used relieve scorpion stings. A paste of the leaf is applied for rheumatism. Seeds are considered anthelmintic.

Cleome viscosa Linnaeus

CHEPANG *ritori* ENGLISH *sticky cleome, wild mustard* MAJHI *hurhule, methi jhar* NEPALI *tori jhar* NEWARI *sui bhanme* THARU *hurhur*

Capparaceae. Viscid, sticky annual herb about 1 m high. Leaves stalked, three- or five-foliate, leaflets subsessile, oblanceolate or elliptic, acute or obtuse, entire, glandular ciliate. Flowers yellow, solitary in the axils of the upper leaves. Fruit a capsule, linear, cylindrical, attenuate toward the apex. Flowers June–August, fruits September–November. Propagated by seeds. Distributed throughout Nepal to about 1200 m in open areas and on uncultivated land; also pantropical.

FOOD. Tender leaves and shoots are cooked as a vegetable. Roasted seeds are used in curries or are pickled. Seed oil is used for cooking in some parts of western Nepal.

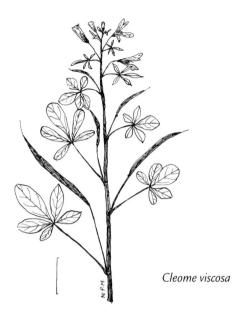

Cleome viscosa

MEDICINE. A paste of the root is applied externally to treat earaches. Seeds are valued as carminative, anthelmintic, and stimulant.

Clerodendrum indicum (Linnaeus) Kuntze

Siphonanthus indica Linnaeus
Clerodendrum siphonanthus R. Brown
Clerodendrum verticillatum Roxburgh ex D. Don

CHEPANG *rauru, syankamale* ENGLISH *tube flower, Turk's turban* MAGAR *ekle bir* NEPALI *bhargi, ekle bir*

Labiatae. Shrub about 2.5 m high with fluted, hollow stems. Leaves stalked, 6–23 cm long, 1–5 cm wide, lanceolate, base narrowed, subentire. Flowers white, fading to yellow, in a terminal panicle. Fruit a drupe, dark blue, supported by the spreading red calyx. Flowers July–August, fruits November–December. Propagated by seeds or stem cuttings. Distributed throughout Nepal at 200–1400 m in open places; also in India, Bhutan, Sri Lanka, southern China, and Southeast Asia.

FOOD. Leaves are used as a potherb.

MEDICINE. Juice of the root, about 6 teaspoons three times a day, is given in cases of cough and colds. Chepangs take the juice for asthma. Juice of the bark, about 4 teaspoons a day, is good for treating malnutrition. Treatment is continued about a month. Juice of the leaf is applied to eruptions on the feet.

Clerodendrum japonicum (Thunberg) Sweet

Volkameria japonica Thunberg
Clerodendrum squamatum Vahl
Volkameria dentata Roxburgh
Volkameria kaempferi Jacquin

CHEPANG *bakan, tingsi* MAGAR *patlange*

Labiatae. Shrub about 2 m high. Leaves stalked, opposite, 5–17 cm long, 3.5–18 cm wide, broadly ovate, acu-

minate, crenulate, base cordate, gland-dotted beneath. Flowers red in large spreading panicles, July–September. Propagated by seeds or stem cuttings. Distributed in eastern and central Nepal to about 1600 m in moist gullies and shady places; also in India and tropical Asia.

FOOD. Young leaves and shoots are cooked as a vegetable or are pickled.

MEDICINE. The squeezed plant is mixed with the feed for animals with diarrhea and dysentery.

Clerodendrum philippinum Schauer

Clerodendrum fragrans var. *plentiflorum* Schauer

NEPALI *raj beli, raj kali* NEWARI *nawa ghyan* TAMANG *tajalhapte, thangapava*

Labiatae. Erect shrub about 1 m high. Leaves stalked, 6–18.5 cm long, 3.8–16 cm wide, ovate or lanceolate to cordate, acute, crenate, hairy on both surfaces. Flowers white, fragrant, on a terminal stalk. Flowers and fruits May–November. Propagated by seeds. Distributed in eastern and central Nepal to about 2000 m in open places; also in India and China.

MEDICINE. Juice of the plant is applied to cuts and wounds. Juice of the bark is applied to burns. Juice of the leaf is used to alleviate boils and pimples.

Clerodendrum serratum (Linnaeus) Moon

Volkameria serrata Linnaeus, *Clerodendrum serratum* (Linnaeus) Sprengel
Clerodendrum divaricatum Jack
Clerodendrum herbaceum Wallich ex Schauer
Clerodendrum macrophyllum Sims
Clerodendrum ornatum Wallich ex Schauer
Clerodendrum ternifolium D. Don

CHEPANG *aabhang* TAMANG *bhusa noba*

Labiatae. Erect subshrub about 1.5 m high. Leaves stalked, opposite, 10–20 cm long, elliptic to oblong, distantly serrate. Flowers bluish white in terminal panicles. Fruit a drupe, obovoid, dark purple when ripe. Flowers May–August, fruits September–November. Propagated by seeds or stem cuttings. Distributed throughout Nepal at 400–1600 m; also in India, Sri Lanka, and Indo-China.

MEDICINE. Juice of the root is given in cases of fever. Shepherds and woodcutters apply the juice of the leaf as an antileech medicine.

Clerodendrum viscosum Ventenat

Clerodendrum castaneaefolium Klotzsch
Clerodendrum infortunatum Linnaeus, *Volkameria infortunata* (Linnaeus) Roxburgh

CHEPANG *bhantilo, pairalo, sarendra, saringro* DANUWAR *bhanti* ENGLISH *glory tree, Turk's turban* GURUNG *daphre, ghancharich, ghatu* MAGAR *bhanti* MOOSHAR *bhaint* NEPALI *bagan, bhat, bhote, chatu, ghantosari, mosane, tite* RAUTE *titya* THARU *bhanth, dhusi*

Labiatae. Deciduous shrub about 2 m high. Leaves stalked, opposite, 7–19 cm long, 3.5–16 cm wide, broadly ovate, acuminate, obscurely denticulate, hairy. Flowers

Clerodendrum viscosum

ery. Flowers white, fragrant, March–July. Fruits September–November. Propagated by seeds. Distributed in western and central Nepal at 1400–2000 m; also in northern India, southeastern Tibet, western China, and northern Myanmar.

MEDICINE. Juice of the bark is applied to cuts and wounds.

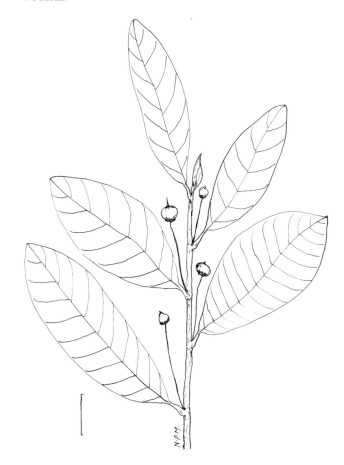

Cleyera japonica

stalked, white, tinged with red. Fruit a drupe, globose, bluish black, enclosed in the leathery calyx. Flowers March–June, fruits July–November. Propagated by seeds or stem cuttings. Distributed throughout Nepal to about 1500 m; also in India, Sri Lanka, China, Myanmar, and Malaysia.

FOOD. Leaves are used as a potherb.

MEDICINE. The root is antiperiodic, vermifuge, and laxative. A paste of the root and leaf is applied for skin diseases. Juice of the root is given to remove worms from the stomachs of animals. The slender stem is used as a toothbrush to relieve toothaches. Juice of the leaf is emetic and has anthelmintic value, too. It is put in cuts and wounds to kill germs. This juice is applied externally to rid livestock of lice. Raizada and Saxena (1978) reported from India that the juice is given for fever and applied to scorpion bites. The juice is dripped into the eyes of cattle with conjunctivitis.

Cleyera japonica Thunberg

Cleyera ochnacea de Candolle
Cleyera ochnacea var. *wallichiana* de Candolle
Ternstroemia lushia Buchanan-Hamilton ex D. Don, *Cleyera ochnacea* var. *lushia* (Buchanan-Hamilton ex D. Don) Dyer
NEPALI *bakal pate*

Theaceae. Tree about 5 m high. Leaves stalked, 2.5–15 cm long, 1.5–5.8 cm wide, elliptic, acuminate, entire, leath-

Clinopodium piperitum (D. Don) Press

Thymus piperitus D. Don, *Satureja piperita* (D. Don) Briquet
Thymus origanifolius D. Don
Clinopodium longicaule Wallich ex Bentham, *Calamintha longicaule* (Wallich ex Bentham) Bentham, *Melissa longicaule* (Wallich ex Bentham) Bentham, *Satureja longicaulis* (Wallich ex Bentham) Banerji
NEPALI *piparmint*

Labiatae. Hairy herb. Leaves stalked, elliptic or lanceolate, entire or crenate, gland-dotted and glabrous beneath, base cuneate. Flowers violet in lax whorls, February–May. Propagated by seeds. Distributed in eastern and central Nepal at 1200–2700 m in moist places; also in Pakistan and India.

MEDICINE. Juice of the leaf is mixed with hot water and the vapor is inhaled to relieve cough and colds.

Clinopodium umbrosum (Marschall von Bieberstein) K. Koch

Melissa umbrosa Marschall von Bieberstein, *Calamintha umbrosa* (Marschall von Bieberstein) Fischer & Meyer
Clinopodium repens Roxburgh, *Melissa repens* (Roxburgh) Bentham, *Thymus repens* (Roxburgh) D. Don
NEPALI *bilajor*

Labiatae. Herb. Leaves stalked, 1.5–3 cm long, 0.5–2 cm wide, ovate, serrate, base rounded or truncate. Flowers pink in axillary and terminal whorls. Fruit a nutlet, subglobose. Flowers and fruits March–October. Propagated by seeds. Distributed throughout Nepal at 180–3400 m in moist places; also in Iran, Afghanistan, Pakistan, India, Bhutan, Sri Lanka, Tibet, China, Taiwan, Myanmar, and Malaysia.

MEDICINE. Juice of the leaf is applied to cuts and wounds.

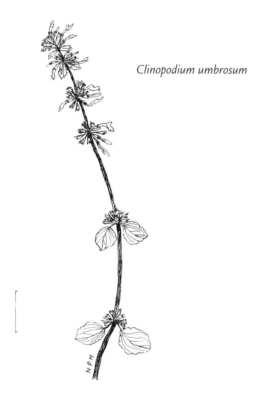

Clinopodium umbrosum

Clintonia udensis Trautvetter & Meyer

Smilacina alpina Royle, *Clintonia alpina* (Royle) Kunth
SHERPA *re chhema*

Convallariaceae. Perennial herb about 1 m high, rootstock creeping. Leaves sessile, oblanceolate, cuspidate, glabrous. Flowers white in terminal racemes, May–June. Propagated by seeds or tubers. Distributed throughout Nepal at 3200–4000 m along the edges of dense forest; also in northern India, western China, and northern Myanmar.

FOOD. Tender shoots and leaves are cooked as a vegetable.

Clintonia udensis

Clitoria ternatea Linnaeus

Ternatea vulgaris Humboldt
ENGLISH *conch-shell flower* NEPALI *aparijita*

Leguminosae. Scandent vine. Leaves stalked, pinnate, leaflets 1.5–4.5 cm long, 0.8–3 cm wide, elliptic to oblong, obtuse, tip needle-like. Flowers solitary, blue with white or yellowish center. Fruit a pod, flat, 6- to 10-seeded. Flowers and fruits November–March. Propagated by seeds. Distributed throughout Nepal to about 250 m in hedges and thickets; also in Pakistan, India, Sri Lanka, Thailand, and South America.

FOOD. Mooshars cook young pods as a vegetable.

MEDICINE. The root is considered diuretic and aperient. A decoction of the root is taken in cases of bronchitis. It is also considered useful for cough and colds. A paste of the leaf is used as a poultice for swollen joints. Juice of the leaf is warmed and applied externally around the ear to treat earaches. Seeds are considered anthelmintic and have emetic, purgative, diuretic, and laxative properties.

Coccinia grandis (Linnaeus) Voigt

Bryonia grandis Linnaeus
Coccinia cordifolia Cogniaux
Coccinia indica Wight & Arnott, *Cephalandra indica* (Wight & Arnott) Naudin
DANUWAR *tilkor* ENGLISH *ivy gourd* MAJHI *tilkot, tilkuti*
MOOSHAR *tilkor* NEPALI *kundri* SATAR *tilkocha*

Cucurbitaceae. Climbing herb. Leaves stalked, alternate, 4–4.5 cm long, 5–5.5 cm wide, generally five-lobed, glandular, margin irregular, base cordate. Flowers stalked, axillary, white. Fruit oblong, red when ripe. Flowers and fruits July–November. Propagated by seeds. Distributed

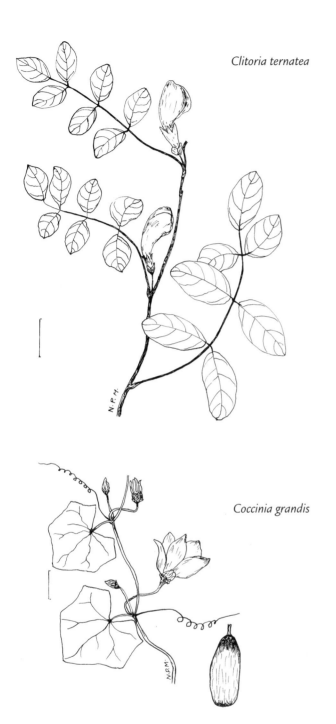

Clitoria ternatea

Coccinia grandis

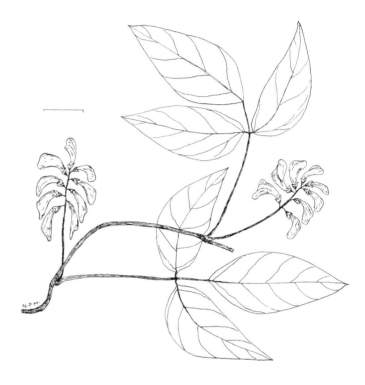

Cochlianthus gracilis

pink in drooping racemes, July–August. Propagated by seeds. Distributed in central Nepal at 1800–2000 m in open places along the margins of forests; also in India, Bhutan, and western China.

MEDICINE. A paste of the bark is applied to boils, pimples, and muscular swellings.

Cocos nucifera Linnaeus

BHOJPURI *nariyar* CHEPANG *nariwal* DANUWAR *nariwal*
ENGLISH *coconut* LEPCHA *naryol* LIMBU *nariyalse* MAGAR *nariwal*
MOOSHAR *gari* NEPALI *nariyal* NEWARI *naikya* RAI *chhudaomsai*
SUNWAR *narwal* TAMANG *nariwal* THARU *gari*

Palmae. Palm about 20 m high with a crown of feather-like leaves at the top. Leaves stalked, 2–5 m long, pinnate, leaflets sessile, 0.3–1.5 m long, wide at the base, with sacking-like tissue attached to the margin. Male and female flowers in the same inflorescence, yellowish, protected by a boat-shaped sheath when young. Fruit a drupe, ovoid. Seeds surrounded by a dense protecting layer of coir, the external layer hard. Propagated by seeds. Distributed throughout Nepal to about 500 m, cultivated.

FOOD. The tender fruit is in demand for its juice, which provides a refreshing and delicious drink. Mature fruits are eaten fresh or dried for future use.

OTHER USES. Leaves are made into mats, fans, and bags. Fiber from the fruits is made into cushions and beds. The hard cover of the fruit is used as bowls.

throughout Nepal to about 1400 m in moist, neglected places, especially on hedges; also pantropical.

FOOD. Tender leaves and shoots are used as a potherb. Ripe fruits are edible.

MEDICINE. The plant is considered good for diabetes. Juice of the stem is dripped into the eyes to treat cataract.

Cochlianthus gracilis Bentham

NEPALI *khasre lahara*

Leguminosae. Twining herb. Leaves stalked, trifoliolate, leaflets ovate, acuminate, entire, pubescent. Flowers

Coelogyne corymbosa Lindley
NEWARI *tuyu kenbu swan*

Orchidaceae. Epiphytic orchid with a short pseudobulb. Leaves sessile, paired, 10–20 cm long, elliptic to lanceolate. Flowers white, fragrant, in a raceme, March–April. Propagated by rhizome cuttings. Distributed in eastern Nepal at 2200–2800 m in sunny places; also in India, Bhutan, southeastern Tibet, and western China.

MEDICINE. Paste of the pseudobulb is applied to the forehead to relieve headache.

Coelogyne cristata Lindley
Cymbidium speciosissimum D. Don
CHEPANG *ban maiser, jhyaupate* NEPALI *chandi gabha*
TAMANG *syabal*

Orchidaceae. Epiphytic orchid. Pseudobulbs oblong, two-leaved. Leaves sessile, lanceolate, acuminate. Flowers white, fragrant, February–March. Propagated by root offshoots. Distributed throughout Nepal at 1000–2000 m on mossy rocks, and tree trunks and branches; also in northern India.

MEDICINE. Juice of the pseudobulb is applied to boils. This juice is also put in wounds on the hooves of animals.

Coelogyne flaccida Lindley
NEPALI *thur gava*

Orchidaceae. Epiphytic orchid with an ovoid to cylindrical pseudobulb 5–15 cm long, sheath papery at the base. Leaves 10–15 cm long, narrowly oblong, pointed. Flowers white in pendulous clusters, April–May. Propagated by seeds. Distributed in central Nepal at 900–2000 m as an epiphyte on trees; also in India and Bhutan.

MEDICINE. Paste of the pseudobulb is applied to the forehead to treat headache, and the juice is taken for indigestion.

Coelogyne flavida Hooker fil. ex Lindley
GURUNG *liso* NEPALI *thurgaujo*

Orchidaceae. Epiphytic orchid. Pseudobulbs ovoid, on a stout rhizome. Leaves in pairs, stalked, 13–20 cm long, 1.5–2 cm wide, oblong to lanceolate, acuminate. Flowers yellow in terminal racemes, May–June. Fruits October–November. Propagated by root offshoots. Distributed in eastern and central Nepal at 1000–2000 m on trees; also in northern India.

MEDICINE. A paste of the pseudobulb is applied to treat backaches.

Coelogyne ochracea Lindley
Coelogyne nitida Lindley
Cymbidium nitidum Wallich ex D. Don
CHEPANG *bhyau pat* ENGLISH *silver orchid* GURUNG *salidha, sanit*
NEPALI *chandi gabha, para phul*

Orchidaceae. Epiphytic orchid. Pseudobulbs oblong.

Leaves sessile, elliptic to lanceolate, entire. Flowers white with dark brown center, on lax racemes, June–July. Propagated by root offshoots. Distributed throughout Nepal at 1300–2400 m on trees; also in northern India, Bhutan, and Myanmar.

MEDICINE. Juice of the pseudobulbs is taken in cases of stomachache.

*Coelogyne
ochracea*

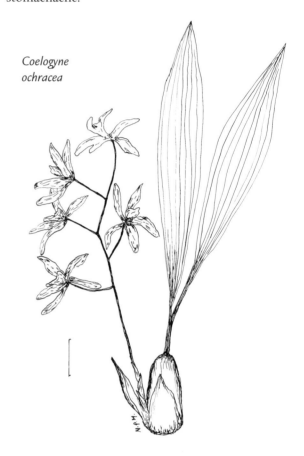

Coix lachryma-jobi Linnaeus
DANUWAR *pitunja, takatoiy, taktriya* ENGLISH *Job's tears,
pearl barley* NEPALI *bhirkaulo, chuis, jabe, lahare chuchcho, lai tuto*
NEWARI *gai pu ya haga* TAMANG *tanki sun*

Gramineae. Stout perennial grass about 2 m high. Leaves lanceolate, acuminate, margin wavy, base cordate. Inflorescence greenish, the racemes fascicled. Fruit a grain. Flowers July–November, fruits December–January. Propagated by seeds or root offshoots. Distributed throughout Nepal to about 2000 m in open, sunny places; also in Pakistan, India, Bhutan, Sri Lanka, Myanmar, and Thailand.

FOOD. The grains serve as a food item for humans.

MEDICINE. The root is boiled with water about 10 minutes and the strained liquid taken as an anthelmintic. The grains are refrigerant, and their paste is used for diarrhea, rheumatism, and bronchitis. Pounded grains, about 2 teaspoons three times a day, is given in cases of urinary trouble.

Coix lachryma-jobi

4 teaspoons twice a day, is given in cases of indigestion. It is also given for fever.

Juice of the leaf is given to treat fever and is applied to the forehead to relieve headaches. It is also applied to wounds to act as an antiseptic. The juice, about 4 teaspoons, is given as an anthelmintic. It is also dripped into the eyes of cattle to treat conjunctivitis. A paste of the leaves is given to treat dysentery. Leaf hairs are put on fresh cuts to stop bleeding and to help heal the wound quickly. Juice of the immature inflorescence, about 6 teaspoons twice a day, is given to treat gastric troubles and is also put in the nose in cases of sinusitis.

OTHER USES. The plant is lopped for fodder. Dried branches are collected for fuel. The inflorescence is sold in urban markets for worshiping during January and February when other flowers are scarce.

Colebrookea oppositifolia

OTHER USES. The grains are used as decorative beads. Leaves and stems are considered good cattle fodder.

Colebrookea oppositifolia Smith

Elsholtzia oppositifolia (Smith) Poiret
Colebrookea ternifolia Roxburgh

CHEPANG *kaichak, noryak, ryak dhyak* DANUWAR *dhursil*
ENGLISH *squirrel's tail, woolly mint* GURUNG *dhursule, hogatani, monjini* MAGAR *bhutra, dhursi* MAJHI *bhutra, dhurseli*
NEPALI *bhogate, dhulsu, dhurseto, dhursi, dhursil, dhusure, dhusyaurli*
SHERPA *nemung* TAMANG *bodebade, bosyol syule, busul sul, koter, libogta, pote pote* THARU *dahi gwala, dhurseta*

Labiatae. Hoary shrub about 3 m high. Leaves stalked, opposite, crowded at the ends of branches, 6–23 cm long, 1.5–9.5 cm wide, oblong to lanceolate, softly pubescent on both surfaces. Flowers small, whitish, densely whorled in panicled spikes, December–February. Fruits March–April. Propagated by seeds. Distributed throughout Nepal to about 1800 m in open, dry, rocky places; also in northern India, Bhutan, southwestern China, and Indo-China.

MEDICINE. Juice of the root is given for epilepsy. This juice, about 2 teaspoons twice a day, is given when blood comes up during cough. The root is boiled with water for 10 minutes, and about 3 teaspoons of the filtered water is given as an anthelmintic. An infusion, about 6 teaspoons three times a day, is given for peptic ulcer. A paste of the root relieves sprain and body pain. Juice of the bark, about

Coleus barbatus (Andrews) Bentham

Plectranthus barbatus Andrews
Plectranthus forskahlaei Aiton, *Coleus forskohlii* Briquet
NEPALI *gandhe jhar*

Labiatae. Perennial herb about 75 cm high. Leaves short-stalked, ovate to oblong, teeth rounded. Flowers pale blue in spikes forming a whorl, September–October. Propagated by seeds or suckers. Distributed throughout Nepal at 1000–2500 m in openings of pine forest; also in western Asia, northern India, Bhutan, Sri Lanka, East Africa, and Madagascar.

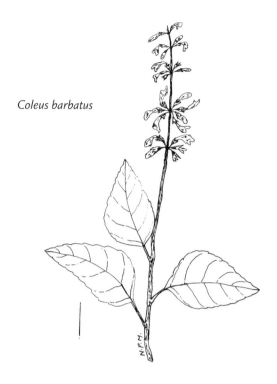

Coleus barbatus

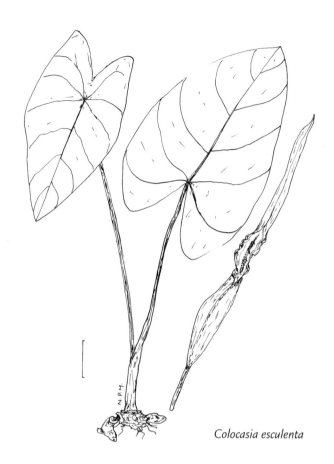

Colocasia esculenta

FOOD. Powdered nutlets are added as flavoring to pickles and roasted foods.

Colocasia esculenta (Linnaeus) Schott

Arum esculentum Linnaeus
Caladium nymphaeafolium Ventenat, *Arum nymphaeifolium* (Ventenat) Roxburgh
Colocasia antiquorum Schott

BHOJPURI *arui, kachchu* CHEPANG *gu* DANUWAR *karkalo, pidalu* ENGLISH *arum, cocoyam, taro* GURUNG *tayo* LEPCHA *slankrilop* LIMBU *yakkhe, yakla* MAGAR *hyak, karkalo* NEPALI *karkalo, pindalu* NEWARI *phakan, saki* RAI *yaksi, yaksitan* SATAR *kanchu* SUNWAR *kagi, raglo* TAMANG *bhangtya, tayabha, tiya* THARU *danth, ghuiya*

Araceae. Rhizomatous herb, rootstock tuberous. Leaves long-stalked, triangular ovate, dark green, blades about 60 cm wide, attached in the middle to the stout leaf stalk. Inflorescence short-stalked, solitary. Spathe yellowish, persistent tube constricted at the mouth. Flowers August–September. Propagated by rhizome bulbils. Distributed throughout Nepal to about 1300 m on moist ground, cultivated; also in Afghanistan, Pakistan, India, and Sri Lanka, and generally in areas with hot climates.

FOOD. The starchy and tuberous rhizomes are edible. Leaves are used as a vegetable.

Colquhounia coccinea Wallich

Colquhounia mollis Schlechtendal

CHEPANG *goikurut* NEPALI *dhuchu, phulpat, phultiso, sano tusare, jhip jhip* TAMANG *kada, kasi, khudu, kurasign, laknda, mrancha, nyakar*

Labiatae. Shrub about 3 m high. Leaves stalked, opposite, 3.5–16.5 cm long, 2.5–7.5 cm wide, ovate, acuminate,

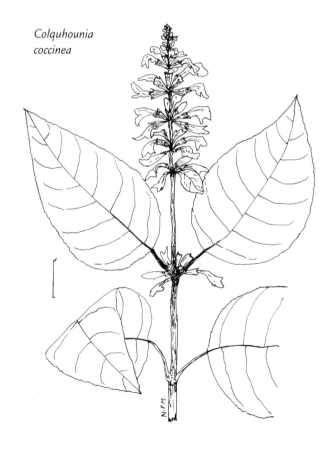

Colquhounia coccinea

dentate or crenate, sparsely tomentose with stellate hairs, base rounded or more or less cordate. Flowers red, whorled in an axillary or terminal spike. Fruit a nutlet, oblong, the compressed tip expanded into a wing. Flowers August–October. Propagated by seeds or cuttings. Distributed throughout Nepal at 1000–2600 m in open, rocky places; also in India, Bhutan, and China.

FOOD. Nectar in the corolla tubes is sucked by village children.

OTHER USES. Leaves and flowers are used in incense. The plant is gathered for fodder.

Combretum roxburghii Sprengel

Combretum decandrum Roxburgh
CHEPANG *dars* MAGAR *jhyaringe* NEPALI *arthunge, thakaule*

Combretaceae. Straggling shrub. Leaves stalked, opposite, 6–18 cm long, 3–8.5 cm wide, oblong to elliptic, entire, glabrous, tip acute or pointed, narrowed toward the base. Flowers greenish white, April–September. Fruits October–January. Propagated by seeds. Distributed throughout Nepal at 200–600 m, common in mixed *Shorea robusta* forest; also in Pakistan, India, western China, and Indo-China.

MEDICINE. Juice of the leaf is applied to wounds between the toes caused by walking barefooted in muddy water, especially during rice planting.

OTHER USES. The plant is lopped for fodder.

Combretum wallichii de Candolle

Combretum chinense Roxburgh
GURUNG *madini*

Combretaceae. Shrub about 6 m high. Leaves stalked, 2.5–16 cm long, 2–9.5 cm wide, elliptic to ovate, entire. Flowers greenish yellow in racemes, April–June. Fruits August–November. Propagated by seeds. Distributed in eastern and central Nepal at 900–1700 m on open ground near rivers; also in India and Bhutan.

MEDICINE. A paste of the seeds is taken in cases of cough and colds.

Commelina benghalensis Linnaeus

ENGLISH *day flower* NEPALI *ban kane, kane jhar* RAUTE *kanema* THARU *kaniya* TAMANG *makai mhendo*

Commelinaceae. Prostrate annual herb. Leaves short-stalked or sessile, 1–10 cm long, 1–4.5 cm wide, elliptic to ovate, entire, parallel veined, more or less succulent, sheathing at the base. Flowers stalked, blue, one to three from each spathe. Fruit a capsule, pear shaped. Flowers and fruits April–October. Propagated by seeds. Distributed throughout Nepal at 900–2000 m in moist places; also in India, eastern China, Japan, Malaysia, the Philippines, and Africa.

FOOD. Young leaves are eaten as a vegetable.

MEDICINE. A paste of the plant is applied to treat burns. Juice of the root, about 2 teaspoons four times a day, is given in cases of indigestion.

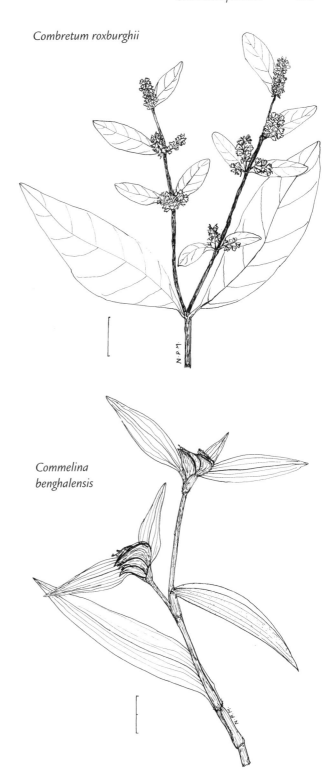

Combretum roxburghii

Commelina benghalensis

Commelina paludosa Blume

Commelina donii A. Dietrich
Commelina obliqua Buchanan-Hamilton ex D. Don,
  Heterocarpus obliquus (Buchanan-Hamilton ex D. Don) Hasskarl
NEPALI *buki*

Commelinaceae. Herb. Leaves 3–7 cm long, 0.8–1.5 cm wide, spatulate, linear. Flowers blue. Flowers and fruits

July–August. Propagated by seeds. Distributed throughout Nepal at 300–3500 m in moist places; also in India, Sri Lanka, Taiwan, and Southeast Asia.

FOOD. The root is boiled and cooked as a vegetable.

Convolvulus arvensis Linnaeus

NEPALI *halinkhur*

Convolvulaceae. Creeping herb. Leaves short-stalked, ovate to lanceolate, base hastate. Flowers pale purple or lilac in cymes. Fruit a capsule, ovoid, glabrous with persistent calyx. Flowers and fruits March–September. Propagated by seeds. Distributed in western and central Nepal at 2600–4100 m in open, dry places; also in temperate regions of the world.

MEDICINE. Juice of the root is given in cases of fever.

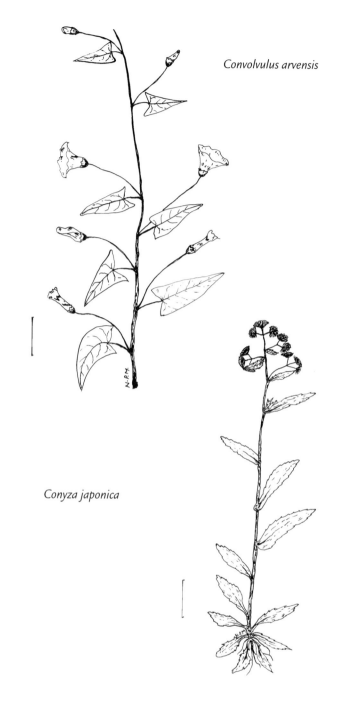

Convolvulus arvensis

Conyza japonica

Conyza bonariensis (Linnaeus) Cronquist

Erigeron bonariensis Linnaeus
Erigeron linifolius Willdenow
DANUWAR *ganhiya*

Compositae. Stout, hirsute herb about 1 m high, stem leafy. Leaves sessile, 5–6.5 cm long, narrowly linear, serrate. Flowers yellowish. Fruit an achene, sparsely silky. Propagated by seeds. Distributed in western and central Nepal at 1400–2800 m as a garden escape or weed; pantropical.

MEDICINE. Juice of the plant is applied to wounds.

Conyza japonica (Roxburgh) Lessing ex de Candolle

Erigeron japonicum Thunberg, *Eschenbachia japonica* (Thunberg) Koster
Conyza multicaulis de Candolle
Conyza stricta Wallich, not Willdenow
Conyza veronicaefolia Wallich ex de Candolle
NEPALI *salaha jhar*

Compositae. Erect herb about 1 m high. Leaves sessile, alternate, oblong to lanceolate, serrate or crenate, villous on both surfaces. Flower heads white, globose. Fruit an achene, compressed, nearly glabrous. Flowers and fruits March–July. Propagated by seeds. Distributed throughout Nepal at 600–2600 m in open places; also in Afghanistan, Pakistan, India, China, Taiwan, Southeast Asia, the Philippines, and Japan.

MEDICINE. Juice of the plant is applied to cuts and wounds.

OTHER USES. Flower heads are used to make *marcha*, a fermenting cake from which liquor is distilled.

Conyza stricta Willdenow

TAMANG *thangsing*

Compositae. Erect herb. Leaves sessile, linear, ovate, irregularly dentate, pubescent on both surfaces. Flower heads yellow in corymbs. Fruit an achene, compressed. Flowers and fruits January–November. Propagated by

seeds. Distributed throughout Nepal at 600–2000 m in open places; also in India, China, Myanmar, and Africa.

MEDICINE. Juice of the root, about 2 teaspoons three times a day, is given in cases of diarrhea and dysentery.

Corallodiscus lanuginosus (Wallich ex de Candolle) B. L. Burtt

Didymocarpus lanuginosus Wallich ex de Candolle, *Didissandra lanuginosus* (Wallich ex de Candolle) C. B. Clarke
TAMANG *dowar*

Gesneriaceae. Trailing herb. Leaves all basal, spreading, ovate or elliptic, obtuse, crenate, hairy on both surfaces, base attenuate. Flowers violet in terminal cymes. Propagated by seeds or by splitting the root offshoots. Distributed throughout Nepal at 1000–3400 m on rocks and in rocky places; also in northern India and Bhutan.

MEDICINE. Juice of the plant is applied to treat measles.

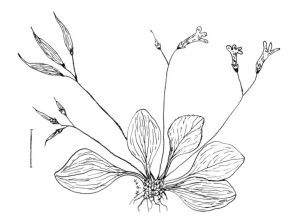

Corallodiscus lanuginosus

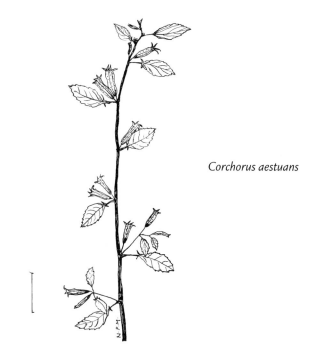

Corchorus aestuans

Corchorus aestuans Linnaeus

Corchorus acutangulus Lamarck
Corchorus fuscus Roxburgh
CHEPANG *lendro* NEPALI *balu jhar, patoi*

Tiliaceae. Shrub. Leaves stalked, ovate to oblong, hairy. Flowers yellow. Flowers and fruits August–October. Propagated by seeds. Distributed in eastern and central Nepal at 400–1000 m on uncultivated land; also pantropical.

FOOD. Tender shoots and leaves are cooked as a vegetable.

MEDICINE. Juice of the root is valued in treating malarial fever.

OTHER USES. Bark from the stem is used to make rope.

Corchorus capsularis Linnaeus

Corchorus maruwa Buchanan-Hamilton
ENGLISH *jute* NEPALI *jut*

Tiliaceae. Erect annual shrub. Leaves stalked, 1–12 cm long, 1.3–3.5 cm wide, ovate to lanceolate. Flowers yellow. Fruit a capsule. Flowers and fruits September–October. Propagated by seeds. Distributed in eastern and central Nepal to about 1200 m, cultivated; also in India and Bangladesh, and cultivated in most tropical countries.

FOOD. Young leaves are eaten as a vegetable.

OTHER USES. Stem bark yields fiber.

Cordia dichotoma Forster fil.

Cordia indica Lamarck
Cordia myxa Linnaeus
ENGLISH *clammy cherry, Indian cherry* NEPALI *bohori, bori*

Boraginaceae. Tree about 15 m high. Leaves stalked, alternate, elliptic to ovate, margin entire or undulate, tip pointed, base rounded. Flowers yellowish in lax panicles. Fruit a drupe, ovoid, yellowish, pulp scanty and stone hard. Flowers March–April, fruits April–June. Propagated by seeds. Distributed in central and eastern Nepal at 300–1400 m; also in western Asia, Pakistan, India, Sri Lanka, eastward to China, southern Taiwan, the Philippines, southern Japan, Polynesia, and Australia.

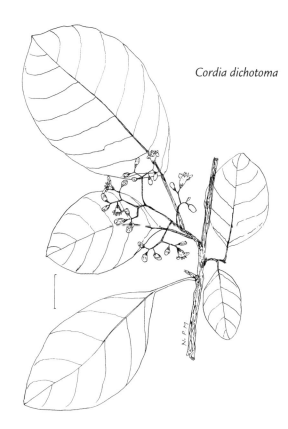

Cordia dichotoma

FOOD. Young leaves and shoots are cooked as a vegetable. Fruits are eaten fresh, and immature ones are pickled.

MEDICINE. Juice of the bark, about 4 teaspoons four times a day, is taken in cases of fever. Juice of the leaf is applied to the forehead to relieve headaches.

OTHER USES. Wood is used for agricultural implements. Fiber from stem bark is used to make twine and cordage.

Coriandrum sativum Linnaeus

BHOJPURI *dhaniya* DANUWAR *dhaniya* ENGLISH coriander GURUNG *dhaniya* LEPCHA *uchung* MAGAR *dhaniya* MOOSHAR *dhaniya* NEPALI *dhaniya* NEWARI *gosangn* RAI *bopchukuksun* SUNWAR *dhaniya* TAMANG *brasyal, dhaniya dhap* THARU *dhaniya* TIBETAN *u-su*

Umbelliferae. Strongly scented annual herb. Leaves pinnate, lower leaflets ovate, lobed, crenate, upper leaflets linear. Flowers white or pinkish in compound umbels. Fruit globose. Flowers and fruits December–April. Propagated by seeds. Distributed throughout Nepal to about 3000 m, cultivated; also in most parts of the world.

FOOD. Dried fruitlets are widely used as a spice and condiment.

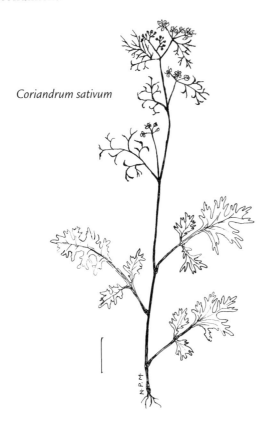

Coriandrum sativum

Coriaria napalensis Wallich

CHEPANG *daurasai, masini* GURUNG *hakupaku, machheno, masyene, unsi* MAGAR *majena* NEPALI *machaino, machhino* SHERPA *aaba* TAMANG *hakupaku, jharose, kaga* TIBETAN *chyarcha*

Coriariaceae. Tree about 5 m high. Leaves subsessile, opposite, 2–10 cm long, 1.5–4 cm wide, oblong to ovate or lanceolate, short-pointed, entire, three-veined, smooth. Flowers sessile, reddish. Fruit black when ripe. Flowers February–March, fruits May–June. Propagated by seeds or stem cuttings. Distributed throughout Nepal at 1000–2800 m in open or shady places; also in northern India, Bhutan, western China, and northern Myanmar.

FOOD. Ripe fruits are eaten fresh.

MEDICINE. Juice of the bark, about 4 teaspoons twice a day, is given in cases of stomachache.

OTHER USES. The wood contains tannin. Branches are used for making baskets. Leaves are poisonous to cattle if eaten in large amounts.

Coriaria napalensis

Cornus capitata Wallich

Benthamia capitata (Wallich) Nakai, *Benthamidia capitata* (Wallich) Hara, *Dendrobenthamia capitata* (Wallich) Hutchinson
Benthamia fragifera Lindley
ENGLISH *Bentham's cornel, dogwood, strawberry tree* NEPALI *damaru, dimmar* TAMANG *bulno*

Cornaceae. Deciduous tree about 10 m high, bark grayish brown. Leaves stalked, opposite, 4–9 cm long, 1.2–3 cm wide, oblong or elliptic, leathery, pale beneath. Flowers yellowish, closely packed in the head. Fruits coalesced into a fleshy strawberry-like head. Flowers April–October, fruits November–January. Propagated by seeds. Distributed throughout Nepal at 1700–2600 m, generally on moist hillsides; also in northern India, Bhutan, western and central China, and northern Indo-China.

FOOD. Fruits are red when ripe and are eaten fresh. They are also brewed to distill alcohol.

OTHER USES. Wood is mainly used for fuel.

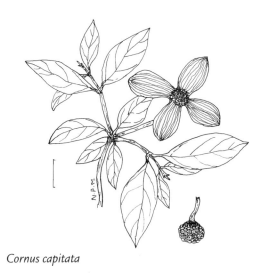

Cornus capitata

Cornus oblonga Wallich

Swida oblonga (Wallich) Soják
Cornus paniculata Buchanan-Hamilton ex D. Don
CHEPANG *sain su sing* NEPALI *chhepasi, daru kath, lato kath, tite*
TAMANG *wa binyauli* TIBETAN *pruna*

Cornaceae. Tree about 10 m high. Leaves short-stalked, 4–16 cm long, 1–5 cm wide, oblong, acuminate, entire, glabrous above, minutely hairy beneath. Flowers white in terminal compound cymes, February–September. Fruits August–September. Propagated by seeds. Distributed throughout Nepal at 1200–2500 m, in forests, mixed with

Cornus oblonga

other species; also in northern India, Bhutan, southern Tibet, western and central China, and Indo-China.

FOOD. Ripe fruits are eaten fresh.

OTHER USES. The plant is lopped for fodder.

Cortia depressa (D. Don) C. Norman

Athamanta depressa D. Don
Cortia nepalensis C. Norman
Cortia lindleyi de Candolle, *Schulzia lindlei* Wallich
NEPALI *bhutkesh* TIBETAN *chynman*

Umbelliferae. Deeply rooted herb. Leaves subsessile, bi- or tripinnate, ultimate segments linear lanceolate, glabrous. Flowers white in an umbel. Fruit compressed. Flowers and fruits July–September. Propagated by seeds. Distributed throughout Nepal at 3300–4500 m in open places; also in northern India, Bhutan, and Tibet.

FOOD. Tender leaves are cooked as a leafy vegetable. Fruitlets are used as a substitute for cumin (*Cuminum cyminum*).

MEDICINE. The root is valued medicinally in folk medicine. Juice of the root, about 2 teaspoons three times a day, is given in cases of fever.

Cortia depressa

Corydalis chaerophylla de Candolle

GURUNG *begar mai* NEPALI *karme jhar, okhre ghans, pahenli, pile*

Fumariaceae. Herb about 1 m high. Cauline leaves pinnate, leaflets pinnatifid, lobes incised, serrate, acute. Flowers yellow in axillary or terminal many-flowered racemes or panicles. Fruit a capsule, ellipsoidal. Flowers July–August, fruits November–December. Propagated by seeds or root offshoots. Distributed throughout Nepal at 2000–4000 m along streams in shady places; also in the Kumaon region of Uttar Pradesh, India, west of Nepal, and Bhutan.

MEDICINE. Juice of the root is mixed with juice of the root of *Cyathula tomentosa* in equal amount, and the mixture is given in doses of about 6 teaspoons three times a day for indigestion and fever. It is also applied to boils. Juice of the plant, about 6 teaspoons three times a day, is given in cases of peptic ulcer.

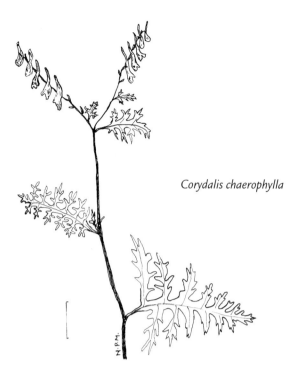

Corydalis chaerophylla

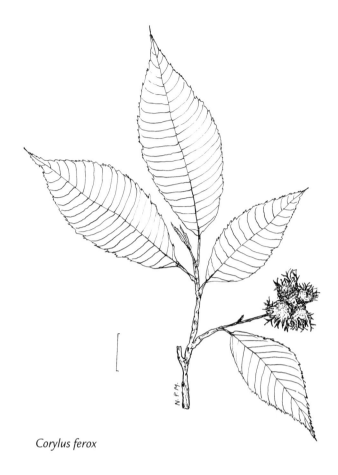

Corylus ferox

Corylus ferox Wallich

NEPALI *lekh katus*

Betulaceae. Tree about 10 m high, young shoots appressed, silky pubescent. Leaves stalked, 4.5–16 cm long, 2.5–7.5 cm wide, elliptic to ovate, acuminate, finely serrate, sparsely pubescent above, glandular hairy, pubescent beneath. Flowers yellowish. Fruit a nut, ovoid, in dense clusters, slightly compressed. Flowers November–December. Propagated by seeds. Distributed in eastern and central Nepal at 2600–3200 m in forest openings; also in northern India, Bhutan, Tibet, western China, and northern Myanmar.

FOOD. The cotyledons are edible.

Costus speciosus (Koenig) Smith

Banksea speciosa Koenig
Costus nepalensis Roscoea
ENGLISH *spiral ginger, white ginger* GURUNG *belauri* NEPALI *betlauri*
TIBETAN *ru-rta*

Zingiberaceae. Herb about 2 m high, with stout stem and tuberous root. Leaves subsessile, spirally arranged, oblong, acuminate, softly pubescent on the lower surface. Flowers white in solitary terminal spikes. Fruit a capsule, ovoid, red, crowded by the persistent calyx. Propagated by splitting the rhizomes. Distributed throughout Nepal at 400–700 m in moist places; also in northern India south to Sri Lanka, Indo-China, Taiwan, Malaysia, and New Guinea.

FOOD. The tuberous roots are edible.

MEDICINE. The plant has antipyretic and diuretic properties. Roots are astringent, purgative, stimulant, digestive, anthelmintic, and aphrodisiac. Root juice is useful for fever, skin disease, worms, dyspepsia, indigestion,

Costus speciosus

cough, and colds. Root paste is applied to snakebites. Juice of the stem, about 4 teaspoons twice a day, is given for diarrhea and dysentery. It is also given in cases of urinary trouble.

OTHER USES. Leaves and stems contain tannin.

Cotoneaster acuminatus Lindley

Cotoneaster rotundifolia Wallich ex Lindley
NEPALI *dave phul, dhalke phul, rains*

Rosaceae. Shrub with shiny dark bluish gray bark. Leaves stalked, 1.5–7 cm long, 0.7–2.5 cm wide, ovate to lanceolate, acuminate, silky pubescent beneath, margin usually ciliate with silky hairs. Flowers white, solitary or in few-flowered axillary cymes. Fruit turbinate, red when ripe. Flowers May–June, fruits June–July. Propagated by seeds. Distributed throughout Nepal at 2500–3500 m on moist, open hillsides; also in northern India, Bhutan, Tibet, and western China.

OTHER USES. Wood is used for making walking sticks.

Cotoneaster acuminatus

Cotoneaster affinis Lindley

Mespilus affinis (Lindley) D. Don, *Cotoneaster frigidus* var. *affinis* (Lindley) Wenzing
NEPALI *kause phul*

Rosaceae. Deciduous shrub. Leaves stalked, elliptic to ovate, obtuse, entire, densely white woolly beneath when young. Flowers white. Fruit reddish. Flowers April–May. Propagated by seeds. Distributed in western and central Nepal at 2200–2800 m in open pastureland; also in Pakistan, India, Bhutan, southeastern Tibet, and western China.

MEDICINE. A paste of the root is applied to treat headaches, and the juice is given in cases of indigestion.

Cotoneaster frigidus Wallich ex Lindley

TIBETAN *chhar*

Rosaceae. Shrub about 5 m high. Leaves short-stalked, 1.5–9 cm long, 1–3.5 cm wide, oblong, acute or obtuse, apiculate, entire, gray tomentose beneath. Flowers white in axillary many-flowered corymbose cymes, June–July. Propagated by seeds. Distributed in western and central Nepal at 2200–3400 m in forest openings; also in northern India, Bhutan, southeastern Tibet, and China.

MEDICINE. Fruits are eaten to replenish blood in cases of deficiency.

Cotoneaster ludlowii Klotzsch

TIBETAN *chhar*

Rosaceae. Shrub about 2 m high. Leaves stalked, 1.5–2.5 cm long, narrowly elliptic, shaggy haired beneath, apex blunt or acute, base wedge shaped. Flowers numerous, white. Fruit red. Flowers May–June. Propagated by seeds. Distributed in western and central Nepal at 1900–4000 m in open places; also in India and Bhutan.

MEDICINE. Ripe fruits are eaten to relieve cough and colds.

Cotoneaster microphyllus Wallich ex Lindley

GURUNG *chyangra, chyar cham, chyengra* NEPALI *burchen, ghangharu, ghari* SHERPA *bharama, kyakpa, pelma* TAMANG *bhoibuju, tharme* TIBETAN *chhar, khenjagan sagnga*

Rosaceae. Much branched evergreen shrub. Leaves short-stalked, 0.3–1.5 cm long, 0.2–0.5 cm wide, ovate or elliptic, acute or obtuse, leathery, glossy dark green above. Flowers solitary, axillary, white. Fruit globose, scarlet when ripe. Flowers April–June, fruits July–August. Propagated by seeds. Distributed throughout Nepal at 1300–3500 m, trailing on grassy hillsides; also in northern India and southwestern China.

FOOD. Ripe fruits are eaten fresh and are watery in taste.

OTHER USES. Leaves are used for incense. In some mountainous regions, the branches are used to make baskets. The plant is used for fences and fuel. It is a good soil binder.

Cotula hemisphaerica (Roxburgh) Wallich ex C. B. Clarke

Artemisia hemisphaerica Roxburgh, *Machlis hemisphaerica* (Roxburgh) de Candolle
NEPALI *galphule*

Compositae. Diffuse annual herb, stem much branched, young branches cottony. Leaves stalked, 1–5 cm long, pinnatifid, segments linear lanceolate, entire, tip needle-like. Flower heads yellow, solitary, on short peduncles. Flowers and fruits January–April. Propagated by seeds. Distributed in central Nepal at 1400–1800 m in moist, open places; also in India and Bhutan.

Cotula hemisphaerica

MEDICINE. Juice of the plant, about 3 teaspoons three times a day, is given for fever. A paste is applied to the forehead to relieve headache.

Craniotome furcata (Link) Kuntze

Ajuga furcata Link
Anisomeles nepalensis Sprengel
Craniotome versicolor Reichenbach, *Nepeta versicolor* (Reichenbach) Treviranus
NEPALI *batuli silam, mirge jhar* TAMANG *umen*

Labiatae. Erect herb. Leaves stalked, 1.5 cm long, 0.7–7 cm wide, ovate, acuminate, densely hirsute, base cordate. Flowers white, pink at the tip, in small stalked cymes. Fruit a nutlet, ellipsoidal. Flowers and fruits June–November. Propagated by seeds. Distributed throughout Nepal at 1000–2400 m in open, moist places; also in Pakistan, northern India, Bhutan, southwestern China, and Indo-China.

MEDICINE. Juice of the plant is applied to cuts and wounds.

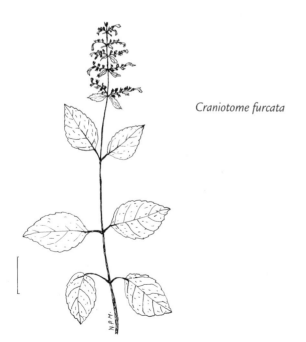

Craniotome furcata

Crassocephalum crepidioides (Bentham) S. Moore

Gynura crepidioides Bentham
CHEPANG *kaikalai, reckname, udumuntu* NEPALI *jhule jhar, namle jhar, salahako jhar, udho munto jhar* TAMANG *lodro, tabra, tirit noba*

Compositae. Erect herb about 75 cm high. Leaves stalked, alternate, 5–15 cm long, ovate to lanceolate, acuminate, margin lyrate or irregularly dentate, glabrous or slightly hairy, base narrowed. Flower heads orange, solitary, peduncle short. Flowers and fruits most of the year. Propagated by seeds. Distributed throughout Nepal at 400–2500 m in open, moist places; also pantropical.

MEDICINE. Juice of the plant is applied to wounds and is used to treat diarrhea.

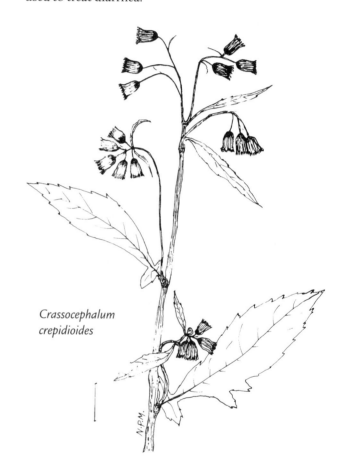

Crassocephalum crepidioides

Crateva unilocularis Buchanan-Hamilton

Crateva religiosa Forster fil.
ENGLISH *sacred garlic pear, three-leaved caper* NEPALI *barun, siplegan, siplekan* NEWARI *khaicho*

Capparaceae. Deciduous tree about 15 m high. Leaves long-stalked, alternate, trifoliolate, leaflets stalked, 5–14 cm long, 1.5–6 cm wide, ovate to lanceolate, acuminate, entire. Flowers stalked, white, fading to yellow, in dense terminal corymbs. Fruit globose, white-dotted with lenticels, fleshy. Flowers March–May, fruits May–October. Propagated by seeds. Distributed throughout Nepal to about 1500 m in open, rocky places; also in northern India, southeastern China, and Indo-China.

FOOD. Tender leaves and buds are boiled and squeezed to lessen the bitterness. They are then prepared as a vegetable or pickle.

MEDICINE. Bark is laxative, stomachic, antiperiodic, and tonic. Juice of the bark is taken to induce appetite and is used for stomachaches. This juice is also taken to decrease the secretion of bile and phlegm. It is also taken in cases of fever and for urinary complaints. Juice of the young leaf has anthelmintic value. A paste of the fruit is applied to treat smallpox.

OTHER USES. The wood is moderately hard and is used for poles and fuel. Bark contains tannin. The plant is lopped for fodder.

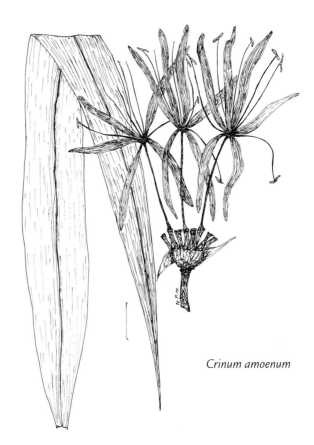

Crinum amoenum

Crateva unilocularis

Crinum amoenum Roxburgh ex Ker-Gawler

NEPALI *haddi jor, hare lasun*

Amaryllidaceae. Herb. Leaves sessile, 25–30 cm long, 2–3.4 cm wide, acuminate. Flowers white in three- to seven-flowered umbels, flowers May–June. Fruits July–August. Propagated by seeds. Distributed in central and eastern Nepal at 500–1700 m in rocky, open places; also in northern India and Myanmar.

MEDICINE. The rhizome is fed to cattle with dysentery.

Crotalaria alata Buchanan-Hamilton ex D. Don

Crotalaria bialata Schrank

CHEPANG *doni, segesai* NEPALI *boksibaja, chhimchhime, sing singe, thulo boksibaja, thulo chheke* TAMANG *sirongon* THARU *ban kurthi*

Leguminosae. Densely hairy subshrub about 1.5 m high, stems winged. Leaves subsessile, 2–10 cm long, 0.7–4.5 cm wide, thin, ovate or elliptic to oblong, acute, entire. Flowers stalked, yellow, in two- or three-flowered racemes. Fruit a pod, oblong, glabrous. Flowers and fruits July–December. Propagated by seeds. Distributed throughout Nepal to about 2000 m; also in northern India, Bhutan, China, and Southeast Asia.

MEDICINE. Juice of the root, about 2 teaspoons twice a day, is given to treat malarial fever and is also useful for bedwetting.

Crotalaria albida Heyne ex Roth

Crotalaria linifolia Linnaeus fil.

CHEPANG *bhuling, matuwa jhar* NEPALI *bhedi phul* RAUTE *kose*

Leguminosae. Diffuse herb about 1.5 m high. Leaves simple, sessile, 1.5–4.5 cm long, 0.2–1 cm wide, linear oblong, gland-dotted. Flowers pinkish yellow in a raceme. Fruit a pod, glabrous. Flowers March–October, fruits November–February. Propagated by seeds. Distributed throughout Nepal at 400–2200 m on open hillsides; also in northern India, Bhutan, China, Taiwan, and Southeast Asia.

MEDICINE. Juice of the root is given for indigestion. Juice of the plant, about 3 teaspoons, is given in cases of bedwetting. A paste of the plant is applied to treat warts, especially those on the sole of the foot.

Crotalaria cytisoides Roxburgh ex de Candolle

Priotropis cytisoides (Roxburgh ex de Candolle) Wight & Arnott
Crotalaria psoralioides D. Don
CHEPANG *naitak, tokale* NEPALI *bakhre ghans, silsile* TAMANG *nagan, ramlagan*

Leguminosae. Deciduous shrub about 2 m high. Leaves stalked, trifoliolate, leaflets 3–8 cm long, elliptic. Flowers yellowish in spike-like clusters. Fruit a pod, flattened, narrowed at both ends. Flowers August–September. Propagated by seeds. Distributed throughout Nepal at 1200–2200 m in open, rocky places; also in northern India, Bhutan, western China, and Myanmar.
OTHER USES. Goats browse the feathery leaves.

Crotalaria ferruginea Graham

CHEPANG *jungraban*

Leguminosae. Shrub. Leaves short-stalked, lanceolate, entire, tip rounded, glabrous above, appressed hairy beneath. Flowers yellowish. Propagated by seeds. Distributed in eastern and central Nepal at 1400–1900 m in open, sunny places; also in India, Sri Lanka, China, and Southeast Asia.
MEDICINE. Juice of the root, about 4 teaspoons three times a day, is given to treat fever.

Crotalaria juncea Linnaeus

ENGLISH *sun hemp* NEPALI *san*

Leguminosae. Shrub about 2 m high, young parts covered with golden yellow hairs. Leaves stalked, linear oblong. Flowers yellow in lateral and terminal racemes. Flowers and fruits September–October. Propagated by seeds. Distributed throughout Nepal to about 1300 m, cultivated; also in tropical regions.
FOOD. The flowers are pickled.
OTHER USES. The stem yields fiber good enough for commerce. Seeds are poisonous to livestock.

Crotalaria prostrata Rottbøll ex Willdenow

Crotalaria hirsuta Willdenow
CHEPANG *segemete* NEPALI *sano boksi baja, sano chheke*
TAMANG *brama, mankero*

Leguminosae. Shrub about 50 cm high, branches yellowish brown hairy. Leaves short-stalked, 1.3–4.5 cm long, 0.5–1.5 cm wide, ovate to oblong, entire, hairy and glandular punctate beneath. Flowers yellow in short, lax racemes. Fruit a pod, oblong. Flowers and fruits March–December. Propagated by seeds. Distributed throughout Nepal at 500–2000 m in open, sunny places; also in northern India, Sri Lanka, and Malaysia.

MEDICINE. Juice of the root, about 2 teaspoons twice a day, is given to treat fever. A paste of the plant is applied to treat gout and also used on cuts and wounds.

Crotalaria sessiliflora Linnaeus

Crotalaria anthylloides Lamarck
Crotalaria napalensis Link
CHEPANG *sokrok* TAMANG *setu phul, sikrebha*

Leguminosae. Erect herb about 60 cm high. Leaves stalked, stipulate, 2–10 cm long, 0.6–1.5 cm wide, oblong to lanceolate, minutely bristly. Flowers nearly sessile, bluish, the upper flowers in a raceme, lower flowers often axillary. Fruit a pod, oblong, glabrous. Flowers August–October, fruits November–December. Propagated by seeds. Distributed throughout Nepal at 200–2800 m in open, grassy places; also in northern India, Bhutan, China, Japan, Southeast Asia, the Philippines, and Java.
MEDICINE. A paste of the plant is used to treat headaches.

Crotalaria spectabilis Roth

Crotalaria leschenaultii de Candolle
Crotalaria retusa Linnaeus
Crotalaria sericea Retzius
NEPALI *bhuban jhar*

Leguminosae. Erect herb about 1.5 m high. Leaves stalked, 2.5–15 cm long, oblanceolate, pubescent beneath. Flowers yellow in terminal racemes. Fruit a pod, short-stalked, oblong. Flowers and fruits August–December. Propagated by seeds. Distributed in eastern and central Nepal to about 200 m in open places; also in the tropics.
FOOD. Flowers are cooked as a vegetable or pickled following boiling.

Crotalaria tetragona Andrews

CHEPANG *bhwan sak, chhan goi* MAGAR *bhwagan*
NEPALI *bhugan, mongan*

Leguminosae. Stiff shrub about 2 m high. Leaves linear or lanceolate, acuminate, membranous, glabrescent. Flowers yellow in a raceme. Fruit a pod, densely dark brown velvety. Flowers September–November, fruits March–June. Propagated by seeds. Distributed throughout Nepal to about 1700 m on open slopes; also in northern India, Bhutan, China, and Southeast Asia.
FOOD. Flowers are cooked as a vegetable.

Croton roxburghii Balakrishnan

Croton oblongifolius Roxburgh
DANUWAR *mahasun* MOOSHAR *mahison* NEPALI *aule*

Euphorbiaceae. Shrub about 2 m high. Leaves stalked, 7–17 cm long, 4–7.5 cm wide, oblong, acute, entire, leathery. Flowers greenish. Propagated by seeds. Distributed throughout Nepal to about 1700 m; also in India, Sri Lanka, southern China, and Indo-China.

Crotalaria tetragona

Croton roxburghii

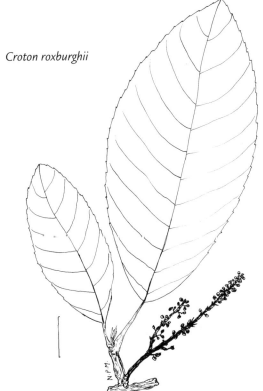

MEDICINE. Juice of the bark, about 2 teaspoon twice a day, is given in cases of malarial fever. Seed oil is used as a laxative.

OTHER USES. Twigs are used for fences. Seed oil is used for fish poison and has an insecticidal property.

Crypsinus hastatus (Thunberg) Copeland

Polypodium hastatum Thunberg, *Phymatodes hastata* (Thunberg) Ching, *Pleopeltis hastatus* (Thunberg) T. Moore

NEPALI *harjor*

Polypodiaceae. Fern. Rhizomes long, creeping, covered with rust-colored falcate scales. Stipes glossy brown. Fronds green, pinnate, pinnae subentire, remotely dentate or notched between the main veins. Sori prominent, brown, round, placed on either side of midrib than the margin. Spores July–August. Propagated by spores or by splitting the rhizome. Distributed in central and western Nepal at 1200–3200 m in mossy rock crevices; also in India, southwestern China, and northern Thailand.

MEDICINE. The rhizome is boiled with water until the amount is reduced by half; then it is given in doses of about 6 teaspoons three times a day to treat fever.

Crypsinus hastatus

Cryptolepis buchananii Roemer & Schultes

Nerium reticulatum Roxburgh, *Cryptolepis reticulata* (Roxburgh) Wallich, *Echites reticulata* (Roxburgh) Roth

DANUWAR *dudhiya, kalo ghuriyo* NEPALI *dudhe, gaisinge, koile ghuriyo*

Asclepiadaceae. Large climber with milky juice. Leaves stalked, oblong to elliptic, acuminate, leathery, glabrous

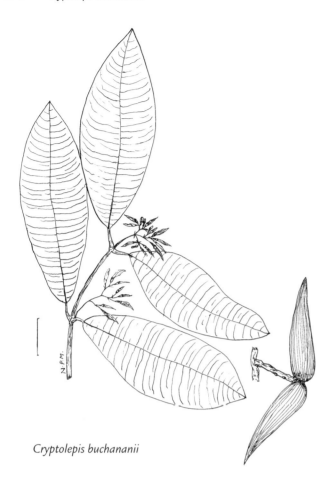

Cryptolepis buchananii

Cryptomeria japonica

and shiny above, glaucous beneath. Flowers stalked, yellowish, in dichotomous cymes. Fruit a follicle, compressed. Flowers May–June, fruits November–December. Propagated by seeds. Distributed throughout Nepal to about 1500 m in open, moist places; also in India, Sri Lanka, western and southern China, and Myanmar.

MEDICINE. Ash of the plant is applied to treat scabies. Latex is applied to treat backaches.

OTHER USES. The plant is lopped for fodder. Bark is used for ropes. Silky fiber from the seed is used to prepare garlands, especially by Gurungs.

Cryptomeria japonica (Linnaeus fil.) D. Don

Cupressus japonica Linnaeus fil.

NEPALI *dhupi*

Taxodiaceae. Coniferous tree about 40 m high, branches spreading or drooping. Leaves sessile, 7–12 cm long, four-angled, incurved, acuminate, broadly and shortly decurrent at the base. Cones yellowish. Seeds narrowly elliptic. Cones March–April. Propagated by seeds. Distributed in eastern and central Nepal at 1300–2600 m; also in India, Bhutan, Myanmar, Malaysia, and Japan.

OTHER USES. Wood is valued for timber. Leaves are used for incense.

Cucumis melo var. *agrestis* Naudin

ENGLISH *small gourd* MOOSHAR *ghurmi* NEPALI *urmi* SATAR *ghurmi* THARU *goihmha*

Cucurbitaceae. Twining annual herb. Leaves stalked, reniform or suborbiculate, three- to six-lobed, denticulate, somewhat roughly textured. Flowers yellowish. Fruit green, ovoid. Flowers July–October, fruits August–October. Propagated by seeds. Distributed throughout Nepal to about 800 m on uncultivated land and in sandy places.

FOOD. Ripe fruit is edible, and immature fruits are cooked as a vegetable.

MEDICINE. A paste of the plant is applied around the navel when there is difficulty in urination.

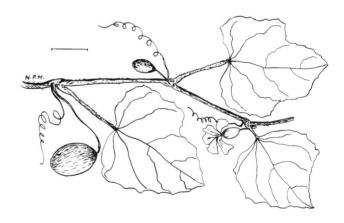

Cucumis melo var. *agrestis*

Cucumis melo Linnaeus var. *melo*

Cucumis utilissimus Roxburgh

ENGLISH *melon* NEPALI *kharbuja* TIBETAN *ma-ru-tse*

Cucurbitaceae. Creeping annual herb. Leaves stalked, orbiculate, about 8 cm in diameter, rough on both surfaces. Flowers yellow in fascicles. Fruit variable in shape, spherical to ovoid or elongated. Flowers and fruits May–September. Propagated by seeds. Distributed throughout Nepal to about 250 m, cultivated; also in most parts of the world.

FOOD. Fruits are edible and rich in sugar and protein.

Cucumis melo var. *momordica* Duthie & Fuller

ENGLISH *snap melon* NEPALI *phut*

Cucurbitaceae. Climber. Leaves stalked, nearly orbiculate, lobed. Flowers yellow. Fruit variable in shape, shortly oval or cylindrical, usually becoming orange when ripe. Flowers and fruits May–September. Propagated by seeds. Distributed throughout Nepal to about 250 m, cultivated.

FOOD. Young fruits are cooked as a vegetable whereas ripe ones eaten fresh.

Cucumis melo var. *utilissimus* Duthie & Fuller

NEPALI *kakari*

Cucurbitaceae. Annual climber. Leaves stalked, orbiculate to cordate. Flowers yellow. Propagated by seeds. Distributed throughout Nepal to about 250 m, cultivated.

FOOD. Ripe fruits are eaten fresh.

Cucumis sativus Linnaeus

ENGLISH *cucumber* GURUNG *lathai* MAGAR *gnyo* NEPALI *kankro* NEWARI *tusi* TAMANG *langai*

Cucurbitaceae. Procumbent annual herb, tendrils simple. Leaves stalked, broadly ovate, palmately three- to five-lobed or angled, cordate, margin undulately crenate, surfaces villous and hispid. Flowers yellow, the male flowers fascicled, female flowers solitary or fascicled. Fruit oblong ovoid, rounded at both ends, with narrow white stripes. Flowers August–September, fruits October–November. Propagated by seeds. Distributed throughout Nepal to about 1600 m, cultivated; also in tropical and subtropical parts of the world.

FOOD. Fruits are eaten fresh, or ripe fruits are preserved as a pickle.

Cucurbita maxima Duchesne ex Poiret

BHOJPURI *kadima* CHEPANG *pharsi* DANUWAR *pharsi* ENGLISH *common gourd, red pumpkin, Spanish gourd, winter squash* GURUNG *onse* LEPCHA *tangat* LIMBU *yakoba* MAGAR *kabali* MOOSHAR *kadima, pharsi* NEPALI *pharsi* NEWARI *phasi* RAI *pharsi* SUNWAR *mupi* TAMANG *pharsi* THARU *konhara*

Cucurbitaceae. Large climber. Leaves stalked, circular to reniform. Flowers yellow, all solitary, large. Fruit large, fleshy. Flowers May–June, fruits November–December.

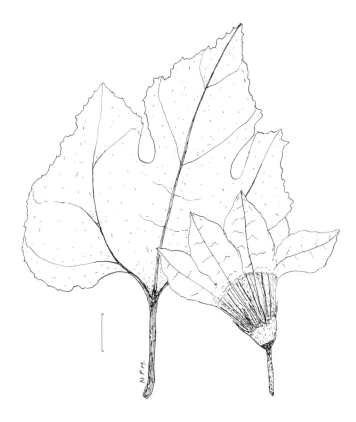

Cucurbita maxima

Propagated by seeds. Distributed throughout Nepal to about 1600 m, cultivated.

FOOD. Tender leaves and fruits are cooked as a vegetable. Ripe fruit can be kept for months.

Cuminum cyminum Linnaeus

BHOJPURI *jira* CHEPANG *jira* DANUWAR *jira* ENGLISH *cumin* GURUNG *jiro* LEPCHA *jyajyurakat* LIMBU *maruk* MAGAR *jira* NEPALI *jira* NEWARI *ji* RAI *jiro* SUNWAR *jira* TIBETAN *go-snyod*

Umbelliferae. Slender annual herb about 30 cm high with angular stems. Lower leaves stalked, upper leaves sessile, segments filiform. Flowers white in compound umbels. Fruit cylindrical, ridged. Flowers and fruits January–March. Propagated by seeds. Distributed in central Nepal to about 400 m, cultivated; native to the Mediterranean region, also found in India.

FOOD. Fruitlets are used as a spice.

MEDICINE. Fruitlets are stimulant and carminative.

OTHER USES. Fruitlets yield 2.5–4.5% essential oil that is used in perfumery and in flavoring beverages.

Cuphea procumbens Cavanilles

NEPALI *sulpha phul*

Lythraceae. Annual herb about 8 cm high. Leaves subsessile, lanceolate, acute, entire, hairy. Flowers mauve-blue or pinkish. Flowers and fruits July–November. Propagated by seeds. Distributed in central Nepal at 1200–1800 m on marshy ground; also in Central America.

OTHER USES. The plant is used for fodder.

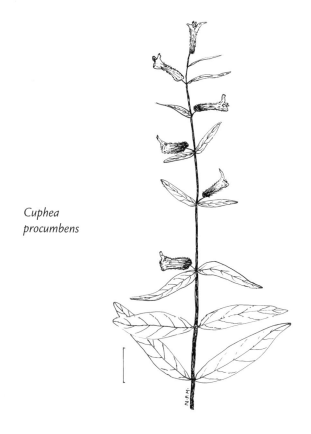

Cuphea procumbens

Cupressus torulosa

Cupressus torulosa D. Don

ENGLISH *Himalayan cypress* NEPALI *dhupi, rani salla*

Cupressaceae. Evergreen coniferous tree about 40 m high with pyramidal crown and drooping branchlets. Leaves scale-like, clasping the stem at their base, triangular, opposite, tips more or less closely appressed, with a gland on either side of the midrib. Male cones terminal, cylindrical, female cones globose, consisting of 6–10 decussate peltate scales. Seeds compressed, with an orbiculate wing. Cones January–February, mature October–November. Propagated by seeds. Distributed in western and central Nepal at 1300–3000 m, commonly in pure stands or associated with other species; also in the rest of the Himalaya.

OTHER USES. Wood is used for framing when constructing huts and other buildings. Leaves are often burned as incense.

Curculigo crassifolia (Baker) Hooker fil.

Molineria crassifolia Baker
NEPALI *dhoti saro*

Hypoxidaceae. Herb. Leaves 30–60 cm long, 5–7 cm wide, spatulate, oblanceolate, woolly hairy beneath. Flow-

ers yellow. Propagated by tubers. Distributed in eastern Nepal at 2200–2800 m in moist, shady places; also in northern India.

MEDICINE. A paste of the root is applied to treat headaches.

Curculigo orchioides Gaertner

CHEPANG *bhakamad* ENGLISH *black musli* NEPALI *musali*
TAMANG *banalhapte, banjari* THARU *musaleri*

Hypoxidaceae. Herb with elongated tuberous rootstock. Leaves subsessile, lanceolate, acuminate, hairy on both surfaces. Flowers yellow, July–August. Propagated by tubers. Distributed throughout Nepal to about 1700 m in moist places in the shade of trees but collection of roots for sale in the trade is a cause of conservation concern; also in northern India, Sri Lanka, eastward to Japan, Malaysia, and Australia.

MEDICINE. Juice of the root is taken to treat diarrhea and dysentery. This juice is also taken in cases of peptic ulcer, hemorrhoids, asthma, jaundice, and gonorrhea.

Curcuma angustifolia Roxburgh

NEPALI *bakhre saro, kachur, kalo besar* THARU *harjor*

Zingiberaceae. Herb about 2 m high with small, globose rootstocks. Leaves short-stalked, 18–35 cm long, 5.5–12.5 cm wide, lanceolate, entire, light brown. Flowers pinkish. Flowers and fruits April–July. Propagated by rhizomes. Distributed in central Nepal to about 1500 m in shade under trees or bamboo; also in northern India.

MEDICINE. A paste of the root is applied in cases of dislocated bone.

Curcuma domestica Valeton

BHOJPURI *hardi* CHEPANG *besar* DANUWAR *besar* ENGLISH *turmeric* GURUNG *urakya* LIMBU *harandi* MAGAR *besar* MOOSHAR *hardi* NEPALI *besar, haledo* NEWARI *halu* RAI *hardithuli* SUNWAR *hardi, hohomich* TAMANG *haldi* THARU *besar* TIBETAN *yungs-ba, ser-po*

Zingiberaceae. Herb about 1 cm high. Leaves in groups of 6–10 on pseudostems, about 40 cm long, broadly lanceolate, acuminate, entire, bright green with distinct mid-

rib, base sheathing. Flowers yellowish in pairs in the axils of the bracts, one opening before the other. Propagated by rhizomes. Distributed throughout Nepal to about 2000 m, cultivated; also in India and China.

FOOD. The rhizome is used for condiments and spices.

MEDICINE. A powder of rhizome, mixed with lemon (*Citrus limon*) and water, is applied to treat swellings caused by inflammation. About half a teaspoon of turmeric powder is boiled with 2 cups of water about 5 minutes and the lukewarm water gargled in cases of cough, colds, and tonsillitis.

Cuscuta reflexa Roxburgh

Cuscuta grandiflora Wallich ex Choisy
Cuscuta verrucosa Sweet

CHEPANG *aakash beli* ENGLISH *dodder* GURUNG *dyo dyoali, kebara, melan mili, tondari* NEPALI *aakash beli, aakashe, sikari lahara*

Convolvulaceae. Parasitic herb with leafless stems. Flowers cream in racemes. Flowers September–October, fruits October–November. Propagated by seeds. Distributed throughout Nepal to about 3000 m; also in Afghanistan, northern India, southwestern China, Myanmar, Thailand, Malaysia, and Indonesia.

MEDICINE. Juice of the plant, mixed with juice of *Saccharum officinarum,* is given in doses of about 4 teaspoons twice a day to treat jaundice. A paste of the plant is prescribed to treat stomachaches, headaches, and rheumatism. This paste is also applied to relieve body pains and itches. A poultice is used to treat swelling of joints and rheumatism. An infusion is used to wash sores. Ash of the plant is applied to cuts and wounds.

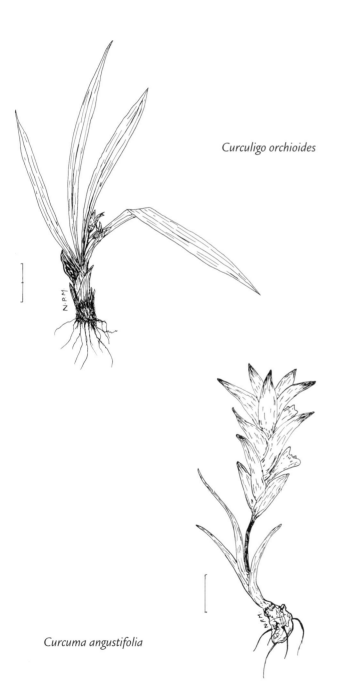

Curculigo orchioides

Curcuma angustifolia

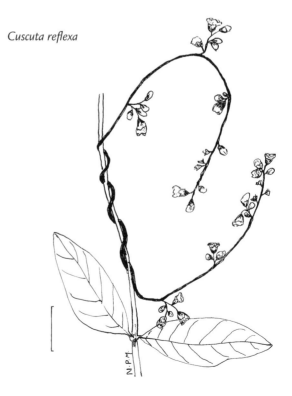

Cuscuta reflexa

Cyananthus lobatus Wallich ex Bentham

NEPALI *nirbisi*

Campanulaceae. Perennial herb about 30 cm high. Leaves short-stalked, obovate, dentate or three-lobed, glabrous above, pubescent beneath. Flowers deep blue, solitary. Propagated by seeds. Distributed throughout Nepal at 3300–4700 m in open fields; also in India, Bhutan, southern Tibet, and western China.

MEDICINE. Juice of the root, mixed with juice of the root of *Valeriana jatamansii* in equal amount, is given in cases of peptic ulcer.

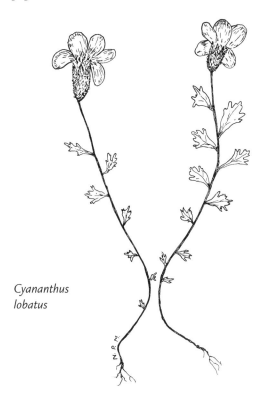

Cyananthus lobatus

Cyathocline purpurea (Buchanan-Hamilton ex D. Don) Kuntze

Tanacetum purpureum Buchanan-Hamilton ex D. Don
Artemisia hirsuta Rottbøll ex Sprengel
Cyathocline lyrata Cassini
NEPALI *galphule, latte jhar, tauke ghans* TAMANG *nas mran*

Compositae. Annual herb about 70 cm high. Leaves stalked, 2.5–12 cm long, lower leaves obovate, upper leaves pinnatifid. Flower heads purple in panicled corymbs. Fruit an achene, oblong, smooth. Flowers and fruits most of the year. Propagated by seeds. Distributed throughout Nepal at 600–1800 m; also in northern India, China, and Indo-China.

MEDICINE. Juice of the root, about 4 teaspoons three times a day, is given for indigestion. Aroma of squeezed plant is inhaled to treat headaches. Juice of the leaves is given in cases of cough and colds.

Cyathula tomentosa (Roth) Moquin-Tandon

Achyranthes tomentosa Roth
Achyranthes sesquax Wallich, *Polyscalis sesquax* (Wallich) Wallich
ENGLISH *cottony chaff flower* GURUNG *tine* NEPALI *aankhle kuro, aulo kuro, bhere kuro, kuro* TAMANG *niketene, tenai, tinet*

Amaranthaceae. Densely tomentose or woolly shrub about 1 m high. Leaves stalked, opposite, 5–17 cm long, elliptic to lanceolate, acuminate, glabrous above, silky tomentose beneath, base narrowed. Flowers greenish in dense globose heads. Fruit ovoid, enclosed in the perianth. Flowers July–August, fruits November–December. Propagated by seeds or root offshoots. Distributed throughout Nepal at 1300–2300 m in moist places; also in India, Bhutan, and western China.

MEDICINE. Juice of the root, about 6 teaspoons three times a day, is taken with water for constipation. It is also given to treat fever and peptic ulcer.

OTHER USES. Squeezed root is used for washing clothes. It is also used to poison fish.

Cycas pectinata Buchanan-Hamilton

NEPALI *thulo nyuro*

Cycadaceae. Coniferous shrub about 2 m high. Leaves stalked, 1.5–2 cm long, pinnate, leaflets numerous, linear lanceolate, 10–18 cm long, 0.5–0.8 cm wide, stiff, leathery. Plants dioecious. Male cones ovoid to cylindrical. Seeds orange, concealed by upwardly turned scaly blades. Propagated by offshoot buds. Distributed throughout Nepal at 500–1400 m, generally planted in gardens and lawns; also in India and Bhutan.

FOOD. Tender leaves are cooked as a vegetable.

Cyclanthera pedata Schrader

NEPALI *barela* NEWARI *barela*

Cucurbitaceae. Herbaceous climber, tendrils bi- to many-fid. Leaves stalked, lobed, dentate. Flowers small, yellowish, the male flowers in panicles, female flowers solitary. Fruit slightly gibbous, oblong, often echinate. Flowers August–September. Propagated by seeds. Distributed throughout Nepal to about 2500 m, cultivated; also in tropical North America, Panama, and Bolivia.

FOOD. Fruits are cooked as a vegetable.

Cymbidium aloifolium (Linnaeus) Swartz

Epidendrum aloifolium Linnaeus
Cymbidium simulans Rolfe
THARU *harjor*

Orchidaceae. Epiphytic orchid. Leaves stalked, 20–60 cm long, 1.3–3.5 cm wide, linear. Flowers yellow with red lip, April–July. Fruits August–November. Propagated by seeds or root offshoots. Distributed in central and eastern Nepal at 300–800 m; also in northern India, Sri Lanka, and Myanmar.

MEDICINE. The plant is emetic and purgative. A paste of the root is applied to set dislocated bones.

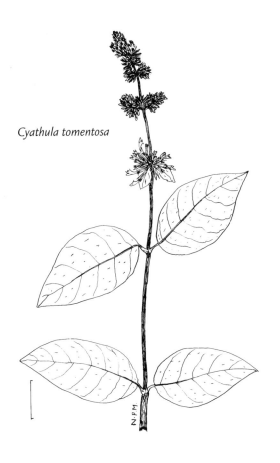

Cyathula tomentosa

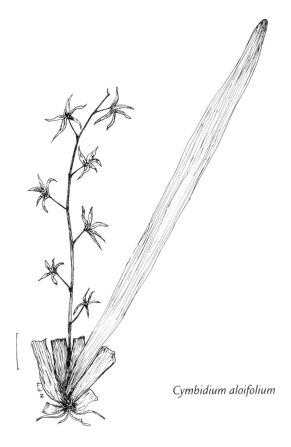

Cymbidium aloifolium

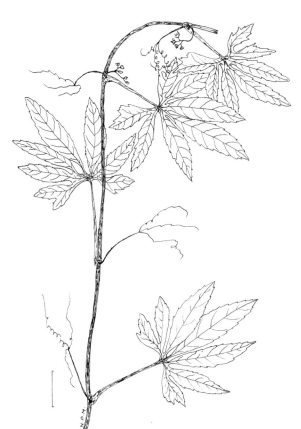

Cyclanthera pedata

Cymbidium devonianum Paxton

NEPALI *thir gava*

Orchidaceae. Epiphytic orchid. Leaves stalked, 14–25 cm long, leathery, entire, narrowed toward the stalk. Flowers reddish yellow, streaked with red. Fruit a capsule, turgidly ellipsoid. Flowers April–June. Propagated by seeds. Distributed in eastern Nepal to about 1500 m in moist, and forested areas; also in India, Bhutan, and Bangladesh.

MEDICINE. Paste of the root is applied to treat boils. The whole plant is boiled with water and some salt till the amount is reduced to half; this liquid, about 6 teaspoons three times a day, is taken in cases of cough and colds.

Cymbopogon jwarancusa (Jones) Schultes

Andropogon jwarancusa Jones
NEPALI *chel*

Gramineae. Tall perennial grass with tufted aromatic roots. Leaves 15–60 cm long, 0.5–1 cm wide, narrowly linear, tip capillary, base filiform. Propagated by seeds or by splitting the root. Distributed in western Nepal at 1600–2000 m in open places; also in India, Bhutan, and Sri Lanka.

MEDICINE. The root is boiled in water until the amount of water is halved, and this water is kept in the mouth 10–15 minutes to treat pyorrhea.

Cymbopogon pendulus (Nees ex Steudel) W. Watson
Andropogon microtheca Hooker fil.
ENGLISH *Jammu lemongrass* NEPALI *pire* TAMANG *tarpanga*

Gramineae. Tufted perennial grass, culms tall. Leaves about 1 m long, linear, margin somewhat roughly textured, bristly with acuminate bristles, glaucous green above, somewhat rough in texture below. Inflorescence greenish. Propagated by seeds or by splitting the root. Distributed in central and eastern Nepal at 500–1800 m in open, rocky places; also in northwestern India.

OTHER USES. The plant has fodder value. It is also used for thatching.

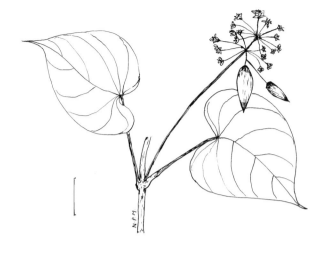

Cynanchum auriculatum

Cymbopogon pendulus

Cynodon dactylon (Linnaeus) Persoon
Panicum dactylon Linnaeus
BHOJPURI *dubh* CHEPANG *dub* DANUWAR *dubo*
ENGLISH *Bahama grass, Bermuda grass, doob grass* GURUNG *no dubo*
LEPCHA *pongmuk* LIMBU *samyok* MAGAR *dubo* MOOSHAR *dubh*
NEPALI *dubo* NEWARI *situ* RAI *hanyunlim* SUNWAR *dubo*
TAMANG *narkhapang, tabang* THARU *dubba* TIBETAN *du-rba*

Gramineae. Prostrate perennial grass, culms slender, with many nodes, forming matted tufts. Leaves, linear, acuminate. Inflorescence green or purplish. Flowers and fruits most of the year. Propagated by splitting of the rooting nodes. Distributed throughout Nepal to about 3000

Cynanchum auriculatum Wight
Endotropis auriculata (Wight) Decaisne
NEPALI *latikoseli*

Asclepiadaceae. Climbing shrub. Leaves stalked, ovate to lanceolate, acuminate, margin undulate, pubescent above with appressed hairs, puberulent on veins beneath, base deeply cordate. Flowers whitish in a many-flowered cyme. Fruit a follicle, spreading widely when open, pointed. Flowers June–August. Propagated by seeds. Distributed throughout Nepal at 1800–3300 m in open places; also in northern India, Bhutan, and China.

FOOD. Young fruits are cooked as a vegetable.

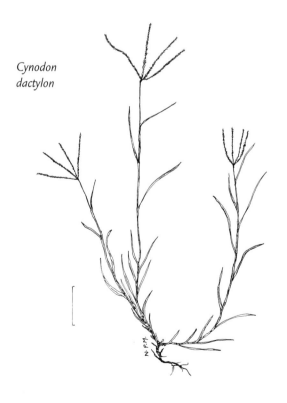

Cynodon dactylon

m, common along trails or on uncultivated land; also widely distributed in countries with warm climates.

MEDICINE. Juice of the plant, about 8 teaspoons at 4-hour intervals, is taken to relieve indigestion. About 4 teaspoons of this juice is mixed with the powder of a clove (*Syzygium aromaticum*) and taken twice a day as an anthelmintic. A paste of the plant is applied to cuts and wounds.

OTHER USES. The plant has good fodder value. Leaves are deemed to be auspicious, playing a role in many rituals.

Cynoglossum glochidiatum Wallich ex Bentham

Cynoglossum denticulatum A. de Candolle
Cynoglossum edgeworthii A. de Candolle
Cynoglossum microcarpum A. Kerner
Cynoglossum vesiculosum Wallich ex G. Don
Cynoglossum wallichii G. Don

DANUWAR *barka chirchiri* NEPALI *bhende kuro, kanike kuro, masine kuro* TAMANG *boke tinai*

Boraginaceae. Erect herb about 75 cm high. Basal leaves stalked, cauline leaves sessile, ovate to lanceolate, entire, hairy, base bulbous. Flowers deep blue in long, one-sided racemes. Fruits nutlets, four, with minutely barbed bristles. Flowers July–October, fruits October–November. Propagated by seeds. Distributed in western and central Nepal at 500–4000 m, common on open uncultivated land; also in Afghanistan, central Asia, Tibet, northern India, and western China.

MEDICINE. Juice of the plant is applied to cuts and wounds. This juice is also used to treat burns and to stop vomiting in infants. Leaves are boiled in water, and the strained water is used to treat the burning sensation of insect bites by washing the affected parts. A paste of the leaf is applied to wounds between the toes caused by walking barefooted in muddy water.

Cynoglossum zeylanicum (Vahl ex Hornemann) Thunberg ex Lehmann

Anchusa zeylanica Vahl ex Hornemann, *Echinospermum zeylanicum* (Vahl ex Hornemann) Lehmann, *Rochelia zeylanica* (Vahl ex Hornemann) Roemer & Schultes
Cynoglossum coeruleum Buchanan-Hamilton ex D. Don
Cynoglossum furcatum Wallich
Myosotis zeylanica Swartz ex Lehmann

CHEPANG *yu muja* ENGLISH *forget-me-not* GURUNG *arkale, khir, tine* NEPALI *bhere kuro, kanike kuro, koda kuro, masino kuro* TAMANG *boke tinai, tine, tilime* TIBETAN *tapa*

Boraginaceae. Erect herb about 70 cm high. Basal leaves stalked, spreading, cauline leaves sessile, alternate, 5–16 cm long, 2–5 cm wide, narrowly lanceolate, acute, densely appressed pilose above, sparsely long pubescent beneath, base bulbous. Flowers blue in long, one-sided racemes. Fruits nutlets, four, with with minutely barbed bristles on all sides. Flowers and fruits April–November. Propagated by seeds. Distributed throughout Nepal at 900–3500 m, common in open places and on uncultivated land; also in Afghanistan, India, Bhutan, Sri Lanka, eastern China, Japan, Thailand, and Malaysia.

Cynoglossum zeylanicum

MEDICINE. Powdered plant mixed with water is applied to treat ringworm. The root, mixed with the root of *Achyranthes bidentata*, is boiled in water about 15 minutes, and the filtered water, about 6 teaspoons twice a day, is given to treat indigestion. Juice of the root is applied to cuts and wounds. A paste of the root is applied around a boil, leaving the central part open to let the pus out, helping the boil heal faster. This paste is also applied to boils on the tongue. Juice of the leaf is used as eyedrops to treat conjunctivitis.

Cyperus distans Linnaeus fil.

NEPALI *mothe*

Cyperaceae. Erect herb about 50 cm high. Leaves sessile, linear. Inflorescence brown. Flowers and fruits June–November. Propagated by seeds or tuberous rhizomes. Distributed throughout Nepal to about 1300 m in open, sunny places; also in tropical and subtropical regions of the eastern and western hemispheres.

MEDICINE. Juice of the root, about 2 teaspoons three times a day, is given to treat fever.

Cyperus rotundus Linnaeus

CHEPANG *moti ban* DANUWAR *motha* ENGLISH *nut grass* GURUNG *bonchho* MOOSHAR *motha* NEPALI *bhada, mothe, kasur* THARU *bhada* TIBETAN *gla-sgang*

Cyperaceae. Erect herb about 40 cm high, rhizomes thickened into ovoid and black tubers which is clothed with scales. Stems three-angled, Leaves linear, smooth with deep midvein. Flowers in spikelets in umbels, brown. Fruit a nut, ellipsoidal. Flowers and fruits June–November. Propagated by seeds or by tuberous rhizomes. Distributed throughout Nepal at 300–2400 m in moist places; also cosmopolitan.

FOOD. Tubers are eaten fresh.

MEDICINE. The tuber is astringent, carminative, sedative, stimulant, and vermifuge. The tuber is mixed with a pounded fruit of black pepper (*Piper nigrum*) and taken to treat stomachaches.

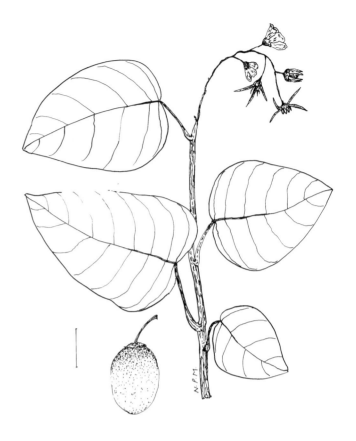

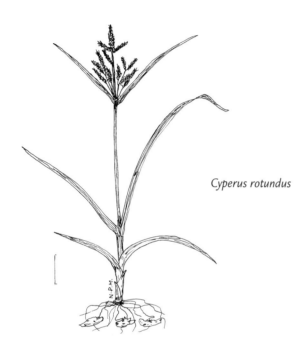

Cyperus rotundus

Cyphomandra betacea

Cyphomandra betacea (Cavanilles) Sendtner

ENGLISH *tree tomato*   NEPALI *tomatar, tyamotar*   NEWARI *antali*

Solanaceae. Erect shrub about 2 m high. Leaves stalked, broadly ovate, acuminate. Flowers pinkish, fragrant. Propagated by seeds. Distributed in eastern and central Nepal at 1000–1400 m in moist, open places, cultivated.

FOOD. Fruits are eaten fresh or, more commonly, stewed.

Cypripedium cordigerum D. Don

NEPALI *jibre*

Orchidaceae. Orchid about 60 cm high. Leaves sessile, about 15 cm long, ovate to lanceolate, acute. Flowers white or pale yellow. Flowers and fruits June–September. Propagated by seeds or by splitting of young buds. Distributed in western and central Nepal at 2000–3800 m in moist, shady places; also in northern India and Bhutan.

FOOD. Tender leaves are cooked as a vegetable.

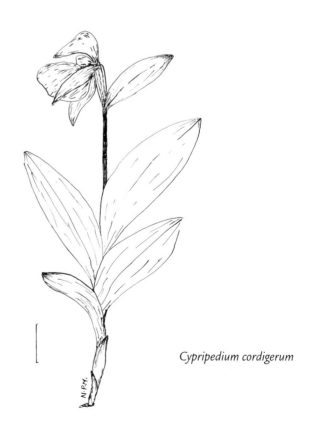

Cypripedium cordigerum

D

Dactylorhiza hatagirea (D. Don) Soó

Orchis hatagirea D. Don
Orchis latifolia Linnaeus
Orchis latifolia var. *indica* Lindley
ENGLISH *marsh orchid, salep* GURUNG *lob, panchaunle*
NEPALI *panchaunle* SHERPA *ongu lakpa* TIBETAN *dbang-po-lag*

Orchidaceae. Orchid about 45 cm high, roots tuberous, slightly flattened and divided into three or five finger-like lobes. Leaves 6–12 cm long, 2–4 cm wide, oblanceolate, base sheathing. Flowers purple, narrowly lanceolate, June–July. Propagated by seeds or tuberous roots. Distributed throughout Nepal at 2800–3800 m in moist places but the gathering of its roots for sale in the trade, even though such collection is banned, and of leaves for local consumption endangers plant populations; also in Pakistan, northern India, Bhutan, and southeastern Tibet.

FOOD. Young leaves and shoots are eaten as a vegetable.

MEDICINE. The root is expectorant, astringent, demulcent, and highly nutritious. Powdered root is spread over wounds to control bleeding. A decoction of the root is given in cases of stomach trouble.

Dalbergia latifolia Roxburgh

Dalbergia emarginata Roxburgh
ENGLISH *rosewood* NEPALI *satisal*

Leguminosae. Tree. Leaves stalked, odd-pinnate, leaflets five or seven, alternate, 3.5–6.5 cm long, orbiculate, obtuse, green above, pale beneath, base cuneate. Flowers white in lax clusters, axillary. Fruit a pod, flat, strap shaped, one- to three-seeded. Propagated by seeds. Distributed throughout Nepal at 300–1000 m; also in northern India and Southeast Asia.

MEDICINE. Juice of the bark is applied to eczema and pimples.

OTHER USES. The tree yields valuable timber. The wood is hard, close-grained, and used for furniture; it takes a beautiful polish.

Dalbergia sisso Roxburgh

CHEPANG *sisau* DANUWAR *sisau* ENGLISH *sisso tree* GURUNG *sisau*
LIMBU *sensosin* MAGAR *sisau* MOOSHAR *siso* NEPALI *sisau*
NEWARI *sisau* RAI *phommi* SUNWAR *sisau* TAMANG *sisau*
THARU *sisava, siso*

Leguminosae. Tree about 20 m high, bark gray, longitudinally furrowed, exfoliating in narrow strips. Leaves stalked, alternate, odd-pinnate, three or five, 2–7 cm long, 1.5–6 cm wide, broadly ovate, acuminate, cuspidate. Flowers sessile, yellowish. Fruit strap shaped, pale brown. Flowers March–June, fruits November–February. Propagated by seeds or root offshoots. Distributed throughout Nepal to about 1400 m in open places; also in western Asia, Afghanistan, Pakistan, India, Bhutan, Bangladesh, and subtropical Africa.

MEDICINE. The root is astringent. Heartwood, which is brown, is boiled in water and taken as an anthelmintic. Squeezed inner bark is boiled in water until the liquid is less than half the original amount. It is then strained and applied to treat gout. After the application, the affected

Dactylorhiza hatagirea

Dalbergia sisso

part is kept in the sun about half an hour. An alternative treatment for gout practiced by the Tharus of Dangdeokhuri district involves application of juice of the bark (Manandhar 1985). The former treatment seems to be more effective; it helps relieve the pain significantly. A decoction of leaves is used for gonorrhea, and the juice is dripped into the eye to treat eye troubles. This juice, mixed with yogurt, is given to treat bloody dysentery. A paste is applied to the forehead to relieve fever.

OTHER USES. Wood is used for various construction purposes. Small branches and bark are used for fuel. Twigs and leaves are lopped for fodder.

Dalbergia stipulacea Roxburgh

NEPALI *tatibari*

Leguminosae. Small tree. Leaves stalked, odd-pinnate, leaflets 17–25, obtuse, green above, glabrous or minutely hairy beneath. Flowers pinkish in copious axillary panicles. Fruit a pod, strap shaped, narrowed toward the base. Propagated by seeds or root offshoots. Distributed in central and eastern Nepal at 200–1300 m; also in northeastern India, Bhutan, Bangladesh, China, and Southeast Asia.

OTHER USES. The root is used as fish poison.

Daphne bholua Buchanan-Hamilton ex D. Don

GURUNG *setabaduwa, syugu mhendo, syu syu*
ENGLISH *Nepalese paper plant* MAGAR *logoto* NEPALI *baruwa, kagatpate, setaberu, setabaduws, syo syo* NEWARI *tayan ki puswan* SHERPA *syu* TAMANG *dyasin, sonsodhogbe* TIBETAN *chu chu, syugu dhangabu*

Thymelaeaceae. Evergreen shrub about 2 m high. Leaves stalked, 2.5–15 cm long, 1–4 cm wide, oblong, entire, leathery. Flowers sessile, white or purplish, fragrant. Fruit an ovoid berry, deep red or rusty when fully ripe, succulent. Flowers November–February, fruits March–May. Propagated by seeds. Distributed throughout Nepal at 1000–3200 m in moist, shady places under trees; also in India and Bhutan.

MEDICINE. Juice of the root, 6 teaspoons with molasses, is given to relieve fever. It is also useful for intestinal troubles. A decoction of the bark is taken to treat fever. Powdered seeds are taken as an anthelmintic.

OTHER USES. Handmade Nepalese paper is prepared from the bark. Rope for carrying loads is also twined from bark. Squeezed bark and leaves are used as fish poison.

Daphne papyracea Wallich ex Steudel

Daphne cannabina Loureiro ex Wallich
Daphne odora Thunberg
NEPALI *kagajpate*

Thymelaeaceae. Much branched evergreen shrub, bark gray, smooth. Leaves short-stalked, 5–12 cm long, narrowly lanceolate, leathery, entire, acuminate. Flowers greenish white, fragrant. Fruit deep red when ripe, fleshy. Flowers and fruits April–November. Propagated by seeds.

Daphne bholua

Distributed in western and central Nepal at 1500–3200 m in shady places in forested areas; also in northwestern India.

OTHER USES. The bark is used to prepare handmade Nepalese paper.

Daphniphyllum himalense (Bentham) Mueller Aargau

Goughia himalensis Bentham
GURUNG *jhaibal, olachi* NEPALI *chandan, rachana, rakta chandan* TAMANG *raksenjen tongbo*

Daphniphyllaceae. Small tree with a stout trunk. Leaves stalked, alternate, oblong to lanceolate, acuminate, entire, glabrous and shiny above, glaucous beneath. Flowers axillary, greenish. Fruit a drupe, oblong. Flowers March–April, fruits June–August. Propagated by seeds. Distributed throughout Nepal at 1600–2500 m on moist hillsides in association with other trees; also in northern India, Bhutan, southern Tibet, and northern Myanmar.

MEDICINE. A paste of the wood is applied to boils.

OTHER USES. Wood is grayish brown and suitable for turnery and carving.

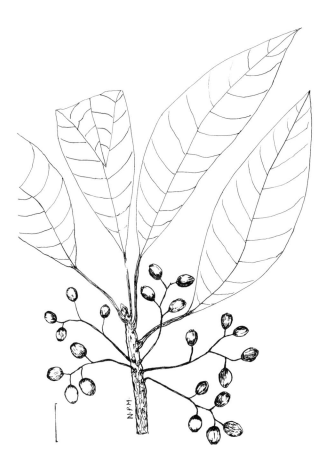

Daphniphyllum himalense

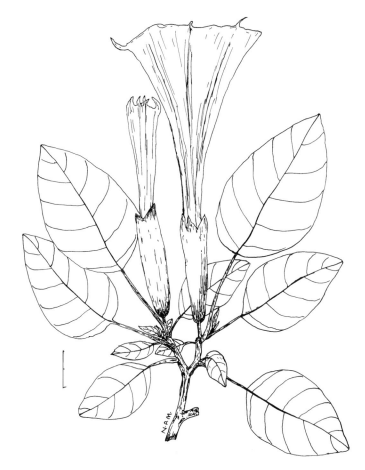

Datura metel

Datura metel Linnaeus

Datura fastuosa Linnaeus

BHOJPURI *dhatura* DANUWAR *dhatur* ENGLISH *dawny datura, thorn apple* GURUNG *dhatur* LEPCHA *sanorip* LIMBU *ningbung* MAGAR *dhatura* MOOSHAR *dhatura* NEPALI *dhatura, kalo dhaturo* NEWARI *kaha swan* RAI *harandukkhakwa* SUNWAR *dhatur* TAMANG *dhatura bish* THARU *dhataur* TIBETAN *man-da-ra-ba*

Solanaceae. Shrub about 2 m high with dichotomous branches. Leaves stalked, 6–26 cm long, 4–14 cm wide, ovate, margin irregularly and shallowly lobed, base with the two sides unequal. Flowers large, solitary, axillary, funnel shaped, purple outside, white within. Fruit a capsule, globose, green, covered with short stout spines. Seeds numerous, closely packed, pale brown. Flowers November–January, fruits January–April. Propagated by seeds. Distributed throughout Nepal to about 1300 m on open uncultivated land; also in Pakistan, India, Bhutan, and Bangladesh.

MEDICINE. A powder of dried leaves or flowers is smoked like cigarettes to treat bronchial asthma. The warmed leaf is applied to rheumatic swellings; it is also useful for swellings caused by some inflammations. A paste of the leaf is applied to treat tumors and sprains. Juice of the leaves is taken in cases of gonorrhea and is also applied externally.

This juice is dropped into the ear to treat earaches and is applied to wounds. Juice of the flower is given for asthma. A decoction of the seed is considered good for earaches and is dropped into the ear as well as applied externally around the ear. Dried seeds are smoked over a fire and the smoke sucked through the mouth to treat toothaches. Large doses of any part of the plant are toxic.

OTHER USES. Seeds have been used by criminals for poisoning.

Datura stramonium Linnaeus

ENGLISH *angel's trumpet, Jamaica thorn apple, jimson weed, stink weed, thorn apple* NEPALI *dhaturo, kalo dhaturo, seto dhaturo* TAMANG *dhaturo* TIBETAN *mdak, rda-rdu-ra*

Solanaceae. Erect shrub about 3 m high, branches spreading. Leaves stalked, pale green, triangular ovate, acuminate, irregularly dentate, glabrous. Flowers white. Fruit a capsule, ovoid, thickly covered with sharp spines. Flowers May–July, fruits June–December. Propagated by seeds. Distributed throughout Nepal at 1000–2500 m on moist, open ground; also in Pakistan, India, Bhutan, and North America.

MEDICINE. A paste of leaves and seeds is applied to boils and sores. Leaves, mixed with leaves of *Cannabis sativa* and *Picrorhiza scrophulariiflora*, are pounded with water and applied to treat headaches. Juice of the flower is dropped into the ear to treat earaches. Juice of the fruit is applied to fight dandruff and hair loss. Seeds are fried in mustard oil, and the smoke emitted is sucked through the mouth to treat dental caries.

OTHER USES. Leaves are used as green manure. Powdered fruit, mixed with rice or bread, is given to kill mad dogs.

Daucus carota Linnaeus

ENGLISH *carrot* NEPALI *gajar* NEWARI *gajar* TIBETAN *shu-mo-za*

Umbelliferae. Annual herb about 3 m high, stem much branched. Leaves stalked, pinnately decompound, segments lanceolate. Flowers white or yellowish in branched and more or less globose umbels. Fruit oblong, with bristly hairs along the ribs. Flowers May–June. Propagated by seeds. Distributed throughout Nepal to about 1700 m, cultivated; also in Pakistan, India, Bhutan, Bangladesh, Sri Lanka, China, Myanmar, Thailand, Malaysia, Indonesia, the Philippines, Australia, and North America.

FOOD. The fleshy taproot is eaten fresh or cooked as a vegetable in soup and curries. It is also pickled.

MEDICINE. An infusion of the root used to treat threadworms. The root is good for easing urination and helping eliminate uric acid. Seeds are aromatic, stimulant, and carminative.

OTHER USES. Green leaves are used for fodder.

Davallia pulchra D. Don

NEPALI *mirmire unyu*

Davalliaceae. Fern with fronds 5–20 cm long, 4–10 cm wide, tripinnate, pinnae with pinnules on a winged rachis, pinnules cut into narrow segments. Sori at the base of the teeth of segments, brown. Propagated by spores. Distributed throughout Nepal at 1300–3500 m in moist, shady places, common; also in India, Bhutan, and China.

MEDICINE. Juice of the rhizome, about 4 teaspoons twice a day, is given in cases of fever.

Debregeasia longifolia (Burman fil.) Weddell

Urtica longifolia Burman fil.
Debregeasia velutina Gaudichaud-Beaupré

CHEPANG *tipromsi* ENGLISH *wild rhea* GURUNG *algudi* MAGAR *chimsai* NEPALI *tusare* TAMANG *kalangu, balwapoungi*

Urticaceae. Small tree. Leaves stalked, acute at the base, linear elliptic, acuminate, serrulate, glabrous and dark green above when mature, ashy tomentose beneath. Plants monoecious, the flowers whitish in small heads. Fruit yellow when ripe, with numerous minute embedded nutlets. Flowers July–August, fruits November–January. Propagated by cuttings or seeds. Distributed throughout Nepal at 500–2200 m along the banks of streams and rivulets; also in northern India, Sri Lanka, western China, and Southeast Asia.

FOOD. Ripe fruits are eaten fresh.

MEDICINE. Juice of the leaves is rubbed on areas affected with scabies.

OTHER USES. Wood is mainly used for fuel. Stem bark yields a strong fiber, making it ideal for ropes. Branches are lopped for fodder.

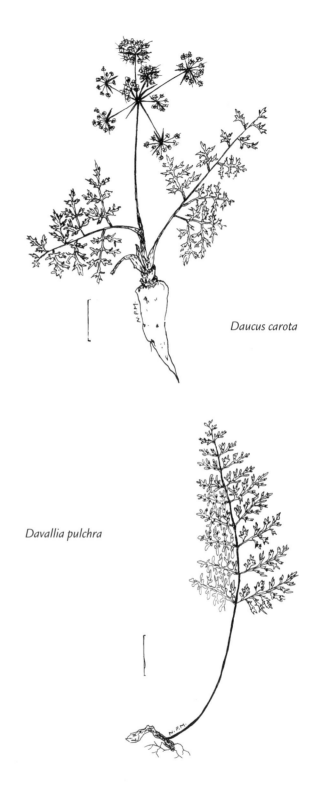

Daucus carota

Davallia pulchra

Debregeasia longifolia

Debregeasia salicifolia (D. Don) Rendle

Boehmeria salicifolia D. Don
Boehmeria hypoleuca Hochstetter ex A. Richard, *Debregeasia hypoleuca* (Hochstetter ex A. Richard) Weddell
Debregeasia bicolor (Roxburgh) Weddell

CHEPANG *ryumsi, tipremsi* GURUNG *kalankugu, kanakhuli*
MAGAR *amilchhe* NEPALI *tusare* TAMANG *kalanguli*

Urticaceae. Tree about 4 m high with pubescent branches. Leaves stalked, alternate, acute or rounded at the base, linear lanceolate, acuminate, serrulate, three-veined, with round elevated dots above, thickly white felted beneath. Plants dioecious, the flowers reddish in sessile or subsessile axillary heads. Fruit amber colored, studded with minute nutlets. Propagated by cuttings or seeds. Distributed throughout Nepal at 1000–2400 m along the banks of streams and watercourses; also in Iran, Afghanistan, and northwestern India.

FOOD. Ripe fruits are sweet in taste and eaten fresh.

OTHER USES. Wood is soft, light, and used mainly for fuel. Fiber from the bark is made into twine and rope. Branches are lopped for fodder.

Delonix regia (Bojer ex Hooker) Rafinesque

Poinciana regia Bojer ex Hooker

ENGLISH *flamboyant, peacock flower, royal poinciana*
NEPALI *gulmohar, siris*

Leguminosae. Tree about 20 m high. Leaves stalked, bipinnate, pinnae in 11–18 pairs, pinnules in 20–30 pairs, elliptic, acuminate, entire. Flowers large, crimson or scarlet-orange. Fruit a pod ending in a short beak. Flowers

April–September, fruits November–April. Propagated by seeds or cuttings. Distributed throughout Nepal to about 1000 m, cultivated in tropical and subtropical regions.

FOOD. Flower buds are eaten as a potherb.

OTHER USES. The plant is cultivated as an avenue tree or in the garden. Wood is soft, white, and used mainly for fuel.

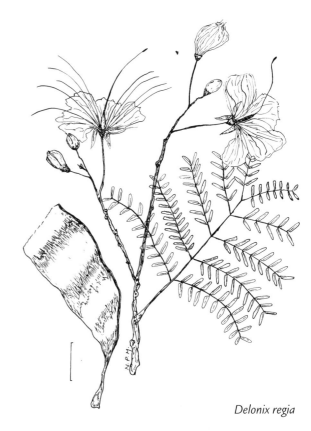

Delonix regia

Delphinium brunonianum Royle

Delphinium jacquemontianum Cambessèdes
Delphinium moschatum Munro ex Hooker fil. & Thomson
NEPALI *kasturi phul*

Ranunculaceae. Herb. Leaves stalked, rounded, deeply lobed, lobes dentate. Flowers blue or purple, with musky odor, July–September. Propagated by seeds or tubers. Distributed in western and central Nepal at 3500–6000 m on open, stony slopes in dry places; also in Afghanistan, Pakistan, and southeastern Tibet.

MEDICINE. Juice of the plant is used to destroy ticks of animals.

Delphinium denudatum Wallich ex

Hooker fil. & Thomson

NEPALI *bish*

Ranunculaceae. Herb about 90 cm high. Lower leaves long-stalked, orbiculate, five- to nine-lobed, dentate, upper leaves few, short-stalked, deeply three- or more-lobed, lobes entire or pinnatifid. Flowers small, blue or violet, with an awl-shaped spur, few in lax racemes. Fruit a follicle, hairy. Flowers and fruits April–November. Propagated by seeds or tubers. Distributed in central Nepal at 2300–3700 m in the margins of fields or along waysides in hilly areas.

MEDICINE. A paste of the root is applied to treat toothaches.

Delphinium himalayai Munz

NEPALI *jaunde mulo, mauro malo, nirabisi*

Ranunculaceae. Erect herb about 1 m high. Leaves stalked, circular, five-lobed, hairy, lobes dentate. Flowers bluish in long, one-sided spikes. Fruit a follicle, densely hairy. Flowers July–August. Propagated by seeds or tubers. Distributed in western and central Nepal at 2000–4000 m on open slopes; endemic.

MEDICINE. Juice of the root is given in cases of cough and colds. An infusion of the root is put in wounds in the hooves of cattle to expel worms or kill germs.

Delphinium himalayai

Delphinium kumaonense Huth

Delphinium grandiflorum var. *kumaonensis* (Huth) Brühl
TIBETAN *chharkang*

Ranunculaceae. Herb about 60 cm high. Leaves stalked, dissected into narrow lobes. Flowers deep blue. Fruit a follicle, densely brown hairy. Flowers July–August.

Propagated by seeds or tubers. Distributed in western and central Nepal at 3000–4500 m on shady, moist slopes; also in northern India.

MEDICINE. A decoction of the plant is applied to treat scabies.

Delphinium scabriflorum D. Don

Delphinium carela Buchanan-Hamilton ex D. Don
Delphinium altissimum Wallich
MAGAR *dokini* NEPALI *bikh, mudulo* TAMANG *toyoring*
TIBETAN *toyoring*

Ranunculaceae. Erect herb about 1 m high. Leaves roundish, five-lobed, dentate. Flowers stalked, blue, densely hairy, August–September. Propagated by seeds or tubers. Distributed throughout Nepal at 1500–2500 m, common on grassy slopes; also in northeastern India and Bhutan.

MEDICINE. An infusion of the plant is applied to remove worms from wounds in the hooves of animals.

Delphinium vestitum Wallich ex Royle

Delphinium rectivenium Royle
NEPALI *atish, maro mulo, maura mulo, mawarmul*

Ranunculaceae. Erect herb about 75 cm high. Basal leaves five- to seven-lobed, lobes rounded, dentate. Flowers blue with incurved conical spur. Fruits three follicles. Flowers and fruits August–October. Propagated by seeds or tubers. Distributed throughout Nepal at 2700–4000 m, generally in shady ravines; also in northern India.

MEDICINE. The root is used as an anthelmintic. It is also used to poison dogs.

Dendranthema nubigenum (Wallich ex de Candolle) Kitamura

Tanacetum nubigenum Wallich ex de Candolle, *Chrysanthemum nubigenum* (Wallich ex de Candolle) Handel-Mazzetti
Artemisia leptophylla D. Don
GURUNG *basant, sun pwaeki phul* NEPALI *sun phul*
TIBETAN *sang khamba, santarkya*

Compositae. Shrub about 20 cm high, stems tufted, densely leafy upward. Leaves sessile, pinnatifid, segments short, linear, acute. Flower heads yellow in terminal corymbs. Fruit an achene. Propagated by seeds. Distributed in western and central Nepal at 2600–4000 m in open, rocky places; also in northern India and Bhutan.

OTHER USES. Leaves contain 0.8% essential oils. A powder of the leaves have lice- and insect-repellent properties. It is also used as incense.

Dendrobium densiflorum Lindley

Dendrobium clavatum Roxburgh
NEPALI *sungabha*

Orchidaceae. Epiphytic orchid with a club-shaped pseudobulb, terete or four-angled, 30–40 cm long. Leaves collected at the apex of the pseudobulb, 10–15 cm long,

Dendranthema nubigenum

Dendrobium longicornu

ovate to lanceolate, acute, leathery. Flowers stalked, yellow with an orange lip, in dense racemes, April–May. Propagated by seeds. Distributed in central Nepal at 600–2000 m on moist rocks, and tree trunks and branches; also in India, Bhutan, and Myanmar.

MEDICINE. Pulp of the pseudobulb is applied to boils and pimples.

OTHER USES. Flowers are used by Rai girls to decorate their heads.

Dendrobium longicornu Lindley

NEPALI *bawar*

Orchidaceae. Epiphytic orchid, stems tufted with black hairs on the sheaths. Leaves sessile, alternate, lanceolate, acute. Flowers white outside, orange inside, October–November. Propagated by splitting of young buds. Distributed in central and western Nepal at 1600–2500 m, generally on tree trunks and branches; also in northern India, Bhutan, and Myanmar.

MEDICINE. Juice of the plant is used to relieve fever. This juice is mixed with lukewarm water to bathe a child suffering from fever. Boiled root is fed to livestock suffering from cough.

Dendrocalamus giganteus Wallich ex Munro

Bambusa gigantea Wallich ex Munro
ENGLISH *giant bamboo* NEPALI *bhalu bans, dhungre bans*

Gramineae. Bamboo about 50 m high. Nodes hairy, internodes 35–40 cm long, 15–25 cm wide, covered with waxy white flakes when young, culm sheath 20–45 cm long, not bristly at the top, hairs few. Leaves short-stalked, 30–35 cm long, 10–12 cm wide, broadly lanceolate, cuspidate, acuminate, ending in a twisted point, rounded at

the base, leaf sheath not hairy, red at the top. Inflorescence a large panicle, drooping. Propagated by culm cuttings. Distributed in eastern and central Nepal at 200–1300 m, cultivated and naturalized in the tropical plains; also in India, Bangladesh, China, and Southeast Asia.

FOOD. Young shoots are used as a vegetable.

MEDICINE. The siliceous secretion of the culm is considered aphrodisiac and tonic.

OTHER USES. Large-diameter culms are used to make containers for storage and pillars for houses. Strips from the culms are used for weaving mats and baskets. Leaves are used for fodder.

Dendrocalamus hamiltonii Nees & Arnott ex Munro

ENGLISH *tufted bamboo* NEPALI *choya bans, tama bans*

Gramineae. Bamboo about 25 m high, forming dense thickets, stems 7–12 cm in diameter, curved downward, nodes marked with root scars, internodes 20–40 cm long, stem sheath triangular, glabrous or with patches of appressed hairs. Leaves narrowly lanceolate, long-pointed, minutely serrulate, smooth above, rough beneath, leaf sheaths with stiff hairs. Inflorescence ovoid, reddish brown or dark pink, glabrous. Fruit a grain, ovoid, beaked, hairy above. Propagated by seeds or by splitting the rhizome. Distributed in central and eastern Nepal at 500–2000 m; also in northern India and Southeast Asia.

FOOD. Young shoots are cooked as a vegetable. They are also preserved in the form of *tama*, fermented shoots.

OTHER USES. Mature bamboo is used to make baskets, mats, screens, and fences. It is thin walled and soft, so it not used much for building purposes. Strips of the bamboo are used for rope.

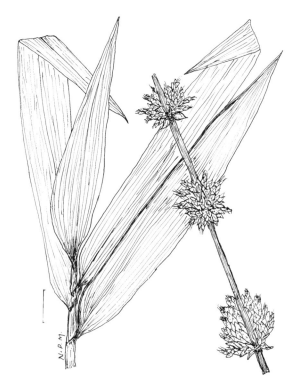

Dendrocalamus hamiltonii

Dendrocalamus hookeri Munro

NEPALI *bhalu bans, kalo bans, tili bans* LEPCHA *patu*

Gramineae. Thin-walled bamboo about 25 m high, culms 12–18 cm long, 7–10 cm wide, culm sheath 15–25 cm long, broad at the base, with black or brown hairs outside, sheaths at the upper nodes narrower, densely covered with black or brown hairs outside, glabrous inside. Leaves short-stalked, 30–40 cm long, oblong to lanceolate, acuminate, ending in a twisted point, hairs scattered near the base, margin rough, base oblique, rounded, leaf sheath striate. Inflorescences large compound panicles. Flowers sporadically. Propagated by culm cuttings. Distributed in eastern and central Nepal at 600–2000 m, common, mainly cultivated in warmer regions of eastern Nepal, also in India, Bhutan, and Bangladesh.

FOOD. Young shoots are used as a vegetable.

OTHER USES. Culms are used for construction, particularly roofing. Strips from the culms are used for weaving. Thin culms are used as walking sticks, and large ones as containers. Leaves are used for fodder.

Dendrocalamus strictus Nees

ENGLISH *male bamboo, solid bamboo* NEPALI *lathi bans, taru bans*

Gramineae. Densely tufted, gregarious bamboo about 13 m high, stems 4–10 cm in diameter, nodes somewhat swollen, lower nodes often rooting, internodes 10–20 cm long, stem sheath hairless or with grayish brown hairs. Leaves narrowly lanceolate, finely hairy on both surfaces. Inflorescences brownish in dense globose heads, usually hairy outside, borne along branched stems. Fruit a grain, ovoid, beaked, hairy above. Flowers October–November, fruits June–July. Propagated by seeds or by splitting the rhizome. Distributed in central and eastern Nepal at 600–1800 m; also in Pakistan, India, and Myanmar.

FOOD. Young shoots are cooked as a vegetable or pickle.

OTHER USES. The stem is used for scaffolding, poles, bridges, and other large bamboo implements. Culms are also used to make walking sticks, furniture, and baskets.

Dendrophthoe falcata (Linnaeus fil.) Ettingshausen

Loranthus falcatus Linnaeus fil.
Loranthus bicolor Roxburgh
Loranthus longiflorus Desroussaux
MOOSHAR *riniya* NEPALI *ainjeru, liso*

Loranthaceae. Parasitic shrub. Leaves stalked, nearly opposite, 3–19 cm long, 1.2–10 cm wide, variable in shape and size, ovate to oblong, entire, smooth, leathery. Flowers stalked, reddish. Fruit a berry, oblong, seated on a green cup-shaped bract. Flowers and fruits May–December. Propagated by seeds. Distributed throughout Nepal to about 2000 m in open places on branches of trees and shrubs; also in northern India, Sri Lanka, Indo-China, and Australia.

FOOD. Ripe fruits are eaten fresh.

MEDICINE. A paste of the bark is applied to boils and helps extract the pus, ultimately hastening healing. A paste of the fruit is applied to set dislocated bone.

Dendrophthoe falcata

Dennstaedtia appendiculata (Wallich ex Hooker) J. Smith

NEPALI *daluko, lute sottar, raunne*

Dennstaedtiaceae. Terrestrial fern. Fronds 25–50 cm long, 10–20 cm wide, bipinnate. Sori small, on the ultimate segment. Propagated by spores or by splitting the rhizome. Distributed throughout Nepal at 1200–2800 m on moist slopes in forested areas; also in northern India and western China.

MEDICINE. Juice of the frond is applied to cuts and wounds.

OTHER USES. Plants are spread in animal sheds for animal bedding at night.

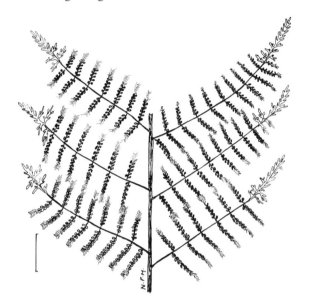

Dennstaedtia appendiculata

Descurainia sophia (Linnaeus) Webb ex Prantl

Sisymbrium sophia Linnaeus
NEPALI *masino tori jhar*

Cruciferae. Erect herb about 40 cm high. Leaves sessile, linear obovate, acuminate. Flowers yellow. Fruit a pod, linear. Flowers and fruits March–May. Propagated by seeds. Distributed in western and central Nepal at 2000–4000 m; also in Afghanistan, India, China, Japan, New Zealand, Europe, North Africa, and North America.

FOOD. Young shoots and leaves are cooked as a vegetable.

Desmodium concinnum de Candolle

Desmodium penduliflorum Wallich
Desmodium pendulum Wallich
NEPALI *gahate jhar, masino bhatamase* TAMANG *nigi miyo*

Leguminosae. Erect deciduous shrub about 2 m high, branches slender, attenuate, bark smooth or brownish,

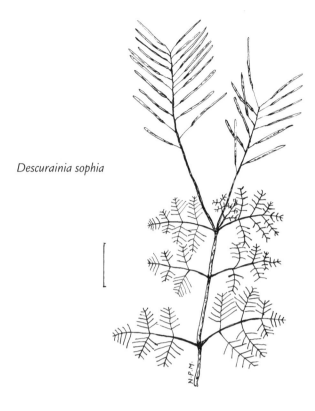

Descurainia sophia

lenticels minute, pale. Leaves stalked, trifoliolate, leaflets 1–7.5 cm long, 0.8–3 cm wide, elliptic to oblong, rounded at both ends, entire, with silky appressed hairs on both sides. Flowers blue in slender axillary and terminal drooping racemes. Fruit a pod. Flowers September–October, fruits November–May. Propagated by seeds. Distributed in eastern and central Nepal at 1300–2200 m in oak forests; also in northern India, western China, and Myanmar.

MEDICINE. Juice of the root, about 2 teaspoons three times a day, is given in cases of indigestion.

Desmodium confertum de Candolle

Hedysarum dioicum Buchanan-Hamilton ex D. Don, *Desmodium dioicum* (Buchanan-Hamilton ex D. Don) de Candolle
CHEPANG *gauza, naitak* DANUWAR *latapatiya* MAJHI *gahate*
NEPALI *bhatamase ghans, bhatako, bhatt* TAMANG *koltechhe, mata syaula, modes, pun pun gosaro, rapha langi, raphalki*

Leguminosae. Shrub about 1 m high. Leaves trifoliolate, leaflets 3–12 cm long, 1.5–8.5 cm wide, elliptic or oblong, entire, leathery, hairy beneath. Flowers purplish in axillary and terminal racemes. Fruit a pod, densely clothed with spreading silky hairs, constricted deeply on the ventral surface. Flowers September–October, fruits October–December. Propagated by seeds. Distributed in central and eastern Nepal at 300–2000 m on dry hillsides; also in northeastern India and Bhutan.

MEDICINE. Juice of the plant, about 2 teaspoons three times a day, is given in cases of amebic dysentery. Juice of the root is given to treat menstrual disorders and gastric troubles. It is also useful for diarrhea and dysentery.

Desmodium elegans de Candolle

Desmodium argenteum Wallich ex Bentham
Desmodium oxphyllum de Candolle
Desmodium serriferum Wallich ex Baker
Hedysarum tiliaefolium D. Don, *Desmodium tiliaefolium* (D. Don)
   Wallich
NEPALI *bakhre ghans, chumlya, rato bakhre ghans, sadan*

Leguminosae. Deciduous shrub about 2 m high. Leaves stalked, trifoliolate, leaflets 2.5–10 cm long, 2–7 cm wide, rhombic to ovate, glabrous above, silky pubescent beneath, apex acute, base crenate or rounded. Flowers pale purple in terminal panicles. Fruit a pod, slightly falcate, with minute, fine, appressed hairs. Flowers August–September, fruits September–December. Propagated by seeds. Distributed in western and central Nepal at 1000–2700 m in oak forests; also in Afghanistan, Pakistan, India, Bhutan, and China.

MEDICINE. The root is carminative, tonic, diuretic, and is used for bilious complaints. People in western Nepal use juice of the root in cases of cholera but in other parts of the country the juice is mixed with bark juice of *Bauhinia malabarica* in equal amount to treat the same disease. Juice of the bark, about 6 teaspoons three times a day, is given for peptic ulcer.

OTHER USES. Goats and sheep browse the leaves.

Desmodium gangetium (Linnaeus) de Candolle

Hedysarum gangetium Linnaeus
Hedysarum collinum Roxburgh
NEPALI *dampate* THARU *gat kosiya*

Leguminosae. Herb. Leaves stalked, 2–19 cm long, 1–6.5 cm wide, oblong to ovate, acuminate, rounded toward the base, entire, glabrous above, hairy underneath. Flowers pinkish. Fruit a pod. Flowers May–July, fruits October–November. Propagated by seeds. Distributed in eastern and central Nepal at 300–1000 m in open as well as shady places; also in northern India, Bhutan, Sri Lanka, China, Southeast Asia, Australia, and tropical Africa.

MEDICINE. Juice of the root, about 2 teaspoons, is given to treat stomach acidity.

Desmodium heterocarpon (Linnaeus) de Candolle

Hedysarum heterocarpon Linnaeus
Desmodium polycarpum (Poiret) de Candolle
GURUNG *bangat, gahate* NEPALI *bakhre ghans, dampate, sakhino jhar, chara pi pi*

Leguminosae. Prostrate subshrub, twigs clothed with long silky hairs. Leaves stalked, trifoliolate, leaflets 1.5–4 cm long, suborbiculate to broadly elliptic, rounded at both ends, glabrous above, appressed silky hairs beneath. Flowers purple in axillary and terminal racemes. Fruit a pod, clothed with minute, hooked, rusty hairs. Flowers July–September, fruits November–December. Propagated by seeds. Distributed throughout Nepal at 400–2100 m in moist or dry places in and about *Shorea robusta* forest;

also in the Kumaon region or Uttar Pradesh, India, west of Nepal, and Bhutan, Sri Lanka, eastward to China, Japan, Malaysia, Australia, and islands of the Pacific Ocean.

MEDICINE. A decoction of the plant is tonic and also useful for coughs. Juice of the root, about 4 teaspoons twice a day, is given for diarrhea and applied for skin diseases. Powdered root, mixed in equal amount with root powder of *Pouzolzia zeylanica*, is taken with water for indigestion.

Desmodium laxiflorum de Candolle

Desmodium elongatum Wallich
Hedysarum recurvatum Roxburgh, *Desmodium recurvatum*
   (Roxburgh) Graham
NEPALI *kuro jhar*

Leguminosae. Deciduous subshrub about 75 cm high, bark reddish brown, lenticels minute. Leaves stalked, trifoliolate, leaflets ovate or broadly lanceolate, acute, entire, hairy above when young, glabrous when mature, glaucous beneath with fine appressed hairs on veins, base narrowed or rounded. Flowers pale yellow in slender, drooping, axillary and terminal racemes. Fruit a pod, clothed with minute hooked hairs. Flowers July–September, fruits October–November. Propagated by seeds. Distributed throughout Nepal at 600–1000 m, gregarious in shady, moist ravines; also in India, China, and Southeast Asia.

OTHER USES. The plant is used for fodder.

Desmodium microphyllum (Thunberg) de Candolle

Hedysarum microphyllum Thunberg
Desmodium parvifolium de Candolle
NEPALI *bute kanike, miriye jhar, sano charimeli*
TAMANG *saritamba ghugi*

Leguminosae. Tufted herb about 1 m high. Leaves stalked, uni- to trifoliolate, leaflets subsessile, elliptic, obtuse to mucronate. Flowers purple in terminal racemes. Fruit a small pod, two- to four-jointed with shallow constrictions. Flowers August–September, fruits October–November. Propagated by seeds. Distributed throughout Nepal at 1000–2000 m in open as well as shady places; also in India, Sri Lanka, southern and eastern Asia including China, Japan, Malaysia, and Australia.

MEDICINE. Juice of the plant is used in cases of headache, cough, and colds. A paste of the plant is applied to boils and blisters. It is also applied to remove pus from wounds.

Desmodium multiflorum de Candolle

Desmodium angulatum de Candolle
Desmodium dubium Lindley
Desmodium nepalense Ohashi
Hedysarum floribundum D. Don, *Desmodium floribundum*
   (D. Don) Sweet
Hedysarum sambuense D. Don
CHEPANG *kardha jhar* MAGAR *bhatte* NEPALI *bakhre ghans, bhatte, bhatmas phul, lahare sajan, til* TAMANG *saritambo ghugi*

Leguminosae. Erect shrub about 1.5 m high. Leaves stalked, trifoliolate, leaflets subsessile, 3–7.5 cm long, 1.5–

3.5 cm wide, elliptic to ovate, obtuse at both ends, usually mucronate, glabrous above, more or less silky haired beneath. Flowers pinkish to purplish in axillary and terminal racemes. Fruit a pod, four- to eight-jointed, densely appressed hairy. Flowers August–September, fruits November–December. Propagated by seeds. Distributed throughout Nepal at 1000–2500 m in open, dry places; also in northern India, Bhutan, and southern and eastern Asia including China.

MEDICINE. Juice of the root, about 3 teaspoons twice a day, is given in cases of peptic ulcer. Powder of the root, about 1 teaspoon, is given for stomach acidity.

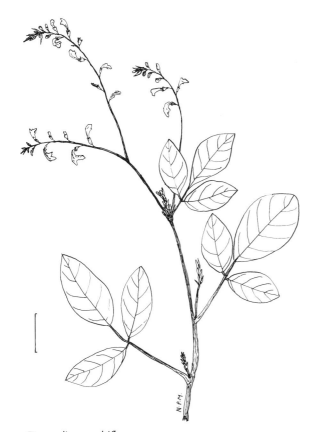

Desmodium multiflorum

Desmodium oojeinense (Roxburgh) Ohashi

Dalbergia oojeinensis Roxburgh
Ougeinia dalbergioides Bentham
DANUWAR *jhonkhimamarkha* NEPALI *sandan* RAUTE *pandang*

Leguminosae. Tree with light brown bark. Leaves stalked, trifoliolate, leaflets short-stalked, 7–14 cm long, 4.5–10 cm wide, entire, glabrous above, slightly brownish beneath, tip obtuse, slightly rounded toward the base. Flowers purplish. Fruit a pod. Flowers February–March, fruits May–July. Propagated by seeds. Distributed in central and western Nepal at 1000–1300 m in mixed forest; also in India.

MEDICINE. Juice of the root, mixed with the powder of two fruits of black pepper (*Piper nigrum*), is taken in cases of eye trouble. A paste of the bark is applied to cuts and wounds.

OTHER USES. The plant is lopped for fodder. Wood is used to make plows and handles of agricultural tools. It is said to withstand termites. Bark is used as fish poison.

Desmodium podocarpum de Candolle

NEPALI *gahare ghans*

Leguminosae. Shrub about 1 m high. Leaves stalked, trifoliolate, terminal leaflet longer, leaflets broadly ovate, entire, membranous, dark green above, glaucous beneath, usually acute at the apex, cuneate at the base. Flowers pinkish in axillary racemes. Fruit a pod, the upper margin straight, lower margin deeply indented. Propagated by seeds. Distributed throughout Nepal at 1500–2000 m in open, dry places; also in northern India, Bhutan, southern and eastern Tibet, China, Korea, and Japan.

MEDICINE. Juice of the root is given in cases of fever.

Desmodium triflorum (Linnaeus) de Candolle

Hedysarum triflorum Linnaeus
DANUWAR *jonki mamarkha* NEPALI *bakhre ghans, bute kanike*
TAMANG *nimphuli*

Leguminosae. Prostrate herb about 20 cm high. Leaves trifoliolate, leaflets 4–7 mm long, cuneate, ovate, apex truncate or emarginate. Flowers pink, axillary. Fruit a pod, three- to five-jointed. Flowers April–September, fruits September–October. Propagated by seeds. Distributed throughout Nepal at 500–2000 m, often in open places along roadsides; also in Pakistan, India, Sri Lanka, southern and eastern Asia including China, Australia, islands of the Pacific Ocean, Africa, and tropical North America.

MEDICINE. Tender leaves or roots are chewed about 10 minutes to alleviate toothaches. Juice of the leaves is recommended in cases of diarrhea and dysentery. It is also applied to heal wounds.

OTHER USES. Twigs are browsed by cattle.

Desmostachya bipinnata (Linnaeus) Stapf

Briza bipinnata Linnaeus
Poa cynosuroides Retzius, *Eragrostis cynosuroides* (Retzius) Palisot de Beauvois
DANUWAR *kush* LEPCHA *tarobongmat* LIMBU *hoyek* MOOSHAR *kush* NEPALI *kush* NEWARI *kush* RAI *yachhamnuma* SUNWAR *ush* TAMANG *ush* THARU *ush* TIBETAN *ku-sha*

Gramineae. Tufted perennial grass about 2 m high. Leaves linear lanceolate, rigid, tip filiform, margin hispid. Inflorescence reddish brown. Flowers and fruits June–October. Propagated by seeds or by splitting the roots. Distributed throughout Nepal to about 300 m in fallow fields and on unused grounds; also in Iran, Afghanistan, Pakistan, India, Arabia, and northern and tropical Africa.

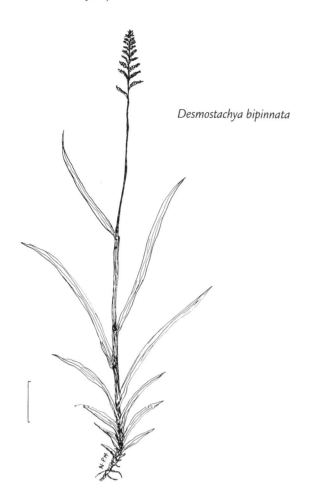

Desmostachya bipinnata

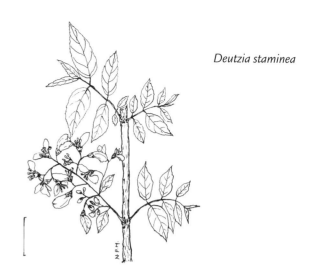

Deutzia staminea

MEDICINE. Juice of the root is given in cases of indigestion. A paste of the root is applied to treat dental caries. Culms are diuretic and used for dysentery.

OTHER USES. Plants are used for thatching and making rope. The plant is used in religious ceremonies such as *shraddha*, that is, rituals and offerings to the dead.

Deutzia staminea R. Brown ex Wallich

Deutzia brunoniana Wallich
NEPALI *sun taule* TAMANG *pana mhendo*

Hydrangeaceae. Shrub about 2 m high, bark pale brown, rather fibrous. Leaves stalked, 0.8–7 cm long, 0.5–3.8 cm wide, lanceolate, minutely serrulate, rough with stellate pubescence, gray beneath. Flowers white, fragrant, in short, trichotomous, terminal panicles. Fruit a capsule, truncated globose, hairy. Flowers April–June. Propagated by seeds or cuttings. Distributed throughout Nepal at 1100–2800 m, usually on sunny hillsides; also in northern India and Bhutan.

MEDICINE. Juice of the root, about 4 teaspoons three times a day, is given to treat fever.

OTHER USES. The plant is gathered for fodder. The Tamangs of Rasuwa district offer flowers to their lineage god.

Dicentra scandens (D. Don) Walpers

Dielytra scandens D. Don
Dactylicapnos thalictrifolia Wallich, *Dicentra thalictrifolia* (Wallich) Hooker fil. & Thomson
GURUNG *barkha jyal, jhapakane, lhan, odal jal, pichikine jhyal*
NEPALI *bichakane, jhilinge, sano pahenli, yarling jhar*

Fumariaceae. Climbing herb. Leaves stalked, decompound, petioles ending in branched tendrils, leaflets subsessile, 0.6–3 cm long, 0.4–2.5 cm wide, elliptic to ovate, acute, entire, membranous. Flowers yellow in racemes opposite to the leaf stalk. Flowers and fruits April–October. Propagated by seeds. Distributed throughout Nepal at 1400–2200 m in open as well as shady places; also in northern India, Bhutan, western China, and Indo-China.

Dicentra scandens

MEDICINE. The plant is fed to livestock as an anthelmintic. Juice of the plant, about 4 teaspoons four times a day, is given to treat fever. Juice of the root is applied to wounds between the toes caused by prolonged walking barefooted in muddy water, especially during the rainy season. Juice of the leaves is dripped into the eyes for eye troubles and is applied to cuts and wounds.

Dichanthium annulatum (Forsskål) Stapf

Andropogon annulatus Forsskål

ENGLISH *marvel grass* NEPALI *apong, seto ranki*

Gramineae. Tufted perennial grass about 1 m high. Leaves linear, bristly. Inflorescence greenish. Flowers and fruits August–January. Propagated by seeds or by splitting the rhizome. Distributed throughout Nepal to about 1100 m on uncultivated land, among hedges, and on roadsides; also in India, Myanmar, and northern and tropical Africa.

OTHER USES. The plant is used as fodder.

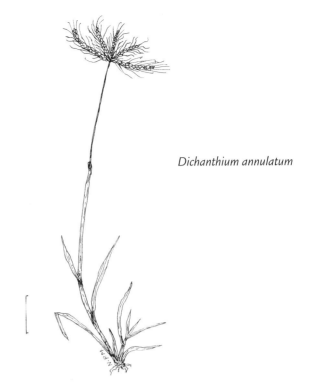

Dichanthium annulatum

Dichroa febrifuga Loureiro

Adamia cyanea Wallich

CHEPANG *basak* ENGLISH *Chinese quinine, fever flower*
GURUNG *kharsata, patre, polokamji, selkainchi* LEPCHA *gebokanak*
MAGAR *basak* NEPALI *bansuli, basak, ganaune pat*
TAMANG *dharmen, mabra*

Hydrangeaceae. Shrub about 3 m high. Leaves stalked, opposite, 4–17 cm long, 1.5–6 cm wide, lanceolate, serrate, tapering toward the stalk. Flowers blue in terminal corymbose panicles. Fruit a berry, ovoid, deep blue. Flowers May–June, fruits October–February. Propagated by seeds or root offshoots. Distributed in central and eastern Nepal at 1000–2500 m in open areas and on neglected ground; also in India, Bhutan, eastward to central China, Malaysia, and Taiwan.

MEDICINE. The root is emetic and febrifuge. Juice of the root, about 2 teaspoons twice a day, is given for fever. It is also considered good for indigestion. Juice of the leaves is given in cases of cough, colds, and bronchitis. A decoction of the leaves, about 4 teaspoons three times a day, is given to treat malarial fever.

OTHER USES. The plant is used as fuel. It is planted as a hedge and has healthy growth on moist, loamy soil.

Dichrocephala benthamii C. B. Clarke

NEPALI *chhiuke jhar*

Compositae. Suberect annual herb. Leaves short-stalked, alternate, obovate, sinuately lobed or spatulate. Flower heads yellowish. Fruit an achene. Flowers and fruits May–June. Propagated by seeds. Distributed in eastern and central Nepal at 600–2500 m in moist, shady places; also in India, Bhutan, China, and Indo-China.

MEDICINE. Juice of the plant is dripped into the nostrils for nasal infections.

Dichroa febrifuga

Dichrocephala integrifolia (Linnaeus fil.) Kuntze

Hippia integrifolia Linnaeus fil.
Cotula bicolor Roth
Grangea latifolia Lamarck, *Dichrocephala latifolia* (Lamarck)
de Candolle
ENGLISH *sneeze weed* GURUNG *bhui khursani, dalidar*
NEPALI *chhyun jhar, goras pan, hachhyun jhar, hachitu, remalime jhar*
TAMANG *bikh*

Compositae. Small herb. Leaves spatulate, irregularly dentate, sparsely hairy on both surfaces. Flower heads small, globose, greenish, on slender divaricating peduncles. Fruit an achene without pappus, compressed. Flowers March–September, fruits August–October. Propagated by seeds. Distributed throughout Nepal to about 3000 m, in open as well as shady places; also in tropical and subtropical Asia, islands of the Pacific Ocean, and Africa.

MEDICINE. Juice of the plant is applied to cuts and wounds. This juice, about 1 teaspoon, is given in cases of malarial fever. It is also put into the nose to treat sinusitis and migraine. When the aroma of squeezed flower heads is inhaled, it induces sneezing, relieving nasal congestion.

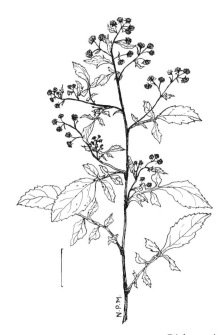

Dichrocephala integrifolia

Dicranostigma lactucoides Hooker fil. & Thomson

Stylophorum lactucoides (Hooker fil. & Thomson) Bentham &
Hooker fil.
TIBETAN *male ponga*

Papaveraceae. Herb with a thick taproot. Lower leaves stalked, upper leaves sessile, pinnate, leaflets broadly ovate, dentate, glaucous beneath. Flowers yellow. Fruit a capsule, oblong or linear, splitting by two or four valves. Flowers June–July. Propagated by seeds. Distributed in

Dicranostigma lactucoides

western and central Nepal at 2700–4000 m on rocky slopes; also in northern India.

MEDICINE. Squeezed root, boiled in water, is given to women who have difficulty in expelling the placenta after childbirth.

Didymocarpus albicalyx C. B. Clarke

Didymocarpus leucocalyx C. B. Clarke
Didymocarpus villosa D. Don
GURUNG *kum kum dhup* NEPALI *kum kum dhup*

Gesneriaceae. Delicate herb about 12 cm high. Leaves stalked, 3–5 cm long, 2–3.5 cm wide, obovate, serrate, villous on both surfaces. Flowers deep purple in long-stalked cymes, July–August. Propagated by seeds or by splitting the rhizome. Distributed in central and eastern Nepal at 1200–1800 m in moist rock crevices; also in northern India and Bhutan.

OTHER USES. The dried leaf base of the plant is burned as incense. Powdered leaves are mixed with vegetable oil and applied to stimulate hair growth.

Didymocarpus aromaticus Wallich ex D. Don

Didymocarpus subalternans Wallich ex R. Brown
NEPALI *pakhanbhetta*

Gesneriaceae. Herb about 30 cm high. Leaves stalked, 2.5–9.5 cm long, 1.5–7.5 cm wide, broadly elliptic, finely dentate, densely woolly hairy. Flowers deep purple. Flowers and fruits June–August. Propagated by seeds or by splitting the rhizome. Distributed throughout Nepal at 1600–3000 m on mossy, wet rocks, and tree trunks and branches; also in northern India and Bhutan.

MEDICINE. The plant is fed to livestock in cases of bovine hematuria.

Didymocarpus cinereus D. Don

Didymocarpus obtusa Wallich ex R. Brown
GURUNG *dhupi* NEPALI *gaurinam, paharo ko kan*

Gesneriaceae. Herb about 20 cm high. Leaves basal, broadly oblong, obtuse, crenate, base cordate, pubescent above and on the veins beneath. Flowers purple in pubescent cymes. Flowers and fruits July–August. Propagated by seeds or by splitting the rhizome. Distributed throughout Nepal to about 2000 m on mossy rocks, and tree trunks and branches; also in northern India and Bhutan.

OTHER USES. Powdered rhizome is used as incense.

Didymocarpus pedicellatus R. Brown

Didymocarpus macrophylla Wallich ex D. Don
NEPALI *kum*

Gesneriaceae. Stemless herb. Leaves all basal, long-stalked, ovate, crenate to serrate, punctate above, gray-white beneath. Flowers purple on a long scape. Fruit a capsule, linear, longitudinally two-valved. Flowers August–September, fruits September–November. Propagated by seeds or by splitting the rhizome. Distributed throughout Nepal at 500–2500 m in moist, shady places; also in northern India.

MEDICINE. Juice of the leaves is given for kidney trouble, most likely when kidney stones are present.

OTHER USES. A powder of the root and rhizome is used as incense.

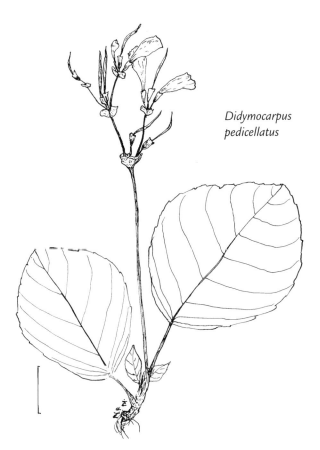

Didymocarpus pedicellatus

Didymocarpus villosus D. Don

NEPALI *kiya*

Gesneriaceae. Herb about 15 cm high. Leaves stalked, ovate, cuneate, obtuse, densely villous above, nearly glabrous beneath. Flowers purplish in many-flowered cymes. Fruit a capsule, the tip curved. Flowers and fruits July–August. Propagated by seeds or by splitting the rhizome. Distributed in eastern and central Nepal at 1000–2400 m in moist rock crevices; also in northern India and Bhutan.

FOOD. Tender stems are cooked as a vegetable, especially when food is scarce.

Digitaria ciliaris (Retzius) Koeler

Panicum ciliare Retzius
Panicum adscendens Kunth, *Digitaria adscendens* (Kunth) Henrard
ENGLISH *crabgrass* NEPALI *banso, chitre banso* TAMANG *pang*

Gramineae. Annual grass about 1 m high. Leaves linear, base contracted. Inflorescence greenish. Flowers and fruits July–November. Propagated by seeds. Distributed in eastern and central Nepal at 600–1500 m in moist places; also in the tropics of the eastern hemisphere.

OTHER USES. The plant provides nutritious animal feed.

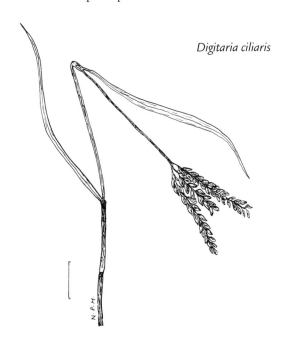

Digitaria ciliaris

Dillenia indica Linnaeus

ENGLISH *elephant apple* LEPCHA *thapru*
NEPALI *chalta, panchaphal, ramphal*

Dilleniaceae. Evergreen tree about 30 m high. Leaves stalked, 15–25 cm long, 5–10 cm wide, oblanceolate, deeply and sharply serrate, parallel veined from the midrib, petiole with sheathing base. Flowers large, solitary, white, fragrant. Fruit circular, hard outside, fleshy inside. Flowers June–July, fruits January–February. Propagated by seeds. Distributed in eastern and central Nepal to about 300 m on moist banks of forest streams; also in India, Sri Lanka, southern China, and Southeast Asia.

FOOD. The fleshy calyx has an agreeable acidic taste and is eaten raw or cooked.

MEDICINE. Bark and leaves are astringent. Fruit is tonic, laxative, and used for abdominal disorders.

Dillenia pentagyna Roxburgh

Dillenia floribunda Hooker fil. & Thomson
CHEPANG *tantari* DANUWAR *tantari* NEPALI *tantari* SATAR *sahad*

Dilleniaceae. Deciduous tree about 20 m high, bark gray, fairly smooth. Leaves stalked, 50-75 cm long, 12–30 cm wide, serrate, narrowed toward the base. Flowers yellow, fragrant, in umbels. Fruit succulent. Flowers March–April, fruits May–June. Propagated by seeds. Distributed in central and eastern Nepal to about 1200 m in open places in the foothills, especially common in *Shorea robusta* forest; also in India, Sri Lanka, southern China, and Southeast Asia.

FOOD. Flower buds and young fruits have a pleasant acidic taste and are eaten raw or pickled.

MEDICINE. A paste of the leaves is applied to treat scorpion bites.

OTHER USES. Wood is used for planking, house posts, and furniture. Bark contains 6% tannin. The inner bark yields fiber for cordage. Leaves are used as green manure.

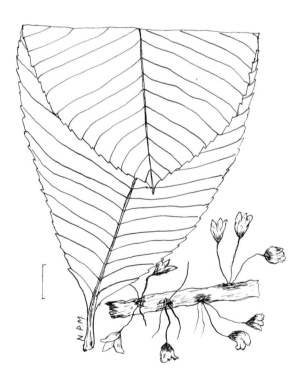

Dillenia pentagyna

Dioscorea bulbifera Linnaeus

Dioscorea sativa Linnaeus
Dioscorea versicolor Buchanan-Hamilton ex Wallich
CHEPANG *pas* DANUWAR *phor* ENGLISH *air potato, potato yam* GURUNG *kamlo, khashyo, kisi* LEPCHA *buk* LIMBU *khe* MAJHI *tarul* NEPALI *ban tarul, bhyakur, githa, kukur tarul* NEWARI *hisaki* RAI *sakkisak* RAUTE *ghar tyaur* SATAR *bengo nari* SHERPA *teme* SUNWAR *kanthamul* THARU *tarul*

Dioscoreaceae. Climbing herb, stems twining to the left, bearing numerous warted bulbils. Leaves stalked, alternate, ovate, acuminate, entire, palmately veined, more or less deeply cordate at the base. Male flowers sessile, bracteate, greenish, drooping, clustered in the leaf axils, female flowers simple, fascicled in the leaf axils. Fruit a capsule, oblong, deeply three-ridged. Flowers June–July, fruits November–December. Propagated by seeds or root tubers. Distributed throughout Nepal to about 2100 m near bushes in moist places; also in the tropics of the eastern hemisphere.

FOOD. The root tubers are boiled and eaten as a vegetable or pickled.

MEDICINE. Juice of the root tubers is taken to expel threadworms. This juice is dripped into wounds to expel worms and germs. This juice, mixed with turmeric powder (*Curcuma domestica*) and local beer, is given in cases of food poisoning.

Dioscorea deltoidea Wallich ex Grisebach

Dioscorea nepalensis Sweet, *Tam(n)us nepalensis* (Sweet) Jacquemont ex Prain & Burkill
CHEPANG *goi* DANUWAR *genthi* ENGLISH *yam* GURUNG *kondro, tentur, thenjo, time* MAGAR *name* NEPALI *bhyakur, gune kauro* NEWARI *tarul* RAI *sakki* SUNWAR *reb* TAMANG *githa, rhideme, temme* THARU *aruwa, kukurak gentha*

Dioscoreaceae. Climbing herb, stems glabrous, twining to the left. Leaves stalked, alternate, 6–12 cm long, 5.5–10 cm wide, variable in size, broadly ovate to cordate, long-pointed, five- or seven-veined. Male flowers solitary, small, white, axillary, only a few arranged alternately on a long stalk, female flowers solitary, slender. Fruit a capsule, deltoid, three-ridged. Flowers April–May, fruits October–November. Propagated by seeds or root tubers. Distributed throughout Nepal at 300–3000 m in moist, open, rocky places but collection of roots for local consumption and sale in the trade is a cause of conservation concern; also in western China and Indo-China.

FOOD. The tuberous root is slightly bitter so villagers boil it, mixing in some wood ash. It is then eaten or cooked as a vegetable (Plate 4).

MEDICINE. Juice of the root tuber, about 10 teaspoons, is given at bedtime to treat for roundworms. It also alleviates constipation. Axillary bulbs from the upper parts of the plant are boiled in water about 10 minutes, and the liquid is taken for gastric trouble. Juice of these bulbs, about 6 teaspoons three times a day, is given for bloody dysentery.

Dioscorea deltoidea

OTHER USES. Squeezed root is mixed with water for washing clothes and is also sprinkled on water to catch fish.

Dioscorea pentaphylla Linnaeus

CHEPANG *hung, jar, gliha* ENGLISH *wild yam* GURUNG *temen, timi* MAGAR *lauka, mangai* NEPALI *chuinyan, jagate bhyakur, tyaguno* SATAR *aser*

Dioscoreaceae. Climbing herb, stems slender, pubescent, twining to the left, prickly toward the base. Leaves stalked, alternate, three- or five-foliolate, sparsely pubescent, earlier leaflets elliptic to lanceolate, acuminate or cuspidate, base usually acute, later leaflets broader, base oblique. Male flowers pale greenish in large panicles, female flowers axillary, solitary or two or three together, pubescent. Fruit a capsule, slightly pubescent. Seeds winged at the tip. Flowers and fruits August–March. Propagated by seeds or root tubers. Distributed throughout Nepal at 600–1500 m in moist, open, rocky places; also in India, China, and Southeast Asia.

FOOD. Root tubers are boiled, peeled, and prepared as a vegetable, curry, and pickle. Generally, boiled roots are eaten like boiled potatoes.

MEDICINE. Juice of the plant is applied to boils.

Diospyros kaki Thunberg

ENGLISH *Japanese persimmon* NEPALI *haluwa bet* TIBETAN *shing-log-a-mra*

Ebenaceae. Deciduous tree about 15 m high, bark corky, greenish brown. Leaves stalked, 5–12.5 cm long, 0.5–5 cm wide, oblanceolate, bluntly acuminate, leathery, glabrous above, pubescent beneath. Flowers yellowish in small cymose clusters. Fruit globose, orange-red or yellow when ripe. Flowers March–May, fruits July–September. Propagated by seeds. Distributed in central and eastern Nepal to about 1200 m, cultivated; also in China, southern Korea, and Japan.

FOOD. Ripe fruits are edible.

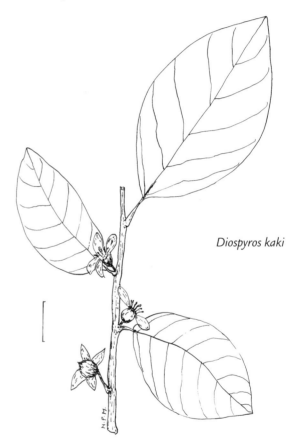

Diospyros kaki

Diplazium esculentum (Retzius) Swartz ex Schrader

NEPALI *pani nyuro* SATAR *ghinki arak*

Dryopteridaceae. Fern about 1 m high. Fronds deep green, 35–85 cm long, 15–35 cm wide, bipinnatifid. Sori oblong, obliquely placed along the veins of the segments. Propagated by spores or by splitting the rhizomes. Distributed throughout Nepal to about 1500 m in moist, shady places; also in India, Bhutan, China, and Thailand.

FOOD. Tender fronds are cooked as a vegetable.

MEDICINE. Juice of the rhizome, about 4 teaspoons twice a day, is given in cases of malarial fever. A paste of the frond is applied to treat scabies and boils.

Diplazium giganteum (Baker) Ching

NEPALI *daunde*

Dryopteridaceae. Fern with erect straw-colored stipe, pinnae 40–50 cm long, 10–15 cm wide, lanceolate, pinnules oblong to lanceolate, cut down to the rachis, lobes elliptic to rhombic. Sori oblong, brown, in two oblique rows on the segments. Propagated by spores or by splitting the rhizomes. Distributed in central and western Nepal at 1000–3000 m in moist, rocky places.

FOOD. Tender fronds are cooked as a vegetable.

Diplazium polypodioides Blume

GURUNG *chyan, chyangan* NEPALI *hare unyu*

Dryopteridaceae. Herbaceous fern. Fronds 40–90 cm long, 15–40 cm wide, tripinnate, pinnae subopposite at the base, opposite above, lanceolate, pinnules serrate. Sori oblong, on either side of the veinlets. Propagated by spores or by splitting the rhizomes. Distributed throughout Nepal at 1300–2500 m on shady forest floor along stream banks.

MEDICINE. Juice of the root is applied to cuts and wounds.

Diplazium stoliczkae

Diplazium stoliczkae Beddome

NEPALI *kalo nyuro*

Dryopteridaceae. Fern with smooth or slightly hairy stipe and rachis. Fronds 10–90 cm long, 15–30 cm wide, pinnate, pinnae many, short-stalked, only a few opposite or subopposite toward the base, other pinnae alternate, gradually tapering toward the apex. Sori linear. Propagated by spores or by splitting the rhizomes. Distributed throughout Nepal between 1500–4000 m in damp places, common.

FOOD. Tender fronds are cooked as a vegetable.

Diplocyclos palmatus (Linnaeus) C. Jeffrey

Bryonia palmata Linnaeus
Bryonia lacinosa Linnaeus, *Bryonopsis lacinosa* (Linnaeus) Naudin
Zehneria erythrocarpa F. Mueller

CHEPANG *garumi lahara, sano ghuru* NEPALI *shivalingi* RAUTE *belo*

Cucurbitaceae. Climber with bifid tendrils. Leaves stalked, palmately five-lobed, lobes 5–8 cm long. Flowers yellowish. Flowers and fruits August–October. Propagated by seeds. Distributed throughout Nepal at 300–1500 m in open, moist places; also in India, Sri Lanka, eastward to southern China, southern Japan, Malaysia, Australia, and Africa.

MEDICINE. A paste of the seed, about 1 teaspoon three times a day, is given to treat fever.

OTHER USES. Seeds are used as soap substitute by village women to wash their heads.

Diplocyclos palmatus

Diplokenma butyracea (Roxburgh) H. J. Lam

Bassia butyracea Roxburgh, *Aesandra butyracea* (Roxburgh) Baehni, *Illipe butyracea* (Roxburgh) Engler, *Madhuca butyracea* (Roxburgh) Macbride

BHOJPURI *chiuli* CHEPANG *alasi sai, yo* DANUWAR *chiuli* ENGLISH *Indian butter tree* LEPCHA *yelpos* LIMBU *imseva* MAGAR *chyuri* NEPALI *chyuri* NEWARI *lhuchhi pu ma* RAI *isi* SUNWAR *chyuri* TAMANG *chiyumli, singmar* THARU *chihuli*

Sapotaceae. Deciduous tree about 20 m high. Leaves stalked, 14–30 cm long, 7.5–16 cm wide, generally crowded near the ends of branches, oblong to ovate, entire, acuminate, hairy beneath, glabrous above. Flowers stalked, crowded at the ends of branches, yellowish. Fruit a berry, pear shaped, with one or two seeds. Flowers November–January, fruits April–July. Propagated by seeds. Distributed throughout Nepal at 300–1500 m on open hillsides but the gathering of wood for fuel and timber, and fruit for sale in the trade, is a cause of conservation concern; also in northern India and Bhutan.

FOOD. Juice of the corolla is boiled into a syrupy liquid, which villagers use like syrupy sugar. Juicy pulp of ripe fruit is eaten fresh. The vegetable butter extracted from seeds is used for cooking and lighting lamps. Chepangs put roasted seeds in a triangular bamboo basket, which is pressed between two wooden planks to extract oil (one end of the planks is fixed and the other end bound tightly).

MEDICINE. Juice of the bark, about 4 teaspoons, is given to treat indigestion. This juice, mixed with bark juice of *Berberis asiatica* in equal amount, is boiled about 10 minutes, and the resultant liquid, about 4 teaspoons twice a day, is given to treat asthma. This juice is also given as an anthelmintic and is applied in cases of rheumatic pain and boils. Seed oil is applied for headache and rheumatism, also to boils, pimples, and burns.

OTHER USES. The plant constitutes an important source of nectar and pollen for bees. It is suitable for controlling soil erosion and provides fodder. According to Gamble (1922), bark has been used for fish poison in Sikkim, India. It is poisonous to chickens as well. Wood is used for furniture and fuel. Leaves are used as plates. In urban areas, vegetable butter extracted from seeds is used to manufacture soap and candles. Oil cake is used to poison fish and as a fertilizer to protect crops from harmful insects and worms.

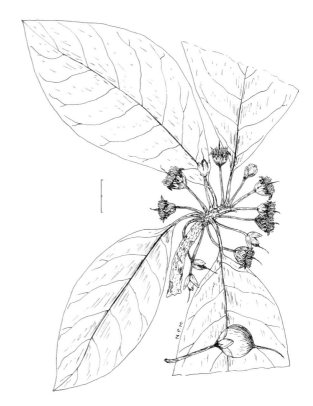

Diplokenma butyracea

Dipsacus inermis Wallich

Virga inermis (Wallich) Holub
Dipsacus mitis D. Don
Dipsacus strictus D. Don

CHEPANG *ban gurdabari* ENGLISH *Nepalese teasel* NEPALI *ban karyal, mula patr* TAMANG *krapodo, riphuli* TIBETAN *khondro, kotanchhin*

Dipsacaceae. Erect herb about 1 m high, covered with stiff hairs. Leaves opposite, 6–20 cm long, ovate to lanceolate, coarsely dentate, basal leaves stalked, upper leaves sessile, bases dilated and united. Flowers white, crowded

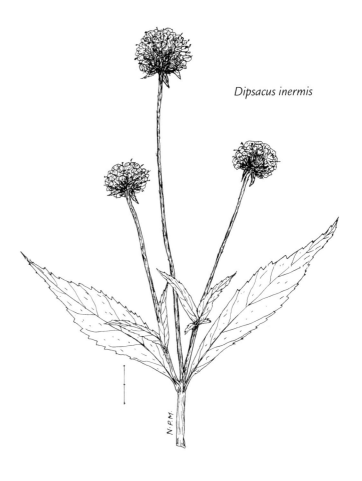

Dipsacus inermis

in hemispheric heads, August–October. Fruits October–November. Propagated by seeds. Distributed in central and western Nepal at 1200–3300 m in open places; also in Afghanistan and northern India.

OTHER USES. The plant provides fodder.

Disporum cantoniense (Loureiro) Merrill

Fritillaria cantoniense Loureiro
Disporum piullum Salisbury
Uvularia chinensis Ker-Gawler
CHEPANG *yom goidung*   NEPALI *mhajari, sano kukurdino*
TAMANG *rajali*

Convallariaceae. Herb about 1 m high. Leaves short-stalked, alternate, lanceolate, acuminate, membranous, base cordate. Flowers greenish white in few-flowered umbels, May–June. Propagated by seeds. Distributed throughout Nepal at 1100–2900 m in shady, cool places; also in northern India and northern Indo-China.

FOOD. Tender leaves and shoots are cooked as a vegetable.

MEDICINE. Juice of the root is given in cases of fever.

Docynia indica (Wallich) Decaisne

Pyrus indica Wallich
Docynia docynioides (C. K. Schneider) Rehder
Docynia griffithiana Decaisne
Docynia hookeriana Decaisne
Docynia rufilolia (Léveillé) Rehder
NEPALI *ekere*

Rosaceae. Tree about 5 m high. Leaves stalked, 3.5–10 cm long, oblong to lanceolate, long acuminate, entire or serrulate, glabrous above, densely woolly beneath. Flowers white, solitary or fascicled. Fruit globose. Propagated by seeds or cuttings. Distributed in eastern Nepal at 1000–2000 m in open places; also in India, Bhutan, China, and Indo-China.

FOOD. Ripe fruits are edible.

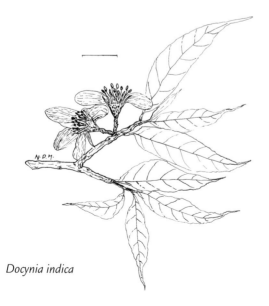

Docynia indica

Dodecadenia grandiflora Nees

Tetranthera grandifora
NEPALI *kaule, pahenli, pawari*

Lauraceae. Evergreen tree about 10 m high, bark with evident lenticels, exfoliating in woody scales. Leaves stalked, 5–18 cm long, 1–4.5 cm wide, oblong to lanceolate, shortly acuminate, leathery, margin undulate, silky tomentose when young, glabrous when mature, dark green above, glaucescent beneath. Flowers stalked, yellowish, axillary, usually solitary, sometimes two together. Fruit a berry, ellipsoidal, purplish black. Flowers March–April, fruits November–December. Propagated by seeds. Distributed throughout Nepal at 1500–2900 m, usually in shady oak forests; also in northern India, southern Tibet, and Myanmar.

OTHER USES. Goats like to browse the leaves.

Dodecadenia grandiflora

Drepanostachyum falcatum (Nees) Keng fil.

Arundinaria falcata Nees, *Chimonobambusa falcata* (Nees) Nakai, *Sinarundinaria falcata* (Nees) C. S. Chao & Renvoize
CHEPANG *saiphing*   ENGLISH *Himalayan bamboo*   GURUNG *kama*
MAGAR *ghure chui*   NEPALI *diu nigalo, ghore nigalo, nigalo, tite nigalo, tithe, tusa*   TAMANG *mha*

Gramineae. Bamboo about 4 m high, culms not straight, about 2 cm in diameter, much branched, stem hollow, smooth, nodes much swollen, slightly hairy, internodes thin walled, branchlets from the nodes in clusters, culm sheaths papery, straw colored, as long as the internodes. Leaves stalked, linear, base sheathing, round, point tapering, slightly hairy, pellucid glands in rows between the veins. Inflorescence on a separate leafless stem, greenish, condensed at the nodes. Propagated by splitting the rhizomes. Distributed in western Nepal at 1000–2000 m in moist, rocky places; also in India, Bangladesh, and Myanmar.

FOOD. Young shoots are cooked as a vegetable. They are also fermented and preserved (*tama* in Nepali). *Tama* is sour and has a very strong flavor; it is sometimes mixed in vegetable curries.

OTHER USES. Stems are used in making baskets, mats, and fishing rods and to line ceilings. It provides useful fodder, especially in winter.

Drepanostachyum intermedium

Drepanostachyum falcatum

Drepanostachyum intermedium (Munro) Keng fil.

Arundinaria intermedia Munro, *Chimonobambusa intermedia* (Munro) Nakai, *Sinarundinaria intermedia* (Munro) C. S. Chao & Renvoize

NEPALI *nigalo bans, tite nigalo*

Gramineae. Resilient bamboo about 4 m high, culm about 2 cm wide, nodes swollen, leaf sheath persistent, auricles with widely spreading bristles, hairy outside and inside, top narrow. Propagated by splitting the rhizome. Distributed in eastern Nepal at 1000–2000 m on open, rocky ground; also in India and Southeast Asia.

OTHER USES. The plant is used for construction, weaving mats and baskets, and walking sticks. Leaves are useful for fodder, especially during winter.

Drosera peltata Smith

ENGLISH *sundew* NEPALI *jhinga jale, makha marne jhar*
TAMANG *nagamichu, panga* TIBETAN *rtag-ngu, sta-nu*

Droseraceae. Herb about 50 m high. Basal leaves stalked, alternate, vanishing rapidly, cauline leaves alternate, peltate, lunate, with long, glandular tentacles. Flowers white in subterminal racemes. Fruit a capsule enclosed within the persistent calyx. Flowers August–September. Propagated by seeds. Distributed throughout Nepal at 1200–3300 m in open places; also in India, southern Tibet, China, Japan, Southeast Asia, Australia, and Tasmania.

MEDICINE. The plant is spread around an ill person to get rid of flies. Leaves are bitter and acidic, and a paste of the leaves is applied to blisters.

Drosera peltata

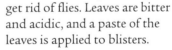

Drymaria cordata (Linnaeus) Willdenow ex Roemer & Schultes

Holosteum cordatum Linnaeus

TAMANG *sadhab*

Caryophyllaceae. Ascending herb. Leaves stalked, 0.8–2 cm long, 0.5–2 cm wide, orbiculate to ovate. Flowers small, white. Fruit a capsule, ovoid, three-angled. Flowers and fruits August–November. Propagated by seeds. Distributed throughout Nepal at 2200–4300 m in open places, along waysides, and on uncultivated land; also in India, southwest China, Taiwan, Southeast Asia, Australia, Africa, and subtropical North America.

FOOD. Tender leaves and shoots are cooked as a vegetable.

MEDICINE. The plant is laxative and gives a cooling effect.

Drymaria diandra Blume

Drymaria cordata subsp. *diandra* (Blume) J. Duke

CHEPANG *aarmale, jalma* GURUNG *aankale, peperano, pipindo, tapke*
NEPALI *abijalo, chhirbire jhar, gorjal, gujale* NEWARI *hichhwalu ghyan*
TAMANG *latapate chhe, nagami chu, tirip mran*

Caryophyllaceae. Diffuse herb. Leaves stalked, 2.5–1 cm long, 0.8–1.8 cm wide, orbiculate or ovate, entire. Flowers small, white, in axillary or terminal clusters. Fruit a capsule. Flowers and fruits most of the year. Propagated by seeds or by nodal rootings. Distributed throughout Nepal to about 2000 m on shady, moist ground; also in northern India, Bhutan, Sri Lanka, western and southern China, Taiwan, southern Japan, Malaysia, Australia, Hawaii, and Africa.

FOOD. Tender portions are eaten as a vegetable.

MEDICINE. Juice of the root is inhaled to treat sinusitis. The plant is laxative and cooling. The plant is heated on the leaf of *Shorea robusta* and the vapor inhaled in cases of headache. The plant, mixed with *Valeriana jatamansii*, is pounded and applied to the stomach of a child suffering from diarrhea and dysentery. A paste of the plant, about 4 teaspoons three times a day, is given for peptic ulcer. This paste is applied to the forehead to treat headaches and ingested to relieve fever caused by cough and colds. Juice of the plant, about 6 teaspoons twice a day, is given for gastric troubles and is also considered useful for indigestion and fever. This juice is also dropped in the eye to treat conjunctivitis.

OTHER USES. The plant is used to make *marcha*, a fermenting cake from which liquor is distilled.

Drymaria villosa Chamisso & Schlechtendal

Drymaria stylosa Backer

NEPALI *abijalo*

Caryophyllaceae. Herb. Leaves short-stalked, 0.3–0.6 cm long, 0.2–0.4 cm wide, ovate, entire, slightly hairy, tip rounded. Flowers white. Propagated by seeds or by nodal rootings. Distributed in eastern and central Nepal at

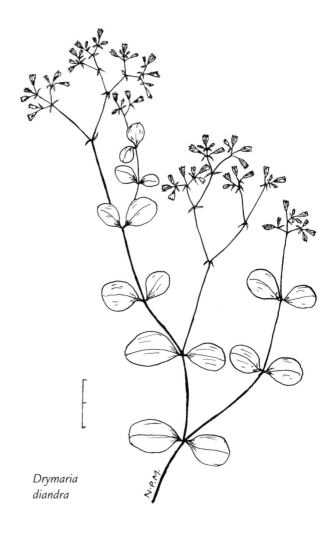

Drymaria diandra

N.P.M.

1000–1900 m in moist, shady places; also in northern India, Malaysia, Africa, and Central and South America.

FOOD. Tender leaves are cooked as a vegetable.

MEDICINE. Juice of the plant, about 6 teaspoons three times a day, is given to treat gastric troubles.

Drynaria mollis Beddome

NEPALI *chyamno*

Polypodiaceae. Epiphytic or terrestrial fern. Rhizome stout, creeping, with bright brown linear scales. Fronds dimorphic, sterile frond 6–15 cm long, 3–4 cm wide, cut three-quarters toward the rachis, spreading, fertile frond 25–40 cm long, 6–10 cm wide, with distinct stipe. Sori conspicuous, bright brown, close together in a row on either side of the midvein. Propagated by spores or by nodal rootings. Distributed throughout Nepal at 1300–3000 m on tree trunks and branches, rocks, and in shady places; also in India and Bhutan.

MEDICINE. A paste of the rhizome is applied to treat backaches. The rhizome is boiled in water until the liquid is half the original amount. It is then used to wash areas around dislocated bones in animals to relieve pain.

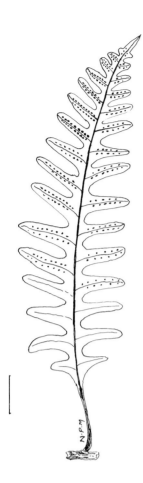

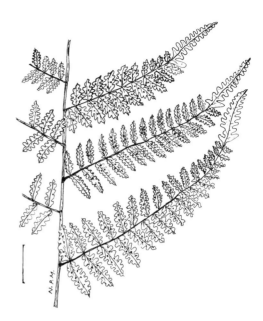

Dryoathyrium boryanum

Drynaria mollis

Drynaria propinqua (Wallich ex Mettenius) J. Smith
NEPALI *kammari* TAMANG *nakabhyak*

Polypodiaceae. Epiphytic or terrestrial fern. Rhizome wide, creeping, with brown, linear lanceolate scales. Fronds glabrous, 30–50 cm long, 15–20 cm wide, with distinct stipe, lobes serrate, reaching down near the rachis. Sori yellowish brown, in a single row along the midvein. Propagated by spores or by nodal rootings. Distributed throughout Nepal at 900–2800 m in shady places near streams; also in northern India, Bhutan, southern and central China, Myanmar, Thailand, and Malaysia.

MEDICINE. A paste of the rhizome is applied to treat backache and dislocated bone. This paste is considered good for sprains and is also applied to the forehead to relieve headaches.

Dryoathyrium boryanum (Willdenow) Ching
NEPALI *bisyau, dunde, ghyu nyuro, kalo nyuro*

Dryopteridaceae. Herbaceous fern. Stipes scaly at the base. Fronds 35 cm long, pinnate, pinnae sessile, deeply cut into oblong pinnules. Sori round, in a row on either side of the veinlet. Propagated by spores or by nodal rootings. Distributed in central and western Nepal at 1400–3000 m in moist places; also in India, Bhutan, Myanmar, Thailand and East Africa.

FOOD. Tender shoots and fronds are cooked as a vegetable.

Dryopteris chrysocoma (C. Christensen) C. Christensen
NEPALI *chyamle*

Dryopteridaceae. Herbaceous fern. Rhizome densely scaly. Fronds 10–25 cm long, 5–8 cm wide, lanceolate, pinnate, pinnae sessile, subopposite, lanceolate, deeply cut down to the rachis, segments serrate. Sori brown, on the basal part of each segment. Propagated by spores or by splitting the rhizomes. Distributed in central Nepal at 1500–3200 m in moist places; also in India, Bhutan, and central China.

MEDICINE. Juice of the rhizome is applied to cuts and wounds.

Dryopteris cochleata (D. Don) C. Christensen
CHEPANG *sete* NEPALI *danthe nyuro, kuthurke* TAMANG *waba degni*

Dryopteridaceae. Terrestrial fern. Stipes tufted, more or less clothed with scales. Fronds 25–80 cm long, pinnate, pinnae short-stalked, lanceolate, crenate. Sori reniform, near the middle on either side of the veinlet. Propagated by spores or by splitting the rhizomes. Distributed in central and western Nepal to about 1600 m on damp forest floor; also in India, China, Myanmar, Thailand, and Malaysia.

FOOD. Tender shoots and fronds are cooked as a green vegetable.

MEDICINE. Juice of the root, about 2 teaspoons twice a day, is given in cases of diarrhea and dysentery.

Dryopteris cochleata

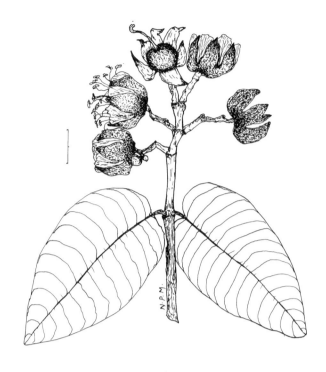

Duabanga grandiflora

Dryopteris sparsa (D. Don) Kuntze

NEPALI *jire nyuro, kuthurke*

Dryopteridaceae. Tufted fern. Fronds light green, 55–80 cm long, 15–25 cm wide, lanceolate, multipinnate. Sori round. Propagated by spores or by splitting the rhizomes. Distributed in central Nepal at 500–2300 m on moist or dry hillsides.

MEDICINE. A paste of the rhizome is applied to boils, cuts, and wounds.

Duabanga grandiflora (Roxburgh ex de Candolle) Walpers

Lagerstroemia grandiflora Roxburgh ex de Candolle,
  Leptospartion grandiflorum (Roxburgh ex de Candolle)
  Griffith
Duabanga sonneratioides Buchanan-Hamilton

CHEPANG *plangasi* NEPALI *lampate, madane, pani saj*

Sonneratiaceae. Tree about 35 m high. Leaves stalked, 8.5–24.5 cm long, 4–11.5 cm wide, broadly lanceolate, entire, glabrous, tip rounded, base cordate. Flowers white, December–March. Fruits May–August. Propagated by seeds. Distributed throughout Nepal to about 1000 m, on the slopes of riverbanks; also in northern India, Bhutan, southeastern Tibet, southwestern China, and Southeast Asia.

FOOD. Fruits are eaten fresh and have a sour taste.

OTHER USES. The plant is lopped for fodder. Wood is used to make household utensils. Bark is used for fish poison.

Duranta repens Linnaeus

Duranta plumieri Jacquin

ENGLISH *golden dewberry, pigeon berry, sky flower* NEPALI *nil kanda*

Verbenaceae. Erect shrub about 4 m high, branches often drooping. Leaves stalked, 1–4.5 cm long, 0.7–2.5 cm wide, elliptic to ovate, acuminate or rounded, dentate

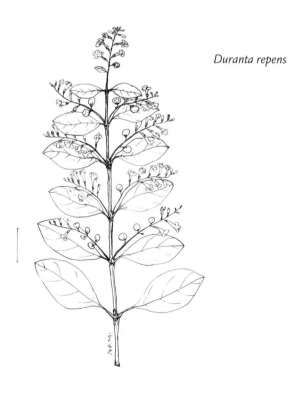

Duranta repens

above the middle, base cuneate. Flowers purplish blue in axillary and terminal racemes. Fruit a berry, ovoid, fleshy, orange when ripe. Flowers and fruits most of the year. Propagated by seeds or cuttings. Distributed throughout Nepal to about 1600 m; also in India, China, Central America, and the West Indies.

MEDICINE. An infusion of the leaves is diuretic and antipyretic. Juice of the fruit is spread on ponds and swampy places as a larvicide.

OTHER USES. The plant is grown as a hedgerow.

E

Echinochloa colona (Linnaeus) Link

Panicum colonum Linnaeus

ENGLISH *barnyard grass* NEPALI *sama*

Gramineae. Annual grass, culms rooting below. Leaves linear, 0.5–0.7 cm wide, narrowed toward the tip. Inflorescence yellowish. Flowers and fruits most of the year. Propagated by seeds. Distributed throughout Nepal at 600–2400 m, cultivated; also in tropical Asia and Africa.

FOOD. The grains are edible.

Echinochloa crus-galli (Linnaeus) Palisot de Beauvois

Panicum crus-galli Linnaeus

Panicum hispidulum Retzius, *Echinochloa hispidula* (Retzius) Nees ex Royle

NEPALI *sama* TAMANG *kuchimran*

Gramineae. Erect grass about 1 m high. Leaves linear, about 1 cm wide. Inflorescence pinkish. Flowers and fruits August–November. Propagated by seeds. Distributed throughout Nepal at 700–2400 m, cultivated in open places; also in India, Sri Lanka, Myanmar, Malaysia, and subtropical Africa.

FOOD. Roasted grains are edible.

OTHER USES. The plant is used for fodder.

Eclipta prostrata (Linnaeus) Linnaeus

Verbesina prostrata Linnaeus, *Eclipta prostrata* (Linnaeus) Roxburgh

Eclipta erecta Linnaeus

Verbesina alba Linnaeus, *Eclipta alba* (Linnaeus) Hasskarl

CHEPANG *chari jhar* DANUWAR *bhangariya* ENGLISH *false daisy* GURUNG *bhiringe* MOOSHAR *gharauriya* NEPALI *aali jhar, bhangeri, bhiringe, bhringaraj, bhiriyo, kal jira, nash jhar* NEWARI *antacha, antali* THARU *bhangarail* TIBETAN *bhri-ga, lug-chhung*

Compositae. Prostrate or suberect herb, often rooting at the nodes. Leaves sessile, 1–5 cm long, 0.4–1 cm wide, oblong to lanceolate, serrate toward the tip, narrowed toward both ends, hairy on both surfaces. Flower heads solitary, axillary, white. Fruit an achene, compressed. Flowers

Echinochloa crus-galli

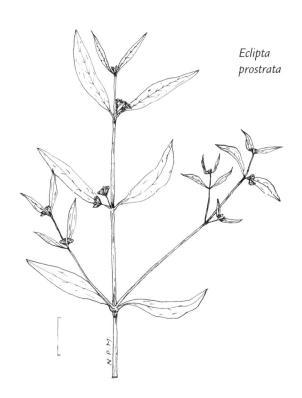

Eclipta prostrata

and fruits most of the year. Propagated by seeds or root offshoots. Distributed throughout Nepal to about 1500 m on moist, neglected ground; also in Pakistan, India, Bhutan, Bangladesh, Sri Lanka, Myanmar, Thailand, and Malaysia.

FOOD. Tender shoots and leaves are cooked as a vegetable.

MEDICINE. A paste of the plant is applied to wounds and skin diseases. In eastern Nepal, the plant is squeezed, mixed in a cup of water, and left a whole night before drinking early the next morning, which is said to purify the blood and give energy to the body. Juice of the plant is applied to fresh cuts to help coagulate blood. The juice is also applied in tatooing, after the skin has been punctured; this helps heal the wound and imparts the desired deep bluish color. The juice helps relieve the burning sensation during urination and ameliorates enlargement of the spleen. The juice, about 6 teaspoons four times a day, is given to treat fever. The root is emetic and purgative, and its juice is applied to cuts, wounds, and pimples. Juice of the root, about 2 teaspoons twice a day, is given in cases of fever. According to N. C. Shah and Joshi (1971), the root is considered a liver tonic. A paste of the seeds is applied to the forehead to treat headaches.

Edgeworthia gardneri (Wallich) Meissner

Daphne gardneri Wallich
ENGLISH *Nepalese paper bush* NEPALI *argeli, arkale pat, pat*
SHERPA *ghyarpati* TAMANG *warpadi*

Thymelaeaceae. Shrub. Leaves short-stalked, crowded near the ends of branches, 2.5–13.5 cm long, 0.6–3.5 cm wide, elliptic to lanceolate, acuminate, glabrous above, pubescent beneath. Flowers yellow, scented, densely crowded in peduncled heads. Flowers and fruits March–November. Propagated by seeds. Distributed in central and eastern Nepal at 3000–3500 m on moist hillsides; also in northern India, western China, and northern Myanmar.

OTHER USES. The inner bark is used to prepare handmade Nepalese paper. Bark and leaf are used as fish poison.

Ehretia acuminata R. Brown

ENGLISH *heliotrope tree* NEPALI *nalsura, seto lodo*

Boraginaceae. Deciduous tree about 20 m high, bark bluish gray, fairly smooth, with deep vertical fissures. Leaves stalked, 3.5–14 cm long, 1–6.3 cm wide, elliptic to oblong, acuminate, serrate, with a few scattered hairs on the upper surface, otherwise glabrous, base narrowed. Flowers sessile, white, fragrant, in terminal panicles. Fruit a drupe, globose, nearly black when ripe. Flowers March–June, fruits June–July. Propagated by seeds or root suckers. Distributed throughout Nepal at 500–1800 m in open areas near streams; also in northern India, southern Tibet, and Myanmar.

MEDICINE. Juice of the bark is given in cases of fever.

Edgeworthia gardneri

Ehretia macrophylla Wallich

NEPALI *lato lodho, seto lodho, thulo lodho*

Boraginaceae. Much branched shrub about 4 m high. Leaves short-stalked, in clusters on short branches, 7.5–29 cm long, 3.5–18 cm wide, oblong to ovate, entire or somewhat dentate, rough on the upper surface. Flowers solitary, axillary, white, fragrant. Fruit rounded, yellow, fleshy, with four-seeded stone. Flowers and fruits April–August. Propagated by seeds or root suckers. Distributed in central and eastern Nepal at 1200–2400 m in thickets in forested areas; also in northern India and Myanmar.

MEDICINE. The root is alterative and is also used for debility and syphilis. Juice of the leaves, about 4 teaspoons three times a day, is taken in cases of diarrhea, dysentery, cough, and colds.

Eichhornia crassipes (Martius) Solms

Pontederia crassipes Martius
DANUWAR *panma* ENGLISH *water hyacinth* NEPALI *teli phul*

Pontederiaceae. Floating aquatic herb, rooting at the nodes. Leaves forming a rosette, spatulate, stalk swollen into a green bladder. Flowers blue-violet in many-flowered spikes. Flowers and fruits September–November. Propagated by suckers or root offshoots. Distributed throughout Nepal at 200–1500 m in moist and boggy areas; also in Pakistan, India, Bhutan, and the Americas.

FOOD. Tender buds are cooked as a vegetable.

Ehretia macrophylla

Eichhornia crassipes

Elaeagnus infundibularis Momiyama

Elaeagnus arborea Roxburgh
Elaeagnus armatus Buchanan-Hamilton ex Schlechter
Elaeagnus conferta Roxburgh
Elaeagnus latifolia Linnaeus

DANUWAR *hyauti*   ENGLISH *bastard oleaster*   GURUNG *khrun, tibru*   NEPALI *gunyelo, kallagir, madilo*   SHERPA *timu*   TAMANG *guaenlo, temign*

Elaeagnaceae. Straggling shrub. Leaves stalked, alternate, 5–11 cm long, 2–4 cm wide, elliptic, acuminate, entire, glabrous above, densely covered with silvery scales beneath. Flowers greenish white or yellowish, with silvery scales outside. Fruit oblong, red with silvery scales, succulent. Flowers August–November, fruits March–June. Propagated by seeds or by layering. Distributed in central and eastern Nepal at 1500–2600 m in forest openings; also in northern India and Bhutan.

FOOD. Ripe fruits are eaten fresh.

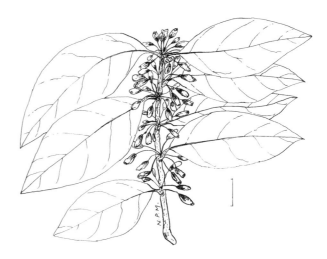

Elaeagnus infundibularis

Elaeagnus kanaii Momiyama

NEPALI *kallageri*

Elaeagnaceae. Shrub about 5 m high. Leaves stalked, 3–6.5 cm long, 0.7–2.5 cm wide, lanceolate, pointed, slightly hairy above, stellately tomentose beneath. Flowers yellowish. Fruits June–July. Propagated by seeds or by layering. Distributed in central and western Nepal at 1400–2700 m in forest openings; also in northern India.

FOOD. Ripe fruits are edible.

Elaeagnus parvifolia Wallich ex Royle

Elaeagnus orientalis Linnaeus
Elaeagnus umbellata Thunberg ex Murray

NEPALI *guyenti*

Elaeagnaceae. Spiny deciduous shrub, young branches covered with silvery scales. Leaves stalked, alternate, 2.5–5 cm long, oblong to elliptic, silvery scaly beneath. Flowers dull white, fragrant, in axillary clusters. Fruit ovoid, covered with silvery scales, fleshy, September–November. Propagated by seeds or by layering. Distributed throughout Nepal at 1300–3000 m in forest openings; also in Afghanistan, northern India, and western China.

FOOD. Ripe fruits are eaten fresh.

MEDICINE. Unripe fruits are eaten in cases of bloody dysentery.

Elaeocarpus lanceifolius Roxburgh

NEPALI *vadrachhya*

Elaeocarpaceae. Tree. Leaves stalked, 10–15 cm long, 4–5 cm wide, broadly lanceolate, serrulate, glabrous, base tapering. Flowers whitish. Fruit a drupe, oblong to ovoid, one-seeded. Propagated by seeds or by layering. Distributed in eastern and central Nepal at 1000–1800 m in open places; also in India, Bhutan, southern China, and Myanmar.

FOOD. Ripe fruits are edible.

OTHER USES. The plant provides fodder.

Elaeocarpus sphaericus (Gaertner) K. Schumacher

Ganitrus sphaericus Gaertner
Elaeocarpus ganitrus Roxburgh
ENGLISH *utrasum bead tree* NEPALI *dana, rudraksha*
TAMANG *rudrachhe*

Elaeocarpaceae. Tree about 20 m high. Leaves stalked, 8–18 cm long, 2.5–6 cm wide, elliptic to lanceolate, rarely serrulate, glabrous. Flowers white, elegantly tubercled, generally with five equidistant grooves, May–June. Fruits August–December. Propagated by seeds. Distributed in eastern and central Nepal at 600–1100 m in open places but the plant's limited natural distribution and gathering of fruit for sale in the trade are causes of conservation concern; also in India, Malaysia, Java, and Sumatra.

FOOD. Pulp of ripe fruit is edible.

MEDICINE. Seeds are valued as a remedy for blood pressure and heart ailments.

OTHER USES. The plant has great religious significance, especially for Hindus. The hard seeds are made into rosaries, necklaces, bracelets, and other ornaments.

Elatostema integrifolium (D. Don) Weddell

Procris integrifolia D. Don
Elatostema sesquifolium (Blume) Hasskarl
Procris punctata Buchanan-Hamilton ex D. Don
Procris sesquifolia Reinwardt ex Blume
NEPALI *lipe jhar*

Urticaceae. Herb. Leaves stalked, 2.5–18 cm long, 1–4 cm wide, elliptic, long-pointed, serrate, hairy on both surfaces, base oblique. Flowers greenish. Flowers and fruits May–November. Propagated by splitting the root. Distributed in central Nepal at 2200–2700 m in moist, shady places; also in India, Bhutan, western China, Myanmar, and Java.

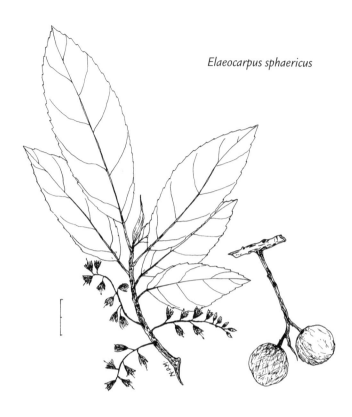

Elaeocarpus sphaericus

MEDICINE. Juice of the root, about 4 teaspoons three times a day, is given in cases of fever.

Elatostema platyphyllum Weddell

GURUNG *til* NEPALI *sano gangleto* TAMANG *tipla*

Urticaceae. Herb about 50 cm high. Leaves stalked, 4–22 cm long, 1.5–9 cm wide, obliquely rhombic, oblong to lanceolate, serrulate, acuminate, glabrous above, slightly pubescent beneath, base auricled. Flowers cream. Fruit an achene, ovoid. Flowers and fruits August–September. Propagated by splitting the root. Distributed in central Nepal at 1100–2000 m in moist, shady places; also in northern India and western China.

FOOD. Tender leaves and shoots are cooked as a green vegetable.

OTHER USES. The plant is used as fodder and is considered nutritious.

Elatostema sessile Forster & Forster fil.

CHEPANG *ledem* GURUNG *til* NEPALI *gagaleto* TAMANG *chhyal, tilio*

Urticaceae. Herb about 60 cm high, stems creeping. Leaves subsessile, 1–20.5 cm long, 0.8–6.3 cm wide, elliptic, acuminate, coarsely and sharply serrate, sparsely appressed pilose, base obliquely cuneate. Flowers greenish white. Fruit an achene, ellipsoidal, angular. Flowers May–August. Propagated by splitting the root. Distributed throughout Nepal at 500–3000 m on wet rocks beside streams; also in northern India, Bhutan, China, Myanmar, and Malaysia.

Elatostema platyphyllum

and stomach troubles. It is also given in cases of blood vomiting, as in tuberculosis. A paste of the root is applied to cuts and wounds as an antiseptic. Juice of the root, about 2 teaspoons three times a day, is given for indigestion. Juice of crushed root is given to treat heart and liver troubles. The root is boiled in water about 10 minutes, and the filtered water is taken for controlling bedwetting. Juice of the leaves is used as applied to wounds and bruises.

OTHER USES. Powdered plant is used to prepare *marcha*, a fermenting cake from which liquor is distilled.

Elephantopus scaber

FOOD. Tender shoots and leaves are cooked as a vegetable.

MEDICINE. Juice of the root is given for stomachache and indigestion. A paste of the root is applied to wounds. A paste of the plant is applied to septic wounds for quick relief.

Elephantopus scaber Linnaeus

CHEPANG *mula pate* DANUWAR *athareti, phurke jhar, tarapasara* ENGLISH *rough elephant's foot* GURUNG *chhetreta, ulphi* NEPALI *buti jhar, chhatre, jande dabai, kankri jhar, mula pate, phulikorne jhar, sahasra buti* TAMANG *gangdap, gobar bramji, thagar* THARU *chotputrya, khasuriya*

Compositae. Herb about 50 cm high. Leaves mostly basal, 5–17 cm long, 2.5–5 cm wide, ovate to oblong, serrate, hairy on both surfaces, cauline leaves sessile, smaller. Flower heads purple, surrounded by three leafy bracts. Fruit an achene, 10-ribbed. Flowers July–December, fruits September–December. Propagated by seeds or root offshoots. Distributed throughout Nepal to about 2000 m, in open as well as shady places; also in Pakistan, India, and Bhutan.

MEDICINE. Tamangs use a paste of the plant for snakebites. Fresh root is chewed to treat cough and colds. A decoction of the root is given for diarrhea, dysentery,

Eleusine coracana (Linnaeus) Gaertner

Cynosurus coracanus Linnaeus

BHOJPURI *maduwa* CHEPANG *kadau* DANUWAR *maduwa* ENGLISH *African millet, finger millet, millet* GURUNG *narau, nare* LEPCHA *mong* LIMBU *mangdok pena* MAGAR *pandare, rankwa* MAJHI *maramcho* MOOSHAR *maruwa* NEPALI *kodo* NEWARI *dusi* RAI *sampicha* SHERPA *gyar* SUNWAR *chirs* TAMANG *sangna* THARU *kodo*

Gramineae. Erect annual grass, culms glabrous, somewhat compressed. Leaves distichous, flat, sheath ciliate. Inflorescence greenish. Fruit a grain, oblong, obtusely three-angled. Flowers and fruits July–October. Propagated by seeds. Distributed throughout Nepal to about 2500 m, cultivated; also in parts of Asia and Africa.

FOOD. The grains are important food items, especially for poor people of Nepal. The local alcoholic beverages, which are considered of good quality, are brewed from the grain.

MEDICINE. Juice of the plant is stimulant and mildly purgative.

Eleusine indica (Linnaeus) Gaertner

Cynosurus indicus Linnaeus

CHEPANG *maisi chaur, syagham* ENGLISH *crowfoot grass, fowl foot* GURUNG *motho* NEPALI *dande, kodo ghans*

Gramineae. Annual grass about 60 cm high, culms glabrous, somewhat compressed. Leaves distichous, flat or folded. Inflorescence greenish. Fruit a grain, oblong, three-angled. Flowers and fruits July–November. Propagated by seeds. Distributed throughout Nepal to about 2600 m in moist, open places; also in tropical and subtropical regions.

OTHER USES. The plant provides fodder.

Eleutherococcus cissifolius (Griffith ex Seemann) Nakai

Aralia cissifolia Griffith ex Seemann, *Acanthopanax cissifolius* (Griffith ex Seemann) Harms

NEPALI *dang dinge*

Araliaceae. Shrub with a weak stem and deflexed prickles. Leaves stalked, digitate, five-lobed, elliptic to lanceolate, acuminate, spinous serrate, pilose above. Flowers yellowish. Propagated by seeds. Distributed throughout Nepal at 3000–4000 m in open places; also in northern India, Bhutan, and western China.

MEDICINE. Juice of the bark is applied to treat eczema.

OTHER USES. Foliage provides fodder.

Elsholtzia blanda (Bentham) Bentham

Aphanochilus blandus Bentham
Perilla elata D. Don

GURUNG *tana* LIMBU *bawage* MAGAR *rudila* NEPALI *ban silam* TAMANG *lhasilam, pangnam, serman, surtenden*

Labiatae. Herb about 1 m high. Leaves stalked, 1.5–12 cm long, 0.7–3.5 cm wide, elliptic to lanceolate, acuminate, serrate, glabrous, gland-dotted beneath. Flowers yellowish, October–November. Propagated by seeds. Distributed throughout Nepal at 300–2500 m in moist, open places; also in northern India, Bhutan, southwestern China, and Southeast Asia.

FOOD. Seeds are pickled.

MEDICINE. Juice of the plant, about 4 teaspoons three times a day, is given to treat headaches. It is also applied to cuts and wounds. Aroma of the squeezed leaf is inhaled to clear congestion of the nostrils because of cough and colds.

OTHER USES. Leaves contain 2% essential oils.

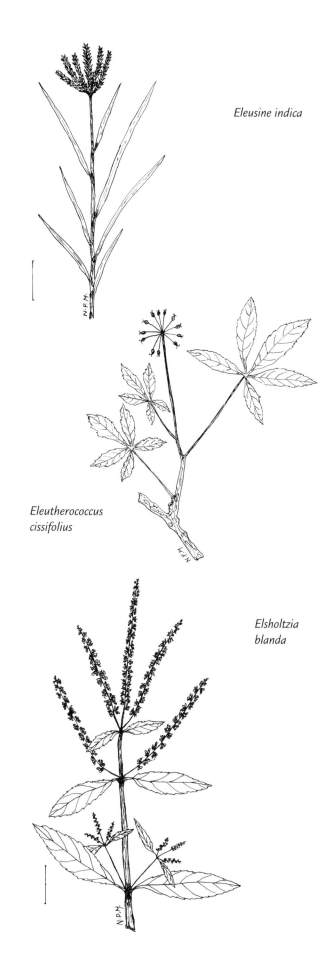

Eleusine indica

Eleutherococcus cissifolius

Elsholtzia blanda

Elsholtzia ciliata (Thunberg) Hylander

Sideritis ciliata Thunberg
Elsholtzia cristata Willdenow
Mentha patrinii Lepechin, *Elsholtzia patrinii* (Lepechin) Garcke
Perilla polystachya D. Don
NEPALI *ban silam*

Labiatae. Erect herb about 60 cm high. Leaves long-stalked, 2–8.5 cm long, 0.8–2.5 cm wide, ovate to lanceolate, serrate, gland-dotted beneath. Flowers purplish in flat spikes, September–October. Propagated by seeds. Distributed throughout Nepal at 1500–3400 m in moist, open places; also in Afghanistan, northern India, Tibet, China, Indo-China, Japan, northern Asia, and Europe.

FOOD. Powdered seeds are used for flavoring foodstuffs.
MEDICINE. The plant is carminative and astringent.

Elsholtzia eriostachya (Bentham) Bentham

Aphanochilus eriostachyus Bentham
Elsholtzia hoffmeisteri Klotzsch
NEPALI *lenja*

Labiatae. Hairy herb about 40 cm high. Leaves short-stalked, oblong, obtuse, denticulate. Flowers yellow in cylindrical spikes. Propagated by seeds. Distributed throughout Nepal at 3000–4800 m in moist, open places; also in northern India, Bhutan, and Tibet.

MEDICINE. Seeds are chewed in cases of cough and colds.

Elsholtzia flava (Bentham) Bentham

Aphanochilus flavus Bentham
NEPALI *ban silam* SHERPA *lenza, nene dhombu* TAMANG *paldungne, palunget* TIBETAN *sop sop*

Labiatae. Erect shrub with sparingly branched stems. Leaves stalked, opposite, 6–20 cm long, 2.8–13 cm wide, elliptic to ovate, acuminate, serrate, base cuneate, rounded, or more or less cordate. Flowers yellow in dense, many-flowered whorls. Fruit a nutlet, ellipsoidal. Flowers September–October. Propagated by seeds. Distributed in central and eastern Nepal at 1600–3000 m in shady ravines and moist places of oak forests; also in northern India and China.

FOOD. Seeds are eaten raw or pickled.
MEDICINE. Leaves are smashed and applied to treat scabies.

Elsholtzia fruticosa (D. Don) Rehder

Perilla fruticosa D. Don
Aphanochilus polystachya Bentham, *Elsholtzia polystachya* (Bentham) Bentham
Colebrookia oppositifolia Loddiges
NEPALI *chhinki* TAMANG *marpchi*

Labiatae. Shrub about 2 m high. Leaves subsessile, 5–15 cm long, 1.5–5.5 cm wide, serrate. Flowers white in long cylindrical spikes, September–October. Fruits November–December. Propagated by seeds. Distributed throughout Nepal at 1800–4200 m in moist areas near stream banks; also in northern India, Bhutan, Tibet, China, and Myanmar.

FOOD. Powdered seeds are used for flavoring foodstuffs. The seed oil is edible.
MEDICINE. Juice of the root, about 3 teaspoons twice a day, is given to relieve headaches.
OTHER USES. Powdered plant is used for incense.

Elsholtzia stachyodes (Link) Raizada & Saxena

Hyptis stachyodes Link
Aphanochilus paniculatus Bentham
Elsholtzia incisa Bentham
Mentha blanda de Candolle
Perilla leptostachya D. Don, *Elsholtzia leptostachya* (D. Don) Bentham
GURUNG *sanse* NEPALI *ban silam*

Labiatae. Much branched annual herb about 1 m high. Leaves stalked, 1.5–5 cm long, 1–3.5 cm wide, broadly ovate, acuminate, coarsely dentate to serrate, lower surface gland-dotted. Flowers white in long cylindrical spikes. Fruit a nutlet, oblong ellipsoidal. Flowers and fruits September–November. Propagated by seeds. Distributed throughout Nepal at 1300–2500 m in moist, open places along stream banks; also in northern India, China, and Myanmar.

FOOD. Seeds are eaten raw or pickled.
MEDICINE. Juice of the plant is put between the toes to treat wounds between the toes caused by walking barefooted in muddy water.

Elsholtzia strobilifera (Bentham) Bentham

Cyclostegia strobilifera Bentham
Elsholtzia exigua Handel-Mazzetti
NEPALI *ban bawari* TAMANG *thagne noba, thongsa*

Labiatae. Herb about 50 cm high. Leaves stalked, 1–3 cm long, ovate. Flowers pinkish in dense cylindrical spikes, July–September. Fruits October–November. Propagated by seeds. Distributed throughout Nepal at 1300–4800 m, occasionally along waysides; also in northern India, Bhutan, Tibet, China, and Myanmar.

FOOD. Powdered seeds are used for flavoring foodstuffs.
MEDICINE. A paste of the plant is applied to the forehead in cases of headache.

Embelia vestita Roxburgh

Embelia nagushia D. Don
NEPALI *amile ghans*

Myrsinaceae. Woody climber. Leaves short-stalked, lanceolate, acute or acuminate, crenate, glabrous. Flowers white in axillary or terminal racemes, November–December. Propagated by seeds. Distributed in central Nepal to about 1700 m in shady places; also in India, Bhutan, China, and Myanmar.

OTHER USES. The plant is used for fodder.

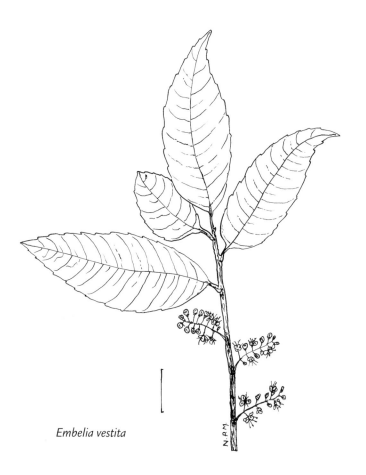

Embelia vestita

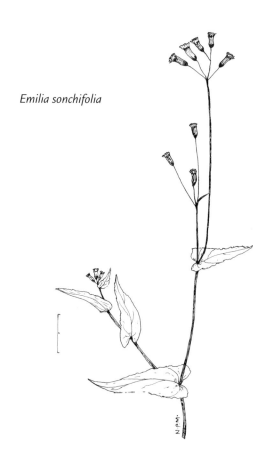

Emilia sonchifolia

Emilia sonchifolia (Linnaeus) de Candolle

Cacalia sonchifolia Linnaeus

CHEPANG *ngangri sag* ENGLISH *tassel flower, shaving brush* MAGAR *toir phule* NEPALI *chaulene jhar, mula pate, tori phul* TAMANG *dhude*

Compositae. Erect, sparingly hairy herb about 40 cm high. Basal leaves stalked, lyrately lobed or sinuately dentate, cauline leaves sessile, somewhat clasping the stem, entire. Flower heads purple in corymbs. Fruit an achene, narrowly oblong, ribbed, the pappus white, soft, copious. Flowers and fruits January–November. Propagated by seeds or root offshoots. Distributed throughout Nepal to about 1700 m, in moist areas and on uncultivated land; also in tropical and subtropical regions of Asia and Africa.

FOOD. Tender leaves and shoots are cooked as a vegetable.

MEDICINE. The plant is astringent, febrifuge, and expectorant. Juice of the plant is applied to cuts and wounds. It is also dripped in the ear to treat earaches. Juice of the root, about 4 teaspoons four times a day, is taken for diarrhea. Juice of the leaves is used in cases of inflammation of the eye and night blindness. Flower heads are chewed and kept in the mouth about 10 minutes to protect teeth from decaying.

OTHER USES. Powdered plant is used to prepare *marcha*, a cake fermented with yeast, from which liquor is distilled.

Engelhardia spicata Leschenault ex Blume

Engelhardia roxburghiana Lindley

CHEPANG *waksi* GURUNG *kal, pli* LIMBU *yakpoma* MAGAR *kane mauwa, lati mauwa, wasing* NEPALI *bhale mauwa, mauwa, seti mauwa* TAMANG *gudu, klowache, wasing*

Juglandaceae. Deciduous tree about 15 m high. Leaves stalked, pinnate, leaflets 5.5–25 cm long, 2.5–8 cm wide, oblong to lanceolate, entire, glabrous. Inflorescence greenish. Flowers and fruits April–November. Propagated by seeds. Distributed throughout Nepal at 500–2000 m on open hillsides; also in Bhutan, Assam in northeastern India, southern Tibet, eastward to western China, and Malaysia.

OTHER USES. Bark is used for tanning. The inner bark gives fiber of low quality. Leaves are valued as green manure. Young leaves are used as fish poison.

Enkianthus deflexus (Griffith) C. K. Schneider

Rhodora deflexa Griffith
Enkianthus himalaicus Hooker fil.

NEPALI *rato angeri*

Ericaceae. Tree about 6 m high. Leaves stalked, mostly in terminal clusters, narrowed at both ends, acute or obtuse, entire or serrulate, pubescent beneath when young. Flowers reddish. Fruit a capsule, globose. Propagated by seeds. Distributed in eastern Nepal at 2500–3300 m in moist places; also in northern India, Bhutan, and northern Myanmar.

MEDICINE. Juice of the bark is applied externally in cases of inflammation of the eye.

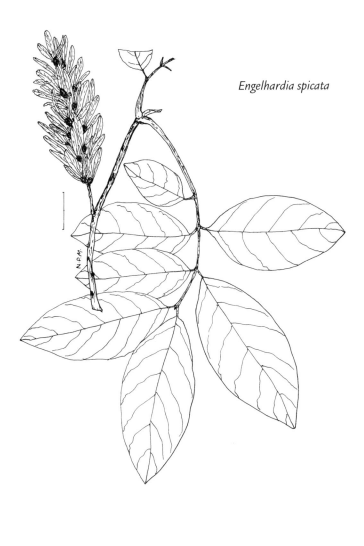

Engelhardia spicata

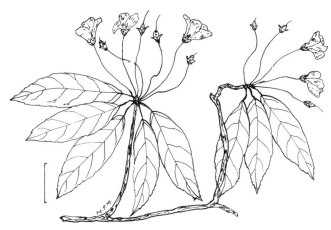

Enkianthus deflexus

Entada phaseoloides (Linnaeus) Merrill

Lens phaseoloides Linnaeus
Mimosa scandens Linnaeus, *Entada scandens* (Linnaeus) Bentham
ENGLISH *nicker bean, St. Thomas bean*   GURUNG *prami, prome*
NEPALI *rukh pangra*   TIBETAN *gla-gor-zho-sha*

Leguminosae. Large woody climber. Leaves stalked, bipinnate, leaflets ovate, acuminate, entire. Flowers yellowish, fragrant, in long narrow spikes. Propagated by seeds. Distributed in central and eastern Nepal at 350–1600 m; also in tropical and subtropical Asia.

MEDICINE. Juice of the bark is used externally to treat ulcers. Seeds are ground and applied to boils, rashes, and itches of the skin, and rubbed on the noses of grazing livestock during the monsoon as a leech repellent. A paste of the cotyledon has anthelmintic value.

OTHER USES. Seeds are used for fish poison and are rubbed on the noses of grazing livestock during the monsoon as a leech repellent.

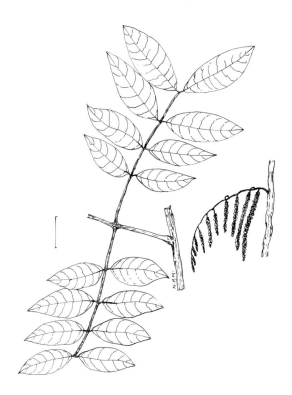

Entada phaseoloides

Ephedra gerardiana Wallich ex Stapf

ENGLISH *ephedrine*   NEPALI *kagcharo, purpurya, somlata*
SHERPA *sang kaba*   TIBETAN *chhe, refesing*

Ephedraceae. Tufted gymnospermous shrub about 1 m high. Stem much branched, branches whorled, spreading. Leaves reduced to two-toothed sheaths. Plants dioecious. Cones yellowish. Ovule ovoid, surrounded by persistent bracts. Cones April–June. Propagated by seeds or branch cuttings. Distributed in central and western Nepal at 2000–5200 m in open, dry, rocky places; also in Afghanistan, Pakistan, India, and Bhutan.

MEDICINE. Squeezed plant is mixed with bathing water to treat skin diseases. Juice of the plant is stimulant for the heart. It is used to treat asthma and hay fever, and is also useful in respiratory infections. This juice is given to children to control bedwetting.

OTHER USES. The plant is used for fuel. Branches are browsed by goats and sheep.

Ephedra gerardiana

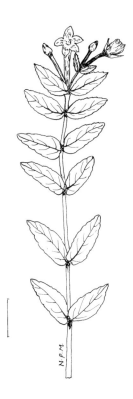

Epilobium sikkimense

Epilobium brevifolium D. Don

TIBETAN *chhyuzii*

Onagraceae. Herb about 25 cm high. Leaves short-stalked, opposite, 0.5–2 cm long, 0.2–0.8 cm wide, elliptic, acute, dentate. Flowers pink. Flowers and fruits August–October. Propagated by seeds. Distributed in central Nepal at 1500–4000 m in wet places along the banks of streams and ditches; also in India, Tibet, China, and Myanmar.

MEDICINE. A paste of the plant is applied to relieve muscular pain.

Epilobium sikkimense Haussknecht

Epilobium alsinifolium Villars
NEPALI *kupate jhar*

Onagraceae. Erect herb about 35 cm high. Lower leaves short-stalked, upper leaves sessile, opposite, lanceolate to elliptic, acute, dentate, narrowed or broadened toward the base. Flowers pink. Flowers and fruits July–August. Propagated by seeds. Distributed throughout Nepal at 1000–4200 m in damp places in partial shade; also in northern India, southern Tibet, and western China.

MEDICINE. Juice of the root is given to treat indigestion.

Epipactis royleana Lindley

Helleborine royleana (Lindley) Soó
Epipactis gigantea Douglas
CHEPANG *chhasakrungai*

Orchidaceae. Orchid about 70 cm high. Leaves clasping the stem, 1–1.5 cm long, ovate to lanceolate. Flowers green, veined with red, the tip reddish, in lax spikes, June–July. Propagated by seeds or by splitting the root off-shoots. Distributed in western and central Nepal at 1600–3500 m in open pastureland; also in Pakistan, northern India, Bhutan, and southeastern Tibet.

FOOD. Boiled roots are eaten by Chepangs.

Equisetum debile Roxburgh ex Vaucher

CHEPANG *yophuli* NEPALI *sime jhar*

Equisetaceae. Spore-bearing herb. Stems erect, cylindrical, hollow, branches long, slender, two or three in a whorl, ribbed, nodes encircled by a tight sheath of connate scale-like leaves. Spikes oblong, at the ends of branches. Spores June–July. Propagated by splitting the rhizomes. Distributed throughout Nepal to about 2600 m, common in moist places; also in India, Sri Lanka, southern China, and Southeast Asia.

Epipactis royleana

MEDICINE. Ash of the plant is applied to treat burns or to treat scabies. Juice of the root, about 1 teaspoon once a day, is given in cases of malarial fever. A paste of the root is applied to treat gonorrhea and dislocation of bones. This paste is taken internally for liver and chest complaints.

OTHER USES. The plant is gathered for fodder.

Equisetum diffusum D. Don

CHEPANG *yophul* DANUWAR *laharjoka* ENGLISH *horsetail*
GURUNG *kurkure no, miduchhi, mithu* NEPALI *aankhle jhar, harjor, kurkure jhar, simdhungri, sime jhar, talche jhar, talgoji*
RAUTE *aankhyailya* TAMANG *gni mran, ibang, thongachhe*

Equisetaceae. Spore-bearing herb. Stems erect, tufted, very rough, branches densely whorled, short, arising from the base of the sheath of scale-like leaves. Spikes short-stalked. Spores June–July. Propagated by splitting the rhizomes. Distributed throughout Nepal to about 3300 m, common in moist places; also in India, Bhutan, and southwestern China.

MEDICINE. Ash of the plant is applied to treat burns and scabies. Juice of the plant is applied to treat sprains and dislocation of bone. A paste of the plant is applied as a remedy for whitlow. Juice of the root, about 4 teaspoons three times a day, is given in cases of fever. It is also used for urinary troubles and indigestion.

Eragrostiella nardoides (Trinius) Bor

Eragarostis nardoides Trinius
NEPALI *chupi*

Gramineae. Slender, tufted grass about 18 cm high. Leaves narrow, convolute, with long, white hairs. Inflorescence brownish. Propagated by seeds or by splitting rhizomes. Distributed throughout Nepal at 400–1800 m; also in India.

OTHER USES. The plant is used for fodder.

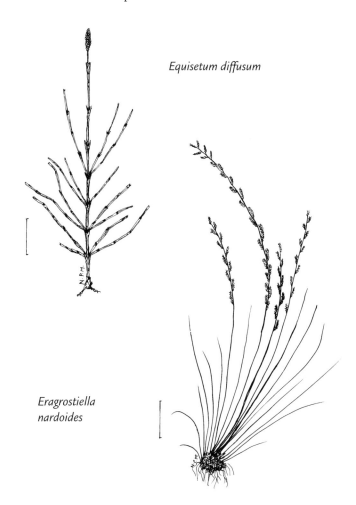

Equisetum diffusum

Eragrostiella nardoides

Eragrostis japonica (Thunberg) Trinius

Poa japonica Thunberg
Eragrostis interrupta var. *tenuissima* Stapf ex Hooker fil.
NEPALI *ranki*

Gramineae. Erect grass, culms erect, slender or stout, simple or branched. Leaves linear, flat, glabrous, smooth. Inflorescences brownish, in panicles. Fruit a grain, ovoid. Flowers and fruits October–March. Propagated by root offshoots. Distributed throughout Nepal to about 1500 m on open, rocky ground; also in tropical Asia, China, Japan, and Malaysia.

OTHER USES. The leaf is used to prepare ropes and cords. Leaves are also used for fodder.

Eragrostis nigra Nees ex Steudel

NEPALI *phurke khar*

Gramineae. Perennial grass about 1 m high. Leaves mostly basal, 10–15 mm long, 2.5–3 mm wide, flat, lanceolate, tapering to a sharp point, margin smooth or slightly rough in texture, base terete, sheaths narrowly terete, mouth barbed. Inflorescences gray in lax panicles. Flowers May–June. Propagated by seeds or by splitting the root offshoots. Distributed throughout Nepal at 900–3000 m on open, rocky ground; also in India, Sri Lanka, China, and Myanmar.

OTHER USES. The plant is a nutritious fodder.

Eragrostis pilosa (Linnaeus) Palisot de Beauvois

Poa pilosa Linnaeus

GURUNG *ki*

Gramineae. Slender grass. Leaves linear lanceolate, acuminate, sheaths bearded at the mouth. Inflorescences blackish, the panicles open with filiform branches, May–July. Propagated by seeds or by splitting the root offshoots. Distributed in eastern Nepal to about 200 m in open places; also in tropical and warm regions of the eastern hemisphere.

OTHER USES. The plant is used for fodder.

Eragrostis tenella (Linnaeus) Palisot de Beauvois ex Roemer & Schultes

Poa tenella Linnaeus
Poa amabilis Linnaeus, *Eragrostis amabilis* (Linnaeus) Wight & Arnott ex Hooker & Arnott
Poa olumosa Retzius

NEPALI *junge banso, charinda*

Gramineae. Annual grass with decumbent culms. Leaves linear, flat. Inflorescence greenish purple. Flowers and fruits July–December. Propagated by seeds or by splitting the root offshoots. Distributed throughout Nepal at 200–1000 m; also in the tropics of the eastern hemisphere.

OTHER USES. The plant is used for fodder.

Eragrostis unioloides (Retzius) Nees ex Steudel

Poa unioloides Retzius

NEPALI *tilke jhar*

Gramineae. Annual grass with decumbent or erect culms. Leaves linear, base rounded or more or less cordate. Inflorescence greenish, often tinged with purple. Flowers and fruits July–December. Propagated by seeds or by splitting the root offshoots. Distributed throughout Nepal to about 3000 m in open, rocky places; also in India and Southeast Asia.

OTHER USES. The plant is used for fodder.

Eriobotrya dubia (Lindley) Decaisne

Photinia dubia Lindley
Crataegus shicola Buchanan-Hamilton ex Lindley
Mespilus tinctoria D. Don

NEPALI *jure kaphal, maya*

Rosaceae. Evergreen tree. Leaves short-stalked, 7–15 cm long, 1.5–4 cm wide, oblanceolate, acuminate, crenate, glabrous, leathery. Flowers small, white. Fruit a drupe, ellipsoidal, orange. Flowers February–March, fruits April–May. Propagated by seeds or cuttings. Distributed in central Nepal at 1300–2000 m in open places around villages; also in northern India and Bhutan.

FOOD. Ripe fruits are eaten fresh.

Eriobotrya japonica (Thunberg) Lindley

Mespilus japonica Thunberg

ENGLISH *Japanese medlar, loquat*   NEPALI *maya*   TIBETAN *zhu-mkhan*

Rosaceae. Evergreen tree about 13 m high. Leaves subsessile, oblanceolate, acuminate, distantly serrate, leath-

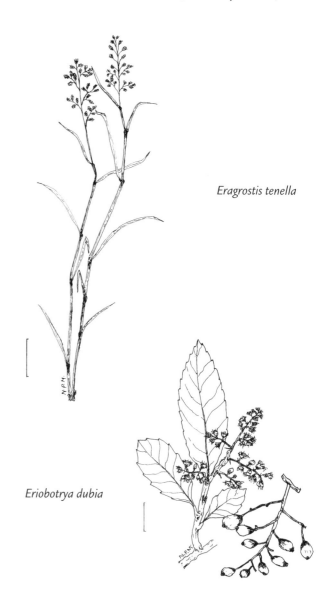

Eragrostis tenella

Eriobotrya dubia

ery, densely woolly, distinctly veined beneath. Flowers dull white, fragrant, in terminal panicles. Fruit pear shaped, succulent, yellow or orange when ripe. Flowers September–December, fruits March–April. Propagated by seeds or cuttings. Distributed in central Nepal at 1300–2000 m, generally planted on private land; also in northern India, China, Japan, Europe, and the Americas.

FOOD. Ripe fruits are edible and are also made into jams, jellies, and sauces.

Eriocaulon nepalense Prescott ex Bongard

NEPALI *bhuri ghans, tauke phul*

Eriocaulaceae. Herb about 15 cm high. Leaves linear or rounded at the tip, narrowed toward the base, opaque or translucent. Flowers whitish, globose, June–November. Fruits September–January. Propagated by seeds. Distributed throughout Nepal at 1300–3000 m in open, moist places; also in northern India.

MEDICINE. A paste of the plant is applied to cuts and wounds.

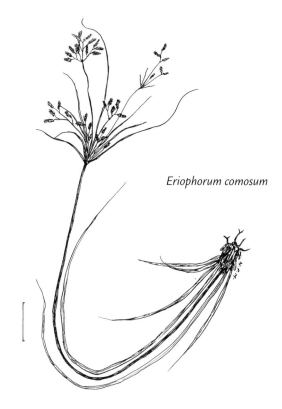

Eriophorum comosum

Eriocaulon nepalense

Eriophorum comosum (Wallich) Wallich

Scirpus comosus Wallich, *Trichophorum comosum* (Wallich) A. Dietrich
Scirpus elongatus Buchanan-Hamilton ex D. Don
NEPALI *pampurya* TAMANG *basalki*

Cyperaceae. Perennial herb, stem tufted, leafy. Leaves numerous, overtopping the stem, narrowly linear, long acuminate, rough in texture. Inflorescences brownish in compound umbels. Propagated by seeds or root offshoots. Distributed throughout Nepal at 500–2600 m, common in rocky places; also in Afghanistan, Pakistan, India, China, and northern Myanmar.

OTHER USES. The plant is used for fodder.

Eriosema himalaicum Ohashi

Crotalaria tuberosa Buchanan-Hamilton ex D. Don, *Eriosema tuberosum* (Buchanan-Hamilton ex D. Don) Wang & Thang
Eriosema chinense Vogel
Rhynchosia virgata Graham
NEPALI *bandar guli*

Leguminosae. Erect herb about 6 cm high. Leaves sessile, 1.4–2 cm long, linear, with a few appressed hairs

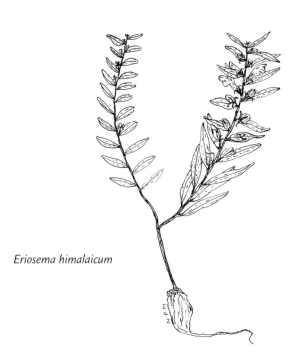

Eriosema himalaicum

above, densely brown hairy beneath. Flowers blue, axillary. Fruit a pod, straight, densely hairy. Flowers and fruits August–September. Propagated by seeds. Distributed throughout Nepal at 900–3000 m in dry places; also in northern India and western China.

FOOD. Tender roots are eaten fresh.

Erodium stephanianum Willdenow

Geranium stephanianum (Willdenow) Poiret

TIBETAN *chyakatu*

Geraniaceae. Annual herb, diffusely branched. Leaves stalked, bipinnatisect, segments decurrent, linear, acute, dentate. Flowers greenish. Propagated by seeds. Distributed in western and central Nepal at 2500–4000 m in open places; also in Afghanistan, India, western Tibet, China, Mongolia, and Siberia.

MEDICINE. A paste of the plant is applied to treat gout.

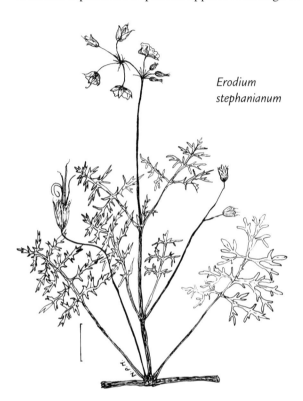

Erodium stephanianum

olate, acute, sinuate and dentate, pubescent with appressed stellate hairs. Flowers yellow. Fruit a pod, many-seeded. Flowers July–August. Propagated by seeds. Distributed throughout Nepal at 1600–3500 m in open, damp grasslands; also in India, Bhutan, Myanmar, central Asia including Mongolia, Siberia, and Europe.

FOOD. Young shoots and leaves are cooked as a vegetable.

Eryngium foetidum

Eryngium foetidum Linnaeus

ENGLISH culantro, fit weed NEPALI *bandhana, brahmdhaniya*

Umbelliferae. Herb. Leaves all basal, 2–16 cm long, 1–3.5 cm wide, lanceolate, serrate, glabrous, tips rounded, each ending in a spine. Flowers yellowish. Flowers and fruits April–December. Propagated by seeds. Distributed in central and eastern Nepal at 700–1200 m in open, rocky places; also widespread in the tropics.

FOOD. Leaves are pickled. Leaves and fruitlets are used as a spice.

MEDICINE. The root is stomachic.

Erysimum hieraciifolium Linnaeus

Erysimum robustum D. Don

NEPALI *ban chansur*

Cruciferae. Pubescent herb about 60 cm high. Lower leaves stalked, upper leaves sessile, lanceolate or oblance-

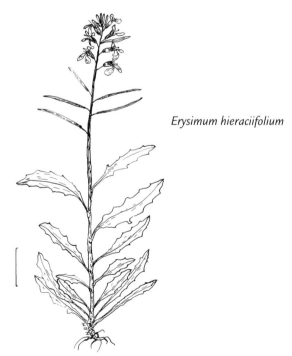

Erysimum hieraciifolium

Erythrina arborescens Roxburgh

ENGLISH *coral tree* LIMBU *kheglema* NEPALI *phaleto, theki kath*

Leguminosae. Tree about 6 m high. Leaves stalked, tri-foliolate, leaflets stalked, 11–23 cm long, 10–24 cm wide, ovate, entire, glabrous above. Flowers scarlet. Fruit a pod, tapering, rusty tomentose. Flowers September–October, fruits October–November. Propagated by seeds. Distributed throughout Nepal at 1500–3000 m in open places, generally around villages; also in northern India, China, and Myanmar.

MEDICINE. Juice of the bark is used for boils. Bark is boiled in water 10 minutes, and the filtered water, about 4 teaspoons, is taken as an anthelmintic.

OTHER USES. Plants are cultivated at the edge of terraced fields with the aim of preventing landslides.

Erythrina stricta Roxburgh

CHEPANG *leksi* NEPALI *phaleto*

Leguminosae. Large tree, trunk and branches covered with sharp, conical, whitish prickles. Leaves stalked, tri-foliolate, leaflets stalked, 5–13 cm long, 3–12 cm wide, broadly ovate, entire. Flowers scarlet in dense spike-like clusters, March–April. Propagated by seeds. Distributed throughout Nepal to about 1600 m, common in cultivated areas; also in India, eastern Tibet, China, and Indo-China.

MEDICINE. Juice of the bark is applied to treat skin diseases.

Eugenia formosa Wallich

Jambosa formosa (Wallich) G. Don

NEPALI *ambake*

Myrtaceae. Tree with widely spreading branches, bark ash colored, marked with the scars of fallen leaves. Leaves stalked, crowded at the ends of branchlets, elliptic to oblong, obtusely acuminate, leathery, shiny above, paler beneath, cordate or tapering at the base. Flowers purple, turning red, in few-flowered racemes. Fruit a berry, subglobose. Propagated by seeds. Distributed in eastern Nepal to 300 m in open places; also in India and Myanmar.

FOOD. Ripe fruits are edible.

Eulaliopsis binata (Retzius) C. E. Hubbard

Andropogon binatus Retzius
Spodiopogon angustifoliius Trinius, *Ischaemum angustifolium* (Trinius) Hackel

CHEPANG *babi* NEPALI *arkhen khar, babiyo, bankasi khar*

Gramineae. Perennial grass about 1 m high, rootstock woody. Leaves linear, tapering toward the tip, base rounded. Inflorescences brown in racemes. Flowers June–November. Propagated by root offshoots. Distributed throughout Nepal at 200–2600 m in open, sunny places; also in northern India, China, Indo-China, and the Philippines.

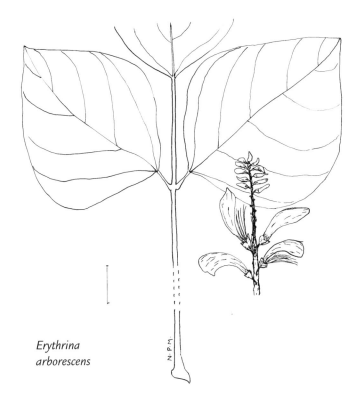

Erythrina arborescens

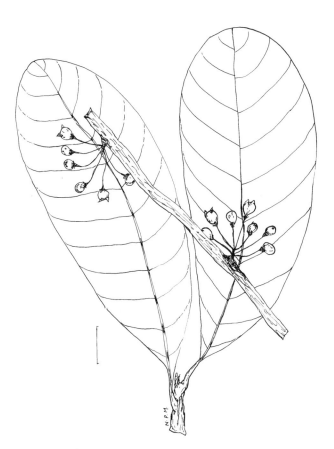

Eugenia formosa

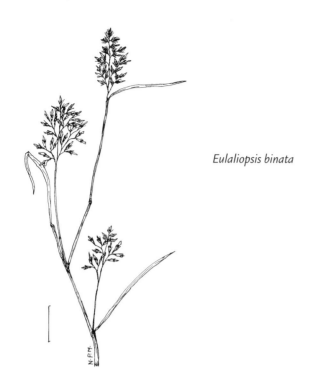

Eulaliopsis binata

Euodia fraxinifolia

OTHER USES. The plant is used to make paper and is also twined into ropes. It is used for thatching roofs.

Euodia fraxinifolia (D. Don) Hooker fil.

Rhus fraxinifolium D. Don, *Philagonia fraxinifolia* (D. Don) Hooker

NEPALI *bokumba, kanukpa*

Rutaceae. Small tree, bark brown or ash gray, young shoots pubescent. Leaves stalked, 20–30 cm long, odd-pinnate, leaflets 9 or 11, 8–20 cm long, 3–7.5 cm wide, oblong to lanceolate, acuminate, crenulate with a gland at each sinus. Flowers yellowish. Fruit a capsule, red. Flowers May–June, fruits February–March. Propagated by seeds. Distributed in central and eastern Nepal at 1000–2400 m on open hillsides; also in India, China, and Southeast Asia.

FOOD. Seeds are used in lentil soup (*daal* in Nepali), fresh pickle, vegetables, and curries for flavor and taste.

OTHER USES. Bark and seeds are used as fish poison.

Euonymus hamiltonianus Wallich

Euonymus atropurpureus Willdenow

ENGLISH *spindle tree* NEPALI *ban chitu, saurah*

Celastraceae. Tree about 10 m high. Leaves stalked, ovate to lanceolate, acuminate, serrulate, membranous, glabrous. Flowers greenish white in axillary cymes, April–May. Propagated by seeds. Distributed throughout Nepal at 500–2500 m in open places around villages; also in Afghanistan, northern India, Bhutan, and northern Myanmar.

OTHER USES. The plant is lopped for fodder. Wood is used to make combs (Plate 46).

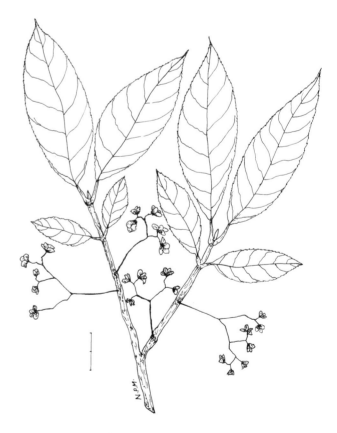

Euonymus hamiltonianus

Euonymus tingens Wallich

TAMANG *pheisign*

Celastraceae. Evergreen tree about 8 m high. Leaves stalked, opposite, 3–7.5 cm long, 1.5–3 cm wide, ovate to lanceolate, serrate, glabrous, dark green above, pale beneath. Flowers greenish in axillary or subterminal dichotomous cymes. Fruit a capsule, pinkish, globose, five-angled. Flowers April–May, fruits September–December. Propagated by seeds. Distributed throughout Nepal at 2300–3300 m in open places and on hillsides; also in northern India, southeastern Tibet, western China, and northern Myanmar.

MEDICINE. Juice of the bark is put into the eye for eye troubles and is also given for constipation.

OTHER USES. Fruits are eaten by monkeys.

Eupatorium adenophorum Sprengel

Eupatorium glandulosum Kunth
Ageratina adenophora (Sprengel) King & H. E. Robinson
CHEPANG *madhuban, mohini* DANUWAR *banmara*
ENGLISH *Crofton weed* MAJHI *sano banmara* NEPALI *banmara,
banmasa* RAUTE *gyane* TAMANG *banmaruwa, kal jhar*

Compositae. Erect shrub. Leaves stalked, opposite, 2–2.5 cm long, 1.5–4.5 cm wide, ovate, coarsely serrate, puberulent beneath, base acute. Flower heads white in terminal corymbs. Fruit an achene, five-angled, black. Flowers and fruits March–October. Propagated by seeds. Distributed in central and eastern Nepal at 500–2400 m in open and deforested areas; a pantropical weed.

MEDICINE. Juice of the plant is applied to minor cuts and wounds. Juice of the root, about 2 teaspoons twice a day, is given in cases of fever. A paste of young leaves is applied to boils. Juice of the leaves is applied to stanch bleeding wounds. The juice is dropped into the eyes to treat insomnia.

OTHER USES. The plant is used as green manure. Leaves contain 6% essential oils.

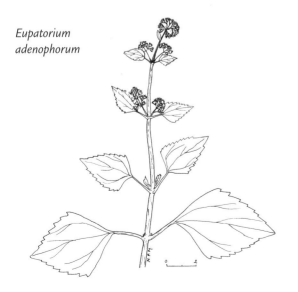

*Eupatorium
adenophorum*

Eupatorium chinense Linnaeus

Conyza longicaulis Wallich, *Eupatorium longicaule* de Candolle
Eupatorium reevesii Wallich ex de Candolle
Eupatorium squamosum Buchanan-Hamilton ex D. Don
Eupatorium viscosum Wallich
Eupatorium wallichii de Candolle
Mikania clematidea Wallich ex de Candolle, *Eupatorium
clematideum* (Wallich ex de Candolle) Schultz Bipontinus
GURUNG *tyapta* NEPALI *banmara* TIBETAN *duk*

Compositae. Hoary pubescent shrub about 1.6 m high. Leaves stalked, opposite, 2–7.5 cm long, 0.5–2.7 cm wide, upper leaves alternate, ovate to lanceolate, coarsely dentate. Flower heads pale purple in spreading panicles. Flowers and fruits July–October. Propagated by seeds. Distributed in central and western Nepal at 2000–2600 m in open and deforested areas; also in India, Bhutan, China, Japan, Taiwan, and the Philippines.

MEDICINE. The milky latex is applied to treat goiter.

OTHER USES. Powdered plant is used to prepare *marcha*, a fermenting cake from which liquor is distilled.

Eupatorium odoratum Linnaeus

Chromolaena odorata (Linnaeus) King & H. E. Robinson
CHEPANG *bhayamara, salah, sing jhar* DANUWAR *bonmara, lohasiya*
ENGLISH *Christmas bush, Siam weed* MAGAR *besi banmara*
MAJHI *thulo banmara* NEPALI *banmara, banmasuwa, chukutenay,
hawi, tite hawi* TAMANG *madhuban*

Compositae. Shrub about 2 m high. Leaves stalked, 2.5–11 cm long, 1.3–6 cm wide, ovate to lanceolate, crenate, slightly hairy above, densely pubescent beneath, tip narrowed, tapering toward the base. Flower heads white. Fruit an achene. Flowers and fruits most of the year. Propagated by seeds. Distributed in central and eastern Nepal to about 1500 m in open and deforested places; also in tropical Asia, and the Americas.

MEDICINE. Juice of the plant is applied to cuts and wounds. It is also considered good for severely chapped hands and feet. Once during fieldwork, I saw a Magar woman of Dhading district pound this plant and then apply it to the wounds of her son. When I asked if it is good for wounds, she replied that her father and grandfather also used the plant and that it had satisfactory results. I have seen villagers throughout Nepal using this plant to treat cuts and wounds.

Euphorbia heterophylla Linnaeus

Poisenttia heterophylla (Linnaeus) Klotzsch & Garcke ex
Klotzsch
Euphorbia geniculata Ortega ex Boissova, *Poinsettia geniculata*
(Ortega ex Boissova) Klotzsch & Garcke ex Klotzsch
CHEPANG *dudhiya* ENGLISH *fire-on-the-mountain*
NEPALI *maitula jhar* TAMANG *nator chhe*

Euphorbiaceae. Herb about 75 cm high. Leaves stalked, alternate, crowded at the apex, entire or sinuate and dentate. Flowers yellowish with pink tip. Fruit a capsule, subglobose. Flowers April–August, fruits July–November.

Propagated by seeds. Distributed throughout Nepal to about 1800 m in open, moist places; a pantropical weed.

MEDICINE. Latex is applied to boils. Juice of the plant is applied to cuts and wounds.

Euphorbia hirta Linnaeus

Chamaesyce hirta (Linnaeus) Millspaugh
Euphorbia pilulifera Linnaeus
CHEPANG *byauli, hanuman, tikapara* DANUWAR *dudhiya jhar*
ENGLISH *asthma weed, garden spurge, pill-bearing spurge, snake weed*
GURUNG *chimphar jhar, taleno* MAGAR *dudhi jhar*
MAJHI *dudhe aainar* MOOSHAR *dudhiya* NEPALI *aankhle jhar,*
chimphar jhar, dudhe, dudhe jhar, jotane jhar, ratango, rhatulo,
kanguil RAI *dudhe, dudhiya* TAMANG *chhumen, dapranchhu,*
gnenoba, makaman, trishubha mran

Euphorbiaceae. Prostrate herb about 60 cm high. Leaves short-stalked, opposite, 2–4 cm long, ovate to oblong, acute, dentate, dark green or reddish above, white or villous beneath. Inflorescence greenish or purplish in axillary cymes. Fruit a capsule, breaking into three cocci, appressed pubescent. Flowers and fruits most of the year. Propagated by seeds or by nodal rooting of the stem. Distributed throughout Nepal to about 1800 m in open, moist places; a pantropical weed.

FOOD. Tender leaves and shoots are cooked as a vegetable.

MEDICINE. A paste of the root is applied to treat dislocated bones and snakebites. The plant has anthelmintic, laxative, and cooling properties and is taken as a useful tonic. A paste of the plant is applied to boils, deeply chapped skin, and also used to relieve body pain. Juice of the plant is used on boils, cuts, wounds, and skin disease and is also used for diarrhea, dysentery, asthma, and bronchial infections. This juice, about 4 teaspoons twice a day, is given to curb fever and is also considered to relieve body pain. The juice is dripped into the ear to clear pus inside the infected ear. Smoke of the dried plant is inhaled to treat asthma. Danuwars, Gurungs, and Mooshars drip the milky juice into the eyes for conjunctivitis and ulcerated cornea. This juice is also applied to abscesses, boils, pimples, cuts, and wounds. Flower heads are chewed fresh to relieve headaches.

Euphorbia milii Des Moulins

Euphorbia splendens Bojer ex Hooker
ENGLISH *crown of thorns* NEPALI *simri*

Euphorbiaceae. Spiny herb, stems angled, armed with needle-like stipular spines. Leaves short-stalked, 2.5–4.5 cm long, 1.2–1.6 cm wide, ovate to oblong, apiculate, glabrous. Flowers red in long-stalked dichotomous cymes. Flowers and fruits most of the year. Propagated by stem cuttings. Distributed throughout Nepal to about 1500 m, in gardens and on walls, cultivated; also in most parts of the world.

MEDICINE. Latex is applied to sprains.

Euphorbia parviflora Linnaeus

Euphorbia hypericifolia Linnaeus
Euphorbia indica Lamarck
Euphorbia tenuis Buchanan-Hamilton
ENGLISH *spurge weed* NEPALI *dudhi, masino dudhi*
THARU *chikini dudhi*

Euphorbiaceae. Herb about 50 cm high. Leaves short-stalked, 1–3.5 cm long, 0.4–2 cm wide, oblong, serrate, glabrous, tip rounded, base oblique. Flowers greenish or pinkish. Flowers and fruits July–October. Propagated by seeds or root offshoots. Distributed in central and western Nepal to about 2000 m in open, stony places or at the edges of cultivated fields; also in northern India and Bhutan.

MEDICINE. Milky latex is applied to wounds and boils.

OTHER USES. Squeezed plant is used for washing clothes.

Euphorbia prostrata Aiton

Chamaesyce prostrata (Aiton) Small
NEPALI *kanike ghans* THARU *dudhai*

Euphorbiaceae. Prostrate herb. Leaves short-stalked, opposite, obliquely oblong, minutely serrate near the tip, glabrous. Flowers reddish. Fruit a capsule, pale yellow. Flowers June–August, fruits August–September. Propagated by seeds. Distributed throughout Nepal at 300–1400 m in moist, open places; native to West Africa, also in India and Mauritius.

MEDICINE. A paste of the plant is applied to snakebites.

Euphorbia pulcherrima Willdenow ex Klotzsch

Poinsettia pulcherrima (Willdenow ex Klotzsch) Graham
BHOJPURI *lalpatta* DANUWAR *lalpate* ENGLISH *Christmas flower,*
poinsettia GURUNG *olat* LEPCHA *lopahirarip* LIMBU *hekaphekwa*
MAGAR *lalpote* NEPALI *lalupate* NEWARI *lalpatya* RAI *halabakabu*
SUNWAR *lalmapha* TAMANG *lalpate mhendo* THARU *lalpate*

Euphorbiaceae. Shrub about 4 m high, branches hollow. Leaves stalked, alternate, elliptic to ovate, acute, sinuate, bracteate leaves bright red or yellow. Flowers red, the involucre bearing large yellow glands on one side. Propagated by stem cuttings. Distributed throughout Nepal at 1000–1400 m in open places; also in most tropical areas of the world.

MEDICINE. Latex is applied to boils. A paste of the leaves is applied for various cutaneous diseases. An infusion of the flower head has a galactagogue property.

OTHER USES. The plant is cultivated as an ornamental.

Euphorbia royleana Boissier

Euphorbia pentagona Royle
CHEPANG *jeri, jeru, syuri* DANUWAR *mahur, parsidha, sidha, syundi*
ENGLISH *cactus spurge* GURUNG *syuri* LIMBU *seritakma, srisin*
MAGAR *dha, mete, simjha* MAJHI *kanpate* MOOSHAR *pasij*
NEPALI *syuri* NEWARI *duru kan* RAI *mukrim, patechurdham*
SHERPA *dhersya* SUNWAR *baro* TAMANG *desya* THARU *seunwahar,*
seuri

Euphorbiaceae. Shrub about 5 m high, branches five- to seven-angled with wavy ridges. Leaves short-stalked, with a pair of spines at the base, entire, fleshy, tip rounded, narrowed toward the base. Flowers yellowish in axillary clusters, June–July. Propagated by stem cuttings. Distributed throughout Nepal to about 2400 m, generally found in open, dry places; also in India and Bhutan.

FOOD. The stem is peeled and the pith boiled and pickled.

MEDICINE. Boiled pith is considered a good appetizer and also useful for stomach disorders and gastric troubles. The leaf is warmed over a fire, pressed, and held on the fontanel of a newborn child to help it harden quicker. A paste of the leaves is applied to cuts and wounds. Juice of the leaves, about 3 teaspoons twice a day, is given to treat fever. It is dripped into the ear to treat the formation of pus inside.

The milky latex is applied to boils, pimples, and mumps. It is also applied to wounds between the toes caused by walking barefooted in muddy water, especially during the rainy season. The latex is warmed over a fire and applied to muscular swellings and sprains. About five to seven drops of latex is mixed in a cup of boiling water and taken in cases of cough and asthma. A teaspoon of milky latex is taken as an anthelmintic. This latex is considered injurious to the eyes.

OTHER USES. The plant is cut into pieces and spread in the water to catch fish. It is grown in an earthen pot and kept on the roof to protect the house from lightning and thunderstorms.

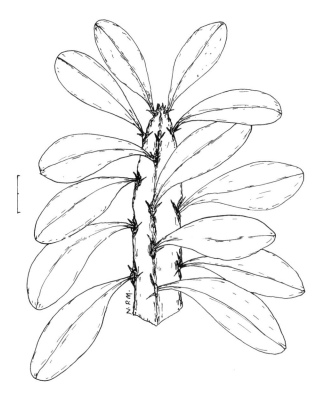

Euphorbia royleana

Euphorbia stracheyi Boissier
Tithymalus stracheyi (Boissier) Hurusawa & Tanaka
TAMANG *sangmen*

Euphorbiaceae. Herb about 10 cm high, rootstock long. Leaves alternate, small, obovate or obtusely ovate, entire. Flowers greenish red in terminal compound umbels. Flowers and fruits May–July. Propagated by seeds. Distributed throughout Nepal at 2800–5000 m on rocky and exposed slopes; also in northern India, Bhutan, Tibet, and southern China.

MEDICINE. A paste of the root is given for diarrhea.

Euphorbia wallichii Hooker fil.
Euphorbia involucrata Wallich
TIBETAN *duk*

Euphorbiaceae. Glabrous or pubescent herb about 1.5 m high, stem glabrous. Leaves sessile, alternate, linear oblong, acute, entire, with silky hairs at the base. Flowers yellowish, April–May. Propagated by seeds. Distributed throughout Nepal at 2300–3700 m in open places with shrubs; also in Afghanistan, northern India, and southwestern China.

MEDICINE. Milky latex is applied to treat goiter.

Euphrasia himalayica Wettstein
NEPALI *hare* TIBETAN *chawa chhiji*

Scrophulariaceae. Erect annual herb about 25 cm high. Leaves sessile, ovate, serrate. Flowers purple in terminal spike-like clusters. Flowers and fruits May–July. Propagated by seeds. Distributed throughout Nepal at 3200–4200 m in open, damp places; also in Afghanistan, India, and Bhutan.

MEDICINE. A paste of the plant is taken to treat profuse menstruation. Juice of the root is applied to boils.

Euphrasia himalayica

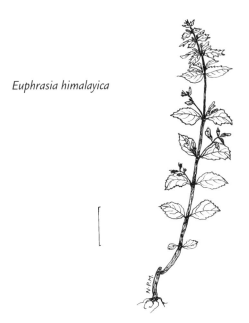

Eurya acuminata de Candolle

Diospyros serrata Buchanan-Hamilton ex D. Don
Eurya japonica Thunberg
Ternstroemia bifaria Buchanan-Hamilton ex D. Don
CHEPANG *chhuisi* GURUNG *chonsi, jhuinsin* NEPALI *bilaune, jhingane, sano jhingane* SHERPA *pajan* TAMANG *tengar*

Theaceae. Evergreen shrub with smooth brown bark. Leaves short-stalked, 1.8–13.5 cm long, 1–4 cm wide, oblong to lanceolate, acuminate, closely serrulate, leathery, usually glabrous above, hairy beneath. Flowers small, yellowish. Fruit globose, crowned by the remains of the styles. Flowers November–December. Propagated by seeds. Distributed throughout Nepal at 1000–2800 m in open places; also in northern India, Sri Lanka, southwestern China, and Malaysia.

OTHER USES. Wood provides an excellent fuel. Foliage is used for fodder.

Eurya acuminata

Eurya cerasifolia (D. Don) Kobuski

Diospyros cerasiolia D. Don
Eurya acuminata Wallich, not de Candolle
Eurya symplocina Blume
Eurya wallichiana Steudel
NEPALI *bhale jhinu, jhigane, thulo jhigane* TAMANG *tengar, tenkar*

Theaceae. Tree about 5 m high. Leaves stalked, 4–13.5 cm long, 2–3.5 cm wide, slightly serrate toward the apex, glabrous, tip rounded. Flowers greenish white, fragrant, September–November. Fruits March–June. Propagated by seeds. Distributed in central and eastern Nepal at 900–2300 m in shady ravines; also in northern India, Bhutan, western China, and Myanmar.

OTHER USES. The plant produces low-quality fodder. It is mildly browsed by sheep. Wood is used for fuel.

Evolvulus alsinoides (Linnaeus) Linnaeus

Convolvulus alsinoides Linnaeus
NEPALI *khunkhune jhar*

Convolvulaceae. Prostrate perennial herb. Leaves sessile or short-stalked, 5–15 mm long, 2.5–6 mm wide, oblong to lanceolate, apex obtuse or mucronate. Flowers bluish purple. Fruit a capsule, globose. Flowers and fruits April–October. Propagated by seeds. Distributed throughout Nepal at 550–1100 m on open hillsides; also in India, Bhutan, southern China, Indo-China, the Philippines, Sunda Isles, tropical Africa, and Madagascar.

MEDICINE. Ash of the plant is spread on boils and pimples. Juice of the plant is taken as a tonic. A powder of dried leaves is smoked to relieve bronchitis and asthma.

Evolvulus alsinoides

Evolvulus nummularius (Linnaeus) Linnaeus

Convolvulus nummularius Linnaeus
THARU *dinghumani phul*

Convolvulaceae. Creeping herb. Leaves short-stalked, alternate, 0.8–2 cm long, 0.6–1.4 cm wide, ovate, entire, rounded at both ends. Flowers white. Flowers and fruits March–November. Propagated by seeds. Distributed in eastern and central Nepal to about 900 m in open, dry places; also in India, Bhutan, tropical Africa, and Madagascar.

MEDICINE. A paste of the plant is applied to treat scabies.

Exbucklandia populnea (R. Brown ex Griffith) R. W. Brown

Bucklandia populnea R. Brown ex Griffith, *Symingtonia populnea* (R. Brown ex Griffith) van Steenis
Bucklandia populifolia Hooker fil. & Thomson
NEPALI *pipli*

Hamamelidaceae. Tree about 25 m high. Leaves stalked, 7–16 cm long, 5–16 cm wide, broadly ovate, leathery, entire, tip narrowed. Propagated by seeds or cuttings. Distributed in eastern Nepal at 1300–2100 m in open places; also in India, Bhutan, eastward to China, southward to Malaysia, and Sumatra.

MEDICINE. A paste of the bark is applied to muscular swellings.

Exbucklandia populnea

acute. Flowers yellowish in axillary and terminal spikes. Fruit a capsule, subglobose. Seeds ovoid, smooth. Flowers April–May, fruits July–December. Propagated by seeds. Distributed in central and western Nepal at 1000–2000 m, common and gregarious in open, stony places; also in northern India.

OTHER USES. Latex is harmful to the skin.

F

Fagopyrum dibotrys (D. Don) Hara

Polygonum dibotrys D. Don
Polygonum cymosum Treviranus, *Fagopyrum cymosum* (Treviranus) Meissner
Polygonum emarginatum Roxburgh
Polygonum triangulare Wallich ex Meissner

GURUNG *tautha, tota* MAGAR *muran* NEPALI *banbhande, barbande, bhande, salsale* TAMANG *tanglai, tanglingbho*

Polygonaceae. Erect pubescent herb about 1 m high. Leaves stalked, 5–11 cm long, 4.5–13 cm wide, triangular, acuminate, entire, veins pubescent, base cordate. Flowers white in axillary and terminal panicled cymes. Fruit a nut, three-angled. Flowers and fruits June–September. Propagated by seeds. Distributed throughout Nepal at 1500–3000 m in shady places; also in northern India, Tibet, and eastward to China.

FOOD. Tender shoots and leaves are cooked as a vegetable.

Excoecaria acerifolia D. F. Didrichsen

Stillingia himalayensis Klotzsch, *Excoecaria himalayensis* (Klotzsch) Mueller Aargau

ENGLISH *blind-your-eyes tree* NEPALI *gadasilo, rajeli*

Euphorbiaceae. Erect deciduous shrub about 2 m high, bark smooth, with scattered, pale, circular lenticels. Leaves stalked, alternate, elliptic to oblong, acuminate, finely crenate to serrate, glabrous, rather glossy above, base usually

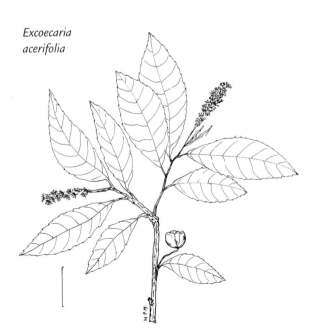

Excoecaria acerifolia

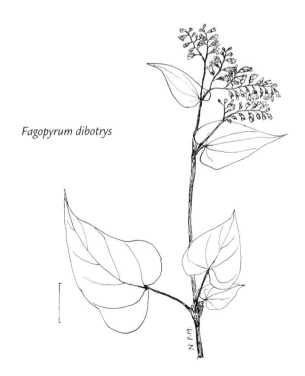

Fagopyrum dibotrys

Fagopyrum esculentum Moench

Fagopyrum sagittatum Gilibert
Polygonum emarginatum Roth
Polygonum fagopyrum Linnaeus

BHOJPURI *phaphar* CHEPANG *phaphar* DANUWAR *paphar*
ENGLISH *buckwheat* GURUNG *bre, ghyabre, phi, tonda*
LEPCHA *karahu* LIMBU *kyobo* MAGAR *phaphar* NEPALI *phaphar*
NEWARI *bhasan* RAI *pempakcha* SHERPA *tau* SUNWAR *bram*
TAMANG *brey, phaphar*

Polygonaceae. Glabrous annual herb about 60 cm high. Upper leaves long-stalked, lower leaves sessile, triangular, acute, cordate, entire. Flowers pink. Flowers and fruits August–November. Propagated by seeds. Distributed in central and eastern Nepal at 1000–2500 m, cultivated; also in central Asia.

FOOD. Tender leaves and shoots are cooked as a vegetable. Fruits are an important food item in the hilly regions of the country.

Fagopyrum tataricum (Linnaeus) Gaertner

Polygonum tataricum Linnaeus

ENGLISH *Tatary buckwheat* NEPALI *tite phaphar* TAMANG *pregyap*
TIBETAN *khra-ma*

Polygonaceae. Annual herb about 1 m high. Leaves stalked, 2.5–12 cm long, 2.5–11.5 cm wide, broadly deltoid, acuminate. Flowers white or pink in branching racemes. Fruit an achene, grooved. Flowers and fruits April–May. Propagated by seeds. Distributed throughout Nepal at 1400–3000 m in open places; indigenous to the Himalayan region, also found in Pakistan, India, Bhutan, central Asia, and Siberia.

FOOD. Tender leaves and shoots are used as a potherb. Flour from the fruits is baked.

Ficus auriculata Loureiro

Ficus roxburghii Wallich

CHEPANG *kaitak* ENGLISH *Eve's apron* GURUNG *paingi*
LIMBU *poyepa* NEPALI *gopa, newaro, nimaro, timila* TAMANG *mako*

Moraceae. Medium-sized tree with warty gray bark, young shoots hollow. Leaves stalked, alternate, 10–25 cm long, 7–23 cm wide, broadly ovate or rounded, acute or mucronate, entire, glabrous or glabrescent above, softly pubescent beneath, base generally deeply cordate. Figs turbinate, depressed, tubercled, longitudinally ribbed, purplish when ripe, ripening April–June. Propagated by seeds or cuttings. Distributed throughout Nepal to about 2000 m on open ground; also in northern Pakistan, northern India, China, and Indo-China.

FOOD. Ripe figs are edible and sweet.

MEDICINE. Latex is applied to cuts and wounds. Roasted figs are prescribed in cases of diarrhea and dysentery.

OTHER USES. The plant is lopped for fodder and is considered nutritious to animals. Leaves are used as plates.

Ficus benghalensis Linnaeus

Urostigma benghalense (Linnaeus) Gaspary
Ficus indica Linnaeus

BHOJPURI *bar* CHEPANG *bar* DANUWAR *bar* ENGLISH *banyan tree*
GURUNG *bar* LEPCHA *kungjyi* LIMBU *lara, paramsing* MAGAR *bar*
MOOSHAR *bar* NEPALI *bar* RAI *bara, dariyongma* SATAR *banidare*
SUNWAR *bar* THARU *bargad* TIBETAN *ni-gro-dha*

Moraceae. Evergreen tree about 35 m high with a spreading canopy, branches with numerous aerial roots that support the widely spreading crown. Leaves stalked, alternate, 10–20 cm long, 5–12.5 cm wide, ovate or elliptic, obtuse, entire, thickly leathery, rounded at the base, glabrescent above. Figs globose, scarlet when ripe, April–May. Propagated by seeds or cuttings. Distributed throughout Nepal to about 1400 m; also in Pakistan, India, Bhutan, and Bangladesh.

FOOD. Ripe figs are eaten fresh, especially by children. Birds and monkeys also eat them greedily.

MEDICINE. An infusion of the bark is a tonic in the treatment of diabetes. Heated young leaves are used as a poultice. The milky latex is applied to bruises and for rheumatism. It is dropped in wounds to kill or expel germs, applied to treat bleeding and swelling of the gums, and mixed with some sugar and given to children suffering from dysentery.

OTHER USES. The plant is used for fodder, but it is a nuisance in the forest because it is impossible for other trees to grow under its dense shade. It is generally planted in the villages and on trailsides for shade. It is considered sacred by the Hindus and it is planted for a religious purpose. Wood is used for poles, cart yokes, and furniture. The wood is water-resistant so planks of it are used to line wells. Leaves and twigs are lopped for fodder, and it is a favorite fodder for cattle and elephants. Aerial roots are used for temporary binding. The latex is made into birdlime.

Ficus benjamina Linnaeus

ENGLISH *golden fig* NEPALI *sarane, swami, sami*

Moraceae. Evergreen tree with some drooping branches. Leaves stalked, 5–11.5 cm long, 2.5–12 cm wide, broadly ovate or elliptic, entire, leathery, tip suddenly tapering to a long point, base rounded. Figs obovate, red when ripe, May–July. Propagated by seeds or cuttings. Distributed throughout Nepal to about 1200 m, generally around villages; also in Pakistan, India, Bangladesh, southern China, Myanmar, Malaysia, and northern Australia.

MEDICINE. The milky latex is applied to boils.

Ficus carica Linnaeus

ENGLISH *fig* NEPALI *anjir*

Moraceae. Medium-sized tree, bark smooth, gray or dull white. Leaves stalked, broadly ovate to cordate, three- or five-lobed, crenate to serrate. Figs solitary or paired, axillary, pear shaped, ripening June–October. Propagated by seeds or cuttings. Distributed throughout Nepal to about 1200 m, cultivated; also in most subtropical countries.

FOOD. Ripe figs are edible.

MEDICINE. Latex is applied to treat hemorrhoids and warts.

Ficus glaberrima Blume

Ficus angustifolia Roxburgh
GURUNG *pakhuri* NEPALI *pakhuri*

Moraceae. Tall tree. Leaves stalked, alternate, 8–22 cm long, 3–7.5 cm wide, ovate to lanceolate or elliptic, blunt to shortly acuminate, leathery, shiny above, glabrescent beneath, with three main veins, lateral veins in 8–10 pairs, base slightly rounded. Figs globose, smooth and orange when ripe, February–March. Propagated by seeds or cuttings. Distributed in central and western Nepal at 600–2000 m along streams in shady places; also in India, southern China, and Southeast Asia.

OTHER USES. Fiber from the inner bark is used to prepare ropes. Leaves and tender shoots are lopped for fodder.

Ficus hederacea Roxburgh

Ficus fruticosa Wallich
Ficus scandens Roxburgh
NEPALI *dudhe lahari*

Moraceae. Trailing shrub. Leaves stalked, 3–12.5 cm long, 1.5–5 cm wide, acute or subacute, entire, leathery, glabrous but slightly rough, base broadly cuneate or rounded. Figs globose, greenish, glabrous, ripe February–May. Propagated by seeds or cuttings. Distributed throughout Nepal at 500–1500 m in subtropical and

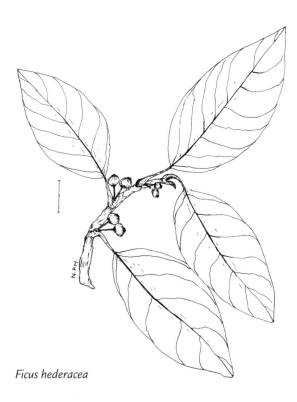

Ficus hederacea

warm, broad-leaved forests; also in northern India, southern China, and Indo-China.

OTHER USES. The inner bark is used for temporary binding. The plant is lopped for fodder.

Ficus hirta Vahl

Ficus hirsuta Roxburgh
Ficus triloba Wallich
DANUWAR *khoksa* RAUTE *khahatya*

Moraceae. Tree about 4 m high. Leaves stalked, 12–40 cm long, 8–35 cm wide, broadly ovate, often three- or five-lobed, acuminate, serrulate, somewhat roughly textured above, densely hirsute beneath, base cordate or rounded. Figs ripening November–February. Propagated by seeds or cuttings. Distributed in central Nepal to about 1000 m in openings in the subtropical forest; also in India, southern China, and Southeast Asia.

FOOD. Ripe figs are eaten fresh.

MEDICINE. Bark of the stem is boiled in water about 10 minutes, and the filtered liquid, about 3 teaspoons three times a day, is given in cases of fever. The milky latex is applied to wounds.

Ficus hispida Linnaeus fil.

Ficus auriculata Trimen, not Loureiro
Ficus daemonum Koenig ex Vahl
Ficus prominens Wallich ex Miquel
CHEPANG *kaitak* ENGLISH *hairy fig, rough-stem fig* GURUNG *khasre, thotne* NEPALI *khasreto, tote* SATAR *setapodo* TAMANG *mugu*

Moraceae. Evergreen tree about 6 m high, bark smooth, pale ash colored, horizontally wrinkled. Leaves stalked, opposite, 2.5–25 cm long, 2–12.5 cm wide, variable in size, ovate to oblong, short acuminate, dentate, somewhat rough in texture, hairy on both surfaces, dark green above, pale beneath, base more or less cordate. Figs turbinate or ovoid, clustered on stout leafless branches, yellow when ripe, July–August. Propagated by seeds or root suckers. Distributed throughout Nepal at 500–1100 m, common in open places along the bases of the foothills; also in India, Sri Lanka, southern China, Southeast Asia, and Australia.

FOOD. Green figs are cooked as a vegetable, and ripe ones are eaten fresh.

MEDICINE. Juice of the root, about 6 teaspoons twice a day, is given in cases of fever. Bark and fruit have an emetic property. The bark is also used as an antiperiodic and tonic. Juice of the figs is taken for liver troubles.

OTHER USES. The inner bark yields fiber that is used for cordage. The plant is lopped for fodder.

Ficus lacor Buchanan-Hamilton

Ficus infestoria Willdenow
ENGLISH *elephant fig, Java fig* MAGAR *kapara* NEPALI *kabhro*

Moraceae. Large evergreen tree with drooping branches, bark brownish gray. Leaves stalked, elliptic to ovate, bluntly acuminate, leathery. Fig globose, in axillary pairs, white when ripe, March–May. Propagated by seeds or cuttings. Distributed throughout Nepal to about 500 m on open hillsides; also in India and Indo-China.

FOOD. Young shoots are cooked as a vegetable or pickled.

MEDICINE. The milky latex is applied to boils.

OTHER USES. Bark gives fiber that is used for rope. The plant is lopped for fodder.

Ficus neriifolia Smith var. *nemoralis*
(Wallich ex Miquel) Corner

CHEPANG *cheksi* GURUNG *gnara, gnta, tauchhi* NEPALI *dudhe, dudhilo* RAI *wakasi* TAMANG *gnehanam, nedhar, nelam*

Moraceae. Small tree with smooth grayish brown bark. Leaves stalked, alternate, 13–15 cm long, 3–6.5 cm wide, lanceolate to elliptic, long acuminate, entire, glabrous, with three main veins, lateral veins in 8–12 pairs, base acute. Figs subglobose, glabrous, reddish when ripe, October–November. Propagated by seeds or cuttings. Distributed throughout Nepal at 500–2200 m in open places; also in India, Bhutan, eastern Tibet, and southwestern China.

FOOD. Ripe figs are edible.

MEDICINE. Latex is applied to boils on the tongue.

OTHER USES. The plant provides nutritious fodder for cattle.

Ficus palmata Forsskål
Ficus caricoides Roxburgh
Ficus virgata Wallich ex Roxburgh
MAGAR *kappa* NEPALI *bedu, beru, berulo*

Moraceae. Tree about 4 m high. Leaves stalked, alternate, 2.5–15 cm long, 3–13.5 cm wide, orbiculate to ovate, acute, dentate or serrate, somewhat roughly textured above, tomentose beneath, lateral veins in six to eight pairs, base truncate or abruptly narrowed toward the petiole. Figs usually solitary, pear shaped, dark purple or pink when ripe, June–October. Propagated by seeds or cuttings. Distributed in western Nepal at 600–2700 m in open places, generally along stream banks; also in Afghanistan, northern Pakistan, northern India, Arabia, and northeastern Africa.

FOOD. Young shoots are cooked as a vegetable. Ripe figs are edible. Latex is used for curdling milk.

MEDICINE. Latex is applied to take out spines lodged deeply in the flesh.

OTHER USES. Leaves are lopped for fodder.

Ficus racemosa Linnaeus
Ficus glomerata Roxburgh
ENGLISH *cluster fig* NEPALI *dumri* DANUWAR *gular* SATAR *loa*

Moraceae. Deciduous tree about 8 m high. Leaves stalked, 7–20 cm long, 2.5–7.5 cm wide, cuneate, elliptic to ovate, entire, leathery. Figs subglobose or pear shaped, on slender, lateral leafless shoots; ripe November–April. Propagated by seeds or cuttings. Distributed in central and western Nepal to about 1000 m in open places; also in Pakistan, India, Sri Lanka, southwestern China, Southeast Asia, and Australia.

FOOD. Ripe figs are eaten fresh.

OTHER USES. Wood is used for minor construction and also as fuelwood. A viscid gum from the stem is made into birdlime. Bark contains tannin. Leaves are lopped for fodder.

Ficus religiosa Linnaeus
BHOJPURI *pipal* CHEPANG *pipal* DANUWAR *pipar* ENGLISH *peepal tree, sacred bo* GURUNG *pipal* LEPCHA *tongjyer* LIMBU *pendi, pirimsing* MAGAR *pipal* MOOSHAR *pipar* NEPALI *pipal* NEWARI *wangal sima* RAI *nayongma, pipola* SUNWAR *pipal* TAMANG *pipal* THARU *pipara* TIBETAN *bo-de-tsa*

Moraceae. Deciduous tree about 35 m high. Leaves stalked, alternate, orbiculate to ovate, entire, undulate, thinly leathery, shiny above, reddish when young, with five to seven main veins, base cordate, rounded. Figs subglobose, dark purple when ripe, April–May. Propagated by seeds or cuttings. Distributed throughout Nepal to about 1500 m, common at the margins of forests or areas of human habitation; also in India and Southeast Asia.

MEDICINE. Bark is astringent and a decoction of it is prescribed to treat gonorrhea. An infusion of the bark is given internally for scabies and is also applied externally. Juice of the bark is given in cases of diarrhea and dysentery and is also used on snakebites. Latex or juice of the plant is used for toothaches and aching gums. Young leaf is boiled in water, filtered, and dripped into the ear to treat earaches. A paste of young leaves or shoots is used for skin disease. Fruits are laxative.

OTHER USES. The plant is held sacred by Hindus and Buddhists and is planted abundantly near temples. It is destructive to forest trees because of the vast shading. Moreover, it does great damage to buildings and walls on which it grows by sending down roots through crevices. Bark is used for dyeing and tanning. Inner bark is used for temporary binding. Leaves and branches are lopped for elephant fodder.

Ficus rumphii Blume
Ficus cordifolia Roxburgh
CHEPANG *wagrans* NEPALI *kathe pipal, pahare pipal* TAMANG *dango, pelka*

Moraceae. Deciduous tree. Leaves stalked, alternate, 8.5–15 cm long, 8.5–10 cm wide, broadly ovate, acuminate, entire, undulate, glabrous, shiny above, lateral veins in three to six pairs, base truncate, rounded, or narrowed. Figs sessile, globose, black when ripe, May–June. Propagated by seeds or cuttings. Distributed in central and western Nepal at 300–1000 m on open slopes; also in India and Southeast Asia.

MEDICINE. The plant is fed to animals with foot-and-mouth disease.

OTHER USES. Leaves and branches are lopped for cattle fodder. Latex is used to trap birds.

Ficus sarmentosa Buchanan-Hamilton ex Smith

Ficus foveolata Wallich ex Miquel
Ficus luducca Wallich ex Roxburgh

MAGAR *aagjara lahara* NEPALI *ban timila, berulo, bhir khanyu, pakhuri*

Moraceae. Scandent shrub with pubescent shoots and rooting branches. Leaves stalked, alternate, 6.5–2–6.5 cm, elliptic to ovate, acuminate, entire, glabrous above, pubescent beneath, lateral veins in 5–10 pairs, base rounded, slightly cuneate. Figs globose, purple when ripe, June–July. Propagated by seeds or cuttings. Distributed throughout Nepal at 1400–2600 m in moist areas, generally along stream banks and rivers; also in India, southern Tibet, China, Taiwan, Southeast Asia, and Japan.

FOOD. Ripe figs are eaten fresh.

OTHER USES. Leaves and twigs are used for fodder.

Ficus semicordata Buchanan-Hamilton ex Smith

Ficus conglomerata Roxburgh
Ficus cunea Buchanan-Hamilton ex Roxburgh

CHEPANG *koksi* DANUWAR *khurhur* GURUNG *khajare, kharne, mauwa, mongu, talsi* LIMBU *khokse* MAGAR *aarkhot* NEPALI *khanyu* RAI *khuksi* RAUTE *kho* SATAR *hor podo* TAMANG *khajare, kosing* THARU *khurhur*

Moraceae. Tree about 10 m high. Leaves stalked, alternate, stipulate, 10–25 cm long, 4–12 cm wide, oblanceolate, long-pointed, roughly textured, neatly dentate in the upper half of the leaf, base unequally bilobed. Figs short-stalked, in pairs or usually clustered on leafless scaly branches, roughly textured, pear shaped or slightly flattened, reddish brown when ripe, September–October. Propagated by seeds or cuttings. Distributed throughout Nepal to about 1800 m in open places; also in India, southern China, and Southeast Asia.

FOOD. Ripe figs are edible.

MEDICINE. Juice of the root is applied to treat headaches and is also recommended for fever and menstrual disorders. Bark, mixed with bark of *Schima wallichii* and *Syzygium cumini*, is pounded, and the juice, about 4 teaspoons four times a day, is given for gastric troubles and peptic ulcer. Immature figs are eaten to treat constipation and a paste of the figs is applied to the forehead to relieve headaches. About five drops of latex is mixed with milk and given to children suffering from fever.

OTHER USES. Bark yields a fiber used in making ropes. Leaves are cut for fodder (Plate 13).

Ficus subincisa Buchanan-Hamilton ex Smith

Ficus caudata Griffith
Ficus chincha Roxburgh
Ficus clavata Wallich

CHEPANG *cheksi* GURUNG *kane chhi* MAGAR *birula, lekho* NEPALI *aankha pakuws, bello, berulo* TAMANG *soror*

Moraceae. Tree about 6 m high, bark reddish brown, covered with minute raised lenticels. Leaves stalked, alternate, 5–10 cm long, 2–5 cm wide, elliptic to lanceolate, acuminate, margin with coarse teeth near the apex, glabrous but rough on both surfaces, base narrowed. Figs ovoid, more or less wrinkled and warted, yellow when ripe, July–September. Propagated by seeds or cuttings. Distributed throughout Nepal to about 1800 m on steep, rocky ground, especially in ravines; also in northern India, southwestern China, and Indo-China.

FOOD. Ripe figs are edible.

OTHER USES. The plant is lopped for fodder.

Fimbristylis dichotoma (Linnaeus) Vahl

ENGLISH *matrush* NEPALI *pani mothe*

Cyperaceae. Annual herb about 40 cm high. Leaves linear, sickle shaped. Inflorescences greenish in compound umbels. Fruit a nutlet, ovoid, whitish. Flowers and fruits July–November. Propagated by seeds or tubers. Distributed in eastern and central Nepal to about 1800 m in open, sunny places; also in tropical and temperate regions of the world.

MEDICINE. A paste of the tuber is applied to treat headaches.

OTHER USES. The plant provides fodder.

Fimbristylis miliacea (Linnaeus) Vahl

Scripus miliaceus Linnaeus
Fimbristylis littoralis Gaudichaud

NEPALI *jwane jhar*

Cyperaceae. Annual herb about 50 cm high, stem slender, four-angled. Leaves all basal, linear. Inflorescences brown in decompound umbels. Fruit a nutlet, obovoid, much of it covered with warts. Flowers and fruits July–November. Propagated by seeds or tubers. Distributed in eastern and central Nepal to about 2000 m in open places; also in tropical and temperate regions of the world.

OTHER USES. The plant provides fodder.

Fimbristylis ovata (Burman fil.) Kern

Carex ovata Burman fil., *Abildgaardia ovata* (Burman fil.) Král
Cyperus monostachyus Linnaeus, *Fimbristylis monostachya* (Linnaeus) Hasskarl

NEPALI *bhulna*

Cyperaceae. Densely tufted herb about 30 cm high. Leaves crowded on the swollen base of the stem, filiform, acute. Inflorescence greenish. Fruit a nut, globosely pear shaped. Flowers and fruits August–December. Propagated by seeds or tubers. Distributed throughout Nepal to about 1000 m in shaded loam of open land; also pantropical.

OTHER USES. The plant provides fodder.

Fimbristylis ovata

Fimbristylis schoenoides (Retzius) Vahl

Scripus schoenoides Retzius
NEPALI *mothe*

Cyperaceae. Annual herb about 45 cm high. Leaves linear, filiform. Inflorescence brownish. Fruit a nut, ovoid, smooth. Flowers and fruits August–November. Propagated by seeds or tubers. Distributed in eastern and central Nepal to about 900 m in open places; also in India, southern China, Southeast Asia, and northern Australia.

OTHER USES. The plant is used for fodder.

Fimbristylis squarrosa Vahl

Fimbristylis comata Nees
NEPALI *jire jhar*

Cyperaceae. Herb about 70 cm high, stem squared. Leaves all basal, linear. Inflorescence brownish. Propagated by seeds or tubers. Distributed throughout Nepal at 500–2000 m in moist, open places; also in tropical and temperate regions of both hemispheres.

MEDICINE. Juice of the plant is applied to treat throat aches.

Flacourtia jangomas (Loureiro) Räuschel

Stigmarota jangomas Loureiro
Flacourtia cataphracta Roxburgh ex Willdenow
CHEPANG *maran* ENGLISH *puneala plum* GURUNG *dhurju pucha*
NEPALI *kareli, paneli*

Flacourtiaceae. Spiny evergreen shrub. Leaves stalked, 5–12 cm long, oblong to lanceolate, acuminate or mucronate, crenate to serrate, shiny on both surfaces. Flowers small, yellowish, in short terminal racemes. Fruit globose, dark purple when ripe. Seeds flattened. Flowers July–August, fruits October–December. Propagated by seeds. Distributed throughout Nepal at 900–1300 m; also in India, Bhutan, Myanmar, Thailand, Malaysia, and East Africa.

FOOD. Ripe fruits are eaten fresh.

MEDICINE. About 4 teaspoons of bark, mixed with half a teaspoon of mustard seed paste, is given twice a day for diarrhea and dysentery.

OTHER USES. The plant is browsed by goats and sheep. Wood is used to make agricultural implements. Walking sticks are prepared from the branches.

Flemingia chappar Buchanan-Hamilton ex Bentham

Moghania chappar (Buchanan-Hamilton ex Bentham) Kuntze
NEPALI *bhatte*

Leguminosae. Gregarious subshrub about 1.5 m high. Leaves stalked, 3–12 cm long, 3–10 cm wide, orbiculate to cordate, acuminate, glabrescent above, more or less pubescent beneath, especially along the veins, three-veined at the base. Flowers yellowish. Fruit a pod, two-seeded. Flowers August–October, fruits November–February. Propagated by seeds. Distributed in central and western Nepal at 150–600 m, generally in open, moist places; also in India and Myanmar.

FOOD. Fresh flowers are chewed by children.

Flemingia macrophylla (Willdenow) Merrill

Crotalaria macrophylla Willdenow, *Moghania macrophylla* (Willdenow) Kuntze
Flemingia congesta Roxburgh ex Aiton
Flemingia semialata Roxburgh
CHEPANG *ghunchuni, myuchuk* LEPCHA *nipitmuk*
NEPALI *bhatamase lahara* TAMANG *mi teptep, ramothe*

Leguminosae. Shrub about 5 m high. Leaves stalked, digitately trifoliolate, leaflets short-stalked, 3.5–19 cm long, 1.5–9.5 cm wide, elliptic to ovate, entire, narrowed toward the tip, base cuneate. Flowers purplish in a raceme.

Flacourtia jangomas

Flemingia macrophylla

Fruit a pod, oblong, tomentose, two-seeded. Flowers and fruits March–December. Propagated by seeds. Distributed throughout Nepal at 300–1700 m in open, dry places; also in India, Sri Lanka, southern and eastern Asia including China, Malaysia, Australia, and Africa.

MEDICINE. A paste of the root is applied to swellings caused by some inflammations.

OTHER USES. The plant provides fodder.

Flemingia strobilifera (Linnaeus) Aiton fil.

Hedysarum strobiliferum Linnaeus, *Moghania strobelifera* (Linnaeus) J. Saint-Hilaire ex Kuntze
Flemingia fruticulosa Wallich ex Bentham, *Moghania fruticulosa* (Wallich ex Bentham) Mukerjee
Hedysarum bracteatum Roxburgh, *Flemingia bracteata* (Roxburgh) Wight, *Moghania bracteata* (Roxburgh) H. L. Li
CHEPANG *grop muja, jyugar, ghari mamarkha, jogbiro*
NEPALI *barkauli jhar, chunetro ghans, duware, gahate, sangle jhar, swata, syano bhatyaula* RAUTE *batya* TAMANG *gahate, mranche*

Leguminosae. Shrub about 3 m high, bark reddish brown, with numerous small lenticels. Leaves stalked, 3–14 cm long, 2.8–4.8 cm wide, simple, ovate to lanceolate, acuminate, glabrous on both surfaces except the midrib, which has appressed rusty hairs. Flowers greenish white in terminal racemes. Fruit a pod, turgid, finely downy. Flowers July–September, fruits January–March. Propagated by seeds. Distributed throughout Nepal at 300–2300 m in open, dry places; also in tropical and subtropical Asia and America.

FOOD. Ripe fruits are eaten fresh.

MEDICINE. A paste of the root, about 2 teaspoons twice a day, is given for indigestion. Juice of the root, about 4 teaspoons four times a day, is given in cases of fever. It is also recommended for epilepsy, diarrhea, and dysentery. Juice of the bark, 4 teaspoons twice a day, is given to treat fever, diarrhea, and dysentery.

Floscopa scandens Loureiro

Aneilema hispidum D. Don, *Commelina hispida* Buchanan-Hamilton ex Sprengel
Commelina hamiltonii Sprengel, *Floscopa hamiltonii* (Sprengel) Hasskarl
Tradescantia paniculata Roxburgh
NEPALI *simkane ghans* RAUTE *kaneuwa*

Commelinaceae. Aquatic herb with creeping stem. Leaves sessile, 5.5–14 cm long, 1.5–4 cm wide, lanceolate, clasping and sheathing the stem at their base, glabrous. Flowers purple in dense panicles. Flowers and fruits September–November. Propagated by seeds or root offshoots. Distributed throughout Nepal at 500–1800 m in moist places; also in India, China, Taiwan, Malaysia, and Australia.

MEDICINE. Juice of the root is applied to the forehead to relieve headaches. The plant is boiled in water until the water is reduced to half the original amount, then filtered. The filtered water, about 6 teaspoons four times a day, is given in cases of cough and colds.

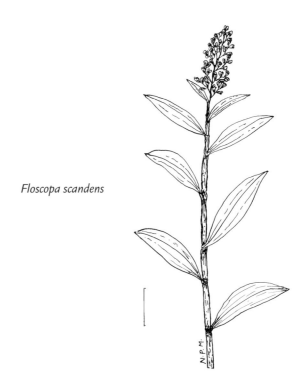

Floscopa scandens

Foeniculum vulgare Miller

DANUWAR *sonp* ENGLISH *fennel, sweet fennel* LEPCHA *sopa* LIMBU *sopa* NEPALI *sonf* NEWARI *sonp* TAMANG *saunf* RAI *somphaphun* SUNWAR *sonp* THARU *sonf* TIBETAN *go-snyod, ze-ra-dkar-po*

Umbelliferae. Glabrous herb. Leaves stalked, divided into filiform segments. Flowers yellowish in compound umbels. Fruit oblong or ellipsoidal, ribbed. Flowers and fruits January–March. Propagated by seeds. Distributed

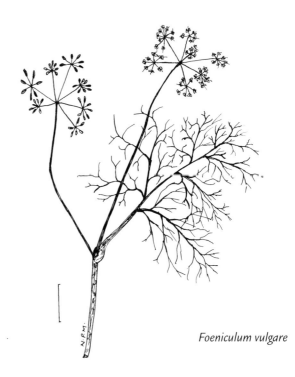

Foeniculum vulgare

throughout Nepal to about 2400 m, cultivated; also in most parts of the world.

FOOD. Seeds are used as spice in cooking and in preparation of pickles, candies, and liqueurs.

MEDICINE. Roots are purgative.

OTHER USES. Seeds contain 2–6.5% essential oil.

Fortunella japonica (Thunberg) Swingle

ENGLISH *kumquat* NEPALI *muntala*

Rutaceae. Thorny evergreen shrub about 4 m high. Leaves simple, entire, leathery. Flowers white. Fruit juicy, divided into three to five compartments. Propagated by seeds. Distributed throughout Nepal at 1000–1500 m, cultivated; also in China and Japan.

FOOD. Ripe fruits may be eaten whole, preserved in syrup, or canned.

Fortunella japonica

Fragaria daltoniana Gay

Fragaria sikkimensis Kurz

GURUNG *nandur* NEPALI *bhuin kaphal*

Rosaceae. Shrub with a stout rootstock. Leaves stalked, trifoliolate, leaflets sessile, 0.5–3.5 cm long, 0.3–2.5 cm wide, obovate or oblong, dentate, hairy on the veins beneath. Flowers white on slender one- or two-flowered peduncles. Fruit globose, red. Flowers May–June, fruits July–September. Propagated by seeds or root suckers. Distributed throughout Nepal at 1000–2800 m in moist, shady places of dense forest; also in northern India and northern Myanmar.

FOOD. Ripe fruits are eaten fresh.

MEDICINE. Juice of the root, about 4 teaspoons three times a day, is given to treat fever.

Fragaria nubicola Lindley ex Lacaita

Fragaria vesca Linnaeus

ENGLISH *Indian strawberry* NEPALI *bhuin ainselu, bhuin kaphal* SHERPA *nhynalang dhambu*

Rosaceae. Herb with filiform runners and stout rootstock. Leaves stalked, trifoliolate, leaflets sessile, 0.7–5 cm long, 0.5–3 cm wide, obovate or orbiculate, dentate, hairy on both surfaces. Flowers white on one- or two-flowered peduncles. Flowers and fruits May–October. Propagated by seeds or root suckers. Distributed throughout Nepal at 1600–4000 m in open grassland; also in Kashmir, Bhutan, northern Myanmar, and western China.

FOOD. Ripe fruits are eaten fresh.

MEDICINE. Juice of the plant, about 4 teaspoons twice a day, is given for profuse menstruation. Unripe fruit is chewed to treat blemishes on the tongue.

Fragaria nubicola

Fraxinus floribunda Wallich

Fraxinus urophylla Wallich ex de Candolle, *Ornus urophylla* G. Don

ENGLISH *Himalayan ash* GURUNG *raunle* LIMBU *khungliba* NEPALI *lankuri* TAMANG *langure*

Oleaceae. Large deciduous tree. Leaves stalked, opposite, pinnate, leaflets seven or nine, stalked, elliptic to lanceolate, acuminate, dentate. Flowers white, fragrant, in terminal panicles. Fruit narrow, winged, one-seeded. Flowers March–April, fruits September–November. Propagated by seeds. Distributed in central and eastern Nepal at 1200–2000 m, generally planted around villages; also in northern India, Bhutan, and eastward to western China.

Fraxinus floribunda

Fritillaria cirrhosa

MEDICINE. Juice of the bark is given to treat stomach disorders of sheep. The bark is boiled in water about 10 minutes, and the strained water, about 2 teaspoons, is given as an anthelmintic. Young shoots have a toxic effect on livestock. These shoots are considered to have an abortifacient property.

OTHER USES. Wood is used for poles and plows.

Fritillaria cirrhosa D. Don

ENGLISH *snake's-head fritillary* NEPALI *kakoli* SHERPA *tak tak* TIBETAN *a-bi-kha-zan-pa*

Liliaceae. Erect herb about 75 cm high. Leaves sessile, linear, lower leaves opposite, upper leaves in a whorl, uppermost with tendril-like tips. Flowers solitary, drooping, yellowish with dark purple spots, May–July. Propagated by bulbs. Distributed throughout Nepal at 3000–4500 m in exposed alpine grassland; also in northern India, Bhutan, southern Tibet, and northern Myanmar.

FOOD. Boiled or roasted roots are edible. The Tamangs of Rasuwa district chew the fresh gynoecium.

MEDICINE. The bulb is heated over a fire and eaten to treat asthma, bronchitis, and bleeding during cough, possibly caused by tuberculosis. A paste of the bulb is applied to check bleeding from wounds and to treat pimples.

Fumaria indica (Haussknecht) Pugsley

Fumaria vaillantii var. *indica* Haussknecht
Fumaria vaillantii Loiseleur-Deslongchamps
NEPALI *dhukure jhar, koire kuro, koirum, shampu phul* RAUTE *maruwa*

Fumariaceae. Much branched, delicate herb about 50 cm high. Leaves stalked, cut two or three times into narrow, pointed segments, ultimate segments linear, apiculate, entire. Flowers pinkish in lax racemes. Fruit a capsule, globose, echinate. Flowers and fruits most of the year. Propagated by seeds. Distributed throughout Nepal

Fumaria indica

to about 1500 m in moist and shady or open places; also in Pakistan, India, Bhutan, and Sri Lanka.

MEDICINE. The plant is diuretic and diaphoretic. Juice of the plant, about 4 teaspoons, is given as an anthelmintic. This juice is also applied to cuts and wounds. Juice of the root is applied to fresh cuts and wounds.

OTHER USES. The plant is gathered for fodder.

Fumaria parviflora Lamarck

ENGLISH *fumitory* NEPALI *kairuwa*

Fumariaceae. Diffuse annual herb. Leaves stalked, pinnatifid, segments deeply lobed, linear, glabrous. Flowers pink in terminal racemes. Fruit globose, one-seeded. Flowers and fruits December–April. Propagated by seeds. Distributed in central Nepal to about 1300 m in moist, shady places; also in central Asia, Europe, and Africa.

MEDICINE. Juice of the plant is applied to cuts and wounds.

G

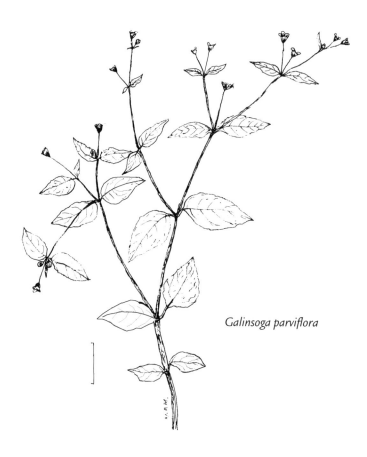

Galinsoga parviflora

Galinsoga parviflora Cavanilles

CHEPANG *chiplange* ENGLISH *gallant soldier* GURUNG *angale, ankale, tinno, ririno* NEPALI *chitlange ghans, gandhe jhar, pire, kharo, rato raunne, taunne* NEWARI *nawa ghyan* SHERPA *gumbo jhyap* TAMANG *balden dhap, mratar, naula, piwa, samden* TIBETAN *hyurma*

Compositae. Erect herb. Leaves stalked, 1.5–3.5 cm long, 0.5–1.8 cm wide, ovate to lanceolate, acuminate, dentate, tapering at the base. Flower heads yellow. Fruit an achene, black. Flowers May–October, fruits August–October. Propagated by seeds. Distributed throughout Nepal to about 3500 m, in open, moist, neglected places; also in most parts of the world.

MEDICINE. Juice of the plant is applied to wounds. It helps coagulate the blood of fresh cuts and wounds.

OTHER USES. The plant is considered poisonous to goats.

Galinsoga quadriradiata Ruiz & Pavón

Adventina ciliata Rafinesque, *Galinsoga ciliata* (Rafinesque) Blake NEPALI *chitlangi, jhuse chitlangi, naulo jhar* NEWARI *nawa ghyan* TAMANG *balde mran, phodi mran* TIBETAN *hyurma*

Compositae. Erect herb about 75 cm high. Leaves stalked, cuneate, elliptic to oblong, acuminate, serrate, hairy on both surfaces, tapering at the base. Flower heads yellow. Fruit an achene. Flowers May–October, fruits August–October. Propagated by seeds. Distributed throughout Nepal to about 2500 m in open, moist, neglected places; also in most parts of the world.

FOOD. Tender leaves and shoots are cooked as a green vegetable by the Tamangs of Rasuwa district.

Galium acutum Edgeworth

Galium himalayense Klotzsch

TAMANG *chyanguya*

Rubiaceae. Prostrate herb. Leaves sessile, four to six in a whorl, 0.2–1.2 cm long, 0.1–0.2 cm wide, elliptic to lanceolate, glabrous, tip spiny. Flowers white. Fruit granulate, glabrous. Flowers October–November. Propagated by seeds. Distributed throughout Nepal at 2000–4100 m in open places; also in northern India, Bhutan, and southern Tibet.

MEDICINE. Juice of the plant is applied to cuts and wounds.

Galium aparine Linnaeus

CHEPANG *chiski* NEPALI *kangre jhar* TAMANG *jajatero*

Rubiaceae. Rambling or climbing herb, stems prickly along the angles. Leaves sessile, five to eight in a whorl, 0.3–1.8 cm long, 0.2–0.5 cm wide, elliptic, tip spiny, midrib and margin minutely prickly. Flowers small, white. Fruit covered with hooked bristles. Flowers and fruits July–August. Propagated by seeds. Distributed in central and western Nepal at 2700–3600 m in open places along rocky tracks; also in western Asia, Europe, and North America.

MEDICINE. Juice of the plant is applied to cuts and wounds. It is also given in doses of about 4 teaspoons three times a day for indigestion.

Galium asperifolium Wallich

Galium mollugo Linnaeus
Galium parviflorum D. Don
CHEPANG *majithi* GURUNG *tiru* NEPALI *khasro jhar, kurkure ghans, pire, sano majitho* TAMANG *bhyarkin, bhyas, chyangkya, tiro*
TIBETAN *gnaharo*

Rubiaceae. Herbaceous creeper. Leaves sessile, six to eight in a whorl, 0.5–2.3 cm long, 0.1–0.7 cm wide, linear to ovate, tip spiny. Flowers yellowish in axillary and terminal cymose panicles. Fruit granulate, glabrous, black when ripe. Flowers and fruits October–December. Propagated by seeds. Distributed throughout Nepal at 1200–3500 m in moist, open places; also in Afghanistan, Pakistan, India, and Thailand.

MEDICINE. Juice of the plant is given in cases of urinary trouble and is put inside the eye to treat reddening of the eyes. This juice is also used on cuts and wounds.

Galium elegans Wallich ex Roxburgh

Galium hamiltonii Sprengel
Galium latifolium Buchanan-Hamilton ex D. Don
Galium rotundifolium Linnaeus
NEPALI *lahare kuro, tinoei* TAMANG *mran*

Rubiaceae. Trailing herb. Leaves sessile or subsessile, four in a whorl, 1–2.5 cm long, 0.5–1.2 cm wide, elliptic to ovate, obtuse, with three prominent veins at the base, hairy above, minutely prickly beneath. Flowers yellowish in axillary and terminal cymes. Fruit smooth. Flowers and fruits May–October. Propagated by seeds. Distributed throughout Nepal at 1400–3000 m in moist, shady places;

also in northern India, Bhutan, western China, Taiwan, northern Myanmar, and Thailand.

MEDICINE. Juice of the plant is applied to cuts and wounds.

OTHER USES. The plant is used as a substitute of fodder.

Galium hirtiflorum Requien ex de Candolle

Galium ciliatum D. Don
NEPALI *lute jhar*

Rubiaceae. Prostrate herb. Leaves sessile, four in whorl, 0.4–2 cm long, 0.1–0.3 cm wide, linear, minutely prickly beneath and on the margin. Flowers small, yellowish, in axillary and terminal cymes. Fruit covered with hooked bristles. Flowers and fruits April–October. Propagated by seeds. Distributed throughout Nepal at 1200–2200 m in moist, shady places; also in northwestern India.

MEDICINE. A paste of the plant is valued in treating scabies.

Garuga pinnata Roxburgh

NEPALI *dabdabe, ramsinghe* RAI *kramtha* THARU *jhengra, jigana*

Burseraceae. Deciduous tree about 25 m high. Leaves stalked, pinnate, leaflets in five to nine pairs, 5–15 cm long, 3–6.5 cm wide, ovate to lanceolate, acuminate, crenate, slightly pubescent. Flowers yellow in large terminal

Galium elegans

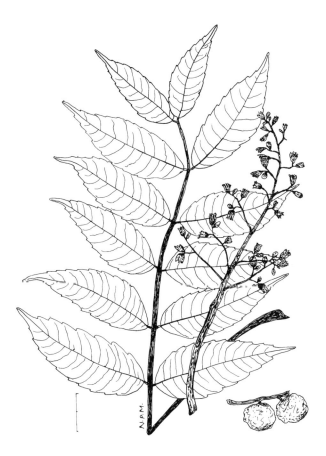

Garuga pinnata

panicles. Fruit a drupe, globose, black, the nutlets generally two, stony. Flowers April–May, fruits June–August. Propagated by seeds or cuttings. Distributed throughout Nepal to about 1200 m in forest scrub and glades; also in India, Bhutan, and Southeast Asia.

FOOD. Fruit is acidic and is eaten fresh or pickled.

MEDICINE. A decoction of the root is useful in treating skin diseases. The bark is stomachic. Juice of the bark is applied to treat dislocated bones and wounds. The bark, mixed with bark of *Ficus semicordata* in equal amount, is squeezed, and the juice, about 2 teaspoons twice a day, is given in cases of stomach disorder.

OTHER USES. Wood is used for house frames, poles, furniture, and other construction. Inner bark yields fiber for making coarse twine. Leaf galls yield tannin.

Gaultheria fragrantissima Wallich

Arbutus laurifolia Buchanan-Hamilton ex D. Don
Gaultheria fragrans D. Don

ENGLISH *fragrant wintergreen, white heather* NEPALI *dhasingar, kalgeri, machino, ogre, padakine, patpate, prava* SHERPA *chele, chenchen* TAMANG *changasai, chainso mererr, chenjuwa* TIBETAN *dawami*

Ericaceae. Shrub about 3 m high. Leaves stalked, 3–13.5 cm long, 1.5–5 cm wide, oblong to lanceolate, acuminate, serrate, leathery, bright green. Flowers whitish, fragrant. Fruit purplish blue when ripe. Flowers March–July, fruits October–December. Propagated by seeds. Distributed throughout Nepal at 1200–2600 m on rocky hillsides in forested areas; also in northern India, Bhutan, Sri Lanka, and northern Myanmar.

FOOD. Ripe fruits are eaten fresh. In 1979, during fieldwork in western Nepal, we made camp at a cowshed near the village of Hansiya, Jajarkot district. The next morning, while we were having our breakfast, five village women were setting off to collect fodder in the forest. They stopped to see what we were eating so I gave each a small piece of cheese. They tasted it but spat it out, saying, Who would eat such rotten things? I remember the first time I ate cheese, I also had the same reaction because I was not used to the taste. They, in turn, gave me ripe fruits of *Gaultheria fragrantissima* and said we should eat fresh fruit but not rotten things. Then they bid farewell, *"pheri bhetaula,"* see you again, in Nepali. The fruits are also distilled locally for alcohol.

MEDICINE. Leaves are aromatic, stimulant, and carminative. Juice of the leaves, mixed with water, is taken for coughs. This juice, about 2 teaspoons, is given as an anthelmintic. It acts as a vermicide on hookworms. Young leaves are also taken as an anthelmintic. Oil extracted from the leaf is applied to treat rheumatism and scabies. Immature fruits are chewed or their paste is given for stomach troubles. Juice of unripe fruit is taken to treat stomachaches.

Gaultheria nummularioides D. Don

NEPALI *bhui ghangharu, bibi phal, bhui kaphal, danphe charo, kali geri* SHERPA *pangsingpu* TAMANG *changasai, dawami, malang, dabrangmi, nobo* TIBETAN *jahari*

Ericaceae. Prostrate herb. Leaves short-stalked, alternate, 0.8–2 cm long, 0.5–2 cm wide, ovate, acute, glabrous above, setulose beneath and on the margin. Flowers solitary, axillary, reddish or white. Flowers and fruits March–December. Propagated by seeds or root offshoots. Distributed throughout Nepal at 2100–4100 m, common in shady places; also in northern India, Bhutan, southern Tibet, and northern Myanmar.

FOOD. Ripe fruits are eaten fresh and are watery in taste.

Gaultheria trichophylla Royle

NEPALI *bhui kaphal*

Ericaceae. Prostrate herb with wiry, hirsute branches. Leaves short-stalked, alternate, 0.5–1.4 cm long, 0.2–0.4 cm wide, elliptic or oblong, acute, crenate. Flowers solitary, axillary, pinkish white. Fruit a capsule, globose, covered with a fleshy and blue calyx. Flowers and fruits May–September. Propagated by seeds or root offshoots. Distributed throughout Nepal at 2700–4500 m in open places; also in northern India, Bhutan, southern Tibet, western China, and northern Myanmar.

FOOD. Ripe fruits are eaten raw.

Geniosporum coloratum (D. Don) Kuntze

Plectranthus colorata D. Don
Geniosporum strobiliferum Bentham

CHEPANG *galaro, sikula* NEPALI *ban bawari, chhale soin, dansupate, mosi jhar, seto tauke, theule* TAMANG *luman, manget, sorchyagne, tagntagngent*

Labiatae. Shrub about 1 m high. Leaves sessile, opposite, 3.5–12 cm long, 1.5–3.5 cm wide, ovate to lanceolate,

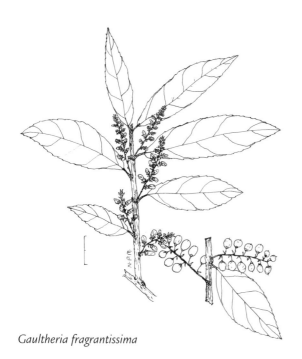

Gaultheria fragrantissima

coarsely serrate, puberulent. Flowers small, purple, in compact whorls. Fruit a nutlet, ellipsoidal, black. Flowers October–November, fruits December–January. Propagated by seeds. Distributed throughout Nepal to about 1600 m in moist places; also in northern India, Bhutan, southwestern China, and Indo-China.

FOOD. Seeds are chewed or pickled.

MEDICINE. Juice of the plant is dropped in the eye to treat inflammation of the eye and is applied for itching of the skin. This juice is also applied to cuts and wounds. A paste of the leaves is applied to cuts and wounds and is also applied in cases of itching.

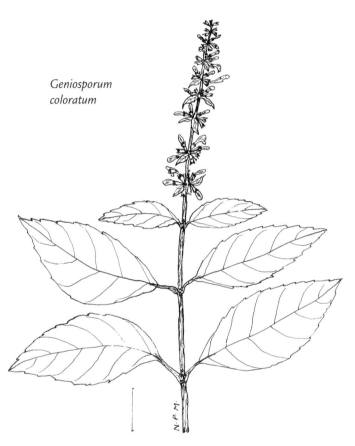

Geniosporum coloratum

Gentiana capitata Buchanan-Hamilton ex D. Don

Ericala capitata (Buchanan-Hamilton ex D. Don) D. Don
NEPALI *ban kauli, hans phul* TIBETAN *pangen mbu*

Gentianaceae. Herb about 10 cm high. Leaves sessile, 2–2.5 cm long, 0.5–1.3 cm wide, ovate, acute or mucronate, entire. Flowers blue, condensed in terminal leafy heads. Fruit a capsule. Flowers and fruits October–May. Propagated by seeds. Distributed in eastern Nepal at 1500–4500 m on open, rocky ground; also in northern India, Bhutan, and northern Myanmar.

MEDICINE. Juice of the plant, about 6 teaspoons four times a day, is given in cases of fever. A paste is given to treat headaches.

Gentiana depressa D. Don

Ericala depressa (D. Don) D. Don ex G. Don, *Gentianodes depressa* (D. Don) Á. & D. Löve, *Pneumonanthe depressa* (D. Don) D. Don
TAMANG *glagengaga*

Gentianaceae. Herb about 4 cm high. Leaves sessile, opposite, 0.5–1.5 cm long, 0.2–0.8 cm wide, spatulate, entire, tapering toward the base, tip rounded. Flowers blue, the corolla pinkish green outside, deep blue inside. Flowers and fruits September–November. Propagated by seeds. Distributed in eastern and central Nepal at 2900–4300 m in open alpine grassland; also in India, Bhutan, and southeastern Tibet.

MEDICINE. Juice of the plant is given in cases of cough and colds.

Gentiana pedicellata (D. Don) Grisebach

Ericala pedicellata D. Don
Ericala procumbens D. Don ex G. Don
Gentiana quadrifria Blume
Gentiana squarrosa Ledebour
NEPALI *chara ko khutta, hans phul, tauke phul* SHERPA *jhyaro kangwa*
TIBETAN *gyanjak, up tikta*

Gentianaceae. Herb about 10 cm high with leafy, decumbent stems. Leaves sessile, opposite, 0.5–2 cm long, 0.2–0.6 cm wide, linear, acute, entire, glabrous. Flowers blue, few, in terminal cymes, April–June. Fruits September–February. Propagated by seeds. Distributed throughout Nepal at 800–3800 m on open slopes; also in northeastern India, Bhutan, Sri Lanka, and Myanmar.

FOOD. Tender portions of the plant are cooked as a vegetable.

MEDICINE. Juice of the plant is given as an anthelmintic.

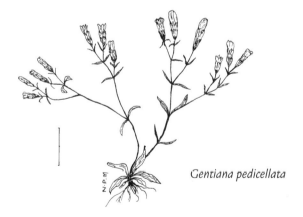

Gentiana pedicellata

Gentiana robusta King ex Hooker fil.

GURUNG *tani ta* NEPALI *bhutkesh* TIBETAN *khije*

Gentianaceae. Erect herb. Lower leaves stalked, 2.5–25 cm long, 0.8–4 cm wide, lanceolate, long-pointed, entire, upper leaves sessile. Flowers cream. Flowers and fruits June–August. Propagated by seeds. Distributed in western and central Nepal at 2500–3600 m in open, dry places; also in northern India and Bhutan.

MEDICINE. Roots and leaves are dried, burned, and the fumes inhaled to treat colds. An infusion is given in cases of fever.

Gentianella moorcroftiana (Wallich ex G. Don) Airy Shaw

Gentiana moorcroftiana Wallich ex G. Don
NEPALI *dhumpu*

Gentianaceae. Much branched annual herb. Leaves sessile, 1.5–3 cm long, lanceolate, entire. Flowers pale blue or dark mauve in lax clusters. Flowers and fruits August–October. Propagated by seeds. Distributed in western and central Nepal at 2900–5200 m on open hillsides; also in northern India.

MEDICINE. An infusion of the plant is applied to the forehead to relieve fever.

Gentianella paludosa (Hooker) H. Smith

TIBETAN *upa tikta*

Gentianaceae. Erect annual herb about 30 cm high. Leaves stalked, 2–4 cm long, narrowly elliptic. Flowers blue or white, July–August. Propagated by seeds. Distributed throughout Nepal at 3000–4600 m on open slopes; also in Pakistan and southwestern China.

MEDICINE. A paste of the root is applied to the forehead to treat headaches. It is also applied to wounds.

Gentianella paludosa

Geranium nepalense Sweet

Geranium radicans de Candolle
CHEPANG *salyang sai* ENGLISH *crane's bill*
NEPALI *chunetro ghans, raktamul*

Geraniaceae. Diffuse herb about 50 cm high, branches villous. Leaves long-stalked, opposite, orbiculate, three- or five-lobed, segments incised. Flowers pink with purple veins. Fruit a capsule, dehiscing from base to apex. Flowers March–August, fruits August–November. Propagated by seeds. Distributed throughout Nepal at 1000–4000 m in moist, shady places along ditches and streams; also in Afghanistan, northern India, Tibet, western China, and Indo-China.

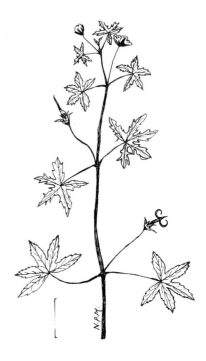

Geranium nepalense

FOOD. Fruits are chewed fresh.

MEDICINE. Juice of the plant is valued for treating renal diseases.

OTHER USES. Roots contain 25–32% tannin.

Geranium ocellatum Cambessèdes

Geranium bicolor Royle
Geranium choorense Royle
Geranium mascatense Boissier
NEPALI *ragatageri*

Geraniaceae. Hoary pubescent herb about 25 cm high. Leaves stalked, orbiculate, palmately five- or seven-lobed, segments three-lobed, dentate. Flowers pinkish, solitary or paired on long axillary peduncles. Fruit a capsule. Flowers and fruits January–May. Propagated by seeds. Distributed in western and central Nepal at 900–2400 m in moist, shady places; also in Afghanistan, northern India, and western China.

MEDICINE. Juice of the plant, about 6 teaspoons three times a day, is given to treat amebic dysentery.

Geranium refractum Edgeworth & Hooker fil.

TAMANG *lhumran*

Geraniaceae. Herb. Leaves stalked, deeply five- or seven-lobed, lobes broadly rhombic, deeply cut, tips rounded. Flowers white with purple veins, nodding. Flowers and fruits June–August. Propagated by seeds. Distributed in eastern and central Nepal at 3500–4800 m on open slopes; also in India, Bhutan, southern Tibet, and northern Myanmar.

MEDICINE. Juice of the root is applied to cuts and wounds. A paste of the plant is applied to boils.

Geranium wallichianum D. Don ex Sweet

NEPALI *rakalamul* TAMANG *polo* TIBETAN *chyaktu, nikyu, yasign*

Geraniaceae. Diffuse herb. Leaves stalked, palmately three- or five-lobed, lobes broadly ovate, hairy, stipules oblong, obtuse. Flowers faint purple on long peduncles. Fruit a capsule, linear. Propagated by seeds. Distributed in western and central Nepal at 2100–4200 m in shady places; also in Afghanistan, Pakistan, northern India, and Bhutan.

MEDICINE. The root, mixed with bark of *Prunus cerasoides*, is boiled and strained, and the liquid, about 4 teaspoons twice a day, is given for peptic ulcer. Juice of the plant is applied to fresh cuts to stop bleeding. A paste is applied to relieve joint pains.

OTHER USES. The plant is gathered for fodder.

Gerbera maxima (D. Don) Palisot de Beauvois

Chaptalia maxima D. Don
Bernieria nepalensis de Candolle
Perdicium semiflosculare D. Don
Tussilago macrophylla Wallich, *Gerbera macrophylla* Wallich ex C. B. Clarke

TAMANG *pangprapa*

Compositae. Herb. Leaves long-stalked, abruptly acuminate, dentate, cottony beneath. Flower heads whitish on a terminal stalk. Fruit an achene, slender, the pappus white. Flowers October–November, fruits December–January. Propagated by seeds. Distributed throughout Nepal at 1900–2900 m in shady places; also in northern India, Bhutan, Tibet, and Thailand.

MEDICINE. Powdered leaves are warmed and put on muscular swellings for quick recovery.

Gerbera nivea (de Candolle) Schultz Bipontinus

Oreoseris nivea de Candolle, *Senecio niveus* Wallich

NEPALI *jhulo*

Compositae. Herb about 35 cm high. Leaves obovate, pinnately lobed, narrowed to a short leafy stalk, glabrous above, white cottony beneath. Flower heads pale yellow, solitary, on a long, cottony, leafless stem. Fruit an achene. Flowers and fruits July–October. Propagated by seeds. Distributed in western and central Nepal at 2800–4500 m on open, rocky hillsides; also in northern India, Bhutan, southern Tibet, and western China.

OTHER USES. Woolly hairs of the leaves are kept with a stone and a piece of iron as a fire-starting kit. When the iron is rubbed against the stone, small sparks start and help light the hairs, which serve as tinder.

Geum elatum Wallich ex G. Don

Acomastylis elata (Wallich ex G. Don) F. Bolle, *Siversia elata* (Wallich ex G. Don) Royle

NEPALI *belochan*

Rosaceae. Herb about 50 cm high. Leaves pinnate, leaflets orbiculate, crenate, sometimes lobed, margin ciliate.

Flowers reddish, usually in pairs. Propagated by seeds. Distributed throughout Nepal at 3000–4200 m in open grassland; also in northern India and southern Tibet.

MEDICINE. Leaves are pounded and applied to wounds.

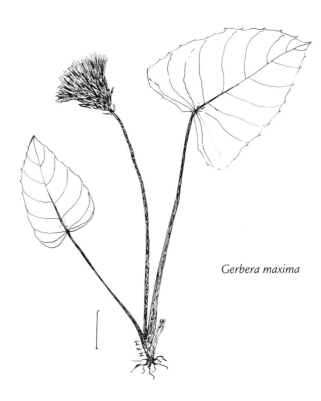

Gerbera maxima

Geum elatum

Girardinia diversifolia (Link) Friis

Urtica diversifolia Link
Girardinia armata Kunth
Girardinia palmata Gaudichaud-Beaupré
Urtica heterophylla Vahl, *Girardinia heterophylla* (Vahl) Decaisne
CHEPANG *malemau* ENGLISH *Himalayan nettle* GURUNG *naipolo, puwa* MAGAR *ghyo* NEPALI *allo, bhyangre sisnu, chalne sisnu, kali sisnu, lekh sisnu, thulo sisno* NEWARI *kisi nhyakan* RAI *potale* SHERPA *lo* SUNWAR *pale* TAMANG *pachyar, pancherpolo*

Urticaceae. Stout herb about 3 m high. Leaves stalked, 10–24 cm long, 7–18 cm wide, palmately and deeply divided, dentate, covered with long, stinging hairs, base three-ribbed. Flowers yellowish, clustered in a panicle, July–September. Propagated by seeds or root offshoots. Distributed throughout Nepal at 1200–3000 m in moist, shady, forested areas; also in northern India, Bhutan, Sri Lanka, eastward to central China, Myanmar, and Malaysia.

FOOD. Young leaves and inflorescences are cooked as a green vegetable. Roasted seeds are pickled.

MEDICINE. Ash of the plant is applied in cases of ringworm and eczema. The root is mixed with *Centella asiatica* and boiled about 10 minutes, strained, and the liquid, about 4 teaspoons twice a day, is given to treat gastric trouble. Juice of the root, about 6 teaspoons twice a day, is given for constipation. Fresh juice of the leaves is applied to treat headaches and joint aches. It is also considered useful for fever.

OTHER USES. The stinging hairs cause dermatitis. Bark of the stem furnishes fine silky fiber used for coarse clothes, bags, nets, fishnets, and ropes (Plate 37).

Girardinia diversifolia

Globba clarkei Baker

NEPALI *devi saro*

Zingiberaceae. Herb about 1 m high. Leaves oblong to lanceolate, long acuminate, slightly hairy above, pubescent beneath. Flowers yellow in long panicles, Septem-

ber–October. Propagated by rhizomes or seeds. Distributed in eastern and central Nepal at 600–1900 m on open, rocky hillsides; also in northern India, Bhutan, and northern Thailand.

MEDICINE. A paste of the root is applied to treat headaches.

Globba racemosa Smith

Globba orixensis Roxburgh
NEPALI *devi saro, harkata, laharepriya ghans, pani saro*

Zingiberaceae. Tall herb. Leaves spatulate, elliptic to lanceolate, acuminate, glabrous above, pubescent beneath. Flowers yellowish in long panicles, July–August. Propagated by rhizomes or seeds. Distributed throughout Nepal to about 1900 m in moist places; also in northern India.

MEDICINE. A paste of the root is applied to treat headaches.

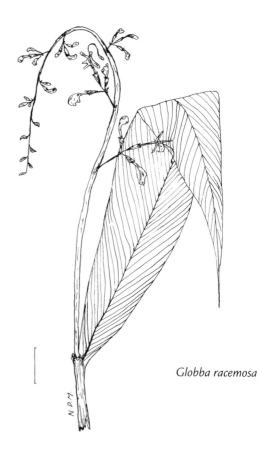

Globba racemosa

Glochidion velutinum Wight

Bradleia ovata Wallich
Phyllanthus nepalensis Mueller Aargau
CHEPANG *maisi* GURUNG *chaulani* NEPALI *bahiro, kane bahiro, kane mauwa, lati kath, mauwa, muse deli* RAUTE *niniya* TAMANG *rabagachhi*

Euphorbiaceae. Small tree. Leaves short-stalked, alternate, orbiculate or elliptic to ovate, acute, thinly leathery, gray tomentose beneath, base rounded or obtuse. Flowers yellowish in axillary clusters. Fruit a capsule, globose, depressed. Seeds red. Flowers and fruits July–September. Propagated by seeds. Distributed throughout Nepal to about 1800 m in open places; also in northern India, Bhutan, and northern Myanmar.

MEDICINE. Juice of the bark is applied to wounds. A paste of the bark is applied externally to treat dislocated bones. A paste of the fruit is applied to pimples.

OTHER USES. The plant is lopped for fodder. Bark yields tannin.

root abortifacient. Leaves are tonic, antiperiodic, and purgative. People in eastern Nepal use juice of the leaves and bulb to treat skin diseases and bowel complaints. Malhotra and Moorthy (1973) reported that the leaf and root are applied externally as an insect poison in India.

Gloriosa superba

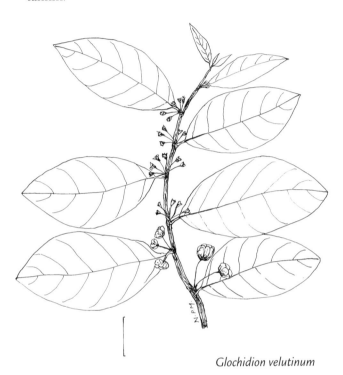

Glochidion velutinum

Gloriosa superba Linnaeus

Gloriosa doniana Schultes & Schultes fil., *Methonica doniana* (Schultes & Schultes fil.) Kunth
Gloriosa simplex D. Don
ENGLISH *climbing lily, glory lily, superb glory, tiger's claw*
NEPALI *haritali phul, kewari*

Colchicaceae. Herb about 2 m high. Leaves sessile or subsessile, 8–19 cm long, 2–3.5 cm wide, oblong to lanceolate, acuminate, spirally twisted, tip linear. Flowers solitary, yellow with a blotch of bright red in the upper portion. Fruit a capsule, oblong. Seeds many, round. Flowers and fruits June–August. Propagated by bulbs or seeds. Distributed throughout Nepal at 500–2000 m in shady places under shrubs and trees; also in India, Bhutan, Bangladesh, Sri Lanka, Myanmar, Malaysia, and tropical Africa.

MEDICINE. The bulb is tonic, antiperiodic, laxative, purgative, and stomachic. Juice of the root is given for hysteria and abdominal disorders. Some people consider the

Glycine max (Linnaeus) Merrill

Phaseolus max Linnaeus, *Soja max* (Linnaeus) Piper
Dolichos soja Linnaeus, *Glycine soja* (Linnaeus) Siebert & Zuccarini
BHOJPURI *bhatmas* CHEPANG *bhatmas* DANUWAR *bhatmas*
ENGLISH *coffee bean, soya bean, soybean* GURUNG *koyapaito*
LEPCHA *salyang* LIMBU *imbing* MAGAR *bhatta* NEPALI *bhatmas*
NEWARI *musya* RAI *khosang* SUNWAR *kolagi* TAMANG *mochhe, mode*
THARU *bharthar*

Leguminosae. Bushy annual, stem with gray hairs. Leaves stalked, alternate, trifoliolate, leaflets stalked, ovate to lanceolate, base rounded, apex acute or obtuse. Flowers white, pinkish, or lilac in axillary racemes. Fruit a pod in a short-stalked cluster. Propagated by seeds. Distributed throughout Nepal to about 1800 m, cultivated.

FOOD. Green pods are boiled and the seeds inside eaten. Green seeds are cooked as a vegetable. Mature seeds are roasted and eaten.

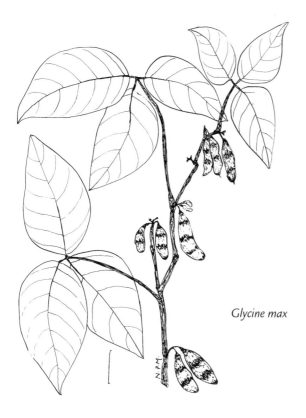

Glycine max

OTHER USES. Seed oil is used for cooking and manufacturing soap and varnish.

Gmelina arborea Roxburgh

Gmelina rheedii Hooker
ENGLISH *comb tree, snapdragon tree, tall beachberry*
NEPALI *gambhari, khamari*

Labiatae. Deciduous tree, bark grayish brown, exfoliating in thin flakes. Leaves stalked, 10–20 cm long, 7.5–14.5 cm wide, broadly ovate to cordate with a shortly cuneate glandular base, acuminate, entire, finely tomentose and glaucous beneath. Flowers brownish yellow in terminal panicles. Fruit a drupe, ovoid or oblong, yellow outside when ripe. Flowers March–April, fruits May–June. Propagated by seeds. Distributed throughout Nepal to about 1100 m in shady places; also in Pakistan, northern India, Bhutan, southern China, and the Philippines.

FOOD. Seeds are edible.

MEDICINE. Juice of the root and bark is applied to swollen necks of bullocks, the swelling caused by use of the yoke.

Gnaphalium affine D. Don

Gnaphalium luteo-album Linnaeus
Gnaphalium multiceps Wallich ex de Candolle
ENGLISH *cudweed* NEPALI *boki jhar, buke phul, husure jhar, jhyapu ghans, kairo jhar* TAMANG *taptap*

Compositae. Woolly herb about 40 cm high. Lower leaves sessile, spatulate, oblong, obtuse, upper leaves lanceolate, acuminate, woolly on both surfaces. Flower heads golden yellow in dense corymbs. Fruit an achene, brown. Flowers and fruits March–November. Propagated by seeds. Distributed throughout Nepal at 600–3500 m, abundant in open places; also in northern India, Tibet, China, Indo-China, Japan, Thailand, the Philippines, Java, and Australia.

OTHER USES. The woolly hairs of dried leaves are used as tinder in making fire.

Gmelina arborea

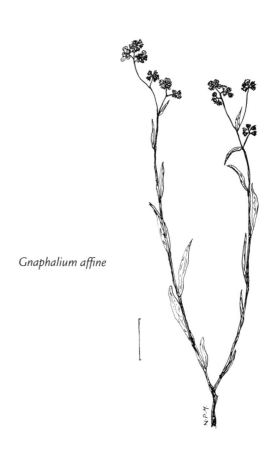

Gnaphalium affine

Gnaphalium hypoleucum de Candolle

TIBETAN *sorka*

Compositae. Herb about 60 cm high. Leaves sessile, 3.5–7.5 cm long, linear, green and hairy above, woolly beneath. Flower heads yellow, many, in dense rounded clusters. Fruit an achene. Flowers and fruits May–September. Propagated by seeds. Distributed in western and central Nepal at 2000–2500 m, common in open places; also in India, China, Indo-China, Thailand, the Philippines, and Japan.

MEDICINE. A paste of the plant is given to relieve cough and backaches. It is also applied externally on affected parts.

Gnaphalium polycaulon Persoon

Gnaphalium indicum Linnaeus
Gnaphalium purpureum Linnaeus
Gnaphalium strictum Roxburgh
ENGLISH *cudweed* NEPALI *boki jhar, husure*

Compositae. Woolly annual herb about 30 cm high. Leaves about 5 cm long, spatulate, linear to ovate, cottony above, densely woolly beneath, apex apiculate, base narrowed. Flower heads yellowish in leafy spikes. Fruit an achene, oblong. Flowers and fruits July–January. Propagated by seeds. Distributed in eastern and central Nepal at 200–1400 m in open pastureland; also pantropical.

MEDICINE. Juice of the leaves is applied to cuts and wounds.

Gnetum montanum Markgraf

Gnetum scandens Roxburgh
NEPALI *pipli*

Gnetaceae. Deciduous gymnospermous climber with compressed stems. Leaves stalked, 15 cm long, 4–6 cm wide, ovate to elliptic, entire, leathery, bluntly acute, base rounded cuneate. Cones yellowish in a terminal cyme. Ovule ellipsoid. Cones April–May, maturing October–November. Propagated by seeds. Distributed in central and eastern Nepal at 300–1800 m in moist forest; also in India, Bhutan, southwestern China, and Thailand.

FOOD. Ripe seeds are edible.

MEDICINE. Seeds are boiled in 4 teaspoons of water about 5 minutes and the liquid is given in doses of 4 teaspoons three times a day for cough and colds.

Gomphrena globosa Linnaeus

ENGLISH *bachelor's button, globe amaranth* NEPALI *makhamali phul, supari phul* NEWARI *gwe swan*

Amaranthaceae. Erect annual herb about 75 cm high. Leaves stalked, 5–10 cm long, 1.6–3 cm wide, elliptic to oblong. Flowers pink or white, globose. Propagated by seeds. Distributed throughout Nepal to about 1500 m on moist ground, cultivated.

OTHER USES. Flowers are valued, especially during Tihar, for Bhai Puja, also known as Bhai Tika because the broth-

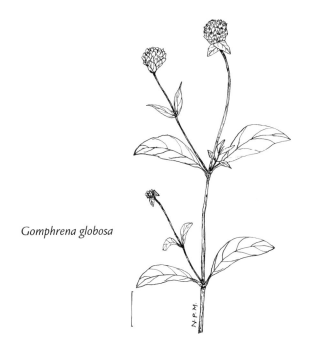

Gomphrena globosa

ers accept *tika*, rice mixed with vermilion and yogurt, from their well-wishing sisters.

Gonostegia hirta (Blume) Miquel

Urtica hirta Blume, *Memorialis hirta* (Blume) Weddell,
  Pouzolzia hirta (Blume) Hasskarl
Memorialis hispida Buchanan-Hamilton ex Weddell
Pouzolzia quinquenervis Bennett, *Memorialis quinquenervis*
  (Bennett) Buchanan-Hamilton ex Weddell
CHEPANG *aaichuli* GURUNG *bhramgoi, ghibrang, syudane*
NEPALI *aterno, atenu, atinno, chiple, chiple lahara, kanguil, mas lahare*
RAUTE *khasaruja* SHERPA *gjunung* TAMANG *blesing, chhojyal, kankri, kraikraing, pingur* TIBETAN *timlagan*

Urticaceae. Decumbent herb. Leaves sessile, opposite, ovate or lanceolate, acuminate, entire. Flowers pinkish in

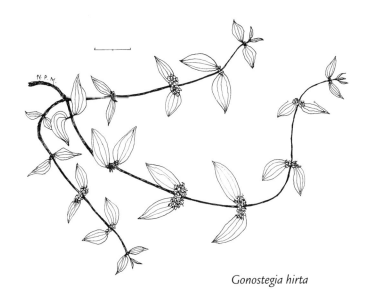

Gonostegia hirta

dense, rounded, axillary clusters. Fruit an achene enclosed in the persistent perianth. Flowers August–September, fruits September–December. Propagated by seeds or root offshoots. Distributed throughout Nepal at 500–2400 m, common in moist, open places; also in northern India, eastward to southern China, southern Japan, Myanmar, Malaysia, and Australia.

FOOD. Fresh root is considered refreshing, especially in summer.

MEDICINE. Fresh root is chewed in cases of cough and colds. A paste of the root is applied to wounds, boils, and muscular swellings. It is also considered useful for chest pain if applied externally. Juice of the plant, mixed in equal amounts with juice of *Centella asiatica* and *Drymaria diandra,* is given in doses of about 4 teaspoons twice a day for diarrhea. The plant is fed to cattle with indigestion.

OTHER USES. Squeezed root, a substitute of soap, is used for washing the head.

Gossypium arboreum Linnaeus

CHEPANG *kapas* ENGLISH *cotton tree* MAGAR *kapas*
NEPALI *kapas ko bot* NEWARI *kapay ma*

Malvaceae. Shrub. Leaves stalked, palmately five- or seven-lobed, shinier above. Flowers yellow or purplish with crimson center. Fruit a capsule, oblong. Flowers and fruits October–November. Propagated by seeds. Distributed throughout Nepal to about 1500 m, cultivated; also in Pakistan, India, Arabia, and Africa.

FOOD. Oil from the seeds is edible.

MEDICINE. Juice of the root is given in cases of fever.

OTHER USES. Fiber obtained from the surface of the seeds is used in the manufacture of textiles and popularly

Gossypium arboreum

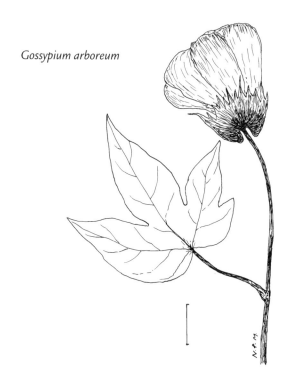

in making wicks for religious oil lamps and incenses. Seed cakes are used as animal feed.

Grangea maderaspatana (Linnaeus) Poiret

Artemisia maderaspatana Linnaeus
Cotula hemisphaerica Wallich, not (Roxburgh) Wallich ex C. B. Clarke
NEPALI *gobre jhar, jhim jhime*

Compositae. Leafy prostrate herb, forming circular patches. Leaves stalked, alternate, sinuately pinnatifid. Flower heads greenish, disk shaped. Fruit an achene. Flowers and fruits most of the year. Propagated by seeds or by splitting the mother plant. Distributed in central and western Nepal to about 2000 m in dry, sandy loam; also in India, China, and Southeast Asia.

FOOD. Tender leaves are cooked as a vegetable.

Grangea maderaspatana

Grevillea robusta A. Cunningham ex R. Brown

ENGLISH *silver oak* MAGAR *sat* NEPALI *kangiyo phul*
NEWARI *kakicha swan* RAI *sakhab bung* SUNWAR *lupse phu*

Proteaceae. Tall tree. Leaves stalked, alternate, pinnate, pinnae deeply pinnatifid, usually lanceolate, margin recurved, nearly glabrous above, silky beneath. Flowers orange in short racemes. Fruit a follicle, oblique. Flowers March–April. Propagated by seeds. Distributed in eastern and central Nepal to about 1500 m, cultivated; also in Australia.

OTHER USES. The plant is grown as an avenue tree. Villagers use the wood as fuel. Flowers are offered in religious rituals to gods and goddesses. It is one of the important plants used in afforestation programs of Nepal.

Grewia disperma Rottbøll

Grewia didyma Roxburgh ex G. Don
Grewia glabra Blume
Grewia laevigata Vahl
Grewia multiflora Jussieu
Grewia sepiaria Roxburgh ex G. Don
CHEPANG *narsin* NEPALI *kharchoti, khari, palcha khari, sarchyat, syal puchhare* TAMANG *dalasin* THARU *gorsyauri*

Tiliaceae. Tree about 6 m high with dark brown bark. Leaves stalked, 7–17 cm long, 2–7 cm wide, serrate, gla-

Grevillea robusta

FOOD. Ripe fruits are eaten fresh.

MEDICINE. Juice of immature fruit is given in cases of diarrhea and dysentery.

OTHER USES. Bark of the stem produces fiber used for twine and rope. The plant is browsed by cattle.

Grewia optiva J. R. Drummond ex Burret

Grewia oppositifolia Buchanan-Hamilton ex D. Don
GURUNG *sitli, syal phosro*   NEPALI *bhima, chiple, phorsa, syal fusro*
TAMANG *dalifarso*

Tiliaceae. Tree about 12 m high with whitish bark. Leaves stalked, ovate to lanceolate, acuminate, serrate, rough above, pubescent beneath, base unequally rounded, usually three-veined. Flowers white, scented, in umbellate cymes. Fruit a drupe, four-lobed, black when ripe, rough with scattered stiff white hairs. Flowers April–June, fruits October–December. Propagated by seeds. Distributed throughout Nepal to about 1800 m, common on open, rocky slopes; also in northern India and Bhutan.

FOOD. Ripe fruits are eaten fresh.

OTHER USES. Bark yields a fiber used for cordage and rope. Branches are used to make handles of axes and sickles. Leaves and tender twigs are lopped for fodder.

Grewia optiva

brescent, three-veined, tapering at both ends. Flowers axillary, white. Fruit a drupe, rugose, black when ripe. Flowers June–September, fruits December–January. Propagated by seeds. Distributed throughout Nepal at 300–1100 m in shady places; also in northern India, Malaysia, Australia, and Africa.

FOOD. Ripe fruits are eaten fresh.

MEDICINE. Juice of the root, about 2 teaspoons twice a day, is given to provide relief from cough and colds. A paste of the bark is applied to boils. Juice of the bark, about 2 teaspoons twice a day, is given in cases of stomach disorder.

OTHER USES. Trees are lopped for fodder. Bark yields a fiber for cordage.

Grewia helicterifolia Wallich ex G. Don

Grewia angustifolia Wallich
Grewia polygama Roxburgh
NEPALI *banmakai, dama*

Tiliaceae. Shrub about 2 m high, young parts pubescent. Leaves stalked, 5–12.5 cm long, 1–2.3 cm wide, narrowly lanceolate, acuminate, closely dentate, stellately pubescent, glabrous above, gray tomentose beneath, base oblique, three-veined. Flowers white. Fruit a drupe, shiny reddish brown when ripe. Flowers October–August, fruits November–January. Propagated by seeds. Distributed in central and western Nepal to about 1500 m, frequent in dry places in forested areas; also in Pakistan, northern India, and Bhutan.

Grewia sapida Roxburgh ex de Candolle

Grewia nana Wallich
Grewia pumila Buchanan-Hamilton
NEPALI *pharsa*

Tiliaceae. Subshrub with woody rootstocks, young shoots shaggy. Leaves stalked, 5–10 cm long, 4–7.5 cm wide, ovate to oblong, doubly serrate, somewhat roughly textured above, softly pubescent beneath, apex rounded or broadly acute, base oblique, five-veined. Flowers yellow.

Fruit a drupe, hirsute. Flowers and fruits March–May. Propagated by seeds. Distributed in eastern and central Nepal at 300–1000 m in open grassland; also in northern India and Bhutan.

OTHER USES. Bark of the stem is used to make rope.

Grewia sclerophylla Roxburgh ex G. Don

Grewia correa Buchanan-Hamilton ex Wallich
Grewia obliqua Jussieu
Grewia scabrophylla Roxburgh
NEPALI *pharso*

Tiliaceae. Shrub about 2 m high, young parts stellately tomentose. Leaves stalked, 11–20 cm long, 6–12.5 cm wide, elliptic to ovate, irregularly dentate, larger teeth often glandular at the tip, base rounded or obtuse, three-veined. Flowers white. Fruit a drupe, globose, stellately hairy. Flowers May–September, fruits October–November. Propagated by seeds. Distributed in central Nepal to about 1200 m in open pastureland; also in northern India and Bhutan.

FOOD. Ripe fruits are eaten fresh.

OTHER USES. Bark yields a fiber used for cordage and rope.

Grewia subinaequalis de Candolle

Grewia asiatica var. *vestita* Wallich ex Masters
CHEPANG *narsin* ENGLISH *phalsa* MAGAR *jalma*
NEPALI *ban kapase, jalmo, pharsa*

Tiliaceae. Small tree. Leaves stalked, 4–17 cm long, 3.5–12.5 cm wide, obliquely ovate, irregularly serrate, densely tomentose beneath. Flowers orange in densely crowded axillary cymes. Fruit globose, dark brown when ripe. Flowers April–May, fruits June–July. Propagated by seeds. Distributed in central and western Nepal at 400–1500 m; also in Pakistan, India, Sri Lanka, and Myanmar.

FOOD. Ripe fruits are edible.

OTHER USES. Leaves are lopped for fodder. Bark of the stem is used to make ropes, cords, and twine.

Guizotia abyssinica (Linnaeus fil.) Cassini

Polymia abyssinica Linnaeus fil.
Verbesina sativa Roxburgh ex Sims
CHEPANG *dakine* ENGLISH *Niger seed* MAGAR *min*
NEPALI *jhuse til, kalo til* TAMANG *chadong, sa*

Compositae. Stout annual herb about 2 m high. Leaves opposite, clasping the stem, dentate, oblong to lanceolate, with a fine apical point. Flower heads yellow in lax, branched, terminal clusters. Fruit an achene, flattened, black. Flowers September–October. Propagated by seeds. Distributed throughout Nepal at 900–2000 m in open places; also in India, Bhutan, and Africa.

FOOD. Seed oil is used in cooking.

MEDICINE. A paste of the seed is applied to treat scabies. Seed oil is applied to burns.

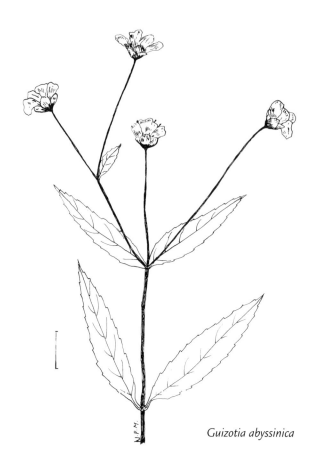

Guizotia abyssinica

Gymnadenia orchidis Lindley

Platanthera orchidis Lindley ex Wallich, *Habenaria orchidis*
(Lindley) Hooker fil., *Peristylus orchidis* (Lindley) Kraenzlin
Gymnadenia cylindrostachya Lindley, *Orchis cylindrostachya*
(Lindley) Kraenzlin
Orchis habenarioides King & Prantl
NEPALI *hati jara, panch aunle* SHERPA *ongbu lakpa*

Orchidaceae. Terrestrial orchid about 50 cm high with lobed pseudobulbs. Leaves sessile, elliptic to lanceolate, acuminate, glabrous. Flowers pink in dense spikes, August–September. Propagated by seeds or pseudobulbs. Distributed throughout Nepal at 3000–4700 m on rocky, shady ground; also in northern India, Bhutan, and southeastern Tibet.

MEDICINE. Powdered pseudobulb is applied to cuts and wounds. A decoction of the pseudobulb, about 6 teaspoons three times a day, is given in cases of stomach trouble.

Gynocardia odorata R. Brown

Chaulmoogra odorata (R. Brown) Roxburgh
NEPALI *gandare, gantay, kadu*

Flacourtiaceae. Crooked evergreen tree. Leaves stalked, 15–25 cm long, 7.5–10 cm wide, linear oblong, abruptly acuminate, shiny above, reticulate beneath. Flowers yellow, fragrant, April–May. Fruits November–January. Prop-

Gymnadenia orchidis

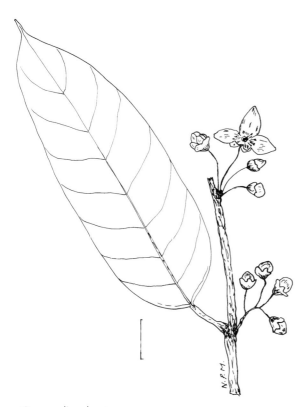

Gynocardia odorata

agated by seeds. Distributed in eastern Nepal at 4000–5000 m, generally along stream banks; also in northern India and Myanmar.

MEDICINE. Oil from the seed is applied to treat skin diseases.

OTHER USES. Bark and fruit are used to intoxicate fish.

Gynura nepalensis de Candolle

Cacalia aurantiaca Wallich
Cacalia foetens Wallich, *Gynura foetens* de Candolle
TAMANG *mangdhong, syang mhendo*

Compositae. Erect shrub about 1 m high, young shoots clothed with pale pubescence. Leaves stalked, 10–23 cm long, 3–10 cm wide, elliptic to lanceolate, acute or acuminate, coarsely dentate, base decurrent. Flower heads orange in open terminal corymbs. Fruit an achene, linear. Flowers April–May, fruits May–July. Propagated by seeds. Distributed throughout Nepal at 250–2000 m in moist, shady ravines; also in India, Bhutan, China, Myanmar, and Thailand.

MEDICINE. Juice of the plant is applied to cuts and wounds.

Gynura nepalensis

H

Habenaria furcifera Lindley

NEPALI *sankalo*

Orchidaceae. Orchid about 50 cm high. Leaves sessile, 8–11 cm long, 2–3.5 cm wide, elliptic to ovate, acuminate. Flowers greenish, August–September. Propagated by seeds or pseudobulbs. Distributed in western and central Nepal at 150–600 m in moist, shady places; also in northern India.

FOOD. Tender shoots and leaves are cooked as a vegetable.

Habenaria intermedia D. Don

NEPALI *thunma*

Orchidaceae. Orchid about 50 cm high. Leaves sessile, 8–18 cm long, ovate, long-pointed. Flowers white, July–August. Propagated by seeds or pseudobulbs. Distributed in western and central Nepal at 2000–3300 m in open grasslands; also in northwestern India and Tibet.

FOOD. Boiled roots are eaten. Tender leaves are cooked as a vegetable.

Habenaria intermedia

Halenia elliptica D. Don

Swertia centrostemma Wallich
Swertia peloris Griffith

NEPALI *gorul tito*   TAMANG *timda, tite*

Gentianaceae. Erect herb about 60 cm high. Lower leaves stalked, opposite, 2.5–5 cm long, ovate, entire, upper leaves sessile. Flowers bluish. Fruit a capsule, ovoid. Flowers and fruits July–September. Propagated by seeds. Distributed throughout Nepal at 1700–4000 m in forest openings; also in northern India, Bhutan, southern Tibet, northern and western China, and Myanmar.

MEDICINE. Juice of the plant, about 4 teaspoons four times a day, is given to relieve fever.

Halenia elliptica

Hedera nepalensis K. Koch

Hedera helix Linnaeus
Hedera himalaica Tobler

ENGLISH *ivy* NEPALI *guhi, pipal pate* TAMANG *krupkrupchhi, tengili*
TIBETAN *khan*

Araliaceae. Vine. Leaves stalked, simple, ovate to cordate, acuminate, entire, leathery, glabrous. Flowers yellowish in panicled umbels. Fruit black, March–April. Propagated by cuttings. Distributed throughout Nepal at

1600–3000 m, occasionally on moist stones or tree stems; also in Afghanistan, northern India, Bhutan, China, and Myanmar.

MEDICINE. A decoction of the plant is used to treat skin diseases.

OTHER USES. The plant is a nutritious fodder for goats and sheep.

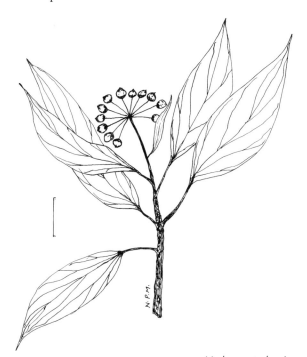

Hedera nepalensis

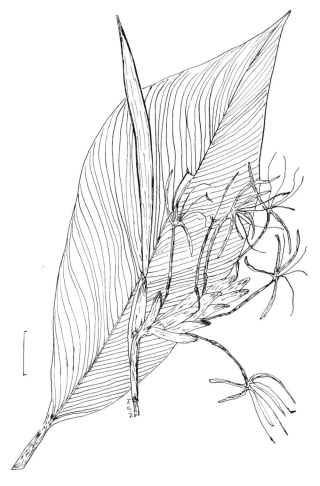

Hedychium ellipticum

Hedychium densiflorum Wallich

Hedychium sino-aureum Stapf
TAMANG *dhungalhapti*

Zingiberaceae. Herb about 1.5 m high. Leaves 16–41 cm long, 4–11 cm wide, spatulate, elliptic, long-pointed. Flowers red, fragrant, in spikes, August–September. Propagated by seeds or rhizomes. Distributed in eastern and central Nepal at 1800–2800 m in moist, shady places; also in northern India and Bhutan.

OTHER USES. Leaves are used as a substitute for plates, and dried leaves are used for animal beds.

Hedychium ellipticum Buchanan-Hamilton ex Smith

Hedychium fastigiatum Wallich
GURUNG *ban besar* NEPALI *rato saro, saro*

Zingiberaceae. Glabrous herb. Leaves elliptic to oblong. Flowers yellow, fragrant, in short, dense, corymbose spikes. Fruit a capsule. Flowers July–September. Propagated by seeds or rhizomes. Distributed throughout Nepal at 500–3000 m in moist, shady places; also in northern India and Bhutan.

MEDICINE. Juice of the rhizome is given in cases of fever.

Hedychium gardnerianum Sheppard ex Ker-Gawler

NEPALI *pankha phul*

Zingiberaceae. Herb about 2.5 m high. Leaves stalked, sheathing, 0.3–1 cm long. Flowers yellowish, fragrant, in a spike. Propagated by splitting the rhizome. Distributed in central and eastern Nepal to about 1900 m, cultivated; also in India, Bhutan, and Bangladesh.

MEDICINE. Juice of the rhizome is given for indigestion and is also considered useful in reducing high fevers.

Hedychium spicatum Smith

Hedychium album Buchanan-Hamilton ex Wallich
CHEPANG *tariya* MAGAR *saisya* NEPALI *pankha phul, seto saro*

Zingiberaceae. Herb about 1 m high. Leaves oblong to lanceolate, acuminate, glabrous. Flowers white, fragrant, in dense spikes. Fruit a capsule, globose. Flowers and fruits July–November. Propagated by seeds or rhizomes. Distributed throughout Nepal at 1600–2400 m in moist, shady places; also in northwestern India.

MEDICINE. Juice of the rhizome is given in cases of fever.

Hedyotis corymbosa (Linnaeus) Lamarck

Oldenlandia corymbosa Linnaeus
NEPALI *piringo*

Rubiaceae. Diffuse annual herb. Leaves sessile, 1–3 cm long, linear, acute, margin recurved. Flowers white or pink in axillary cymes. Fruit a capsule. Flowers July–September, fruits August–November. Propagated by seeds. Distributed throughout Nepal at 200–2400 m; also in India, Sri Lanka, and tropical and subtropical Asia, Africa, and America.

MEDICINE. Juice of the root is given in cases of indigestion. The juice is also applied to the forehead to relieve headaches.

Hedyotis diffusa Willdenow

Oldenlandia diffusa (Willdenow) Roxburgh
Oldenlandia brachypoda de Candolle
NEPALI *majithe jhar*

Rubiaceae. Annual herb. Leaves sessile, 1–2 cm long, linear, acute, margin recurved, glabrous. Flowers solitary, axillary, white. Fruit a capsule, subglobose. Flowers May–September, fruits August–November. Propagated by seeds. Distributed in eastern and central Nepal at 600–1000 m in open, sunny places; also in India, tropical and subtropical eastern Asia, southern China, Malaysia, and Japan.

MEDICINE. Juice of the root is given in cases of indigestion.

Hedyotis lineata Roxburgh

Hedyotis ulmifolia Wallich, *Exallage ulmifolia* (Wallich) Bremekamp
NEPALI *charpate jhar, nimane jhar*

Rubiaceae. Herb. Leaves stalked, 1.5–5.5 cm long, 0.5–2 cm wide, acuminate, entire. Flowers white in axillary cymes. Flowers and fruits August–September. Propagated by seeds or root offshoots. Distributed throughout Nepal at 1000–1800 m in open or shady places; also in northeastern India, Bangladesh, and Myanmar.

MEDICINE. Juice of the root is given to treat stomachaches.

Hedyotis scandens Roxburgh

Oldenlandia scandens (Roxburgh) Kuntze
Hedyotis volubilis R. Brown
CHEPANG *buke lahara, mahadeorat* GURUNG *tibe nori*
NEPALI *aankhle jhar, bakhri lahara, boke lahara, dudhe lahara, nimane jhar, tite* TAMANG *chimte ghans, ganusa ablamban, ghugi, jingan, nalimran, phirphire*

Rubiaceae. Climber. Leaves sessile, elliptic or lanceolate, acuminate, entire, glabrous. Flowers purplish green in axillary and terminal cymes, July–August. Propagated by seeds or root offshoots. Distributed in central and western Nepal at 500–2000 m in shady places; also in northeastern India, Bhutan, and Indo-China.

MEDICINE. A paste of the root, about 1 teaspoon once a day, is given for indigestion and is applied externally in cases of gout. Juice of the root, about 4 teaspoons three times a day, is given to treat peptic ulcer. It is also useful for gastric troubles. A paste of the plant is applied to treat gout and is also used as a leech repellent. The bark, mixed with bark of *Lyonia ovalifolia,* is boiled in water, and the strained liquid, about 2 teaspoons three times a day, is given for stomach disorder.

OTHER USES. Leaves and twigs are collected to provide fodder for stall feeding, as they enhance the secretion of milk. Squeezed plant is used for fish poison.

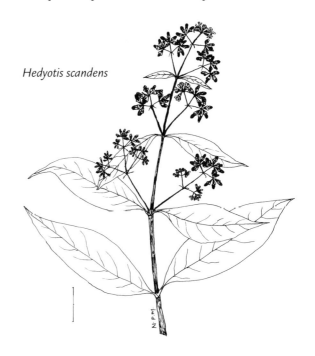

Hedyotis scandens

Helianthus annuus Linnaeus

ENGLISH *sunflower* NEPALI *suryamukhi phul*

Compositae. Erect annual herb about 2.5 m high, stems usually unbranched. Leaves stalked, 10–30 cm long, 5–20 cm wide, ovate, sinuate and dentate, with soft appressed hairs on both surfaces, tip acute or acuminate. Flower heads yellow. Fruit an achene, obovoid, compressed, four-angled. Propagated by seeds. Distributed throughout Nepal to about 600 m, cultivated; also in India, Russia, Romania, Italy, the United States, Canada, and Argentina.

FOOD. The seed contains 22–32% oil, which is used in salads and cooking. Roasted seeds are eaten.

OTHER USES. Seed oil also used in soap, lubricant, paint, and for treating wool.

Helicia nilagirica Beddome

Helicia erratica Hooker fil.
NEPALI *bandre*

Proteaceae. Tree about 7 m high. Leaves stalked, 8–24 cm long, 2.5–7 cm wide, oblong to elliptic, acute, distantly

Helianthus annuus

serrate, glabrous, tapering toward the base. Flowers yellowish. Flowers and fruits June–August. Propagated by seeds. Distributed in eastern Nepal at 450–1400 m on open slopes; also in India, Bhutan, southwestern China, and Indo-China.

MEDICINE. Juice of the bark is applied to treat muscular swellings and is also applied to cuts and wounds.

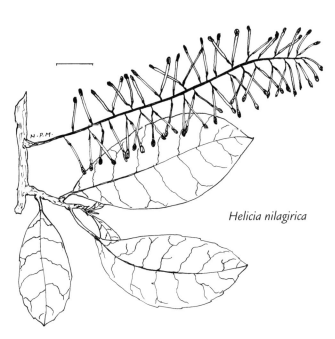

Helicia nilagirica

Helicteres isora Linnaeus
ENGLISH *East Indian screw tree* NEPALI *mrigasinghi*

Sterculiaceae. Shrub with gray bark, young parts covered with stellate hairs. Leaves stalked, 6–18 cm long, 3.5–15 cm wide, broadly ovate, acuminate, often lobed, obliquely cordate or rounded at the base, irregularly dentate, rough above, pubescent beneath. Flowers stalked, axillary, red, turning lead color at maturity. Fruit cylindrical, pubescent, composed of five spirally twisted carpels. Flowers April–August, fruits September–November. Propagated by seeds. Distributed throughout Nepal to about 300 m, generally gregarious in open places; also in India, eastward to southern China, Malaysia, and Australia.

MEDICINE. Juice of the bark is given in cases of diarrhea and dysentery. The fruit is considered good for the twisting pain of colic.

OTHER USES. Fiber of the bark is used for making ropes and cordage. Branches are used for fences and thatch frames. Leaves are slightly browsed by goats.

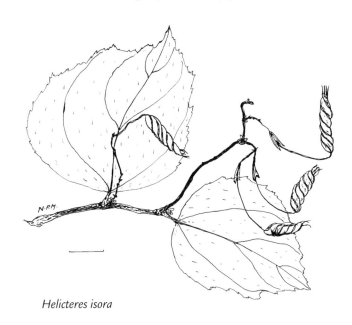

Helicteres isora

Heliotropium indicum Linnaeus
Tiaridium indicum (Linnaeus) Lehmann
NEPALI *kuro*

Boraginaceae. Annual herb about 50 cm high. Leaves stalked, opposite or alternate, ovate to oblong, acuminate, hairy, base decurrent. Flowers all on one side of the inflorescence, pale lavender. Fruit a nutlet. Propagated by seeds. Distributed in eastern and central Nepal to about 150 m on uncultivated land; also in India, eastern to southwestern China, Myanmar, the Ryukyu Islands, Malaysia, and North America.

MEDICINE. A decoction of the root and inflorescence is emmenagogue. Juice of the plant is given for cough and asthma and is also used as eyedrops for conjunctivitis. Juice of the leaves is applied to cuts, wounds, boils, and pimples.

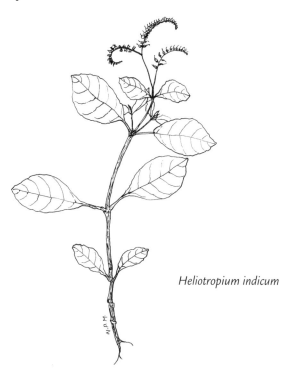

Heliotropium indicum

Helixanthera ligustrina

Heliotropium strigosum Willdenow
subsp. brevifolium (Wallich) Kazmi

Heliotropium brevifolium Wallich
Heliotropium compactum D. Don
NEPALI *mrigaraj*

Boraginaceae. Prostrate herb about 25 cm high. Leaves stalked, 0.5–2 cm long, linear lanceolate, margin slightly revolute. Flowers small, white, in axillary or terminal spikes. Fruit a nutlet, dark gray-brown. Flowers and fruits June–September. Propagated by seeds. Distributed throughout Nepal to about 1400 m in open, dry places; also in Afghanistan, India, Bhutan, southern China, Myanmar, and Thailand.

MEDICINE. A paste of the root is applied to cuts and wounds.

Helixanthera ligustrina (Wallich) Danser

Loranthus ligustrinus Wallich
GURUNG *bhrunge* MAGAR *ainjheru* NEPALI *ainjeru*

Loranthaceae. Woody parasite. Leaves stalked, 2–8 cm long, 0.8–3 cm wide, lanceolate, acuminate, glabrous on both surfaces. Flowers orange in few-flowered racemes, April–May. Propagated by seeds. Distributed in central and western Nepal at 1000–2000 m on trees and shrubs; also in India, Bhutan, and Myanmar.

FOOD. Ripe fruits are eaten fresh.

Helminthostachys zeylanica Linnaeus

NEPALI *kamraj*

Ophioglossaceae. Erect fern. Fronds 25–35 cm long, 12–20 cm wide, three-parted, segments lobed. Fertile frond producing a spike at the distal end of the frond between the segments. Propagated by splitting the rhizomes. Distributed throughout Nepal to about 500 m in open or shady places but very rare; also in India, southern China, Myanmar, Malaysia, the Philippines, and Japan.

FOOD. Young fronds are cooked as a vegetable.

MEDICINE. Juice of the rhizome is given in cases of fever.

Hemigraphis hirta (Vahl) T. Anderson

Ruellia hirta Vahl
Ruellia sarmentosa Nees
THARU *banpan*

Acanthaceae. Herb. Leaves sessile, 0.7–3 cm long, 0.5–2 cm wide, ovate, acuminate, dentate, hairy on both surfaces. Flowers light violet. Flowers and fruits April–June. Propagated by seeds. Distributed throughout Nepal to about 300 m in open, dry places; also in Pakistan, India, and Bhutan.

MEDICINE. Juice of the plant is applied in cases of throat pain.

Hemiphragma heterophyllum Wallich

NEPALI *lahare phul, nash jhar, rato geri* TAMANG *tangar, taprangmi*

Scrophulariaceae. Prostrate herb, frequently rooting at the nodes. Leaves dimorphic, those on main stem short-stalked, opposite, ovate to orbiculate, obtuse, crenate,

Helminthostachys zeylanica

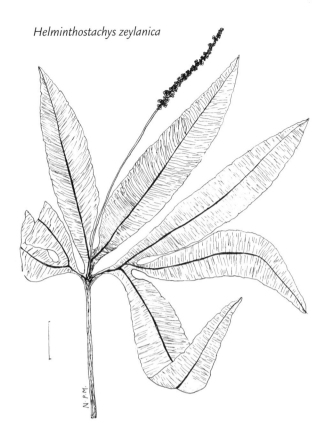

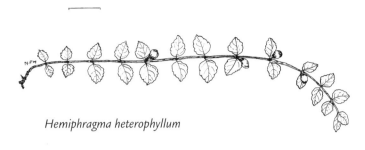

Hemiphragma heterophyllum

Heracleum nepalense D. Don

Heracleum nepalense var. *bivittata* C. B. Clarke
NEPALI *ban timur, budho aushadhi, bhut kesh, chhatare, chinne jhar*
TAMANG *nhajyangaman*   TIBETAN *chyowa, phaki*

Umbelliferae. Herb about 2 m high. Leaves stalked, pinnate, pinnae irregularly serrate, slightly hairy. Flowers, stalked, bracteate, white. Fruit flat, ovate, rigid, the lateral edges expanded into membranous wings. Flowers June–July, fruits August–November. Propagated by seeds. Distributed throughout Nepal at 1800–3700 m, frequent in moist, shady places; also in northern India and Bhutan.

FOOD. Powdered fruitlets are used as a spice in lentil soup (*daal* in Nepali), vegetables, and roasted food items.

MEDICINE. Juice of the root, about 2 teaspoons twice a day, is given in cases of diarrhea. Roasted fruitlets are chewed to treat cough, diarrhea, and dysentery.

Hemigraphis hirta

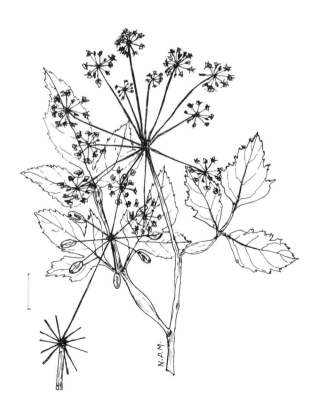

those on branchlets fascicled, needle shaped. Flowers pink. Fruit a berry, turning bright red at maturity. Flowers and fruits March–July. Propagated by seeds or cuttings. Distributed throughout Nepal at 1800–4000 m on dry slopes; also in northern India, Bhutan, western and central China, Myanmar, Taiwan, and the Philippines.

FOOD. Ripe fruits are eaten fresh.

MEDICINE. Juice of the plant is applied to cuts and wounds.

Heracleum nepalense

Herpetospermum pedunculosum (Seringe) Baillon

Bryonia pedunculosa Seringe
Herpetospermum caudigerum Wallich ex C. B. Clarke
Rampinia herpetospermoides C. B. Clarke
NEPALI *kurkure kankro, murmure, pitta kangri*   TAMANG *phongo*

Cucurbitaceae. Weak climber with bifid tendrils. Leaves ovate to cordate, acuminate, caudate, crenulate to dentate, sparsely pilose. Flowers yellow, the calyx hairy. Flowers and fruits July–October. Propagated by seeds. Distributed throughout Nepal at 1000–3000 m, common along forest edges, especially along trails; also in northern India, Bhutan, southern Tibet, and southwestern China.

FOOD. Fried seeds are edible.

MEDICINE. Pounded root, about 6 teaspoons three times a day, is given to treat troubles of the bile ducts.

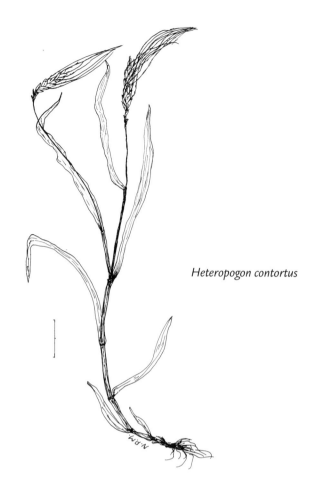

Heteropogon contortus

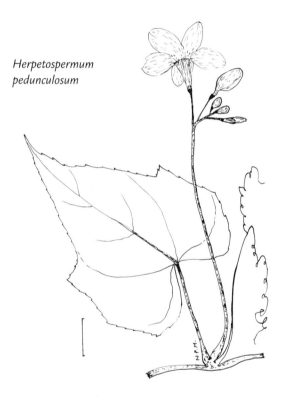

Herpetospermum pedunculosum

Heteropogon contortus (Linnaeus) Palisot de Beauvois ex Roemer & Schultes

Andropogon contortus Linnaeus
Andropogon melanocarpus Elliott
NEPALI *arthunge, dapsu khar, gaj*

Gramineae. Erect perennial grass. Leaves linear, flat. Inflorescences brownish in terminal racemes. Flowers and fruits October–January. Propagated by seeds or by splitting the rhizomes. Distributed throughout Nepal at 400–2600 m in dry places; also widely distributed in the tropics.

OTHER USES. The plant is used for roof thatching. It is also eaten voraciously by cattle before the appearance of inflorescences.

Hibiscus cannabinus Linnaeus

ENGLISH *bhimli jute*   NEPALI *hati phul*

Malvaceae. Shrub. Lower leaves stalked, cordate, entire, upper leaves palmately lobed, lobes narrow, serrate. Flowers yellow with crimson center. Fruit a capsule, globose, pointed. Flowers August–November, fruits January–February. Propagated by seeds or root offshoots. Distributed in eastern and central Nepal to about 500 m in open places, cultivated; mostly in tropical countries.

OTHER USES. Bark of the stem furnishes fiber for cords and ropes.

Hibiscus mutabilis Linnaeus

NEPALI *nalu*

Malvaceae. Large, much branched, tomentose shrub. Leaves stalked, broadly ovate, three- or five-lobed, lobes triangular, acute, shallowly crenate or dentate. Flowers white or pink. Fruit a capsule, subglobose, hirsute. Flowers and fruits most of the year. Propagated by seeds or root offshoots. Distributed in eastern and central Nepal to about 1200 m, frequent in gardens; also in southern China, Taiwan, and southern Japan, and widely cultivated in tropical regions of the world.

OTHER USES. Bark from the stem is used to make cords and ropes.

Hibiscus rosa-sinensis Linnaeus

ENGLISH *Chinese rose, shoe flower*   MOOSHAR *urhur*
NEPALI *ghanti phul*   NEWARI *malta swan*
TAMANG *bala mhendo, lata pucha*

Malvaceae. Evergreen shrub. Leaves stalked, ovate to lanceolate, more or less acuminate, serrate, glabrous and shiny, base three-veined. Flowers red or scarlet, solitary, in a terminal raceme, flowers most of the year. Propagated by cuttings. Distributed throughout Nepal to about 1400 m in open, moist places; also widely cultivated in the tropics and subtropics.

FOOD. Mooshar children eat the fresh flower ovary.

MEDICINE. Juice of the root, about 3 teaspoons four times a day, is given in cases of cough and colds. A paste of the root is used to treat venereal disease. Leaves have a laxative property. An infusion of the flower is given as a cooling drink to ill persons.

OTHER USES. The plant is occasionally cultivated for ornamental purposes, and the flowers are offered to the gods and goddesses. Petals are used for dye.

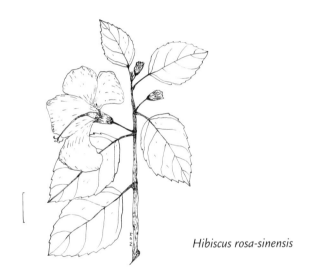

Hibiscus rosa-sinensis

Hibiscus sabdariffa Linnaeus

CHEPANG *shrok*   ENGLISH *Jamaica sorrel, Java jute, red sorrel, roselle*
NEPALI *belchadna, patuwa*

Malvaceae. Shrub about 2 m high. Leaves variable in shape, deeply three- or five-lobed, lobes oblong to lanceolate. Flowers pinkish, calyx somewhat hairy, connate below the middle, forming a fleshy cup. Fruit ovoid, pointed, hairy, enclosed by the enlarged, fleshy, acidic calyx. Propagated by seeds. Distributed throughout Nepal at 1000–1500 m in open places; also cultivated in the tropics.

FOOD. Young leaves are cooked as a vegetable. The red fleshy calyx, which surrounds the fruit, is eaten raw or pickled.

OTHER USES. The stem yields a strong fiber used for various household purposes. The fiber is also sold by villagers.

Himalayacalamus brevinodus Stapleton

NEPALI *malinge nigalo*

Gramineae. Bamboo about 9 m high, internodes about 20 cm long, 2.5 cm wide, culm sheath with narrow tip and long blade, without hairs or bristles. Propagated by splitting the rhizome. Distributed in eastern Nepal at 1800–2200 m in open places; also in India.

FOOD. Tender shoots are cooked as a vegetable.

OTHER USES. The plant provides weaving materials but is not of superior quality because of the relatively short length between nodes. Leaves provide useful fodder.

Himalayacalamus falconeri (Hooker fil. ex Munro) Keng fil.

Arundinaria falconeri (Hooker fil. ex Munro) Bentham & Hooker fil. ex Duthie, *Drepanostachyum falconeri* (Hooker fil. ex Munro) J. J. N. Campbell ex D. C. McClintock, *Thamnocalamus falconeri* Hooker fil. ex Munro
Fargesia collaris T. P. Yi
NEPALI *singhane, thudi nigalo*

Gramineae. Bamboo, often striped with yellow and purple, culm sheath bullet shaped, without hairs, spines, or auricles. Propagated by splitting the rhizome. Distributed in eastern and central Nepal at 2000–2500 m, common in cool, broad-leaved forests; also in India.

FOOD. Tender shoots are cooked as a vegetable.

OTHER USES. Stems are good for weaving bamboo goods.

Himalayacalamus fimbriatus Stapleton

NEPALI *tite nigalo*

Gramineae. Bamboo, culm sheath with dense orange-brown hairs at the base, sheath rough on the inside sur-

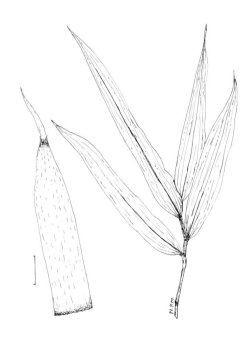

Himalayacalamus fimbriatus

face, tip narrow. Propagated by splitting the rhizome. Distributed in eastern and western Nepal at 1100–1800 m in open slopes, cultivated; also in India and Southeast Asia.

FOOD. Tender shoots are cooked as a vegetable.

OTHER USES. The plant is used for weaving mats, making walls for huts, and as walking sticks. Leaves are used for fodder.

Himalayacalamus hookerianus (Munro) Stapleton

Arundinaria hookeriana Munro, *Chimonobambusa hookeriana* (Munro) Nakai, *Drepanostachyum hookerianum* (Munro) Keng fil., *Sinarundinaria hookeriana* (Munro) C. S. Chao & Renvoize

NEPALI *nibha, padang*

Gramineae. Bamboo about 7 m high, culms with fewer branches toward the base. Propagated by splitting the rhizome or by culm cuttings. Distributed in eastern Nepal at 2000–2500 m in gullies, on open land, and at the edges of terraced fields; commonly cultivated, also in India, Myanmar, and Thailand.

OTHER USES. Stems are used for making baskets because the long internodes are easier to split into strips for weaving. Leaves provide fodder.

Hippophae salicifolia D. Don

Elaeagnus salicifolia (D. Don) A. Nelson
Hippophae conferta Wallich

NEPALI *chichi*

Elaeagnaceae. Deciduous tree about 10 m high, bark reddish brown with deep longitudinal furrows. Leaves stalked, oblong to lanceolate, stellately pubescent above. Flowers yellowish, appearing before or with the young leaves. Fruit ovoid, yellow with scattered scales, acidic. Flowers April–May, fruits October–March. Propagated by seeds. Distributed in central and western Nepal at 2200–3500 m, common on riverbanks; also in northern India and southern Tibet.

FOOD. Ripe fruits are eaten fresh or are pickled.

Hippophae tibetana Schlechter

Hippophae rhamnoides Linnaeus
ENGLISH *sand thorn, sea buckthorn* GURUNG *phirchi*
NEPALI *armalito, asuk, taro* TAMANG *chugo* TIBETAN *kirpu, star bu*

Elaeagnaceae. Thorny deciduous shrub about 50 cm high. Leaves subsessile, alternate or opposite, 1–2 cm long, 0.2–0.6 cm wide, linear lanceolate, somewhat leathery, densely clothed with silvery brown scales on both surfaces. Flowers yellow in axillary clusters, appearing with the new leaves. Fruit oblong or globose, orange or bright scarlet when ripe. Flowers May–June, fruits August–September. Propagated by seeds. Distributed in eastern and central Nepal at 3800–4200 m on rocky and sandy ground; also in Afghanistan, northern India, Bhutan, southern Tibet, and northwestern China.

FOOD. The acidic fruit is eaten raw or pickled.

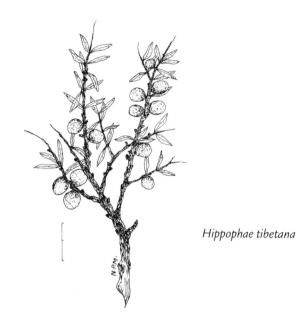

Hippophae tibetana

OTHER USES. The plant is used for fuel, and dry branches are gathered for use as fences. Ripe fruit is the source of a red cosmetic.

Holarrhena pubescens (Buchanan-Hamilton) Wallich ex G. Don

Echites pubescens Buchanan-Hamilton
Holarrhena codaga G. Don
Nerium antidysentericum Linnaeus, *Echites antidysenterica* (Linnaeus) Roxburgh ex Fleming, *Holarrhena antidysenterica* (Linnaeus) Wallich ex de Candolle

CHEPANG *dutyalo, khirsi, mauchherchi* DANUWAR *korahiya*
ENGLISH *conessi bark, Easter tree, ivory tree* KHALING *khaksalap*
MAGAR *dude khirma* MAJHI *dhudhe* NEPALI *indrajau, karingi, khirro, kura, kurchi, madise khirro, sano khirro* TAMANG *dedon*
TIBETAN *tug-mo-nyung*

Apocynaceae. Deciduous small tree about 2 m high. Leaves stalked, opposite, ovate to oblong, acuminate, entire. Flowers white or cream, fragrant, in terminal corymbose cymes. Fruit a follicle, usually covered with white specks. Flowers May–June, fruits September–December. Propagated by seeds. Distributed throughout Nepal to about 1500 m; also in India and Southeast Asia.

MEDICINE. Juice of the bark is taken for chronic dysentery. This juice, about 1 teaspoon twice a day, is given to relieve fever. Bark is boiled in water about 15 minutes and the filtered water taken as an anthelmintic. Fruit is ground and given in doses of about 2 teaspoons twice a day to treat malarial fever. A paste of the seeds is applied to boils on the tongue.

Holboellia latifolia Wallich

MAGAR *charigophala* NEPALI *bagul, guphala, seto guphala*
TAMANG *chhyamba*

Lardizabalaceae. Trailing shrub. Leaves stalked, opposite, digitate, leaflets stalked, 3–12.5 cm long, 0.8–6 cm

Holarrhena pubescens

wide, oblong or elliptic, acuminate, entire, leathery. Flowers stalked, white, fragrant, in few-flowered racemes. Fruit a berry, red when ripe. Flowers March–April, fruits May–July. Propagated by seeds. Distributed throughout Nepal at 1500–2800 m in open as well as shady places; also in northern India, western China, and Myanmar.

FOOD. Ripe fruits are eaten fresh.

Holmskioldia sanguinea Retzius

Hastingia coccinea Smith
Hastingia scandens Roxburgh

CHEPANG *chuttaparat, kuphin* ENGLISH *Chinese hat plant, cup and saucer plant, mandarin's hat, parasol flower, sombrero flower* NEPALI *aputo, ghanti phu, jhule phul* TAMANG *langad, chili*

Labiatae. Straggling shrub. Leaves stalked, opposite, 3.5–11 cm long, 2.5–7.5 cm wide, ovate, acuminate, generally crenate, pubescent, base truncately cuneate. Flowers red. Fruit a drupe, obovoid, deeply four-lobed at the apex. Flowers October–December. Propagated by seeds or cuttings. Distributed throughout Nepal at 300–1500 m in open, moist places; also in northern India and Bhutan.

OTHER USES. The plant is a good substitute fodder, especially for goats. It is also planted for ornamental purposes.

Holboellia latifolia

Holmskioldia sanguinea

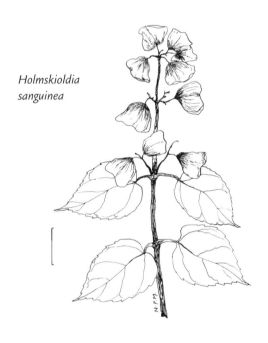

Homalium napaulense (de Candolle) Bentham

Blackwellia napaulensis de Candolle

MAGAR *bakremala* NEPALI *hade, kuphre, tite* TAMANG *pasing, nagpasi*

Flacourtiaceae. Tree about 8 m high. Leaves stalked, ovate, acuminate, dentate, glabrous. Flowers small, short-stalked, greenish white, November–December. Propagated by seeds. Distributed throughout Nepal at 700–1900 m in mixed woodlands; endemic.

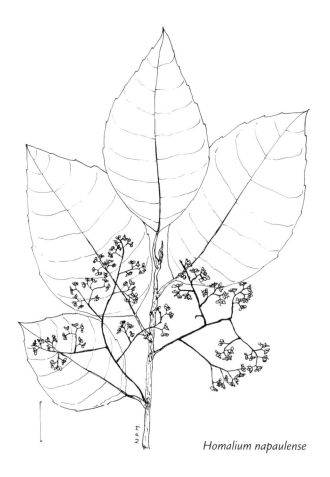

Homalium napaulense

Hordeum vulgare

Houttuynia cordata

MEDICINE. Juice of the bark, about 2 teaspoons three times a day, is given in cases of stomachache.

OTHER USES. Wood is used for construction. Leaves are used for compost.

Hordeum vulgare Linnaeus

ENGLISH *barley* NEPALI *jau*

Gramineae. Erect annual grass. Leaves linear, biauriculate. Inflorescence greenish. Fruit a grain, ovoid, narrowly oblong. Flowers and fruits January–March. Propagated by seeds. Distributed throughout Nepal to about 3500 m, cultivated; also in most parts of the world.

FOOD. The grains are edible.

Houttuynia cordata Thunberg

Polypara cochinchinensis Loureiro

ENGLISH *fishwort* NEPALI *ganaune jhar, gande, gane, ban bhande, kukurpaile* NEWARI *kalancha* TAMANG *kalme*

Saururaceae. Herb about 40 cm high. Leaves stalked, alternate, stipulate, 3–6 cm long, 2–4 cm wide, broadly ovate or cordate, acuminate. Flowers stalked, white, May–August. Propagated by seeds. Distributed throughout Nepal at 700–2500 m in moist, shady places; also in northern India, southern Tibet, eastward to China, Thailand, and Japan.

FOOD. Tender shoots and leaves are cooked as a vegetable and also pickled.

MEDICINE. Juice of the root is given for indigestion, applied for skin diseases, and dripped in the eye to treat eye troubles. Juice of the plant is dripped into the wounds of animals to rid them of worms and accelerate healing.

Hoya lanceolata Wallich ex D. Don

NEPALI *kurkure jhar*

Asclepiadaceae. Epiphytic shrub with long, pendulous branches. Leaves stalked, 2–5.5 cm long, 0.7–1.5 cm wide, lanceolate, acuminate, fleshy, midrib very obscure, base acute. Flowers white with red center, in axillary and terminal umbellate cymes. Fruit a follicle, slender. Flowers and fruits May–July. Propagated by seeds. Distributed throughout Nepal at 500–2000 m, on tree trunks and branches in shady places; also in northern India, Bhutan, and northern Myanmar.

Hoya lanceolata

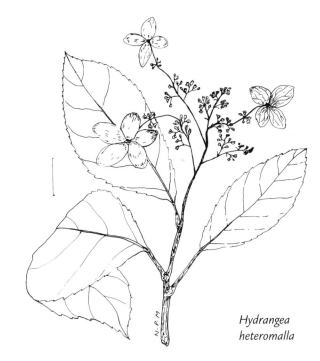

Hydrangea
heteromalla

MEDICINE. A powder of dried plant, mixed with clarified butter, is given in doses of 6 teaspoons three times a day to treat backaches.

Hydrangea heteromalla D. Don

Hydrangea vestita Wallich
NEPALI *phusre kath*

Hydrangeaceae. Tree about 5 m high, young branches hairy. Leaves stalked, elliptic, acute, serrate, densely gray tomentose beneath. Flowers reddish white in terminal corymbs. Propagated by cuttings. Distributed throughout Nepal at 2400–3300 m; also in India, southern Tibet, China, and Indo-China.

MEDICINE. Juice of the bark is given in cases of cough and colds.

OTHER USES. The plant is browsed by goats and sheep.

Hydrilla verticillata (Linnaeus fil.) Royle

Serpicula verticillata Linnaeus fil.
DANUWAR *khasi*

Hydrocharitaceae. Aquatic herb, stems submersed, rooting from the lower nodes. Leaves sessile, in whorls of three to eight, variable in shape and size, linear to lanceolate, apiculate, serrate, translucent. Flowers whitish, March–April. Propagated by seeds or by rooting the branches. Distributed throughout Nepal to about 1400 m, immersed in water or in boggy places; also in Southeast Asia, Australia, southeastern Europe, Africa, and North America.

MEDICINE. Among Danuwars and Tharus, a dried powder of the plant is applied to cuts and wounds to help accelerate healing.

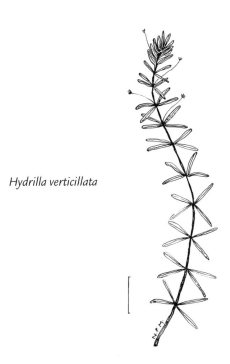

Hydrilla verticillata

Hydrocotyle himalaica P. K. Mukherjee

Hydrocotyle podantha Molkenboer
NEPALI *seto tapre*

Umbelliferae. Herb. Leaves stalked, 0.6–2 cm long, 0.8–3 cm wide, reniform to circular, dentate, glabrous. Flowers greenish white. Flowers and fruits September–November. Propagated by nodal rootings. Distributed throughout Nepal at 1500–2500 m in moist places beside streams; also in northern India and Bhutan.

MEDICINE. Juice of the plant, about 3 teaspoons three times a day, is given in cases of indigestion and fever. It is also considered good for asthma.

OTHER USES. Juice of the plant is mixed with water and taken as refreshment, especially during summer. Squeezed plant is used as fish poison.

Hydrocotyle nepalensis Hooker

Hydrocotyle hispida Buchanan-Hamilton ex D. Don
Hydrocotyle polycephala Wight & Arnott
CHEPANG *ghortapre* GURUNG *pelnti* NEPALI *hathi paila, jhar timur, kukur paile, sano ghortapre* TAMANG *dowa chilim, lumeng, tilikosyo*

Umbelliferae. Prostrate herb. Leaves stalked, 1.5–3 cm long, 2.5–6.5 cm wide, lobed, cordate, crenate. Flowers greenish in many-flowered umbels. Fruit an achene, compressed. Flowers and fruits July–November. Propagated by nodal rootings. Distributed throughout Nepal at 1000–700 m in shady places; also in northern India, Bhutan, Tibet, and Myanmar.

MEDICINE. Juice of the plant, about 4 teaspoons twice a day, is given in cases of fever and cough and is also applied to boils. This juice, mixed with water, is used to bathe children suffering from fever.

ers greenish white in umbels. Flowers and fruits most of the year. Propagated by nodal rootings. Distributed throughout Nepal at 600–2500 m in open, moist places and marshy places; also widespread in the tropics of the eastern hemisphere.

MEDICINE. Juice of the plant, about 2 teaspoons twice a day, is given to treat fever. A paste of the plant is applied to wounds and boils.

Hydrolea zeylanica (Linnaeus) Vahl

Hydrolea inermis Loureiro
Nama javana Linnaeus
Steris aquatica Burman fil.
DANUWAR *dhauka* THARU *gohuwa*

Hydrophyllaceae. Herb about 35 cm high. Leaves stalked, alternate, 1–6 cm long, 0.2–1.3 cm wide, elliptic, acute, entire, glabrous, narrowed toward the base. Flowers blue. Flowers and fruits March–November. Propagated by root offshoots. Distributed in eastern and central Nepal to about 1200 m in moist places near ditches; also in India, Sri Lanka, western and southern China, Taiwan, Malaysia, and tropical Africa.

FOOD. Young leaves are cooked as a vegetable.

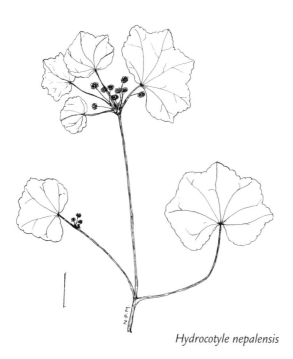

Hydrocotyle nepalensis

Hydrolea zeylanica

Hydrocotyle sibthorpioides Lamarck

Hydrocotyle nitidula A. Richard
Hydrocotyle rotundifolia Roxburgh ex de Candolle
Hydrocotyle tenella D. Don
GURUNG *sano ghortapre* NEPALI *sano tapre, tike ghortapre*
TAMANG *tili kosyo*

Umbelliferae. Creeping herb. Leaves stalked, peltate, blade circular to five-angled, deeply cordate, crenate. Flow-

Hygrophila auriculata (Schumacher) Heine

Barleria auriculata Schumacher
Barleria longifolia Linnaeus, *Asteracantha longifolia* (Linnaeus) Nees, *Ruellia longifolia* (Linnaeus) Roxburgh
Hygrophila spinosa T. Anderson
DANUWAR *khokala* NEPALI *gokhala, makhan, tal makhana*

Acanthaceae. Erect gregarious subshrub. Leaves sessile, whorled on short axillary branchlets, 2.5–17 cm long, 0.5–2 cm wide, oblanceolate. Flowers bright blue. Fruit a capsule, linear oblong. Flowers and fruits October–January.

Hygrophila auriculata

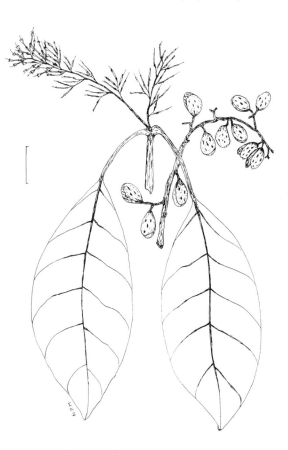

Hymenodictyon excelsum

Propagated by seeds or root offshoots. Distributed throughout Nepal at 200–1700 m in shallow ditches along roads; also in India and Southeast Asia.

MEDICINE. A decoction of the root is valued as a diuretic and is also used for jaundice and diseases of the urogenital tract. A paste of the plant is applied to muscular swellings.

Hymenodictyon excelsum (Roxburgh) Wallich

Cinchona excelsa Roxburgh
Cinchona thyrsiflora Roxburgh
NEPALI *bhurkul, lati karam*

Rubiaceae. Deciduous tree about 25 m high, bark dark gray, divided into small, polygonal, corky scales. Leaves stalked, opposite, 7.5–23 cm long, 4–11.5 cm wide, ovate to oblong, acuminate, membranous, pubescent on both surfaces, base narrowed. Flowers white, fragrant. Fruit a capsule, ellipsoidal. Seeds surrounded by a membranous reticulate wing. Flowers June–August, fruits January–March. Propagated by seeds or by planting stumps. Distributed in eastern and central Nepal to about 400 m, common in dry mixed forest; also in India and Southeast Asia.

MEDICINE. The bark is febrifuge.

OTHER USES. Bark yields tannin. Leaves afford fodder for buffalo.

Hyoscyamus niger Linnaeus var. *agrestis* (Kitaibel) G. Beck

Hyoscyamus agrestis Kitaibel, *Hyoscyamus niger* subsp. *agrestis* (Kitaibel) Hultén
ENGLISH *henbane* NEPALI *bajar bhanga, khursani ajawan* SHERPA *parasika yabani* TIBETAN *lang-thang-tse, lang-thang-rtsi*

Solanaceae. Hairy erect herb. Lower leaves long-stalked, upper leaves sessile, 6.5–8.5 cm long, 3.4.5 cm wide, ob-

Hyoscyamus niger var. *agrestis*

long to ovate, sinuate and dentate. Flowers yellowish with deep purple venation. Flowers and fruits May–August. Propagated by seeds. Distributed in western and central Nepal at 2000–3500 m in open, moist places; also in southwestern and central China, Europe, North Africa, and North America.

MEDICINE. Juice of the leaves is given in cases of asthma and whooping cough.

Hypericum choisianum Wallich ex Robinson

Hypericum hookeranum var. *leschenaultii* (Choisy) Dyer,
    Norysca hookeriana var. *leschenaultii* (Choisy) Y. Kimura
NEPALI *doli phul*

Guttiferae. Much branched shrub about 2 m high. Leaves short-stalked, ovate to lanceolate, acuminate. Flowers yellow. Propagated by seeds. Distributed throughout Nepal at 2100–3500 m in open, rocky places; also in Pakistan, India, Bhutan, and southwestern China.

MEDICINE. Juice of the root is used to relieve fever.
OTHER USES. The plant provides fodder.

Hypericum cordifolium Choisy

Eremanthe cordifolia (Choisy) K. Koch, *Norysca cordifolia*
    (Choisy) Blume
Hypericum bracteatum Buchanan-Hamilton ex D. Don
Hypericum lungusum Buchanan-Hamilton ex D. Don
GURUNG *pyaunli* MAGAR *areli, chaite, gorkhali, odhale* MAJHI *sli pate*
NEPALI *areli, areto, mali phul, pyaunli, urauli phul* TAMANG *chaita, gangelang, kelang, kyakalan, mamhendo, numpa mhendo, saplang*

Guttiferae. Shrub about 2 m high. Leaves sessile, lanceolate, acute, entire, leathery, base cordate, clasping the stem. Flowers yellow in dense cymes, February–April. Propagated by seeds. Distributed throughout Nepal at 900–1900 m on open slopes; endemic.

MEDICINE. Juice of the plant, about 2 teaspoons twice a day, is given for menstrual disorders. Juice of the bark, mixed in equal amount with juice of *Diplokenma butyracea*, is applied in cases of backache and dislocation of bone. Juice of the root is given to treat diarrhea and dysentery.

OTHER USES. The plant is appreciated for its flowers, which are used as offering in religious places. Young leaves are poisonous to cattle.

Hypericum elodeoides Choisy

Hypericum adenophorum Wallich
Hypericum napaulense Choisy
Hypericum nervosum D. Don
Hypericum pallens D. Don
GURUNG *tida* MAGAR *tida* NEPALI *jibre ghans* TAMANG *babatimta, jaben* TIBETAN *tida*

Guttiferae. Erect herb. Leaves sessile, clasping the stem, ovate to lanceolate, acute, entire, closely pellucid punctate. Flowers small, yellow, in many-flowered terminal cymes, November–December. Propagated by seeds. Distributed throughout Nepal at 1200–3000 m on dry slopes

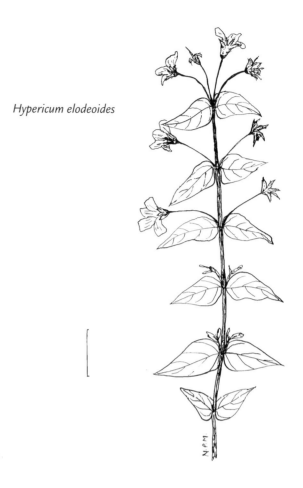

Hypericum elodeoides

along trails; also in southern and northern India, Bhutan, southwestern China, and Myanmar.

MEDICINE. A paste of the root is given in cases of fever.
OTHER USES. The plant is gathered for fodder.

Hypericum japonicum Thunberg ex Murray

Brathys laxa Blume, *Hypericum laxum* (Blume) Koidzumi,
    Sarothra laxa (Blume) Y. Kimura
Brathys nepalensis Blume
Hypericum calyculatum Jacquemont ex Dyer
Hypericum chinense Osbeck
Hypericum dichotomum Buchanan-Hamilton ex D. Don
NEPALI *boksi jhar, chalak jhar, kanike ghans, kugute jhar, nake jhar*
TAMANG *nacha mhendo, syawal nowa, ur mhendo*

Guttiferae. Herb about 20 cm high. Leaves elliptic or ovate, clasping the stem, acute, three-veined. Flowers yellow in dichotomous cymes, June–July. Propagated by seeds. Distributed throughout Nepal to about 2600 m on open, rocky ground; also in southern India, Sri Lanka, southeastern China, southern Korea, Japan, southern and southeastern Australia, New Zealand, and Hawaii.

MEDICINE. Juice of the plant is used for asthma and dysentery. This juice, about 4 teaspoons three times a day, is given in cases of indigestion. Juice of the root is put in the nose to treat severe headaches. This juice, about 2 teaspoons three times a day, is given for fever.

Hypericum oblongifolium Choisy

Hypericum putulum var. *oblongifolium* (Choisy) Koehne
Hypericum cernuum Roxburgh ex D. Don
Hypericum speciosum Wallich
TAMANG *kalan*

Guttiferae. Glabrous shrub with terete branches. Leaves sessile, 2–3 cm long, elliptic or ovate to lanceolate, entire, glaucous beneath, tip acute or rounded. Flowers bright yellow in a short terminal cyme. Fruit a capsule. Flowers and fruits April–October. Propagated by seeds. Distributed in western and central Nepal at 800–2100 m in open places along riverbanks or among shrubs; also in Pakistan and India.

MEDICINE. Juice of the leaves is considered to be an antidote against snakebites.

OTHER USES. The plant is gathered for fodder. The flower has aesthetic value.

Hypericum podocarpoides N. Robson

Hypericum acutum Wallich
TAMANG *chali mhendo, miriri*

Guttiferae. Branched shrub about 1.5 m high, stems reddish, four-angled. Leaves 3–5 cm long, clasping the stem, linear lanceolate, pointed. Flowers yellow in terminal branched clusters, April–July. Fruits September–October. Propagated by seeds. Distributed in western and central Nepal at 800–2100 m on open hillsides; also in northern India.

MEDICINE. Juice of the root is applied to cuts and wounds.

OTHER USES. The plant is used as fodder.

Hypericum uralum Buchanan-Hamilton ex D. Don

Norysca urala (Buchanan-Hamilton ex D. Don) K. Koach
Hypericum patulum Thunberg ex Murray
Hypericum patulum var. *attenuatum* Choisy
TAMANG *kelang, yatsing*

Guttiferae. Herb about 1 m high, branchlets four-angled, arching. Leaves short-stalked, 1.5–3 cm long, ovate, entire. Flowers yellow. Propagated by seeds. Distributed in western and central Nepal at 1200–3600 m on open hillsides; also in India, Bhutan, southern China, Thailand, and Sumatra.

OTHER USES. The plant is lopped for fodder.

Hyptis suaveolens (Linnaeus) Poiteau

Ballota suaveolens Linnaeus
CHEPANG *bhaise selang, namse jhar, simthi* DANUWAR *bawari*
ENGLISH *bush tea, West Indian spikenard* MAGAR *silame* MAJHI *silam*
NEPALI *ban bawari, thulo mirre*

Labiatae. Hairy aromatic herb about 2 m high. Leaves stalked, ovate, acute, serrate. Flowers bluish, axillary, on a long stalk. Nutlets flat, mucilaginous. Flowers and fruits October–February. Propagated by seeds. Distributed in eastern and central Nepal to about 1400 m on open uncultivated land; also in most parts of Asia and the Americas.

MEDICINE. Juice of the plant is applied to wounds. Danuwars drip this juice in the ear in cases of ear trouble. A decoction of the root is emmenagogue. Juice of the root is given to treat menstrual disorder. A paste of the leaves is applied to the forehead to relieve headaches. Juice of the leaves is used to treat wounds, boils, pimples, and ringworm. A decoction of the leaves is antirheumatic and antispasmodic.

OTHER USES. The plant is used as an insecticide, especially for bedbugs and mosquitoes. The plant yields essential oil.

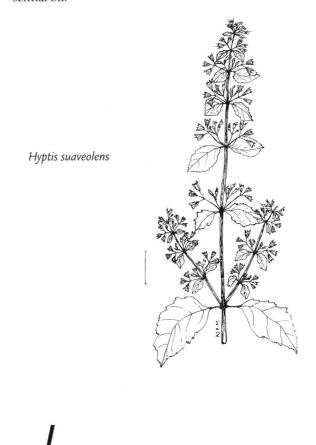

Hyptis suaveolens

I

Ichnocarpus frutescens (Linnaeus) R. Brown

Apocynum frutescens Linnaeus
MOOSHAR *dudh latti* NEPALI *dudhe lahara, parari ghans*
TAMANG *nagara*

Apocynaceae. Trailing shrub. Leaves stalked, 2.8–10 cm long, 0.8–6 cm wide, elliptic to oblong or lanceolate, acute or acuminate, glabrous and dark green above, more or less pubescent beneath. Flowers white, scented, in axillary and terminal leafy cymose panicles. Fruit a follicle, cylindrical, slender. Flowers August–November, fruits February–April. Propagated by seeds or cuttings. Distributed throughout Nepal at 150–900 m, common in open as well as shady places; also in Afghanistan, Pakistan, India, and Southeast Asia.

FOOD. Ripe fruits are edible.

MEDICINE. A decoction of the root, mixed with a powdered fruit of black pepper (*Piper nigrum*), is given to women after childbirth to promote lactation. Latex is applied to boils and pimples.

OTHER USES. Thin branches are used for making baskets and for temporary binding. Tharus used the branches to make fishing traps.

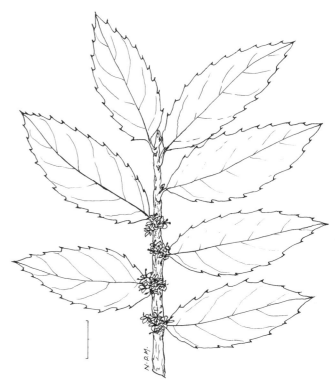

Ilex dipyrena

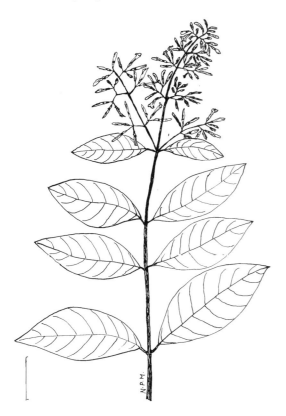

Ichnocarpus frutescens

Ilex dipyrena Wallich

ENGLISH *Himalayan holly* GURUNG *puchu* NEPALI *kaliso, lekh chotra, liso, seto khasru* SHERPA *therma* TAMANG *kerpa, nai, nichhi* TIBETAN *chherma, prak prak*

Aquifoliaceae. Evergreen tree about 10 m high with rough, dark gray bark. Leaves stalked, elliptic to ovate or lanceolate, acute, spinous serrate on young parts, nearly entire when fully mature. Flowers greenish white in round axillary clusters. Fruit a drupe, globose when ripe, the stones longitudinally grooved. Flowers April–June, fruits August–October. Propagated by seeds. Distributed throughout Nepal at 2000–3300 m, common in forested areas; also in northern India, western China, and northern Myanmar.

FOOD. Ripe fruits are eaten fresh.

OTHER USES. Wood is white and close-grained, but it cracks on drying and is chiefly used for fuel.

Ilex excelsa (Wallich) Hooker fil.

Cassine excelsa Wallich
Ilex doniana de Candolle
Ilex elliptica D. Don
Ilex exsulca Wallich
Ilex nepalensis Sprengel
Ilex rotunda Thunberg
Ilex umbellulata Loesener
NEPALI *nir syaul, puwanle*

Aquifoliaceae. Medium-sized tree. Leaves stalked, elliptic to lanceolate, acuminate, entire, leathery, glabrous. Flowers whitish, crowded in umbels. Fruit a drupe, globose, red. Flowers May–June, fruits September–October. Propagated by seeds. Distributed throughout Nepal at 600–2000 m in mixed forest; also in northern India, western China, and Indo-China.

FOOD. Ripe fruits are eaten fresh.

OTHER USES. The plant is lopped for fodder.

Impatiens balsamina Lindley

Impatiens coccinea Sims
ENGLISH *balsam* NEPALI *padake*

Balsaminaceae. Succulent erect herb about 1 m high. Leaves stalked, alternate, lanceolate, acuminate, serrate, glabrous or pubescent. Flowers axillary, pink, red, white, or purple. Fruit pubescent. Propagated by seeds. Distributed throughout Nepal at 1200–1900 m, a common garden plant; also in Southeast Asia.

MEDICINE. Squeezed plant is applied for painful inflammation, carbuncles, and bruises. Flowers are mucilaginous and cooling, and their juice is applied to treat snakebites. Powdered seeds are given during labor pains to provide strength.

Impatiens bicornuta Wallich

TAMANG *raja bubu*

Balsaminaceae. Much branched herb. Leaves stalked, 10–27 cm long, 3–5.5 cm wide, elliptic or oblong to lanceolate, acuminate, crenate. Flowers pinkish mauve in long-stalked racemes. Flowers and fruits July–October. Propagated by seeds. Distributed throughout Nepal at 1900–2600 m in moist, shady places, generally along stream banks.

FOOD. Tender leaves and shoots are cooked as a vegetable.

Impatiens falcifer Hooker fil.

Impatiens serrata Bentham

TAMANG *raja bu bu*

Balsaminaceae. Erect herb about 40 cm high. Leaves stalked, alternate, elliptic to ovate, acute, serrate, membranous, glabrous. Flowers solitary, axillary, yellow, the spur as long as the rest of the flower. Fruit a capsule. Flowers and fruits July–October. Propagated by seeds. Distributed in central and eastern Nepal at 2200–3400 m in moist, shady places; also in northern India and Bhutan.

FOOD. Tender shoots are cooked as a vegetable.

Impatiens puberula de Candolle

Impatiens hispidula Bentham
Impatiens mollis Wallich

NEPALI *bhenda ghans, masino ratanaulo*

Balsaminaceae. Pubescent herb. Leaves stalked, alternate, elliptic to lanceolate, acuminate, crenate, hairy on both surfaces. Flowers solitary, purple, the spur long, incurved. Flowers and fruits July–October. Propagated by seeds. Distributed in central and eastern Nepal at 1500–2700 m in moist, shady places; also in northern India and Bhutan.

FOOD. Seeds are pickled.

Impatiens racemosa de Candolle

Impatiens laxiflora Edgeworth
Impatiens micrantha D. Don
Impatiens microsciadia Hooker fil.
Impatiens tingens Edgeworth

GURUNG *nuki phoko* NEPALI *anchirna, mauphul*

Balsaminaceae. Much branched glabrous herb. Leaves stalked, alternate, elliptic, acuminate, crenate. Flowers yellow, the spur globose. Fruit a capsule, club shaped. Flowers and fruits July–October. Propagated by seeds. Distrib-

Impatiens puberula

uted throughout Nepal at 1300–3900 m in damp places; also in northern India, Bhutan, and southern Tibet.

FOOD. Seeds are pickled.

OTHER USES. The plant is browsed by goats and sheep.

Impatiens scabrida de Candolle

Impatiens calycina Wallich
Impatiens cristata Wallich
Impatiens hamiltoniana D. Don
Impatiens praetermissa Hooker fil.
Impatiens tricornis Lindley

NEPALI *mujyaro, phatakya, tyure* TAMANG *frek* TIBETAN *neki po*

Balsaminaceae. Erect glabrous herb about 50 cm high. Leaves stalked, alternate, elliptic to lanceolate, serrate, base narrowed into a stalk. Flowers yellow, usually on two-flowered axillary peduncles, the spur short, slightly curved. Fruit a capsule. Flowers and fruits May–October. Propagated by seeds. Distributed throughout Nepal at 1000–3600 m in shade in rocky areas; also in Kashmir and Bhutan.

FOOD. Seeds are pickled or eaten raw.

MEDICINE. The plant is fed to cattle in cases of fever.

OTHER USES. A paste of the seeds is mixed with other natural coloring agents to make the color permanent.

Impatiens sulcata Wallich

Impatiens gigantea Edgeworth
NEPALI *mujero*

Balsaminaceae. Annual herb about 1 m high. Leaves stalked, opposite, dentate, tip pointed. Flowers pink. Flowers and fruits May–October. Propagated by seeds. Distributed throughout Nepal at 1700–4000 m, common in moist places; also in Kashmir and Bhutan.

FOOD. Ripe fruits are eaten fresh, and seeds are pickled.

Imperata cylindrica (Linnaeus) Palisot de Beauvois

Lagurus cylindricus Linnaeus
Imperata arundinacea Cirillo
CHEPANG *kiyon* DANUWAR *davar* ENGLISH *alang-alang, cogon grass, cotton grass, thatch grass* GURUNG *salame* LIMBU *nurigba* MOOSHAR *phulki* NEPALI *dhaki banso, siru* SHERPA *chaharu* THARU *churki*

Gramineae. Erect perennial grass about 50 cm high. Leaves linear, acuminate, flat, entire, base sheathing. Inflorescences white in panicles. Flowers and fruits April–November. Propagated by splitting the root. Distributed throughout Nepal to about 2400 m in open fields; a weed also in Afghanistan, Pakistan, India, Bhutan, Tibet, central Asia, Myanmar, and the Mediterranean region.

MEDICINE. The root is boiled in water about 15 minutes, and the filtered water is taken as an anthelmintic. A decoction of the root, about 6 teaspoons three times a day, is taken in cases of diarrhea and dysentery and is also used for indigestion and gastric troubles. It is astringent, diuretic, and tonic. Juice of the root is used for asthma, jaundice, dropsy, and nosebleed. A paste of the root is taken for fever. A paste of the inflorescence is applied to cuts and wounds and acts as a sedative when taken internally.

OTHER USES. The plant is used for thatching roofs and is gathered for fodder. It is also used for temporary binding.

Imperata cylindrica

Inflorescences are valued for stuffing pillows and cushions. The dried inflorescence is soaked in mustard oil and burned during religious performances. The plant is a good sand binder.

Incarvillea arguta (Royle) Royle

Amphicome arguta Royle
Incarvillea diffusa Royle, *Amphicome diffusa* (Royle) Sprague
Incarvillea emodi Wallich
NEPALI *maruwa pani*

Bignoniaceae. Perennial shrub, often pendulous. Leaves stalked, pinnate, leaflets five to nine, short-stalked, 2–3 cm long, elliptic, serrate. Flowers pink in long terminal clusters. Fruit a capsule, linear. Flowers and fruits June–August. Propagated by seeds. Distributed in central and western Nepal at 1300–3000 m on stony slopes; also in northern India, eastern Tibet, and western China.

MEDICINE. Juice of the plant is applied to treat toothaches.

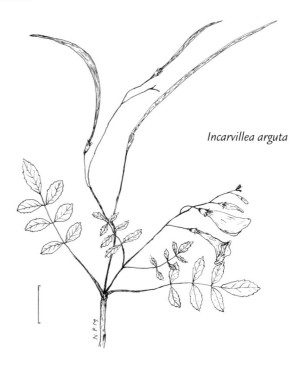

Incarvillea arguta

Indigofera atropurpurea Buchanan-Hamilton ex Hornemann

Indigofera cassioides Rottler ex de Candolle
Indigofera elliptica Roxburgh
Indigofera hamiltonii Graham ex Duthie & Prain
Indigofera leptostachya de Candolle
Indigofera violacea Roxburgh
NEPALI *sagino* RAUTE *hakunya*

Leguminosae. Shrub with glabrescent branchlets. Leaves stalked, odd-pinnate, ovate, membranous, glabrescent, dark green. Flowers pinkish in racemes. Fruit a pod, linear, turgid. Flowers April–August. Propagated by seeds. Distributed throughout Nepal at 700–3200 m on open hill-sides; also in India, Bhutan, and China.

FOOD. Flowers are boiled and pickled.

MEDICINE. Flowers are boiled in water until the liquid is half the original amount, and the liquid is then taken in cases of diarrhea and dysentery.

Indigofera dosua Buchanan-Hamilton ex D. Don

Indigofera virgata Roxburgh
NEPALI *phusre ghans* NEWARI *dusi swan* TAMANG *chipro, kurna*

Leguminosae. Shrub about 2 m high. Leaves stalked, odd-pinnate, leaflets 15–23, narrowly oblong, obtuse to mucronate, entire, densely pubescent. Flowers pink in axillary racemes. Fruit a pod, cylindrical, tomentose. Flowers April–May, fruits July–August. Propagated by seeds. Distributed throughout Nepal at 1000–3000 m in hedges along trails; also in Pakistan, India, and Bhutan.

FOOD. Flowers are pickled.

Indigofera hebepetala Bentham ex Baker

CHEPANG *roiro*

Leguminosae. Shrub about 5 m high. Leaves stalked, pinnate, leaflets opposite, oblong to ovate, with short, appressed, bristly hairs on both sides. Flowers pink in many-flowered racemes. Fruit a pod, glabrous. Flowers May–June, fruits July–August. Propagated by seeds. Distributed throughout Nepal at 1600–2800 m, common in open places; also in northern India and Bhutan.

FOOD. Flowers and tender fruits are cooked as vegetables or pickled.

OTHER USES. Goats browse the leaves.

Indigofera heterantha Wallich ex Brandis

Indigofera gerardiana var. *heterantha* (Wallich ex Brandis) Baker
Indigofera gerardiana Wallich
NEPALI *sakhino*

Leguminosae. Shrub with brown bark. Leaves short-stalked, pinnate, leaflets opposite, ovate, mucronate, somewhat leathery, clothed with short white hairs above, pale gray beneath. Flowers pink in short-stalked racemes. Fruit a pod, cylindrical, with a few scattered hairs. Flowers May–June, fruits September–November. Propagated by seeds. Distributed in central and western Nepal at 600–3100 m in open, moist places; also in Pakistan, India, and Bhutan.

FOOD. Flowers are boiled and pickled.

OTHER USES. The plant is gathered for fodder.

Indigofera pulchella Roxburgh

Indigofera arborea Roxburgh
Indigofera purpurascens Roxburgh
CHEPANG *chisro, roiro* NEPALI *phusre ghans, rato mirmire, sakhino*

Leguminosae. Straggling shrub about 3 m high. Leaves stalked, alternate, odd-pinnate, leaflets short-stalked, ob-long to ovate, obtuse to mucronate, entire, tomentose above, with soft, appressed, gray hairs beneath. Flowers pink or violet in axillary racemes. Flowers September–March, fruits July–August. Propagated by seeds. Distributed throughout Nepal at 300–1900 m in open, dry places; also in northern India and Bhutan.

FOOD. Flowers are either pickled or eaten as a vegetable.

MEDICINE. A decoction of the root is given in cases of cough.

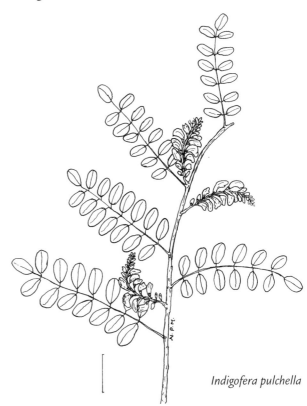

Indigofera pulchella

Inula cappa (Buchanan-Hamilton ex D. Don) de Candolle

Conyza cappa Buchanan-Hamilton ex D. Don
Conyza eriophora Wallich, *Inula eriophora* de Candolle
Conyza lanuginosa Wallich
CHEPANG *danesar, ridang, toreban* ENGLISH *elecampane, sheep's ear*
GURUNG *donrah, gukpa, tigaji, tiware ta* MAJHI *gaitihare*
NEPALI *bakhra kane, dware phul, gaitihare, guru tiware, kanpate, madane, tihare phul* SHERPA *lhapi karpo* TAMANG *ranabhyang*
TIBETAN *guri namcho, lhapti karku*

Compositae. Erect shrub about 2 m high. Leaves stalked, alternate, 7–15 cm long, 2–3.5 cm wide, oblong to lanceolate, narrowed at both ends, distantly dentate, softly tomentose beneath. Flower heads yellow in corymbs. Fruit an achene, silky, the hairs thickened at the ends. Flowers September–October. Propagated by seeds. Distributed throughout Nepal to about 2500 m on open, sunny hillsides; also in northern India, Bhutan, China, Myanmar, Thailand, Malaysia, and Java.

MEDICINE. Juice of the root, about 4 teaspoons three times a day, is given for peptic ulcer. This juice, about 2 teaspoons three times a day, is given in cases of indigestion and is also used for gastric troubles. Pounded root is applied to the forehead to treat headaches. A decoction of the root, about 2 teaspoons twice a day, is given for fever. This decoction is mixed with water for bathing to relieve body aches caused by heavy physical work. Juice of the bark, mixed with bark juice of *Ficus semicordata* and *Myrica esculenta* in equal amounts, is given to treat menstrual disorder.

OTHER USES. The plant is used to make *marcha*, a fermenting cake from which liquor is distilled.

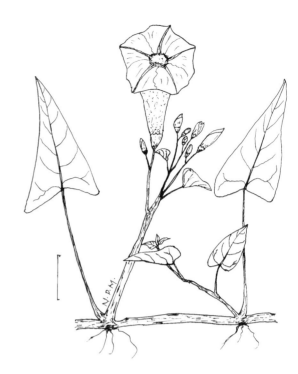

Ipomoea aquatica

Inula cappa

Ipomoea aquatica Forsskål

ENGLISH *swamp cabbage, water spinach*   NEPALI *kalmi sag, karmi*
SATAR *karmi*   THARU *karamuwan*

Convolvulaceae. Annual herb with hollow, trailing stems, rooting at the nodes. Leaves stalked, alternate, oblong to ovate, acute, entire, base cordate or hastate. Flowers stalked, axillary, purple, on a one- or two-flowered stalk. Flowers and fruits October–February. Propagated by stem cuttings. Distributed throughout Nepal to about 500 m, common in ponds, ditches, and muddy places; also pantropical.

FOOD. Young shoots and leaves are eaten as a vegetable.

MEDICINE. Young leaves are mildly laxative and used by diabetic patients. A decoction of the leaves, about 6 teaspoons twice a day, is suggested for cough by native healers. A paste of buds is applied for ringworm.

Ipomoea batatas (Linnaeus) Lamarck

Convolvulus batatas Linnaeus

CHEPANG *lahar goi*   DANUWAR *aruwa*   ENGLISH *sweet potato*
MAJHI *syuthani*   NEPALI *sakarkhand*   NEWARI *chakuhi*
TAMANG *sakar time*

Convolvulaceae. Prostrate herb with tuberous roots. Leaves stalked, triangular or ovate, usually irregularly lobed, base more or less cordate. Flowers purple. Propagated by stem cuttings. Distributed throughout Nepal to about 2200 m in open places, cultivated.

FOOD. The tuberous root provides a nutritious food. Tender leaves and shoots are cooked as a vegetable by Chepangs and Mooshars.

Ipomoea carnea Jacquin subsp. *fistulosa*
(Martius ex Choisy) D. Austin

Ipomoea fistulosa Martius ex Choisy
Ipomoea crassicaulis (Bentham) B. L. Robinson
NEPALI *ajamari, behaya, thechar*   THARU *behaya, bishram*

Convolvulaceae. Shrub about 2 m high. Leaves long-stalked, elliptic, long-pointed, base cordate. Flowers pink or white, May–June. Propagated by seeds or cuttings. Distributed throughout Nepal to about 1000 m, often gregarious; also in most tropical regions of the world.

MEDICINE. Juice of the plant is applied to wounds between the toes caused by prolonged walking barefooted in muddy water. The milky latex is applied to cuts and wounds.

OTHER USES. The plant is cultivated as a hedge.

Ipomoea muricata (Linnaeus) Jacquin

Convolvulus muricatus Linnaeus, *Calonyction muricatum*
  (Linnaeus) G. Don
Ipomoea turbinata Lagasca
NEPALI *lahare sag*

Convolvulaceae. Glabrous climber. Leaves stalked, broadly ovate, entire, base cordate. Flowers purple on one- to five-flowered axillary peduncles. Fruit a capsule, ovoid. Flowers August–September, fruits September–November. Propagated by seeds. Distributed in central Nepal at 900–1400 m, along waysides on shrubs and thickets; also in Pakistan, India, Bhutan, China, Japan, tropical Africa, the southern United States, Mexico, Colombia, Brazil, and the West Indies.

FOOD. Tender leaves and shoots are cooked as a vegetable.

MEDICINE. A paste of the seed is used for snakebites.

Ipomoea nil (Linnaeus) Roth

Convolvulus nil Linnaeus, *Pharbitis nil* (Linnaeus) Choisy
Ipomoea hederacea of authors, not Jacquin
MAJHI *siyunri*

Convolvulaceae. Annual twiner. Leaves stalked, broadly ovate to cordate, three-lobed, rarely entire. Flowers pinkish on axillary peduncles. Fruit a capsule, ovoid. Flowers July–October, fruits September–November. Propagated by seeds. Distributed in central and western Nepal at 760–2000 m in moist places; also pantropical.

MEDICINE. The plant is pounded and used to wash the head to remove lice.

Ipomoea quamoclit Linnaeus

THARU *chotaki gurubans*

Convolvulaceae. Slender climber. Leaves numerous, stalked, pinnate, leaflets needle-like. Flowers long-stalked, crimson or white. Fruit a capsule, ovoid, with long, persistent styles. Flowers and fruits August–October. Propagated by seeds. Distributed throughout Nepal to about 1400 m in moist places; also in tropical Asia and widespread.

MEDICINE. A decoction of the plant, about half a teaspoon, is given in cases of vomiting blood. A paste of the leaf is applied to treat hemorrhoids.

Iris clarkei Baker ex Hooker fil.

Iris himalaica Dykes
NEPALI *bojho jhar*

Iridaceae. Herb with a stout, creeping rhizome. Leaves variable, linear, long-pointed, glossy above, glaucous beneath. Flowers bright lilac with yellow throat. Fruit cylindrical. Flowers June–July. Propagated by seeds or root tubers. Distributed in eastern and central Nepal at 3000–3500 m in wet meadows; also in northern India and Bhutan.

MEDICINE. A paste of the root is applied to cuts and wounds.

Ischaemum rugosum Salisbury var. *segetum* (Trinius) Hackel

Ichaemum segetum Trinius
NEPALI *banso, madilo*

Gramineae. Annual grass, culms erect or ascending, nodes rooting at the base. Leaves linear lanceolate, acuminate, narrowed into a short stalk at the base. Inflores-

Iris clarkei

Ischaemum rugosum var. *segetum*

cence greenish. Flowers and fruits July–November. Propagated by seeds. Distributed throughout Nepal to about 800 m in moist places; also in India, China, and Southeast Asia.

OTHER USES. The plant is used for fodder.

Isodon coetsa (Buchanan-Hamilton ex D. Don)

Plectranthus coetsa Buchanan-Hamilton ex D. Don, *Rabdosia coetsa* (Buchanan-Hamilton ex D. Don) Hara

CHEPANG *kontyong, rangiya* NEPALI *jwahane jhar, mirre* TAMANG *chyandre, surchendro*

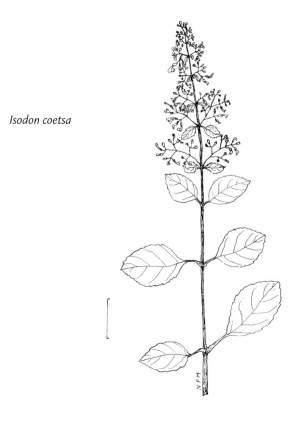

Isodon coetsa

Labiatae. Shrub about 1 m high. Leaves stalked, 1.5–6 cm long, 1–3 cm wide, ovate to lanceolate, acuminate, serrate, pubescent. Flowers bluish in axillary and terminal panicles. Flowers and fruits July–December. Propagated by seeds. Distributed throughout Nepal at 600–3400 m along trails, in hedges or wet places; also in northern India, Bhutan, Sri Lanka, western China, and Indo-China.

MEDICINE. Juice of the plant is applied to boils. Juice of the root is dripped in the eye as an ophthalmic medicine. Juice of the leaves, about 6 teaspoons three times a day, is given for fever.

Isodon lophanthoides (Buchanan-Hamilton ex D. Don) Hara

Hyssopus lophanthoides Buchanan-Hamilton ex D. Don, *Rabdosia lophanthoides* (Buchanan-Hamilton ex D. Don) Hara *Plectranthus striatus* Bentham, *Isodon striatus* (Bentham) Kudô

CHEPANG *cha jahr* NEPALI *masino chapate* TAMANG *chhiku dhap, kambaman, lha bawari, sarbhen mhendo*

Labiatae. Shrub about 2 m high. Leaves stalked, ovate, acuminate, crenate, reddish purple beneath. Flowers pinkish in cymes. Propagated by seeds. Distributed throughout Nepal at 1300–2700 m along tracks in moist gullies; also in northern India, Bhutan, China, and Indo-China.

MEDICINE. Juice of the plant is applied to the forehead to relieve headaches.

Ixeris polycephala Cassini

Chondrilla fontinalis Wallich, *Ixeris fontinalis* de Candolle *Lactuca polycephala* (Cassini) C. B. Clarke

NEPALI *muli buti, nangasari*

Compositae. Erect herb. Basal leaves stalked, lanceolate, acuminate, sinuate and dentate, cauline leaves sessile, auricled. Flower heads yellow in terminal corymbs. Fruit an achene, ribbed, narrowed into a slender brown beak. Flowers and fruits most of the year. Propagated by seeds. Distributed in central and western Nepal at 700–2100 m in moist, shady places; also in Japan.

MEDICINE. Juice of the plant, about 2 teaspoons twice a day, is given in cases of fever. A paste of the flower heads is applied to treat scabies.

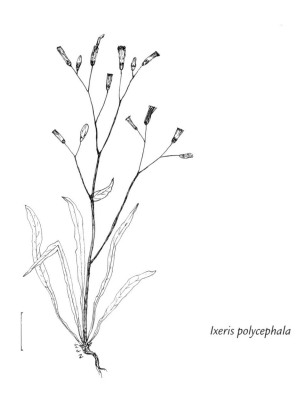

Ixeris polycephala

J

Jacaranda mimosifolia D. Don

Jacaranda ovalifolia R. Brown
NEPALI *jakaranda* NEWARI *chakhuncha swan*

Bignoniaceae. Tree about 15 m high. Leaves stalked, alternate, bipinnate, pinnae 9–15, alternate or nearly opposite, each pinna bearing 14–24 pinnules, pinnules sessile, opposite or subopposite, tip pointed, terminal pinnule larger. Flowers blue in terminal panicles. Fruit a capsule, suborbicular. Seeds winged. Flowers April–May. Propagated by seeds. Distributed in central Nepal at 1000–1400 m, cultivated; also in India, the Philippines, tropical America, and Argentina.

MEDICINE. An infusion of the bark is administered to treat mucous discharge and syphilis. A paste of the leaves is applied to cuts and wounds.

OTHER USES. The plant is cultivated as an avenue tree.

Jasminum gracile Andrews

NEPALI *chameli* NEWARI *dhawa swan*

Oleaceae. Much branched shrub. Leaves stalked, 1–3 cm long, 2–3 cm wide, simple, ovate, glossy above, entire. Flowers stalked, white, fragrant, in a branched panicle. Flowers and fruits most of the year. Propagated by cuttings. Distributed throughout Nepal to about 1400 m, cultivated; also in India, Bhutan, China, Southeast Asia, Australia, and Bermuda.

MEDICINE. Juice of the root is applied to treat ringworm. Juice of the flower is considered good for indigestion.

Jasminum humile Linnaeus

Jasminum humile var. *glabrum* (de Candolle) Kobuski
Jasminum inodorum Jacquemont ex Decaisne
Jasminum wallichianum Lindley
BHOJPURI *jai* DANUWAR *jai* ENGLISH *Nepal jasmine, yellow jasmine* LEPCHA *riyakat* LIMBU *idatphung* NEPALI *jai phul, lahare jai, masino jai* NEWARI *aji swan* RAI *jai* SUNWAR *jai* TAMANG *jai, jail mhendo* THARU *jai*

Oleaceae. Diffuse shrub about 3 m high. Leaves stalked, alternate, odd-pinnate, leaflets three to seven, ovate to lanceolate, entire, terminal leaflet larger. Flowers golden yellow in umbels, February–May. Fruits September–December. Propagated by seeds or root offshoots. Distributed throughout Nepal at 1200–3400 m in moist places; also in Afghanistan, Pakistan, India, Bhutan, Tibet, western China, Myanmar, Mauritius, Italy, Great Britain, and Paraguay.

MEDICINE. Juice of the root is applied to treat ringworm. A paste of the flowers is considered good for intestinal problems.

OTHER USES. The plant is cultivated as a hedge plant.

Jasminum multiflorum (Burman fil.) Andrews

Nyctanthes multiflora Burman fil.
Jasminum bracteatum Wight
Jasminum hirsutum Willdenow
Nyctanthes pubescens Retzius, *Jasminum pubescens* (Retzius) Willdenow
CHEPANG *mausuni* ENGLISH *Chinese jasmine, hairy jasmine* NEPALI *ban beli, chameli* NEWARI *dapswan*

Oleaceae. Scandent shrub, young branches velvety pubescent. Leaves stalked, opposite, ovate, entire. Flowers white, fragrant, in short-stalked cymes. Fruit globose, black when ripe. Flowers December–April. Propagated by seeds or root offshoots. Distributed in western and central Nepal to about 1300 m in moist, shady places; also in Pakistan, India, Sri Lanka, China, and Myanmar.

MEDICINE. A powder of dried leaves is used to treat ulcers. A paste of the fruit is applied to wounds between the toes caused by walking barefooted in muddy water.

OTHER USES. The plant is grown as an ornamental. It is used to adorn the water jar in Newar religious rites.

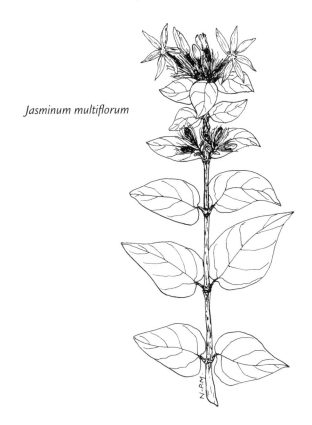

Jasminum multiflorum

Jasminum sambac [Solander in] Aiton

ENGLISH *Arabian jasmine, Tuscan jasmine* NEPALI *beli phul*

Oleaceae. Spreading shrub about 1 m high. Leaves stalked, ovate, glossy, tip blunt or pointed, base rounded or tapering. Flowers white, fragrant, in an axillary or terminal inflorescence. Propagated by splitting the root. Distributed throughout Nepal to about 1400 m, cultivated.

MEDICINE. A poultice of the root is applied to sprains and fractures. A decoction of the root is employed in bronchitis and asthma. Juice of the leaves is applied to cuts and wounds; about 4 teaspoons of this juice is given to treat fever. A paste of the flower is applied to the breast as a galactagogue. Juice of the flower is applied externally for eye inflammation.

Jatropha curcas Linnaeus

CHEPANG *dhuching, nirguri* DANUWAR *akakgachha, arari* ENGLISH *physic nut, purging nut* GURUNG *rajani giri, sajin, satiman* MAGAR *ratyun* MAJHI *aren, aril* MOOSHAR *baghandi* NEPALI *arin, kadam, nimte, sajyon* RAI *kadam* RAUTE *dekiro* TAMANG *desya, gara, gyagar desya* THARU *ratanjot*

Euphorbiaceae. Soft-wooded tree about 4 m high. Leaves stalked, 4–13 cm long, 3.5–13 cm wide, blade angled or three- or five-lobed, orbiculate, glabrous, base cordate. Flowers yellowish in cymes. Fruit three-lobed, oblong, yellowish when ripe. Seeds oblong, dark brown, smooth, oily. Flowers April–October, fruits November–January. Propagated by seeds. Distributed throughout Nepal to about 1300 m in open places, generally around villages; also in Pakistan, India, Bhutan, Sri Lanka, and Myanmar.

FOOD. Tender shoots are cooked as a vegetable.

MEDICINE. Juice of the root is applied to boils and pimples. Fresh bark is cut into pieces and chewed or kept inside the mouth 1–2 hours to treat pyorrhea. A paste of the bark is applied inside the mouth around the gums to treat wounds and swelling of the gums. The paste is left there about an hour, and this process is continued three or four times a day. Juice of the bark, about 1 teaspoon three times a day, is taken with milk or hot water in cases of malarial fever and is also helpful in relieving swelling of parts of the body caused by inflammation. This juice also relieves burns and is used for scabies, eczema, and ringworm.

In 1977, I was on my way to Mugu district, one of the most remote areas of western Nepal. After 3 days' walk from Nepalganj, a Nepalese town near the Indian border, I reached the village of Chhinchu, Surkhet district, at 4 p.m. I was tired and decided to stay there for the night. As I changed the papers of the plant specimens, some villagers gathered and asked the reason for collecting such specimens as these plants were available everywhere. When I asked the uses of the plants, they said they were hardly useful plants (*jharpat* in Nepali). Anyway, I wanted to create a diversion to get some information on the plants already collected. I started singing and dancing although I am at best an awkward dancer. The villagers were laughing and after some time, I was convinced, they would take interest in my queries. I asked them what they would do if someone in the village fell ill or got cut or wounded. They talked of one woman healer in the village who prescribed plant-based drugs. I visited the healer, who was about 60 years of age. A small girl of about 12 was on the bed, crying. I asked the woman why the girl was crying.

Jatropha curcas

She said that the girl was her granddaughter and had burned herself 3 days ago, below her navel, but that she was treating the girl, who was getting better. She showed me the latex she had collected in a small bottle and pointed out the plant (*Jatropha curcas*) she had grown as a hedge near her house. She provided further information on about 50 species of plants that she prescribed to patients. After a month, I returned through Chhinchu. The girl was playing and her burns were all healed. On another occasion in 1978, at the village of Manthali, Dolkha district in central Nepal, I saw a villager rubbing the same latex on a sprain. He explained further that the latex is also useful for boils and pimples. In most parts of the country, it is used for pyorrhea and rheumatic pain.

Thin twigs are used as a toothbrush to treat toothaches, and when I grew up, entire villages used the twigs this way. The twigs are considered especially good for bleeding and swollen gums. Juice of the leaves is applied to cuts and wounds and is used for treating decayed teeth. Oil from the seed is purgative and emetic and is applied for herpes, itches, eczema, and boils. Warmed oil is applied to burns. One cotyledon twice a day is given to ease constipation. A paste of the cotyledon is taken as an appetizer.

OTHER USES. Seeds contain 20–40% nonvolatile oil that is also used for lighting. The cotyledons serve as candles for villagers. The plant makes an excellent hedge.

Jatropha gossypifolia Linnaeus

DANUWAR *chhotaka baghandi* ENGLISH *bellyache bush,
red physic nut bush* MOOSHAR *lal baghandi* NEPALI *bepane danti*

Euphorbiaceae. Much branched shrub, stems gray-white, with brown lenticels, young parts deep purple. Leaves stalked, three- or five-lobed, covered with numerous fascicled, branched, glandular bristles. Flowers crimson or purple in corymbose cymes. Fruit a capsule, oblong, brownish, truncate at both ends. Flowers and fruits July–September. Propagated by seeds. Distributed throughout Nepal to about 600 m on uncultivated land along roadsides; also in tropical regions.

MEDICINE. Small, soft branches are used as toothbrushes for pyorrhea. Latex is applied in cases of toothache. This latex is applied to wounds caused by walking barefooted in muddy water during the rainy season.

Juglans regia Linnaeus var. kamaonia C. de Candolle

Juglans kamaonia (C. de Candolle) Dode

BHOJPURI *okhar* CHEPANG *okhar* DANUWAR *okhar* ENGLISH *walnut* GURUNG *akhor, katu* LEPCHA *kolpot* LIMBU *khayusing, khejik* MAGAR *okhar* NEPALI *okhar* NEWARI *khonsi* RAI *khaisi* SHERPA *kotasi* SUNWAR *phoro* TAMANG *kado, kato* THARU *okhar* TIBETAN *star-ga*

Juglandaceae. Deciduous tree about 30 m high. Leaves stalked, odd-pinnate, leaflets 11–13, subsessile, 10–25 cm long, 3–10 cm wide, ovate to lanceolate, acuminate, those in a pair somewhat unequal. Flowers unisexual, greenish. Fruit a nut, ellipsoidal, green, thick shelled in the wild form, distinctly two-valved, containing irregularly corrugated, two-lobed, oily cotyledons. Flowers February–April, fruits May–September. Propagated by seeds. Distributed throughout Nepal at 1200–3000 m on open hillsides but the plant's limited natural distribution is a cause of conservation concern; also in Afghanistan, northern India, Bhutan, southern Tibet, Myanmar, and the species commonly cultivated in Europe and the Americas.

FOOD. Seed oil is used for culinary purposes and illumination. The kernel is eaten raw. The people of Jumla district eat the oil cake.

MEDICINE. Juice of the bark has an anthelmintic property. Leaves are astringent and tonic. Oil cake is applied to the forehead to treat headaches.

OTHER USES. Wood is moderately hard and used for making furniture, wooden utensils, and gun stocks. It is also used for construction. Bark and the rind of unripe fruit yield dye and tannin and are also used as fish poison. Leaves are lopped to furnish winter fodder.

Juniperus indica Bertoloni

Juniperus pseudosabina Fischer & Meyer
Juniperus wallichiana Hooker fil. & Thomson ex Parlatore
NEPALI *dhupi, pamo* SHERPA *syukapa* TAMANG *syukpa*

Cupressaceae. Evergreen coniferous shrub about 2 m high. Leaves closely appressed, overlapping, decussate. Cone berry-like, ovoid, blue, one-seeded. Cones May–June.

Propagated by seeds. Distributed throughout Nepal at 2100–4300 m on open alpine slopes; also in northern India, southeastern Tibet, and western China.

MEDICINE. Fruits are eaten to cure fever and headaches.
OTHER USES. Leaves are used as incense.

Juniperus recurva Buchanan-Hamilton ex D. Don

Juniperus excelsa Marschall von Bieberstein
Juniperus macropoda Boissier
ENGLISH *juniper, weeping blue juniper* NEPALI *dhup* SHERPA *syukpa* TAMANG *dhang ling* TIBETAN *chher syukpa*

Cupressaceae. Evergreen coniferous shrub, procumbent stems curling upward at the tips. Leaves in whorls of

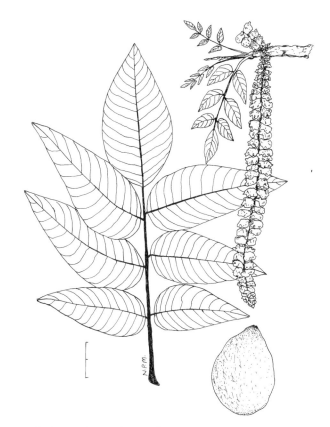

Juglans regia var. *kamaonia*

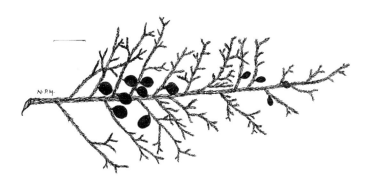

Juniperus indica

three, lanceolate, sharply pointed, loosely imbricated, incurved, base not jointed, decurrent, with a large gland on the decurrent portion. Cones yellowish in terminal, short, lateral branches. Seed cone ovoid, black. Cones June–July, mature November the following year. Propagated by seeds. Distributed throughout Nepal at 3300–4600 m in open, rocky places in alpine regions; also in northern India, western China, and Myanmar.

OTHER USES. Wood and leaves are used as incense. Leaves contain 1.7% essential oils.

Juniperus squamata Buchanan-Hamilton ex D. Don

NEPALI *dhupi* TIBETAN *phar*

Cupressaceae. Prostrate evergreen coniferous shrub about 2 m high. Leaves in whorls of three, linear, somewhat narrowed at the base, flat and bluish green above, convex and light green beneath, often incurved. Cones yellowish. Seed cone berry-like, oblong, dark purple, smooth, shiny when ripe. Seeds solitary, oblong, not winged. Cones June–July, mature August–October the following year. Propagated by seeds. Distributed throughout Nepal at 3300–4400 m in dry, open, alpine regions; also in Afghanistan, Pakistan, India, western China, and northern Myanmar.

MEDICINE. Powdered plant is mixed in water and kept for half an hour; it is then used for bathing in cases of skin disease.

OTHER USES. The plant is chiefly used for fuel. Leaves are used as incense.

Jurinea dolomiaea Boissier

Carduus macrocephalus Wallich, *Dolomiaea macrocephala* Royle, *Jurinea macrocephala* (Royle) C. B. Clarke

NEPALI *ukhin dukhin jhyau*

Compositae. Perennial herb. Leaves stalked, arising in a rosette from a stout taproot, oblong, blunt in outline, pinnately lobed, lobes dentate or shallow, white woolly beneath. Flowers bluish purple, July–September. Propagated by seeds. Distributed throughout Nepal at 3200–4300 m on open slopes; also in northern India.

MEDICINE. Juice of the root is given in cases of fever.

OTHER USES. The plant is used for incense.

Justicia adhatoda Linnaeus

Adhatoda vasica Nees

BHOJPURI *asuro* DANUWAR *asura* ENGLISH *Malabar nut*
GURUNG *aasuri* NEPALI *asuro, kalo basak* NEWARI *alahan ma*
RAI *asura, nakhunbun* RAUTE *washing* SUNWAR *riwa*
TAMANG *basak* THARU *rus* TIBETAN *ba-sha-ka*

Acanthaceae. Shrub about 2 m high. Leaves stalked, 7–19 cm long, 6–4 cm wide, elliptic to lanceolate, acuminate, entire. Flowers sessile, white. Fruit a capsule, longitudinally channeled, four-seeded. Propagated by seeds or branch cuttings. Distributed throughout Nepal to about

Jurinea dolomiaea

2700 m in open areas and on uncultivated land; also in India and Southeast Asia.

FOOD. Tender leaves and flowers are cooked as a vegetable.

MEDICINE. Juice of the plant, mixed with juice of *Dichroa febrifuga* and *Vitex negundo,* is boiled and is given in doses of 4 teaspoons twice a day in cases of fever. Leaves are boiled in water, filtered, and the liquid is boiled again till a sticky gelatinous mass is formed. It is then cooled and a pea-

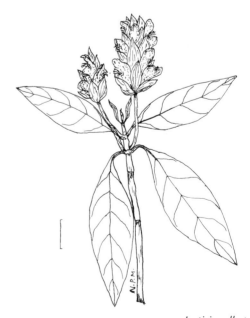

Justicia adhatoda

sized tablet is prepared. About 2 tablets three times a day are given for stomach acidity. Juice of the leaves is used for cough, bronchitis, and asthma. This juice is given to relieve malarial fever, about 2 teaspoons three times a day, and intermittent fever, about 4 teaspoons three times a day. It is also applied externally to relieve joint ache, especially during fever. Juice of the flower is valued as an ophthalmic medicine.

OTHER USES. Leaves are used as green compost. They also have insecticidal properties and are mixed with manure to keep harmful insects away from the field.

Justicia procumbens Linnaeus var. *simplex* (D. Don) Yamazaki

Justicia mollissima Wallich
Rostellaria rotundifolia Nees
CHEPANG *aangdyan jhar* GURUNG *kyubo* NEPALI *bisaune jhar, khursani jhar, phuli jhar* TAMANG *gyuru puju, ping mhendo*

Acanthaceae. Much branched herb. Leaves stalked, 0.8–4 cm long, 0.4–3 cm wide, elliptic or ovate, acute, entire, hairy on both surfaces. Flowers pinkish. Fruit a capsule, elliptic. Flowers and fruits April–November. Propagated by seeds. Distributed throughout Nepal at 700–2500 m in moist, open places; also in India, Bhutan, Sri Lanka, Myanmar, Thailand, Malaysia, and East Africa.

MEDICINE. Juice of the plant is given for cough and colds. It is also valued as an ophthalmic medicine. A paste of the plant is applied to treat rheumatism, backache, flatulence, cuts, and wounds. Juice of the root, about 2 teaspoons three times a day, is given to treat blood mixed with cough.

K

Kalanchoe spathulata de Candolle

Kalanchoe varians Haworth
MAJHI *bhalu musa* NEPALI *ajamari jhar* TAMANG *desi, mainabing*
TIBETAN *bhangu aamcho*

Crassulaceae. Erect herb about 1 m high. Leaves stalked, opposite, 16–26 cm long, 6–8 cm wide, spatulate, oblong, crenate. Flowers yellow in terminal corymbs. Fruit a follicle, many-seeded, enclosed in the dry, persistent calyx and corolla. Flowers September–October, fruits October–November. Propagated by seeds. Distributed in central and eastern Nepal to about 1300 m in dry, sandy, open places; also in Kashmir, Bhutan, China, Myanmar, Java, South Africa, and Brazil.

MEDICINE. A paste of the leaves is applied to sprains, burns, eczema, and boils. Juice of the leaves, about 4 teaspoons three times a day, is given for diarrhea and dysen-

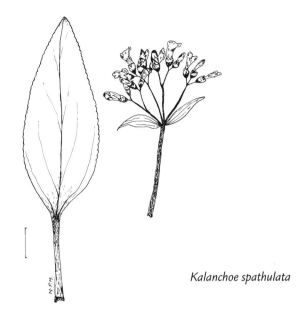

Kalanchoe spathulata

tery. This juice is applied to sprains. A heated leaf is placed on the lower part of the abdomen for dysuria.

OTHER USES. The plant is poisonous to cattle.

Knoxia corymbosa Willdenow

Cuncea trifida Buchanan-Hamilton ex D. Don
Knoxia mollis R. Brown ex Wallich
Spermacoce exserta Roxburgh
Spermacoce teres Roxburgh
TAMANG *goli*

Rubiaceae. Erect herb about 1.5 m high. Leaves short-stalked, opposite, 2.5–12 cm long, 0.8–3 cm wide, ovate to lanceolate, entire. Flowers white-purple in terminal cor-

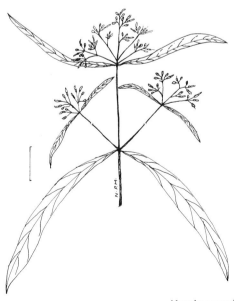

Knoxia corymbosa

ymbs. Fruit four-angled. Flowers August–September, fruits September–October. Propagated by seeds. Distributed throughout Nepal to about 1100 m in open places; also in Sri Lanka, China, and tropical Australia.

FOOD. Ripe fruits are eaten fresh.

Kohautia gracilis (Wallich) de Candolle

Hedyotis gracilis Wallich, *Oldenlandia gracilis* (Wallich) Hooker fil.
Hedyotis fusca Buchanan-Hamilton ex D. Don
Hedyotis stricta Wallich
NEPALI *majithe jhar*

Rubiaceae. Erect herb. Leaves stalked, 2–5 cm long, linear, acuminate, glabrous. Flowers brownish, April–August. Propagated by seeds. Distributed in western and central Nepal to about 1500 m in open, sunny places; also in India.

MEDICINE. Juice of the root is given to treat fever and indigestion.

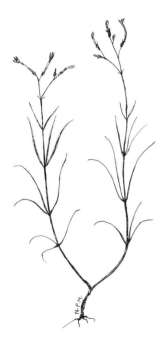

Kohautia gracilis

Kydia calycina Roxburgh

NEPALI *pulia*

Malvaceae. Medium-sized deciduous tree, bark gray, exfoliating in long strips. Leaves stalked, nearly rounded, base cordate, with scattered hairs above, downy and pale beneath. Flowers white in much branched axillary or terminal panicles. Fruit a capsule, subglobose. Flowers July–October, fruits December–February. Propagated by seeds. Distributed throughout Nepal to about 900 m in open places around villages; also in India, Bhutan, southeastern China, Myanmar, and Thailand.

OTHER USES. The plant is lopped for fodder. Bark of the stem is used for binding bundles of sticks in the forest.

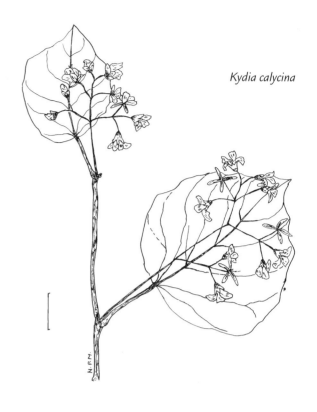

Kydia calycina

L

Lablab purpureus (Linnaeus) Sweet

Dolichos purpureus Linnaeus
Dolichos lablab Linnaeus
Lablab niger Medikus
CHEPANG *rinchhai* ENGLISH *bonavist bean, hyacinth bean, lablab bean* NEPALI *hiunde simi, simi* NEWARI *khocha simi*

Leguminosae. Twining herb. Leaves stalked, trifoliolate, leaflets broadly ovate, acuminate, entire. Flowers white or purple. Fruit a pod, flat, green or greenish brown, incurved with the remains of the persistent style. Propagated by seeds. Distributed throughout Nepal to about 2500 m, cultivated; also in most tropical, subtropical, and temperate regions.

FOOD. Pods and seeds are cooked as a vegetable.
MEDICINE. Seeds are febrifuge, stomachic, and antiseptic.
OTHER USES. The plant is used for fodder.

Lactuca graciliflora de Candolle

Lactuca rostrata (Blume) Kuntze
Prenanthes graciliflora Wallich
NEPALI *phule jhar* TAMANG *lhasmin*

Compositae. Leafy herb. Basal leaves pinnatifid, terminal lobe hastate, acuminate, irregularly dentate, upper

Lablab purpureus

Lagenaria siceraria (Molina) Standley

Cucurbita siceraria Molina
Cucurbita lagenaria Linnaeus
Cucurbita leucantha Duchesne, *Lagenaria leucantha* (Duchesne)
    Rusby
Lagenaria vulgaris Seringe

BHOJPURI *lauki* CHEPANG *dum* ENGLISH *bottle gourd,*
calabash cucumber LEPCHA *jomatapheng* LIMBU *tembephutra*
MAGAR *lauka* NEPALI *lauka* NEWARI *lauka* RAI *wachekalasi*
SUNWAR *lauka* TAMANG *lauka* THARU *lauka* TIBETAN *ka-bed*

Curcurbitaceae. Scandent herb with bifid tendrils.
Leaves stalked, three- or five-lobed, softly pubescent. Flowers large, white. Fruit variable in size and shape, usually
dumbbell shaped. Flowers and fruits during the rainy season, July–September. Propagated by seeds. Distributed
throughout Nepal to about 2200 m, cultivated; also in
tropical Asia and Africa.

FOOD. Fruit is cooked as a vegetable.

MEDICINE. Pulp of the fruit is emetic and purgative. Juice
of the fruit is given in cases of stomach acidity, indigestion, and ulcers.

Lactuca graciliflora

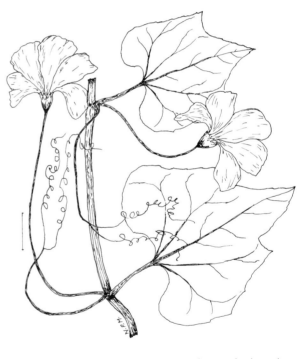

Lagenaria siceraria

Lagerstroemia indica Linnaeus

ENGLISH *crepe myrtle* NEPALI *asare phul* NEWARI *sinajya swan*

Lythraceae. Deciduous shrub. Leaves stalked, 2.5–5 cm
long, oblong, glabrous. Flowers pink, purple, or white.
Fruit a capsule. Flowers and fruits March–September.
Propagated by cuttings. Distributed throughout Nepal to
about 1500 m, planted in gardens and lawns.

MEDICINE. A paste of the flower is applied to cuts and
wounds.

leaves ovate. Flower heads purple in large drooping panicles. Fruit an achene, narrowly oblong. Propagated by
seeds. Distributed throughout Nepal at 2000–3700 m in
wet places of the forest; also in northern India, Bhutan,
Tibet, western China, and Myanmar.

MEDICINE. Juice of the plant is dripped in the eye to treat
inflammation of the eye.

OTHER USES. Women of the village like to put a bunch of the flowers on their heads as decoration.

Lagerstroemia parviflora Roxburgh

Fatioa napaulensis de Candolle, *Lagerstroemia parviflora* subsp. *napaulensis* (de Candolle) Koehne

CHEPANG *chyansi, sis, sindhal*   DANUWAR *banjhi*
ENGLISH *crepe myrtle*   MAGAR *guguri, mibhajharek*   MAJHI *siddhe*
NEPALI *bahidaro, budho dhayaro, dhauti, hade, manjhi, rukh dhayaro*
TAMANG *jhangal, jangathan, phili*   THARU *asith*

Lythraceae. Large deciduous tree with smooth, ash-colored bark. Leaves stalked, oblong, acute, leathery, glabrous above, glaucous and reticulate beneath. Flowers white, fragrant, axillary, in terminal panicles. Fruit a capsule, ovoid. Flowers May–July, fruits July–August. Propagated by seeds or cuttings. Distributed throughout Nepal to about 1300 m, common in *Shorea robusta* forest; also in India, Bhutan, and Myanmar.

MEDICINE. Leaves are boiled, and the filtered water, about 3 teaspoons twice a day, is given for fever.

OTHER USES. Wood is used to make agricultural implements and for construction. Bark and leaves are used for tannin and dye. Leaves are fed to goats.

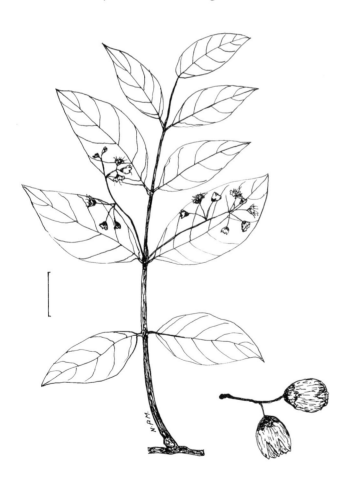

Lagerstroemia parviflora

Laggera alata (D. Don) Schultz Bipontinus ex Oliver

Erigeron alatum D. Don, *Blumea alata* (D. Don) de Candolle, *Conyza alata* (D. Don) Roxburgh
Conyza cernua Wallich

NEPALI *manange jhar*

Compositae. Herb about 1 m high, stem robust, winged. Leaves sessile, oblong, acuminate, serrate, base decurrent. Flower heads purple in axillary racemes. Fruit an achene, hairy, the pappus white. Flowers October–November. Propagated by seeds. Distributed throughout Nepal at 800–2500 m; also in India, Bhutan, China, Indo-China, Java, the Philippines, and Africa.

MEDICINE. Juice of the plant is ingested or applied to the back and chest for cough and colds. A paste of the root is applied to boils.

Laggera alata

Lannea coromandelica (Houttuyn) Merrill

DANUWAR *jingar*   NEPALI *dabadabe, halalunde*   TAMANG *bhel dhap*

Anacardiaceae. Medium-sized deciduous tree. Leaves stalked, odd-pinnate, leaflets 5–11, 6–15 cm long, 3–8 cm wide, ovate to oblong, acuminate, entire, pubescent when young, glabrous at maturity. Flowers greenish yellow, crowded in cymes, appearing when the tree is leafless. Fruit a drupe, ovoid, succulent. Flowers March–April, fruits May–July. Propagated by seeds. Distributed throughout Nepal at 100–1400 m in moist, open places; also in India, Sri Lanka, and Southeast Asia.

MEDICINE. Juice of the bark and leaf is given for ulcers.

OTHER USES. The plant is used for fodder. Bark yields tannin.

Lannea coromandelica

Lantana camara

Lantana camara Linnaeus

ENGLISH *English sage bush, red sage bush, wild sage, yellow sage*
NEPALI *masino kanda, sitaji phul* TAMANG *polung, thangbua*

Verbenaceae. Straggling shrub about 2 m high with re-curved spines on the branches. Leaves stalked, opposite, 1.5–8.5 cm long, 0.8–6 cm wide, ovate to oblong, acuminate, serrate, somewhat roughly textured on both surfaces, base more or less cordate. Flowers stalked, orange, crimson, and purple. Fruit a drupe, black when ripe, one-seeded. Flowers and fruits most of the year. Propagated by seeds. Distributed throughout Nepal to about 1500 m, in moist areas and on uncultivated land, also planted as a hedge; also in India, Myanmar, China, Southeast Asia, and the Philippines.

FOOD. Children eat the ripe black fruits.

MEDICINE. A decoction of the plant is used in cases of rheumatism. About 2 teaspoons of juice of the plant is given three times a day to treat malarial fever. A decoction of the root is used for influenza, cough, and mumps. Juice of the leaves is used as an external wash for eczema. A paste of the leaves is applied for sprains. Flowers are diaphoretic and stimulant, and an infusion of them is used for cough, colds, fever, and jaundice.

OTHER USES. The plant is grown as a hedge. The stems contain tannin. Leaves are believed to be poisonous to cattle.

Larix griffithiana Carrière

Abies griffithiana Hooker fil., *Pinus griffithiana* (Hooker fil.) Voss
Larix griffithii Hooker fil. & Thomson, *Pinus griffithii* (Hooker fil. & Thomson) Parlatore

ENGLISH *east Himalayan larch* NEPALI *talis patra*

Pinaceae. Coniferous tree about 20 m high. Bark thick, brown. Leaves 25–40 mm long, 0.7 mm wide, pale green,

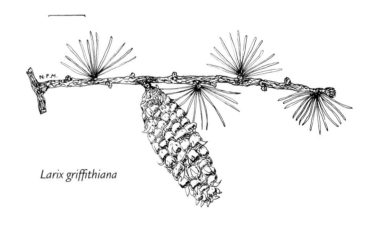

Larix griffithiana

subacute, margin revolute, in clusters of 30–50 on short lateral shoots. Cones erect, cylindrical, yellowish. Seeds ovoid, the wing broadly ovate. Cones May–June. Propagated by seeds. Distributed in eastern and central Nepal at 1400–3900 m on cool and northern slopes; also in northeastern India, Bhutan, and southeastern China.

OTHER USES. Wood is valued as timber and fuelwood.

Lathyrus aphaca Linnaeus

ENGLISH *grass pea, wild pea, yellow vetchling*
NEPALI *akare, jangali matar, pitpir*

Leguminosae. Trailing annual herb. Stipules in pairs, leaf-like, appressed to the stem, truncate, hastate, rachis ending in a tendril, leaflets none. Flowers yellow, solitary. Fruit a pod, linear oblong. Flowers and fruits February–May. Propagated by seeds. Distributed throughout Nepal to about 1300 m; also in western Asia, Afghanistan, Pakistan, India, Bhutan, Bangladesh, Myanmar, Thailand, Europe, and North Africa.

OTHER USES. The plant is used as cattle fodder.

Lathyrus aphaca

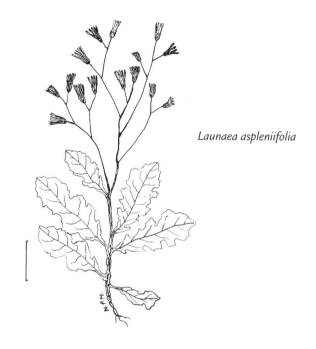

Launaea aspleniifolia

Lathyrus sativus Linnaeus

ENGLISH *chickling vetch, grass pea* NEPALI *khesari*

Leguminosae. Annual herb with winged stem. Leaves stalked, trifoliolate, leaflets short-stalked, 2–5.5 cm long, entire, tendrils branching. Flowers blue or reddish purple. Fruit a pod, flat. Flowers and fruits February–April. Propagated by seeds. Distributed throughout Nepal to about 1100 m in open, moist fields; also cultivated in the eastern hemisphere.

FOOD. Seeds are eaten.

OTHER USES. The plant provides fodder.

Launaea aspleniifolia (Willdenow) Hooker fil.

Prenanthes aspleniifolia Willdenow, *Microrhynchus asplenifolius* (Willdenow) de Candolle

CHEPANG *naki jhar* NEPALI *dudhe jhar* TAMANG *bel dhap*

Compositae. Perennial herb about 40 cm high. Basal leaves sinuately lobed or pinnatifid. Flower heads yellow. Fruit an achene, angled, ribbed. Flowers and fruits October–February. Propagated by seeds. Distributed in eastern and central Nepal to about 1500 m, frequently in open places; also in India, Bhutan, and Myanmar.

FOOD. Tender leaves and shoots are cooked as a vegetable.

MEDICINE. A paste of the plant is applied to treat itching. The milky latex is applied to boils.

Launaea secunda (C. B. Clarke) Hooker fil.

Microrhynchus secunda C. B. Clarke

NEPALI *chaule jhar, mula pate*

Compositae. Glabrous herb. Leaves all basal, runcinate or lyrate, lobes irregularly dentate. Flower heads yellow in small clusters. Fruit an achene, oblong, truncate. Flowers and fruits October–November. Propagated by seeds. Distributed in western and central Nepal at 500–3400 m in moist places; also in Afghanistan, Pakistan, and India.

FOOD. Tender shoots and leaves are cooked as a vegetable.

MEDICINE. Juice of the plant, about 4 teaspoons four times a day, is given in cases of fever and dysuria.

Lawsonia inermis Linnaeus

Lawsonia alba Lamarck

BHOJPURI *mehandi* DANUWAR *mehandi* ENGLISH *camphire, Egyptian privet, henna plant, mignonette tree* GURUNG *tiure* LIMBU *palphung* MAGAR *tihure* MOOSHAR *mehandi* NEPALI *mehandi, tyure* NEWARI *laincha* RAI *tanbalaksun* SUNWAR *tyuri* TAMANG *tiuri* THARU *mehandi* TIBETAN *bri-mog*

Lythraceae. Shrub with thin grayish brown bark, branchlets sometimes spiny. Leaves short-stalked, opposite, elliptic, acute at both ends, entire, leathery. Flowers greenish white, fragrant, in large, cymously branched, terminal panicles. Fruit a capsule, globose, one-celled. Flowers and fruits most of the year. Propagated by cuttings or by seeds. Distributed throughout Nepal to about 600 m in open places; also in Pakistan, India, and central Asia.

MEDICINE. Bark of the stem is chewed and kept between the teeth about 25 minutes to treat toothaches. Juice of the leaves is applied to wounds between the toes caused by prolonged walking barefooted in muddy water. A paste of the

Lawsonia inermis

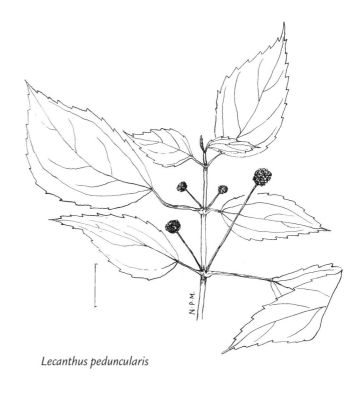

Lecanthus peduncularis

leaves is applied to itches and other skin diseases. Leaves are pounded with mustard oil and applied to burns.

OTHER USES. The plant is grown as a hedge. Leaves are used to dye hands and feet.

Lecanthus peduncularis (Wallich ex Royle) Weddell

Procris peduncularis Wallich ex Royle
Procris obtusa Royle, *Lecanthus obtusus* (Royle) Handel-Mazzetti
Elatostema ovatum Wight
Lecanthus wallichii Willdenow
Lecanthus wightii Willdenow

DANUWAR *tili* GURUNG *baulacha, gaulat, til* NEPALI *gakaleti, ganthe golia, goliko, khole jhar, khole sag* TAMANG *tilo*

Urticaceae. Weak herb. Leaves stalked, opposite, 1.8–1.5 cm long, 1–6 cm wide, elliptic to ovate, acuminate, coarsely dentate, glabrous. Flowers greenish on a long stalk, axillary, the receptacle saucer shaped. Flowers and fruits July–November. Propagated by seeds or root offshoots. Distributed throughout Nepal at 1200–3000 m, common in wet, shady places; also in India, western and central China, Taiwan, Indo-China, and Java.

FOOD. Tender portions are eaten as a vegetable.

MEDICINE. The root is ground and applied to sprains. The plant is mixed with bark of *Saurauia napaulensis* in equal amount and is pounded; the resultant juice, about 4 teaspoons three times a day, is given to relieve fever.

OTHER USES. The plant is fed to cattle as a galactagogue.

Leea crispa van Royen ex Linnaeus

Leea aspera Edgeworth
Leea edgeworthii Santapau

CHEPANG *dhakkar* NEPALI *galena, harva, lahasune, ranabas*

Leeaceae. Erect shrub about 1 m high. Leaves stalked, bipinnate, upper leaves with five to seven leaflets, 7.5–20 cm long, long acuminate, elliptic to oblong, serrate. Flowers white with yellow tinge in subterminal corymbose cymes. Fruit a berry, greenish. Flowers July–August, fruits August–October. Propagated by seeds. Distributed throughout Nepal at 400–1500 m on open hillsides; also in India, Bhutan, Bangladesh, China, Myanmar, Thailand, and Cambodia.

FOOD. Ripe fruits are edible.

MEDICINE. Juice of the leaves is applied to wounds.

Leea macrophylla Roxburgh ex Hornemann

Leea aspera Wallich ex Roxburgh
Leea robusta Roxburgh
Leea diffusa Lawson

CHEPANG *dhakkar* LEPCHA *pantom* NEPALI *bhuin charchare, galagala, galena, lahasune* TAMANG *mlamran*

Leeaceae. Shrub about 2.5 m high. Leaves stalked, pinnate, leaflets stalked, 5–20.5 cm long, 2–8.5 cm wide, elliptic to oblong, pointed, serrate, glabrous above, slightly hairy on the veins beneath, base rounded. Flowers white. Fruit globose. Flowers June–July, fruits August–December. Propagated by seeds. Distributed in central and eastern Nepal at 300–1700 m in moist, shady places; also in India, Bhutan, and Indo-China.

FOOD. Ripe fruits are eaten fresh.

MEDICINE. A paste of the root is applied to snakebites. Juice of the root is used for ringworm. A paste of the leaf is applied to cuts and wounds.

Leea macrophylla

Leersia hexandra Swartz

NEPALI *karante jhar*

Gramineae. Perennial grass, culms decumbent at the base, rooting at the nodes. Leaf spatulate, linear, blades curling when dry. Inflorescence yellowish. Flowers and fruits September–November. Propagated by seeds. Distributed in eastern Nepal to about 300 m in moist parts of rice fields; also in the tropics.

MEDICINE. Juice of the plant is applied to boils and pimples.

Lens culinaris Medikus

Ervum lens Linnaeus, *Cicer lens* (Linnaeus) Willdenow
Lens esculenta Moench

BHOJPURI *masur* CHEPANG *musuro* DANUWAR *musuro*
ENGLISH *lens seed, lentil* LEPCHA *dalhari, kalhahir* LIMBU *hekkari*
MAGAR *masuro* MOOSHAR *musar* NEPALI *masuro* NEWARI *musu*
RAI *mututchya* SUNWAR *mosor* TAMANG *musuri masye*
THARU *masari*

Leguminosae. Pubescent erect herb about 40 cm high. Leaves stalked, even-pinnate, leaflets 8–12, linear oblong, rachis ending in a short tendril. Flowers bluish white in axillary racemes. Fruit a pod, oblong rhombic. Seeds black or gray. Flowers February–March, fruits March–April. Propagated by seeds. Distributed throughout Nepal to about 1000 m, cultivated.

FOOD. Seeds are used for lentil soup (*daal* in Nepali).

OTHER USES. Straw of the plant is much valued as fodder.

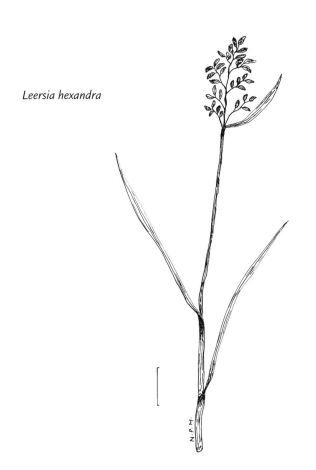

Leersia hexandra

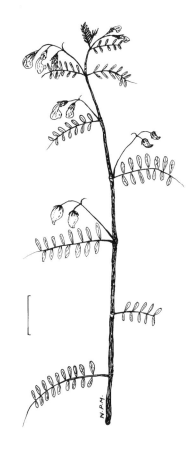

Lens culinaris

Leonurus cardiaca Linnaeus

ENGLISH *common motherwort* NEPALI *kalo miri*

Labiatae. Erect herb about 1 m high. Leaves stalked, 4–8 cm long, 2–5.5 cm wide, ovate to lanceolate, lower leaves irregularly cut into several dentate lobes, upper leaves narrow, lobed. Flowers pink or white, crowded in axillary whorls, July–September. Propagated by seeds. Distributed in western and central Nepal at 2000–2900 m in open, rocky places; also in northwestern Asia and Europe.

MEDICINE. Juice of the plant is diaphoretic and stomachic. Pounded leaf is applied to wounds between the toes caused by prolonged walking barefooted in muddy water.

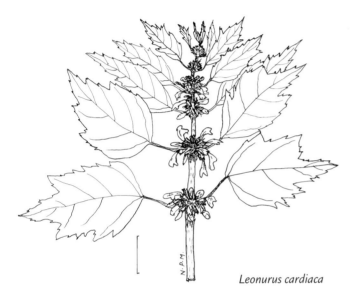

Leonurus cardiaca

Lepidagathis incurva Buchanan-Hamilton ex D. Don

Lepidagathis semiherbacea Nees
Reullia dependens Roxburgh

NEPALI *kande, seto phuli*

Acanthaceae. Perennial herb about 50 cm high. Leaves minutely viscid pubescent, lower leaves ovate, upper leaves narrower. Flowers white or pinkish, in dense spikes forming terminal heads. Fruit a capsule. Flowers January–April, fruits April–May. Propagated by seeds. Distributed throughout Nepal at 200–1400 m in moist, shady places; also in Pakistan, India, Bhutan, eastward to southern China, Myanmar, Malaysia, and the Philippines.

MEDICINE. A paste of leaf buds is applied to cuts and wounds.

Lepidium sativum Linnaeus

BHOJPURI *chamsur* DANUWAR *chansur* ENGLISH *garden cress* LEPCHA *sumari* LIMBU *nodi* MAGAR *chansur* NEPALI *chamsur* NEWARI *chasu* RAI *sichanphun* SUNWAR *chamasur* TAMANG *chamsur dhap* THARU *chansur*

Cruciferae. Erect herb. Basal leaves long-stalked, entire or pinnatifid, cauline leaves sessile, entire, ovate or oblong.

Flowers white. Fruit a pod, ovate or oblong, deeply notched. Flowers and fruits February–April. Propagated by seeds. Distributed throughout Nepal at 200–3000 m in moist places, cultivated.

FOOD. Tender foliage is cooked as a vegetable.

Lepidagathis incurva

Lepidium sativum

Leptodermis lanceolata Wallich

Hamiltonia fruticosa D. Don
NEPALI *bakhre biri, ghure, guhya bir, gunaune* TAMANG *rumsing*
TIBETAN *maru*

Rubiaceae. Erect deciduous shrub about 3 m high, bark smooth, pale brown, with scattered lenticels. Leaves ovate to lanceolate, acuminate, variable in size, somewhat roughly textured on both surfaces with short stiff hairs, base narrowed. Flowers sessile, bluish. Fruit a capsule, subcylindrical. Seeds with loose fibrous covering. Flowers June–October, fruits November–January. Propagated by seeds. Distributed throughout Nepal at 1000–3000 m, common on open uncultivated land; also in India and Bhutan.

MEDICINE. Juice of the plant is used on cuts and wounds.

OTHER USES. The plant is browsed by animals, especially goats. A powder of leaves and flowers is used for incense.

Lespedeza juncea

Leptodermis lanceolata

Leucaena leucocephala (Lamarck) de Wit

Mimosa leucocephala Lamarck
Mimosa glauca Linnaeus, *Acacia glauca* (Linnaeus) Bentham
Mimosa latisiliqua Linnaeus, *Leucaena latisiliqua* (Linnaeus) Gillis
ENGLISH *coffee bush* NEPALI *epil*

Leguminosae. Tree about 6 m high. Leaves stalked, evenly bipinnate, pinnae 8–16, pinnules in 10–15 pairs, linear oblong, dark or dull green above, glaucous beneath.

Lespedeza juncea (Linnaeus fil.) Persoon

Hedysarum junceum Linnaeus fil.
NEPALI *bhainsaino*

Leguminosae. Rigid subshrub about 60 cm high. Leaves stalked, trifoliolate, leaflets subsessile, 1–1.8 cm long, 0.2–0.5 cm wide, cuneate, linear, glabrous above, silky beneath, apex truncate. Flowers white-purple, axillary. Fruit a pod, suborbicular, thinly silky, one-seeded. Flowers August–October, fruits October–November. Propagated by seeds. Distributed in western and central Nepal at 1000–2000 m, common in open places; also in Afghanistan, India, China, Korea, eastern Siberia, Japan, northern Myanmar, and northern Australia.

MEDICINE. Juice of the root is given to treat diarrhea and dysentery.

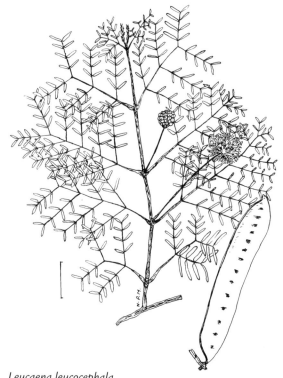

Leucaena leucocephala

Flowers white in axillary or terminal pairs. Fruit a pod, thin, flat, strap shaped. Seeds 15–25, elliptic, compressed, shiny brown. Flowers June–August. Propagated by seeds. Distributed in central and western Nepal to about 1400 m in open places; also in India and the Philippines.

FOOD. Tender pods and shoots are cooked as a vegetable. A powder of roasted seeds is used as a substitute for coffee, and the powder is also pickled, adding salt and spices.

MEDICINE. A decoction of bark and root is abortifacient. Roasted seeds are emollient.

OTHER USES. Bark is a source of brown dye. Foliage provides fodder.

Leucas cephalotes (Roth) Sprengel

Phlomis cephalotes Roth
Leucas capitata Desfontaines
CHEPANG *talang tolo* DANUWAR *julphi* ENGLISH *spiderwort* MAJHI *phoke jhar, tauke jahar* MOOSHAR *guma* NEPALI *kanthe jhar, rudraghanti, tauke jhar* THARU *gum*

Labiatae. Erect herb about 50 cm high. Leaves short-stalked, 2.5–10 cm long, 0.8–3.5 cm wide, ovate to lanceolate, acute, serrate, hairy on both surfaces. Flowers white in globose whorls. Flowers and fruits July–November. Propagated by seeds. Distributed throughout Nepal to about 2400 m in open places; also in Afghanistan, Pakistan, India, and Bhutan.

FOOD. Tender leaves and shoots are cooked as a vegetable.

MEDICINE. The plant is boiled in water about 15 minutes, filtered, and the liquid, about 4 teaspoons three times a day, is given for malarial fever. A paste of the plant is boiled with mustard oil and applied to boils. Juice of the plant is given in cases of urinary complaint. Dried inflorescences are smoked, and the smoke is expelled through the nose to treat nosebleed.

Leucas cephalotes

Leucas indica (Linnaeus) R. Brown ex Vatke

Leonurus indicus Linnaeus
Leucas lavandulifolia Smith
Phlomis linifolia Roth, *Leucas linifolia* (Roth) Sprengel
DANUWAR *julphi jhar*

Labiatae. Herb about 35 m high. Leaves short-stalked, 1.3–5.5 cm long, 0.2–1.4 cm wide, linear, acute, slightly dentate, narrowed toward the base. Flowers white in condensed heads. Flowers and fruits January–June. Propagated by seeds. Distributed in eastern and central Nepal to about 1000 m in open places; also in India, Bhutan, Bangladesh, Malaysia, and Mauritius.

MEDICINE. Juice of the plant, about 3 teaspoons twice a day, is given in cases of malarial fever. A paste of the plant is applied to fresh cuts and wounds.

Leucas mollissima Wallich ex Bentham

MAJHI *sano bhattu* NEPALI *dhusure khar, jhunke ghans* TAMANG *chilimran*

Labiatae. Straggling herb about 1.5 m high. Leaves stalked, 1.3–7 cm long, 0.4–2.5 cm wide, ovate to lanceolate, acute, serrate. Flowers white, July–August. Fruits August–September. Propagated by seeds. Distributed throughout Nepal at 500–2400 m, frequent in moist, shady places; also in northern India, Bhutan, Sri Lanka, China, and Myanmar.

MEDICINE. A paste of the flower heads, about 3 teaspoons twice a day, is given to alleviate fever.

Leucas plukenetii (Roth) Sprengel

Phlomis plukenetii Roth
Leucas aspera Link
NEPALI *gumpate*

Labiatae. Hispid annual herb about 60 cm high. Leaves short-stalked, 2.5–8 cm long, linear or oblong to lanceolate, obtuse, entire or obscurely crenate, pubescent on both surfaces, base narrow. Flowers white. Fruit a nutlet, smooth, brown. Flowers and fruits June–July. Propagated by seeds. Distributed in central Nepal to about 1000 m in open places; also in Pakistan, India, Bangladesh, Southeast Asia, and Mauritius.

MEDICINE. Juice of the plant is given in cases of fever, cough, and colds.

Leucosceptrum canum Smith

Clerodendrum leucosceptrum D. Don
Comanthosphace nepalensis Kitamura & Murata
Teucrium macrostachyum Wallich ex Bentham
CHEPANG *syogatong* GURUNG *naurusa* NEPALI *bhusure, dhusre* TAMANG *badarsing, mechchhen, phosyang, torbo*

Labiatae. Tree about 5 m high. Leaves stalked, 9–25 cm long, 2.5–12 cm wide, elliptic to lanceolate, acuminate, serrulate, glabrous above, densely silvery tomentose beneath. Flowers white or light pink, whorled, in dense terminal spikes, June–September. Fruits November–February. Propagated by seeds. Distributed throughout Nepal at 1000–2800 m in open places; also in northern India, Bhutan, southwestern China, and Myanmar.

FOOD. Ripe fruits are eaten by village children.

OTHER USES. The plant is not a good fodder and is collected only when other fodder species are scanty.

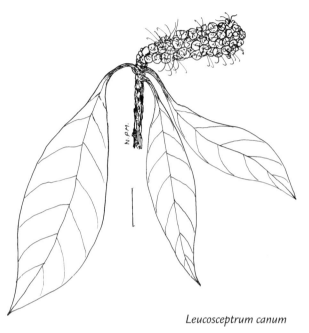

Leucosceptrum canum

Leucostegia immersa

Leucostegia immersa (Wallich ex Hooker) K. Presl

NEPALI *chamsure unyu*

Davalliaceae. Herbaceous fern. Fronds yellowish, 30–40 cm long, 10–20 cm wide, multipinnatifid. Sori brown, on each of the ultimate segments. Propagated by spores or by splitting the rhizomes. Distributed in eastern and central Nepal at 1200–2900 m in moist rock crevices or on mossy tree trunks and branches; also in India, southwestern China, Taiwan, Indo-China, New Guinea, and the Philippines.

MEDICINE. A paste of the rhizome is applied to boils.

Ligularia amplexicaulis de Candolle

Senecio amplexicaulis Wallich
Ligularia corymbosa de Candolle
NEPALI *bijauri, nangreu*

Compositae. Tall robust herb. Lower leaves stalked, upper leaves sessile with broad sheathing wings, orbiculate or reniform to cordate, irregularly dentate. Flowers heads yellow in corymbose racemes. Fruit an achene. Propagated by seeds. Distributed throughout Nepal at 2700–3600 m on moist, rocky slopes, generally beside streams; also in northern India and Bhutan.

MEDICINE. Pounded root is applied to treat dislocated bone. It is also used in cases of sprain.

Ligularia fischeri (Ledebour) Turczaninow

Cineraria fischeri Ledebour
Ligularia racemosa de Candolle, *Senecio racemosus* Wallich
Senecio ligularia Hooker fil.
Senecio sibiricus Linnaeus fil.
TAMANG *simaudya*

Compositae. Herb about 1.5 m high. Leaves stalked, 5–23 cm long, 6–30 cm wide, reniform or orbiculate, incised, base cordate. Flower heads yellow. Fruit an achene. Flowers and fruits July–October. Propagated by seeds. Distributed throughout Nepal at 2200–4600 m in moist, open places beside streams; also in northern India, Bhutan, China, Mongolia, Korea, Japan, eastern Siberia, and Myanmar.

FOOD. Tender leaves are cooked as a vegetable.

Ligustrum compactum (Wallich ex de Candolle) Hooker fil. & Thomson ex Brandis

Olea compacta Wallich ex de Candolle
ENGLISH *privet* GURUNG *onili* NEPALI *kanike phul*

Oleaceae. Small tree with gray bark. Leaves stalked, 3–10 cm long, 1–4 cm wide, elliptic to oblong, entire, leathery, shiny above. Flowers subsessile, white, in compound racemes. Fruits numerous, cylindrical, slightly curved. Flowers April–June, fruits November–February. Propagated by seeds or cuttings. Distributed in western and central Nepal at 2000–2300 m in shady places on riverbanks; also in Northern India, Bhutan, and western China.

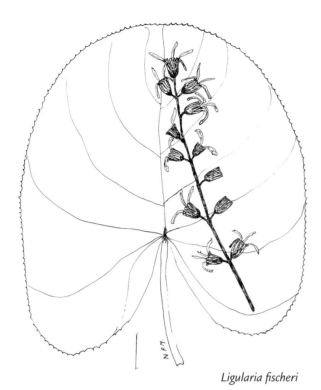

Ligularia fischeri

OTHER USES. The plant is lopped for fodder. Stems are used to make the walls of huts.

Ligustrum confusum Decaisne

Olea robustum Wallich
NEPALI *bardanti, kanike*

Oleaceae. Shrub, twigs with evident lenticels. Leaves stalked, 3–8 cm long, 1.5–3 cm wide, ovate to lanceolate, acuminate, entire, leathery, rounded at the base. Flowers white, fragrant, in terminal panicles. Fruit a berry, ovoid. Flowers April–July, fruits September–October. Propagated by seeds or cuttings. Distributed throughout Nepal at 800–2600 m in open, sunny places; also in northern India, western China, and Indo-China.

MEDICINE. Bark of the stem is chewed and kept between the teeth about 20 minutes to relieve toothaches.

Lilium nepalense D. Don

Lilium ochroleucum Wallich ex Baker
NEPALI *ban lasun, khiraule* THARU *puna*

Liliaceae. Herb about 1.5 m high. Leaves sessile, alternate, opposite, or whorled, 3–12.5 cm long, 1–3 cm wide, lanceolate, acute. Flowers large, creamy yellow with purple dots, drooping, solitary, June–July. Fruits September–October. Propagated by seeds or bulbs. Distributed throughout Nepal at 2200–3400 m in moist places; also in northern India.

FOOD. Boiled bulbs are eaten.
MEDICINE. The bulb is used as a tonic.

Lilium wallichianum Schultes & Schultes fil.

Lilium batisua Buchanan-Hamilton ex D. Don
Lilium japonicum Thunberg
Lilium longiflorum Wallich
CHEPANG *gaibin* NEPALI *tite pidalu*

Liliaceae. Herb about 1.5 m high. Leaves sessile, alternate, 7.5–15 cm long, 0.5–0.8 cm wide, linear, acuminate. Flowers white, fragrant, large, solitary, September–November. Propagated by seeds or bulbs. Distributed in western and central Nepal at 1100–2000 m in moist, shady places; also in northern India.

FOOD. Boiled and roasted bulbs are eaten.

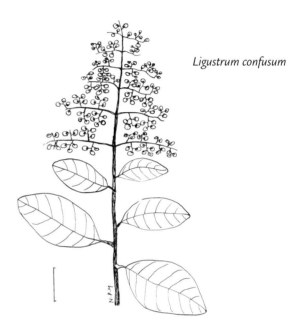

Ligustrum confusum

Lilium nepalense

Lindenbergia grandiflora (Buchanan-Hamilton ex D. Don) Bentham

Stemodia grandiflora Buchanan-Hamilton ex D. Don
CHEPANG *nani bakyo ro, pyuling* NEPALI *bhedi phul, binas, dhurset* TAMANG *luman, nakachchu, punkiya*

Scrophulariaceae. Rambling herb. Leaves stalked, 1.5–13 cm long, 0.8–4.8 cm wide, ovate, acute, coarsely serrate or crenate, pubescent. Flowers yellow in terminal lax spikes, September–March. Propagated by seeds. Distributed throughout Nepal at 700–2400 m in open, moist places; also in India, Bhutan, Tibet, western China, and Myanmar.

MEDICINE. Juice of the leaves is applied to cuts, wounds, and boils.

Lindenbergia grandiflora

Lindenbergia indica (Linnaeus) Vatke

GURUNG *mamui* NEPALI *baghmukhe ghans, ban bawari, binas*

Scrophulariaceae. Diffuse annual herb. Leaves stalked, opposite, 1–5.5 cm long, 0.5–3 cm wide, oblong to lanceolate, crenate to serrate. Flowers yellow, axillary. Fruit a capsule, beaked, slightly exerted from the calyx. Flowers and fruits July–November. Propagated by seeds. Distributed throughout Nepal at 300–2600 m along waysides and on uncultivated land and hillsides; also in Afghanistan, China, and Myanmar.

MEDICINE. Juice of the plant is used to treat cuts, wounds, and chronic bronchitis. This juice is dropped in the ear to remove pus blocked inside. The juice, mixed in equal amount with juice of the rhizome of turmeric (*Curcuma domestica*), is applied to skin eruptions.

Lindera neesiana (Wallich ex Nees) Kurz

Tetranthera neesiana Wallich, *Benzoin neesianum* Wallich ex Nees, *Aperula neesiana* (Wallich ex Nees) Blume
GURUNG *katu, kutung, siltimuri* NEPALI *siltimur* TAMANG *kutumb*

Lauraceae. Tree about 4 m high. Leaves stalked, 2.5–19 cm long, 1.5–9 cm wide, ovate, glabrous. Flowers yellow. Fruit globose. Flowers October–November, fruits March–June. Propagated by seeds. Distributed in central and eastern Nepal at 700–2600 m in openings along ravines in forests; also in northeastern India, Bhutan, and Myanmar.

MEDICINE. Fruits are chewed in cases of diarrhea, toothache, nausea, and flatulence and are also given to cattle if they eat poisonous plants. Oil from the seed is applied for boils and scabies.

Lindera pulcherrima (Nees) Bentham ex Hooker fil.

Daphnidium pulcherrima Nees, *Tetranthera pulcherrima* Wallich
NEPALI *kharane, kirkito, phusuro, pipiri, serga, sisi* SHERPA *ping tak tak* TAMANG *pibil, piwi* TIBETAN *pipi*

Lauraceae. Tree about 7 m high. Leaves stalked, 6–17 cm long, 1.5–5.3 cm wide, elliptic to lanceolate, caudate-acuminate, entire, thinly leathery, finely reticulate and pale beneath. Flowers yellow, crowded, in umbels, March–April. Fruits May–August. Propagated by seeds. Distributed throughout Nepal at 1400–2700 m on open slopes in mixed oak forest; also in southwestern China.

OTHER USES. The plant is used as fodder and collected for animal bedding. Wood is used for fuel.

Lindernia nummularifolia (D. Don) Wettstein

NEPALI *kankre jhar, pitmare jhar*

Scrophulariaceae. Herb about 8 cm high. Leaves subsessile, opposite, suborbiculate or ovate, serrate. Flowers pinkish, axillary. Fruit a capsule, ellipsoidal. Flowers and fruits August–November. Propagated by seeds. Distributed throughout Nepal at 1000–2900 m in moist places on hillsides; also in India and Myanmar.

MEDICINE. Juice of the plant is given in cases of fever.

Linum usitatissimum Linnaeus

BHOJPURI *aalas* CHEPANG *aalas* DANUWAR *aalas* ENGLISH *flax seed, linseed* LEPCHA *tisinam* LIMBU *thange* MAGAR *aalas* MOOSHAR *tisi* NEPALI *alsi* NEWARI *tisi* RAI *aakawa yob* SUNWAR *ankejil guib* THARU *arasi*

Linaceae. Erect annual herb. Leaves short-stalked, linear lanceolate, entire. Flowers blue. Fruit a capsule, spherical, five-celled. Flowers and fruits January–March. Propagated by seeds. Distributed throughout Nepal to about 1000 m, cultivated; also in Pakistan, India, and Tibet.

MEDICINE. Juice of the plant is applied to fresh wounds. A paste of the seed is applied to boils remove pus and for quick relief.

OTHER USES. Bark of the plant yields flax fiber and linen. Oil extracted from the seed is used for various domestic purposes.

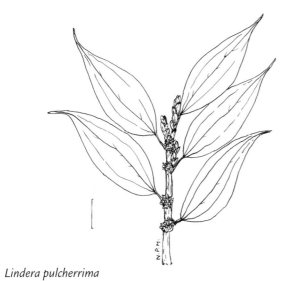

Lindera pulcherrima

Lindernia nummularifolia

Litchi chinensis Sonnerat

ENGLISH *litchi* MOOSHAR *luchi* NEPALI *lichi* NEWARI *lichi*

Sapindaceae. Evergreen tree with grayish brown bark. Leaves stalked, alternate, leaflets in two or three pairs, 5–16 cm long, 2.5–4 cm wide, oblong to elliptic or lanceolate, acuminate, leathery, shiny above. Flowers yellowish in terminal panicles. Fruit globose, covered with pointed tubercles, red when ripe. Flowers April–May, fruits May–June. Propagated by seeds. Distributed throughout Nepal to about 1200 m, cultivated; also in India, Bangladesh, China, Myanmar, Thailand, and the Americas.

FOOD. The aril of the fruit is edible.

Lithocarpus elegans (Blume) Hatusima ex Soepadmo

Quercus elegans Blume, *Lithocarpus spicata* var. *elegans* (Blume) A. Camus
Quercus grandifolia D. Don
Quercus spicata Smith
Quercus squamata Roxburgh

NEPALI *arkhaulo* TAMANG *botdung*

Fagaceae. Tree about 16 m high. Leaves stalked, 8–35 cm long, 3–10 cm wide, elliptic to lanceolate, acuminate, leathery, base cuneate or rounded. Flowers yellowish in clusters. Fruit an acorn. Flowers May–July. Propagated by seeds. Distributed throughout Nepal at 1400–2000 m in forests on hillsides; also in India, Bhutan, southern China, and Southeast Asia.

FOOD. Bears like the seeds; roasted seeds are edible by people.

MEDICINE. Oil from the seed is applied to treat scabies.

OTHER USES. The plant is lopped for fodder.

Lithocarpus elegans

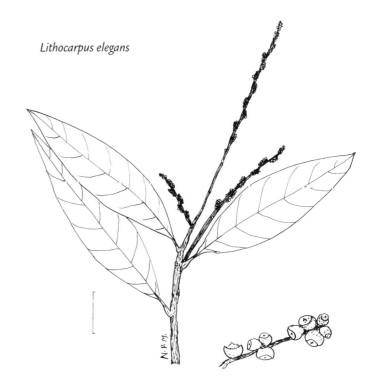

Linum usitatissimum

Lithocarpus pachyphylla (Kurz) Rehder

Quercus pachyphylla Kurz
NEPALI *sungure katus*

Fagaceae. Tree. Leaves stalked, 9–5 cm long, 2–5 cm wide, elliptic to lanceolate, long-pointed, entire, glabrous above, with stellate hairs on midrib and veins beneath. Fruit an acorn. Flowers May–June. Propagated by seeds. Distributed in eastern Nepal at 2100–2800 m on moist hillsides; also in northeastern India and Myanmar.

MEDICINE. Bark is astringent.

OTHER USES. The plant is lopped for fodder.

Litsea doshia (Buchanan-Hamilton ex D. Don) Kostermans

Tetranthera doshia Buchanan-Hamilton ex D. Don
Tetranthera oblonga Wallich ex Nees, *Litsea oblonga* (Wallich ex Nees) Hooker fil.
CHEPANG *rimchi* GURUNG *jhankri chhe* NEPALI *jhankre, kathe kaula, paheli, patake* TAMANG *humjing, using*

Lauraceae. Evergreen tree. Leaves stalked, 10–18 cm long, elliptic or oblong to lanceolate, leathery, shiny above, glaucous beneath. Flowers yellowish in an axillary cluster of three to six flowers. Fruit cylindrical, dark purple when ripe. Flowers October–November. Propagated by seeds. Distributed throughout Nepal at 1300–2700 m on open hillsides; also in northern India and Myanmar.

OTHER USES. The plant provides fodder.

Litsea monopetala (Roxburgh) Persoon

Tetranthera monopetala Roxburgh
Litsea polyantha Jussieu
Tetranthera macrophylla Roxburgh
Tetranthera quadriflora Roxburgh
CHEPANG *puchhi* GURUNG *kuturke* NEPALI *kutmero, ratomutne* TAMANG *chaput, chhatalhapte, gobarchi*

Lauraceae. Tree about 12 m high. Leaves stalked, alternate, oblong to ovate, tip obtuse or rounded, base acute, rounded, or cordate. Flowers yellow. Fruit black when ripe. Propagated by seeds. Distributed in eastern and central Nepal at 400–2200 m in open places around villages or on private land; also in India, eastern Pakistan, southwestern China, and Myanmar.

OTHER USES. The plant is lopped for fodder.

Litsea sericea (Wallich ex Nees) Hooker fil.

Tetranthera sericea Wallich ex Nees
NEPALI *pahele*

Lauraceae. Medium-sized deciduous tree, young parts with silky hairs. Leaves stalked, 7.5–12.5 cm long, 2–3.7 cm wide, elliptic to lanceolate, acuminate, somewhat leathery, clothed with brown silky tomentum. Flowers yellowish in umbels. Fruit subglobose. Flowers April–May, fruits October–November. Propagated by seeds. Distributed in eastern and central Nepal at 2500–3000 m in open

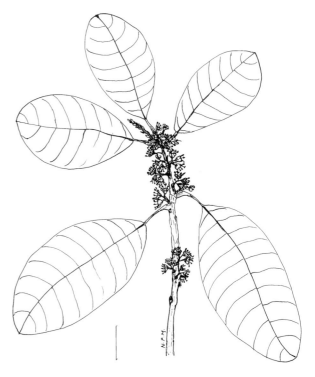

Litsea monopetala

places; also in northern India, Bhutan, western and central China, and Myanmar.

OTHER USES. Leaves are used for fodder.

Lobelia nummularia Lamarck

Pratia nummularia (Lamarck) A. Brown & Ascherson
Lobelia begonifolia Wallich, *Pratia begonifolia* (Wallich) Lindley
NEPALI *boxi ko makai, dhikur ko makai, jale chorto, lal geri, malagiri, nilo ghortapre* TAMANG *maru geda, tili koshyo*

Campanulaceae. Small, creeping herb. Leaves short-stalked, ovate to cordate, dentate. Flowers axillary, purple striped. Fruit a berry, ellipsoidal, black. Flowers August–September. Propagated by seeds. Distributed throughout Nepal at 800–2500 m in moist, shady places; also in India, eastward to China, Myanmar, and Malaysia.

FOOD. Ripe fruits are edible.

MEDICINE. A paste of the plant is applied to treat muscular swellings. A paste of the fruit, about 2 teaspoons three times a day, is taken to treat diarrhea and dysentery. This paste is also applied to cuts and wounds.

Lobelia pyramidalis Wallich

Lobelia nicotianaefolia Roth
Rapuntium wallichianum K. Presl, *Lobelia wallichana* (K. Presl) Hooker fil. & Thomson
GURUNG *ek phale bikh* NEPALI *eklebir* TAMANG *eklebir*

Campanulaceae. Erect herb about 2 m high. Leaves sessile or subsessile, linear lanceolate, acuminate, finely ser-

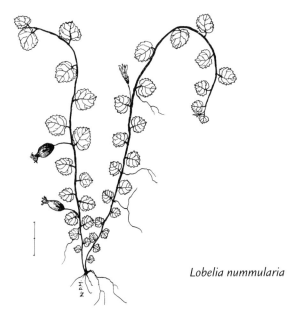

Lobelia nummularia

rate, glabrous above. Flowers stalked, purplish, March–October. Propagated by seeds. Distributed in central and western Nepal at 1100–2300 m in open, moist places; also in northern India and Indo-China.

MEDICINE. The plant is boiled in water about 10 minutes, and the strained water, about 4 teaspoons three times a day, is given to treat fever. The leaf and flower have antispasmodic properties.

Lobelia pyramidalis

Lonicera angustifolia Wallich ex de Candolle
NEPALI *nani kaphal*

Caprifoliaceae. Straggling shrub with smooth gray bark, exfoliating in long papery flakes. Leaves short-stalked, oblong to lanceolate, glabrous beneath. Flowers pinkish in pairs on slender axillary peduncles. Fruit globose, bright ruby. Flowers May–June, fruits July–August. Propagated by seeds. Distributed throughout Nepal at 2600–3800 m in moist, open places; also in northern India and Tibet.

FOOD. Ripe fruits are edible.

OTHER USES. Walking sticks are prepared from stems.

Lonicera angustifolia

Lonicera hypoleuca Decaisne
Lonicera bicolor var. *glabrata* Hara
Lonicera elliptica Royle
THARU *chichi*

Caprifoliaceae. Erect shrub about 2 m high, stems much branched, forming a dense bush. Leaves stalked, broadly ovate, thick, glandular and pubescent on both surfaces, apex obtuse or rounded, base more or less cordate. Flowers stalked, yellow, fragrant, hairy. Fruit a berry, globose, orange-red, glandular hairy. Flowers May–June, fruits August–September. Propagated by seeds. Distributed in central and western Nepal at 3000–4200 m, common among boulders or stones in open places.

FOOD. Ripe fruits are edible.

MEDICINE. A paste of the plant is given in cases of kidney trouble.

Lonicera macarantha (D. Don) Sprengel
Caprifolium macaranthum D. Don
Lonicera japonica Thunberg
Xylosteum scandens Buchanan-Hamilton ex D. Don
NEPALI *ban juhi*

Caprifoliaceae. Twining shrub. Leaves short-stalked, oblong to lanceolate, acuminate, entire, leathery above, villous beneath. Flowers yellow, February–April. Propagated by seeds. Distributed throughout Nepal at 1500–2100 m in shady places; also in India, Bhutan, China, Taiwan, and Myanmar.

FOOD. Ripe fruits are edible.

Loranthus odoratus Wallich

Hyphear odoratum (Wallich) Danser
NEPALI *ainjeru* TAMANG *donglanais*

Loranthaceae. Parasitic shrub. Leaves stalked, subopposite, elliptic to lanceolate, often falcate, fleshy, narrowed toward the base. Flowers yellowish, fragrant, in a fascicled spike. Fruit a berry, ellipsoidal, glabrous. Propagated by seeds. Distributed throughout Nepal 1300–2400 m on branches of trees; also in northern India and Myanmar.

MEDICINE. Fruits are chewed in cases of indigestion.

Lotus corniculatus Linnaeus

Lotus corniculatus var. *minor* Baker
NEPALI *nakhar simbi*

Leguminosae. Perennial herb. Leaves stalked, pinnate, leaflets sessile, ovate or oblong, glabrous. Flowers yellow in axillary umbels. Fruit a pod, cylindrical. Propagated by seeds. Distributed in western and central Nepal at 3000–3700 m in moist, open places; also in central and western Asia, India, Australia, Europe, and Africa.

OTHER USES. The plant provides a nutritious fodder.

Loxogramme involuta (D. Don) Presl

NEPALI *parpare*

Polypodiaceae. Epiphytic fern. Rhizome creeping, clothed with rust-colored lanceolate scales. Frond broad, lanceolate, acuminate, entire, lower part gradually narrowed into a short stipe, leathery. Sori brown, in parallel oblique lines from the midrib to the edge. Propagated by spores. Distributed throughout Nepal to about 3500 m on mossy tree trunks and branches; also in India, Sri Lanka, and Indo-China.

MEDICINE. Juice of the rhizome is used to treat cuts and wounds.

Luculia gratissima (Wallich) Sweet

Cinchona gratissima Wallich
Mussaenda luculia Buchanan-Hamilton ex D. Don

CHEPANG *dukuna* GURUNG *kyonsin* NEPALI *asare phui, ban kangiyo, darabari, dwari, gai phul* TAMANG *bhramendo, bungamjo, surati*

Rubiaceae. Shrub 2–5 m high. Leaves stalked, 5–18 cm long, 1.5–1.5 cm wide, elliptic to lanceolate, acuminate, glabrous, pubescent beneath on the veins, narrowed toward the base of the petiole. Flowers short-stalked, pink in many-flowered terminal corymbs. Fruit a capsule, narrowly obovoid, pubescent. Flowers September–October, fruits November–December. Propagated by seeds. Distributed throughout Nepal at 1000–2100 m in shady

Lotus corniculatus

Loxogramme involuta

places; also in India, Bhutan, Tibet, southwestern China, and Indo-China.

MEDICINE. Juice of the root is applied to the forehead to treat headache. Juice of the bark is given to cattle to remove parasitic worms from the stomach. Juice of leaf is used for cuts and wounds. Juice of the fruit, about 2 teaspoons three times a day, is given in cases of indigestion.

OTHER USES. Flowers are offered to gods and goddesses.

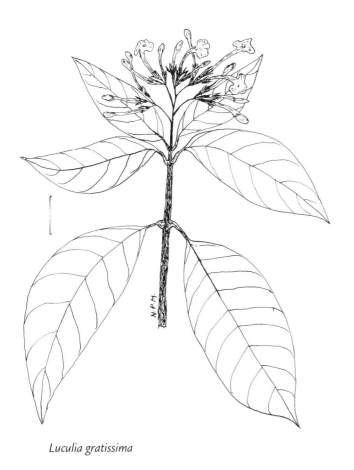

Luculia gratissima

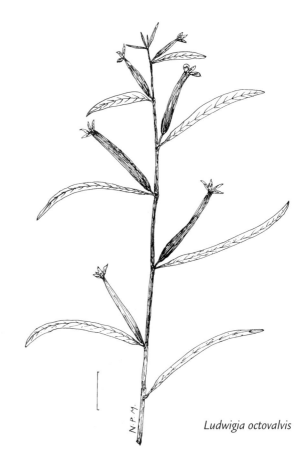

Ludwigia octovalvis

Ludwigia adscendens (Linnaeus) Hara

Jussiaea adscendens Linnaeus
Jussiaea repens Linnaeus
ENGLISH *alligator primrose-willow* NEPALI *poke jhar*

Onagraceae. Annual herb, stem creeping, rooting at the nodes. Leaves stalked, 1–7 cm long, ovate to lanceolate, obtuse, with yellow glands at the acute base. Flowers solitary, axillary, white or cream. Fruit a capsule, cylindrical, ribbed. Flowers and fruits November–February. Propagated by seeds. Distributed throughout Nepal at 200–600 m in moist and boggy places; also in India, China, Malaysia, and Australia.

MEDICINE. A paste of the plant is applied to treat headaches and is also applied to cuts and wounds.

Ludwigia octovalvis (Jacquin) Raven

Oenothera octovalvis Jacquin
Jussiaea suffruticosa Linnaeus
ENGLISH *Mexican primrose-willow* THARU *bihi*

Onagraceae. Herb about 60 cm high. Leaves stalked, alternate, 1.3–12 cm long, 0.5–1.4 cm wide, oblanceolate, entire, glabrous, tip narrowed. Flowers and fruits September–December. Propagated by seeds. Distributed throughout Nepal at 2100–900 m in damp places; also in India, eastward to Japan, Malaysia, Polynesia, Australia, Africa, and the Americas.

MEDICINE. Juice of the plant is applied to heal wounds between the toes caused by prolonged walking barefooted in muddy water.

Ludwigia perennis Linnaeus

Ludwigia parviflora Roxburgh
NEPALI *lwang jhar*

Onagraceae. Annual herb about 7 cm high. Leaves stalked, 1.5–9 cm long, 0.3–2 cm wide, lanceolate, acute or subacute. Flowers solitary, axillary, yellow. Fruit a capsule, obscurely four-angled. Flowers and fruits August–November. Propagated by seeds. Distributed throughout Nepal at 200–1400 m in moist places; also in Afghanistan, India, Japan, Malaysia, Australia, New Caledonia, and Africa.

MEDICINE. Juice of the plant is applied to heal wounds between the toes caused by prolonged walking barefooted in muddy water.

Luffa acutangula (Linnaeus) Roxburgh

ENGLISH *loofah, dishcloth gourd, ribbed gourd, vegetable sponge*
GURUNG *geronl* NEPALI *pate ghiraunla* NEWARI *silin poloncha*
TIBETAN *kosh-ta-ki*

Cucurbitaceae. Trailing herb, stems round in cross section or five-angled, tendrils trifid. Leaves stalked, five- or seven-lobed, deeply cordate. Flowers yellow. Fruit linear, ridged. Flowers and fruits July–November. Propagated by seeds. Distributed throughout Nepal at 1000–1600 m on moist ground, cultivated.

FOOD. Green fruit is eaten as a vegetable.

MEDICINE. Seeds are emetic and purgative.

Luffa cylindrica (Linnaeus) Roemer

Momordica cylindrica Linnaeus
Luffa aegyptiaca Miller
Luffa pentandra Roxburgh
Luffa racemosa Roxburgh

BHOJPURI *ghyura* CHEPANG *porali* DANUWAR *ghiraunla* ENGLISH *dishrag gourd, luffa, vegetable sponge* GURUNG *toragy* LEPCHA *kalhubi* LIMBU *toryang* MAGAR *gharaunla* MOOSHAR *ghyura* NEPALI *ghiraunla* NEWARI *polancha* RAI *wachitbob* SUNWAR *ghiraunla* TAMANG *porol* THARU *ghiwaha torai*

Cucurbitaceae. Annual climber with bifid or trifid tendrils. Leaves stalked, about 10 cm in diameter, orbiculate or reniform, palmately lobed, dentate, punctate on both surfaces. Flowers yellow. Fruit cylindrical, smooth. Flowers and fruits July–October. Propagated by seeds. Distributed throughout Nepal to about 1700 m, cultivated; also in the tropics of the eastern hemisphere.

FOOD. Tender fruits are eaten as vegetables.

OTHER USES. Dried fruit, with its fabric of fiber, is used as a sponge for bathing.

Luisia zeylanica Lindley

Luisia teretifolia Gaudichaud-Beaupré
CHEPANG *bori jhyau* NEPALI *kauwa ko kera*

Orchidaceae. Epiphytic orchid. Leaves sessile, alternate, 4–16 cm long, cylindrical, fleshy. Flowers greenish with purple lip, April–May. Fruits June–July. Propagated by seeds. Distributed in western and central Nepal at 700–1400 m on tree trunks and branches in sunny places; also in northern India, Bhutan, and Sri Lanka.

MEDICINE. The stem is emollient for abscesses and burns. Juice of the leaves is applied to boils and is also used as an anthelmintic.

Lycopersicon esculentum Miller

Solanum lycopersicum Linnaeus
BHOJPURI *golbhanta* CHEPANG *hamali, rani bhenta* DANUWAR *tamatar* ENGLISH *tomato* GURUNG *golbenda* LEPCHA *birupot* LIMBU *chaphenda* MAGAR *rhamatyak* MOOSHAR *golbhant* NEPALI *golbhera* NEWARI *golbhyara* RAI *bendasi, tumsun* SUNWAR *ranbhera* TAMANG *ghyagar banda* THARU *golbhera*

Solanaceae. Erect herb, stems covered with long hairs. Leaves stalked, odd-pinnate with small leaflets interposed, leaflets ovate to oblong, acuminate, irregularly dentate. Flowers yellow. Fruit a berry, red or yellow when ripe. Flowers and fruits most of the year. Propagated by seeds. Distributed throughout Nepal to about 1400 m; also in most parts of the world.

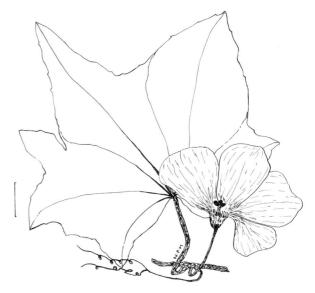

Luffa cylindrica

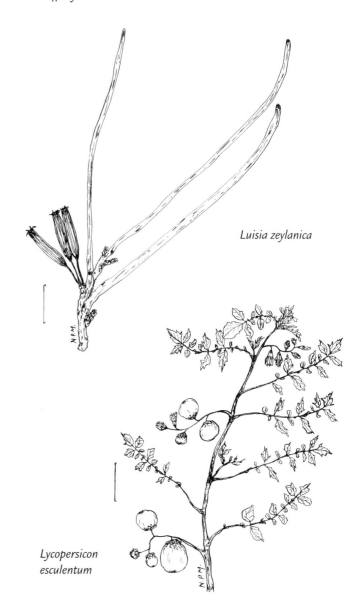

Luisia zeylanica

Lycopersicon
esculentum

FOOD. The fruit is rich in vitamins A and C. Fruits are cooked as a vegetable or used in salads, pickle, and many other foods. Large quantities of the fruit are canned.

Lycopodium clavatum Linnaeus

ENGLISH *club moss* GURUNG *khajuri, maisindur* MAJHI *sindur* NEPALI *ban mala, lahare jhyu, nagbeli* SHERPA *chhe mehendo* TAMANG *chhemhendo, chongi langdu, pangsen daima, syebal, tamda, thapsang, urgen langdu*

Lycopodiaceae. Trailing, spore-bearing herb, usually branching dichotomously. Leaves many, scaly, crowded, linear, awl shaped. Spike yellowish, terminal, elongated. Propagated by spores or by splitting plants. Distributed throughout Nepal at 1600–3600 m in damp, shady places; also in India and Bhutan.

MEDICINE. Spores are diuretic, antispasmodic, and used for rheumatism. A paste of the spores is applied to wounds, cracks, and fissures.

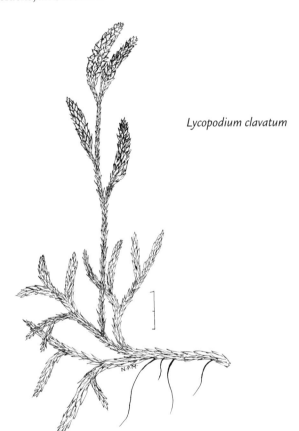

Lycopodium clavatum

Lygodium japonicum (Thunberg) Swartz

MAJHI *ukuse jhar* NEPALI *aankhle jhar, bahun lahara, janai lahara, luto jhar, pinase*

Lygodiaceae. Herbaceous fern. Fronds bright green, decompound, sterile lamina broader. Sporangia large, in two rows on each ultimate lobe. Propagated by spores. Distributed throughout Nepal at 1000–3900 m in moist, shady places; also in India, China, Malaysia, the Philippines, and Japan.

FOOD. Tender fronds are cooked as a vegetable.

MEDICINE. Juice of the plant is applied for boils, wounds, whitlow, scabies, and herpes. A paste of the plant is applied to treat joint aches.

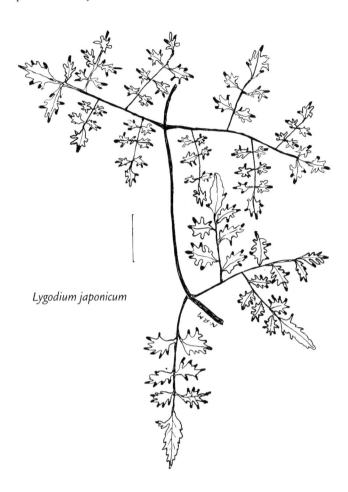

Lygodium japonicum

Lyonia ovalifolia (Wallich) Drude

Andromeda ovalifolia Wallich, *Xolisma ovalifolia* (Wallich) Rehder *Andromeda lanceolata* Wallich, *Pieris lanceolata* (Wallich) D. Don *Andromeda squamulosa* D. Don

CHEPANG *prayesi* GURUNG *chyarsi, chyaryo, chesin* MAGAR *angare, pakasing* NEPALI *anger, anyar, thaune, thainyar* SHERPA *rongle* TAMANG *domsing* TIBETAN *chwayme*

Ericaceae. Deciduous tree about 5 m high. Leaves short-stalked, ovate or elliptic, acuminate, entire. Flowers white in simple, axillary, terminal racemes, March–May. Propagated by seeds. Distributed throughout Nepal at 1300–3300 m; also in northern India, Bhutan, Tibet, eastward to China, Myanmar, Malaysia, and Indonesia.

MEDICINE. Juice of the leaves is applied to treat scabies and itching.

OTHER USES. The plant provides a poor-quality fuel. Leaves are poisonous to animals.

Lyonia ovalifolia

June–August. Propagated by seeds. Distributed throughout Nepal at 1100–2400 m in shady places; also in northern India, Bhutan, and Myanmar.

MEDICINE. Juice of the plant is inhaled to treat sinusitis.

M

Macaranga denticulata (Blume) Mueller Aargau

Mappa denticulata Blume
RAUTE *indolya*

Euphorbiaceae. Medium-sized evergreen tree, young parts rusty tomentose, bark greenish brown. Leaves stalked, 14–22 cm long, 11–16 cm wide, broadly ovate, acuminate, denticulate or entire, glabrescent above, glaucescent and dotted with minute orbicular glands beneath. Flowers reddish. Fruit a capsule, blackish, clothed with minute, waxy, orbicular glands. Flowers March–May, fruits May–July. Propagated by seeds. Distributed in eastern and central Nepal at about 1400 m in open places; also in India, southern China, Myanmar, Thailand, and Malaysia.

MEDICINE. A paste of the bark is applied to swellings and bruises.

OTHER USES. The plant is lopped for fodder.

Macaranga pustulata King ex Hooker fil.

CHEPANG *pahasingh* GURUNG *kala, khorsani chhi*
NEPALI *banare, mallato*

Euphorbiaceae. Medium-sized tree, young shoots clothed with rusty tomentum. Leaves stalked, alternate, 7–16 cm long, 4.5–11 cm wide, orbiculate to ovate, acuminate, rusty tomentose on both surfaces, base truncate. Flowers small, greenish red, in axillary tomentose panicles. Fruit a capsule, oblong, grooved between the two cocci. Seeds two, globose, black. Flowers September–November, fruits May–July. Propagated by seeds. Distributed throughout Nepal at 700–1800 m on open hillsides; also in northern India.

MEDICINE. Juice of the bark is applied to boils and pimples.

OTHER USES. Wood is used for fuel. Leaves are used as plates and wrappings for foodstuffs.

Lysimachia alternifolia Wallich

Lysimachia glandulosa Edgeworth
Lysimachia quinquangularis Buchanan-Hamilton ex D. Don
Lysimachia tetragona D. Don
NEPALI *butte ghans, pinase jhar*

Primulaceae. Herb about 15 cm high. Leaves sessile or short-stalked, 1.5–2 cm long, 0.8–1.5 cm wide, elliptic to lanceolate, acute. Flowers solitary, axillary, yellowish,

Lysimachia alternifolia

Maclura cochinchinensis (Loureiro) Corner

Vanieria cochinchinensis Loureiro, *Cudrania cochinchinensis* (Loureiro) Kudô & Masamune
Cudrania javanensis Trécul
MAGAR *dhyabbar, gwakhar* NEPALI *amali, damaru, dewar, gai dimmar*

Moraceae. Trailing shrub. Leaves stalked, 2–8 cm long, 1–4 cm wide, elliptic to ovate, entire, glabrous, apex

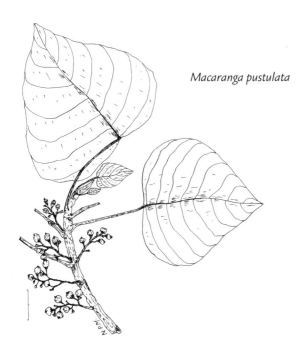

Macaranga pustulata

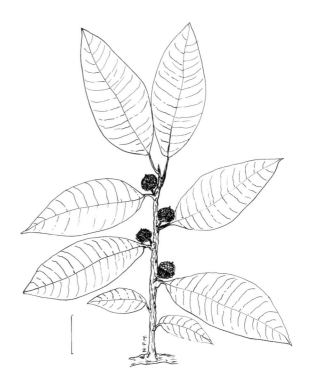

Maclura cochinchinensis

rounded or acute. Fruit a fleshy aggregation of fruitlets, globose, solitary, red when ripe, May–June. Propagated by cuttings. Distributed throughout Nepal at 600–1200 m, frequent on the outer edges of forested areas.

FOOD. Ripe fruits are eaten fresh.

MEDICINE. Juice of the bark, about 6 teaspoons twice a day, is given to treat peptic ulcer. The heartwood is used for promoting parturition. Latex is applied to boils.

Macropanax dispermus (Blume) Kuntze

Aralia disperma Blume, *Hedera disperma* (Blume) de Candolle
Macropanax oreophilus Miquel
Panax serratum Wallich ex de Candolle
NEPALI *ninde*

Araliaceae. Tree about 7 m high. Leaves stalked, pinnate, leaflets stalked, lanceolate, acuminate, crenate, glabrous, glossy above. Flowers yellowish in compound spreading panicles, August–September. Propagated by seeds or cuttings. Distributed in eastern and central Nepal at 1200–2200 m, along the margins of forests; also in northern India, Bhutan, western and central China, and Southeast Asia.

FOOD. Tender leaves and shoots are cooked as a vegetable or pickled.

Macropanax undulatus (Wallich ex G. Don) Seemann

Hedera undulatus Wallich ex G. Don
Panax assamicus Banerjee
Panax sikkimensis Banerjee
NEPALI *chinde*

Araliaceae. Small tree, bark smooth, pale gray, with large, prominent, raised lenticels. Leaves stalked, pinnate,

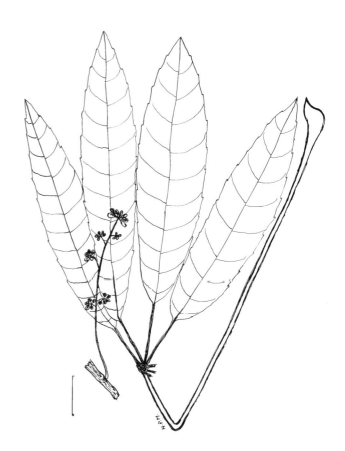

Macropanax dispermus

leaflets stalked, 6–12 cm long, 2–5 cm wide, oblong to elliptic, acuminate, entire or with fine distant teeth, glabrous, shiny above. Flowers yellowish. Fruit ovoid. Flowers August–September, fruits February–March. Propagated by cuttings. Distributed in eastern Nepal at 2200–2900 m on open hillsides; also in northeastern India, Bhutan, western China, Myanmar, and Thailand.

FOOD. Young leaves are cooked as a vegetable.

OTHER USES. The plant provides fodder.

Madhuca longifolia (Koenig) Macbride

Bassia longifolia Koenig

BHOJPURI *mahuwa* CHEPANG *mahuwa* DANUWAR *mahuwa* ENGLISH *mohwa tree* GURUNG *mhain* LEPCHA *mawapot* LIMBU *yakpanpa* MOOSHAR *mahuwa* NEPALI *mahuwa* NEWARI *mauwa* RAI *chhokwa* TAMANG *mahuwa airag* THARU *mahuwa*

Sapotaceae. Deciduous tree about 20 m high. Leaves stalked, oblong to elliptic, acuminate, entire. Flowers stalked, cream, succulent. Fruit ovoid, fleshy, one- or two-seeded. Flowers February–April, fruits June–August. Propagated by seeds. Distributed throughout Nepal to about 200 m in open places at the margins of subtropical forest

but forest depletion and the gathering of its wood and flowers endanger plant populations; also in subtropical or tropical parts of the Himalaya, India, and Sri Lanka.

FOOD. The succulent flowers, which taste sweet, are eaten fresh, but excessive amounts can be intoxicating. People prepare alcohol from the flowers, and it is considered the best local alcoholic beverage. Seed oil is used for cooking.

MEDICINE. A decoction of the bark is given to diabetic patients. In India, it is used for itches and bleeding gums (Jain 1965). Flowers are cooling, tonic, and nutritive. Alcohol distilled from the flower is astringent, tonic, and appetizing as well. A decoction of the flowers, about 3 teaspoons three times a day, is taken in cases of cough and colds. Oil from the seed is used for skin diseases.

OTHER USES. Wood is used for construction, furniture, and fuel. Bark yields tannin. Oil cake is valued for poisoning fish.

Maesa argentea (Wallich) A. de Candolle

Baeobotrys argentea Wallich

NEPALI *bhogate*

Myrsinaceae. Shrub about 4 m high. Leaves stalked, alternate, 7–17 cm long, 3.5–7.5 cm wide, broadly elliptic, long-pointed, serrate, glabrous. Flowers white, April–June. Fruits October–November. Propagated by seeds. Distributed throughout Nepal at 1700–2100 m in moist areas of mixed forest; also in northern India, western China, and northern Myanmar.

OTHER USES. Squeezed leaves are used to poison fish.

Maesa chisia Buchanan-Hamilton ex D. Don

Maesa dioica A. de Candolle

CHEPANG *bilauni* GURUNG *chhotne, chhyonre, tushi* LIMBU *yongjigwa* MAGAR *bilauni* NEPALI *bilauni, kanige, thinke* TAMANG *bhijin, busing* TIBETAN *khemona*

Myrsinaceae. Shrub about 7 m high. Leaves stalked, 3–15 cm long, 1–5 cm wide, elliptic to lanceolate, acuminate, crenate, glabrous. Flowers white in simple axillary racemes. Fruit globose. Flowers and fruits March–January. Propagated by seeds. Distributed throughout Nepal at 900–1900 m on shady slopes; also in northern India, Bhutan, and northern Myanmar.

MEDICINE. Bark is boiled in water about 10 minutes, and the filtered water is taken as an anthelmintic. Juice of the bark is applied to treat ringworm. A paste of ripe fruit is applied to treat scabies.

OTHER USES. The plant is lopped for fodder and is important when other species are scarce, especially during winter. Root and bark are used as fish poison. Bark, root, and leaf have insecticidal properties. The plant is an undesirable fuelwood because the smoke causes eye infections, headaches, and giddiness. Villagers cover pots of locally made alcohol and beer with the leaves, believing they add good taste to the beverage.

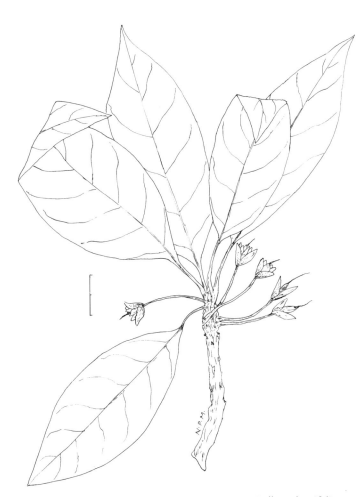

Madhuca longifolia

Maesa macrophylla (Wallich) A. de Candolle

Baeobotrys macrophylla Wallich
Maesa tomentosa D. Don
CHEPANG *dhusi* DANUWAR *bhogate* MAGAR *bhogate* NEPALI *bhogate, paha phal* TAMANG *bhogate*

Myrsinaceae. Shrub about 3 m high. Leaves stalked, 3.5–17.5 cm long, 2.5–14 cm wide, orbiculate, denticulate, softly hairy on both surfaces. Flowers white in branched racemes. Fruit small, globose. Flowers April–May, fruits June–July. Propagated by seeds. Distributed in eastern and central Nepal at 500–1800 m in open, moist places; also in northwestern India and Bhutan.

MEDICINE. Bark paste is applied to boils, pimples; bark juice is mixed in equal amount with that of *Trichilia connaroides*, warmed, and given, 3 teaspoons three times a day, for diarrhea, dysentery (Plate 2). Leaves are roasted in an earthen pot and powdered to apply to boils. Juice of the fruit is given in cases of diphtheria of cattle, and is applied to treat scabies.

OTHER USES. The leaf is used to poison fish.

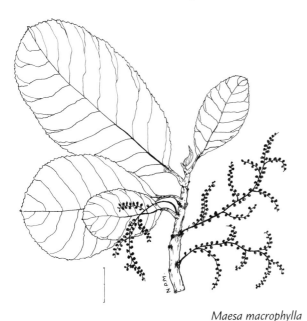

Maesa macrophylla

Maesa montana A. de Candolle

Baeobotrys indica Roxburgh, *Maesa indica* Wallich ex C. B. Clarke
Baeobotrys nemoralis Willdenow
Maesa elongata (A. de Candolle) Mez
NEPALI *thinke*

Myrsinaceae. Shrub about 3.5 m high. Leaves stalked, 3–15.5 cm long, 1.5–7 cm wide, elliptic, serrate, glabrous, tip narrowed, tapering toward the base. Flowers whitish. Flowers and fruits April–December. Propagated by seeds. Distributed throughout Nepal at 250–1500 m in moist hill forests; also in northwestern India, Bhutan, and western China.

FOOD. Ripe fruit is edible.

Magnolia campbellii Hooker fil. & Thomson

NEPALI *ghode chanp* NEWARI *chobasi*

Magnoliaceae. Tree about 12 m high. Leaves stalked, 8.5–28 cm long, 3.8–15.5 cm wide, elliptic to ovate, acuminate, entire, glabrous above, rusty tomentose beneath. Flowers white, March–April. Fruits June–October. Propagated by seeds. Distributed in eastern and central Nepal at 2250–2700 m in open, disturbed forest; also in northern India, Bhutan, southeastern Tibet, southwestern China, and northern Myanmar.

OTHER USES. Timber is used for construction and furniture.

Magnolia globosa Hooker fil. & Thomson

NEPALI *khukie chanp*

Magnoliaceae. Tree about 8 m high. Leaves stalked, ovate, dark glossy green above, rusty felted beneath. Fruit cylindrical, crimson. Flowers May–June. Propagated by seeds. Distributed in eastern Nepal at 3200–3400 m; also in India, Bhutan, southeastern Tibet, eastward to western China, and northern Myanmar.

OTHER USES. The plant is used for timber.

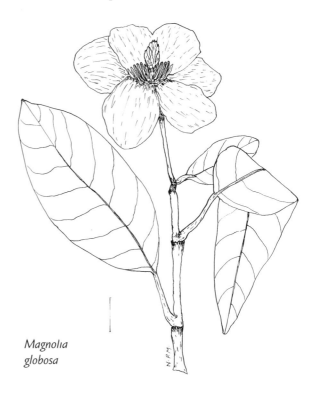

Magnolia globosa

Magnolia grandiflora Linnaeus

ENGLISH *bull bay* NEPALI *rukh kamal*

Magnoliaceae. Evergreen tree with rusty pubescent buds and branchlets. Leaves stalked, elliptic to oblong, thick and firm, shiny above, rusty pubescent beneath. Flowers large, white, fragrant, May–June. Propagated by seeds. Distributed in central Nepal at 900–1700 m, often planted in gardens; also in India and North America.

OTHER USES. Flowers are offered to gods and goddesses.

Maharanga bicolor (Wallich ex G. Don) A. de Candolle

Onosma bicolor Wallich ex G. Don

NEPALI *jhuske, maharangi*

Boraginaceae. Hispid herb about 30 cm high. Leaves sessile or short-stalked, oblong, acute, entire. Flowers blue-pink in axillary and terminal cymes. Propagated by seeds. Distributed in western and central Nepal at 2000–3000 m in open fields; also in northern India, Bhutan, and southern Tibet.

MEDICINE. Juice of the rhizome is applied as a hair tonic.

Maharanga bicolor

Maharanga emodi (Wallich) A. de Candolle

Onosma emodi Wallich
Onosma vestitum Wallich ex G. Don

NEPALI *maharangi*

Boraginaceae. Hispid herb about 30 cm high. Leaves oblanceolate, acute, entire, hispid on both surfaces. Flowers pink in axillary and terminal cymes. Propagated by seeds. Distributed throughout Nepal at 2200–4500 m on open, rocky ground; also in India, Bhutan, and southern Tibet.

MEDICINE. Juice of the rhizome is applied as a hair tonic.

Mahonia acanthifolia G. Don

NEPALI *kesari*

Berberidaceae. Shrub about 3 m high. Leaves stalked, odd-pinnate, leaflets 17–21, ovate to oblong, acuminate, spinous dentate, glossy. Flowers yellow in dense racemes, November–December. Propagated by seeds. Distributed

in western and central Nepal at 2200–2800 m in moist, shady places; also in northern India, Bhutan, China, and Malaysia.

FOOD. Ripe fruit is eaten fresh and also pickled.

MEDICINE. Juice of the bark is dropped in the eye to treat inflammation of the eye.

Mahonia napaulensis de Candolle

Berberis nepalensis (de Candolle) Sprengel
Berberis miccia Buchanan-Hamilton ex D. Don

CHEPANG *bajardanti* GURUNG *komo* NEPALI *bhote chotro, jamanemandro, mandre chotro* TAMANG *bokipan, chachan, kerpal*

Berberidaceae. Evergreen shrub about 3 m high. Leaves stalked, alternate, pinnate, leaflets sessile, ovate to lanceolate, sharply spinous dentate, base oblique. Flowers stalked, yellow. Fruit a berry, dark blue when ripe. Flowers February–March, fruits May–June. Propagated by seeds. Distributed throughout Nepal at 1400–2900 m in the forest with other shrubs and trees; also in northern India.

FOOD. Ripe fruit is edible fresh or pickled.

MEDICINE. Juice of the bark is boiled, cooled, and dripped in the eye to treat inflammation of the eye. Fruit is diuretic and demulcent.

OTHER USES. Bark yields a dye.

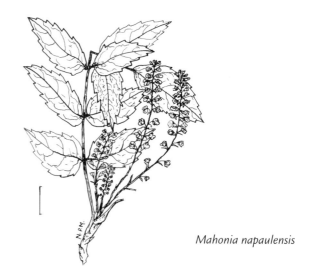

Mahonia napaulensis

Maianthemum fuscum (Wallich) LaFrankie

Smilacina fusca Wallich, *Tovaria fusca* (Wallich) Baker
Smilacina divaricata Wallich, *Medora divaricata* Kunth
Tovaria finitima W. W. Smith, *Smilacina finitima* (W. W. Smith) Wang & Tang

NEPALI *seto jara*

Convallariaceae. Shrub. Leaves stalked, 7.5–15 cm long, ovate to cordate, acuminate, membranous, five- or seven-veined, glabrous or sparsely pilose beneath. Flowers brown-purple. Fruit a berry, one- to three-seeded. Propagated by seeds or root offshoots. Distributed in eastern and central Nepal at 1200–400 m in moist, shady places; also in India, Bhutan, western China, and northern Myanmar.

MEDICINE. A paste of the root is applied to treat dislocation of bone.

Maianthemum purpureum (Wallich) LaFrankie

Smilacina purpurea Wallich, *Jocaste purpurea* (Wallich) Kunth, *Tovaria purpurea* (Wallich) Baker
Smilacina pallida Royle
ENGLISH *false Solomon's seal* NEPALI *sikari sag* SHERPA *rukpa*
TAMANG *nar-dhap*

Convallariaceae. Perennial herb about 60 cm high, rootstock stout, creeping. Leaves sessile or subsessile, 5–12 cm long, broadly ovate, acuminate, distinctly ciliate on the margin, pubescent beneath. Flowers deep brown in terminal, many-flowered racemes. Flowers and fruits April–June. Propagated by seeds or root offshoots. Distributed throughout Nepal at 2600–4200 m in dense *Betula* and *Sorbus* forests; also in northern India, southern Tibet, and western China.

FOOD. Tender leaves and shoots are cooked as a vegetable.

Malaxis cylindrostachya (Lindley) Kuntze

Dienia cylindrostachya Lindley, *Microstylis cylindrostachya* (Lindley) Reichenbach fil.
NEPALI *tukuna*

Orchidaceae. Orchid about 15 cm high. Leaves solitary, 5–11 cm long, 2–4 cm wide, elliptic, obtuse, base sheathing. Flowers minute, greenish, July–August. Propagated by seeds or tubers. Distributed throughout Nepal at 2100–3500 m, frequent in rocky soil; also in India, Tibet, and Myanmar.

FOOD. Boiled roots are edible.

Mallotus philippensis (Lamarck) Mueller Aargau

Croton philippense Lamarck
CHEPANG *dusi, paras, sindurya* DANUWAR *sunphunari*
ENGLISH *Kamala dye tree* GURUNG *sindare* LEPCHA *puroa, tukla*
MAGAR *sinduri* NEPALI *rohini, roina, singure* NEWARI *kamila*
RAUTE *rohinya* TAMANG *pyongla, sililin, sindri* THARU *rohini*

Euphorbiaceae. Tree about 10 m high. Leaves stalked, alternate, 4–24 cm long, 2–10 cm wide, oblong to ovate, acuminate, entire or sinuate, glabrous above, rusty tomentose beneath. Inflorescence many-flowered, the flowers unisexual, axillary, yellowish. Fruit a capsule, globose, densely covered with red or crimson powder. Flowers August–November, fruits December–January. Propagated by seeds. Distributed throughout Nepal to about 1800 m, common in *Shorea robusta* forest with other trees and shrubs; also in Pakistan, India, Bhutan, Sri Lanka, China, Southeast Asia, the Philippines, Australia, and Polynesia.

MEDICINE. Juice of the root is applied for body pains caused by fever. The root is boiled in water about 20 minutes, and the filtered water, about 4 teaspoons, is taken as

an anthelmintic. A decoction of the bark is used for typhoid, bronchitis, and meningitis. Juice of the bark is given for diarrhea and, in doses of about 3 teaspoons four times a day, to relieve indigestion. Juice of the leaves is applied to fungal infections of the skin. This juice, about 2

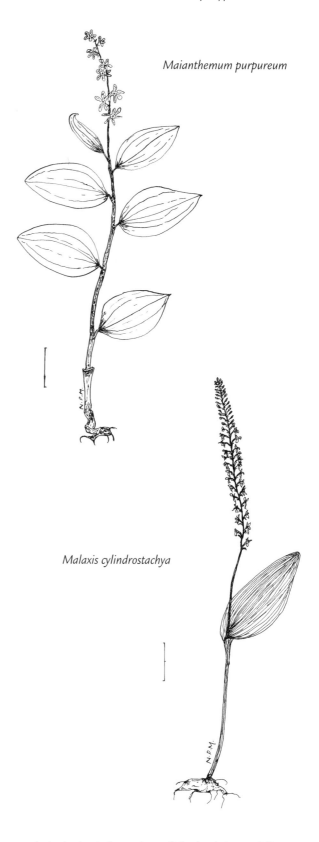

Maianthemum purpureum

Malaxis cylindrostachya

teaspoons twice a day, is given for constipation. The red powder covering the fruit is vermifuge and purgative.

OTHER USES. The plant is lopped for fodder. Stems and branches are used to build temporary huts. Leaves contain tannin. The red glandular powder of the fruit is used as a dye. According to Kapur and Sarin (1984), seeds contain 1.4–3.7% oil.

Malus baccata

Mallotus philippensis

Malus baccata (Linnaeus) Borkhausen

Pyrus baccata Linnaeus
Malus manshurica (Maximowicz) Komarov
Malus pallasiana Juzepczuk
Malus rockii Rehder
Malus sachalinensis Juzepczuk

ENGLISH *Manchurian crab apple* NEPALI *hare chyuli*

Rosaceae. Small deciduous tree. Leaves stalked, 4–8 cm long, elliptic, pointed, finely blunt dentate. Flowers white, fragrant. Fruit small, globose, red or scarlet. Flowers April–June. Propagated by seeds. Distributed in western and central Nepal at 1800–3600 m in open, forested areas; also in northern India, Bhutan, Tibet, China, Mongolia, Siberia, and Japan.

MEDICINE. A paste of the fruit is applied to the forehead to relieve headaches.

Malva verticillata Linnaeus

Malva alchemillaefolia Wallich
Malva neilgherrensis Wight

ENGLISH *Chinese mallow, large mallow* GURUNG *tangajang*
NEPALI *majaino* TAMANG *chyatalama, jhamolumo*
TIBETAN *chyatalama*

Malvaceae. Erect herb about 1 m high. Leaves stalked, suborbiculate to cordate, three- or five-lobed, lobes rounded, crenate. Flowers subsessile, pinkish white,

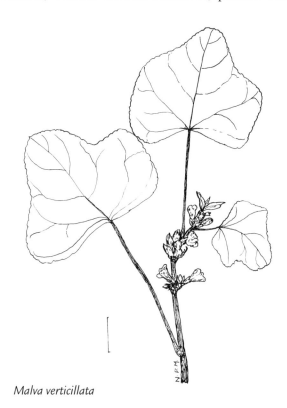

Malva verticillata

crowded in the axil. Flowers and fruits February–August. Propagated by seeds. Distributed throughout Nepal at 2000–3500 m on moist ground around villages; also in northern India, Bhutan, northeastern Asia including China, Europe, and Egypt.

FOOD. Tender leaves and shoots are eaten as a potherb.

Mangifera indica Linnaeus

CHEPANG *taksai* DANUWAR *yam* ENGLISH *mango* GURUNG *aanp* LIMBU *ambe* MAGAR *aabo* MAJHI *aam* MOOSHAR *aam* NEPALI *aanp* NEWARI *an* RAI *aamba* TAMANG *amba, kyungwa* TIBETAN *shing-tog*

Anacardiaceae. Large evergreen tree with rough, thick, dark gray bark. Leaves stalked, alternate, crowded at the ends of branches, ovate to lanceolate, entire, leathery, dark green, margin wavy, base acute. Flowers yellowish, fragrant, in terminal panicles. Fruit a drupe, ovoid, laterally compressed. Flowers March–April, fruits June–July. Propagated by seeds and by grafting and budding. Distributed throughout Nepal to about 1300 m in open places; also in subtropical parts of the Himalaya, India, Sri Lanka, and Southeast Asia.

FOOD. Pulp of ripe fruit is delicious. The pulp is made into marmalade and can be preserved for a long time. Unripe fruit is pickled, and dried slices are also made into pickle.

MEDICINE. The root has diuretic properties. Juice of the bark is boiled in water, which is used to wash the body and legs to provide relief from jaundice. Bark juice is heated and applied for rheumatism. This juice, about 6 teaspoons three times a day, is given to treat peptic ulcer. Slender branches are used as toothbrushes to treat toothaches. An infusion of the leaves is taken in cases of hoarseness, cough, and bronchial tube disease. Juice of the leaves, about 3 teaspoons three times a day, is given for bloody

dysentery. Ash of the leaves is applied to burns for quick recovery. Latex is applied to treat gingivitis. Gum mixed with mustard oil is applied for scabies, warts, and other skin diseases. Ripe fruit is laxative. The seed is vermifuge. A paste of the cotyledon is given for diarrhea.

OTHER USES. Wood is gray, light, and used for furniture and implements. Planks are made into boxes for packing. Bark contains tannin.

Manglietia insignis (Wallich) Blume

NEPALI *ban kamal*

Magnoliaceae. Medium-sized evergreen tree. Leaves stalked, 15–20 cm long, 5–8 cm wide, elliptic to lanceolate, acute, leathery, glabrous, shiny above. Flowers axillary, solitary, pinkish, fragrant. Propagated by seeds. Distributed in central Nepal at 1500–2700 m in open, sunny places but forest depletion, the plant's limited natural distribution, and the gathering of its wood endanger plant populations; also in India, southeastern Tibet, southwestern China, and northern Myanmar.

OTHER USES. Wood is extensively used for fuel.

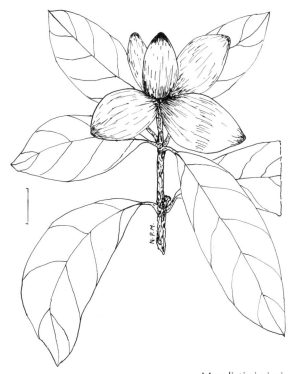

Manglietia insignis

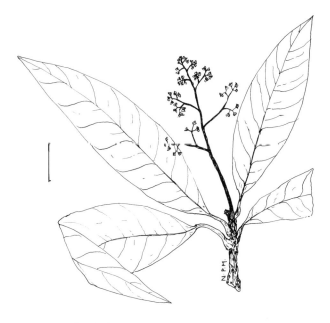

Mangifera indica

Manilkara zapota (Linnaeus) van Royen

Achras zapota Linnaeus

ENGLISH *chiku tree, sapodilla plum* NEPALI *sapatu*

Sapotaceae. Evergreen tree about 10 m high with spreading crown. Leaves stalked, oblong to ovate, entire, acute, narrowed toward the base. Flowers white, rusty pubescent outside. Fruit ovoid, brown, fleshy. Flowers

March–June, fruits August–September. Propagated by seeds or layering, budding, and grafting. Distributed throughout Nepal to about 250 m on rich or well-manured sandy loam, cultivated; also in India, tropical America, and the tropics and subtropics of the eastern hemisphere.

FOOD. The thin-skinned and sweet-fleshed fruit is edible.

MEDICINE. A decoction of the bark is given to treat diarrhea and fever. Fruits are astringent, and the juice is used for biliousness. Seeds are aperient and diuretic.

OTHER USES. Villagers mix the plant with the latex of *Ficus religiosa,* boil the mixture, and apply it to a bamboo trapper to catch birds. Leaves contain tannin.

Maoutia puya (Hooker) Weddell

Urtica puya Buchanan-Hamilton ex Wallich, *Boehmeria puya* Hooker

CHEPANG *hilang, kul* GURUNG *kalan kuli* NEPALI *nani palo, putaleso, puwa* TAMANG *nani palo*

Urticaceae. Shrub with pubescent branches. Leaves stalked, alternate, elliptic to lanceolate, caudate-acuminate, coarsely dentate, somewhat roughly textured above, white woolly beneath. Flowers greenish in axillary cymes. Flowers and fruits May–November. Propagated by seeds or root offshoots. Distributed throughout Nepal at 900–1700 m in open places; also in northern India, Bhutan, southwestern China, and Indo-China.

MEDICINE. In 1986, I met a Tamang couple practicing native medicine in the village of Chyangli, Dhading district. The wife learned herbal treatment from her grandfather, who asked her to collect herbal plants when she went to the forest to gather fodder. She practiced herbal medicine in and around her village. She believed that only one part of a plant can be effective if the treatment is done at the beginning of disease. For example, she prescribed juice of the root of *Agrimonia pilosa* to treat peptic ulcer. The husband, on the other hand, learned his healing art from the native healers of his village. He thought that the healing business was a good source of income and generally treated patients outside his village, where one had to walk 4 hours to a full day. Unlike his wife, he believed that an admixture of parts of plants is good for treatment. For example, root of *Maoutia puya* mixed with root of *Boehmeria platyphylla* and bark of *Psidium guajava* are pounded and applied to cuts and wounds. Most of the uses of plants used by the couple are practiced in other parts of Nepal. A paste of the root, about 1 teaspoon, is given in cases of indigestion. Juice of the root, about 3 teaspoons three times a day, is given for indigestion.

OTHER USES. Bark yields a fine white fiber used to make fishnets, twine, and clothes. Leaves provide fodder for cattle.

Mariscus sumatrensis (Retzius) T. Koyama

Kyllinga sumatrensis Retzius
Mariscus sieberianus Nees ex Steudel
Scirpus cyperoides Linnaeus, *Cyperus cyperoides* (Linnaeus) Kuntze

NEPALI *guja, nagarmothe*

Cyperaceae. Herb about 40 cm high. Leaves linear, flat. Inflorescence brownish, supported by three unequal leaves. Flowers June–August. Propagated by seeds. Distributed

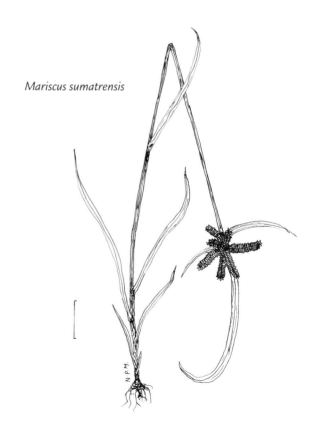

Mariscus sumatrensis

Maoutia puya

throughout Nepal at 100–2400 m in open, moist places; also in tropical and subtropical regions of the eastern hemisphere.

MEDICINE. Juice of the root is taken to treat cough and fever. Ash of the plant is applied to cuts and wounds.

Marsdenia lucida Edgeworth ex Madden

CHEPANG *jharang*

Asclepiadaceae. Evergreen climber with dextrorse stem, bark pale brown, lenticels circular. Leaves stalked, 9–19 cm long, 5–10 cm wide, ovate to oblong, acute or acuminate, dark glossy green above, pale yellowish green beneath, base rounded or cordate. Flowers purplish red, fragrant, in many-flowered axillary umbels. Fruit a follicle, solitary, straight, beaked, glabrous. Flowers July–October, fruits March–April. Propagated by layering or by cuttings. Distributed throughout Nepal at 2100–2700 m, usually in dense oak forests; also in northern India and Bhutan.

OTHER USES. The plant is used for fencing kitchen gardens. Stems are used as house beams.

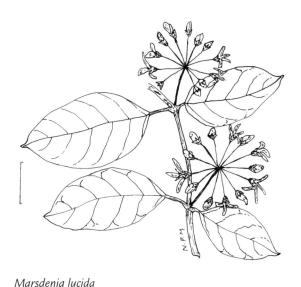

Marsdenia lucida

Marsdenia roylei Wight

NEPALI *dudhe lahara, jogi lahara*

Asclepiadaceae. Twining shrub with milky latex. Leaves stalked, broadly ovate, acuminate, entire, base deeply cordate. Flowers orange, crowded in axillary umbellate cymes. Fruit a follicle with a beak-like tip. Flowers May–July, fruits September–October. Propagated by layering or by cuttings. Distributed throughout Nepal at 1400–2400 m in shady places; also in northern India, Bhutan, and Myanmar.

MEDICINE. Juice of the stem, about 4 teaspoons three times a day, is given in cases of gastric trouble and peptic ulcer.

OTHER USES. Bark yields silky white fiber used for fishing lines and other similar purposes.

Martynia annua Linnaeus

Martynia diandra Gloxin

ENGLISH *tiger's claw* NEPALI *boksi kanda, gau chuchcho, goru singe*

Pedaliaceae. Glandular pubescent shrub about 2 m high. Leaves stalked, opposite, 15–36 cm long, 15–20 cm wide, broadly ovate, acute, sinuate, pubescent, base slightly cordate. Flowers pinkish in axillary racemes. Fruit a beaked berry crowned by two strong, claw-like, sharp hooks, woody. Flowers August–September, fruits October–November. Propagated by seeds. Distributed throughout Nepal to about 1200 m in forested areas; also in Pakistan, India, Myanmar, Malaysia, tropical and subtropical America, and Queensland, Australia.

MEDICINE. Juice of the leaves is mixed with hot water, which is used as a gargle in cases of sore throat. Juice of the fruit is given to treat inflammation of the stomach.

Martynia annua

Maytenus rufa (Wallich) Hara

Celastrus rufa Wallich, *Catha rufa* (Wallich) G. Don, *Gymnosporia rufa* (Wallich) Lawson

CHEPANG *tang* NEPALI *kande khasru, kesari* TAMANG *mama bhuzu, mole maran, pipal geda, pipa pa*

Celastraceae. Thorny shrub about 2 m high. Leaves stalked, elliptic to lanceolate, acute, serrate, glabrous. Flowers white in fascicled cymes. Propagated by seeds. Distributed throughout Nepal at 1000–2200 m in open, rocky places; also in northern India.

MEDICINE. Juice of the root, about 3 teaspoons three times a day, is given in cases of cough.

Maytenus rufa

Mazus pumilus (Burman fil.) van Steenis

Lobelia pumila Burman fil.
Gratiola goodenifolia Hornemann, *Mazus goodenifolia* (Hornemann) Pennell
Lindernia japonica Thunberg, *Mazus japonicus* (Thunberg) Kuntze
Mazus rugosus Loureiro
TAMANG *moemran*

Scrophulariaceae. Small herb. Lower leaves stalked, upper leaves sessile, 1–5.5 cm long, 0.7–2 cm wide, elliptic, acute, dentate, narrowed toward the base. Flowers white. Flowers and fruits most of the year. Propagated by seeds or root offshoots. Distributed in eastern and central Nepal at 200–1600 m in moist places; also in India, Bhutan, eastward to western China, Malaysia, Korea, and Japan.

MEDICINE. Juice of the plant, about 4 teaspoons twice a day, is given in cases of typhoid.

Mazus surculosus D. Don

Mazus harmandii Bonati
NEPALI *khasre buti*

Scrophulariaceae. Trailing herb. Basal leaves spatulate, ovate, crenate, sparsely hairy, apex rounded, upper leaves sessile, slightly crenate. Flowers purple in terminal racemes. Flowers and fruits February–August. Propagated by seeds or root offshoots. Distributed throughout Nepal at 900–3000 m in moist places; also in India, Tibet, and western China.

Mazus surculosus

MEDICINE. Juice of the plant, about 2 teaspoons twice a day, is given to treat stomach acidity. This juice is also applied to cuts and wounds.

Meconopsis grandis Prain

ENGLISH *blue poppy* NEPALI *childar, kyasar* SHERPA *shinnakpa*

Papaveraceae. Hairy herb about 1 m high. Leaves oblanceolate, slightly dentate, covered with stiff golden hairs. Flowers blue, solitary, June–July. Fruits October–November. Propagated by seeds. Distributed throughout Nepal at 3000–5000 m in shady places among shrubs; also in northern India, southeastern Tibet, western China, and northern Myanmar.

FOOD. Seeds are roasted and pickled by Sherpas and Tamangs of the mountainous region.

Medicago lupulina Linnaeus

ENGLISH *hop clover* NEPALI *jhupe pyaunli*

Leguminosae. Prostrate annual herb about 30 cm high. Leaves stalked, trifoliolate, leaflets short-stalked, 0.4–1 cm long, pale yellow. Flowers yellowish in dense ovoid heads. Fruit a pod, pubescent, black at maturity. Flowers and fruits March–June. Propagated by seeds. Distributed in western and central Nepal at 1000–1400 m in open places, generally as a weed in wheat and maize fields; also in western and central Asia, Europe, Africa, and the Americas.

OTHER USES. The plant provides fodder.

Megacarpaea polyandra Bentham

NEPALI *rubi ko sag*

Cruciferae. Robust perennial herb about 2 m high. Lower leaves deeply pinnately lobed, lobes in five to nine pairs, 10–20 cm long, oblong to lanceolate, teeth pointed, upper leaves linear, entire. Flowers yellowish. Fruit winged, one-seeded. Flowers June–July. Propagated by seeds. Distributed in western and central Nepal at 2700–

Meconopsis grandis

Medicago lupulina

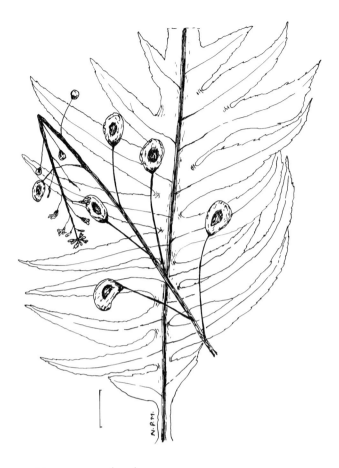

Megacarpaea polyandra

4500 m on open slopes in light forest; also in northwestern India, and western Tibet.

FOOD. Young leaves and shoots are cooked as vegetables.

Megacodon stylophorus (C. B. Clarke) H. Smith

Gentiana stylophora C. B. Clarke
NEPALI pile jhar

Gentianaceae. Herb about 30 cm high. Leaves shortstalked, 10–30 cm long, elliptic, acuminate. Flowers stalked, axillary, yellowish. Fruit a capsule, cylindrical. Flowers June–July. Propagated by seeds. Distributed in eastern Nepal at 3000–4000 m on moist ground among shrubs; also in India, southern Tibet, and southwestern China.

FOOD. Tender leaves are cooked as a vegetable.

MEDICINE. A paste of the root is applied to wounds and swellings.

Melastoma malabathricum Linnaeus

CHEPANG diklak, gabrasai DANUWAR koilar
ENGLISH Indian rhododendron GURUNG anguri, tun kaphal
NEPALI angeri, kali angeri, thulo anyar, thulo chulesi SATAR chulesi
TAMANG lemlang

Melastomataceae. Shrub about 2 m high. Leaves stalked, 3.5–10 cm long, 1.4–3 cm wide, broadly lanceolate, appressed hairy above, slightly hairy between the veins beneath. Flowers purple. Fruit ovoid, truncate. Flowers March–June, fruits November–December. Propagated by

Melastoma malabathricum

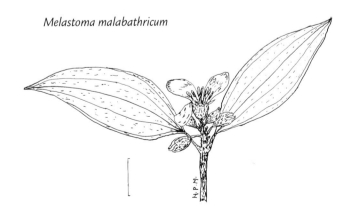

seeds or root offshoots. Distributed in eastern and central Nepal at 200–1600 m in open as well as shady places; also in India, Sri Lanka, Southeast Asia, and Australia.

FOOD. Ripe fruits are eaten fresh.

MEDICINE. Juice of the plant, about 4 teaspoons three times a day, is given in cases of cough and colds.

OTHER USES. A purple dye is obtained from the fruits.

Melastoma normale D. Don

Melastoma malabaricum Linnaeus
Melastoma nepalensis Loddiges
Melastoma wallichii de Candolle
NEPALI *chulesi, kali angeri*

Melastomataceae. Shrub with branches densely shaggy. Leaves subsessile, lanceolate, entire, acuminate, villous on both surfaces, three-veined. Flowers pink, clustered, July–August. Propagated by seeds or root offshoots. Distributed in eastern and central Nepal at 900–1800 m; also in northern India, Bhutan, China, Southeast Asia, and New Caledonia.

FOOD. Ripe fruits are eaten fresh.

Melia azedarach Linnaeus

BHOJPURI *bakain* CHEPANG *bakaina* DANUWAR *bakainu* ENGLISH *bread tree, China berry, Persian lilac* GURUNG *bakainu* LEPCHA *rakaskung* LIMBU *raksasing* MAGAR *bakainu* MAJHI *bakainu* NEPALI *bakaino* NEWARI *khaibasi* RAI *chhachharima, chhayal* SUNWAR *bakaina* TAMANG *bakaina, bakasyitong, chanyal, gorakha mal* THARU *bakain, bakyan* TIBETAN *smag sing*

Meliaceae. Deciduous tree about 10 m high. Leaves stalked, large, bi- or tripinnate, leaflets 3–11 in each pinna, short-stalked, 3–9 cm long, 0.8–2.5 cm wide, ovate to lanceolate, acuminate, serrate or subentire, glabrous. Flowers lilac-blue, fragrant. Fruit a drupe, ellipsoidal, yellowish when ripe, wrinkled and remaining long on the tree after ripening. Flowers March–May, fruits June–July. Propagated by seeds or branch cuttings. Distributed throughout Nepal at 700–1700 m in open places around villages; also in Iran, Afghanistan, Pakistan, India, Bhutan, and eastward to western China.

MEDICINE. Juice of the bark is anthelmintic, stimulant, and antispasmodic. A paste of the bark is applied to relieve headaches and rheumatic pain. Juice of the leaves has an antiseptic property. A decoction of the flower is applied to the head to remove lice. Fruit, boiled in water, is used for washing hands and feet, especially for chapped skin. Powdered fruit, about 2 teaspoons, is taken as an anthelmintic.

OTHER USES. The plant is fast-growing so it is a good substitute for fuelwood trees. Wood is also used for furniture. Leaves are lopped for fodder. Seeds are strung into necklaces and rosaries.

Melilotus alba Medikus

ENGLISH *sweet clover, white melilot* NEPALI *methi jhar*

Leguminosae. Glabrous herb about 1 m high. Leaves stalked, trifoliolate, lateral leaflets nearly sessile, terminal

Melia azedarach

Melilotus alba

leaflet stalked, oblong, upper part dentate. Flowers white in axillary and terminal slender racemes. Fruit a pod, one-seeded. Flowers June–July. Propagated by seeds. Distributed throughout Nepal at 200–1000 m in open pastureland; also in Pakistan, India, Tibet, China, Mongolia, Siberia, Malaysia, Australia, and the Americas.

OTHER USES. The plant provides fodder.

Melilotus indica (Linnaeus) Allioni

Trifolium indica Linnaeus
Melilotus parviflora Desfontaines
NEPALI *methi jhar*

Leguminosae. Annual herb about 70 cm high. Leaves stalked, trifoliolate, leaflets sessile, to 2 cm long, ovate to lanceolate, dentate, glabrous. Flowers yellow in long racemes. Fruit a pod, ovoid to ellipsoidal, apiculate, ribbed. Flowers and fruits April–August. Propagated by seeds. Distributed in central Nepal at 2700–3600 m in moist, open places; also in India, Bhutan, western and central Asia, Myanmar, Thailand, Malaysia, Australia, Europe, Africa, and North America.

OTHER USES. The plant provides fodder.

Meliosma dilleniifolia (Wallich ex Wight & Arnott)
Walpers

Millingtonia dilleniifolia Wallich ex Wight & Arnott
NEPALI *kode khabde*

Sabiaceae. Tree about 3 m high. Leaves stalked, obovate, acuminate, coarsely dentate, rusty pubescent beneath, narrowed toward the base. Flowers greenish in spreading panicles, July–August. Propagated by seeds. Distributed throughout Nepal at 1800–2900 m in open, grassy places along trails; also in India, Bhutan, Tibet, and Myanmar.

OTHER USES. The plant is used for fodder.

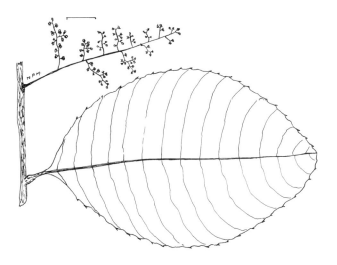

Meliosma dilleniifolia

Melissa axillaris (Bentham) Bakhuizen fil.

Geniosporum axillare Bentham
Melissa parviflora Bentham
GURUNG *charpate, lomai*

Labiatae. Herb about 60 cm high. Leaves stalked, 1–5 cm long, 0.5–2.8 cm wide, lanceolate, pointed, serrate, glabrous. Flowers white. Flowers and fruits July–December. Propagated by seeds or suckers. Distributed throughout Nepal at 1000–3600 m in open, grassy places along trails; also in northern India, Bhutan, southern China, Taiwan, Myanmar, and Malaysia.

MEDICINE. Juice of the plant is applied to cuts and wounds.

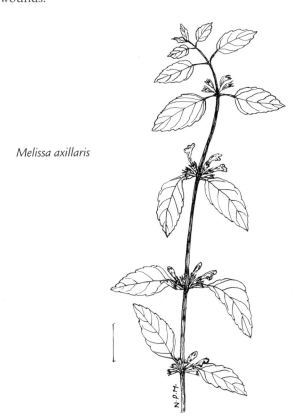

Melissa axillaris

Melochia corchorifolia Linnaeus

ENGLISH *wild mallow*　NEPALI *ban pate, patuwa jhar*

Sterculiaceae. Erect annual herb about 1 m high. Leaves stalked, 2–7.5 cm long, 1–4.5 cm wide, ovate to lanceolate, acute, irregularly incised, base cordate or rounded. Flowers white with a yellowish blotch. Fruit a capsule, depressed globose. Flowers and fruits August–December. Propagated by seeds. Distributed in eastern and central Nepal to about 1300 m in open areas and maize fields as a weed; pantropical.

FOOD. Tender leaves and shoots are cooked as a vegetable.

MEDICINE. A paste of the root is applied to boils and pimples.

Melochia corchorifolia

Mentha spicata

Mesua ferrea

Mentha spicata Linnaeus

Mentha crispa Linnaeus
Mentha pudina Buchanan-Hamilton ex Bentham
Mentha sativa Roxburgh
Mentha viridis (Linnaeus) Linnaeus

BHOJPURI *pudina* CHEPANG *tursiro* ENGLISH *spearmint*
GURUNG *bawari* LEPCHA *ribirip* LIMBU *ondong* MAGAR *daunne*
MOOSHAR *pudina* NEPALI *bawari, pudina, patina*
NEWARI *nawa ghyan* RAI *thompa* SUNWAR *padena* TAMANG *bawari*
THARU *bawari*

Labiatae. Herb about 50 cm high. Leaves short-stalked, 2–3.5 cm long, 1.5–2.5 cm wide, ovate, serrate, aromatic, tip round. Flowers white in a whorl of many-flowered spikes, June–August. Propagated by seeds or suckers. Distributed throughout Nepal to about 2500 m in moist, open places; also in Afghanistan, Pakistan, India, Tibet, Europe, and North America.

FOOD. Leaves are pickled.

MEDICINE. Juice of the leaves is taken to treat bloody dysentery. Leaves are also chewed for boils on the tongue. Seeds are soaked in water and taken in cases of fever.

Mesua ferrea Linnaeus

Calophyllum nagassarium Burman fil.
Mesua nagassarium (Burman fil.) Kostermans
Mesua roxburghii Wight

ENGLISH *Ceylon ironwood, ironwood tree* NEPALI *nagkeshar, narisal*
TIBETAN *ana-ga-ge-ser*

Guttiferae. Evergreen tree about 20 m high. Leaves stalked, linear to ovate, acuminate, entire, leathery. Flow-ers stalked, white or yellow. Fruit ovoid. Flowers April–June, fruits July–December. Propagated by seeds. Distributed in eastern and central Nepal at 400–900 m in open places around villages; also in India, Sri Lanka, Thailand, Vietnam, and Malaysia.

MEDICINE. The flower has astringent and stomachic properties. A paste of the flowers, about 2 teaspoons once a day, is given in cases of amebic dysentery. Fruit is stimulant and alterative; a paste of it is applied to boils. Seed oil is applied for itches, sores, and scabies.

OTHER USES. Oil from the seed is used for lighting.

Michelia champaca Linnaeus

Michelia aurantiaca Wallich
ENGLISH *champak, sapu* LIMBU *soyemba* NEPALI *champa*
RAI *lukbhung* TAMANG *chempe* TIBETAN *tsam-pa-ka*

Magnoliaceae. Tree about 20 m high with dark gray bark. Leaves stalked, 15–20 cm long, 5–8 cm wide, oblong to lanceolate, acuminate, entire, leathery, shiny dark green above, base acute. Flowers solitary, axillary, yellow, fragrant. Fruit subsessile, dark with white specks. Flowers June–July. Propagated by seeds. Distributed in central Nepal at 600–1300 m, planted on private land; also in India, southern Yunnan province in China, and Indo-China.

MEDICINE. Seeds are used to treat badly chapped skin.

OTHER USES. Wood is durable, polishes well, and is mainly used for furniture. Flowers are used in some religious activities and are indispensable on certain occasions. The flower produces a yellow dye.

Michelia doltsopa Buchanan-Hamilton ex de Candolle

Magnolia excelsa Wallich, *Michelia excelsa* (Wallich) Blume ex Wallich, *Sampacca excelsa* (Wallich) Kuntze
NEPALI *rani chanp*

Magnoliaceae. Large deciduous tree. Leaves stalked, 7–18 cm long, ovate to oblong, dark glossy green above, glaucous beneath. Flowers solitary, axillary, pale yellow or white, fragrant, March–April. Propagated by seeds. Distributed in eastern and central Nepal at 2100–2500 m; also in northern India, southeastern Tibet, southeastern China, and northern Myanmar.

OTHER USES. Trees provide timber and fuelwood. Foliage is used for fodder.

Michelia kisopa Buchanan-Hamilton ex de Candolle

Sampacca kisopa (Buchanan-Hamilton ex de Candolle) Kuntze
Michelia tila Buchanan-Hamilton ex Wallich
NEPALI *kaula, seto chanp*

Magnoliaceae. Tree about 20 m high. Leaves stalked, oblong to lanceolate, acuminate, leathery, glabrous above, pubescent beneath. Flowers solitary, axillary at the tips of branches, yellow, October–November. Propagated by seeds. Distributed throughout Nepal at 1200–2200 m; also in northern India and Bhutan.

FOOD. Powdered bark, mixed with corn flour (*Zea mays*), is baked to make delicious bread.

OTHER USES. The plant provides fodder.

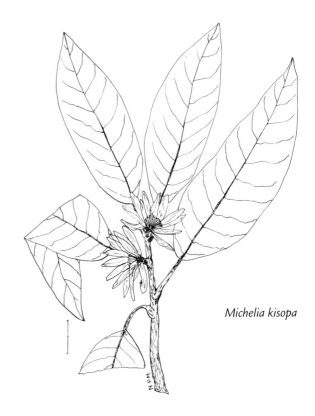

Michelia kisopa

Microlepia speluncae (Linnaeus) T. Moore

NEPALI *hare unyu*

Dennstaedtiaceae. Herbaceous fern. Fronds 40–65 cm long, 20–35 cm wide, ovate to deltoid lanceolate, tripinnate, pinnae linear, deeply cut into segments. Sori large, near the bases of the segments. Propagated by spores. Dis-

Microlepia speluncae

tributed in central Nepal to about 2000 m, common in the shade under forest trees; also in India, Sri Lanka, southwestern China, Taiwan, Southeast Asia, the Philippines, Polynesia, and Hawaii.

OTHER USES. The plant is used for animal bedding.

Micromeria biflora (Buchanan-Hamilton ex D. Don) Bentham

Thymus biforus Buchanan-Hamilton ex D. Don, *Satureja biflora* (Buchanan-Hamilton ex D. Don) Briquet

ENGLISH *lemon-scented thyme* GURUNG *jimuno* NEPALI *buchke ghans, jotane jhar, mishri jhar, majaito, pinase jhar, sinka jhar*
TAMANG *setero*

Labiatae. Perennial herb about 20 cm high with a woody rootstock. Leaves sessile, 4–6 mm long, ovate or oblong, entire, gland-dotted. Flowers pinkish or white in one- to four-flowered cymes. Fruit a nutlet, reddish brown, smooth, April–July. Propagated by seeds. Distributed throughout Nepal at 600–4000 m in open places; also in Afghanistan, northern India, Bhutan, and Myanmar.

FOOD. Leaves and flowers are used as tea. A powder of leaves and flowers is used to flavor lentil soup (*daal* in Nepali) and curries.

MEDICINE. A paste of the root is pressed between the jaws to treat toothaches. The plant is rubbed and inhaled to stop nosebleed. A paste of the plant is applied to wounds. Juice of the plant, about 1 teaspoon, is taken to treat sinusitis, and this juice is also inhaled for the same illness.

OTHER USES. The plant is used as fodder, especially during rainy season. It is also burned as an incense.

Microsorum hymenodes (Kuntze) Ching

NEPALI *lahare unyu*

Polypodiaceae. Epiphytic fern. Rhizome creeping, with brown scales. Fronds 10–20 cm long, 2–3 cm wide, lanceolate, entire, tapering toward both ends. Sori globose, brown, on either side of the midvein. Propagated by spores. Distributed in central Nepal at 1200–2500 m on mossy tree trunks and branches.

MEDICINE. Juice of the plant, about 4 teaspoons three times a day, is given in cases of fever.

Microstegium ciliatum (Trinius) A. Camus

Pollinia ciliata Trinius
NEPALI *khunkhune*

Gramineae. Annual or perennial grass about 1 m high. Leaves sessile, linear lanceolate, finely acuminate, thin, flat, narrowed at the base, margin somewhat roughly textured, with a few tubercle-based hairs on the upper surface, sheath somewhat rough. Inflorescence pale green. Propagated by seeds. Distributed throughout Nepal at 500–2000 m on open, rocky ground; also in India, Bhutan, China, Taiwan, Myanmar, and Thailand.

OTHER USES. The plant is used for fodder.

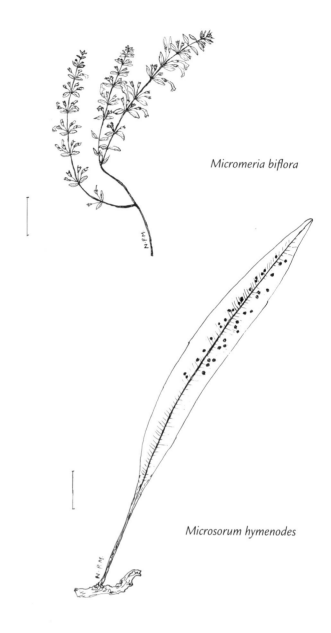

Micromeria biflora

Microsorum hymenodes

Millettia extensa (Bentham) Baker

Otosema extensa Bentham
Millettia auriculata Baker ex Brandis
Robinia macrophylla Roxburgh, *Otosema macrophylla* (Roxburgh) Bentham

CHEPANG *bhaising, burban* GURUNG *pirpite* MAJHI *gausho*
NEPALI *gaujo* RAUTE *gaujo*

Leguminosae. Woody climber. Leaves stalked, pinnate, leaflets 5–19 cm long, 3.5–11 cm wide, ovate, entire. Flowers dull white. Fruit a pod, brown tomentose. Flowers June–July, fruits August–November. Propagated by seeds. Distributed throughout Nepal to about 1000 m in deciduous forests of the subtropical belt; also in northern India, Bhutan, and Indo-China.

MEDICINE. Juice of the bark is applied to treat scabies.

OTHER USES. Juice of the plant is applied to the bodies of cattle to rid them of lice and parasitic worms. Root and

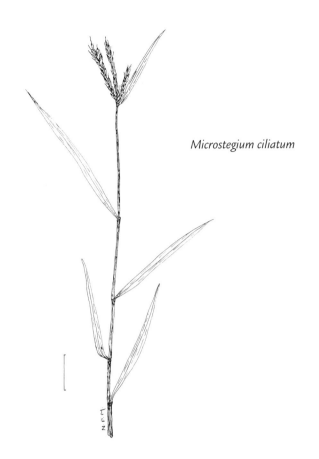

Microstegium ciliatum

bark are used as fish poison. Bark from the branches provides a coarse fiber used for rough cordage. Leaves and twigs are lopped for fodder.

Millettia fruticosa (de Candolle) Bentham ex Baker

Tephrosea fruticosa de Candolle, *Otosema fruticosa* (de Candolle) Bentham
Robinia fruticosa Roxburgh
NEPALI *tantari*

Leguminosae. Woody climber, young shoots silky tomentose. Leaves stalked, crowded at the ends of branchlets, pinnate, leaflets ovate to oblong, acuminate, minutely pubescent beneath. Flowers reddish in short axillary racemes. Fruit a pod, glabrous when mature. Flowers April–June, fruits November–December. Propagated by seeds. Distributed in eastern and central Nepal at 300–1000 m in broad-leaved forest, climbing on trees and shrubs; also in India.

MEDICINE. Juice of the plant is applied to wounds between the toes caused by prolonged walking barefooted in muddy water. A paste of the leaves is applied to treat gout.

OTHER USES. Bark and leaves are used as fish poison.

Millettia pinnata (Linnaeus) Panigrahi

Cytisus pinnatus Linnaeus, *Pongamia pinnata* (Linnaeus) Pierre
ENGLISH *Indian beach tree, pongam* NEPALI *kersingi, sadum*
THARU *kanju* TIBETAN *jam-bras*

Leguminosae. Tree about 18 m high, bark grayish green, often mottled with dark brown dots. Leaves stalked,

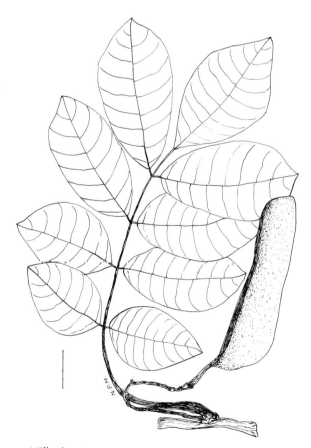

Millettia extensa

*Millettia
pinnata*

odd-pinnate, leaflets five to seven, elliptic, acuminate, entire. Flowers pinkish, fragrant, in axillary racemes. Fruit a pod, woody, smooth, compressed, with a short, curved beak. Flowers April–June. Propagated by seeds or cuttings. Distributed throughout Nepal to about 600 m; also in India, Sri Lanka, southern China, Malaysia, tropical Australia, Polynesia, and Fiji.

MEDICINE. Juice of the root, with juice of the green fruit of coconut, is taken for gonorrhea. Bark is boiled in water and gargled in cases of cough and colds. Juice of the bark is given in cases of mental disorder. Juice of the flower is taken for diabetes and cough and colds. A paste of the seed, mixed with the seed of *Cassia tora*, is applied to treat skin diseases. Seed oil is reputed to have antiseptic value in treating scabies and other skin diseases.

OTHER USES. Plants are lopped for fodder, and leaves are used as green manure. Leaves and seeds are used as fish poison. Seeds yield 30–40% oil, which is burned in lamps.

Mimosa pudica Linnaeus

CHEPANG *kama muja* DANUWAR *lajauni* ENGLISH *humble plant, sensitive plant* GURUNG *mhaira* MOOSHAR *lajauni* NEPALI *bhuin lahara, buhari jhar, lajamani jhar, lajanti jhar, lajjawati, lajyati, lalati jhar, nidaune jhar, nani jhar, nani kanda* RAI *lajuwa* TAMANG *pebamran*

Leguminosae. Diffuse herb, stems sparingly armed with recurved prickles. Leaves stalked, sensitive, digitate, pinnae in one or two pairs, 4 cm long, leaflets in 12–22 pairs, sessile, narrowly oblong, acute into a pointed tip. Flowers pinkish in globose heads. Fruit a pod, flat, slightly curved, jointed, the margin spinous, bristly. Flowers August–November, fruits November–December. Propagated by seeds. Distributed throughout Nepal to about 1500 m, common in open, moist areas and on uncultivated land; also pantropical.

MEDICINE. A paste of the plant is applied for gout. Juice of the plant is considered antiasthmatic and is also applied to treat gout. The root has emetic and aphrodisiac properties. It is considered efficacious in treating asthma, fever, cough, dysentery, and vaginal troubles. Juice of the root, about 4 teaspoons twice a day, is given to treat inflammation during urination. A paste of leaves and roots is used for hemorrhoids and kidney troubles. Juice of the leaves is given for dysentery and kidney troubles. A paste of the leaves is applied to glandular swellings. Burned leaf mixed with kerosene is applied to treat skin diseases. Seeds are chewed for sore throat.

Mimosa rubicaulis Lambert subsp. himalayana
(Gamble) Ohashi

Mimosa himalayana Gamble

CHEPANG *mairang, rangchu* MAGAR *arkhu, jhukre* MAJHI *arali* NEPALI *arari, areli kanda, boksi ghans, tirinkhe* TAMANG *arai, hunrapa puju, marang puju, warkopuchu*

Leguminosae. Straggling shrub. Leaves stalked, bipinnate, pinnae in 8–12 pairs, pinnules in 16–20 pairs, 2.5–7

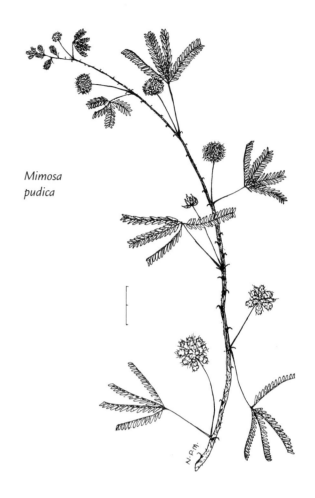

*Mimosa
pudica*

mm long, oblong, unequally sided, obtuse to mucronate. Flowers pink, fading to white, in axillary fascicles. Fruit a pod, falcate, glabrous, remaining long on the tree. Flowers August–October, fruits October–January. Propagated by seeds. Distributed throughout Nepal to about 1900 m in open places; also in Afghanistan, northern India, and Bhutan.

MEDICINE. Juice of the plant, about 2 teaspoons twice a day, is given to treat peptic ulcer. Powdered root is given for vomiting as a result of weakness. A paste of the root is applied to sprains and backaches. It is also used to reset dislocated bone. A paste of the leaves is used in cases of hemorrhoids. Pounded seeds are given for fever.

OTHER USES. Dried plants are used as fences. Charcoal from the wood is used to prepare explosives.

Mirabilis jalapa Linnaeus

GURUNG *maritidha, nakajali* ENGLISH *four o'clock plant, marvel of Peru* NEPALI *lankaphul, lankasoni, malati* TAMANG *labujana, langasani* THARU *barka gurubands*

Nyctaginaceae. Herb about 1 m high with a tuberous root. Leaves stalked, opposite, 3.5–7.5 cm long, 1.5–5 cm wide, unequal, narrowly ovate, acuminate, base often subtruncate. Flowers pink, white, or yellow, the corolla tube elongated. Fruit narrowly ovoid, black, finely ribbed.

Flowers and fruits July–November. Propagated by splitting the root or by seeds. Distributed throughout Nepal to about 1800 m in moist, open places; also mainly in tropical regions of the world.

FOOD. Tender leaves are cooked as a vegetable.

MEDICINE. The root is purgative and aphrodisiac, and a paste of it is applied for scabies and muscular swelling. Juice of the root, about 4 teaspoons twice a day, is given in cases of diarrhea and is also considered good for fever. This juice, about 3 teaspoons twice a day, is given to treat indigestion. Powder of the root, mixed with corn flour (*Zea mays*), is baked and given in cases of menstrual disorder. A paste of the root is applied to treat scabies. The leaf is diuretic and used for dropsy. A paste of the leaf is applied to abscesses and boils.

Mitragyna parvifolia (Roxburgh) Korthals

Nauclea parvifolia Roxburgh, *Stephegyne parvifolia* (Roxburgh) Korthals
THARU *tekui*

Rubiaceae. Deciduous tree about 15 m high, bark pale gray, covered with small circular lenticels, exfoliating in thick woolly pieces. Leaves stalked, opposite, 5–15 cm long, 4–10 cm wide, elliptic to orbiculate, rounded or bluntly acuminate at the apex, glabrous above, minutely pubescent beneath, base rounded or more or less cordate. Flowers greenish yellow, fragrant, in globose heads. Fruit a capsule, splitting into two dehiscent cocci. Flowers June–July, fruits May–June. Propagated by seeds. Distributed throughout Nepal to about 250 m in forest openings; also in India and Sri Lanka.

OTHER USES. The plant is lopped for fodder.

Mollugo pentaphylla Linnaeus

Mollugo stricta Linnaeus
Mollugo triphylla Loureiro
ENGLISH *carpet weed* NEPALI *nyauli*

Molluginaceae. Prostrate annual herb about 30 cm high. Leaves stalked, 1–5 cm long, 0.2–1 cm wide, linear lanceolate, acute or obtuse. Flowers whitish in axillary or terminal cymes. Fruit a capsule, ellipsoidal. Flowers and fruits May–November. Propagated by seeds. Distributed in central and eastern Nepal at 450–110 m on moist ground in pastureland, also in India, China, Japan, Malaysia, Australia, and Melanesia.

MEDICINE. A paste of the plant is applied to cuts and wounds.

Momordica balsamina Linnaeus

ENGLISH *balsam apple* NEPALI *barela*

Cucurbitaceae. Glabrous herb. Leaves stalked, 4–7.5 cm in diameter, orbiculate, palmately three- or five-lobed, lobes acutely lanceolate, punctate on both surfaces. Flowers yellowish. Fruit ovoid, narrowed toward both ends, smooth. Propagated by seeds or tubers. Distributed in

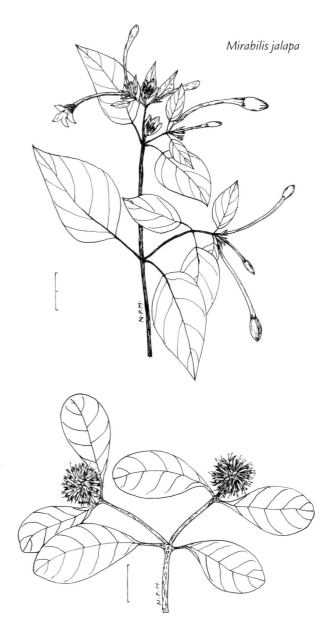

Mirabilis jalapa

Mitragyna parvifolia

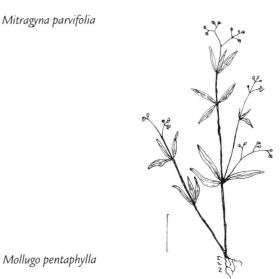

Mollugo pentaphylla

western and central Nepal to about 600 m, cultivated; also in western Asia, India, China, Malaysia, eastern Australia, Africa, and the Americas.

FOOD. Fruit is cooked as a vegetable.

Momordica charantia Linnaeus

Cucumis africanus Lindley
Momordica muricata de Candolle

BHOJPURI *karaila* DANUWAR *karaila* ENGLISH *African cucumber, bitter gourd, bitter squash, carilla fruit, leprosy gourd* LEPCHA *khakatik* LIMBU *takrukse* MAGAR *karela* MOOSHAR *karela* NEPALI *karela* NEWARI *kakacha* RAI *khukshi, phekwasi* SUNWAR *karela* TAMANG *kareli, karilo* THARU *karaila*

Cucurbitaceae. Annual vine with simple tendrils. Leaves stalked, rounded, oblong to ovate, cut to near the base into five or seven lobes, lobes variously dentate, cordate at the base. Flowers long-stalked, yellow, axillary. Fruit cylindrical, oblong, ribbed and wrinkled, pointed at both ends. Seeds oblong, compressed, the margins corrugated. Propagated by seeds. Distributed throughout Nepal to about 2100 m, cultivated; also in tropical Asia and Africa.

FOOD. Immature fruits are cooked as a vegetable or pickled.

MEDICINE. Juice of the plant is used to treat chronic ulcers of the stomach, skin diseases, and diabetes. It is also useful to treat sterility in women. The root is abortifacient and has an astringent property. Juice of the leaves is applied to treat inflammation of the sole. This juice, about 5 teaspoons three times a day, is given in cases of cough and colds. A paste of the leaves is applied to cuts and wounds. Juice of green fruit is applied to treat burns; it is also a remedy for inflammation of the intestine and bacillary dysentery.

Momordica dioica Roxburgh ex Willdenow

ENGLISH *small bitter gourd* NEPALI *chatel* NEWARI *chatali* SATAR *kanchan arak*

Cucurbitaceae. Perennial climber with a tuberous root. Leaves stalked, 3.5–10 cm long, ovate to cordate, acuminate, three- or five-lobed, distantly denticulate. Flowers whitish. Fruit short beaked, densely covered with soft spines. Flowers June–August. Propagated by seeds. Distributed in eastern and central Nepal to about 1300 m, cultivated; also in northern India, Sri Lanka, eastward to western China, Myanmar, and Malaysia.

FOOD. Young fruit and the tuberous root are cooked as a vegetable.

Monochoria hastata (Linnaeus) Solms

Pontederia hastata Linnaeus
Monochoria hastaefolia K. Presl

ENGLISH *pickerel weed* NEPALI *nilo jaluke*

Pontederiaceae. Perennial herb, rhizomes covered with the remains of the leaf sheaths. Leaves stalked, 3.5–25 cm long, ovate or triangular, base hastate or sagittate. Flowers

Momordica dioica

blue in short-stalked racemes, May–December. Propagated by seeds. Distributed in eastern and central Nepal to about 200 m in marshy or boggy places; also in tropical and subtropical Asia.

FOOD. Tender leaves are cooked as a vegetable.

Monochoria vaginalis (Burman fil.) K. Presl

Pontederia vaginalis Burman fil.
Pontederia plantaginea Roxburgh

DANUWAR *karboni* ENGLISH *duke's tongue* NEPALI *dhape jhar, hans jhar, karkale jhar, kumbhi*

Pontederiaceae. Aquatic herb with spongy a rootstock. Leaves stalked, 3.5–4 cm long, 3–4 cm wide, ovate to cordate, acuminate. Flowers blue in racemes, September–October. Propagated by seeds. Distributed throughout Nepal to about 1800 m on the margins of ponds and ditches; also in India, Bhutan, eastward to western China, Malaysia, and Japan.

FOOD. Tender leaves and buds are cooked as a vegetable. The flower is eaten raw.

MEDICINE. The root is chewed to treat toothaches. The flower is refrigerant.

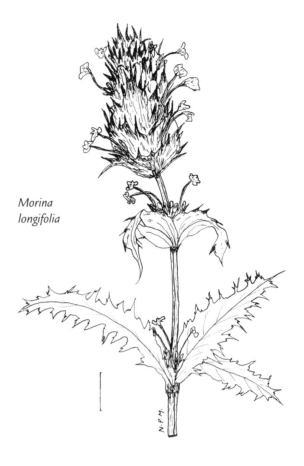

Morina
longifolia

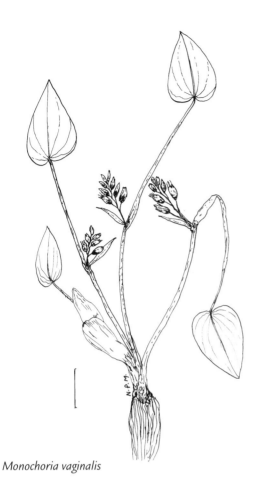

Monochoria vaginalis

Moringa oleifera

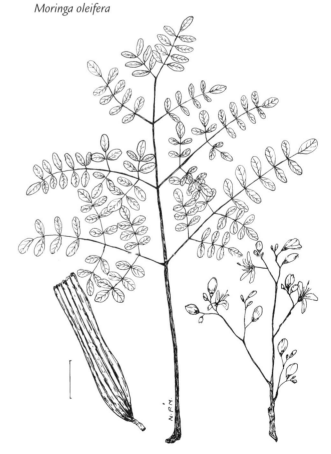

Morina longifolia Wallich ex de Candolle

NEPALI *kanda masi, thakaili kanda* TIBETAN *pitsir tserma*

Morinaceae. Prickly herb about 75 cm high. Leaves in whorls of three, oblong, acuminate, doubly spinous dentate, glabrous. Flowers purple, condensed in heads. Propagated by seeds. Distributed throughout Nepal at 3000–4200 m, common on moist ground along trials; also in northern India and Bhutan.

OTHER USES. The plant is used as incense.

Moringa oleifera Lambert

Guilandina moringa Linnaeus
Moringa pterygosperma (Linnaeus) Gaertner

CHEPANG *amaris* DANUWAR *munga* ENGLISH *drumstick tree, horseradish tree* MOOSHAR *sohijan* NEPALI *sajyon* SATAR *munga* TIBETAN *na-sha*

Moringaceae. Tree about 10 m high with corky bark. Leaves stalked, alternate, tripinnate, pinnae in four to six pairs, leaflets short-stalked, elliptic to ovate, thin, entire, pale beneath. Flowers white, fragrant. Fruit a pod, three-angled, nine-ribbed. Seeds three-angled, winged on the angles. Propagated by seeds or branch cuttings. Distributed throughout Nepal to about 1100 m, cultivated; also in India, Bhutan, Thailand, Malaysia, and the Philippines.

FOOD. Green fruits and tender leaves are cooked as a vegetable. The plant is a source of dietary iron.

MEDICINE. A paste of the root is applied to snakebites. It is purgative and stimulant. A decoction of the root is considered useful in asthma, gout, and liver troubles. Leaves are purgative and galactagogue. A paste of leaves is applied to glandular swellings. A paste of the gum, mixed with some molasses, is given to children suffering from dysentery. Fruits have anthelmintic properties.

OTHER USES. Leaf and stem contain tannin.

Morus australis Roxburgh

Morus indica Linnaeus
CHEPANG *chanaru* NEPALI *kimu* SATAR *kodaz*

Moraceae. Medium-sized deciduous tree. Leaves stalked, ovate to lanceolate, acuminate, dentate or serrate, glabrous above, slightly pubescent on veins and midribs beneath, base rounded or truncate. Flowers unisexual, yellowish. Fruit slender, white or dark purple. Flowers March–April, fruits May–June. Propagated by seeds or root offshoots. Distributed throughout Nepal at 900–2400 m; also in northern India, Bhutan, western China, and Myanmar.

FOOD. Ripe fruits are eaten fresh.

MEDICINE. The root is boiled in water about 10 minutes, and the filtered water, about 2 teaspoons, is given as an anthelmintic. A paste of the bark is applied to treat gingivitis.

OTHER USES. The plant is generally cultivated on private land or grown as an avenue tree.

Morus macroura Miquel

Morus laevigata Wallich ex Brandis, *M. alba* var. *laevigata* (Wallich ex Brandis) Bureau
ENGLISH *mulberry, white mulberry* NEPALI *kimu*

Moraceae. Tree about 15 m high. Leaves stalked, 8–20 cm long, 6–15 cm wide, usually unlobed, finely serrate, soft pubescent. Inflorescence greenish. Fruit white or purple, sweet when ripe. Flowers and fruits March–April. Propagated by seeds or root offshoots. Distributed throughout Nepal at 1000–2000 m on open hillsides; also in northern India, Bhutan, western and southern China, and Indo-China.

FOOD. Ripe fruits are edible.

MEDICINE. Juice of the bark is applied to cuts and wounds.

OTHER USES. Wood is used for building houses and furniture. Leaves are a source of food for silkworms.

Morus serrata Roxburgh

Morus alba var. *serrata* (Roxburgh) Bureau
Morus pabularia Decaisne
CHEPANG *chanaru* ENGLISH *Himalayan mulberry* MAGAR *kimbu* NEPALI *kimu*

Moraceae. Tree about 20 m high, bark dark gray, exfoliating in irregular woody scales. Leaves variable, broadly ovate, acuminate, deeply three- or five-lobed, coarsely and sharply serrate, teeth usually unequal and cuspidate, base truncate. Flowers greenish. Fruit an achene, pinkish or purplish when ripe. Flowers April–May, fruits May–June. Propagated by seeds or root offshoots. Distributed in central and western Nepal at 1500–2400 m in open places around villages; also in northwestern India.

FOOD. Ripe fruits are edible.

MEDICINE. Juice of the root, about 6 teaspoons, is taken at bedtime as an anthelmintic.

Mucuna nigricans (Loureiro) Steudel

Citta nigricans Loureiro
Carpopogon imbricatum Roxburgh, *Mucuna imbricata* (Roxburgh) de Candolle, *Stizolobium imbricatum* (Roxburgh) Kuntze
NEPALI *baldhendro, dhoireti* SATAR *atkir, etka*

Leguminosae. Woody climber with hollow branches. Leaves stalked, trifoliolate, leaflets 10–18 cm long, ovate to oblong, lateral leaflets oblique. Flowers dark purple in axillary racemes. Fruit a pod, oblong, clothed with deciduous, brownish yellow, irritating bristles. Flowers August–September, fruits November–December. Propagated by seeds. Distributed in central and eastern Nepal at 600–1200 m, climbing on shrubs and trees in broad-leaved forest; also in northern India, China, Southeast Asia, and the Ryukyu Islands.

OTHER USES. Foliage provides fodder. Seeds are used as a substitute for gum.

Mukia maderaspatana (Linnaeus) M. J. Roemer

Cucumis maderaspatana Linnaeus, *Melothria maderaspatana* (Linnaeus) Cogniaux
Bryonia scabrella Linnaeus fil., *Mukia scabrella* (Linnaeus fil.) Arnott
DANUWAR *moti jhar* TAMANG *nagilangai*

Cucurbitaceae. Climbing annual herb. Leaves stalked, three- to seven-lobed, dentate, roughly textured, deeply

Morus macroura

Mucuna nigricans

cordate. Flowers yellowish. Fruit a berry, globose. Flowers and fruits August–February. Propagated by seeds. Distributed in eastern and central Nepal to about 1200 m in shady places; also in India, Bhutan, China, Taiwan, Myanmar, Malaysia, Australia, and New Zealand.

MEDICINE. Squeezed plant is applied to treat scabies of animals. The root is chewed about 15 minutes to relieve toothaches. A decoction of the root is useful for flatulence and is also applied to treat toothaches.

Murdannia japonica (Thunberg) Faden

Commelina japonica Thunberg
Aneilema latifolium Wight
Commelina elata Vahl, *Aneilema elatum* (Vahl) Kunth, *Murdannia elata* (Vahl) Bruckner
Commelina herbacea Roxburgh, *Aneilema herbaceum* (Roxburgh) Wallich
Commelina lineolata Blume, *Aneilema lineolatum* (Blume) Kunth, *Murdannia lineolata* (Blume) J. K. Morton

NEPALI *nigale gava* TAMANG *gangdol*

Commelinaceae. Erect herb. Leaves sessile, 6–16 cm long, 1–2 cm wide, narrowly oblong, acuminate, margin roughly textured, base cuneate, rounded. Flowers purplish. Fruit a capsule, ellipsoidal. Flowers and fruits August–September. Propagated by seeds. Distributed in eastern and central Nepal at 400–2000 m in shady places; also in India, Bhutan, China, Myanmar, and Malaysia.

FOOD. Boiled roots are eaten like potatoes.

MEDICINE. The root, which is exported as a crude drug, is also sold in local markets.

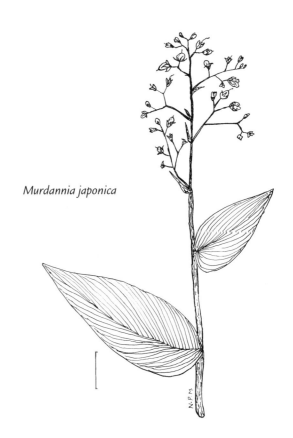

Murdannia japonica

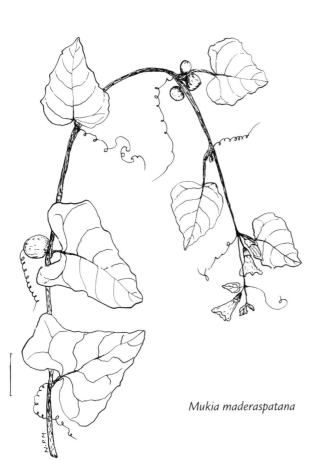

Mukia maderaspatana

Murdannia nudiflora (Linnaeus) Brenan

Commelina nudiflora Linnaeus, *Aneilema nudiflorum* (Linnaeus)
Wallich
Tradescantia malabarica Linnaeus, *Murdannia malabarica*
(Linnaeus) Bruckner
Aneilema radicans D. Don, *Commelina radicans* (D. Don)
Sprengel
NEPALI *kane jhar, masino kane*

Commelinaceae. Erect annual herb. Leaves sessile, linear lanceolate, acute, glabrous, base more or less cordate
or rounded. Flowers purplish in lax cymose panicles. Fruit
a capsule, subglobose. Flowers and fruits August–
November. Propagated by seeds. Distributed throughout
Nepal to about 1500 m in moist places; also in India,
China, Myanmar, Malaysia, southern Japan, and Africa.

FOOD. Tender leaves are cooked as a vegetable.

MEDICINE. A paste of the root is applied to treat headaches.

Murdannia scapiflora (Roxburgh) Royle

Commelina scapiflora Roxburgh, *Aneilema scapiflorm* (Roxburgh)
Kosteletzky
Aneilema serotinum D. Don ex C. B. Clarke
NEPALI *nigale gava, pate phul*

Commelinaceae. Tufted herb about 70 cm high with
elongated tuberous roots. Leaves all basal, erect, 4–10 cm
long, finely acuminate. Flowers small, pale mauve. Fruit a
capsule, ellipsoidal, three-angled, mucronate. Propagated
by seeds. Distributed throughout Nepal to about 2000 m,
frequent in moist places; also in India, Sri Lanka, and
Myanmar.

FOOD. Boiled roots are eaten like potatoes.

MEDICINE. Juice of the root is given in cases of fever.

Murraya koenigii (Linnaeus) Sprengel

Bergera koenigii Linnaeus, *Chalcas koenigii* (Linnaeus)
Millspaugh
DANUWAR *bhuin jamun* ENGLISH *curry leaf tree* NEPALI *baugureti,
bogaino, bokini* THARU *bhenri*

Rutaceae. Deciduous shrub about 3 m high. Leaves
stalked, pinnate, leaflets stalked, alternate, obliquely
ovate, entire, gland-dotted. Flowers stalked, white, in terminal panicles, May–April. Fruits June–August. Propagated by seeds or stem cuttings. Distributed throughout
Nepal to about 1400 m in open, dry places; also in India,
Sri Lanka, China, and Indo-China.

FOOD. Leaves are used to flavor curry dishes. Ripe fruits
are eaten fresh.

MEDICINE. Roots are stimulant. A paste of the bark is
applied to the bites of poisonous insects and other animals. Leaves are stomachic and chewed for diarrhea and
dysentery.

OTHER USES. The plant is fast-growing and good for soil
binding.

Murraya koenigii

Murraya paniculata (Linnaeus) Jack

Chalcas paniculata Linnaeus
Murraya exotica Linnaeus, *Chalcas exotica* (Linnaeus)
Millspaugh
NEPALI *bajardante*

Rutaceae. Evergreen shrub with gray corky bark. Leaves
stalked, three- to nine-foliolate; leaflets short-stalked, 2.5–
7.5 cm long, 1.5–2.5 cm wide, obliquely rhombic, more or
less acuminate, entire, leathery when mature, shiny above.
Flowers white, fragrant, in axillary or terminal corymbs.
Fruit a berry, narrowed at both ends, bright red or dark
red when ripe, two-seeded. Flowers March–September,
fruits October–February. Propagated by seeds or stem cuttings. Distributed in eastern and central Nepal at 400–
1100 m in open, dry places; also in India, Sri Lanka, China,
and Southeast Asia.

MEDICINE. Fresh leaves are chewed for toothaches.

Musa paradisiaca Linnaeus

BHOJPURI *kera* CHEPANG *maisai* DANUWAR *kera* ENGLISH *banana*
GURUNG *mach* LEPCHA *kardung* LIMBU *tetlase* MAGAR *mocha*
MOOSHAR *kera* NEPALI *kera* NEWARI *kera* RAI *gnksi* SUNWAR *mugi*
TAMANG *moje* THARU *kera*

Musaceae. Tall stoloniferous plant. Leaves large, erect
or ascending, spirally arranged, oblong, bases successively
sheathing, forming the trunk. Inflorescence drooping.
Fruit oblong, yellowish green when ripe, sweet. Flowers
and fruits most of the year. Propagated by root buds. Distributed throughout Nepal to about 1800 m, planted in
orchards and gardens; also in most tropical countries.

FOOD. Flowers are boiled and eaten like pickles. Ripe
fruits are edible. They have a high content of carbohy-
drates with some fats and proteins. Green bananas may
be cooked as a vegetable.

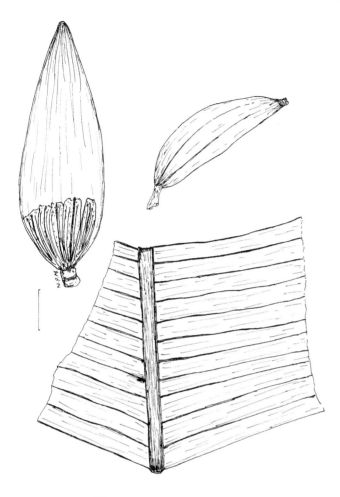

Musa paradisiaca

Mussaenda macrophylla

MEDICINE. Flowers are astringent.

OTHER USES. Leaves are used as plates. The leaf sheath is used for temporary binding.

Mussaenda frondosa Linnaeus

NEPALI *asari*

Rubiaceae. Straggling shrub about 3 m high. Leaves stalked, 7–13 cm long, broadly elliptic, cuspidate, more or less pubescent above, pubescent on veins beneath. Flowers orange or yellowish in terminal cymes. Fruit a berry, subglobose. Flowers June–July, fruits November–December. Propagated by seeds or cuttings. Distributed in central Nepal to about 1200 m; also in India and Sri Lanka.

MEDICINE. Juice of the root is applied to treat blemishes on the tongue. This juice, about 5 teaspoons mixed with half a teaspoon of cow's urine, is given three times a day for jaundice. Juice of the bark is given in cases of body ache, diarrhea, and dysentery. Flowers are diuretic, and juice of them is given in cases of cough.

OTHER USES. The shrub is cultivated in gardens as an ornamental.

Mussaenda macrophylla Wallich

Mussaenda hispida D. Don

CHEPANG *dhobi jhar* GURUNG *nanimaiso, tarkheta*
NEPALI *asari, dhobini, dware*

Rubiaceae. Shrub with hirsute branches. Leaves stalked, broadly elliptic, acuminate, hirsute. Flowers orange or yellowish, crowded in cymes, the showy bracts very bright. Fruit a berry, broadly ellipsoidal, hairy. Flowers March–April, fruits July–August. Propagated by seeds or cuttings. Distributed in central and eastern Nepal to about 1800 m in moist places in association with herbs and other shrubs; also in northern India, southeastern China, and Myanmar.

MEDICINE. Juice of the root, about 6 teaspoons three times a day, is given in cases of fever. It is also considered good for stomach acidity and is also given to diabetic patients.

Mussaenda roxburghii Hooker fil.

Mussaenda corymbosa Wallich

GURUNG *nanimaso*

Rubiaceae. Shrub. Leaves stalked, 4–15 cm long, 2–7 cm wide, oblanceolate, narrowed at both ends, smooth on both sides. Flowers yellow in many-flowered cymes. Fruit a berry, oval, glabrous, crowned with the persistent calyx teeth. Propagated by seeds or cuttings. Distributed in eastern and central Nepal at 200–1200 m in moist, shady places; also in India, Bhutan, Bangladesh, and Myanmar.

MEDICINE. A paste of the root is applied to boils on the tongue.

Myriactis nepalensis Lessing

Lavenia dentata Wallich
Lavenia sphaerantha Wallich
Myriactis wallichii Lessing
NEPALI *thuke phul* TAMANG *sabromo*

Compositae. Herb about 50 cm high. Leaves stalked, alternate, ovate to lanceolate, acute, coarsely serrate, hairy or glabrous. Flower heads yellowish in slender panicles. Fruit an achene. Propagated by seeds. Distributed throughout Nepal at 1400–3900 m in open places along trails, weedy; also in Iran, Afghanistan, India, western China, Indo-China, and Indonesia.

FOOD. Roasted fruits are pickled.

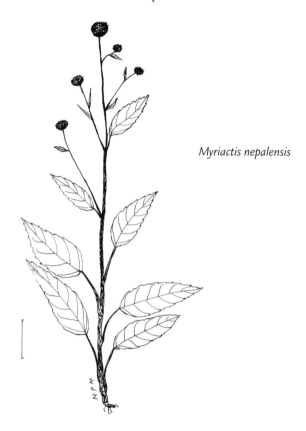

Myriactis nepalensis

Myrica esculenta Buchanan-Hamilton ex D. Don

Myrica farquhariana Wallich
Myrica integrifolia Roxburgh
Myrica nagi Thunberg
Myrica sapida Wallich

BHOJPURI *kaphal* CHEPANG *brionung* DANUWAR *kaphal*
ENGLISH *bay berry, box myrtle* GURUNG *kaphal* KHALING *jheremsi*
LEPCHA *lhothampot* LIMBU *lalise* MAGAR *kaphal* NEPALI *kaphal*
NEWARI *kobasi* RAI *chakchansi* SUNWAR *phechchi* SHERPA *karbisi*
TAMANG *karbija, karpasi, kharbusya, namun* THARU *kaphal*
TIBETAN *kat-pha-la*

Myricaceae. Evergreen tree about 12 m high. Leaves stalked, 3–15 cm long, 1–4.5 cm wide, oblanceolate, obtuse or acute, nearly entire, glabrous above, with resinous dots beneath, base acute. Flowers unisexual, greenish or slightly reddish. Fruit ellipsoidal, reddish when ripe. Flowers July–October, fruits March–May. Propagated by seeds. Distributed throughout Nepal at 1300–2100 m in open places; also in northern India, Bhutan, Myanmar, western and southern China, and Southeast Asia.

FOOD. Ripe fruits are edible; they are also sold in markets.

MEDICINE. The bark is stimulant, carminative, and astringent, and its juice is applied to treat rheumatism. Juice of the bark is applied to cuts and wounds. This juice is also taken for catarrh and headaches and is applied to treat body aches. A decoction of bark is boiled to form a gelatinous mass that is applied to sprains. The decoction is taken for fever, asthma, and diarrhea. In eastern Nepal, a paste of the bark is applied to the forehead to treat headaches. In the Dhankuta district of eastern Nepal, people boil the bark with bark of *Quercus lanata* about 10 minutes, and the filtered liquid is taken in cases of dysentery. Powdered bark, about 2 teaspoons three times a day, is given for gastric troubles. This powder is also used to relieve headaches and nasal congestion. Bark of the stem or root is kept pressed between the teeth to treat dental caries. Juice of unripe fruit, about 2 teaspoons, is taken as an anthelmintic.

OTHER USES. Wood is mainly used for fuel but in some places it is also used for making poles for construction. Squeezed bark is spread on the water to intoxicate fish. Bark yields a yellow dye and contains 60–80% tannin.

Myrica esculenta

Myricaria rosea W. W. Smith

Myricaria prostrata Hooker fil. & Thomson ex Bentham &
Hooker fil., *M. germinaca* var. *prostrata* (Hooker fil. &
Thomson ex Bentham & Hooker fil.) Dyer

TIBETAN *humpu*

Tamaricaceae. Trailing shrub, young shoots glaucous green or reddish. Leaves small, crowded, oblong to lanceolate, acute or obtuse. Flowers violet-purple in dense spikes, March–August. Fruits September–November. Propagated by seeds. Distributed in eastern and central Nepal at 3300–4500 m in open as well as shady places along streams; also in India, Bhutan, southern Tibet, and western China.

MEDICINE. A paste of the plant is taken to treat colds and is applied to relieve backaches.

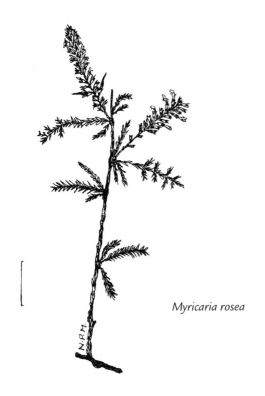

Myricaria rosea

Myrsine capitellata Wallich

Rapanea capitellata (Wallich) Mez
Myrsine excelsa D. Don

NEPALI *bakal pate, phalam kath, seti kath*   TAMANG *gharma*

Myrsinaceae. Tree about 9 m high. Leaves stalked, crowded at the tips of branches, 7–13 cm long, elliptic to lanceolate, narrowed at both ends, entire, leathery, glabrous. Flowers white, fascicled on short branches, November–December. Fruits March–April. Propagated by seeds. Distributed in eastern and central Nepal at 900–1800 m on moist hillsides with other plants; also in Afghanistan, northern India, Bhutan, and Indo-China.

FOOD. Ripe fruits are edible.

Myrsine capitellata

Myrsine semiserrata Wallich

Myrsine acuminata Royle
Myrsine sessilis D. Don
Myrsine subspinosa D. Don

NEPALI *phalame*

Myrsinaceae. Small tree with ash-colored bark. Leaves stalked, 12–18 cm long, 5–7.5 cm wide, ovate to oblong, short acuminate, undulate, sometimes serrulate, usually rusty pubescent beneath, base cuneate. Flowers small, white. Fruit a berry, clustered, globose, shiny red. Flowers and fruits November–January. Propagated by seeds. Distributed throughout Nepal at 1200–2700 m on open hillsides; also in northern India, Bhutan, Tibet, western and central China, and northern Myanmar.

OTHER USES. Wood is used for construction. Leaves are gathered for fodder.

N

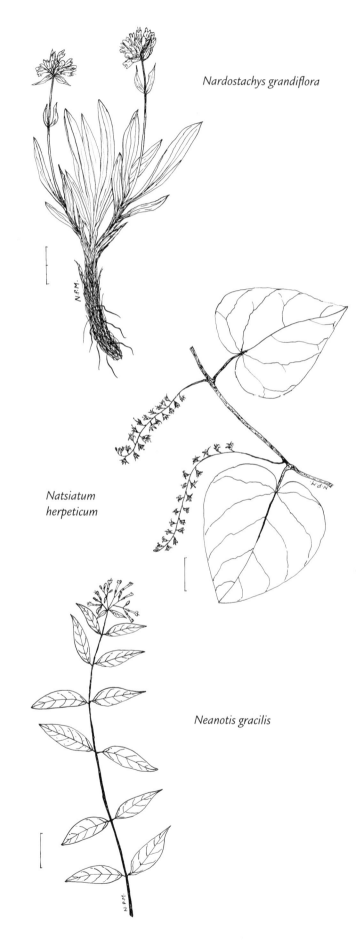

Nardostachys grandiflora

Nardostachys grandiflora de Candolle

Fedia grandiflora Wallich ex de Candolle
Nardostachys gracilis Kitamura
Patrinia jatamansi D. Don, *Nardostachys jatamansi* (D. Don)
de Candolle

ENGLISH *spikenard* GURUNG *jatamansi* KHALING *naorochi* NEPALI
bhultya, jatamansi NEWARI *naswan* SHERPA *pangbu* TAMANG *poi*
TIBETAN *spang-spos*

Valerianaceae. Perennial herb about 35 cm high, rootstock stout, covered with fibrous stalks of withered leaves. Basal leaves lanceolate, longitudinally veined, glabrous or slightly hairy, cauline leaves sessile. Flowers bluish white, June–August. Fruits October–November. Propagated by seeds or rhizomes. Distributed throughout Nepal at 3200–5000 m on rocky hillsides but collection of rhizomes for sale in the trade is a cause of conservation concern; also in northern India, Bhutan, Tibet, and western China.

MEDICINE. A paste of the rhizome is applied to treat hemorrhoids.

OTHER USES. Dried leaves are used as incense.

Natsiatum herpeticum Buchanan-Hamilton ex
Arnott

Sicyos pentandra Wallich
CHEPANG *khasre lahara* NEPALI *kali lahara*

Natsiatum herpeticum

Icacinaceae. Herbaceous climber with tuberous roots, shoots densely strigose. Leaves stalked, 7.5–15 cm long, 5–12.5 cm wide, broadly ovate, acute or acuminate, dentate, somewhat roughly textured, with appressed soft white hairs, base truncate or cuneate. Flowers greenish yellow in axillary racemes. Fruit a drupe, somewhat oblique, rugose. Flowers December–January, fruits January–February. Propagated by seeds. Distributed throughout Nepal at 250–1400, trailing on hedges in sunny places; also in India, Bhutan, and Indo-China.

FOOD. Tender leaves and shoots are cooked as a vegetable by Rautes.

OTHER USES. The plant is used to make *marcha,* a fermenting cake from which liquor is distilled.

Neanotis gracilis (Hooker fil.) W. H. Lewis

Anotis gracilis Hooker fil.
NEPALI *sim ghans*

Neanotis gracilis

Rubiaceae. Straggling herb. Leaves short-stalked, opposite, about 5 cm long, lanceolate, acuminate, entire, pubescent. Flowers white in subterminal and terminal cymes, August–September. Propagated by seeds. Distributed in eastern and central Nepal at 1500–2000 m on moist hillsides with other plants; also in India and Bhutan.

MEDICINE. Juice of the plant is given in cases of indigestion.

Neillia thyrsiflora D. Don

Neillia virgata Wallich
GURUNG *bhogla* TAMANG *pheli, rawagen, saplung*

Rosaceae. Shrub about 2 m high. Leaves stalked, alternate, trifoliolate, leaflets ovate to lanceolate, caudate-acuminate, sharply dentate, pubescent on the vein beneath. Flowers white in axillary and terminal panicles, July–August. Fruits September–November. Propagated by seeds. Distributed in central and eastern Nepal at 1600–2100 m on exposed slopes along streams; also in northern India, China, Myanmar, and western Sumatra.

FOOD. Ripe fruits are edible.

Neillia thyrsiflora

Nelumbo nucifera Gaertner

Nelumbium speciosum Willdenow
Nymphaea nelumbo Linnaeus
BHOJPURI *kamal* DANUWAR *kamal* ENGLISH *lotus* GURUNG *kamal*
LEPCHA *pemariy* LIMBU *sumjiriphung* MAGAR *kamal* NEPALI *kamal*
NEWARI *pal swan* RAI *chakwa phoma* SUNWAR *kamal*
TAMANG *kamal mhendo* THARU *kamal* TIBETAN *sa-bras*

Nelumbonaceae. Aquatic herb. Leaves long-stalked, circular, attached to the stalk beneath near the middle, blade glaucous. Flowers white or rose, carried above the water surface. Fruit top shaped, flat-topped. Propagated by seeds or rhizomes. Distributed throughout Nepal to about 800 m in marshy areas and in the bottoms of ponds; also in India and northern China.

FOOD. Rhizome, young leaves, and seeds are cooked as a vegetable. Seeds are also eaten raw.

MEDICINE. Flowers are astringent and used for fever, diarrhea, and liver diseases.

OTHER USES. Leaves are used as plates. The plant is held in high regard by Buddhists and Hindus.

Neohymenopogon parasiticus (Wallich)
S. S. R. Bennet

Hymenopogon parasiticus Wallich
Mussaenda cuneifolia D. Don
NEPALI *banbiri, bangaja, biri, danta biri, gobre kath, hansaraj*

Rubiaceae. Deciduous tree about 5 m high. Leaves stalked, crowded toward the ends of branches, 4.5–21 cm long, 2–8 cm wide, ovate or elliptic, acute, pubescent on both surfaces. Flowers white in terminal trichotomous corymbs. Fruit a capsule, turbinate. Flowers May–August, fruits September–October. Propagated by seeds or by planting stumps. Distributed throughout Nepal at 160–2500 m on mossy rocks; also in the Kumaon region of Uttar Pradesh, India, west of Nepal, and Bhutan, western China, and Indo-China.

MEDICINE. A paste of the fruit is applied to treat toothaches.

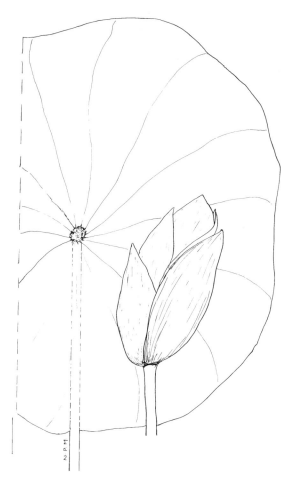

Nelumbo nucifera

OTHER USES. Wood is used for agricultural and domestic purposes. Bark yields tannin. Villagers, especially youngsters, chew the seeds to decorate their teeth. When chewed, seeds leave black marks between the teeth, which is considered beautiful.

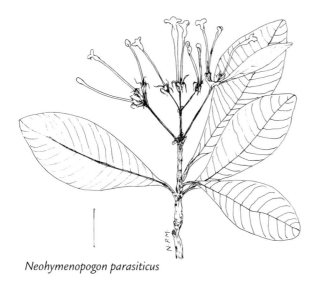

Neohymenopogon parasiticus

Neolamarckia cadamba (Roxburgh) Bosser

Nauclea cadamba Roxburgh, *Anthocephalus cadamba* (Roxburgh) Miquel, *Sarcocephalus cadamba* (Roxburgh) Kurz
Anthocephalus indicus A. Richard
Cephalanthus chinensis Lamarck, *Anthocephalus chinensis* (Lamarck) A. Richard ex Walpers
LEPCHA *kodum* MOOSHAR *kadam* NEPALI *kadam*

Rubiaceae. Evergreen tree about 15 m high. Leaves stalked, opposite, 7–15 cm long, 4–6 cm wide, elliptic to oblong, entire, smooth, acuminate. Flowers condensed in terminal and solitary heads, orange, June–October. Prop-

agated by seeds or shoot cuttings. Distributed throughout Nepal to about 1000 m in open places; also in India, Sri Lanka, southern China, and Southeast Asia.

FOOD. Flower heads are eaten raw or pickled.

MEDICINE. Flower heads are boiled in water about 10 minutes, and the resultant liquid, about 4 teaspoons three times a day, is taken in cases of diarrhea and dysentery.

OTHER USES. Wood is used as ceiling material and for light construction work.

Neolitsea cuipala (Buchanan-Hamilton ex D. Don) Kostermans

Tetranthera cuipala Buchanan-Hamilton ex D. Don, *Litsea cuipala* (Buchanan-Hamilton ex D. Don) Balakrishnan
Tetradenia lanuginosa Nees, *Litsea lanuginosa* (Nees) Nees, *Neolitsea lanuginosa* (Nees) Gamble, *Tetranthera lanuginosa* Wallich
GURUNG *kalchhe*

Lauraceae. Tree about 10 m high. Leaves stalked, 12–32 cm long, 2.5–7 cm wide, elliptic to lanceolate, acuminate, entire, distinctly three-veined. Flowers yellowish in many-flowered umbels. Fruit a berry. Flowers and fruits April–September. Propagated by seeds. Distributed in eastern and central Nepal at 900–2100 m in association with subtropical forest trees; also in northern India and northern Myanmar.

MEDICINE. Seed oil is applied to boils and scabies.

Neolamarckia cadamba

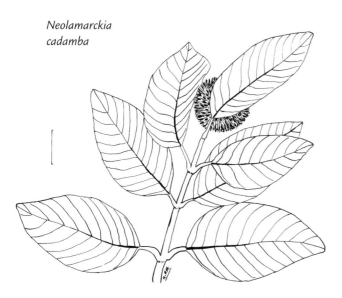

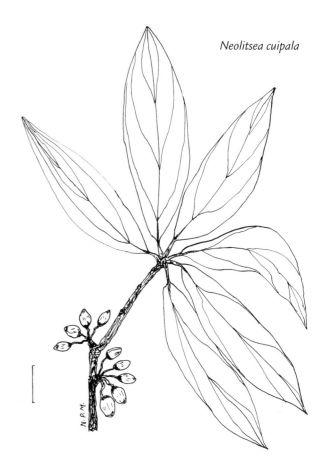

Neolitsea cuipala

Nepeta leucophylla Bentham

NEPALI *kankarne* THARU *gandheli gharra*

Labiatae. Erect herb about 1 m high. Leaves short-stalked, 0.9–3.5 cm long, 0.4–2.3 cm wide, ovate, often cordate at the base, crenate, glabrescent above, densely tomentose beneath. Flowers purplish in spikes. Flowers and fruits August–October. Propagated by seeds. Distributed in western and central Nepal at 2000–3900 m, often abundant along trails or on uncultivated land; also in Afghanistan, Pakistan, and northern India.

MEDICINE. A decoction of the plant is applied to boils. Juice of the root, about 4 teaspoons three times a day, is given to relieve fever.

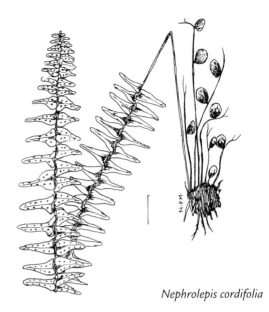

Nephrolepis cordifolia

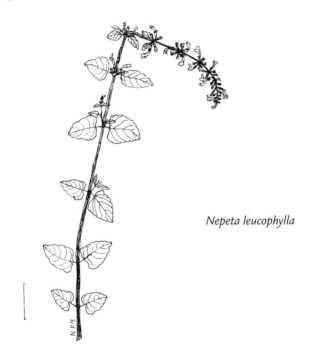

Nepeta leucophylla

Nerium indicum Miller

Nerium odoratum Lamarck
Nerium odorum Solander

ENGLISH *oleander* NEPALI *kaner, karbir* NEWARI *bau swan*

Apocynaceae. Evergreen shrub about 3 m high. Leaves stalked, in whorls of three or four, linear lanceolate, acuminate, entire. Flowers pink or white, fragrant, in a terminal inflorescence. Fruit cylindrical, in pairs, slightly twisted. Seeds compressed, with silky hairs. Flowers and fruits most of the year. Propagated by stem cuttings. Distrib-

Nephrolepis cordifolia (Linnaeus) K. Presl

GURUNG *amala, kyudabi, kyu phun, napre, tyubi* MAGAR *pani amala*
NEPALI *pani amala, pani saro* NEWARI *lasi* RAI *lolobabung*
TAMANG *ambali, bekalang, bhuin kalang, tui amala*

Dryopteridaceae. Terrestrial or epiphytic fern about 75 cm high. Roots often bearing tubers. Stipes stiff, brown, slightly scaly. Fronds pinnately divided, pinnae numerous, sessile, alternate, bases overlapping, entire or slightly crenate, rounded or bluntly pointed. Sori reniform. Propagated by root tubers or by splitting the mother plant. Distributed throughout Nepal at 500–2400 m in moist, shady places; also in tropical and subtropical regions of the world.

FOOD. Root tubers are eaten to quench thirst. Boiled root tubers are edible.

MEDICINE. Juice of root tubers is taken to treat fever, indigestion, headache, and hematuria. This juice is also considered effective for headaches, cough, and colds.

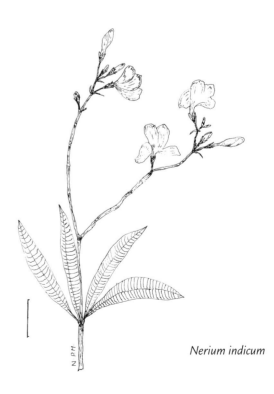

Nerium indicum

uted throughout Nepal to about 1000 m; also in Afghanistan and northern and central India.

MEDICINE. The plant is poisonous and it is important to be cautious in its use. A paste of root bark is used for skin diseases such as ringworm and herpes. Pounded paste of leaves and bark is used on snakebites and also has insecticidal properties.

OTHER USES. The plant is cultivated in gardens as a hedge or for its ornamental flowers. Pounded paste of leaves and bark has insecticidal properties.

Neyraudia reynaudiana (Kunth) Keng ex
A. S. Hitchcock

Arundo reynaudiana Kunth
Arundo zollingeri Buese
CHEPANG *lese ghans*

Gramineae. Perennial grass about 4 m high, culms thick, terete, smooth. Leaves 20–60 cm long, 1–2.5 cm wide, narrowed and subinvolute, sheaths woolly at the throat. Inflorescences silvery olive-gray in nodding panicles. Propagated by seeds by splitting the rhizomes. Distributed in eastern and central Nepal at 400–900 m in open, rocky places; also in northeastern India, China, Taiwan, Myanmar, and Malaysia.

OTHER USES. The plant is used as fodder. It is essential in the worship of the lineage god of Chepangs.

Nicandra physalodes (Linnaeus) Gaertner

Atropa physalodes Linnaeus
NEPALI *isamgoli*

Solanaceae. Herb about 1.5 m high. Leaves stalked, alternate, ovate to lanceolate, acuminate, sinuately lobed. Flowers solitary, axillary, bluish. Fruit a berry, globose. Flowers and fruits June–October. Propagated by seeds. Distributed throughout Nepal at 750–2600 m in open places; also in North and Central America.

MEDICINE. Seeds, about 1 teaspoon, are boiled with a cup of water, and the filtered liquid is taken in cases of fever.

Nicotiana tabacum Linnaeus

CHEPANG *chyakhala, gaderi, kacha pat, sira* ENGLISH *tobacco* GURUNG *tamahun, tamausu, tampo* MAGAR *bhusa* NEPALI *surti, tambaku* NEWARI *surti* TAMANG *bhusa*

Solanaceae. Erect herb about 1.5 m high. Leaves sessile or short-stalked, elliptic to ovate, base narrowed. Flowers pinkish. Fruit a capsule, ovoid. Propagated by seeds. Distributed throughout Nepal to about 1800 m; widely cultivated, also in the Americas.

MEDICINE. Leaves are sedative, narcotic, emetic, antiseptic, purgative, and stimulant. The leaf is heated and put on the abdomen for colic. It is also used for rheumatic swellings and skin diseases. Juice of the leaf is anthelmintic and is also put on scorpion bites. Powder of dried leaf is applied to treat itching and ringworm. It is also used for

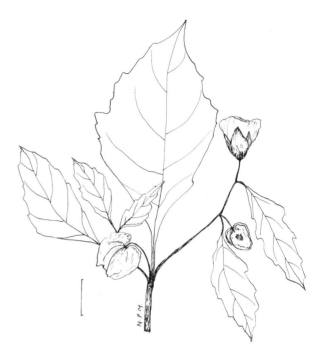

Nicandra physalodes

Nicotiana tabacum

brushing teeth to treat swelling of the gums. This powder is applied to fresh cuts and wounds because it helps coagulate blood and protect cuts from germs.

OTHER USES. Leaves are soaked in water and sprayed on vegetables as an insecticide. Dried leaves are used for smoking. Seeds are considered nutritious feed for animals.

Nyctanthes arbor-tritis Linnaeus

CHEPANG *jargat, jathra* DANUWAR *harsingar* ENGLISH *tree of sorrow, night-flowering jasmine* MOOSHAR *kamcha* NEPALI *chitachinki, chitaina, parijat, kharso* NEWARI *palija swan* TAMANG *khosorya*

Oleaceae. Tree about 5 m high. Leaves stalked, opposite, 6.5–15 cm long, 3–8.5 cm wide, ovate, rough in texture. Flowers white with orange corolla tube, fragrant. Fruit a capsule, compressed, two-seeded. Flowers and fruits September–November. Propagated by seeds. Distributed throughout Nepal to about 1300 m on open, dry hillsides; also in Pakistan, India, Bhutan, Thailand, and Indonesia.

MEDICINE. A paste of the bark is applied to treat dislocated bones. Juice of the bark is applied to snakebites. Juice of the leaves is laxative. It is boiled about 10 minutes, and the filtered water is taken for fever and rheumatism. This juice, mixed with sugar, is given to children as a rem-

Nyctanthes arbor-tritis

edy for intestinal worms. A decoction of the leaves is considered good for obstinate sciatica.

OTHER USES. The plant is considered sacred and is also planted in kitchen gardens for its flowers. The corolla tube yields orange dye.

O

Ocimum basilicum Linnaeus

Ocimum caryophyllatum Roxburgh
Ocimum thyrsiflorum Linnaeus, *O. basilicum* var. *thyrsiflorum* (Linnaeus) Bentham
NEPALI *bawari*

Labiatae. Erect herb about 1 m high. Leaves stalked, 2.5–4.5 cm long, 1–2.5 cm wide, ovate, acuminate, gland-dotted beneath. Flowers purplish white in racemes. Fruit a nutlet, smooth. Flowers August–September. Propagated by seeds. Distributed in eastern and central Nepal at 300–1500 m in open, sunny places; also in India, Bhutan, southern China, Taiwan, Myanmar, Malaysia, and Polynesia.

MEDICINE. The plant is pounded with the roots of *Achyranthes aspera* and applied to snakebites.

Ocimum tenuiflorum Linnaeus

Ocimum sanctum Linnaeus

BHOJPURI *tulsi* DANUWAR *tulsi* GURUNG *tulsi* ENGLISH *sacred basil* LEPCHA *tulsi* LIMBU *achhaphun* NEPALI *tulsi* NEWARI *tulsi* RAI *tompanamma* SUNWAR *tulsi* TAMANG *tulsi* THARU *tulsi*

Labiatae. Shrub about 80 cm high. Leaves stalked, 2.5–6 cm long, 1–3 cm wide, elliptic to oblong, acute at both ends. Flowers purplish in racemes, September–October. Fruits November–December. Propagated by seeds. Distributed throughout Nepal to about 1600 m in open places, generally planted around houses and sacred places; also in Pakistan, India, Bhutan, Bangladesh, China, Myanmar, Thailand, Malaysia, Australia, and the Philippines.

MEDICINE. The plant is stimulant, diaphoretic, and expectorant. A decoction of the root, about 4 teaspoons three times a day, is given for fever. The decoction is applied to treat gonorrhea and used as a bath for rheumatism and paralysis. Juice of the leaves is applied to treat ringworm and other cutaneous diseases and is taken in cases of gastric trouble. This juice is also dripped in the ear to relieve earaches. Fresh leaves are chewed or boiled in water until the amount is reduced to half, and the liquid is taken for cough, colds, and bronchial infection. Seeds have demulcent properties. They are soaked in water about 10 hours and taken with water for disorders of the genitourinary system.

OTHER USES. The plant is considered sacred to the god Vishnu, one of the most revered gods of the Hindu reli-

Ocimum
tenuiflorum

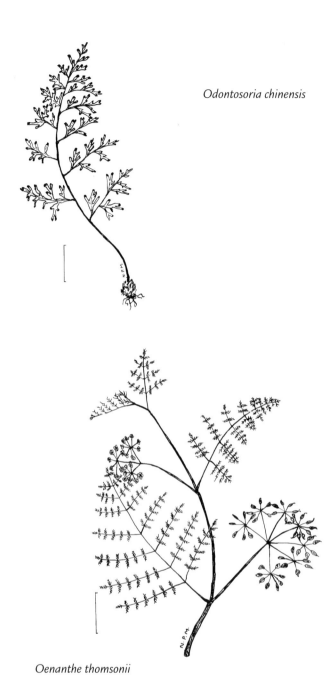

Odontosoria chinensis

Oenanthe thomsonii

gion. The small beads of the root or stem are made into rosaries worn by followers of Vishnu, the Vaishanavs. The stem and leaf contain tannin.

Odontosoria chinensis (Linnaeus) Small

Trichomanes chinense Linnaeus, *Sphenomeris chinensis* (Linnaeus) Maxon

NEPALI *sano unyu*

Dennstaedtiaceae. Terrestrial fern. Fronds deep green, 30–45 cm long, 5–15 cm wide, decompound, segments lanceolate. Sori on the upper part of the margin of the segment. Propagated by spores. Distributed in eastern and central Nepal to about 2400 m, frequent along shady trails; also in India, Sri Lanka, southern central China, Taiwan, Japan, Malaysia, the Philippines, Polynesia, and Madagascar.

MEDICINE. A paste of the plant is applied to cuts and wounds.

Oenanthe thomsonii C. B. Clarke

NEPALI *sup jhar*

Umbelliferae. Erect herb. Leaves stalked, pinnate or bipinnate, leaflets ovate to lanceolate, dentate, sometimes lobed. Flowers white in compound umbels, June–August. Propagated by seeds. Distributed in eastern and central Nepal at 1600–2500 m in moist places; also in India and Southeast Asia.

MEDICINE. Seeds are boiled in water and the vapor is inhaled through the nose for cough and colds.

Oenothera rosea L'Héritier ex Aiton

NEPALI *pitambar phul*

Onagraceae. Erect herb about 60 cm high. Leaves stalked, alternate, lanceolate, acute, margin wavy or dentate. Flowers pink. Fruit a capsule. Flowers April–July, fruits May–October. Propagated by seeds. Distributed in western and central Nepal at 1100–2500 m; also in India, Myanmar, Europe, and the Americas.

OTHER USES. The plant is used for fodder.

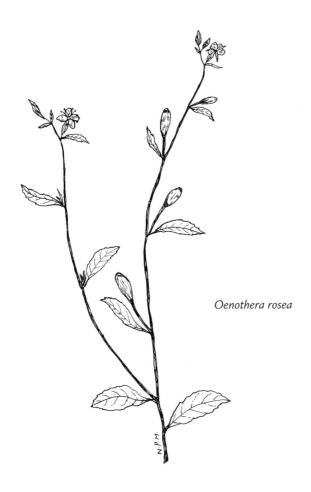

Oenothera rosea

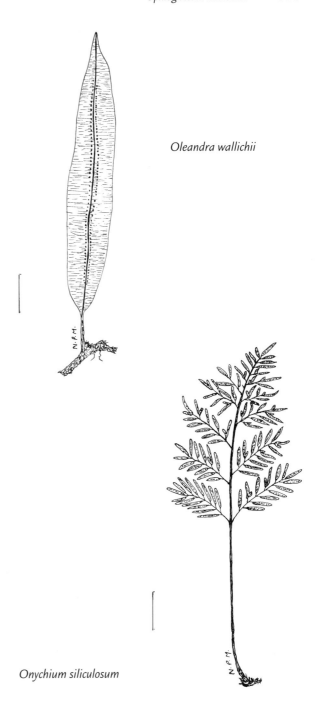

Oleandra wallichii

Onychium siliculosum

Oleandra wallichii (Hooker) Presl

NEPALI *jibre unyu* TAMANG *bhalenakabhyak*

Dryopteridaceae. Epiphytic or terrestrial fern. Rhizome creeping, stout, with linear brown scales. Fronds 15–30 cm long, 2–4 cm wide, oblong to elliptic, membranous, acuminate. Sori brown, on either side of and close to the midrib. Propagated by spores. Distributed throughout Nepal at 1300–3100 m on mossy tree trunks and branches; also in India, western China, Taiwan, and Southeast Asia.

MEDICINE. A paste of the rhizome is applied to the forehead to treat headaches and is used to treat dislocation of bones.

Onychium siliculosum (Desvaux) C. Christensen

NEPALI *kangiyo sotar, seto sinki*

Pteridaceae. Terrestrial fern. Rhizome tufted with brown linear scales. Stipe naked. Fronds bright green, 18–30 cm long, four-pinnatifid, segments numerous. Sori marginal, yellow. Propagated by spores. Distributed throughout Nepal at 500–1700 m in open, rocky places; also in India, western China, Taiwan, Southeast Asia, New Guinea, the Philippines, and Polynesia.

MEDICINE. Juice of the rhizome, about 4 teaspoons three times a day, is given to relieve fever.

Ophioglossum nudicaule Linnaeus fil.

ENGLISH *adder's tongue* NEPALI *jibre sag* TAMANG *ledap* THARU *aek patiya*

Ophioglossaceae. Herbaceous fern. Rhizomes small, slightly tuberous. Fronds distinct, sterile fronds 2.5–7 cm long, 2–3.5 cm wide, linear to ovate, fertile frond about 2.5 cm long, spike greenish. Spores March–October. Propagated by spores. Distributed throughout Nepal to about 1800 m in moist, shady places.

FOOD. Fronds are cooked as a vegetable.

MEDICINE. A paste of the root is applied to wounds.

Ophioglossum reticulatum Linnaeus

NEPALI *jibre sag*

Ophioglossaceae. Herbaceous fern. Rhizome cylindrical, with many fibrous roots. Stipes 3–8 cm long. Fronds distinct, sterile fronds 3.5 cm long, 2 cm wide, ovoid, base cordate, fertile frond 2–2.5 cm long, on slender stalk arising from the base of the sterile frond. Spores March–April. Propagated by spores. Distributed throughout Nepal to about 1400 m in moist, shady places.

FOOD. Fronds are cooked as a vegetable.

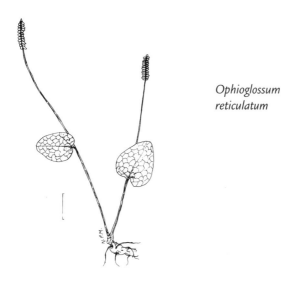

Ophioglossum reticulatum

Ophiorrhiza fasciculata D. Don

Ophiorrhiza bracteolata R. Brown
Ophiorrhiza mungo Linnaeus

ENGLISH *mongoose plant* GURUNG *yagon* NEPALI *gardaino*

Rubiaceae. Erect herb. Leaves stalked, 2–16 cm long, elliptic to ovate or oblanceolate. Flowers white in axillary and terminal cymes. Fruit a capsule, compressed. Flowers and fruits July–September. Propagated by spores. Distributed throughout Nepal at 500–2100 m in rock crevices; also in northern India and Malaysia.

MEDICINE. Juice of the plant is applied to boils and pimples. A paste of the plant is applied in cases of angular stomatitis.

Oplismenus burmannii (Retzius) Palisot de Beauvois

Panicum burmannii Retzius

NEPALI *ote ghans*

Gramineae. Annual grass, culms often rooting at the nodes. Leaves spatulate, acute or acuminate, with tubercle-based hairs. Inflorescence yellowish. Flowers and fruits August–November. Propagated by seeds or cuttings of culms. Distributed in eastern and central Nepal at 200–1800 m, on open, moist ground as a weed in rice and maize fields; also in the tropics.

OTHER USES. The plant is used for fodder.

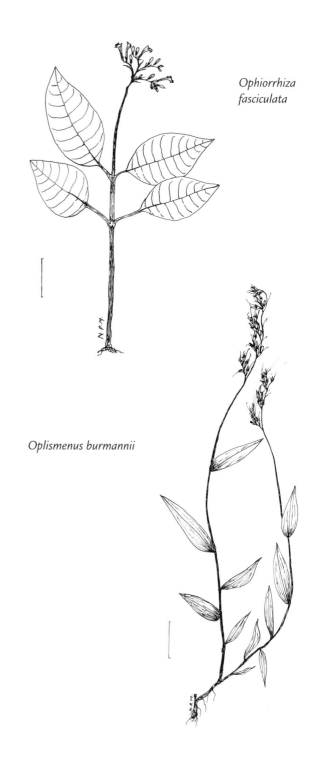

Ophiorrhiza fasciculata

Oplismenus burmannii

Opuntia monacantha (Willdenow) Haworth

Opuntia vulgaris of authors, not Miller

ENGLISH *prickly pear* NEPALI *nagphani kanda*

Cactaceae. Spiny, leafless shrub, stem succulent, with oblong jointed segments, covered with needle-like spines about 5 cm long. Flowers golden yellow, May–August. Fruits September–October. Propagated by splitting the jointed stems. Distributed throughout Nepal to about 1400 m in open, dry places; also in India and Africa.

FOOD. Ripe fruits are eaten fresh.

Oreocnide frutescens (Thunberg) Miquel

Urtica frutescens Thunberg, *Boehmeria frutescens* (Thunberg)
    Thunberg, *Villebrunea frutescens* (Thunberg) Blume
Boehmeria frondosa D. Don
Boehmeria fruticosa Gaudichaud-Beaupré, *Oreocnide fruticosa*
    (Gaudichaud-Beaupré) Handel-Mazzetti, *Villebrunea*
    fruticosa (Gaudichaud-Beaupré) Nakai
Morocarpus microcephalus Bentham

CHEPANG *lyandru*   GURUNG *keme, peda, pleta*   MAGAR *chiple*
NEPALI *chail, chiple ghans, gaulanto, lise kuro, nite*
TAMANG *chhyal, pungi, syo tolo*

Urticaceae. Shrub about 3 m high. Leaves stalked, 8–15
cm long, 3.5–5 cm wide, ovate to lanceolate, acuminate,
serrate, pubescent and often pale beneath, base rounded.
Inflorescence yellowish. Propagated by seeds. Distributed
throughout Nepal at 500–2200 m on rocky soil in warm,
broad-leaved forest; also in northern India, Bhutan, western and southern China, Indo-China, and southern Japan.

FOOD. Powdered root is mixed with flour of rice (*Oryza*
sativa) or wheat (*Triticum aestivum*) and baked to add softness to the taste of the bread. Tender leaves and shoots
are cooked as a vegetable.

MEDICINE. The root is fed to animals; it is believed to
counter constipation. A paste of the leaves is applied to
boils.

OTHER USES. Powdered root is mixed with clay to mop
floors, adding durability to the floor. Bark fiber is used to
make fishnets and sacks.

Origanum majorana Linnaeus

Majorana hortensis Moench
Origanum wallichianum Bentham

ENGLISH *sweet marjoram*   NEPALI *maruwa phul*   NEWARI *mu swan*

Labiatae. Herb about 28 cm high. Leaves stalked, 1–1.5
cm long, 0.5–0.8 cm wide, ovate, entire, glabrous, tip
slightly rounded. Flowers pinkish white, May–July. Propagated by seeds. Distributed in central Nepal to about
1300 m, planted in moist places; also in southwestern
Asia, Europe, and North Africa.

MEDICINE. The plant is antispasmodic, digestive, expectorant, and diuretic.

OTHER USES. The plant is used to disinfect beehives. It is
offered to gods and goddesses.

Origanum vulgare Linnaeus

Origanum laxiflora Royle
Origanum normale D. Don

ENGLISH *delight of the mountain, wild marjoram*
NEPALI *bishmaro, ramtulsi*   TIBETAN *akino, tano*

Labiatae. Erect herb about 1 m high. Leaves stalked,
1–3 cm long, 0.5–1.5 cm wide, broadly ovate, entire, rarely
dentate. Flowers white or pink, crowded in numerous
four-sided spikes, July–September. Fruits October–November. Propagated by seeds. Distributed in central and
western Nepal at 1000–4000 m in open, sunny places; also
throughout Asia, and in Europe and North America.

FOOD. Leaves and flowers are consumed as a condiment
and spice. Leaves and flowers are mixed in boiled water
and used as tea. Leaves and seeds are pickled.

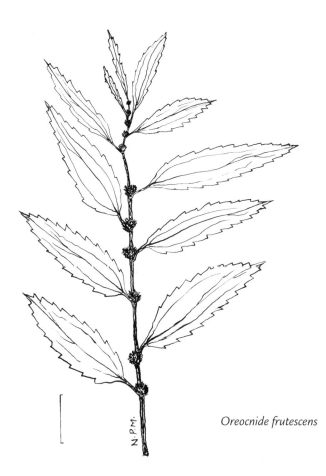

Oreocnide frutescens

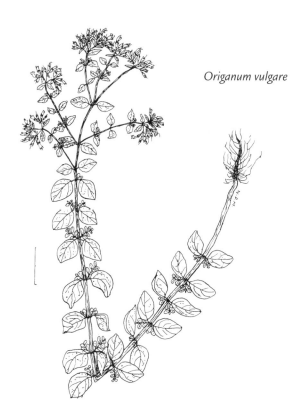

Origanum vulgare

MEDICINE. Volatile oil from the plant is given for colic, diarrhea, and hysteria and is applied for rheumatism, toothaches, and earaches. An infusion of the plant is given to promote menstrual flow if it is disturbed or suppressed by cold or other reasons. It is also used for toothaches and earaches. Ash of the bark is applied to wounds. Leaves are chewed to prevent tooth decay.

OTHER USES. Dried leaves are used as a substitute of incense.

Orobanche aegyptiaca Persoon

Phelipaea aegyptiaca (Persoon) Beck ex Lojacono
Orobanche indica Buchanan-Hamilton ex Roxburgh, *Phelipaea indica* (Buchanan-Hamilton ex Roxburgh) G. Don
ENGLISH *broomrape* NEPALI *nilo jhar*

Orobanchaceae. Parasitic annual herb with a brownish stem. Leaves scaly. Flowers bluish purple with cream corolla tube, in lax spikes. Fruit a capsule. Flowers and fruits December–February. Propagated by seeds. Distributed in western and central Nepal to about 3000 m as a weed in maize fields; also in Pakistan, India, the Mediterranean region, and North Africa.

MEDICINE. Juice of the root is applied to treat eczema and ringworm.

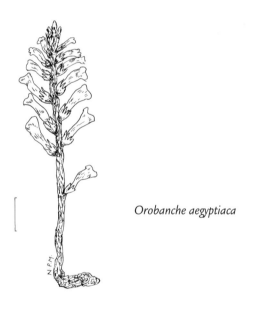

Orobanche aegyptiaca

Oroxylum indicum (Linnaeus) Kurz

Bignonia indica Linnaeus, *Calosanthes indica* (Linnaeus) Blume
BHOJPURI *sonpat* CHEPANG *dakhin, phalako, pharaka, tatalasi* DANUWAR *totala* ENGLISH *broken bones, Indian trumpet flower* GURUNG *krimtata* LEPCHA *totola* LIMBU *yabasim* MAGAR *tatal* NEPALI *mai tato, mal tata, saune tatal, tatelo* NEWARI *bachi, tarwar sima* RAI *bunbet* SHERPA *mendochampa* SUNWAR *poltata* TAMANG *nhangali, tare mendo, thuman mhendo* THARU *sauna, sontata*

Bignoniaceae. Deciduous tree about 10 m high. Leaves stalked, opposite, bipinnate, leaflets stalked, 6–16 cm

long, 4–7 cm wide, broadly ovate, entire. Flowers pinkish, fetid. Fruit a capsule, flat. Seeds with papery wings. Flowers May–June, fruits October–November. Propagated by seeds. Distributed throughout Nepal to about 1300 m; also in India, western and southern China, and Southeast Asia.

MEDICINE. Juice of the bark is applied for body pain, especially during fever, and also applied to burns and wounds. Tamangs take juice of bark for diarrhea and dysentery. A decoction of the bark is a coolant and given for fever and jaundice. Paste of the seed is applied to wounds.

OTHER USES. The papery and winged seeds are strung together to offer to gods and goddesses, especially by Buddhists.

Orthosiphon incurvus Bentham

NEPALI *ratapate, tite*

Labiatae. Small shrub. Leaves stalked, ovate to lanceolate, coarsely crenate, narrowed toward the winged stalk. Flowers purple in loose whorls. Fruit a nutlet, broadly ellipsoidal, dark brown. Flowers May–June, fruits July–August. Propagated by seeds. Distributed throughout Nepal at 300–900 m in cool places; also in northern India and Myanmar.

MEDICINE. Juice of the plant, mixed with juice of *Justicia adhatoda*, is given in doses of about 2 teaspoons three times a day to treat malarial fever.

Oryza sativa Linnaeus

BHOJPURI *dhan* CHEPANG *yam* DANUWAR *dha* ENGLISH *paddy plant, rice* GURUNG *lhma, mlda* LEPCHA *jo* LIMBU *ya* MAGAR *chho, chhosan* MOOSHAR *dhan* NEPALI *dhan* NEWARI *wa* RAI *cha* SUNWAR *buru* TAMANG *sun* THARU *dhan* TIBETAN *bras, mi-tong-kar-la*

Gramineae. Annual grass about 1 m high. Leaves linear, hairy, narrowed toward the tip. Inflorescences yellowish or brownish in panicles. Propagated by seeds. Distributed throughout Nepal to about 2800 m, cultivated; also in most tropical and subtropical countries of the world.

FOOD. The grains, rice, are the staple food of the majority of the population of the world (Plate 9). Local beer and liquor are made from fermented rice.

MEDICINE. Rice is soaked in water about an hour and strained, and this liquid is drunk for inflammation of the heart; it is also considered good for indigestion.

OTHER USES. Rice straw is used for weaving (Plate 47).

Osbeckia nepalensis Hooker

Osbeckia chulesis D. Don
Osbeckia speciosa D. Don
CHEPANG *presi* GURUNG *anger* NEPALI *angeri, arbale, chulsi, galphule, kali angeri, late angeri, sano angeri, seto chulsi, thoro angeri* TAMANG *aarbale, aarpati, ambal bambul, lemlong, surate, tauning*

Melastomataceae. Shrub about 2 m high. Leaves sessile, 2.8–12 cm long, oblanceolate, hairy on both surfaces.

Oroxylum indicum

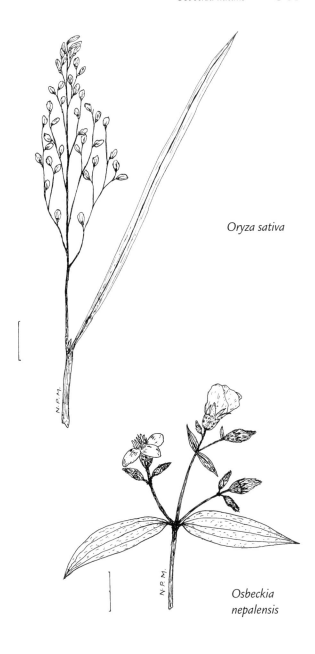

Oryza sativa

*Osbeckia
nepalensis*

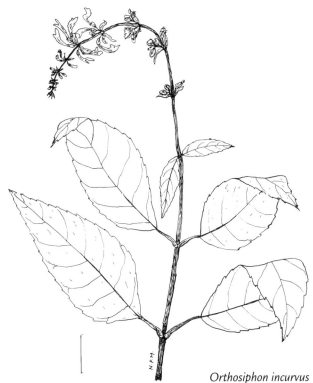

Orthosiphon incurvus

Flowers purple in corymbs. Fruit a capsule with persistent scales. Flowers and fruits January–November. Propagated by seeds. Distributed in eastern and central Nepal at 500–2300 m in damp places; also in northern India, western China, and Southeast Asia.

FOOD. Ripe fruits are eaten fresh.

MEDICINE. Juice of the plant, about 1 teaspoon twice a day, is given for indigestion. This juice is also considered efficacious in treating typhoid. Juice of the leaves is applied to cuts and wounds.

Osbeckia nutans Wallich ex C. B. Clarke

NEPALI *sano angeri* GURUNG *rathi*

Melastomataceae. Shrub. Leaves stalked, opposite, narrowly lanceolate, acute, entire, three-veined, rough on the veins beneath. Flowers pinkish in few-flowered terminal corymbs. Propagated by seeds. Distributed in eastern and central Nepal at 1000–1400 m in open, sandy places; also in northern India and northern Myanmar.

MEDICINE. Juice of the root, about 2 teaspoons three times a day, is given in cases of stomach disorder.

Osbeckia sikkimensis Craib

Osbeckia crinita Bentham ex Naudin, *O. stellata* var. *crinita* (Bentham ex Naudin) Hansen
NEPALI *galphule*

Melastomataceae. Shrub about 1.5 m high. Leaves stalked, 3.5–14 cm long, 1–5 cm wide, oblanceolate, entire, five-veined, tip narrowed, hairy on both surfaces. Flowers pinkish in panicles, July–September. Fruits October–November. Propagated by seeds. Distributed in eastern and central Nepal at 1700–2100 m on open, grassy slopes; also in northern India.

MEDICINE. A paste of the root is applied to treat goiter.

Osbeckia stellata Buchanan-Hamilton ex D. Don

CHEPANG *gaurak lyangsai, ikalaksap* GURUNG *paglya jhar*
NEPALI *angeri, asare phul, leto, pagalya jhar, phul pati, rato chulsi, shanirwar, thulo chulesi* TAMANG *aarbale, aarbote, aarpati, lemlang*

Melastomataceae. Hairy shrub about 2 m high. Leaves stalked, lanceolate, five-veined, with short hairs on both surfaces. Flowers pink-purple. Fruit ovoid, the outside felted. Flowers August–October. Propagated by seeds. Distributed throughout Nepal at 800–2600 m, common in open places; also in Pakistan and northern India.

FOOD. Ripe fruits are eaten fresh.

MEDICINE. Juice of the root, about 3 teaspoons twice a day, is given to treat diarrhea and dysentery. A decoction of the plant is also used as an antidote when domestic animals happen to eat poisonous plants. Juice of the plant is applied to treat scabies.

Osmanthus fragrans Loureiro var. *longifolia* (de Candolle) Hara

Olea fragrans var. *longifolia* (de Candolle) Blume
Notelaea posua D. Don
Olea acuminata Wallich ex G. Don, *O. fragrans* var. *acuminata* (Wallich ex G. Don) Blume, *Osmanthus acuminatus* (Wallich ex G. Don) Nakai
ENGLISH *fragrant olive, sweet olive* NEPALI *bakalpate, siringe*

Oleaceae. Tree about 15 m high. Leaves stalked, elliptic to lanceolate, acuminate, entire or serrate, glabrous. Flowers white or yellowish in axillary fascicles, fragrant, September–October. Fruits March–April. Propagated by seeds. Distributed in western and central Nepal at 1300–3000 m in the forest in association with *Ilex dipyrena* and *Castanopsis* trees; also in northern India, Bhutan, western China, northern Myanmar, and northern Thailand.

MEDICINE. A paste of stem or bark is used for boils, carbuncles, whooping cough, and retinitis.

Osmanthus fragrans var. *longifolia*

Osmunda claytoniana Linnaeus

ENGLISH *interrupted fern* NEPALI *kuthurke*

Osmundaceae. Terrestrial fern. Fronds 20–35 cm long, 10–15 cm wide, pinnatifid, segments sessile, subopposite, glabrous. Propagated by spores. Distributed throughout Nepal at 1400–3300 m in shady places.

FOOD. Tender portions are cooked as a vegetable.

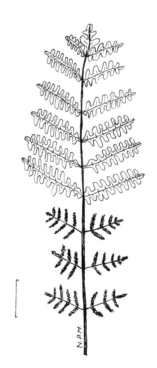

Osmunda claytoniana

Ostodes paniculata Blume

NEPALI *bepari*

Euphorbiaceae. Tree with a spreading crown, bark grayish, mottled brown inside, leaf scars distinct. Leaves crowded at the ends of branchlets, 12–25 cm long, 7–15 cm wide, ovate, acuminate, distantly serrate, dark green above, pale beneath, base truncate or rounded. Flowers pinkish. Fruit a capsule, subglobose. Flowers March–April, fruits July–August. Propagated by seeds. Distributed in eastern Nepal at 500–1400 m; also in northern India, Bhutan, southern China, and Southeast Asia.

MEDICINE. Oil from the seed is applied for muscular swellings.

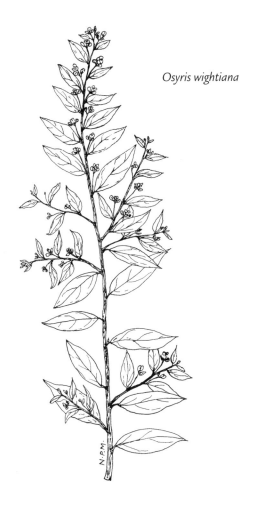

Osyris wightiana

Ostodes paniculata

Osyris wightiana Wallich ex Wight

Osyris arborea Wallich ex de Candolle
Osyris nepalensis Griffith

CHEPANG *chiyarani, nokhrek* GURUNG *chawang, dalima*
MAGAR *bakhre darim, kim* MAJHI *panle* NEPALI *bakhre khursani, ban chiyapate, banjhari, bhorekhayar, dalle pate, mane, muse sakeno, nundhik, nune, wodar* TAMANG *bhuinakato, borsajini, dhong, khayar, krepsin, mamjari, menje, rokawala*

Santalaceae. Shrub about 3 m tall. Leaves subsessile, alternate, 2–7 cm long, 0.5–3 cm wide, ovate, entire, tip acute. Flowers stalked, small, greenish. Fruit a drupe, nearly circular, orange when ripe. Flowers and fruits most of the year. Propagated by seeds. Distributed throughout Nepal at 900–2500 m, generally in open, sunny places; also in northern India, Bhutan, Sri Lanka, western China, and Myanmar.

FOOD. Leaves are steamed, dried in the shade, and used as tea.

MEDICINE. Bark is boiled in water, strained, and boiled again to form a gelatinous mass that is applied to set dislocated bone and put in the eye to relieve inflammation. About 1 teaspoon of this preparation, three times a day, is given to persons suffering from bloody dysentery. Juice of the bark is applied to the forehead to relieve headaches, but in some places a paste of the fruit is applied for headache. Juice of the bark, about 4 teaspoons three times a day, is given in cases of indigestion. A paste of the bark is applied to sprains.

The root is boiled in water about 10 minutes, cooled, strained, and the liquid, about 10 teaspoons three times a day, is given to the mother after childbirth to control bleeding and to boost energy. A paste of leaf buds is applied to cuts and wounds. Magars of western Nepal take juice of the fruit, about 4 teaspoons four times a day, to relieve headache. Immature fruits and leaves have emetic properties.

OTHER USES. Young leaves are poisonous to goats.

Oxalis corniculata Linnaeus

Oxalis pusilla Salisbury
Oxalis repens Thunberg

BHOJPURI *amaraundha* CHEPANG *kanthamal* DANUWAR *chari amilo*
ENGLISH *creeping sorrel* GURUNG *chino, kyuba, khursan, kyunpro,
nawamle, nawar kyun, nwakyumro, syu, tumdusyu*
LEPCHA *namachyormuk* LIMBU *charamma* MAGAR *chari amilo*
MAJHI *chariumal* MOOSHAR *amati* NEPALI *amili, boksi jhar,
chari amilo, khorsane jhar, kugute jhar* NEWARI *pam pam ghyan,
paughyan, wauncha ghyan* RAI *chachng, nachrim* RAUTE *chalmaro*
SATAR *tandi chatum arak* SUNWAR *charamlo*
TAMANG *khurcheni mran, kunya dhap, nakhachu kungwa,
nakhrupan gyan, tintinchung* THARU *amchaucha, kanthamalai jhar*

Oxalidaceae. Small procumbent herb. Leaves stalked, alternate, trifoliolate, leaflets subsessile, deeply lobed at the apex, entire, base cuneate. Flowers small, solitary or two on an axillary stalk, yellow. Fruit linear oblong, five-angled, short-beaked. Seeds numerous, brown. Flowers and fruits most of the year. Propagated by seeds or by nodal rooting of prostrate branches. Distributed throughout Nepal to about 2900 m in moist, shady places; also in Pakistan, India, Bhutan, Sri Lanka, and Bangladesh.

FOOD. Leaves are chewed like gum when fresh, or pickled; fresh leaves are a good source of vitamin C.

MEDICINE. Juice of the plant, mixed with butter, is applied to muscular swellings, boils, and pimples. This juice, about 6 teaspoons three times a day, is prescribed in cases of stomach acidity, peptic ulcer, diarrhea, and dysentery and is dropped in the eye to treat inflammation of the eye and conjunctivitis. Leaves are acidic, coolant, and stomachic. They are considered a good appetite inducer and are useful for dyspeptic patients. Juice of the leaves is taken for dysentery, fever, hemorrhoids, and anemia and is dropped in the eye for conjunctivitis, in the ear for tympanitis. This juice is also dropped in the ear to treat earaches of cattle.

Oxalis latifolia Kunth

NEPALI *thulo chari amilo*

Oxalidaceae. Erect herb about 30 cm high. Leaves all basal, long-stalked, trifoliolate, leaflets triangular, membranous, usually notched at the apex. Flowers pink in lax umbels, June–October. Fruits October–November. Propagated by seeds. Distributed in eastern and central Nepal at 1200–1600 m, in patches in moist places; also in India, Malaysia, southern Europe, and the Americas.

FOOD. Young leaves are pickled.
OTHER USES. The root is mixed with natural colors to make the colors fast.

Oxyria digyna (Linnaeus) Hill

Rumex digynus Linnaeus
Oxyria elatior R. Brown

GURUNG *thonra* NEPALI *banbare, barmale* TIBETAN *kyurba*

Polygonaceae. Erect herb about 40 cm high, with a stout rootstock. Leaves mostly basal, very few cauline, long-stalked, orbiculate to ovate, entire or slightly dentate. Flowers reddish in terminal panicles, May–June. Propagated by seeds. Distributed throughout Nepal at 2400–5200 m, generally along stream banks; also in northern India, Bhutan, Tibet, western and central Asia, western China, Japan, Europe, North America, and Greenland.

MEDICINE. Roots, stems, and leaves are cooked and eaten by villagers to treat dysentery.

Oxyspora paniculata (D. Don) de Candolle

Arthorstemma paniculatum D. Don
Oxyspora vagans Wallich

CHEPANG *gauraksai, mhemjusai* NEPALI *angerig, bakhra kane,
chulesi jhar* TAMANG *aarpate, lemlang*

Melastomataceae. Shrub about 3 m high. Leaves stalked, ovate, acute, crenate, base round. Flowers small, deep pink. Fruit a capsule, elliptic with truncate end. Flowers September–October. Propagated by seeds. Distributed in central and eastern Nepal at 1300–2000 m, common in wet ravines; also in northern India, western China, and Indo-China.

FOOD. Ripe fruits are edible.
OTHER USES. Leaves are gathered for fodder.

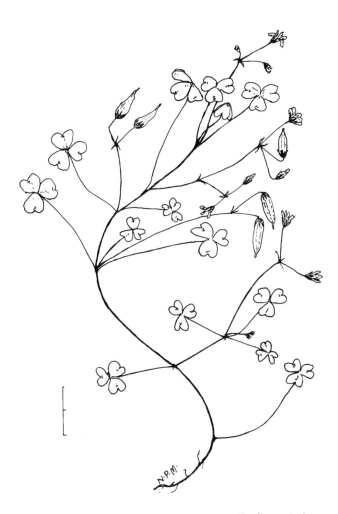

Oxalis corniculata

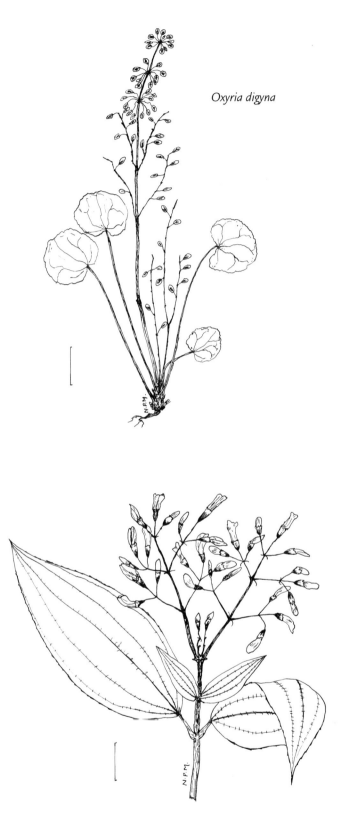

Oxyria digyna

Oxyspora paniculata

P

Paederia foetida Linnaeus

NEPALI *biri*

Rubiaceae. Climber with fetid odor when rubbed. Leaves stalked, opposite, ovate to lanceolate, acuminate, entire, base more or less cordate. Flowers purple in axillary and terminal, branched, panicled cymes. Fruit oblong. Flowers May–October. Propagated by seeds. Distributed in central and eastern Nepal at 300–1800 m in moist, rocky places; also in central and eastern India and Southeast Asia.

MEDICINE. Juice of the root is given in cases of indigestion. A paste of the leaves is applied to cuts and wounds.

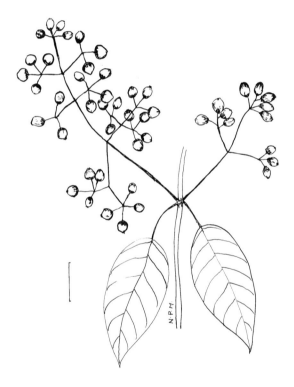

Paederia foetida

Paeonia emodi Wallich ex Royle

Paeonia officinalis Linnaeus

ENGLISH *Himalayan peony, peony* NEPALI *sungure aunle*

Paeoniaceae. Robust perennial herb about 1.5 m high. Leaves long-stalked, alternate, lanceolate, deeply lobed. Flowers pinkish. Fruit a follicle, hairy or hairless. Flowers April–June, fruits June–July. Propagated by seeds. Distributed in western Nepal at 1900–2400 m in moist, shady places but forest depletion and extensive use of the plant

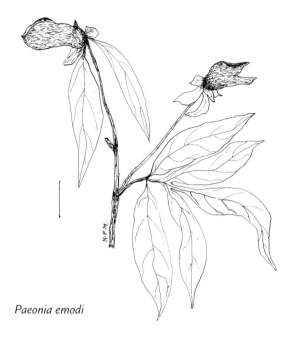

Paeonia emodi

Panax pseudoginseng

endanger plant populations; also in Afghanistan and northwestern India.

MEDICINE. A paste of root tubers is considered efficacious in uterine and nervous diseases. Seeds are purgative and emetic.

Panax pseudoginseng Wallich

Aralia pseudoginseng (Wallich) Bentham ex C. B. Clarke,
    A. quinquefolia var. *pseudoginseng* (Wallich) Burkill
Panax schin-seng var. *nepalensis* Nees
ENGLISH *Himalayan ginseng* NEPALI *mangen, nadar*

Araliaceae. Herb about 60 cm high with a tuberiferous rootstock. Leaves stalked, digitate, leaflets subsessile, 5–15 cm long, 0.8–6 cm wide, lanceolate, narrowly acuminate, minutely serrate, with scattered bristly hairs on both surfaces. Flowers white, May–June. Fruits July–September. Propagated by seeds. Distributed throughout Nepal at 2000–3300 m, frequent in moist, shady places; also in northern India, Bhutan, southeastern Tibet, Bhutan, western China, northern Myanmar, and Thailand.

FOOD. Young leaves and shoots are cooked as a vegetable.

MEDICINE. The root is aphrodisiac, stimulant, and expectorant. It is used to treat indigestion and vomiting. An infusion of the root is taken in cases of fever.

Pandanus nepalensis St. John

Pandanus diodon Martelli
Pandanus furcatus Roxburgh
Pandanus furcatus var. *indica* Kurz
NEPALI *keura, tarika*

Pandanaceae. Erect, much branched shrub about 5 m high. Leaves spirally crowded toward the ends of branches,

long, linear lanceolate, acuminate, leathery, glaucous. Flowers yellowish. Propagated by seeds. Distributed in eastern and central Nepal at 700–1100 m in moist, shady places; also in Pakistan, India, and Bhutan.

FOOD. Juice of the fruit is sucked.

OTHER USES. Stems are used as poles in construction. Leaves are used to make cots, mats, and for thatching.

Panicum miliaceum Linnaeus

ENGLISH *broomcorn millet, common millet, hog millet, proso millet*
NEPALI *chino* TIBETAN *khra-ma*

Gramineae. Annual grass with a fibrous root, culms tufted, round, pubescent at the base and on the nodes. Leaves 30–50 cm long, 1–5 cm wide, linear, flat, margin slightly rough with a few long cilia at the swollen, slightly rounded base. Inflorescence yellowish. Fruit a grain. Propagated by seeds. Distributed throughout Nepal to about 2200 m, cultivated; also in northwestern India.

FOOD. The grains have food value.

Paris polyphylla Smith

Paris daisua Buchanan-Hamilton ex D. Don
ENGLISH *love apple* GURUNG *satuwa* NEPALI *kalchun, satuwa*

Trilliaceae. Herb about 60 cm high. Leaves stalked, in a whorl at the top of the stem, 5–16 cm long, 1.5–4 cm wide,

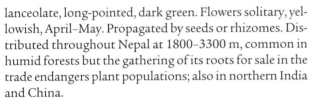

Panicum miliaceum

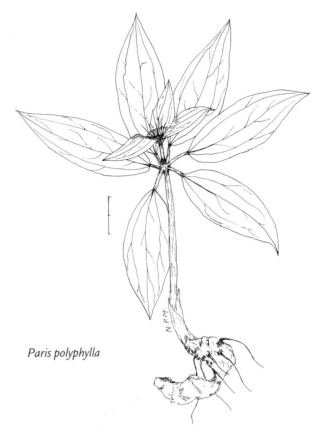

Paris polyphylla

lanceolate, long-pointed, dark green. Flowers solitary, yellowish, April–May. Propagated by seeds or rhizomes. Distributed throughout Nepal at 1800–3300 m, common in humid forests but the gathering of its roots for sale in the trade endangers plant populations; also in northern India and China.

MEDICINE. A paste of the root is applied to cuts and wounds. Pieces of the root are fed to cattle with diarrhea and dysentery. Juice of the root is taken as an anthelmintic.

Parnassia nubicola Wallich ex Royle

ENGLISH *grass of Parnassus* NEPALI *mamira, nirabisi, nirmasi*

Parnassiaceae. Glabrous herb about 50 cm high. Lower leaves stalked, oblong to ovate to slightly cordate, acute, upper leaves sessile, clasping the stem at their base. Flowers white, solitary, in a terminal scape. Fruit a capsule, ovoid, September–October. Propagated by seeds or root offshoots. Distributed throughout Nepal at 2800–4000 m on wet ground; also in Afghanistan, northern India, Bhutan, and southern Tibet.

MEDICINE. Juice of the root is applied to wounds.

Parochetus communis Buchanan-Hamilton ex D. Don

Parochetus major D. Don
Parochetus oxalidifolia Royle
NEPALI *chengi phul*

Leguminosae. Herb. Leaves stalked, trifoliolate, leaflets sessile, 0.5–2.8 cm long, deeply lobed at the apex, entire or

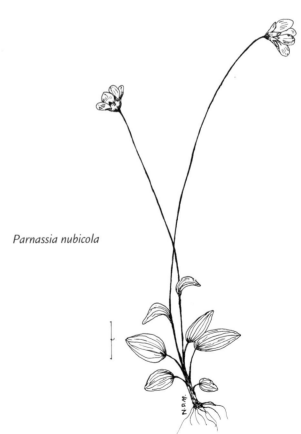

Parnassia nubicola

minutely dentate near the tip, slightly pubescent. Flowers bluish, solitary or in pairs at the end of the stalk. Fruit a pod, glabrous, linear, tipped with a persistent style. Flowers March–November, fruits November–July. Propagated by seeds. Distributed throughout Nepal at 900–4000 m in open, sunny places; also in India, Bhutan, Sri Lanka, China, Southeast Asia, and Africa.

MEDICINE. Juice of the leaves is applied to boils, cuts, and wounds.

OTHER USES. The plant is used as fodder.

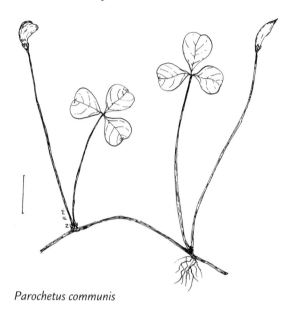

Parochetus communis

Parthenocissus himalayana (Royle) Planchon

Ampelopsis himalayana Royle, *Vitis himalayana* (Royle)
    C. K. Schneider
NEPALI *charchare*

Vitaceae. Large climber. Leaves stalked, trifoliolate, leaflets stalked, ovate, long-pointed, sharply dentate, dark green above, pale beneath. Flowers yellowish. Fruit a berry, black when ripe. Flowers April–May. Propagated by seeds. Distributed in eastern and central Nepal at 2100–3200 m in open, moist places; also in India, western China, Myanmar, and Thailand.

OTHER USES. The plant is gathered for fodder.

Parthenocissus semicordata (Wallich) Planchon

Vitis semicordata Wallich, *V. himalayana* var. *semicordata*
    (Wallich) Lawson
GURUNG *simal jel* NEPALI *barkhe lahara, charchare, parenu*
TAMANG *gungap*

Vitaceae. Climber with small warts on the stem. Leaves long-stalked, trifoliolate, leaflets sessile, 2–14.5 cm long, 1.5–9.5 cm wide, lateral leaflets oblique, ovate, terminal leaflet ovate, acuminate, serrate, upper surface nearly glabrous, hispid on the veins beneath. Flowers greenish in

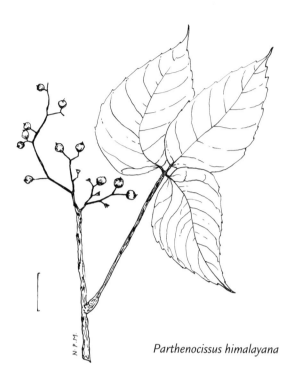

Parthenocissus himalayana

much branched cymes, March–July. Fruits August–September. Propagated by seeds. Distributed in central and western Nepal at 1000–2600 m in moist places in forested areas; also in northern India and Bhutan.

MEDICINE. A poultice of the root is applied to help set dislocated bones.

OTHER USES. The plant provides fodder.

Paspalum conjugatum Bergius

NEPALI *janai ghans*

Gramineae. Perennial grass with creeping culms, rooting at the nodes. Leaves oblong to lanceolate, subacute or obtuse, base cordate. Inflorescence greenish white. Flowers and fruits September–December. Propagated by seeds or by splitting the mother plant. Distributed in eastern Nepal at 300–700 m in moist, open places; also in India, Bhutan, Africa, and the Americas.

OTHER USES. The plant provides fodder.

Paspalum distichum Linnaeus

ENGLISH *knotgrass, water couch, wild dallis grass* NEPALI *janai ghans, pani dubo, tar ghans* THARU *panduba*

Gramineae. Rhizomatous perennial grass, rhizome long, forming loose mats. Leaves linear, ascending, glabrous. Inflorescence greenish, the stigmas black. Flowers and fruits June–September. Propagated by seeds or by splitting the mother plant. Distributed throughout Nepal to about 2000 m in moist places near canals, ponds, and ditches; also in the tropics and subtropics of the eastern hemisphere.

OTHER USES. The plant provides fodder.

Paspalum distichum

Passiflora edulis

Paspalum scrobiculatum Linnaeus

Paspalum commersonii Lamarck
Paspalum longifolium Roxburgh
Paspalum orbiculare Forster fil.
ENGLISH *kodo millet* NEPALI *banso, janai ghans, kode banso*

Gramineae. Annual grass with decumbent culms. Leaves linear lanceolate, white margined. Inflorescences greenish in racemes. Flowers and fruits July–December. Propagated by seeds or by splitting the mother plant. Distributed throughout Nepal to about 2400 m on open, sandy ground; also in Southeast Asia, Polynesia, Australia, and North America.

OTHER USES. The plant provides fodder.

Passiflora edulis Sims

ENGLISH *purple granadilla* NEPALI *aul aanp*

Passifloraceae. Trailing vine. Leaves stalked, 5–17.5 cm long, three-lobed, dentate, glabrous. Flowers large, white. Flowers and fruits June–October. Propagated by seeds. Distributed in eastern and central Nepal at 1200–1700 m in open places; also in Brazil.

FOOD. Ripe fruit is edible.

Pavetta tomentosa Roxburgh ex Smith

Ixora tomentosa Roxburgh
NEPALI *kangiyo*

Rubiaceae. Large shrub with brownish gray bark. Leaves stalked, opposite, 3–16.5 cm long, 1.3–9.5 cm wide,

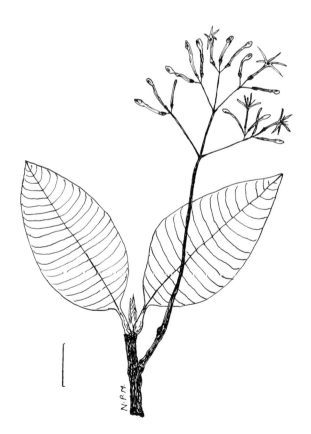

Pavetta tomentosa

broadly ovate, acuminate, tomentose on both surfaces. Flowers white, fragrant, in trichotomous corymbs. Fruit a berry, about the size of a pea. Flowers April–May, fruits September–November. Propagated by seeds. Distributed in eastern and central Nepal at 200–1000 m in moist places among shrubs in secondary growth; also in India and Indo-China.

MEDICINE. Juice of the root or bark is given in cases of fever.

Pedicularis longiflora Rudolph var. *tubiformis*
(Klotzsch) Tsoong

Pedicularis tubiformis Klotzsch
Pedicularis tubiflora Hooker fil.

TIBETAN *minje*

Scrophulariaceae. Herb about 15 cm high. Basal leaves long-stalked, cauline leaves short-stalked, pinnatifid, lobes crenate, nearly glabrous. Flowers bright yellow, fragrant, May–August. Fruits September–October. Propagated by seeds. Distributed throughout Nepal at 2500–4100 m in marshy and damp places; also in northern India, Bhutan, southeastern Tibet, and western China.

MEDICINE. The plant is boiled in water and the filtered water used to wash diseased skin.

Pedicularis longiflora
var. *tubiformis*

Pedicularis siphonantha D. Don

Pedicularis hookeriana Wallich ex Bentham

NEPALI *ponki*

Scrophulariaceae. Pubescent herb. Leaves stalked, alternate, oblong to linear, pinnatisect, lobes crenate. Flowers pink in terminal racemes. Propagated by seeds. Distributed throughout Nepal at 3000–4500 m in marshy and damp areas of alpine meadows; also in northern India, Bhutan, and southern Tibet.

MEDICINE. A paste of the plant is applied to boils and pimples.

Pennisetum flaccidum Grisebach

TAMANG *pang*

Gramineae. Tufted perennial grass about 1.5 m high, with thick rhizomes. Leaves linear, 5–38 cm long, flat. Inflorescences pinkish in panicles. Flowers and fruits August–November. Propagated by seeds or by splitting the rhizomes. Distributed in western and central Nepal at 1700–4300 m in rocky, open places; also in India and Tibet.

OTHER USES. The plant is a good source of fodder, especially during winter when most fodder plants are dormant.

Pennisetum flaccidum

Pennisetum polystachion (Linnaeus) Schultes

Panicum polystachion Linnaeus
Panicum barbatum Roxburgh
Panicum setosum Richard

CHEPANG *yam jhar*

Gramineae. Perennial grass about 2 m high, culms stout, erect or ascending and bent like a knee, rooting at the lower nodes. Leaves 10–45 cm long, 3–15 cm wide, spatulate, linear lanceolate, acute, flat, flaccid, with small, raised roughnesses, margin ciliate at the base, otherwise densely pilose with tubercle-based hairs, base rounded or narrowed. Inflorescence reddish brown or orange-brown. Propagated by seeds or by splitting the rhizomes. Distributed in eastern and central Nepal at 300–1600 m in open places; also in the tropics.

OTHER USES. The plant provides fodder.

Pentanema indicum (Linnaeus) Ling

Inula indica Linnaeus, *Vicoa indica* (Linnaeus) de Candolle
Vicoa auriculata Cassini
NEPALI *pahenlo jhurjhuri*

Compositae. Pubescent herb about 1 m high. Leaves sessile, alternate, 1.5–5 cm long, 0.4–0.8 cm wide, clasping the stem, lanceolate, entire or serrate, margin recurved when dry, usually somewhat rough in texture above. Flower heads yellow, on long slender peduncles. Fruit an achene. Flowers and fruits August–October. Propagated by seeds. Distributed in western and central Nepal at 250–2000 m in *Shorea robusta* forest; also in India, Bhutan, western China, Southeast Asia, and tropical Africa.

MEDICINE. Juice of the root is taken in cases of indigestion.

Peperomia pellucida (Linnaeus) Kunth

Piper pellucidum Linnaeus
Piper exiguum Blume, *Peperomia exigua* (Blume) Miquel
CHEPANG *jhyun jhyuro* NEPALI *latapate*

Piperaceae. Annual herb, stems thick, rounded, pale green. Leaves stalked, 0.8–3.5 cm long, 0.6–2.8 cm wide, ovate, obtuse, shiny pale green, base cordate. Flowers yellowish. Flowers and fruits January–September. Propagated by seeds. Distributed throughout Nepal to about 2000 m in shady, damp places; also in India, Bhutan, Myanmar, Malaysia, West Africa, and tropical America.

FOOD. Tender leaves and shoots are cooked as a vegetable.

Perilla frutescens (Linnaeus) Britton

Ocimum frutescens Linnaeus
Mentha perilloides Willdenow
Perilla ocimoides Linnaeus
CHEPANG *namche* DANUWAR *silam* ENGLISH *beefsteak plant, purple perilla* NEPALI *silam* TAMANG *tangnam*

Labiatae. Villous annual herb. Leaves stalked, 2–15 cm long, 0.8–12 cm wide, ovate, acuminate, dentate, hairy on both surfaces. Flowers white in erect axillary and terminal racemes, August–September. Fruits September–October. Propagated by seeds. Distributed throughout Nepal at 600–2400 m, cultivated; also in northern India, Bhutan, China, Myanmar, Malaysia, and Japan.

FOOD. Roasted seeds are pickled. Seed oil is an ingredient in cookery.

MEDICINE. Juice of the leaves is applied to cuts and wounds. It contains 1.6% essential oils.

Periploca calophylla (Wight) Falconer

Streptocaulon calophyllum Wight
GURUNG *tuisingri* NEPALI *shikari lahara* TAMANG *bhasipsip*

Asclepiadaceae. Trailing shrub. Leaves stalked, 3.5–8.5 cm long, 0.3–1.7 cm wide, lanceolate, long acuminate, leathery, shiny. Flowers pinkish in lax cymes. Fruit a follicle, cylindrical. Flowers April–May, fruits November–

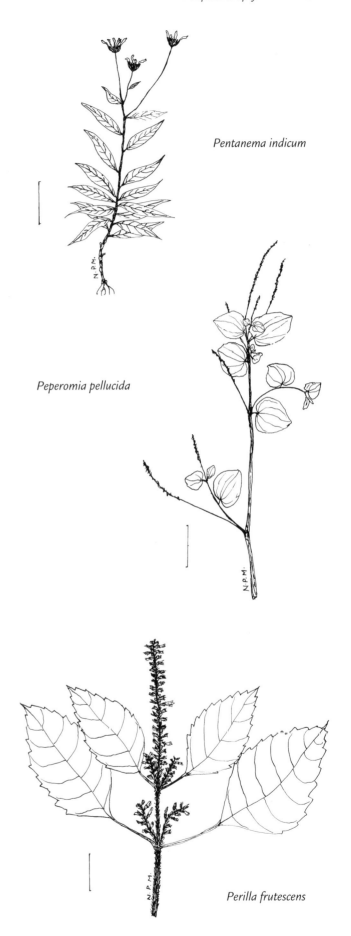

Pentanema indicum

Peperomia pellucida

Perilla frutescens

January. Propagated by seeds. Distributed throughout Nepal at 1500–2100 m in shady places; also in northern India, Bhutan, Tibet, and western and central China.

MEDICINE. A paste of the plant is applied to set dislocated bones. I observed Magar healers carry out this process in Dhading district. The paste is heated about 10 minutes and plastered over dislocated parts of bone. The affected part is wrapped with handmade Nepalese paper, then tied using three or four pieces of bamboo strips as splints. The plaster is kept on 2–3 weeks, depending on the nature of the dislocation, then the bamboo splints are removed, followed by removal of the paper a week later. The affected area is then hot compressed with the help of a soft cloth immersed in hot water. The healer also showed me a bone he had treated in a patient who was proud to show the fully healed bone.

OTHER USES. The plant is a nutritious fodder.

Peristrophe speciosa

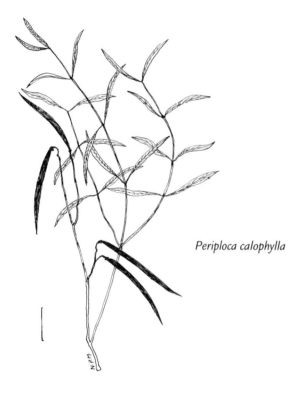

Periploca calophylla

Peristrophe speciosa (Roxburgh) Nees

Justicia speciosa Roxburgh
CHEPANG *kom jhar*

Acanthaceae. Shrub with weak stems, twigs terete, clothed with gray hairs. Leaves stalked, opposite, 10–20 cm long, 5–10 cm wide, elliptic, acuminate, base cuneate. Flowers magenta-pink in large, terminal, leafy panicles, January–March. Propagated by seeds. Distributed in eastern and central Nepal at 1500–2100 m, more or less gregarious in moist, shady places; also in northern India and Bhutan.

OTHER USES. The plant is used for fodder.

Persea bombycina (King ex Hooker fil.) Kostermans

Machilus bombycina King ex Hooker fil.
Laurus sericea Wallich, *Ocotea sericea* Nees, *Machilus sericea* (Nees) Blume
CHEPANG *runsi* NEPALI *kaula*

Lauraceae. Tree about 20 m high. Leaves stalked, 4.5–18 cm long, 2–6 cm wide, oblanceolate, entire, glabrous, tip pointed, narrowed toward the base. Flowers yellowish, March–June. Propagated by seeds. Distributed throughout Nepal at 1200–1800 m in wet forest areas; also in northern India.

FOOD. Powder of the inner bark is mixed with flour to bake bread in the belief that the powder helps develop the taste of the bread.

Persea gamblei (King ex Hooker fil.) Kostermans

Machilus gamblei King ex Hooker fil.
NEPALI *kathe kaulo*

Lauraceae. Tree about 7 m high. Leaves stalked, elliptic, acute, entire, glabrous beneath. Flowers yellowish in lax panicles, April–May. Propagated by seeds. Distributed in western and central Nepal at 750–900 m in mixed forest; also in India and Bhutan.

OTHER USES. The plant is used for fodder.

Persea gammieana (King ex Hooker fil.) Kostermans

Machilus gammieana King ex Hooker fil.
NEPALI *seto kaulo*

Lauraceae. Tree about 15 m high. Leaves stalked, lanceolate, acute, somewhat leathery. Flowers yellowish,

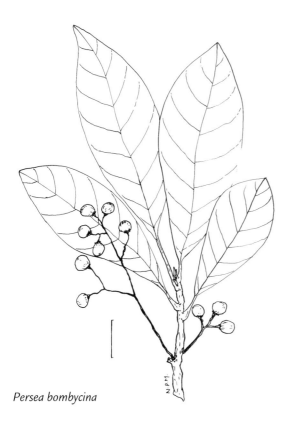

Persea bombycina

slightly fragrant, in panicles, March–April. Propagated by seeds. Distributed in eastern Nepal at 2000–2600 m in broad-leaved forests; also in northeastern India.

OTHER USES. The plant provides fodder.

Persea odoratissima (Nees) Kostermans

NEPALI *lali*

Lauraceae. Medium-sized evergreen tree. Leaves stalked, 7.5–20 cm long, 1.5–4.8 cm wide, lanceolate, acute or long-pointed, narrowed toward the base, bright green above. Flowers yellowish in lax, branched clusters. Fruit purple, ellipsoidal, supported by the persistent perianth. Flowers March–April. Propagated by seeds. Distributed throughout Nepal at 1000–2000 m in moist, open places; also in northern India, Bhutan, and Southeast Asia.

OTHER USES. Foliage is cut for fodder.

Persicaria barbata (Linnaeus) Hara

Polygonum barbatum Linnaeus
Polygonum hispidum Buchanan-Hamilton ex D. Don
DANUWAR *bhakundo, bishalari* ENGLISH *joint weed, knotweed*
NEPALI *khursani jhar, mirmiri, semchare ghans, thulo pirya, tote jhar*
THARU *piriya*

Polygonaceae. Erect herb about 75 cm high, stems terete, thickened on the nodes. Leaves stalked, 4.5–20 cm long, 0.6–4 cm wide, oblong to lanceolate, acuminate, appressed pubescent, base acute. Flowers white. Fruit a nut, ovoid to ellipsoidal, three-angled. Flowers and fruits July–

December. Propagated by seeds. Distributed throughout Nepal to about 1200 m in moist places; also in western Asia, India, Bhutan, eastern China, southern Japan, Malaysia, Australia, and tropical Africa.

FOOD. Tender shoots and leaves are cooked as a vegetable.

MEDICINE. A paste of the root is applied to treat scabies.

OTHER USES. The plant is used as fish poison.

Persicaria campanulata (Hooker fil.) Ronse Decraene

Polygonum campanulatum Hooker fil., *Aconogonum campanulatum* (Hooker fil.) Hara, *Reynoutria campanulata* (Hooker fil.) Moldenke
Polygonum crispatum C. B. Clarke
NEPALI *rapre ghans*

Polygonaceae. Prostrate herb. Leaves short-stalked, elliptic to lanceolate, entire, acuminate, pubescent above, woolly beneath. Flowers white in branched terminal panicles. Propagated by seeds or root offshoots. Distributed in eastern and central Nepal at 2100–4000 m in moist, open places; also in northern India, Bhutan, and northern Myanmar.

FOOD. Tender shoots are boiled and cooked as a vegetable.

Persicaria capitata (Buchanan-Hamilton ex D. Don) H. Gross

Polygonum capitatum Buchanan-Hamilton ex D. Don
Polygonum repens Wallich ex Meissner
GURUNG *khurseno, maisoti phul* NEPALI *pire jhar, pitle, ratnaulo*
TAMANG *phulimhendo, kyumbamran, tungdhap*

Polygonaceae. Trailing herb, stems rooting at the nodes. Leaves stalked, 1–3.8 cm long, 0.4–2.3 cm wide, elliptic, acute, ciliate, biauriculate at the base. Flowers pink in terminal heads. Flowers and fruits June–November. Propagated by seeds. Distributed throughout Nepal at

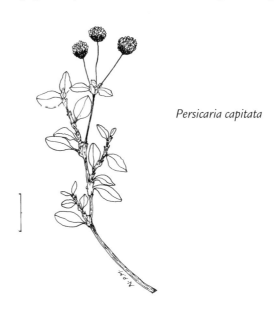

Persicaria capitata

600–2400 m on open, moist ground; also in northern India, Bhutan, Tibet, and eastern and western China.

MEDICINE. A paste of the plant is applied to boils and wounds. Juice of the plant is given in cases of stomach disorder.

OTHER USES. The plant is gathered for fodder.

Persicaria chinensis (Linnaeus) H. Gross

Polygonum chinense Linnaeus, *Ampelygonum chinense* (Linnaeus) Lindley
Coccoloba crispata Buchanan-Hamilton ex Roxburgh
Polygonum auriculatum Meissner
Polygonum brachiatum Lamarck
Polygonum patens D. Don
GURUNG *musa thotane* NEPALI *bakhre thotne, kurkur thotane, ratnaulo* TAMANG *lahapangyu*

Polygonaceae. Herb. Leaves stalked, 2.5–14 cm long, 1.3–8 cm wide, oblong to lanceolate, acuminate, entire, glabrous above, pubescent on the midvein beneath, base truncate. Flowers white in axillary or terminal panicled heads. Fruit a nut, three-angled. Propagated by seeds. Distributed throughout Nepal at 700–2200 m in moist, open places; also in India, Bhutan, eastern China, southern Japan, and Malaysia.

FOOD. Tender leaves and shoots are pickled.

Persicaria glabra (Willdenow) M. Gómez de la Maza

Polygonum glabrum Willdenow
ENGLISH *joint weed* NEPALI *seto pire*

Polygonaceae. Perennial herb about 70 cm high. Leaves stalked, 5–20 cm long, 0.5–4 cm wide, linear lanceolate, acuminate, gland-dotted. Flowers pinkish in racemes. Fruit a nut, compressed, ovoid. Flowers and fruits October–March. Propagated by seeds. Distributed in western and central Nepal at 200–900 m; also in Afghanistan, India, southern China, Malaysia, southern Japan, and Africa.

OTHER USES. The plant is used to poison fish.

Persicaria hydropiper (Linnaeus) Spach

Polygonum hydropiper Linnaeus
ENGLISH *smartweed, water pepper* NEPALI *pire khai, ratnaulo* TAMANG *kurangamhendo, tungbhrambra*

Polygonaceae. Erect herb about 1 m high. Leaves short-stalked, 1.3–12.5 cm long, 0.3–2 cm wide, lanceolate, acuminate, entire, hairy on the midvein. Flowers pinkish in terminal racemes, June–October. Fruits November–December. Propagated by seeds. Distributed throughout Nepal to about 2500 m along the stream-side thickets; also in India, eastern China, Japan, Malaysia, Europe, North Africa, and North America.

MEDICINE. The plant is boiled in water about 10 minutes, and the filtered water, about 4 teaspoons, is taken as an anthelmintic.

OTHER USES. The plant is used to poison fish.

Persicaria lapathifolia (Linnaeus) S. F. Gray var. *lanata* (Roxburgh) Hara

Polygonum lanatum Roxburgh
Polygonum lanigerum R. Brown
DANUWAR *phelwa bhakundo*

Polygonaceae. Glabrous herb about 2 m high. Leaves short-stalked, 6–17 cm long, 1–2 cm wide, lanceolate, acuminate, white woolly beneath. Flowers white or pink in drooping racemes. Fruit an achene, compressed, blackish. Flowers and fruits July–November. Propagated by seeds. Distributed in central Nepal to about 1500 m on marshy ground; also in India, Bhutan, Myanmar, Malaysia, and Taiwan.

MEDICINE. The plant produces a soft white mass, a froth like that of soap, which Danuwars apply to burns. It is also used for bathing and washing clothes.

Persicaria microcephala (D. Don) H. Gross

Polygonum microcephalum D. Don
Polygonum graciale Hooker fil.
Polygonum podocephalum Klotzsch
Polygonum sphaerocephalum Wallich
Polygonum staticiflorum Wallich ex Meissner
Polygonum wallichii Meissner
GURUNG *dhetubro* NEPALI *ban pire, dhunga lahara, masino thotne* TAMANG *tebya, tunglhap*

Polygonaceae. Decumbent herb. Leaves stalked, 1.3–11 cm long, 0.8–5.5 cm wide, ovate to lanceolate, acuminate, entire, base abruptly narrowed into a winged petiole. Flowers white or pink in terminal panicles. Flowers and fruits April–November. Propagated by seeds. Distributed in central and eastern Nepal at 1200–1800 m in moist, open places; also in northern India and northern Myanmar.

FOOD. Tender portions are cooked as a vegetable.

OTHER USES. The plant is good fodder.

Persicaria mollis (D. Don) Gross

Polygonum molle D. Don, *Aconogonum molle* (D. Don) Hara, *Ampelygonum molle* (D. Don) Roberty & Vautier
Coccoloba totnea Buchanan-Hamilton ex D. Don
ENGLISH *vegetable smartweed* GURUNG *tibu* NEPALI *chanwale, thotane* NEWARI *pathu* SHERPA *nyalo* TAMANG *painjugn, painkyum, panjyun*

Polygonaceae. Erect, stout herb about 2 m tall with a straggling stem. Leaves stalked, alternate, 5–20 cm long, 2–7 cm wide, stipulate, elliptic to lanceolate, entire, acuminate, silky hairs below. Flowers sessile, white or pinkish. Flowers May–September, fruits October–November. Propagated by seeds or root offshoots. Distributed in eastern and central Nepal at 1200–2400 m in moist, open places; also in northern India eastward to western China.

FOOD. Tender shoots are boiled and cooked as a vegetable or pickled; their taste is sour.

Persicaria mollis

Persicaria nepalensis (Meissner) H. Gross

Polygonum nepalense Meissner
Polygonum alatum Buchanan-Hamilton ex Sprengel
Polygonum punctatum Buchanan-Hamilton ex D. Don
GURUNG *tungro, kyubrisi* MAGAR *ratan daure* NEPALI *ratanaulo, priya ghans, raunne* TAMANG *kyurchumba, tunglhapchhi, tungdhap*

Polygonaceae. Erect herb. Leaves stalked, 1–6 cm long, 0.6–1 cm wide, ovate, acute, entire, sparsely hairy, petiole winged and auricled at the base. Flowers pink in axillary or terminal heads. Flowers and fruits May–November. Propagated by seeds. Distributed throughout Nepal at 1200–4000 m on exposed rocky slopes in forested areas; also in Afghanistan, India, eastern China, Malaysia, Japan, and tropical Africa.

FOOD. Tender leaves and shoots are cooked as a vegetable.

MEDICINE. Juice of the root, about 3 teaspoons three times a day, is given in cases of fever. A paste of the root is applied to fresh wounds.

OTHER USES. The plant is considered poisonous to animals. Squeezed plant is used for washing clothes.

Persicaria perfoliata (Linnaeus) H. Gross

Polygonum perfoliatum Linnaeus, *Ampelygonum perfoliatum* (Linnaeus) Roberty & Vautier, *Truellum perfoliatum* (Linnaeus) Sojak
NEPALI *bakhre aankhla, phaphre jhar*

Polygonaceae. Trailing annual herb. Leaves stalked, deltoid, obtuse, with recurved prickles. Flowers yellowish in terminal racemes, June–October. Fruits July–October. Propagated by seeds. Distributed in central and eastern Nepal at 900–1400 m on moist, open uncultivated land; also in India, eastern China, Korea, Japan, and Malaysia.

FOOD. Tender leaves and shoots are cooked as vegetables. Ripe fruits are eaten fresh, especially by children.

MEDICINE. Juice of the leaves is taken in cases of backache.

OTHER USES. The plant provides fodder for animals in stalls.

Persicaria posumbu (Buchanan-Hamilton ex D. Don) H. Gross

Polygonum posumbu Buchanan-Hamilton ex D. Don
Polygonum caespitosum Blume
NEPALI *seto pire*

Polygonaceae. Annual herb with a creeping stem. Leaves stalked, 2–8.7 cm long, elliptic to lanceolate, acute or acuminate, hairy. Flowers yellow or pinkish white. Fruit a nut, three-angled. Seeds smooth, shiny. Flowers and fruits most of the year. Propagated by seeds. Distributed in eastern and central Nepal at 200–2000 m in moist, open places; also in India, Bhutan, China, and Southeast Asia.

MEDICINE. A paste of the leaves is applied to muscular swellings.

Persicaria pubescens (Blume) Hara

Polygonum pubescens Blume
Polygonum flaccidum Roxburgh
NEPALI *pire*

Polygonaceae. Perennial herb about 75 cm high. Leaves stalked, 3.5–10 cm long, 0.7–2 cm wide, lanceolate, acuminate, setulose or pubescent on veins beneath. Flowers pinkish in drooping racemes. Fruit an achene, three-angled. Flowers and fruits May–November. Propagated by seeds. Distributed throughout Nepal at 800–2100 m on moist ground; also in India, eastern China, Malaysia, Australia, and Japan.

OTHER USES. The plant is used for fish poison.

Persicaria runcinata (Buchanan-Hamilton ex D. Don) H. Gross

Polygonum runcinatum Buchanan-Hamilton ex D. Don
NEPALI *kapre sag*

Polygonaceae. Trailing herb. Leaves stalked, 2–18.5 cm long, 1.7–7.5 cm wide, runcinate, glabrous or bristly hairy on the midvein above, terminal lobe triangular ovate, acuminate, ciliate. Flowers white or pink in few-headed terminal panicles. Flowers and fruits May–November. Propagated by seeds. Distributed in eastern and central Nepal at 1600–3600 m in moist, shady places; also in northern India, Bhutan, Tibet, eastern China, and Malaysia.

FOOD. Young shoots and leaves are cooked as a vegetable.

Persicaria tenella (Blume) Hara var. *kawagoeana* (Makino) Hara

Polygonum kawagoeanum Makino
Polygonum micranthum Meissner, *P. minus* subsp. *micranthum* (Meissner) Danser, *Persicaria minor* subsp. *micrantha* (Meissner) Soják
Polygonum minus Hudson
NEPALI *pire jhar*

Polygonaceae. Erect herb about 25 cm high. Leaves subsessile, 2.5–7 cm long, 0.4–0.6 cm wide, narrowly elliptic to lanceolate, acuminate, bearing minute bristles and scaly glands beneath, base attenuate. Flowers pinkish in racemes. Fruit an achene, biconvex. Flowers and fruits April–December. Propagated by seeds. Distributed throughout Nepal at 600–2100 m in moist places; also in India, Bhutan, eastward to China, Japan, and Malaysia.

OTHER USES. Squeezed plant is spread on water to poison fish.

Persicaria viscosa (Buchanan-Hamilton ex D. Don) Nakai

Polygonum viscosum Buchanan-Hamilton ex D. Don
NEPALI *rato pire*

Polygonaceae. Annual herb, stems hirsute with spreading bristly hairs. Leaves short-stalked, alternate, lanceolate, acuminate, strigose. Flowers pink in axillary or terminal racemes, April–June. Fruits June–October. Propagated by seeds. Distributed in central Nepal at 1200–1800 m on moist, open ground; also in India, Bhutan, China, Korea, and Japan.

MEDICINE. Juice of the root is taken in cases of indigestion.

Phalaris minor Retzius

Phalaris nepalensis Trinius
NEPALI *ragate jhar, saun* NEWARI *hi ghyan*

Gramineae. Erect or decumbent grass, culms branched, nodes swollen. Leaves linear lanceolate, acuminate, glabrous. Inflorescence greenish. Flowers and fruits January–April. Propagated by seeds. Distributed in central and western Nepal at 1000–1600 m, as a weed in crop fields; also in the northwestern Himalaya.

OTHER USES. The plant is used as fodder.

Phalaris minor

Phaseolus aconitifolius Jacquin

Vigna aconitifolia (Jacquin) Maréchal
BHOJPURI *kelai* DANUWAR *masyang* ENGLISH *dew gram, moth bean* GURUNG *masyaunro* LIMBU *ke* MAGAR *siltung* NEPALI *masyang* NEWARI *masyan* RAI *sapsibob* SUNWAR *masyang* TAMANG *latamran* THARU *mung*

Leguminosae. Slender, diffuse, slightly hairy herb. Leaves stalked, deeply three-lobed, lobes linear or lanceolate, acute. Flowers yellow, usually in capitate racemes. Fruit a pod, usually seven- or eight-seeded. Flowers and fruits July–October. Propagated by seeds. Distributed throughout Nepal to about 1000 m, cultivated; also in Pakistan, India, Sri Lanka, China, Myanmar, and the Americas.

FOOD. Seeds are used as lentil soup (*daal* in Nepali).
OTHER USES. The plant is used as fodder.

Phaseolus aureus Roxburgh

BHOJPURI *mung* DANUWAR *mungi* ENGLISH *green gram, golden gram, mung* LEPCHA *mungkalha* LIMBU *soikari* MAGAR *mugi* NEPALI *mung* NEWARI *mu* RAI *masiduchong* SUNWAR *mugi* TAMANG *mungi* THARU *mung*

Leguminosae. Hirsute annual shrub. Leaves stalked, pinnate, leaflets deltoid or rounded at the base. Flowers yellow in capitate racemes. Fruit a pod clothed with long silky hairs. Flowers and fruits September–October. Propagated by seeds. Distributed throughout Nepal to about 1000 m, cultivated; also in Pakistan, India, Bangladesh, and Myanmar.

FOOD. Soup (*daal* in Nepali) made from the seeds is much valued, especially for sick people because it is easily digested.
OTHER USES. The plant provides cattle fodder.

Phaseolus vulgaris Linnaeus

ENGLISH *dwarf bean, field bean, French bean, garden bean, haricot bean, kidney bean* NEPALI *rajama*

Leguminosae. Glabrous annual herb. Leaves stalked, trifoliolate. Flowers white, pink, or lilac. Fruit a pod, straight, turgid, glabrous. Flowers and fruits February–April. Propagated by seeds. Distributed throughout Nepal to about 1200 m, cultivated; also in tropical and temperate regions.

FOOD. Tender fruits and seeds are used for vegetable and lentil soup (*daal* in Nepali).

Phlogacanthus thyrsiformis (Roxburgh ex Hardwicke) Mabberley

Justicia thyrsiformis Roxburgh ex Hardwicke
Justicia thyrsiflorus Roxburgh, *Phlogacanthus thyrsiflorus* (Roxburgh) Nees
CHEPANG *chutap* NEPALI *tite*

Acanthaceae. Shrub about 2 m high, branches four-angled. Leaves stalked, 15–20 cm long, oblanceolate, drooping. Flowers orange or brick red in spike-like terminal thyrses. Fruit a capsule, subquadrangular, deeply grooved

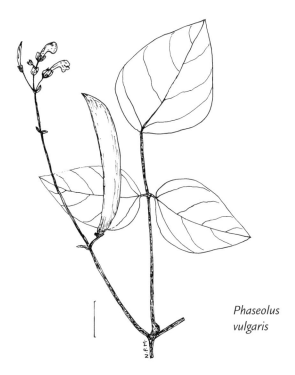

Phaseolus vulgaris

Phoenix humilis Royle ex Beccari & Hooker fil.

CHEPANG *nahi* ENGLISH *date palm* MOOSHAR *khajur*
NEPALI *khajuri, thakal*

   Palmae. Erect, unbranched palm, stems densely covered with the remains of old leaf stalks. Leaves stalked, pinnately divided, stalk armed with slender yellow spines, leaflets linear, pointed, folded on the flattened rachis, leathery, shiny. Flowers unisexual, fragrant, the male flowers alternate, pale yellow, female flower covered with large bracts. Fruit oblong, sessile, smooth, fleshy, brown when ripe, sweet. Flowers October–December, fruits February–May. Propagated by seeds. Distributed throughout Nepal to about 1000 m in open, dry places; also in India, Sri Lanka, China, and Indo-China.

   FOOD. Ripe fruits are eaten fresh.

   MEDICINE. Mooshars boil the leaf with some salt about 15 minutes, filter the water, and use it to gargle in cases of toothache.

   OTHER USES. Leaves are plaited into mats and are used for thatching. The base of the leaf is used as a brush for cleaning walls, windows, or floors, as a substitute for a broom. This brush is also used for rough painting of walls and ceilings. The stalk of the leaves is used for fuel.

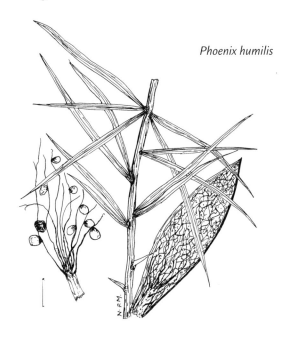

Phoenix humilis

on the back. Flowers February–April, fruits March–May. Propagated by seeds. Distributed in eastern and central Nepal at 200–1700 m in open fields; also in northern India, Bhutan, and Myanmar.

   FOOD. Flowers are used as a vegetable.

   MEDICINE. Juice of the leaf, 4 teaspoons three times a day for a week, is given for cough and colds.

   OTHER USES. The plant is used for fodder.

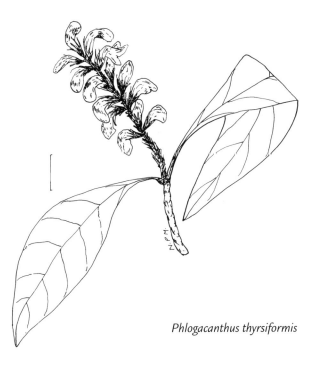

Phlogacanthus thyrsiformis

Pholidota griffithii Hooker fil.

Pholidota auriculata var. *griffithii* (Hooker fil.) King & Pantling
TAMANG *syabe lamda, timpuno*

   Orchidaceae. Epiphytic orchid with a jointed stem. Leaves in pairs, 5.5–8 cm long, 1.5–3 cm wide, oblong to lanceolate, acute. Flowers white in terminal racemes, April–May. Propagated by seeds or root offshoots. Distributed throughout Nepal at 800–1400 m on tree trunks and branches; also in northeastern India.

MEDICINE. A paste of the pseudobulb is applied to treat dislocated bones.

Pholidota griffithii

Pholidota imbricata Hooker

Coelogyne imbricata (Hooker) Reichenbach fil.
Cymbidium imbricatum Roxburgh, *Ornithidium imbricatum*
  Wallich ex Hooker fil.
Ptilocnema bracteatum D. Don
TAMANG *syalamba, timyuno*

Orchidaceae. Epiphytic orchid with elongated pseudo-bulbs. Leaves solitary, 7.5–36 cm long, 2.3–6.5 cm wide, elliptic to lanceolate, acuminate. Flowers brownish white. Fruit a capsule, ellipsoidal, greenish black. Flowers June–July, fruits February–March. Propagated by seeds or root offshoots. Distributed in eastern and central Nepal at 600–2900 m on tree trunks and branches; also in India, Sri Lanka, China, Myanmar, Malaysia, and Australia.

MEDICINE. Squeezed pseudobulbs are applied to boils.

Photinia integrifolia Lindley

Photinia eugenifolia Lindley
Pyrus integerrima D. Don
Photinia notoniana Wight & Arnott
NEPALI *lahare bakal pate, gaj phul*

Rosaceae. Tree about 6 m high. Leaves stalked, oblan-ceolate, acuminate, entire, glabrous. Flowers white in large spreading corymbs, June–July. Propagated by seeds. Distributed throughout Nepal at 1300–2800 m in forest openings; also in northern India, Bhutan, China, and Indo-China.

OTHER USES. Goats browse the leaves.

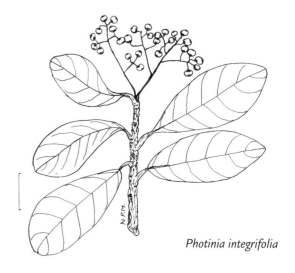

Photinia integrifolia

Phragmites karka (Retzius) Trinius ex Steudel

Arundo karka Retzius
Phragmites maxima (Forsskål) Chiovenda
NEPALI *narkat* TAMANG *bhordonbo*

Gramineae. Stout grass about 1 m high. Leaves broadly lanceolate. Inflorescences greenish in panicles, the in-volucral glumes subequal, hyaline. Flowers October–Feb-ruary. Propagated by seeds or by splitting the mother plant. Distributed in central Nepal at 1400–2000 m in open, dry places; also in India, Sri Lanka, Southeast Asia, and Australia.

OTHER USES. The plant is gathered for fodder.

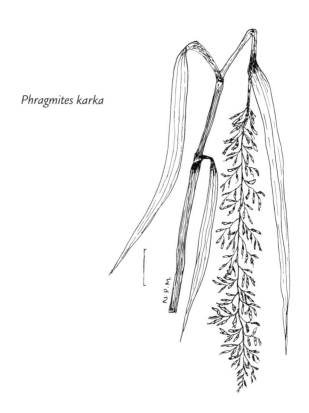

Phragmites karka

Phyla nodiflora (Linnaeus) Greene

Verbena nodiflora Linnaeus, *Lippia nodiflora* (Linnaeus) Michaux
CHEPANG *kamani* DANUWAR *ganhiya, jharmaruwa*
ENGLISH *cape weed, fog fruit, Godet's weed, link weed, lippia grass, sprain bush, mat grass, toad's stool* NEPALI *akamar, kurkur, phuli jhar* THARU *kokaina*

Verbenaceae. Creeping, much branched herb. Leaves subsessile, opposite, spatulate, elliptic, entire toward the base, serrulate at the rounded apex, minutely appressed hairy on both surfaces. Flowers pinkish in dense, globose, peduncled, axillary heads. Flowers and fruits April–November. Propagated by seeds or by nodal rooting of the stems. Distributed throughout Nepal to about 1400 m on moist or dry places; also in India, Bhutan, Sri Lanka, China, Japan, Myanmar, Malaysia, Africa, and North and South America.

MEDICINE. The plant is demulcent and is used as a cooling drug. Juice of the plant, about 2 teaspoons three times a day, is given to relieve fever. This juice is also given for cough and colds. The plant is squeezed and its aroma inhaled for cough and colds. Or the squeezed plant is put in water overnight, and the next morning the filtered water, about half a teaspoon, is given in cases of headache. Juice of the root, about 4 teaspoons twice a day, is given for gastric troubles.

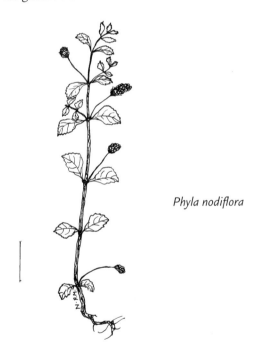

Phyla nodiflora

Phyllanthus acidus (Linnaeus) Skeels

Averrhoa acida Linnaeus
Cicca disticha Linnaeus, *Phyllanthus distichus* (Linnaeus) Mueller Aargau
DANUWAR *aura*

Euphorbiaceae. Deciduous tree about 10 m high. Leaves stalked, crowded at the ends of branches, pinnate, leaflets short-stalked, alternate, 5–9 cm long, 2.5–4 cm wide, ovate, acuminate, base rounded or cuneate. Flowers yellowish. Fruit globose, slightly flat at the top, usually with deep ribs. Propagated by seeds. Distributed in eastern and central Nepal to about 250 m, cultivated; also in India, Malaysia, Madagascar, Florida, and Brazil.

FOOD. Fruits are eaten fresh or pickled.

Phyllanthus amarus Schumacher

Phyllanthus niruri Linnaeus
ENGLISH *fly roost* NEPALI *bhui amala* THARU *chhotaki dahigola*

Euphorbiaceae. Erect annual herb about 60 cm high. Leaves stalked, oblong, distichous, often overlapping. Flowers yellowish, axillary. Fruit a capsule, smooth, rounded or somewhat flattened. Flowers and fruits June–November. Propagated by seeds. Distributed throughout Nepal to about 1000 m, as a weed in cultivated fields; also pantropical.

MEDICINE. An infusion of the root is febrifuge and diuretic. A decoction of the plant is stomachic, emmenagogue, febrifuge, and diuretic. Bark has a purgative property. Juice of the leaves is applied to pimples, cuts, and wounds and is also useful for swellings caused by some inflammations.

Phyllanthus emblica Linnaeus

Emblica officinalis Gaertner
Phyllanthus taxifolius D. Don
CHEPANG *tausi* DANUWAR *rikhiya* ENGLISH *emblica myrobalans* GURUNG *kyun, titi* KHALING *korosi* LIMBU *aagra* MAGAR *aaunlesa, ghwarbhet* MAJHI *amala* MOOSHAR *rikhiya* NEPALI *amala* NEWARI *amba* RAI *chimbak, jurse* RAUTE *aurya* TAMANG *amble, harimnal, tebu* THARU *aura* TIBETAN *kyu-ru-ra*

Euphorbiaceae. Deciduous tree about 15 m high. Leaves subsessile, 1–1.5 cm long, 0.2–0.3 cm wide, oblong, acute and apiculate, entire, base rounded. Flowers small, yellowish, densely clustered on the branches, the male flowers numerous, female flowers few, both sexes on the same branchlets. Fruit globose, smooth, fleshy, with six longitudinal faint lines. Flowers March–May, fruits October–February. Propagated by seeds. Distributed throughout Nepal to about 1600 m; also in India, Bhutan, Sri Lanka, southern China, and Southeast Asia.

FOOD. Fruit is eaten fresh or pickled; fresh fruit is rich in vitamin C (Plate 17).

MEDICINE. Juice of the bark, about 3 teaspoons twice a day, is given in cases of amebic dysentery. Rautes warm the juice and use it to massage relieve body aches caused by heavy physical work. Juice of the leaves, about 2 teaspoons twice a day, is given for constipation. The fruit is acidic, astringent, diuretic, laxative, stomachic, and useful for diarrhea, dysentery, dyspepsia, menorrhagia, hemorrhage, inflammation of the eye, and troubles of the uterus. The juice is also cooling and is, therefore, useful for treating burning sensations of the heart and during urinary discharge, thirst, also diseases of the heart, liver complaints, and eye troubles. Dried fruit is valued in treating hemorrhage, jaundice, dyspepsia, diarrhea, and dysentery.

The fruit is one of the ingredients of *triphala* (Nepali and Sanskrit for three fruits) of Ayurvedic medicine, the infusion of three myrobalans: emblica (*Phyllanthus emblica*), belleric (*Terminalia bellirica*), and chebulic (*T. chebula*). *Triphala* is stomachic, cooling, and a good tonic. In cases of stomach disorder, the fruit of *P. emblica* is crushed with that of *T. chebula* and taken with milk.

OTHER USES. Bark and leaves are used for tanning in different parts of Nepal. Dried fruits have detergent properties and are used for washing the head in some places in the midlands of Nepal.

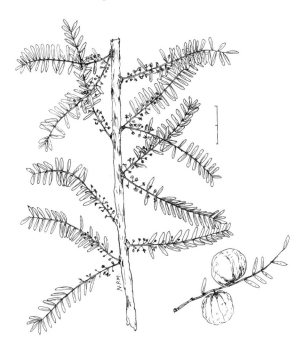

Phyllanthus emblica

Phyllanthus parvifolius Buchanan-Hamilton ex D. Don

Phyllanthus juniperinus Wallich ex Mueller Aargau
CHEPANG *khareto* GURUNG *nabhya* MAJHI *khargaja* NEPALI *khareto, paitei, sunpate* TAMANG *khagan, maimanthara, mirman, ramhagam, ramalakan, rawagan, wasipsip*

Euphorbiaceae. Straggling shrub about 1.5 m high. Leaves short-stalked, 0.4–1.3 cm long, 0.2–0.6 cm wide, ovate, elliptic, or oblong, entire, glabrous, glaucous beneath, apex rounded. Flowers small, solitary, axillary, brown-purple. Fruit a capsule, depressed, globose, dull black when ripe. Flowers September–October. Propagated by seeds. Distributed in central and eastern Nepal at 1000–2200 m, on the open land of waysides; also in northern India and Bhutan.

MEDICINE. A paste of the plant is applied to boils and pimples. Powdered plant is put on obstinate wounds to encourage healing. Powdered leaves are used to remove dandruff and lice from the head.

Phyllanthus reticulatus Poiret

Kirganelia reticulata (Poiret) Baillon
Cicca microcarpa Bentham, *Kirganelia microcarpa* (Bentham) Hurusawa & Y. Tanaka, *Phyllanthus microcarpa* (Bentham) Mueller Aargau
MOOSHAR *sikat* NEPALI *nundhik* TAMANG *khayal*

Euphorbiaceae. Straggling shrub with grayish, warty bark. Leaves distichous, 1.5–5 cm long, 0.8–2.5 cm wide, ovate to oblong, obtuse or acute, entire, glabrous, dark green above, pale beneath. Flowers solitary, axillary, yellowish, in few-flowered fascicles. Fruit a berry, purplish. Seeds triquetrous. Flowers December–March, fruits March–July. Propagated by seeds. Distributed in central and eastern Nepal to about 800 m; also in northern India, Bhutan, Sri Lanka, southern China, Southeast Asia, and tropical Africa.

FOOD. Ripe fruits are edible.

MEDICINE. Juice of the bark is applied to treat swellings caused by some inflammations. The leaf is diuretic and cooling. A paste of the leaves, mixed with some soil of the *chulo*, the traditional earthen hearth, is applied to wounds.

Phyllanthus urinaria Linnaeus

NEPALI *bhuin amala*

Euphorbiaceae. Annual herb about 50 cm high. Leaves sessile, 1–1.5 cm long, oblong, obtuse or apiculate, base rounded. Flowers solitary, axillary, reddish to yellowish white. Fruit a capsule, depressed, globose. Flowers and fruits June–December. Propagated by seeds. Distributed throughout Nepal to about 760–1700 m in moist, open places; also pantropical.

MEDICINE. A paste of the plant is applied to boils.

Phyllanthus virgatus Forster fil.

Phyllanthus simplex Retzius
NEPALI *amala jhar*

Euphorbiaceae. Herb about 50 cm high. Leaves stalked, 1–2 cm long, oblong, obtuse to mucronate. Flowers yellowish, axillary. Fruit a capsule, depressed, globose. Flowers and fruits June–November. Propagated by seeds. Distributed throughout Nepal to about 1400 m in moist, open places; also in India, Bhutan, southern China, Southeast Asia, and Polynesia.

MEDICINE. Juice of the leaves is applied to boils and pimples.

Phyllodium pulchellum (Linnaeus) Desvaux

Hedysarum pulchellum Linnaeus, *Desmodium pulchellum* (Linnaeus) Bentham, *Dicerma pulchellum* (Linnaeus) de Candolle
MAJHI *bhatte*

Leguminosae. Deciduous shrub about 2 m high, bark smooth, reddish brown, with minute pale lenticels. Leaves stalked, trifoliolate, leaflets oblong to lanceolate, obtuse or subacute, entire, glabrous or dull green above, finely downy beneath, base rounded. Flowers white, tinged with pink, in erect axillary and terminal racemes. Fruit a pod. Flowers July–September, fruits December–February. Propagated by seeds. Distributed throughout Nepal to about 500 m, gregarious in *Shorea robusta* forest; also in India, Bhutan, Sri Lanka, China, Southeast Asia, the Ryukyu Islands, and northern Australia.

MEDICINE. Among Majhis, a paste of the seeds is given in cases of fever and applied to the forehead to relieve headaches.

Physalis divaricata

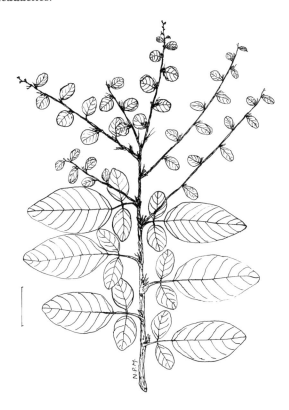

Phyllodium pulchellum

Physalis divaricata D. Don

Physalis minima Linnaeus
CHEPANG *phongretel* ENGLISH *ground cherry, sun berry, wild husk*
NEPALI *isamgoli, jangali mewa, patpate* THARU *gal bhomra*

Solanaceae. Pubescent annual herb about 1 m high. Leaves stalked, 1.5–6 cm long, 1.5–4 cm wide, ovate, sinuate, angular or scarcely lobed, base rounded or cuneate. Flowers yellow, solitary. Fruit a berry, globose. Flowers and fruits June–November. Propagated by seeds. Distributed throughout Nepal to about 600 m in open places; also in Afghanistan, Pakistan, and northern India.

FOOD. Ripe fruit is eaten fresh.

MEDICINE. The plant is tonic and diuretic.

Physalis peruviana Linnaeus

Physalis edulis Sims
Physalis pubescens Linnaeus
NEPALI *jangali mewa* TAMANG *kyungba*

Solanaceae. Stout herb about 1 m high. Leaves stalked, 1.5–19 cm long, 1–9 cm wide, ovate, sinuate, angular. Flowers solitary, axillary, light blue. Fruit a berry, globose, included within the membranous calyx. Flowers July–August, fruits September–November. Propagated by seeds. Distributed in central Nepal at 900–2200 m in wetlands of cultivated fields; also in tropical South America.

FOOD. Roasted seeds are pickled.

Phytolacca acinosa Roxburgh

Pircunia latbenia Moquin-Tandon, *Phytolacca latbenia* (Moquin-Tandon) H. Walter
Rivina latbenia Buchanan-Hamilton ex Wallich
ENGLISH *poker weed, sweet belladona* NEPALI *jariongo sag*
TIBETAN *thang-phrom*

Phytolaccaceae. Succulent herb about 1 m high. Leaves stalked, alternate, 12–26 cm long, 5–10 cm wide, elliptic to ovate, narrowed toward the petiole, smooth. Flowers stalked, greenish, June–August. Fruits September–November. Propagated by seeds or root offshoots. Distributed in central and western Nepal at 2200–3200 m in the shade of forest trees; also in northern India, western China, and Laos.

FOOD. Tender leaves and shoots are cooked as a green vegetable.

Phytolacca acinosa

Picea smithiana (Wallich) Boissier

Pinus smithiana Wallich

ENGLISH *spruce* NEPALI *jhunde salla*

Pinaceae. Coniferous tree about 40 m high. Bark grayish, shallowly furrowed into rounded or four-sided scales. Leaves 2.5–3.7 cm long, pungent, spirally arranged. Male cones solitary, erect, female cones pendulous, bright green when young, brownish when ripe. Cones mature October–November. Propagated by seeds. Distributed in western Nepal at 2400–2900 m, often in association with *Abies, Cedrus,* and *Pinus.*

OTHER USES. Wood is used for planks, boxes, construction, and household purposes.

Picea smithiana

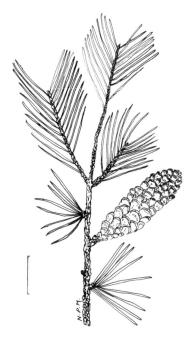

Picrasma quassioides (Buchanan-Hamilton ex D. Don) Bennett

Simaba quassioides Buchanan-Hamilton ex D. Don

NEPALI *nim kath*

Simaroubaceae. Climbing shrub with bitter bark. Leaves stalked, odd-pinnate, leaflets subopposite, rusty tomentose, oblong to lanceolate, long acuminate, serrate, lowest pair of leaflets smallest, penultimate pair largest. Flowers greenish in axillary panicles. Fruit a drupe, black when ripe. Flowers April–June, fruits July–September. Propagated by seeds. Distributed in western and central Nepal at 2000–3000 m in shady ravines; also in northern India, Bhutan, China, Taiwan, Korea, and Japan.

MEDICINE. Juice of the bark is used as a tonic. A paste of the leaves is applied to treat itches.

Picrasma quassioides

Picris hieracioides Linnaeus subsp. kaimaensis Kitamura

Picris hieracioides var. *indica* Wight

NEPALI *ban dudhe*

Compositae. Herb. Lower leaves stalked, oblong or lanceolate, sinuate and dentate, upper leaves smaller, clasping the stem at their base. Flower heads yellow, on long peduncles. Fruit an achene, spindle shaped, brown. Flowers and fruits May–October. Propagated by seeds. Distributed throughout Nepal at 1200–3800 m in wet places; also in northern India, China, and Korea.

MEDICINE. The plant is mixed and pounded with *Swertia pedicellata* and applied to the forehead to treat headaches.

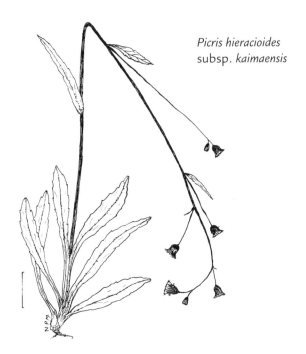

Picris hieracioides
subsp. *kaimaensis*

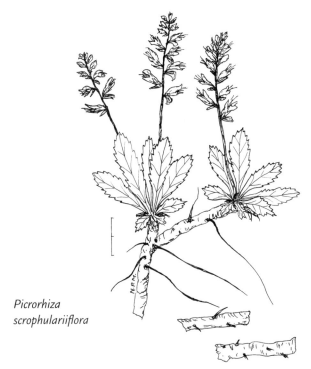

*Picrorhiza
scrophulariiflora*

Picrorhiza scrophulariiflora Pennell

Picrorhiza kurrooa Royle ex Bentham
Veronica lindleyana Wallich

GURUNG *kutaki* NEPALI *kutaki* SHERPA *hodling* TAMANG *kuraki*
TIBETAN *gorki, hong-len*

Scrophulariaceae. Herb about 10 cm high. Leaves sub-sessile, aggregated at the base, 1.5–5 cm long, 0.5–1.2 cm wide, acuminate, serrate, stalk winged. Flowers pinkish, July–August. Fruits October–November. Propagated by seeds or rhizomes. Distributed throughout Nepal at 3500–4800 m on open, rocky pastureland but the gathering of its rhizomes for sale in the trade endangers plant populations; also in northern India, Bhutan, southeastern Tibet, western China, and northern Myanmar.

MEDICINE. The rhizome is bitter, cathartic, stomachic, and purgative. Juice of the rhizome is given for fever, stomachache, and dropsy. A paste of the rhizome is used for cough and colds.

Pieris formosa (Wallich) D. Don

Andromeda formosa Wallich, *Lyonia formosa* (Wallich) Handel-Mazzetti

GURUNG *padake* NEPALI *chimal, gineri, pote, prake, temal*
SHERPA *praba* TAMANG *bra bu ba, chanjiwa, pra*

Ericaceae. Small tree. Leaves short-stalked, 6.5–12 cm long, 1.3–4 cm wide, lanceolate, acuminate, serrate, glabrous. Flowers white in terminal panicles, April–June. Fruits July–November. Propagated by seeds or root offshoots. Distributed in central and eastern Nepal at 2000–3300 m in shady places; also in northern India, Bhutan, and Myanmar.

MEDICINE. Juice of the leaves is applied to treat scabies.
OTHER USES. The plant is poisonous to livestock.

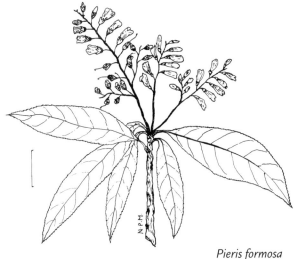

Pieris formosa

Pilea anisophylla Weddell

Urtica anisophylla Wallich

CHEPANG *begelau* TAMANG *chhal, syalamba, tɪmyuno, tɪple*

Urticaceae. Herb. Leaves stalked, 0.7–16 cm long, 0.4–5.5 cm wide, oblanceolate, slightly serrate toward the upper part, glossy above, slightly hairy beneath, base oblique. Inflorescence greenish. Flowers and fruits August–November. Propagated by seeds or root offshoots. Distributed in eastern and central Nepal at 900–2000 m on damp, mossy rocks beside streams; also in India, Bhutan, western China, and Taiwan.

MEDICINE. Juice of the root is used to wash the head to remove dandruff.
OTHER USES. The plant is considered nutritious fodder.

Pilea glaberrima (Blume) Blume

Urtica glaberrima Blume
Pilea goglado Blume, *Urtica goglado* Buchanan-Hamilton
ex Wallich
Pilea smilacifolia Weddell
CHEPANG *ledem, tankan* NEPALI *hare gageleto*
TAMANG *chhyal, pakha chhal*

Urticaceae. Herb about 1 m high. Leaves stalked, elliptic to lanceolate, acuminate, entire, three-veined, narrowed toward the base. Inflorescence yellowish. Fruit an achene, smooth. Propagated by seeds or root offshoots. Distributed in central and eastern Nepal at 300–2000 m in moist, rocky places; also in northern India, Bhutan, Myanmar, and Java.

FOOD. Tender leaves and shoots are cooked as a vegetable.

Pilea racemosa (Royle) Tuyama

Procris racemosa Royle
Pilea subalpina Handel-Mazzetti
NEPALI *lede sag*

Urticaceae. Herb about 10 cm high. Leaves crowded at the top of the stem, ovate, acute, serrate, base rounded. Flowers reddish, terminal, the receptacle peduncled, June–August. Propagated by seeds or root offshoots. Distributed throughout Nepal at 2000–3800 m in moist areas and on mossy tree trunks and branches; also in northern India, southern Tibet, and western China.

FOOD. Soft leaves and shoots are cooked as a vegetable.

Pilea symmeria Weddell

Pilea wightii Weddell
CHEPANG *aailanta* NEPALI *chiple, gagaleto, ganthe, gharlahi,
lali ghans, kamle* TAMANG *chhal*

Urticaceae. Creeping herb. Leaves stalked, opposite, 2–19.5 cm long, 0.8–7 cm wide, oblong to lanceolate, long acuminate, distantly serrate, glabrous, base acute. Flowers small, greenish, in axillary panicles. Flowers and fruits May–November. Propagated by seeds or root offshoots. Distributed throughout Nepal at 1600–3000 m in crevices of rocks in moist places; also in northern India, Bhutan, and western and central China.

FOOD. Tender shoots and leaves are cooked as a vegetable.

OTHER USES. The plant is collected for stall feeding, especially for goats.

Pilea umbrosa Blume

Urtica umbrosa Wallich
Pilea cordifolia Hooker fil.
Pilea producta Blume
NEPALI *chholyang*

Urticaceae. Herb about 50 cm high. Leaves stalked, 5–15 cm long, 4–8 cm wide, ovate, acuminate, pubescent, coarsely serrate, base rounded or subcuneate. Flowers

Pilea symmeria

greenish. Fruit an achene. Flowers and fruits May–September. Propagated by seeds or root offshoots. Distributed throughout Nepal at 1200–2500 m in moist, rocky places; also in India, Bhutan, western China, and Myanmar.

FOOD. Tender leaves and shoots are cooked as a vegetable.

Pimpinella achilleifolia (de Candolle) C. B. Clarke

Ptychotis achilleifolia de Candolle
Athamanta achilleifolia Wallich
GURUNG *najo* TAMANG *semal*

Umbelliferae. Herb about 50 cm high. Lower leaves stalked, glabrous, tripinnate, leaflets dissected, ultimate segments linear lanceolate. Upper leaves reduced. Flowers white in compound umbels. Propagated by seeds. Distributed throughout Nepal at 1200–3200 m on open, grassy slopes; also in northern India.

FOOD. Tender shoots are cooked as a vegetable.

Pimpinella aniseum Linnaeus

ENGLISH *anise* GURUNG *anise* NEPALI *sonph*

Umbelliferae. Annual herb about 60 cm high. Basal leaves stalked, pinnate or bipinnate. Flowers yellowish white. Fruit grayish brown, curved, with short hairs. Propagated by seeds. Distributed throughout Nepal to about 3000 m, cultivated; also in Asia Minor, India, northeastern United States, Mexico, and South America.

FOOD. Seeds are used as a spice.

MEDICINE. Fruits are carminative, diuretic, and used to prevent flatulence.

Pimpinella achilleifolia

Pinus roxburghii Sargent

Pinus longifolia Roxburgh ex Lambert
CHEPANG *metang* GURUNG *siuri* ENGLISH *chir pine,
Himalayan long-leaved pine* LIMBU *aang* MAGAR *aragi*
NEPALI *aule salla, jumlo salla, rani salla, salla dhup* RAI *angma*
TAMANG *thamsingdong*

Pinaceae. Evergreen coniferous tree. Leaves in bundles of three, 10–20 cm long, filiform, pointed. Male cones cylindrical, yellowish, female cones brownish. Seeds nearly 1 cm long. Cones May–February, mature September–November. Propagated by seeds. Distributed throughout Nepal at 800–1400 m on dry slopes; also in Afghanistan, northern India, and Bhutan.

FOOD. Seeds are roasted and eaten.

MEDICINE. The resin, in the form of a paste, is applied to hasten healing of cuts and wounds. Resin the size of a pea is given six times a day in cases of gastric trouble.

OTHER USES. Wood has value as timber and is also used for furniture and construction. Needles provide resin and turpentine, and their sharpness is put to use in protecting stored grain from rodents (Plate 18).

Pinus wallichiana A. B. Jackson

Pinus chylla Loddiges
Pinus dicksonii Carrière
Pinus excelsa Wallich ex D. Don
Pinus griffithii M'Clelland
Pinus nepalensis de Chambray
ENGLISH *blue pine* NEPALI *gobre salla*

Pinaceae. Evergreen coniferous tree about 50 m high. Leaves in bundles of five, needle-like, about 20 cm long. Female cones pendulous, cylindrical, about 30 cm long, yellowish. Propagated by seeds. Distributed throughout Nepal at 1800–2300 m in open mountainous areas; also in Afghanistan and northwestern India.

OTHER USES. Wood is used as timber. Resin is extracted for commercial purposes.

Piper longum Linnaeus

ENGLISH *long pepper* NEPALI *lahare pan, pipla* NEWARI *pipi*
RAI *yakham* THARU *murjhanga* TIBETAN *pi-pi-ling*

Piperaceae. Twining herb, creeping, and rooting below, often minutely tomentose. Leaves stalked, 3–8 cm long, 2–8 cm wide, broadly ovate to cordate, shortly acuminate, glabrous, lower leaves long-stalked, upper leaves sessile,

Pinus roxburghii

Piper longum

clasping the stem at their base, usually five-veined at the base. Flowers greenish in spikes. Fruit a berry, crowded in cylindrical spikes. Flowers September October, fruits November–December. Propagated by seeds or root offshoots. Distributed throughout Nepal to about 800 m in shady places; also in northern India, Bhutan, Sri Lanka, and Malaysia.

FOOD. Fruits are used as condiments.

MEDICINE. Water boiled with two or three dried fruits is taken in cases of cough and colds.

Piper mullesua D. Don

Chavica mullesua (D. Don) Miquel
Chavica sphaerostachya Miquel
Piper brachystachyum Wallich ex Hooker fil.
Piper guigual D. Don
NEPALI *chabo, pipala*

Piperaceae. Trailing herb, stems swollen at the joints. Leaves stalked, 5.3–14 cm long, 2–8 cm wide, elliptic, acuminate, entire, five-veined, glabrous. Flowers yellowish. Fruit a berry, small, crowded. Flowers November–December, fruits May–October. Propagated by seeds or root offshoots. Distributed throughout Nepal at 400–2500 m on mossy tree trunks and branches; also in northern India and Bhutan.

FOOD. Ripe fruits are eaten fresh. Flowers are added to vegetables and meat curries for flavor.

MEDICINE. Juice of ripe fruits is boiled to reduce the amount to half, and about 5 teaspoons of the resultant liquid juice is taken twice a day for cough and colds. Magars of western Nepal eat roasted fruit to treat cough and colds.

Piper nepalense Miquel

NEPALI *pipli*

Piperaceae. Slender climber. Leaves stalked, 4–13.5 cm long, 1.5–8 cm wide, ovate to lanceolate, caudate-acuminate, thinly leathery, base rounded, nearly oblique. Flowers greenish in solitary, more or less interrupted spikes. Fruit a berry, ovoid, pointed, granulate. Flowers May–July, fruits August–September. Propagated by seeds or root offshoots. Distributed in eastern and central Nepal at 200–2000 m in steep, rocky, shady places; also in India and Bhutan.

FOOD. Fruits are used as spices.

Piper peepuloides Roxburgh

NEPALI *ban pipla*

Piperaceae. Woody climber. Leaves stalked, ovate or elliptic to lanceolate, entire, acuminate. Flowers yellowish. Fruit a berry, black when ripe. Flowers September–October, fruits January–February. Propagated by seeds or root offshoots. Distributed in eastern Nepal at 400–1500 m on moist, shady ground; also in India, Bhutan, western China, and Myanmar.

FOOD. Dried fruits are used to flavor vegetables and curries.

MEDICINE. Two or three fruits are chewed once a day in cases of cough and colds.

Piper wallichii (Miquel) Handel-Mazzetti

Chavica wallichii Miquel
Piper aurantiacum Wallich
CHEPANG *tang* TAMANG *pipal*

Piperaceae. Climber. Leaves stalked, 3.5–10 cm long, 2–9.5 cm wide, broadly ovate, acute, entire, five-veined, glabrous, base cordate. Flowers greenish, September–October. Fruits December–January. Propagated by seeds or root offshoots. Distributed in eastern and central Nepal at 700–2800 m in moist, shady places; also in northern India, Bhutan, western China, and Myanmar.

MEDICINE. Juice of the root or fruit, about 2 teaspoons three times a day, is given to treat intermittent fever.

Piptanthus nepalensis (Hooker) D. Don

Baptisia nepalensis Hooker
Anagyris nepalensis Graham
Piptanthus bicolor Craib
Piptanthus bombycinus Marquand
Piptanthus concolor Harrow ex Craib
Piptanthus forrestii Craib
Piptanthus leiocarpus O. Stapf
Thermopsis laburnifolia D. Don
Thermopsis nepaulensis de Candolle
NEPALI *suga phul, siksike*

Leguminosae. Shrub about 4 m high. Leaves stalked, digitately trifoliolate, leaflets sessile, lanceolate, acuminate, entire, dark green above, pale beneath, gray pubescent when young, later glabrous and shiny. Flowers yellow in compact hairy racemes. Fruit a pod, flat, narrowed at both ends. Flowers April–June, fruits August–September. Propagated by seeds. Distributed throughout Nepal at 2000–3800 m on open hillsides; also in India, Bhutan, western China, and Myanmar.

OTHER USES. Stems are used as beams in the construction of huts. They are also used to make walking sticks. Bark and leaves are used as fish poison. Leaves are gathered for fodder.

Pisum sativum Linnaeus

BHOJPURI *matar* CHEPANG *kerau* DANUWAR *kerau, matar*
ENGLISH *garden pea, pea* GURUNG *tangar* LEPCHA *takabyit* LIMBU *ke*
MAGAR *mocha* MOOSHAR *matar* NEPALI *kerau, matar*
NEWARI *kachhe, keyagu* RAI *khubasalanwa* RAUTE *kalaun*
SUNWAR *kar* TAMANG *kerau, tangar* THARU *kerau*

Leguminosae. Annual herb. Leaves stalked, pinnate, leaflets ovate to oblong, entire. Flowers white or violet on long peduncles. Fruit a pod. Seeds round, white. Flowers and fruits January–March. Propagated by seeds. Distributed throughout Nepal to about 3500 m, cultivated; also in most regions of the world.

Piptanthus nepalensis

FOOD. Young buds and leaves are cooked as a vegetable. Seeds are used for various purposes in the diet.

MEDICINE. Rautes take juice of the root, about 4 teaspoons twice a day, in cases of fever.

OTHER USES. The plant is used for fodder.

Pithecellobium dulce (Roxburgh) Bentham

Mimosa dulce Roxburgh

ENGLISH *Madras thorn, Manila tamarind, monkey pod* NEPALI *jalebi*

Leguminosae. Thorny shrub about 7 m high, branches armed with short, sharp, stipular spines. Leaves short-stalked, evenly bipinnate, each pinna with a single pair of oblique, ovate to oblong, obtuse, entire leaflets. Flowers white in dense heads. Fruit a pod, turgid, twisted, often spiral. Seeds six to eight, embedded in a whitish pulpy aril. Flowers February–March, fruits June–August. Propagated by seeds or cuttings. Distributed throughout Nepal to about 700 m in open, dry places; also in Pakistan, India, Bhutan, Bangladesh, the Philippines, southern United States, and Mexico.

FOOD. The sweet aril is edible. Roasted seeds are edible, or they are mixed with curries.

MEDICINE. Juice of root bark, about 2 teaspoons twice a day, is taken in cases of diarrhea and dysentery. A paste of the leaves is applied to treat muscular swellings caused by some inflammations. Juice of the leaves, about 2 teaspoons three times a day, is taken for indigestion; in some places in Nepal an excess dose of this juice is used for abortion.

OTHER USES. Bark of the stem contains 25% tannin.

Pithecellobium dulce

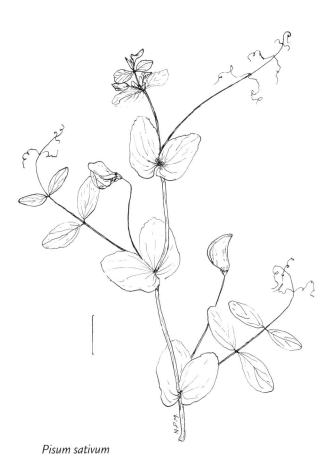

Pisum sativum

Pityrogramma calomelanos (Linnaeus) Link

NEPALI *dankerno*

Pteridaceae. Terrestrial fern. Rhizome stout, clothed with narrow, light brown, peltate scales. Stipes glossy dark purplish. Fronds bipinnate, narrowly oblong, pinnae short-stalked, subopposite, linear lanceolate, pinnules narrowly deltoid, margin dentate. Sori along the veins. Spores July–August. Propagated by spores. Distributed in eastern and central Nepal at 250–1100 m in open, rocky places; also in India, Malaysia, Africa, and tropical America.

MEDICINE. Juice of the frond, about 4 teaspoons three times a day, is given to relieve stomach acidity.

Plantago erosa Wallich

Plantago major var. *angusta* (Pilger) Yamazaki
ENGLISH *greater plantain, Englishman's foot, way bread, white man's foot* GURUNG *kanchai jhar* MAGAR *sano dhable*
NEPALI *bijauni phul, esapgol, gahun jhar, khete sag, pothi sahasrabuti*
TAMANG *nyamnyung* SHERPA *gangdhap, syong* TIBETAN *fuchi amcho*

Plantaginaceae. Perennial herb with fibrous roots. Leaves all basal, stalked, 2–11 cm long, 0.8–5.5 cm wide, ovate, entire. Flowers greenish in slender spikes. Fruit a capsule, two-celled, with four to eight small black seeds. Flowers and fruits March–November. Propagated by seeds. Distributed throughout Nepal at 2000–4600 m on open, moist uncultivated land; also in India, Bhutan, Sri Lanka, southeastern Tibet, western China, and Myanmar.

FOOD. Tender leaves are cooked as a vegetable.

MEDICINE. Juice of the whole plant, about 4 teaspoons

Plantago erosa

three times a day, is given for malarial fever and leukorrhea. A paste of the plant is applied to boils. The root is astringent and its juice is used as mouthwash for inflammation of the gums. Powdered root, about 2 teaspoons, is taken as an anthelmintic. Juice of the leaves is applied to bruises and given to children with fever. The juice is boiled to reduce the amount to half and taken in cases of diarrhea and dysentery. A paste of the leaves is applied to boils, carbuncles, and used for other skin diseases. This paste is also applied to insect bites. Seeds are boiled and the liquid is given for whooping cough.

Plantago lanceolata Linnaeus

Plantago attenuata Wallich
NEPALI *isapgol*

Plantaginaceae. Perennial herb. Leaves stalked, 2.5–30 cm long, lanceolate, acuminate, entire or dentate. Flowers yellowish, May–July. Propagated by seeds. Distributed in eastern and central Nepal to about 1700 m on open, sandy ground; also in India, Bhutan, eastern Asia, Europe, and North America.

FOOD. Tender leaves are cooked as a vegetable.

Platanthera clavigera Lindley

Habenaria clavigera (Lindley) Dandy
Habenaria densa Wallich ex Lindley, *Platanthera densa*
  (Wallich ex Lindley) Soó
NEPALI *kanga*

Orchidaceae. Orchid about 1 m high. Leaves 7.5–12.5 cm long, 2.5–5 cm wide, ovate or oblong, acuminate, base sheathing. Flowers greenish. Propagated by seeds. Distributed throughout Nepal at 2000–4600 m; also in northern India and Bhutan.

FOOD. Boiled root is edible.

Plectranthus mollis (Aiton) Sprengel

Ocimum molle Aiton
Plectranthus cordifolia D. Don
Plectranthus incanus Link
NEPALI *guhya silam*

Labiatae. Pubescent herb. Leaves stalked, 2–10.5 cm long, 1–9.5 cm wide, ovate, acuminate, crenate, pubescent. Flowers bluish in lax cymes. Fruit a nutlet, globose, brown. Flowers and fruits July–November. Propagated by seeds. Distributed throughout Nepal at 800–1500 m in open places; also in northern India and Sri Lanka.

MEDICINE. Juice of the leaves is used to treat wounds.

Pleione humilis (Smith) D. Don

Epidendrum humile Smith, *Coelogyne humilis* (Smith) Lindley,
  Cymbidium humile (Smith) Lindley
NEPALI *hathi tauke*

Orchidaceae. Epiphytic orchid with tufted roots, pseudobulbs flagon shaped. Leaves elliptic. Flowers purplish, October–November. Propagated by seeds or root off-

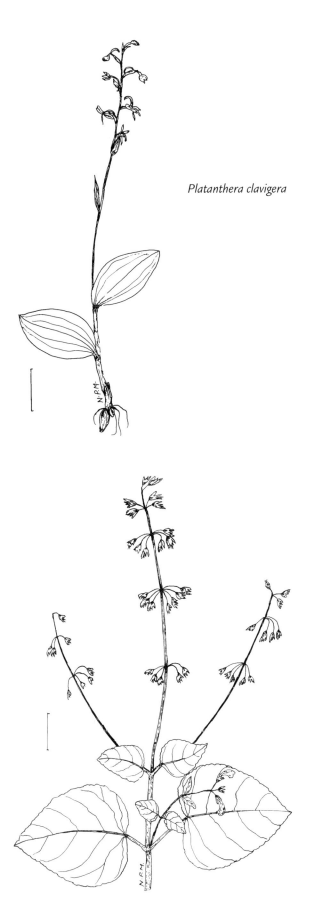

Platanthera clavigera

shoots. Distributed in central Nepal at 2400–3000 m in moist, shady places; also in India, Bhutan, and eastern Tibet.

MEDICINE. A paste of the pseudobulb is applied to cuts and wounds.

Pleione praecox (Smith) D. Don

Epidendrum praecox Smith, *Coelogyne praecox* (Smith) Lindley, *Cymbidium praecox* (Smith) Lindley
Coelogyne wallichiana Lindley
NEPALI *lasun pate*

Orchidaceae. Terrestrial orchid, pseudobulbs depressed, conical, greenish. Flowers mauve on a one-flowered stalk about 1.5 m high, October–November. Propagated by seeds or root offshoots. Distributed in eastern and central Nepal at 2000–2400 m on moist, rocky ground; also in northern India, western China, Myanmar, and Thailand.

MEDICINE. A paste of the pseudobulb is applied to cuts and wounds.

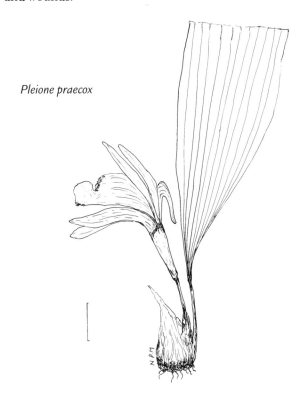

Pleione praecox

Pleurospermum angelicoides (de Candolle) C. B. Clarke

Hymenolaena angelicoides de Candolle, *Pterocyclus angelicoides* (de Candolle) Klotzsch, *Ligusticum angelicoides* Wallich
NEPALI *jwane*

Umbelliferae. Annual herb about 1 m high. Leaves stalked, pinnate or bipinnate, pinnae 7–15 cm long, narrowly lanceolate, entire. Flowers white. Fruit narrowly ob-

Plectranthus mollis

long. Propagated by seeds. Distributed throughout Nepal at 2500–4000 m; also in northern India, Bhutan, Tibet, and southeastern China.

FOOD. Tender leaves and shoots are cooked as a vegetable. Fruitlets are used as a substitute for cumin seeds (*Cuminum cyminum*).

Pleurospermum hookeri C. B. Clarke

NEPALI *bhuset, chhatare* TIBETAN *phaki*

Umbelliferae. Herb with a thick rootstock. Leaves stalked, tripinnate, leaflets dissected, top segments broad, serrate. Bracteoles linear lanceolate, entire, margins membranous, hairy. Flowers white in compound umbels. Propagated by seeds. Distributed throughout Nepal to about 1300 m on exposed hillsides; also in northern India, Tibet, and western China.

FOOD. Seeds are pickled and also used as a spice.

MEDICINE. The root is used in the treatment of dyspepsia, rheumatism, diarrhea, hemorrhoids, and certain skin diseases.

Pleurospermum hookeri

Plumbago zeylanica Linnaeus

Plumbago rosea Linnaeus

CHEPANG *abijale* ENGLISH *Ceylon leadwort, frangipani* GURUNG *negnmaitam* MAGAR *chitu* NEPALI *chitu, seto kuro* THARU *kalamnath*

Plumbaginaceae. Shrub about 1 m high with striate green twigs. Leaves stalked, alternate, 3.5–10 cm long, 1.5–5.5 cm wide, ovate, acuminate, entire, somewhat glaucous beneath, stalk often auricled. Flowers white in terminal spikes. Fruit a capsule, oblong, pointed. Flowers and fruits most of the year. Propagated by seeds or root offshoots. Distributed throughout Nepal to about 1300 m in open, moist places; also in India, Sri Lanka, Malaysia, and tropical Africa.

MEDICINE. A paste of the root is valued for skin diseases, hemorrhoids, and rheumatic pains. Juice of the root, about 2 teaspoons twice a day, is given for diarrhea, dysentery, and to treat boils; an excess dose is not good for health.

Plumbago zeylanica

Plumeria rubra Linnaeus

Plumeria acuminata Aiton
Plumeria acutifolia Poiret

CHEPANG *chuwa, chuwaro* ENGLISH *frangipani, temple tree* GURUNG *galainchi* MAGAR *golaichi* MAJHI *chyan phul* NEPALI *chuwa, galaichi, galaichon, golanchi* NEWARI *chaswan* RAI *chuwa* TAMANG *chuwa, wala*

Apocynaceae. Soft-wooded deciduous tree about 5 m high. Leaves stalked, 14–36 cm long, 4–13 cm wide, oblong to lanceolate, acuminate, glabrous. Flowers white with yellow center, fragrant. Fruit a follicle. Seeds winged. Flowers September–June. Propagated by branch cuttings. Distributed throughout Nepal to about 1200 m; also in Pakistan, India, Bhutan, Bangladesh, Sri Lanka, Myanmar, and tropical America.

MEDICINE. Bark is purgative and its juice is considered effective for gonorrhea and venereal sores. Juice of the bark, about half a teaspoon twice a day, is given to treat amebic dysentery. This juice has an abortifacient property. A poultice of leaves is applied to treat muscular swellings. The milky juice is employed in cases of boils and rheumatic pain. It is also applied to remove worms or germs from wounds.

OTHER USES. Bark is used as fish poison.

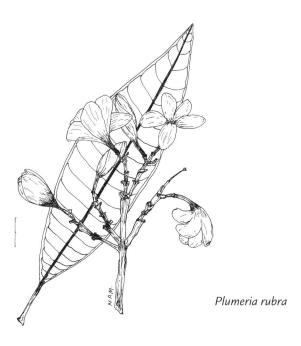

Plumeria rubra

Poa annua

*Podocarpus
neriifolius*

Poa annua Linnaeus

NEPALI *pode ghans*

Gramineae. Annual grass with decumbent culms. Leaves linear, subobtuse, glabrous. Inflorescence brownish. Flowers and fruits January–October. Propagated by seeds or by splitting the mother plant. Distributed in eastern and central Nepal at 2300–3500 m in open pastureland; also in most regions of the world.

OTHER USES. The plant can be provided as fodder.

Podocarpus neriifolius D. Don

Podocarpus macrophyllus Wallich

NEPALI *gunsi*

Podocarpaceae. Coniferous tree about 10 m high. Leaves 5–12 cm long, 0.8–1.5 cm wide, narrowly elliptic, acuminate, leathery, base narrowed. Cones yellowish. Seed cone red, fleshy. Seeds globose, surrounded by yellow or orange, fleshy scale. Propagated by seeds. Distributed in eastern and central Nepal at 900–1300 m in humid subtropical regions; also in India, Bhutan, China, Myanmar, Malaysia, Taiwan, New Guinea, and Fiji.

OTHER USES. The plant produces high-quality timber.

Podophyllum hexandrum Royle

Podophyllum emodi var. *hexandrum* (Royle) R. Chatterjee & Mukerjee
Podophyllum emodi Wallich ex Hooker fil. & Thomson, *P. hexandrum* var. *emodi* (Wallich ex Hooker fil. & Thomson) Selivan
Podophyllum hexandrum var. *bhootanense* (R. Chatterjee & Mukerjee) Browicz

ENGLISH *May apple* NEPALI *ban bhanta, laghu patra*

Berberidaceae. Herb about 40 cm high. Leaves long-stalked, orbiculate to cordate, deeply three-lobed, lobes obovate, acuminate, serrate. Flowers pinkish. Fruit a berry, solitary, terminal, drooping. Flowers May–June, fruits July–September. Propagated by seeds. Distributed throughout Nepal at 3000–4500 m in moist soil beneath cliffs near streams but the gathering of its rhizomes for

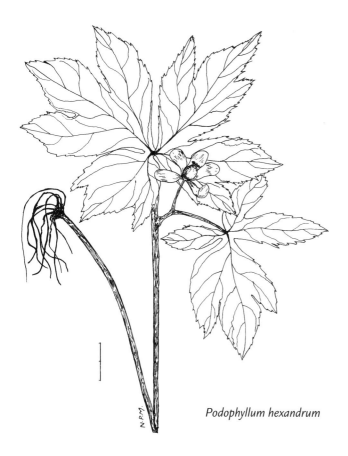

Podophyllum hexandrum

Flowers and fruits June–December. Propagated by seeds or root offshoots. Distributed throughout Nepal at 900–3200 m, common in shady places; also in India, Sri Lanka, China, Taiwan, Thailand, and Southeast Asia.

OTHER USES. The plant is gathered for fodder.

Pogostemon amarantoides Bentham

TAMANG *rasangan*

Labiatae. Tall herb. Leaves stalked, oblong, acuminate, margin incised, serrate, glabrous. Flowers white in dense whorls, January–March. Propagated by seeds. Distributed in eastern and central Nepal at 900–2100 m in open, moist places; also in India and Bhutan.

MEDICINE. Juice of the root, 4 teaspoons three times a day, is taken to treat cough and indigestion. This juice is also applied to the forehead to relieve headaches.

Pogostemon benghalensis (Burman fil.) Kuntze

Ocimum benghalensis Burman fil.
Pogostemon plectranthoides Desfontaines

CHEPANG *basdamrat, nampani, senghas* DANUWAR *utajara*
NEPALI *kalo asuro, rudilo* TAMANG *lutiri* THARU *kohabar*

Labiatae. Aromatic shrub about 1 m high, stems dark purple, gray tomentose when young. Leaves stalked, opposite, 1.5–16 cm long, 0.8–8 cm wide, ovate, acuminate, doubly serrate, base rounded. Flowers faint violet, crowded in a cylindrical spike. Fruit a nutlet, dark brown when ripe. Flowers and fruits most of the year. Propagated

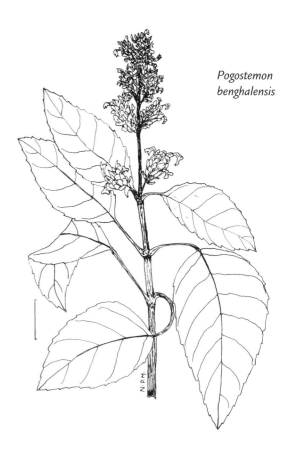

Pogostemon benghalensis

sale in the trade endangers plant populations. Also in Afghanistan, northern India, Bhutan, southern Tibet, and western China.

MEDICINE. Rhizomes are stimulant and purgative.

Pogonatherum crinitum (Thunberg) Kunth

Andropogon crinitum Thunberg

GURUNG *masino kharuto* NEPALI *bhuse khari, kharuki, muse jhar*

Gramineae. Tufted grass. Leaves linear lanceolate, about 4 cm long. Inflorescence brown. Flowers June–July. Propagated by seeds or root offshoots. Distributed throughout Nepal at 500–1700 m in open, sandy soil; also in India, Bhutan, China, Southeast Asia, and Japan.

OTHER USES. The plant provides fodder.

Pogonatherum paniceum (Lamarck) Hackel

Saccharum paniceum Lamarck
Perotis polystachya Willdenow, *Pogonatherum polystachyum* (Willdenow) Roemer & Schultes
Pogonatherum saccharoideum Palisot de Beauvois

TAMANG *pabg*

Gramineae. Tufted perennial grass, culms 10–50 cm tall, in dense tufts, with numerous nodes, culm sheath lax, subcompressed. Leaves 2–7 cm long, 1–4 cm wide, spreading, linear lanceolate, acuminate, pale green, base rounded, abruptly contracted. Inflorescence whitish.

by seeds. Distributed throughout Nepal to about 1400 m in moist, shady places; also in India.

MEDICINE. Juice of the plant is given in cases of cough and colds. This juice, mixed with old cow dung, is given to cattle suffering from diarrhea. The plant is boiled in water for bathing to relieve fever. Juice of the root, mixed with water, is used to bathe a child suffering from fever.

OTHER USES. Powdered dried leaves or ash of the plant is used as manure in plant nurseries.

Pogostemon glaber Bentham

CHEPANG *braj damre* GURUNG *khole dhyak* NEPALI *rudilo* TAMANG *darakhyang*

Labiatae. Shrub. Leaves stalked, 2–15 cm long, 1–8 cm wide, ovate to lanceolate, acuminate, doubly serrate, glabrous. Flowers white in dense spikes, February–March. Propagated by seeds. Distributed in western and central Nepal at 300–1900 m in open, sunny places; also in northern India, China, and Indo-China.

MEDICINE. Juice of the plant is applied to the forehead to relieve headaches. Juice of the root is given in cases of indigestion. Juice of the leaves, about 1 teaspoon three times a day, is given to relieve fever, and a warmed leaf is put to the forehead for the same problem.

Polyalthia longifolia (Sonnerat) Thwaites

ENGLISH *Indian fir, mast tree* NEPALI *ashok, nakali ashok*

Annonaceae. Evergreen tree about 15 m high. Leaves stalked, 7.5–22.5 cm long, 1.3–3.8 cm wide, lanceolate, narrowly tapering, pointed, shiny, margin wavy or crinkled. Flowers yellowish. Fruit ovate, rounded at both ends, smooth, black when ripe. Propagated by seeds. Distributed throughout Nepal to about 600 m, planted around villages; also in India and Sri Lanka.

OTHER USES. The plant is grown for shade or as an avenue tree. Wood is light and suitable for boxes and barrels. Bark furnishes fiber suitable for cordage. Bats like the fruits.

Polygala arillata Buchanan-Hamilton ex D. Don

Chamaebuxus arillata (Buchanan-Hamilton ex D. Don) Hasskarl

LEPCHA *clem-som-crem* NEPALI *luinche phul*

Polygalaceae. Erect shrub about 2 m high. Leaves stalked, oblong to lanceolate, acuminate, entire, glabrous. Flowers yellow in racemes. Fruit a capsule, reniform. Flowers June–July, fruits August–September. Propagated by seeds. Distributed in eastern and central Nepal at 1500–2700 m in open, moist places; also in India, Bhutan, southern Tibet, China, and Southeast Asia.

MEDICINE. Juice of the plant, mixed with turmeric powder (*Curcuma domestica*), is applied to treat muscular swellings. The root is used as a purgative, and a paste of it is applied to the forehead to treat headache.

Polyalthia longifolia

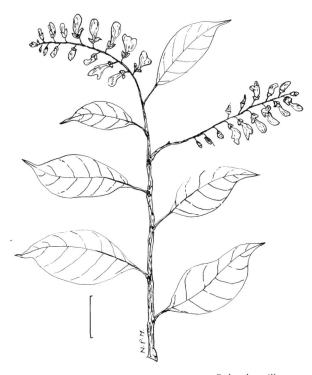

Polygala arillata

Polygala persicariifolia de Candolle

Polygala buchanani D. Don
Polygala wallichiana Wight
CHEPANG *bijakanne*

Polygalaceae. Pubescent annual herb about 45 cm high. Leaves subsessile, oblong to lanceolate, entire. Flowers yellow in axillary and terminal racemes. Fruit a capsule, elliptic to oblong, emarginate. Flowers and fruits August–November. Propagated by seeds. Distributed throughout Nepal at 700–1900 m in shady places; also in India, China, Southeast Asia, New Guinea, Australia, the Philippines, and Africa.

OTHER USES. The plant is used to make *marcha,* a fermenting cake from which liquor is distilled.

Polygala tartarinowii Regel

Polygala triphylla Buchanan-Hamilton ex D. Don
NEPALI *kurkure jhar, phabare ghans*

Polygalaceae. Erect herb about 10 cm high. Leaves stalked, broadly elliptic, obtuse, entire, ciliate. Flowers pinkish in many-flowered terminal racemes. Fruit a capsule, compressed, orbicular, slightly winged. Propagated by seeds. Distributed in western and central Nepal at 1800–2900 m on grassy hillsides; also in India, Bhutan, southeastern Tibet, China, northern Myanmar, the Philippines, and Japan.

MEDICINE. Juice of the plant is given in cases of fever caused by common colds.

Polygonatum cirrhifolium (Wallich) Royle

Convallaria cirrhifolia Wallich
Polygonatum sibiricum Redouté
ENGLISH *Solomon's seal* GURUNG *printa* NEPALI *ramsikia*
SHERPA *rhanisekya* THARU *kairuwa* TIBETAN *ra-mnye*

Convallariaceae. Herb about 1 m high, stem grooved. Leaves sessile, in whorls of three to six, 12–16.5 cm long, 0.2–0.7 cm wide, linear lanceolate, circinate at the tip, glaucous beneath, margin rolled in. Flowers white in racemes, May–July. Fruits August–September. Propagated by seeds or root tubers. Distributed throughout Nepal at 1700–4600 m on moist ground in the forest; also in northern India, Bhutan, southern Tibet, and western China.

FOOD. Tender leaves and shoots are cooked as a vegetable.

MEDICINE. The root tuber is given as tonic, especially to ill persons.

Polygonatum verticillatum (Linnaeus) Allioni

Convallaria verticillata Linnaeus
Convallaria leptophulla D. Don, *Polygonatum leptophullum*
    (D. Don) Royle
NEPALI *khirangalo, khirlung* TAMANG *ma dhap*

Convallariaceae. Herb about 1 m high, stem angled, grooved. Leaves sessile, three to eight in a whorl, linear lanceolate, glaucous beneath, margin ciliate, slightly rolled in, tip acuminate. Flowers white in peduncled axillary pairs, May–July. Fruits August–September. Propagated by seeds or root tubers. Distributed throughout Nepal at 2000–4000 m in open places among shrubs; also in Tibet, central and western Asia including western China, and Europe.

FOOD. Tender leaves and shoots are cooked as a vegetable.

MEDICINE. A paste of the root tuber is given to debilitated dogs as a health tonic.

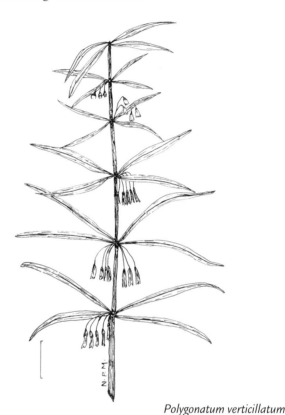

Polygonatum verticillatum

Polygonum plebejum R. Brown

Polygonum aviculare Linnaeus
Polygonum cliffortioides Meissner
Polygonum dryandri Sprengel
Polygonum elegans [Dryander in] Aiton
Polygonum herniarioides Delile
Polygonum roxburghii Meissner
DANUWAR *maseno sag* NEPALI *baluni sag, bethe, latte jhar, sain sag, sukul jhar* TIBETAN *nene*

Polygonaceae. Prostrate herb with very diffuse branches. Leaves sessile, stipulate, small, linear, acute, entire. Flowers small, sessile, pink, in axillary clusters. Flowers and fruits most of the year. Propagated by seeds or root suckers. Distributed throughout Nepal to about 3200 m in open places; also in western Asia eastward to China, India, Malaysia, Australia, and Africa.

FOOD. Soft and tender parts are cooked as a vegetable.

Polygonum plebejum

MEDICINE. The plant is boiled in water about 15 minutes, and the strained water, about 4 teaspoons twice a day, is given in cases of bloody dysentery. A paste of the plant is applied to heal wounds between the toes caused by prolonged walking barefooted in muddy water. Juice of the root is given for stomach trouble.

Polypodium amoenum Wallich ex Mettenius

NEPALI *bish phej*

Polypodiaceae. Epiphytic or terrestrial fern. Rhizome wide, creeping, with brown linear scales. Fronds 30–65 cm long, 8–15 cm wide, glabrous or slightly pubescent, cut down to the rachis into numerous, minutely dentate pinnae, pinnae gradually narrowed toward the base. Sori globose, brown. Propagated by spores. Distributed throughout Nepal at 1300–2700 m in moist, shady places; also in India, China, Taiwan, and Indo-China.

MEDICINE. Powdered rhizome, mixed with corn flour (*Zea mays*), is roasted, and about 8 teaspoons of this powder, three times a day, is given to relieve backaches.

Polypodium lachnopus Wallich ex Hooker

NEPALI *harber unyu*

Polypodiaceae. Epiphytic fern. Rhizome creeping, with deep brown fine scales. Fronds 12–35 cm long, 3–6 cm wide, broad, cut down to the rachis into spreading, small-toothed pinnae. Sori globose, orange. Propagated by spores. Distributed throughout Nepal at 1200–3200 m in moist, shady places, generally near streams; also in northern and southwestern India.

MEDICINE. Juice of the plant is applied to treat itches on the skin.

Polypodium microrhizoma C. B. Clarke

NEPALI *daluko*

Polypodiaceae. Epiphyte or terrestrial fern. Rhizome creeping, with blackish brown linear scales. Fronds 25–50 cm long, 3–9 cm wide, lanceolate, pinnate, pinnae in 25–45 pairs, lanceolate, acute, distantly incised. Sori yellowish, in a single row on either side of the midvein. Propagated by spores. Distributed throughout Nepal at 1400–3300 m on mossy tree trunks and branches.

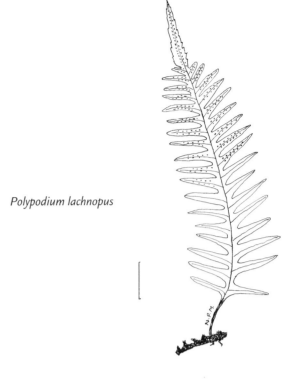

Polypodium lachnopus

MEDICINE. A paste of the plant is applied to cuts and wounds.

Polypogon fugax Nees ex Steudel

Polypogon higegaweri Steudel, *P. littoralis* var. *higegaweri* (Steudel) Hooker fil.

NEPALI *jhyaple ghans*

Gramineae. Annual grass, culms creeping, rooting at the nodes. Leaves lanceolate, about 1 cm wide. Inflorescence greenish. Flowers and fruits February–June. Propagated by seeds. Distributed in western and central Nepal

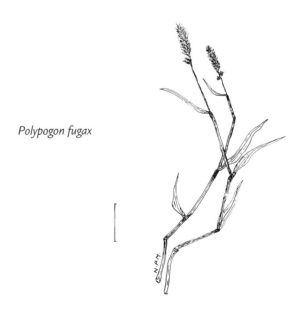

Polypogon fugax

at 1500–3600 m in open, sunny places; also in India, China, Korea, and Japan.

OTHER USES. The plant is supplied as fodder.

Polystichum squarrosum (D. Don) Fée

NEPALI *bhyagute nyuro, phusre nyuro, rato unyu, thulo nyuro*
TIBETAN *idum-bu-re-ral*

Dryopteridaceae. Herbaceous fern. Stipe erect, tufted, densely scaly, rachis rust colored, with fine scales. Fronds 5–70 cm long, ovate to lanceolate, bipinnate, pinnae numerous, lanceolate, pinnules oblong, unequal at the base, auricled on the upper side, margin with small spines. Sori brown, in a single row on either side of the main vein. Propagated by spores. Distributed throughout Nepal at 1000–3000 m in shady places; also in India and China.

FOOD. Tender portions are cooked as a vegetable.

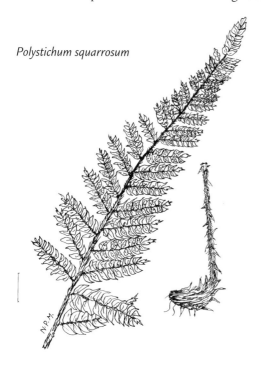

Polystichum squarrosum

Populus ciliata Wallich ex Royle

Populus pyriformis Royle
ENGLISH *Himalayan poplar* NEPALI *bange kath, bangikot, bhote pipal, lahare pipal* TIBETAN *chyangma*

Salicaceae. Lofty tree. Leaves stalked, 5–25 cm long, 4–15 cm wide, broadly ovate, acuminate, finely dentate, margin glandular ciliate, base usually cordate, stalk compressed above. Flowers greenish in lateral catkins. Fruit a capsule, long, ovoid. Flowers March–April, fruits May–June. Propagated by seeds or root offshoots. Distributed throughout Nepal at 2000–3600 m in open places; also in northern India, Bhutan, southwestern China, and northern Myanmar.

MEDICINE. A paste of the bark, mixed with the ash of cow dung, is applied to treat muscular swellings.

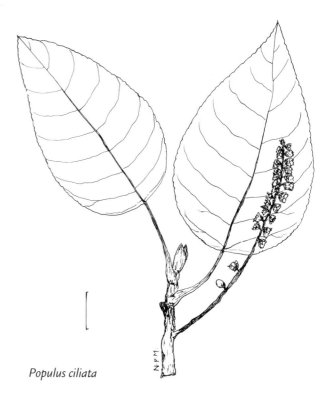

Populus ciliata

OTHER USES. The plant is grown along roadsides. Leaves are valued as fodder for goats.

Porana grandiflora Wallich

Dinetopsis grandiflora (Wallich) Roberty
Ipomoea cuspidata D. Don
NEPALI *chamero laharo*

Convolvulaceae. Pubescent climber. Leaves stalked, ovate, acuminate, entire, pubescent, base deeply cordate. Flowers pink in axillary racemes, September–October. Propagated by seeds. Distributed in eastern and central Nepal at 1900–2500 m in shady places; also in India and Bhutan.

MEDICINE. A paste of the root is applied to treat dislocated bone.

Porana paniculata Roxburgh

NEPALI *kubhinde lahara*

Convolvulaceae. Woody twiner. Leaves stalked, 3–12 cm long, 2.5–8 cm wide, ovate to cordate, entire. Flowers white in many-flowered lateral to terminal panicles. Fruit a capsule, ovoid to globose. Flowers November–January, fruits February–April. Propagated by seeds. Distributed throughout Nepal to about 1900 m in open places, climbing on shrubs and thickets; also in northern India and Myanmar.

OTHER USES. Twigs are used for temporary binding and to make baskets.

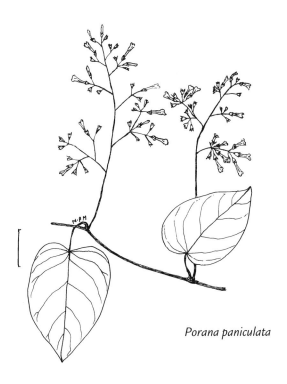

Porana paniculata

Portulaca oleracea Linnaeus

CHEPANG *basupaku, pakchho* ENGLISH *purslane* GURUNG *dhap, khate jhar* MOOSHAR *nuniya sag* NEPALI *garyaunla jhar, nundhiki, paite jhar* TAMANG *salimran*

Portulacaceae. Prostrate, much branched, annual herb. Leaves short-stalked, 1–1.4 cm long, 0.3–0.5 cm wide, oblong to lanceolate, obtuse, fleshy, flat, base cuneate. Flowers yellow in sessile, axillary and terminal, few-flowered

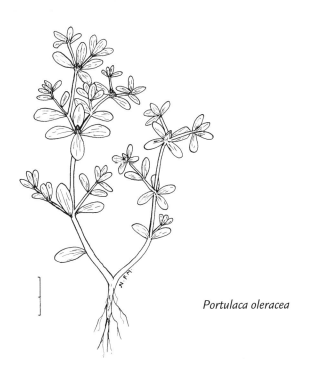

Portulaca oleracea

heads. Flowers and fruits most of the year. Propagated by seeds or root offshoots. Distributed throughout Nepal to about 1600 m on uncultivated land; also pantropical.

FOOD. Tender leaves and shoots are used as a potherb; leaves are also boiled and pickled.

Potentilla argyrophylla Wallich ex Lehmann

Potentilla cataclines Lehmann
Potentilla insignis Royle
Potentilla jacquemontiana Cambessèdes
Potentilla leucochroa Lindley
NEPALI *aate* TAMANG *dapse*

Rosaceae. Perennial herb with a stout rootstock. Leaves digitately trifoliolate, leaflets sessile, elliptic to ovate, oblong, serrate, finely hairy above, white tomentose beneath. Flowers red in terminal few-flowered cymes. Flowers and fruits May–October. Propagated by seeds. Distributed throughout Nepal at 2300–4600 m on exposed slopes in oak forests; also in Afghanistan, Pakistan, and northern India.

MEDICINE. Juice or a paste of the root is applied to treat toothaches.

Potentilla fruticosa Linnaeus

Dasiphora fruticosa (Linnaeus) Rydberg
ENGLISH *bush cinquefoil* NEPALI *bhairung pate, chiniya phal, sebaro* TIBETAN *pama*

Rosaceae. Erect shrub about 1 m high. Leaves pinnate, leaflets three to seven, sessile, 0.6–1.8 cm long, 0.2–0.6 cm wide, oblong to lanceolate, apiculate, entire, densely silky haired above, glabrous beneath. Flowers yellow, usually solitary, terminal. Flowers and fruits June–October. Propagated by seeds or root offshoots. Distributed throughout Nepal at 2400–4600 m in rocky grassland; also in northern India, Bhutan, and China.

FOOD. Leaves are used as tea substitute by people living at higher elevations.

MEDICINE. Juice of the root is given in cases of indigestion.

OTHER USES. Powdered plant is used as incense.

Potentilla fulgens Wallich ex Hooker

Potentilla fulgens var. *intermedia* Hooker fil.
Potentilla siemersiana Lehmann
Potentilla splendens Wallich ex D. Don

ENGLISH *Himalayan cinquefoil* GURUNG *hosre* NEPALI *bagajari, bajra danti, dantaman, kanthamun, mulapate, panpate, phosre* TAMANG *dapakya, dapse, nawali, phusure, tap tap* TIBETAN *sen ge zil pa*

Rosaceae. Herb about 50 cm high. Leaves stalked, odd-pinnate, leaflets numerous, 0.5–5.5 cm long, 0.5–3 cm wide, alternately large and small, diminishing in size from the uppermost downward, ovate, silky tomentose beneath. Flowers yellow, July–August. Fruits September–November. Propagated by seeds or root offshoots. Distributed throughout Nepal at 1700–3800 m in open, moist places; also in northern India and Bhutan.

MEDICINE. Juice of the plant is taken to treat stomachaches, cough, and colds. Powdered root is kept inside the mouth about 2 hours to relieve toothaches. The powder, about 4 teaspoons twice a day, is given with water for stomach disorders. Villagers of the districts of Rasuwa and Nuwakot chew fresh root in cases of cough and colds. Juice of the root is taken as an anthelmintic. It is also taken to treat peptic ulcer. The juice, mixed with root juice of *Valeriana jatamansii* in equal amount, is given in doses of about 2 teaspoons twice a day to treat dysuria. The leaf is considered useful for pyorrhea.

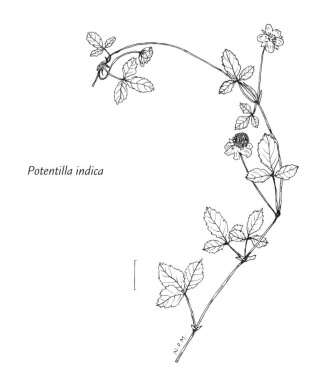

Potentilla indica

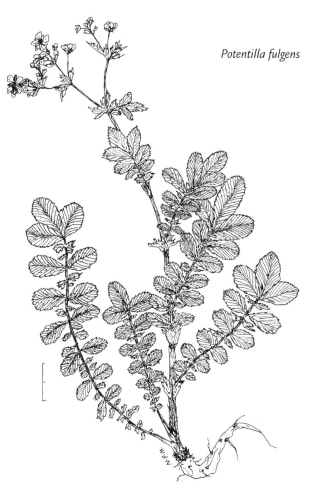

Potentilla fulgens

Potentilla indica (Andrews) Wolf

Fragaria indica Andrews, *Duchesnea indica* (Andrews) Focke
Duchesnea fragiformis Smith
Potentilla denticulosa Seringe
Potentilla wallichiana Seringe, not Delile ex Lehmann (see
    P. kleiniana)

ENGLISH *mock strawberry* GURUNG *sapala* MAJHI *chhepara kaphal, gare kaphal* NEPALI *bhuin ainselu, bhuin kaphal, chhepra kaphal, gare kaphal, jogi ainselu, kukur ainselu, pahenlo ainselu, rato ainselu, sarpa ko kaphal* TAMANG *sapulung*

Rosaceae. Creeping herb. Leaves stalked, alternate, stipulate, trifoliolate, leaflets sessile, 1–2.5 cm long, 1–1.8 cm wide, dentate, hairy, the middle leaflet larger than the others. Flowers stalked, solitary, yellow. Fruit round, red, succulent. Flowers March–April, fruits May–July. Propagated by seeds. Distributed throughout Nepal at 500–2600 m in moist places; also in Afghanistan, Pakistan, India, eastward to China, Japan, and Malaysia.

FOOD. Fresh fruits, which are insipid, watery, and entirely destitute of flavor, are edible.

Potentilla kleiniana Wight

Potentilla wallichiana Delile ex Lehmann, not Seringe (see
    P. indica)

GURUNG *jhyume* MAGAR *bhui kaphal* NEPALI *kauwa kaphal, maraute jhar* TAMANG *tilipalang*

Rosaceae. Annual herb. Leaves stalked, digitately five-foliolate, leaflets sessile, 0.7–3 cm long, 0.8–1.7 cm wide, oblong, serrate, nearly glabrous above, hairy on the veins beneath. Flowers yellow in terminal corymbose cymes. Flowers and fruits most of the year. Propagated by seeds or root offshoots. Distributed throughout Nepal at 800–2500 m, scattered in moist, open places; also in northern India, Bhutan, Sri Lanka, China, and Java.

FOOD. Ripe fruits are edible.

MEDICINE. Juice of the plant, about 2 teaspoons three times a day, is given in cases of fever.

Potentilla leschenaultiana Seringe

NEPALI *hyumi*

Rosaceae. Hairy herb. Leaves stalked, pinnate, leaflets five to nine, sessile, 0.7–2.7 cm long, 0.6–1.2 cm wide, broadly elliptic, serrate, hairy above, white, villous on the veins beneath. Flowers white in panicled corymbs, July–August. Propagated by seeds or root offshoots. Distributed in central and western Nepal at 1800–3000 m in open, sunny places; also in northern India.

FOOD. Ripe fruits are edible.

Potentilla leuconota D. Don

NEPALI *sakkali jhare jaro*

Rosaceae. Prostrate herb. Leaves stalked, pinnate, leaflets sessile, 0.3–1.8 cm long, 0.2–0.6 cm wide, oblong, serrate, hairy above, silvery beneath, tip narrowed. Flowers yellow. Flowers and fruits June–August. Propagated by seeds or root offshoots. Distributed throughout Nepal at 3300–3800 m in open meadows; also in India, Bhutan, China, and Borneo.

MEDICINE. An infusion of the root is given in cases of indigestion.

Potentilla monanthes Wallich ex Lehmann

Potentilla cryptantha Klotzsch
Potentilla monanthes var. *sibthorpioides* Hooker fil.
CHEPANG *salyangsai* TAMANG *saplang*

Rosaceae. Herb. Leaves stalked, trifoliolate, leaflets short-stalked, 0.5–2 cm long, 0.3–1.5 cm wide, spatulate, crenate, narrowed toward the base. Flowers yellow. Flowers and fruits May–June. Propagated by seeds or root offshoots. Distributed throughout Nepal at 3000–4500 m among tufts of grasses on open slopes; also in northern India and Bhutan.

FOOD. Ripe fruits are edible.

Potentilla peduncularis D. Don

Potentilla peduncularis var. *clarkei* Hooker fil.
Potentilla peduncularis var. *obscura* Hooker fil.
Potentilla velutina Wallich
NEPALI *kali ainselu, mula jhar* TAMANG *nagabhya*

Rosaceae. Herb about 30 cm high with a long, stout rootstock. Leaves uniformly pinnate, leaflets numerous, sessile, 0.7–2.5 cm long, 0.2–0.6 cm wide, oblong, serrate, silky haired above, densely white hairy beneath. Flowers yellow in few-flowered corymbs. Flowers and fruits July–November. Propagated by seeds or root offshoots. Distributed throughout Nepal at 3000–4700 m on open, moist ground; also in northern India, Bhutan, and China.

MEDICINE. A paste of the root is given to treat profuse menstruation. Leaf buds are boiled in water to use for bathing in cases of fever.

Potentilla supina Linnaeus

Comarum flavum Buchanan-Hamilton ex Roxburgh
Potentilla paradoxa Nuttall, *P. supina* var. *paradoxa* (Nuttall) Wold
NEPALI *bajra danti*

Rosaceae. Prostrate annual herb. Lower leaves larger, with more leaflets, upper leaves smaller, with fewer leaf-lets, leaflets subsessile, ovate, cuneate, coarsely serrate, appressed hairy. Flowers yellowish. Fruit an achene, ovoid, smooth. Flowers and fruits March–June. Propagated by seeds or root offshoots. Distributed throughout Nepal at 1000–1400 m in open pastureland; also in western Asia, India, Mongolia, Europe, North Africa, and North America.

MEDICINE. Pieces of the root are kept in the mouth about 1–2 hours to relieve toothaches. Juice of the root, about 3 teaspoons three times a day, is given in cases of indigestion.

Pouzolzia sanguinea (Blume) Merrill

Urtica sanguinea Blume, *Boehmeria sanguinea* (Blume) Hasskarl
Boehmeria viminea Blume, *Pouzolzia viminea* (Blume) Weddell, *Urtica viminea* Wallich
Pouzolzia ovalis Miquel
NEPALI *lipe* TAMANG *pungi, syutelo*

Urticaceae. Shrub about 3 m high with a reddish stem. Leaves stalked, alternate, 5–15 cm long, 1–5 cm wide, acuminate, serrate or crenate, glabrous above, white tomentose beneath, base rounded or cuneate. Inflorescence yellowish, clustered, mostly axillary. Fruit an achene, ellipsoidal, compressed, ovate to lanceolate. Flowers and fruits June–July. Propagated by seeds. Distributed in eastern and central Nepal at 900–3000 m, common on rocky ground;

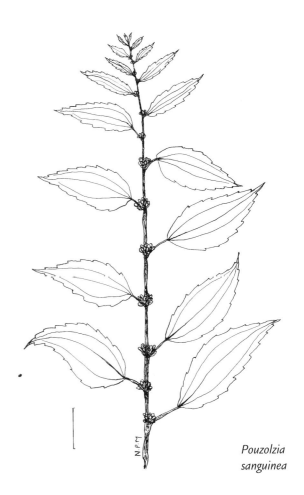

Pouzolzia sanguinea

also in northern India, Bhutan, southeastern China, Taiwan, Myanmar, and Malaysia.

FOOD. Tender leaves and shoots are cooked as a vegetable.

MEDICINE. A paste of the root is applied to boils.

Pouzolzia zeylanica (Linnaeus) J. Bennett & Brown

Parietaria zeylanica Linnaeus
Boehmeria nana Buchanan-Hamilton ex D. Don
Parietaria indica Linnaeus, *Pouzolzia indica* (Linnaeus)
  Gaudichaud-Beaupré
DANUWAR *nicha sag* GURUNG *pedano, saki* NEPALI *ban pate, barbere, bhere kuro, chiple jhar, moiso jhar* THARU *dardhuli*

Urticaceae. Erect, pubescent herb about 50 cm high. Leaves short-stalked, opposite, 0.6–3.5 cm long, 0.2–2.5 cm wide, ovate to lanceolate, acuminate, entire, three- or five-veined, base rounded. Flowers greenish in axillary clusters. Fruit an achene, ovoid, ribbed. Flowers and fruits July–December. Propagated by seeds. Distributed throughout Nepal to about 2400 m in dry, open, rocky places; also in India, Bhutan, Sri Lanka, China, Myanmar, Malaysia, and southern Japan.

FOOD. Tender leaves and shoots are cooked as a vegetable.

MEDICINE. Juice of the plant is used to treat boils, dysentery, fever, toothaches, and urinary troubles. A paste of the plant is applied to cuts and wounds. Juice of the root, about 4 teaspoons three times a day, is given in cases of indigestion.

Premna barbata Wallich ex Schauer

Premna cana Wallich
NEPALI *gineri* TAMANG *ginar*

Labiatae. Deciduous tree about 5 m high. Leaves stalked, ovate to lanceolate, caudate-acuminate, generally dentate, pubescent beneath and on the veins above. Flowers white in terminal corymbose panicles. Fruit globose. Propagated

by seeds. Distributed throughout Nepal at 700–1500 m on open hillsides; also in northern India and Bhutan.

FOOD. Ripe fruits are eaten fresh.

MEDICINE. A paste of the wood is applied to cuts and wounds. Juice of the bark, about 6 teaspoons three times a day, is taken for fever and chilblain.

OTHER USES. The plant is lopped for fodder. Bark fiber is made into coarse rope.

Prenanthes brunoniana Wallich

Cicerbita brunoniana (Wallich ex de Candolle) Tuisl ex
  Rechinger, *Lactuca brunoniana* (Wallich ex de Candolle)
  C. B. Clarke
Prenanthes hispidula de Candolle
TIBETAN *chakatik*

Compositae. Erect perennial herb about 2 m high. Leaves stalked with a winged base, 10–20 cm long, dissected into lobes, lobes further cut into lobules or dentate. Flower heads blue or purple in lax, terminal, branched clusters. Fruit an achene. Flowers and fruits July–October. Propagated by seeds. Distributed in western and central Nepal at 2300–3800 m in meadows or shrubby areas of forests; also in Afghanistan, Pakistan, and India.

MEDICINE. A paste of flower and leaf is taken to relieve fever.

Prenanthes violaefolia Decaisne

Cicerbita violaefolia (Decaisne) Beauverd, *Lactuca violaefolia*
  (Decaisne) C. B. Clarke
NEPALI *ghortapre*

Compositae. Erect herb about 50 cm high. Leaves stalked, alternate, 2.5–6 cm long, 2–6 cm wide, ovate or

Premna barbata

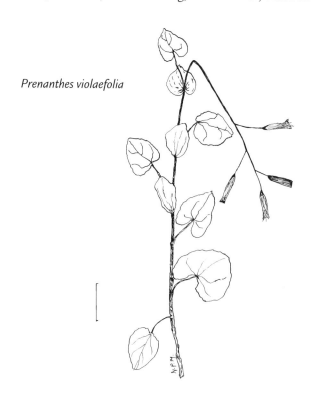

Prenanthes violaefolia

triangular to cordate, entire or minutely dentate. Flower heads purple. Fruit an achene, contracted at both ends. Flowers and fruits October–November. Propagated by seeds. Distributed in western and central Nepal at 2200–4600 m in moist, open places; also in northern India, Bhutan, and Myanmar.

MEDICINE. A paste of the plant is applied to the forehead to relieve headaches.

Primula irregularis Craib

Primula petiolaris var. *nana* Hooker fil.
NEPALI *bhuinchampa phul*

Primulaceae. Herb. Lower leaves long-stalked, upper leaves sessile, oblanceolate, irregularly serrate, tip rounded. Flowers pink. Propagated by seeds. Distributed throughout Nepal at 2800–3400 m, common in moist places; also in northern India.

OTHER USES. The plant is browsed by domestic animals.

Prinsepia utilis Royle

NEPALI *dhatelo, gotyalo, khilkanda, kurkur paile* SHERPA *yormang* TAMANG *bechar, melingo, melonm, mom puju* TIBETAN *tischa, tisya*

Rosaceae. Deciduous shrub about 2 m high, branches armed with stout spines. Leaves stalked, alternate, 6–7 cm long, 0.5–3 cm wide, lanceolate, acuminate, slightly serrate, glabrous. Flowers stalked, white, in short axillary racemes. Fruit a drupe, oblong, purple when ripe. Flowers February–March, fruits April–May. Propagated by seeds or branch cuttings. Distributed throughout Nepal at 1300–2900 m in sunny, open places; also in northern India, Bhutan, southern Tibet, and western China.

FOOD. Children of Dolpa, Jumla, and Mugu districts eat the ripe fruits. Seed oil is used for cooking and lighting.

MEDICINE. Oil from the seed is rubefacient and applied for rheumatism and muscular pain caused by heavy work. This oil is also applied to the forehead and temples in cases of cough and colds. Heated oil cake is applied to the abdomen for stomachaches. A paste of this cake is applied to treat ringworm or eczema.

OTHER USES. Plants are used for making fences, and the leaves are browsed by goats. The plant is good for soil binding. The people of Jumla district use the oil cake for washing clothes. A deep purple color is prepared from the fruits and is generally used for painting windows and walls. Seeds contain 20% fatty oil that is also used for lighting.

Prunella vulgaris Linnaeus

TIBETAN *lugro mhumpo*

Labiatae. Herb about 25 cm high. Leaves stalked, 1–6 cm long, 0.6–2.8 cm wide, ovate or oblong, acute, dentate. Flowers purplish in cylindrical terminal spikes, June–July. Propagated by seeds. Distributed throughout Nepal at 1200–3800 m in moist, open places; also in temperate Asia, and Europe.

MEDICINE. A paste of the plant is applied to treat backaches.

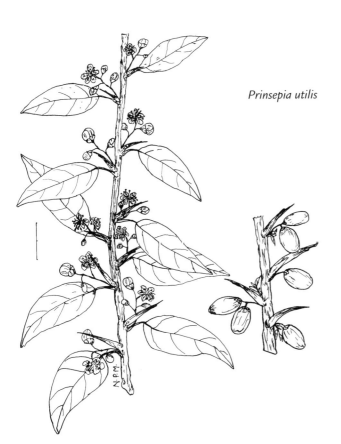

Prinsepia utilis

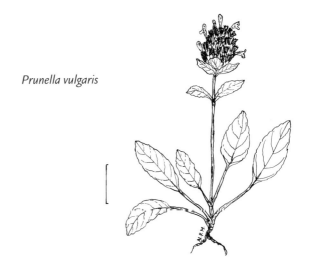

Prunella vulgaris

Prunus armeniaca Linnaeus

Armeniaca vulgare Lamarck
ENGLISH *apricot* NEPALI *khurpani* NEWARI *khorpani* TIBETAN *kham-bu*

Rosaceae. Tree. Leaves stalked, broadly ovate, acuminate, crenate. Flowers white or pinkish. Fruit ovoid or orbicular, the stone smooth. Propagated by seeds. Distributed in central Nepal at 2500–3500 m, cultivated; also in China.

FOOD. Ripe fruits are edible. Seed oil is used for cooking.

OTHER USES. Seed oil is also used for burning.

Prunus cerasoides D. Don

Cerasus phoshia Buchanan-Hamilton ex D. Don
Cerasus puddum Roxburgh ex de Candolle, *Prunus puddum*
  (Roxburgh ex de Candolle) Roxburgh ex Brandis
Maddenia pedicellata Hooker fil.

ENGLISH *wild Himalayan cherry* GURUNG *chyarbu, payem*
LIMBU *funsigma* MAGAR *pange* NEPALI *ban paiyun, paiyun*
TAMANG *birsing, byuru* TIBETAN *takpa, shing-shug-pa*

Rosaceae. Deciduous tree about 15 m high. Leaves stalked, alternate, 6–12.5 cm long, 2–5 cm wide, ovate to lanceolate, pointed, finely serrate, smooth. Flowers stalked, bracteate, pink. Fruit ovoid, fleshy. Flowers October–February, fruits March–May. Propagated by seeds. Distributed throughout Nepal at 1300–2400 m in open places; also in northern India, Bhutan, southern Tibet, western China, and Myanmar.

FOOD. Ripe fruits are eaten fresh.

MEDICINE. Juice of the bark is applied to treat backaches. Fruits are astringent.

OTHER USES. The plant is lopped for fodder. Branches are used for making walking sticks. Seeds are made into rosaries and necklaces.

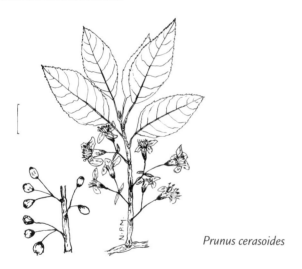

Prunus cerasoides

Prunus cornuta (Wallich ex Royle) Steudel

Cerasus cornuta Wallich ex Royle, *Padus cornuta* (Wallich
  ex Royle) Carrière
Prunus padus Linnaeus

ENGLISH *wild peach* NEPALI *aarupate, aarya, lekh aaru, thulo aare*

Rosaceae. Medium-sized tree with gray-brown bark. Leaves stalked, 2.5–17 cm long, 1–7.5 cm wide, oblanceolate, long-pointed, closely and finely dentate. Flowers white in long, drooping clusters. Fruit globose, dark purple or black when ripe. Flowers April–May, fruits June–Au-

gust. Propagated by seeds. Distributed throughout Nepal at 2100–3500 m in deciduous forests on shady slopes; also in Afghanistan, northern India, Bhutan, southern Tibet, and western China.

FOOD. Ripe fruits are eaten fresh and used in brewing local liquor.

OTHER USES. Foliage is cut for fodder.

Prunus domestica Linnaeus

BHOJPURI *aalubakhara* DANUWAR *aaru* ENGLISH *queen's plum*
GURUNG *aalbokhra* LEPCHA *aarura* LIMBU *kankhombrek*
MAGAR *aalu bakhara* NEPALI *aaru bakhara* NEWARI *aalucha*
RAI *wakholausi* SUNWAR *lapkyu* TAMANG *aalu bakhara*
THARU *aalu bakhar* TIBETAN *star-bu*

Rosaceae. Small tree, young twigs pubescent. Leaves stalked, alternate, 2–7 cm long, 0.7–3.5 cm wide, ovate, acuminate, finely serrate, base rounded. Flowers white, usually in clusters. Fruit globose, golden yellow, greenish, or red and dark purple, the stone large, rough or pitted. Propagated by seeds or cuttings. Distributed throughout Nepal at 1200–2000 m, cultivated.

FOOD. Ripe fruits are eaten fresh.

MEDICINE. Ripe fruits are laxative and cooling.

OTHER USES. Bark contains tannin. Foliage is cut for fodder.

Prunus napaulensis (Seringe) Steudel

Cerasus napaulensis Seringe
Cerasus glaucifolia Wallich

ENGLISH *Nepalese cherry* GURUNG *khawai, puri* NEPALI *aaru pate,
jangali aaru* TAMANG *kaul duse*

Rosaceae. Tree about 7 m high. Leaves stalked, oblong to lanceolate, acuminate, serrate, glabrous. Flowers white in terminal elongated racemes, April–May. Fruits July–August. Propagated by seeds. Distributed throughout Nepal at 1600–3000 m in mixed forest; also in northern India, Bhutan, western China, and northern Myanmar.

FOOD. Ripe fruits are eaten fresh.

OTHER USES. Wood can be used for timber and fuel. Young leaves and shoots are poisonous to cattle.

Prunus persica (Linnaeus) Batsch

BHOJPURI *arul* CHEPANG *bagal* DANUWAR *aru* ENGLISH *peach*
GURUNG *kholo* LEPCHA *takbopot* LIMBU *khombrekpa* MAGAR *ghorli*
NEPALI *aaru* NEWARI *basi* RAI *bonkolong* SUNWAR *labgyur*
TAMANG *khale* THARU *aru* TIBETAN *kham-bu*

Rosaceae. Tree. Leaves stalked, oblong to lanceolate, serrate. Flowers white. Fruit variable in shape and size, yellow when ripe, the stone deeply furrowed. Propagated by seeds. Distributed throughout Nepal at 1100–2000 m, cultivated.

FOOD. Ripe fruits are edible. Seed oil is used for cooking and lighting.

MEDICINE. Juice of the leaves is put in wounds as an anthelmintic. Flowers are diuretic and purgative.

OTHER USES. Seed oil is also used for lighting.

Psidium guajava Linnaeus

Psidium pomiferum Linnaeus
Psidium pyriferum Linnaeus

BHOJPURI *latam* CHEPANG *amba* DANUWAR *belauki* ENGLISH *guava* GURUNG *bilauti* LEPCHA *lambu* LIMBU *aambak, lupro* MAGAR *belauti* MAJHI *amba* MOOSHAR *latam* NEPALI *amba* NEWARI *amasi* RAI *lattam* SUNWAR *ambhok* TAMANG *amba, ambaru*

Myrtaceae. Tree about 8 m high, young branches four-angled. Leaves stalked, opposite, oblong to elliptic, apex pointed, base usually rounded. Flowers white, solitary or two or three together. Fruit ovoid, rounded, yellow-green when ripe. Seeds many, embedded in pink or white pulp. Propagated by seeds. Distributed throughout Nepal to about 1400 m, planted in gardens or orchards; also in tropical Asia and America.

FOOD. Fruit is edible and contains acid, sugar, and pectin; it is a rich source of vitamins A and B. It is used for making jellies, jams, and pastes.

MEDICINE. Bark is mixed with the roots of *Achyranthes aspera* and *Urena lobata,* pounded, and the extracted juice, 4 teaspoons three times a day, is given to treat diarrhea and dysentery. A decoction of the plant is astringent, vulnerary, febrifuge, antispasmodic, and is also used as mouthwash to alleviate swollen gums. Juice of the root, about 2 teaspoons twice a day, is given for dysentery. Juice of the bark is also given in cases of dysentery. A paste of unripe fruit is also given to treat dysentery. An infusion of the leaves is considered useful in treating inflammation of kidney. A paste of the leaves is applied for rheumatism, and to cuts and wounds. Leaf buds are chewed to treat fever and headaches.

OTHER USES. Bark is used for tanning. It is also used to make *marcha,* a fermenting cake from which liquor is distilled.

Pteracanthus alatus (Wallich ex Nees) Bremekamp

Ruellia alata Wallich ex Nees
Strobilanthes wallichii Nees
NEPALI *ankhle*

Acanthaceae. Perennial herb about 1 m high. Lower leaves stalked, opposite, 6.5–15 cm long, 2.5–7 cm wide, elliptic, long-pointed, crenate to serrate, base rounded or cordate. Flowers purple in panicled spikes. Fruit a capsule, cylindrical. Flowers June–August, fruits October–November. Propagated by seeds. Distributed throughout Nepal at 2700–3500 m, along waysides on hillsides; also in Afghanistan, India, and Bhutan.

OTHER USES. The plant is gathered for fodder.

Pteridium aquilinum (Linnaeus) Kunth

Pteris aquilina Linnaeus
NEPALI *ainu*

Dennstaedtiaceae. Terrestrial fern. Rhizome long, creeping, clothed with fine, pale brown hairs. Fronds large, three- or four-pinnate, lowest pair of pinnae larger than the others, ultimate segments narrow. Sori marginal. Spores July–August. Propagated by spores. Distributed in western and central Nepal at 1200–3400 m on open, damp hillsides; also in India, Sri Lanka, Malaysia, Taiwan, and the Philippines.

FOOD. Tender fronds are cooked as a vegetable.

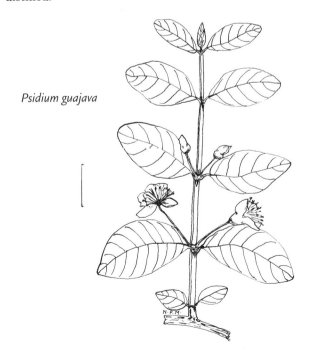

Psidium guajava

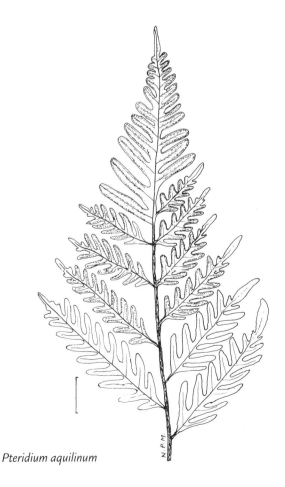

Pteridium aquilinum

OTHER USES. The plant is spread in animal sheds for their use as bedding.

Pteris aspericaulis Wallich ex J. Agardh

Pteris quadriaurita var. *aspericaulis* (Wallich ex J. Agardh) Beddome
NEPALI *guhya sattar, mauro, pire unyu* TAMANG *tamda*

Pteridaceae. Terrestrial fern. Rhizome short, creeping, clothed with deep brown linear scales. Stipes reddish or pinkish, glossy. Fronds ovate to lanceolate, bipinnate, pinnae opposite, lanceolate, segments linear oblong. Sori marginal, rarely extending to the apex. Spores June–July. Propagated by spores. Distributed throughout Nepal at 400–3200 m in moist, shady places; also in India, southeastern China, and northern Myanmar.

MEDICINE. Juice of the rhizome is given in cases of diarrhea and dysentery. A paste of the rhizome is applied to boils, cuts, and muscular swellings. Tender parts of the rhizome are fried in clarified butter and taken for backache.

Pteris biaurita Linnaeus

Campteria biaurita (Linnaeus) Hooker
NEPALI *hade unyu*

Pteridaceae. Terrestrial fern. Fronds 30–50 cm long, 15–25 cm wide, bipinnate, pinnae subopposite or alternate, cut down to the rachis, segments oblong. Sori along the margin of the segments, protected by the reflexed margin. Propagated by spores. Distributed in western and central Nepal to about 2500 m in shady places.

MEDICINE. A paste of the frond is applied to cuts and wounds. Juice of the frond, about 4 teaspoons once a day, is given to sterile women to aid conception.

Pteris geminata Wallich

NEPALI *thadho unyu*

Pteridaceae. Herbaceous fern. Rhizome erect, stout, with light brown scales. Stipes erect, glossy dark purplish. Fronds large, pinnate, pinnae subopposite, lanceolate, terminal segments long. Sori marginal but lacking at the apical and basal parts of the segments. Spores July–September. Propagated by spores. Distributed in western and central Nepal at 250–3000 m, common on the forest floor; also in India.

MEDICINE. Juice of the frond is applied to cuts and wounds.

Pteris quadriaurita Retzius

NEPALI *mauro*

Pteridaceae. Terrestrial fern. Rhizome stout, clothed with reddish brown linear scales. Stipes pinkish at the base, brownish above. Fronds ovate to lanceolate, pinnate, pinnae linear lanceolate, subopposite. Sori linear, partly along the margin. Spores July–August. Propagated by spores. Distributed throughout Nepal at 700–2600 m in shady, moist parts of forests; also in India, Sri Lanka, and Malaysia.

MEDICINE. A paste of the rhizome is applied to boils.

Pteris vittaria Linnaeus

CHEPANG *sechik* NEPALI *unigar*

Pteridaceae. Terrestrial fern. Rachis scaly. Fronds 35–65 cm long, 10–35 cm wide, pinnate, pinnae sessile, subopposite, linear, acuminate. Sori linear, marginal. Propagated by spores. Distributed in eastern and central Nepal at 400–3000 m in shady places; also in tropical and subtropical regions of the world.

OTHER USES. Plants are used as fodder and for thatching roofs.

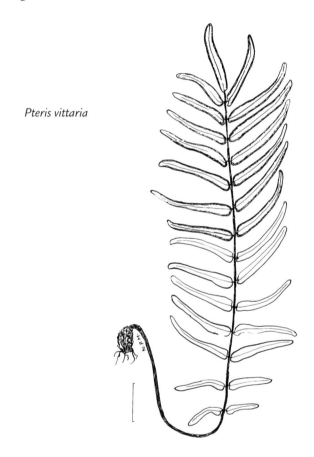

Pteris vittaria

Pteris wallichiana Agardh

NEPALI *dalumo*

Pteridaceae. Terrestrial fern. Fronds 40–90 cm long, 20–30 cm wide, bipinnate, pinnae numerous, subopposite, linear lanceolate, deeply cut, segments obtuse, glossy. Sori linear, marginal. Propagated by spores. Distributed throughout Nepal at 1200–3200 m, common in open places; also in India, southern China, Taiwan, Japan, Malaysia, the Philippines, and the Samoa Islands.

MEDICINE. The plant is fed to animals with indigestion.

Pterocephalus hookeri (C. B. Clarke) Diels

Scabiosa hookeri C. B. Clarke

TIBETAN *panze*

Dipsacaceae. Herb about 65 cm high with a woody rootstock. Leaves all basal, 3–30 cm long, spatulate, lanceolate, pinnately lobed, slightly hairy. Flowers white in dense globose heads, July–September. Propagated by seeds. Distributed in western and central Nepal at 3000–4500 m in open alpine meadows; also in India and Bhutan.

MEDICINE. Juice of the root is taken in cases of fever.

Pulicaria dysenterica

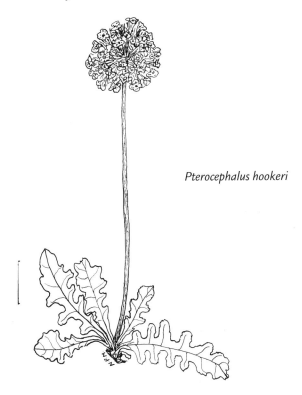

Pterocephalus hookeri

Pulicaria dysenterica (Linnaeus) Gaertner

THARU *gandhaiya*

Compositae. Perennial herb. Leaves half-clasping the stem at their base, oblong to cordate, margin wavy and dentate. Flower heads densely woolly, whitish. Fruit an achene. Propagated by seeds. Distributed in central Nepal at 250–2000 m in open places; also in India, Bhutan, Myanmar, Britain, and Algeria.

MEDICINE. A paste of the plant is applied to wounds.

Punica granatum Linnaeus

BHOJPURI *anar* DANUWAR *darim* ENGLISH *pomegranate* GURUNG *darim* LEPCHA *anar* LIMBU *lalimse* MAGAR *darim* MOOSHAR *anar* NEPALI *anar* NEWARI *dhale* RAI *kanthakasi* SUNWAR *darim* TAMANG *darim* THARU *anar* TIBETAN *se-bru*

Punicaceae. Shrub about 3 m high with dark gray bark, branchlets often spiny. Leaves stalked, subopposite or clustered, oblanceolate, obtuse, entire, glabrous, shiny,

Punica granatum

narrowed toward the base. Flowers terminal, bright red, solitary or in three-flowered cymes, April–May. Fruits July–September. Propagated by seeds or branch cuttings. Distributed throughout Nepal to about 2700 m, planted around homesteads in open, moist places; also in Afghanistan, Iran, India, Thailand, Malaysia, the Philippines, and central and southern Europe.

FOOD. Seeds are edible and are cooling. Their juice is thirst quenching and is taken to alleviate fever.

MEDICINE. Bark of the root is astringent and vermifuge. A paste of stem bark is used to treat hemorrhoids. Leaf paste is applied to burns to relieve the inflammation or burning sensation. Powdered flower buds are taken for bronchitis. A decoction of the rind of the fruit is taken as an anthelmintic, and juice of the rind, about 5 teaspoons twice a day, is taken in cases of diarrhea and dysentery. Seeds are cooling. Their juice is thirst quenching and is taken to alleviate fever.

OTHER USES. Bark of the stem and rind of the fruit are used for tanning. Flowers give a red dye.

Pycreus sanguinolentus (Vahl) Nees ex C. B. Clarke

Cyperus sanguinolentus Vahl
Cyperus albidus Lamarck
Cyperus cruentus Retzius
Cyperus eragrostis Vahl
Cyperus neurotropia Steudel
NEPALI *jhuse mothe, ragate mothe*

Cyperaceae. Annual herb with a creeping base. Leaves linear. Inflorescences greenish brown in a simple umbel of spikes or a compound umbel. Fruit a nutlet, obovoid, dark brown. Flowers and fruits July–December. Propagated by seeds or by splitting the roots. Distributed in eastern and central Nepal at 800–2900 m in open, rocky places; also in India, Bhutan, central Asia including China, Malaysia, and Africa.

OTHER USES. The plant is used for fodder.

Pyracantha crenulata (D. Don) M. Roemer

Mespilus crenulata D. Don, *Crataegus crenulata* (D. Don) Roxburgh
ENGLISH *firethorn, Nepalese white thorn*   GURUNG *bhon pujo, chento, rishin pojo*   MAGAR *ghangaru*   NEPALI *ghangaru, kanime, kath gedi*   SHERPA *mharu*   TAMANG *chherne kanda, ghangaru*

Rosaceae. Spiny evergreen shrub about 3 m high. Leaves stalked, crowded on short lateral branches, 1.5–5.5 cm long, 0.8–1.8 cm wide, oblong to ovate, narrowed toward the base, crenate, smooth. Flowers stalked, white. Fruit globose, red. Propagated by seeds. Distributed throughout Nepal at 1000–2500 m on open hillsides among other shrubs; also in northern India, Bhutan, Tibet, China, and Myanmar.

FOOD. Ripe fruits are eaten fresh.

MEDICINE. Powdered dry fruit, about 4 teaspoons mixed with half a cup of yogurt, is taken in cases of bloody dysentery.

OTHER USES. The plant makes an excellent hedge. Branches are used as walking sticks.

Pyrrosia mollis (Kuntze) Ching

Niphobolus mollis Kuntze
NEPALI *harparo*

Polypodiaceae. Epiphytic fern. Rhizome long, creeping, covered with lanceolate scales. Fronds simple, gradually attenuate downward from the middle. Sori in a few rows close on either side of the midrib. Spores June–July. Propagated by spores. Distributed throughout Nepal at 1200–2000 on tree trunks and branches, or rocks; also in India, Sri Lanka, and China.

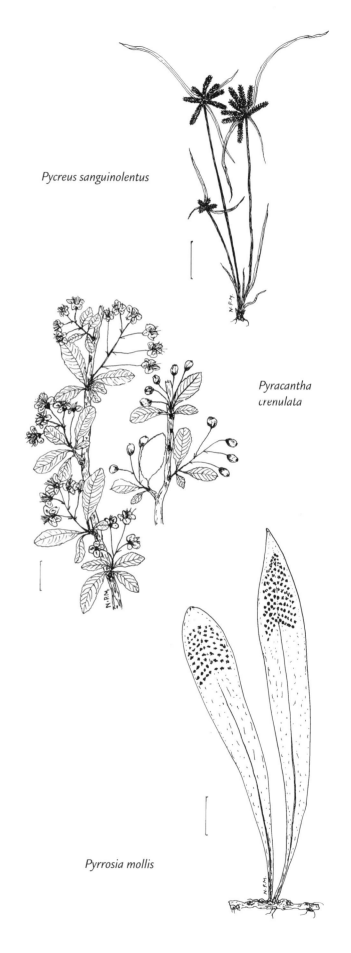

Pycreus sanguinolentus

Pyracantha crenulata

Pyrrosia mollis

MEDICINE. The rhizome, mixed with the root of *Agrimonia pilosa,* is powdered and given in doses of about 2 teaspoons once a day as a tonic to women after delivery.

Pyrularia edulis (Wallich ex Roxburgh) de Candolle

Sphaerocarya edulis Wallich ex Roxburgh
NEPALI *amphi*

Santalaceae. Medium-sized, deciduous tree. Leaves stalked, 5–15 cm long, 1.5–6.5 cm wide, elliptic to oblong, acuminate, entire, crenulate toward the apex. Flowers yellowish. Fruit a drupe, pear shaped, narrowed into a stout stalk. Flowers March–June, fruits August–November. Propagated by seeds. Distributed throughout Nepal at 1600–1800 m in open, forested areas; also in India, Bhutan, China, and Myanmar.

FOOD. Ripe fruits are eaten fresh.

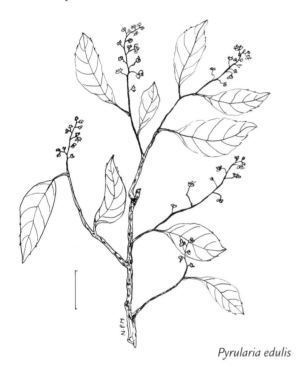

Pyrularia edulis

Pyrus communis Linnaeus

BHOJPURI *nashpati* CHEPANG *nashpati* DANUWAR *nashpati* ENGLISH *pear* GURUNG *nashpati* LEPCHA *pirise* LIMBU *lipot* MAGAR *nashpati* NEPALI *nashpati* NEWARI *pasi* RAI *lembasi* SUNWAR *nashpati* TAMANG *nashpati*

Rosaceae. Deciduous tree. Leaves stalked, 5–14 cm long, 4–9 cm wide, elliptic to lanceolate, acuminate, finely serrate, glossy dark green above. Flowers white on short terminal shoots. Fruit pear shaped, rough with close, raised specks, yellowish green when ripe, the pulp very gritty. Propagated by spores or by graftings. Distributed throughout Nepal at 700–1900 m, cultivated; also in western Asia and Europe.

FOOD. The fruit is edible.

Pyrus malus Linnaeus

BHOJPURI *seb* DANUWAR *syau* ENGLISH *apple* LEPCHA *lipot* LIMBU *nagnse* MAGAR *syau* MOOSHAR *seb* NEPALI *syau* NEWARI *syau* RAI *sapukawasi* SUNWAR *syau* TAMANG *syau* THARU *seb* TIBETAN *amra*

Rosaceae. Deciduous tree. Leaves stalked, ovate, acuminate, crenate, glabrous above, tomentose beneath. Flowers pink tinged. Fruit a pome, globose. Flowers March–May, fruits July–August. Propagated by seeds or by grafting. Distributed throughout Nepal to about 2200 m, cultivated.

FOOD. Fruits are edible.

Pyrus pashia Buchanan-Hamilton ex D. Don

Pyrus kumaoni Decaisne ex Hooker fil.
Pyrus nepalensis hort. ex Decaisne
ENGLISH *Nepalese wild pear* LIMBU *thumro* MAGAR *mel* NEPALI *mayal* TAMANG *nai, pana* TIBETAN *tayana*

Rosaceae. Deciduous tree about 8 m high. Leaves stalked, 3–7 cm long, 1.5–3 cm wide, ovate to lanceolate, acuminate, crenate, glabrous, shiny, often woolly beneath on young plants. Flowers stalked, white. Fruit globose, covered with white dots. Flowers March–April, fruits September–October. Propagated by seeds or cuttings. Distributed throughout Nepal at 700–2600 m in open, rocky places; also in northern India, Bhutan, western China, and Myanmar.

FOOD. Ripe fruits are edible.

MEDICINE. Juice of ripe fruit is put in the eye of animals to treat conjunctivitis. This juice, about 6 teaspoons twice a day, is given to treat diarrhea.

OTHER USES. Wood is used for making walking sticks and for fuel. Leaves and twigs are lopped for fodder.

Pyrus pashia

Q

Quercus floribunda Lindley ex A. Camus

Quercus dilatata Lindley
Quercus himalayana Bahadur
NEPALI *midho* TAMANG *belekhar mhenso*

Fagaceae. Tree. Leaves stalked, about 8 cm long, elliptic to lanceolate, margin spiny or smooth. Flowers yellowish. Fruit an acorn, ovoid with a fine point. Flowers April–May. Propagated by seeds. Distributed in western and central Nepal at 2100–2700 m in moist, forested areas on mountain slopes; also in eastern Afghanistan and northwestern India.

OTHER USES. The plant is lopped for fodder. The wood is strong and used for many purposes.

Quercus glauca Thunberg

Quercus annulata Smith
Quercus phullata Buchanan-Hamilton ex D. Don
NEPALI *phalat*

Fagaceae. Large evergreen tree, bark blackish gray, glandular, warty. Leaves stalked, 6.5–12.5 cm long, 1.5–5 cm wide, oblong to lanceolate, acuminate, sharply serrate, leathery, glabrous above, glaucous beneath. Flowers in solitary, unisexual, axillary spikes, the female spike two- to five-flowered. Fruit an acorn. Flowers March–May, fruits October–December. Propagated by seeds. Distributed throughout Nepal at 450–3100 m on hillsides with other oaks; also in northern India, China, Korea, Japan, Taiwan, and Indo-China.

OTHER USES. The plant is lopped for fodder. Wood is mainly used for fuel.

Quercus lamellosa Smith

Quercus imbricata Roxburgh
Quercus lamellata Roxburgh
ENGLISH *bull oak* GURUNG *nhansi* LEPCHA *buk* NEPALI *bansi, phalant* TAMANG *banchet*

Fagaceae. Evergreen tree, young parts tomentose. Leaves stalked, 17.5–23 cm long, 6.5–11.5 cm wide, oblong, acuminate, sharply serrate toward the apex, leathery, glabrous above, glaucous beneath except the veins. Flowers in axillary spikes, the male spike solitary, shorter than the leaves, female spike very short, three- or four-flowered. Fruit an acorn. Flowers July–August, fruits January–March. Propagated by seeds. Distributed in central and eastern Nepal at 1600–2800 m on hillsides; also in northeastern India, Bhutan, Tibet, southwestern China, and northern Myanmar.

OTHER USES. The plant is lopped for fodder. Wood is used to make the handles of agricultural equipment.

Quercus lanata Smith

Quercus lanuginosa D. Don
Quercus nepaulensis Desfontaines
CHEPANG *sarasi* MAGAR *huk* MAJHI *banjho* NEPALI *banjh, khar banjh, phalant* RAI *wari* TAMANG *berkap, pepkar, sulsing* TIBETAN *beghar*

Fagaceae. Tree about 6 m high. Leaves stalked, alternate, elliptic or oblong to ovate, acute, dentate, leathery, glabrous above, densely woolly beneath. Male flower spike long, slender, drooping, yellow. Fruit an acorn. Flowers April–May. Propagated by seeds. Distributed throughout Nepal at 1000–2600 m; also in northern India and Indo-China.

FOOD. Resin of the plant is boiled in water and taken as tea.

MEDICINE. Juice of the bark, mixed with bark juice of *Betula alnoides,* is applied for sprains. Resin is useful for soothing body aches caused by heavy physical work. Powdered dry resin, about 2 teaspoons twice a day, is given to treat bloody dysentery. A paste of the cotyledon is applied to scorpion bites.

OTHER USES. The plant is lopped for cattle fodder. Wood is used make the handles of agricultural equipment and for construction, and it provides good fuel.

Quercus leucotrichophora A. Camus

Quercus incana Roxburgh
NEPALI *banjhi, rainj, khasarant, tikhe bhanjh* TAMANG *sulsing*

Fagaceae. Evergreen tree. Leaves stalked, ovate to lanceolate, acuminate, serrate, leathery, dark green, glabrous above, densely white or gray pubescent beneath. Male flower spikes slender, drooping, female spikes sessile, axillary. Fruit an acorn, solitary. Flowers April–May, fruits August–October. Propagated by seeds. Distributed throughout Nepal at 1500–2700 m in forested areas in association with *Rhododendron arborea;* also in Pakistan, northern India, Sri Lanka, and Myanmar.

OTHER USES. The plant is lopped for fodder. Wood is used for building purposes and is a good fuel. Bark contains 6–20% tannin. Acorns are generally eaten by bears.

Quercus semecarpifolia Smith

Quercus cassura Buchanan-Hamilton ex D. Don
Quercus obtusiloba D. Don
ENGLISH *kharshu oak* GURUNG *bheno, pyena* NEPALI *kharsu, thinke dar* RAI *dhenu* SHERPA *bhelo, tadumpa* TAMANG *bena*

Fagaceae. Tree about 20 m high. Leaves stalked, alternate, oblong, obtuse, entire, glabrous on both sides when old, sparsely stellate hairy above, densely pubescent beneath when young. Male flower spikes, long, slender, densely pubescent, drooping, yellowish, female spikes short, few-flowered. Fruit an acorn, solitary or in pairs. Flowers May–June. Propagated by seeds. Distributed throughout Nepal at 700–3800 m on hillsides; also in Afghanistan, Pakistan, northern India, southern Tibet, southern China, and Myanmar.

FOOD. Sap of the plant is drunk as tea.

MEDICINE. Juice of the bark is applied to relieve muscular pains.

OTHER USES. Wood is used for building purposes and is a good fuelwood. Bark contains tannin. Leaves are lopped for fodder.

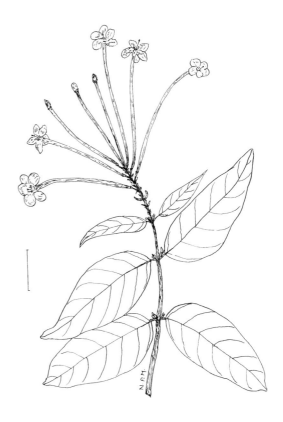

Quisqualis indica

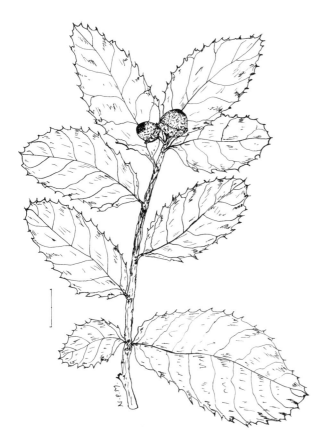

Quercus semecarpifolia

Quisqualis indica Linnaeus

ENGLISH *Rangoon creeper* NEPALI *asare phul*

Combretaceae. Trailing shrub, young parts rusty pubescent. Leaves stalked, oblong to elliptic, acute, base rounded. Flowers red, white, or pink in a drooping cluster. Fruit narrowly ellipsoidal, five-angled or -winged. Propagated by seeds or cuttings. Distributed throughout Nepal to about 600 m, cultivated; also pantropical.

MEDICINE. Pieces of the plant are boiled in water, strained, and boiled again until the liquid is half the amount, and 4 teaspoons of the liquid are taken twice a day for cough and colds. A paste of the leaves is applied to the temples to relieve headaches. In some places of Banke, Kailali, Salyan, and Surkhet districts of western Nepal, five to seven seeds are chewed as an anthelmintic.

OTHER USES. The plant has ornamental value. Leaves contain tannin.

R

Randia tetrasperma (Roxburgh) Bentham & Hooker fil. ex Brandis

Gardenia tetrasperma Roxburgh, *Aidia tetrasperma* (Roxburgh) Yamazaki, *Himalrandia tetrasperma* (Roxburgh) Yamazaki
Gardenia densa Wallich
Gardenia rigida Buchanan-Hamilton ex D. Don
GURUNG *thadhu* NEPALI *bajarjanti, bakhre kanda, basante kanda, ghari, hade, pahenlo nundhiki, rukh ghari* TAMANG *chermang, dajerbhu, mangtar sipuju*

Rubiaceae. Shrub about 40 cm high with stiff gray branches. Leaves crowded at the ends of the branchlets, oblanceolate, narrowed into a short stalk, glabrous. Flowers sessile, yellowish, fragrant. Fruit a berry, globose, four-seeded. Flowers April–May, fruits June–July. Propagated by seeds or cuttings. Distributed throughout Nepal at 800–2400 m, in open, dry places; also in northern India.

MEDICINE. The plant is burned and a paste of the charcoal is applied to extract spines that have penetrated deeply into the flesh.

OTHER USES. The plant is collected for fuel. It is planted for fences. Goats browse its leaves. Straight branches are used for walking sticks.

Randia tetrasperma

Ranunculus diffusus de Candolle

Ranunculus hydrocotyloides Wallich
Ranunculus mollis Wallich
Ranunculus obtectus Wallich
Ranunculus vitifolius Royle ex D. Don
GURUNG *sun phul* NEPALI *mardi jahr, narapolo, sano saro*
TAMANG *brimomhendo, ganumen, nakori*

Ranunculaceae. Perennial herb about 60 cm high. Lower leaves stalked, ovate to cordate, deeply three-lobed, lobes sharply dentate, upper leaves short-stalked, smaller. Flowers long-stalked, yellow. Fruit an achene, flat, minutely dotted. Flowers April–July, fruits July–October. Propagated by seeds. Distributed throughout Nepal at 1000–3500 m, common in open, wet places; also in northern India, Bhutan, northern Myanmar, and Indonesia.

FOOD. Tender leaves and shoots are dried about 4 hours, then cooked as a vegetable. They are also fermented for making *gundruk*.

MEDICINE. Pounded root is used to treat cuts and wounds. Juice of the root, about 6 teaspoons three times a day, is given in cases of stomachache.

Ranunculus scleratus Linnaeus

Ranunculus umbellatus Roxburgh ex Willdenow
ENGLISH *celery-leaved crowfoot* GURUNG *sunphul* NEPALI *nagakor, nakuri phul, shamphu jhar, tharuni* THARU *nakapolwa*
TIBETAN *ram-pa*

Ranunculaceae. Erect annual herb about 75 cm high. Basal leaves stalked, 1.5–3 cm long, 2.5–4 cm wide, reniform, three-lobed, upper leaves narrowly oblong, three-lobed. Flowers yellow. Fruits achenes, numerous, apiculate. Flowers and fruits most of the year. Propagated by seeds or root offshoots. Distributed throughout Nepal to about 2500 m, common in fields, on neglected, moist ground, and along irrigation channels; also in northern India, Bhutan, central Asia including Pakistan, China, Mongolia, and Siberia, also Japan, Europe, and North America.

FOOD. The plant is very acrid and poisonous, producing violent irritant effects if taken internally. Therefore, tender shoots are first boiled, then cooked as a vegetable. The plant is an ingredient in the preparation of *gundruk*.

MEDICINE. Juice of the plant is dripped into the eyes of livestock suffering from conjunctivitis. A piece of cloth soaked in the juice and is spread over the abdomen for gastric inflammation. A bruised leaf is applied to blisters.

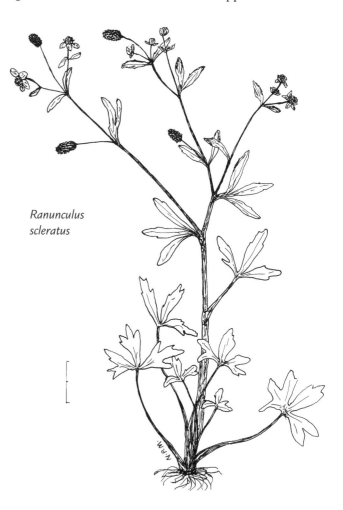

Ranunculus scleratus

Raphanus sativus Linnaeus

BHOJPURI *murai* CHEPANG *lakhan* DANUWAR *murai* ENGLISH *radish* GURUNG *labu* LEPCHA *labak* LIMBU *labonk* MAGAR *mula* MOOSHAR *murai* NEPALI *mula* NEWARI *lain* RAI *pundlukwa* SHERPA *lau* SUNWAR *mula* TAMANG *labu* THARU *murai* TIBETAN *la-phug*

Cruciferae. Annual herb with long, thick, fleshy roots. Leaves lyrate or pinnate. Flowers white or lilac with purple veins. Fruit a pod, terete, indehiscent, more or less constricted between the seeds. Flowers March–April. Propagated by seeds. Distributed throughout Nepal to about 3500 m, cultivated.

FOOD. Roots and leaves are cooked as a vegetable or fermented for making *gundruk*; young leaves are eaten raw. Roots and seeds are pickled.

Rauvolfia serpentina

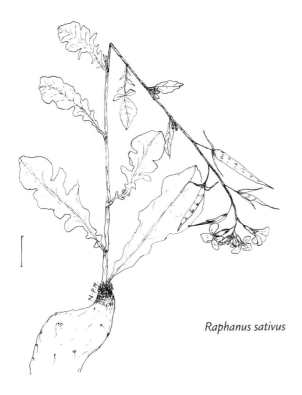

Raphanus sativus

Rauvolfia serpentina (Linnaeus) Bentham ex Kurz

Ophioxylon serpentinum Linnaeus

CHEPANG *chyarungro* ENGLISH *serpentine* NEPALI *chandamaruwa, phulchiso, sarpagandha* THARU *dhaldhaliya*

Apocynaceae. Erect shrub about 50 cm high. Leaves stalked, opposite or three or four leaves in a whorl, oblong, tapering toward the stalk. Flowers pinkish. Fruit globose, dark purple or blackish when ripe. Flowers November–January, fruits May–July. Propagated by seeds. Distributed throughout Nepal to about 1000 m but the gathering of its roots for sale in the trade endangers plant populations; also in India, Sri Lanka, Myanmar, Malaysia, and Indonesia.

MEDICINE. Juice of the root has sedative and hypnotic properties and is also used to treat dysentery and fever.

Reinwardtia indica Dumortier

Linum repens Buchanan-Hamilton ex D. Don, *Reinwardtia repens* (Buchanan-Hamilton ex D. Don) Planchon
Linum trigynum Roxburgh, *Reinwardtia trigyna* (Roxburgh) Planchon

CHEPANG *methi jhar, niphar, niphin, tiribo* ENGLISH *winter flax, yellow flax* GURUNG *gyumi, hyumi, nime pa, syal kainj* MAGAR *gebatisar* NEPALI *bakhre ghans, pyaunli* TAMANG *najachhe, nakachyu, nakchhi, singalangdu, ubherndo*

Linaceae. Erect perennial herb about 1 m high. Leaves short-stalked, ovate to lanceolate, obtuse or acute, entire or minutely crenate to serrate. Flowers yellow, mostly solitary and axillary. Fruit a capsule, depressed, globose. Flowers January–March, fruits March–April. Propagated by root offshoots. Distributed throughout Nepal at 300–2300 m; also in northern India, Bhutan, China, and Indo-China.

Reinwardtia indica

MEDICINE. A paste of the root is applied to boils, and to the forehead to treat headaches. Juice of the root, about 2 teaspoons three times a day, is given to treat fever and indigestion. Juice of the plant is applied to treat scabies and wounds. Leaves, flowers, and stems are crushed and applied to bee stings, insect bites, and thorn stabs.

Reissantia arborea (Roxburgh) Hara

Hippocratea arborea Roxburgh, *Pristimaria arborea* (Roxburgh) A. C. Smith

CHEPANG *masyangri, trakchh* NEPALI *chatapate, chilbile, phirke, putalil kath* MAGAR *thinke*

Celastraceae. Woody climber. Leaves stalked, 5.5–16.5 cm long, 2.7–9 cm wide, elliptic, pointed, distantly serrate, glabrous. Flowers yellowish, May–August. Fruits November–December. Propagated by seeds. Distributed throughout Nepal to about 1100 m in open places; also in northern India, Bhutan, western China, and northern Myanmar.

MEDICINE. A paste of the root is applied to treat headaches. This paste, about 2 teaspoons twice a day, is ingested and also applied externally to treat swellings of the throat. Juice of the bark, about 2 teaspoons once a day, is given to treat inflammation of the heart.

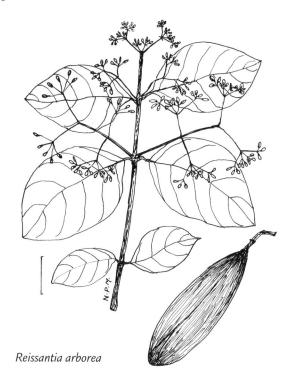

Reissantia arborea

Remusatia pumila (D. Don) H. L. Li & A. Hay

Caladium pumilum D. Don, *Colocasia pumila* (D. Don) Kunth, *Gonatanthus pumilus* (D. Don) Engler & Krause *Gonanthus sarmentosus* Klotzsch & Otto

GURUNG *chaglo* NEPALI *gagata, jaluka*

Araceae. Tuberous herb. Leaves ovate to cordate, peltate, acuminate, dark green. Spathe yellowish, purplish

beneath. Flowers June–August. Propagated by corms. Distributed throughout Nepal at 1000–2400 m on mossy rocks; also in northern India, western China, and Indo-China.

FOOD. Tender leaves are cooked as a vegetable.

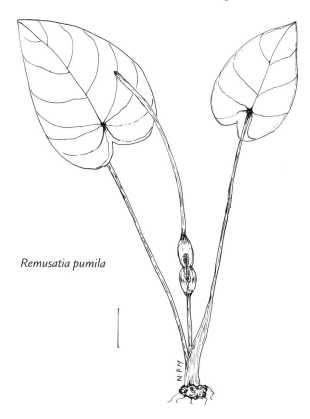

Remusatia pumila

Remusatia vivipara (Roxburgh) Schott

Arum viviparum Roxburgh

GURUNG *gawa* NEPALI *jaluka, kalo pidalu* NEWARI *hyangu saki* RAUTE *pinda*

Araceae. Tuberous herb about 30 cm high. Leaves long-stalked, orbiculate to ovate, acuminate, glabrous. Spathe pinkish. Propagated by seeds or by splitting the rhizomes. Distributed throughout Nepal at 1000–2600 m in moist, shady places; also in India, Sri Lanka, China, Indo-China, Java, and West Africa.

FOOD. Young leaves are cooked as a vegetable.

MEDICINE. In western parts of Nepal, a paste of the rhizome is applied to muscular swellings. Juice of the rhizome is dripped in wounds to expel germs and worms.

Rhamnus nepalensis (Wallich) Lawson

Ceanothus nepalensis Wallich

NEPALI *chille kath*

Rhamnaceae. Tree. Leaves stalked, 7.5–15 cm long, 3–5 cm wide, oblong to lanceolate, acuminate, serrate, glabrous above, softly hairy on the vein beneath. Flowers greenish. Fruit small, turning dark blue. Flowers July–

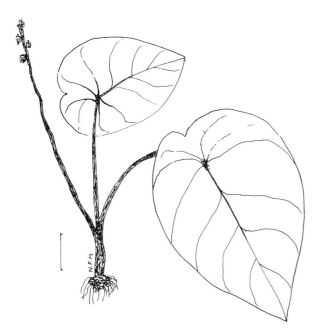

Remusatia vivipara

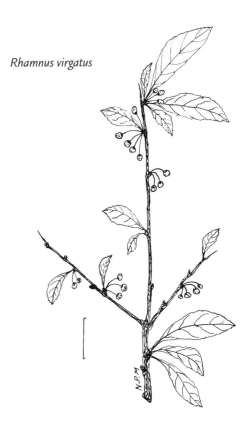

Rhamnus virgatus

August, fruits March–April. Propagated by seeds. Distributed in eastern and central Nepal at 600–1700 m; also in northern India, Bhutan, China, and Southeast Asia.

OTHER USES. The plant provides fodder.

Rhamnus triqueter Wallich

Ceanothus triquetra Wallich
NEPALI *haledo* TAMANG *tamda*

Rhamnaceae. Evergreen tree about 7 m high. Leaves stalked, 5–15 cm long, 2.5–6 cm wide, ovate to oblong, somewhat leathery. Flowers yellowish green in axillary racemes. Fruit globose. Flowers May–July, fruits July–November. Propagated by seeds. Distributed in western and central Nepal at 1200–3000 m at the margins of forests among shrubs; also in Pakistan and India.

MEDICINE. Juice of the bark is given in cases of diarrhea and dysentery.

OTHER USES. Charcoal from the plant is used to prepare explosives.

Rhamnus virgatus Roxburgh

Rhamnus dahuricus Pallas
Rhamnus flavidus Momiyama
CHEPANG *adum* MAGAR *chariwal* NEPALI *bhalu kanda, kande painyu, phalame* TAMANG *thurmang*

Rhamnaceae. Shrub about 2 m high, branches terminating into spines. Leaves short-stalked, alternate, elliptic to lanceolate, acuminate, serrate, glabrous or sparsely hairy. Flowers yellowish. Fruit globose. Flowers April–May, fruits July–August. Propagated by seeds. Distributed throughout Nepal at 1000–3000 m in open places along

the margin of the forest; also in northern India, Bhutan, western China, and northern Myanmar.

MEDICINE. Fruits are used as a purgative.

OTHER USES. Goats browse the leaves.

Rhaphidophora glauca (Wallich) Schott

Pothos glaucus Wallich, *Monstera glauca* (Wallich) K. Koch ex Ender, *Scindapsus glaucus* (Wallich) Schott
NEPALI *haddi jor, kanchiruwa*

Araceae. Tall climber with succulent stems. Leaves stalked, 15–30 cm long, 12–23 cm wide, elliptic to ovate, acuminate, somewhat leathery, green above, glaucous beneath. Spathe variable in size, fleshy, ovate to oblong, cuspidate. Spadix pale yellow, cylindrical. Flowers January–February. Propagated by seeds or corms. Distributed throughout Nepal at 300–1900 m in damp places in the hills; also in northern India and Bhutan.

MEDICINE. A paste of the plant is used to treat wounds.

Rheum acuminatum Hooker fil.

TAMANG *pongaju*

Polygonaceae. Herb about 1 m high. Lower leaves 15–30 cm long and wide, ovate, shortly acuminate, base cordate, pubescent beneath, upper leaves smaller. Flowers reddish in axillary or terminal panicles. Fruit an achene, orbicular, notched at the base and apex. Flowers and fruits June–August. Propagated by seeds or root offshoots. Distributed in eastern and central Nepal at 3300–4200 m in open, rocky places; also in northern India, Bhutan, and northern Myanmar.

FOOD. Petioles are pickled.

Rheum australe D. Don

Rheum emodi Wallich ex Meissner
ENGLISH *rhubarb* GURUNG *khaghyun* NEPALI *akase chuk, chulthi amilo, padamchal* SHERPA *atvhowa, chyurcha* TAMANG *kyunpa-rim* TIBETAN *gyasa*

Polygonaceae. Herb about 1.5 m high, rootstock woody. Leaves stalked, orbiculate or broadly ovate, cordate, entire, glabrous above, sparsely hairy on the veins beneath. Flowers dark purple. Fruit oblong ovoid, purple, winged, notched at the apex. Flowers June–July, fruits August–September. Propagated by seeds or root offshoots. Distributed throughout Nepal at 3200–4200 m on open, rocky ground but the gathering of its rhizomes for sale in the trade and leaf stalks for local consumption endangers plant populations; also in northern India and southern Tibet.

FOOD. Petioles are pickled, mostly after drying.

MEDICINE. The rhizome is purgative, astringent, tonic, aperient, and stomachic.

OTHER USES. The rhizome yields a bright yellow dye.

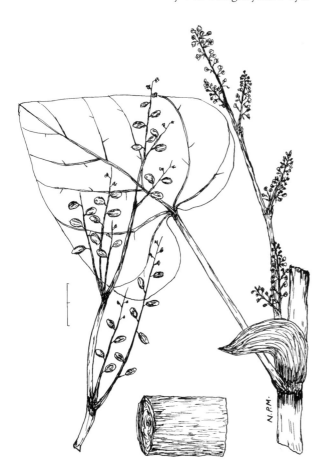

Rheum australe

Rheum moorcroftianum Royle

GURUNG *keje, kesa*

Polygonaceae. Dwarf herb. Leaves stalked, large, orbiculate, leathery, glabrous above, stellately puberulent beneath. Flowers magenta in racemes arising from the rootstock, June–July. Propagated by seeds or root offshoots. Distributed in western and central Nepal at 3600–4400 m on rocky hillsides above streams; also in northern India.

MEDICINE. Dried leaves are smoked in a pipe to treat sinusitis.

Rheum nobile Hooker fil. & Thomson

NEPALI *chulthi amilo*

Polygonaceae. Herb about 1.5 m high, densely covered with pale reflexed bracts. Leaves stalked, about 30 cm long and wide, ovate or orbiculate, obtuse, base rounded or cordate. Flowers cream in racemes concealed by bracts. Fruit an achene, ovoid. Flowers and fruits June–August. Propagated by seeds or root offshoots. Distributed in eastern Nepal at 3900–4300 m on open, rocky ground; also in northeastern India and Bhutan.

FOOD. Peeled petioles are eaten raw or pickled.

Rhododendron anthopogon D. Don

NEPALI *guraunsi phul, sunpati* SHERPA *balu changsing, balu kapo, masur*

Ericaceae. Shrub about 30 cm high. Leaves stalked, elliptic to ovate, obtuse to mucronate, upper surface slightly scaly, lower surface densely scaly. Flowers yellow. Fruit a capsule, ovoid, enclosed in the persistent calyx. Flowers June–July, fruits October–November. Propagated by seeds. Distributed throughout Nepal at 3300–4600 m on open, moist hillsides; also in northern India, Bhutan, and Tibet.

FOOD. Flowers are used as a substitute of tea.

MEDICINE. Leaves are boiled and the vapor is inhaled to relieve cough and colds.

OTHER USES. Dried leaves are used as incense. Leaves contain 0.2% essential oils.

Rhododendron arboreum Smith

Rhododendron puniceum Roxburgh

CHEPANG *takro* DANUWAR *gurans* GURUNG *porota, pota* LEPCHA *tokariya* LIMBU *thokpheklaphun* MAGAR *lalisar, palsai, patak, patgasar* NEPALI *guras, laliguras* NEWARI *takaswan* RAI *dakbun, tokse* SHERPA *kalma, tangu* SUNWAR *tosel* TAMANG *paramhendo, pat* THARU *guras* TIBETAN *tag ma sin me, tangu, tog damr po*

Ericaceae. Tree about 15 m high. Leaves stalked, crowded toward the ends of branches, 4.5–16 cm long, 1.5–6 cm wide, oblong to lanceolate, narrowed at both ends, entire, silvery beneath. Flowers red, white, or pink, crowded in large rounded corymbs. Fruit a capsule about 2.5 cm long, cylindrical, longitudinally ribbed. Flowers March–April, fruits May–June. Propagated by seeds. Distributed throughout Nepal at 1400–3300 m on hillsides in mixed oak forests but the gathering of wood is a cause of conservation concern; also in northern India, Bhutan, southern Tibet, and Myanmar.

FOOD. Villagers eat the flower petals. Chepangs and Rautes pickle the flower simply by mixing it with salt and chili (*Capsicum annuum*).

MEDICINE. Juice of the bark, about 3 teaspoons twice a day, is taken in cases of diarrhea and dysentery. This juice, about 1 teaspoon twice a day, is given for cough. Lepchas and Limbus of eastern Nepal apply a paste of young leaves to the temples to relieve headaches. When a fish bone gets stuck in the throat, people eat the petals to help extract the bone. Juice of the flower is also taken to treat menstrual disorder. Five to seven corollas are chewed three times a day to treat bloody dysentery. The flower is boiled in water about 10 minutes, and the filtered water, about 6 teaspoons, is given to check vomiting tendencies, especially during loss of appetite.

OTHER USES. Wood is used to prepare household utensils. It is also used for building small houses and fences around kitchen gardens. Planks of the wood are nicely carved to make boxes, drawers, cupboards, and other furniture. The wood provides long-lasting heat, hence it is extensively used for firewood. Using the wood, villagers stealthily prepare charcoal in the forest and sell it to the blacksmiths and goldsmiths.

Immature leaves are used as fish poison. Tender leaves are poisonous to cattle. Dried leaves are collected as a substitute for firewood and to prepare compost for the field.

Rhododendron arboreum

The people of Doti district spread juice of the leaves on cots and beds to get rid of bugs. Village women like to use the flowers on their heads as ornament, and similarly, flowers are used to decorate the main gates and windows of houses. Flowers are also offered to gods and goddesses, especially around March when other flowers are scarce. Nowadays, villagers sell flowers in urban markets and earn a good income. It is the national flower of Nepal.

Rhododendron barbatum Wallich ex G. Don

Rhododendron lancifolium Hooker fil.
ENGLISH *giant blood rhododendron* GURUNG *ryapu*
NEPALI *gurans, chimal, lal chimal*

Ericaceae. Tree about 10 m high. Leaves stalked, 10–20 cm long, 4–7 cm wide, elliptic to lanceolate, acute, rugulose above, margin reflexed, stalk covered with bristles. Flowers scarlet in dense, many-flowered heads, April–June. Propagated by seeds. Distributed throughout Nepal at 2400–3600 m, common in subalpine forest; also in northern India and Bhutan.

OTHER USES. Young leaves and shoots are poisonous to livestock. Nectar is also toxic.

Rhododendron campanulatum D. Don

Rhododendron aeruginosum Hooker fil.
GURUNG *syapu* NEPALI *cherailu, chimalo, nilo chimal*
SHERPA *khamapu, sok* TAMANG *bel*

Ericaceae. Much branched shrub about 3 m high. Leaves stalked, 7–15 cm long, 3–6 cm wide, elliptic or ovate, acute or obtuse, glabrous and rugulose above, rusty brown or with felted covering of hairs beneath. Flowers white or light purple in a lax raceme. Fruit a capsule, curved. Flowers April–June. Propagated by seeds. Distributed throughout Nepal at 2800–4400 m on open slopes along the tracks; also in northern India, Bhutan, and southwestern Tibet.

MEDICINE. Juice of leaves is used in cases of rheumatic pain and syphilis. This juice, mixed with tobacco (*Nicotiana tabacum*), is used as snuff.

OTHER USES. The plant provides excellent fuelwood. Young leaves and shoots are poisonous to livestock.

Rhododendron cinnabarinum Hooker fil.

GURUNG *ryapu* NEPALI *gurans, sanu chimal*

Ericaceae. Much branched shrub about 2 m high, branches purple. Leaves stalked, 5–7.5 cm long, 2.5–4 cm wide, elliptic to ovate, lower surface densely scaly, apex rounded. Flowers reddish. Fruit a capsule, densely scaly. Flowers April–June, fruits August–November. Propagated by seeds. Distributed in eastern Nepal at 3200–3800 m on rocky mountain slopes; also in northeastern India, Bhutan, and southern Tibet.

OTHER USES. The plant is used as fuel. Young leaves and shoots are poisonous to livestock.

Rhododendron dalhousiae Hooker fil.

NEPALI *lahare chimal*

Ericaceae. Epiphytic shrub about 3 m high. Leaves stalked, 6–15 cm long, 2.5–6 cm wide, ovate to lanceolate, entire, densely scaly beneath, apex obtuse, base cuneate. Flowers white, tinged with rose outside, fragrant, in a five-flowered stalk. Fruit a capsule with persistent calyx. Flowers May–June, fruits October–November. Propagated by seeds. Distributed in eastern and central Nepal at 1800–2500 m on rocky mountain slopes; also in northeastern India.

MEDICINE. Juice of tender leaves is applied to wounds of cattle.

Rhododendron falconeri Hooker fil.

NEPALI *khorlinga, seto gurans*

Ericaceae. Tree about 15 m high, young shoots with gray tomentum. Leaves stalked, 20–30 cm long, 5–15 cm wide, elliptic to ovate, upper surface smooth, lower surface densely rusty tomentose, apex obtuse to rounded, base more or less cordate. Flowers yellowish with purple spots on the throat. Fruit a capsule, large, woody, obliquely set, ridged and warted. Flowers April–June, fruits October–December. Propagated by seeds. Distributed in eastern Nepal at 2700–3000 m on rocky slopes; also in northeastern India and Bhutan.

OTHER USES. Wood is used for fuel. Young leaves are poisonous to animals.

Rhododendron fulgens Hooker fil.

NEPALI *chimal, korlingo*

Ericaceae. Shrub about 3 m high. Leaves stalked, 6–11 cm long, 5–7 cm wide, ovate to oblong, entire, glossy on the upper surface, densely woolly on the lower surface, apex rounded, base slightly cordate. Flowers deep red or scarlet, May–June. Propagated by seeds. Distributed in eastern Nepal at 3300–4100 m on rocky slopes; also in northeastern India, Bhutan, and southern Tibet.

OTHER USES. Wood is used for fuel. Leaves are poisonous to livestock.

Rhododendron grande Wight

Rhododendron argenteum Hooker fil., *Waldemaria argentea* (Hooker fil.) Klotzsch
Rhododendron longifolium Nuttall
NEPALI *chimal, patu korlingo, seto gurans*

Ericaceae. Tree about 14 m high. Leaves stalked, 15–35 cm long, oblanceolate, deep green above, covered with a thin layer of silvery white hairs beneath. Flowers white with purple blotches at the base, in large rounded clusters. Fruit a capsule, woody, with a persistent calyx. Flowers March–April. Propagated by seeds. Distributed in eastern Nepal at 1700–2900 m on rocky slopes; also in Bhutan and southeastern Tibet.

OTHER USES. The plant is mainly used for fuelwood.

Rhododendron hodgsonii Hooker fil.

NEPALI *korlingo*

Ericaceae. Tree about 8 m high, bark pinkish. Leaves stalked, about 30 cm long, oblong to elliptic, leathery, dark dull green above, brown woolly beneath. Flowers magenta-pink, usually with a few darker blotches inside, in compact clusters, April–May. Propagated by seeds. Distributed in eastern Nepal at 3000–3800 m on alpine slopes; also in India, Bhutan, and southeastern Tibet.

OTHER USES. The plant is used as fuelwood.

Rhododendron lepidotum Wallich ex G. Don

Rhododendron salignum Hooker fil.
NEPALI *bhale sunpati, saluma, sebaro, sunpati* TAMANG *balu mhendo* TIBETAN *bhalunakpo*

Ericaceae. Shrub about 1.5 m high. Leaves stalked, 2.5–4 cm long, narrowly lanceolate, lower surface densely covered with fleshy scales. Flowers pink or purple. Fruit a capsule, densely scaly, covered with a persistent calyx. Flowers April–June, fruits October–November. Propagated by seeds. Distributed throughout Nepal at 1900–4700 m; also in northern India, southeastern Tibet, southwestern China, and northern Myanmar.

MEDICINE. The people of Manang district, central Nepal, take the juice of the plant, believing it purifies the blood. Pounded leaves are boiled in water and spread on cots, beds, and mats to kill bugs.

OTHER USES. Dried leaves are used as incense.

Rhododendron lindleyi T. Moore

Rhododendron bhotanicum C. B. Clarke
NEPALI *lahare chimal*

Ericaceae. Epiphytic shrub. Leaves stalked, 6–15 cm long, 1.7–3 cm wide, oblong elongate, rounded at both ends, glaucous beneath. Flowers pale yellow or white, slightly fragrant, April–June. Fruits December–January. Propagated by seeds. Distributed in eastern Nepal at 2100–3300 m in shady places; also in India, Bhutan, southern Tibet, and Myanmar.

OTHER USES. Young leaves are poisonous to livestock.

Rhododendron lowndesii Davidian

TAMANG *barjhum mhendo*

Ericaceae. Creeping shrub about 10 cm high, twigs slender, hairy, sparsely covered with scales. Leaves stalked, 1–2 cm long, 0.5–0.1 cm wide, margin hairy, upper surface with or without scales, lower surface sparsely covered with hairs and greenish scales, apex rounded and pointed, base obtuse or cuneate. Flowers yellowish, June–July. Propagated by seeds. Distributed in western and central Nepal at 3200–4500 m in mountain forests; endemic.

MEDICINE. A paste of the bark is applied to boils and pimples.

Rhododendron setosum D. Don

SHERPA *silu, siru*

Ericaceae. Shrub about 30 cm high, branches densely setose. Leaves 8–15 cm long, 4–6 cm wide, oblong to elliptic, glandular scaly on upper surface, densely scaly and setose beneath. Flowers bright purple or pink. Fruit a capsule, ovoid. Flowers April–June, fruits October–November. Propagated by seeds. Distributed in eastern and central Nepal at 3700–5600 m in mountain forests; also in India, Bhutan, and southern Tibet.

FOOD. Sherpas use dried petals as a substitute for tea.

Rhododendron triflorum Hooker fil.

NEPALI *phenla chimal*

Ericaceae. Shrub about 3 m high, branches with black glands. Leaves stalked, 3–8 cm long, 1.5–3 cm wide, oblong to lanceolate, upper surface glabrous, lower surface densely glandular scaly, apex acute, base obtuse or rounded. Flowers light yellow, green-spotted, fragrant. Fruit a capsule covered with scales. Flowers May–July, fruits November–January. Propagated by seeds. Distributed in eastern Nepal at 2400–3300 m; also in northeastern India, Bhutan, and southern Tibet.

OTHER USES. Wood is used for fuel. Young leaves are considered poisonous to livestock.

Rhododendron wightii Hooker fil.

NEPALI *radu*

Ericaceae. Tree about 4 m high, young branches gray floccose, older branches glabrous. Leaves stalked, 12–18 cm long, 5–7 cm wide, oblanceolate, upper surface bright green, lower surface grayish, apex obtuse or acute, base rhombic. Flowers pale yellow. Fruit a capsule, cylindrical, slightly curved. Flowers May–June. Propagated by seeds. Distributed in eastern Nepal at 3300–4100 m on open alpine slopes; also in northeastern India, Bhutan, and southwestern Tibet.

OTHER USES. Wood is used for fuel.

Rhus javanica Linnaeus

Rhus amela D. Don
Rhus bucki-amela Roxburgh
Rhus chinensis Miller
Rhus semialata Murray, *Toxicodendron semialatum* (Murray) Kuntze

BHOJPURI *aanwala* CHEPANG *rusi* DANUWAR *bhakiamilo* ENGLISH *Nepalese sumac* GURUNG *tibu* LEPCHA *tanghrilchyor* LIMBU *iseba, isi* MAGAR *muruk* NEPALI *amilo, bhaki amilo, bhangil, chugo, chuk amilo, dudhe bhalayo* NEWARI *supchun* RAI *mahada, mara* SUNWAR *bhakari, kursinglo* TAMANG *tibro, tipru* THARU *amil* TIBETAN *thaksin*

Anacardiaceae. Deciduous tree about 8 m high. Leaves stalked, odd-pinnate, leaflets sessile, opposite, 5–16 cm long, 3–8 cm wide, oblong, acuminate, coarsely dentate, pubescent above, tomentose beneath. Flowers small, yellowish, in large terminal panicles. Fruit a drupe, compressed, orbicular, red when mature. Flowers September–October, fruits November–March. Propagated by seeds. Distributed throughout Nepal at 1000–2600 m on open hillsides; also in northern India, Bhutan, Sri Lanka, eastward to China, Korea, Japan, and Myanmar.

FOOD. Ripe fruits are eaten either raw or pickled.

MEDICINE. A paste of the galls on the plant is applied to treat swellings and wounds, and according to Kirtikar and Basu (1935), it is given to treat paralysis. Fruit is considered appetite inducing; it is also chewed in cases of stomachache. Powdered fruit is given to treat profuse menstruation. The powder is mixed with double the amount of yogurt and taken for bloody dysentery. A decoction of the fruit is given to animals with foot-and-mouth disease.

OTHER USES. The plant provides fodder and fuelwood.

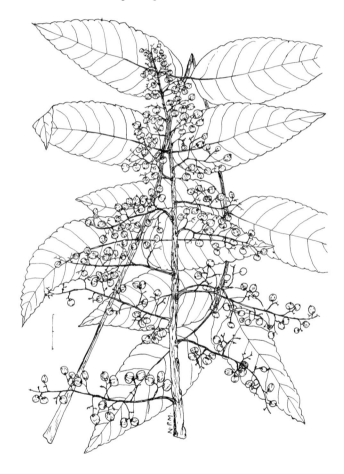

Rhus javanica

Rhus parviflora Roxburgh

Toxicodendron parviflorum (Roxburgh) Kuntze
ENGLISH *sumac* MAGAR *madan* NEPALI *dantya, datakano, satibayar* TAMANG *satibro*

Anacardiaceae. Much branched shrub. Leaves stalked, alternate, trifoliolate, lower pair of leaflets smaller, ovate, irregularly crenate, hairy on both surfaces, tip rounded, gradually tapering toward the base. Flowers yellowish, fragrant. Fruit small, round, red when ripe. Flowers August–November, fruits December–April. Propagated by seeds. Distributed throughout Nepal at 700–1400 m on open, dry hillsides; also in northern India, Bhutan, and Sri Lanka.

FOOD. Ripe fruits are eaten fresh or pickled. They are sour in taste. Fruits are also sold in the market (Plate 17).

MEDICINE. A paste of the bark is applied to treat muscular swellings caused by some inflammations and injuries.

OTHER USES. Leaves are used with tobacco (*Nicotiana tabacum*) for smoking and are considered tasty. Leaves are also used for cattle beds and compost.

Rhus succedanea Linnaeus

Toxicodendron succedaneum (Linnaeus) Kuntze
Rhus acuminata de Candolle, *R. succedanea* var. *acuminata* (de Candolle) Hooker fil.
Rhus succedanea var. *himalaica* Hooker fil.
Rhus succedanea var. *sikkimensis* Hooker fil.

ENGLISH *Japanese wax tree, Japan tallow, wild varnish tree* GURUNG *bhayo* MAGAR *ban amre* NEPALI *bhalayo, kag bhalayo, rani bhalayo* TAMANG *krosying*

Anacardiaceae. Tree about 10 m high. Leaves stalked, odd-pinnate, leaflets seven, ovate to oblong, acuminate, entire, glabrous, often reddish. Flowers greenish in axillary panicles. Fruit a drupe, brown, oblique. Flowers May–June. Propagated by seeds. Distributed throughout Nepal at 1300–2400 m, occasional in open places; also in northern India, Bhutan, Tibet, eastward to China, Myanmar, and Thailand.

FOOD. The acidic pulp of the fruit is edible.

OTHER USES. Latex is acrid and forms blisters on the skin.

Rhus wallichii Hooker fil.

Rhus juglandifolium Wallich ex D. Don
Rhus vernicifera Willdenow

GURUNG *chalaya, thulo mayal* NEPALI *thulo bhalayo* TAMANG *grosing*

Anacardiaceae. Tree about 8 m high, branches softly and densely tomentose. Leaves stalked, odd-pinnate, leaflets seven or nine, ovate to oblong, acuminate, entire, densely tomentose beneath. Flowers greenish white in axillary panicles, densely tomentose. Fruit a drupe, globose. Flowers May–June, fruits September–October. Propagated by seeds. Distributed throughout Nepal at 300–2500 m in shady as well as open places; also in northern India and Bhutan.

OTHER USES. Wood is used to make the handle of the *khukuri*, the Nepalese curved knife. Juice of bark and leaves is corrosive and vesicant.

Rhynchosia himalensis Bentham ex Baker

NEPALI *ban bhata*

Leguminosae. Trailing, more or less hairy shrub. Leaves stalked, trifoliolate, leaflets stalked, lateral leaflets nearly sessile, ovate. Flowers yellow, purple veined, in long axillary racemes. Fruit a pod, oblong, slightly curved, pubescent, November–December. Propagated by seeds. Distributed in western Nepal at 1000–2800 m in open places; also in northern India and China.

FOOD. Young fruits are cooked as a vegetable.

MEDICINE. A paste of the root is applied to the forehead to treat headaches.

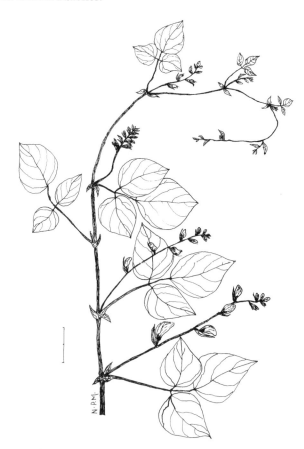

Rhynchosia himalensis

Rhynchostylis retusa (Linnaeus) Blume

Epidendrum retusum Linnaeus
Aerides guttatum Roxburgh
Aerides spicatum D. Don
Epidendrum hippium Buchanan-Hamilton ex D. Don
Sarcanthus guttatus Lindley, *Saccolabium guttatum* (Lindley) Lindley

GURUNG *gam* NEPALI *ghoge gava, thur*

Orchidaceae. Epiphytic orchid with stout, creeping stem, pseudobulbs absent. Leaves deeply channeled, keeled, notched at the apex, the bases imbricated. Flowers pinkish in dense racemes, May–June. Propagated by seeds. Distributed throughout Nepal at 500–1500 m, generally on tree trunks; also in northern India, Bhutan, Sri Lanka, and Myanmar.

MEDICINE. Juice of the root is applied to cuts and wounds.

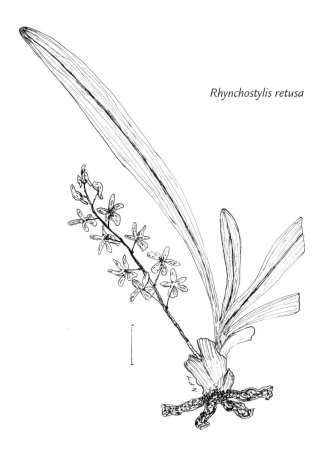

Rhynchostylis retusa

Ribes himalense Royle ex Decaisne

Ribes emodense Rehder
Ribes rubrum Linnaeus
NEPALI *khamar, paunro* TIBETAN *se-rgod-ras*

Grossulariaceae. Erect shrub. Leaves stalked, three- or five-lobed, 3–7.5 cm long, dentate, cordate, tip pointed. Flowers greenish yellow. Fruit a berry, red. Flowers and fruits April–June. Propagated by seeds. Distributed throughout Nepal at 2700–3900 m in drier places in shrubby areas of forests; also in northern India, Bhutan, and western and central China.

FOOD. Ripe fruits are edible.

MEDICINE. Juice of the leaf is given for diarrhea and dysentery, and a paste of it is applied to cuts and wounds.

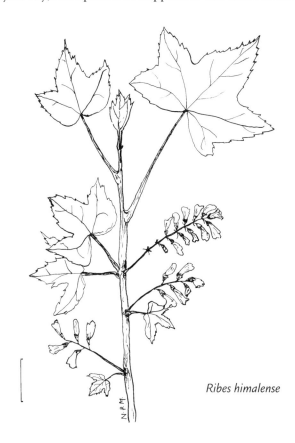

Ribes himalense

Ribes alpestre Wallich ex Decaisne

Ribes grossularia Linnaeus
Ribes himalensis Royle
ENGLISH *European gooseberry* NEPALI *masino kimu*

Grossulariaceae. Much branched shrub about 2 m high, stem prickly, one to three spines at each node. Leaves long-stalked, rounded, with blunt teeth, slightly hairy. Flowers solitary, bell shaped, white. Fruit a berry, ovoid, dull red, glandular hairy. Flowers May–June. Propagated by seeds. Distributed in central and western Nepal at 3200–3600 m on dry, open slopes; also in Afghanistan, northern India, Bhutan, Tibet, and western and central China.

FOOD. Ripe fruits are edible and also preserved as jams, jellies, and sauces.

Ribes glaciale Wallich

NEPALI *tanfu* SHERPA *nhekha, takoi* TIBETAN *domaru*

Grossulariaceae. Shrub about 3 m high. Leaves stalked, ovate, acuminate, three- or five-lobed, crenate to serrate, cordate, scattered hairy on both surfaces. Flowers pinkish. Fruit a berry, orange when ripe, May–July. Propagated by seeds. Distributed throughout Nepal at 2400–4400 m, occasional in open places; also in northern India, southern Tibet, Bhutan, and western China.

FOOD. Ripe fruits are edible.

Ribes takare D. Don

Ribes acuminatum Wallich
NEPALI *dhusurlo, tanfu*

Grossulariaceae. Shrub about 2 m high. Leaves stalked, cordate, softly pubescent, three- or five-lobed, lobes acuminate, serrate. Flowers pinkish. Fruit a berry, red, glandular hairy. Flowers April–June. Propagated by seeds. Distributed throughout Nepal at 2200–3300 m in open woodlands; also in northern India, Tibet, western and central China, and northern Myanmar.

FOOD. Ripe fruits are edible.

Ricinus communis Linnaeus

CHEPANG *areth, ater, kukat, lidis* DANUWAR *andi*
ENGLISH *castor-oil plant* GURUNG *yanyan* MAJHI *madhishe aril*
MOOSHAR *andi* NEPALI *arend, arer, aaril* NEWARI *aa ma* RAI *daldo*
RAUTE *indeyo* TAMANG *dandarobi, thatur* THARU *reyar*
TIBETAN *dan-khra, dar-ta, e-ra*

Euphorbiaceae. Shrub about 5 m high. Leaves long-stalked, alternate, palmately lobed, lobes oblong to lanceolate, acuminate, irregularly serrate. Plants monoecious, yellowish, the male flowers crowded in the upper portion of the inflorescence, female flowers below. Fruit a capsule, ovoid, covered with fleshy spines. Seeds three, elliptic, glossy, black or usually mottled gray, black, brown, or white. Propagated by seeds. Distributed throughout Nepal to about 2400 m on open uncultivated land around villages; also in Pakistan, India, Bhutan, Myanmar, Thailand, Malaysia, the Philippines, and most tropical regions.

MEDICINE. The root has purgative effects. Juice of the root is taken in cases of diarrhea and dysentery, and applied for cutaneous skin diseases. A powder of dried root is given for jaundice and nervous disorders. A paste of the bark is employed to treat cuts and wounds. A warmed leaf or its poultice is put on the forehead to relieve fever and headaches. It is also applied to treat boils, rheumatic pains, and over the breast to stimulate milk. Some Gurungs take juice of the leaves for diarrhea and dysentery, and apply it to burns.

A paste of the flowers is applied to obstinate wounds. Seeds are purgative. Oil from the seed is used for hemorrhoids, liver complaints, rheumatism, and cutaneous diseases like ringworm. It is also used in treating acute diarrhea. A paste of the seed is valued in treating gout. It is also applied to swollen parts of the body and chapped skin. In the Terai of Nepal, one cotyledon per day is taken after menstruation for birth control. A cotyledon, crushed with sugar or sugarcane juice, is given to infants as an anthelmintic. A paste of the cotyledon is applied to treat scabies and gout. Cotyledons are fried in mustard oil and the smoke emitted by this process is inhaled through the mouth, which is kept closed about 10 minutes for dental caries.

OTHER USES. The dried plant is a good source of fuel but it gives only mild heat. The stem contains tannin. Seeds are used for poisoning mad dogs. Seed oil is used for lighting and as a lubricant. The seed contains 35–55% oil.

Rorippa indica (Linnaeus) Hiern

Sisymbrium indicum Linnaeus, *Nasturtium indicum* (Linnaeus) de Candolle
Nasturtium heterophyllum D. Don
Nasturtium montanum Wallich ex Hooker fil. & Thomson
NEPALI *tori ghans*

Cruciferae. Erect annual herb about 60 cm high. Basal leaves pinnatifid, lobes dentate, cauline leaves lyrate. Flowers yellow in long, many-flowered racemes. Fruit a pod, cylindrical, narrow. Flowers and fruits July–August. Propagated by seeds. Distributed in western and central Nepal at 150–200 m in moist places; also in India, eastward to China, Malaysia, and Japan.

FOOD. Tender shoots and leaves are cooked as a vegetable.

Rorippa nasturtium-aquaticum (Linnaeus) Hayek

Sisymbrium nasturtium-aquaticum Linnaeus
Nasturtium officinale R. Brown
ENGLISH *watercress* NEPALI *lahure sag, pani sag, sim sag*
RAUTE *dubakya* TAMANG *syaudhap*

Cruciferae. Herb. Leaves stalked, odd-pinnate, acuminate, smooth. Flowers white. Fruit a pod, linear, curved upward slightly. Flowers and fruits most of the year. Propagated by seeds. Distributed in central and eastern Nepal at 1300–2100 m on moist ground; also in temperate Asia, Europe, and North America.

FOOD. Tender portions are cooked as a vegetable.

MEDICINE. The plant is digestive and diuretic. Juice of the plant, about 6 teaspoons three times a day, is given for fever. Tender parts of the plant are boiled in water about 10 minutes, and the filtered liquid is given to sick persons to help them regain strength and vigor.

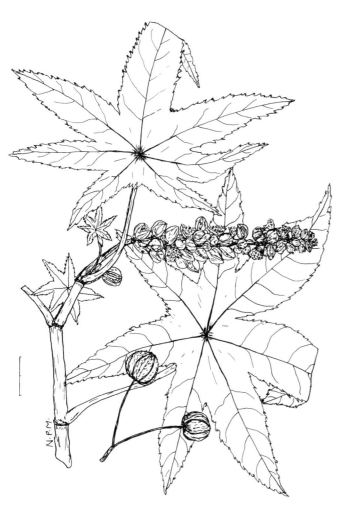

Ricinus communis

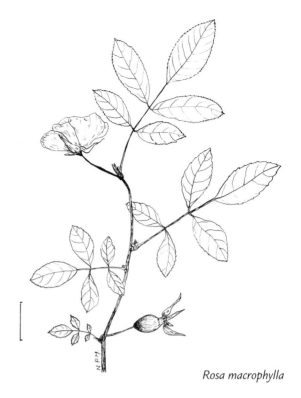

Rosa macrophylla

Rorippa nasturtium-aquaticum

Rosa brunonii Lindley

Rosa moschata Miller

MAGAR *domala* NEPALI *bhainsi kanda, gulab* TAMANG *tawar buju*

Rosaceae. Straggling shrub. Leaves stalked, odd-pinnate, leaflets seven or nine, subsessile, elliptic to oblong, acute, serrate, glabrous above, hairy on veins underneath. Flowers white in terminal corymbs, April–June. Propagated by seeds or cuttings. Distributed throughout Nepal at 1500–2700 m in open, rocky places; also in northern India, Bhutan, western China, and Myanmar.

FOOD. Ripe fruits are edible.

Rosa macrophylla Lindley

Rosa hookeriana Wallich

NEPALI *jangali gulab* TIBETAN *siya*

Rosaceae. Shrub about 2 m high, prickles few, straight with a broad, dilated base. Leaves stalked, odd-pinnate, leaflets five to nine, sessile, elliptic, acute, finely serrate, glabrous above, hairy beneath. Flowers large, solitary, terminal, pinkish red, June–July. Propagated by seeds or cuttings. Distributed throughout Nepal at 2100–3800 m in open, rocky places; also in northern India and Bhutan.

FOOD. Ripe fruits are edible.

MEDICINE. A paste of the fruit is ingested in the belief that it helps eyesight.

OTHER USES. The plant makes a good hedge. Leaves are browsed by goats and sheep.

Rosa sericea Lindley

Rosa tetrasepala Royle

ENGLISH *Himalayan rose* NEPALI *darimpate, kharaute, rhyuli* TAMANG *gjama, sema* TIBETAN *aalo tanso, se-ba*

Rosaceae. Spiny, much branched shrub about 2 m high, prickles brown, straight. Leaves stalked, odd-pinnate, leaflets seven or nine, subsessile, elliptic to oblong, obtuse or acute, serrate toward the tip, villous on both surfaces or only on the veins beneath. Flowers axillary, solitary on lateral shoots, white or yellowish. Fruit globose or pear shaped, red. Flowers May–July. Propagated by seeds or cuttings. Distributed throughout Nepal at 1700–4200 m in exposed places; also in northern India, Bhutan, Tibet, western China, and northern Myanmar.

FOOD. Ripe fruit is edible.

MEDICINE. A paste of the flower is applied to treat headaches and given for liver complaints.

OTHER USES. The plant makes a good hedge. Leaves are browsed by goats and sheep.

Roscoea alpina Royle

NEPALI *bharda*

Zingiberaceae. Erect herb about 10 cm high. Leaves sessile, 2.5–5 cm long, oblong to lanceolate. Flowers whitish, the limb purple. Flowers and fruits June–July. Propagated by tubers. Distributed throughout Nepal at 2400–3100 m in moist areas and forest openings; also in India, Bhutan, and Tibet.

OTHER USES. The tuber is considered poisonous.

Roscoea purpurea Smith

Roscoea exilis Smith ex Horaninow, *R. purpurea* var. *exilis* (Smith ex Horaninow) Baker
NEPALI *bhordaya, bhuin saro, kokoli, rasgari, themni*

Zingiberaceae. Erect herb about 50 cm high. Leaves sheathing, lanceolate, acuminate. Flowers violet, July–September. Propagated by tubers. Distributed in eastern and central Nepal at 1500–3000 m in open, moist places; also in northern India and Bhutan.

FOOD. Boiled tubers are edible.

MEDICINE. The Tamangs of Rasuwa district give the tuber to animals with indigestion.

Roscoea purpurea

Rotala indica (Willdenow) Koehne

Peplis indica Willdenow, *Ameletia indica* (Willdenow) de Candolle
Ameletia polystachya Wallich
Ammania nana Roxburgh
Ammania peploides Sprengel
NEPALI *belaiti jhar*

Lythraceae. Annual herb about 30 cm high. Leaves subsessile, opposite, 0.5–2 cm long, 0.2–0.5 cm wide, oblong, obtuse, base narrowed. Flowers pinkish on long leafy spikes. Fruit a capsule, ellipsoidal, red. Flowers and fruits

September–January. Propagated by seeds. Distributed in eastern and central Nepal at 200–1400 m in moist places; also in western Asia, India, China, Malaysia, and Japan.

MEDICINE. Juice of the root is applied to cuts and wounds.

Rotala rotundifolia (Buchanan-Hamilton ex Roxburgh) Koehne

Ammannia rotundifolia Buchanan-Hamilton ex Roxburgh
NEPALI *sim jhar*

Lythraceae. Procumbent herb about 25 cm high. Leaves sessile, decussate, 3–11 cm long, 2.5–10 cm wide, orbiculate to broadly elliptic. Flowers pink in dense terminal spikes. Fruit a capsule, ellipsoidal. Flowers February–March. Propagated by seeds. Distributed throughout Nepal at 300–3000 m in moist, open places around water in subtropical forests; also in India, Sri Lanka, eastward to China, Taiwan, and southern Japan.

FOOD. Tender leaves and shoots are cooked as a vegetable.

Rotala rotundifolia

Rubia manjith Roxburgh ex Fleming

Rubia cordifolia of authors, not Linnaeus
Rubia munijista Roxburgh, *R. cordifolia* var. *munijista* (Roxburgh) Miquel
CHEPANG *mijuki* ENGLISH *Indian madder* KHALING *kat*
LIMBU *sunggingba* NEPALI *majitho, tiro lahara* SHERPA *chwe*
TAMANG *tinet, tinru* TIBETAN *bhada, rtsod*

Rubiaceae. Trailing herb, stems and branches four-angled, minutely prickly. Leaves stalked, ovate to cordate, long-pointed, basal veins prominent. Flowers dark red. Fruit globose, succulent. Flowers June–October, fruits

November–December. Propagated by seeds. Distributed throughout Nepal at 1200–2300 m in moist, open places; also in northern India.

MEDICINE. The root is alterative, astringent, and tonic. A paste of the stem is applied to scorpion bites.

OTHER USES. The root is used for dye.

Rubia manjith

Rubus acuminatus Smith

Rubus acaenocalyx Hara
NEPALI *phurse kanda, rato ainselu* TAMANG *mamapolang*

Rosaceae. Scandent shrub. Leaves stalked, ovate to lanceolate, caudate-acuminate, serrate, base rounded. Flowers white in axillary and terminal panicles. Fruit globose, bright red. Flowers July–August, fruits September–October. Propagated by root offshoots or seeds. Distributed throughout Nepal at 1000–2300 m as part of the secondary forest layer, in moist, shady places; also in northern India, western China, and Indo-China.

FOOD. Ripe fruits are eaten raw.

MEDICINE. Juice of the bark, about 4 teaspoons twice a day, is given in cases of indigestion.

Rubus biflorus Buchanan-Hamilton ex Smith

NEPALI *kalo ainselu, sanu gulpha*

Rosaceae. Large, spreading shrub, branches white, with sharp, strong prickles. Leaves stalked, three- or five-foliolate, leaflets subsessile, 5–8.5 cm long, ovate to lanceolate, obscurely lobed, doubly serrate or dentate, hairy above,

densely white tomentose beneath. Flowers white on slender, drooping peduncles. Fruit a drupe, globose, yellow. Flowers April–May, fruits May–June. Propagated by root offshoots or seeds. Distributed throughout Nepal at 1700–3300 m in moist, rocky places; also in northern India, Tibet, and western China.

FOOD. Ripe fruits are eaten fresh.

Rubus calycinus Wallich ex D. Don

Rubus lobatus Wallich
ENGLISH *wild raspberry* NEPALI *bhuin ainselu*

Rosaceae. Prostrate herb. Leaves stalked, alternate, stipulate, 1.5–2.5 cm long, 2.5–3.5 cm wide, leaflets circular, serrate, slightly hairy. Flowers solitary, white. Fruit globose, red. Flowers April–May, fruits June–July. Propagated by root offshoots or seeds. Distributed in central and eastern Nepal at 2200–2800 m in moist, shady places; also in northern India, western China, and northern Myanmar.

FOOD. Ripe fruits are eaten fresh.

Rubus ellipticus Smith

Rubus flavus Buchanan-Hamilton ex D. Don
Rubus gowreephul Roxburgh
Rubus rotundifolius Wallich

CHEPANG *lyangsai, thangsai* DANUWAR *ainselu*
ENGLISH *false blackberry, golden evergreen raspberry, Himalayan yellow raspberry, oval-leaved bramble, yellow bramble*
GURUNG *melanchi, palan* LEPCHA *kashyampot* LIMBU *tingwase*
MAGAR *dhewasi, dewasin, juis* MAJHI *jyaunsi, melanchi*
NEPALI *ainselu* NEWARI *isi ma* RAI *bansi* SHERPA *nanyungma*
SUNWAR *khrumich* TAMANG *polang, pulung, urpolang*
THARU *ainselu* TIBETAN *chherma, mapalang, nhyalang*

Rosaceae. Straggling shrub about 5 m high, with rusty brown bristles. Leaves stalked, pinnately trifoliolate, leaflets short-stalked, 1.5–9 cm long, 1–7 cm wide, terminal leaflet largest, elliptic to ovate, serrate, hoary pubescent beneath, apex rounded. Flowers white in dense axillary and terminal panicles. Fruit an aggregate of drupelets, yellow. Flowers December–March, fruits May–July. Propagated by root offshoots or seeds. Distributed throughout Nepal at 1600–2300 m on open slopes; also in northern India, Sri Lanka, eastern and western China, Myanmar, and the Philippines.

FOOD. Ripe fruits are eaten fresh or made into preserves. These fruits are sold in local markets and are a good source of protein, fat, and minerals.

MEDICINE. The plant is astringent. The root, mixed with root of *Girardinia diversifolia* and bark of *Lagerstroemia parviflora*, is boiled in water, and the filtered water, about 2 teaspoons twice a day, is given in cases of fever. Juice of the root, about 6 teaspoons four times a day, is given for fever, gastric trouble, diarrhea, and dysentery. A paste of the root is applied to wounds. A decoction of the root in water is taken as febrifuge. Roots descending from the branches are pounded and given in doses of about 2 teaspoons three times a day for indigestion. The root and

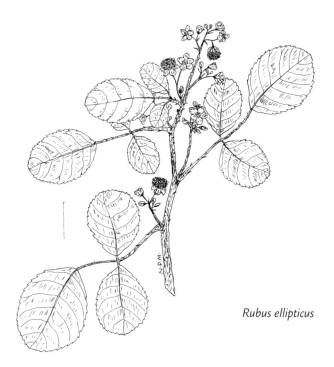

Rubus ellipticus

young shoot are considered good for colic. Leaf buds mixed in equal amounts with leaves of *Centella asiatica* and *Cynodon dactylon,* are pounded, and the juice, about 6 teaspoons three times a day, is given for peptic ulcer. Juice of the fruit is given for colic, fever, and sore throat; it is also considered useful for cough.

OTHER USES. The plant is grown to deter soil erosion and is good for soil conservation. Leaves are browsed by goats and sheep.

Rubus fockeanus Kurz

Rubus nutans var. *fockeanus* (Kurz) Kuntze
ENGLISH *Himalayan wild raspberry* NEPALI *ainselu, bhuin ainselu*
TAMANG *laya polang, pan polang*

Rosaceae. Prostrate herb. Leaves stalked, stipulate, trifoliolate, leaflets subsessile, 0.8–2.5 cm long, 0.5–2 cm wide, orbiculate, finely dentate, smooth or slightly hairy. Flowers stalked, white. Fruit globose, red. Propagated by root offshoots or seeds. Distributed throughout Nepal at 2100–2900 m in moist, shady places; also in northeastern India, southern Tibet, western and central China, and northern Myanmar.

FOOD. Ripe fruits are eaten raw.

Rubus foliolosus D. Don

Rubus microphyllus D. Don
Rubus parvifolius Linnaeus
Rubus pedunculosus D. Don
Rubus roylei Klotzsch
NEPALI *kalo ainselu*

Rosaceae. Small trailing shrub. Leaves stalked, alternate, stipulate, pinnate, leaflets subsessile, ovate, acumi-

nate, finely serrate, white tomentose beneath. Flowers stalked, bracteate, pink. Fruit black when ripe. Flowers and fruits March–May. Propagated by root offshoots or seeds. Distributed in western and central Nepal at 2100–2900 m in moist, shady places; also in northern India.

FOOD. Ripe fruits are eaten fresh.

MEDICINE. Immature fruit is chewed to relieve headaches.

Rubus griffithii Hooker fil.

Rubus hexagynus Roxburgh
NEPALI *bhuin ainselu, bhalu kanda, kalo ainselu*

Rosaceae. Trailing, prickly shrub. Leaves stalked, alternate, stipulate, pinnate, leaflets three or five, subsessile, ovate, acute, finely serrate, white tomentose beneath. Flowers stalked, pinkish. Fruit black when ripe. Flowers and fruits March–July. Propagated by root offshoots or seeds. Distributed in eastern Nepal at 1400–2400 m in moist, shady places; also in northern India.

FOOD. Ripe fruits are eaten fresh.

Rubus hypargyrus Edgeworth

Rubus niveus var. *hypargyrus* (Edgeworth) Hooker fil.,
R. *pedunculosus* var. *hypargyrus* (Edgeworth) Kitamura
GURUNG *marphulang* NEPALI *kali ainselu*

Rosaceae. Straggling, spiny shrub about 2 m high. Leaves stalked, trifoliolate, leaflets ovate, long-pointed, doubly dentate, white hoary beneath. Flowers pinkish. Fruit red or orange. Flowers and fruits May–August. Propagated by root offshoots or seeds. Distributed in central and western Nepal at 2400–2700 m in moist places in forested areas; also in northern India.

FOOD. Ripe fruits are eaten fresh.

MEDICINE. Juice of the leaves, about 2 teaspoons three times a day, is given for fever.

Rubus macilentus Cambessèdes

Rubus uncatus Wallich
GURUNG *ghoya palan, mhenpalan* NEPALI *jogi ainselu*
TAMANG *aachung*

Rosaceae. Trailing shrub, stem nearly glabrous, shiny. Leaves stalked, digitately trifoliolate, leaflets stalked, variable in shape and size, ovate to lanceolate, doubly crenate, glabrous, prickly along the midribs. Flowers white. Fruit a berry, globose, deep orange. Flowers April–May, fruits June–July. Propagated by root offshoots or seeds. Distributed throughout Nepal at 1800–2800 m in damp places in forested areas; also in northern India, southern Tibet, and western China.

FOOD. Ripe fruits are eaten fresh.

Rubus nepalensis (Hooker fil.) Kuntze

Rubus barbatus Edgeworth
Rubus nutans Wallich ex G. Don
Rubus nutantiflorus Hara
SHERPA *nhyalang*

Rosaceae. Herb with creeping stems. Leaves stalked, trifoliolate, leaflets broadly ovate, long-pointed, doubly dentate, hairy on both surfaces. Flowers white, nodding. Fruit scarlet. Flowers May–July, fruits September–November. Propagated by root offshoots or seeds. Distributed throughout Nepal at 2100–3200 m on rocky ground along riverbanks; also in northern India.

FOOD. Ripe fruits are edible.

Rubus niveus Thunberg

Rubus distans D. Don
Rubus lasiocarpus Smith
Rubus pauciflorus Wallich ex Lindley
Rubus pinnatus D. Don
Rubus rosaeflorus Roxburgh
ENGLISH *woolly-berried bramble* NEPALI *kalo ainselu*
TIBETAN *kan-ta-ka-ri*

Rosaceae. Straggling shrub. Leaves stalked, trifoliolate, leaflets stalked, ovate, lobed, generally doubly serrate, often cordate. Flowers pinkish in few-flowered, corymbose, terminal cymes. Fruit a drupe, globose. Flowers April–May, fruits May–June. Propagated by root offshoots or seeds. Distributed throughout Nepal at 1900–2900 m in open places; also in Afghanistan, northern India, Bhutan, and Southeast Asia.

FOOD. Ripe fruits are eaten raw.

Rubus paniculatus Smith

CHEPANG *dhusilo* GURUNG *mhoplan, palha* NEPALI *bhalu ainselu, boksi kanda, kalo ainselu, phusre kanda, rukh ainselu* SHERPA *anselo* TAMANG *mebulang, sipolan, timju polan, timu gra*

Rosaceae. Straggling shrub about 5 m high. Leaves stalked, alternate, 6–14 cm long, 5–10.5 cm wide, broadly ovate to cordate, long-pointed, irregularly serrate, softly white hairy underneath. Flowers stalked, bracteate, white. Fruit red or black. Flowers and fruits June–September. Propagated by root offshoots or seeds. Distributed throughout Nepal at 1700–2900 m on open hillsides; also in northern India.

FOOD. Ripe fruits are edible.

MEDICINE. A paste of the bark is applied for scabies and other rashes. A paste of the leaves is applied to sprains.

Rubus pentagonus Wallich ex Focke

Rubus alpestris Blume
NEPALI *lekh ainselu, rato ainselu*

Rosaceae. Straggling, prickly shrub. Leaves stalked, three- or five-foliolate; leaflets subsessile, elliptic, acuminate, crenate to serrate, white pubescent beneath. Flowers white or pinkish. Fruit red, succulent, July–August. Propagated by root offshoots or seeds. Distributed throughout Nepal at 2000–3000 m in moist, rocky places; also in northern India, western China, and northern Myanmar.

FOOD. Ripe fruits are eaten fresh.

Rubus reticulatus Wallich ex Hooker fil.

CHEPANG *molangsai* GURUNG *palang, tarpucho* MAGAR *ghyampa jyaunsi* NEPALI *ainselu, ban ainselu, gada ainselu, kalo ainselu* TAMANG *maphro polang, me polang*

Rosaceae. Straggling shrub with woolly tomentose branchlets. Leaves stalked, alternate, orbiculate or ovate to cordate, five- to nine-lobed, acuminate, distinctly reticulate, glabrous above, finely downy beneath. Flowers white in short terminal panicles. Fruit orange. Propagated by root offshoots or seeds. Distributed in eastern and central Nepal at 2000–3000 m on exposed hillsides; also in northern India and southern Tibet.

FOOD. Ripe fruits are edible.

MEDICINE. Juice of the fruit is given in cases of stomach disorder.

Rubus rugosus Smith

Rubus hamiltonianus Seringe
Rubus moluccanus Linnaeus
ENGLISH *raspberry* NEPALI *ban ainselu, goru ainselu* TAMANG *gol buju, mewalang*

Rosaceae. Scandent shrub. Leaves stalked, ovate, five- or seven-lobed, irregularly dentate, deeply cordate, rugose above, clothed with yellowish tomentum beneath. Flowers pink or white in axillary and terminal panicles, September–October. Propagated by root offshoots or seeds. Distributed in central and eastern Nepal at 1000–2000 m in open, rocky places; also in northern India.

FOOD. Ripe fruits are eaten fresh.

Rubus splendidissimus Hara

Rubus andersonii Hooker fil.
NEPALI *chande ainselu*

Rosaceae. Shrub about 2.5 m high. Leaves stalked, trifoliolate, leaflets sessile, 1.5–14 cm long, 1–7 cm wide, elliptic, pointed, incised, glabrous above, silky pubescent beneath. Flowers white. Fruit red. Flowers September–October, fruits October–November. Propagated by root offshoots or seeds. Distributed in eastern and central Nepal at 2400–3000 m in moist areas and forest openings; also in northern India and Bhutan.

FOOD. Ripe fruits are edible.

Rubus thomsonii Focke

NEPALI *ainselu*

Rosaceae. Straggling shrub. Leaves stalked, alternate, trifoliolate, leaflets short-stalked, 1.2–12.5 cm long, 0.8–6 cm wide, broadly ovate, acuminate, lateral leaflets cuneate or serrate. Flowers pinkish. Fruit red. Flowers September–October, fruits October–November. Propagated by root offshoots or seeds. Distributed in eastern Nepal at 2600–2900 m in shady places on the forest floor; also in northeastern India and Bhutan.

FOOD. Ripe fruits are edible.

Rubus treutleri Hooker fil.

NEPALI *thulo ainselu*

Rosaceae. Straggling shrub about 2 m high. Leaves stalked, alternate, 3–12.5 cm long, 2.7–19.5 cm wide, orbiculate, lobed, margin incised, slightly hairy on both surfaces, base cordate. Flowers white. Fruit red. Flowers June–August, fruits September–November. Propagated by root offshoots or seeds. Distributed throughout Nepal at 2200–3000 m in thickets in shady places at the edge of the forest; also in northern India, Bhutan, and western China.

FOOD. Ripe fruits are edible.

Rumex acetosa Linnaeus

ENGLISH *dock sorrel, garden sorrel, sheep's sorrel* GURUNG *tarpujo* NEPALI *hale* TIBETAN *sho-mang-ri-sho*

Polygonaceae. Perennial herb with a fibrous root. Basal leaves stalked, 5–15 cm long, oblong, cordate to hastate, cauline leaves sessile, serrate. Flowers reddish, June–August. Propagated by tubers. Distributed in western and central Nepal at 2100–4100 m; also in western Asia, northern India, Bhutan, Tibet, China, Japan, Siberia, Europe, and North America.

MEDICINE. A paste of the root is applied to set dislocated bones.

Rumex dentatus Linnaeus subsp. *klotzschianus*

(Meissner) Reichenbach fil.

Rumex klotzschianus Meissner

NEPALI *ban palungo*

Polygonaceae. Erect annual herb about 70 cm high. Lower leaves stalked, 3–20 cm long, 0.6–5 cm wide, oblong, obtuse, base rounded or cordate, upper leaves smaller. Flowers greenish yellow in distinct, axillary, leafy whorls. Fruit a nut, triquetrous. Flowers and fruits January–August. Propagated by seeds or tubers. Distributed in eastern Nepal at 1200–1400 m on moist, neglected ground; also in Iran, Afghanistan, India, Bhutan, and China.

FOOD. Tender leaves are cooked as a vegetable.

Rumex hastatus D. Don

MAGAR *birgan* NEPALI *adimaro, amili, charemala, kapu*

Polygonaceae. Much branched herb about 1 m high with reddish brown stem. Leaves stalked, 1.3–5 cm, long, variable in size, flattened, hastate with central lobe linear oblong or deltoid, fleshy, glaucous. Flowers red in small clusters in racemes. Fruit a nut enclosed by the enlarged inner perianth segments. Flowers April–June, fruits October–March. Propagated by seeds or tubers. Distributed in western and central Nepal at 1000–2600 m on shady slopes or in dry streambeds; also in Afghanistan, northern India, Bhutan, and western China.

FOOD. Tender leaves and shoots are pickled or mixed with other vegetables for a sour taste.

MEDICINE. Juice of the plant, about 6 teaspoons twice a day, is given in cases of bloody dysentery. Fresh tuber is chewed for throat ache.

OTHER USES. Semidried leaves are given to animals as feed. The root contains 25–30% tannin.

Rumex nepalensis Sprengel

ENGLISH *dock, sheep sorrel* GURUNG *albi, haleto, olvi, ulphi* MAGAR *kelai* NEPALI *hale, halhale, soma* NEWARI *hyamakho ghyan, paswan* SHERPA *dampshima, syoma* TAMANG *albi, alpipi, halil* THARU *dhaldhaliya* TIBETAN *sho-mang, sho-ma-rtsa-ba, syamolhapti, syusodesing*

Polygonaceae. Herb about 1 m high with a stout rootstock. Leaves stalked, 3.5–14 cm long, 1–9 cm wide, entire, lower leaves long-stalked, upper leaves sessile, elliptic to ovate. Flowers bisexual, reddish, in whorls of long racemes. Fruit a nut, brown, fringed with comb-like hooked teeth. Flowers and fruits March–October. Propagated by seeds. Distributed throughout Nepal to about 3300 m, common in open, moist places; also in western Asia, Pakistan, India, Bhutan, Bangladesh, western and central China, southwestern Europe, and Africa.

FOOD. Tender leaves and shoots are cooked as a vegetable or fermented for making *gundruk* (Plate 21).

MEDICINE. The plant is boiled in water about 10 minutes and the filtered water used to wash the body to alleviate body pain. The root is purgative and used as an antidote to food poisoning in cattle. It is boiled with some water, strained, and boiled again until the liquid is about a quarter the original amount, then applied to the area of dislocated bone, which is wrapped with a piece of cloth and bound with four or five strips of bamboo as a splint. Water boiled with the root is dripped into the eye to treat eye troubles. A decoction of the root is given to cattle with diarrhea. Juice of the root, about 4 teaspoons, is given as an anthelmintic and is also useful for cough and colds. A paste of the root is applied to swollen gums.

Juice of the leaves is applied to relieve headaches, but in Bhutan it is used to treat eczema (Anonymous 1973). Squeezed leaves are rubbed slightly over muscular swellings and boils. A paste of the leaves is applied to treat swelling of the gums. In India, leaves are rubbed over the stings of nettles, which inject formic acid (Chopra et al. 1958). According to Coburn (1984), Gurungs of western Nepal boil the leaves and eat them in cases of nausea or dysentery.

OTHER USES. The root contains 5–13% tannin.

Rungia parviflora (Retzius) Nees

Justicia parviflora Retzius
Justicia pectinata Linnaeus
Rungia repens Nees

CHEPANG *chithi, khari jhar, khorseng, pangali jhar* MAJHI *ali jhar* NEPALI *bisaune jhar, kurkure, musaleri, ukuche jhar* NEWARI *ipicha ghyan* TAMANG *kharseni nowa*

Acanthaceae. Diffuse herb. Leaves subsessile, 1.5–5 cm long, 0.5–1.6 cm wide, elliptic to ovate, acute, entire. Flow-

Rumex nepalensis

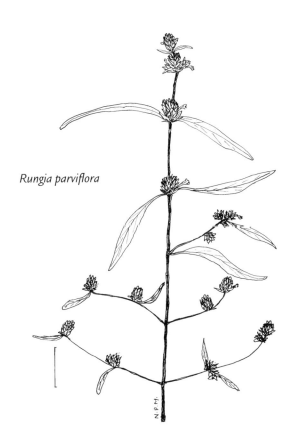

Rungia parviflora

ers blue in axillary and terminal subsessile spikes. Fruit a capsule, ovoid. Flowers and fruits most of the year. Propagated by seeds. Distributed throughout Nepal to about 2000 m in open places and rock crevices; also in India, Sri Lanka, southern China, and Southeast Asia.

FOOD. Young buds are cooked as a vegetable.

MEDICINE. Juice of the plant is applied to cuts and wounds.

OTHER USES. The plant is used to make *marcha,* a fermenting cake from which liquor is distilled.

S

Saccharum officinarum Linnaeus

BHOJPURI *unkh* DANUWAR *ukhu* ENGLISH *sugarcane* GURUNG *usyu* LEPCHA *pam* LIMBU *soo, sotalang* MAGAR *khum* MAJHI *aankhu* MOOSHAR *uinkh* NEPALI *ukhu* NEWARI *tu* RAI *uduwa* SHERPA *gursing* SUNWAR *bich* TAMANG *ukhu, usyup* THARU *khujhi* TIBETAN *bu-ram, ka-ra*

Gramineae. Tall grass, stems with many nodes. Leaves long, linear lanceolate, acuminate, rigid, drooping at the tip. Inflorescence brownish, surrounded by dense silky white hairs. Flowers and fruits October–January. Propagated by cuttings of culms. Distributed throughout Nepal to about 1400 m, cultivated; also in most parts of the world.

FOOD. Juice from the culms is used in the sugar industry. The juice is also drunk and considered good for the stomach.

Saccharum spontaneum Linnaeus

Saccharum canaliculatum Roxburgh
Saccharum semidecumbens Roxburgh
NEPALI *kans*

Gramineae. Perennial grass with erect culms. Leaves linear to filiform. Inflorescence white, about 45 cm long. Flowers and fruits September–November. Propagated by seeds or root offshoots. Distributed throughout Nepal to about 1700 m; also in warmer regions of the world (p. 408).

OTHER USES. The plant is used for thatching and fodder.

Sacciolepis indica (Linnaeus) Chase

Aira indica Linnaeus, *Panicum indicum* (Linnaeus) Linnaeus
NEPALI *kaune banso*

Gramineae. Annual grass with decumbent culms, rooting from the nodes. Leaves linear, with a contracted base. Inflorescence greenish. Flowers and fruits July–December. Propagated by seeds or root offshoots. Distributed in eastern and central Nepal at 200–2100 m in open, sandy places; also in India, tropical Asia, Polynesia, and tropical Australia, Africa, and America (p. 408).

OTHER USES. The plant provides fodder.

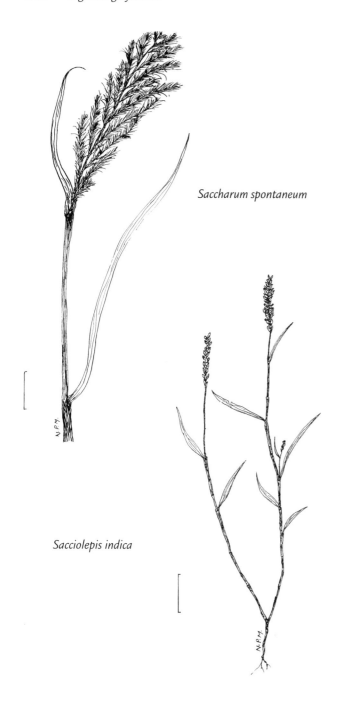

Saccharum spontaneum

Sacciolepis indica

Sagittaria guayanensis

Sagittaria guayanensis Kunth

Liphotocarpus guayanensis (Kunth) Durand & Schinz,
    Lophiocarpus guayanensis (Kunth) Micheli
Alisma hamiltonianum Wallich
Alisma lappula Buchanan-Hamilton ex D. Don
Sagittaria cordifolia Roxburgh
Sagittaria lappula D. Don
Sagittaria triflora Norton
THARU *banarbhega*

Alismataceae. Aquatic herb. Leaves stalked, 2.5–5 cm long, broadly ovate to deeply cordate, obtuse, floating. Flowers white in few irregular whorls. Fruit an achene. Propagated by seeds. Distributed throughout Nepal to about 1300 m on marshy ground; also in India, southern China, Taiwan, Myanmar, Malaysia, and tropical Australia.

MEDICINE. Juice of the plant is applied over the body to normalize fever.

Salix babylonica Linnaeus

Salix japonica Thunberg
NEPALI *bains*

Salicaceae. Medium-sized tree with long, slender, pendulous branches. Leaves stalked, 7–12 cm long, 1–1.7 cm wide, linear lanceolate, acuminate, pubescent when young. Flowers yellowish, February–March. Propagated by seeds or cuttings. Distributed throughout Nepal at 1400–3600 m, generally along stream banks; also in temperate regions of the world.

OTHER USES. The plant has a soil-binding capacity and is used for soil conservation. Thin branches are used to make baskets.

Salix denticulata Anderson

Salix elegans Wallich ex Andersson
Salix himalensis Klotzsch ex Andersson
Salix kamaunensis Lindley
GURUNG *bains* NEPALI *buiset, pasa kath*

Salicaceae. Tree about 6 m high, young stems pubescent. Leaves stalked, alternate, oblong, acuminate, distantly serrulate, glaucous beneath. Inflorescences greenish brown in long spikes. Fruit a capsule, glabrous. Flowers April–May. Propagated by seeds or cuttings. Distributed throughout Nepal at 2400–3000 m along stream banks; also in Afghanistan and northern India.

OTHER USES. The plant is poisonous to sheep.

Salix denticulata

Salomonia cantoniensis Loureiro

Salomonia edentula de Candolle
Salomonia petiolata Buchanan-Hamilton
NEPALI *methi ghans*

Polygalaceae. Annual herb about 20 cm high, stems narrowly winged. Leaves short-stalked, 1–2 cm long, ovate, acuminate, base more or less cordate. Flowers cream or pale violet. Fruit a capsule, ovoid. Flowers July–August,

Salomonia cantoniensis

fruits September–November. Propagated by seeds. Distributed in eastern and central Nepal at 700–1600 m in moist places; also in India, Bhutan, China, northern Myanmar, and Malaysia.

MEDICINE. Juice of the leaves is given in cases of fever.

Salvia hians Royle ex Bentham

TIBETAN *aaibe, ajibe*

Labiatae. Herb about 1 m high, viscidly hairy. Leaves long-stalked, 3.5–11.5 cm long, 2–9 cm wide, ovate to cordate, dentate. Flowers yellowish, July–August. Propagated by seeds. Distributed throughout Nepal at 2600–4100 m in open places at the margins of forested areas; also in Afghanistan and northern India.

FOOD. Pith of tender stems is pickled. Flowers are chewed and have a sweet taste. Roasted seeds are edible.

Salvia nubicola Wallich ex Sweet

Salvia glutinosa subsp. *nubicola* (Wallich ex Sweet) Murata
NEPALI *dhampu, gobre* TIBETAN *aaibe*

Labiatae. Herb about 75 cm high, viscidly hairy. Leaves stalked, 1.5–11.5 cm long, 1.3–6 cm wide, ovate to oblong, acuminate, dentate, hairy, base hastate. Flowers yellow in large spreading panicles. Flowers and fruits June–August. Propagated by seeds. Distributed in western and central Nepal at 2100–3600 m on open, rocky ground; also in Afghanistan, Pakistan, northern India, Bhutan, and Tibet.

FOOD. Roasted seeds are pickled.

MEDICINE. Juice of the root, about 3 teaspoons three times a day, is given in cases of fever.

Salvia officinalis Linnaeus

ENGLISH *sage* NEWARI *kapu swan*

Labiatae. Shrub about 70 cm high. Leaves stalked, opposite, 4–7 cm long, 1.3–2.5 cm wide, lanceolate to cordate, acuminate, minutely dentate, greenish above, white beneath. Flowers purplish or blue-violet. Flowers and fruits March–April. Propagated by seeds. Distributed in central Nepal at 1200–1400 m, planted in kitchen gardens.

MEDICINE. The plant is digestive, carminative, and emmenagogue. Dried leaves can be smoked to give relief in asthma attacks.

Salvia plebeia R. Brown

Salvia brachiata Roxburgh
Salvia parviflora Roxburgh
CHEPANG *ban namsai* NEPALI *ban bawari, kalo pati*

Labiatae. Annual herb about 50 cm high. Leaves stalked, 1.6–8 cm long, 0.7–4 cm wide, ovate to lanceolate, obtuse, crenate to serrate, pubescent or glabrous. Flowers bluish in terminal racemes. Fruit a nutlet, minute, ovoid. Flowers and fruits December–January. Propagated by seeds. Distributed throughout Nepal at 100–1000 m on open, moist ground; also in Afghanistan, Pakistan, northern India, Bhutan, China, Japan, Malaysia, and Australia.

MEDICINE. A paste of the plant is applied to wounds between the toes caused by prolonged walking barefooted in muddy water.

Salvia plebeia

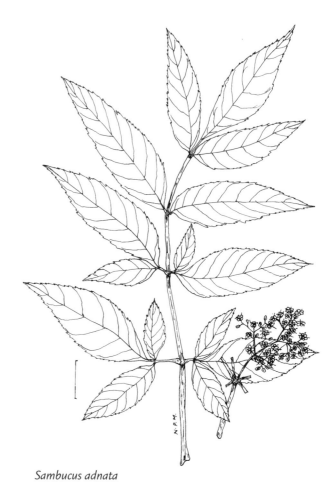

Sambucus adnata

Sambucus adnata Wallich ex de Candolle

ENGLISH *red elderberry* NEPALI *mayakot, moti phul*
NEWARI *jali swan, moti swan* TAMANG *domjo*

Caprifoliaceae. Shrub about 3 m high. Leaves stalked, odd-pinnate, leaflets short-stalked, oblong to lanceolate, acuminate, serrate, puberulent. Flowers white in spreading terminal corymbs. Flowers and fruits May–September. Propagated by cuttings. Distributed throughout Nepal at 2000–3700 m in open places; also in northern India, Bhutan, southern Tibet, and western China.

FOOD. Young shoots and leaves are cooked as a vegetable. Ripe fruits are eaten fresh.

Sanicula elata Buchanan-Hamilton ex D. Don

Sanicula europaea var. *elata* (Buchanan-Hamilton ex D. Don) H. Wolff
Sanicula hermaphrodita Buchanan-Hamilton ex D. Don
CHEPANG *kanchurene* TAMANG *meman*

Umbelliferae. Erect herb about 70 cm high. Leaves long-stalked, palmately divided into three or five segments, segments serrate to crenate, mucronate. Flowers white in umbels. Flowers and fruits May–July. Propagated by seeds. Distributed throughout Nepal at 1600–3500 m

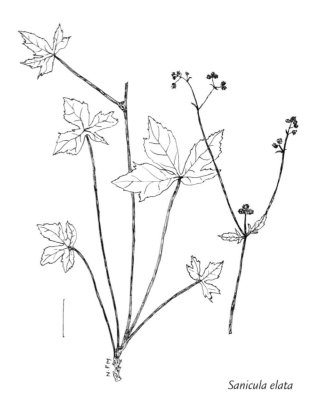

Sanicula elata

in moist, shady places; also in India, Bhutan, China, Malaysia, Europe, and tropical Africa.

MEDICINE. Juice of the root, about 4 teaspoons twice a day, is given in cases of indigestion.

Sapindus mukorossi Gaertner

BHOJPURI *ritha* CHEPANG *ritha* DANUWAR *ritha* ENGLISH *Chinese soap berry, soap nut tree* MAGAR *jharlyang* NEPALI *ritha* NEWARI *hathan* RAI *bhakri, makalawa* SHERPA *chhopra* SUNWAR *kalalgera* TAMANG *gundarasi, ritha* THARU *ritha*

Sapindaceae. Deciduous tree about 10 m high. Leaves stalked, pinnate, leaflets short-stalked, alternate or sub-opposite, 5.5–13 cm long, 2–4 cm wide, lanceolate, entire, smooth, base oblique. Flowers yellowish or purplish. Fruit globose, fleshy, saponaceous. Flowers February–May, fruits October–February. Propagated by seeds. Distributed throughout Nepal at 600–1300 m in open, rocky places; also in northern India, Bhutan, China, Taiwan, Korea, Japan, and Indo-China.

MEDICINE. A lather of the fruit is used to treat burns.

OTHER USES. A common practice among villagers of remote places is to use squeezed fruit mixed in water to wash clothes (Plate 48).

Sapium baccatum Roxburgh

NEPALI *ban pipal*

Euphorbiaceae. Tree with milky sap. Leaves short-stalked, alternate, elliptic, recurved. Flowers greenish. Propagated by seeds or cuttings. Distributed in eastern and central Nepal at 300–1200 m, often planted in gardens and near temples; also in India, Bhutan, Sri Lanka, southern China, and Southeast Asia.

MEDICINE. Latex mixed with mustard oil is applied to muscular swellings.

Sapium insigne (Royle) Bentham ex Hooker fil.

Falconeria insignis Royle
Falconeria wallichiana Royle

CHEPANG *rangati* MAGAR *khirra, mibalang* MAJHI *khirra* NEPALI *khirro* TAMANG *dese, khalung, khyuru*

Euphorbiaceae. Deciduous tree about 10 m high, bark rough, divided into deeply sided furrows with corky ridges. Leaves stalked, crowded toward the ends of branches, 20–35 cm long, 6–13 cm wide, elliptic to oblong, acuminate, serrate, glabrous, glossy on both surfaces, base acute. Flowers yellowish in stout erect spikes. Fruit a capsule. Flowers February–March. Propagated by seeds or cuttings. Distributed throughout Nepal at 500–1800 m among loose rocks or on steep, rocky ground; also in northern India, Sri Lanka, China, and Southeast Asia.

Sapium insigne

Sapindus mukorossi

MEDICINE. Juice of the plant is applied around the navel of a child suffering from diarrhea. Juice of the root is given to cattle with stomach disorders. Juice of the bark is dropped in the wounds of livestock to dispel worms or germs and, therefore, accelerate healing. The milky latex, about two or three drops mixed with a cup of water, is given in cases of indigestion.

OTHER USES. Bark and leaf are used as fish poison.

Saraca asoca (Roxburgh) de Wilde

Jonesia asoca Roxburgh
Saraca indica Linnaeus
NEPALI *ashok*

Leguminosae. Evergreen tree. Leaves stalked, pinnate, leaflets in three to six pairs, stalked, oblong to lanceolate, glabrous. Flowers scarlet in dense corymbs. Fruit a pod, flat. Flowers March–April. Propagated by seeds. Distributed in eastern and central Nepal to about 1400 m, often planted in gardens and near temples; also in India, Sri Lanka, Myanmar, and Malaysia.

MEDICINE. A decoction of bark is astringent and used for urinary infection and menorrhagia. A paste of the flower with water is taken for dysentery.

OTHER USES. The plant is sacred to Buddhists and Hindus.

Sarcococca coriacea (Hooker) Sweet

Sarcococca pruniformis Lindley
Tricera napalensis Wallich, in part
GURUNG *shhyura, radi*   NEPALI *bakhre ghans, fitifiya, telparo*
TAMANG *patape, pibi*

Buxaceae. Shrub about 2 m high. Leaves short-stalked, 2–15 cm long, 0.8–5.5 cm wide, narrowly lanceolate, caudate-acuminate, glabrous. Flowers creamy white in short axillary racemes. Fruit ellipsoidal, black. Flowers January–February, fruits July–August. Propagated by seeds. Distributed in eastern and central Nepal at 600–2000 m in moist, shady places; also in northern India and northern Myanmar.

MEDICINE. Juice of the root, about 2 teaspoons twice a day, is given to treat fever.

OTHER USES. The plant is browsed by goats.

Sarcococca hookeriana Baillon

Sarcococca pruniformis var. *hookeriana* (Baillon) Hooker fil.
GURUNG *chhyanda, chhyudha*   NEPALI *ghyu phul, khursani pate, phirphire, phiti bhi*

Buxaceae. Shrub with green, terete branches. Leaves stalked, alternate, 4–10 cm long, 1–2.5 cm wide, linear lanceolate, acuminate, base acute. Flowers white in racemes. Fruit globose. Flowers and fruits March–September. Propagated by seeds. Distributed throughout Nepal at 1800–3500 m in shady places, sometimes in open pastureland; also in northern India, Bhutan, southern Tibet, and western China.

Saraca asoca

Sarcococca coriacea

MEDICINE. Powdered root is boiled in water and applied in cases of gout.

Sarcococca saligna (D. Don) Mueller Aargau

Buxus saligna D. Don
Sarcococca pruniformis of authors, not Lindley (see *S. coriacea*)
Sarcococca pruniformis var. *angustifolia* Lindley
Tricera napalensis Wallich, in part
GURUNG *chhyunta* NEPALI *fiti fiya*

Buxaceae. Evergreen shrub about 2 m high, bark smooth, green. Leaves stalked, 6–14 cm long, 0.8–2.5 cm wide, lanceolate, long acuminate, glabrous, dark green above, base narrow. Flowers yellowish, fragrant, in short axillary racemes. Fruit a drupe, ovoid, black when ripe. Flowers March–May, fruits June–August. Propagated by seeds. Distributed in western and central Nepal at 1900–2300 m in shady places in oak forests; also in Afghanistan and northern India.

OTHER USES. The plant provides fodder to goats.

Satyrium nepalense D. Don

CHEPANG *kasyegoi* NEPALI *gamdol, thamni* TAMANG *okhal, prabading*

Orchidaceae. Terrestrial orchid. Leaves oblong, acute, base sheathing. Flowers pink, fragrant, September–October. Propagated by seeds or pseudobulbs. Distributed throughout Nepal at 600–4600 m in moist places; also in

northern India, Bhutan, eastern Tibet, Sri Lanka, western China, and northern Myanmar.

FOOD. Pseudobulbs are boiled and eaten. Villagers in Jumla district cook the tender leaves as a vegetable.

Saurauia napaulensis de Candolle

Saurauia paniculata Wallich
Ternstroemia racemosa D. Don
CHEPANG *amsi* GURUNG *gokane, gugun, ona, ondo* MAGAR *gogan, gowan* NEPALI *gogane* RAI *lekbu* TAMANG *aandro, amjur, hamiur*

Actinidiaceae. Tree about 7 m high. Leaves stalked, oblanceolate, sharply acuminate, serrate, rusty tomentose beneath. Flowers stalked, pinkish. Fruit a berry, yellow when ripe. Flowers April–August, fruits January–February. Propagated by seeds or cuttings. Distributed throughout Nepal at 800–2100 m in open places; also in northern India, western China, and Indo-China.

FOOD. Ripe fruits are edible.

MEDICINE. Juice of the bark, about 6 teaspoons four times a day, is given to treat fever. Juice of the fruit, about 6 teaspoons once a day, is given for cough and colds.

OTHER USES. Leaves and twigs are lopped for fodder.

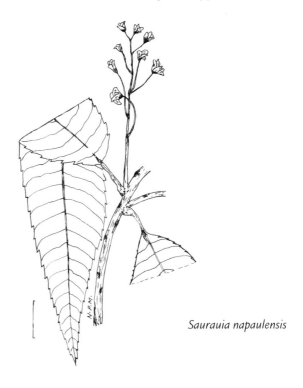

Saurauia napaulensis

Satyrium nepalense

Sauromatum brevipes (Hooker fil.) N. E. Brown

Typhonium brevipes Hooker fil.
Typhonium pedatum Schott
NEPALI *ban karkal*

Araceae. Herb with a tuberous root. Leaves solitary, stalked, divided into lobes, appearing after the flowers. Spathe purplish. Fruit a berry. Flowers July–August. Propagated by tubers. Distributed in western and central Nepal

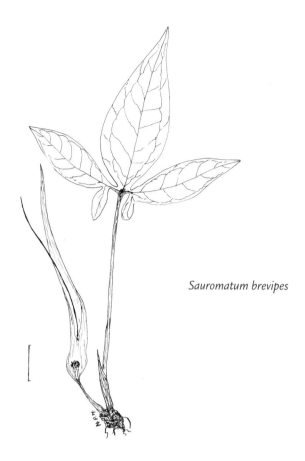

Sauromatum brevipes

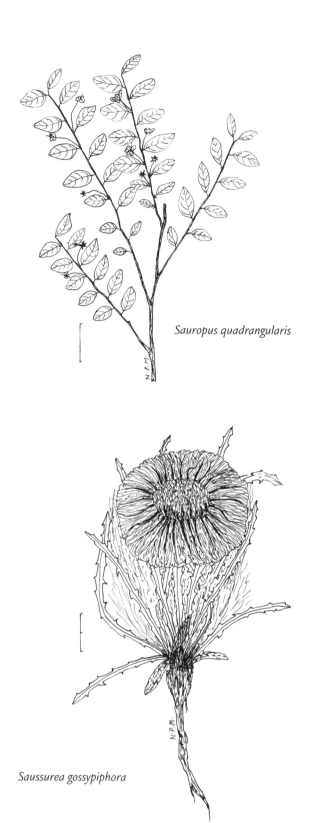

Sauropus quadrangularis

Saussurea gossypiphora

at 2200–2800 m in shady, mossy places; also in northern India.

FOOD. The spathe is cooked as a vegetable, adding some lime juice (*Citrus aurantifolia*), tamarind pulp (*Tamarindus indica*), or other sour substance.

Sauropus quadrangularis (Willdenow) Mueller Aargau

Phyllanthus quadrangularis Willdenow
Sauropus compressus Mueller Aargau
NEPALI *pyaunli*

Euphorbiaceae. Shrub about 1.5 m high. Leaves short-stalked, alternate, elliptic, obtuse or apiculate, entire, glabrous. Flowers solitary, axillary, greenish. Propagated by seeds. Distributed in eastern and central Nepal to about 2100 m in moist places along foot trails; also in northern India, Bhutan, and Indo-China.

MEDICINE. Dried leaf is smoked for tonsillitis.

OTHER USES. Young leaves are poisonous to animals.

Saussurea gossypiphora D. Don

Saussurea gossypina Wallich, *Aplotaxis gossypina* (Wallich) de Candolle
NEPALI *kapase phul* SHERPA *khabal*

Compositae. Annual herb about 30 cm high, rootstock perennial. Leaves sessile, 5–15 cm long, 0.5–1.5 cm wide, lanceolate, distantly dentate or runcinate, usually glabrous above, densely woolly beneath, tapering toward the base. Flower heads purple, concealed by woolly hairs. Fruit an achene. Flowers July–October. Propagated by seeds. Distributed throughout Nepal at 3800–5200 m in open alpine pastureland; also in northern India, Bhutan, southern Tibet, and southwestern China.

MEDICINE. Juice of the root is given to treat fever, cough, asthma, and dysentery. It is also considered to have an appetizing property.

OTHER USES. The plant is considered sacred by Nepalese people, especially Buddhist Lamas of the alpine region.

Saussurea heteromalla (D. Don) Handel-Mazzetti

Cnicus heteromallus D. Don
Aplotaxis candicans de Candolle, *Saussurea candicans* (de Candolle) Schultz Bipontinus
NEPALI *bhukur*

Compositae. Herb about 1.5 cm high. Basal leaves ovate to oblong, lyrate, narrowed into a short stalk, sinuately dentate, white tomentose beneath, cauline leaves sessile, smaller, oblanceolate, white tomentose beneath. Flower heads pink in panicled corymbs. Fruit an achene. Flowers and fruits March–June. Propagated by seeds. Distributed in western and central Nepal at 600–4000 m in open places; also in Afghanistan, northern Pakistan, northwestern India, and Bhutan.

MEDICINE. Juice of the root is given in cases of diarrhea and dysentery. Seeds are carminative.

Saussurea roylei (de Candolle) Schultz Bipontinus

Aplotaxis roylei de Candolle
TIBETAN *lhapcha*

Compositae. Herb. Leaves short-stalked or sessile, 7–19 cm long, 2–5 cm wide, linear lanceolate, long-pointed, white woolly beneath. Flower heads dark purple. Fruit an achene. Flowers and fruits July–September. Propagated by seeds. Distributed in western and central Nepal at 3000–4900 m in open slopes; also in northern India.

MEDICINE. A paste of the plant is applied to relieve joint aches.

Schefflera venulosa (Wight & Arnott) Harms

Paratropia venulosa Wight & Arnott, *Heptapleurum venulosum* (Wight & Arnott) Seemann
Aralia digitata Roxburgh
Schefflera elliptica Harms
NEPALI *dang dinge, kursimal*

Araliaceae. Climbing evergreen shrub. Leaves long-stalked, alternate, three- or five-foliolate, leaflets short-stalked, 8–20 cm long, 3–8.5 cm wide, elliptic to oblong, entire, glabrous, middle leaflet largest. Flowers cream in globose umbels. Fruit globose, yellow. Flowers January–February, fruits April–May. Propagated by seeds or cuttings. Distributed throughout Nepal at 300–1800 m in open, sunny places; also in India, Bhutan, western and southern China, and Southeast Asia.

FOOD. Ripe fruits are eaten fresh, especially by children.

MEDICINE. Leaves are given as feed fed to animals with conjunctivitis and other eye troubles.

OTHER USES. The plant provides fodder.

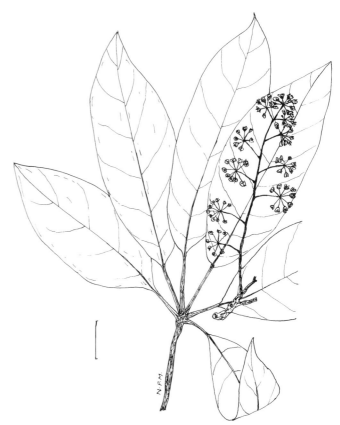

Schefflera venulosa

Schima wallichii (de Candolle) Korthals

Gordonia wallichii de Candolle
Gordonia chilaunea Buchanan-Hamilton ex D. Don
CHEPANG *chyangsi* ENGLISH *needle wood* GURUNG *kyosin, nash* LIMBU *yangsingba* MAGAR *hyansing* NEPALI *chilaune, nini* NEWARI *gwechasim* RAI *yangsung* TAMANG *kyasim*

Theaceae. Evergreen tree 25 m high. Leaves stalked, 5–18 cm long, 2–8 cm wide, oblong to lanceolate, acuminate, entire, glabrous above, pubescent beneath. Flowers white, fragrant. Fruit a capsule, globose, supported by the persistent calyx. Flowers March–July, fruits July–January. Propagated by seeds. Distributed throughout Nepal at 700–2100 m in open places; also in northern India, Bhutan, southern Tibet, Bangladesh, eastward to western China, Myanmar, and Sumatra.

MEDICINE. On my field trip in 1985, I slipped down a big rock on my way to the village of Bhainse, Kaski district, and was bleeding from my left leg because of the fall. My porters had gone ahead to prepare food, carrying all my belongings except my camera, including the few emergency medicines I had. A villager passing by told me that such wounds were quite common for him and said he would look for a plant-based medicine. In a way I was afraid, but at the same time I was curious to know about his treatment. He brought bark of *Schima wallichii*,

Schima wallichii

but with small distant teeth. Flowers stalked, drooping, white, fragrant. Fruit globose, sessile, red, fleshy, two-seeded. Flowers April–May, fruits August–October. Propagated by seeds or cuttings. Distributed throughout Nepal at 1700–3300 m, frequent in mixed forest; also in northern India and Bhutan.

MEDICINE. Ripe fruits are edible.

Schisandra grandiflora

pounded it with his sickle on a stone (Plate 29), and gently applied the paste to my wound. He also told me to keep the affected part dry and to remove the paste when the wound healed, which would take about a week. Indeed, the wound was cured within a week, and there is still a small scar on my leg. This treatment for cuts and wounds is prevalent in most parts of Nepal.

Powdered bark is given to animals to treat liver flukes. Juice of the plant is taken in cases of gastric trouble and peptic ulcer. It is also applied for gonorrhea. The juice, mixed with bark juice of *Plumeria rubra*, is given to cattle with stomach disorders. This juice is given to animals as an anthelmintic in the eastern part of Nepal. Coburn (1984) reported that Gurungs of western Nepal apply crushed root to scorpion bites. Storrs and Storrs (1984) reported that young leaves and roots are used for fever.

OTHER USES. Wood is moderately hard and used as timber for construction and many other useful purposes. It is also used for fuel, hence villagers are interested in planting this tree on their private land. Bark and leaf are used as fish poison. Flowers are used to make *marcha*, a fermenting cake from which liquor is distilled.

Schisandra grandiflora (Wallich) Hooker fil. & Thomson

Kadsura grandiflora Wallich, *Sphaerostema grandiflora* (Wallich) Blume

NEPALI *pahenlo singulto, singhata lahara, theki phul*

Schisandraceae. Trailing herb. Leaves stalked, alternate or clustered, ovate or oblanceolate, pointed, nearly entire

Schisandra propinqua (Wallich) Baillon

Kadsura propinqua Wallich, *Sphaerostema propinqua* (Wallich) Blume

NEPALI *pahinlo singulto*

Schisandraceae. Woody climber. Leaves stalked, alternate, oblanceolate, serrate, glabrous. Flowers yellow, solitary, July–August. Propagated by seeds or cuttings. Distributed in eastern and central Nepal at 1600–2100 m in moist, open places; also in India.

MEDICINE. Juice of the root is given in cases of fever.

Schleichera oleosa (Loureiro) Oken

Pistacia oleosa Loureiro
Schleichera trijuga Willdenow

ENGLISH *Ceylon oak, jacassar, lac tree* NEPALI *kusum* SATAR *baru*

Sapindaceae. Tree about 25 m high. Leaves stalked, pinnate, leaflets in two to four pairs, subsessile, 6–26 cm long, 3–9 cm wide, oblong to elliptic, entire, glabrous. Flowers short-stalked, yellowish, in lateral racemes appearing with new purple foliage. Fruit ovoid, greenish when ripe. Flowers February–March, fruits June–August. Propagated by seeds. Distributed throughout Nepal to about 300 m in mixed *Shorea robusta* forest; also in Afghanistan, Pakistan, India, Myanmar, Sri Lanka, Thailand, and Malaysia.

FOOD. The pulpy aril of ripe fruit is edible and has a pleasant acidic taste. Seed oil is used for cooking and for lighting.

MEDICINE. Juice of the bark is used for leprotic ruptures, skin diseases, and ulcers. Pulp of the fruit is astringent and appetite inducing. Oil from the seed is applied for skin diseases, rashes on the skin, and is supposed to be good for massaging in cases of rheumatism. G. L. Shah and Gopal (1982) reported from India that the oil promotes growth of hair lost through baldness and relieves headaches and colds.

OTHER USES. The plant is lopped for fodder. Wood is very hard and used for construction, furniture, and many other household purposes.

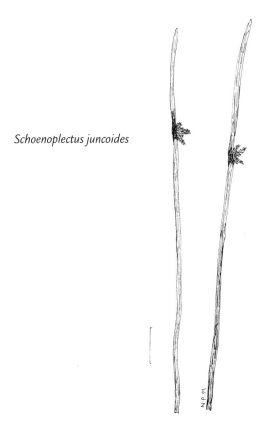

Schoenoplectus juncoides

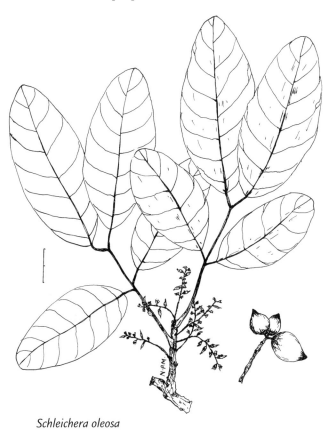

Schleichera oleosa

Schoenoplectus juncoides (Roxburgh) Palla

Scripus juncoides Roxburgh
Scripus erectus Poiret
Scripus junciformis Nees
NEPALI *arbaje jhar, dadu jhar, pani mothe*

Cyperaceae. Annual or perennial herb about 50 cm high, stem terete, sheaths punctate with red dots, throat oblique. Leaves short, linear, blade red-dotted, midvein distinct. Inflorescence greenish or brown. Fruit a nut, obovoid, straw colored. Flowers and fruits June–December. Propagated by seeds or root offshoots. Distributed throughout Nepal to about 2700 m in marshy and sunny places; also in India, China, Southeast Asia, and Japan.

OTHER USES. The plant is used to weave mats and provides fodder.

Schoenoplectus mucronatus (Linnaeus) Palla

Scripus mucronatus Linnaeus
Scripus javanus Nees
Scripus muticatus D. Don
Scripus triangulatus Roxburgh
NEPALI *thulo mothe*

Cyperaceae. Tufted herb about 75 cm high, stems stout, triquetrous, nearly leafless. Leaves like continuations of the stem, three-angled. Inflorescence chestnut color. Fruit a nut, obovoid, somewhat compressed, unequally three-angled, shiny black. Propagated by seeds or root offshoots. Distributed in eastern and central Nepal at 400–2000 m in moist, open places; also in India, China, Southeast Asia, and Japan.

OTHER USES. The plant is used to prepare mats and provides fodder.

Scindapsus officinalis (Roxburgh) Schott

Pothos officinalis Roxburgh
CHEPANG *yuk maisai* NEPALI *kanchini, kanchirru* TAMANG *chipalan, magar muja, mam derga*

Araceae. Epiphyte climbing shrub, rooting freely from the stem, marked with annular scars of fallen leaves. Leaves stalked, 12–25 cm long, 7–15 cm wide, elliptic to ovate, caudate-acuminate, entire, sheathing at the base, base obliquely rounded or more or less cordate. Flowers yellowish. Fruit a berry, fleshy. Flowers July–August, fruits September–November. Propagated by seeds or root offshoots. Distributed throughout Nepal to about 1200 m, trailing on tree trunks and branches; also in India and Indo-China.

FOOD. Roasted seeds are edible.

MEDICINE. Juice of the stem is applied externally around the ear to treat swellings of the ear. Juice of the fruit is given to calves as an anthelmintic.

Scleria biflora

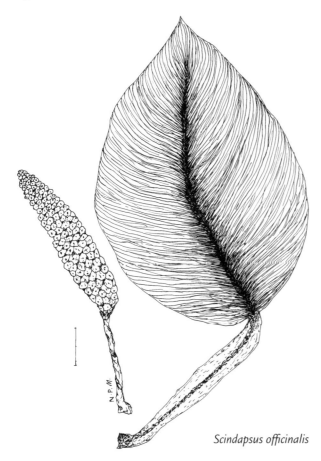

Scindapsus officinalis

Scoparia dulcis

Scleria biflora Roxburgh

NEPALI *karante jhar*

Cyperaceae. Annual herb about 50 cm high, stem triquetrous. Leaves rosulate at the base, linear, 4–22 cm long, flat. Sheaths three-sided, loosely surrounding the culm, narrowly winged. Inflorescence brownish. Fruit a nutlet. Flowers and fruits August–September. Propagated by seeds or root offshoots. Distributed in central Nepal at 800–1000 m in open places; also in India, Sri Lanka, southern China, the Ryukyu Islands, and Indo-China.

OTHER USES. The plant provides fodder.

Scoparia dulcis Linnaeus

CHEPANG *man* DANUWAR *bonphula, chinijhar, nang*
ENGLISH *sweet broom* NEPALI *chini jhar, mirmire jhar, salle jhar*
TAMANG *chini mran*

Scrophulariaceae. Erect shrub about 1 m high. Leaves short-stalked, 0.8–4 cm long, 0.2–1.8 cm wide, ternately whorled, sometimes opposite, lanceolate, serrate. Flowers white. Fruit a capsule, subglobose. Flowers and fruits most of the year. Propagated by seeds. Distributed throughout Nepal to about 1300 m, common on uncultivated land; also in tropical Asia.

MEDICINE. Juice of the plant, about 2 teaspoons three times a day, is given to treat blood-mixed cough, and the juice is also considered useful for fever. A paste of the plant boiled in mustard oil is applied to boils. A paste of the root, about 2 teaspoons twice a day, is given for fever and dysentery. Juice of the leaves is applied to the forehead to treat headaches.

Scopolia stramonifolia (Wallich) T. B. Shrestha

Physalis stramonifolia Wallich
Anisodus luridus Link & Otto, *Scopolia lurida* (Link & Otto) Dunal
Nicandra anomala Link & Otto
NEPALI *wangal* TIBETAN *langtang kabo*

Solanaceae. Erect herb. Leaves stalked, 5–27 cm long, 2–15 cm wide, ovate to lanceolate, acute at both ends, membranous, stellately hairy beneath. Flowers greenish, nodding, June–July. Propagated by seeds. Distributed throughout Nepal at 2500–3800 m in open, moist grasslands; also in northern India, Bhutan, and southwestern China.

MEDICINE. Some seeds are cast onto the fire and the smoke emitted is inhaled to treat wounds inside the nose.

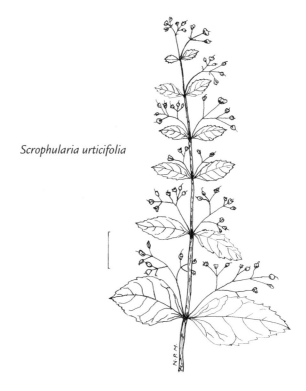

Scrophularia urticifolia

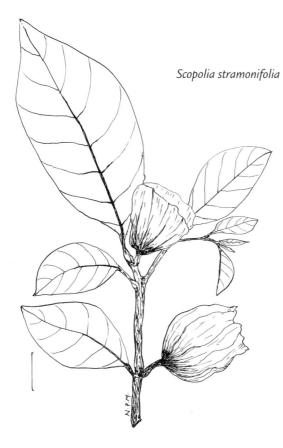

Scopolia stramonifolia

Scurrula elata (Edgeworth) Danser

Loranthus elatus Edgeworth
NEPALI *ainjero* TAMANG *nai*

Loranthaceae. Woody parasite. Leaves stalked, 3.5–12.5 cm long, 1–5 cm wide, ovate, acute, glabrous. Flowers red, umbellate or fascicled, the peduncles short, October–November. Propagated by seeds. Distributed throughout Nepal at 1600–2700 m, generally on shrubs and trees; also in India, Bhutan, Tibet, and western China.

FOOD. Ripe fruits are edible.

Scrophularia urticifolia Wallich ex Bentham

NEPALI *bandar puchhare, mokhi ghan* TAMANG *nowa, slitanghape*

Scrophulariaceae. Shrub about 1 m high. Leaves stalked, opposite, cordate to ovate, acuminate, coarsely dentate. Flowers white in axillary and terminal cymes, July–August. Propagated by seeds. Distributed throughout Nepal at 1500–2800 m in moist, open pastureland; also in India and Bhutan.

MEDICINE. Juice of the leaves is applied to boils and wounds.

Scurrula elata

Scurrula parasitica Linnaeus

Loranthus scurrula Linnaeus

CHEPANG *tinet* MAGAR *hajar* NEPALI *ainjeru, liso* TAMANG *nai*

Loranthaceae. Parasitic shrub, young parts tomentose. Leaves stalked, opposite, 1.5–3 cm long, 0.5–1.5 cm wide, elliptic or ovate to oblong, obtuse or acute, leathery, rusty tomentose on both surfaces when young, glabrous above at maturity. Flowers red in dense axillary fascicles. Fruit pear shaped. Flowers and fruits November–April. Propagated by seeds. Distributed throughout Nepal to about 2200 m on forest trees; also in northern India, Bhutan, Sri Lanka, China, and Southeast Asia.

FOOD. Ripe fruits are edible and sweet.

Scutellaria barbata D. Don

Scutellaria peregrina Roxburgh
Scutellaria ruvularis Wallich ex Bentham

NEPALI *babre ghans, nilo butte ghans* TAMANG *dhapre*

Labiatae. Rambling herb about 30 cm high. Lower leaves stalked, upper leaves sessile, 0.6–2.5 cm long, 0.2–1.4 cm wide, ovate or lanceolate, obtuse, entire, minutely hairy on the margin. Flowers axillary, blue, in slender spikes. Fruit a nutlet, black, granular. Flowers and fruits April–August. Propagated by seeds. Distributed in eastern and central Nepal at 1300–1500 m in moist places; also in India, Bhutan, China, and Myanmar.

MEDICINE. Juice of the plant is applied to cuts and wounds.

Scutellaria discolor Colebrooke

Scutellaria indica Blume

CHEPANG *ghunro* ENGLISH *skull cup* GURUNG *ratopate*
NEPALI *dampate, nil pate, parbata phul, ratapate*
TAMANG *bala mran, mambu wala, surchenti, uttim noba, wala mran*

Labiatae. Herb about 35 cm high. Leaves basal, stalked, 2–5 cm long and wide, broadly elliptic, orbiculate, crenate, tip rounded. Flowers violet in long slender racemes. Flowers and fruits May–November. Propagated by seeds. Distributed throughout Nepal at 700–2400 m; also in northern India, Bhutan, southwestern China, and Southeast Asia.

MEDICINE. Juice of the plant is applied to wounds between the toes caused by prolonged walking barefooted in muddy water during the rainy season. This juice, about 2 teaspoons twice a day, is given in cases of fever. Root, mixed with leaves of *Cynodon dactylon* and *Justicia adhatoda*, is boiled in water about 15 minutes, and the filtered water, about 4 teaspoons twice a day, is given for fever. Juice of the root, about 4 teaspoons twice a day, is given to treat indigestion and gastric trouble.

Scutellaria repens Buchanan-Hamilton ex D. Don

Scutellaria cana Wallich ex Bentham
Scutellaria wallichiana A. Hamilton

NEPALI *charpate* TAMANG *aamnyai, kudu mran, nakchhi sursomba*

Labiatae. Shrub about 2 m high. Leaves stalked, 0.8–2.5 cm long, ovate, acuminate, lower leaves usually coarsely

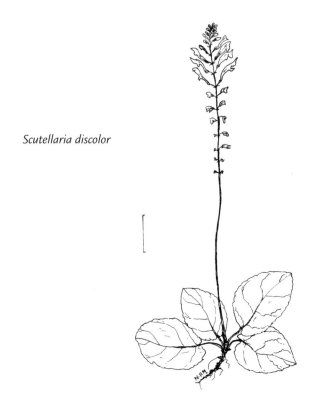

Scutellaria discolor

crenate, upper leaves entire, minutely hairy beneath, base acute. Flowers yellowish, tinged with pink, axillary in bracts of the leaves. Fruit a nutlet, minute, blue. Flowers February–April, fruits July–August. Propagated by seeds. Distributed throughout Nepal at 600–2100 m in open areas in rock crevices; also in northern India, Bhutan, and Myanmar.

FOOD. Fresh roots are chewed by wood-cutters and shepherds. Tender shoots and leaves are cooked as a vegetable.

MEDICINE. Juice of the plant, about 6 teaspoons three times a day, is given in cases of fever.

Scutellaria scandens Buchanan-Hamilton ex D. Don

Scutellaria angulosa Bentham
Scutellaria celtidifolia A. Hamilton

NEPALI *charpate, kankarne, miro, pani jhar* TAMANG *nal sal*

Labiatae. Herb with diffuse branches. Leaves short-stalked, 1.5–8 cm long, 0.6–4.5 cm wide, ovate to lanceolate, coarsely crenate. Flowers yellowish in lax axillary and terminal racemes, March–May. Propagated by seeds. Distributed throughout Nepal at 1200–3000 m in shady places; also in northwestern India.

MEDICINE. Juice of the plant is applied to cuts and wounds, and dropped in the ear to relieve earaches. This juice, about 3 teaspoons three times a day, is given to treat fever and stomachaches. Juice of the root is applied for backache. It is also fed to domestic animals to prevent miscarriage.

Scutellaria violacea Heyne ex Bentham

Scutellaria violacea var. *sikkimensis* Hooker fil.
NEPALI *kalo bheri*

Labiatae. Herb. Leaves stalked, 1.8–5.5 cm long, 0.6–3 cm wide, lanceolate, acute, dentate, glabrous, rounded toward the base. Flowers yellowish. Flowers and fruits April–August. Propagated by seeds. Distributed throughout Nepal at 1400–3000 m on exposed slopes in pine forest; also in northern India, Bhutan, and Sri Lanka.

MEDICINE. Juice of the plant is applied to cuts and wounds.

Sechium edule (Jacquin) Swartz

Chayota edulis Jacquin
ENGLISH *chayote, cho cho, christophine* MAGAR *desi name*
NEPALI *iskus* NEWARI *iskul* TAMANG *kadilo*

Cucurbitaceae. Climber with a perennial rootstock. Leaves stalked, orbiculate. Flowers yellow. Fruit pear shaped, with a distal short spine. Flowers and fruits July–November. Propagated by seeds. Distributed throughout Nepal to about 2000 m, planted on moist ground; also in the tropics.

FOOD. Boiled root tubers are eaten like yams. Fruits are cooked as a vegetable.

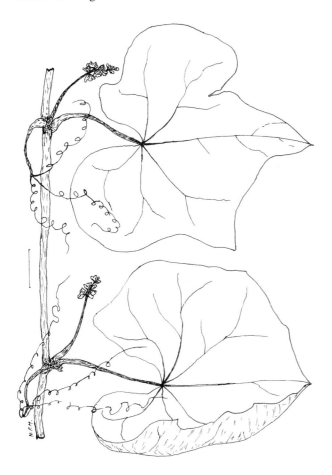

Sechium edule

Securinega virosa (Roxburgh ex Willdenow) Baillon

Phyllanthus virosus Roxburgh ex Willdenow
Fluggea microcarpa Blume
Phyllanthus glauca Wallich
Phyllanthus griseus Wallich
CHEPANG *wakarang* NEPALI *nundhiki, paileti, sano nundhiki*

Euphorbiaceae. Straggling shrub about 5 m high. Leaves stalked, alternate, elliptic to ovate, glabrous. Flowers yellowish in axillary clusters. Fruit a capsule, ovoid, fleshy. Flowers and fruits May–June. Propagated by seeds. Distributed throughout Nepal to about 1800 m in subtropical forest; also in northern India, Bhutan, Sri Lanka, Japan, Southeast Asia, Polynesia, Australia, and tropical Africa.

FOOD. Ripe fruits are eaten fresh.

MEDICINE. The bark is astringent.

OTHER USES. Squeezed bark is spread on stagnant water to intoxicate fish.

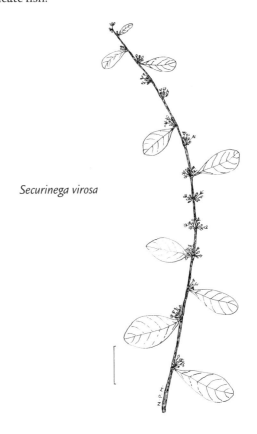

Securinega virosa

Sedum wallichianum Hooker

Rhodiola wallichiana (Hooker) Fu
Sedum asiaticum de Candolle
Sedum crassipes Wallich ex Hooker fil. & Thomson,
    Chamaerhodiola crassipes (Wallich ex Hooker fil. & Thomson)
    Nakai ex Nakai & Kitagawa, *Rhodiola crassipes* (Wallich
    ex Hooker fil. & Thomson) A. Borissova
TAMANG *amba singh*

Crassulaceae. Tufted herb about 35 cm high, with a thick rootstock. Leaves 0.5–3.5 cm long, 1–2 cm wide, linear, acute, entire, glabrous. Flowers yellow in dense corymbose cymes. Propagated by seeds. Distributed throughout Nepal to about 3300–4200 m in moist places, generally under shrubs and trees; also in India, Bhutan, and Tibet.

MEDICINE. Juice of the plant is applied to burns and wounds.

Sedum wallichianum

Selaginella involvens

Selaginella chrysocaulos (Hooker & Greville) Spring
TAMANG *kaldar*

Selaginellaceae. Spore-bearing herb. Stem slender, bright yellow, usually rooting at the stoloniferous base, branches short, pinnately decompound. Leaves oblique, ovate, bright green, membranous, finely serrulate. Spikes short, at the tips of branches. Sporophylls crowded, with large cups. Spores June–July. Propagated by spores. Distributed throughout Nepal at 300–2600 m in shady places.

MEDICINE. A paste of the plant is applied to cuts and wounds.

Selaginella involvens (Swartz) Spring
GURUNG *tana* NEPALI *simrik jhar*

Selaginellaceae. Spore-bearing herb. Stem slender, weak. Leaves scaly, ovate, pointed. Spikes at the tips of branches. Sporophylls crowded. Propagated by spores. Distributed throughout Nepal at 1000–3200 m on mossy tree trunks and branches, or rocks; also in India, Bhutan, and southern China.

OTHER USES. A powder of the spores is used on the forehead of a Nepalese woman, signifying her status as married, as a substitute for vermilion powder (*sindur* in Nepali).

Selinum candollii de Candolle
Peucedanum wallichianum de Candolle, *Selinum wallichianum* (de Candolle) Raizada & Saxena
NEPALI *bhutkesh, chhatadre* TIBETAN *nanicha*

Umbelliferae. Herb about 1 m high. Leaves stalked, bipinnate, leaflets deeply lobed, glabrous, spiny. Flowers white, July–August. Fruits October–November. Propagated by seeds. Distributed throughout Nepal at 3000–3800 m among bamboo and shrubs on steep slopes; also in northern India.

FOOD. Seeds are used as a spice.

OTHER USES. Roots are used for incense.

Selinum tenuifolium Wallich ex C. B. Clarke
Oreocome filicifolia Edgeworth
Selinum candollii Edgeworth, not de Candolle
NEPALI *ban sampu, bhut kesh, jwane ghans* TIBETAN *manancha*

Umbelliferae. Herb about 1.5 m high. Leaves stalked, tripinnate, leaflets pinnatifid, ultimate segments lanceolate, acute to mucronate. Bracts linear, densely hairy. Flowers white in compound umbels. Flowers and fruits July–November. Propagated by seeds. Distributed throughout Nepal at 2500–4800 m in open, rocky places; also in northern India and Tibet.

FOOD. Tender leaves and shoots are cooked as a vegetable. Seeds are used as a spice in place of coriander (*Coriandrum sativum*) and cumin (*Cuminum cyminum*).

MEDICINE. A paste of the root mixed with water is taken to relieve body pain and fever.

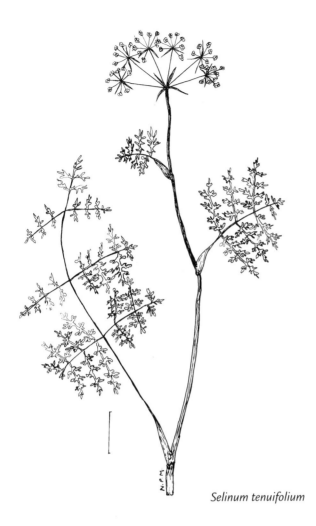

Selinum tenuifolium

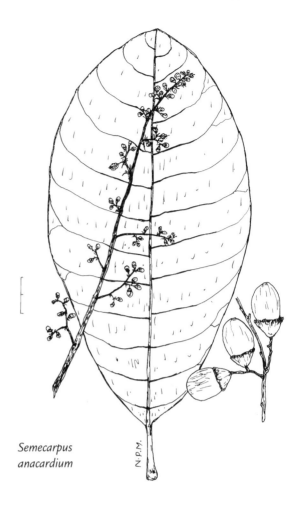

Semecarpus anacardium

Semecarpus anacardium Linnaeus fil.

CHEPANG *tingsi* ENGLISH *marking nut tree* GURUNG *khur dan* LEPCHA *konghi* MAJHI *bhalay* NEPALI *bhalayo* RAI *kholaksi* SATAR *soso* TAMANG *baral* THARU *bhela, kumbh* TIBETAN *bse-shing*

Anacardiaceae. Tree about 10 m high. Leaves stalked, alternate, 13–45 cm long, 6–26 cm wide, ovate to oblong, entire, glabrous, apex rounded, narrowed toward the base. Flowers yellowish in simple terminal panicles. Fruit a drupe, oblong, black, shiny when ripe, seated on a fleshy orange cup. Flowers May–October, fruits November–March. Propagated by seeds. Distributed throughout Nepal to about 1700 m; also in India, Bhutan, Bangladesh, Myanmar, and northern Australia.

FOOD. Roasted fruit rinds are eaten by local people.

MEDICINE. A paste or juice of the fruit is used for bronchitis, dysentery, fever, asthma, and hemorrhoids. Juice of the root is considered good in causing sterility in women. Latex is applied to treat headaches, skin diseases, and scabies. Ripe fruits are digestive, stimulant, and aphrodisiac. According to Damle (1977), juice of the kernels has been tested as a possible anticancer agent. A paste of the seed mixed with honey, 2 teaspoons twice a day, is taken to treat gastric troubles. Juice of the seed is applied in cases of ringworm and severely chapped feet. Oil from the seed is used to treat skin eruptions.

OTHER USES. Seeds yield tannin and juice of the seed, mixed with powdered burned shells of a mollusk (*chun* in Nepali), is used as a clothes-marking ink by washermen.

Senecio cappa Buchanan-Hamilton ex D. Don

Senecio densiflorus Wallich ex de Candolle
NEPALI *barkhe kane*

Compositae. Perennial shrub about 2 m high. Leaves stalked, broadly elliptic, hairy above, margin dentate. Flower heads yellow, in terminal branched clusters. Fruit an achene. Flowers and fruits September–November. Propagated by seeds. Distributed in eastern and central Nepal at 1300–2900 m, common in shrubby areas of forests; also in northern India, Bhutan, western China, and northern Myanmar.

MEDICINE. Juice of the root, about 4 teaspoons three times a day, is given to treat fever. A paste of the leaves is applied to treat boils.

OTHER USES. The plant is used to make *marcha*, a fermenting cake from which liquor is distilled.

Senecio chrysanthemoides de Candolle

Senecio jacobaea Linnaeus
NEPALI *bijauri phul*

Compositae. Herb about 2 m high. Leaves clasping the stem, alternate, 3–15 cm long, lyrate, irregularly lobed or dentate. Flower heads yellow in large terminal corymbs. Fruit an achene, glabrous. Flowers and fruits August–October. Propagated by seeds. Distributed throughout Nepal at 1400–4000 m in moist, shady places; also in northwestern Pakistan, India, and southern China.

MEDICINE. An infusion of the root is given in cases of indigestion.

Senecio diversifolius Wallich ex de Candolle

Senecio raphanifolius Wallich ex de Candolle
NEPALI *marcha* TAMANG *chenti, kadik mhendo, pramji*

Compositae. Shrub about 1 m high. Leaves all cauline, sessile, lyrate, lobes oblong, acute. Flower heads yellow in a corymb. Fruit an achene. Flowers and fruits October–February. Propagated by seeds. Distributed throughout Nepal at 2300–4000 m in moist, shady places; also in northern India, Bhutan, and northern Myanmar.

OTHER USES. The plant is used for animal beds. It is also used to prepare *marcha,* a cake fermented with yeast, from which liquor is distilled.

Senecio wallichii de Candolle

Senecio detataus Wallich
NEPALI *mohini jhar* TAMANG *banno ba* TIBETAN *tasyu*

Compositae. Herb about 50 cm high. Leaves all basal, long-stalked, ovate to cordate, sinuate and dentate, acuminate, sparsely hairy. Flower heads yellow in corymbs. Fruit an achene. Flowers and fruits September–November. Propagated by seeds. Distributed in eastern and central Nepal at 1500–3300 m in moist, shady places under trees; also in northern India, Bhutan, and northern Myanmar.

MEDICINE. A paste of the root is applied to treat headaches and joint aches.

Sesamum orientale Linnaeus

Sesamum indicum Linnaeus
CHEPANG *nimso* ENGLISH *benne, gingelly, sesame* MAGAR *min*
MAJHI *til* NEPALI *til* NEWARI *hamo* TAMANG *grangasa*
TIBETAN *spri-nag, ti-la-dkar, zar-ma*

Pedaliaceae. Annual herb about 1.5 m high. Leaves stalked, opposite or alternate, ovate to oblong. Flowers solitary, axillary, pinkish white. Fruit a capsule. Flowers July–August. Propagated by seeds. Distributed throughout Nepal to about 2400 m in open, sunny places, cultivated; also in Pakistan, India, Bhutan, Sri Lanka, eastern Asia, and warm regions of the world.

FOOD. Seeds are eaten in the form of sweetmeats, and roasted seeds are used in pickles. Oil from the seeds is used for culinary purposes.

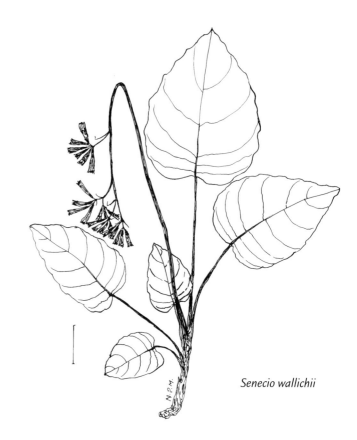

Senecio wallichii

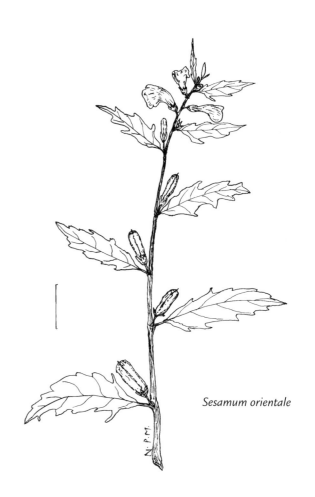

Sesamum orientale

MEDICINE. A paste of the seeds is used in cases of hemorrhoids. Seed oil is valued for treating dysentery and urinary complaints.

OTHER USES. Oil from the seeds is used for lighting and manufacture of soap.

Sesbania grandiflora (Linnaeus) Poiret

Robinia grandiflora Linnaeus, *Aeschynomene grandiflora* (Linnaeus) Linnaeus, *Agati grandiflora* (Linnaeus) Desvaux
NEPALI *agasti phul, dhaincha* TIBETAN *po-son-cha*

Leguminosae. Shrub about 10 m high. Leaves stalked, pinnate, leaflets in 20–40 pairs, short-stalked, entire. Flowers large, white or pinkish. Fruit a pod, linear, somewhat curved, many-seeded. Flowers December–January. Propagated by seeds. Distributed in eastern and central parts of Nepal to about 250 m, cultivated; also in Pakistan, India, Bhutan, Myanmar, Thailand, Indonesia, northern Australia, the Philippines, Mauritius, and tropical Africa.

FOOD. Young leaves, flowers, and pods are eaten as a vegetable and pickled.

MEDICINE. A paste of the root is applied for rheumatism. Bark is astringent and febrifuge, and the juice, about 4 teaspoons three times a day, is given in cases of fever, diarrhea, and dysentery. The leaf is aperient and diuretic. Juice of leaves and flowers is taken for nasal catarrh and headaches. The flower is emollient and laxative.

OTHER USES. Bark yields tannin.

Sesbania sesban (Linnaeus) Merrill

Aeschynomene sesban Linnaeus
Sesbania aegyptiacus Poiret, *Sesban aegyptiacus* Persoon
NEPALI *dhandiain, jaita* NEWARI *laxmi swan*

Leguminosae. Soft-wooded, short-lived shrub about 5 m high with short terete branches. Leaves stalked, 7.5–15 cm long, even-pinnate, leaflets in 8–20 pairs, short-stalked, 1.5–2.5 cm long, 0.3–0.5 cm wide, linear oblong, glabrous, pale green. Flowers pale yellow, axillary, in 6- to 10-flowered racemes. Fruit a pod, torulose, twisted, 20- to 30-seeded. Flowers August–September, fruits December–February. Propagated by seeds. Distributed in eastern Nepal at 200–400 m in moist places; also in tropical Asia and Africa.

MEDICINE. A paste of the leaves is applied for rheumatism and muscular swelling. Juice of the seed is used for itches and other skin diseases.

OTHER USES. The plant is used as green manure. Fiber from the bark is used to make ropes. Leaves and tender branches serve as cattle fodder. The flower or leaf is offered to the goddess Laxmi during the festival of Tihar.

Setaria glauca (Linnaeus) Palisot de Beauvois

Panicum glaucum Linnaeus, *Pennisetum glaucum* (Linnaeus) R. Brown
CHEPANG *aayam muja* ENGLISH *cattail millet* NEPALI *bale banso, bandra ghans, kut banso* THARU *banara* TIBETAN *ma-ma-sgog-lchags*

Gramineae. Annual grass about 30 cm high. Leaves ciliate at the base, hairy on the upper surface, glaucous

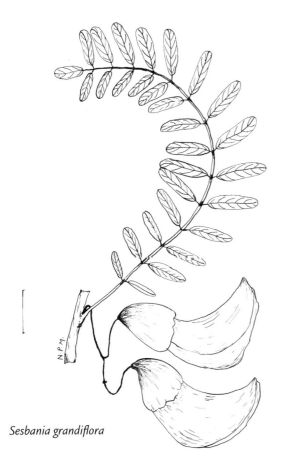

Sesbania grandiflora

Setaria glauca

beneath. Inflorescence brown. Flowers April–November. Propagated by seeds or root offshoots. Distributed throughout Nepal to about 2300 m, on open, sandy ground; also in Australia, other areas in the eastern hemisphere, and the Americas.

OTHER USES. The plant is used as fodder.

Setaria italica (Linnaeus) Palisot de Beauvois

Panicum italicum Linnaeus
ENGLISH *foxtail millet, Italian millet* MOOSHAR *kauni*
NEPALI *kaguno, sama* THARU *sawan* TIBETAN *khre*

Gramineae. Erect, tufted, annual grass, culms long, branched, rooting toward the base. Leaves linear lanceolate, acuminate, margin retrorse, hispid, sheath densely ciliated on the margin and mouth. Inflorescences greenish in panicles. Fruit a grain. Flowers and fruits August–October. Propagated by seeds or stolons. Distributed throughout Nepal to about 1800 m, cultivated; also in most warm and tropical regions.

FOOD. The grains are eaten like millet (*Eleusine coracana*).

Setaria pallidefusca (Schumacher) Stapf &
C. E. Hubbard

Panicum pallidefuscum Schumacher
ENGLISH *kavatta grass* NEPALI *buis*

Gramineae. Grass about 50 cm high. Leaves long, linear. Inflorescences greenish, cylindrical, in spike-like panicles. Fruits August–September. Propagated by seeds or root offshoots. Distributed throughout Nepal to about 2100 m in open, rocky soil; also in the tropics of the eastern hemisphere.

OTHER USES. The plant provides fodder.

Shorea robusta Gaertner

BHOJPURI *sakhuwa* CHEPANG *jin, raksi* DANUWAR *sankhu*
ENGLISH *sal tree* GURUNG *jhesin, sal* LEPCHA *takralakung*
LIMBU *sosin* MAGAR *agras, phoksing* MOOSHAR *sakhuwa*
NEPALI *agrath, sal* NEWARI *dhusin, sisi* RAI *chhuma, salan*
SUNWAR *sal* TAMANG *agrakh, jersing* THARU *chimar*
TIBETAN *spos-dkar*

Dipterocarpaceae. Subdeciduous tree about 50 m high, bark rough, reddish brown, with long, deep, wide vertical fissures. Leaves stalked, 10–20 cm long, 5–13 cm wide, ovate to oblong, entire, leathery, acuminate, glabrous and shiny when mature, base cordate or rounded. Flowers yellowish in axillary and terminal panicles. Fruit ovoid, indehiscent, pubescent, with wing-like sepals at the base. Flowers March–May, fruits May–July. Propagated by seeds. Distributed throughout Nepal to about 1400 m in open sub-Himalayan tracts and on outer ridges of the hills when it is the main tree of the forest, but the gathering of wood for fuel and timber, and leaves for fodder, is a cause of conservation concern; also in India.

FOOD. Roasted seeds are eaten.

MEDICINE. The resin is valued for dysentery, gonorrhea, boils, and toothaches. A warmed leaf is applied to swollen parts of the body for its quick effect. Among Danuwars, a young leaf is heated over the fire and pressed against the stomach of a child suffering from dysentery. Juice of the leaf is also given to treat the same ailment. Seed oil is applied in cases of skin disease.

OTHER USES. Wood is an important source of timber and firewood. Bark is used for tanning. Leaves are used as fodder, plates, and for wrapping (Plate 3). Oil from the seed is used for illumination.

Shorea robusta

Shuteria involucrata (Wallich) Wight & Arnott

Glycine involucrata Wallich
TAMANG *dongsing noba*

Leguminosae. Hairy twiner. Leaves stalked, trifoliolate, leaflets 2.5–7 cm long, 2–4 cm wide, ovate to oblong, glabrous above, somewhat hairy beneath. Flowers pink in axillary racemes. Fruit a pod, linear oblong, hairy. Flowers October–November, fruits December–January. Propagated by seeds. Distributed in eastern and central Nepal at 1000–2500 m, often climbing over shrubs and trees; also in India, Bhutan, Sri Lanka, China, and Southeast Asia.

MEDICINE. A paste of the plant is applied to set dislocated bones.

Shuteria involucrata

Sida acuta Burman fil.

Sida carpinifolia Linnaeus
CHEPANG *mechhedami, thangara* DANUWAR *bariyar*
NGLISH *broom weed* NEPALI *balu, kuro, sano chilya*

Malvaceae. Erect shrub about 1 m high, bark smooth, greenish, with numerous small lenticels. Leaves stalked, 4–8 cm long, 1.5–4 cm wide, serrate, stellately hairy beneath when young, glabrous when mature, dull green above, base narrow. Flowers yellow, solitary or in pairs, August–December. Propagated by seeds. Distributed throughout Nepal to about 2700 m, on uncultivated land and in open places; also pantropical.

MEDICINE. Juice of the plant, about 2 teaspoons three times a day, is given for indigestion. A decoction of the root, about 2 teaspoons twice a day, is given in cases of fever.

OTHER USES Bark yields a good fiber for making ropes, canvas, and fishnets. Twigs are made into brooms.

Sida cordata (Burman fil.) Borssum Waalkes

Melochia cordata Burman fil.
Sida humilis Willdenow
Sida multicaulis Cavanilles
Sida nervosa Wallich
Sida veronicifolia Lamarck
CHEPANG *ghakatek* DANUWAR *chirchira, laharjoka* MAJHI *kaule jhar*
MOOSHAR *jari jhar* NEPALI *balu, bish khapre* TAMANG *begabu, mesi*
THARU *bish khopra*

Malvaceae. Diffuse herb, branches trailing, with long, spreading hairs. Leaves stalked, 6–12 cm long, ovate to cordate, acuminate, crenate to serrate, membranous, sparsely clothed with stellate hairs. Flowers yellow. Flowers and fruits March–November. Propagated by seeds. Distributed throughout Nepal to about 1800 m, on uncultivated land and as undergrowth in forest scrub; also pantropical.

MEDICINE. Juice of the plant is applied to boils and pimples. Juice of the root, about 4 teaspoons twice a day, is given in cases of indigestion. A paste of the root is applied to remove pus from boils and wounds. The paste, mixed with caustic soda and butter made from cow milk, is applied to treat gonorrhea and other venereal diseases. A decoction of the root is given as a tonic. Juice of the leaves is used to treat cuts and wounds.

OTHER USES. Bark of the stem is used to make cords, ropes, and twine.

Sida rhombifolia Linnaeus

Sida compressa Wallich
CHEPANG *machhedham* DANUWAR *bariyar* ENGLISH *broom jute, Canary Islands tea plant, sida hemp* GURUNG *pendro no, thadho balu* NEPALI *balu jhar, barera, channaino, sano chilya* NEWARI *sinamani ghyan* RAI *dallo kuro* TAMANG *syodal, tilbi*

Malvaceae. Erect deciduous shrub about 2 m high, branches stellately hairy. Leaves stalked, variable is shape and size, lower leaves 2.5–6.5 cm long, rhombic, serrate, often entire toward the base, stellately pubescent beneath, base cuneate, upper leaves narrowly rhombic. Flowers axillary, yellow, in a panicle-like inflorescence, August–Sep-

Sida rhombifolia

tember. Fruits October–November. Propagated by seeds. Distributed throughout Nepal to about 1500 m, common on uncultivated land and in open areas in *Shorea robusta* forest; also pantropical.

MEDICINE. Juice of the plant, about 2 teaspoons three times a day, is given to treat intermittent fever. A paste of the plant is applied to treat headaches, boils, cramps, rheumatism, toothaches, chapped lips, and pimples. This paste is also taken for indigestion. A paste of the root is applied to boils.

OTHER USES. Fiber from the bark is used to prepare ropes and twine.

Siegesbeckia orientalis Linnaeus

Siegesbeckia brachiata Roxburgh
Siegesbeckia glutinosa Wallich
CHEPANG *bhogate muja, drap muja, sati muja* ENGLISH *divine herb* GURUNG *dhumre, dhungre* NEPALI *duche jhar, gobre jhar, kuro, telaile, thulo piryu* TAMANG *chhyukutinai, thangabima*

Compositae. Erect annual herb about 2 m high. Leaves stalked, opposite, 1.5–15 cm long, 0.5–9 cm wide, ovate or broadly triangular, irregularly dentate, cuneate. Flower heads yellow. Fruit an achene. Flowers and fruits July–December. Propagated by seeds. Distributed throughout Nepal at 400–2700 m, common on uncultivated land and in open places; also in India, China, southern Japan, Southeast Asia, Australia, Oceania, and Africa.

MEDICINE. Juice of the plant is applied to treat ringworm and other parasitic infections. This juice is considered a heart tonic. A paste of the plant is used to treat wounds between the toes caused by prolonged walking barefooted in muddy water. Juice of the root is applied to wounds. A paste of the root is given to treat indigestion. Leaves are bitter and febrifuge.

Siegesbeckia orientalis

Silene stracheyi Edgeworth

TIBETAN *nyamsisi*

Caryophyllaceae. Herb. Leaves subsessile, lanceolate, entire, acuminate, sparsely hairy. Flowers brownish, pendant, in lax cymes. Propagated by seeds. Distributed in western and central Nepal at 2000–3500 m, occasional in open pastureland; also in northern India and Bhutan.

OTHER USES. Powdered root is used as a substitute for soap.

Sinarundinaria maling (Gamble) C. S. Chao & Renvoize

Arundinaria maling Gamble
Arundinaria racemosa Munro
NEPALI *dhana bans, malingo* TAMANG *machhe*

Gramineae. Tufted bamboo about 9 m high, culms slender, hollow, culm sheaths striate. Leaves 5–10 cm long, 0.8–2 cm wide, papery, linear lanceolate, glabrous on both surfaces, base attenuate into a short stalk, apex terminating in a bristly acuminate point, margin minutely rough. Inflorescence brownish. Propagated by splitting the rhizomes. Distributed in eastern and central Nepal at 1000–3000 m in open, rocky places; also in northeastern India.

FOOD. Young shoots are cooked as a vegetable or pickled.

OTHER USES. Strips from the culms are used to make mats, fishing equipment, and baskets. Culms are also used for roofing and fences. Leaves are used for fodder.

Skimmia laureola (de Candolle) Siebert & Zuccarini ex Walpers

Limonia laureola de Candolle
NEPALI *aranth, narapati*

Rutaceae. Erect evergreen shrub about 2 m high, bark smooth. Leaves stalked, crowded at the ends of branches,

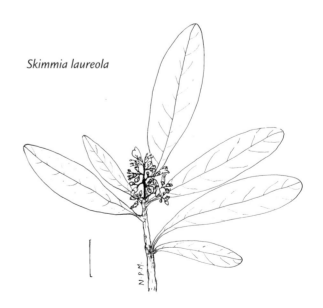

Skimmia laureola

7–15 cm long, 2–4 cm wide, oblong to lanceolate, acuminate, leathery, gland-dotted. Flowers greenish yellow, fragrant, in panicles. Fruit a drupe, ovoid, red when ripe. Flowers April–May, fruits October–November. Propagated by seeds or cuttings. Distributed in western Nepal at 2400–3100 m in shady areas of the forest, forming dense patches; also in Afghanistan, Pakistan, India, and Bhutan.

FOOD. Leaves are used as a condiment.

OTHER USES. Wood is often used to make handles of farming implements such as hoes and axes. The leaf and flower are used for decorative purposes by women. An essential oil is obtained from the leaf.

Smilax aspera Linnaeus

Smilax capitata Buchanan-Hamilton ex D. Don
Smilax fulgens Wallich
Smilax maculata Roxburgh ex D. Don
ENGLISH *Italian smilax, prickly greenbrier* GURUNG *naikhre, nayukre* MAGAR *jogi dang* NEPALI *syal daino, kubi ghanino* SHERPA *pregemgyalting* TAMANG *nagret, nakikre*

Smilacaceae. Twining shrub. Leaves stalked, alternate, 5–9 cm long, 4–7 cm wide, ovate or lanceolate to cordate, mucronate, entire, smooth, stalk bearing a pair of long, slender tendrils near the base. Flowers stalked, white, fragrant, September–October. Fruits March–April. Propagated by seeds. Distributed throughout Nepal at 1200–2900 m on forest trees in moist places; also in India, Sri Lanka, the Mediterranean region, and East Africa.

FOOD. Tender shoots and leaves are cooked as a vegetable.

MEDICINE. Ripe fruits are squeezed and applied in cases of scabies.

Smilax ferox Wallich ex Kunth

NEPALI *kukurdaino*

Smilacaceae. Trailing shrub, branches with prickles. Leaves stalked, 2.5–5 cm long, 0.6–2 cm wide, elliptic to ovate, acuminate or mucronate, leathery, base cuneate or rounded. Flowers greenish in umbels. Fruit a berry, one- or two-seeded. Flowers April–May, fruits June–July. Propagated by seeds. Distributed in eastern and central Nepal at 1100–2700 m in forests and shrubby areas; also in northern India.

FOOD. Young shoots and leaves are cooked as a vegetable. Ripe fruits are eaten fresh.

Smilax glaucophylla Klotzsch

Smilax elegans Wallich ex Kunth, and A. de Candolle, not Wallich ex Hooker fil. (see *S. menispermoides*)
Smilax longibracteolata Hooker fil.
Smilax parvifolia Wallich ex Hooker fil.
TAMANG *chatalang*

Smilacaceae. Thorny climber, branches flat, zigzag. Leaves stalked, 1.5–3.5 cm long, 0.4–0.8 cm wide, ovate to lanceolate, acuminate, three- or five-veined, glaucous beneath, base rounded. Flowers greenish in few-flowered

umbels, April–May. Fruits June–July. Propagated by seeds. Distributed throughout Nepal at 1500–2700 m, trailing on bushes in the forest; also in northeastern India, Tibet and western China.

FOOD. Tender leaves and shoots are cooked as a vegetable.

Smilax lanceifolia Roxburgh

NEPALI *kubiraina*

Smilacaceae. Thorny, twining shrub. Leaves stalked, orbiculate to lanceolate, acuminate, stalk obscurely winged. Flowers small, yellowish, in many-flowered umbels. Fruit a berry, green when young. Flowers March–April, fruits April–June. Propagated by seeds. Distributed in central Nepal to about 2000 m in moist places in forested areas; also in northeastern India and Indo-China.

FOOD. Young shoots and leaves are cooked as a vegetable. Ripe fruits are eaten fresh.

Smilax menispermoides A. de Candolle

Smilax elegans Wallich ex Hooker fil., not Wallich ex Kunth, nor A. de Candolle (see *S. glaucophylla*)
NEPALI *hade kukurdaino, karyang, kukurdaino, kurung* TAMANG *gatlang, nagikhre*

Smilacaceae. Thorny climber with slender, wiry stems, stem blackish toward the base, smooth, twigs terete. Leaves stalked, 2–4 cm long, 1.5–3 cm wide, broadly ovate, entire, acuminate, base rounded truncate. Flowers deep brown in axillary pendent umbels. Fruit a berry, subglobose, black. Seeds pale brown. Flowers May–June, fruits

Smilax menispermoides

October–November. Propagated by seeds. Distributed throughout Nepal at 1600–3400 m in openings in oak forests; also in northwestern India, southwestern China, and Indo-China.

FOOD. Tender leaves and shoots are boiled and pickled by Tamangs. Ripe fruits are eaten fresh.

Smilax ovalifolia Roxburgh ex D. Don

Smilax columnifera Buchanan-Hamilton ex D. Don
Smilax macrophylla Roxburgh
Smilax prolifera Wallich
Smilax retusa Roxburgh
CHEPANG *jakrak* NEPALI *kukurdaino, nadar*
TAMANG *nagikhre, nakre, yo lhapte*

Smilacaceae. Twining shrub armed with some prickles. Leaves stalked, 10–20 cm long, 3.5–15 cm wide, ovate or orbiculate, acuminate, entire. Flowers yellowish. Fruit a berry, globose. Propagated by seeds. Distributed in eastern and central Nepal to about 1400 m in moist places in forested areas; also in India and northern Indo-China.

FOOD. Tender leaves and shoots are cooked as a vegetable. Ripe fruits are eaten fresh.

OTHER USES. Thin stems are used for temporary binding.

Smilax perfoliata Loureiro

Smilax laurifola Willdenow
Smilax prolifera Roxburgh
NEPALI *kukurdaino*

Smilacaceae. Trailing, prickly shrub. Leaves stalked, ovate, acuminate, stalk winged and auricled. Flowers axillary, yellowish, January–March. Propagated by seeds. Distributed throughout Nepal at 500–900 m, trailing on shrubs in open areas; also in northern India, southern China, and Indo-China.

FOOD. Tender leaves and shoots are cooked as a vegetable.

OTHER USES. Thin stems are used for temporary binding.

Smilax rigida Wallich ex Kunth

NEPALI *putali jhar*

Smilacaceae. Erect, much branched shrub. Leaves stalked, 1.6–2.5 cm long, 1.2–2.5 cm wide, orbiculate to ovate, acuminate or apiculate, leathery. Flowers small, greenish. Fruit a berry, black when ripe. Flowers February–March, fruits April–June. Propagated by seeds. Distributed in eastern and central Nepal at 2100–2900 m in temperate forest; also in northern India and Bhutan.

FOOD. Tender shoots are cooked as a vegetable.

Smithia ciliata Royle

TAMANG *narimurago*

Leguminosae. Erect herb about 25 cm high. Leaves stalked, even-pinnate, leaflets in three to six pairs, 5–12 mm long, narrowly oblong, bristly, sensitive. Flowers bluish, crowded on an axillary stalk. Fruit a pod, six- to

eight-jointed. Flowers August–September, fruits September–November. Propagated by seeds. Distributed throughout Nepal at 1200–2800 m on open, shady, often stony ground; also in India, Bhutan, China, Japan, and Southeast Asia.

OTHER USES. According to the Tamangs of Dhading district, if a man happens to eat this plant, it would cause impotency.

Smithia sensitiva Aiton

DANUWAR *amti*

Leguminosae. Much branched shrub about 75 cm high. Leaves stalked, pinnate, leaflets generally 10–30 cm long, 0.5–10 cm wide, linear, fringed with bristles. Flowers yellow with a brown band in the throat, in axillary racemes. Fruit a pod, densely papillate on the faces. Flowers and fruits October–December. Propagated by seeds. Distributed throughout Nepal to about 1200 m in open grassland; also in India, Bhutan, China, Southeast Asia, and Australia.

MEDICINE. Juice of the root, about 2 teaspoons three times a day, is given in cases of fever.

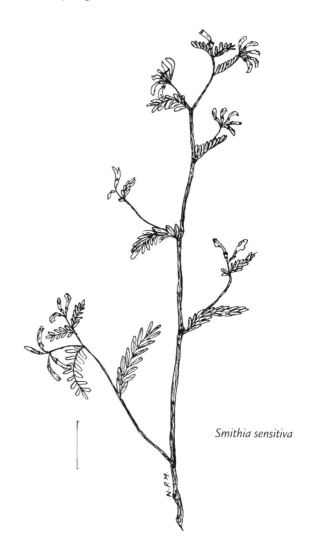

Smithia sensitiva

Solanum aculeatissimum Jacquin

CHEPANG *chuisai* DANUWAR *barka regmi* GURUNG *golbhera puju, saplunme* MAGAR *kantageri, kanthakumari* MOOSHAR *kataiya* NEPALI *bhalkanda, bhel, dhalde, indreni, kalchauda kanda, kanthakari, thulo lunden* RAUTE *ban baikal* TAMANG *bhel, golambi, kambalo, kantakari, kyakar binda, niki bhenta, ri bhenta, sabhulung*

Solanaceae. Spiny shrub. Leaves stalked, alternate, 2–14 cm long, 1.5–12 cm wide, ovate to cordate, acute, sinuate, upper surface densely hairy, lower surface with stellate hairs. Flowers white, axillary, in cymes. Fruit a berry, globose. Flowers and fruits July–September. Propagated by seeds. Distributed throughout Nepal to about 2000 m in open areas and on uncultivated land; also in Pakistan, India, Bhutan, Sri Lanka, and the Americas.

MEDICINE. Pounded roots are applied to treat swelling of the gums and toothaches; powdered dried fruit is also smoked to treat these diseases. Squeezed fruit is applied to the forehead to relieve headaches. Seeds are chewed to treat toothaches and dental caries. Squeezed seeds are applied in cases of headache.

OTHER USES. Fruits are used as fish poison. Squeezed fruit is used for washing clothes.

Solanum anguivi Lamarck

Solanum indicum Linnaeus

ENGLISH *large eggplant* GURUNG *krichinte* NEPALI *bihi, nilo bihi, thulo bihi* TAMANG *gramji*

Solanaceae. Much branched shrub about 2 m high, branches stellate tomentose, armed with somewhat recurved prickles. Leaves stalked, ovate, acuminate, subentire, base cuneate or truncate, often unequally sided. Flowers violet or blue, in extra-axillary racemose cymes. Fruit a berry, globose, supported by the persistent calyx, yellow when ripe. Propagated by seeds. Distributed throughout Nepal to about 2300 m on uncultivated land, and frequent on rocky banks bordering streams and rivers; also in India, Bhutan, Southeast Asia, Taiwan, and the Philippines.

MEDICINE. Young shoots are eaten as a vegetable to treat insomnia. A paste of leaves or fruit is applied to the forehead to treat headaches.

OTHER USES. Fruit is used for washing clothes.

Solanum erianthum D. Don

Solanum pubescens Willdenow
Solanum verbascifolium Linnaeus
RAUTE *khauda*

Solanaceae. Shrub about 4 m high, bark bright gray. Leaves stalked, alternate, 5.5–30 cm long, 1.5–12.5 cm wide, oblanceolate, acute, entire, slightly stellately hairy above, densely so beneath, with a fetid odor when bruised. Flowers white in few, woolly, dichotomous cymes. Fruit a berry supported by the persistent calyx. Flowers and fruits June–September. Propagated by seeds. Distributed throughout Nepal at 200–1400 m, fairly common in moist, shady places; also in India, Southeast Asia, northern Australia, and tropical America.

MEDICINE. A paste of the fruit is applied to boils and pimples.

Solanum melongena Linnaeus

Solanum insanum Linnaeus

BHOJPURI *baigan* DANUWAR *bhanta* ENGLISH *brinjal, eggplant* GURUNG *bhyanta* LEPCHA *kandu* LIMBU *paranda* MAGAR *bhanta* MOOSHAR *bhanta* NEPALI *bhanta* NEWARI *bhyanta* RAI *bombob* SUNWAR *bhenta* TAMANG *bhanta* THARU *bhanta*

Solanaceae. Annual herb about 1 m high, somewhat prickly or unarmed. Leaves stalked, oblong to ovate, irregularly and shallowly lobed, stellately pubescent beneath. Flowers axillary, purplish or bluish. Fruit variable in shape, globose to oblong, purple, smooth, fleshy. Propagated by seeds. Distributed throughout Nepal to about 1500 m, cultivated; also in most tropical and temperate regions of the world.

FOOD. Fruits are cooked as a vegetable or pickled in various ways, according to the recipe.

MEDICINE. Powdered whole plant is boiled in water and used for washing sores and boils. A decoction of the root is stimulant. Juice of the leaves is a remedy for throat aches and stomach troubles. A poultice of green fruit is used for cough and colds, also in cases of loss of appetite.

OTHER USES. Leaves contain tannin.

Solanum nigrum Linnaeus

DANUWAR *bhutung* ENGLISH *black nightshade* GURUNG *khursani jhar, pimnendo* MAGAR *ninaura, pitimgan* MAJHI *kali gedi* MOOSHAR *bhutaka* NEPALI *bihi, kaligeri, kalikuiyan, kamai, kamari jhar, kawai, khursene, paire golbhera* NEWARI *haku pasi* RAUTE *khajima* SATAR *sano bini* TAMANG *cangsani, chema* TIBETAN *u-lu-zan-pa*

Solanaceae. Erect herb about 50 cm high. Leaves stalked, 1.3–9 cm long, 0.5–6 cm wide, oblong, acuminate, entire or undulately lobed, base acute. Flowers white in an umbel. Fruit a berry, globose, red or black when ripe. Flowers and fruits most of the year. Propagated by seeds. Distributed throughout Nepal to about 2900 m in open, moist areas and on uncultivated land; also in Afghanistan, India, Bhutan, and temperate and tropical regions of the world.

FOOD. Tender shoots and leaves are cooked as a vegetable. Ripe berries are eaten fresh.

MEDICINE. The plant is alterative, aphrodisiac, diuretic, laxative, febrifuge, stimulant, and tonic. A paste of the plant is applied to the forehead to relieve headaches and is also used for pain of joints. A juice of the plant is used to treat enlargement of the liver, hemorrhoids, dysentery, fever, wounds, and inflammation of the urinary bladder. It is also applied to the forehead to relieve headaches and is dripped into the eye in cases of inflammation of the eye. Juice of the root, mixed with the powder of two fruits of black pepper (*Piper nigrum*), is given to relieve fever.

Ripe fruit is alterative, diuretic, laxative, and aphrodisiac. It is useful for diarrhea, eye diseases, and rabies. Juice of the fruit, about 2 teaspoons three times a day, is prescribed to treat fever. A paste of unripe fruit is applied to treat ringworm and is also applied to the forehead to relieve headaches.

Solanum nigrum

Solanum pseudocapsicum Linnaeus

NEPALI *bihi*

Solanaceae. Erect shrub about 1 m high, branches spreading. Leaves stalked, 2–9 cm long, 0.8–2.8 cm wide, oblanceolate, entire, bright green, base attenuate. Flowers white or purple in few-flowered umbellate cymes. Fruit a berry, globose, bright red when ripe. Flowers July–August, fruits May–June. Propagated by seeds. Distributed in eastern and central Nepal at 1300–1500 m in moist, shady places; also in India, Bhutan, and North America.

MEDICINE. Fruits are squeezed and applied to the forehead to relieve headaches.

Solanum surattense Burman fil.

Solanum diffusum Roxburgh
Solanum jacquinii Willdenow
Solanum xanthocarpum Schrader & Wendland

DANUWAR *regmi* MOOSHAR *gurmi kant* NEPALI *kantakari*
THARU *kacharehat* TIBETAN *kan-ta-ka-ri*

Solanaceae. Diffuse herb, covered all over with straight yellow prickles. Leaves stalked, 2–9 cm long, ovate, oblong or elliptic, deeply lobed, armed with numerous long prickles. Flowers blue. Fruit a berry, yellow blotched with green. Flowers and fruits April–October. Propagated by seeds. Distributed throughout Nepal to about 1600 m in dry, sunny places; also in northern India, Southeast Asia, Australia, and Polynesia.

MEDICINE. The plant is used to treat toothaches, fever, cough, chest ailment, rheumatism, dropsy, and gonorrhea. Juice of the root is used in cases of asthma. A paste of the fruit is applied to treat toothaches. Dried powder of the fruit is smoked like cigarettes and the smoke is kept in the mouth about 5 minutes for dental caries.

Solanum torvum Swartz

Solanum stramonifolium Jacquin

CHEPANG *kamsar kambar, chusai* DANUWAR *bihi* NEPALI *ban bihi, bihi, seti bihi, thulo bihi* SATAR *henji*

Solanaceae. Shrub about 2 m high with few pickles on the branches. Leaves stalked, 4–18.5 cm long, 2–15 cm wide, ovate, acuminate, sinuate, base more or less cordate, sparsely stellately tomentose above, densely so beneath. Flowers white in dichotomous cymes. Fruit a berry, globose, yellowish when ripe. Flowers December–March. Propagated by seeds. Distributed in eastern and central Nepal to about 1000 m on open, moist ground; also in Afghanistan, India, Sri Lanka, Myanmar, Malaysia, northern Australia, tropical Africa, and North America.

FOOD. Unripe fruits are pickled.

MEDICINE. Juice of the plant is used to treat fever, cough, asthma, chest ailments, rheumatism, dropsy, and gonorrhea. Juice of the root is given to treat vomiting caused by weakness. Juice of the flower, mixed with salt, is dropped in watery eyes. A paste of mature fruit is applied to the forehead to treat headaches.

OTHER USES. Leaves and fruits are used to make *marcha*, a fermenting cake from which liquor is distilled.

Solanum tuberosum Linnaeus

BHOJPURI *aalu* CHEPANG *aallu* DANUWAR *allu* ENGLISH *potato* GURUNG *aalu* LEPCHA *aalubuk* LIMBU *khamakhe* MOOSHAR *allu* NEPALI *aalu* NEWARI *aalu* RAI *aalu* SHERPA *riki* SUNWAR *reb* TAMANG *teme*

Solanaceae. Herb about 30 cm high, bearing underground tubers. Leaves stalked, odd-pinnate, leaflets entire. Flowers white or bluish in terminal cymes, January–March. Propagated by tubers. Distributed throughout Nepal to about 3000 m, cultivated; also in Pakistan, India, South America, and most parts of the world.

FOOD. Tubers are important items of food. Tender leaves are cooked as a vegetable by Danuwars and Mooshars.

MEDICINE. A fine paste of the tuber is applied to burns to relieve inflammation; it also prevents the formation of boils.

Solena heterophylla Loureiro

Melothria heterophylla (Loureiro) Cogniaux
Bryonia hastata Loureiro
Bryonia nepalensis Seringe, *Zehneria umbellata* var. *nepalensis*
  (Seringe) C. B. Clarke
Bryonia umbellata Klein ex Willdenow, *Karivia umbellata*
  (Klein ex Willdenow) Arnott, *Momordica umbellata*
  (Klein ex Willdenow) Roxburgh, *Zehneria umbellata*
  (Klein ex Willdenow) Thwaites
CHEPANG *kremsai, tirketa, kryakata* GURUNG *thankaja, tsuputu*
NEPALI *ban kankri, golkankri* TAMANG *tangsar kato*

Cucurbitaceae. Perennial climber. Leaves stalked, 3.5–17 cm long, 2–14 cm wide, three- or five-lobed, sometimes deeply, margin denticulate, ashy and glabrous beneath, tendrils simple or branched. Flowers yellow. Fruit bright red, obovoid. Flowers and fruits July–September. Propagated by seeds. Distributed throughout Nepal at 600–3000 m; also in Afghanistan, India, Bhutan, Sri Lanka, southwestern China, Taiwan, Southeast Asia, Java, and Australia.

FOOD. Ripe fruits are eaten fresh.

MEDICINE. Juice of the plant, about 6 teaspoons twice a day, is given to treat stomachaches. A paste of the fruit or root is taken in cases of indigestion.

OTHER USES. The plant is considered a nutritious feed and also helps increase milk production of cows and buffalo.

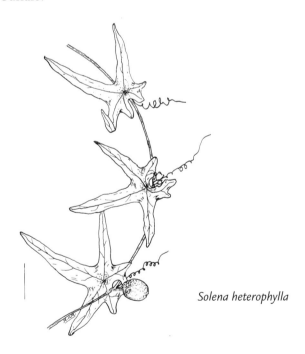

Solena heterophylla

Sonchus asper (Linnaeus) Hill

Sonchus oleraceus var. *asper* Linnaeus
Sonchus ferox Wallich
TAMANG *gnedhap*

Compositae. Herb about 1 m high, sparsely glandular in the upper part. Leaves half-clasping the stem at their base with rounded appressed auricles, margin entire, spiny, or dentate. Flower heads yellow, crowded in an irregular umbel. Fruit an achene. Flowers and fruits March–May. Propagated by seeds. Distributed in eastern and central Nepal at 1000–1800 m on moist, neglected ground; also found in most areas of the world.

FOOD. Tender leaves and shoots are cooked as a vegetable.

MEDICINE. The plant is fed to animals for proper development of the fetus. A paste of the plant is applied to wounds and boils.

OTHER USES. The plant is nutritious fodder and helps increase milk production.

Sonchus asper

Sonchus oleraceus Linnaeus

ENGLISH *sow thistle* NEPALI *chote jhar, dudhi kanda* TIBETAN *gnete*

Compositae. Annual herb with milky latex. Leaves sessile, half-clasping the stem at their base, lanceolate, entire or pinnatifid. Flower heads crowded, yellow. Fruit an achene, compressed, three-ribbed. Flowers and fruits February–November. Propagated by seeds. Distributed in central and western Nepal at 2000–2800 m; also found in most places of the world.

FOOD. Tender shoots and leaves are cooked as a vegetable.

Sonchus wightianus de Candolle

Sonchus arvensis Linnaeus
NEPALI *ban rayo, bhale mulapate* TIBETAN *gnete*

Compositae. Erect perennial herb about 1 m high. Lower leaves rosulate, deeply pinnately lobed, lobes mucronate, shortly spinous and dentate, upper leaves smaller, oblong, spatulate, lyrate or pinnately lobed. Flower heads yellow. Fruit an achene, oblong, five-ribbed. Flowers and fruits April–November. Propagated by seeds. Distributed throughout Nepal at 600–2500 m in moist, shady places; also in Afghanistan, Pakistan, India, Sri Lanka, China, and Southeast Asia.

FOOD. Young leaves and shoots are cooked as a vegetable.

MEDICINE. Juice of the plant, about 4 teaspoons twice a day, is given in cases of fever, indigestion, typhoid, and dysuria. Juice of the root, 4 teaspoons three times a day, is given to treat troubles of the bile ducts.

Sophora moorcroftiana (Bentham) Bentham ex

Baker var. *nepalensis* Kitamura

TIBETAN *ghansinmen*

Leguminosae. Much branched spiny shrub about 1 m high. Leaves stalked, pinnate, leaflets many, ovate, silky haired. Flowers bluish or yellow. Fruit a pod, constricted between the seeds, five- or six-seeded. Flowers May–June. Propagated by seeds. Distributed in central Nepal at 2800–3900 m on rocky slopes; also in northern India.

MEDICINE. A paste of the seeds is given in cases of gastric trouble, and to animals as an antidote if they happen to eat poisonous plants.

OTHER USES. The plant is used for firewood where trees are scanty.

Sophora moorcroftiana
var. *nepalensis*

Sopubia trifida Buchanan-Hamilton ex D. Don

Gerardia scabra Wallich
Gerardia sopubia Bentham
NEPALI *salcha*

Scrophulariaceae. Erect herb about 70 cm high. Leaves sessile, narrowly linear, mostly fascicled and three-parted, lower leaves opposite or clustered, upper leaves undivided, alternate. Flowers yellow in terminal racemes. Fruit a capsule, ovoid. Flowers and fruits September–December. Propagated by seeds. Distributed throughout Nepal at 1500–3600 m; also in northern India, Bhutan, Sri Lanka, western and central China, Southeast Asia, the Philippines, and tropical Africa.

MEDICINE. Juice of the leaves is applied to the forehead in cases of headache.

Sopubia trifida

Sorbaria tomentosa (Lindley) Rehder

Schizonotus tomentosus Lindley
Spiraea lindleyana Wallich
Spiraea sorbifolia (Linnaeus) A. Brown
TIBETAN *kantakari*

Rosaceae. Tall shrub. Leaves stalked, pinnate, leaflets 2.5–11 cm long, 0.8–3 cm wide, long lanceolate, doubly serrate, sparsely pubescent beneath. Flowers white, May–

July. Propagated by seeds. Distributed in western and central Nepal at 2100–2900 m in moist places; also in Afghanistan, India, and central Asia.

MEDICINE. Juice of the seeds is given for liver troubles.

Sorbaria tomentosa

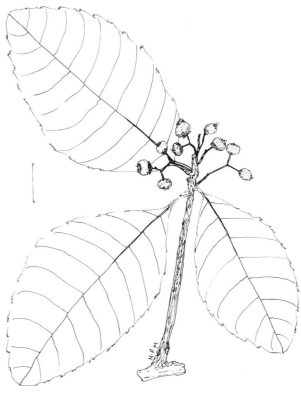

Sorbus cuspidata

June, fruits August–October. Propagated by seeds. Distributed in eastern Nepal at 2500–3200 m in moist places in the forest; also in northeastern India and Bhutan.

FOOD. Ripe fruits are eaten fresh.

Sorbus cuspidata (Spach) Hedlund

Crataegus cuspidata Spach
Pyrus crenata D. Don
Pyrus vestita Wallich ex Hooker fil.
Sorbus crenata K. Koch
NEPALI *chyuli* SHERPA *nhajhel*

Rosaceae. Tree about 15 m high. Leaves short-stalked, 5–17 cm long, 2–9 cm wide, elliptic, acute, lobulate and serrulate, densely woolly beneath. Flowers yellowish in corymbs, May–June. Fruits July–August. Propagated by seeds. Distributed throughout Nepal at 2500–3700 m in mixed forested areas; also in northern India, Bhutan, western China, Taiwan, and Southeast Asia.

FOOD. Ripe fruits are edible.

Sorbus hedlundii C. K. Schneider

NEPALI *najhil*

Rosaceae. Tree about 6 m high. Leaves stalked, 9–18 cm long, 5–12.5 cm wide, elliptic or ovate, acute, obscurely lobulate, dentate, glabrous above, white tomentose beneath. Flowers white. Fruit globose, warted. Flowers May–

Sorbus lanata (D. Don) Schauer

Pyrus lanata D. Don
Pyrus kumaonensis Wallich
NEPALI *mhelcha, nalam, pangmhe* TAMANG *denga*

Rosaceae. Medium-sized tree. Leaves stalked, 5–19 cm long, 3–11.5 cm wide, ovate, irregularly serrate, grayish white beneath, narrowing toward the base, base cuneate. Flowers white, fragrant, in clusters. Fruit yellow when ripe. Flowers April–May. Propagated by seeds. Distributed in western and central Nepal at 2200–3400 m; also in Afghanistan, Pakistan, and northwestern India.

FOOD. Ripe fruits are eaten fresh.

OTHER USES. The plant is lopped for fodder.

Sorbus microphylla Wenzig

Pyrus microphylla Wallich ex Hooker fil.
SHERPA *bajhar*

Rosaceae. Tree about 7 m high. Leaves stalked, odd-pinnate, leaflets sessile, subopposite, 1–3.5 cm long, 0.5–1 cm wide, oblong, acute, finely serrate, base oblique. Flowers pink in lax corymbs. Propagated by seeds. Distributed throughout Nepal at 3000–4500 m in open, sunny places; also in India and Bhutan.

OTHER USES. The plant is lopped for fodder.

Sorbus ursina (Wallich ex G. Don) S. Schauer

Pyrus ursina Wallich ex G. Don
Sorbus foliolosa Wallich
NEPALI *ghuro*

Rosaceae. Tree about 7 m high. Leaves stalked, pinnate, leaflets subsessile, 0.7–4.3 cm long, 0.3–1.2 cm wide, linear oblong, sharply dentate, midribs with red hairs. Flowers white or pinkish, May–June. Propagated by seeds. Distributed throughout Nepal at 2900–4300 m in shrubby areas of the forest; also in India, Bhutan, Tibet, and Myanmar.

MEDICINE. A paste of the leaves is applied to treat boils.

Spatholobus parviflorus (Roxburgh) Kuntze

Butea parviflora Roxburgh
Spatholobus roxburghii Bentham
NEPALI *debre lahara, mokare*

Leguminosae. Woody climber. Leaves stalked, trifoliolate, leaflets stalked, 8–26 cm long, 4–17.5 cm wide, elliptic to ovate, acuminate, entire, glabrous. Flowers cream. Fruit a pod covered with brown hairs. Flowers September–October, fruits December–April. Propagated by seeds. Distributed throughout Nepal to about 2000 m, climbing on trees in sunny places; also in India, China, and Southeast Asia.

OTHER USES. Fiber from the bark is used to prepare ropes. Leaves are used for fodder.

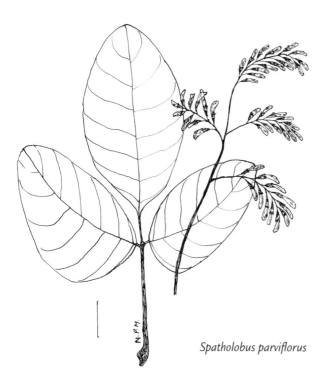

Spatholobus parviflorus

Spergula arvensis Linnaeus

NEPALI *jhyau jhar*

Caryophyllaceae. Suberect annual herb about 30 cm high. Leaves short-stalked, opposite, 1–3 cm long, linear, acute, glandular pubescent. Flowers white in terminal cymes. Fruit a capsule, ovoid. Flowers and fruits most of the year. Propagated by seeds. Distributed in western Nepal to about 300 m in moist places; also found in most areas of the world.

OTHER USES. The plant is used for fodder.

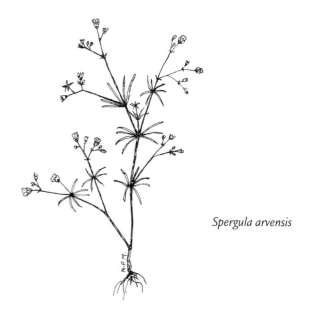

Spergula arvensis

Spermadictyon suaveolens Roxburgh

Hamiltonia suaveolens (Roxburgh) Roxburgh
Hamiltonia propinqua Decaisne
Hamiltonia scabra D. Don
Spermadictyon azureum Wallich
CHEPANG *klibharok, michhano, tugasage* MAJHI *bakhre*
NEPALI *bakhara pire, biri, guhya biri, karkare ghans, patare*
TAMANG *bhakhre, khidang*

Rubiaceae. Shrub about 2 m high. Leaves stalked, opposite, 7–22 cm long, 3–10 cm wide, elliptic to oblong. Flowers blue, fascicled in panicles. Fruit a capsule, ellipsoidal, five-seeded. Flowers and fruits March–December. Propagated by seeds. Distributed throughout Nepal at 600–2300 m on open hillsides; also in northern India, Bhutan, and China.

FOOD. Tender leaves and shoots are eaten as a vegetable.

MEDICINE. Juice of the root is given for diarrhea and cholera. A paste of the root is useful for diabetes and carbuncles. Juice of the bark, about 1 teaspoon twice a day, is given to treat fever and indigestion. It is also given to animals with coughs and colds. Juice of the leaves is applied to wounds between the toes caused by prolonged walking barefooted in muddy water.

OTHER USES. The plant is lopped for fodder.

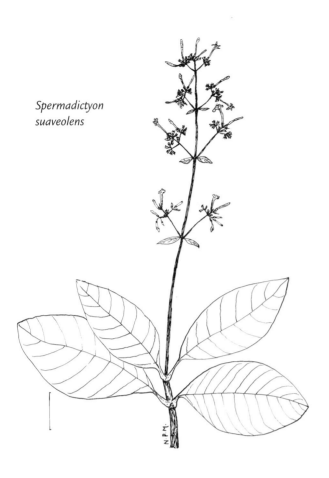

*Spermadictyon
suaveolens*

Sphaeranthus indicus

Sphaeranthus indicus Linnaeus

Sphaeranthus hirtus Willdenow
Sphaeranthus mollis Roxburgh

ENGLISH *globe thistle*   DANUWAR *bon supari, supari jhar*
NEPALI *supare jhar*

Compositae. Procumbent herb about 50 cm high. Leaves sessile, alternate, 2.5–5 cm long, oblong, mucronate, dentate, base cuneate. Flower heads purple. Fruit an achene, glandular hairy. Flowers and fruits November–January. Propagated by seeds. Distributed throughout Nepal at 200–800 m; also in India, Bhutan, Sri Lanka, Myanmar, Malaysia, and Australia.

MEDICINE. The plant is considered a good tonic. A paste is applied externally and put in the mouth to treat toothaches.

OTHER USES. Flower heads are squeezed and mixed with water to spread on cots and mats to drive away fleas and bugs.

Sphenoclea zeylanica Gaertner

Pongatium indicum Lamarck
Rapinia herbacea Loureiro
Sphenoclea pongatium de Candolle

NEPALI *panimarich*   THARU *dhansejuwa*

Sphenocleaceae. Herb about 50 cm high, stems much branched, hollow. Leaves stalked, alternate, 2.5–7.5 cm long, lanceolate, entire. Flowers white. Fruit a capsule, wedge shaped, enclosed in the persistent calyx. Flowers and fruits August–October. Propagated by seeds. Distributed in eastern and central Nepal to about 1600 m, common in swampy areas along canals and ditches; also in central Asia, India, Sri Lanka, eastward to China, Taiwan, Southeast Asia, and tropical Africa.

FOOD. Tender leaves are cooked as a vegetable.

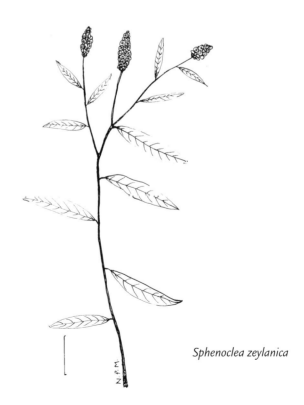

Sphenoclea zeylanica

Spilanthes paniculata Wallich ex de Candolle

Spilanthes acmella var. *paniculata* (Wallich ex de Candolle)
C. B. Clarke
Spilanthes acmella (Linnaeus) Murray

CHEPANG *saru, pire, sampur* DANUWAR *bon supari, ganhuwa*
ENGLISH *Brazil cress, toothache plant* GURUNG *khursani jhar*
MAGAR *marati* NEPALI *bhuin timur, gorakh ban, lato ghans, maretho*
TAMANG *saprumo*

Compositae. Herb. Leaves stalked, opposite, ovate to
lanceolate, acuminate, serrate, sparsely hairy. Flower
heads yellow. Fruit an achene, flattened. Propagated by
spores. Distributed in western and central Nepal to about
1800 m; also in India, Bhutan, China, and Southeast Asia.

FOOD. Tender parts are used as a potherb. Seeds are
used in pickles and curries.

MEDICINE. A paste of the plant is applied to snakebites.
Flower heads are pungent and chewed in cases of toothache. Juice of the flower heads is given for stomach pain.

OTHER USES. The plant is used as fish poison.

Spinacia oleracea Linnaeus

ENGLISH *spinach* NEPALI *palungo sag* NEWARI *pala*

Chenopodiaceae. Smooth annual herb. Basal leaves
large, cauline leaves smaller, lanceolate. Flowers greenish
in spikes or panicles. Flowers and fruits most of the year.
Propagated by seeds. Distributed in eastern and central
Nepal to about 1400 m, cultivated.

FOOD. Leaves are much used as a vegetable; they are rich
in mineral salts and proteins.

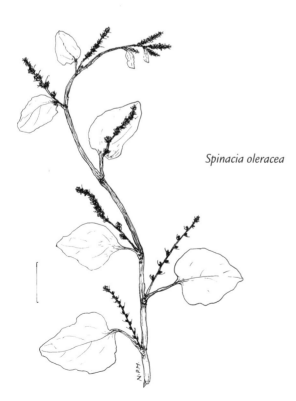

Spinacia oleracea

Spiraea bella Sims

Spiraea expansa Wallich
NEPALI *seto khareto*

Rosaceae. Shrub about 2 m high. Leaves short-stalked,
alternate, about 4 cm long, ovate to lanceolate, acute or
acuminate, crenate toward the tip, glabrous. Flowers
white in a terminal corymb. Propagated by seeds. Distributed throughout Nepal at 1900–4200 m in forest openings; also in northern India, southern Tibet, and western
China.

OTHER USES. The plant is browsed by goats and sheep.

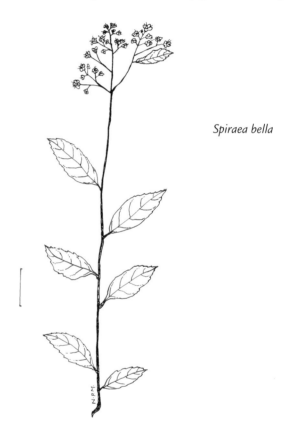

Spiraea bella

Spiraea canescens D. Don

Spiraea cuneifolia Wallich ex Cambessèdes
NEPALI *jhilleti*

Rosaceae. Deciduous shrub about 5 m high, branches
usually arching and densely pubescent when young, bark
reddish brown, with some circular lenticels. Leaves
stalked, 0.3–0.5 cm long, elliptic to ovate, entire or slightly
dentate near the tip, densely pubescent on both surfaces,
apex rounded, base cuneate. Flowers white in cymose panicles, May–June. Fruits October–November. Propagated
by seeds. Distributed throughout Nepal at 1500–2200 m
on exposed areas in secondary growth of forest scrub; also
in northern India, Bhutan, and Tibet.

OTHER USES. The plant is browsed by goats and sheep.

Spondias pinnata (Linnaeus fil.) Kurz

Mangifera pinnata Linnaeus fil.
Spondias mangifera Willdenow
ENGLISH *golden apple, hog plum tree* NEPALI *amara, amato, khallu*

Anacardiaceae. Medium-sized tree. Leaves stalked, alternate, odd-pinnate, leaflets 7–11, short-stalked, opposite, 7.5–17 cm long, 3.5–7.5 cm wide, elliptic to oblong, entire, glabrous. Flowers greenish white in spreading terminal panicles. Fruit a drupe, greenish yellow, oblong. Flowers March–April, fruits June–September. Propagated by seeds. Distributed throughout Nepal at 300–1400 m on open hillsides; also in India, Sri Lanka, Thailand, Malaysia, and elsewhere in tropical Asia.

FOOD. The acidic fruit is eaten fresh or pickled.

MEDICINE. Juice of the bark is given for dysentery and rheumatism.

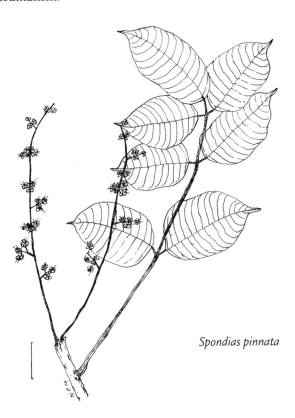

Spondias pinnata

Stachys melissaefolia Bentham

Stachys oblongifolia Wallich ex Bentham
Stachys splendens Wallich
NEPALI *migina*

Labiatae. Erect, woolly, perennial shrub. Leaves stalked, oblong, cordate, dentate. Flowers pink with purple spots, in many-flowered whorls. Flowers and fruits June–August. Propagated by seeds. Distributed throughout Nepal at 2100–4000 m on open slopes in forest clearings; also in India, Bhutan, and southeastern Tibet.

FOOD. The plant is used as a condiment.

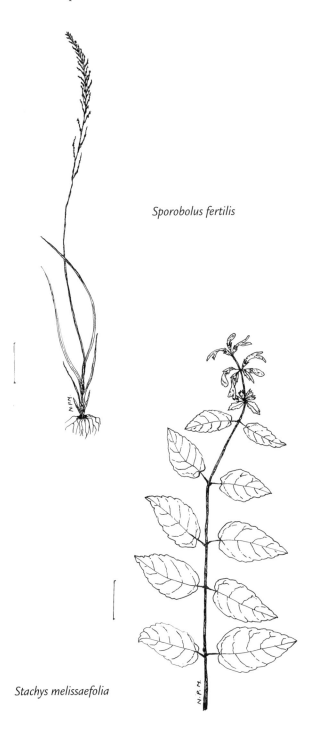

Sporobolus fertilis

Stachys melissaefolia

Sporobolus fertilis (Steudel) W. D. Clayton

Agrostis fertilis Steudel
Sporobolus indicus (Linnaeus) R. Brown
CHEPANG *bachau* NEPALI *bandhan jhar, ghobe*

Gramineae. Perennial grass. Leaves linear. Inflorescence greenish. Fruit a utricle, brownish, ellipsoidal to ovoid. Flowers May–November. Propagated by seeds or root offshoots. Distributed throughout Nepal at 900–2400 m on open, rocky ground; also in India, Sri Lanka, China, Japan, and Southeast Asia.

OTHER USES. The plant is used for fodder and for thatching roofs.

Stachyurus himalaicus Hooker fil. & Thomson ex Bentham

NEPALI *lahare chunetro*

Stachyuraceae. Shrub about 3 m high. Leaves stalked, ovate to lanceolate, acuminate, serrate. Flowers yellowish in erect spikes, March–April. Propagated by seeds. Distributed in eastern and central Nepal at 1300–3000 m in open as well as shady places; also in India, Bhutan, southern Tibet, and western and central China.

OTHER USES. The plant is used for fodder.

Stachyurus himalaicus

Stellaria media (Linnaeus) Villars

NEPALI *armale jhar* TAMANG *sandhap*

Caryophyllaceae. Procumbent annual herb. Lower leaves stalked, upper leaves sessile, ovate or elliptic, shortly acuminate, glossy above, pale beneath. Flowers purple in axillary or terminal cymes. Fruit a capsule, ovoid. Flowers and fruits November–July. Propagated by seeds. Distributed in western and central Nepal at 1800–2700 m, often gregarious on waysides and in open places; also in India, western Tibet, Sri Lanka; also found in most areas of the world.

FOOD. Tender shoots and leaves are cooked as a vegetable.

MEDICINE. A paste of the plant is employed as a plaster for broken bones and swellings.

Stellaria monosperma Buchanan-Hamilton ex D. Don

Stellaria crispata Wallich ex Edgeworth & Hooker fil.

NEPALI *jethi madhu, mhanjari, sanhali sag* TAMANG *ban mran*

Caryophyllaceae. Herb about 50 cm high. Leaves sessile, opposite, 11–16 cm long, 1–3 cm wide, lanceolate, cordate, long-pointed, crispate, glabrous. Flowers white, stalked, the stalk hairy, gland-dotted, August–September. Propagated by seeds. Distributed in western and central at 2200–3200 m in moist, shady places; also in northern India.

FOOD. Tender shoots and leaves are cooked as a vegetable.

MEDICINE. Juice of the root is given to cattle with diarrhea.

Stellaria monosperma

Stellaria sikkimensis Hooker fil. ex Edgeworth & Hooker fil.

NEPALI *lesya kuro*

Caryophyllaceae. Herb, forming matted tufts. Leaves short-stalked, ovate to lanceolate, rarely cordate, hairy on both surfaces. Flowers white in many-flowered cymes. Fruit a capsule, elongate ovoid. Propagated by seeds. Distributed throughout Nepal at 2000–3500 m in moist places; also in northern India and Bhutan.

MEDICINE. Juice of the plant is given in cases of fever. A paste is applied to the forehead to relieve headaches.

Stellaria vestita Kurz

Stellaria hamiltoniana Majumdar
Stellaria saxatilis Buchanan-Hamilton ex D. Don
Stellaria stellato-pilosa Hayata
NEPALI *armane, kharane jhar* TAMANG *tarma*

Caryophyllaceae. Stellately pubescent herb. Leaves sessile, 0.5–3 cm long, 0.3–1 cm wide, ovate, acuminate, base rounded. Flowers white in loose cymes. Fruit a capsule. Flowers and fruits May–July. Propagated by seeds. Distributed throughout Nepal at 1500–2500 m in moist, open places; also in India, Bhutan, western China, Taiwan, and Southeast Asia.

FOOD. Tender shoots and leaves are cooked as a vegetable.

MEDICINE. Juice of the plant is applied to cuts and wounds.

Stellera chamaejasme Linnaeus

Wikstroemia chamaejasme (Linnaeus) Domke
NEPALI *daurali phul, jogi phul* TAMANG *kolte mhendo*
TIBETAN *re-lchag*

Thymelaeaceae. Herb about 30 cm high with a thick rhizome. Leaves numerous, sessile, 1.5–2 cm long, overlapping, elliptic to lanceolate, long-pointed. Flowers pinkish, fragrant. Flowers and fruits May–September. Propagated by seeds. Distributed in western and central Nepal at 2700–4200 m on stony slopes or in abandoned terraced fields; also in northern India, Bhutan, northern China, Mongolia, and eastern Siberia.

MEDICINE. The root is boiled in water until the amount is reduced to half, and this liquid is applied to aching joints. A decoction of bark is applied in cases of sprain.

OTHER USES. Root fiber is used to make cords and twine.

Stephania glandulifera Miers

Stephania rotunda Loureiro
CHEPANG *janjulung, toro lahara* NEPALI *biralgano, gujurgano, mataro gano* TAMANG *gundri gano, miku langu*

Menispermaceae. Twining herb. Leaves stalked, broadly ovate, obtuse, peltate, entire, base truncate. Flowers yellowish or purplish in axillary branched umbels, July–August. Propagated by seeds. Distributed throughout Nepal at 1100–2500 m on moist ground, climbing on hedges and shrubs; also in northern India.

MEDICINE. Juice of the root is applied to sprains and muscular swellings. The tuberous roots are considered nutritious and pieces of them are given to cattle with diarrhea.

Stephania japonica (Thunberg) Miers

Menispermum japonicum Thunberg
NEPALI *batulpate*

Menispermaceae. Slender climber. Leaves peltate, ovate, acuminate to mucronate, leathery, glaucous beneath, base truncate or cordate. Flowers yellowish. Fruit a drupe, small ovoid, red when ripe. Flowers May–October, fruits October–December. Propagated by seeds. Distributed in eastern Nepal at 1800–2600 m on moist ground, trailing on hedges; also in India, Sri Lanka, western China, Malaysia, Taiwan, and Japan.

MEDICINE. Juice of the root is given for fever, diarrhea, and urinary troubles, and a paste is given in cases of stomach trouble.

Stellera chamaejasme

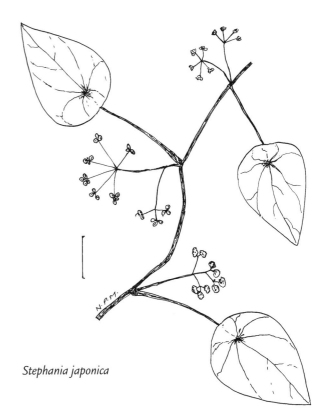

Stephania japonica

Sterculia foetida Linnaeus

ENGLISH *hill coconut, wild almond* NEPALI *kaju*

Sterculiaceae. Deciduous tree about 20 m high. Leaves stalked, crowded at the ends of branches, compound, leaflets seven to nine, borne in a whorl at the end of the stalk, 10–18 cm long, 3.8–5 cm wide. Flowers orange-red or purplish. Fruit large, ovoid, woody, 10- to 15-seeded. Flowers January–March. Propagated by seeds. Distributed in eastern and central Nepal to about 300 m, occasional in *Shorea robusta* forest; also in India, Sri Lanka, Myanmar, northern Australia, and tropical Africa.

FOOD. Roasted seeds are edible.

MEDICINE. Seed oil is laxative and carminative.

Sterculia villosa Roxburgh ex Smith

CHEPANG *botasi, man, manchhi* ENGLISH *elephant rope tree* MAGAR *phirphire* MAJHI *odal* NEPALI *marila, odal* RAI *knowang* TAMANG *tat*

Sterculiaceae. Deciduous tree about 10 m high. Leaves long-stalked, cordate, deeply five- or seven-lobed, lobes entire, stellately hairy above, with intermixed, spreading hairs beneath. Flowers stalked, yellowish, in rusty tomentose panicles, March–April. Fruits June–July. Propagated by seeds. Distributed throughout Nepal at 300–600 m in open places; also in northern India.

FOOD. Powdered root is mixed with rice flour to prepare a bread-like donut (*sel* in Nepali). It makes the bread soft and tasty.

OTHER USES. Wood is soft and may be used as paper pulp. Bark yields a coarse but very strong fiber that is made into ropes and bags.

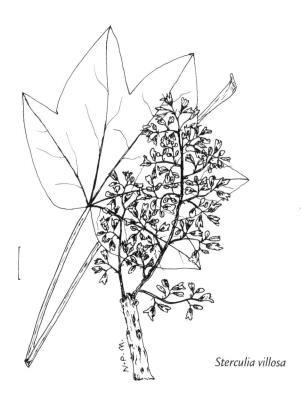

Sterculia villosa

Stereospermum chelonoides (Linnaeus fil.) de Candolle

Bignonia chelonoides Linnaeus fil.
Bignonia suaveolens Roxburgh, *Stereospermum suaveolens* (Roxburgh) de Candolle
NEPALI *dudhe ghirle, padari*

Bignoniaceae. Tree about 15 m high. Leaves stalked, pinnate, leaflets stalked, 6–16 cm long, 3–10 cm wide, elliptic, acuminate, entire, slightly hairy on both surfaces. Flowers yellow. Fruit long cylindrical, covered with many lenticular spots. Flowers June–August, fruits September–December. Propagated by seeds. Distributed throughout Nepal to about 700 m on open land of forest margins; also in India, Bhutan, Sri Lanka, Myanmar, and Java.

MEDICINE. Juice of the bark is given in cases of indigestion.

OTHER USES. Wood is used for furniture.

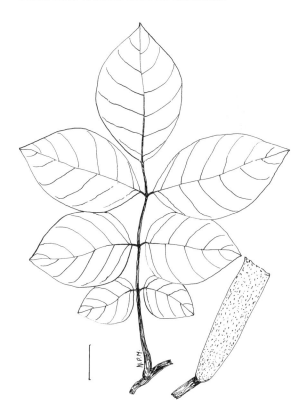

Stereospermum chelonoides

Stranvaesia nussia (Buchanan-Hamilton ex D. Don) Decaisne

Pyrus nussia Buchanan-Hamilton ex D. Don
Cotoneaster affinis Wallich, not Lindley
Crataegus glauca Wallich
Stranvaesia glaucescens Lindley
NEPALI *jure mayel* TAMANG *phaising*

Rosaceae. Tree about 15 m high. Leaves short-stalked, elliptic, oblanceolate, or narrowly lanceolate, acute to apiculate, serrate, leathery, glabrous above, woolly beneath. Flowers white, fragrant, in corymbose panicles. Fruit globose, orange-yellow. Flowers May–June, fruits September–October. Propagated by seeds. Distributed in western and central Nepal at 1000–2500 m in mixed forest; also in northern India, Myanmar, Thailand, Laos, and the Philippines.

FOOD. Ripe fruits are eaten fresh.

OTHER USES. The plant provides fodder.

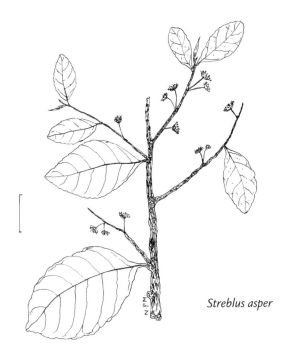

Streblus asper

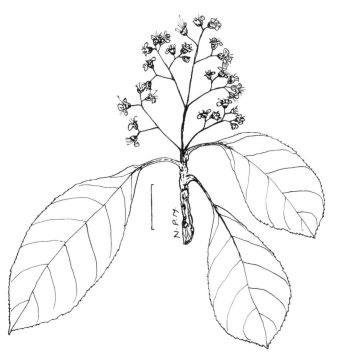

Stranvaesia nussia

Strobilanthes atropurpureus Nees

Ruellia atropurpurea Wallich
NEPALI *angare, jaro buti, kagadil*

Acanthaceae. Subshrub about 2 m high with a stout, woody rootstock. Leaves stalked, 5–11 cm long, 2.5–4.5 cm wide, elliptic to oblong, acuminate, serrate or dentate, base narrowed into a winged stalk. Flowers violet or dark purple in axillary and terminal one-sided spikes. Fruit a capsule, glabrous. Seeds hairy. Flowers June–August, fruits October–November. Propagated by seeds. Distrib-

Streblus asper Loureiro

Trophis asper Retzius
DANUWAR *sahora* ENGLISH *crooked rough brush* MAJHI *datung*
MOOSHAR *sahora* NEPALI *khaksi pate* SATAR *sada*

Moraceae. Evergreen tree about 15 m high. Leaves stalked, 2–8 cm long, 1–4 cm wide, oblong to ovate, obtuse to acuminate, somewhat roughly textured, finely dentate, base narrowed. Flowers yellowish, April–May. Propagated by seeds. Distributed throughout Nepal to about 500 m, along margins of *Shorea robusta* forest; also in northern India, Bhutan, Sri Lanka, southern China, and Southeast Asia.

FOOD. Ripe fruit is edible.

MEDICINE. Juice of the bark is used in cases of skin disease and chapped hands. This juice is also applied to treat gingivitis.

OTHER USES. Stem bark is used for cords, ropes, and twine. Twigs are used as toothbrushes. Leaves are browsed by cattle and goats.

Strobilanthes atropurpureus

uted throughout Nepal at 1100–2400 m in moist, shady places; also in northwestern India.

MEDICINE. Juice of the plant is applied to cuts and wounds.

Strobilanthes colorata (Nees) T. Anderson

Goldfussia colorata Nees, *Diflugossa colorata* (Nees) Bremekamp
Ruellia colorata Wallich
Ruellia hamiltoniana Steudel
Strobilanthes laevigatus C. B. Clarke

TAMANG *tiple*

Acanthaceae. Herb about 1 m high. Leaves stalked, opposite, 5–16 cm long, 2–8 cm wide, ovate to lanceolate, serrate, dark green, slightly hairy on both surfaces, tip pointed, base slightly oblique. Flowers white. Flowers and fruits September–November. Propagated by seeds. Distributed in eastern and central Nepal at 400–1500 m in forest ravines; also in northern India and Bhutan.

OTHER USES. The plant provides fodder.

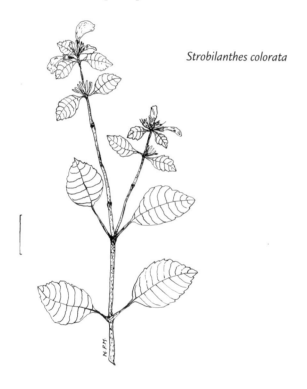

Strobilanthes colorata

Strobilanthes pentastemonoides (Nees)
T. Anderson

Goldfussia pentastemonoides Nees
Ruellia capitata Buchanan-Hamilton ex D. Don
Ruellia cephalotes Wallich
Ruellia penstemonoides Wallich

NEPALI *gathe, kebu* MAGAR *ghurya* TAMANG *dare, dhade, daprangi*

Acanthaceae. Much branched shrub. Leaves stalked, elliptic, long-pointed, finely dentate, the stalk winged. Flowers pink in axillary stalks of round heads. Fruit a capsule, cylindrical. Propagated by seeds. Distributed throughout

Nepal at 1200–2500 m in moist places; also in northern India, Bhutan, western and central China, and Indo-China.

OTHER USES. The plant is poisonous to livestock.

Strobilanthes pentastemonoides

Swertia angustifolia Buchanan-Hamilton ex D. Don

Ophelia angustifolia (Buchanan-Hamilton ex D. Don) G. Don

DANUWAR *chireta* NEPALI *chiraito, goru tite* TAMANG *kampman*

Gentianaceae. Erect herb about 60 cm high with a four-angled stem. Leaves short-stalked, opposite, 4–8 cm long, 1.5–2.2 cm wide, narrowly lanceolate, entire, base narrowed. Flowers yellowish with deep purple dots. Fruit a capsule, oblong. Flowers and fruits May–December. Propagated by seeds. Distributed throughout Nepal at 1300–2500 m on open, grassy slopes; also in northern India, southern China, and Myanmar.

MEDICINE. Juice of the root, about 4 teaspoons twice a day, is given in cases of fever.

Swertia chirayita (Roxburgh ex Fleming) Karsten

Gentiana chirayita Roxburgh ex Fleming
Agathotes chirayta D. Don ex G. Don, *Ophelia chirayta* D. Don ex G. Don
Swertia purpurascens (D. Don) C. B. Clarke

ENGLISH *chiretta* GURUNG *tento* LIMBU *sungkhingba* MAGAR *rauka* NEPALI *chiraito, tito* TAMANG *timda* TIBETAN *tig-ta*

Gentianaceae. Annual herb about 1.5 m high. Leaves sessile, opposite, 3–10 cm long, 0.6–3.5 cm wide, elliptic,

Swertia chirayita

Swertia multicaulis D. Don

NEPALI *sharma guru* SHERPA *hogling*

Gentianaceae. Tufted herb about 15 cm high. Leaves 3–8 cm long, 0.3–1.5 cm wide, linear oblong, acute, entire, base decurrent, forming a winged stalk. Flowers blue in terminal compound cymes. Flowers and fruits June–September. Propagated by seeds. Distributed in eastern and central Nepal at 4000–4900 m in open alpine meadows or on rocky slopes; also in northern India, Bhutan, and southeastern Tibet.

MEDICINE. Juice of the rhizome is used in cases of fever, cough, and colds. The plant is boiled in water about 10 minutes, and the filtered water, about 4 teaspoons, is taken as an anthelmintic.

Swertia nervosa (G. Don) C. B. Clarke

Agathotes nervosa G. Don, *Ophelia nervosa* (G. Don) Grisebach
NEPALI *tite*

Gentianaceae. Erect herb about 1 m high with a four-angled stem. Leaves short-stalked, 4–8 cm long, 1.5–2.2 cm wide, elliptic to lanceolate, base narrow. Flowers yellowish, purple veined, in many-flowered panicles. Fruit a capsule, ovoid. Flowers and fruits October–November. Propagated by seeds. Distributed throughout Nepal at 700–3000 m on open, moist ground; also in northern India and western China.

MEDICINE. The whole plant is boiled in water about 15 minutes, and the filtered water, about 6 teaspoons twice a day, is given in cases of malarial fever.

Swertia pedicellata Banerji

Swertia purpurascens var. *ramosa* Burkill
TIBETAN *syumju tikta*

Gentianaceae. Herb about 35 cm high, stem square. Leaves sessile, opposite, 0.3–3 cm long, 0.2–0.5 cm wide, acute, entire, glabrous. Flowers brownish. Flowers and fruits August–October. Propagated by seeds. Distributed in eastern Nepal at 2500–3500 m in open places; also in northeastern India.

MEDICINE. A paste of the plant is given with water to relieve headaches.

Swertia racemosa (Grisebach) C. B. Clarke

Ophelia racemosa Grisebach, *Kingdon-wardia racemosa*
(Grisebach) T. N. He
Kingdon-wardia codonopsidoides Marquand
NEPALI *chiraito*

Gentianaceae. Erect herb. Leaves subsessile, opposite, 1–6 cm long, 0.3–2.5 cm wide, elliptic to lanceolate, acuminate, entire, glabrous. Flowers blue, axillary, in two- or three-flowered fascicles. Flowers and fruits August–October. Propagated by seeds. Distributed throughout Nepal at 3000–5000 m, common on mossy scree slopes; also in northern India, Bhutan, and southeastern Tibet.

entire, tip pointed. Flowers yellowish or greenish, July–November. Propagated by seeds. Distributed in eastern and central Nepal at 1500–2500 in moist areas and forest openings but the gathering of plants for sale in the trade is a cause of conservation concern; also in northern India and Bhutan.

MEDICINE. The plant is tonic, stomachic, febrifuge, and laxative. It is boiled in water, filtered, and about 4 teaspoons is given three times a day in cases of fever and headache. A paste of the plant is applied to treat skin diseases such as eczema and pimples.

Swertia kingii Hooker fil.

NEPALI *chiraito*

Gentianaceae. Glabrous herb about 60 cm high. Lower leaves stalked, elliptic, acute, narrowed into a broad stalk, upper leaves sessile, opposite, half-clasping the stem at their base, oblong to elliptic. Flowers yellowish green in axillary and terminal cymes. Propagated by seeds. Distributed in central and eastern Nepal at 3100–4500 m in moist places along stream banks; also in India, Bhutan, and southeastern Tibet.

MEDICINE. Juice of the leaves is given in cases of fever.

MEDICINE. The plant is tonic, stomachic, febrifuge, and laxative. It is boiled in water, filtered, and about 4 teaspoons is given three times a day in cases of fever and headache. A paste of the plant is applied to treat skin diseases such as eczema and pimples.

Symplocos dryophila C. B. Clarke

Symplocos laurina Wallich ex G. Don
Symplocos spicata Roxburgh
NEPALI *kholme*

Symplocaceae. Tree about 12 m high. Leaves stalked, 4–16.5 cm long, 1.5–5 cm wide, elliptic to ovate, acuminate, entire, glabrous. Flowers cream. Fruit black when ripe. Flowers March–May, fruits June–September. Propagated by seeds. Distributed in eastern and central Nepal at 2000–2900 m in forest openings; also in northeastern India, southeastern Tibet, southwestern China, and Indo-China.

MEDICINE. Oil from the seed is applied to treat skin diseases such as eczema and ringworm.

Symplocos paniculata (Thunberg) Miquel

Prunus paniculata Thunberg, *Symplocos paniculata* (Thunberg) Wallich ex D. Don
Myrtus chinensis Loureiro, *Symplocos chinensis* (Loureiro) Druce
Symplocos crataegioides Buchanan-Hamilton ex D. Don
ENGLISH *saphire berry* NEPALI *nakulal, sano lodo*

Symplocaceae. Tree about 3 m high. Leaves short-stalked, 2–9 cm long, 1–5 cm wide, ovate or elliptic, acute, serrulate, pubescent beneath. Flowers white, fragrant, in many-flowered pubescent panicles, May–June. Propagated by seeds. Distributed throughout Nepal at 1000–2700 m on sunny hillsides; also in northern India, China, Korea, Japan, and Indo-China.

MEDICINE. Juice of the bark is applied to sprains and muscular swellings.

OTHER USES. Bark yields yellow dye.

Symplocos pyrifolia Wallich ex G. Don

Symplocos nervosa A. de Candolle
NEPALI *ghole, kali kath, kholme, pipiri, seti birauli, seti kath*
SHERPA *khole* TAMANG *sadiwal, syugan*

Symplocaceae. Tree about 10 m high. Leaves stalked, 10–13 cm long, 2–4.5 cm wide, elliptic to lanceolate, acuminate, leathery. Flowers white, fragrant. Fruit cylindrical to ellipsoidal. Flowers and fruits March–February. Propagated by seeds. Distributed in eastern and central Nepal at 1000–2500 m in wet temperate forests; also in northeastern India.

MEDICINE. Oil from the seed is applied to burns and boils.

Symplocos ramosissima Wallich ex G. Don

GURUNG *dhonsi* NEPALI *dabdabe, kauli, kharane, thabthabe*
TAMANG *chunkee, kali geri, syugen*

Symplocaceae. Tree about 15 m high. Leaves stalked, alternate, lanceolate, acuminate, glabrous, serrate. Flowers stalked, bracteate, yellowish. Fruit ellipsoidal. Flowers April–June, fruits June–August. Propagated by seeds. Distributed throughout Nepal at 1400–3000 m in mixed forest; also in northern India, southwestern China, and Indo-China.

FOOD. Seed oil is used for cooking.

MEDICINE. Bark is boiled about 15 minutes, and the strained water is applied to treat dislocated bones.

Symplocos ramosissima

Symplocos theifolia D. Don

Symplocos lucida Siebert & Zuccarini
Symplocos phyllocalyx C. B. Clarke
NEPALI *ghole, hakulal*

Symplocaceae. Tree about 10 m high. Leaves stalked, oblong to lanceolate, acuminate, serrate. Flowers yellowish. Fruit ellipsoidal, glabrous. Flowers July–September, fruits January–February. Propagated by seeds. Distributed throughout Nepal at 1500–3000 m in mixed forest; also in India, Bhutan, southwestern China, and Southeast Asia.

MEDICINE. Oil from the seed is applied to treat scabies.

Synedrella nodiflora (Linnaeus) Gaertner

Verbesina nodiflora Linnaeus
MAJHI *silame ghans* NEPALI *hare jhar*

Compositae. Herb about 50 cm high. Leaves stalked, opposite, 1.3–10 cm long, 0.6–6.5 cm wide, elliptic, pointed, serrate, hairy on both surfaces. Flower heads yellow. Fruit an achene. Flowers and fruits May–December. Propagated by seeds. Distributed in eastern and central Nepal at 400–1400 m on moist ground in the shade of trees; a pan-tropical weed.

MEDICINE. A paste of the plant is applied to cuts and wounds.

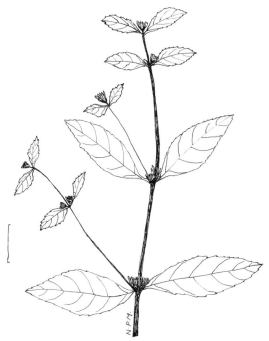

Synedrella nodiflora

Syzygium cumini (Linnaeus) Skeels

Myrtus cumini Linnaeus, *Eugenia cumini* (Linnaeus) Druce
Eugenia jambolana Lamarck, *Syzygium jambolana* (Lamarck)
   de Candolle

BHOJPURI *jamun* CHEPANG *phanrid* DANUWAR *jamuno*
ENGLISH *blackberry, black olum tree, jambolan plum, Java plum, Malabar plum, pitanga* GURUNG *jamuna* LEPCHA *mangret*
LIMBU *makalimse* MAGAR *jamunu* MAJHI *phandil* MOOSHAR *jamun*
NEPALI *jamun, jamuna, kalo jamun, phanir* NEWARI *jamun*
RAI *jamuna, pitlemsi, pitumse, yuyam* SUNWAR *jamuna* SATAR *sokod*
TAMANG *gandijambu, jabu, jamun, jamuna* THARU *jam*
TIBETAN *dzum bu, li shi*

Myrtaceae. Tree about 30 m high. Leaves stalked, 4.5–16.5 cm long, 2–8 cm wide, elliptic to oblong, acuminate, entire, leathery. Flowers creamy white in trichotomous panicles. Fruit a berry, ovoid, dark purple, juicy, one-seeded. Flowers April–May, fruits June–July. Propagated easily by seeds. Distributed throughout Nepal to about 1400 m in open places; also in India, Sri Lanka, China, Myanmar, Malaysia, Australia, and the Philippines.

FOOD. Ripe fruits are eaten fresh and sold in urban markets.

MEDICINE. Juice of the bark or leaf, about 4 teaspoons three times a day, is taken in cases of diarrhea and dysen-tery. Bark juice is also considered good for treating wounds and enlargement of the spleen. In some places in eastern Nepal, diabetics take juice of the bark. Ripe fruit is astringent and is taken as effective remedy for diabetes. In the Terai, diabetic patients chew about 10–15 seeds a day.

OTHER USES. The wood is hard and durable in water, so villagers use planks of it instead of bricks and stones in wells. Wood is resistant to termites and is used to make carts, furniture, handles for agricultural tools, and household articles; it is also used as fuelwood. Bark contains 13–19% tannin and is much used for tanning and dyeing.

Syzygium cumini

Syzygium jambos (Linnaeus) Alston

Eugenia jambos Linnaeus
Jambosa vulgaris de Candolle

CHEPANG *phanrid* ENGLISH *rose apple* NEPALI *gulab jamun*

Myrtaceae. Tree about 6 m high. Leaves stalked, opposite, 8.5–20 cm long, 2–4 cm wide, narrowly lanceolate, acuminate, entire, leathery. Flowers greenish white in terminal cymes. Propagated by seeds. Distributed in eastern and central Nepal at 600–1400 m in open places, generally around villages; also in tropical Asia and Australia.

FOOD. Ripe fruits are eaten fresh.

MEDICINE. Bark is astringent.

OTHER USES. The plant is grown as avenue tree.

T

Tabernaemontana divaricata (Linnaeus)
R. Brown ex Roemer & Schultes

Nerium divaricatum Linnaeus, *Ervatamia divaricata* (Linnaeus) Burkill
Nerium coronarium Jacquin, *Tabernaemontana coronaria* (Jacquin) Aiton
NEPALI *kagate phul*

Apocynaceae. Evergreen shrub about 3 m high. Leaves elliptic to lanceolate, undulate. Flowers white in few-flowered cymes. Fruit a follicle, usually paired but sometimes single, spreading widely when open, cylindrical, fleshy. Propagated by seeds. Distributed in eastern and central Nepal at 250–1200 m, fairly common on uncultivated land; also in tropical Asia.

MEDICINE. The root is chewed to treat toothaches. The milky juice is applied to relieve inflammation of the eye.

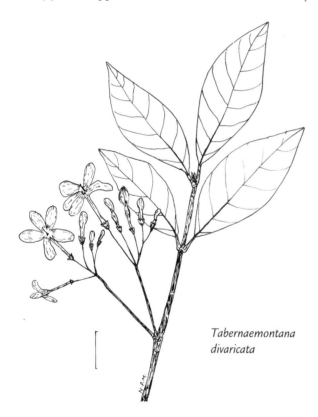

Tabernaemontana divaricata

Tadehaji triquetrum (Linnaeus) Ohashi

Hedysarum triquetrum Linnaeus, *Desmodium triquetrum* (Linnaeus) de Candolle, *Pteroloma triquetrum* (Linnaeus) Bentham
Desmodium pseudotriquetrum de Candolle
NEPALI *sano bhatte, sangle jhar, sulsule*   TAMANG *golamen*

Leguminosae. Shrub. Leaves stalked, winged, 2.5–11 cm long, 1–4.5 cm wide, lanceolate, acuminate, entire,

slightly hairy on the upper surface, hairy on the veins beneath, base rounded. Flowers purplish, July–August. Fruits September–November. Propagated by seeds. Distributed throughout Nepal at 500–1500 m in openings in *Shorea robusta* forest; also in northern India, China, and the Philippines.

MEDICINE. Juice of the plant, about 4 teaspoons twice a day, is given in cases of diarrhea.

Tadehaji triquetrum

Tagetes erecta Linnaeus

ENGLISH *African marigold*   NEPALI *sayapatri*   NEWARI *taphwa swan*   TAMANG *phole mhendo*

Compositae. Erect shrub about 1 m high. Leaves deeply pinnatifid, lobes lanceolate, coarsely and sharply dentate. Flower heads solitary, long-stalked, yellow. Fruit an achene. Propagated by seeds. Distributed throughout Nepal to about 2200 m, cultivated; also in most parts of the world.

FOOD. The fresh receptacle is eaten by Mooshar children.

MEDICINE. Juice of the plant is used for rheumatic pains, colds, and bronchitis. The root has a laxative property. A paste of the leaves is applied to treat boils, carbuncles, and earaches. A decoction of the flowers is carminative, diuretic, and vermifuge. Juice of the flowers is applied externally for inflammation of the eye and to treat skin diseases.

Tagetes erecta

cm wide, oblong, obtuse. Flowers yellow with pink streaks, in racemes. Fruit a pod, oblong, thickened, slightly compressed, the mesocarp pulpy, acidic. Flowers March–May, fruits April–June. Propagated by seeds. Distributed throughout Nepal to about 1200 m in open places around villages; also in Pakistan, India, Bhutan, Thailand, and tropical Africa.

FOOD. Ripe or immature fruits are eaten fresh or pickled. A marmalade is also made from the pulp of ripe fruits.

MEDICINE. Bark is astringent and tonic. Juice of the bark is boiled and the liquid is used externally for sores and boils; it is taken internally for asthma and as a febrifuge. A paste of young leaves is applied for rheumatism, inflammation of ankles and other joints, sores, and wounds. Boiled juice of young leaves is dripped into the eye to treat conjunctivitis and is also taken in doses of about 4 teaspoons three times a day for cough and colds. Water boiled with the leaf is used as a wash to relieve joint pains and body aches. Pulp of the fruit is a mild laxative. A powder of the seeds is taken in cases of diarrhea and dysentery.

OTHER USES. Bark and leaves contain tannin.

OTHER USES. The plant has an ornamental value, and flower heads are offered to gods and goddesses. The plant provides a good source of income for villagers who sell the flower heads and garlands in urban markets, especially during Dasain, Tihar, and other ceremonial occasions.

Talauma hodgsonii Hooker fil. & Thomson

Magnolia hodgsonii (Hooker fil. & Thomson) Keng fil.
NEPALI *bhalu kath*

Magnoliaceae. Evergreen tree to 12 m high. Leaves stalked, 25–30 cm long, 10–16 cm wide, alternate, ovate to oblong, acute, entire, glabrous. Flowers large, terminal, white or pinkish, fragrant, April–May. Fruits August–September. Propagated by seeds. Distributed in central and eastern Nepal at 900–1800 m, mostly in forested areas, but habitat destruction, the plant's limited natural distribution, and the gathering of its wood for sale in the trade endanger plant populations; also India, Bhutan, Myanmar, and Thailand.

OTHER USES. Wood is used for the handle of the *khukuri*, the Nepalese curved knife. It is also extensively used for fuelwood. Stipules are chewed by village girls to blacken their teeth and gums.

Tamarindus indica Linnaeus

Tamarindus officinalis Hooker
DANUWAR *imali, tetor, tetara* ENGLISH *tamarind* MAJHI *titari*
MOOSHAR *imali* NEPALI *tate amilo, titari* NEWARI *titis paun*
RAI *titari* SATAR *jojo* TIBETAN *bse-yab*

Leguminosae. Tree about 25 m high. Leaves stalked, even-pinnate, leaflets short-stalked, 1–2 cm long, 0.5–0.8

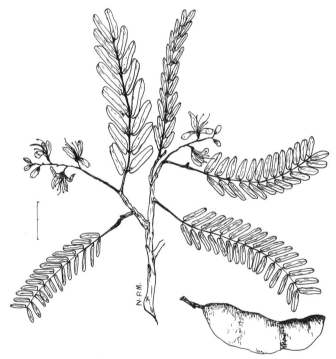

Tamarindus indica

Tanacetum dolichophyllum (Kitamura) Kitamura

Chrysanthemum dolichophyllum Kitamura
Tanacetum longifolium Wallich ex de Candolle
NEPALI *bojhari*

Compositae. Erect perennial shrub about 30 cm high. Lower leaves long-stalked, upper leaves sessile, 12–25 cm long, oblong, twice cut into linear segments. Flower heads yellow. Fruit an achene. Flowers and fruits July–September. Propagated by seeds. Distributed in western and central Nepal at 3000–4400 m, common on open slopes; also in India and China.

MEDICINE. A paste of the root is given in cases of indigestion.

Taraxacum officinale (Linnaeus) Weber

ENGLISH *dandelion* GURUNG *neta dha* NEPALI *dudhe jhar, karnaphuli, phuli jhar, tuki phul* TAMANG *hyo mran, nedhap, dini mhendo* TIBETAN *khur-mang-mang, kojate*

Compositae. Herb about 10 cm high. Leaves all basal, variable in shape, narrowly oblong, irregularly pinnatifid, dentate. Flower heads yellow, solitary, on a hollow leafless stalk. Fruit an achene. Flowers March–November. Propagated by seeds. Distributed throughout Nepal at 1000–4000 m, common in moist or dry places.

FOOD. Tender leaves are valued as a potherb.

MEDICINE. Roots are diuretic, aperient, and tonic. Juice of the root, about 2 teaspoons three times a day, is given to treat stomach disorders.

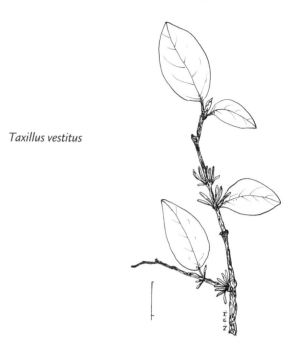

Taxillus vestitus

Taraxacum officinale

Taxillus vestitus (Wallich) Danser

Loranthus vestitus Wallich

NEPALI *nai*

Loranthaceae. Woody parasitic shrub, branches stout, terete, with evident lenticels. Bark brown, young parts softly tomentose. Leaves stalked, 4–7.5 cm long, 1.5–4 cm wide, elliptic to lanceolate, obtuse, leathery, glabrous above, brown tomentose beneath, base rounded or obtuse. Flowers reddish in axillary fascicles. Fruit ellipsoidal, orange, glabrous. Propagated by seeds. Distributed through-

out Nepal to about 2100 m on the branches of trees and shrubs; also in northern India.

FOOD. Ripe fruits are edible.

MEDICINE. The plant is boiled in water to prepare a gelatinous mass that is applied to sprains and muscular swellings.

Taxus baccata Linnaeus subsp. *wallichiana* (Zuccarini) Pilger

Taxus wallichiana Zuccarini

ENGLISH *common yew, English yew* GURUNG *salin* NEPALI *barma salla, bham salla, bung, luinth, pate salla, silangi, thingre salla* NEWARI *la swan* SHERPA *chyangsing* TAMANG *sigi*

Taxaceae. Evergreen coniferous tree about 12 m high. Bark reddish brown, rough, exfoliating in irregular papery

Taxus baccata subsp. *wallichiana*

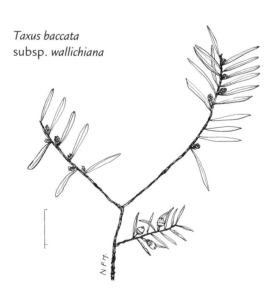

scales. Leaves short-stalked, 2.5–4 cm long, linear, flattened, distichous, acute, shiny dark green above, rusty beneath, narrowed toward the base. Cones yellowish, axillary. Seed cones red. Seeds olive green. Cones April–May, mature November–December. Propagated by seeds. Distributed throughout Nepal at 2200–3400 m on exposed slopes but the gathering of its leaves for sale in the trade is a cause of conservation concern; also in Afghanistan, Pakistan, northern India, western China, and Southeast Asia.

FOOD. The red and fleshy cup-shaped aril that surrounds the seed is eaten by villagers.

MEDICINE. Juice of leaves is given for cough, bronchitis, and asthma. Leaves are sold in the trade as a cancer cure.

Tectaria macrodonta (Fée) C. Christensen

CHEPANG *gorgan* GURUNG *yolpa kuta, kuturge* NEPALI *kali nyuro, kali kuthurke, rani sinka* TAMANG *toplign degni*

Dryopteridaceae. Erect fern about 70 cm high. Fronds 25–35 cm long, 14–20 cm wide, subdeltoid, apex pinnatifid. Sori prominent, brown, in two rows near the main vein. Propagated by spores or by splitting the rhizomes. Distributed throughout Nepal at 1000–2500 m, common in moist, shady places; also in India and Bhutan.

FOOD. Tender fronds are cooked as a vegetable.

MEDICINE. Juice of the rhizome, about 4 teaspoons three times a day, is given for diarrhea and dysentery. This juice, mixed with the juice of *Ageratum conyzoides* in equal amount, is applied to cuts and wounds. A paste of the rhizome is applied to treat throat aches and headaches.

Telosma pallida (Roxburgh) Craib

Asclepias pallida Roxburgh, *Pergularia pallida* (Roxburgh) Wight & Arnott

NEPALI *asare phul*

Asclepiadaceae. Twining shrub, bark pale brown, somewhat corky. Leaves stalked, 4–9.5 cm long, 1–2.5 cm wide, lanceolate to cordate, acuminate, entire, dull dark green above, pale beneath. Flowers yellowish in umbellate cymes. Fruit a follicle, lanceolate, longitudinally wrinkled, tapering to a blunt point. Flowers May–July, fruits September–November. Propagated by seeds. Distributed throughout Nepal at 300–900 m in moist, open places, climbing on shrubby hedges; also in India, Indo-China, and Taiwan.

FOOD. Flowers are fried and are eaten as a vegetable.

Terminalia alata Heyne ex Roth

Pentaptera tomentosa Roxburgh, *Terminalia tomentosa* (Roxburgh) Wight & Arnott

CHEPANG *darsing* DANUWAR *asana* ENGLISH *Indian laurel* NEPALI *asana, saj* TAMANG *sas*

Combretaceae. Large deciduous tree, bark brown or gray, young parts rusty tomentose. Leaves stalked, subopposite, 10–14 cm long, oblong or ovate, obtuse, entire, unequal and somewhat cordate at the base. Flowers cream

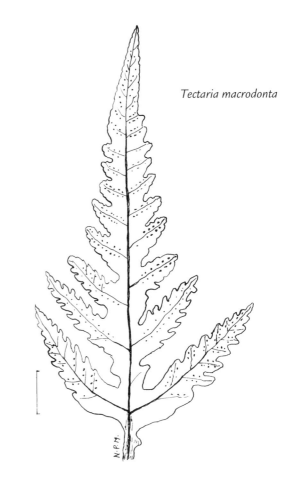

Tectaria macrodonta

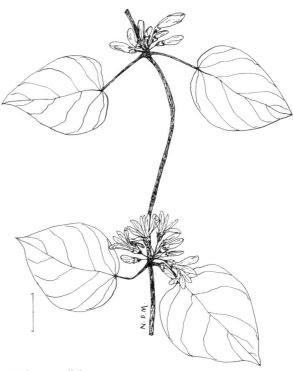

Telosma pallida

in panicled lax spikes. Fruit five-winged. Flowers May–July, fruits August–November. Propagated by seeds. Distributed throughout Nepal at 200–1400 m, common in *Shorea robusta* forest; also in India, Sri Lanka, and Indo-China.

MEDICINE. Juice of the bark is applied to cuts and wounds. This juice is boiled and is rubbed on the head to remove dandruff. A paste of the gum is applied to burns and is also used to treat swellings caused by inflammation.

OTHER USES. The plant is lopped for fodder. Wood has timber value and provides excellent fuelwood for heat and wood for making charcoal.

Terminalia arjuna Beddome

NEPALI *arjun*

Combretaceae. Large deciduous tree, bark whitish, smooth. Leaves stalked, subopposite, 10–20 cm long, 4.5–6.5 cm wide, ovate to oblong, crenate, slightly pointed at the tip, base rounded or unequally sided. Flowers yellowish. Fruit with five leathery wings, tan when dry. Flowers April–May, fruits November–December. Propagated by seeds. Distributed throughout Nepal to about 1000 m in mixed forest; also in India, Bangladesh, Sri Lanka, and Myanmar.

MEDICINE. Juice of the bark is given as tonic.

OTHER USES. Wood is used for agricultural implements. Bark contains tannin. Leaves are lopped for fodder.

Terminalia bellirica (Gaertner) Roxburgh

Myrobalanus bellirica Gaertner

BHOJPURI *bahare* CHEPANG *lisi, tupchi, tumsai* DANUWAR *barro* ENGLISH *belleric myrobalans* GURUNG *barro* LEPCHA *samylapot* LIMBU *tamajise* NEPALI *barro* NEWARI *bala* RAI *thushasansi, tuktam* RAUTE *sidha* SUNWAR *barro* THARU *asidha* TIBETAN *ba-ru*

Combretaceae. Deciduous tree about 30 m high. Leaves long-stalked, alternate, 9–26 cm long, 5–14 cm wide, mostly at the ends of branches, elliptic to ovate, leathery, entire, base narrowed and unequal. Flowers sessile, yellowish, in axillary slender spikes, the odor offensive. Fruit a drupe, obovoid, gray velvety. Flowers April–June, fruits July–December. Propagated by seeds. Distributed throughout Nepal to about 1100 m in mixed *Shorea robusta* forest but the gathering of its wood for timber and fuel and its fruit for sale in the trade are causes of conservation concern; also in India, Sri Lanka, and Southeast Asia.

FOOD. Kernels of the fruit are edible.

MEDICINE. The fruit is anthelmintic, astringent, digestive, laxative, and purgative; it is also considered tonic. It is one of the important constituents of the *triphala* of Ayurvedic medicine (as explained under *Phyllanthus emblica*). The fruit is boiled in water about 15 minutes, and the filtered water is taken to ameliorate asthma, bronchitis, and respiratory trouble. Rautes take juice of immature fruit to relieve fever.

OTHER USES. Wood is valued as fuelwood and timber for construction. Bark is used for dye. It is also used for mak-

ing agricultural implements and other domestic articles. Leaves are lopped for fodder. Fruits contain tannin.

Terminalia chebula Retzius

CHEPANG *tupchi, lisai* ENGLISH *chebulic myrobalans* LIMBU *hangsep* NEPALI *harro* NEWARI *hala* SHERPA *arubharelu* TIBETAN *a-ru, a-ru-ra*

Combretaceae. Deciduous tree about 30 m high, young branches covered with rusty brown hairs. Leaves stalked, opposite or alternate, 6–17 cm long, 3.5–12 cm wide, oblong to ovate, acuminate, entire, smooth. Flowers sessile, yellowish, the odor offensive, in terminal spikes. Fruit a nut, ellipsoidal, thick and hard with a rough surface. Flowers April–June, fruits December–March. Propagated by seeds. Distributed throughout Nepal to about 1100 m in openings in *Shorea robusta* forest but the gathering of its wood for timber and fuel and its fruit for sale in the trade are causes of conservation concern; also in India, Sri Lanka, Myanmar, and Malaysia.

FOOD. Kernels of the fruit are edible.

MEDICINE. Bark has diuretic properties. The fruit is alterative, astringent, carminative, purgative, and stomachic. It is one of the important constituents of the *triphala* of Ayurvedic medicine (as explained under *Phyllanthus emblica*). A paste of the fruit is used for asthma and hemorrhoids. Juice of the fruit is valued for eye, heart, and spleen diseases. Powdered fruit is taken with water to treat cough.

OTHER USES. Wood is used for construction, agricultural implements, furniture, and other domestic purposes, including fuel. Leaves are lopped for fodder. Fruit and bark have tannin.

Terminalia chebula

Terminalia myriocarpa Heurck & Mueller Aargau

ENGLISH *hallock* NEPALI *pani saj, saj*

Combretaceae. Deciduous tree about 30 m high, bark rough, grayish brown, exfoliating in longitudinal flakes. Leaves stalked, oblong or elliptic, acute, glabrous. Flowers pinkish. Fruit shiny yellow, with two very broad wings and one narrow wing. Flowers October–November, fruits March–June. Propagated by seeds. Distributed in eastern and central Nepal at 200–1200 m in moist situations, usually near streams; also in India, Bhutan, western China, Indo-China, and northern Sumatra.

MEDICINE. Juice of the bark is applied to cuts and wounds.

OTHER USES. Wood is used to make furniture, household articles, doors, and windows.

Tetrastigma serrulatum (Roxburgh) Planchon

Cissus serrulata Roxburgh
Cissus napaulensis de Candolle
Tetrastigma indicum M. Maulik
Vitis affinis Gagnepain ex Osmaston, *Tetrastigma affine* (Gagnepain ex Osmaston) Raizada & Saxena
Vitis capriolata D. Don, *Cissus capriolata* (D. Don) Royle

CHEPANG *arthunge* NEPALI *baragaunlo, barkhyu lahara, charchare lahara, chatake, cuchi, makuri, pani lahara, thulo makure lahara* TAMANG *chijlangdu, ghugi, hukki, landu bramji*

Vitaceae. Evergreen climber, stems climbing by means of adventitious roots and tendrils. Leaves stalked, trifoli-

olate, leaflets 1.5–9 cm long, 0.6–3 cm wide, elliptic to lanceolate, acuminate, cuspidately serrate, glabrous. Flowers yellowish in umbellate cymes. Fruit globose, black when ripe. Flowers July–September, fruits November–February. Propagated by seeds. Distributed throughout Nepal to about 2400 m in open, moist places; also in India, Bhutan, Bangladesh, western China, and Indo-China.

FOOD. Ripe fruits are eaten fresh.

MEDICINE. Juice of the plant, about 6 teaspoons twice a day, is given in cases of fever. A paste of the plant is applied to aid setting of dislocated bone.

OTHER USES. Plants are gathered to feed animals in stalls. Squeezed plant is used for washing the head. Thin stems and branches are used for temporary binding.

Teucrium quadrifarium Buchanan-Hamilton ex D. Don

CHEPANG *siongwan* NEPALI *bhatarya pat, kalo rudilo*

Labiatae. Erect herb about 1 m high. Leaves shortstalked, 2.5–12 cm long, 2–4.5 cm wide, oblong to ovate or cordate, serrate. Flowers pink in terminal panicled racemes, August–October. Fruits November–December. Propagated by seeds. Distributed in western and central Nepal at 1000–2400 m on open, sunny hillsides and in grassland; also in India, Bhutan, China, and Southeast Asia.

MEDICINE. Juice of the plant is applied to wounds between the toes caused by prolonged walking barefooted in muddy water.

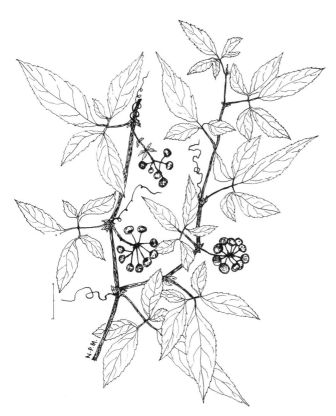

Tetrastigma serrulatum

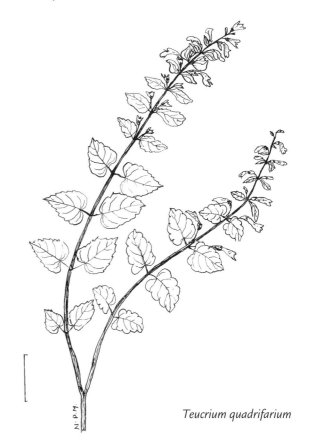

Teucrium quadrifarium

Thalictrum elegans Wallich ex Royle

SHERPA *kuner* TIBETAN *chyaksep*

Ranunculaceae. Erect herb about 30 cm high. Leaves stalked, tripinnate, leaflets small, often three-lobed. Flowers whitish. Fruit an achene, obliquely ovoid, membranous with a winged ventral surface. Flowers and fruits July–September. Propagated by seeds. Distributed throughout Nepal at 3100–4100 m in exposed, sunny areas on rocky ground; also in India, Bhutan, and Tibet.

MEDICINE. A paste of the plant is applied to treat joint aches.

Thalictrum foliolosum de Candolle

Thalictrum falconeri Lecoyer

CHEPANG *bangpahar, bathure, bhajuri* GURUNG *bekar mai, pajeni* MAGAR *bajuri* NEPALI *bajara, bansuli, chhate, dampati, mamira, penyale* TAMANG *bathuri, nangsewamen, phalkichhe* TIBETAN *kremiye*

Ranunculaceae. Shrub about 1.5 m high. Leaves stalked, pinnately decompound, leaflets subsessile, 0.5–2.5 cm long, 0.5–2 cm wide, orbiculate or ovate to oblong, dentate. Flowers purplish, whitish, or yellowish, in branched panicles, June–August. Fruits September–November. Prop-

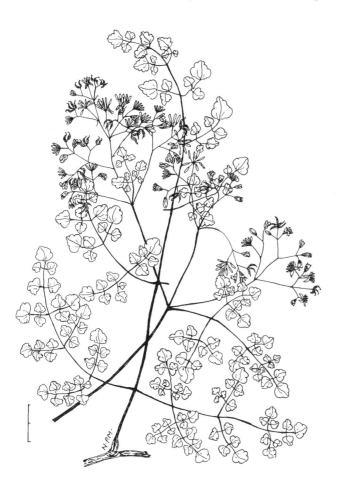

Thalictrum foliolosum

agated by seeds or root offshoots. Distributed throughout Nepal at 1300–3400 m; also in northern India, Bhutan, Tibet, northern Myanmar, Africa, and Europe.

MEDICINE. Juice of the root is a valuable remedy for ophthalmia and is febrifuge, diuretic, and purgative. The juice, about 6 teaspoons twice a day, is given for fever and peptic ulcer. It is also useful in cases of indigestion, toothache, hemorrhoids, and earache. A paste of the root is applied to set dislocated bones of animals and is useful in soothing itching. Juice of the leaves is applied to boils and pimples.

Thalictrum javanicum Blume

Thalictrum glyphocarpum Wight & Arnott

GURUNG *saipatin* NEPALI *guhya pati*

Ranunculaceae. Shrub about 1 m high. Leaves stalked, ternately divided, leaflets 0.7–2 cm long, 0.5–1.5 cm wide, ovate, obtusely three- to seven-lobed, glaucous beneath. Flowers white or purplish in branched panicles, often at the ends of branches. Fruit an achene, short beaked. Flowers July–October, fruits October–November. Propagated by seeds or root offshoots. Distributed in western and central Nepal at 2100–3000 m on moist, rocky ground in shady places; also in northern India, Tibet, Sri Lanka, western China, and Java.

MEDICINE. Juice of the plant is applied to boils and pimples. A decoction of the root, about 1 teaspoon twice a day, is given to treat fever.

Thamnocalamus aristatus (Gamble) E. G. Camus

Arundinaria aristata Gamble

NEPALI *ghore nigalo*

Gramineae. Bamboo of short stature, with robust culms, culms mealy white, nodes hardly inflated, culm sheath broad at the base, gradually narrowed toward the top. Leaves in groups of two or three at the tops of branchlets, oblong to lanceolate, terminating in a bristly point, shorter toward the base, sparsely hairy below, the surface somewhat rough. Inflorescence whitish. Fruit a grain, linear oblong, dark brown, furrowed on one side. Propagated by splitting the rhizomes. Distributed in eastern Nepal at 2200–3100 m on open, rocky ground; also in northeastern India.

OTHER USES. Culms are suitable for making walking sticks. Leaves are used for fodder.

Thelypteris ciliata (Wallich ex Bentham) Ching

NEPALI *jire nyuro, tore nyuro*

Thelypteridaceae. Erect fern. Stipes about 25 cm long, covered with fine, soft hairs. Fronds pinnate, pinnae nearly sessile. Sori small, brown, marginal. Available for use June–July. Propagated by spores or by splitting the rhizomes. Distributed throughout Nepal at 500–2400 m in moist, rocky places.

FOOD. Tender fronds are cooked as a vegetable.

Thamnocalamus aristatus

Thelypteris multilineata

MEDICINE. Juice of the rhizome, about 3 teaspoons twice a day, is given to treat fever.

Thelypteris esquirolii (H. Christ) Ching

NEPALI *danthe unyu*

Thelypteridaceae. Fern. Stipes erect, covered with scattered brown scales. Fronds pinnate, pinnae numerous, sessile, lanceolate, subopposite, deeply cut down to the rachis into oblong segments. Sori close to the margin on either side of the midvein. Spores July–August. Propagated by spores or by splitting the rhizomes. Distributed in central Nepal at 1200–2200 m, frequent in shady places in temperate forest; also in India, China, and Japan.

MEDICINE. Juice of the rhizome, about 4 teaspoons three times a day, is given in cases of stomach disorder.

Thelypteris multilineata (Wallich ex Hooker) Morton

NEPALI *koche*

Thelypteridaceae. Herbaceous fern. Stipes about 60 cm long. Fronds pinnate, pinnae many, short-stalked, 10–20 cm long, distantly serrate. Sori brown, in a row on either side of the veinlet. Available for use June–July. Propagated by spores or by splitting the rhizomes. Distributed throughout Nepal at 300–1500 m in moist places; also in India, Bhutan, Malaysia, and Polynesia.

FOOD. Tender fronds are cooked as a vegetable.

MEDICINE. Juice of the rhizome, about 3 teaspoons twice a day, is given in cases of diarrhea and dysentery.

Thelypteris paludosa (Blume) K. Iwatsuki

NEPALI *kalare unyu*

Thelypteridaceae. Terrestrial fern. Stipes slender, glossy purplish brown. Fronds large, bipinnate, pinnae numerous, lanceolate, opposite, deeply cut. Sori small, on lateral veins. Spores July–August. Propagated by spores or by splitting the rhizomes. Distributed in eastern and central Nepal at 1200–2800 m, frequent in shady places; also in India, Bhutan, Taiwan, Malaysia, and Polynesia.

MEDICINE. Juice of the rhizome, about 4 teaspoons twice a day, is given in cases of indigestion.

Thelypteris subpubescens (Blume) K. Iwatsuki

NEPALI *tyamno*

Thelypteridaceae. Terrestrial fern. Fronds pinnate, pinnae in few pairs, linear lanceolate, subopposite, deeply cut down to the rachis, margin reflexed. Sori in a row on either side of the main vein. Spores July–August. Propagated by spores or by splitting the rhizomes. Distributed in central Nepal at 1000–2500 m in shady places in forested areas; also in India, Bhutan, and Southeast Asia.

MEDICINE. The plant is spread in the animal shed as bedding.

Thespesia lampas (Cavanilles) Dalzell & Gibson

Azanza lampas Cavanilles, *Hibiscus lampas* (Cavanilles) Alefeld
Hibiscus tetralocularis Roxburgh

MAGAR *ban kapas* NEPALI *ban kapas, kapase*
TAMANG *khamari, syang*

Malvaceae. Shrub about 3 m high. Leaves stalked, 6–19 cm long, 4.5–17.5 cm wide, ovate, palmately three-lobed, roughly entire, stellately pilose above, tomentose beneath. Flowers yellow in axillary cymes. Fruit a capsule, ovoid, pointed. Flowers August–September, fruits October–January. Propagated by seeds. Distributed throughout Nepal at 200–1100 m in moist, shady places on rocky ground; also in southern Asia, Southeast Asia, and Africa.

MEDICINE. Juice of the root, about 4 teaspoons twice a day, is given for indigestion. A paste of the root and fruit is used in cases of gonorrhea and syphilis.

OTHER USES. Bark yields white fiber used for temporary binding.

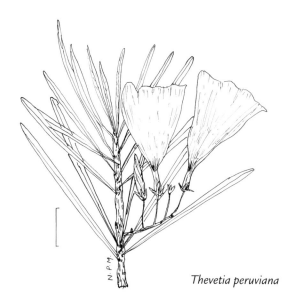

Thevetia peruviana

Thespesia lampas

Thevetia peruviana (Persoon) K. Schumann

Cerbera peruviana Persoon
Cerbera thevetia Linnaeus, *Cascabela thevetia* (Linnaeus) Lippold
NEPALI *sano karbir* THARU *kandail*

Apocynaceae. Evergreen shrub. Leaves stalked, spirally arranged, 7.5–15 cm long, linear, glossy green, margin recurved. Flowers yellow, fragrant, in few-flowered cymes. Fruit nearly globose, longitudinally constricted, fleshy. Flowers and fruits most of the year. Propagated by seeds. Distributed throughout Nepal at 130–1000 m; also in India, Bhutan, and tropical America.

MEDICINE. Bark is febrifuge and antiperiodic. Extreme caution is used in these remedies as parts of the plant are poisonous.

OTHER USES. The fruit and its latex are poisonous.

Thlaspi arvensis Linnaeus

NEPALI *tite*

Cruciferae. Erect annual herb about 40 cm high. Lower leaves ovate to lanceolate, dentate, upper leaves clasping the stem at their base. Flowers white. Fruit a pod, flattened. Flowers March–May. Propagated by seeds. Distributed in western and central Nepal at 2100–4500 m in open or shady places along riverbanks; also in temperate Eurasia.

FOOD. Tender shoots are cooked as a vegetable.

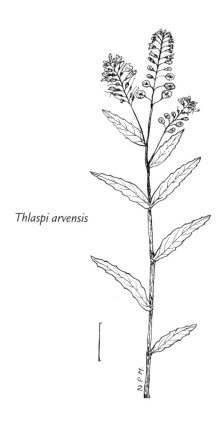

Thlaspi arvensis

Thunbergia coccinea Wallich ex D. Don

Hexacentris coccinea (Wallich ex D. Don) Nees
CHEPANG *basekre* GURUNG *kaka lahara* NEPALI *kanase,
singarne lahara, ullu khar* TAMANG *gau lahara, kaulun thunga*

Acanthaceae. Branched climber, bark pale brown, reddish. Leaves stalked, 7.5–15 cm long, 4–7.5 cm wide, ovate to oblong, acuminate, margin sinuate or bluntly dentate, base cordate or rounded. Flowers yellow, tinged with red outside, in terminal drooping racemes. Fruit a capsule. Flowers December–March. Propagated by seeds. Distributed throughout Nepal at 300–1800 m in moist, shady places; also in northern India, Bhutan, western China, and Indo-China.

FOOD. Flowers are cooked as a vegetable.

MEDICINE. Juice of the plant is applied to cuts and wounds. The root is chewed to treat boils on the tongue.

OTHER USES. The vine is used for binding.

Thunbergia grandiflora Roxburgh

Flemingia grandiflora Roxburgh ex Rottler
DANUWAR *kag phuli, kauwa latti* NEPALI *kag chuchche*
TAMANG *gau lahara, kaulun thunga*

Acanthaceae. Large woody climber. Leaves stalked, 3–20 cm long, 2.5–17 cm wide, orbiculate or ovate, thick, fleshy, upper leaves lanceolate, 6–20 cm long, deeply cordate, dentate or lobed. Flowers light blue in racemes. Fruit a capsule. Flowers and fruits September–December. Propagated by seeds. Distributed in eastern and central Nepal at 300–1300 m, cultivated, or naturalized in moist places; also in India, Bhutan, southern China, and Indo-China.

MEDICINE. Juice of the leaves and root is used to treat cuts and wounds.

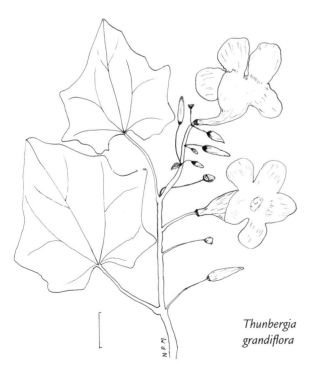

Thunbergia grandiflora

OTHER USES. The plant is grown as an ornamental on fences.

Thunia alba (Lindley) Reichenbach

Phaius albus Lindley
Limodorum bracteatum Roxburgh, *Thunia bracteata* (Roxburgh) Schlechter
NEPALI *chhade phul, golaino*

Orchidaceae. Epiphytic orchid without pseudobulbs. Leaves sessile, 15–25 cm long, 2–3.5 cm wide, elliptic to lanceolate, acuminate, glaucous beneath, sheathing at the base. Flowers white in terminal racemes, May–July. Propagated by seeds or root offshoots. Distributed throughout Nepal at 500–1800 m in sunny places; also in northern India and Myanmar.

MEDICINE. A paste of the plant is applied to set dislocated bone.

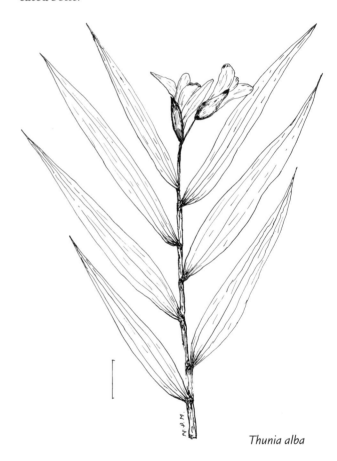

Thunia alba

Thymus linearis Bentham

Thymus himalayicus Ronniger
Thymus quinquecostatus Čelakovsky
Thymus serpylim Linnaeus
ENGLISH *mother-of-thyme, serpyllum, thyme* GURUNG *ban jawan*
NEPALI *ghora marcha* TAMANG *teno* TIBETAN *rgya-spos*

Labiatae. Aromatic herb with procumbent stem, twigs clothed with short white hairs. Leaves short-stalked, opposite, 0.5–1.5 cm long, 0.2–0.5 cm wide, ovate to oblong, gland-dotted on both surfaces. Flowers purplish in globose terminal spikes, July–October. Propagated by seeds. Distributed in western and central Nepal at 2400–4500 m on open slopes; also in Afghanistan, Pakistan, northern India, Tibet, China, and Japan.

FOOD. Leaves and flowers are pickled and also used as a spice and condiment.

MEDICINE. Juice of the plant is given for stomach and liver complaints. It is mixed with warm water for bathing to relieve body pains. The plant is boiled in water about 10 minutes, and the filtered water, about 3 teaspoons, is given as an anthelmintic.

OTHER USES. The plant contains 1.4% essential oils and is burned for incense.

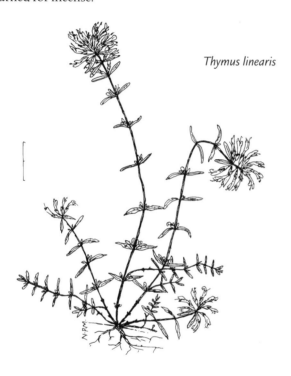

Thymus linearis

Thysanolaena maxima (Roxburgh) Kuntze

Agrostis maxima Roxburgh
Melica latiflia Roxburgh
Thysanolaena acarifera Arnott & Nees
Thysanolaena agrostis Nees
CHEPANG *chyas, gerai*   ENGLISH *tiger grass*   GURUNG *mra, mro kucha*
LIMBU *sellosang*   MAGAR *huk, phurke*   NEPALI *amreso, amrisau*
NEWARI *tuphi*   TAMANG *karauti chhe, phys, sarsi*

Gramineae. Perennial grass about 3 m high, culms terete, smooth, glabrous, solid rather than hollow. Leaves large, linear lanceolate, leathery, tapering to a fine point, cordate at the base. Inflorescence brownish. Fruit a grain, minute. Flowers and fruits November–February. Propagated by seeds or by splitting the mother plant. Distributed in eastern and central Nepal at 300–2000 m in open, rocky places; also in India, China, and Southeast Asia.

FOOD. Chepangs eat fresh leaf buds.

MEDICINE. A paste of the root is applied to boils.

OTHER USES. The inflorescence is used for brooms, which many villagers sell in the urban markets.

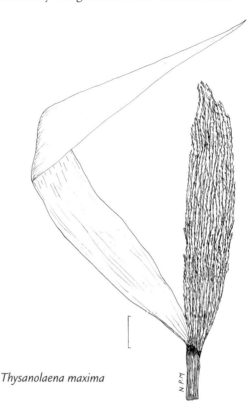

Thysanolaena maxima

Tiarella polyphylla D. Don

NEPALI *sisne jhar*

Saxifragaceae. Erect herb about 30 cm high. Lower leaves long-stalked, broadly ovate to cordate, crenate, upper leaves short-stalked, smaller. Flowers whitish in terminal racemes. Propagated by seeds. Distributed in eastern and central Nepal at 2000–4000 m; also in India, Bhutan, southeastern Tibet, western and central China, and Japan.

MEDICINE. Juice of the root, about 4 teaspoons twice a day, is given in cases of fever. Juice of the leaves is applied as a hot compression to treat muscular swellings.

Tinospora sinensis (Loureiro) Merrill

Campylus sinensis Loureiro
Cocculus tomentosus Colebrooke, *Menispermum tomentosum* (Colebrooke) Roxburgh, *Tinospora tomentosa* (Colebrooke) Hooker fil. & Thomson
Menispermum malabaricum Lamarck, *Tinospora malabarica* (Lamarck) Hooker fil. & Thomson
Tinospora cordifolia (Willdenow) Hooker fil. & Thomson
MOOSHAR *guruj*   NEPALI *banwar, gurjo*   NEWARI *galay*
TIBETAN *se-tres*

Menispermaceae. Deciduous climber with rambling stems, bark smooth, peeling off in papery pieces, with scattered wart-like lenticels, bright green underneath the papery bark. Leaves stalked, 7.5–20 cm long, 7.5–17.5 cm wide, orbiculate, acuminate, entire, soft pubescent on both surfaces, greenish above, venation prominent beneath, base cordate. Flowers yellowish in racemes. Fruit a drupe, ellipsoidal, red when ripe. Flowers March–April. Propagated by seeds or cuttings. Distributed throughout Nepal to about 500 m in moist areas and in the shade of trees; also in India, Bhutan, Sri Lanka, southern China, Myanmar, Thailand, Vietnam, and Malaysia.

MEDICINE. Juice of the plant is used as a tonic and febrifuge and is also given for urinary troubles and stomach ailments. Pieces of the stems are fed to cattle with cough.

Tithonia diversifolia (Hemsley) A. Gray

Mirasoria diversifolia Hemsley
TAMANG *lahure mhendo*

Compositae. Shrub about 3 m high. Leaves stalked, alternate, ovate or orbiculate, entire or three- or five-lobed, crenate. Flower heads golden yellow. Fruit an achene, quadrangular. Flowers November–December. Propagated by seeds. Distributed in eastern Nepal at 800–1500 m, gregarious on uncultivated land; also in India, the Philippines, Florida, Mexico, and Central America.

MEDICINE. Juice of the plant is applied to cuts and wounds.

OTHER USES. The plant is often grown as an ornamental.

Tiarella polyphylla

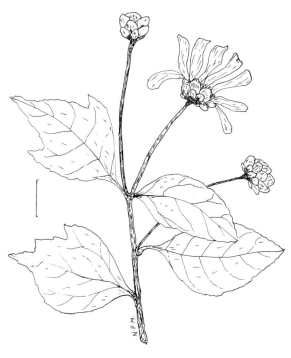

Tithonia diversifolia

Tinospora sinensis

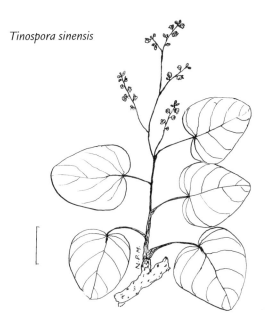

Toona ciliata M. Roemer

Cedrela toona Roxburgh ex Rottler & Willdenow
ENGLISH *Moulmain cedar, red cedar, toon tree* GURUNG *tuni*
LEPCHA *poma, henduri poma* NEPALI *tuni*

Meliaceae. Deciduous tree about 50 m high. Leaves stalked, even-pinnate, leaflets 8–30, subopposite, 3–19.5 cm long, 1–6.5 cm wide, ovate to lanceolate, acuminate, entire to faintly sinuate, base oblique. Flowers yellowish, fragrant, in drooping panicles. Fruit a capsule, oblanceolate, dark brown. Seeds with numerous wings at both ends. Flowers and fruits April–September. Propagated by seeds. Distributed throughout Nepal to about 1700 m in open places; also in Afghanistan, Pakistan, India, Bhutan, Sri Lanka, eastward to China, Malaysia, and Australia.

MEDICINE. Bark is astringent and is used in chronic dysentery; it is also febrifuge and yields a resinous gum that is applied to boils.

OTHER USES. Wood is moderately hard and forms moderately durable timber used for interior boards and planks. It is also used for making furniture and carving. It contains about 7–12% tannin. Leaves are lopped for fodder and contain about 15% crude protein.

Toona ciliata

Toona serrata (Royle) M. Roemer

Cedrela serrata Royle
NEPALI *tuni*

Meliaceae. Deciduous tree. Leaves stalked, usually odd-pinnate, leaflets opposite, 1.5–12.5 cm long, 0.5–4 cm wide, ovate to lanceolate, acuminate, serrate, base oblique. Flowers yellowish, tinged with pink, in large drooping panicles. Fruit a capsule, ovoid, five-valved. Seeds with nu-

merous wings at the upper end only. Flowers May–June, fruits July–August. Propagated by seeds. Distributed in western and central Nepal at 2100–2300 m along riverbanks; also in northern India and Myanmar.

OTHER USES. Wood is hard and forms moderately durable timber used for interior boards and planks. It is also used for making furniture and carving. The plant provides a low- to medium-quality fodder.

Torenia cordifolia Roxburgh

Torenia indica Saldanha
NEPALI *pidhamari*

Scrophulariaceae. Annual herb about 20 cm high. Leaves stalked, opposite, ovate, sharply serrate. Flowers solitary, axillary, purplish white. Fruit a capsule, oblong, enclosed in the persistent calyx. Flowers July–October, fruits October–November. Propagated by seeds. Distributed throughout Nepal at 1000–1600 m in moist places; also in India, Bhutan, eastward to western China, Myanmar, Java, and the Philippines.

MEDICINE. Juice of the plant is applied to cuts and wounds.

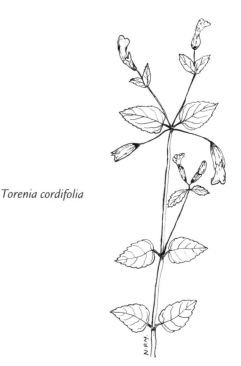

Torenia cordifolia

Toricellia tiliifolia de Candolle

Sambucus tiliaefolia Wallich
NEPALI *lekh bhogate*

Cornaceae. Tree about 6 m high. Leaves stalked, broadly ovate or suborbiculate, dentate, pubescent on both surfaces, base cordate. Flowers greenish in drooping terminal panicles. Fruit ovoid, whitish. Propagated by seeds. Distributed in western and central Nepal at 1600–

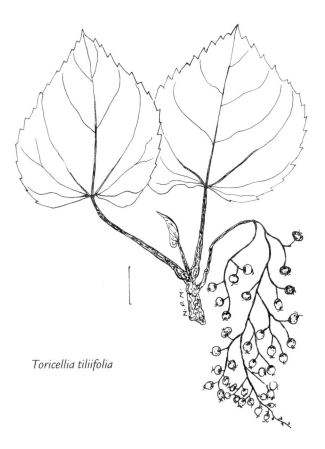

Toricellia tiliifolia

Torilis japonica

Trachelospermum lucidum

2500 m in oak and rhododendron forest; also in India, Bhutan, and western and southern China.

MEDICINE. A paste of the fruit is applied to the forehead to relieve headaches.

Torilis japonica (Houttuyn) de Candolle

Caucalis elata D. Don
Tordylium anthriscus Linnaeus, *Caucalis anthriscus* (Linnaeus) Hudson
NEPALI *chhatare*

Umbelliferae. Pubescent herb about 1 m high. Leaves stalked, pinnate, leaflets lanceolate, pinnately divided, segments acute, entire or serrate. Flowers pinkish in long-stalked umbels. Fruit ovoid, covered with hooked bristles. Flowers and fruits July-August. Propagated by seeds. Distributed throughout Nepal at 500–3000 m in moist places; also in temperate Eurasia.

MEDICINE. Juice of the root is given in cases of indigestion.

Trachelospermum lucidum (D. Don) K. Schumann

Alstonia lucida D. Don
Ichnocarpus fragrans Wallich ex G. Don, *Trachelospermum fragrans* (Wallich ex G. Don) Hooker fil.
NEPALI *dudhe lahara, lahare bedule, salikal*

Apocynaceae. Climbing shrub. Leaves short-stalked, opposite, elliptic to lanceolate, acuminate, leathery, glabrous. Flowers white, fragrant, in axillary or terminal cymes, May-June. Propagated by seeds or cuttings. Distributed throughout Nepal at 300–2200 m in dry, open places and trailing on shrubs; also in Pakistan and northern India.

MEDICINE. Juice of the root is given in cases of fever.

OTHER USES. Thin stems or branches are used for temporary binding.

Trachyspermum ammi (Linnaeus) Sprague

Sison ammi Linnaeus
Athamanta ajowan Wallich, *Ptychotis ajowan* de Candolle
Carum copticum C. B. Clarke
Ligusticum ajawain Roxburgh ex Fleming
BHOJPURI *jawain* CHEPANG *jwanu* DANUWAR *jwanu*
ENGLISH caraway, lovage LEPCHA *jyajyurakata* LIMBU *maruk*
MAGAR *jwanu* NEPALI *jwan* NEWARI *imu* RAI *juwano*
SUNWAR *jwanu* TAMANG *jhuwan* THARU *jawain* TIBETAN *la-la-phud*

Umbelliferae. Herb about 50 cm high. Leaves stalked, bi- or tripinnate, ultimate segments linear oblong. Flowers white in compound umbels, September–October. Propagated by seeds. Distributed throughout Nepal to about 1500 m, cultivated; also in Pakistan, India, Bhutan, Bangladesh, Europe, and Egypt.

FOOD. Fruits yield essential oils and are used as a spice.

Trapa bispinosa

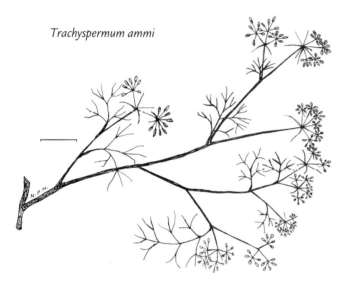

Trachyspermum ammi

Trapa bispinosa Roxburgh

ENGLISH *singhara nut, water chestnut* NEPALI *singhara*
SATAR *paniphalz*

Trapaceae. Aquatic herb with ascending stems. Leaves floating, rosulate, often three-lobed, rhombic, broader than long, stalk spongy. Flowers white, solitary. Fruit a nut, angled, short beaked at the apex, with a sharp spiny horn on either side. Flowers and fruits September–December. Propagated by seeds or rhizomes. Distributed throughout Nepal to about 600 m, cultivated.

FOOD. Cotyledons, which are fleshy, white, and rich in starch, are edible.

Trema cannabina Loureiro

Trema amboinensis (Willdenow) Blume
CHEPANG *cheksi* ENGLISH *sandpaper* MAJHI *thagsi* NEPALI *khaksi, khore* TAMANG *sorongrong, khosre*

Ulmaceae. Shrub with smooth, thin, grayish bark with numerous lenticels. Leaves stalked, 1.5–16 cm long, 0.8–

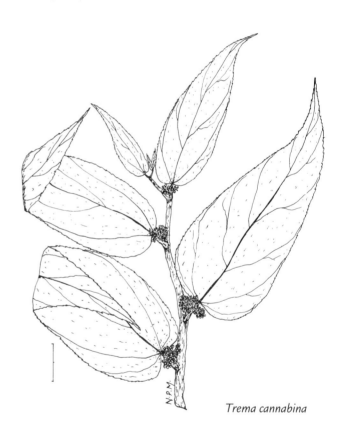

Trema cannabina

7.5 cm wide, ovate to oblong, acuminate, serrulate, somewhat roughly textured above, soft tomentose beneath. Flowers greenish. Fruit a drupe, ovoid, black when ripe. Flowers February–April, fruits June–August. Propagated by seeds. Distributed throughout Nepal at 300–2000 m, generally in moist, open places; also in India, southern China, and Malaysia.

OTHER USES. Bark yields strong fiber for cordage. Leaves are lopped for fodder.

Trema orientalis (Linnaeus) Blume

Celtis orientalis Linnaeus

ENGLISH *charcoal tree*   NEPALI *khaksi*   SATAR *sitaindu*

Ulmaceae. Small tree, bark thin, grayish, with numerous lenticels. Leaves stalked, 7.5–15 cm long, 5–9 cm wide, ovate to oblong, acuminate, crenate, membranous, somewhat roughly textured above, soft tomentose beneath, base cordate. Flowers greenish. Fruit a drupe, ovoid, black when ripe. Flowers February–April, fruits June–August. Propagated by seeds. Distributed in eastern and central Nepal at 200–1200 m in open places on hillsides; also in northern India, Bhutan, Sri Lanka, western and southern China, Indo-China, Australia, and Polynesia.

OTHER USES. The plant is lopped for fodder. Charcoal from the wood is used for gunpowder. Bark yields fiber used for cords and ropes.

Trevesia palmata (Roxburgh) Visiani

Gastonia palmata Roxburgh

GURUNG *moputachhe*   NEPALI *chuletro, loriya*

Araliaceae. Tree about 3 m high, branches armed with incurved, short, sharp prickles, young shoots rusty pubescent. Leaves stalked, 25–33 cm long, orbiculate, deeply palmatifid, lobes acuminate, serrate, glabrous, leathery. Flowers white in umbels. Fruit fleshy, crowded. Flowers

February–April, fruits May–June. Propagated by seeds. Distributed in eastern and central Nepal to about 2500 m, generally grown around villages; also in northeastern India, western China, Myanmar, and Malaysia.

FOOD. Flower buds are cooked as a vegetable.

OTHER USES. The plant is lopped for fodder.

Trewia nudiflora Linnaeus

DANUWAR *pithari*   MOOSHAR *pitho*   NEPALI *belar, gamari, gutel, gule kapasi, rambrero, ramritha, ranipha*

Euphorbiaceae. Deciduous tree about 20 m high, bark smooth, yellowish brown, exfoliating in irregular pieces. Leaves stalked, 15–22 cm long, 11–16 cm wide, broadly ovate to cordate, acuminate, five- or seven-veined at the base, glabrous. Flowers yellowish in axillary racemes, appearing before the leaves. Fruit a berry, globose. Seeds four, black, smooth. Flowers February–April, fruits November–December. Propagated by seeds. Distributed throughout Nepal to about 1800 m in damp places and ravines; also in northern India, Sri Lanka, southern China, and Indo-China.

MEDICINE. Juice of the root is given in cases of stomach complaints such as indigestion, diarrhea, and dysentery.

OTHER USES. Wood is soft, light, and used for carving and for cheap planking. It is also used in the match and paper industries. Leaves are lopped for fodder and contain 12.6% crude protein (Jackson 1987).

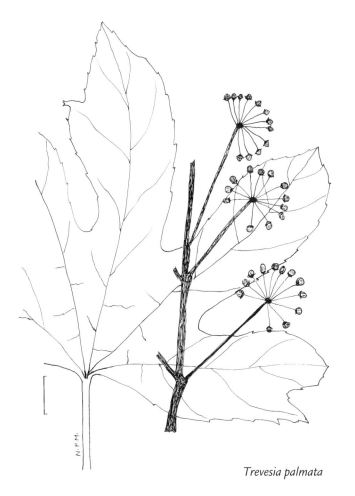

Trevesia palmata

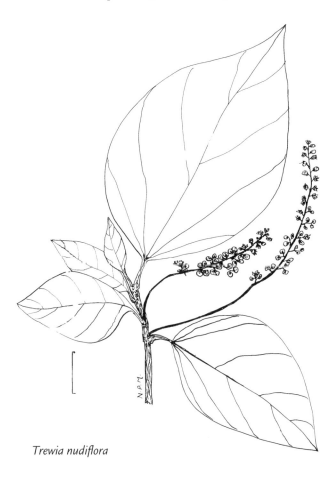

Trewia nudiflora

Trianthema portulacastrum Linnaeus

Trianthema monogyna Linnaeus
ENGLISH *horse purslane* MAJHI *kharkande*
NEPALI *gadapurina, kharkandf*

Aizoaceae. Prostrate succulent herb. Leaves stalked, opposite, unequally paired, 0.8–4 cm long, 0.4–3.4 cm wide, nearly ovate, entire, smooth, tip rounded. Flowers small, solitary, axillary, subsessile, white or pinkish. Flowers and fruits June–December. Propagated by seeds. Distributed throughout Nepal to about 300 m, common in moist and unused areas; also pantropical.

FOOD. Tender shoots and leaves are cooked as a vegetable.

Trianthema portulacastrum

Trichilia connaroides

Trichilia connaroides (Wight & Arnott) Bentvelzen

Zanthoxylum connaroides Wight & Arnott
Heynea trijuga Roxburgh, *Walsura trijuga* (Roxburgh) Kurz
GURUNG *aankhatare* NEPALI *aankhataruwa, komal siule, tantari*
TAMANG *aakhataro, tailung* THARU *tantari*

Meliaceae. Tree about 10 m high. Leaves stalked, opposite, pinnate, leaflets stalked, 5–20 cm long, 2–10 cm wide, ovate to oblong, entire. Flowers white in a panicled inflorescence. Fruit a capsule, one-celled, two-valved. Flowers August–May, fruits June–February. Propagated by seeds. Distributed throughout Nepal at 700–2400 m, sometimes in *Shorea robusta* forest, also in *Castanopsis* and *Schima* forests at higher altitudes; also in northeastern India, Bhutan, eastward to China, and Malaysia.

MEDICINE. Juice of the root, about 2 teaspoons once a day, is given as an anthelmintic. Juice of the bark is mixed with bark juice of *Schima wallichii* or *Maesa macrophylla* in equal amount and given in cases of stomach trouble. Oil from the seed is applied to treat scabies and is also put in the wound to prevent pus formation.

OTHER USES. Wood is mostly used for fuel. Seed oil is used for burning.

Trichodesma indicum (Linnaeus) R. Brown

Borago indica Linnaeus
NEPALI *kanike kuro*

Boraginaceae. Erect annual herb, stems densely hispid. Leaves subsessile, oblong to lanceolate, thinly hairy above, densely hairy beneath with tubercle-based hairs, base slightly clasping the stem or more or less cordate. Flowers white in many-flowered racemes. Flowers and fruits May–October. Propagated by seeds. Distributed in western and central Nepal to about 900 m; also in Afghanistan, India, Myanmar, the Philippines, and Mauritius.

MEDICINE. Juice of the leaves is applied to boils and also massaged on muscular swellings.

Trichosanthes anguina Linnaeus

BHOJPURI *chichura* DANUWAR *chichindo* ENGLISH *snake gourd*
LEPCHA *bubi* LIMBU *natirakwa* MAGAR *chichinda* NEPALI *chichindo*
NEWARI *chichinda, polancha* RAI *lemkansi* SUNWAR *chichinda*
TAMANG *chichinda* THARU *kaitha*

Cucurbitaceae. Large trailing herb. Leaves stalked, five- or seven-lobed. Flowers white. Fruit variable in shape and size, usually spindle shaped, long, bright orange when ripe. Flowers and fruits July–October. Propagated by

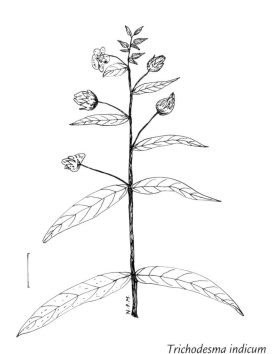

Trichodesma indicum

seeds. Distributed throughout Nepal at 1000–1800 m, cultivated.

FOOD. Fruits are cooked as a vegetable.

Trichosanthes dioica Roxburgh

BHOJPURI *parwal* DANUWAR *parbar* ENGLISH *patol, wild snake gourd* LEPCHA *parwal* LIMBU *tampait* MOOSHAR *paror* NEPALI *parwal* NEWARI *parwal* RAI *bopchom* SUNWAR *parwal* TAMANG *parwal* THARU *pador* TIBETAN *pa-to-la*

Cucurbitaceae. Herbaceous climber, stems slender, angled, with soft hairs, tendrils two- to four-fid. Leaves stalked, 5–10 cm long, oblong to ovate or cordate, acute, sinuate and dentate, rigid, rough on both surfaces. Flowers unisexual, white. Fruit oblong or pointed on both sides, orange-red when ripe. Seeds slightly compressed. Flowers and fruits July–November. Propagated by seeds. Distributed throughout Nepal to about 600 m, cultivated; also in India.

FOOD. Fruits are cooked as a vegetable.

Trichosanthes tricuspidata Loureiro

Involucraria lepiniana Naudin, *Trichosanthes lepiniana* (Naudin) Cogniaux
Medecca bracteata Lamarck, *Trichosanthes bracteata* (Lamarck) Voigt
Trichosanthes palmata Roxburgh
Trichosanthes pubera Blume
Trichosanthes quinquangulata A. Gray
NEPALI *indreni*

Cucurbitaceae. Herbaceous climber with branched tendrils. Leaves stalked, 5–20 cm long, deeply three- to seven-lobed, cordate. Flowers white, petals conspicuously long-fringed. Fruit globose, orange striped. Seeds embedded in

dark green pulp. Flowers and fruits May–August. Propagated by seeds. Distributed throughout Nepal at 1200–2300 m, trailing on shrubs in shady places; also in India, China, Japan, Malaysia, and tropical Australia.

MEDICINE. Juice of the fruit is given in cases of liver trouble.

Trichosanthes wallichiana (Seringe) Wight

Involucraria wallichiana Seringe
Trichosanthes multiloba Miquel
NEPALI *ban pharsi, indrayani*

Cucurbitaceae. Climber. Leaves stalked, suborbiculate, upper surface villous, lower surface glabrous, palmately three- to nine-lobed, lobes oblong to lanceolate, acuminate, crenate or dentate. Flowers unisexual, white. Fruit ovoid. Flowers May–July. Propagated by seeds. Distributed throughout Nepal at 600–2700 m in moist, shady places; also in northern India, Bhutan, China, and Southeast Asia.

FOOD. Seeds are pickled.

MEDICINE. Juice of the root or fruit is given in cases of fever.

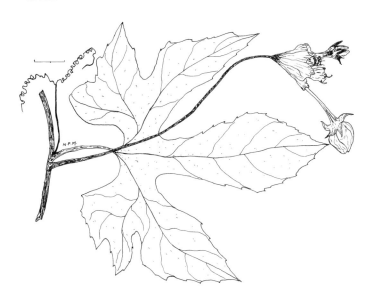

Trichosanthes wallichiana

Tridax procumbens Linnaeus

DANUWAR *thikuri* CHEPANG *dhankan sar, khurmure, marhathi, paira jhar, pamsali ban, ryop jhar* ENGLISH *Australian daisy weed* MAJHI *churmure* NEPALI *bulake jhar, hur sure jhar, kamale jhar, kurkure jhar, phuli no, pyanle phul, thunke jhar* TAMANG *chopachhi, chopoma, hanuman, hyan mran, kokor mran, rabarep* THARU *dhuseri, maraute jhar*

Compositae. Hispid herb about 50 cm high. Leaves stalked, 1–5 cm long, 0.5–2 cm wide, lanceolate, coarsely dentate, with bulbous based hairs on both surfaces. Flower heads solitary, yellow, on long stalks. Fruit an ach-

Tridax procumbens

Trifolium repens

ene. Flowers and fruits most of the year. Propagated by seeds. Distributed throughout Nepal to about 1500 m in open, dry places; a pantropical weed.

MEDICINE. The plant is mixed with feed to treat hemorrhagic septicemia of animals. A paste of the plant is applied to boils. Juice of the plant, about 2 teaspoons twice a day, is given to relieve fever. This juice is dripped into the eye to treat cataracts. Leaf juice is also dripped into the eye to treat cataracts. Fresh leaves are chewed to counter toothaches. Flower heads are chewed in cases of cough and colds.

OTHER USES. The plant is used to make *marcha,* a fermenting cake from which liquor is distilled.

Trifolium repens Linnaeus

ENGLISH *white clover* NEPALI *seto behuli*

Leguminosae. Prostrate annual herb. Leaves stalked, trifoliolate, leaflets sessile, ovate, tip rounded. Flowers condensed in a globose head, white or tinged pink. Flowers and fruits March–December. Propagated by seeds or root offshoots. Distributed in central Nepal at 1300–2500 m on moist ground in pastureland; also in India, western and central Asia, Europe, and North Africa.

OTHER USES. The plant is considered nutritious animal feed and is given especially to increase milk production.

Trigonella foenum-graecum Linnaeus

BHOJPURI *methi* CHEPANG *methi* DANUWAR *methi*
ENGLISH *bird's foot, fenugreek, Greek hay seed* GURUNG *methi*
LEPCHA *bikrim* LIMBU *khiknodi* MAGAR *methi* MOOSHAR *methi*
NEPALI *methi* NEWARI *micha* RAI *khakwaphun* SUNWAR *methi*
TAMANG *mothi* THARU *methi*

Leguminosae. Annual herb about 60 cm high. Leaves stalked, trifoliolate, leaflets sessile, 1.3–2.7 cm long, 0.5–1.7 cm wide, spatulate, dentate, tip rounded, narrowed toward the base. Flowers white. Fruit a pod, long, slender, with pronounced beak. Propagated by seeds. Distributed throughout Nepal to about 2500 m, cultivated; also in Asia and Europe.

FOOD. Leaves are used as vegetables, seeds as spice.

MEDICINE. Seeds are rubbed on a brass plate with mustard oil and put in the eye to treat inflammation of the eye.

Trigonella gracilis Bentham

TIBETAN *jyaso serpo*

Leguminosae. Prostrate herb with a stout rootstock. Leaves stalked, trifoliolate, leaflets short-stalked, 0.5–1.7 cm long, 0.2–1 cm wide, spatulate, serrate, glabrous, tip rounded, narrowed toward the base. Flowers yellow. Flowers and fruits May–August. Propagated by seeds. Distributed in western and central Nepal at 2200–3400 m on open, rocky ground; also in northern India.

MEDICINE. A paste of the plant is applied to treat skin diseases.

Triticum aestivum Linnaeus

Triticum vulgare Villars

BHOJPURI *gahun* CHEPANG *gahun* DANUWAR *gahun* ENGLISH *wheat* GURUNG *gahun* LEPCHA *kakyo* LIMBU *si* MAGAR *gahun* MOOSHAR *gahum* NEPALI *gahun* NEWARI *chhow* RAI *luncha* SHERPA *ta* SUNWAR *cherbi* TAMANG *kwa* THARU *gehun* TIBETAN *gro*

Gramineae. Annual grass. Leaves linear lanceolate, acuminate, flat. Inflorescence greenish. Fruit a grain, oblong, ventrally grooved. Flowers and fruits January–March. Propagated by seeds. Distributed throughout Nepal to about 3000 m, cultivated; also in most parts of the world.

FOOD. The grains are edible (Plate 15).

OTHER USES. Wheat straw is used in the paper industry.

Triticum aestivum

Triumfetta pilosa Roth

Triumfetta oblonga Wallich ex D. Don

NEPALI *ban kuro, masino kuro*

Tiliaceae. Bristly herb. Leaves stalked, 2.5–12 cm long, 1–7 cm wide, ovate to lanceolate, acuminate, unequally dentate, stellately hairy on both surfaces. Flowers yellow, August–September. Propagated by seeds. Distributed throughout Nepal at 1000–1700 m in moist, open places; also in India, Indo-China, and Africa.

OTHER USES. Bark of the stem is used to make ropes and twine.

Triumfetta rhomboides Jacquin

Bartramia indica Linnaeus
Triumfetta bartramia Linnaeus

CHEPANG *talmuja* GURUNG *balu* MAJHI *ciple* NEPALI *balu kuro, ban kuro, bishkhapre, dalle kuro, kurepat* TAMANG *ghyutinet*

Tiliaceae. Shrub about 1 m high. Leaves stalked, 1–7 cm long, 0.8–6 cm wide, broadly ovate or rhombic to ovate,

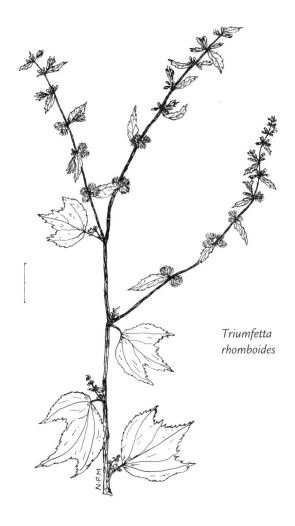

Triumfetta rhomboides

three-lobed, irregularly serrate. Flowers yellow in dense axillary cymes or fascicled, forming a long, terminal, spike-like inflorescence. Fruit globose, spinous. Flowers and fruits August–November. Propagated by seeds. Distributed throughout Nepal to about 1500 m in moist, open places; also in India, eastward to China, and Malaysia.

MEDICINE. Juice of the plant is applied to boils and pimples. Juice of the root, about 2 teaspoons twice a day, is given to control bedwetting. It is also given in cases of indigestion. A paste of the root, about 2 teaspoons twice a day, is given for indigestion and is also applied to wounds.

OTHER USES. Bark of the stem is a source of soft, glossy fiber.

Tsuga dumosa (D. Don) Eichler

Pinus dumosa D. Don, *Abies dumosa* (D. Don) Mirbel
Pinus brunoniana Wallich, *Abies brunoniana* (Wallich) Lindley, *Tsuga brunoniana* (Wallich) Carrière

ENGLISH *hemlock* NEPALI *chune salla, gobre salla, thingre salla* TAMANG *chesing, ji, kising* TIBETAN *ke*

Pinaceae. Evergreen coniferous tree about 40 m high, branches drooping. Leaves subsessile, about 2.5 cm long, linear, entire, more or less distichous, apex obtuse. Cones

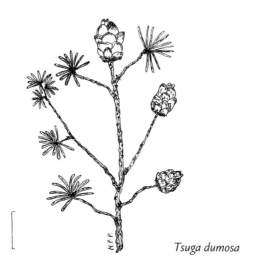

Tsuga dumosa

ovoid. Propagated by seeds. Distributed throughout Nepal at 2000–3600 m on open hillsides; also in northern India and northern Myanmar.

OTHER USES. Wood is used for construction though it is not of good quality. Leaves are used as incense.

Typhonium diversifolium Wallich ex Schott

Heterostalis diversifolia (Wallich ex Schott) Schott
NEPALI *talu*

Araceae. Tuberous herb. Leaves one or two, long-stalked, deeply three-lobed. Spathe purplish. Flowers June–July. Propagated by corms. Distributed throughout Nepal at 2400–4300 m in shady, wet places; also in northern India, Bhutan, and southern Tibet.

FOOD. Young leaves are cooked as a vegetable.

Typhonium diversifolium

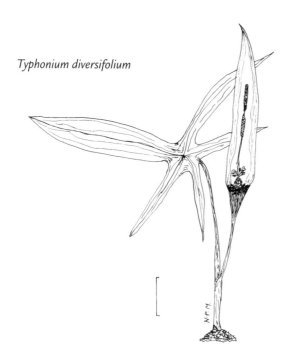

U

Ulmus wallichiana Planchon

NEPALI *dhamina*

Ulmaceae. Tree about 20 high. Leaves stalked, alternate, 4–9 cm long, 1.5–5 cm wide, ovate, margin incised, tip pointed, base narrowed. Flowers greenish. Fruits April–May. Propagated by seeds. Distributed in western and central Nepal to about 250 m in mixed *Shorea robusta* forest; also in India.

OTHER USES. Bark and leaf are used as fish poison.

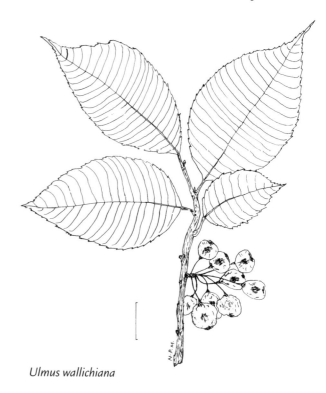

Ulmus wallichiana

Uraria lagopodioides (Linnaeus) Desvaux ex de Candolle

Hedysarum lagopodioides Linnaeus
Uraria lagopoides de Candolle
MAJHI *jhuse* NEPALI *sano bhatte* THARU *odarbau*

Leguminosae. Herb, stems trailing, densely tufted, woolly, slender. Leaves stalked, pinnate, leaflets small, orbiculate or oblong, obtuse, glabrous above, finely downy below, broadly rounded at the base. Flowers purplish. Propagated by seeds. Distributed throughout Nepal at 150–1700 m in open, sandy soil; also in India, China, Australia, and Polynesia.

MEDICINE. A paste of the plant, boiled in mustard oil, is applied to boils. Juice of the plant, mixed with the juice of

Uraria lagopodioides

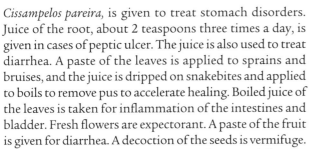

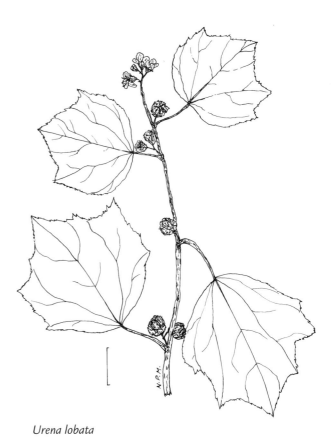

Urena lobata

Cissampelos pareira, is given to treat stomach disorders. Juice of the root, about 2 teaspoons three times a day, is given in cases of peptic ulcer. The juice is also used to treat diarrhea. A paste of the leaves is applied to sprains and bruises, and the juice is dripped on snakebites and applied to boils to remove pus to accelerate healing. Boiled juice of the leaves is taken for inflammation of the intestines and bladder. Fresh flowers are expectorant. A paste of the fruit is given for diarrhea. A decoction of the seeds is vermifuge.

OTHER USES. Bark of the stem provides a good fiber for rope and twine. Stem and leaf yield tannin.

Urena lobata Linnaeus

CHEPANG *taurmuja* DANUWAR *chhotaka chidchidhi, chiraita* ENGLISH *aramina, cadillo, Caesar weed, duck foot* GURUNG *goya, fusre pamale* MAGAR *bishkhapre* MAJHI *soranto* MOOSHAR *bariyar* NEPALI *bhere jhar, bishmaro, chiple, dalle kuro, katahare kuro, kuro, lise kuro, nalu kuro* TAMANG *jarsai, tinai*

Malvaceae. Erect shrub about 2.5 m high. Leaves stalked, ovate or orbiculate, cordate, more or less dentate or somewhat lobed, acute. Flowers axillary, solitary or somewhat fascicled, pinkish. Fruit globose, covered with short, retrorsely barbed spines. Propagated by seeds. Distributed throughout Nepal to about 1600 m; a pantropical weed.

MEDICINE. The root is mixed with that of *Achyranthes aspera* and bark of *Psidium guajava*, pounded, and the extracted juice, 4 teaspoons three times a day, is given to treat diarrhea and dysentery. A paste of the plant is applied to treat skin diseases and rheumatism. The root is diuretic and colic; its juice is used to treat tonsillitis and

dysentery. Leaf paste is applied to sprains and bruises, and leaf juice is dripped onto snakebites. Boiled juice of the leaf is taken for inflammation of the intestine and bladder. Fresh flowers are expectorant. A decoction of the seeds is vermifuge.

OTHER USES. Bark of the stem provides a good fiber for making rope and twine. Stem and leaf yield tannin.

Urtica dioica Linnaeus

BHOJPURI *sisnu* CHEPANG *nelau* DANUWAR *sisnu* ENGLISH *stinging nettle* GURUNG *polo, pulu* LEPCHA *kajyang* LIMBU *sikya* MAGAR *dhyo, hyo* NEPALI *sisnu* NEWARI *nhyakan* RAI *chhoku, chutle* SHERPA *jhaduk, syak* SUNWAR *chule* TAMANG *polo* THARU *sisna* TIBETAN *satu, za-chhag, zwa*

Urticaceae. Stinging shrub about 2 m high, clothed with bristly stinging hairs with hooked protrusions that irritate when they contact skin. Leaves stalked, opposite, 4–15 cm long, 1–7 cm wide, stipulate, ovate and cordate or lanceolate, long-pointed, serrate, both surfaces covered with stiff hairs that produce the burning sensation. Flowers unisexual, sessile, greenish. Flowers and fruits June–November. Propagated by seeds or root offshoots. Distributed throughout Nepal at 500–4500 m, common in moist areas and on uncultivated land; also in northern India, Bhutan, Tibet, central Asia including western China, western Siberia, Europe, and North Africa.

FOOD. The plant is an important food for the people of remote hilly regions. Tender shoots and leaves are collected with the help of bamboo or iron pincers, and cooked as a vegetable or soup. The plant is boiled with maize (*Zea mays*), millet (*Eleusine coracana*), or wheat (*Triticum aestivum*) flour, adding salt and chili (*Capsicum annuum*), to make a sort of porridge, which is a favorite food item of the villagers.

MEDICINE. The root is mixed with bark of *Castanopsis indica, Pyrus pashia, Rhododendron arboreum,* and *Woodfordia fruticosa* in equal amounts and boiled in water until a quarter of the amount of syrupy liquid is left; it is given in doses of about 2 teaspoons three times a day to relieve cough and colds. The plant has different medicinal uses depending on the communities using it. In many places, a decoction of the root is given for asthma. People of Jajarkot district chew the root and keep it in their mouth about an hour for dental caries. They apply a paste of the root to dog bites. The Tamangs of Sindhupalchok district add sparrow and rat droppings to paste of the root to treat cuts and wounds, whereas the Tharus of Dangdeokhuri district simply apply the paste to cuts and wounds. Danuwars and Magars apply a paste of the root, and bark of *Pinus roxburghii,* to reset dislocated bones. Among Rautes, juice of the root is given in cases of bile disease. Juice of the root, about 4 teaspoons three times a day, is given for fever. The root is boiled in water about 10 minutes and the filtered water is taken as an anthelmintic. Pounded root is applied to wounds; a decoction is given for asthma.

Juice of the stem, about 4 teaspoons three times a day, is given in cases of fever. Squeezed leaves are warmed and applied to cuts, wounds, and boils. Leaves are boiled in water to reduce the amount to half, and about a cup of this liquid, three times a day, is given to women after childbirth to help regain energy. A decoction of the leaves is given to treat menstrual disorder or jaundice. A paste of the leaves, about 3 teaspoons three times a day, is given for diarrhea and dysentery. Villagers in eastern Nepal boil tender leaves and eat them plain, without salt, chile, or spice, for cough and colds. A paste of the fruits is applied to treat dislocated bones.

OTHER USES. The plant is considered good for binding soil. Plants are nutritious fodder and help increase milk production in animals. Dried plants are a good substitute for animal feed as they are rich in protein. The plant is put on the main door of a house to ward off witches and evil spirits; it also has insecticidal properties. Stem fiber is widely used to make cords, clothes, bags, sacks, and fishnets. Twigs are put on foodstuffs to protect them from flies.

Utricularia aurea Loureiro

Utricularia confervaefolia D. Don
Utricularia fasciculata Roxburgh
Utricularia flexuosa Vahl
Utricularia macrocarpa Wallich
NEPALI *sim ghans*

Lentibulariaceae. Aquatic herb about 30 cm high. Leaves stalked, divided into many thread-like segments, with a bladder at each leaf-like segment. Flowers yellow. Fruit a capsule, globose. Flowers and fruits August-December. Propagated by seeds. Distributed in eastern and

Urtica dioica

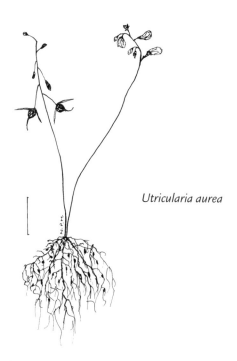

Utricularia aurea

central Nepal at 200–1400 m; also in the tropics and subtropics of the eastern hemisphere from India to Japan, and Australia.

MEDICINE. Powdered dried plant is put on cuts and wounds. It helps stanch the bleeding by coagulating blood and also aids the healing.

V

Valeriana hardwickii Wallich

Valeriana acuminata Royle
Valeriana elata D. Don
Valeriana repens Wallich
ENGLISH *valerian* LEPCHA *chammaha* NEPALI *nakli jatamansi*

Valerianaceae. Herb about 1.5 m high. Basal leaves long-stalked, cauline leaves opposite, odd-pinnate, leaflets 1–10 cm long, 0.3–4.5 cm wide, oblong to lanceolate, terminal segment largest. Flowers small, white, in compound corymbs. Flowers and fruits June–November. Propagated by seeds or root offshoots. Distributed throughout Nepal at 1000–3500 m in moist, shady places; also in northern India, Bhutan, eastward to western China, northern Myanmar, Sumatra, and Java.

MEDICINE. The root is bitter, stimulant, expectorant, carminative, and diuretic. It is used as a nerve tonic and for epilepsy, hysteria, rheumatism, and low blood pressure. Pounded root or leaves are used for boils.

OTHER USES. The plant contains essential oils.

Valeriana jatamansii Jones

Valeriana spica Vahl
Valeriana villosa Wallich
Valeriana wallichii de Candolle

ENGLISH *valerian* GURUNG *poti* NEPALI *samaya, sugandhawal*
NEWARI *naswan* SHERPA *nhakapai* TAMANG *albi, daling*
THARU *samaya* TIBETAN *nagbo*

Valerianaceae. Herb about 50 cm high with a thick rootstock. Basal leaves long-stalked, ovate, acuminate, dentate or sinuate, cauline leaves short-stalked, opposite, small. Flowers white or tinged with pink, in terminal corymbs, March–June. Propagated by seeds or root offshoots. Distributed throughout Nepal at 1300–3300 m in moist, shady places but the gathering of its rhizomes for sale in the trade is a cause of conservation concern; also in Afghanistan, northern India, Bhutan, Tibet, western and central China, and Myanmar.

MEDICINE. A paste of the plant is applied to boils. Roots are carminative, stimulant, and used for hysteria, insomnia, nausea, pimples, rheumatism, and cholera. Juice of the root is applied for headaches and is dripped in the eye for eye troubles.

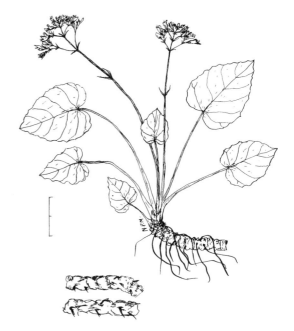

Valeriana jatamansii

OTHER USES. The plant is used in the preparation of incense. Root and rhizome are a source of essential oils, which constitute about 0.8% of them.

Vanda cristata Lindley

Aerides cristatum Wallich ex Hooker fil.
Vanda alpina Wallich ex Lindley
NEPALI *bhyagute phul*

Orchidaceae. Epiphytic orchid, stem stout. Leaves long and narrow, channeled. Flowers yellowish, usually in short erect clusters, May–June. Propagated by seeds or root offshoots. Distributed in central and eastern Nepal at

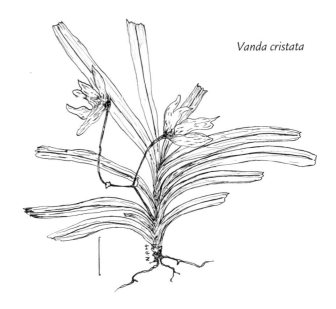

Vanda cristata

1300–2000 m, common on tree trunks and branches; also in northern India, Bhutan, and Tibet.

MEDICINE. A paste of the plant is applied to cuts and wounds. A paste of the root is applied to boils; it is also used to treat dislocated bones.

Vanda teres Lindley

Dendrobium teres Roxburgh
GURUNG *harjor* NEPALI *harjor, thurjo*

Orchidaceae. Epiphytic orchid. Leaves linear, entire, channeled. Flowers purplish, fragrant, May–June. Propagated by seeds or root offshoots. Distributed in eastern and central Nepal at 400–600 m on tree trunks and branches; also in northern India and Myanmar.

MEDICINE. A paste of the plant is applied to treat dislocated bones.

Verbascum thapsus Linnaeus

Verbascum indicum Wallich
ENGLISH *Aaron's rod, Jacob's staff, mullein* NEPALI *bandar puchhare, bugi, guna puchhar, guntho* TAMANG *banban* TIBETAN *hikusing, sin gi gser bye*

Scrophulariaceae. Herb about 2 m high. Leaves sessile, alternate, 10–20 cm long, 3.5–6 cm wide, ovate to oblong, entire, woolly. Flowers sessile, yellow, April–September. Fruits September–November. Propagated by seeds. Distributed throughout Nepal at 1500–4000 m on open, rocky ground; also in Afghanistan, northern India, Bhutan, Tibet, and western and central China.

MEDICINE. A poultice of the root is applied to treat muscular swellings. It is mixed with some locally distilled liquor, warmed, and taken for diarrhea. A paste of the plant is employed to treat asthma, pulmonary diseases, coughs, constipation, and bowel complaints. The paste is applied to wounds.

Kirtikar and Basu (1935) mentioned that in Germany, dried leaves were smoked like cigarettes to treat asthma and spasmodic cough. Verbascum tea can clear away bronchial troubles, and it can be applied in cases of inflammation of the eyes, wounds, skin rashes, and burns, as mentioned by Loewenfeld and Back (1974).

OTHER USES. The plant is used as a fish poison.

Verbena officinalis Linnaeus

Verbena sororia Roxburgh ex D. Don
ENGLISH *Juno's tears, vervain* NEPALI *bhekpadi, pittamari*

Verbenaceae. Erect perennial herb about 1 m high. Leaves stalked, pinnatifid, variously lobed, upper leaves sessile, usually three-parted. Flowers sessile, faint violet, in long slender spikes. Fruit dry, included in the calyx. Flowers April–August. Propagated by seeds. Distributed throughout Nepal to about 2400 m along waysides and on uncultivated land, usually in moist places; also in northern India, Bhutan, China, Japan, Indo-China, Europe, Africa, and North and South America.

MEDICINE. The plant is stomachic and antineuralgic. A paste of the root is applied to the forehead to treat headaches.

Verbascum thapsus

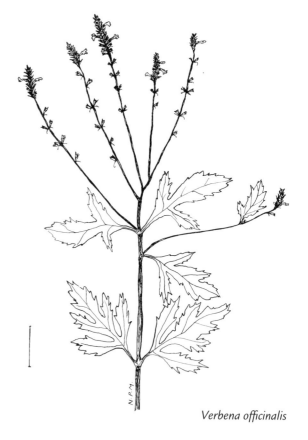

Verbena officinalis

Vernonia cinerea (Linnaeus) Lessing

Conyza cinerea Linnaeus, *Cyanthillium cinereum* (Linnaeus)
   H. E. Robinson
Vernonia cinerea var. *parviflora* (Reinwardt) de Candolle
CHEPANG *osaru, panthan* ENGLISH *iron weed, ash-colored fleabane*
GURUNG *pukpa, phuli jhar, musalindi, teptha* MAJHI *dampra*
NEPALI *marche jhar, musaledi, phuli jhar, phurke jhar, sodemode*
TAMANG *mamabramji, pramaimran, pramalaman* THARU *sahadeya*

Compositae. Perennial herb about 75 cm high. Leaves stalked, alternate, 1.2–7.5 cm long, 0.4–4 cm wide, ovate, pointed at both ends, slightly dentate, hairy on both sides. Flower heads purple, in an open lax corymb. Fruit an achene. Flowers and fruits February–June. Propagated by seeds. Distributed throughout Nepal to about 2300 m, common in open, dry places; also in India, Bhutan, China, Thailand, Malaysia, Australia, the Philippines, Africa, and Florida.

MEDICINE. An infusion of the plant, about 6 teaspoons twice a day, is taken in cases of cough and colds. A paste of the plant is applied to cuts, wounds, and skin diseases. An infusion of the plant is applied to the forehead to lower the temperature of an ill person. A decoction is also used to reduce body temperature during a fever. Juice of the root, about 4 teaspoons three times a day, is given for diarrhea and stomach disorders, and is also used for hemorrhoids. In some places it is valued as an anthelmintic: the root is boiled in water about 5 minutes, and the filtered water, about 4 teaspoons, is taken. A paste of the root is applied to boils. A poultice of the leaves is applied for headaches. Juice of the flower heads is used for conjunctivitis. A paste of the seeds is taken as an anthelmintic.

OTHER USES. Powdered plant is used to prepare *marcha,* a fermenting cake from which liquor is distilled. Flower heads have religious value in different communities.

Vernonia squarrosa (D. Don) Lessing

Acilepis squarrosa D. Don
Vernonia rigida Wallich
Vernonia rigiophylla de Candolle
Vernonia teres Wallich ex de Candolle
CHEPANG *cheklo* NEPALI *phule jhar*

Compositae. Shrub. Leaves subsessile, 2–12.5 cm long, 2.5–5 cm wide, oblong to lanceolate, acute, somewhat rough on both surfaces, base cordate. Flower heads purple. Fruit an achene, silky. Propagated by seeds. Distributed in western and central Nepal to about 2000 m in open places; also in India, China, and Indo-China.

MEDICINE. Juice of the root, about 4 teaspoons twice a day, is given to treat peptic ulcer.

OTHER USES. The plant is used to prepare *marcha,* a fermenting cake from which liquor is distilled.

Veronica anagallis-aquatica Linnaeus

Veronica secunda Pennell
NEPALI *dhapre jhar, tite* TIBETAN *bhatik tikta*

Scrophulariaceae. Herb about 50 cm high. Leaves sessile, 5–15 cm long, linear oblong, entire or serrate. Flowers

Vernonia cinerea

Veronica anagallis-aquatica

white or pinkish in lax slender racemes. Fruit a capsule, compressed, glabrous. Flowers and fruits January–April. Propagated by seeds. Distributed throughout Nepal at 500–3500 m near ditches, stream banks, and on marshy ground; also in India, Bhutan, western and central Asia including China, Korea, temperate Europe, and Africa.

FOOD. Seeds are pickled.

MEDICINE. Juice of the plant, about 6 teaspoons twice a day, is prescribed for malarial fever; a decoction is taken in cases of stomach acidity.

Veronica baccabunga Linnaeus

ENGLISH *brooklime* NEPALI *khole sag*

Scrophulariaceae. Herb with creeping hollow stem. Leaves stalked, 3–5 cm long, elliptic to oblong, glossy. Flowers blue in few-flowered axillary clusters. Flowers and fruits May–September. Propagated by nodal rootings. Distributed in western Nepal at 2200–3100 m in damp places; also in India, Bhutan, eastward to western China, temperate Eurasia, and North Africa.

FOOD. Tender leaves and shoots are cooked as a vegetable.

MEDICINE. Juice of the plant is given in cases of fever.

Vetiveria zizanioides (Linnaeus) Nash

ENGLISH *vetiver* NEPALI *khas*

Gramineae. Perennial grass about 2 m high with aromatic rhizomes. Leaves erect, 30–90 cm long, 0.5–2 cm wide, linear, acute, firm or somewhat spongy, usually gla-

Vetiveria zizanioides

brous, pale green. Inflorescence violet-brown or purplish. Flowers July–November. Propagated by seeds or by splitting the rhizomes. Distributed throughout Nepal to about 1000 m in open, dry places; also in Pakistan, India, Sri Lanka, and Southeast Asia.

OTHER USES. The rhizome is used for its aroma, especially during summer. Vetiver oil used in perfumery in many countries.

Viburnum cylindricum Buchanan-Hamilton ex D. Don

Viburnum capitellatum Wight & Arnott
Viburnum coriaceum Blume

CHEPANG *kharane* ENGLISH *arrow wood* GURUNG *crepsing* MAGAR *kharane* NEPALI *bakalpati, ghai jure, gharaghuri, ghorekhari, gorakuri, pithochor* TAMANG *badbada, mam pranet, podo, prabobho, twang twang*

Caprifoliaceae. Small tree. Leaves stalked, opposite, 8.5–20 cm long, 2.5–6 cm wide, oblong to lanceolate, acuminate, leathery, glabrous. Flowers white in terminal corymbs. Fruit a drupe, orange when ripe. Flowers May–July, fruits July–September. Propagated by seeds or cuttings. Distributed throughout Nepal at 1000–2500 m in open, rocky places; also in India, Sri Lanka, China, and Southeast Asia.

FOOD. Oil from the seeds is used for cooking.

MEDICINE. Seed oil is applied to itchy skin.

Viburnum erubescens Wallich ex de Candolle

CHEPANG *chyorosai* GURUNG *chhyonde, gneko, mhenko, narko* NEPALI *ban chulo, bhamar, chilam kath, ganamane, narga, nyage, purkhe kath* NEWARI *byancha sin* TAMANG *darmen, naiki chedang, namsing, themasin, chelem lundu, kasinkalo*

Caprifoliaceae. Tree about 6 m high. Leaves stalked, opposite, 2–13.5 cm long, 1–6.5 cm wide, oblong, acuminate, serrate, glabrous with a few scattered hairs above, hairy beneath. Flowers white or pinkish. Fruit a drupe, ellipsoidal, red. Flowers and fruits April–July. Propagated by seeds or cuttings. Distributed throughout Nepal at 1300–3300 m in open places; also in northern India, Bhutan, southeastern Tibet, western and central China, and northern Myanmar.

FOOD. Ripe fruits are edible.

MEDICINE. Juice of the root is prescribed in cases of cough.

Viburnum grandiflorum Wallich ex de Candolle

NEPALI *ganhaune, goli* TAMANG *phok phok*

Caprifoliaceae. Shrub about 3 m high. Leaves stalked, 8–10 cm long, elliptic, dentate, hairy on veins beneath. Flowers pinkish, fragrant. Fruit red, then black, ellipsoidal. Flowers April–May. Propagated by seeds or cuttings. Distributed in western and central Nepal at 3000–3700 m in forested areas; also in northern India, Bhutan, and southern Tibet.

FOOD. Ripe fruits are eaten fresh.

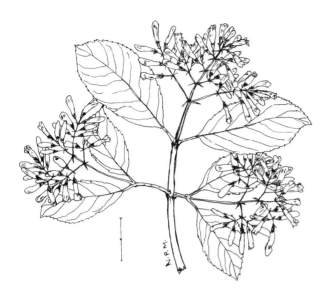

Viburnum erubescens

Viburnum mullaha Buchanan-Hamilton ex D. Don

Viburnum involucratum Wallich ex de Candolle, *V. stellulatum*
    var. *involucratum* (Wallich ex de Candolle) C. B. Clarke
Viburnum stellulatum Wallich ex de Candolle

CHEPANG *malayo* GURUNG *aasingra dhun, aasinkra*
NEPALI *kanda malau, mahelo, malagiri, maler, malewa, malyo, molo,*
narko TAMANG *aasingdhap, kasingal* TIBETAN *bramse*

Caprifoliaceae. Tree about 9 m high. Leaves stalked, opposite, 6–14 cm long, 3–5.5 cm wide, ovate to lanceolate,
acuminate, dentate, stellately pubescent beneath. Flowers
white in terminal cymes. Fruit a drupe, oblong, bright red.
Flowers September–October. Propagated by seeds or cuttings. Distributed throughout Nepal at 1600–2700 m in
moist, shady places in oak forests; also in northern India
and Indo-China.

FOOD. Ripe fruits are acidic and are eaten fresh.

MEDICINE. Fruits are crushed and ingested as a stimulant. Their juice, about 6 teaspoons twice a day, is given in
cases of indigestion.

OTHER USES. Straight branches are made into walking
sticks. Fruits yield a dye.

Viburnum nervosum D. Don

Viburnum acuminatum Wallich ex de Candolle
TAMANG *guldung*

Caprifoliaceae. Shrub with stout gray branches. Leaves
stalked, 6–10 cm long, 3–4 cm wide, oblong to elliptic,
acuminate, serrate, glabrous above, hairy on the veins beneath. Flowers white. Fruit a drupe, ellipsoidal. Flowers
April–May, fruits May–July. Propagated by seeds or cuttings. Distributed throughout Nepal at 2600–3500 m on
open slopes; also in northern India, Bhutan, southeastern
Tibet, western China, and northern Myanmar.

FOOD. Ripe fruits are eaten fresh.

Vicia angustifolia Linnaeus

Vicia sativa var. *angustifolia* (Linnaeus) Wahlenberg
ENGLISH *clover vetch* NEPALI *kuteli kosa*

Leguminosae. Weedy herb. Leaves stalked, pinnatifid,
ending in branched tendrils, leaflets sessile, opposite, 0.7–
2.3 cm long, 0.4–1 cm wide, lanceolate, mucronate, entire,
hairy on both surfaces. Flowers violet, September–November. Fruits December–February. Propagated by seeds.
Distributed throughout Nepal at 200–4000 m in moist,
open places; also in Asia, Australia, Europe, and Africa.

FOOD. Tender leaves and shoots are cooked as a vegetable. Green seeds are eaten fresh.

OTHER USES. The plant provides fodder.

Vicia bakeri Ali

Vicia pallida Turczaninow
Vicia sylvatica Linnaeus
NEPALI *bunkala*

Leguminosae. Shrub about 3 m high. Leaves stalked,
pinnatifid, ending with branched tendrils, leaflets many,
oblong to lanceolate. Flowers pale lilac, drooping. Fruit a
pod. Flowers and fruits July–September. Propagated by
seeds. Distributed in western and central Nepal at 2500–
3200 m with other shrubs on mountain slopes; also in
Pakistan and northern India.

FOOD. Tender fruits are boiled and pickled.

Vicia faba Linnaeus

ENGLISH *broad bean, garden bean, horse bean, fava bean, Scotch bean,*
Windsor bean NEPALI *bakala* NEWARI *bakula* TIBETAN *mon-sran*

Leguminosae. Erect annual herb, stems quadrangular.
Leaves stalked, pinnate, leaflets four to six, ovate, entire.

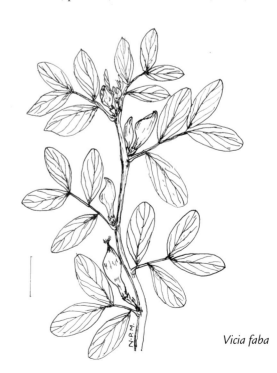

Vicia faba

Flowers dull white with a large purplish spot. Fruit a pod, turgid, glabrous, beaked. Flowers and fruits December–February. Propagated by seeds. Distributed throughout Nepal to about 1800 m, cultivated in the cold season.

FOOD. Tender pods and seeds are eaten as a vegetable.

Vicia hirsuta (Linnaeus) S. F. Gray

Ervum hirsutum Linnaeus
ENGLISH *vetch* NEPALI *jhuse kutelikosa, munmun* MOOSHAR *ankara*

Leguminosae. Annual herb about 60 cm high, tendril apical, branched. Leaves stalked, 2–5 cm long, pinnate, leaflets in 5–10 pairs, short-stalked, 0.8–1.5 cm long, oblong, entire, base rounded. Flowers white or tinged with purple. Fruit a pod, oblong, two-seeded. Flowers December–March, fruits April–May. Propagated by seeds. Distributed throughout Nepal to about 2700 m, a weed in crop fields; also in Pakistan, India, Bhutan, Bangladesh, Myanmar, Australia, Europe, Africa, and the Americas.

FOOD. Tender leaves, shoots, and fruits are cooked as a vegetable.

Vigna mungo (Linnaeus) Hepper

Phaseolus mungo Linnaeus, *Azukia mungo* (Linnaeus) Masamune
ENGLISH *black gram* NEPALI *mas* NEWARI *may*

Leguminosae. Annual herb about 80 cm high with reddish brown hairs. Leaves stalked, trifoliolate, leaflets short-stalked, 5–10 cm long, ovate to lanceolate, entire. Flowers yellow, axillary, in a cluster of five or six at the top of a stalk. Fruit a pod, dark brown when mature. Propagated by seeds. Distributed throughout Nepal to about 2000 m, cultivated; also in tropical Asia and Africa.

FOOD. The seeds are eaten as lentil soup (*daal* in Nepali), parched and ground into flour to prepare porridge, or baked into bread.

OTHER USES. The plant provides fodder. The husks and straw are used as cattle feed.

Vigna unguiculata (Linnaeus) Walpers

ENGLISH *asparagus bean, cowpea* GURUNG *bod* NEPALI *bori* NEWARI *bhuti*

Leguminosae. Suberect annual herb. Leaves stalked, trifoliolate, leaflets short-stalked, 7–15 cm long, broadly or narrowly ovate, entire or slightly lobed. Flowers yellow or reddish in subcapitate racemes. Fruit a pod, linear, slightly depressed between the seeds. Flowers and fruits June–October. Propagated by seeds. Distributed throughout Nepal to about 1800 m, cultivated during the rainy season, mixed with millet (*Eleusine coracana*) and other crops.

FOOD. Tender fruits and seeds are edible.

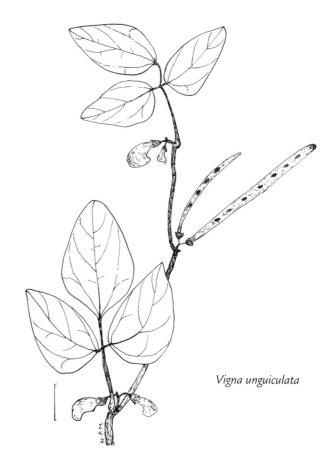

Vigna unguiculata

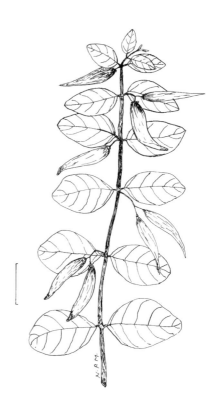

Vincetoxicum hirundinaria subsp. *glaucum*

Vincetoxicum hirundinaria Medikus
subsp. *glaucum* (Wallich ex Wight) Hara
Cynanchum glaucum Wallich ex Wight, *Vincetoxicum glaucum* (Wallich ex Wight) Rechinger fil.
NEPALI *latikoseli*

Asclepiadaceae. Erect perennial herb about 25 cm high. Leaves short-stalked, opposite, about 5 cm long, broadly elliptic to ovate, acute, base rounded. Flowers yellowish green in axillary and terminal umbels. Flowers and fruits May–July. Propagated by seeds. Distributed in western and central Nepal at 2300–3600 m on open slopes; also in western Asia, Pakistan, India, Bhutan, southeastern Tibet, and Europe.

MEDICINE. Juice of the plant is applied to boils and pimples.

Viola pilosa Blume
Viola aspera Gingins ex de Candolle
Viola buchaniana de Candolle ex D. Don
Viola palmaris Buchanan-Hamilton ex D. Don
Viola serpens Wallich ex Gingins
GURUNG *patendo* NEPALI *aankhle, gatha ghans, rate jhar, ti kaphal*
TAMANG *aule ghor, tilikosyo*

Violaceae. Perennial herb with a stout rootstock. Leaves all basal, stalked, 1.4–4 cm long, 0.8–4 cm wide, broadly ovate to deeply cordate, crenate. Flowers light blue or white, usually solitary, on long axillary stalks. Fruit a capsule, ovoid, opening horizontally by three boat-shaped valves. Flowers February–March. Propagated by seeds. Distributed throughout Nepal at 900–3000 m in open, moist places; also in Afghanistan, Pakistan, northern India, Bhutan, western China, and Southeast Asia.

MEDICINE. Juice of the plant is applied to cuts and wounds; it is given in doses of about 3 teaspoons three times a day in cases of fever. A paste of the plant is applied to boils on joints of the fingers. Juice of the root is applied to boils; it is given in doses of about 4 teaspoons three

times a day to relieve fever. Fresh flowers are chewed to treat biliousness and lung trouble.

Viscum album Linnaeus
Viscum stellatum D. Don
ENGLISH *birdlime, mistletoe* GURUNG *harjor* NEPALI *ainjeru, harchur*

Viscaceae. Parasitic shrub. Leaves sessile, oblong, cuneate, with two to five longitudinal veins. Flowers reddish. Fruit ellipsoidal, white, transparent, smooth. Flowers March–May, fruits September–November. Propagated by seeds. Distributed in western and central Nepal at 600–2300 m on tree trunks; also in India.

FOOD. Ripe fruits are edible.

MEDICINE. A paste of the root, bark, leaves, and fruit is used to treat sprains, bruises, dislocated bones, boils, and wounds. Juice of the bark is applied to muscular swellings and is also used on boils and wounds.

OTHER USES. Viscid pulp of the fruit is made into birdlime.

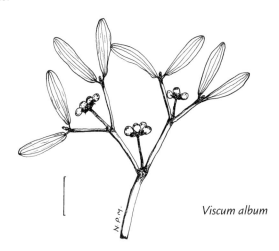
Viscum album

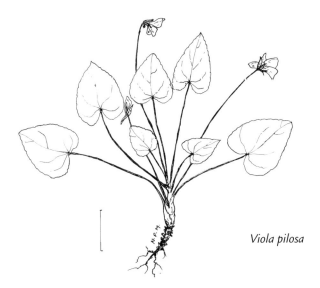
Viola pilosa

Vitex negundo Linnaeus
CHEPANG *siwanli* ENGLISH *Chinese chaste tree* GURUNG *tara*
NEPALI *simali* RAI *simali* TAMANG *sinyal* THARU *semali, simli*

Labiatae. Shrub about 3 m high. Leaves stalked, trifoliolate, leaflets lanceolate, acuminate, entire, nearly glabrous above, white tomentose beneath. Flowers bluish in cymes forming the terminal panicles, July–August. Propagated easily by cuttings. Distributed throughout Nepal to about 1600 m; also in Afghanistan, India, Bhutan, Sri Lanka, China, Southeast Asia, and Africa.

MEDICINE. Juice of squeezed leaves is given to treat cough, colds, and fever. This juice is also inhaled to treat sinusitis. Dried leaves are smoked like tobacco to relieve headaches. Roasted leaf powder, about 2 teaspoons twice a day, is given with water in cases of stomach disorder. Juice of the leaves is applied to rheumatic swellings of joints. This juice, about 2 teaspoons twice a day, is given for fever. Juice of young leaves is taken for gastric troubles. Crushed seeds are given with water to cure animals with cough and colds.

OTHER USES. The plant is good for countering land-slides. Juice of the plant is applied to remove lice and other ectoparasites from chickens. Branches and twigs are made into baskets and brooms, and also used as toothbrushes.

Vitex negundo

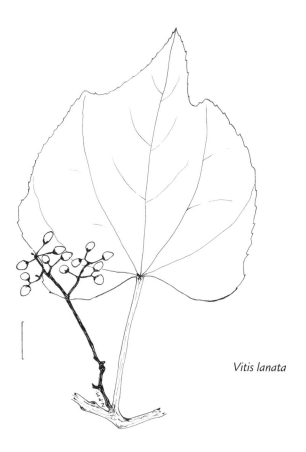

Vitis lanata

Vitis lanata Roxburgh

Cissus vitiginea Linnaeus
ENGLISH *mountain splitter, wild grape* GURUNG *kakryon, kangri jhar, krakryon, purni* NEPALI *bhim lahara, pureni* TAMANG *gangap*

Vitaceae. Large woody climber, branches and leaves covered with brown felted tomentum. Leaves stalked, 6.5–22 cm long, 5.5–27 cm wide, ovate or suborbiculate to cordate, acuminate, dentate, more densely tomentose beneath than above. Flowers yellowish, fragrant, in large compound panicles opposite the leaves. Fruit globose, usually one-seeded. Flowers April–June, fruits August–November. Propagated by seeds or root offshoots. Distributed throughout Nepal at 900–2100 m, common in moist, open, rocky places; also in India, Bhutan, western China, and Myanmar.

FOOD. Woodcutters and shepherds cut the stem and drink the watery sap to quench thirst. Ripe fruits are edible.

MEDICINE. Watery sap of the stem is dripped in the eye to relieve inflammation of the eye.

Vitis parvifolia Roxburgh

NEPALI *pureni* TAMANG *gongap*

Vitaceae. Slender woody climber. Leaves stalked, 2.5–9 cm long, 1.5–6 cm wide, triangular ovate, acuminate, distantly serrate, sometimes lobed, glabrous. Flowers yellowish in slender umbels. Fruit globose, black when ripe. Flowers April–May, fruits June–August. Propagated by seeds. Distributed in western and central Nepal at 1200–2100 m in moist, open places; also in northwestern India, western and central China, and Indo-China.

FOOD. Ripe fruits are eaten fresh.

MEDICINE. Fresh plant is cut and the watery sap is dripped in the eye to treat inflammation of the eye.

Vitis repanda Wight & Arnott

NEPALI *jhuleti*

Vitaceae. Large climber with ribbed branches, tendril forked. Leaves stalked, 7.5–12.5 cm long, 6.5–10 cm wide, ovate to cordate, acuminate, crenate with a sharp point, rusty tomentose beneath when young, glabrescent when old. Flowers cream in slender umbel-bearing cymes. Fruit pear shaped, tipped with the persistent style. Flowers May–June, fruits July–August. Propagated by seeds. Distributed in western and central Nepal at 1400–2500 m in open, rocky places.

FOOD. Ripe fruits are eaten fresh.

Vitis vinifera Linnaeus

ENGLISH *grape* NEPALI *angur, dakh* NEWARI *dakh*
TIBETAN *rgun-brum*

Vitaceae. Large woody climber with bifid tendrils. Leaves stalked, suborbiculate to cordate, more or less deeply five-lobed, margin unequally cut into acute teeth, glabrous above, clothed beneath with gray deciduous tomentum. Flowers yellowish in umbel-like cymes, March–April. Fruits August–October. Propagated by seeds or by grafting. Distributed throughout Nepal to about 1400 m, cultivated; also in Pakistan, India, Myanmar, Thailand, Malaysia, Europe, Africa, North America, Argentina, and Chile.

FOOD. Ripe fruits are edible and contain sugar, minerals such as calcium and iron, and vitamin B.

Vittaria elongata Swartz

NEPALI *daluko*

Vittariaceae. Epiphytic fern. Rhizome creeping, densely covered with blackish brown, hair-like, pointed scales. Fronds linear, sometimes needle-like because of the reflexed margins. Sori sunken in an inward-facing marginal groove, partially covered with revolute margins. Spores July–August. Propagated by spores. Distributed throughout Nepal at 1300–2600 m on mossy tree trunks and branches in forested areas; also in India, Sri Lanka, southern China, Taiwan, Southeast Asia, the Philippines, Polynesia, and tropical Australia and Africa.

MEDICINE. A paste of the plant is applied to sprains and swellings caused by some inflammations and injuries.

Vittaria elongata

W

Wahlenbergia marginata (Thunberg) A. de Candolle

Campanula marginata Thunberg
Campanula agrestis Wallich, *Wahlenbergia agrestis* (Wallich) A. de Candolle
Campanula dehiscens Roxburgh
Wahlenbergia gracilis A. de Candolle, *Lightfootia gracilis* (A. de Candolle) Miquel

NEPALI *nilo tike*

Campanulaceae. Annual herb with a stout taproot. Lower leaves sessile, ovate to oblong, obtuse or rounded, serrate, slightly hairy, base narrowed. Flowers white or pale violet. Fruit a capsule. Flowers and fruits December–May. Propagated by seeds. Distributed throughout Nepal at 600–1400 m in moist places as a weed; also in India, China, southern Japan, Malaysia, Australia, and New Zealand.

MEDICINE. Juice of the root is applied to cuts and wounds.

Wendlandia coriacea (Wallich) de Candolle

Rondeletia coriacea Wallich

CHEPANG *korosi, syaruj* MAGAR *kangio* NEPALI *ban kanyu, garuli, kane ghans, kangio phul, kanike phul, lampate*

Rubiaceae. Tree about 4 m high. Leaves stalked, opposite, 3–18 cm long, 1–5.5 cm wide, lanceolate, acuminate, entire, leathery, glabrous. Flowers white, fragrant, in dense

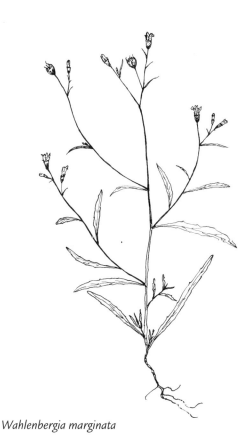

Wahlenbergia marginata

panicles, February–March. Propagated by seeds. Distributed throughout Nepal at 200–1900 m in shady places in the forest; also in northern India.

OTHER USES. The plant is used for dyeing. Branches are used for construction.

Wendlandia exserta (Roxburgh) de Candolle

Rondeletia exserta Roxburgh
Rondeletia cinerea Wallich, *Wendlandia cinerea* (Wallich) de Candolle
NEPALI *neware pati*

Rubiaceae. Deciduous shrub, bark rough, longitudinally cracked and exfoliating in long strips. Leaves stalked, 4–9 cm long, 1–3.5 cm wide, ovate to lanceolate, acuminate, leathery, glabrous above, densely pubescent beneath. Flowers sessile, yellowish, fragrant. Fruit a capsule, white tomentose. Flowers March–April, fruits June–July. Propagated by seeds. Distributed throughout Nepal at 150–1400 m along trails and on landslides; also in northeastern India.

OTHER USES. This shrub is considered excellent for soil binding and is lopped for fodder. Wood is hard and used for construction and to make handles of household implements.

Wendlandia pendula (Wallich) de Candolle

Rondeletia pendula Wallich
CHEPANG *goldarin* MAJHI *sansi dhauli*
NEPALI *paredhayaro, rani dhayaro*

Rubiaceae. Straggling shrub. Leaves short-stalked or sessile, opposite, 3–10.5 cm long, 0.8–4.3 cm wide, lance-olate, long-pointed, entire, rough, slightly hairy beneath. Flowers yellowish. Flowers and fruits September–November. Propagated by seeds. Distributed in eastern and central Nepal at 900–1100 m in open places; also in northern India, Bhutan, southeastern China, and Myanmar.

OTHER USES. The plant is used for fodder.

Wendlandia puberula de Candolle

Wendlandia sikkimensis Cowan
NEPALI *ban kanyu*

Rubiaceae. Tree about 3 m high. Leaves stalked, elliptic to lanceolate, acute or acuminate, pubescent. Flowers white in terminal panicles. Fruit a capsule, globose, black. Propagated by seeds. Distributed throughout Nepal at 700–2000 m in open places; also in northern India and Myanmar.

MEDICINE. Juice of the bark is applied to cuts and wounds.
OTHER USES. The plant is used for fodder.

Wikstroemia canescens Meissner

Daphne canescens Wallich
Daphne sericea D. Don
NEPALI *kalo logte, kalo chaulayo, lul lule, pati, phurke pati*
TAMANG *grepti, warpati*

Thymelaeaceae. Shrub with a few slender branches. Leaves stalked, 1.5–8 cm long, 0.5–2.5 cm wide, oblong to lanceolate, acuminate, entire, membranous, often pubescent. Flowers subsessile, yellow, in few-flowered cymes. Fruit narrowly ovoid, silky. Flowers April–June, fruits October–November. Propagated by seeds or root offshoots. Distributed throughout Nepal at 1800–3200 m in open places; also in Afghanistan, northern India, Sri Lanka, and China.

OTHER USES. Fiber from bark of the stem is used to prepare handmade Nepalese paper.

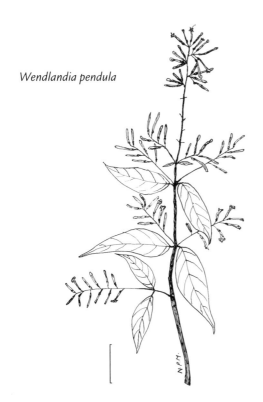

Wendlandia pendula

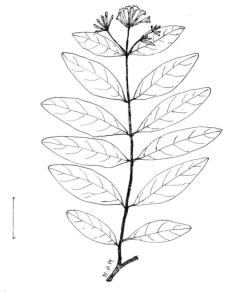

Wikstroemia canescens

Woodfordia fruticosa (Linnaeus) Kurz

Lythrum fruticosum Linnaeus
Grislea tomentosa Roxburgh
Woodfordia floribunda Salisbury
CHEPANG *daring* DANUWAR *bajhiya, chyuhuwa* GURUNG *dhanyar*
MAGAR *dhainra* MAJHI *dhauli* NEPALI *anare phul, dhanyaro,
sano dhayaro* RAI *chenchev, sano dhayaro* RAUTE *dhaya*
TAMANG *birukanda, dhayaro, jamjasa, syakte* THARU *ghayaro*
TIBETAN *dha-ta-ki*

Lythraceae. Spreading shrub about 3 m high with drooping branches. Leaves sessile, opposite, sometimes in whorls of three, 5–12 cm long, 1.5–4 cm wide, oblong to lanceolate, acuminate, entire, upper surface green, lower surface velvety, with black dots. Flowers short-stalked, scarlet, in few-flowered axillary cymes. Fruit a capsule, ellipsoidal, included in the persistent calyx tube, many-seeded. Flowers and fruits March–June. Propagated by seeds or root offshoots. Distributed throughout Nepal at 200–2000 m in open, dry places, but habitat destruction is a cause of conservation concern; also in western Asia, Afghanistan, India, Bhutan, Sri Lanka, eastward to China, Myanmar, Australia, and Africa.

MEDICINE. Bark is chewed to treat boils on the tongue. Juice of the bark is taken for gastric trouble. A paste of the bark is applied externally to treat angular stomatitis; a decoction is applied to sprains and swellings. Flowers, boiled in water, are taken in cases of profuse menstruation and to treat fever. A juice of the flower, about 6 teaspoons three times a day, is given for fever. A paste of the flower, about 3 teaspoons twice a day, is given in cases of indigestion and bloody dysentery. Juice of the fruit, about 4 teaspoons three times a day, is given to treat urinary troubles.

OTHER USES. The plant is commonly used for fuel. Bark, leaves, and flowers contain tannin. Villagers of Rolpa district like to smoke tobacco (*Nicotiana tabacum*) mixed with dried leaves of the plant for a milder taste. Flowers yield a red dye and are sold in the trade (Plate 30).

Woodwardia unigemmata (Makino) Nakai

NEPALI *danthe unyu*

Blechnaceae. Terrestrial fern. Fronds deep green, 60–90 cm long, 20–45 cm wide, bipinnate, pinnae broadly lanceolate, deeply cut into segments. Sori oblong, along the veins. Propagated by spores or by splitting rhizomes. Distributed in central Nepal at 1300–2600 m in rock crevices or shady, moist places; also in India, China, Taiwan, Japan, and the Philippines.

OTHER USES. The plant is used as cattle fodder.

*Woodwardia
unigemmata*

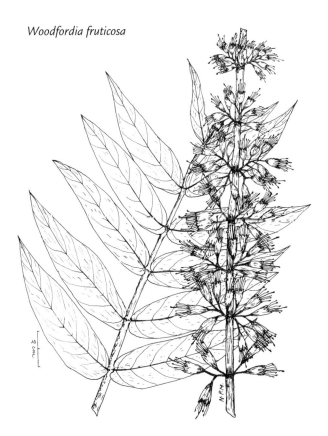

Woodfordia fruticosa

Wrightia arborea (Dennstaedt) Mabberley

Periploca arborea Dennstaedt
Wrightia mollissima Wallich
Wrightia tomentosa Roemer & Schultes, *Nerium tomentosum*
  (Roemer & Schultes) Roxburgh
NEPALI *rani khirro*

Apocynaceae. Deciduous tree about 10 m high. Leaves stalked, opposite, 7.5–15 cm long, 2.5–7.5 cm wide, ellip-

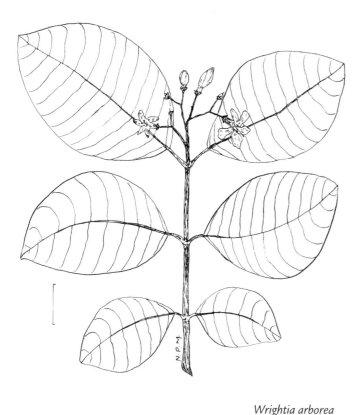

Wrightia arborea

Wulfenia amherstiana

tic to lanceolate, acuminate, velvety hairy on both surfaces, base acute or somewhat rounded. Flowers white. Fruit a follicle, cylindrical, with a groove on each side at the junction of the carpels. Propagated by seeds. Distributed in eastern and central Nepal at 450–950 m in open places; also in India, Sri Lanka, southern China, and Indo-China.

MEDICINE. Juice of the bark is given in cases of gastritis.

OTHER USES. Wood is used in making combs and other household goods by carving and turning. Juice of the plant yields a yellow dye.

Wulfenia amherstiana Bentham

Wulfeniopsis amherstiana (Bentham) Hong
Paederota amherstiana Wallich
NEPALI *batule*

Scrophulariaceae. Herb about 10 cm high. Leaves stalked, 1.5–11 cm long, 1–4 cm wide, oblong to ovate, lobed or coarsely crenate, apex round. Flowers mauve-blue in dense racemes. Flowers and fruits March–December. Propagated by seeds. Distributed in western and central Nepal at 1300–3000 m in shady rock crevices; also in Afghanistan and northwestern India.

MEDICINE. Juice of the root is prescribed in cases of stomachache.

X

Xanthium strumarium Linnaeus

CHEPANG *taulamuja* DANUWAR *chirchiri* ENGLISH *burweed, sheep bur* GURUNG *tene* MAJHI *badake chorant*
MOOSHAR *khanghara* NEPALI *bhende kuro, dagne kuro, jumli kuro*
THARU *kangres, kuchakuchiye*

Compositae. Shrub about 1 m high. Leaves stalked, 7–13 cm long, 4–14 cm wide, triangular, acuminate, cordate, irregularly dentate and incised. Flower heads unisexual, greenish, in single or clustered axillary heads. Fruit an achene. Flowers and fruits August–November. Propagated by seeds. Distributed throughout Nepal to about 2500 m, common in open areas and on uncultivated land; also in Pakistan, India, Bhutan, and Bangladesh.

MEDICINE. Juice of the root is taken as a tonic. A paste of the root is applied to treat swollen bones, especially by Chepangs. In 1988, I saw a Chepang apply the paste over a very swollen bone of his left leg. He told me it was cancer. I was surprised when he said the word cancer, which he said he had heard from two foreigners (*bideshi* in Nepali) who had told him his affliction was cancer. He said that the skin was swollen, difficult to heal, and that the affected part grew very slowly. In 1990, I met the same Chepang patient; the swelling was gone but there was a black spot and I knew the position of bone was not normal, and he was limping.

A paste of the plant is sedative, diuretic, and diaphoretic. According to Raizada and Saxena (1978), the fruit is demulcent and given to treat smallpox. Charred fruit is powdered and mixed with coconut oil to apply on chapped skin. This treatment is prevalent among Danuwars, Mooshars, and Tharus.

OTHER USES. Leaves are poisonous to cattle. Seeds contain 15.7–24% essential oils.

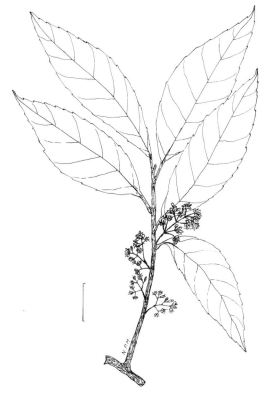

Xylosma controversum

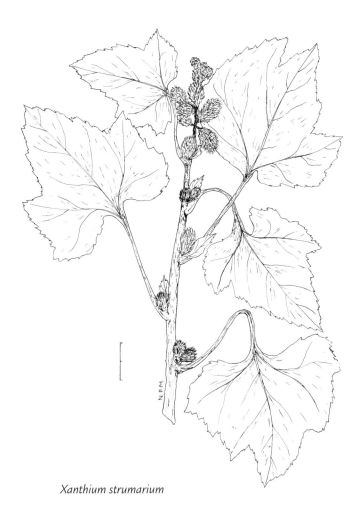

Xanthium strumarium

Xylosma controversum Clos

NEPALI *dande kanda*

Flacourtiaceae. Tree about 3 m high. Leaves stalked, elliptic to oblong, acute, serrate, glabrous. Flowers purplish white, March–April. Propagated by seeds. Distributed in central Nepal at 300–1700 m; also in India and western China.

OTHER USES. The plant is browsed by goats and sheep.

Y

Youngia japonica (Linnaeus) de Candolle

Prenanthes japonica Linnaeus, *Crepis japonica* (Linnaeus) Bentham
Youngia napifolia Wight
NEPALI *chaulane, dudhe* RAUTE *goibi*

Compositae. Annual herb about 60 cm high with milky latex. Basal leaves stalked, 5–10 cm long, lyrate, dentate, cauline leaves sessile or subsessile, smaller. Flower heads pinkish in lax terminal panicled corymbs. Fruit an achene, spindle shaped, slightly curved, brown, ribbed. Flowers February–July, fruits May–November. Propagated by seeds. Distributed throughout Nepal at 230–2900 m; also in Pakistan, northern India, Bhutan, Sri Lanka, China, Southeast Asia, the Philippines, Japan, and Hawaii.

FOOD. In September 1979, two expedition staff and I flew to Chaurjhari by light twin-engine aircraft on our way to my destination in the Dolpa district. We had our lunch in the house of a *kami* (blacksmith, an untouchable caste) because his place was spacious and the flowers were in full bloom in the surrounding area. When we were having our meal, his neighbors, of higher caste, were shocked that we were having a meal in the house of a *kami*. Which caste do I belong to?, the *kami*'s neighbors asked, to which I replied that we have no caste. The *kami* brought a bunch of tender shoots of *Youngia japonica* and said he had nothing to offer but said, "You all are my guests and it is my duty to offer you something to eat." I was not sure whether the wild plant was edible, but at the same time I did not want to appear rude so I accepted the greens and thanked him. He said that after lunch we would have to climb a steep mountain ridge and the vegetable would give us energy. He further added that if we were afraid to eat it, he would eat it uncooked in front us and started eating two or three shoots. Later, I also got the same information on its food value from the Rautes of western Nepal. Although I have tasted 80% of the food plants mentioned in this book, most of the time I ask the informants to taste first.

MEDICINE. Juice of the leaves, about 4 teaspoons three times a day, is given in cases of indigestion.

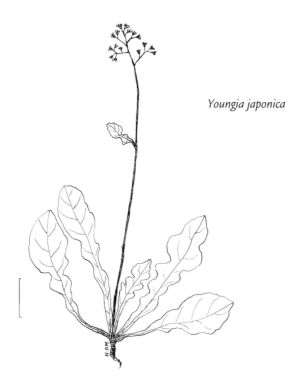

Youngia japonica

Yucca gloriosa Linnaeus

ENGLISH *Spanish dagger plant* NEPALI *ketuki*

Agavaceae. Shrub with a woody trunk. Leaves 50–70 cm long, 3–5 cm wide, sword shaped, lanceolate, margin reddish with spiny points, tip narrowed to a spine. Flowers white, July–November. Propagated by suckers. Distributed throughout Nepal to about 1400 m in open places; also in India and Bhutan.

OTHER USES. Fiber from the leaf is used for twine and other binding purposes. Juice from the squeezed leaf is spread in stagnant water as fish poison.

Z

Zanthoxylum acanthopodium de Candolle

Zanthoxylum alatum Wallich

NEPALI *bhote timur, jangali timur, timur* TIBETAN *te-dza-ni, par-pa-ta*

Rutaceae. Spiny shrub, young branches densely pubescent. Leaves stalked, odd-pinnate, leaflets sessile, 1.5–5 cm long, 0.8–2 cm wide, oblong to lanceolate, acuminate, crenate, pubescent on both surfaces, with one or two spines on the midvein. Flowers dark purple. Fruit reddish, globose, in dense clusters. Seeds shiny black. Flowers April–August, fruits September–October. Propagated by seeds or branch cuttings. Distributed throughout Nepal at 1600–2800 m in rocky places and hanging from cliffs; also in northern India, Bhutan, eastward to China.

FOOD. Seeds are pickled. A powder of dried seeds is used for flavoring foodstuffs.

OTHER USES. Seeds contain essential oils.

Zanthoxylum armatum de Candolle

Zanthoxylum alatum Roxburgh
Zanthoxylum hostile Wallich
Zanthoxylum violaceum Wallich

BHOJPURI *timur* CHEPANG *timpur, umpur* DANUWAR *timur, tirkene* ENGLISH *Nepal pepper, prickly ash bark* GURUNG *prumo* LEPCHA *sungrukung, timbur* LIMBU *midimba, warekpa* MAGAR *timur* MAJHI *timur* NEPALI *bhale timur, timur* NEWARI *tebu* RAI *khakchan, terkane* SHERPA *yerma* SUNWAR *sekkren* TAMANG *prumo* THARU *timur* TIBETAN *gyer-ma*

Rutaceae. Spiny shrub about 3 m high, with corky bark and strong prickles on the branches. Leaves stalked, alternate, slightly winged, with stipular spines at the base, odd-pinnate, leaflets three to nine, 2–10 cm long, 1.5–2.5 cm wide, sessile, lanceolate, entire, gland-dotted. Flowers small, whitish, in loose clusters. Fruit spherical, red when mature, splitting into two valves. Seeds solitary, shiny black. Flowers April–May, fruits July–November. Propagated by seeds or branch cuttings. Distributed throughout Nepal at 1100–2900 m in open places or in forest undergrowth but habitat destruction is a cause of conservation concern; also in northern India, Bhutan, eastward to China, Taiwan, Korea, Japan, the Philippines, and the Lesser Sunda Islands.

FOOD. Fresh fruits are pickled and also used as spice.

MEDICINE. The root is boiled in water about 20 minutes and the filtered water is taken as an anthelmintic. Branches are used for brushing teeth in cases of toothache. Juice of the leaves is taken to treat abdominal pains, and a paste of the leaves is applied for leukoderma. A paste of immature fruits is applied to cuts and wounds. This paste is also taken in cases of cough. Two or three seeds and a small clove of garlic are chewed for indigestion. A paste of the seeds is kept between the teeth about 10 minutes to relieve toothaches. Crushed seeds are boiled in water and taken for fever and cough. Powdered seeds are taken to treat roundworm. Seeds are roasted in clarified butter and taken for stomach troubles.

OTHER USES. Bark and leaf are used to intoxicate fish. A paste of the fruit is mixed with water and sprayed on vegetables as an insecticide. Fruits contain 2.5–3% essential oils and are sold in the trade.

Zanthoxylum armatum

Zanthoxylum nepalense Babu

NEPALI *ban timur*

Rutaceae. Shrub with corky bark and numerous straight spines. Leaves stalked, pinnatifid, rachis winged, leaflets short-stalked, 1–3 cm long, ovate, dentate, gland-dotted. Flowers yellowish. Fruit a capsule, globose, red, wrinkled. Flowers May–June. Propagated by seeds or branch cuttings. Distributed in eastern and central Nepal at 2100–2800 m in open, rocky slopes; also in northern India and Myanmar.

MEDICINE. A paste of immature fruit is kept between the teeth about 10 minutes to relieve toothaches.

Zanthoxylum oxyphyllum Edgeworth

Fagara oxyphylla (Edgeworth) Engler
NEPALI *ban timur*

Rutaceae. Shrub with hooked prickles. Leaves stalked, odd-pinnate, leaflets usually seven, 2–11.5 cm long, 0.5–

4.5 cm wide, elliptic, acuminate, serrulate, gland-dotted beneath. Flowers stalked, purplish, in branched cymes, April–May. Fruits June–September. Propagated by seeds or branch cuttings. Distributed in eastern and central Nepal at 2100–2800 m on open, rocky slopes; also in northern India and Myanmar.

FOOD. Fruits are pickled and also used as spice.

MEDICINE. A paste of immature fruit is kept between the teeth about 10 minutes to relieve toothaches.

Zea mays Linnaeus

BHOJPURI *makai* CHEPANG *makai* DANUWAR *makai* ENGLISH *corn, maize* GURUNG *makai* LEPCHA *kanachung* LIMBU *maki* MAGAR *makaina* MAJHI *makai* MOOSHAR *makai* NEPALI *makai* NEWARI *kani* RAI *yobabacha* SUNWAR *aank* TAMANG *makai* THARU *makai*

Gramineae. Grass about 5 m high. Leaves 30–50 cm long, narrow, broadly lanceolate, flat, hairy on both surfaces, margin wavy. Inflorescence yellowish. Fruit a grain, covered, shiny. Flowers and fruits September–October. Propagated by seeds. Distributed throughout Nepal to about 3000 m, cultivated; also widely cultivated in regions with warm climates.

FOOD. The grains are important as food (Plates 10, 18).

OTHER USES. Husks are used to make roughly woven goods (Plate 11).

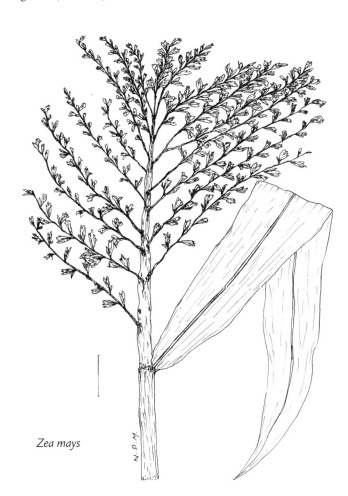

Zea mays

Zingiber officinale Roscoe

CHEPANG *semmar* ENGLISH *ginger* GURUNG *adab* MAGAR *chhebok* NEPALI *aduwa* NEWARI *palu* TAMANG *kingra, tunga* TIBETAN *sga, sman-sga*

Zingiberaceae. Erect herb about 1 m high, rising from an aromatic rootstock. Leaves distichous, linear lanceolate. Scape erect, covered with distant imbricated bracts. Inflorescence ovoid, dense, greenish with a small dark purple or purplish black tip. Propagated by splitting rhizomes. Distributed throughout Nepal to about 2500 m, cultivated.

FOOD. The rhizome is used as a condiment.

MEDICINE. The rhizome is carminative, astringent, stimulant, diuretic, and diaphoretic. It is chewed to treat sore throat, hoarseness, and loss of voice. Roasted rhizome is chewed in cases of cough and colds, toothaches, and bleeding gums. A paste of the rhizome is applied for rheumatism and has rubefacient properties. A paste of the leaves is applied to bruises.

OTHER USES. Lepchas use the plant in all their religious observances.

Zingiber officinale

Ziziphus incurva Roxburgh

CHEPANG *gaisi* GURUNG *kande puju* MAGAR *hare bayer* NEPALI *hade bayer, raju kanda* NEWARI *koko pasi* TAMANG *banger, dangding*

Rhamnaceae. Medium-sized tree. Leaves stalked, 2–11.5 cm long, 1.5–6 cm wide, ovate or oblong, acuminate, serrate, three-veined, glabrous. Flowers small, yellowish, in axillary cymes. Fruits August–January. Propagated by seeds or root suckers. Distributed in eastern and central Nepal at 800–1900 m in open places along with other trees and shrubs; also in northern India, Bhutan, eastward to western China, and Myanmar.

FOOD. Ripe fruits are edible.

OTHER USES. The plant is a useful fodder.

Ziziphus mauritiana Lamarck

Rhamnus jujuba Linnaeus, *Ziziphus jujuba* (Linnaeus) Gaertner

CHEPANG *bayar, dabar, dame, onai* DANUWAR *bayar* ENGLISH *Chinese date, jujube* GURUNG *baher, bhayar* MAJHI *boyar* NEPALI *bayer* NEWARI *bayali, bayer* SATAR *janum* TAMANG *bayar* THARU *bayer* TIBETAN *gya-shug*

Rhamnaceae. Deciduous tree about 6 m high, stems armed with paired thin spines, young branches covered with whitish woolly hairs. Leaves stalked, alternate, 3.5–6 cm long, 2–3.8 cm wide, ovate or oblong, serrate, generally three-veined, dorsally hairy, base oblique. Flowers stalked, crowded, yellowish, in dense axillary cymes. Fruit spherical on wild plants, ovoid on cultivated plants, reddish brown or yellowish when ripe. Flowers August–September, fruits October–March. Propagated by seeds or root suckers. Growth is very fast. Distributed throughout Nepal to about 1200 m in open areas; also in Afghanistan, India, Bhutan, China, Australia, and Africa.

FOOD. Fruits are eaten fresh and have a high content of vitamin C. They are also dried for selling and for use during the off-season.

MEDICINE. A decoction of the root is given in cases of fever. Juice of the root is given for menstrual disorders. This juice, about 2 teaspoons once a day, is given for indigestion and is also considered good for peptic ulcer. A paste of the root is applied for backaches. Juice of the bark, about 6 teaspoons three times a day, is given to treat diarrhea and dysentery. Fresh leaf is chewed to treat bleeding gums. Juice of the leaf is given for liver complaints and diarrhea. Danuwars drip juice in the eye to treat conjunctivitis.

According to the villagers, immature fruits cause cough and colds, especially when eaten in the evening. When eaten during the daytime, they increase thirst. Pulp of ripe fruits is considered useful for fever, ulcer, and wounds. It is said to purify the blood and aid digestion. Gurungs mix a paste of the seed with goat milk and apply it to blemishes. The seed is burned and its ash, mixed with coconut oil, is applied to remove scars left by burns. A powder of the plant gall, about 1 teaspoon three times a day, is given in cases of dysentery.

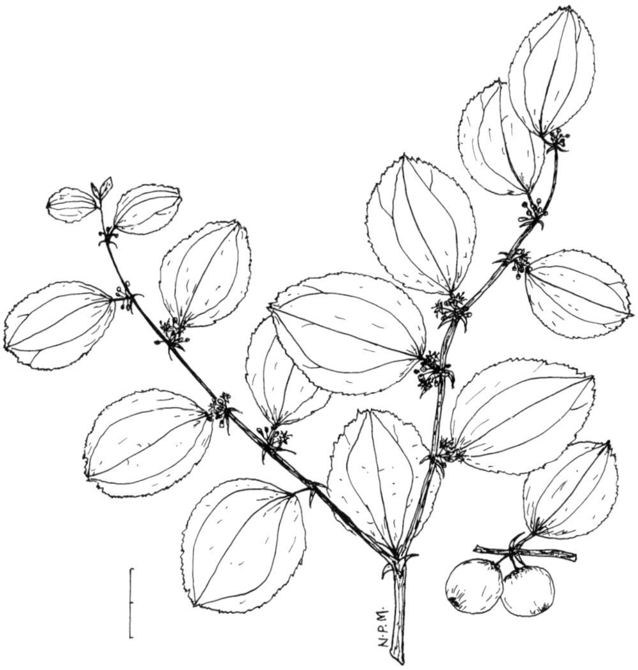

Ziziphus mauritiana

OTHER USES. Wood is hard and used to make handles of tools and agricultural implements. It also is much used for fuel. Bark contains tannin. The thorny branches are used for fences. Leaves are used for fodder and contain 12.6–16.9% crude protein (Jackson 1987). Goats browse the young leaves.

Ziziphus oenoplia (Linnaeus) Miller

Rhamnus oenoplia Linnaeus
Ziziphus albens Roxburgh
Ziziphus napeca Willdenow

MAJHI *koli* NEPALI *aule bayar, boksi bayar, sita bayar* TAMANG *bayar* THARU *bayar*

Rhamnaceae. Thorny shrub about 5 m high with straggling branches. Leaves short-stalked, 2.3–5.5 cm long, 1.3–3 cm wide, ovate to lanceolate, acuminate, crenate to serrate, pubescent above, softly rusty tomentose beneath, oblique at the base. Flowers yellowish. Fruit a drupe, ovoid, yellowish when fully ripe, the scanty mealy pulp acidic. Flowers June–August, fruits September–January. Propagated by seeds. Distributed in western and central Nepal to about 1600 m, common along the margins of subtropical forests; also in India, Sri Lanka, Malaysia, and Australia.

FOOD. Ripe fruits are eaten fresh, and dried for off-season use or for sale.

MEDICINE. Juice of the root is applied to fresh cuts and wounds. A paste of inner bark is applied to obstinate wounds. A decoction of the fruit is taken in cases of indigestion.

OTHER USES. Bark contains tannin. Branches are used for fences, and the plant is also grown as a hedge. Seeds are made into rosaries.

Ziziphus rugosa Lamarck

Ziziphus glabra Roxburgh
Ziziphus latifolia Roxburgh
Ziziphus xylopyrus (Retzius) Willdenow

NEPALI *gamarai* SATAR *sekra*

Rhamnaceae. Tree about 5 m high, bark dark gray, deeply cracked into thick rectangular scales. Leaves stalked, 5.5–13 cm long, 3–11 cm wide, suborbiculate, ovate, or elliptic, subacute, closely serrulate, dark green and glabrous above, thickly gray or rusty felted beneath, obliquely rounded at the base. Flowers yellowish in long axillary or terminal panicles. Fruit a drupe, globose or pear shaped. Flowers March–April, fruits December–February. Propagated by seeds or root suckers. Distributed throughout Nepal to about 1200 m in *Shorea robusta* forest or along the rivers in association with *Acacia catechu*; also in India, Sri Lanka, and Myanmar.

FOOD. The meaty pulp of ripe fruits is edible.

MEDICINE. A paste of the bark is applied to treat swellings of the gums or toothaches.

OTHER USES. Wood is used for fuel. Branches are used for fences. Leaves are lopped for fodder.

Plants According to Use

The genera of plants are grouped under the three main categories of use: food, medicine, and other uses. The particular species used may be found in Chapter 4, where the plants are listed alphabetically.

FOOD

Food plants are listed according to their use as vegetables, as the fermented vegetable preparations *gundruk* and *tama*, and as fresh fruit, oil, spices or flavorings, alcoholic beverages, other beverages, and other food uses. Plants used for fodder or other animal food are listed under Other Uses.

Vegetables. *Abelmoschus, Abrus, Abutilon, Aesculus, Allium, Alternanthera, Amaranthus, Amorphophallus, Anagallis, Anemone, Anogeissus, Antidesma, Arachis, Araucaria, Arisaema, Arthromeris, Artocarpus, Asparagus, Averrhoa, Bambusa, Barbarea, Basella, Bauhinia, Begonia, Benincasa, Berberis, Bergenia, Bidens, Bistorta, Blyxa, Boehmeria, Boerhavia, Bombax, Botrychium, Brachycorythis, Brassica, Cajanus, Camellia, Campylotropis, Canavalia, Cannabis, Capparis, Capsella, Caragana, Cardamine, Cardiospermum, Carica, Carissa, Carum, Cassia, Castanopsis, Catunaregam, Cautleya, Celosia, Centella, Chaerophyllum, Chenopodium, Chlorophytum, Choerospondias, Citrus, Clematis, Cleome, Clerodendrum, Clintonia, Clitoria, Coccinia, Colocasia, Commelina, Corchorus, Cordia, Cortia, Corylus, Costus, Crateva, Crotalaria, Cucumis, Cucurbita, Cycas, Cyclanthera, Cynanchum, Cyperus, Cyphomandra, Cypripedium, Dactylorhiza, Daucus, Delonix, Dendrocalamus, Descurainia, Didymocarpus, Dillenia, Dioscorea, Diplazium, Disporum, Drepanostachyum, Drymaria, Dryoathyrium, Dryopteris, Eclipta, Eichhornia, Elatostema, Elsholtzia, Emilia, Epipactis, Eriosema, Eryngium, Erysimum, Euphorbia, Fagopyrum, Ficus, Fortunella, Fritillaria, Galinsoga, Garuga, Geniosporum, Gentiana, Girardinia, Glycine, Gmelina, Gonostegia, Grangea, Habenaria,* *Helminthostachys, Hibiscus, Himalayacalamus, Hippophae, Houttuynia, Hydrolea, Impatiens, Indigofera, Ipomoea, Jatropha, Justicia, Lablab, Lagenaria, Lathyrus, Launaea, Lecanthus, Lens, Lepidium, Leucaena, Leucas, Ligularia, Lilium, Luffa, Lycopersicon, Lygodium, Macropanax, Mahonia, Mahonia, Maianthemum, Malaxis, Malva, Mangifera, Megacarpaea, Megacodon, Melochia, Mentha, Mirabilis, Momordica, Monochoria, Moringa, Murdannia, Musa, Myriactis, Natsiatum, Nelumbo, Nephrolepis, Ophioglossum, Oreocnide, Osmunda, Oxalis, Panax, Peperomia, Perilla, Persicaria, Phaseolus, Phlogacanthus, Phyllanthus, Phytolacca, Pilea, Pimpinella, Pisum, Plantago, Platanthera, Pleurospermum, Polygonatum, Polygonum, Polystichum, Portulaca, Pouzolzia, Pteridium, Ranunculus, Raphanus, Remusatia, Rheum, Rhus, Rhynchosia, Rorippa, Roscoea, Rotala, Rumex, Rungia, Sambucus, Satyrium, Sauromatum, Scutellaria, Sechium, Selinum, Sesbania, Sinarundinaria, Smilax, Solanum, Sonchus, Spermadictyon, Sphenoclea, Spilanthes, Spinacia, Spondias, Stellaria, Tamarindus, Taraxacum, Tectaria, Telosma, Thelypteris, Thlaspi, Thunbergia, Thymus, Thysanolaena, Trevesia, Trianthema, Trichosanthes, Trigonella, Typhonium, Urtica, Veronica, Vicia, Vigna, Youngia*

Gundruk. *Arisaema, Brassica, Ranunculus, Raphanus, Rumex*

Tama. *Bambusa, Drepanostachyum, Dendrocalamus*

Fresh Fruit. *Actinidia, Aegle, Agapetes, Ampelocissus, Ananas, Annona, Antidesma, Ardisia, Artocarpus, Averrhoa, Berberis, Berchemia, Bischofia, Bridelia, Buchanania, Callicarpa, Capparis, Capsicum, Carica, Carissa, Catunaregam, Choerospondias, Cipadessa, Cissus, Citrullus, Citrus, Clausena, Cleistocalyx, Coccinia, Cocos, Cordia, Coriaria, Cornus, Cotoneaster, Cucumis, Cyphomandra, Debregeasia, Dendrophthoe, Dillenia, Diospyros, Diplokenma, Docynia, Duabanga, Elaeagnus, Elaeocarpus, Eriobotrya, Eugenia, Ficus, Flacourtia, Flemingia, Fortunella, Fragaria, Garuga, Gaultheria, Geranium, Grewia, Helixanthera, Hemiphragma, Hippophae, Hol-*

[Fresh Fruit]

boellia, Ichnocarpus, Ilex, Impatiens, Knoxia, Lantana, Leea, Leuscoceptrum, Lobelia, Lonicera, Lycopersicon, Maclura, Maesa, Mahonia, Mangifera, Manilkara, Melastoma, Morus, Murraya, Musa, Myrica, Myrsine, Neillia, Opuntia, Osbeckia, Oxyspora, Pandanus, Passiflora, Persicaria, Phoenix, Phyllanthus, Physalis, Piper, Potentilla, Premna, Prinsepia, Prunus, Psidium, Pyracantha, Pyrularia, Pyrus, Rhus, Ribes, Rosa, Rubus, Sambucus, Saurauia, Schefflera, Schleichera, Scurrula, Securinega, Smilax, Solanum, Solena, Sorbus, Spondias, Stranvaesia, Streblus, Syzygium, Tamarindus, Taxillus, Tetrastigma, Viburnum, Viscum, Vitis, Ziziphus

Oil. *Arachis, Brassica, Camellia, Cleome, Diplokenma, Elsholtzia, Gossypium, Guizotia, Helianthus, Juglans, Madhuca, Perilla, Prinsepia, Prunus, Schleichera, Sesamum, Symplocos, Viburnum*

Spices or Flavorings. *Acorus, Allium, Amomum, Capsicum, Carum, Cinnamomum, Cipadessa, Coleus, Coriandrum, Cortia, Cuminum, Curcuma, Diplokenma, Elsholtzia, Eryngium, Euodia, Foeniculum, Heracleum, Micromeria, Murraya, Origanum, Pimpinella, Piper, Pleurospermum, Saccharum, Salvia, Selinum, Sesamum, Sinarundinaria, Skimmia, Spilanthes, Stachys, Thymus, Trachyspermum, Trigonella, Zanthoxylum, Zingiber*

Alcoholic Beverages. *Aerva, Artocarpus, Blumea, Blumeopsis, Capsicum, Clematis, Conyza, Cornus, Drymaria, Elephantopus, Eleusine, Emilia, Eupatorium, Inula, Madhuca, Natsiatum, Oryza, Polygala, Prunus, Psidium, Rungia, Schima, Senecio, Solanum, Tridax, Vernonia*

Other Beverages. *Camellia, Cassia, Centella, Citrus, Cocos, Gaultheria, Hydrocotyle, Leucaena, Micromeria, Origanum, Osyris, Potentilla, Quercus, Rhododendron, Saccharum, Vitis*

Other Food Uses. *Areca, Avena, Boehmeria, Cannabis, Castanopsis, Chesneya, Cicer, Cirsium, Citrus, Coix, Colquhounia, Echinochloa, Eleusine, Elsholtzia, Fagopyrum, Flemingia, Gnetum, Helianthus, Herpetospermum, Hibiscus, Hordeum, Impatiens, Juglans, Litchi, Lithocarpus, Madhuca, Meconopsis, Michelia, Monochoria, Nelumbo, Neolamarckia, Nephrolepis, Oreocnide, Oryza, Oxalis, Panicum, Persea, Physalis, Pinus, Pithecellobium, Punica, Rhododendron, Salvia, Scindapsus, Semecarpus, Setaria, Shorea, Sterculia, Tagetes, Taxus, Terminalia, Trapa, Trichosanthes, Triticum, Veronica, Vicia, Vigna, Zanthoxylum, Zea, Ziziphus*

MEDICINE

Medicinal plants are listed alphabetically by their properties, the diseases treated, or the organs affected, except that the following categories have been intercalated to group certain uses together: eye medicines, fever medicines, gastrointestinal medicines, gynecological medicines, injury medicines, liver medicines, lung medicines, mouth medicines, pain medicines, parasite medicines, skin and mucous membrane medicines, tumor medicines, urinary system medicines, and venereal dis-

ease medicines. The various kinds of medicines used for animals are grouped under veterinary medicines. Obviously, there is a certain amount of overlap between some of the categories, but it has been thought helpful to do some grouping.

Alteratives. *Alstonia, Arctium, Argemone, Asparagus, Bauhinia, Ehretia, Mesua, Rubia, Solanum, Terminalia*

Antiperiodics. *Abrus, Alstonia, Cassia, Clerodendrum, Crateva, Ficus, Gloriosa, Thevetia*

Antiseptics. *Adina, Allium, Areca, Artemisia, Arthromeris, Asparagus, Azadirachta, Betula, Boenninghausenia, Carissa, Cissampelos, Clerodendrum, Colebrookea, Delphinium, Dioscorea, Elephantopus, Ficus, Lablab, Melia, Millettia, Nicotiana, Plumeria, Remusatia, Sapium*

Antispasmodics. *Artemisia, Asparagus, Chenopodium, Hyptis, Lobelia, Lycopodium, Melia, Origanum, Psidium*

Aphrodisiacs. *Abrus, Bambusa, Acorus, Artocarpus, Asparagus, Bauhinia, Costus, Dendrocalamus, Mimosa, Mirabilis, Panax, Semecarpus, Solanum*

Astringents. *Acacia, Achyranthes, Aegle, Aesculus, Agrimonia, Aloe, Anisomeles, Annona, Asparagus, Averrhoa, Bauhinia, Brachycorythis, Caesalpinia, Capsella, Careya, Costus, Cyperus, Dactylorhiza, Dalbergia, Dillenia, Elsholtzia, Emilia, Ficus, Imperata, Juglans, Lithocarpus, Madhuca, Manilkara, Mesua, Momordica, Musa, Myrica, Nelumbo, Phyllanthus, Plantago, Prunus, Psidium, Punica, Rheum, Rubia, Rubus, Saraca, Schleichera, Securinega, Sesbania, Syzygium, Tamarindus, Terminalia, Toona, Zingiber*

Cholera. *Achyranthes, Aconitum, Allium, Alstonia, Desmodium, Spermadictyon, Valeriana*

Coagulants. *Boehmeria, Eclipta, Galinsoga, Nicotiana, Utricularia*

Coughs, Colds, or Sore Throats (see also lung medicines, and skin and mucous membrane medicines). *Abies, Abrus, Abutilon, Acacia, Acorus, Adiantum, Agrimonia, Ajuga, Aletris, Allium, Aloe, Anaphalis, Anemone, Anogeissus, Artemisia, Azadirachta, Bergenia, Bombax, Caesalpinia, Cajanus, Calotropis, Cannabis, Careya, Carum, Cassia, Centella, Centipeda, Chrozophora, Cinnamomum, Cipadessa, Cirsium, Cissampelos, Cleistocalyx, Clematis, Clerodendrum, Clinopodium, Clitoria, Colebrookea, Combretum, Costus, Cotoneaster, Curcuma, Cyathocline, Cymbidium, Delphinium, Dendrobium, Desmodium, Dichroa, Ehretia, Elephantopus, Elsholtzia, Euphorbia, Fimbristylis, Floscopa, Fritillaria, Gaultheria, Gentiana, Gnaphalium, Gnetum, Gonostegia, Grewia, Heliotropium, Hemigraphis, Heracleum, Hibiscus, Hydrangea, Hydrocotyle, Hyoscyamus, Indigofera, Ipomoea, Justicia, Laggera, Lantana, Leucas, Madhuca, Mangifera, Mariscus, Martynia, Maytenus, Melastoma, Millettia, Mimosa, Momordica, Mussaenda, Nephrolepis, Ocimum, Oenanthe, Osmanthus, Phlogacanthus, Phyla, Picrorhiza, Piper, Plantago, Pogostemon, Potentilla, Prinsepia, Quisqualis, Reissantia, Rhododendron, Rubus, Rumex, Saurauia, Saussurea,*

Scoparia, Solanum, Spermadictyon, Swertia, Tamarindus, Taxus, Tectaria, Terminalia, Tinospora, Tridax, Urtica, Verbascum, Vernonia, Viburnum, Vitex, Zanthoxylum, Zingiber, Ziziphus

Diabetes. *Cassia, Coccinia, Ficus, Ipomoea, Madhuca, Millettia, Momordica, Mussaenda, Spermadictyon, Syzygium*

Diphtheria. *Maesa*

Dislocated Bones. *Ageratum, Alangium, Ampelocissus, Betula, Calanthe, Caragana, Cardiocrinum, Cassia, Cissampelos, Cissus, Curcuma, Cymbidium, Dendrophthoe, Drynaria, Euphorbia, Garuga, Glochidion, Ligularia, Mimosa, Nyctanthes, Osyris, Parthenocissus, Periploca, Pholidota, Porana, Rumex, Shuteria, Symplocos, Tetrastigma, Thalictrum, Thunia, Urtica, Vanda, Viscum*

Dropsy. *Aloe, Anagallis, Argemone, Capsella, Cardiospermum, Cassia, Imperata, Mirabilis, Picrorhiza, Solanum*

Epilepsy. *Anagallis, Asparagus, Colebrookea, Flemingia, Valeriana*

Eye Medicines

Cataracts. *Coccinia, Tridax*

Conjunctivitis. *Artemisia, Begonia, Berberis, Clematis, Clerodendrum, Colebrookea, Cynoglossum, Euphorbia, Heliotropium, Oxalis, Pyrus, Ranunculus, Schefflera, Tamarindus, Vernonia, Ziziphus*

Ophthalmia. *Thalictrum*

Retinitis. *Osmanthus*

Other Eye Problems. *Abrus, Aegle, Anemone, Argemone, Berberis, Brassica, Caesalpinia, Chenopodium, Cirsium, Clematis, Clerodendrum, Coccinia, Colebrookea, Cynoglossum, Dalbergia, Desmodium, Dicentra, Emilia, Enkianthus, Euonymus, Eupatorium, Euphorbia, Galium, Geniosporum, Heliotropium, Houttuynia, Isodon, Jasminum, Justicia, Lactuca, Maesa, Mahonia, Osyris, Oxalis, Phyllanthus, Pyrus, Ranunculus, Rosa, Rumex, Schefflera, Solanum, Tabernaemontana, Tagetes, Tamarindus, Terminalia, Tridax, Trigonella, Valeriana, Verbascum, Vitis, Ziziphus*

Fever Medicines

Antipyretics. *Costus, Duranta*

Febrifuges. *Adina, Aegle, Alstonia, Amaranthus, Averrhoa, Azadirachta, Cassia, Dichroa, Emilia, Hymenodictyon, Justicia, Lablab, Phyllanthus, Psidium, Rubus, Sesbania, Siegesbeckia, Solanum, Swertia, Tamarindus, Thalictrum, Thevetia, Tinospora, Toona*

Fever (see also malaria under parasite medicines). *Abrus, Abutilon, Acacia, Achyranthes, Adiantum, Aeginetia, Aegle, Aloe, Alstonia, Alternanthera, Alysicarpus, Amaranthus, Ammannia, Anagallis, Anemone, Artemisia, Averrhoa, Azadirachta, Berberis, Bergenia, Biophytum, Bistorta, Blumea, Boenninghausenia, Boer-*

havia, Bombax, Borreria, Buddleja, Butea, Caesalpinia, Callicarpa, Calotropis, Cardiospermum, Carissa, Cassia, Catunaregam, Cedrus, Celastrus, Centella, Cicerbita, Cirsium, Cissampelos, Cleome, Clerodendrum, Colebrookea, Convolvulus, Cordia, Cortia, Corydalis, Costus, Cotula, Crateva, Crotalaria, Crypsinus, Cyathula, Cyperus, Dalbergia, Daphne, Davallia, Dendrobium, Desmodium, Deutzia, Dicentra, Dichroa, Diplocyclos, Disporum, Eclipta, Ehretia, Elatostema, Ephedra, Equisetum, Eupatorium, Euphorbia, Ficus, Flemingia, Fragaria, Gentiana, Gentianella, Girardinia, Gossypium, Halenia, Hedychium, Helminthostachys, Holarrhena, Hydrocotyle, Hypericum, Impatiens, Imperata, Inula, Isodon, Ixeris, Jasminum, Juniperus, Jurinea, Justicia, Kohautia, Lagerstroemia, Lantana, Launaea, Lecanthus, Leucas, Lindernia, Lobelia, Mallotus, Manilkara, Mariscus, Mentha, Microsorum, Mimosa, Mirabilis, Murdannia, Mussaenda, Myrica, Nelumbo, Nepeta, Nephrolepis, Nicandra, Nyctanthes, Ocimum, Onychium, Oroxylum, Oxalis, Panax, Pavetta, Persicaria, Phyla, Phyllodium, Picrorhiza, Piper, Pisum, Plantago, Pogostemon, Polygala, Potentilla, Pouzolzia, Premna, Prenanthes, Psidium, Pterocephalus, Punica, Rauvolfia, Reinwardtia, Ricinus, Rorippa, Rubus, Sagittaria, Salomonia, Salvia, Sarcococca, Saurauia, Saussurea, Schima, Schisandra, Scoparia, Scutellaria, Selinum, Semecarpus, Senecio, Sesbania, Sida, Smithia, Solanum, Sonchus, Spermadictyon, Stellaria, Stephania, Swertia, Terminalia, Tetrastigma, Thalictrum, Thelypteris, Tiarella, Trachelospermum, Trichosanthes, Tridax, Urtica, Vernonia, Veronica, Viola, Vitex, Woodfordia, Zanthoxylum, Ziziphus

Gastrointestinal Medicines

Aperients (see also constipation, and laxatives). *Clitoria, Manilkara, Rheum, Sesbania, Taraxacum*

Carminatives (see also flatulence). *Abies, Acorus, Allium, Amorphophallus, Anisomeles, Artemisia, Belamcanda, Betula, Boerhavia, Callicarpa, Carum, Cedrus, Cleome, Cuminum, Cyperus, Daucus, Desmodium, Elsholtzia, Gaultheria, Myrica, Pimpinella, Salvia, Saussurea, Sterculia, Tagetes, Terminalia, Valeriana, Zingiber*

Colic. *Achyranthes, Aechmanthera, Arisaema, Averrhoa, Bergenia, Cinnamomum, Cissampelos, Helicteres, Nicotiana, Origanum, Rubus, Urena*

Constipation (see also laxatives). *Aloe, Amaranthus, Boschniakia, Cirsium, Cissampelos, Cyathula, Dioscorea, Euonymus, Ficus, Girardinia, Mallotus, Oreocnide, Phyllanthus, Verbascum*

Diarrhea. *Acacia, Achyranthes, Acorus, Aechmanthera, Aegle, Agrimonia, Ajuga, Albizia, Allium, Alstonia, Amaranthus, Annona, Artemisia, Artocarpus, Asparagus, Astilbe, Bauhinia, Berberis, Bergenia, Bistorta, Boehmeria, Bombax, Buddleja, Caesalpinia, Cajanus, Callicarpa, Calotropis, Campanula, Cannabis, Capsella, Cardiospermum, Carissa, Caryopteris, Cassia, Castanopsis, Catharanthus, Catunaregam, Cinnamomum, Clematis, Clerodendrum, Coix, Conyza, Costus, Crassocephalum, Curculigo, Desmodium, Dioscorea, Dryopteris, Ehretia, Elephantopus, Emilia, Euphorbia, Ficus, Flacourtia, Flemingia, Gono-*

[Diarrhea]

stegia, Grewia, Helicteres, Heracleum, Hypericum, Imperata, Indigofera, Kalanchoe, Lespedeza, Lindera, Lobelia, Maesa, Mallotus, Mangifera, Manilkara, Mirabilis, Murraya, Mussaenda, Myrica, Nelumbo, Neolamarckia, Origanum, Oroxylum, Osbeckia, Oxalis, Paris, Phyllanthus, Pithecellobium, Plantago, Pleurospermum, Plumbago, Pogostemon, Psidium, Pteris, Punica, Pyrus, Quercus, Rhamnus, Rhododendron, Ribes, Ricinus, Rubus, Rumex, Sapium, Saussurea, Sesbania, Solanum, Spermadictyon, Stellaria, Stephania, Syzygium, Tadehaji, Tamarindus, Tectaria, Thelypteris, Trewia, Trichilia, Uraria, Urena, Urtica, Verbascum, Vernonia, Woodfordia, Ziziphus

Digestives. Achyranthes, Aegle, Carica, Citrus, Costus, Origanum, Rorippa, Salvia, Semecarpus, Terminalia

Dysentery. Acacia, Achyranthes, Acorus, Adiantum, Aegle, Agrimonia, Ajuga, Albizia, Alstonia, Alternanthera, Amaranthus, Amorphophallus, Anemone, Annona, Artemisia, Artocarpus, Asparagus, Astilbe, Azadirachta, Bauhinia, Bistorta, Boehmeria, Bombax, Buddleja, Caesalpinia, Cajanus, Callicarpa, Callistephus, Calotropis, Campanula, Cannabis, Cardiospermum, Carissa, Caryopteris, Cassia, Catunaregam, Centella, Chenopodium, Citrus, Clematis, Clerodendrum, Colebrookea, Conyza, Costus, Crinum, Curculigo, Dalbergia, Desmodium, Desmostachya, Dioscorea, Dryopteris, Ehretia, Elaeagnus, Elephantopus, Euphorbia, Ficus, Flacourtia, Flemingia, Geranium, Grewia, Helicteres, Heracleum, Holarrhena, Hypericum, Imperata, Indigofera, Kalanchoe, Lespedeza, Lobelia, Maesa, Mangifera, Mentha, Mesua, Mimosa, Momordica, Moringa, Murraya, Mussaenda, Myrica, Neolamarckia, Oroxylum, Osbeckia, Osyris, Oxalis, Oxyria, Paris, Phyllanthus, Pithecellobium, Plantago, Plumbago, Plumeria, Polygonum, Pouzolzia, Psidium, Pteris, Punica, Pyracantha, Quercus, Rauvolfia, Rhamnus, Rhododendron, Rhus, Ribes, Ricinus, Rubus, Rumex, Saraca, Saussurea, Scoparia, Semecarpus, Sesamum, Sesbania, Shorea, Solanum, Spondias, Syzygium, Tamarindus, Tectaria, Thelypteris, Toona, Trewia, Trichilia, Urena, Urtica, Woodfordia, Ziziphus

Dyspepsia. Artemisia, Asparagus, Capsicum, Carum, Costus, Oxalis, Phyllanthus, Pleurospermum

Emetics (see also vomiting). Abrus, Achyranthes, Cardiospermum, Catunaregam, Clerodendrum, Clitoria, Cymbidium, Dichroa, Eclipta, Ficus, Lagenaria, Luffa, Mimosa, Nicotiana, Osyris, Paeonia

Flatulence (see also carminatives). Asparagus, Justicia, Lindera, Mukia, Pimpinella

Indigestion. Acacia, Achyranthes, Adiantum, Aloe, Amaranthus, Ardisia, Aster, Barleria, Bauhinia, Bergenia, Blumea, Bombax, Breynia, Callicarpa, Careya, Cassia, Castanopsis, Celastrus, Celtis, Centella, Cheilanthes, Cipadessa, Cirsium, Cissampelos, Clematis, Coelogyne, Colebrookea, Commelina, Corydalis, Costus, Cotoneaster, Crotalaria, Cyathocline, Cynodon, Cynoglossum, Desmodium, Desmostachya, Dichroa, Diplokenma, Elatostema, Elephantopus, Epilobium, Equisetum, Flemingia, Galium, Gonostegia, Hedychium, Hedyotis, Houttuynia, Hydrocotyle,

Hypericum, Imperata, Inula, Jasminum, Kohautia, Lagenaria, Loranthus, Luculia, Mallotus, Maoutia, Mirabilis, Neanotis, Nephrolepis, Oryza, Osbeckia, Osyris, Paederia, Panax, Pentanema, Persicaria, Pithecellobium, Pogostemon, Potentilla, Pouzolzia, Pteris, Reinwardtia, Roscoea, Rubus, Sanicula, Sapium, Scutellaria, Senecio, Sida, Siegesbeckia, Solena, Sonchus, Spermadictyon, Stereospermum, Tanacetum, Thalictrum, Thelypteris, Thespesia, Torilis, Trewia, Triumfetta, Viburnum, Woodfordia, Youngia, Zanthoxylum, Ziziphus

Laxatives (see also aperients, and constipation). Abutilon, Achyranthes, Aegle, Agave, Aloe, Argemone, Artocarpus, Asparagus, Averrhoa, Berberis, Cardiospermum, Cassia, Chenopodium, Clerodendrum, Clitoria, Crateva, Croton, Dillenia, Drymaria, Euphorbia, Ficus, Gloriosa, Hibiscus, Ipomoea, Mangifera, Nyctanthes, Phyllanthus, Prunus, Sesbania, Solanum, Sterculia, Swertia, Tagetes, Tamarindus, Terminalia

Nausea. Lindera, Rumex, Valeriana

Peptic Ulcer. Agrimonia, Aloe, Astilbe, Begonia, Berberis, Bridelia, Catunaregam, Cheilanthes, Chenopodium, Cissampelos, Clematis, Colebrookea, Corydalis, Curculigo, Cyananthus, Cyathula, Desmodium, Ficus, Geranium, Hedyotis, Inula, Lagenaria, Maclura, Mangifera, Marsdenia, Mimosa, Momordica, Oxalis, Potentilla, Rubus, Schima, Thalictrum, Uraria, Vernonia, Ziziphus

Purgatives. Abrus, Achyranthes, Aloe, Ananas, Annona, Areca, Azadirachta, Cassia, Catharanthus, Clitoria, Costus, Cymbidium, Eclipta, Eleusine, Foeniculum, Gloriosa, Lagenaria, Luffa, Mallotus, Mirabilis, Moringa, Nicotiana, Paeonia, Phyllanthus, Picrorhiza, Plumeria, Podophyllum, Polygala, Prunus, Rhamnus, Rheum, Ricinus, Rumex, Terminalia, Thalictrum

Stomachaches and Other Gastric, Abdominal, or Intestinal Troubles. Achyranthes, Aconitum, Adiantum, Agrimonia, Amaranthus, Artemisia, Bauhinia, Berberis, Boerhavia, Bombax, Botrychium, Caesalpinia, Callicarpa, Cassia, Castanopsis, Catunaregam, Cautleya, Centella, Cheilanthes, Cirsium, Citrus, Clematis, Coelogyne, Colebrookea, Coriaria, Crateva, Cuscuta, Cyperus, Dactylorhiza, Daphne, Desmodium, Dillenia, Dioscorea, Drymaria, Elatostema, Elephantopus, Euphorbia, Ficus, Fraxinus, Garuga, Gaultheria, Girardinia, Gloriosa, Grewia, Gymnadenia, Hedyotis, Homalium, Imperata, Inula, Jasminum, Justicia, Lagenaria, Luculia, Marsdenia, Mazus, Momordica, Mussaenda, Myrica, Nyctanthes, Ocimum, Osbeckia, Oxalis, Persicaria, Phyla, Phyllanthus, Picrorhiza, Pinus, Pityrogramma, Polygonum, Potentilla, Prinsepia, Ranunculus, Rhus, Rubus, Sapium, Schima, Scutellaria, Semecarpus, Shorea, Solanum, Solena, Sophora, Spilanthes, Stephania, Taraxacum, Thelypteris, Thymus, Tinospora, Trewia, Trichilia, Uraria, Urena, Vernonia, Veronica, Vitex, Woodfordia, Wrightia, Wulfenia, Zanthoxylum

Stomachics. Achyranthes, Aegle, Amorphophallus, Artemisia, Asparagus, Boerhavia, Capsicum, Cardiospermum, Carissa, Carum, Cassia, Citrus, Crateva, Eryngium, Garuga, Gloriosa, Lablab, Leonurus, Mesua, Murraya, Oxalis, Phyllanthus, Picrorhiza, Rheum, Swertia, Terminalia, Verbena

Vomiting (see also emetics). *Amaranthus, Cynoglossum, Elephantopus, Ipomoea, Mimosa, Panax, Rhododendron, Solanum*

Goiter. *Eupatorium, Euphorbia, Osbeckia*

Gout. *Bergenia, Chlorophytum, Crotalaria, Dalbergia, Erodium, Hedyotis, Millettia, Mimosa, Moringa, Ricinus, Sarcococca*

Gynecological Medicines

Abortifacients. *Ananas, Areca, Artemisia, Averrhoa, Caesalpinia, Catunaregam, Fraxinus, Gloriosa, Leucaena, Momordica, Pithecellobium, Plumeria*

Amenorrhea. *Asparagus*

Emmenagogues. *Artemisia, Averrhoa, Heliotropium, Hyptis, Phyllanthus, Salvia*

Galactagogues. *Alstonia, Amaranthus, Asparagus, Averrhoa, Bambusa, Euphorbia, Hedyotis, Ichnocarpus, Jasminum, Lecanthus, Moringa, Ricinus, Solena, Sonchus, Trifolium, Urtica*

Leukorrhea. *Acacia, Boerhavia, Plantago*

Menorrhagia. *Amaranthus, Artemisia, Phyllanthus, Saraca*

Menstruation. *Abroma, Adiantum, Aloe, Alternanthera, Artemisia, Arundo, Astilbe, Desmodium, Euphrasia, Ficus, Fragaria, Hypericum, Hyptis, Inula, Mirabilis, Origanum, Potentilla, Rhododendron, Rhus, Ricinus, Urtica, Woodfordia, Ziziphus*

Other Gynecological Medicines. *Acacia, Achyranthes, Aeschynanthus, Alstonia, Anisomeles, Asparagus, Astilbe, Begonia, Betula, Careya, Carum, Cissampelos, Dicranostigma, Hygrophila, Ichnocarpus, Impatiens, Osyris, Paeonia, Phyllanthus, Pteris, Pyrrosia*

Hair Loss. *Aloe, Datura, Didymocarpus, Schleichera*

Heart. *Elaeocarpus, Elephantopus, Ephedra, Oryza, Phyllanthus, Reissantia, Siegesbeckia, Terminalia*

Hemorrhage. *Acacia, Artemisia, Astilbe, Phyllanthus, Tridax*

Injury Medicines

See also astringents.

Bruise. *Ageratum, Cedrus, Elephantopus, Ficus, Impatiens, Macaranga, Plantago, Uraria, Urena, Viscum, Zingiber*

Burn. *Acacia, Alnus, Aloe, Amaranthus, Ananas, Areca, Argemone, Azadirachta, Bacopa, Betula, Clerodendrum, Commelina, Cynoglossum, Diplokenma, Equisetum, Guizotia, Jatropha, Kalanchoe, Lawsonia, Luisia, Mangifera, Momordica, Oroxylum, Persicaria, Punica, Ricinus, Sapindus, Sedum, Solanum, Symplocos, Terminalia, Verbascum, Ziziphus*

Cut. *Abelmoschus, Acacia, Acrocephalus, Adiantum, Adina, Ageratum, Agrostemma, Albizia, Alternanthera, Ampelocissus,*

Anaphalis, Anemone, Artemisia, Artocarpus, Aster, Aster, Bauhinia, Betula, Bidens, Bistorta, Blumeopsis, Boehmeria, Boenninghausenia, Bombax, Breynia, Caesulia, Callicarpa, Cannabis, Catunaregam, Centella, Centranthera, Ceropegia, Cheilanthes, Clematis, Clerodendrum, Cleyera, Clinopodium, Colebrookea, Conyza, Craniotome, Crotalaria, Cuscuta, Cynodon, Cynoglossum, Dennstaedtia, Desmodium, Dicentra, Dichrocephala, Diplazium, Dryopteris, Eclipta, Elephantopus, Elsholtzia, Emilia, Eriocaulon, Eupatorium, Euphorbia, Ficus, Fumaria, Galinsoga, Galium, Geniosporum, Geranium, Gnaphalium, Gymnadenia, Gynura, Helicia, Heliotropium, Hemiphragma, Hydrilla, Hypericum, Imperata, Ipomoea, Iris, Jacaranda, Jasminum, Justicia, Lagerstroemia, Leea, Lepidagathis, Leptodermis, Leucas, Lindenbergia, Lobelia, Loxogramme, Luculia, Ludwigia, Maoutia, Mariscus, Mazus, Melissa, Mollugo, Momordica, Morus, Myrica, Nicotiana, Odontosoria, Osbeckia, Osyris, Paederia, Paris, Parochetus, Perilla, Phyllanthus, Pinus, Pleione, Polypodium, Pouzolzia, Premna, Psidium, Pteris, Ranunculus, Rhynchostylis, Ribes, Ricinus, Rotala, Rungia, Schima, Scutellaria, Selaginella, Sida, Stellaria, Strobilanthes, Synedrella, Tectaria, Terminalia, Thunbergia, Tithonia, Torenia, Urtica, Utricularia, Vanda, Vernonia, Viola, Wahlenbergia, Wendlandia, Zanthoxylum, Ziziphus

Scorpion Bite. *Ampelocissus, Carica, Cassia, Cleome, Clerodendrum, Dillenia, Nicotiana, Quercus, Rubia, Schima*

Snakebite. *Achyranthes, Ageratum, Agrimonia, Amaranthus, Ampelocissus, Arisaema, Cassia, Cissampelos, Costus, Elephantopus, Euphorbia, Ficus, Hypericum, Impatiens, Ipomoea, Leea, Moringa, Nerium, Nyctanthes, Ocimum, Spilanthes, Uraria, Urena*

Other Bites. *Achyranthes, Cynoglossum, Murraya, Plantago, Reinwardtia, Urtica*

Sprain. *Abelmoschus, Acacia, Ampelocissus, Astilbe, Caesalpinia, Calotropis, Canna, Cardiospermum, Colebrookea, Datura, Drynaria, Equisetum, Euphorbia, Jasminum, Kalanchoe, Lantana, Lecanthus, Ligularia, Mimosa, Myrica, Osyris, Quercus, Rubus, Stellera, Stephania, Symplocos, Taxillus, Uraria, Urena, Viscum, Vittaria, Woodfordia*

Vulneraries. *Cajanus, Psidium*

Wound. *Abelmoschus, Abutilon, Acacia, Acrocephalus, Adenocaulon, Adiantum, Adina, Ageratum, Agrimonia, Agrostemma, Albizia, Alternanthera, Ampelocissus, Anaphalis, Anemone, Arisaema, Artemisia, Arthromeris, Artocarpus, Aster, Azadirachta, Bauhinia, Betula, Bidens, Bistorta, Blumeopsis, Boehmeria, Boenninghausenia, Boerhavia, Bombax, Breynia, Caesulia, Cajanus, Callicarpa, Calotropis, Cannabis, Carissa, Carpesium, Catunaregam, Centella, Centranthera, Ceropegia, Cheilanthes, Chrysopogon, Cissampelos, Clematis, Clerodendrum, Cleyera, Clinopodium, Coelogyne, Colebrookea, Combretum, Conyza, Craniotome, Crassocephalum, Crotalaria, Cuscuta, Cynodon, Cynoglossum, Dactylorhiza, Datura, Delphinium, Dennstaedtia, Desmodium, Dicentra, Dichrocephala, Dioscorea, Diplazium, Dryopteris, Eclipta, Elatostema, Elephantopus, Elsholtzia, Emilia, Eriocaulon, Eupatorium, Euphorbia, Ficus, Fritillaria,*

[Wound]

Fumaria, Galinsoga, Galium, Garuga, Geniosporum, Gentianella, Geranium, Geum, Glochidion, Gnaphalium, Gonostegia, Gymnadenia, Gynura, Helicia, Heliotropium, Hemiphragma, Houttuynia, Hydrilla, Hydrocotyle, Hypericum, Hyptis, Imperata, Ipomoea, Iris, Jacaranda, Jasminum, Jatropha, Justicia, Lagerstroemia, Lawsonia, Leea, Leonurus, Lepidagathis, Leptodermis, Leucas, Lindenbergia, Linum, Lobelia, Loxogramme, Luculia, Ludwigia, Lycopodium, Lygodium, Maoutia, Mariscus, Mazus, Megacodon, Melissa, Micromeria, Millettia, Mollugo, Momordica, Morus, Myrica, Nicotiana, Odontosoria, Ophioglossum, Origanum, Oroxylum, Osbeckia, Osyris, Paederia, Paris, Parnassia, Parochetus, Perilla, Persicaria, Phyllanthus, Pinus, Plectranthus, Pleione, Plumeria, Polygonum, Polypodium, Pouzolzia, Premna, Prunus, Psidium, Pteris, Pulicaria, Ranunculus, Reinwardtia, Remusatia, Rhaphidophora, Rhododendron, Rhus, Rhynchostylis, Ribes, Ricinus, Rotala, Rubus, Rungia, Salvia, Sapium, Schima, Scopolia, Scrophularia, Scutellaria, Sedum, Selaginella, Sida, Siegesbeckia, Solanum, Sonchus, Spermadictyon, Stellaria, Strobilanthes, Synedrella, Syzygium, Tamarindus, Tectaria, Terminalia, Teucrium, Thunbergia, Tithonia, Torenia, Triumfetta, Urtica, Utricularia, Vanda, Verbascum, Vernonia, Viola, Viscum, Wahlenbergia, Wendlandia, Zanthoxylum, Ziziphus

Insomnia. *Eupatorium, Solanum, Valeriana*

Liver Medicines

Bile. *Abrus, Ajuga, Anagallis, Asparagus, Boerhavia, Crateva, Desmodium, Herpetospermum, Manilkara, Sonchus, Urtica, Viola*

Liver. *Aloe, Belamcanda, Bupleurum, Centella, Eclipta, Elephantopus, Equisetum, Ficus, Moringa, Nelumbo, Phyllanthus, Ricinus, Rosa, Schima, Solanum, Sorbaria, Thymus, Trichosanthes, Ziziphus*

Lung Medicines

See also coughs, colds, or sore throats, and skin and mucous membrane medicines.

Asthma. *Abies, Abrus, Achyranthes, Acorus, Artemisia, Averrhoa, Bergenia, Boerhavia, Calotropis, Cardiospermum, Carica, Cassia, Clerodendrum, Curculigo, Datura, Diplokenma, Ephedra, Euphorbia, Evolvulus, Fritillaria, Heliotropium, Hydrocotyle, Hyoscyamus, Hypericum, Imperata, Jasminum, Justicia, Mimosa, Moringa, Myrica, Salvia, Saussurea, Semecarpus, Solanum, Tamarindus, Taxus, Terminalia, Urtica, Verbascum*

Bronchitis. *Abelmoschus, Abies, Acorus, Barleria, Clitoria, Coix, Dichroa, Euphorbia, Evolvulus, Fritillaria, Jasminum, Justicia, Lindenbergia, Mallotus, Mangifera, Ocimum, Punica, Semecarpus, Tagetes, Taxus, Terminalia, Verbascum*

Expectorants. *Abies, Abrus, Amaranthus, Ananas, Artemisia, Asparagus, Belamcanda, Brachycorythis, Cajanus, Capparis, Cedrus, Dactylorhiza, Emilia, Ocimum, Origanum, Panax, Uraria, Urena, Valeriana*

Tuberculosis. *Abrus, Agrimonia, Elephantopus, Fritillaria*

Whooping Cough. *Cassia, Hyoscyamus, Osmanthus, Plantago*

Other Lung Problems. *Cedrus, Verbascum, Viola*

Meningitis. *Mallotus*

Mouth Medicines

See also skin and mucous membrane medicines, and tonsillitis.

Gingivitis. *Mangifera, Morus, Streblus*

Gums. *Acacia, Albizia, Azadirachta, Cipadessa, Cissampelos, Ficus, Jatropha, Madhuca, Nicotiana, Plantago, Psidium, Rumex, Solanum, Zingiber, Ziziphus*

Pyorrhea. *Achyranthes, Cymbopogon, Jatropha, Potentilla*

Stomatitis. *Ophiorrhiza, Woodfordia*

Toothache or Dental Caries. *Abelmoschus, Abrus, Acacia, Achyranthes, Anemone, Azadirachta, Berberis, Boenninghausenia, Cassia, Catharanthus, Clematis, Clerodendrum, Datura, Delphinium, Desmodium, Desmostachya, Ficus, Incarvillea, Jatropha, Lawsonia, Ligustrum, Lindera, Mangifera, Micromeria, Monochoria, Mukia, Murraya, Myrica, Neohymenopogon, Origanum, Phoenix, Potentilla, Pouzolzia, Shorea, Sida, Solanum, Sphaeranthus, Spilanthes, Streblus, Tabernaemontana, Thalictrum, Tridax, Urtica, Vitex, Zanthoxylum, Zingiber, Ziziphus*

Mumps. *Antidesma, Euphorbia, Lantana*

Narcotics. *Aesculus, Cannabis, Nicotiana*

Nosebleed. *Acacia, Cerastium, Cirsium, Imperata, Leucas, Micromeria*

Pain Medicines

Anodyne. *Averrhoa*

Backache. *Acacia, Aeschynanthus, Aglaomorpha, Bergenia, Boerhavia, Coelogyne, Cryptolepis, Drynaria, Gnaphalium, Hoya, Hypericum, Justicia, Mimosa, Myricaria, Persicaria, Polypodium, Prunella, Prunus, Pteris, Scutellaria, Ziziphus*

Earache. *Alstonia, Bergenia, Betula, Brassica, Calotropis, Cassia, Cleome, Clitoria, Datura, Emilia, Ficus, Ocimum, Origanum, Oxalis, Scutellaria, Tagetes, Thalictrum*

Headache. *Abrus, Acacia, Adiantum, Adina, Aesculus, Agrimonia, Amaranthus, Anemone, Annona, Artemisia, Artemisia, Arundo, Averrhoa, Azadirachta, Begonia, Boenninghausenia, Boerhavia, Bombax, Botrychium, Cassia, Cedrus, Centella, Cerastium, Chamabainia, Clematis, Coelogyne, Colebrookea, Cordia, Cotoneaster, Cotula, Crotalaria, Curculigo, Cuscuta, Cyathocline, Datura, Desmodium, Dichrocephala* (migraine), *Diplokenma, Drynaria, Eclipta, Elsholtzia, Euphorbia, Ficus, Fim-*

bristylis, Floscopa, Gentiana, Gentianella, Girardinia, Globba, Hedyotis, Hypericum, Hyptis, Inula, Isodon, Juglans, Juniperus, Luculia, Ludwigia, Maesa, Malus, Melia, Murdannia, Myrica, Nephrolepis, Oleandra, Osyris, Phyla, Phyllodium, Picris, Pogostemon, Polygala, Prenanthes, Psidium, Quisqualis, Reinwardtia, Reissantia, Rhododendron, Rhynchosia, Ricinus, Rosa, Rubus, Rumex, Schleichera, Scoparia, Semecarpus, Senecio, Sesbania, Sida, Solanum, Sopubia, Stellaria, Swertia, Tectaria, Toricellia, Valeriana, Verbena, Vernonia, Vitex

Neuralgia. *Aconitum, Verbena*

Sciatica. *Abrus, Nyctanthes*

Other Pain. *Abrus, Acacia, Achyranthes, Acorus, Adiantum, Agrimonia, Alnus, Aloe, Alstonia, Anemone, Artemisia, Boehmeria, Bombax, Bromus, Callicarpa, Calotropis, Caragana, Cardiospermum, Carum, Cassia, Catunaregam, Cedrus, Centella, Cirsium, Cissampelos, Clematis, Colebrookea, Cuscuta, Dalbergia, Diplokenma, Drynaria, Epilobium, Euphorbia, Fimbristylis, Geranium, Girardinia, Gonostegia, Helianthus, Helicteres, Hemigraphis, Impatiens, Inula, Justicia, Lygodium, Mallotus, Melia, Mussaenda, Myrica, Oroxylum, Phoenix, Plumbago, Plumeria, Prinsepia, Quercus, Rhododendron, Ricinus, Rumex, Saussurea, Selinum, Senecio, Solanum, Spilanthes, Tagetes, Tamarindus, Tectaria, Thalictrum, Thymus, Zanthoxylum*

Paralysis. *Abrus, Ocimum, Rhus*

Parasite Medicines

Anthelmintics and Vermifuges. *Aesculus, Albizia, Alstonia, Ananas, Anemone, Annona, Areca, Arisaema, Artemisia, Asclepias, Asparagus, Averrhoa, Azadirachta, Bauhinia, Bergenia, Boenninghausenia, Butea, Caesalpinia, Cajanus, Cannabis, Capparis, Carica, Carissa, Cassia, Catunaregam, Centella, Chenopodium, Cipadessa, Cissampelos, Clematis, Cleome, Clerodendrum, Clitoria, Coix, Colebrookea, Costus, Crateva, Cynodon, Cynoglossum, Cyperus, Dalbergia, Daphne, Daucus, Delphinium, Dicentra, Dioscorea, Diplokenma, Entada, Erythrina, Euphorbia, Ficus, Fraxinus, Fumaria, Gaultheria, Gentiana, Girardinia, Holarrhena, Houttuynia, Hyptis, Imperata, Ipomoea, Jasminum, Jatropha, Juglans, Luculia, Luisia, Maesa, Mallotus, Mangifera, Melia, Millettia, Moringa, Morus, Myrica, Nerium, Nicotiana, Nyctanthes, Ocimum, Orobanche, Paris, Persicaria, Plantago, Plumeria, Potentilla, Prinsepia, Prunus, Punica, Quisqualis, Remusatia, Ricinus, Rumex, Sapium, Schima, Scindapsus, Semecarpus, Siegesbeckia, Solanum, Swertia, Symplocos, Tagetes, Terminalia, Thymus, Trichilia, Uraria, Urena, Urtica, Vernonia, Zanthoxylum*

Malaria. *Abrus, Berberis, Corchorus, Crotalaria, Croton, Dichroa, Dichrocephala, Diplazium, Equisetum, Holarrhena, Jatropha, Justicia, Lantana, Leucas, Orthosiphon, Plantago, Swertia, Veronica*

Ringworm. *Artemisia, Averrhoa, Cassia, Centella, Cynoglossum, Girardinia, Hyptis, Ipomoea, Jasminum, Jatropha, Leea, Maesa, Nerium, Nicotiana, Ocimum, Orobanche, Prinsepia, Ricinus, Semecarpus, Siegesbeckia, Solanum, Symplocos*

Scabies. *Acacia, Acorus, Ageratum, Albizia, Alternanthera, Anemone, Boenninghausenia, Cassia, Cryptolepis, Debregeasia, Delphinium, Diplazium, Elsholtzia, Equisetum, Evolvulus, Ficus, Galium, Gaultheria, Guizotia, Ixeris, Jatropha, Lindera, Lithocarpus, Lygodium, Lyonia, Maesa, Mangifera, Mesua, Millettia, Mirabilis, Mukia, Neolitsea, Osbeckia, Persicaria, Pieris, Reinwardtia, Ricinus, Rubus, Semecarpus, Smilax, Symplocos, Trichilia*

Septicemia. *Tridax*

Rabies. *Achyranthes, Anagallis, Solanum*

Refrigerants. *Abutilon, Amaranthus, Asparagus, Averrhoa, Berberis, Bombax, Cissampelos, Coix, Drymaria, Euphorbia, Gonostegia, Hibiscus, Impatiens, Madhuca, Monochoria, Phyla, Phyllanthus, Prunus, Punica*

Rheumatism. *Abies, Abrus, Achyranthes, Aconitum, Acorus, Aesculus, Ageratum, Aloe, Alstonia, Asparagus, Callicarpa, Capparis, Cardiospermum, Carica, Cassia, Catunaregam, Cedrus, Celastrus, Cleome, Coix, Cuscuta, Datura, Diplokenma, Ficus, Gaultheria, Hyptis, Justicia, Lantana, Lycopodium, Mangifera, Melia, Myrica, Nicotiana, Nyctanthes, Ocimum, Origanum, Pleurospermum, Plumbago, Plumeria, Prinsepia, Psidium, Rhododendron, Ricinus, Schleichera, Sesbania, Sida, Solanum, Spondias, Tagetes, Tamarindus, Urena, Valeriana, Vitex, Zingiber*

Sedatives. *Albizia, Cajanus, Cannabis, Citrus, Cyperus, Imperata, Nicotiana, Rauvolfia, Xanthium*

Skin and Mucous Membrane Medicines

See also coughs, colds, or sore throats, injury medicines, lung medicines, and tonsillitis.

Blister. *Desmodium, Drosera, Ranunculus, Rhus*

Boils. *Abelmoschus, Abrus, Abutilon, Acacia, Acer, Achyranthes, Adiantum, Ageratum, Ajuga, Alstonia, Amaranthus, Ammannia, Ananas, Anaphalis, Androsace, Arctium, Artemisia, Arthromeris, Artocarpus, Asclepias, Aster, Barleria, Basella, Bauhinia, Bergenia, Betula, Boehmeria, Botrychium, Bupleurum, Butomopsis, Cajanus, Callicarpa, Calotropis, Ceropegia, Cheilanthes, Chrysopogon, Clerodendrum, Cochlianthus, Coelogyne, Corydalis, Cymbidium, Cynoglossum, Daphniphyllum, Datura, Dendrobium, Dendrophthoe, Desmodium, Dioscorea, Diplazium, Diplokenma, Dryopteris, Entada, Erythrina, Eupatorium, Euphorbia, Euphrasia, Evolvulus, Ficus, Geranium, Gonostegia, Grewia, Heliotropium, Holarrhena, Hydrocotyle, Hyptis, Ichnocarpus, Isodon, Jatropha, Kalanchoe, Laggera, Launaea, Leersia, Leucas, Leucostegia, Lindenbergia, Lindera, Linum, Luisia, Lygodium, Macaranga, Maclura, Maesa, Melochia, Mentha, Mesua, Mirabilis, Mussaenda, Neolitsea, Nepeta, Ophiorrhiza, Oreocnide, Osmanthus, Oxalis, Parochetus, Pedicularis, Persicaria, Pholidota, Phyllanthus, Plantago, Plumbago, Plumeria, Pouzolzia, Pteris, Reinwardtia, Rhododendron, Ricinus, Rumex, Scoparia, Scrophularia, Senecio, Shorea, Sida, Solanum, Sonchus,*

[**Boils**]
Sorbus, Symplocos, Tagetes, Tamarindus, Thalictrum, Thunbergia, Thysanolaena, Toona, Trichodesma, Tridax, Triumfetta, Uraria, Urtica, Valeriana, Vanda, Vernonia, Vincetoxicum, Viola, Viscum, Woodfordia

Carbuncle. *Impatiens, Osmanthus, Plantago, Spermadictyon, Tagetes*

Catarrh. *Aegle, Basella, Myrica, Sesbania*

Chilblain. *Premna*

Demulcents. *Abutilon, Argemone, Artocarpus, Asparagus, Cardiospermum, Dactylorhiza, Mahonia, Ocimum, Phyla, Xanthium*

Diaphoretics. *Abrus, Aconitum, Arctium, Cardiospermum, Cedrus, Fumaria, Lantana, Leonurus, Ocimum, Xanthium, Zingiber*

Eczema. *Amaranthus, Cassia, Centella, Dalbergia, Eleutherococcus, Girardinia, Jatropha, Kalanchoe, Lantana, Orobanche, Prinsepia, Rumex, Swertia, Symplocos*

Emollients. *Amaranthus, Leucaena, Luisia, Sesbania*

Hemorrhoid. *Abutilon, Acacia, Achyranthes, Agrimonia, Albizia, Aloe, Amorphophallus, Azadirachta, Bergenia, Cardiospermum, Cedrus, Curculigo, Ficus, Ipomoea, Mimosa, Nardostachys, Oxalis, Pleurospermum, Plumbago, Punica, Ricinus, Semecarpus, Sesamum, Solanum, Terminalia, Thalictrum, Vernonia*

Herpes. *Lygodium, Nerium*

Jaundice. *Aloe, Argemone, Averrhoa, Berberis, Betula, Boerhavia, Centella, Curculigo, Cuscuta, Hygrophila, Imperata, Lantana, Mangifera, Mussaenda, Oroxylum, Phyllanthus, Ricinus, Urtica*

Leprosy. *Abutilon, Aconitum, Ageratum, Alstonia, Azadirachta, Calotropis, Cassia, Celastrus, Centella*

Leukoderma. *Abrus, Cassia, Zanthoxylum*

Pimple. *Acer, Ajuga, Amaranthus, Ammannia, Artocarpus, Asparagus, Barleria, Calotropis, Centella, Ceropegia, Clerodendrum, Cochlianthus, Dalbergia, Dendrobium, Diplokenma, Eclipta, Euphorbia, Evolvulus, Fritillaria, Glochidion, Heliotropium, Hyptis, Ichnocarpus, Jatropha, Leersia, Macaranga, Maesa, Melochia, Ophiorrhiza, Oxalis, Pedicularis, Phyllanthus, Rhododendron, Sida, Solanum, Swertia, Thalictrum, Triumfetta, Valeriana, Vincetoxicum*

Rubefacients. *Basella, Capsicum, Cardiospermum, Prinsepia, Zingiber*

Sinusitis. *Anemone, Calotropis, Cleistocalyx, Clematis, Colebrookea, Dichrocephala, Lysimachia, Micromeria, Rheum, Vitex*

Skin. *Abrus, Acacia, Achyranthes, Aconitum, Acorus, Aesculus, Ageratum, Aloe, Alstonia, Areca, Argemone, Artemisia, Azadirachta, Buddleja, Caesalpinia, Callicarpa, Calotropis, Carica, Cassia, Cedrus, Centella, Centipeda, Cheilanthes, Cissampelos, Clerodendrum, Costus, Desmodium, Eclipta, Entada, Ephedra,*

Erythrina, Euphorbia, Excoecaria, Ficus, Garuga, Geniosporum, Gloriosa, Gynocardia, Hedera, Houttuynia, Juniperus, Lawsonia, Lindenbergia, Madhuca, Mallotus, Mangifera, Melia, Michelia, Millettia, Mimosa, Momordica, Nerium, Nicotiana, Ocimum, Pedicularis, Plantago, Pleurospermum, Plumbago, Polypodium, Rhus, Ricinus, Schleichera, Semecarpus, Sesbania, Shorea, Streblus, Swertia, Symplocos, Tagetes, Trigonella, Urena, Verbascum, Vernonia, Viburnum, Xanthium

Sore. *Adina, Carpesium, Combretum, Cuscuta, Cynoglossum, Datura, Dicentra, Elsholtzia, Euphorbia, Ipomoea, Jasminum, Jatropha, Lawsonia, Leonurus, Ludwigia, Mesua, Millettia, Polygonum, Salvia, Scutellaria, Siegesbeckia, Solanum, Spermadictyon, Tamarindus, Teucrium*

Vesicant. *Rhus*

Wart. *Asclepias, Crotalaria, Ficus, Mangifera*

Whitlow. *Equisetum, Lygodium*

Spleen. *Eclipta, Syzygium, Terminalia*

Stimulants. *Acorus, Albizia, Artemisia, Averrhoa, Capsicum, Cleome, Costus, Cuminum, Cyperus, Daucus, Fleusine, Ephedra, Gaultheria, Lantana, Melia, Mesua, Moringa, Murraya, Myrica, Nicotiana, Ocimum, Panax, Podophyllum, Semecarpus, Solanum, Valeriana, Viburnum, Zingiber*

Swelling. *Abrus, Acacia, Acer, Adiantum, Aegle, Ajuga, Alnus, Ampelocissus, Artocarpus, Astilbe, Azadirachta, Basella, Boehmeria, Caesalpinia, Calotropis, Canna, Cardiospermum, Carum, Centella, Centipeda, Cinnamomum, Cipadessa, Cissampelos, Cleistocalyx, Clematis, Clitoria, Cochlianthus, Curcuma, Cuscuta, Datura, Euphorbia, Exbucklandia, Ficus, Flemingia, Gerbera, Gmelina, Gonostegia, Helicia, Hygrophila, Jatropha, Lobelia, Macaranga, Megacodon, Mimosa, Mirabilis, Moringa, Nicotiana, Ostodes, Oxalis, Persicaria, Phyllanthus, Pithecellobium, Plumeria, Polygala, Populus, Psidium, Pteris, Reissantia, Remusatia, Rhus, Ricinus, Rumex, Sapium, Scindapsus, Sesbania, Shorea, Solanum, Stellaria, Stephania, Symplocos, Taxillus, Terminalia, Tiarella, Trichodesma, Verbascum, Viscum, Vitex, Vittaria, Woodfordia, Xanthium, Ziziphus*

Tonics (see also hair tonics, listed under washing clothes or bathing, under Other Uses). *Aconitum, Acorus, Agrimonia, Alstonia, Anisomeles, Artemisia, Asparagus, Bambusa, Bauhinia, Berberis, Bombax, Brachycorythis, Caesulia, Callicarpa, Capparis, Cardiospermum, Carum, Cassia, Centella, Chenopodium, Cissampelos, Citrus, Crateva, Dendrocalamus, Desmodium, Dillenia, Eclipta, Euphorbia, Evolvulus, Ficus, Gloriosa, Imperata, Juglans, Lilium, Madhuca, Phyllanthus, Physalis, Picrasma, Polygonatum, Pyrrosia, Rheum, Rubia, Sida, Siegesbeckia, Solanum, Sphaeranthus, Swertia, Swertia, Tamarindus, Taraxacum, Terminalia, Tinospora, Valeriana, Xanthium*

Tonsillitis. *Curcuma, Sauropus, Urena*

Tranquilizer. *Albizia*

Tumor Medicines

Cancer. *Semecarpus, Taxus, Xanthium*

Tumor. *Datura*

Tympanitis. *Oxalis*

Urinary System Medicines

Bedwetting. *Bischofia, Crotalaria, Elephantopus, Ephedra, Triumfetta*

Diuretics. *Achyranthes, Aconitum, Agave, Agrimonia, Amaranthus, Arctium, Artemisia, Arundo, Asparagus, Bombax, Capsella, Cassia, Cedrus, Centella, Cissampelos, Clitoria, Costus, Desmodium, Desmostachya, Duranta, Fumaria, Hygrophila, Imperata, Lycopodium, Mahonia, Mangifera, Manilkara, Mirabilis, Mussaenda, Origanum, Phyllanthus, Physalis, Pimpinella, Prunus, Rorippa, Sesbania, Solanum, Tagetes, Taraxacum, Terminalia, Thalictrum, Urena, Valeriana, Xanthium, Zingiber*

Dysuria. *Alternanthera, Kalanchoe, Launaea, Potentilla, Sonchus*

Hematuria. *Agrimonia, Cassia, Didymocarpus, Nephrolepis*

Other Urinary Problems. *Aloe, Alternanthera, Amaranthus, Areca, Asparagus, Azadirachta, Bergenia, Boerhavia, Bombax, Centella, Chenopodium, Cirsium, Cissampelos, Coix, Costus, Crateva, Cucumis, Daucus, Didymocarpus, Eclipta, Equisetum, Galium, Geranium, Hygrophila, Leucas, Lonicera, Mimosa, Ocimum, Phyllanthus, Pouzolzia, Psidium, Saraca, Sesamum, Solanum, Stephania, Tinospora, Woodfordia*

Venereal Disease Medicines

Gonorrhea. *Aloe, Amaranthus, Asparagus, Bombax, Cardiospermum, Carum, Cissampelos, Curculigo, Dalbergia, Datura, Equisetum, Ficus, Millettia, Ocimum, Plumeria, Schima, Shorea, Sida, Solanum, Thespesia*

Syphilis. *Cassia, Ehretia, Jacaranda, Rhododendron, Thespesia*

Other Venereal Problems. *Alternanthera, Cassia, Hibiscus, Plumeria, Sida*

Veterinary Medicines. *Aconitum, Adina, Aesculus, Alstonia, Anemone, Arisaema, Artemisia, Asparagus, Astragalus, Azadirachta, Bambusa, Boehmeria, Boenninghausenia, Bupleurum, Carissa, Centella, Clausena, Cleistocalyx, Clematis, Clerodendrum, Colebrookea, Coriaria, Crinum, Crotalaria, Datura, Delphinium, Dendrobium, Dicentra, Didymocarpus, Diplokenma, Entada, Fraxinus, Gonostegia, Hypericum, Impatiens, Kalanchoe, Lantana, Lecanthus, Lindera, Luculia, Maesa, Millettia, Oxalis, Paris, Pogostemon, Polygonatum, Prunus, Ranunculus, Rhododendron, Ricinus, Rumex, Salix, Sapium, Schima, Solena, Stellaria, Stephania, Strobilanthes, Tinospora, Urtica, Vitex, Xanthium*

OTHER USES

Plants can be put to many kinds of uses other than food or medicine. Here, plants are grouped according to some of these uses.

Dyes. *Acacia, Alnus, Artocarpus, Bauhinia, Begonia, Berberis, Bischofia, Bixa, Butea, Catunaregam, Eclipta, Ficus, Hibiscus, Impatiens, Juglans, Lagerstroemia, Lawsonia, Leucaena, Mahonia, Mallotus, Melastoma, Michelia, Myrica, Nyctanthes, Oxalis, Prinsepia, Punica, Rheum, Rubia, Selaginella, Semecarpus, Symplocos, Syzygium, Terminalia, Viburnum, Wendlandia, Woodfordia, Wrightia*

Fibers (see also paper). *Abelmoschus, Abroma, Abrus, Abutilon, Agave, Bauhinia, Bixa, Boehmeria, Butea, Calamus, Calotropis, Cannabis, Careya, Chonemorpha, Cissampelos, Cocos, Corchorus, Cordia, Coriaria, Cotoneaster, Crotalaria, Cryptolepis, Daphne, Debregeasia, Dendrocalamus, Desmostachya, Dillenia, Engelhardia, Eragrostis, Eulaliopsis, Ficus, Garuga, Girardinia, Gossypium, Grewia, Helicteres, Hibiscus, Ichnocarpus, Imperata, Kydia, Linum, Luffa, Maoutia, Marsdenia, Millettia, Musa, Oreocnide, Pandanus, Phoenix, Polyalthia, Porana, Premna, Salix, Schoenoplectus, Sesbania, Sida, Sinarundinaria, Smilax, Spatholobus, Stellera, Sterculia, Streblus, Tetrastigma, Thespesia, Thunbergia, Trachelospermum, Trema, Triumfetta, Uraria, Urena, Urtica, Vitex, Wikstroemia, Yucca*

Fish Poisons. *Acacia, Agave, Albizia, Anagallis, Anemone, Annona, Buddleja, Careya, Casearia, Catunaregam, Croton, Cyathula, Dalbergia, Daphne, Desmodium, Dioscorea, Diplokenma, Duabanga, Edgeworthia, Engelhardia, Entada, Euodia, Euphorbia, Gynocardia, Hedyotis, Hydrocotyle, Juglans, Madhuca, Maesa, Millettia, Myrica, Persicaria, Piptanthus, Plumeria, Sapium, Schima, Securinega, Solanum, Spilanthes, Ulmus, Verbascum, Yucca, Zanthoxylum*

Fodder or Other Animal Food. *Acacia, Acer, Aechmanthera, Aegle, Aesculus, Albizia, Alnus, Alstonia, Andropogon, Antidesma, Apluda, Arachis, Argyreia, Arisaema, Artemisia, Artocarpus, Arundinella, Avena, Bambusa, Bauhinia, Berberis, Betula, Boehmeria, Brachiaria, Brassaiopsis, Brassica, Bridelia, Bromus, Buddleja, Bulbostylis, Cajanus, Callicarpa, Capillipedium, Caragana, Cardamine, Carex, Caryopteris, Cassia, Castanopsis, Catunaregam, Celastrus, Celtis, Chenopodium, Chirita, Chrysopogon, Cicer, Cissus, Clematis, Coix, Colebrookea, Colquhounia, Combretum, Cornus, Crateva, Crotalaria, Cryptolepis, Cuphea, Cymbopogon, Cynodon, Dalbergia, Daucus, Debregeasia, Dendrocalamus, Desmodium, Deutzia, Dichanthium, Diplokenma, Dipsacus, Dodecadenia, Drepanostachyum, Duabanga, Echinochloa, Elaeocarpus, Elatostema, Eleusine, Eleutherococcus, Embelia, Ephedra, Equisetum, Eragrostiella, Eragrostis, Eriophorum, Euonymus, Eurya, Ficus, Fimbristylis, Flacourtia, Flemingia, Fumaria, Galium, Gaultheria, Geranium, Glochidion, Grewia, Hedera, Hedyotis, Helicteres, Heteropogon, Himalayacalamus, Holmskioldia, Hydrangea, Hymenodictyon, Hypericum, Ilex, Impatiens, Imperata, Indigofera, Ischaemum, Juglans, Kydia, Lablab, Lagerstroemia, Lannea, Lathyrus, Lecanthus, Lens, Leptodermis, Leucaena, Leucosceptrum, Ligustrum, Lindera, Lithocarpus, Litsea, Lotus, Macaranga, Macropanax, Maesa, Mallotus,*

[Fodder or Other Animal Food]
Maoutia, Medicago, Melia, Melilotus, Meliosma, Michelia, Micromeria, Microstegium, Millettia, Mitragyna, Morus, Mucuna, Myrsine, Neyraudia, Oenothera, Oplismenus, Oxyspora, Parochetus, Parthenocissus, Paspalum, Pennisetum, Periploca, Peristrophe, Persea, Persicaria, Phalaris, Phaseolus, Phlogacanthus, Photinia, Phragmites, Pilea, Piptanthus, Pisum, Poa, Pogonatherum, Polyalthia, Polypogon, Populus, Premna, Primula, Prinsepia, Prunus, Pteracanthus, Pteris, Pycreus, Pyrus, Quercus, Randia, Rhamnus, Rhus, Rosa, Rubus, Saccharum, Sacciolepis, Sarcococca, Saurauia, Schefflera, Schleichera, Schoenoplectus, Scleria, Sesbania, Setaria, Shorea, Sinarundinaria, Solena, Sonchus, Sorbus, Spatholobus, Spergula, Spermadictyon, Spiraea, Sporobolus, Stachyurus, Stranvaesia, Streblus, Strobilanthes, Terminalia, Tetrastigma, Thamnocalamus, Toona, Trema, Trevesia, Trewia, Urtica, Vicia, Vigna, Wendlandia, Woodwardia, Xylosma, Ziziphus

Fuel or Charcoal. *Abies, Acacia, Acer, Albizia, Alnus, Callicarpa, Callistemon, Calotropis, Caragana, Cassia, Castanopsis, Cedrus, Colebrookea, Cotoneaster, Crateva, Dalbergia, Debregeasia, Delonix, Dichroa, Diplokenma, Ephedra, Eurya, Ficus, Grevillea, Hippophae, Juniperus, Larix, Lyonia, Macaranga, Madhuca, Maesa, Manglietia, Melia, Michelia, Mimosa, Myrica, Prunus, Pyrus, Quercus, Randia, Rhamnus, Rhododendron, Rhus, Ricinus, Schima, Shorea, Sophora, Syzygium, Talauma, Terminalia, Trema, Trichilia, Woodfordia, Ziziphus*

Gums or Resins. *Acacia, Aegle, Anogeissus, Areca, Ficus, Mucuna, Oxalis, Pinus*

Insecticides or Miticides. *Acorus, Ageratum, Anaphalis, Anemone, Annona, Arisaema, Artemisia, Azadirachta, Boenninghausenia, Clausena, Clerodendrum, Croton, Delphinium, Dendranthema, Hyptis, Ipomoea, Justicia, Maesa, Melia, Millettia, Nerium, Nicotiana, Phyllanthus, Sphaeranthus, Urtica, Vitex, Zanthoxylum*

Incense. *Abies, Artemisia, Betula, Colquhounia, Cotoneaster, Cryptomeria, Cupressus, Dendranthema, Didymocarpus, Elsholtzia, Gossypium, Juniperus, Jurinea, Leptodermis, Micromeria, Morina, Nardostachys, Origanum, Potentilla, Rhododendron, Selinum, Thymus, Tsuga, Valeriana*

Oil (other than food). *Abies, Acorus, Aesculus, Amomum, Anisomeles, Annona, Argemone, Artemisia, Azadirachta, Boenninghausenia, Brassica, Buchanania, Cedrus, Celastrus, Chenopodium, Cinnamomum, Croton, Cuminum, Dendranthema, Diplokenma, Elsholtzia, Eupatorium, Foeniculum, Gaultheria, Glycine, Guizotia, Helianthus, Hyptis, Jatropha, Juglans, Juniperus, Lindera, Linum, Madhuca, Mallotus, Mesua, Millettia, Neolitsea, Origanum, Perilla, Prinsepia, Prunus, Rhododendron, Ricinus, Schleichera, Semecarpus, Sesamum, Shorea, Skimmia, Sterculia, Thymus, Trachyspermum, Trichilia, Valeriana, Vetiveria, Viburnum, Xanthium, Zanthoxylum*

Paper. *Daphne, Edgeworthia, Eulaliopsis, Sterculia, Trewia, Triticum, Wikstroemia*

Perfume. *Cinnamomum, Cuminum, Vetiveria*

Religious or Ritualistic Uses. *Achyranthes, Aegle, Aeschynomene, Anaphalis, Aster, Buddleja, Callistemon, Cannabis, Carex, Colebrookea, Cynodon, Desmostachya, Deutzia, Elaeocarpus, Ficus, Gomphrena, Gossypium, Grevillea, Hibiscus, Hypericum, Imperata, Jasminum, Luculia, Magnolia, Michelia, Neyraudia, Nyctanthes, Ocimum, Origanum, Oroxylum, Saraca, Saussurea, Sesbania, Tagetes, Vernonia, Zingiber*

Smoking or Snuff. *Adina, Bauhinia, Calotropis, Castanopsis, Cleistocalyx, Datura, Euphorbia, Evolvulus, Leucas, Nicotiana, Rheum, Rhododendron, Rhus, Salvia, Sauropus, Scopolia, Solanum, Verbascum, Vitex, Woodfordia*

Tannin or Tanning. *Acacia, Alnus, Anogeissus, Artocarpus, Bauhinia, Belamcanda, Bergenia, Bridelia, Buchanania, Caesalpinia, Capsicum, Careya, Cassia, Coriaria, Costus, Crateva, Dillenia, Engelhardia, Ficus, Garuga, Geranium, Glochidion, Hymenodictyon, Juglans, Lagerstroemia, Lannea, Lantana, Madhuca, Mallotus, Mangifera, Manilkara, Moringa, Myrica, Neohymenopogon, Ocimum, Phyllanthus, Pithecellobium, Prunus, Psidium, Punica, Quercus, Quisqualis, Ricinus, Rumex, Semecarpus, Sesbania, Shorea, Solanum, Syzygium, Tamarindus, Terminalia, Toona, Uraria, Urena, Woodfordia, Ziziphus*

Thatch. *Abies, Apluda, Arundinella, Arundo, Bauhinia, Cajanus, Cymbopogon, Desmostachya, Eulaliopsis, Helicteres, Heteropogon, Imperata, Pandanus, Phoenix, Pteris, Saccharum, Sinarundinaria, Sporobolus*

Timber or Other Construction. *Abies, Acacia, Acer, Actinodaphne, Adina, Albizia, Alnus, Anogeissus, Artocarpus, Arundo, Averrhoa, Bambusa, Bauhinia, Betula, Bischofia, Buchanania, Calamus, Careya, Castanopsis, Cedrus, Celtis, Cordia, Cryptomeria, Cupressus, Dalbergia, Dendrocalamus, Dillenia, Diplokenma, Drepanostachyum, Ficus, Flacourtia, Garuga, Himalayacalamus, Homalium, Juglans, Lagerstroemia, Larix, Madhuca, Magnolia, Mangifera, Marsdenia, Melia, Michelia, Morus, Myrica, Myrsine, Neolamarckia, Pandanus, Picea, Pinus, Piptanthus, Podocarpus, Polyalthia, Prunus, Quercus, Rhododendron, Schima, Schleichera, Shorea, Sinarundinaria, Skimmia, Stereospermum, Syzygium, Talauma, Terminalia, Thamnocalamus, Toona, Tsuga, Wendlandia, Ziziphus*

Walking Sticks. *Bauhinia, Cotoneaster, Dendrocalamus, Flacourtia, Himalayacalamus, Lonicera, Piptanthus, Prunus, Pyracantha, Pyrus, Randia, Sinarundinaria, Thamnocalamus, Viburnum*

Washing Clothes or Bathing (including hair tonics). *Acacia, Achyranthes, Albizia, Anagallis, Asparagus, Boenninghausenia, Catunaregam, Cicer, Cyathula, Dendrobium, Dioscorea, Ephedra, Euphorbia, Gonostegia, Hydrocotyle, Inula, Juniperus, Luffa, Maharanga, Melia, Persicaria, Phyllanthus, Pogostemon, Potentilla, Prinsepia, Solanum, Tetrastigma, Thymus*

Plants According to Ethnic Community

For each ethnic community or language included in *Plants and People of Nepal*, those genera that have at least one species that has been given a common name are listed. The application of common names serves as a guide to plant use by the ethnic communities. The particular species named and used by each ethnic community may be found in Chapter 4, where the plants are listed alphabetically.

Bhojpuri. *Allium, Arundo, Azadirachta, Bauhinia, Benincasa, Brassica, Buddleja, Camellia, Cannabis, Capsicum, Carica, Castanopsis, Centella, Choerospondias, Cinnamomum, Citrus, Cocos, Colocasia, Coriandrum, Cucurbita, Cuminum, Curcuma, Cynodon, Datura, Diplokenma, Eleusine, Euphorbia, Fagopyrum, Ficus, Glycine, Jasminum, Juglans, Justicia, Lagenaria, Lawsonia, Lens, Lepidium, Linum, Luffa, Lycopersicon, Madhuca, Melia, Mentha, Mmordica, Musa, Myrica, Nelumbo, Ocimum, Oroxylum, Oryza, Oxalis, Phaseolus, Pisum, Prunus, Psidium, Punica, Pyrus, Raphanus, Rhus, Saccharum, Sapindus, Shorea, Solanum, Syzygium, Terminalia, Trachyspermum, Trichosanthes, Trigonella, Triticum, Urtica, Zanthoxylum, Zea*

Chepang. *Abelmoschus, Abrus, Acacia, Achyranthes, Acorus, Adiantum, Adina, Aechmanthera, Aegle, Ageratum, Agrimonia, Albizia, Allium, Alnus, Alstonia, Alternanthera, Amaranthus, Ampelocissus, Anemone, Apluda, Arachis, Arisaema, Artemisia, Artocarpus, Arundinella, Arundo, Asparagus, Aster, Avena, Azadirachta, Bauhinia, Benincasa, Bidens, Boehmeria, Boenninghausenia, Boerhavia, Bombax, Brassica, Bridelia, Buddleja, Butea, Cajanus, Callicarpa, Calotropis, Cannabis, Capillipedium, Capsicum, Cardiospermum, Careya, Cassia, Castanopsis, Catunaregam, Celosia, Celtis, Centella, Choerospondias, Chrysopogon, Cipadessa, Cissampelos, Citrus, Clausena, Clematis, Cleome, Clerodendrum, Cocos, Coelogyne, Colebrookea, Colocasia, Colquhounia, Combretum, Corchorus, Coriaria, Cornus, Crassocephalum, Crotalaria, Cucurbita, Cuminum, Curculigo, Curcuma, Cuscuta, Cynodon, Cynoglossum,* *Cyperus, Dalbergia, Debregeasia, Desmodium, Dichroa, Dillenia, Dioscorea, Diplocyclos, Diplokenma, Dipsacus, Disporum, Drepanostachyum, Drymaria, Dryopteris, Duabanga, Eclipta, Elatostema, Elephantopus, Eleusine, Emilia, Engelhardia, Epipactis, Equisetum, Erythrina, Eulaliopsis, Eupatorium, Euphorbia, Eurya, Fagopyrum, Ficus, Flacourtia, Flemingia, Galinsoga, Galium, Geniosporum, Geranium, Girardinia, Glochidion, Glycine, Gonostegia, Gossypium, Grewia, Guizotia, Hedychium, Hedyotis, Hibiscus, Holarrhena, Holmskioldia, Hydrocotyle, Hyptis, Imperata, Indigofera, Inula, Ipomoea, Isodon, Jasminum, Jatropha, Juglans, Justicia, Lablab, Lagenaria, Lagerstroemia, Launaea, Leea, Lens, Leucas, Leucosceptrum, Lilium, Lindenbergia, Linum, Litsea, Luculia, Luffa, Luisia, Lycopersicon, Lyonia, Macaranga, Madhuca, Maesa, Mahonia, Mallotus, Mangifera, Maoutia, Marsdenia, Maytenus, Melastoma, Melia, Mentha, Millettia, Mimosa, Moringa, Morus, Musa, Mussaenda, Myrica, Natsiatum, Neyraudia, Nicotiana, Nyctanthes, Oreocnide, Oroxylum, Oryza, Osbeckia, Osyris, Oxalis, Oxyspora, Pennisetum, Peperomia, Perilla, Peristrophe, Persea, Phlogacanthus, Phoenix, Phyla, Phyllanthus, Physalis, Pilea, Pinus, Piper, Pisum, Plumbago, Plumeria, Pogostemon, Polygala, Portulaca, Potentilla, Prunus, Psidium, Pteris, Pyrus, Quercus, Raphanus, Rauvolfia, Reinwardtia, Reissantia, Rhamnus, Rhododendron, Rhus, Ricinus, Rubia, Rubus, Rungia, Salvia, Sanicula, Sapindus, Sapium, Satyrium, Saurauia, Schima, Scindapsus, Scoparia, Scurrula, Scutellaria, Securinega, Semecarpus, Sesamum, Setaria, Shorea, Sida, Siegesbeckia, Smilax, Solanum, Solena, Spermadictyon, Spilanthes, Sporobolus, Stephania, Sterculia, Syzygium, Tectaria, Terminalia, Tetrastigma, Teucrium, Thalictrum, Thunbergia, Thysanolaena, Trachyspermum, Trema, Tridax, Trigonella, Triticum, Triumfetta, Urtica, Vernonia, Viburnum, Vitex, Wendlandia, Woodfordia, Xanthium, Zanthoxylum, Zea, Zingiber, Ziziphus*

Danuwar. *Abrus, Acacia, Achyranthes, Acorus, Adina, Aegle, Ageratum, Allium, Aloe, Alstonia, Alternanthera, Amaranthus, Ananas, Annona, Anogeissus, Arachis, Areca, Argemone, Artemisia, Arto-*

carpus, Artocarpus, Arundo, Asparagus, Avena, Azadirachta, Bauhinia, Benincasa, Blumea, Blumeopsis, Boerhavia, Bombax, Borreria, Brassica, Bridelia, Buchanania, Buddleja, Butea, Caesulia, Cajanus, Calotropis, Camellia, Cannabis, Capsicum, Careya, Carica, Carissa, Cassia, Castanopsis, Catunaregam, Centella, Chenopodium, Chlorophytum, Choerospondias, Chrysopogon, Cinnamomum, Cirsium, Citrus, Clausena, Cleistocalyx, Clerodendrum, Coccinia, Cocos, Coix, Colebrookea, Colocasia, Colocasia, Conyza, Coriandrum, Croton, Cryptolepis, Cucurbita, Cuminum, Curcuma, Cynodon, Cynoglossum, Cyperus, Dalbergia, Datura, Desmodium, Desmostachya, Dillenia, Dioscorea, Diplokenma, Eclipta, Eichhornia, Elaeagnus, Elephantopus, Eleusine, Equisetum, Eupatorium, Euphorbia, Fagopyrum, Ficus, Foeniculum, Glycine, Holarrhena, Hydrilla, Hydrolea, Hygrophila, Hyptis, Imperata, Ipomoea, Jasminum, Jatropha, Juglans, Justicia, Lagerstroemia, Lannea, Lawsonia, Lecanthus, Lens, Lepidium, Leucas, Linum, Luffa, Lycopersicon, Madhuca, Maesa, Mallotus, Mangifera, Melastoma, Melia, Mimosa, Momordica, Monochoria, Moringa, Mukia, Murraya, Musa, Myrica, Nelumbo, Nyctanthes, Ocimum, Oroxylum, Oryza, Oxalis, Perilla, Persicaria, Phaseolus, Phyla, Phyllanthus, Pisum, Pogostemon, Polygonum, Pouzolzia, Prunus, Psidium, Punica, Pyrus, Raphanus, Rhododendron, Rhus, Ricinus, Rubus, Saccharum, Sapindus, Scoparia, Shorea, Sida, Smithia, Solanum, Sphaeranthus, Spilanthes, Streblus, Swertia, Syzygium, Tamarindus, Terminalia, Thunbergia, Trachyspermum, Trewia, Trichosanthes, Tridax, Trigonella, Triticum, Urena, Urtica, Woodfordia, Xanthium, Zanthoxylum, Zea, Ziziphus

Gurung. Abrus, Acacia, Achyranthes, Aconitum, Acorus, Ageratum, Allium, Alnus, Aloe, Amaranthus, Anaphalis, Anemone, Areca, Arisaema, Artemisia, Artocarpus, Arundo, Asclepias, Asparagus, Avena, Azadirachta, Bauhinia, Begonia, Benincasa, Berberis, Bergenia, Betula, Bidens, Boehmeria, Boenninghausenia, Bombax, Brassaiopsis, Brassica, Buddleja, Butea, Callicarpa, Camellia, Campanula, Cannabis, Capillipedium, Capsicum, Cardiocrinum, Carica, Castanopsis, Catunaregam, Cautleya, Centella, Centipeda, Cheilanthes, Chenopodium, Chlorophytum, Choerospondias, Chonemorpha, Chrysopogon, Cicer, Cinnamomum, Cipadessa, Cissampelos, Citrus, Cleistocalyx, Clematis, Clerodendrum, Coelogyne, Colebrookea, Colocasia, Combretum, Coriandrum, Coriaria, Corydalis, Costus, Cotoneaster, Cucumis, Cucurbita, Cuminum, Curcuma, Cuscuta, Cyathula, Cynodon, Cynoglossum, Cyperus, Dactylorhiza, Dalbergia, Daphne, Daphniphyllum, Datura, Debregeasia, Dendranthema, Desmodium, Dicentra, Dichroa, Dichrocephala, Didymocarpus, Dioscorea, Diplazium, Drepanostachyum, Drymaria, Eclipta, Elaeagnus, Elatostema, Elephantopus, Eleusine, Elsholtzia, Engelhardia, Entada, Equisetum, Eragrostis, Eupatorium, Euphorbia, Eurya, Fagopyrum, Ficus, Flacourtia, Fragaria, Fraxinus, Galinsoga, Galium, Gentiana, Girardinia, Glochidion, Glycine, Gonostegia, Grewia, Hedychium, Hedyotis, Helixanthera, Hippophae, Hydrocotyle, Hypericum, Ilex, Impatiens, Imperata, Inula, Jatropha, Juglans, Justicia, Lawsonia, Lecanthus, Leucosceptrum, Ligustrum, Lindenbergia, Lindera, Litsea, Lobelia, Luculia, Luffa, Lycopersicon, Lycopodium, Lyonia, Macaranga, Madhuca, Maesa, Mahonia, Mallotus, Malva, Mangifera, Maoutia, Melastoma, Melia, Melissa, Mentha, Micromeria, Millettia, Mimosa, Mirabilis, Musa, Mussaenda, Myrica, Nar-

dostachys, Neillia, Nelumbo, Neolitsea, Nephrolepis, Nicotiana, Ocimum, Ophiorrhiza, Oreocnide, Oroxylum, Oryza, Osbeckia, Osyris, Oxalis, Oxyria, Paris, Parthenocissus, Periploca, Persicaria, Phaseolus, Phyllanthus, Picrorhiza, Pieris, Pimpinella, Pinus, Pisum, Plantago, Plumbago, Plumeria, Pogonatherum, Pogostemon, Polygonatum, Portulaca, Potentilla, Pouzolzia, Prunus, Psidium, Punica, Pyracantha, Pyrus, Quercus, Randia, Ranunculus, Raphanus, Reinwardtia, Remusatia, Rheum, Rhododendron, Rhus, Rhynchostylis, Ricinus, Rubus, Rumex, Saccharum, Salix, Sarcococca, Saurauia, Schima, Scutellaria, Selaginella, Semecarpus, Shorea, Sida, Siegesbeckia, Smilax, Solanum, Solena, Spilanthes, Swertia, Symplocos, Syzygium, Taraxacum, Taxus, Tectaria, Terminalia, Thalictrum, Thunbergia, Thymus, Thysanolaena, Toona, Trevesia, Trichilia, Trigonella, Triticum, Triumfetta, Urena, Urtica, Valeriana, Vanda, Vernonia, Viburnum, Vigna, Viola, Viscum, Vitex, Vitis, Woodfordia, Xanthium, Zanthoxylum, Zea, Zingiber, Ziziphus

Khaling. Bombax, Holarrhena, Myrica, Nardostachys, Phyllanthus, Rubia

Lepcha. Abrus, Acacia, Acorus, Aegle, Agapetes, Allium, Aloe, Amaranthus, Arachis, Areca, Artocarpus, Arundo, Asparagus, Avena, Bauhinia, Benincasa, Brassica, Buddleja, Butea, Camellia, Cannabis, Capsicum, Carica, Castanopsis, Catharanthus, Centella, Choerospondias, Cinnamomum, Citrus, Cocos, Coelogyne, Colocasia, Coriandrum, Cucurbita, Cuminum, Cynodon, Datura, Dendrocalamus, Desmostachya, Dichroa, Dillenia, Dioscorea, Diplokenma, Eleusine, Euphorbia, Fagopyrum, Ficus, Foeniculum, Glycine, Jasminum, Juglans, Lagenaria, Leea, Lens, Lepidium, Linum, Luffa, Lycopersicon, Madhuca, Mallotus, Melia, Mentha, Momordica, Musa, Myrica, Nelumbo, Neolamarckia, Ocimum, Oroxylum, Oryza, Oxalis, Phaseolus, Pisum, Prunus, Psidium, Punica, Pyrus, Quercus, Raphanus, Rhododendron, Rhus, Rubus, Saccharum, Shorea, Solanum, Syzygium, Terminalia, Trachyspermum, Trichosanthes, Trigonella, Triticum, Urtica, Zanthoxylum, Zea

Limbu. Acacia, Acorus, Aegle, Allium, Alnus, Aloe, Amaranthus, Arachis, Areca, Artocarpus, Arundo, Avena, Azadirachta, Bauhinia, Benincasa, Bombax, Brassica, Buddleja, Camellia, Cannabis, Capsicum, Carica, Castanopsis, Celtis, Centella, Choerospondias, Cinnamomum, Citrus, Cleistocalyx, Cocos, Colocasia, Cucurbita, Cuminum, Curcuma, Cynodon, Dalbergia, Datura, Desmostachya, Dioscorea, Diplokenma, Eleusine, Elsholtzia, Engelhardia, Erythrina, Euphorbia, Fagopyrum, Ficus, Foeniculum, Fraxinus, Glycine, Imperata, Jasminum, Juglans, Lagenaria, Lawsonia, Lens, Lepidium, Linum, Luffa, Lycopersicon, Madhuca, Maesa, Mangifera, Melia, Mentha, Michelia, Momordica, Musa, Myrica, Nelumbo, Ocimum, Oroxylum, Oryza, Oxalis, Phaseolus, Phyllanthus, Pinus, Pisum, Prunus, Psidium, Punica, Pyrus, Raphanus, Rhododendron, Rhus, Rubia, Rubus, Saccharum, Schima, Shorea, Solanum, Swertia, Syzygium, Terminalia, Thysanolaena, Trachyspermum, Trichosanthes, Trigonella, Triticum, Urtica, Zanthoxylum, Zea

Magar. Abrus, Acacia, Acer, Achyranthes, Acorus, Agave, Ageratum, Albizia, Allium, Aloe, Amaranthus, Ampelocissus, Anemone, Arachis, Areca, Arisaema, Artemisia, Artocarpus, Asclepias, Avena,

Azadirachta, Bauhinia, Begonia, Benincasa, Berberis, Boehmeria, Boerhavia, Bombax, Brassica, Bridelia, Buddleja, Bupleurum, Butea, Callicarpa, Camellia, Cannabis, Capsella, Capsicum, Carica, Cassia, Castanopsis, Catunaregam, Celtis, Centella, Centipeda, Chenopodium, Cinnamomum, Cipadessa, Citrus, Cleistocalyx, Clematis, Clerodendrum, Cocos, Colebrookea, Colocasia, Colocasia, Combretum, Coriandrum, Coriaria, Crotalaria, Cucumis, Cucurbita, Cuminum, Curcuma, Cynodon, Dalbergia, Daphne, Datura, Debregeasia, Delphinium, Desmodium, Dichroa, Dioscorea, Diplokenma, Drepanostachyum, Eleusine, Elsholtzia, Emilia, Engelhardia, Eupatorium, Euphorbia, Fagopyrum, Ficus, Girardinia, Glycine, Gossypium, Grevillea, Grewia, Guizotia, Hedychium, Helixanthera, Holarrhena, Holboellia, Homalium, Hypericum, Hyptis, Jatropha, Juglans, Lagenaria, Lagerstroemia, Lawsonia, Lens, Lepidium, Linum, Luffa, Lycopersicon, Lyonia, Maclura, Maesa, Mallotus, Mangifera, Melia, Mentha, Mimosa, Momordica, Morus, Musa, Myrica, Nelumbo, Nephrolepis, Nicotiana, Oreocnide, Oroxylum, Oryza, Osyris, Oxalis, Persicaria, Phaseolus, Phyllanthus, Pinus, Pisum, Plantago, Plumbago, Plumeria, Potentilla, Prunus, Psidium, Punica, Pyracantha, Pyrus, Quercus, Raphanus, Reinwardtia, Reissantia, Rhamnus, Rhododendron, Rhus, Rosa, Rubus, Rumex, Saccharum, Sapindus, Sapium, Saurauia, Schima, Scurrula, Sechium, Sesamum, Shorea, Smilax, Solanum, Spilanthes, Sterculia, Strobilanthes, Swertia, Syzygium, Thalictrum, Thespesia, Thysanolaena, Trachyspermum, Trichosanthes, Trigonella, Triticum, Urena, Urtica, Viburnum, Wendlandia, Woodfordia, Zanthoxylum, Zea, Zingiber, Ziziphus

Majhi. *Abrus, Abutilon, Acacia, Achyranthes, Aegle, Amaranthus, Ananas, Annona, Argemone, Arthromeris, Artocarpus, Bauhinia, Bidens, Boerhavia, Bombax, Caesulia, Cajanus, Capsicum, Carica, Cassia, Catunaregam, Chenopodium, Cipadessa, Cissampelos, Cleome, Coccinia, Colebrookea, Desmodium, Dioscorea, Eleusine, Eupatorium, Euphorbia, Holarrhena, Hypericum, Hyptis, Inula, Ipomoea, Jatropha, Kalanchoe, Lagerstroemia, Leucas, Lycopodium, Lygodium, Mangifera, Melia, Millettia, Mimosa, Osyris, Oxalis, Phyllanthus, Phyllodium, Plumeria, Potentilla, Psidium, Quercus, Ricinus, Rubus, Rungia, Saccharum, Sapium, Semecarpus, Sesamum, Sida, Solanum, Spermadictyon, Sterculia, Streblus, Synedrella, Syzygium, Tamarindus, Trema, Trianthema, Tridax, Triumfetta, Uraria, Urena, Vernonia, Wendlandia, Woodfordia, Xanthium, Zanthoxylum, Zea, Ziziphus*

Mooshar. *Abrus, Achyranthes, Adina, Aegle, Ageratum, Allium, Alstonia, Alternanthera, Amaranthus, Anagallis, Annona, Areca, Argemone, Artocarpus, Asparagus, Azadirachta, Bauhinia, Benincasa, Bombax, Brassica, Bridelia, Calotropis, Capsicum, Carica, Carissa, Cassia, Centella, Centipeda, Chenopodium, Chrysopogon, Cicer, Citrus, Clerodendrum, Coccinia, Cocos, Coriandrum, Croton, Cucumis, Cucurbita, Curcuma, Cynodon, Cyperus, Dalbergia, Datura, Dendrophthoe, Desmostachya, Eclipta, Eleusine, Euphorbia, Ficus, Hibiscus, Ichnocarpus, Imperata, Jatropha, Lawsonia, Lens, Leucas, Linum, Litchi, Luffa, Lycopersicon, Madhuca, Mangifera, Mentha, Mimosa, Momordica, Moringa, Musa, Neolamarckia, Nyctanthes, Oryza, Oxalis, Phoenix, Phyllanthus, Pisum, Portulaca, Psidium, Punica, Pyrus, Raphanus, Ricinus, Saccharum, Setaria,*

Shorea, Sida, Solanum, Streblus, Syzygium, Tamarindus, Tinospora, Trewia, Trichosanthes, Trigonella, Triticum, Urena, Vicia, Xanthium, Zea

Nepali. *Abelmoschus, Abies, Abroma, Abrus, Abutilon, Acacia, Acer, Achyranthes, Aconitum, Acorus, Acrocephalus, Actinidia, Actinodaphne, Adiantum, Adina, Aechmanthera, Aeginetia, Aegle, Aerva, Aeschynanthus, Aeschynomene, Aesculus, Agapetes, Agave, Ageratum, Aglaomorpha, Agrimonia, Agrostemma, Ajuga, Alangium, Albizia, Allium, Alnus, Aloe, Alstonia, Alternanthera, Alysicarpus, Amaranthus, Ammannia, Amomum, Amorphophallus, Ampelocissus, Anagallis, Ananas, Anaphalis, Andropogon, Anemone, Anisomeles, Annona, Anogeissus, Antidesma, Apluda, Arachis, Araucaria, Arctium, Ardisia, Areca, Argemone, Argyreia, Arisaema, Artemisia, Arthromeris, Artocarpus, Arundinella, Arundo, Asclepias, Asparagus, Aster, Astilbe, Avena, Averrhoa, Azadirachta, Bacopa, Bambusa, Barbarea, Barleria, Basella, Bauhinia, Begonia, Belamcanda, Benincasa, Berberis, Berchemia, Bergenia, Betula, Bidens, Biophytum, Bischofia, Bistorta, Bixa, Blumea, Blyxa, Boehmeria, Boenninghausenia, Boerhavia, Bombax, Borreria, Botrychium, Brachiaria, Brachycorythis, Brassaiopsis, Brassica, Breynia, Bridelia, Buchanania, Buddleja, Bulbostylis, Bupleurum, Butea, Butomopsis, Caesalpinia, Caesulia, Cajanus, Calamus, Calanthe, Callicarpa, Callistemon, Calotropis, Caltha, Camellia, Campanula, Campylotropis, Canavalia, Canna, Cannabis, Capillipedium, Capparis, Capsella, Capsicum, Caragana, Cardamine, Cardiospermum, Carex, Careya, Carica, Carissa, Carpesium, Carum, Caryopteris, Casearia, Cassia, Castanopsis, Catharanthus, Catunaregam, Cautleya, Cedrus, Celastrus, Celosia, Celtis, Centella, Centipeda, Centranthera, Cerastium, Ceropegia, Cestrum, Chamabainia, Cheilanthes, Chenopodium, Chesneya, Chirita, Chlorophytum, Choerospondias, Chonemorpha, Chrysopogon, Cicer, Cinnamomum, Cipadessa, Cirsium, Cissampelos, Cissus, Citrullus, Citrus, Cleistocalyx, Clematis, Cleome, Clerodendrum, Cleyera, Clinopodium, Clitoria, Coccinia, Cochlianthus, Cocos, Coelogyne, Coix, Colebrookea, Coleus, Colocasia, Colquhounia, Combretum, Commelina, Convolvulus, Conyza, Corchorus, Cordia, Coriandrum, Coriaria, Cornus, Cortia, Corydalis, Corylus, Costus, Cotoneaster, Cotula, Craniotome, Crassocephalum, Crateva, Crinum, Crotalaria, Croton, Crypsinus, Cryptolepis, Cryptomeria, Cucumis, Cucurbita, Cuminum, Cuphea, Cupressus, Curculigo, Curcuma, Cuscuta, Cyananthus, Cyathocline, Cyathula, Cycas, Cyclanthera, Cymbidium, Cymbopogon, Cynanchum, Cynodon, Cynoglossum, Cyperus, Cyphomandra, Cypripedium, Dactylorhiza, Dalbergia, Daphne, Daphniphyllum, Datura, Daucus, Davallia, Debregeasia, Delonix, Delphinium, Dendranthema, Dendrobium, Dendrocalamus, Dendrophthoe, Dennstaedtia, Descurainia, Desmodium, Desmostachya, Deutzia, Dicentra, Dichanthium, Dichroa, Dichrocephala, Didymocarpus, Digitaria, Dillenia, Dioscorea, Diospyros, Diplazium, Diplocyclos, Diplokenma, Dipsacus, Disporum, Docynia, Dodecadenia, Drepanostachyum, Drosera, Drymaria, Drymaria, Drynaria, Dryoathyrium, Dryopteris, Duabanga, Duranta, Echinochloa, Eclipta, Edgeworthia, Ehretia, Eichhornia, Elaeagnus, Elaeocarpus, Elatostema, Elephantopus, Eleusine, Eleutherococcus, Elsholtzia, Embelia, Emilia, Engelhardia, Enkianthus, Entada, Ephedra, Epilobium, Equisetum, Eragrostiella, Eragrostis, Eriobotrya, Eriocaulon, Eriophorum, Eriosema, Eryngium, Erysi-*

mum, Erythrina, Eugenia, Eulaliopsis, Euodia, Euonymus, Eupatorium, Euphorbia, Euphrasia, Eurya, Evolvulus, Exbucklandia, Excoecaria, Fagopyrum, Ficus, Fimbristylis, Flacourtia, Flemingia, Floscopa, Foeniculum, Fortunella, Fragaria, Fraxinus, Fritillaria, Fumaria, Galinsoga, Galium, Garuga, Gaultheria, Geniosporum, Gentiana, Gentianella, Geranium, Gerbera, Geum, Girardinia, Globba, Glochidion, Gloriosa, Glycine, Gmelina, Gnaphalium, Gnetum, Gomphrena, Gonostegia, Gossypium, Grangea, Grevillea, Grewia, Guizotia, Gymnadenia, Gynocardia, Habenaria, Halenia, Hedera, Hedychium, Hedyotis, Helianthus, Helicia, Helicteres, Heliotropium, Helixanthera, Helminthostachys, Hemiphragma, Heracleum, Herpetospermum, Heteropogon, Hibiscus, Himalayacalamus, Hippophae, Holarrhena, Holboellia, Holmskioldia, Homalium, Hordeum, Houttuynia, Hoya, Hydrangea, Hydrocotyle, Hygrophila, Hymenodictyon, Hyoscyamus, Hypericum, Hyptis, Ichnocarpus, Ilex, Impatiens, Imperata, Incarvillea, Indigofera, Inula, Ipomoea, Iris, Ischaemum, Isodon, Ixeris, Jacaranda, Jasminum, Jatropha, Juglans, Juniperus, Jurinea, Justicia, Kalanchoe, Kohautia, Kydia, Lablab, Lactuca, Lagenaria, Lagerstroemia, Laggera, Lannea, Lantana, Larix, Lathyrus, Launaea, Lawsonia, Lecanthus, Leea, Leersia, Lens, Leonurus, Lepidagathis, Lepidium, Leptodermis, Lespedeza, Leucaena, Leucas, Leucosceptrum, Leucostegia, Ligularia, Ligustrum, Lilium, Lindenbergia, Lindera, Lindernia, Linum, Litchi, Lithocarpus, Litsea, Lobelia, Lonicera, Loranthus, Lotus, Loxogramme, Luculia, Ludwigia, Luffa, Luisia, Lycopersicon, Lycopodium, Lygodium, Lyonia, Lysimachia, Macaranga, Maclura, Macropanax, Madhuca, Maesa, Magnolia, Maharanga, Mahonia, Maianthemum, Malaxis, Mallotus, Malus, Malva, Mangifera, Manglietia, Manilkara, Maoutia, Mariscus, Marsdenia, Martynia, Maytenus, Mazus, Meconopsis, Medicago, Megacarpaea, Megacodon, Melastoma, Melia, Melilotus, Meliosma, Melochia, Mentha, Mesua, Michelia, Microlepia, Micromeria, Microsorum, Microstegium, Millettia, Mimosa, Mirabilis, Mollugo, Momordica, Monochoria, Morina, Moringa, Morus, Mucuna, Murdannia, Murraya, Musa, Mussaenda, Myriactis, Myrica, Myrsine, Nardostachys, Natsiatum, Neanotis, Nelumbo, Neohymenopogon, Neolamarckia, Nepeta, Nephrolepis, Nerium, Nicandra, Nicotiana, Nyctanthes, Ocimum, Odontosoria, Oenanthe, Oenothera, Oleandra, Onychium, Onychium, Ophioglossum, Ophiorrhiza, Oplismenus, Opuntia, Oreocnide, Origanum, Orobanche, Oroxylum, Orthosiphon, Oryza, Osbeckia, Osmanthus, Osmunda, Ostodes, Osyris, Oxalis, Oxyria, Oxyspora, Paederia, Paeonia, Panax, Pandanus, Panicum, Paris, Parnassia, Parochetus, Parthenocissus, Paspalum, Passiflora, Pavetta, Pedicularis, Pentanema, Peperomia, Perilla, Periploca, Persea, Persicaria, Phalaris, Phaseolus, Phlogacanthus, Phoenix, Photinia, Phragmites, Phyla, Phyllanthus, Physalis, Phytolacca, Picea, Picrasma, Picris, Picrorhiza, Pieris, Pilea, Pimpinella, Pinus, Piper, Piptanthus, Pisum, Pithecellobium, Pityrogramma, Plantago, Platanthera, Plectranthus, Pleione, Pleurospermum, Plumbago, Plumeria, Poa, Podocarpus, Podophyllum, Pogonatherum, Pogostemon, Polyalthia, Polygala, Polygonatum, Polygonum, Polypodium, Polypogon, Polystichum, Populus, Porana, Portulaca, Potentilla, Pouzolzia, Premna, Prenanthes, Primula, Prinsepia, Prunus, Psidium, Pteracanthus, Pteridium, Pteris, Punica, Pycreus, Pyracantha, Pyrrosia, Pyrularia, Pyrus, Quercus, Quisqualis, Randia, Ranunculus, Raphanus, Rauvolfia, Reinwardtia, Reissantia, Remusatia,

Rhamnus, Rhaphidophora, Rheum, Rhododendron, Rhus, Rhynchosia, Rhynchostylis, Ribes, Ricinus, Rorippa, Rosa, Roscoea, Rotala, Rubia, Rubus, Rumex, Rungia, Saccharum, Sacciolepis, Salix, Salomonia, Salvia, Sambucus, Sapindus, Sapium, Saraca, Sarcococca, Satyrium, Saurauia, Sauromatum, Sauropus, Saussurea, Schefflera, Schima, Schisandra, Schleichera, Schoenoplectus, Scindapsus, Scleria, Scoparia, Scopolia, Scrophularia, Scurrula, Scutellaria, Sechium, Securinega, Selaginella, Selinum, Semecarpus, Senecio, Sesamum, Sesbania, Setaria, Shorea, Sida, Siegesbeckia, Sinarundinaria, Skimmia, Smilax, Solanum, Solena, Sonchus, Sopubia, Sorbus, Spatholobus, Spatholobus, Spergula, Spermadictyon, Sphaeranthus, Sphenoclea, Spilanthes, Spinacia, Spiraea, Spondias, Sporobolus, Stachys, Stachyurus, Stellaria, Stellera, Stephania, Sterculia, Stereospermum, Stranvaesia, Streblus, Strobilanthes, Swertia, Symplocos, Synedrella, Syzygium, Tabernaemontana, Tadehaji, Tagetes, Talauma, Tamarindus, Tanacetum, Taraxacum, Taxillus, Taxus, Tectaria, Telosma, Terminalia, Tetrastigma, Teucrium, Thalictrum, Thamnocalamus, Thelypteris, Thespesia, Thevetia, Thlaspi, Thunbergia, Thunia, Thymus, Thysanolaena, Tiarella, Tinospora, Toona, Torenia, Toricellia, Torilis, Trachelospermum, Trachyspermum, Trapa, Trema, Trevesia, Trewia, Trianthema, Trichilia, Trichodesma, Trichosanthes, Tridax, Trifolium, Trigonella, Triticum, Triumfetta, Tsuga, Typhonium, Ulmus, Uraria, Urena, Urtica, Utricularia, Valeriana, Vanda, Verbascum, Verbena, Vernonia, Veronica, Vetiveria, Viburnum, Vicia, Vigna, Vincetoxicum, Viola, Viscum, Vitex, Vitis, Vittaria, Wahlenbergia, Wendlandia, Wikstroemia, Woodfordia, Woodwardia, Wrightia, Wulfenia, Xanthium, Xylosma, Youngia, Yucca, Zanthoxylum, Zea, Zingiber, Ziziphus

Newari. Abelmoschus, Abrus, Acacia, Acorus, Aegle, Ageratum, Allium, Aloe, Amaranthus, Amomum, Annona, Arachis, Areca, Artemisia, Artocarpus, Arundo, Asclepias, Asparagus, Avena, Azadirachta, Bauhinia, Benincasa, Berberis, Boehmeria, Bombax, Brassica, Buddleja, Butea, Callistemon, Camellia, Cannabis, Capsicum, Carica, Castanopsis, Catharanthus, Celtis, Centella, Centipeda, Chenopodium, Choerospondias, Cinnamomum, Cirsium, Citrus, Cleome, Clerodendrum, Cocos, Coelogyne, Coix, Colocasia, Coriandrum, Crateva, Cucumis, Cucurbita, Cuminum, Curcuma, Cyclanthera, Cymbidium, Cynodon, Cyphomandra, Dalbergia, Daphne, Datura, Daucus, Desmostachya, Dioscorea, Diplokenma, Drymaria, Eclipta, Eleusine, Euphorbia, Fagopyrum, Ficus, Foeniculum, Galinsoga, Girardinia, Glycine, Gomphrena, Gossypium, Grevillea, Hibiscus, Houttuynia, Indigofera, Ipomoea, Jacaranda, Jasminum, Juglans, Justicia, Lablab, Lagenaria, Lagerstroemia, Lawsonia, Lens, Lepidium, Linum, Litchi, Luffa, Lycopersicon, Madhuca, Magnolia, Mallotus, Mangifera, Melia, Mentha, Momordica, Musa, Myrica, Nardostachys, Nelumbo, Nephrolepis, Nerium, Nicotiana, Nyctanthes, Ocimum, Origanum, Oroxylum, Oryza, Oxalis, Persicaria, Phalaris, Phaseolus, Phyllanthus, Piper, Pisum, Plumeria, Prunus, Psidium, Punica, Pyrus, Raphanus, Remusatia, Rhododendron, Rhus, Ricinus, Rubus, Rumex, Rungia, Saccharum, Salvia, Sambucus, Sapindus, Schima, Sechium, Sesamum, Sesbania, Shorea, Sida, Solanum, Spinacia, Syzygium, Tagetes, Tamarindus, Taxus, Terminalia, Thysanolaena, Tinospora, Trachyspermum, Trichosanthes, Trigonella, Triticum, Urtica, Valeriana, Viburnum, Vicia, Vigna, Vitis, Zanthoxylum, Zea, Zingiber, Ziziphus

Rai. *Abrus, Acacia, Achyranthes, Acorus, Aegle, Allium, Alnus, Aloe, Alstonia, Amaranthus, Arachis, Areca, Arundo, Asparagus, Avena, Azadirachta, Bauhinia, Benincasa, Boerhavia, Bombax, Brassaiopsis, Brassica, Bridelia, Buddleja, Butea, Camellia, Cannabis, Capsicum, Carica, Cassia, Castanopsis, Catunaregam, Centella, Chenopodium, Choerospondias, Cinnamomum, Citrus, Cleistocalyx, Cocos, Colocasia, Coriandrum, Cucurbita, Cuminum, Curcuma, Cynodon, Dalbergia, Datura, Desmostachya, Dioscorea, Diplokenma, Eleusine, Euphorbia, Fagopyrum, Ficus, Foeniculum, Garuga, Girardinia, Glycine, Grevillea, Jasminum, Jatropha, Juglans, Justicia, Lagenaria, Lawsonia, Lens, Lepidium, Linum, Luffa, Lycopersicon, Madhuca, Mangifera, Melia, Melia, Mentha, Michelia, Mimosa, Momordica, Musa, Myrica, Nelumbo, Nephrolepis, Ocimum, Oroxylum, Oryza, Oxalis, Phaseolus, Phyllanthus, Pinus, Piper, Pisum, Plumeria, Prunus, Psidium, Punica, Pyrus, Quercus, Raphanus, Rhododendron, Rhus, Ricinus, Rubus, Saccharum, Sapindus, Saurauia, Schima, Semecarpus, Shorea, Sida, Solanum, Sterculia, Syzygium, Tamarindus, Terminalia, Trachyspermum, Trichosanthes, Trigonella, Triticum, Urtica, Vitex, Woodfordia, Zanthoxylum, Zea*

Raute. *Ageratum, Amaranthus, Ardisia, Boehmeria, Calotropis, Cannabis, Cassia, Celastrus, Centella, Cissampelos, Clerodendrum, Commelina, Crotalaria, Desmodium, Dioscorea, Diplocyclos, Equisetum, Eupatorium, Ficus, Flemingia, Floscopa, Fumaria, Glochidion, Gonostegia, Indigofera, Jatropha, Justicia, Macaranga, Mallotus, Millettia, Oxalis, Phyllanthus, Pisum, Remusatia, Ricinus, Rorippa, Solanum, Terminalia, Woodfordia, Youngia*

Satar. *Aegle, Amaranthus, Amorphophallus, Ampelocissus, Capparis, Chenopodium, Cleome, Coccinia, Colocasia, Cucumis, Dillenia, Dioscorea, Diplazium, Ficus, Ipomoea, Melastoma, Momordica, Morina, Morus, Mucuna, Oxalis, Schleichera, Semecarpus, Solanum, Streblus, Syzygium, Tamarindus, Trapa, Trema, Ziziphus*

Sherpa. *Abies, Albizia, Allium, Alnus, Anemone, Arisaema, Artemisia, Asparagus, Berberis, Berchemia, Bergenia, Betula, Boehmeria, Boerhavia, Botrychium, Brassica, Bupleurum, Caragana, Carum, Centella, Cheilanthes, Chenopodium, Clintonia, Colebrookea, Coriaria, Cotoneaster, Dactylorhiza, Daphne, Dioscorea, Edgeworthia, Elaeagnus, Eleusine, Elsholtzia, Ephedra, Euphorbia, Eurya, Fagopyrum, Fragaria, Fritillaria, Galinsoga, Gaultheria, Gentiana, Girardinia, Gonostegia, Gymnadenia, Hyoscyamus, Ilex, Imperata, Inula, Juglans, Juniperus, Lindera, Lycopodium, Lyonia, Maianthemum, Meconopsis, Myrica, Nardostachys, Oroxylum, Persicaria, Picrorhiza, Pieris, Polygonatum, Prinsepia, Pyracantha, Quercus, Raphanus, Rheum, Rhododendron, Ribes, Rubia, Rubus, Rumex, Saccharum, Sapindus, Saussurea, Smilax, Solanum, Sorbus, Swertia, Symplocos, Taxus, Terminalia, Thalictrum, Triticum, Urtica, Valeriana, Zanthoxylum*

Sunwar. *Acacia, Acorus, Aegle, Allium, Aloe, Amaranthus, Arachis, Areca, Artemisia, Artocarpus, Arundo, Asparagus, Avena, Azadirachta, Benincasa, Brassica, Buddleja, Butea, Camellia, Cannabis, Capsicum, Carica, Celtis, Centella, Choerospondias, Cinnamomum, Citrus, Cleistocalyx, Cocos, Colocasia, Coriandrum, Cucurbita, Cuminum, Curcuma, Cynodon, Dalbergia, Datura, Desmostachya, Dioscorea, Diplokenma, Eleusine, Euphorbia, Fagopyrum, Ficus, Foeniculum, Girardinia, Glycine, Grevillea, Jasminum, Juglans, Justicia, Lagenaria, Lawsonia, Lens, Lepidium, Linum, Luffa, Lycopersicon, Melia, Mentha, Momordica, Musa, Myrica, Nelumbo, Ocimum, Oroxylum, Oryza, Oxalis, Phaseolus, Pisum, Prunus, Psidium, Punica, Pyrus, Raphanus, Rhododendron, Rhus, Rubus, Saccharum, Sapindus, Shorea, Solanum, Syzygium, Terminalia, Trachyspermum, Trichosanthes, Trigonella, Triticum, Urtica, Zanthoxylum, Zea*

Tamang. *Abelmoschus, Abies, Acacia, Achyranthes, Aconitum, Acorus, Adiantum, Adina, Aechmanthera, Aegle, Aeschynanthus, Ageratum, Agrimonia, Ajuga, Aletris, Allium, Alnus, Aloe, Alternanthera, Amaranthus, Ananas, Anaphalis, Anemone, Annona, Antidesma, Arachis, Arctium, Areca, Arisaema, Artemisia, Artocarpus, Arundo, Asparagus, Aster, Astilbe, Avena, Azadirachta, Bauhinia, Begonia, Benincasa, Berberis, Bergenia, Betula, Bidens, Boehmeria, Boenninghausenia, Bombax, Borreria, Botrychium, Brassaiopsis, Brassica, Bridelia, Buchanania, Buddleja, Bupleurum, Butea, Caesalpinia, Cajanus, Callicarpa, Camellia, Canavalia, Cannabis, Capillipedium, Capsella, Capsicum, Caragana, Cardamine, Carex, Carica, Caryopteris, Cassia, Castanopsis, Catunaregam, Celtis, Centella, Chaerophyllum, Cheilanthes, Chenopodium, Chlorophytum, Choerospondias, Chrysopogon, Cinnamomum, Cipadessa, Cirsium, Cissampelos, Cissus, Citrus, Cleistocalyx, Clematis, Clerodendrum, Cocos, Coelogyne, Coix, Colebrookea, Colocasia, Colquhounia, Commelina, Conyza, Corallodiscus, Coriandrum, Coriaria, Cornus, Cotoneaster, Craniotome, Crassocephalum, Crotalaria, Cucumis, Cucurbita, Curculigo, Curcuma, Cyathocline, Cyathula, Cymbopogon, Cynodon, Cynoglossum, Dalbergia, Daphne, Daphniphyllum, Datura, Debregeasia, Delphinium, Desmodium, Desmostachya, Deutzia, Dichroa, Dichrocephala, Digitaria, Dioscorea, Diplokenma, Dipsacus, Disporum, Drepanostachyum, Drosera, Drymaria, Drynaria, Dryopteris, Echinochloa, Edgeworthia, Elaeagnus, Elaeocarpus, Elatostema, Elephantopus, Eleusine, Elsholtzia, Emilia, Engelhardia, Equisetum, Eriophorum, Euonymus, Eupatorium, Euphorbia, Eurya, Fagopyrum, Ficus, Flemingia, Foeniculum, Fraxinus, Galinsoga, Galium, Gaultheria, Geniosporum, Gentiana, Geranium, Gerbera, Girardinia, Glochidion, Glycine, Gnaphalium, Gonostegia, Grewia, Guizotia, Gynura, Halenia, Hedera, Hedychium, Hedyotis, Hemiphragma, Heracleum, Herpetospermum, Hibiscus, Hippophae, Holarrhena, Holboellia, Holmskioldia, Homalium, Houttuynia, Hydrocotyle, Hypericum, Ichnocarpus, Ilex, Impatiens, Indigofera, Inula, Ipomoea, Isodon, Jasminum, Jatropha, Juglans, Juniperus, Justicia, Kalanchoe, Knoxia, Lactuca, Lagenaria, Lagerstroemia, Lannea, Lantana, Launaea, Lawsonia, Lecanthus, Leea, Lens, Lepidium, Leptodermis, Leucas, Leucosceptrum, Ligularia, Lindenbergia, Lindera, Lithocarpus, Litsea, Lobelia, Loranthus, Luculia, Luffa, Lycopersicon, Lycopodium, Lyonia, Madhuca, Maesa, Mahonia, Maianthemum, Mallotus, Malva, Mangifera, Maoutia, Maytenus, Mazus, Melastoma, Melia, Mentha, Michelia, Micromeria, Mimosa, Mirabilis, Momordica, Mukia, Murdannia, Musa, Myriactis, Myrica, Myrsine, Nardostachys, Neillia, Nelumbo, Nephrolepis, Nicotiana, Nyctanthes, Ocimum, Oleandra, Ophioglossum, Oreocnide, Oroxylum, Oryza, Osbeckia, Osyris, Oxalis, Oxyspora, Par-*

thenocissus, Pennisetum, Perilla, Periploca, Persicaria, Phaseolus, Pholidota, Phragmites, Phyllanthus, Physalis, Picrorhiza, Pieris, Pilea, Pimpinella, Pinus, Piper, Pisum, Plantago, Plumeria, Pogonatherum, Pogostemon, Polygonatum, Portulaca, Potentilla, Pouzolzia, Premna, Prinsepia, Prunus, Psidium, Pteris, Punica, Pyracantha, Pyrus, Quercus, Randia, Ranunculus, Raphanus, Reinwardtia, Rhamnus, Rheum, Rhododendron, Rhus, Ricinus, Rorippa, Rosa, Rubia, Rumex, Rungia, Saccharum, Sambucus, Sanicula, Sapindus, Sapium, Sarcococca, Satyrium, Saurauia, Schima, Scindapsus, Scoparia, Scrophularia, Scurrula, Scutellaria, Sechium, Sedum, Selaginella, Semecarpus, Senecio, Sesamum, Shorea, Shuteria, Sida, Siegesbeckia, Sinarundinaria, Smilax, Smithia, Solanum, Solena, Sonchus, Sorbus, Spermadictyon, Spilanthes, Stellaria, Stellera, Stephania, Sterculia, Stranvaesia, Strobilanthes, Swertia, Symplocos, Syzygium, Tadehaji, Tagetes, Taraxacum, Taxus, Tectaria, Terminalia, Tetrastigma, Thalictrum, Thespesia, Thunbergia, Thymus, Thysanolaena, Tithonia, Trachyspermum, Trema, Trichilia, Trichosanthes, Tridax, Trigonella, Triticum, Triumfetta, Tsuga, Urena, Urtica, Valeriana, Verbascum, Vernonia, Viburnum, Viola, Vitex, Vitis, Wikstroemia, Woodfordia, Zanthoxylum, Zea, Zingiber, Ziziphus

Tharu. Abrus, Acacia, Achyranthes, Adiantum, Aegle, Allium, Aloe, Alternanthera, Amaranthus, Arachis, Areca, Argemone, Artemisia, Artocarpus, Arundinella, Arundo, Asparagus, Avena, Azadirachta, Bauhinia, Benincasa, Boehmeria, Boerhavia, Bombax, Borreria, Brassica, Buddleja, Butea, Cajanus, Calotropis, Camellia, Cannabis, Capsicum, Carica, Carissa, Cassia, Castanopsis, Catunaregam, Celtis, Centella, Cheilanthes, Chlorophytum, Choerospondias, Chrozophora, Chrysopogon, Citrus, Cleome, Clerodendrum, Cocos, Colebrookea, Colocasia, Commelina, Coriandrum, Crotalaria, Cucumis, Cucurbita, Curculigo, Curcuma, Cymbidium, Cynodon, Cyperus, Dalbergia, Datura, Desmodium, Desmostachya, Dioscorea, Diplokenma, Eclipta, Elephantopus, Eleusine, Euphorbia, Evolvulus, Ficus, Foeniculum, Garuga, Glycine, Grewia, Hemigraphis, Hydrolea, Imperata, Ipomoea, Jasminum, Jatropha, Juglans, Justicia, Lagenaria, Lagerstroemia, Lawsonia, Lens, Lepidium, Leucas, Lilium, Linum, Lonicera, Ludwigia, Luffa, Lycopersicon, Madhuca, Mallotus, Melia, Mentha, Millettia, Mirabilis, Mitragyna, Momordica, Murraya, Musa, Myrica, Nelumbo, Nepeta, Ocimum, Ophioglossum, Oroxylum, Oryza, Oxalis, Paspalum, Persicaria, Phaseolus, Phyla, Phyllanthus, Physalis, Piper, Pisum, Plumbago,

Pogostemon, Polygonatum, Pouzolzia, Prunus, Pulicaria, Punica, Pyrus, Ranunculus, Raphanus, Rauvolfia, Rhododendron, Rhus, Ricinus, Rubus, Rumex, Saccharum, Sagittaria, Sapindus, Semecarpus, Setaria, Shorea, Sida, Solanum, Sphenoclea, Syzygium, Terminalia, Thevetia, Trachyspermum, Trichilia, Trichosanthes, Tridax, Trigonella, Triticum, Uraria, Urtica, Valeriana, Vernonia, Vitex, Woodfordia, Xanthium, Zanthoxylum, Zea, Ziziphus

Tibetan. Achyranthes, Adenocaulon, Ajuga, Allium, Amomum, Anaphalis, Androsace, Anemone, Arctium, Areca, Artemisia, Asparagus, Astragalus, Azadirachta, Benincasa, Berberis, Bergenia, Betula, Bistorta, Bombax, Boschniakia, Brassica, Bromus, Buddleja, Bupleurum, Butea, Cajanus, Callicarpa, Calotropis, Camellia, Campanula, Cannabis, Capsella, Capsicum, Caragana, Carum, Cassia, Catunaregam, Cedrus, Chenopodium, Cicerbita, Cinnamomum, Cissampelos, Citrullus, Citrus, Clematis, Coriandrum, Coriaria, Cornus, Cortia, Costus, Cotoneaster, Cucumis, Cuminum, Curcuma, Cynodon, Cynoglossum, Cyperus, Dactylorhiza, Daphne, Datura, Daucus, Delphinium, Dendranthema, Desmostachya, Dicranostigma, Diospyros, Dipsacus, Drosera, Eclipta, Elsholtzia, Entada, Ephedra, Epilobium, Eriobotrya, Erodium, Eupatorium, Euphorbia, Euphrasia, Fagopyrum, Ficus, Foeniculum, Fritillaria, Galinsoga, Galium, Gaultheria, Gentiana, Gentianella, Geranium, Gnaphalium, Gonostegia, Hedera, Heracleum, Hippophae, Holarrhena, Hyoscyamus, Hypericum, Ilex, Impatiens, Inula, Juglans, Juniperus, Justicia, Kalanchoe, Lagenaria, Lawsonia, Leptodermis, Lindera, Luffa, Lyonia, Maesa, Malva, Mangifera, Melia, Mesua, Michelia, Millettia, Morina, Moringa, Myrica, Myricaria, Nardostachys, Nelumbo, Origanum, Oryza, Oxyria, Panicum, Pedicularis, Phyllanthus, Phytolacca, Picrorhiza, Piper, Plantago, Pleurospermum, Polygonatum, Polygonum, Polystichum, Populus, Potentilla, Prenanthes, Prinsepia, Prunella, Prunus, Pterocephalus, Punica, Pyrus, Quercus, Ranunculus, Raphanus, Rheum, Rhododendron, Rhus, Ribes, Ricinus, Rosa, Rubia, Rubus, Rumex, Saccharum, Salvia, Saussurea, Scopolia, Selinum, Semecarpus, Senecio, Sesamum, Sesbania, Setaria, Shorea, Silene, Solanum, Sonchus, Sophora, Sorbaria, Stellera, Swertia, Syzygium, Tamarindus, Taraxacum, Terminalia, Thalictrum, Thymus, Tinospora, Trachyspermum, Trichosanthes, Trigonella, Triticum, Tsuga, Urtica, Valeriana, Verbascum, Veronica, Viburnum, Vicia, Vitis, Woodfordia, Zanthoxylum, Zingiber, Ziziphus

Glossary

abortifacient. Causes abortion or miscarriage

abscess. Localized collection of pus in body tissue

achene. Small dry fruit that does not split to release its single seed

acuminate. Tapering to a prolonged point

acute. Tapering to a narrow angle, less than a right angle

alterative. Substance that gradually restores health

amenorrhea. Abnormal suppression of menses

annual. Completing its life cycle within a year, flowering once only

anodyne. Drug that allays pain

anthelmintic. Expels worms from the intestine; compare vermifuge

antiperiodic. Prevents the return of recurring diseases such as malaria

antipyretic. Drug that reduces fever

antiseptic. Destroys microorganisms that produce disease

antispasmodic. Preventing or relieving convulsions

aperient. Mild laxative

aphrodisiac. Stimulates sexual desire

apiculate. With a short, pointed tip

appressed. Closely pressed against

aril. Appendage borne on a seed

asthma. Chronic disease that causes difficulty in breathing

astringent. Causes contraction of tissues and prevents secretion of fluids from wounds

attenuate. Narrow and gradually tapering

auricle. Ear-shaped projection, at the top of a sheath in grasses

axillary. Bearing flowers at the angle between leaf and twig

berry. Juicy fruit with seeds in the middle of the pulp

bile. Yellow or greenish liquid secreted by the liver that aids in absorption or digestion

biliousness. Disturbance in the digestive system as a result of improper functioning of the liver

blade. Expanded part of a leaf

blister. Elevation of the skin containing watery liquid

boil. Hard, inflamed, suppurating tumor

bracteate. With leaf-like bracts, like those of *Euphorbia*

bronchitis. Inflammation of the air passages

bulbil. Small bulb, usually axillary

calyx. Outer whorl of flower parts, the sepals

capillary. Hair-like, very slender

capitate. In the form of a head

capsule. Dry fruit splitting by two or more valves

carbuncle. Acute suppurative inflammation of the skin and tissues under the skin, rapidly spreading around the original point of infection

carminative. Expels gas from the stomach and intestine

carpel. One of the units of a compound gynoecium

cataract. Clouded condition in the lens of the eye, resulting the blurred vision

catarrh. Inflammation of a mucous membrane, especially the nose and other air passages

cauline. Borne on the stem

chilblain. Inflammatory swelling or sore, resulting in defective circulation of the blood and caused by damp cold

cholera. Disease characterized by severe gastrointestinal symptoms caused by a bacterial toxin

ciliate. With hairs on the margin

circinate. Coiled, as in an immature fern frond

cladode. Flattened stem in the form of a leaf

coagulant. Coagulates blood, helping stop bleeding

coccus (plural, cocci). One of the one-seeded units of a compound fruit

colic. Pain resulting from spasmodic contraction of the abdomen

conjunctivitis. Inflammation of the inner surface of the eyelid

constipation. Abnormally infrequent passage of usually hardened feces

convolute. Rolled, with overlapping margins

cordate. Heart shaped

cornea. Tough transparent outer membrane protecting the iris of the eyeball

corolla. Inner whorl of laminar floral parts, the petals

corymb. Short, broad, more or less flat-topped indeterminate inflorescence, the outer flowers opening first; compare cyme

cotyledon. Seed leaves of the embryo

crenate. Shallowly round-toothed, scalloped

crenulate. Diminutively round-toothed, scalloped

crispate. Extremely undulate

culm. Stem of a grass

cuneate. Wedge shaped

cuspidate. Tip abruptly notched but ending in a sharp tip

cutaneous. Relating to the skin

cyme. Short, broad, more or less flat-topped determinate inflorescence, the central flowers opening first; compare corymb

deciduous. Shedding leaves annually

decoction. Extract of crude drug obtained by boiling in water

decompound. More than once compound

decumbent. Lying on the ground but with the tip ascending

decurrent. Extending down and pressed against the stem

decussate. Leaves in four rows on the stem with opposite pairs at right angles

deflexed. Bent downward; compare reflexed

dehiscent. A fruit that opens at maturity

demulcent. Agent that has a soothing effect on skin and mucous membranes

dentate. Toothed

dextrorse. Twining upward toward the right

diabetes. Wasting disease that affects metabolism; in one form, excessive sugar is present continuously in the urine, in the other form overabundant sugar is not present but there is excessive discharge of urine pale in color and of low specific gravity

diaphoretic. Increases perspiration

diarrhea. Abnormally frequent evacuation of the bowel with more or less fluid feces

diffuse. Loosely branched

digestive. Aids digestion

digitate. A compound leaf with leaflets arising from one point

dilated. Expanded

dimorphic. Of two forms, as in ferns with differently formed vegetative and reproductive fronds

dioecious. Male and female flowers borne on separate plants

diphtheria. Acute feverish disease characterized by formation of a false membrane, especially in the throat

distichous. Leaves in two rows on the stem and in the same plane

diuretic. Increases secretion and discharge of urine

divaricate. Spreading widely apart

dropsy. Disease marked by excessive collection of watery fluid in the tissue or cavities of the body

drupe. Fruit with a thin outer layer, fleshy inner layer, and a hard casing around the seed

dysentery. Severe diarrhea with passage of mucus and blood

dyspepsia. Indigestion characterized by nausea

dysuria. Difficulty in discharge of urine

echinate. With stout prickles

eczema. Skin disease characterized by redness, itching, and formation of scales and crusts

elliptic. Oval with rounded to narrowed ends

emarginate. Notched at the tip

emetic. Induces vomiting

emmenagogue. Promotes menstruation

emollient. Softening and soothing to the skin

entire. Margin smooth, not divided

epilepsy. Disorder of the central nervous system, usually marked by convulsive attacks

epiphyte. Plant that grows on another plant but not parasitically

expectorant. Promotes ejection of fluid from the lungs and trachea

falcate. Sickle shaped

febrifuge. Agent used for reducing fever

-fid. Suffix meaning cleft; compare -sect

filiform. Thread-like, long and slender

flaccid. Limp, not stiff

flatulence. Disorder in which there is excessive collection of gas in the stomach or intestine

floccose. Bearing tufts of soft hair

-foliate. Suffix denoting number of leaves

-foliolate. Suffix denoting number of leaflets in a leaf

follicle. Many-seeded fruit opening along one suture only

frond. Leaf of, usually, a fern

galactagogue. Promotes secretion and flow of milk

gingivitis. Inflammation of gums around the teeth

glabrescent. Nearly glabrous or becoming so with age

glabrous. Without hairs

glaucescent. Slightly glaucous

glaucous. Covered with a waxy coating that rubs off

globose. Approximately spherical

glume. A bract in the inflorescence of a grass or similar plant

goiter. Chronic enlargement of the thyroid gland

gonorrhea. Infectious venereal disease marked by an inflammatory discharge from the genital organs

gout. Disease marked by painful inflammation of the joints

gynoecium. Female organs of the flower

hastate. Spearhead shaped with pointed basal lobes at right angles to the petiole

hematuria. Presence of blood in the urine

hemorrhage. Heavy or uncontrolled bleeding

hemorrhoid. Inflamed condition of the veins in the rectal region

herb. A plant with annual stems and perennial roots

herpes. Disease of the skin or mucous membranes characterized by blisters caused by herpesvirus

hirsute. With rough hairs

hispid. With stiff hairs

hoary. With closely set whitish pubescence

hyaline. Translucent and colorless

imbricated. Overlapping

indehiscent. A fruit that remains closed at maturity

inflorescence. Arrangement of flowers on a plant

infusion. Liquid extract resulting from steeping a substance in water

insomnia. Inability to sleep

internode. Section of a culm between two nodes

involucre. Whorl or whorls of bracts beneath a flower or inflorescence

involute. Rolled inward toward the upper side

itch. Uneasy sense of irritation in the skin

jaundice. Disease that causes yellowness of the skin, eyes, and body fluids along with disturbed vision

juice. Liquid expressed from a plant or part of a plant

laciniate. Cut into narrow pointed lobes

lamina. Blade of a leaf, especially that of a fern

lanceolate. Lance shaped

laxative. Gentle bowel stimulant

lenticel. Lens-shaped corky spot on bark

leprosy. Disease characterized by enlarged lumps or patches of skin and caused by a bacterium

leukoderma. Disease causing deterioration or loss of skin pigments

leukorrhea. Whitish, purulent, mucous discharge from the vagina and uterine canal

lobulate. With small lobes

lunate. Crescent shaped

lyrate. Pinnatifid, with a large lobe at the tip and smaller lower lobes

malaria. Disease caused by parasitic sporozoa in red blood cells, characterized by periodic attacks of chills and fever

masticatory. Substance chewed to increase flow of saliva

meningitis. Contagious disease causing inflammation of the membrane covering the brain and lungs

menorrhagia. Abnormally profuse menstrual flow

mesocarp. Middle layer of a pericarp

migraine. Periodic attack of headache affecting one side of the head

monoecious. Separate male and female flowers borne on the same plant

mucronate. Abruptly terminating in a short, straight, stiff, sharp point

mumps. Inflammation of the parotid glands

narcotic. Induces drowsiness

nausea. Feeling of having to vomit

neuralgia. Pain felt along a nerve

node. Raised ring on a culm; position on the stem where a leaf is borne

nut. Hard one-seeded fruit, not splitting open

ob-. Prefix meaning inversely; for example, oblanceolate, lance shaped but with the broader end distal to he point of attachment; oblong, rectangular and at least twice as long as broad; obovate, ovate but attached at the narrow end; obovoid, egg shaped but attached at the narrow end

oblique. Unequally sided

oblong. Much longer than broad, with nearly parallel sides

obtuse. Tip blunt, rounded

ophthalmia. Inflammation of the eye or membrane lining the inner surface of the eyelid

opposite. Leaves on either side of the stem at the same node

orbiculate. Circular, disk shaped

ovary. Ovule-bearing part of the gynoecium

ovate. Egg shaped

palea. Upper bract in a grass flower

palmate. Lobed in a digitate fashion

panicle. Loose flower cluster

papilla. Small pimple-like protruberance

pappus. Outer perianth of Compositae, composed of bristles or scales

paralysis. Loss of sensation caused by injury to or disease of the nerves, brain, or spinal cord

paste. Any material or preparation of a soft or plastic mass

peduncle. Stalk of a flower or inflorescence

pellucid. Clear, almost transparent

peltate. Attached to the stalk inside the margin

perennial. Plant that lives for more than 2 years

perianth. The two whorls of the outer flower parts, the calyx and corolla

pericarp. Outer wall of a fruit; compare mesocarp

petiole. Leaf stalk

petiolule. Leaflet stalk

phlegm. Thick, slimy substance secreted by the mucous membrane of the respiratory passages

pilose. Thinly hairy with long, soft hairs

pimple. Small, solid, round tumor of the skin

pinna. Primary leaflet of a pinnate leaf; compare pinnule

pinnate. Compound leaf with leaflets on either side of the rachis

pinnatifid. Pinnately rather than palmately divided

pinnatisect. Pinnately cleft to the midrib but not compound

pinnule. Secondary leaflet of a bi- or tripinnate leaf; compare pinna

pod. Dry, dehiscent fruit with more than one seed

poultice. Soft, usually heated preparation spread on a cloth and applied to an inflammation

procumbent. Lying its whole length on the ground

prolapse. Slippage of a body part from its usual position

prostrate. Lying on the ground; compare decumbent, procumbent

pseudobulb. Swollen stem of certain orchids

puberulent. Minutely pubescent

pubescent. With short, downy hairs

punctate. With dots

purgative. Causing evacuation, as from the bowels

pyorrhea. Disease marked by discharge of pus from the gums accompanied by loosening of the teeth

rabies. Disease of the nervous system caused by a virus and characterized by increased salivation, abnormal behavior, and eventual paralysis and death

raceme. Undivided inflorescence with a long rachis bearing essentially equally stalked flowers

rachis. Part of an axis that bears leaflets or flowers

receptacle. Enlarged end of a flowering stem bearing parts of the flower or, in inflorescences, the flowers (as in Compositae)

recurved. Bent or curved downward or backward

reflexed. Abruptly deflexed at more than a right angle

refrigerant. Relieves feverishness or produces a feeling of coolness

reniform. Kidney shaped

retinitis. Inflammation of the retina

retrorse. Turned over backward or downward

revolute. Rolled inward from the margin or apex

rheumatism. Disease characterized by inflammation of joints, muscles, or connective tissue

rhizome. Underground creeping stem

ringworm. Parasitic skin disease usually marked by red circular patches

rosulate. In a rosette

rubefacient. External skin application causing redness to the skin

rugose. Wrinkled

rugulose. Finely wrinkled

runcinate. Coarsely serrate

sagittate. Spearhead shaped with pointed basal lobes pointed downward toward the petiole

samara. Indehiscent winged fruit of *Acer*

scabies. Itching skin disease caused by a mite

scandent. Climbing without tendrils

scape. Leafless stalk rising from the ground and bearing one or more flowers

sciatica. Pain along a nerve in the lower back or adjoining areas

scurfy. With a scaly surface

-sect. Suffix meaning deeply cleft; compare -fid

sedative. Sleep inducing

septicemia. Infection of the blood by virulent microorganisms, usually characterized by chills or fever

serrate. Saw-toothed, teeth pointing forward

serrulate. Minutely serrate

sessile. Without a stalk

setose. With bristles

setulose. With fine bristles or hairs

sheath. Tubular or rolled portion of a leaf

simple. Leaves with a single blade, not compound

sinuate. Margin deeply wavy

sinusitis. Inflammation of a sinus of the head

smooth. Surface without roughness

sorus (plural, sori). Cluster of sporangia on a fern frond

spadix. Spike with a fleshy axis

spathe. Bract enclosing an inflorescence

spatulate. Spoon shaped

spicate. Spike-like

spike. Raceme in which flowers are sessile

spinous. With spines

sporophyll. Spore-bearing leaf

stellate. Star-like, of hairs with radiating branches

stimulant. Energy producing

stipe. Petiole of a fern frond

stipule. Basal appendage of a petiole

stolon. Creeping stem at or above the ground

stomachic. Strengthens the stomach and promotes its action

stomatitis, angular. Inflammation of the corners of the mouth

striate. With thin longitudinal lines or furrows

strigose. With sharp, appressed, straight, stiff hairs

sub- . Prefix meaning somewhat; for example, subshrub, small but truly woody shrub

syphilis. Chronic venereal disease

tendril. Modified leaf or similar structure, often coiled like a spring and helping a climbing plant cling to what it is climbing

terete. Round in cross section

terminal. Bearing flowers at the end of a branch

ternate. In threes

thyrse. Compact, more or less compound panicle

tomentose. Densely pubescent with short, soft, tangled hairs

tomentum. Covering of hairs

tonic. Substance taken to strengthen, usually in the absence of disease

tonsillitis. Inflammation of the tonsils, lymphoid masses in the throat

torulose. Irregularly knobby

tranquilizing. Relieves mental tension or anxiety

trichotomous. Divided into threes

triquetrous. Three-angled in cross section

truncate. Ending abruptly as if the end had been cut off

tumor. Abnormal tissue growth on or in the body

tympanitis. Otitis media, inflammation of the middle ear

ulcer. Open sore on the skin or mucous membrane

umbel. Umbrella-shaped inflorescence

undulate. Wavy up and down instead of in and out

urticle. One-celled, one-seeded fruit with thin, somewhat loose pericarp

vermifuge. Kills worms in wounds, boils, etc.; compare anthelmintic

vesicant. Induces blistering

villous. With long, soft, unmatted hairs

vulnerary. Useful in healing wounds

wart. Hypertrophy of or growth on the skin

whitlow. Septic inflammation of the tissues surrounding the nail, toe, or bone of the distal joint of a finger

whooping cough. Disease, especially of children, characterized by a convulsive cough sometimes followed by a wheezing intake of breath

References

Anonymous. 1973. Materials for the flora of Bhutan. Records of the Botanical Survey of India 20(2): 1–278.

Anonymous. 1998. Statistical Information on Nepalese Agriculture 1997–98. Agricultural Statistics Division, Ministry of Agriculture, Kathmandu.

Banerji, M. L. 1955. Some edible and medicinal plants from east Nepal. Journal of the Bombay Natural History Society 53: 153–155.

Baral, A. 1997 (2 August). Rai jati ko sanskar [customs and culture of the Rai community]. Kantipur (Nepali daily newspaper, Kathmandu).

Basnyat, K. 1995 (2 December). Animal husbandry and pasture development: two sides of a coin. The Rising Nepal (English daily newspaper, Kathmandu).

Bhatta, D. D. 1970. Natural History and Economic Botany of Nepal. Department of Information, His Majesty's Government of Nepal, Kathmandu.

Bhatta, D. D. 1977. Natural History and Economic Botany of Nepal. Orient Longman, New Delhi.

Bista, D. B. 1980. People of Nepal. Ratna Pustak Bhandar, Kathmandu.

Carson, B. 1985. Erosion and sedimentation process in the Nepalese Himalaya. Occasional Paper 1. ICIMOD, Kathmandu.

Central Bureau of Statistics. 2000. Statistical Pocket Book—Nepal. His Majesty's Government of Nepal, Kathmandu.

Chopra, R. N., I. C. Chopra, K. L. Handa, and L. D. Kapoor. 1958. Chopra's Indigenous Drugs of India. U. N. Dhur and Sons, Calcutta.

Coburn, B. 1984. Some native medicinal plants of western Gurung. Kailash 11(1–2): 55–88.

Damle, N. V. 1977 (16 October). A cure for cancer? Illustrated Weekly of India. New Delhi.

Dobremez, J. F. 1972. Mise au Point d'une Méthode Cartographique d'Étude des Montagnes Tropicales. Le Nepal, Écologie et Phytogeographie. Thèse, Université Scientifique et Médicale, Grenoble.

Dobremez, J. F. 1976. Exploitation and prospects of medicinal plants in eastern Nepal. In Mountain Environment and Development. Swiss Association for Technical Assistance in Nepal, Kathmandu.

Gamble, J. S. 1922 (reprinted 1972). A Manual of Indian Timbers (reprinted by Bishen Singh Mahendra Pal Singh, Dehra Dun, India).

Gillam, S. 1989. The traditional healer as village health worker. Journal of the Institute of Medicine 11: 67–76.

Gorkhapatra News. 1992 (22 December). 21 pratishat bhubhag ma matra jangal [only 21% of the total land area is covered by forest]. Gorkhapatra (Nepali daily newspaper, Kathmandu).

Hagen, T. 1960. Nepal. Kummerly and Frey, Graphical Institute, Berne, Switzerland.

Ives, J. D., and B. Messerli. 1989. The Himalayan Dilemma: Reconciling Development and Conservation. Routledge, London.

Jackson, J. K. 1987. Manual of Afforestation in Nepal. Nepal-United Kingdom Forestry Research Project. Department of Forests, His Majesty's Government of Nepal, Kathmandu.

Jain, S. K. 1965. On prospects of some new or less known medicinal plant resources. Indian Medical Journal 59(12): 270–272.

Joshi, L., and S. L. Sherpa. 1992. Preliminary results of some fodder research activities at Pakhribas Agriculture Centre. In Proceedings, Fourth Meeting of the Working Group on Fodder Trees, Forest Fodder and Leaf Litter. Forest Research Division, Occasional Paper 1/92, Department of Forests, Kathmandu.

Joshi, P. 1986. Fish stupefying plants employed by tribals of southern Rajasthan—a probe. Current Science 55(14): 647–650.

Kapur, S. K., and Y. K. Sarin. 1984. Plant resources exploitation and their utilization in Trikata Hills of Jammu provinces (J. and K. state). Journal of Economic and Taxonomic Botany 5: 1143–1158.

Karki, J. B. S. 1992. Forest and fodder: a historical perspective. Banko Jankari 3 (3): 1–8.

Karki, T., H. Itoh, S. Nikkuni, and M. Kozaki. 1986. Improvement of *gundruk* processing by selected lactic stains. Journal of Food Science and Technology (Nippon Shokuhin Kogyo Gakkaishi) 33(10): 734–739.

Kirtikar, K. P., and B. D. Basu. 1935. Indian Medicinal Plants. L. M. Basu, Allahabad, India.

Koelz, W. N. 1979. Notes on ethnobotany of Lahul, a province of the Punjab. Quarterly Journal of Crude Drug Research 17(1): 1–56.

Lacoul, P. 1995. Biogeography and protected areas in Nepal. *In* Souvenir, Second International Workshop cum Seminar on Legume Database of South Asia. Central Department of Botany, Tribhuvan University, Kathmandu.

Lal, K. 1983. The Tharus. The Rising Nepal (English daily newspaper, Kathmandu) 20(233): 3.

Loewenfeld, C., and P. Back. 1974. The Complete Book of Herbs and Spices. Putnam, New York.

Mahat, T. B. S., D. M. Griffin, and R. K. Shephard. 1986. Human impact on some forests of the middle hills of Nepal. Forestry in the context of the traditional resources of the state. Mountain Research and Development 6(3): 223–232.

Majumdar, R., K. C. Tiwari, S. Bhattacharjee, and A. K. Nair. 1978. Some folklore medicine from Assam and Meghalaya. Quarterly Journal of Crude Drug Research 16(4): 185–198.

Malhotra, S. K., and S. Moorthy. 1973. Some useful and medicinal plants of Chandrapur district (Maharashtra state). Bulletin of the Botanical Survey of India 15(1–2): 13–21.

Malla, L. 1993. The Natural Dyes of Nepal. Research Centre for Applied Science and Technology, Tribhuvan University, Kathmandu.

Manandhar, D. N., and D. M. Shakya. 1996. Climate and Crops of Nepal. Nepal Agricultural Research Council, Swiss Agency for Development and Cooperation, Kathmandu.

Manandhar, N. P. 1980a. Medicinal Plants of Nepal Himalaya. Ratna Pustak Bhandar, Kathmandu.

Manandhar, N. P. 1980b. Some less known medicinal plants of Rasuwa district (Nepal). Quarterly Journal of Crude Drug Research 18(3): 147–151.

Manandhar, N. P. 1982. An ethnobotanical study of Nuwakot. Pages 72–79 *in* Proceedings of First National Science and Technology Congress. National Council for Science and Technology, Kirtipur, Kathmandu.

Manandhar, N. P. 1985. Ethnobotanical notes on certain medicinal plants used by Tharus of Dangdeokhuri district, Nepal. International Journal of Crude Drug Research 23(4): 153–159.

Manandhar, N. P. 1986a. A contribution to the ethnobotany of Mooshar tribes of Dhanusha district, Nepal. Journal of Natural History Museum (Kathmandu) 10(1–4): 53–64.

Manandhar, N. P. 1986b. Ethnobotany of Jumla district, Nepal. International Journal of Crude Drug Research 24(2): 81–89.

Manandhar, N. P. 1989. Useful Wild Plants of Nepal. Nepal Research Centre Publications 14. Franz Steiner Verlag, Stuttgart.

Manandhar, N. P. 1990. Traditional phytotherapy of Danuwar tribes of Kamlakhonj in Sindhuli district, Nepal. Fitoterapia 61(4): 325–332.

Manandhar, N. P. 1991. Medicinal plant-lore of Tamang tribes of Kabhrepalanchok district, Nepal. Economic Botany 45(1): 58–71.

Manandhar, N. P. 1994. Ethnobotanical note on *bhorla* (*Bauhinia vahlii* Wight & Arn.). Pages 599–602 *in* Proceedings of Second National Conference on Science and Technology. Royal Nepal Academy of Science and Technology, Kathmandu.

Manandhar, N. P. 1997. Ethnobotany in Nepal. Pages 20–27 *in* Proceedings of the National Training Workshop in Nepal—Ethnobotany for Conservation and Community Development. Kathmandu.

Manandhar, N. P. 1998. Native phytotherapy among Raute tribes of Dadeldhura district, Nepal. Journal of Ethnopharmacology 60: 199–206.

Moench, M., and J. Bandyopadhyay 1986. People-forest interaction: a neglected parameter in Himalayan forest management. Mountain Research and Development 6(1): 3–16.

Pandey, B. D. 1964. The wealth of medicinal plants of Nepal. Pages 183–140 *in* Peking Symposium, China.

Pandey, R. S. 1982 (5 March). Pashu dhanko arthik mahatwa [economic value of cattle]. Gorkhapatra (Nepali daily newspaper, Kathmandu).

Poudel, K. 1992 (5 November). Forest protection efforts—people at the centre. The Rising Nepal (English daily newspaper, Kathmandu).

Poudel, M. M. 1986. Drive Against Poverty, Nepal. Ultra Research Centre, Gairidhara, Kathmandu.

Pudasaini, S. P. 1992 (26 August). Environment crisis—integrated action required. The Rising Nepal (English daily newspaper, Kathmandu).

Raizada, M. B., and H. O. Saxena. 1978 (reprinted 1984). Flora of Mussoorie, Volume 1 (reprinted by Periodical Expert Book Agency, Delhi).

Reinhard, J. 1976. The Ban Raja—a vanishing Himalayan tribe. Contribution to Nepalese Studies 4: 1–21.

Rimal, D. N. 1967. A Guide to Mineral Resources in Nepal. Bureau of Mines, Kathmandu.

Sacherer, J. 1979. The high altitude ethnobotany of Rolwaling Sherpa. Contribution to Nepalese Studies 6(2): 45–64.

Sarin, Y. K., and L. D. Kapoor 1962. Survey of medicinal weeds. Bulletin of Regional Research Laboratory, Jammu 1(1): 25–29.

Schweinfurth, U. 1957. Die horizontale und vertikale Verbreitung der Vegetation im Himalaya. Bonner Geographische Abhandlungen 20.

Shah, G. L., and G. U. Gopal. 1982. An ethnobotanical profile of the Dangils. Journal of Economic and Taxonomic Botany 3(2): 355–364.

Shah, N. C., and M. C. Joshi. 1971. An ethnobotanical study of the Kumaon regions of India. Economic Botany 25(4): 414–422.

Shakya, P. R., and R. M. Joshi. 1995. Biodiversity database in Nepal. *In* Souvenir, Second International Workshop cum Seminar on Legume Database of South Asia. Central Department of Botany, Tribhuvan University, Kathmandu.

Shrestha, K., and K. Nobuo. 1995–1996. Ethnobotanical knowledge of *Pongamia pinnata* (L.) Pierre in the Ranataru tribe in Kanchanpur district of far western Nepal. Natural History Society of Nepal Bulletin 5–6(1–4): 28–31.

Shrestha, S. 1992. Present energy situation in Nepal and some possibilities for the future. Banko Jankari 3(2): 17–19.

Shrestha, T. B. 1979. Traditional medicine and native plants of Nepal. *In* Proceedings of the Seminar on Traditional Medicines and Role of Medicinal Plants, August 2–3. Kathmandu.

Singh, S. C. 1960. Some wild plants of food value in Nepal. Journal of Tribhuvan University 4(1): 50–56.

Singh, V. 1976. A taxonomic study of the genus *Cassia* Linn. in Rajasthan. Bulletin of the Botanical Survey of India 18(1–4): 85–101.

Stainton, J. D. A. 1972. Forests of Nepal. John Murray, London.

Stearn, W. T. 1960. *Allium* and *Milula* in the central and eastern Himalaya. Bulletin of the British Museum (Natural History), Botany 2: 161–191.

Stiller, L. F. 1993. Nepal: Growth of a Nation. Human Resources Development Research Centre, Kathmandu.

Storrs, A., and J. Storrs 1984. Discovering Trees. Sahayogi Press, Kathmandu.

Swan, L. W., and A. E. Leviton. 1962. Herpetology of Nepal. Proceedings of the California Academy of Sciences 32(6): 103–142.

Uprety, L. P. 1985 (3 August). An indispensable component of livestock: farming fodder. The Rising Nepal (English daily newspaper, Kathmandu).

Watt, G. 1889–1896 (reprinted 1972). A Dictionary of the Economic Products of India (reprinted by Periodical Experts, Delhi).

World Bank. 1979. Nepal Development Performance and Prospects, a World Bank Country Study. South Asia Regional Office, World Bank, Washington, D.C.

World Bank. 1995. World Development Report. Oxford University Press, New York.

World Health Organization. 1993. State of Environment in South-east Asia, Health and Environment. The Growing Challenge (Information Kit), March, New Delhi, India.

Yatri, P. P. 1983. Raute lok jivan [folk life of the Rautes]. Ministry of Communication, His Majesty's Government of Nepal, Kathmandu.

Index of Common Names

Cross-references are given from common names to scientific names of the plants, which are listed alphabetically in Chapter 4. The genera of conifers, fern allies, and ferns are also listed here under those names. References to page numbers are given in the Index of Scientific Names.

aaba (Sherpa), see *Coriaria napalensis*
aabhang (Chepang), see *Clerodendrum serratum*
aabo (Magar), see *Mangifera indica*
aachung (Tamang), see *Rubus macilentus*
aagjara lahara (Magar), see *Ficus sarmentosa*
aagra (Limbu), see *Phyllanthus emblica*
aaibe (Tibetan), see *Salvia hians, S. nubicola*
aaichuli (Chepang), see *Gonostegia hirta*
aailanta (Chepang), see *Pilea symmeria*
aajising (Limbu), see *Bauhinia variegata*
aakash beli (Chepang, Nepali), see *Cuscuta reflexa*
aakashe (Nepali), see *Cuscuta reflexa*
aakawa yob (Rai), see *Linum usitatissimum*
aakhataro (Tamang), see *Trichilia connaroides*
aakwabob (Rai), see *Brassica napus*
aalas (Bhojpuri, Chepang, Danuwar, Magar), see *Linum usitatissimum*
aalbokhra (Gurung), see *Prunus domestica*
aali jhar (Nepali), see *Eclipta prostrata*
aallu (Chepang), see *Solanum tuberosum*
aalo tanso (Tibetan), see *Rosa sericea*
aaltano (Tamang), see *Arisaema jacquemontii*
aalu (Bhojpuri, Gurung, Nepali, Newari, Rai), see *Solanum tuberosum*
aalu bakhar (Tharu), see *Prunus domestica*
aalubakhara (Bhojpuri), aalu bakhara (Magar, Tamang), see *Prunus domestica*
aalubuk (Lepcha), see *Solanum tuberosum*
aalucha (Newari), see *Prunus domestica*
aam (Majhi, Mooshar), see *Mangifera indica*
aa ma (Newari), see *Ricinus communis*
a-ama-bhe-da (Tibetan), see *Bergenia ciliata*
aamali (Newari), see *Choerospondias axillaris*
aamba (Gurung), see *Bauhinia malabarica*
aamba (Rai), see *Mangifera indica*

aambak (Limbu), see *Psidium guajava*
aambu (Tamang), see *Bauhinia malabarica*
aamnyai (Tamang), see *Scutellaria repens*
aampruk (Chepang), see *Abelmoschus moschatus*
aamrora (Mooshar), see *Anagallis arvensis*
aanbu (Tamang), see *Bauhinia variegata*
aanda kaule (Nepali), see *Brassica oleracea* var. *gemmifera*
aandro (Tamang), see *Saurauia napaulensis*
aang (Limbu), see *Pinus roxburghii*
aangdyan jhar (Chepang), see *Justicia procumbens* var. *simplex*
aank (Nepali), see *Calotropis gigantea*
aank (Sunwar), see *Zea mays*
aankale (Gurung), see *Drymaria diandra*
aankha pakuws (Nepali), see *Ficus subincisa*
aankhatare (Gurung), see *Trichilia connaroides*
aankhataruwa (Nepali), see *Trichilia connaroides*
aankhle (Nepali), see *Chirita urticifolia, Viola pilosa*
aankhle jhar (Nepali), see *Alternanthera sessilis, Equisetum diffusum, Euphorbia hirta, Hedyotis scandens, Lygodium japonicum*
aankhle kuro (Nepali), see *Cyathula tomentosa*
aankhu (Majhi), see *Saccharum officinarum*
aankhyailya (Raute), see *Equisetum diffusum*
aankuri bankuri (Nepali), see *Aeginetia indica*
aanp (Gurung, Nepali), see *Mangifera indica*
aant (Majhi, Tamang), see *Annona squamata*
aanta (Danuwar, Mooshar), see *Annona reticulata*
aanti (Nepali), see *Annona reticulata*
aanwala (Bhojpuri), see *Rhus javanica*
aarbale (Tamang), see *Osbeckia nepalensis, O. stellata*
aarbote (Tamang), see *Osbeckia stellata*
aaril (Nepali), see *Ricinus communis*
aarkhot (Magar), see *Ficus semicordata*
aarmale (Chepang), see *Drymaria diandra*
Aaron's rod (English), see *Verbascum thapsus*
aarpate (Tamang), see *Oxyspora paniculata*
aarpati (Tamang), see *Osbeckia nepalensis, O. stellata*
aaru (Danuwar), see *Prunus domestica*
aaru (Nepali), see *Prunus persica*
aaru bakhara (Nepali), see *Prunus domestica*
aarupate (Nepali), see *Prunus cornuta*
aaru pate (Nepali), see *Prunus napaulensis*
aarura (Lepcha), see *Prunus domestica*

aarya (Nepali), see *Prunus cornuta*
aasingdhap (Tamang), see *Viburnum mullaha*
aasingra dhun (Gurung), see *Viburnum mullaha*
aasinkra (Gurung), see *Viburnum mullaha*
aasuri (Gurung), see *Justicia adhatoda*
aasyangpolo (Tamang), see *Boehmeria platyphylla*
aate (Nepali), see *Potentilla argyrophylla*
aaunlesa (Magar), see *Phyllanthus emblica*
aayam muja (Chepang), see *Setaria glauca*
abijale (Chepang), see *Plumbago zeylanica*
abijalo (Nepali), see *Drymaria diandra, D. villosa*
a-bi-kha-zan-pa (Tibetan), see *Fritillaria cirrhosa*
a-bi-sa (Tibetan), see *Cajanus cajan*
abroma, cotton (English), see *Abroma angusta*
acacia, Persian (English), see *Albizia julibrissin*
acacia, sweet (English), see *Acacia farnesiana*
achhaphun (Limbu), see *Ocimum tenuiflorum*
aconite (English), see *Aconitum ferox*
aconite, Nepal (English), see *Aconitum spicatum*
adab (Gurung), see *Zingiber officinale*
adder's tongue (English), see *Ophioglossum nudicaule*
adimaro (Nepali), see *Rumex hastatus*
aduwa (Nepali), see *Zingiber officinale*
aek patiya (Tharu), see *Ophioglossum nudicaule*
agalai (Gurung), see *Acacia pennata*
agasti phul (Nepali), see *Sesbania grandiflora*
agela (Nepali), see *Acacia pennata*
agrakh (Tamang), see *Shorea robusta*
agras (Magar), see *Shorea robusta*
agrath (Nepali), see *Shorea robusta*
agrimony (English), see *Agrimonia pilosa*
agrimony, bastard (English), see *Ageratum conyzoides*
agrimony, common (English), see *Agrimonia pilosa*
aikh (Nepali), see *Aconitum spicatum*
ailo bikh (Nepali), see *Aconitum spicatum*
ainjero (Nepali), see *Scurrula elata*
ainjeru (Nepali), see *Dendrophthoe falcata, Helixanthera ligustrina,
    Loranthus odoratus, Scurrula parasitica, Viscum album*
ainjheru (Magar), see *Helixanthera ligustrina*
ainselu (Danuwar), see *Rubus ellipticus*
ainselu (Nepali), see *Rubus ellipticus, R. fockeanus, R. reticulatus, R.
    thomsonii*
ainselu (Tharu), see *Rubus ellipticus*
ainu (Nepali), see *Pteridium aquilinum*
airi lahara (Nepali), see *Ampelocissus rugosa*
ajamari (Nepali), see *Ipomoea carnea* subsp. *fistulosa*
ajamari jhar (Nepali), see *Kalanchoe spathulata*
ajibe (Tibetan), see *Salvia hians*
aji swan (Newari), see *Jasminum humile*
akakgachha (Danuwar), see *Jatropha curcas*
akamar (Nepali), see *Phyla nodiflora*
akamaro (Nepali), see *Achyranthes aspera*
akare (Nepali), see *Lathyrus aphaca*
akase chuk (Nepali), see *Rheum australe*
akhor (Gurung), see *Juglans regia* var. *kamaonia*
akino (Tibetan), see *Origanum vulgare*
akolkrim (Lepcha), see *Asparagus racemosus*
akolkrim khikkithuk (Lepcha), see *Asparagus racemosus*
akon (Danuwar, Mooshar), see *Calotropis gigantea*
alahan ma (Newari), see *Justicia adhatoda*
alang-alang (English), see *Imperata cylindrica*
alasi sai (Chepang), see *Diplokenma butyracea*
albi (Gurung), see *Rumex nepalensis*
albi (Tamang), see *Rumex nepalensis, Valeriana jatamansii*
alder, Nepalese (English), see *Alnus nepalensis*
algudi (Gurung), see *Debregeasia longifolia*
allo (Nepali), see *Girardinia diversifolia*

allu (Danuwar, Mooshar), see *Solanum tuberosum*
almond, Cuddapah (English), see *Buchanania latifolia*
almond, wild (English), see *Sterculia foetida*
aloe (English), see *Aloe vera*
aloe, Barbados (English), see *Aloe vera*
alpipi (Tamang), see *Rumex nepalensis*
alsi (Nepali), see *Linum usitatissimum*
amala (Gurung), see *Nephrolepis cordifolia*
amala (Majhi, Nepali), see *Phyllanthus emblica*
amala jhar (Nepali), see *Cassia mimosoides, Phyllanthus virgatus*
amali (Nepali), see *Antidesma acidum, Maclura cochinchinensis*
amaltas (Nepali), see *Cassia fistula*
amara (Nepali), see *Spondias pinnata*
amaranth, globe (English), see *Gomphrena globosa*
amaranth, prickly (English), see *Amaranthus spinosus*
amaraundha (Bhojpuri), see *Oxalis corniculata*
amaris (Chepang), see *Moringa oleifera*
amasi (Newari), see *Psidium guajava*
amati (Mooshar), see *Oxalis corniculata*
amato (Nepali), see *Spondias pinnata*
amba (Chepang, Majhi, Nepali), see *Psidium guajava*
amba (Newari), see *Phyllanthus emblica*
amba (Tamang), see *Mangifera indica, Psidium guajava*
ambake (Nepali), see *Eugenia formosa*
ambal bambul (Tamang), see *Osbeckia nepalensis*
ambali (Tamang), see *Nephrolepis cordifolia*
ambar (Nepali), see *Ammannia baccifera*
ambaru (Tamang), see *Psidium guajava*
amba singh (Tamang), see *Sedum wallichianum*
ambe (Limbu), see *Mangifera indica*
ambhok (Sunwar), see *Psidium guajava*
amble (Tamang), see *Phyllanthus emblica*
amchaucha (Tharu), see *Oxalis corniculata*
amil (Tharu), see *Rhus javanica*
amilchhe (Magar), see *Debregeasia salicifolia*
amile ghans (Nepali), see *Embelia vestita*
amili (Nepali), see *Oxalis corniculata, Rumex hastatus*
amilo (Nepali), see *Rhus javanica*
amjur (Tamang), see *Saurauia napaulensis*
ammarak (Chepang), see *Boehmeria platyphylla*
amphi (Nepali), see *Pyrularia edulis*
amra (Tibetan), see *Pyrus malus*
amreso (Nepali), see *Thysanolaena maxima*
amrisau (Nepali), see *Thysanolaena maxima*
amsi (Chepang), see *Saurauia napaulensis*
amti (Danuwar), see *Smithia sensitiva*
an (Newari), see *Mangifera indica*
ana-ga-ge-ser (Tibetan), see *Mesua ferrea*
anajamse (Limbu), see *Aegle marmelos*
anar (Bhojpuri, Lepcha, Mooshar, Nepali, Tharu), see *Punica
    granatum*
anare phul (Nepali), see *Woodfordia fruticosa*
anchirna (Nepali), see *Impatiens racemosa*
andi (Danuwar, Mooshar), see *Ricinus communis*
anemone, common wild (English), see *Anemone rivularis*
anemone, grape-leaved (English), see *Anemone vitifolia*
angale (Gurung), see *Galinsoga parviflora*
angale no (Gurung), see *Ageratum conyzoides*
angare (Magar), see *Lyonia ovalifolia*
angare (Nepali), see *Strobilanthes atropurpureus*
angel's trumpet (English), see *Datura stramonium*
anger (Gurung), see *Osbeckia nepalensis*
anger (Nepali), see *Lyonia ovalifolia*
angeri (Nepali), see *Melastoma malabathricum, Osbeckia nepalensis,
    O. stellata*
angerig (Nepali), see *Oxyspora paniculata*
angma (Rai), see *Pinus roxburghii*

angur (Nepali), see *Vitis vinifera*
anguri (Gurung), see *Melastoma malabathricum*
anise (English, Gurung), see *Pimpinella aniseum*
anjir (Nepali), see *Ficus carica*
ankale (Gurung), see *Galinsoga parviflora*
ankalw (Gurung), see *Drymaria diandra*
ankara (Mooshar), see *Vicia hirsuta*
ankejil guib (Sunwar), see *Linum usitatissimum*
anket (Raute), see *Calotropis gigantea*
ankhle (Nepali), see *Pteracanthus alatus*
ankkhen (Limbu), see *Allium ascalonicum*
annatto (English), see *Bixa orellana*
anselo (Sherpa), see *Rubus paniculatus*
antacha (Newari), see *Eclipta prostrata*
antali (Newari), see *Cyphomandra betacea, Eclipta prostrata*
anyar (Nepali), see *Lyonia ovalifolia*
anyi-ba (Tibetan), see *Chenopodium album*
aparijita (Nepali), see *Clitoria ternatea*
apong (Nepali), see *Dichanthium annulatum*
appa grass (English), see *Ageratum conyzoides*
apple (English), see *Pyrus malus*
apple, balsam (English), see *Momordica balsamina*
apple, custard (English), see *Annona reticulata, A. squamata*
apple, elephant (English), see *Dillenia indica*
apple, golden (English), see *Spondias pinnata*
apple, love (English), see *Paris polyphylla*
apple, May (English), see *Podophyllum hexandrum*
apple, rose (English), see *Syzygium jambos*
apple, sugar (English), see *Annona reticulata, A. squamata*
apple, thorn (English), see *Datura metel, D. stramonium*
apricot (English), see *Prunus armeniaca*
aputo (Nepali), see *Holmskioldia sanguinea*
aragi (Magar), see *Pinus roxburghii*
arai (Tamang), see *Mimosa rubicaulis* subsp. *himalayana*
arali (Majhi), see *Mimosa rubicaulis* subsp. *himalayana*
arali (Nepali), see *Acacia rugata*
aramina (English), see *Urena lobata*
aranth (Nepali), see *Skimmia laureola*
arari (Danuwar), see *Jatropha curcas*
arari (Nepali), see *Mimosa rubicaulis* subsp. *himalayana*
arasi (Tharu), see *Linum usitatissimum*
arbaje jhar (Nepali), see *Schoenoplectus juncoides*
arbale (Nepali), see *Osbeckia nepalensis*
archal (Nepali), see *Antidesma acidum*
areca nut tree (English), see *Areca catechu*
areli (Magar, Nepali), see *Hypericum cordifolium*
areli kanda (Nepali), see *Mimosa rubicaulis* subsp. *himalayana*
aren (Majhi), see *Jatropha curcas*
arend (Nepali), see *Ricinus communis*
arer (Nepali), see *Ricinus communis*
areri (Nepali), see *Acacia pennata*
areth (Chepang), see *Ricinus communis*
areto (Nepali), see *Hypericum cordifolium*
a-rga (Tibetan), see *Calotropis gigantea*
argeli (Nepali), see *Edgeworthia gardneri*
argho (Danuwar), see *Cassia fistula*
aril (Majhi), see *Jatropha curcas*
arile kanda (Nepali), see *Caesalpinia decapetala*
arin (Nepali), see *Jatropha curcas*
arjun (Nepali), see *Terminalia arjuna*
arkale (Gurung), see *Cynoglossum zeylanicum*
arkale pat (Nepali), see *Edgeworthia gardneri*
arkhaulo (Nepali), see *Lithocarpus elegans*
arkhen khar (Nepali), see *Eulaliopsis binata*
arkhu (Magar), see *Acacia intsia, Mimosa rubicaulis* subsp. *himalayana*
arkhu (Nepali), see *Acacia intsia, A. pennata*

armale (Nepali), see *Anagallis arvensis*
armale jhar (Nepali), see *Stellaria media*
armalito (Nepali), see *Hippophae tibetana*
armane (Nepali), see *Stellaria vestita*
arnema (Mooshar), see *Carica papaya*
arphu (Nepali), see *Acacia pennata*
arrow wood (English), see *Viburnum cylindricum*
arthunge (Chepang), see *Tetrastigma serrulatum*
arthunge (Nepali), see *Bidens pilosa* var. *minor, Combretum roxburghii, Heteropogon contortus*
aru (Danuwar, Tharu), see *Prunus persica*
a-ru (Tibetan), see *Terminalia chebula*
arubharelu (Sherpa), see *Terminalia chebula*
arui (Bhojpuri), see *Colocasia esculenta, Prunus persica*
arum (English), see *Colocasia esculenta*
a-ru-ra (Tibetan), see *Terminalia chebula*
aruwa (Danuwar), see *Ipomoea batatas*
aruwa (Tharu), see *Dioscorea deltoidea*
asana (Danuwar, Nepali), see *Terminalia alata*
asanyam (Chepang), see *Clausena excavata*
asare (Nepali), see *Cipadessa baccifera*
asare (Satar), see *Aegle marmelos*
asare phui (Nepali), see *Luculia gratissima*
asare phul (Nepali), see *Lagerstroemia indica, Osbeckia stellata, Quisqualis indica, Telosma pallida*
asari (Nepali), see *Mussaenda frondosa, M. macrophylla*
asaria (Satar), see *Capparis spinosa*
aser (Satar), see *Dioscorea pentaphylla*
ash, Himalayan (English), see *Fraxinus floribunda*
ashok (Nepali), see *Polyalthia longifolia, Saraca asoca*
ashok (Tharu), see *Cassia fistula*
asidha (Tharu), see *Terminalia bellirica*
asinam sai (Chepang), see *Cipadessa baccifera*
asith (Tharu), see *Lagerstroemia parviflora*
asparagus, wild (English), see *Asparagus racemosus*
aster, China (English), see *Callistephus chinensis*
asthma weed (English), see *Euphorbia hirta*
asuk (Nepali), see *Hippophae tibetana*
asura (Danuwar, Rai), see *Justicia adhatoda*
asuro (Bhojpuri, Nepali), see *Justicia adhatoda*
atenu (Nepali), see *Gonostegia hirta*
ater (Chepang), see *Ricinus communis*
aterno (Nepali), see *Gonostegia hirta*
athareti (Danuwar), see *Elephantopus scaber*
atibish (Nepali), see *Aconitum spicatum*
atinno (Nepali), see *Gonostegia hirta*
atish (Nepali), see *Delphinium vestitum*
atkir (Satar), see *Mucuna nigricans*
atvhowa (Sherpa), see *Rheum australe*
aul aanp (Nepali), see *Passiflora edulis*
aul chotra (Nepali), see *Berberis asiatica*
aule (Nepali), see *Croton roxburghii*
aule bayar (Nepali), see *Ziziphus oenoplia*
aule ghor (Tamang), see *Viola pilosa*
aule sag (Nepali), see *Boerhavia diffusa*
aule salla (Nepali), see *Pinus roxburghii*
aulo kuro (Nepali), see *Cyathula tomentosa*
aura (Danuwar), see *Phyllanthus acidus*
aura (Tharu), see *Phyllanthus emblica*
aurya (Raute), see *Phyllanthus emblica*
axle wood (English), see *Anogeissus latifolius*
babatimta (Tamang), see *Hypericum elodeoides*
babi (Chepang), see *Eulaliopsis binata*
babiyo (Nepali), see *Eulaliopsis binata*
babre ghans (Nepali), see *Scutellaria barbata*
babul (Nepali), see *Acacia nilotica*
bach (Newari), see *Acorus calamus*

bachau (Chepang), see *Sporobolus fertilis*
bachelor's button (English), see *Gomphrena globosa*
bachi (Newari), see *Oroxylum indicum*
bachinampa (Rai), see *Acorus calamus*
bacon weed (English), see *Chenopodium album*
badake chorant (Majhi), see *Xanthium strumarium*
badaki ganhuwa (Danuwar), see *Blumea lacera*
badam (Chepang, Danuwar, Lepcha, Magar, Nepali, Sunwar, Tamang), see *Arachis hypogaea*
badam (Mooshar), see *Cicer arietinum*
badar (Chepang), see *Artocarpus lakoocha*
badarsing (Tamang), see *Leucosceptrum canum*
badbada (Tamang), see *Viburnum cylindricum*
bagajari (Nepali), see *Potentilla fulgens*
bagal (Chepang), see *Prunus persica*
bagan (Nepali), see *Clerodendrum viscosum*
bagani dhap (Tamang), see *Amaranthus spinosus, A. viridis*
bagarni (Danuwar), see *Calotropis gigantea*
baghandi (Mooshar), see *Jatropha curcas*
baghjunge (Magar), see *Clematis buchananiana*
baghjwen (Nepali), see *Clematis buchananiana*
bagh mukhe (Nepali), see *Capparis spinosa*
baghmukhe ghans (Nepali), see *Lindenbergia indica*
bagh paile (Nepali), see *Anemone rivularis*
bagul (Nepali), see *Holboellia latifolia*
bahare (Bhojpuri), see *Terminalia bellirica*
baher (Gurung), see *Ziziphus mauritiana*
bahidaro (Nepali), see *Lagerstroemia parviflora*
bahiro (Nepali), see *Glochidion velutinum*
bahun lahara (Nepali), see *Lygodium japonicum*
baigan (Bhojpuri), see *Solanum melongena*
bail fruit tree (English), see *Aegle marmelos*
bains (Gurung), see *Salix denticulata*
bains (Nepali), see *Salix babylonica*
baisi (Rai), see *Castanopsis indica*
bajara (Nepali), see *Thalictrum foliolosum*
bajar bhanga (Nepali), see *Hyoscyamus niger* var. *agrestis*
bajardante (Nepali), see *Murraya paniculata*
bajardanti (Chepang), see *Mahonia napaulensis*
bajarjanti (Nepali), see *Randia tetrasperma*
bajhar (Sherpa), see *Sorbus microphylla*
bajhiya (Danuwar), see *Woodfordia fruticosa*
bajra danti (Nepali), see *Potentilla fulgens, P. supina*
bajuri (Magar), see *Thalictrum foliolosum*
bakain (Bhojpuri, Tharu), see *Melia azedarach*
bakaina (Chepang, Sunwar, Tamang), see *Melia azedarach*
bakaino (Nepali), see *Melia azedarach*
bakainu (Danuwar, Gurung, Magar, Majhi), see *Melia azedarach*
bakala (Nepali), see *Vicia faba*
bakal pate (Nepali), see *Cleyera japonica, Myrsine capitellata*
bakalpate (Nepali), see *Osmanthus fragrans* var. *longifolia*
bakalpati (Nepali), see *Viburnum cylindricum*
bakan (Chepang), see *Clerodendrum japonicum*
bakan (Newari), see *Amaranthus spinosus*
bakarphawa khangn (Rai), see *Brassica oleracea* var. *capitata*
bakasyitong (Tamang), see *Melia azedarach*
bakhara pire (Nepali), see *Spermadictyon suaveolens*
bakhra kane (Nepali), see *Inula cappa, Oxyspora paniculata*
bakhre (Majhi), see *Spermadictyon suaveolens*
bakhre aankhla (Nepali), see *Persicaria perfoliata*
bakhre biri (Nepali), see *Leptodermis lanceolata*
bakhre darim (Magar), see *Osyris wightiana, Desmodium elegans, D. heterocarpon, D. multiflorum, D. triflorum, Reinwardtia indica, Sarcococca coriacea*
bakhre ghans (Nepali), see *Crotalaria cytisoides*
bakhre kanda (Nepali), see *Randia tetrasperma*
bakhre khursani (Nepali), see *Osyris wightiana*

bakhre saro (Nepali), see *Curcuma angustifolia*
bakhre thotne (Nepali), see *Persicaria chinensis*
bakhri lahara (Nepali), see *Hedyotis scandens*
bakremala (Magar), see *Homalium napaulense*
baktusing (Limbu), see *Arundo donax*
bakucha ghyan (Newari), see *Centella asiatica*
bakula (Newari), see *Vicia faba*
bakyan (Tharu), see *Melia azedarach*
bala (Newari), see *Terminalia bellirica*
bala mhendo (Tamang), see *Hibiscus rosa-sinensis*
bala mran (Tamang), see *Scutellaria discolor*
balba pungi (Tamang), see *Boehmeria platyphylla*
balde mran (Tamang), see *Galinsoga quadriradiata*
balden dhap (Tamang), see *Galinsoga parviflora*
baldhendro (Nepali), see *Mucuna nigricans*
bale banso (Nepali), see *Setaria glauca*
balloon vine (English), see *Cardiospermum halicacabum*
balsam (English), see *Impatiens balsamina*
balsam apple (English), see *Momordica balsamina*
balu (Gurung), see *Triumfetta rhomboides*
balu (Nepali), see *Sida acuta, S. cordata*
balu changsing (Sherpa), see *Rhododendron anthopogon*
balu jhar (Nepali), see *Corchorus aestuans, Sida rhombifolia*
balu kapo (Sherpa), see *Rhododendron anthopogon*
balu kuro (Nepali), see *Triumfetta rhomboides*
balu mhendo (Tamang), see *Rhododendron lepidotum*
baluni sag (Nepali), see *Polygonum plebejum*
balwapoungi (Tamang), see *Debregeasia longifolia*
bamboo, giant (English), see *Dendrocalamus giganteus*
bamboo, Himalayan (English), see *Drepanostachyum falcatum*
bamboo, male (English), see *Dendrocalamus strictus*
bamboo, solid (English), see *Dendrocalamus strictus*
bamboo, tufted (English), see *Dendrocalamus hamiltonii*
bamboo reed (English), see *Arundo donax*
banada kopi (Sunwar), see *Brassica oleracea* var. *capitata*
ban ainselu (Nepali), see *Rubus reticulatus, R. rugosus*
banalhapte (Tamang), see *Curculigo orchioides*
ban amre (Magar), see *Rhus succedanea*
banana (English), see *Musa paradisiaca*
banara (Tharu), see *Setaria glauca*
banarbhega (Tharu), see *Sagittaria guayanensis*
banare (Nepali), see *Macaranga pustulata*
banarsota (Danuwar), see *Cassia fistula*
ban baikal (Raute), see *Solanum aculeatissimum*
banban (Tamang), see *Verbascum thapsus*
ban bans (Nepali), see *Bambusa balcooa*
banbare (Nepali), see *Oxyria digyna*
ban bawari (Nepali), see *Elsholtzia strobilifera, Geniosporum coloratum, Hyptis suaveolens, Lindenbergia indica, Salvia plebeia*
ban beli (Nepali), see *Jasminum multiflorum*
ban besar (Gurung), see *Hedychium ellipticum*
ban besar (Nepali), see *Cautleya spicata*
banbhande (Nepali), see *Fagopyrum dibotrys*
ban bhande (Nepali), see *Houttuynia cordata*
ban bhanta (Nepali), see *Podophyllum hexandrum*
ban bhart (Tharu), see *Cajanus scarabaeoides*
ban bhata (Nepali), see *Rhynchosia himalensis*
ban bheri (Nepali), see *Abelmoschus moschatus*
ban bihi (Nepali), see *Solanum torvum*
banbiri (Nepali), see *Neohymenopogon parasiticus*
ban bori (Chepang), see *Cajanus scarabaeoides*
ban chansur (Nepali), see *Erysimum hieraciifolium*
banchet (Tamang), see *Quercus lamellosa*
ban chichinda (Chepang), see *Cardiospermum halicacabum*
ban chitu (Nepali), see *Euonymus hamiltonianus*
ban chiya (Nepali), see *Camellia kissi*
ban chiyapate (Nepali), see *Osyris wightiana*

ban chulo (Nepali), see *Viburnum erubescens*

ban chutro (Chepang), see *Berberis aristata*

banda (Nepali, Newari), see *Brassica oleracea* var. *capitata*

banda gobi (Gurung, Tamang), see *Brassica oleracea* var. *capitata*

banda kaule (Nepali), see *Brassica oleracea* var. *capitata*

banda kobhi (Magar), see *Brassica oleracea* var. *capitata*

banda kobi (Bhojpuri, Danuwar), see *Brassica oleracea* var. *capitata*

banda kobi (Nepali), see *Brassica oleracea* var. *capitata*

bandani (Nepali), see *Amaranthus spinosus*

bandar guli (Nepali), see *Eriosema himalaicum*

bandar puchhare (Nepali), see *Scrophularia urticifolia, Verbascum thapsus*

bande kuro (Nepali), see *Barleria cristata*

bandhana (Nepali), see *Eryngium foetidum*

bandhan jhar (Nepali), see *Sporobolus fertilis*

bandra ghans (Nepali), see *Setaria glauca*

bandre (Nepali), see *Helicia nilagirica*

ban dudhe (Nepali), see *Picris hieracioides* subsp. *kaimaensis*

ban gahate (Nepali), see *Cajanus scarabaeoides*

bangaja (Nepali), see *Neohymenopogon parasiticus*

bangat (Gurung), see *Desmodium heterocarpon*

bange kath (Nepali), see *Populus ciliata*

banger (Tamang), see *Ziziphus incurva*

bangikot (Nepali), see *Populus ciliata*

bangpahar (Chepang), see *Thalictrum foliolosum*

ban gurdabari (Chepang), see *Dipsacus inermis*

banidare (Satar), see *Ficus benghalensis*

banjari (Tamang), see *Curculigo orchioides*

ban jawan (Gurung), see *Thymus linearis*

banjh (Nepali), see *Quercus lanata*

banjhari (Nepali), see *Osyris wightiana*

banjhi (Danuwar), see *Lagerstroemia parviflora*

banjhi (Nepali), see *Annona squamata, Quercus leucotrichophora*

banjho (Majhi), see *Quercus lanata*

ban juhi (Nepali), see *Lonicera macarantha*

ban kamal (Nepali), see *Manglietia insignis*

ban kane (Nepali), see *Commelina benghalensis*

ban kangiyo (Nepali), see *Luculia gratissima*

ban kankri (Nepali), see *Solena heterophylla*

ban kanyu (Nepali), see *Wendlandia coriacea, W. puberula*

ban kapas (Magar), see *Thespesia lampas*

ban kapas (Nepali), see *Abelmoschus manihot, A. moschatus, Thespesia lampas*

ban kapase (Nepali), see *Grewia subinaequalis*

ban karkal (Nepali), see *Sauromatum brevipes*

ban karyal (Nepali), see *Dipsacus inermis*

bankasi khar (Nepali), see *Eulaliopsis binata*

ban kauli (Nepali), see *Gentiana capitata*

bankhor (Nepali), see *Aesculus indica*

banko (Nepali), see *Arisaema flavum, A. tortuosum*

banku (Chepang), see *Arisaema consanguineum*

ban kuro (Nepali), see *Triumfetta pilosa, T. rhomboides*

ban kurthi (Danuwar), see *Cajanus scarabaeoides*

ban kurthi (Tharu), see *Crotalaria alata*

ban lasun (Nepali), see *Abelmoschus manihot, Allium wallichii, Lilium nepalense*

ban lunde (Nepali), see *Amaranthus lividus*

banlunde (Nepali), see *Amaranthus spinosus*

ban maiser (Chepang), see *Coelogyne cristata*

banmakai (Nepali), see *Grewia helicterifolia*

ban mala (Nepali), see *Lycopodium clavatum*

banmara (Danuwar), see *Eupatorium adenophorum*

banmara (Nepali), see *Eupatorium adenophorum, E. chinense, E. odoratum*

banmaruwa (Tamang), see *Eupatorium adenophorum*

banmasa (Nepali), see *Eupatorium adenophorum*

banmasuwa (Nepali), see *Eupatorium odoratum*

ban mran (Tamang), see *Stellaria monosperma*

ban namsai (Chepang), see *Salvia plebeia*

banno ba (Tamang), see *Senecio wallichii*

ban paiyun (Nepali), see *Prunus cerasoides*

ban palungo (Nepali), see *Rumex dentatus* subsp. *klotzschianus*

banpan (Tharu), see *Hemigraphis hirta*

ban pate (Nepali), see *Melochia corchorifolia, Pouzolzia zeylanica*

ban pharsi (Nepali), see *Trichosanthes wallichiana*

ban pipal (Nepali), see *Sapium baccatum*

ban pipla (Nepali), see *Piper peepuloides*

ban pire (Nepali), see *Persicaria microcephala*

ban pyaj (Nepali), see *Chlorophytum nepalense*

ban rayo (Nepali), see *Sonchus wightianus*

ban sampu (Nepali), see *Bupleurum hamiltonii, Selinum tenuifolium*

ban semi (Nepali), see *Ceropegia pubescens*

bansi (Nepali), see *Quercus lamellosa*

bansi (Rai), see *Rubus ellipticus*

ban silam (Nepali), see *Elsholtzia blanda, E. ciliata, E. flava, E. stachyodes*

banso (Nepali), see *Digitaria ciliaris, Ischaemum rugosum* var. *segetum, Paspalum scrobiculatum*

banspate (Nepali), see *Brachiaria ramosa*

bansuli (Nepali), see *Dichroa febrifuga, Thalictrum foliolosum*

ban tarul (Nepali), see *Dioscorea bulbifera*

ban timila (Nepali), see *Ficus sarmentosa*

ban timur (Nepali), see *Heracleum nepalense, Zanthoxylum nepalense, Z. oxyphyllum*

ban tori (Danuwar), see *Blumeopsis flava*

banwar (Nepali), see *Tinospora sinensis*

banyan tree (English), see *Ficus benghalensis*

bar (Bhojpuri, Chepang, Danuwar, Gurung, Magar, Mooshar, Nepali, Sunwar), see *Ficus benghalensis*

bara (Rai), see *Ficus benghalensis*

baragaunlo (Nepali), see *Tetrastigma serrulatum*

barahar (Danuwar, Mooshar, Nepali), see *Artocarpus lakoocha*

baral (Gurung), see *Artocarpus lakoocha*

baral (Tamang), see *Semecarpus anacardium*

baranha (Newari), see *Arachis hypogaea*

barbanda (Tharu), see *Argemone mexicana*

barbande (Nepali), see *Fagopyrum dibotrys*

barbere (Nepali), see *Pouzolzia zeylanica*

barberry (English), see *Berberis aristata, B. asiatica*

bardanti (Nepali), see *Ligustrum confusum*

barela (Nepali), see *Cyclanthera pedata, Momordica balsamina*

barela (Newari), see *Cyclanthera pedata*

barera (Nepali), see *Sida rhombifolia*

bargad (Tharu), see *Ficus benghalensis*

barhamase chutro (Nepali), see *Berberis aristata, B. wallichiana*

barhamase phul (Nepali), see *Catharanthus roseus*

bariyar (Danuwar), see *Sida acuta, S. rhombifolia*

bariyar (Mooshar), see *Urena lobata*

barjhum mhendo (Tamang), see *Rhododendron lowndesii*

barka chirchiri (Danuwar), see *Cynoglossum glochidiatum*

barka gurubands (Tharu), see *Mirabilis jalapa*

barka regmi (Danuwar), see *Solanum aculeatissimum*

barkauli jhar (Nepali), see *Flemingia strobilifera*

barkaunle (Nepali), see *Arisaema tortuosum*

barkha jyal (Gurung), see *Dicentra scandens*

barkhe kane (Nepali), see *Senecio cappa*

barkhe lahara (Nepali), see *Parthenocissus semicordata*

barkhyu lahara (Nepali), see *Tetrastigma serrulatum*

barkichakor (Danuwar), see *Cassia occidentalis*

barley (English), see *Hordeum vulgare*

barley, pearl (English), see *Coix lachryma-jobi*

barmale (Nepali), see *Oxyria digyna*

barma salla (Nepali), see *Taxus baccata* subsp. *wallichiana*

barno (Sunwar), see *Buddleja asiatica*

baro (Sunwar), see *Euphorbia royleana*
barro (Danuwar, Gurung, Nepali, Sunwar), see *Terminalia bellirica*
baru (Satar), see *Schleichera oleosa*
ba-ru (Tibetan), see *Terminalia bellirica*
barun (Nepali), see *Crateva unilocularis*
baruwa (Nepali), see *Daphne bholua*
basak (Chepang, Magar, Nepali), see *Dichroa febrifuga*
basak (Tamang), see *Justicia adhatoda*
basalki (Tamang), see *Eriophorum comosum*
basana (Nepali), see *Cestrum nocturnum*
basant (Gurung), see *Dendranthema nubigenum*
basante kanda (Nepali), see *Randia tetrasperma*
basdamrat (Chepang), see *Pogostemon benghalensis*
basekre (Chepang), see *Thunbergia coccinea*
ba-sha-ka (Tibetan), see *Justicia adhatoda*
basi (Newari), see *Prunus persica*
basil, sacred (English), see *Ocimum tenuiflorum*
bas phul (Nepali), see *Caesalpinia pulcherrima*
basupaku (Chepang), see *Portulaca oleracea*
batal (Gurung), see *Artocarpus lakoocha*
batan gobi (Nepali), see *Brassica oleracea* var. *gemmifera*
bathu (Nepali), see *Chenopodium album*
bathure (Chepang), see *Thalictrum foliolosum*
bathuri (Tamang), see *Thalictrum foliolosum*
bathuwa (Danuwar, Mooshar), see *Chenopodium album*
batule (Nepali), see *Wulfenia amherstiana*
batuli silam (Nepali), see *Craniotome furcata*
batulpate (Majhi), see *Cissampelos pareira*
batulpate (Nepali), see *Cissampelos pareira, Stephania japonica*
batya (Raute), see *Flemingia strobilifera*
baugureti (Nepali), see *Murraya koenigii*
bauhinia, variegated (English), see *Bauhinia variegata*
baulacha (Gurung), see *Lecanthus peduncularis*
bau swan (Newari), see *Nerium indicum*
bawage (Limbu), see *Elsholtzia blanda*
bawar (Nepali), see *Dendrobium longicornu*
bawari (Danuwar), see *Hyptis suaveolens*
bawari (Gurung, Tamang, Tharu), see *Mentha spicata*
bawari (Nepali), see *Mentha spicata, Ocimum basilicum*
bay, bull (English), see *Magnolia grandiflora*
bayakhra (Nepali), see *Botrychium multifidum*
bayali (Newari), see *Ziziphus mauritiana*
bayar (Chepang, Danuwar), see *Ziziphus mauritiana*
bayar (Tamang), see *Ziziphus mauritiana, Z. oenoplia*
bayar (Tharu), see *Ziziphus oenoplia*
bay berry (English), see *Myrica esculenta*
bayer (Nepali, Newari, Tharu), see *Ziziphus mauritiana*
beachberry, tall (English), see *Gmelina arborea*
beach tree, Indian (English), see *Millettia pinnata*
bead tree, utrasum (English), see *Elaeocarpus sphaericus*
bead vine (English), see *Abrus precatorius*
bean, asparagus (English), see *Vigna unguiculata*
bean, bonavist (English), see *Lablab purpureus*
bean, broad (English), see *Vicia faba*
bean, dwarf (English), see *Phaseolus vulgaris*
bean, fava (English), see *Vicia faba*
bean, field (English), see *Phaseolus vulgaris*
bean, French (English), see *Phaseolus vulgaris*
bean, garden (English), see *Phaseolus vulgaris, Vicia faba*
bean, haricot (English), see *Phaseolus vulgaris*
bean, horse (English), see *Canavalia cathartica, Vicia faba*
bean, hyacinth (English), see *Lablab purpureus*
bean, jack (English), see *Canavalia cathartica*
bean, jequirith (English), see *Abrus precatorius*
bean, kidney (English), see *Phaseolus vulgaris*
bean, lablab (English), see *Lablab purpureus*
bean, licorice (English), see *Abrus precatorius*

bean, moth (English), see *Phaseolus aconitifolius*
bean, nicker (English), see *Entada phaseoloides*
bean, St. Thomas (English), see *Entada phaseoloides*
bean, Scotch (English), see *Vicia faba*
bean, soya (English), see *Glycine max*
bean, sword (English), see *Canavalia cathartica*
bean, Windsor (English), see *Vicia faba*
beauty berry (English), see *Callicarpa macrophylla*
bebali kanda (Nepali), see *Caragana brevispina*
bechar (Tamang), see *Prinsepia utilis*
bedango (Nepali), see *Astilbe rivularis*
bedu (Nepali), see *Ficus palmata*
beefsteak plant (English), see *Perilla frutescens*
begabu (Tamang), see *Sida cordata*
begar mai (Gurung), see *Corydalis chaerophylla*
begelau (Chepang), see *Pilea anisophylla*
beggar's button (English), see *Arctium lappa*
beggar's stick (English), see *Bidens pilosa* var. *minor*
beggar's-ticks, hairy (English), see *Bidens pilosa* var. *minor*
beghar (Tibetan), see *Quercus lanata*
behaya (Nepali, Tharu), see *Ipomoea carnea* subsp. *fistulosa*
bekalang (Tamang), see *Nephrolepis cordifolia*
bekar mai (Gurung), see *Thalictrum foliolosum*
bel (Danuwar, Majhi, Mooshar, Nepali, Rai, Sunwar, Tharu), see
   Aegle marmelos
bel (Tamang), see *Aegle marmelos, Rhododendron campanulatum*
belaiti jhar (Nepali), see *Rotala indica*
belakhan (Rai), see *Cinnamomum tamala*
belar (Nepali), see *Trewia nudiflora*
belasi (Chepang), see *Aegle marmelos*
belauki (Danuwar), see *Psidium guajava*
belauri (Gurung), see *Costus speciosus*
belauti (Magar), see *Psidium guajava*
belchadna (Nepali), see *Hibiscus sabdariffa*
bel dhap (Tamang), see *Launaea aspleniifolia*
belekhar mhenso (Tamang), see *Quercus floribunda*
beli phul (Nepali), see *Jasminum sambac*
belladona, sweet (English), see *Phytolacca acinosa*
bello (Nepali), see *Ficus subincisa*
bellyache bush (English), see *Jatropha gossypifolia*
belo (Raute), see *Diplocyclos palmatus*
belochan (Nepali), see *Geum elatum*
belpit (Lepcha), see *Aegle marmelos*
bena (Tamang), see *Quercus semecarpifolia*
bendasi (Rai), see *Lycopersicon esculentum*
bengo nari (Satar), see *Dioscorea bulbifera*
benne (English), see *Sesamum orientale*
bepane danti (Nepali), see *Jatropha gossypifolia*
bepari (Nepali), see *Ostodes paniculata*
berkap (Nepali), see *Castanopsis indica*
berkap (Tamang), see *Castanopsis indica, Quercus lanata*
beru (Nepali), see *Ficus palmata*
berulo (Nepali), see *Ficus palmata, F. sarmentosa, F. subincisa*
besar (Chepang, Danuwar, Magar, Nepali, Tharu), see *Curcuma*
   domestica
besi banmara (Magar), see *Eupatorium odoratum*
besya (Tamang), see *Buddleja asiatica*
betel nut palm (English), see *Areca catechu*
bethe (Gurung), see *Chenopodium album*
bethe (Nepali), see *Polygonum plebejum*
bethe gan (Magar), see *Chenopodium album*
bethu arak (Satar), see *Chenopodium album*
betlauri (Nepali), see *Costus speciosus*
betu (Tamang), see *Chenopodium ambrosoides*
bhada (Nepali, Tharu), see *Cyperus rotundus*
bhada (Tibetan), see *Rubia manjith*
bhadal (Nepali), see *Catunaregam spinosa*

bhainsaino (Nepali), see *Lespedeza juncea*

bhainse laharo (Nepali), see *Clematis connata*

bhainsi kanda (Gurung), see *Catunaregam spinosa*

bhainsi kanda (Nepali), see *Rosa brunonii*

bhaint (Mooshar), see *Clerodendrum viscosum*

bhairung pate (Nepali), see *Potentilla fruticosa*

bhaise selang (Chepang), see *Hyptis suaveolens*

bhaising (Chepang), see *Millettia extensa*

bhaisya marelo (Magar), see *Anemone vitifolia*

bhaji (Magar), see *Brassica juncea* var. *cuneifolia*

bhajuri (Chepang), see *Thalictrum foliolosum*

bhakamad (Chepang), see *Curculigo orchioides*

bhakari (Sunwar), see *Rhus javanica*

bhakhre (Tamang), see *Spermadictyon suaveolens*

bhakiamilo (Danuwar), bhaki amilo (Nepali), see *Rhus javanica*

bhakmat (Chepang), see *Calotropis gigantea*

bhakri (Rai), see *Sapindus mukorossi*

bhakundo (Danuwar), see *Persicaria barbata*

bhalay (Majhi), see *Semecarpus anacardium*

bhalayo (Nepali), see *Rhus succedanea, Semecarpus anacardium*

bhale bhringaraj (Nepali), see *Alternanthera sessilis*

bhale jhinu (Nepali), see *Eurya cerasifolia*

bhale mauwa (Nepali), see *Engelhardia spicata*

bhale mulapate (Nepali), see *Sonchus wightianus*

bhalenakabhyak (Tamang), see *Oleandra wallichii*

bhale sunpati (Nepali), see *Rhododendron lepidotum*

bhale timur (Nepali), see *Zanthoxylum armatum*

bhalkanda (Nepali), see *Solanum aculeatissimum*

bhalu ainselu (Nepali), see *Rubus paniculatus*

bhalu bans (Nepali), see *Bambusa balcooa, Dendrocalamus giganteus, D. hookeri*

bhalu kanda (Nepali), see *Rhamnus virgatus, Rubus griffithii*

bhalu kath (Nepali), see *Talauma hodgsonii*

bhalu musa (Majhi), see *Kalanchoe spathulata*

bhalunakpo (Tibetan), see *Rhododendron lepidotum*

bhalu paile (Nepali), see *Alangium chinense*

bhamar (Nepali), see *Viburnum erubescens*

bham salla (Nepali), see *Taxus baccata* subsp. *wallichiana*

bhan bhaniya (Danuwar), see *Clausena excavata*

bhande (Nepali), see *Fagopyrum dibotrys*

bhang (Nepali), see *Cannabis sativa*

bhanga (Raute), see *Cannabis sativa*

bhangarail (Tharu), see *Eclipta prostrata*

bhangariya (Danuwar), see *Eclipta prostrata*

bhangeri (Nepali), see *Eclipta prostrata*

bhangil (Nepali), see *Rhus javanica*

bhango (Magar, Nepali), see *Cannabis sativa*

bhangtya (Tamang), see *Colocasia esculenta*

bhangu aamcho (Tibetan), see *Kalanchoe spathulata*

bhanta (Danuwar, Magar, Mooshar, Nepali, Tamang, Tharu), see *Solanum melongena*

bhanth (Tharu), see *Clerodendrum viscosum*

bhanti (Danuwar, Magar), see *Clerodendrum viscosum*

bhantilo (Chepang), see *Clerodendrum viscosum*

bharama (Sherpa), see *Cotoneaster microphyllus*

bharaun (Nepali), see *Boehmeria polystachya*

bharda (Nepali), see *Roscoea alpina*

bhargi (Nepali), see *Clerodendrum indicum*

bharla (Rai), see *Bauhinia vahlii*

bharthar (Tharu), see *Glycine max*

bhasan (Newari), see *Fagopyrum esculentum*

bhasin (Chepang), see *Castanopsis indica*

bhasipsip (Tamang), see *Periploca calophylla*

bhaska (Tamang), see *Cipadessa baccifera*

bhat (Nepali), see *Clerodendrum viscosum*

bhatako (Nepali), see *Desmodium confertum*

bhatamase ghans (Nepali), see *Desmodium confertum*

bhatamase lahara (Nepali), see *Flemingia macrophylla*

bhatarya pat (Nepali), see *Teucrium quadrifarium*

bhatik tikta (Tibetan), see *Veronica anagallis-aquatica*

bhatmas (Bhojpuri, Chepang, Danuwar, Nepali), see *Glycine max*

bhatmas phul (Nepali), see *Desmodium multiflorum*

bhatt (Nepali), see *Desmodium confertum*

bhatta (Magar), see *Glycine max*

bhatte (Magar), see *Desmodium multiflorum*

bhatte (Majhi), see *Phyllodium pulchellum*

bhatte (Nepali), see *Cassia floribunda, Desmodium multiflorum, Flemingia chappar*

bhattemla (Nepali), see *Anemone rivularis*

bhayamara (Chepang), see *Eupatorium odoratum*

bhayar (Gurung), see *Ziziphus mauritiana*

bhayo (Gurung), see *Rhus succedanea*

bhedi phul (Nepali), see *Crotalaria albida, Lindenbergia grandiflora*

bhekpadi (Nepali), see *Verbena officinalis*

bhel (Nepali, Tamang), see *Solanum aculeatissimum*

bhela (Tharu), see *Semecarpus anacardium*

bhel dhap (Tamang), see *Lannea coromandelica*

bhelo (Sherpa), see *Quercus semecarpifolia*

bhenda ghans (Nepali), see *Impatiens puberula*

bhende kuro (Nepali), see *Cynoglossum glochidiatum, Xanthium strumarium*

bheno (Gurung), see *Quercus semecarpifolia*

bhenri (Tharu), see *Murraya koenigii*

bhenta (Sunwar), see *Solanum melongena*

bhera jhar (Nepali), see *Ageratum conyzoides*

bherakuro (Nepali), see *Agrimonia pilosa*

bhere jhar (Nepali), see *Urena lobata*

bhere kuro (Nepali), see *Clematis grewiiflora, Cyathula tomentosa, Cynoglossum zeylanicum, Pouzolzia zeylanica*

bheri (Chepang), see *Abelmoschus esculentus*

bhijin (Tamang), see *Maesa chisia*

bhima (Nepali), see *Grewia optiva*

bhim lahara (Nepali), see *Vitis lanata*

bhimpati (Tharu), see *Buddleja asiatica*

bhimsenpati (Bhojpuri, Danuwar, Magar, Nepali), see *Buddleja asiatica*

bhimsen pati (Chepang), see *Buddleja paniculata*

bhiringe (Gurung, Nepali), see *Eclipta prostrata*

bhiringi jhar (Nepali), see *Alternanthera sessilis*

bhiriyo (Nepali), see *Eclipta prostrata*

bhirkaulo (Nepali), see *Coix lachryma-jobi*

bhir khanyu (Nepali), see *Ficus sarmentosa*

bhisa (Tamang, Tibetan), see *Buddleja asiatica*

bhlan chhing (Tamang), see *Boehmeria rugulosa*

bhogat (Magar), see *Citrus margarita*

bhogate (Danuwar, Magar), see *Maesa macrophylla*

bhogate (Nepali), see *Citrus margarita, Colebrookea oppositifolia, Maesa argentea, M. macrophylla*

bhogate (Tamang), see *Citrus margarita, Maesa macrophylla*

bhogate (Tharu), see *Citrus margarita*

bhogate muja (Chepang), see *Siegesbeckia orientalis*

bhogati (Gurung), see *Cardiocrinum giganteum*

bhogatya (Newari), see *Citrus margarita*

bhogla (Gurung), see *Neillia thyrsiflora*

bhoibuju (Tamang), see *Cotoneaster microphyllus*

bhojapatra (Nepali), see *Betula utilis*

bhok (Chepang), see *Arundo donax*

bhokat (Danuwar), see *Citrus margarita*

bhokate (Sunwar), see *Citrus margarita*

bhon pujo (Gurung), see *Pyracantha crenulata*

bhordaya (Nepali), see *Roscoea purpurea*

bhordonbo (Tamang), see *Phragmites karka*

bhorekhayar (Nepali), see *Osyris wightiana*

bhorla (Majhi, Nepali), see *Bauhinia vahlii*

bhorle (Nepali), see *Careya arborea*

bhote (Nepali), see *Clerodendrum viscosum*

bhote chotro (Nepali), see *Mahonia napaulensis*

bhote pipal (Nepali), see *Populus ciliata*

bhote timur (Nepali), see *Zanthoxylum acanthopodium*

bhramendo (Tamang), see *Luculia gratissima*

bhramgoi (Gurung), see *Gonostegia hirta*

bhramlaman (Tamang), see *Clematis grewiiflora*

bhraun (Nepali), see *Boehmeria macrophylla*

bhri-ga (Tibetan), see *Eclipta prostrata*

bhringaraj (Nepali), see *Eclipta prostrata*

bhrunge (Gurung), see *Helixanthera ligustrina*

bhuban jhar (Nepali), see *Crotalaria spectabilis*

bhugan (Nepali), see *Crotalaria tetragona*

bhui amala (Nepali), see *Phyllanthus amarus*

bhui ghangharu (Nepali), see *Gaultheria nummularioides*

bhui kaphal (Magar), see *Potentilla kleiniana*

bhui kaphal (Nepali), see *Gaultheria nummularioides, G. trichophylla*

bhui khursani (Gurung), see *Dichrocephala integrifolia*

bhuin ainselu (Nepali), see *Fragaria nubicola, Potentilla indica, R. calycinus, R. fockeanus, R. griffithii*

bhuinakato (Tamang), see *Osyris wightiana*

bhuin amala (Nepali), see *Phyllanthus urinaria*

bhuinchampa phul (Nepali), see *Primula irregularis*

bhuinchapo (Nepali), see *Canna chinensis*

bhuin charchare (Nepali), see *Leea macrophylla*

bhuin jamun (Danuwar), see *Murraya koenigii*

bhuin jhar (Chepang), see *Centella asiatica*

bhuin kalang (Tamang), see *Nephrolepis cordifolia*

bhuin kaphal (Nepali), see *Fragaria daltoniana, F. nubicola. Potentilla indica*

bhuin katahar (Danuwar), see *Ananas comosus*

bhuin kathar (Nepali), see *Ananas comosus*

bhuin lahara (Nepali), see *Mimosa pudica*

bhuin saro (Nepali), see *Roscoea purpurea*

bhuin timur (Nepali), see *Spilanthes paniculata*

bhuj (Nepali), see *Betula utilis*

bhuje bho lha (Magar), see *Butea buteiformis*

bhujetro (Nepali), see *Butea buteiformis*

bhuko (Nepali), see *Anaphalis contorta*

bhukur (Nepali), see *Saussurea heteromalla*

bhuletro (Nepali), see *Butea buteiformis*

bhuling (Chepang), see *Aechmanthera gossypina, Crotalaria albida*

bhulingaro (Chepang), see *Aster trinervius*

bhulna (Nepali), see *Fimbristylis ovata*

bhultya (Nepali), see *Nardostachys grandiflora*

bhunru (Tharu), see *Benincasa hispida*

bhuri ghans (Nepali), see *Eriocaulon nepalense*

bhurkul (Nepali), see *Hymenodictyon excelsum*

bhusa (Magar, Tamang), see *Nicotiana tabacum*

bhusa noba (Tamang), see *Clerodendrum serratum*

bhuse khari (Nepali), see *Pogonatherum crinitum*

bhuset (Nepali), see *Pleurospermum hookeri*

bhuspat (Gurung), see *Betula utilis*

bhusure (Nepali), see *Leucosceptrum canum*

bhutaka (Mooshar), see *Solanum nigrum*

bhuti (Newari), see *Vigna unguiculata*

bhutkesh (Nepali), see *Cortia depressa, Gentiana robusta, Selinum candollii*

bhut kesh (Nepali), see *Heracleum nepalense, Selinum tenuifolium*

bhutra (Magar, Majhi), see *Colebrookea oppositifolia*

bhutung (Danuwar), see *Solanum nigrum*

bhuyu phasi (Newari), see *Benincasa hispida*

bhwagan (Magar), see *Crotalaria tetragona*

bhwan sak (Chepang), see *Crotalaria tetragona*

bhyagute nyuro (Nepali), see *Polystichum squarrosum*

bhyagute phul (Nepali), see *Vanda cristata*

bhyakur (Nepali), see *Dioscorea bulbifera, D. deltoidea*

bhyangre sisnu (Nepali), see *Girardinia diversifolia*

bhyanta (Gurung, Newari), see *Solanum melongena*

bhyarkin (Tamang), see *Galium asperifolium*

bhyas (Tamang), see *Galium asperifolium*

bhyau pat (Chepang), see *Coelogyne ochracea*

bibi phal (Nepali), see *Gaultheria nummularioides*

bich (Sunwar), see *Saccharum officinarum*

bichakane (Nepali), see *Dicentra scandens*

bihi (Danuwar), see *Solanum torvum*

bihi (Nepali), see *Solanum anguivi, S. nigrum, S. pseudocapsicum, S. torvum*

bihi (Tharu), see *Ludwigia octovalis*

bijakanne (Chepang), see *Polygala persicariifolia*

bijauni phul (Nepali), see *Plantago erosa*

bijauri (Nepali), see *Ligularia amplexicaulis*

bijauri phul (Nepali), see *Senecio chrysanthemoides*

bikh (Nepali), see *Aconitum ferox, Delphinium scabriflorum*

bikh (Tamang), see *Aconitum ferox, Dichrocephala integrifolia*

bikrim (Lepcha), see *Trigonella foenum-graecum*

bilajor (Nepali), see *Clinopodium umbrosum*

bilaune (Nepali), see *Eurya acuminata*

bilauni (Chepang, Magar, Nepali), see *Maesa chisia*

bilauti (Gurung), see *Psidium guajava*

bil-ba (Tibetan), see *Citrus medica*

bimara (Tamang), see *Citrus medica*

bimiro (Danuwar, Nepali), see *Citrus medica*

bin (Chepang), see *Allium sativum*

binas (Nepali), see *Lindenbergia grandiflora, L. indica*

bipyu kanda (Majhi), see *Achyranthes aspera*

bir (Magar), see *Citrus limon*

biralgano (Nepali), see *Stephania glandulifera*

bir banko (Nepali), see *Arisaema tortuosum*

birch (English), see *Betula alnoides*

birch, Himalayan silver (English), see *Betula utilis*

birdlime (English), see *Viscum album*

bird's foot (English), see *Trigonella foenum-graecum*

birgan (Magar), see *Rumex hastatus*

biri (Nepali), see *Neohymenopogon parasiticus, Paederia foetida, Spermadictyon suaveolens*

birosi (Rai), see *Capsicum annuum*

birsing (Tamang), see *Prunus cerasoides*

birukanda (Tamang), see *Woodfordia fruticosa*

birula (Magar), see *Ficus subincisa*

birupot (Lepcha), see *Lycopersicon esculentum*

bisaune jhar (Nepali), see *Alternanthera sessilis, Justicia procumbens* var. *simplex, Rungia parviflora*

bish (Nepali), see *Aconitum gammiei, A. heterophyllum, Delphinium denudatum*

bishalari (Danuwar), see *Persicaria barbata*

bish kabre (Nepali), see *Cheilanthes rufa*

bishkhapre (Magar), see *Urena lobata*

bish khapre (Nepali), see *Sida cordata*

bishkhapre (Nepali), see *Triumfetta rhomboides*

bish khopra (Tharu), see *Sida cordata*

bishmaro (Nepali), see *Origanum vulgare, Urena lobata*

bishop wood (English), see *Bischofia javanica*

bish phej (Nepali), see *Polypodium amoenum*

bishram (Tharu), see *Ipomoea carnea* subsp. *fistulosa*

bisiri (Tamang), see *Catunaregam spinosa*

bisyau (Nepali), see *Dryoathyrium boryanum*

blackberry (English), see *Syzygium cumini*

blackberry, false (English), see *Rubus ellipticus*

bladderwort (English), see *Butomopsis latifolia*

blesing (Tamang), see *Gonostegia hirta*

blind-your-eyes tree (English), see *Excoecaria acerifolia*

blood flower (English), see *Asclepias curassavica*

bo, sacred (English), see *Ficus religiosa*
boba (Rai), see *Brassica rapa*
bod (Gurung), see *Vigna unguiculata*
bodebade (Tamang), see *Colebrookea oppositifolia*
bo-de-tsa (Tibetan), see *Ficus religiosa*
bodi (Chepang), see *Acorus calamus*
bogaino (Nepali), see *Murraya koenigii*
bohori (Nepali), see *Cordia dichotoma*
bojhari (Nepali), see *Tanacetum dolichophyllum*
bojho (Danuwar, Gurung, Magar, Nepali, Sunwar), see *Acorus calamus*
bojho jhar (Nepali), see *Iris clarkei*
boke (Nepali), see *Ageratum conyzoides*
boke lahara (Nepali), see *Hedyotis scandens*
boke tinai (Tamang), see *Cynoglossum glochidiatum, C. zeylanicum*
boki jhar (Nepali), see *Gnaphalium affine, G. polycaulon*
bokini (Nepali), see *Murraya koenigii*
bokipan (Tamang), see *Mahonia napaulensis*
bokro mran (Tamang), see *Agrimonia pilosa*
boksiambo (Rai), see *Catunaregam spinosa*
boksibaja (Nepali), see *Crotalaria alata*
boksi bayar (Nepali), see *Ziziphus oenoplia*
boksi ghans (Nepali), see *Mimosa rubicaulis* subsp. *himalayana*
boksi jhar (Nepali), see *Hypericum japonicum, Oxalis corniculata*
boksi kanda (Nepali), see *Caesalpinia bonduc, Martynia annua, Rubus paniculatus*
bokumba (Nepali), see *Euodia fraxinifolia*
bombob (Rai), see *Solanum melongena*
bomosyo (Magar), see *Benincasa hispida*
bomsin (Tamang), see *Alnus nepalensis*
bonchho (Gurung), see *Cyperus rotundus*
bongsalim (Rai), see *Asparagus racemosus*
bonkolong (Rai), see *Prunus persica*
bonmara (Danuwar), see *Eupatorium odoratum*
bonphula (Danuwar), see *Scoparia dulcis*
bon supari (Danuwar), see *Sphaeranthus indicus, Spilanthes paniculata*
bopchom (Rai), see *Trichosanthes dioica*
bopchukuksun (Rai), see *Coriandrum sativum*
bori (Nepali), see *Cordia dichotoma, Vigna unguiculata*
bori jhyau (Chepang), see *Luisia zeylanica*
borsajini (Tamang), see *Osyris wightiana*
borso tene (Gurung), see *Bidens pilosa* var. *minor*
bosyol syule (Tamang), see *Colebrookea oppositifolia*
botasi (Chepang), see *Sterculia villosa*
botdung (Tamang), see *Lithocarpus elegans*
bottlebrush (English), see *Callistemon citrinus*
boxi ko makai (Nepali), see *Lobelia nummularia*
boyar (Majhi), see *Ziziphus mauritiana*
bra bu ba (Tamang), see *Pieris formosa*
brahmdhaniya (Nepali), see *Eryngium foetidum*
braj damre (Chepang), see *Pogostemon glaber*
braju (Tamang), see *Begonia picta*
bram (Sunwar), see *Fagopyrum esculentum*
brama (Tamang), see *Clematis buchananiana, Crotalaria prostrata*
bramble, oval-leaved (English), see *Rubus ellipticus*
bramble, woolly-berried (English), see *Rubus niveus*
bramble, yellow (English), see *Rubus ellipticus*
bramse (Tibetan), see *Viburnum mullaha*
bras (Tibetan), see *Oryza sativa*
brasyal (Tamang), see *Coriandrum sativum*
bratar (Tamang), see *Ageratum conyzoides*
bre (Gurung), see *Fagopyrum esculentum*
bread tree (English), see *Melia azedarach*
bregal (Tamang), see *Begonia rubella*
bregyal (Tamang), see *Bergenia ciliata*
brey (Tamang), see *Fagopyrum esculentum*

briksha (Chepang), see *Cassia fistula*
bri-mog (Tibetan), see *Lawsonia inermis*
brimomhendo (Tamang), see *Ranunculus diffusus*
brinjal (English), see *Solanum melongena*
brionung (Chepang), see *Myrica esculenta*
broken bones (English), see *Oroxylum indicum*
brooklime (English), see *Veronica baccabunga*
broom, sweet (English), see *Scoparia dulcis*
broomrape (English), see *Aeginetia indica, Orobanche aegyptiaca*
broom weed (English), see *Sida acuta*
Brussels sprouts (English), see *Brassica oleracea* var. *gemmifera*
bse-shing (Tibetan), see *Semecarpus anacardium*
bse-yab (Tibetan), see *Tamarindus indica*
btsong (Tibetan), see *Allium cepa*
bubi (Lepcha), see *Trichosanthes anguina*
buchke ghans (Nepali), see *Micromeria biflora*
buckthorn, sea (English), see *Hippophae tibetana*
buckwheat (English), see *Fagopyrum esculentum*
buckwheat, Tatary (English), see *Fagopyrum tataricum*
budho aushadhi (Nepali), see *Astilbe rivularis, Heracleum nepalense*
budho dhayaro (Nepali), see *Lagerstroemia parviflora*
bugaino (Nepali), see *Cipadessa baccifera*
bugi (Nepali), see *Blumea lacera, Verbascum thapsus*
buhari jhar (Nepali), see *Mimosa pudica*
buis (Nepali), see *Setaria pallidefusca*
buiset (Nepali), see *Salix denticulata*
buk (Lepcha), see *Dioscorea bulbifera, Quercus lamellosa*
buke lahara (Chepang), see *Hedyotis scandens*
buke phul (Nepali), see *Gnaphalium affine*
buki (Nepali), see *Commelina paludosa*
buki phul (Nepali), see *Anaphalis adnata, A. contorta*
bulake jhar (Nepali), see *Tridax procumbens*
bullock's heart (English), see *Annona reticulata*
bulno (Tamang), see *Cornus capitata*
bunbet (Rai), see *Oroxylum indicum*
bunbobhu (Rai), see *Brassica oleracea* var. *botrytis*
bung (Nepali), see *Taxus baccata* subsp. *wallichiana*
bunga (Newari), see *Brassica oleracea* var. *botrytis*
bungamjo (Tamang), see *Luculia gratissima*
bunga salla (Nepali), see *Abies spectabilis*
bunkala (Nepali), see *Vicia bakeri*
bu-ram (Tibetan), see *Saccharum officinarum*
burban (Chepang), see *Millettia extensa*
burchen (Nepali), see *Cotoneaster microphyllus*
burdock (English), see *Arctium lappa*
buru (Sunwar), see *Oryza sativa*
burweed (English), see *Xanthium strumarium*
busing (Tamang), see *Maesa chisia*
busul sul (Tamang), see *Colebrookea oppositifolia*
bute kanike (Nepali), see *Desmodium microphyllum*
bute kanike (Nepali), see *Desmodium triflorum*
buti jhar (Nepali), see *Elephantopus scaber*
butte ghans (Nepali), see *Lysimachia alternifolia*
butterfly bush (English), see *Buddleja asiatica*
butter tree, Indian (English), see *Diplokenma butyracea*
button tree (English), see *Anogeissus latifolius*
bya (Newari), see *Aegle marmelos*
byahagan (Magar), see *Bauhinia variegata*
byancha sin (Newari), see *Viburnum erubescens*
byauli (Chepang), see *Euphorbia hirta*
byi-bzung (Tibetan), see *Arctium lappa*
byid-zung (Tibetan), see *Arctium lappa*
byuru (Tamang), see *Prunus cerasoides*
cabbage (English), see *Brassica oleracea* var. *capitata*
cabbage, bud-bearing (English), see *Brassica oleracea* var. *gemmifera*
cabbage, swamp (English), see *Ipomoea aquatica*
cadillo (English), see *Urena lobata*

Caesar weed (English), see *Urena lobata*
calabash cucumber (English), see *Lagenaria siceraria*
Calumpang nut tree (English), see *Buchanania latifolia*
camel's foot climber (English), see *Bauhinia vahlii*
camphire (English), see *Lawsonia inermis*
camphor tree (English), see *Cinnamomum camphora*
cane, donax (English), see *Arundo donax*
cane, Provence (English), see *Arundo donax*
cangsani (Tamang), see *Solanum nigrum*
caper (English), see *Capparis spinosa*
caper, three-leaved (English), see *Crateva unilocularis*
cape weed (English), see *Phyla nodiflora*
carambola (English), see *Averrhoa carambola*
caraway (English), see *Carum carvi, Trachyspermum ammi*
cardamom, greater (English), see *Amomum subulatum*
cardamom, Nepalese (English), see *Amomum subulatum*
carilla fruit (English), see *Momordica charantia*
carpet weed (English), see *Mollugo pentaphylla*
carrot (English), see *Daucus carota*
cassia, dwarf (English), see *Cassia mimosoides*
cassia, fetid (English), see *Cassia tora*
cassia, purging (English), see *Cassia fistula*
cassia lignea, Indian (English), see *Cinnamomum tamala*
cassie flower (English), see *Acacia farnesiana*
castor-oil plant (English), see *Ricinus communis*
catechu, black (English), see *Acacia catechu*
catechu palm or tree (English), see *Areca catechu*
cauliflower (English), see *Brassica oleracea* var. *botrytis*
cedar, Himalayan (English), see *Cedrus deodara*
cedar, Himalayan black (English), see *Alnus nitida*
cedar, Java (English), see *Bischofia javanica*
cedar, Moulmain (English), see *Toona ciliata*
cedar, red (English), see *Toona ciliata*
cha (Rai), see *Oryza sativa*
chabo (Nepali), see *Piper mullesua*
chachan (Tamang), see *Mahonia napaulensis*
chachng (Rai), see *Oxalis corniculata*
chad (Gurung), see *Camellia sinensis*
chadong (Tamang), see *Guizotia abyssinica*
chadu (Nepali), see *Bupleurum candollii*
chadu (Tamang), see *Bupleurum hamiltonii*
chaff flower, cottony (English), see *Cyathula tomentosa*
chaff flower, prickly (English), see *Achyranthes aspera*
chaglo (Gurung), see *Remusatia pumila*
chah (Tharu), see *Camellia sinensis*
chaharu (Sherpa), see *Imperata cylindrica*
chail (Nepali), see *Oreocnide frutescens*
chainso mererr (Tamang), see *Gaultheria fragrantissima*
chaita (Tamang), see *Hypericum cordifolium*
chaite (Magar), see *Hypericum cordifolium*
cha jahr (Chepang), see *Isodon lophanthoides*
chakatik (Tibetan), see *Prenanthes brunoniana*
chakchansi (Rai), see *Myrica esculenta*
chakhuncha swan (Newari), see *Jacaranda mimosifolia*
chaklebtutwa (Rai), see *Aloe vera*
chakon (Tharu), see *Cassia tora*
chakor (Danuwar, Mooshar), see *Cassia tora*
chakramandi (Nepali), see *Cassia tora*
chakuhi (Newari), see *Ipomoea batatas*
chakwa phoma (Rai), see *Nelumbo nucifera*
chakyal (Chepang), see *Castanopsis indica*
chalak jhar (Nepali), see *Hypericum japonicum*
chalaya (Gurung), see *Rhus wallichii*
chali dhap (Tamang), see *Chlorophytum nepalense*
chali mhendo (Tamang), see *Hypericum podocarpoides*
chalmaro (Raute), see *Oxalis corniculata*
chalne (Nepali), see *Capsella bursa-pastoris*

chalnesisnu (Nepali), see *Boehmeria platyphylla*
chalne sisnu (Nepali), see *Girardinia diversifolia*
chalta (Nepali), see *Dillenia indica*
chamasur (Sunwar), see *Lepidium sativum*
chameli (Nepali), see *Jasminum gracile, J. multiflorum*
chamero laharo (Nepali), see *Porana grandiflora*
chammaha (Lepcha), see *Valeriana hardwickii*
champa (Nepali), see *Michelia champaca*
champak (English), see *Michelia champaca*
chamsur (Bhojpuri, Nepali), see *Lepidium sativum*
chamsur dhap (Tamang), see *Lepidium sativum*
chamsure ghans (Nepali), see *Cardamine loxostemonoides, C. scutata*
    subsp. *flexuosa*
chamsure unyu (Nepali), see *Leucostegia immersa*
chana (Gurung, Nepali), see *Cicer arietinum*
chanaru (Chepang), see *Morus australis, M. serrata*
chandamaruwa (Nepali), see *Rauvolfia serpentina*
chandan (Nepali), see *Daphniphyllum himalense*
chande ainselu (Nepali), see *Rubus splendidissimus*
chandi gabha (Nepali), see *Coelogyne cristata, C. ochracea*
chandre (Tamang), see *Artemisia indica*
changasai (Tamang), see *Gaultheria fragrantissima, G.*
    nummularioides
chanjiwa (Tamang), see *Pieris formosa*
channaino (Nepali), see *Sida rhombifolia*
chansur (Danuwar, Magar, Tharu), see *Lepidium sativum*
chanwale (Nepali), see *Persicaria mollis*
chanyal (Tamang), see *Melia azedarach*
chaphenda (Limbu), see *Lycopersicon esculentum*
chaput (Tamang), see *Litsea monopetala*
chara ko khutta (Nepali), see *Gentiana pedicellata*
charamlo (Sunwar), see *Oxalis corniculata*
charamma (Limbu), see *Oxalis corniculata*
chara pi pi (Nepali), see *Desmodium heterocarpon*
charas (Nepali), see *Cannabis sativa*
charchare (Nepali), see *Clematis buchananiana, Parthenocissus*
    himalayana, P. semicordata
charchare lahara (Nepali), see *Tetrastigma serrulatum*
charcoal tree (English), see *Trema orientalis*
charemala (Nepali), see *Rumex hastatus*
chari amilo (Danuwar, Magar, Nepali), see *Oxalis corniculata*
chari banko (Nepali), see *Arisaema tortuosum*
charigophala (Magar), see *Holboellia latifolia*
chari jhar (Chepang), see *Eclipta prostrata*
charinda (Nepali), see *Eragrostis tenella*
chariumal (Majhi), see *Oxalis corniculata*
chariwal (Magar), see *Rhamnus virgatus*
charpate (Gurung), see *Melissa axillaris*
charpate (Nepali), see *Scutellaria repens, S. scandens*
charpate jhar (Nepali), see *Hedyotis lineata*
chaste tree, Chinese (English), see *Vitex negundo*
chasu (Newari), see *Lepidium sativum*
chaswan (Newari), see *Plumeria rubra*
chatake (Nepali), see *Tetrastigma serrulatum*
chatalang (Tamang), see *Smilax glaucophylla*
chatali (Newari), see *Momordica dioica*
chatapate (Nepali), see *Reissantia arborea*
chatel (Nepali), see *Momordica dioica*
chatu (Nepali), see *Clerodendrum viscosum*
chatu (Sherpa), see *Bupleurum hamiltonii*
chaturo (Tamang), see *Berberis asiatica*
chaulane (Nepali), see *Youngia japonica*
chaulani (Gurung), see *Glochidion velutinum*
chaule jhar (Nepali), see *Launaea secunda*
chaulene jhar (Nepali), see *Emilia sonchifolia*
chawa chhiji (Tibetan), see *Euphrasia himalayica*
chawang (Gurung), see *Osyris wightiana*

chay (Bhojpuri), see *Camellia sinensis*
chayote (English), see *Sechium edule*
cheklo (Chepang), see *Boehmeria platyphylla, Vernonia squarrosa*
chekru (Chepang), see *Acacia intsia*
cheksi (Chepang), see *Ficus neriifolia* var. *nemoralis, F. subincisa, Trema cannabina*
chel (Nepali), see *Cymbopogon jwarancusa*
chele (Sherpa), see *Gaultheria fragrantissima*
chelem lundu (Tamang), see *Viburnum erubescens*
chema (Tamang), see *Solanum nigrum*
chempe (Tamang), see *Michelia champaca*
chenchen (Sherpa), see *Gaultheria fragrantissima*
chenchev (Rai), see *Woodfordia fruticosa*
chengi phul (Nepali), see *Parochetus communis*
chenji (Tamang), see *Artemisia indica*
chenjuwa (Tamang), see *Gaultheria fragrantissima*
chenti (Tamang), see *Artemisia indica, Senecio diversifolius*
chento (Gurung), see *Pyracantha crenulata*
cherailu (Nepali), see *Rhododendron campanulatum*
cherbi (Sunwar), see *Triticum aestivum*
chermang (Tamang), see *Randia tetrasperma*
cherry, clammy (English), see *Cordia dichotoma*
cherry, ground (English), see *Physalis divaricata*
cherry, Indian (English), see *Cordia dichotoma*
cherry, Nepalese (English), see *Prunus napaulensis*
cherry, wild Himalayan (English), see *Prunus cerasoides*
chesin (Gurung), see *Lyonia ovalifolia*
chesing (Tamang), see *Tsuga dumosa*
chestnut (English), see *Castanopsis hystrix*
chestnut, hill (English), see *Castanopsis tribuloides*
chestnut, horse (English), see *Aesculus indica*
chestnut, Indian (English), see *Castanopsis indica*
chestnut, water (English), see *Trapa bispinosa*
chha (Newari), see *Allium ascalonicum*
chhachharima (Rai), see *Melia azedarach*
chhade phul (Nepali), see *Thunia alba*
chhal (Tamang), see *Pilea anisophylla, P. symmeria*
chhalam (Lepcha), see *Citrus aurantium*
chhale soin (Nepali), see *Geniosporum coloratum*
chhambowsi (Rai), see *Citrus aurantifolia*
chhan goi (Chepang), see *Crotalaria tetragona*
chhapa (Limbu), see *Camellia sinensis*
chhaphung (Tibetan), see *Artemisia indica*
chhar (Tibetan), see *Cotoneaster frigidus, C. ludlowii, C. microphyllus*
chhargu lhapti (Tamang), see *Butea buteiformis*
chharkang (Tibetan), see *Delphinium kumaonense*
chhasakrungai (Chepang), see *Epipactis royleana*
chhatadre (Nepali), see *Selinum candollii*
chhatalhapte (Tamang), see *Litsea monopetala*
chhatamain (Mooshar), see *Alstonia scholaris*
chhatare (Nepali), see *Heracleum nepalense, Pleurospermum hookeri, Torilis japonica*
chhataun (Chepang), see *Alstonia scholaris*
chhate (Nepali), see *Thalictrum foliolosum*
chhatiwan (Danuwar), see *Alstonia scholaris*
chhatiwan (Nepali), see *Alstonia scholaris*
chhatre (Nepali), see *Elephantopus scaber*
chhayal (Rai), see *Melia azedarach*
chhe (Tibetan), see *Ephedra gerardiana*
chhebok (Magar), see *Zingiber officinale*
chhechhedungma (Rai), see *Brassaiopsis hainla*
chhelem langdu (Tamang), see *Cissampelos pareira*
chhe mehendo (Sherpa), see *Lycopodium clavatum*
chhemhendo (Tamang), see *Lycopodium clavatum*
chhepara kaphal (Majhi), see *Potentilla indica*
chhepare unyu (Nepali), see *Arthromeris wallichiana*
chhepasi (Nepali), see *Cornus oblonga*

chhepra kaphal (Nepali), see *Potentilla indica*
chherma (Tibetan), see *Ilex dipyrena, Rubus ellipticus*
chhermang (Sherpa), see *Brassica juncea* var. *cuneifolia*
chherne kanda (Tamang), see *Pyracantha crenulata*
chher syukpa (Tibetan), see *Juniperus recurva*
chhetreta (Gurung), see *Elephantopus scaber*
chhigu (Gurung), see *Aloe vera*
chhiku dhap (Tamang), see *Isodon lophanthoides*
chhima (Tibetan), see *Cannabis sativa*
chhimchhime (Nepali), see *Crotalaria alata*
chhimile (Sherpa), see *Centella asiatica*
chhimnva (Gurung), see *Callicarpa arborea*
chhimra (Mooshar), see *Chrysopogon aciculatus*
chhinchhie (Nepali), see *Cassia floribunda*
chhinchhine (Nepali), see *Cassia occidentalis, C. tora*
chhindari (Gurung), see *Chrysopogon aciculatus*
chhin jhar (Nepali), see *Centipeda minima*
chhinki (Nepali), see *Elsholtzia fruticosa*
chhiple (Tibetan), see *Bupleurum hamiltonii*
chhirbire jhar (Nepali), see *Drymaria diandra*
chhirlinge (Nepali), see *Cassia floribunda*
chhischchar jhar (Magar), see *Centipeda minima*
chhiuke jhar (Nepali), see *Centipeda minima, Dichrocephala benthamii*
chho (Magar), see *Oryza sativa*
chhojyal (Tamang), see *Gonostegia hirta*
chhokawasi (Rai), see *Citrus aurantium*
chhoku (Rai), see *Urtica dioica*
chhokwa (Rai), see *Madhuca longifolia*
chholyang (Nepali), see *Pilea umbrosa*
chhomlokasi (Rai), see *Benincasa hispida*
chhong (Rai), see *Avena sativa*
chhopra (Sherpa), see *Sapindus mukorossi*
chhosan (Magar), see *Oryza sativa*
chhotaka baghandi (Danuwar), see *Jatropha gossypifolia*
chhotaka chidchidhi (Danuwar), see *Urena lobata*
chhotaki dahigola (Tharu), see *Phyllanthus amarus*
chhotang nau (Tamang), see *Boenninghausenia albiflora*
chhotne (Gurung), see *Maesa chisia*
chhow (Newari), see *Triticum aestivum*
chhudaomsai (Rai), see *Cocos nucifera*
chhuisi (Chepang), see *Eurya acuminata*
chhulumase (Tamang), see *Berberis asiatica*
chhuma (Rai), see *Shorea robusta*
chhumen (Tamang), see *Euphorbia hirta*
chhyal (Tamang), see *Boehmeria platyphylla, Elatostema sessile, Oreocnide frutescens, Pilea glaberrima*
chhyamba (Tamang), see *Holboellia latifolia*
chhyanda (Gurung), see *Sarcococca hookeriana*
chhyapi (Bhojpuri, Danuwar, Nepali, Sunwar, Tamang), see *Allium ascalonicum*
chhyapim (Magar), see *Allium ascalonicum*
chhyo (Lepcha), see *Camellia sinensis*
chhyonde (Gurung), see *Viburnum erubescens*
chhyonre (Gurung), see *Maesa chisia*
chhyudha (Gurung), see *Sarcococca hookeriana*
chhyukutinai (Tamang), see *Siegesbeckia orientalis*
chhyun jhar (Nepali), see *Centipeda minima, Dichrocephala integrifolia*
chhyunta (Gurung), see *Sarcococca saligna*
chhyuzii (Tibetan), see *Epilobium brevifolium*
chibung (Rai), see *Bauhinia variegata*
chichi (Nepali), see *Hippophae salicifolia*
chichi (Tharu), see *Lonicera hypoleuca*
chichinda (Magar, Newari, Sunwar, Tamang), see *Trichosanthes anguina*
chichindo (Danuwar, Nepali), see *Trichosanthes anguina*

chichura (Bhojpuri), see *Trichosanthes anguina*
chickpea (English), see *Cicer arietinum*
chicory weed (English), see *Caesulia axillaris*
chihuli (Tharu), see *Diplokenma butyracea*
chijlangdu (Tamang), see *Tetrastigma serrulatum*
chikap (Rai), see *Castanopsis indica*
chikini dudhi (Tharu), see *Euphorbia parviflora*
chikli (Gurung), see *Amaranthus spinosus, A. viridis*
chiku tree (English), see *Manilkara zapota*
chilahariyak thond (Tharu), see *Abrus precatorius*
chilam kath (Nepali), see *Viburnum erubescens*
chilaune (Nepali), see *Schima wallichii*
chilbile (Nepali), see *Reissantia arborea*
chilbile (Tharu), see *Cassia tora*
childar (Nepali), see *Meconopsis grandis*
chile (English), see *Capsicum annuum*
chili (English), see *Capsicum annuum*
chili (Tamang), see *Holmskioldia sanguinea*
chilimran (Tamang), see *Leucas mollissima*
chille kath (Nepali), see *Rhamnus nepalensis*
chillo batulpate (Nepali), see *Cissampelos pareira*
chilmile (Danuwar), see *Cassia occidentalis*
chimal (Nepali), see *Pieris formosa, R. barbatum, R. fulgens, R. grande*
chimalo (Nepali), see *Rhododendron campanulatum*
chimar (Tharu), see *Shorea robusta*
chimbak (Rai), see *Phyllanthus emblica*
chimbers (Satar), see *Ampelocissus latifolia*
chimphar jhar (Gurung, Nepali), see *Euphorbia hirta*
chimsai (Magar), see *Debregeasia longifolia*
chimte ghans (Tamang), see *Hedyotis scandens*
China berry (English), see *Melia azedarach*
chinde (Nepali), see *Macropanax undulatus*
Chinese hat plant (English), see *Holmskioldia sanguinea*
chinijhar (Danuwar), chini jhar (Nepali), see *Scoparia dulcis*
chini mran (Tamang), see *Scoparia dulcis*
chiniya phal (Nepali), see *Potentilla fruticosa*
chinne (Nepali), see *Abroma angusta, Adina cordifolia*
chinne jhar (Nepali), see *Heracleum nepalense*
chino (Gurung), see *Oxalis corniculata*
chino (Nepali), see *Panicum miliaceum*
chipalan (Tamang), see *Scindapsus officinalis*
chiplange (Chepang), see *Galinsoga parviflora*
chiple (Magar), see *Oreocnide frutescens*
chiple (Nepali), see *Gonostegia hirta, Grewia optiva, Pilea symmeria, Urena lobata*
chiple ghans (Nepali), see *Oreocnide frutescens*
chiple jhar (Nepali), see *Pouzolzia zeylanica*
chiple lahara (Nepali), see *Gonostegia hirta*
chipro (Tamang), see *Indigofera dosua*
chiraita (Danuwar), see *Urena lobata*
chiraito (Nepali), see *Swertia angustifolia, S. chirayita, S. kingii, S. racemosa*
chirchira (Danuwar), see *Sida cordata*
chirchiri (Danuwar), see *Chrysopogon aciculatus, Xanthium strumarium*
chirchiri (Mooshar), see *Achyranthes aspera*
chireta (Danuwar), see *Swertia angustifolia*
chiretta (English), see *Swertia chirayita*
chirs (Sunwar), see *Eleusine coracana*
chiski (Chepang), see *Galium aparine*
chisro (Chepang), see *Indigofera pulchella*
chitachinki (Nepali), see *Nyctanthes arbor-tritis*
chitaina (Nepali), see *Nyctanthes arbor-tritis*
chithi (Chepang), see *Rungia parviflora*
chitlange ghans (Nepali), see *Galinsoga parviflora*
chitlangi (Nepali), see *Galinsoga quadriradiata*
chitre banso (Nepali), see *Digitaria ciliaris*

chitu (Magar, Nepali), see *Plumbago zeylanica*
chituwa nimur (Magar), see *Clematis buchananiana*
chiuli (Bhojpuri, Danuwar), see *Diplokenma butyracea*
chiya (Danuwar, Magar, Nepali), see *Camellia sinensis*
chiya pate (Nepali), see *Camellia kissi*
chiyarani (Chepang), see *Osyris wightiana*
chiyumli (Tamang), see *Diplokenma butyracea*
chobasi (Newari), see *Magnolia campbellii*
cho cho (English), see *Sechium edule*
chokam (Tamang), see *Cirsium verutum*
chom (Tamang), see *Cardamine scutata* subsp. *flexuosa*
chomchhadersi (Rai), see *Carica papaya*
chongi langdu (Tamang), see *Lycopodium clavatum*
chongonchhi (Gurung), see *Bombax ceiba*
chonsi (Gurung), see *Eurya acuminata*
chopachhi (Tamang), see *Tridax procumbens*
chopoma (Tamang), see *Tridax procumbens*
chorato (Majhi), see *Achyranthes aspera*
chotaki gurubans (Tharu), see *Ipomoea quamoclit*
chotaki hunkatath (Tharu), see *Chrozophora rottleri*
chote jhar (Nepali), see *Sonchus oleraceus*
choto (Nepali), see *Berberis chitria*
choto (Sherpa), see *Bupleurum candollii*
choto pichar (Tamang), see *Berberis chitria*
chotputiya (Tharu), see *Elephantopus scaber*
chotr (Gurung), see *Berberis asiatica*
chotra (Nepali), see *Berberis aristata*
chotro (Nepali), see *Berberis asiatica*
choya bans (Nepali), see *Bambusa nepalensis, Dendrocalamus hamiltonii*
choya phul (Nepali), see *Celosia argentea*
Christmas bush (English), see *Eupatorium odoratum*
Christmas flower (English), see *Euphorbia pulcherrima*
christophine (English), see *Sechium edule*
chu chu (Tibetan), see *Daphne bholua*
chuchuriya (Tharu), see *Boerhavia diffusa*
chugo (Nepali), see *Rhus javanica*
chugo (Tamang), see *Hippophae tibetana*
chuinyan (Nepali), see *Dioscorea pentaphylla*
chuis (Nepali), see *Coix lachryma-jobi*
chuisai (Chepang), see *Solanum aculeatissimum*
chuk amilo (Nepali), see *Rhus javanica*
chukutenay (Nepali), see *Eupatorium odoratum*
chule (Sunwar), see *Urtica dioica*
chulesi (Nepali), see *Melastoma normale*
chulesi (Satar), see *Melastoma malabathricum*
chulesi jhar (Nepali), see *Oxyspora paniculata*
chuletro (Nepali), see *Trevesia palmata*
chulsi (Nepali), see *Osbeckia nepalensis*
chulthi amilo (Nepali), see *Rheum australe, R. nobile*
chumlya (Nepali), see *Desmodium elegans*
chune salla (Nepali), see *Tsuga dumosa*
chunetro ghans (Nepali), see *Flemingia strobilifera, Geranium nepalense*
chunkee (Tamang), see *Symplocos ramosissima*
chupi (Nepali), see *Eragrostiella nardoides*
churki (Tharu), see *Imperata cylindrica*
churmure (Majhi), see *Tridax procumbens*
churut jhar (Chepang), see *Achyranthes aspera*
chusai (Chepang), see *Solanum torvum*
chutap (Chepang), see *Phlogacanthus thyrsiformis*
chutle (Rai), see *Urtica dioica*
chutra (Magar), see *Berberis asiatica*
chutro (Gurung, Magar), see *Berberis aristata*
chutro (Nepali), see *Berberis aristata, B. chitria*
chuttaparat (Chepang), see *Holmskioldia sanguinea*
chuwa (Chepang, Nepali, Rai, Tamang), see *Plumeria rubra*

chuwaro (Chepang), see *Plumeria rubra*
chwakan (Newari), see *Cirsium wallichii*
chwayme (Tibetan), see *Lyonia ovalifolia*
chwe (Sherpa), see *Rubia manjith*
chya (Newari, Tamang), see *Camellia sinensis*
chyabra (Sunwar), see *Asparagus racemosus*
chyakatu (Tibetan), see *Erodium stephanianum*
chyakhala (Chepang), see *Nicotiana tabacum*
chyaksep (Tibetan), see *Thalictrum elegans*
chyaktu (Tibetan), see *Geranium wallichianum*
chyali (Nepali), see *Chesneya nubigena*
chyali (Tamang), see *Chlorophytum khasianum*
chyamle (Nepali), see *Dryopteris chrysocoma*
chyamno (Nepali), see *Drynaria mollis*
chyan (Gurung), see *Diplazium polypodioides*
chyandhen (Tamang), see *Artemisia indica*
chyandre (Tamang), see *Isodon coetsa*
chyangan (Gurung), see *Diplazium polypodioides*
chyangkya (Tamang), see *Galium asperifolium*
chyangma (Tibetan), see *Populus ciliata*
chyangra (Gurung), see *Cotoneaster microphyllus*
chyangsi (Chepang), see *Callicarpa arborea, Schima wallichii*
chyangsing (Sherpa), see *Taxus baccata* subsp. *wallichiana*
chyanguya (Tamang), see *Galium acutum*
chyanmangre (Tamang), see *Clematis buchananiana*
chyan phul (Majhi), see *Plumeria rubra*
chyansi (Chepang), see *Lagerstroemia parviflora*
chyarangro (Chepang), see *Rauvolfia serpentina*
chyarbi (Gurung), see *Betula alnoides*
chyarbu (Gurung), see *Prunus cerasoides*
chyarcha (Tibetan), see *Coriaria napalensis*
chyar cham (Gurung), see *Cotoneaster microphyllus*
chyarsi (Gurung), see *Lyonia ovalifolia*
chyaryo (Gurung), see *Lyonia ovalifolia*
chyas (Chepang), see *Thysanolaena maxima*
chyatalama (Tamang, Tibetan), see *Malva verticillata*
chyate (Tibetan), see *Cicerbita macrorhiza*
chyaun (Tamang), see *Chaerophyllum villosum*
chyau phul (Nepali), see *Bistorta amplexicaulis, B. macrophylla*
chyengra (Gurung), see *Cotoneaster microphyllus*
chyenti (Tamang), see *Artemisia japonica*
chynman (Tibetan), see *Cortia depressa*
chyongapolo (Tamang), see *Boehmeria platyphylla*
chyonre (Gurung), see *Artemisia indica*
chyonthe (Gurung), see *Artemisia indica*
chyorosai (Chepang), see *Viburnum erubescens*
chyowa (Tibetan), see *Heracleum nepalense*
chyucha (Sherpa), see *Bergenia ciliata*
chyuhuwa (Danuwar), see *Woodfordia fruticosa*
chyuli (Nepali), see *Sorbus cuspidata*
chyungba (Tamang), see *Berberis asiatica*
chyurcha (Sherpa), see *Rheum australe*
chyuri (Magar, Nepali, Sunwar), see *Diplokenma butyracea*
chyurpu (Sherpa), see *Bergenia ciliata*
cinnamon, Nepalese (English), see *Cinnamomum tamala*
cinquefoil, bush (English), see *Potentilla fruticosa*
cinquefoil, Himalayan (English), see *Potentilla fulgens*
cin-tsh (Tibetan), see *Cinnamomum camphora*
ciple (Majhi), see *Triumfetta rhomboides*
citron (English), see *Citrus medica*
clem-som-crem (Lepcha), see *Polygala arillata*
cleome, sticky (English), see *Cleome viscosa*
clover, hop (English), see *Medicago lupulina*
clover, sweet (English), see *Melilotus alba*
clover, white (English), see *Trifolium repens*
club moss (English), see *Lycopodium clavatum*
cobra plant (English), see *Arisaema nepenthoides*

cocklebur (English), see *Agrimonia pilosa*
coconut (English), see *Cocos nucifera*
coconut, hill (English), see *Sterculia foetida*
cocoyam (English), see *Colocasia esculenta*
coffee, Negro (English), see *Cassia occidentalis*
coffee, wild (English), see *Cassia occidentalis*
coffee bean (English), see *Glycine max*
coffee bush (English), see *Leucaena leucocephala*
coffee senna (English), see *Cassia occidentalis*
cogon grass (English), see *Imperata cylindrica*
colza, Indian (English), see *Brassica campestris* var. *sarson*
comb tree (English), see *Gmelina arborea*
conch-shell flower (English), see *Clitoria ternatea*
conessi bark (English), see *Holarrhena pubescens*
conifers, see *Abies, Araucaria, Cedrus, Cryptomeria, Cupressus, Cycas, Ephedra, Gnetum, Larix, Picea, Pinus, Podocarpus, Taxus, Tsuga*
coral tree (English), see *Erythrina arborescens*
coriander (English), see *Coriandrum sativum*
corn (English), see *Zea mays*
cornel, Bentham's (English), see *Cornus capitata*
cotton, devil's (English), see *Abroma angusta*
cotton tree (English), see *Gossypium arboreum*
cotton tree, silk (English), see *Bombax ceiba*
cowpea (English), see *Vigna unguiculata*
crab apple, Manchurian (English), see *Malus baccata*
crabgrass (English), see *Digitaria ciliaris*
crab's eye (English), see *Abrus precatorius*
crane's bill (English), see *Geranium nepalense*
crepe myrtle (English), see *Lagerstroemia indica, L. parviflora*
crepsing (Gurung), see *Viburnum cylindricum*
cress, Brazil (English), see *Spilanthes paniculata*
cress, garden (English), see *Lepidium sativum*
Crofton weed (English), see *Eupatorium adenophorum*
crooked rough brush (English), see *Streblus asper*
crowfoot, celery-leaved (English), see *Ranunculus sceleratus*
crown of thorns (English), see *Euphorbia milii*
cuchi (Nepali), see *Tetrastigma serrulatum*
cuckoo flower (English), see *Cardamine loxostemonoides*
cucumber (English), see *Cucumis sativus*
cucumber, African (English), see *Momordica charantia*
cucumber, calabash (English), see *Lagenaria siceraria*
cudweed (English), see *Gnaphalium affine, G. polycaulon*
culantro (English), see *Eryngium foetidum*
cumin (English), see *Cuminum cyminum*
cup and saucer plant (English), see *Holmskioldia sanguinea*
curassavian swallow wort (English), see *Asclepias curassavica*
curry leaf tree (English), see *Murraya koenigii*
cutch, black (English), see *Acacia catechu*
cutch tree (English), see *Acacia catechu*
cypress, Himalayan (English), see *Cupressus torulosa*
dabadabe (Nepali), see *Lannea coromandelica*
dabar (Chepang), see *Ziziphus mauritiana*
dabdabe (Nepali), see *Garuga pinnata, Symplocos ramosissima*
dable sag (Nepali), see *Allium wallichii*
dabrangmi (Tamang), see *Gaultheria nummularioides*
dadu jhar (Nepali), see *Schoenoplectus juncoides*
dagger plant, Spanish (English), see *Yucca gloriosa*
dagne kuro (Nepali), see *Xanthium strumarium*
dahi gwala (Tharu), see *Colebrookea oppositifolia*
dahijalo (Nepali), see *Callicarpa macrophylla*
dahikaula (Nepali), see *Callicarpa macrophylla*
daindali (Nepali), see *Callicarpa macrophylla*
daisy, false (English), see *Eclipta prostrata*
daisy weed, Australian (English), see *Tridax procumbens*
dajerbhu (Tamang), see *Randia tetrasperma*
dakbun (Rai), see *Rhododendron arboreum*
dakh (Nepali, Newari), see *Vitis vinifera*

dakhin (Chepang), see *Oroxylum indicum*
dakine (Chepang), see *Guizotia abyssinica*
dalasin (Tamang), see *Grewia disperma*
dalchini (Nepali, Tamang), see *Cinnamomum tamala*
daldo (Rai), see *Ricinus communis*
dalhari (Lepcha), see *Lens culinaris*
dalidar (Gurung), see *Dichrocephala integrifolia*
dalidare (Gurung), see *Ageratum conyzoides*
dalifarso (Tamang), see *Grewia optiva*
dalima (Gurung), see *Osyris wightiana*
daling (Tamang), see *Valeriana jatamansii*
dalle kuro (Nepali), see *Triumfetta rhomboides, Urena lobata*
dalle pate (Nepali), see *Osyris wightiana*
dalli laharo (Majhi), see *Cissampelos pareira*
dallis grass, wild (English), see *Paspalum distichum*
dallo kuro (Rai), see *Sida rhombifolia*
daluko (Nepali), see *Adiantum caudatum, A. venustum, Dennstaedtia appendiculata, Polypodium microrhizoma, Vittaria elongata*
dalumo (Nepali), see *Pteris wallichiana*
dalwa bungi (Tamang), see *Boehmeria ternifolia*
dama (Nepali), see *Grewia helicteriifolia*
damai phal (Nepali), see *Ardisia macrocarpa, A. solanacea*
damaru (Nepali), see *Cornus capitata, Maclura cochinchinensis*
dame (Chepang), see *Ziziphus mauritiana*
damini sinka (Nepali), see *Cheilanthes albomarginata*
dampate (Nepali), see *Boenninghausenia albiflora, Desmodium gangetium, D. heterocarpon, Scutellaria discolor*
dampati (Nepali), see *Thalictrum foliolosum*
dampra (Majhi), see *Vernonia cinerea*
dampshima (Sherpa), see *Rumex nepalensis*
dana (Nepali), see *Elaeocarpus sphaericus*
danamusi (Gurung), see *Callicarpa arborea, C. macrophylla*
dandarobi (Tamang), see *Ricinus communis*
dande (Nepali), see *Eleusine indica*
dande kanda (Nepali), see *Xylosma controversum*
dandelion (English), see *Taraxacum officinale*
danesar (Chepang), see *Inula cappa*
dangding (Tamang), see *Ziziphus incurva*
dangdinge (Nepali), see *Brassaiopsis polyacantha*
dang dinge (Nepali), see *Eleutherococcus cissifolius, Schefflera venulosa*
dango (Tamang), see *Ficus rumphii*
dankerno (Nepali), see *Pityrogramma calomelanos*
dankernu (Nepali), see *Cheilanthes albomarginata*
dan-khra (Tibetan), see *Ricinus communis*
danphe charo (Nepali), see *Gaultheria nummularioides*
dan sinki (Nepali), see *Adiantum caudatum*
dansupate (Nepali), see *Geniosporum coloratum*
danta biri (Nepali), see *Neohymenopogon parasiticus*
dantaman (Nepali), see *Potentilla fulgens*
danth (Tharu), see *Colocasia esculenta*
danthe nyuro (Nepali), see *Dryopteris cochleata*
danthe unyu (Nepali), see *Thelypteris esquirolii, Woodwardia unigemmata*
danti sag (Danuwar), see *Chlorophytum nepalense*
dantya (Nepali), see *Rhus parviflora*
dapakya (Tamang), see *Potentilla fulgens*
dapchhe (Tamang), see *Agrimonia pilosa*
daphre (Gurung), see *Clerodendrum viscosum*
dapranchhu (Tamang), see *Euphorbia hirta*
daprangi (Tamang), see *Strobilanthes pentastemonoides*
dapse (Tamang), see *Potentilla argyrophylla, P. fulgens*
dapsu khar (Nepali), see *Heteropogon contortus*
dapswan (Newari), see *Jasminum multiflorum*
dar (Gurung, Magar, Nepali, Tamang), see *Boehmeria rugulosa*
darabari (Nepali), see *Luculia gratissima*
darakhyang (Tamang), see *Pogostemon glaber*
dardhuli (Tharu), see *Pouzolzia zeylanica*

dare (Tamang), see *Strobilanthes pentastemonoides*
darim (Danuwar, Gurung, Magar, Sunwar, Tamang), see *Punica granatum*
darimpate (Nepali), see *Rosa sericea*
daring (Chepang), see *Woodfordia fruticosa*
dariyongma (Rai), see *Ficus benghalensis*
darmen (Tamang), see *Viburnum erubescens*
dars (Chepang), see *Combretum roxburghii*
darsing (Chepang), see *Terminalia alata*
dar-ta (Tibetan), see *Ricinus communis*
daru kath (Nepali), see *Cornus oblonga*
datakano (Nepali), see *Rhus parviflora*
date, Chinese (English), see *Ziziphus mauritiana*
date palm (English), see *Phoenix humilis*
datil (Chepang), see *Achyranthes aspera*
datiwan (Magar, Nepali, Tamang), see *Achyranthes bidentata*
datung (Majhi), see *Streblus asper*
datura, dawny (English), see *Datura metel*
daunde (Nepali), see *Diplazium giganteum*
daunne (Magar), see *Mentha spicata*
daurali phul (Nepali), see *Stellera chamaejasme*
daurasai (Chepang), see *Coriaria napalensis*
davar (Danuwar), see *Imperata cylindrica*
dave phul (Nepali), see *Cotoneaster acuminatus*
dawami (Tamang), see *Gaultheria nummularioides*
dawami (Tibetan), see *Gaultheria fragrantissima*
day flower (English), see *Commelina benghalensis*
dbang-po-lag (Tibetan), see *Dactylorhiza hatagirea*
debre lahara (Nepali), see *Spatholobus parviflorus*
dedon (Tamang), see *Holarrhena pubescens*
degani (Tamang), see *Botrychium lanuginosum*
dekiro (Raute), see *Jatropha curcas*
delight of the mountain (English), see *Origanum vulgare*
denga (Tamang), see *Sorbus lanata*
dengsin (Tamang), see *Alnus nepalensis*
dese (Tamang), see *Sapium insigne*
desi (Tamang), see *Kalanchoe spathulata*
desi name (Magar), see *Sechium edule*
desya (Tamang), see *Euphorbia royleana, Jatropha curcas*
deudar (Nepali), see *Cedrus deodara*
devil's cotton (English), see *Abroma angusta*
devil's tree (English), see *Alstonia scholaris*
devi saro (Nepali), see *Globba clarkei, G. racemosa*
dewar (Nepali), see *Maclura cochinchinensis*
dewasin (Magar), see *Rubus ellipticus*
dewberry, golden (English), see *Duranta repens*
dha (Danuwar), see *Oryza sativa*
dha (Magar), see *Euphorbia royleana*
dha (Sherpa), see *Botrychium lanuginosum*
dhadale (Nepali), see *Boehmeria ternifolia*
dhade (Tamang), see *Strobilanthes pentastemonoides*
dhaincha (Nepali), see *Sesbania grandiflora*
dhainra (Magar), see *Woodfordia fruticosa*
dhakani (Majhi), see *Cissampelos pareira*
dhaki banso (Nepali), see *Imperata cylindrica*
dhakkar (Chepang), see *Leea crispa, L. macrophylla*
dhalde (Nepali), see *Solanum aculeatissimum*
dhaldhaliya (Tharu), see *Rauvolfia serpentina, Rumex nepalensis*
dhale (Newari), see *Punica granatum*
dhale katus (Nepali), see *Castanopsis indica*
dhalke khar (Nepali), see *Andropogon munroi, Apluda mutica*
dhalke phul (Nepali), see *Cotoneaster acuminatus*
dhalya (Nepali), see *Amaranthus spinosus*
dhamina (Nepali), see *Ulmus wallichiana*
dhampu (Nepali), see *Salvia nubicola*
dhamura ghans (Nepali), see *Centranthera nepalensis*
dhan (Bhojpuri, Mooshar, Nepali, Tharu), see *Oryza sativa*

dhana bans (Nepali), see *Arundinaria maling*
dhandiain (Nepali), see *Sesbania sesban*
dhanero (Nepali), see *Anemone elongata, A. vitifolia*
dhang ling (Tamang), see *Juniperus recurva*
dhaniya (Bhojpuri, Danuwar, Gurung, Magar, Mooshar, Nepali,
    Sunwar, Tharu), see *Coriandrum sativum*
dhaniya dhap (Tamang), see *Coriandrum sativum*
dhankan sar (Chepang), see *Tridax procumbens*
dhansejuwa (Tharu), see *Sphenoclea zeylanica*
dhanseri (Gurung), see *Cipadessa baccifera*
dhanu bans (Nepali), see *Bambusa balcooa*
dhanyar (Gurung), see *Woodfordia fruticosa*
dhanyaro (Nepali), see *Woodfordia fruticosa*
dhap (Gurung), see *Portulaca oleracea*
dhape jhar (Nepali), see *Monochoria vaginalis*
dhaple ghans (Nepali), see *Chrysopogon gryllus*
dhapre (Tamang), see *Scutellaria barbata*
dhapre jhar (Nepali), see *Veronica anagallis-aquatica*
dharmen (Tamang), see *Dichroa febrifuga*
dharni (Nepali), see *Castanopsis indica*
dharpat (Magar), see *Butea buteiformis*
dhasingar (Nepali), see *Gaultheria fragrantissima*
dha-ta-ki (Tibetan), see *Woodfordia fruticosa*
dhataur (Tharu), see *Datura metel*
dhatelo (Nepali), see *Prinsepia utilis*
dhatur (Danuwar, Gurung, Sunwar), see *Datura metel*
dhatura (Bhojpuri, Magar, Mooshar, Nepali), see *Datura metel*
dhatura bish (Tamang), see *Datura metel*
dhaturo (Nepali, Tamang), see *Datura stramonium*
dhauka (Danuwar), see *Hydrolea zeylanica*
dhauli (Majhi), see *Woodfordia fruticosa*
dhausi (Chepang), see *Artocarpus lakoocha*
dhauti (Nepali), see *Anogeissus latifolius, Lagerstroemia parviflora*
dhawa (Danuwar), see *Anogeissus latifolius*
dhawa swan (Newari), see *Jasminum gracile*
dhaya (Raute), see *Woodfordia fruticosa*
dhayaro (Tamang), see *Woodfordia fruticosa*
dhenu (Rai), see *Quercus semecarpifolia*
dhersya (Sherpa), see *Euphorbia royleana*
dhetubro (Gurung), see *Persicaria microcephala*
dhewasi (Magar), see *Rubus ellipticus*
dhikur ko makai (Nepali), see *Lobelia nummularia*
dhobi jhar (Chepang), see *Mussaenda macrophylla*
dhobini (Nepali), see *Mussaenda frondosa, M. macrophylla*
dhode kanda (Nepali), see *Cirsium verutum*
dhoh (Newari), see *Allium wallichii*
dhohalni (Tharu), see *Arundinella nepalensis*
dhoireti (Nepali), see *Mucuna nigricans*
dhokai (Magar), see *Arisaema utile*
dhokaya (Nepali), see *Arisaema utile*
dhondia (Nepali), see *Aeschynomene asper*
dhong (Tamang), see *Osyris wightiana*
dhoni (Tharu), see *Allium wallichii*
dhonsi (Gurung), see *Symplocos ramosissima*
dhoti saro (Nepali), see *Curculigo crassifolia*
dhuching (Chepang), see *Jatropha curcas*
dhuchu (Nepali), see *Colquhounia coccinea*
dhude (Tamang), see *Emilia sonchifolia*
dhudhe (Majhi), see *Holarrhena pubescens*
dhukure jhar (Nepali), see *Fumaria indica*
dhulsu (Nepali), see *Colebrookea oppositifolia*
dhumpu (Nepali), see *Gentianella moorcroftiana*
dhumre (Gurung), see *Siegesbeckia orientalis*
dhunga lahara (Nepali), see *Persicaria microcephala*
dhungalhapti (Tamang), see *Hedychium densiflorum*
dhungre (Gurung), see *Siegesbeckia orientalis*
dhungre bans (Nepali), see *Dendrocalamus giganteus*

dhungri ko jara (Nepali), see *Bergenia ciliata*
dhunsi (Gurung), see *Alnus nepalensis*
dhun swan (Newari), see *Artemisia indica*
dhup (Nepali), see *Juniperus recurva*
dhupi (Gurung), see *Didymocarpus cinereus*
dhupi (Nepali), see *Cryptomeria japonica, Cupressus torulosa,
    Juniperus indica, J. squamata*
dhurju pucha (Gurung), see *Flacourtia jangomas*
dhurseli (Majhi), see *Colebrookea oppositifolia*
dhurset (Nepali), see *Lindenbergia grandiflora*
dhurseta (Tharu), see *Colebrookea oppositifolia*
dhurseto (Nepali), see *Colebrookea oppositifolia*
dhursi (Magar, Nepali), see *Colebrookea oppositifolia*
dhursil (Danuwar, Nepali), see *Colebrookea oppositifolia*
dhursule (Gurung), see *Colebrookea oppositifolia*
dhuseri (Tharu), see *Tridax procumbens*
dhusi (Chepang), see *Citrus margarita, Maesa macrophylla*
dhusi (Tharu), see *Clerodendrum viscosum*
dhusilo (Chepang), see *Rubus paniculatus*
dhusin (Newari), see *Shorea robusta*
dhusre (Nepali), see *Leucosceptrum canum*
dhusure (Nepali), see *Colebrookea oppositifolia*
dhusure khar (Nepali), see *Leucas mollissima*
dhusurlo (Nepali), see *Ribes takare*
dhusyaurli (Nepali), see *Colebrookea oppositifolia*
dhutighans (Nepali), see *Amaranthus spinosus*
dhyabbar (Magar), see *Maclura cochinchinensis*
dhyapinu (Nepali), see *Caryopteris bicolor*
dhyo (Magar), see *Urtica dioica*
dibhar (Chepang), see *Butea buteiformis*
diklak (Chepang), see *Melastoma malabathricum*
dimmar (Nepali), see *Cornus capitata*
dinghumani phul (Tharu), see *Evolvulus nummularius*
dini mhendo (Tamang), see *Taraxacum officinale*
dita bark tree (English), see *Alstonia scholaris*
diu nigalo (Nepali), see *Drepanostachyum falcatum*
divine herb (English), see *Siegesbeckia orientalis*
diyar (Nepali), see *Cedrus deodara*
dobapongi (Tamang), see *Boehmeria platyphylla*
dock (English), see *Rumex nepalensis*
dock sorrel (English), see *Rumex acetosa*
dodder (English), see *Cuscuta reflexa*
dogwood (English), see *Cornus capitata*
dokini (Magar), see *Delphinium scabriflorum*
dokni (Danuwar), see *Centella asiatica*
doli phul (Nepali), see *Hypericum choisianum*
domala (Magar), see *Rosa brunonii*
domaru (Tibetan), see *Ribes glaciale*
domchhedama (Rai), see *Arachis hypogaea*
domjo (Tamang), see *Sambucus adnata*
domsing (Tamang), see *Lyonia ovalifolia*
dond (Magar), see *Allium wallichii*
dong-ga (Tibetan), see *Cassia fistula*
donglanais (Tamang), see *Loranthus odoratus*
dongsing noba (Tamang), see *Shuteria involucrata*
doni (Chepang), see *Crotalaria alata*
donrah (Gurung), see *Inula cappa*
dori phul (Gurung), see *Asclepias curassavica*
dowa chilim (Tamang), see *Hydrocotyle nepalensis*
dowar (Tamang), see *Corallodiscus lanuginosus*
drap muja (Chepang), see *Siegesbeckia orientalis*
drumstick (English), see *Cassia fistula*
drumstick tree (English), see *Moringa oleifera*
du (Sunwar), see *Capsicum annuum*
dub (Chepang), see *Cynodon dactylon*
dubakya (Raute), see *Rorippa nasturtium-aquaticum*
dubba (Tharu), see *Cynodon dactylon*

dube jhar (Nepali), see *Alternanthera sessilis*

dubh (Bhojpuri, Mooshar), see *Cynodon dactylon*

dubo (Danuwar, Magar, Nepali, Sunwar), see *Cynodon dactylon*

duche jhar (Nepali), see *Siegesbeckia orientalis*

duck foot (English), see *Urena lobata*

dude khirma (Magar), see *Holarrhena pubescens*

dudhai (Tharu), see *Euphorbia prostrata*

dudhe (Nepali), see *Cryptolepis buchananii, Euphorbia hirta, Ficus neriifolia* var. *nemoralis, Youngia japonica*

dudhe (Rai), see *Euphorbia hirta*

dudhe aainar (Majhi), see *Euphorbia hirta*

dudhe bhalayo (Nepali), see *Rhus javanica*

dudhe ghirle (Nepali), see *Stereospermum chelonoides*

dudhe jhar (Nepali), see *Euphorbia hirta, Launaea aspleniifolia, Taraxacum officinale*

dudhe lahara (Nepali), see *Hedyotis scandens, Ichnocarpus frutescens, Marsdenia roylei, Trachelospermum lucidum*

dudhe lahari (Nepali), see *Ficus hederacea*

dudhi (Nepali), see *Euphorbia parviflora*

dudhi jhar (Magar), see *Euphorbia hirta*

dudhi kanda (Nepali), see *Sonchus oleraceus*

dudhilo (Nepali), see *Ficus neriifolia* var. *nemoralis*

dudhiya (Chepang), see *Euphorbia heterophylla*

dudhiya (Danuwar), see *Cryptolepis buchananii*

dudhiya (Mooshar, Rai), see *Euphorbia hirta*

dudhiya jhar (Danuwar), see *Euphorbia hirta*

dudh latti (Mooshar), see *Ichnocarpus frutescens*

duk (Tibetan), see *Eupatorium chinense, Euphorbia wallichii*

duke's tongue (English), see *Monochoria vaginalis*

dukuna (Chepang), see *Luculia gratissima*

dulphi (Danuwar), see *Borreria alata*

dum (Chepang), see *Lagenaria siceraria*

dum kalleti (Nepali), see *Cheilanthes albomarginata*

dumri (Nepali), see *Ficus racemosa*

dunda (Danuwar), see *Allium wallichii*

dunde (Nepali), see *Dryoathyrium boryanum*

dundu (Nepali), see *Allium wallichii*

dundudhap (Tamang), see *Allium wallichii*

dundunge (Rai), see *Allium hypsistum*

dung dungbi (Lepcha), see *Allium ascalonicum*

du-rba (Tibetan), see *Cynodon dactylon*

duru kan (Newari), see *Euphorbia royleana*

dusi (Chepang), see *Mallotus philippensis*

dusi (Newari), see *Eleusine coracana*

dusi swan (Newari), see *Indigofera dosua*

dutyalo (Chepang), see *Holarrhena pubescens*

duwane sinka (Tharu), see *Cheilanthes albomarginata*

duware (Nepali), see *Flemingia strobilifera*

dware (Nepali), see *Mussaenda macrophylla*

dware phul (Nepali), see *Inula cappa*

dwari (Nepali), see *Luculia gratissima*

dyasin (Tamang), see *Daphne bholua*

dyo dyoali (Gurung), see *Cuscuta reflexa*

dzam-bu (Tibetan), see *Syzygium cumini*

Easter tree (English), see *Holarrhena pubescens*

ebony, Malabar (English), see *Bauhinia malabarica*

ebony, mountain (English), see *Bauhinia malabarica, B. variegata*

eggplant (English), see *Solanum melongena*

eggplant, large (English), see *Solanum anguivi*

eka aankhle phul (Nepali), see *Caltha palustris*

ekere (Nepali), see *Docynia indica*

ekle bir (Magar, Nepali), see *Clerodendrum indicum*

eklebir (Nepali, Tamang), see *Lobelia pyramidalis*

ek phale bikh (Gurung), see *Lobelia pyramidalis*

elderberry, red (English), see *Sambucus adnata*

elecampane (English), see *Inula cappa*

elephant foot yam (English), see *Amorphophallus campanulatus*

elephant rope tree (English), see *Sterculia villosa*

elephant's foot, rough (English), see *Elephantopus scaber*

emau phanjau (Tibetan), see *Clematis graveolens*

emetic nut (English), see *Catunaregam spinosa*

Englishman's foot (English), see *Plantago erosa*

ephedrine (English), see *Ephedra gerardiana*

epil (Nepali), see *Leucaena leucocephala*

e-ra (Tibetan), see *Ricinus communis*

esapgol (Nepali), see *Plantago erosa*

etka (Satar), see *Mucuna nigricans*

Eve's apron (English), see *Ficus auriculata*

fat hen (English), see *Chenopodium album*

fava bean (English), see *Vicia faba*

fennel (English), see *Foeniculum vulgare*

fennel, sweet (English), see *Foeniculum vulgare*

fenugreek (English), see *Trigonella foenum-graecum*

fern, grape (English), see *Botrychium lanuginosum*

fern, interrupted (English), see *Osmunda claytoniana*

fern allies, see *Equisetum, Lycopodium*

ferns, see *Adiantum, Aglaomorpha, Arthromeris, Botrychium, Cheilanthes, Crypsinus, Davallia, Dennstaedtia, Diplazium, Drynaria, Dryoathyrium, Dryopteris, Helminthostachys, Leucostegia, Loxogramme, Lygodium, Microlepia, Microsorum, Nephrolepis, Odontosoria, Oleandra, Onychium, Ophioglossum, Osmunda, Pityrogramma, Polypodium, Polystichum, Pteridium, Pteris, Pyrrosia, Selaginella, Tectaria, Thelypteris, Vittaria, Woodwardia*; see also fern allies

fever flower (English), see *Dichroa febrifuga*

fever nut (English), see *Caesalpinia bonduc*

fever weed (English), see *Cassia tora*

fig (English), see *Ficus carica*

fig, cluster (English), see *Ficus racemosa*

fig, elephant (English), see *Ficus lacor*

fig, golden (English), see *Ficus benjamina*

fig, hairy (English), see *Ficus hispida*

fig, Java (English), see *Ficus lacor*

fig, rough-stem (English), see *Ficus hispida*

fir, Himalayan silver (English), see *Abies spectabilis*

fir, Indian (English), see *Polyalthia longifolia*

fire-on-the-mountain (English), see *Euphorbia heterophylla*

firethorn (English), see *Pyracantha crenulata*

fishwort (English), see *Houttuynia cordata*

fitifiya (Nepali), see *Sarcococca coriacea*

fiti fiya (Nepali), see *Sarcococca saligna*

fit weed (English), see *Eryngium foetidum*

flamboyant (English), see *Delonix regia*

flame of the forest (English), see *Butea monosperma*

flax, winter (English), see *Reinwardtia indica*

flax, yellow (English), see *Reinwardtia indica*

flax seed (English), see *Linum usitatissimum*

fleabane, ash-colored (English), see *Vernonia cinerea*

flea plant (English), see *Boenninghausenia albiflora*

fly roost (English), see *Phyllanthus amarus*

fog fruit (English), see *Phyla nodiflora*

forget-me-not (English), see *Cynoglossum zeylanicum*

four o'clock plant (English), see *Mirabilis jalapa*

fowl foot (English), see *Eleusine indica*

frangipani (English), see *Plumbago zeylanica, Plumeria rubra*

frek (Tamang), see *Impatiens scabrida*

fritillary, snake's-head (English), see *Fritillaria cirrhosa*

fuchi amcho (Tibetan), see *Plantago erosa*

fumitory (English), see *Fumaria parviflora*

funsigma (Limbu), see *Prunus cerasoides*

fusre pamale (Gurung), see *Urena lobata*

gabrasai (Chepang), see *Melastoma malabathricum*

ga-bur (Tibetan), see *Cinnamomum camphora*

gada ainselu (Nepali), see *Rubus reticulatus*

gadapurena (Danuwar), see *Boerhavia diffusa*
gadapurina (Nepali), see *Trianthema portulacastrum*
gadasilo (Nepali), see *Excoecaria acerifolia*
gaderi (Chepang), see *Nicotiana tabacum*
gagaleto (Nepali), see *Elatostema sessile, Pilea symmeria*
gagata (Nepali), see *Remusatia pumila*
gagleto (Nepali), see *Cautleya spicata*
gahare ghans (Nepali), see *Desmodium podocarpum*
gahat (Danuwar), see *Cassia occidentalis*
gahate (Chepang), see *Cajanus scarabaeoides*
gahate (Gurung), see *Desmodium heterocarpon*
gahate (Majhi), see *Desmodium confertum*
gahate (Nepali, Tamang), see *Flemingia strobilifera*
gahate jhar (Majhi), see *Cajanus scarabaeoides*
gahate jhar (Nepali), see *Desmodium concinnum*
gahum (Mooshar), see *Triticum aestivum*
gahun (Bhojpuri, Chepang, Danuwar, Gurung, Magar, Nepali),
    see *Triticum aestivum*
gahun jhar (Nepali), see *Plantago erosa*
gaibin (Chepang), see *Lilium wallichianum*
gaibyai (Nepali), see *Aeginetia indica*
gai dimmar (Nepali), see *Maclura cochinchinensis*
gaidung (Chepang), see *Asparagus racemosus*
gainda kande (Nepali), see *Cirsium arvense*
gai phul (Nepali), see *Luculia gratissima*
gai pu ya haga (Newari), see *Coix lachryma-jobi*
gaisi (Chepang), see *Ziziphus incurva*
gaisinge (Nepali), see *Cryptolepis buchananii*
gaitihare (Majhi), see *Inula cappa*
gaitihare (Nepali), see *Inula cappa*
gaiyo (Danuwar), see *Bridelia retusa*
gaj (Nepali), see *Heteropogon contortus*
gajar (Nepali, Newari), see *Daucus carota*
gaj phul (Nepali), see *Photinia integrifolia*
gakaleti (Nepali), see *Lecanthus peduncularis*
galagala (Nepali), see *Leea macrophylla*
galaichi (Nepali), see *Plumeria rubra*
galaichon (Nepali), see *Plumeria rubra*
galainchi (Gurung), see *Plumeria rubra*
galaro (Chepang), see *Geniosporum coloratum*
galay (Newari), see *Tinospora sinensis*
gal bhomra (Tharu), see *Physalis divaricata*
galena (Nepali), see *Leea crispa, L. macrophylla*
galeni (Nepali), see *Arisaema tortuosum*
gallant soldier (English), see *Galinsoga parviflora*
galphule (Nepali), see *Caesulia axillaris, Cotula hemisphaerica,
    Cyathocline purpurea, Osbeckia nepalensis, O. sikkimensis*
gam (Gurung), see *Rhynchostylis retusa*
gamarai (Nepali), see *Ziziphus rugosa*
gamari (Nepali), see *Trewia nudiflora*
gambhari (Nepali), see *Gmelina arborea*
Gamble's man (English), see *Bridelia retusa*
gamdol (Nepali), see *Satyrium nepalense*
ganamane (Nepali), see *Ageratum conyzoides, Viburnum erubescens*
ganaune jhar (Nepali), see *Ageratum conyzoides, Houttuynia cordata*
ganaune pat (Nepali), see *Dichroa febrifuga*
ganchhyung mran (Tamang), see *Astilbe rivularis*
gandare (Nepali), see *Gynocardia odorata*
gande (Gurung, Magar), see *Ageratum conyzoides*
gande (Nepali), see *Ageratum conyzoides, Houttuynia cordata*
gandhaiya (Tharu), see *Pulicaria dysenterica*
gandhe jhar (Nepali), see *Ageratum houstonianum, Coleus barbatus,
    Galinsoga parviflora*
gandheli gharra (Tharu), see *Nepeta leucophylla*
gandijambu (Tamang), see *Syzygium cumini*
gandri (Majhi), see *Amaranthus spinosus, A. viridis*
gane (Nepali), see *Houttuynia cordata*

ganegeri (Nepali), see *Caesalpinia bonduc*
gane gurjo (Nepali), see *Astilbe rivularis*
gane jhar (Chepang), see *Boenninghausenia albiflora*
ganele jhar (Nepali), see *Borreria articularis*
gangap (Tamang), see *Vitis lanata*
gangdap (Tamang), see *Elephantopus scaber*
gangdol (Nepali), see *Brachycorythis obcordata*
gangdol (Tamang), see *Murdannia japonica*
gangelang (Tamang), see *Hypericum cordifolium*
ganhaune (Nepali), see *Viburnum grandiflorum*
ganheri (Danuwar), see *Amaranthus viridis*
ganhiya (Danuwar), see *Conyza bonariensis, Phyla nodiflora*
ganhiya jhar (Danuwar), see *Ageratum conyzoides*
ganhuwa (Danuwar), see *Spilanthes paniculata*
ganja (Bhojpuri, Chepang, Danuwar, Gurung, Nepali, Sunwar,
    Tharu), see *Cannabis sativa*
ganja (Tamang), see *Canavalia cathartica, Cannabis sativa*
ganki (Mooshar), see *Ageratum conyzoides*
ganne jhar (Nepali), see *Ageratum conyzoides*
ganobuti (Nepali), see *Campanula pallida*
gantay (Nepali), see *Gynocardia odorata*
gantemula (Danuwar), see *Brassica rapa*
gante mula (Magar), see *Brassica rapa*
gantemula (Nepali, Tamang), see *Brassica rapa*
gantha phula (Tharu), see *Alternanthera sessilis*
ganthe (Nepali), see *Pilea symmeria*
ganthe golia (Nepali), see *Lecanthus peduncularis*
ganthe jhar (Nepali), see *Agrimonia pilosa*
ganumen (Tamang), see *Ranunculus diffusus*
ganusa ablamban (Tamang), see *Hedyotis scandens*
gara (Tamang), see *Jatropha curcas*
gardaino (Nepali), see *Ophiorrhiza fasciculata*
gardenia, brilliant (English), see *Catunaregam uliginosa*
gare kaphal (Majhi, Nepali), see *Potentilla indica*
gargalo (Nepali), see *Boehmeria platyphylla*
gari (Mooshar, Tharu), see *Cocos nucifera*
garlic (English), see *Allium sativum*
garlic, wild (English), see *Allium wallichii*
garri (Tharu), see *Alternanthera sessilis*
garuli (Nepali), see *Wendlandia coriacea*
garumi lahara (Chepang), see *Diplocyclos palmatus*
garyaunla jhar (Nepali), see *Portulaca oleracea*
gatha ghans (Nepali), see *Viola pilosa*
gathe (Nepali), see *Strobilanthes pentastemonoides*
gat kosiya (Tharu), see *Desmodium gangetium*
gatlang (Tamang), see *Smilax menispermoides*
gau chuchcho (Nepali), see *Martynia annua*
gaujo (Nepali, Raute), see *Millettia extensa*
gau lahara (Tamang), see *Thunbergia coccinea, T. grandiflora*
gaulanto (Nepali), see *Oreocnide frutescens*
gaulat (Gurung), see *Lecanthus peduncularis*
gaurak lyangsai (Chepang), see *Osbeckia stellata*
gauraksai (Chepang), see *Oxyspora paniculata*
gauri dhan (Nepali), see *Carex nivalis*
gaurinam (Nepali), see *Didymocarpus cinereus*
gausho (Majhi), see *Millettia extensa*
gauza (Chepang), see *Desmodium confertum*
gawa (Gurung), see *Remusatia vivipara*
gayo (Magar, Nepali), see *Bridelia retusa*
gayongma (Rai), see *Bombax ceiba*
gebatisar (Magar), see *Reinwardtia indica*
gebokanak (Lepcha), see *Dichroa febrifuga*
gehun (Tharu), see *Triticum aestivum*
genthi (Danuwar), see *Dioscorea deltoidea*
gerai (Chepang), see *Thysanolaena maxima*
geronl (Gurung), see *Luffa acutangula*
ge-ser (Tibetan), see *Bombax ceiba*

gethi (Raute), see *Boehmeria rugulosa*

ghai jure (Nepali), see *Viburnum cylindricum*

ghakatek (Chepang), see *Sida cordata*

ghancharich (Gurung), see *Clerodendrum viscosum*

ghangaru (Magar, Nepali, Tamang), see *Pyracantha crenulata*

ghangharu (Nepali), see *Cotoneaster microphyllus*

ghangol (Magar), see *Ampelocissus divaricata*

ghansinmen (Tibetan), see *Sophora moorcroftiana* var. *nepalensis*

ghante phul (Nepali), see *Clematis buchananiana*

ghanti phu (Nepali), see *Holmskioldia sanguinea*

ghanti phul (Nepali), see *Hibiscus rosa-sinensis*

ghantosari (Nepali), see *Clerodendrum viscosum*

gharaghuri (Nepali), see *Viburnum cylindricum*

gharaunla (Magar), see *Luffa cylindrica*

gharauriya (Mooshar), see *Eclipta prostrata*

ghari (Nepali), see *Cotoneaster microphyllus*, *Randia tetrasperma*

ghari mamarkha (Chepang), see *Flemingia strobilifera*

gharlahi (Nepali), see *Pilea symmeria*

gharma (Tamang), see *Myrsine capitellata*

ghar tyaur (Raute), see *Dioscorea bulbifera*

ghatu (Gurung), see *Clerodendrum viscosum*

ghayaro (Tharu), see *Woodfordia fruticosa*

ghibinduri (Gurung), see *Chonemorpha fragrans*

ghibrang (Gurung), see *Gonostegia hirta*

ghinki arak (Satar), see *Diplazium esculentum*

ghiraunla (Danuwar, Nepali, Sunwar), see *Luffa cylindrica*

ghiwaha torai (Tharu), see *Luffa cylindrica*

ghobe (Nepali), see *Sporobolus fertilis*

ghode chanp (Nepali), see *Magnolia campbellii*

ghoge gava (Nepali), see *Rhynchostylis retusa*

ghoke ghans (Nepali), see *Ajuga macrosperma*

ghole (Nepali), see *Symplocos pyrifolia*, *S. theifolia*

ghora marcha (Nepali), see *Thymus linearis*

ghore dubo (Nepali), see *Chrysopogon aciculatus*

ghorekhari (Nepali), see *Viburnum cylindricum*

ghore nigalo (Nepali), see *Drepanostachyum falcatum*, *Thamnocalamus aristatus*

ghorli (Magar), see *Prunus persica*

ghortap (Mooshar), see *Centella asiatica*

ghortapa (Danuwar), see *Centella asiatica*

ghortapre (Bhojpuri, Magar, Sunwar, Tamang, Tharu), see *Centella asiatica*

ghortapre (Chepang), see *Hydrocotyle nepalensis*

ghortapre (Nepali), see *Centella asiatica*, *Prenanthes violaefolia*

ghortaprya (Chepang), see *Centella asiatica*

ghoryu (Nepali), see *Chonemorpha fragrans*

ghoya palan (Gurung), see *Rubus macilentus*

ghozel (Tamang), see *Alnus nepalensis*

ghruksu (Khaling), see *Bombax ceiba*

ghugi (Sherpa), see *Berchemia flavescens*

ghugi (Tamang), see *Hedyotis scandens*, *Tetrastigma serrulatum*

ghuiya (Tharu), see *Colocasia esculenta*

ghumen (Sherpa), see *Centella asiatica*

ghunchuni (Chepang), see *Flemingia macrophylla*

ghunro (Chepang), see *Scutellaria discolor*

ghunyalo (Nepali), see *Callicarpa arborea*

ghure (Nepali), see *Leptodermis lanceolata*

ghure chui (Magar), see *Drepanostachyum falcatum*

ghurmi (Mooshar, Satar), see *Cucumis melo* var. *agrestis*

ghuro (Nepali), see *Sorbus ursina*

ghurya (Magar), see *Strobilanthes pentastemonoides*

ghuyu (Tamang), see *Areca catechu*

ghwarbhet (Magar), see *Phyllanthus emblica*

ghyabre (Gurung), see *Fagopyrum esculentum*

ghyagar banda (Tamang), see *Lycopersicon esculentum*

ghyampa jyaunsi (Magar), see *Rubus reticulatus*

ghyani (Gurung), see *Arisaema utile*

ghyarpati (Sherpa), see *Edgeworthia gardneri*

ghyo (Magar), see *Girardinia diversifolia*, *Urtica dioica*

ghyudangdi (Tamang), see *Berberis asiatica*

ghyukumari (Danuwar, Magar, Nepali, Sunwar, Tamang), see *Aloe vera*

ghyukuwanr (Tharu), see *Aloe vera*

ghyu nyuro (Nepali), see *Dryoathyrium boryanum*

ghyu phul (Nepali), see *Sarcococca hookeriana*

ghyura (Bhojpuri, Mooshar), see *Luffa cylindrica*

ghyutinet (Tamang), see *Triumfetta rhomboides*

giddha pwankhe (Nepali), see *Cirsium falconeri*

ginar (Tamang), see *Premna barbata*

gineri (Nepali), see *Pieris formosa*, *Premna barbata*

gingelly (English), see *Sesamum orientale*

ginger (English), see *Zingiber officinale*

ginger, spiral (English), see *Costus speciosus*

ginger, white (English), see *Costus speciosus*

ginseng, Himalayan (English), see *Panax pseudoginseng*

githa (Nepali), see *Boehmeria rugulosa*, *Dioscorea bulbifera*

githa (Tamang), see *Dioscorea deltoidea*

gjama (Tamang), see *Rosa sericea*

gjunung (Sherpa), see *Gonostegia hirta*

glagengaga (Tamang), see *Gentiana depressa*

gla-gor-zho-sha (Tibetan), see *Entada phaseoloides*

glantu (Gurung), see *Aconitum spicatum*

gla-sgang (Tibetan), see *Cyperus rotundus*

glausi (Chepang), see *Bombax ceiba*

gle mhendo (Tamang), see *Cassia fistula*

gliha (Chepang), see *Dioscorea pentaphylla*

glinji (Gurung), see *Arisaema utile*

glory tree (English), see *Clerodendrum viscosum*

gnaharo (Tibetan), see *Galium asperifolium*

gnaji (Newari), see *Cannabis sativa*

gnalep (Tibetan), see *Adenocaulon himalaicum*

gnara (Gurung), see *Ficus neriifolia* var. *nemoralis*

gnedhap (Tamang), see *Sonchus asper*

gnehanam (Tamang), see *Ficus neriifolia* var. *nemoralis*

gneko (Gurung), see *Viburnum erubescens*

gnenoba (Tamang), see *Euphorbia hirta*

gnete (Tibetan), see *Sonchus oleraceus*, *S. wightianus*

gni mran (Tamang), see *Equisetum diffusum*

gnksi (Rai), see *Musa paradisiaca*

gnta (Gurung), see *Ficus neriifolia* var. *nemoralis*

gnyo (Magar), see *Cucumis sativus*

goat weed (English), see *Ageratum conyzoides*

gobar bramji (Tamang), see *Elephantopus scaber*

gobarchi (Tamang), see *Litsea monopetala*

gobarya (Nepali), see *Carpesium nepalense*

gobre (Nepali), see *Salvia nubicola*

gobre jhar (Nepali), see *Grangea maderaspatana*, *Siegesbeckia orientalis*

gobre kath (Nepali), see *Neohymenopogon parasiticus*

gobre salla (Nepali), see *Abies spectabilis*, *Pinus wallichiana*, *Tsuga dumosa*

gochhchhi (Chepang), see *Bauhinia malabarica*

Godet's weed (English), see *Phyla nodiflora*

gogal (Bhojpuri), see *Citrus margarita*

gogan (Magar), see *Saurauia napaulensis*

gogane (Nepali), see *Saurauia napaulensis*

gogpa (Sherpa), see *Allium sativum*

gohuwa (Tharu), see *Hydrolea zeylanica*

goi (Chepang), see *Dioscorea deltoidea*

goibi (Raute), see *Youngia japonica*

goihamro (Chepang), see *Buddleja asiatica*

goihmha (Tharu), see *Cucumis melo* var. *agrestis*

goikurut (Chepang), see *Colquhounia coccinea*

gokane (Gurung), see *Saurauia napaulensis*

gokhala (Nepali), see *Hygrophila auriculata*
gokpa (Sherpa), see *Allium wallichii*
golaichi (Magar), see *Plumeria rubra*
golaino (Nepali), see *Thunia alba*
golambi (Tamang), see *Solanum aculeatissimum*
golamen (Tamang), see *Tadehaji triquetrum*
golanchi (Nepali), see *Plumeria rubra*
golbenda (Gurung), see *Lycopersicon esculentum*
golbhant (Mooshar), see *Lycopersicon esculentum*
golbhanta (Bhojpuri), see *Lycopersicon esculentum*
golbhera (Nepali, Tharu), see *Lycopersicon esculentum*
golbhera puju (Gurung), see *Solanum aculeatissimum*
golbho (Tamang), see *Callicarpa arborea*
golbhyara (Newari), see *Lycopersicon esculentum*
gol buju (Tamang), see *Rubus rugosus*
goldar (Nepali), see *Callicarpa macrophylla*
goldar (Tamang), see *Callicarpa arborea*
goldarin (Chepang), see *Wendlandia pendula*
golden shower (English), see *Cassia fistula*
goldharni (Majhi), see *Catunaregam spinosa*
goli (Nepali), see *Viburnum grandiflorum*
goli (Tamang), see *Knoxia corymbosa*
goliko (Nepali), see *Lecanthus peduncularis*
golkankri (Nepali), see *Solena heterophylla*
golpat (Nepali), see *Centella asiatica*
gome (Gurung), see *Berberis aristata*
gongap (Tamang), see *Cissus javanica, Vitis parvifolia*
gooseberry, European (English), see *Ribes alpestre*
goosefoot, white (English), see *Chenopodium album*
gopa (Nepali), see *Ficus auriculata*
gorakha mal (Tamang), see *Melia azedarach*
gorakh ban (Nepali), see *Spilanthes paniculata*
gorakuri (Nepali), see *Viburnum cylindricum*
goras pan (Nepali), see *Dichrocephala integrifolia*
gorer (Danuwar), see *Catunaregam spinosa*
gorgan (Chepang), see *Tectaria macrodonta*
gorjal (Nepali), see *Drymaria diandra*
gorkhali (Magar), see *Hypericum cordifolium*
gorki (Tibetan), see *Picrorhiza scrophulariiflora*
gorsava (Tharu), see *Achyranthes aspera*
gorsyauri (Tharu), see *Grewia disperma*
goru ainselu (Nepali), see *Rubus rugosus*
gorul tito (Nepali), see *Halenia elliptica*
goru singe (Nepali), see *Martynia annua*
goru tite (Nepali), see *Swertia angustifolia*
gosangn (Newari), see *Coriandrum sativum*
go-snyod (Tibetan), see *Carum carvi, Cuminum cyminum, Foeniculum vulgare*
gothala phul (Nepali), see *Chonemorpha fragrans*
gotsai sag (Chepang), see *Bauhinia purpurea*
gotyalo (Nepali), see *Prinsepia utilis*
gourd, bitter (English), see *Momordica charantia*
gourd, bottle (English), see *Lagenaria siceraria*
gourd, common (English), see *Cucurbita maxima*
gourd, dishcloth (English), see *Luffa acutangula*
gourd, dishrag (English), see *Luffa cylindrica*
gourd, ivy (English), see *Coccinia grandis*
gourd, leprosy (English), see *Momordica charantia*
gourd, ribbed (English), see *Luffa acutangula*
gourd, small (English), see *Cucumis melo* var. *agrestis*
gourd, small bitter (English), see *Momordica dioica*
gourd, snake (English), see *Trichosanthes anguina*
gourd, Spanish (English), see *Cucurbita maxima*
gourd, white (English), see *Benincasa hispida*
gourd, wild snake (English), see *Trichosanthes dioica*
gowan (Magar), see *Saurauia napaulensis*
goya (Gurung), see *Urena lobata*

goyne (Sherpa), see *Carum carvi*
go-yu (Tibetan), see *Areca catechu*
gram (English), see *Cicer arietinum*
gram, black (English), see *Vigna mungo*
gram, dew (English), see *Phaseolus aconitifolius*
gram, golden (English), see *Phaseolus aureus*
gram, green (English), see *Phaseolus aureus*
gram, red (English), see *Cajanus cajan*
gramji (Tamang), see *Solanum anguivi*
gramsachhe (Tamang), see *Bridelia retusa*
granadilla, purple (English), see *Passiflora edulis*
grangasa (Tamang), see *Sesamum orientale*
grape (English), see *Vitis vinifera*
grape, wild (English), see *Vitis lanata*
grass, appa (English), see *Ageratum conyzoides*
grass, Bahama (English), see *Cynodon dactylon*
grass, barnyard (English), see *Echinochloa colona*
grass, Bermuda (English), see *Cynodon dactylon*
grass, China (English), see *Boehmeria platyphylla*
grass, cogon (English), see *Imperata cylindrica*
grass, cotton (English), see *Imperata cylindrica*
grass, crowfoot (English), see *Eleusine indica*
grass, doob (English), see *Cynodon dactylon*
grass, kavatta (English), see *Setaria pallidefusca*
grass, lippia (English), see *Phyla nodiflora*
grass, marvel (English), see *Dichanthium annulatum*
grass, mat (English), see *Phyla nodiflora*
grass, nut (English), see *Cyperus rotundus*
grass, quail (English), see *Celosia argentea*
grass, shepherd's weather (English), see *Anagallis arvensis*
grass, signal (English), see *Brachiaria ramosa*
grass, thatch (English), see *Imperata cylindrica*
grass, tiger (English), see *Thysanolaena maxima*
grass, wild dallis (English), see *Paspalum distichum*
grass, worm (English), see *Chenopodium ambrosoides*
grass of Parnassus (English), see *Parnassia nubicola*
greenbrier, prickly (English), see *Smilax aspera*
grepti (Tamang), see *Wikstroemia canescens*
gro (Tibetan), see *Triticum aestivum*
grop muja (Chepang), see *Flemingia strobilifera*
grosing (Tamang), see *Rhus wallichii*
ground nut (English), see *Arachis hypogaea*
gu (Chepang), see *Colocasia esculenta*
guaenlo (Tamang), see *Elaeagnus infundibularis*
guava (English), see *Psidium guajava*
gudi (Nepali), see *Bridelia retusa*
gudu (Tamang), see *Engelhardia spicata*
gugu (Tamang), see *Chenopodium album*
gugun (Gurung), see *Saurauia napaulensis*
guguri (Magar), see *Lagerstroemia parviflora*
guhi (Nepali), see *Hedera nepalensis*
guhya bir (Nepali), see *Leptodermis lanceolata*
guhya biri (Nepali), see *Spermadictyon suaveolens*
guhyapati (Nepali), see *Artemisia sieversiana*
guhya pati (Nepali), see *Thalictrum javanicum*
guhya sattar (Nepali), see *Pteris aspericaulis*
guhya silam (Nepali), see *Plectranthus mollis*
guja (Nepali), see *Mariscus sumatrensis*
gujale (Nepali), see *Drymaria diandra*
gujurgano (Nepali), see *Stephania glandulifera*
gukpa (Gurung), see *Inula cappa*
gulab (Nepali), see *Rosa brunonii*
gulab jamun (Nepali), see *Syzygium jambos*
gular (Danuwar), see *Ficus racemosa*
gulaure (Nepali), see *Camellia kissi*
guldung (Tamang), see *Viburnum nervosum*
gule kapasi (Nepali), see *Trewia nudiflora*

gulmohar (Nepali), see *Delonix regia*
gum (Tharu), see *Leucas cephalotes*
guma (Mooshar), see *Leucas cephalotes*
gumbo jhyap (Sherpa), see *Galinsoga parviflora*
gum ghatti (English), see *Anogeissus latifolius*
gumpate (Nepali), see *Leucas plukenetii*
guna puchhar (Nepali), see *Verbascum thapsus*
gunaune (Nepali), see *Leptodermis lanceolata*
gundarasi (Tamang), see *Sapindus mukorossi*
gundri gano (Tamang), see *Stephania glandulifera*
gune kauro (Nepali), see *Dioscorea deltoidea*
gungap (Tamang), see *Parthenocissus semicordata*
gunsi (Nepali), see *Podocarpus neriifolius*
guntho (Nepali), see *Verbascum thapsus*
gunyelo (Nepali), see *Elaeagnus infundibularis*
guphala (Nepali), see *Holboellia latifolia*
gurans (Danuwar), see *Rhododendron arboreum*
gurans (Nepali), see *Rhododendron barbatum, R. cinnabarinum*
guras (Nepali, Tharu), see *Rhododendron arboreum*
guraunsi phul (Nepali), see *Rhododendron anthopogon*
guren (Gurung), see *Callicarpa arborea, C. macrophylla*
guren (Nepali), see *Callicarpa arborea*
guri namcho (Tibetan), see *Inula cappa*
gurjo (Nepali), see *Tinospora sinensis*
gurmi (Nepali), see *Cucumis melo* var. *agrestis*
gurmi kant (Mooshar), see *Solanum surattense*
gursing (Sherpa), see *Saccharum officinarum*
gurubuti (Gurung), see *Cissampelos pareira*
gurubuti (Nepali), see *Clematis alternata*
guruj (Mooshar), see *Tinospora sinensis*
guru tiware (Nepali), see *Inula cappa*
gutel (Nepali), see *Trewia nudiflora*
guyela (Magar), see *Callicarpa arborea*
guyenlo (Nepali), see *Callicarpa macrophylla*
guyenti (Nepali), see *Elaeagnus parvifolia*
gu-yu (Tibetan), see *Areca catechu*
gwakhar (Magar), see *Maclura cochinchinensis*
gwame jhar (Nepali), see *Boenninghausenia albiflora*
gwaye (Newari), see *Areca catechu*
gwechasim (Newari), see *Schima wallichii*
gwe swan (Newari), see *Gomphrena globosa*
gyagar desya (Tamang), see *Jatropha curcas*
gyaine (Raute), see *Ageratum conyzoides*
gyane (Raute), see *Eupatorium adenophorum*
gyanjak (Tibetan), see *Gentiana pedicellata*
gyansin (Tamang), see *Alnus nepalensis*
gyantaka swan (Newari), see *Callistephus chinensis*
gyanth kauli (Newari), see *Brassica oleracea* var. *caulorapa*
gyanth kobi (Nepali), see *Brassica oleracea* var. *caulorapa*
gyar (Sherpa), see *Eleusine coracana*
gyasa (Tibetan), see *Rheum australe*
gya-shug (Tibetan), see *Ziziphus mauritiana*
gyer-ma (Tibetan), see *Zanthoxylum armatum*
gyumi (Gurung), see *Reinwardtia indica*
gyuru puju (Tamang), see *Justicia procumbens* var. *simplex*
hachhyun ghyan (Newari), see *Centipeda minima*
hachhyun jhar (Nepali), see *Centipeda minima, Dichrocephala integrifolia*
hachitu (Nepali), see *Dichrocephala integrifolia*
hackberry (English), see *Celtis tetrandra*
haddi jor (Nepali), see *Crinum amoenum, Rhaphidophora glauca*
hade (Nepali), see *Anogeissus latifolius, Homalium napaulense, Lagerstroemia parviflora, Randia tetrasperma*
hade bayer (Nepali), see *Ziziphus incurva*
hade kukurdaino (Nepali), see *Smilax menispermoides*
hade unyu (Nepali), see *Pteris biaurita*
hajar (Magar), see *Scurrula parasitica*

hakulal (Nepali), see *Symplocos theifolia*
hakunya (Raute), see *Indigofera atropurpurea*
hakupaku (Gurung, Tamang), see *Coriaria napalensis*
haku pasi (Newari), see *Solanum nigrum*
hala (Newari), see *Terminalia chebula*
halabakabu (Rai), see *Euphorbia pulcherrima*
hala lunde (Nepali), see *Ardisia solanacea*
halalunde (Nepali), see *Lannea coromandelica*
haldi (Tamang), see *Curcuma domestica*
hale (Nepali), see *Rumex acetosa, R. nepalensis*
haledo (Nepali), see *Curcuma domestica, Rhamnus triqueter*
haledu (Nepali), see *Adina cordifolia*
haleto (Gurung), see *Rumex nepalensis*
halhale (Nepali), see *Rumex nepalensis*
halil (Tamang), see *Rumex nepalensis*
halinkhur (Nepali), see *Convolvulus arvensis*
hallock (English), see *Terminalia myriocarpa*
halu (Newari), see *Curcuma domestica*
haluwa bet (Nepali), see *Diospyros kaki*
halyune (Raute), see *Ardisia solanacea*
hamali (Chepang), see *Lycopersicon esculentum*
hamiur (Tamang), see *Saurauia napaulensis*
hammal kanda (Nepali), see *Chonemorpha fragrans*
hamo (Newari), see *Sesamum orientale*
hangsep (Limbu), see *Terminalia chebula*
hansaraj (Nepali), see *Neohymenopogon parasiticus*
hans jhar (Nepali), see *Monochoria vaginalis*
hans phul (Nepali), see *Gentiana capitata, G. pedicellata*
hanuman (Chepang), see *Euphorbia hirta*
hanuman (Nepali), see *Ageratum conyzoides*
hanuman (Tamang), see *Tridax procumbens*
hanyunlim (Rai), see *Cynodon dactylon*
happa myan (Tamang), see *Bidens pilosa* var. *minor*
harandi (Limbu), see *Curcuma domestica*
harandukkhakwa (Rai), see *Datura metel*
harandupunwa (Rai), see *Cannabis sativa*
harber unyu (Nepali), see *Polypodium lachnopus*
harchur (Nepali), see *Aglaomorpha coronans, Arthromeris wallichiana, Viscum album*
hardi (Bhojpuri, Mooshar, Sunwar), see *Curcuma domestica*
hardithuli (Rai), see *Curcuma domestica*
hare (Nepali), see *Euphrasia himalayica*
hare bayer (Magar), see *Ziziphus incurva*
hare chyuli (Nepali), see *Malus baccata*
hare gageleto (Nepali), see *Pilea glaberrima*
hare jhar (Nepali), see *Synedrella nodiflora*
hare lasun (Nepali), see *Crinum amoenum*
hare unyu (Nepali), see *Diplazium polypodioides, Microlepia speluncae*
harimnal (Tamang), see *Phyllanthus emblica*
haritali phul (Nepali), see *Gloriosa superba*
harjor (Gurung), see *Vanda teres, Viscum album*
harjor (Nepali), see *Crypsinus hastatus, Equisetum diffusum, Vanda teres*
harjor (Tharu), see *Curcuma angustifolia, Cymbidium aloifolium*
harkata (Nepali), see *Globba racemosa*
harparo (Nepali), see *Pyrrosia mollis*
harro (Nepali), see *Terminalia chebula*
harshi (Chepang), see *Alnus nepalensis*
harsingar (Danuwar), see *Nyctanthes arbor-tritis*
harva (Nepali), see *Leea crispa*
hasina (Nepali), see *Cestrum nocturnum*
hasung (Rai), see *Bridelia retusa*
hathan (Newari), see *Sapindus mukorossi*
hathi paila (Nepali), see *Hydrocotyle nepalensis*
hathi tauke (Nepali), see *Pleione humilis*
hati jara (Nepali), see *Gymnadenia orchidis*
hati paila (Nepali), see *Brassaiopsis hainla*

hati phul (Nepali), see *Hibiscus cannabinus*
hawi (Nepali), see *Eupatorium odoratum*
hay seed, Greek (English), see *Trigonella foenum-graecum*
heather, white (English), see *Gaultheria fragrantissima*
hekaphekwa (Limbu), see *Euphorbia pulcherrima*
hekkari (Limbu), see *Lens culinaris*
hekse (Limbu), see *Cleistocalyx operculatus*
heliotrope tree (English), see *Ehretia acuminata*
hemlock (English), see *Tsuga dumosa*
hemp (English), see *Cannabis sativa*
hemp, sida (English), see *Sida rhombifolia*
hemp, soft (English), see *Cannabis sativa*
hemp, sun (English), see *Crotalaria juncea*
henbane (English), see *Hyoscyamus niger* var. *agrestis*
henduri poma (Lepcha), see *Toona ciliata*
henji (Satar), see *Solanum torvum*
henna plant (English), see *Lawsonia inermis*
hichhwalu ghyan (Newari), see *Drymaria diandra*
hi ghyan (Newari), see *Phalaris minor*
hikusing (Tibetan), see *Verbascum thapsus*
hilang (Chepang), see *Maoutia puya*
himal churi (Nepali), see *Antidesma acidum*
hinguwa (Nepali), see *Camellia kissi*
hiralal (Nepali), see *Asclepias curassavica*
hisaki (Newari), see *Dioscorea bulbifera*
hiunde simi (Nepali), see *Lablab purpureus*
hodling (Sherpa), see *Picrorhiza scrophulariiflora*
hogatani (Gurung), see *Colebrookea oppositifolia*
hogling (Sherpa), see *Swertia multicaulis*
hog weed (English), see *Boerhavia diffusa*
hohomich (Sunwar), see *Curcuma domestica*
holly, Himalayan (English), see *Ilex dipyrena*
hong-len (Tibetan), see *Picrorhiza scrophulariiflora*
hongma summ (Limbu), see *Avena sativa*
honrkandma (Rai), see *Arundo donax*
hor podo (Satar), see *Ficus semicordata*
horseradish tree (English), see *Moringa oleifera*
horsetail (English), see *Equisetum diffusum*
hoshadawaku (Sunwar), see *Camellia sinensis*
hoyek (Limbu), see *Desmostachya bipinnata*
hoyobama (Rai), see *Butea monosperma*
hubek (Rai), see *Chenopodium album*
huisache (English), see *Acacia farnesiana*
huk (Magar), see *Quercus lanata, Thysanolaena maxima*
hukki (Tamang), see *Tetrastigma serrulatum*
humble plant (English), see *Mimosa pudica*
humjing (Tamang), see *Litsea doshia*
humpu (Tibetan), see *Myricaria rosea*
hung (Chepang), see *Dioscorea pentaphylla*
hunrapa puju (Tamang), see *Mimosa rubicaulis* subsp. *himalayana*
hurhule (Majhi), see *Cleome viscosa*
hurhur (Tharu), see *Cleome viscosa*
hur sure jhar (Nepali), see *Tridax procumbens*
husure (Nepali), see *Gnaphalium polycaulon*
husure jhar (Nepali), see *Gnaphalium affine*
hyacinth, water (English), see *Eichhornia crassipes*
hyak (Magar), see *Colocasia esculenta*
hyamakho ghyan (Newari), see *Rumex nepalensis*
hyangu saki (Newari), see *Remusatia vivipara*
hyan mran (Tamang), see *Tridax procumbens*
hyansing (Magar), see *Schima wallichii*
hyauti (Danuwar), see *Elaeagnus infundibularis*
hyo mran (Tamang), see *Taraxacum officinale*
hyssop, water (English), see *Bacopa monnieri*
hyumi (Gurung), see *Reinwardtia indica*
hyumi (Nepali), see *Potentilla leschenaultiana*
hyurma (Tibetan), see *Galinsoga parviflora, G. quadriradiata*

hyurpuju (Tamang), see *Achyranthes aspera*
ibang (Tamang), see *Equisetum diffusum*
ibarara (Tibetan), see *Asparagus racemosus*
ice vine (English), see *Cissampelos pareira*
idatphung (Limbu), see *Jasminum humile*
idum-bu-re-ral (Tibetan), see *Polystichum squarrosum*
ika (Newari), see *Brassica campestris* var. *sarson*
ikalaksap (Chepang), see *Osbeckia stellata*
ikancha (Newari), see *Chenopodium album*
imali (Danuwar, Mooshar), see *Tamarindus indica*
imbing (Limbu), see *Glycine max*
imseva (Limbu), see *Diplokenma butyracea*
imu (Newari), see *Trachyspermum ammi*
indeyo (Raute), see *Ricinus communis*
Indian butter tree (English), see *Diplokenma butyracea*
Indian cassia lignea (English), see *Cinnamomum tamala*
Indian colza (English), see *Brassica campestris* var. *sarson*
indolya (Raute), see *Macaranga denticulata*
indrajau (Nepali), see *Holarrhena pubescens*
indrayani (Nepali), see *Trichosanthes wallichiana*
indreni (Nepali), see *Solanum aculeatissimum, Trichosanthes tricuspidata*
ipecac, false (English), see *Asclepias curassavica*
iron weed (English), see *Vernonia cinerea*
ironwood, Ceylon (English), see *Mesua ferrea*
ironwood tree (English), see *Mesua ferrea*
isamgoli (Nepali), see *Nicandra physalodes, Physalis divaricata*
isapgol (Nepali), see *Plantago lanceolata*
iseba (Limbu), see *Rhus javanica*
isi (Limbu), see *Rhus javanica*
isi (Rai), see *Diplokenma butyracea*
isi ma (Newari), see *Rubus ellipticus*
iskul (Newari), see *Sechium edule*
iskus (Nepali), see *Sechium edule*
ivory tree (English), see *Holarrhena pubescens*
ivy (English), see *Hedera nepalensis*
jabe (Nepali), see *Coix lachryma-jobi*
jaben (Tamang), see *Hypericum elodeoides*
jabu (Tamang), see *Syzygium cumini*
jacassar (English), see *Schleichera oleosa*
jackfruit (English), see *Artocarpus heterophyllus*
jack-in-the-pulpit (English), see *Arisaema tortuosum*
Jacob's staff (English), see *Verbascum thapsus*
jadum (Chepang), see *Rhamnus virgatus*
jagate bhyakur (Nepali), see *Dioscorea pentaphylla*
jahari (Tibetan), see *Gaultheria nummularioides*
jai (Bhojpuri, Danuwar, Rai, Sunwar, Tamang, Tharu), see *Jasminum humile*
jail mhendo (Tamang), see *Jasminum humile*
jai phul (Nepali), see *Jasminum humile*
jait (Nepali), see *Acacia farnesiana*
jaita (Nepali), see *Sesbania sesban*
jajatero (Tamang), see *Galium aparine*
jakaranda (Nepali), see *Jacaranda mimosifolia*
jakrak (Chepang), see *Smilax ovalifolia*
jalebi (Nepali), see *Pithecellobium dulce*
jale chorto (Nepali), see *Lobelia nummularia*
jali swan (Newari), see *Sambucus adnata*
jalma (Chepang), see *Drymaria diandra*
jalma (Magar), see *Grewia subinaequalis*
jalmo (Nepali), see *Grewia subinaequalis*
jaluka (Nepali), see *Remusatia pumila, R. vivipara*
jaluko (Nepali), see *Botrychium lanuginosum, Cissampelos pareira*
jam (Tharu), see *Syzygium cumini*
jamanemandro (Nepali), see *Mahonia napaulensis*
jambolan plum (English), see *Syzygium cumini*
jam-bras (Tibetan), see *Millettia pinnata*

jamdi (Nepali), see *Achyranthes aspera*

jamjasa (Tamang), see *Woodfordia fruticosa*

jamjite (Magar), see *Achyranthes aspera*

jamun (Bhojpuri, Mooshar, Nepali, Newari, Tamang), see *Syzygium cumini*

jamuna (Gurung, Nepali, Rai, Sunwar, Tamang), see *Syzygium cumini*

jamuno (Danuwar), see *Syzygium cumini*

jamunu (Magar), see *Syzygium cumini*

janai ghans (Nepali), see *Paspalum conjugatum, P. distichum, P. scrobiculatum*

janai lahara (Gurung), see *Abrus precatorius*

janai lahara (Nepali), see *Lygodium japonicum*

jande dabai (Nepali), see *Elephantopus scaber*

jangali aaru (Nepali), see *Prunus napaulensis*

jangali gulab (Nepali), see *Rosa macrophylla*

jangali jau (Nepali), see *Avena fatua*

jangali jira (Nepali), see *Carum carvi*

jangali matar (Nepali), see *Lathyrus aphaca*

jangali mewa (Nepali), see *Physalis divaricata, P. peruviana*

jangali timur (Nepali), see *Zanthoxylum acanthopodium*

jangathan (Tamang), see *Lagerstroemia parviflora*

janjulung (Chepang), see *Stephania glandulifera*

janum (Satar), see *Ziziphus mauritiana*

jar (Chepang), see *Dioscorea pentaphylla*

jarayu (Nepali), see *Ammannia auriculata*

jargat (Chepang), see *Nyctanthes arbor-tritis*

jari jhar (Mooshar), see *Sida cordata*

jariongo sag (Nepali), see *Phytolacca acinosa*

jaro buti (Nepali), see *Strobilanthes atropurpureus*

jarsai (Tamang), see *Urena lobata*

jasmine, Arabian (English), see *Jasminum sambac*

jasmine, Chinese (English), see *Jasminum multiflorum*

jasmine, hairy (English), see *Jasminum multiflorum*

jasmine, Nepal (English), see *Jasminum humile*

jasmine, night-flowering (English), see *Nyctanthes arbor-tritis*; see also jessamine

jasmine, Tuscan (English), see *Jasminum sambac*

jasmine, yellow (English), see *Jasminum humile*

jasundo (Gurung), see *Centella asiatica*

jatamansi (Gurung, Nepali), see *Nardostachys grandiflora*

jatengu (Chepang), see *Achyranthes aspera*

jathra (Chepang), see *Nyctanthes arbor-tritis*

jau (Chepang, Danuwar, Gurung, Magar, Tamang, Tharu), see *Avena sativa*

jau (Nepali), see *Avena sativa, Hordeum vulgare*

jaunde mulo (Nepali), see *Delphinium himalayai*

jawain (Bhojpuri, Tharu), see *Trachyspermum ammi*

jembir (Nepali), see *Bupleurum hamiltonii*

jeri (Chepang), see *Euphorbia royleana*

jersing (Tamang), see *Shorea robusta*

jeru (Chepang), see *Euphorbia royleana*

Jerusalem thorn (English), see *Acacia catechu*

jessamine, night (English), see *Cestrum nocturnum*; see also jasmine

jethi madhu (Nepali), see *Stellaria monosperma*

jhaduk (Sherpa), see *Urtica dioica*

jhaibal (Gurung), see *Daphniphyllum himalense*

jhamolumo (Tamang), see *Malva verticillata*

jhangal (Tamang), see *Lagerstroemia parviflora*

jhankre (Nepali), see *Litsea doshia*

jhankri chhe (Gurung), see *Litsea doshia*

jhapakane (Gurung), see *Dicentra scandens*

jhar (Danuwar, Mooshar, Tharu), see *Ammannia baccifera*

jhar (Nepali), see *Alysicarpus vaginalis*

jharang (Chepang), see *Marsdenia lucida*

jhare jara (Nepali), see *Anemone trullifolia*

jharlyang (Magar), see *Sapindus mukorossi*

jharmaruwa (Danuwar), see *Phyla nodiflora*

jharose (Tamang), see *Coriaria napalensis*

jhar timur (Nepali), see *Hydrocotyle nepalensis*

jhengra (Tharu), see *Garuga pinnata*

jheremsi (Khaling), see *Myrica esculenta*

jhesin (Gurung), see *Shorea robusta*

jhigane (Nepali), see *Eurya cerasifolia*

jhilinge (Nepali), see *Dicentra scandens*

jhilleri (Nepali), see *Boehmeria platyphylla*

jhilleti (Nepali), see *Spiraea canescens*

jhim jhime (Nepali), see *Grangea maderaspatana*

jhinga jale (Nepali), see *Drosera peltata*

jhinga jhar (Nepali), see *Boenninghausenia albiflora*

jhingane (Nepali), see *Eurya acuminata*

jhingucha (Newari), see *Allium hypsistum*

jhip jhip (Nepali), see *Colquhounia coccinea*

jhiru (Magar), see *Castanopsis indica*

jhomasin (Tibetan), see *Boschniakia himalaica*

jhonkhimamarkha (Danuwar), see *Desmodium oojeinense*

jhuinsin (Gurung), see *Eurya acuminata*

jhukre (Magar), see *Mimosa rubicaulis* subsp. *himalayana*

jhule jhar (Nepali), see *Crassocephalum crepidioides*

jhule phul (Nepali), see *Holmskioldia sanguinea*

jhuleti (Nepali), see *Vitis repanda*

jhulo (Nepali), see *Gerbera nivea*

jhunde salla (Nepali), see *Picea smithiana*

jhunke ghans (Nepali), see *Leucas mollissima*

jhupe pyaunli (Nepali), see *Medicago lupulina*

jhuse (Majhi), see *Uraria lagopodioides*

jhuse chitlangi (Nepali), see *Galinsoga quadriradiata*

jhuse jhar (Nepali), see *Bulbostylis densa*

jhuse kutelikosa (Nepali), see *Vicia hirsuta*

jhuse mothe (Nepali), see *Pycreus sanguinolentus*

jhuse til (Nepali), see *Guizotia abyssinica*

jhuske (Nepali), see *Maharanga bicolor*

jhuwan (Tamang), see *Trachyspermum ammi*

jhyaple ghans (Nepali), see *Polypogon fugax*

jhyapmuja (Chepang), see *Bidens pilosa* var. *minor*

jhyapu ghans (Nepali), see *Gnaphalium affine*

jhyaringe (Magar), see *Combretum roxburghii*

jhyaro kangwa (Sherpa), see *Gentiana pedicellata*

jhyasuk (Tibetan), see *Ajuga lupulina*

jhyau jhar (Nepali), see *Spergula arvensis*

jhyaupate (Chepang), see *Coelogyne cristata*

jhyaure kanda (Nepali), see *Caragana brevispina*

jhyume (Gurung), see *Potentilla kleiniana*

jhyun jhyuro (Chepang), see *Peperomia pellucida*

ji (Newari), see *Cuminum cyminum*

ji (Tamang), see *Tsuga dumosa*

jibre (Nepali), see *Cypripedium cordigerum*

jibre ghans (Nepali), see *Hypericum elodeoides*

jibre pate (Nepali), see *Alternanthera sessilis*

jibre sag (Nepali), see *Ophioglossum nudicaule, O. reticulatum*

jibre unyu (Nepali), see *Oleandra wallichii*

jigana (Tharu), see *Garuga pinnata*

jimbu (Bhojpuri, Danuwar, Gurung, Lepcha, Nepali, Sunwar, Tamang, Tharu), see *Allium hypsistum*

jimbu jhar (Nepali), see *Allium wallichii*

jimson weed (English), see *Datura stramonium*

jimuno (Gurung), see *Micromeria biflora*

jin (Chepang), see *Shorea robusta*

jinchhi (Gurung), see *Buddleja paniculata*

jingan (Tamang), see *Hedyotis scandens*

jingar (Danuwar), see *Lannea coromandelica*

jira (Bhojpuri, Chepang, Danuwar, Magar, Nepali, Sunwar), see *Cuminum cyminum*

jire jahr (Nepali), see *Fimbristylis squarrosa*
jire nyuro (Nepali), see *Dryopteris sparsa, Thelypteris ciliata*
jiro (Gurung, Rai), see *Cuminum cyminum*
jo (Lepcha), see *Oryza sativa*
Job's tears (English), see *Coix lachryma-jobi*
jodung (Chepang), see *Asparagus racemosus*
jogbiro (Chepang), see *Flemingia strobilifera*
jogi ainselu (Nepali), see *Potentilla indica, Rubus macilentus*
jogi dang (Magar), see *Smilax aspera*
jogi lahara (Nepali), see *Cissus javanica, Marsdenia roylei*
jogi phul (Nepali), see *Stellera chamaejasme*
joi chaiba damphu (Sunwar), see *Allium wallichii*
joint weed (English), see *Persicaria barbata, P. glabra*
jojo (Satar), see *Tamarindus indica*
jomatapheng (Lepcha), see *Lagenaria siceraria*
jomosing (Tibetan), see *Caragana brevispina*
jonki mamarkha (Danuwar), see *Desmodium triflorum*
jorbhok (Chepang), see *Asparagus racemosus*
jotane jhar (Nepali), see *Euphorbia hirta, Micromeria biflora*
juga chutro (Nepali), see *Berberis chitria*
juis (Magar), see *Rubus ellipticus*
jujube (English), see *Ziziphus mauritiana*
juku (Tibetan), see *Bromus tectorum*
julphi (Danuwar), see *Leucas cephalotes*
julphi jhar (Danuwar), see *Leucas indica*
jumalo (Nepali), see *Boenninghausenia albiflora*
jumarijhar (Nepali), see *Boenninghausenia albiflora*
jumli kuro (Nepali), see *Xanthium strumarium*
jumlo salla (Nepali), see *Pinus roxburghii*
junge banso (Nepali), see *Eragrostis tenella*
junge lahara (Nepali), see *Clematis barbellata, C. buchananiana, C. gouriana*
jungraban (Chepang), see *Crotalaria ferruginea*
juniper (English), see *Juniperus recurva*
juniper, weeping blue (English), see *Juniperus recurva*
Juno's tears (English), see *Verbena officinalis*
jure kaphal (Nepali), see *Eriobotrya dubia*
jure mayel (Nepali), see *Stranvaesia nussia*
jurse (Rai), see *Phyllanthus emblica*
jut (Nepali), see *Corchorus capsularis*
jute (English), see *Corchorus capsularis*
jute, bhimli (English), see *Hibiscus cannabinus*
jute, broom (English), see *Sida rhombifolia*
jute, Java (English), see *Hibiscus sabdariffa*
juwano (Rai), see *Trachyspermum ammi*
jwahane jhar (Nepali), see *Isodon coetsa*
jwan (Nepali), see *Trachyspermum ammi*
jwane (Nepali), see *Pleurospermum angelicoides*
jwane ghans (Nepali), see *Selinum tenuifolium*
jwane jhar (Nepali), see *Boenninghausenia albiflora, Fimbristylis miliacea*
jwanu (Chepang, Danuwar, Magar, Sunwar), see *Trachyspermum ammi*
jyajyurakat (Lepcha), see *Cuminum cyminum*
jyajyurakata (Lepcha), see *Trachyspermum ammi*
jyammu (Magar), see *Allium hypsistum*
jyaso serpo (Tibetan), see *Trigonella gracilis*
jyaunsi (Majhi), see *Rubus ellipticus*
jyugar (Chepang), see *Flemingia strobilifera*
kabali (Magar), see *Cucurbita maxima*
ka-bed (Tibetan), see *Citrullus lanatus, Lagenaria siceraria*
kabhro (Nepali), see *Ficus lacor*
kable (Nepali), see *Agrimonia pilosa*
kachanar (Bhojpuri), see *Bauhinia variegata*
kacha pat (Chepang), see *Nicotiana tabacum*
kacharehat (Tharu), see *Solanum surattense*
kachchhe (Lepcha), see *Citrus medica*

kachchu (Bhojpuri), see *Colocasia esculenta*
kachhe (Newari), see *Pisum sativum*
kachur (Nepali), see *Curcuma angustifolia*
kachyer (Lepcha), see *Avena sativa*
kada (Tamang), see *Colquhounia coccinea*
kadam (Mooshar), see *Neolamarckia cadamba*
kadam (Nepali), see *Jatropha curcas, Neolamarckia cadamba*
kadam (Rai), see *Jatropha curcas*
kadau (Chepang), see *Eleusine coracana*
kadik mhendo (Tamang), see *Senecio diversifolius*
kadilo (Tamang), see *Sechium edule*
kadima (Bhojpuri, Mooshar), see *Cucurbita maxima*
kado (Tamang), see *Juglans regia* var. *kamaonia*
kadu (Nepali), see *Gynocardia odorata*
kaga (Tamang), see *Coriaria napalensis*
kagadil (Nepali), see *Strobilanthes atropurpureus*
kagajpate (Nepali), see *Daphne papyracea*
kagarete (Nepali), see *Anemone rivularis*
kagat (Tamang), see *Citrus aurantifolia*
kagate phul (Nepali), see *Tabernaemontana divaricata*
kagati (Chepang, Danuwar, Magar, Nepali, Newari, Tharu), see *Citrus aurantifolia*
kagatpate (Nepali), see *Daphne bholua*
kag bhalayo (Nepali), see *Rhus succedanea*
kagcharo (Nepali), see *Ephedra gerardiana*
kag chuchche (Nepali), see *Thunbergia grandiflora*
kagdhong (Tamang), see *Bombax ceiba*
kagi (Sunwar), see *Colocasia esculenta*
kag phuli (Danuwar), see *Thunbergia grandiflora*
kaguno (Nepali), see *Setaria italica*
kaha swan (Newari), see *Datura metel*
kaichak (Chepang), see *Colebrookea oppositifolia*
kaikalai (Chepang), see *Crassocephalum crepidioides*
kainjalo (Nepali), see *Bischofia javanica*
kairo jhar (Nepali), see *Gnaphalium affine*
kairun (Nepali), see *Cirsium verutum*
kairuwa (Nepali), see *Fumaria parviflora*
kairuwa (Tharu), see *Polygonatum cirrhifolium*
kaitak (Chepang), see *Ficus auriculata, F. hispida*
kaitha (Tharu), see *Trichosanthes anguina*
kaja (Nepali), see *Bridelia retusa*
kaju (Nepali), see *Sterculia foetida*
kajyang (Lepcha), see *Urtica dioica*
kakacha (Newari), see *Momordica charantia*
kaka lahara (Gurung), see *Thunbergia coccinea*
kakari (Nepali), see *Cucumis melo* var. *utilissimus*
kakati (Sunwar), see *Citrus aurantifolia*
kakicha swan (Newari), see *Grevillea robusta*
kakoli (Nepali), see *Fritillaria cirrhosa*
kakryon (Gurung), see *Vitis lanata*
kakyo (Lepcha), see *Triticum aestivum*
kal (Gurung), see *Engelhardia spicata*
kal (Nepali), see *Arisaema consanguineum*
kala (Gurung), see *Macaranga pustulata*
kalalgera (Sunwar), see *Sapindus mukorossi*
kalama (Chepang), see *Adina cordifolia*
kalambo (Chepang), see *Adina cordifolia*
kalamnath (Tharu), see *Plumbago zeylanica*
kalan (Gurung), see *Choerospondias axillaris*
kalan (Tamang), see *Hypericum oblongifolium*
kalancha (Newari), see *Houttuynia cordata*
kalang (Tamang), see *Choerospondias axillaris*
kalangu (Tamang), see *Debregeasia longifolia*
kalanguli (Tamang), see *Debregeasia salicifolia*
kalankugu (Gurung), see *Debregeasia salicifolia*
kalan kuli (Gurung), see *Maoutia puya*
kalare unyu (Nepali), see *Thelypteris paludosa*

kalaun (Raute), see *Pisum sativum*

kalchauda kanda (Nepali), see *Solanum aculeatissimum*

kalchhe (Gurung), see *Neolitsea cuipala*

kalchun (Nepali), see *Paris polyphylla*

kaldar (Tamang), see *Selaginella chrysocaulos*

kalgeri (Nepali), see *Gaultheria fragrantissima*

kalhahir (Lepcha), see *Lens culinaris*

kalhubi (Lepcha), see *Luffa cylindrica*

kali ainselu (Nepali), see *Potentilla peduncularis, Rubus hypargyrus*

kali angeri (Nepali), see *Melastoma malabathricum, M. normale, Osbeckia nepalensis*

kali gedi (Majhi), see *Solanum nigrum*

kali geri (Nepali), see *Cipadessa baccifera, Gaultheria nummularioides*

kaligeri (Nepali), see *Solanum nigrum*

kali geri (Tamang), see *Symplocos ramosissima*

kali jhar (Majhi), see *Rungia parviflora*

kali jhar (Nepali), see *Achyranthes aspera*

kali kath (Magar), see *Cipadessa baccifera*

kali kath (Nepali), see *Symplocos pyrifolia*

kalikuiyan (Nepali), see *Solanum nigrum*

kali kuthurke (Nepali), see *Tectaria macrodonta*

kali lahara (Nepali), see *Natsiatum herpeticum*

kali nyuro (Nepali), see *Tectaria macrodonta*

kalising (Sherpa, Tamang), see *Cheilanthes albomarginata*

kali sinka (Nepali), see *Cheilanthes tenuifolia*

kali sisnu (Nepali), see *Girardinia diversifolia*

kaliso (Nepali), see *Ilex dipyrena*

kal jhar (Tamang), see *Eupatorium adenophorum*

kal jira (Nepali), see *Eclipta prostrata*

kalki phul (Nepali), see *Callistemon citrinus*

kalki swan (Newari), see *Callistemon citrinus*

kallageri (Nepali), see *Elaeagnus kanaii*

kallagir (Nepali), see *Elaeagnus infundibularis*

kalma (Sherpa), see *Rhododendron arboreum*

kalme (Tamang), see *Houttuynia cordata*

kalmi sag (Nepali), see *Ipomoea aquatica*

kalo ainselu (Nepali), see *Rubus biflorus, R. foliolosus, R. griffithii, R. niveus, R. paniculatus, R. reticulatus*

kalo asuro (Nepali), see *Pogostemon benghalensis*

kalo bans (Nepali), see *Dendrocalamus hookeri*

kalo basak (Nepali), see *Justicia adhatoda*

kalo besar (Nepali), see *Curcuma angustifolia*

kalo bethe (Nepali), see *Chenopodium murale*

kalo bharaun (Nepali), see *Boehmeria platyphylla*

kalo bheri (Nepali), see *Scutellaria violacea*

kalo bikh (Nepali), see *Aconitum laciniatum*

kalo chaulayo (Nepali), see *Wikstroemia canescens*

kalo dhaturo (Nepali), see *Datura metel, D. stramonium*

kalo ghuriyo (Danuwar), see *Cryptolepis buchananii*

kalo gojale (Nepali), see *Anagallis arvensis*

kalo jamun (Nepali), see *Syzygium cumini*

kalo kuro (Nepali), see *Bidens pilosa* var. *minor*

kalo logte (Nepali), see *Wikstroemia canescens*

kalo miri (Nepali), see *Leonurus cardiaca*

kalo nyuro (Nepali), see *Diplazium stoliczkae, Dryoathyrium boryanum*

kalo pati (Nepali), see *Salvia plebeia*

kalo pidalu (Nepali), see *Remusatia vivipara*

kalo rudilo (Nepali), see *Teucrium quadrifarium*

kalo siris (Nepali), see *Albizia chinensis, A. lebbeck*

kalo til (Nepali), see *Guizotia abyssinica*

kalo tori (Nepali), see *Brassica nigra*

kalsinkha (Nepali), see *Cheilanthes albomarginata*

kalta (Tamang), see *Abies spectabilis*

kama (Gurung), see *Drepanostachyum falcatum*

kamai (Nepali), see *Solanum nigrum*

kamal (Bhojpuri, Danuwar, Gurung, Magar, Nepali, Sunwar, Tharu), see *Nelumbo nucifera*

Kamala dye tree (English), see *Mallotus philippensis*

kamale jhar (Nepali), see *Tridax procumbens*

kamal mhendo (Tamang), see *Nelumbo nucifera*

kama muja (Chepang), see *Mimosa pudica*

kamani (Chepang), see *Phyla nodiflora*

kamarakh (Nepali), see *Averrhoa carambola*

kamari jhar (Nepali), see *Solanum nigrum*

kambalo (Tamang), see *Solanum aculeatissimum*

kambaman (Tamang), see *Isodon lophanthoides*

kambari jhar (Nepali), see *Acrocephalus indicus*

kamcha (Mooshar), see *Nyctanthes arbor-tritis*

kamila (Newari), see *Mallotus philippensis*

kamla (Nepali), see *Callicarpa macrophylla*

kamle (Magar), see *Boehmeria platyphylla, B. ternifolia, Pilea symmeria*

kamlo (Gurung), see *Dioscorea bulbifera*

kammari (Nepali), see *Drynaria propinqua*

kampman (Tamang), see *Swertia angustifolia*

kamraj (Nepali), see *Helminthostachys zeylanica*

kamsar kambar (Chepang), see *Solanum torvum*

kanachung (Lepcha), see *Zea mays*

kanakhuli (Gurung), see *Debregeasia salicifolia*

kanase (Nepali), see *Thunbergia coccinea*

kanchai jhar (Gurung), see *Plantago erosa*

kanchan arak (Satar), see *Momordica dioica*

kanchini (Nepali), see *Scindapsus officinalis*

kanchiro (Nepali), see *Acer acuminatum, A. caesium*

kanchirru (Nepali), see *Scindapsus officinalis*

kanchiruwa (Nepali), see *Rhaphidophora glauca*

kanchu (Satar), see *Colocasia esculenta*

kanchuli (Nepali), see *Cirsium wallichii*

kanchurene (Chepang), see *Sanicula elata*

kandail (Tharu), see *Thevetia peruviana*

kanda malau (Nepali), see *Viburnum mullaha*

kanda masi (Nepali), see *Morina longifolia*

kandar (Nepali), see *Aesculus indica*

kande (Nepali), see *Amaranthus spinosus, Argemone mexicana, Lepidagathis incurva*

kande (Rai), see *Amaranthus spinosus*

kande khasru (Nepali), see *Maytenus rufa*

kande painyu (Nepali), see *Rhamnus virgatus*

kande puju (Gurung), see *Ziziphus incurva*

kandu (Lepcha), see *Solanum melongena*

kane bahiro (Nepali), see *Glochidion velutinum*

kane chhi (Gurung), see *Ficus subincisa*

kane ghans (Nepali), see *Wendlandia coriacea*

kane jhar (Nepali), see *Commelina benghalensis, Murdannia nudiflora*

kanema (Raute), see *Commelina benghalensis*

kane mauwa (Magar), see *Engelhardia spicata*

kane mauwa (Nepali), see *Glochidion velutinum*

kaner (Nepali), see *Nerium indicum*

kaneuwa (Raute), see *Floscopa scandens*

kanga (Nepali), see *Platanthera clavigera*

kangaraito phul (Nepali), see *Aechmanthera gossypina*

kangarata (Nepali), see *Anemone rivularis*

kangio (Magar), see *Wendlandia coriacea*

kangio phul (Nepali), see *Wendlandia coriacea*

kangiyo (Nepali), see *Abutilon indicum, Pavetta tomentosa*

kangiyo phul (Nepali), see *Grevillea robusta*

kangiyo sotar (Nepali), see *Onychium siliculosum*

kangre jhar (Nepali), see *Galium aparine*

kangres (Tharu), see *Xanthium strumarium*

kangri jhar (Gurung), see *Vitis lanata*

kanguil (Nepali), see *Euphorbia hirta, Gonostegia hirta*

kani (Newari), see *Zea mays*

kanige (Nepali), see *Maesa chisia*
kanike (Nepali), see *Ligustrum confusum*
kanike chutro (Nepali), see *Berberis everstiana*
kanike ghans (Nepali), see *Euphorbia prostrata, Hypericum japonicum*
kanike kuro (Nepali), see *Cynoglossum glochidiatum, C. zeylanicum, Trichodesma indicum*
kanike phul (Nepali), see *Ligustrum compactum, Wendlandia coriacea*
kanime (Nepali), see *Pyracantha crenulata*
kani unyun (Nepali), see *Adiantum philippense*
kaniya (Tharu), see *Commelina benghalensis*
kanja (Nepali), see *Caesalpinia bonduc*
kanjhi (Danuwar, Mooshar), see *Bridelia retusa*
kanju (Tharu), see *Millettia pinnata*
kankarne (Nepali), see *Nepeta leucophylla, Scutellaria scandens*
kankhombrek (Limbu), see *Prunus domestica*
kankre jhar (Nepali), see *Lindernia nummularifolia*
kankri (Tamang), see *Gonostegia hirta*
kankri jhar (Nepali), see *Elephantopus scaber*
kankro (Nepali), see *Cucumis sativus*
kanpate (Majhi), see *Euphorbia royleana*
kanpate (Nepali), see *Inula cappa*
kanre mate (Nepali), see *Amaranthus spinosus*
kanre salla (Nepali), see *Araucaria bidwillii*
kans (Nepali), see *Saccharum spontaneum*
kanta (Danuwar), see *Cirsium wallichii*
kantageri (Magar), see *Solanum aculeatissimum*
kantakari (Nepali), see *Solanum surattense*
kantakari (Tamang), see *Solanum aculeatissimum*
kan-ta-ka-ri (Tibetan), see *Rubus niveus, Solanum surattense*
kantakari (Tibetan), see *Sorbaria tomentosa*
kanthakari (Nepali), see *Solanum aculeatissimum*
kanthakasi (Rai), see *Punica granatum*
kanthakumari (Magar), see *Solanum aculeatissimum*
kanthamal (Chepang), see *Oxalis corniculata*
kanthamalai jhar (Tharu), see *Oxalis corniculata*
kanthamale (Majhi), see *Caesulia axillaris*
kanthamul (Sunwar), see *Dioscorea bulbifera*
kanthamun (Nepali), see *Potentilla fulgens*
kanthe jhar (Nepali), see *Leucas cephalotes*
kantiya (Tharu), see *Amaranthus spinosus, A. viridis*
kanukpa (Nepali), see *Euodia fraxinifolia*
kanur (Tamang), see *Bauhinia purpurea*
kanyong (Lepcha), see *Brassica rapa*
kapara (Magar), see *Ficus lacor*
kapas (Chepang, Magar), see *Gossypium arboreum*
kapase (Nepali), see *Anemone vitifolia, Thespesia lampas*
kapase phul (Nepali), see *Saussurea gossypiphora*
kapas ko bot (Nepali), see *Gossypium arboreum*
kapay ma (Newari), see *Gossypium arboreum*
kaphal (Bhojpuri, Danuwar, Gurung, Magar, Nepali, Tharu), see *Myrica esculenta*
kapiphung (Limbu), see *Brassica oleracea* var. *botrytis*
kappa (Magar), see *Ficus palmata*
kapre sag (Nepali), see *Persicaria runcinata*
kapu (Nepali), see *Rumex hastatus*
kapu ma (Newari), see *Cinnamomum camphora*
kapur (Bhojpuri, Danuwar, Gurung, Lepcha, Magar, Nepali, Sunwar, Tamang), see *Cinnamomum camphora*
kapu swan (Newari), see *Salvia officinalis*
kar (Sunwar), see *Pisum sativum*
ka-ra (Tibetan), see *Saccharum officinarum*
karahu (Lepcha), see *Fagopyrum esculentum*
karai (Nepali), see *Cirsium wallichii*
karaila (Bhojpuri, Danuwar, Tharu), see *Momordica charantia*
karam (Danuwar, Nepali, Tamang), see *Adina cordifolia*
karama (Mooshar), see *Adina cordifolia*

karamuwan (Tharu), see *Ipomoea aquatica*
karanda (English), see *Carissa carandas*
karante jhar (Nepali), see *Leersia hexandra, Scleria biflora*
karaunte (Nepali), see *Carissa carandas*
karauti chhe (Tamang), see *Thysanolaena maxima*
karbija (Tamang), see *Myrica esculenta*
karbir (Nepali), see *Nerium indicum*
karbisi (Sherpa), see *Myrica esculenta*
karboni (Danuwar), see *Monochoria vaginalis*
kardha jhar (Chepang), see *Desmodium multiflorum*
kardung (Lepcha), see *Musa paradisiaca*
karela (Magar, Mooshar, Nepali, Sunwar), see *Momordica charantia*
kareli (Nepali), see *Cirsium verutum, Flacourtia jangomas*
kareli (Tamang), see *Momordica charantia*
karilo (Tamang), see *Momordica charantia*
karingi (Nepali), see *Holarrhena pubescens*
karjani (Mooshar), see *Abrus precatorius*
karkale jhar (Nepali), see *Butomopsis latifolia, Monochoria vaginalis*
karkalo (Danuwar, Magar, Nepali), see *Colocasia esculenta*
karkare ghans (Nepali), see *Spermadictyon suaveolens*
karkera (Nepali), see *Caesalpinia bonduc*
karme jhar (Nepali), see *Corydalis chaerophylla*
karmi (Nepali, Satar), see *Ipomoea aquatica*
karna (Nepali), see *Boenninghausenia albiflora*
karnaphuli (Nepali), see *Taraxacum officinale*
karona (Danuwar, Mooshar), see *Carissa carandas*
karonda (Nepali, Tharu), see *Carissa carandas*
karpasi (Tamang), see *Myrica esculenta*
karu (Nepali), see *Aesculus indica*
karyang (Nepali), see *Smilax menispermoides*
kasaili (Mooshar), see *Areca catechu*
kashyampot (Lepcha), see *Rubus ellipticus*
kashyopot (Lepcha), see *Castanopsis indica*
kasi (Tamang), see *Colquhounia coccinea*
kasing (Tamang), see *Camellia kissi*
kasingal (Tamang), see *Viburnum mullaha*
kasinkalo (Tamang), see *Viburnum erubescens*
kasintu (Gurung), see *Castanopsis indica*
kaski lang (Chepang), see *Buddleja asiatica*
kasturi (Nepali), see *Abelmoschus moschatus*
kasturi phul (Nepali), see *Delphinium brunonianum*
kastus (Nepali), see *Castanopsis indica*
kasur (Nepali), see *Cyperus rotundus*
kasyegoi (Chepang), see *Satyrium nepalense*
kat (Khaling), see *Rubia manjith*
katageni (Danuwar), see *Amaranthus spinosus, A. viridis*
katahar (Danuwar, Magar, Nepali, Tharu), see *Artocarpus heterophyllus*
katahare kuro (Nepali), see *Urena lobata*
kataiya (Mooshar), see *Solanum aculeatissimum*
katar (Majhi), see *Artocarpus heterophyllus*
katar (Mooshar), see *Amaranthus spinosus*
katara (Danuwar), see *Argemone mexicana*
katare (Nepali), see *Bidens pilosa* var. *minor*
kathar (Sunwar), see *Artocarpus heterophyllus*
kathe kaula (Nepali), see *Litsea doshia*
kathe kaulo (Nepali), see *Persea gamblei*
kathe pipal (Nepali), see *Ficus rumphii*
kath gedi (Nepali), see *Pyracantha crenulata*
kati (Gurung), see *Campanula pallida*
kato (Tamang), see *Juglans regia* var. *kamaonia*
kat-pha-la (Tibetan), see *Myrica esculenta*
katu (Gurung), see *Juglans regia* var. *kamaonia, Lindera neesiana*
katus (Bhojpuri, Chepang, Danuwar, Tamang, Tharu), see *Castanopsis indica*
katus (Nepali), see *Castanopsis tribuloides*
kaula (Nepali), see *Michelia kisopa, Persea bombycina*

kaul duse (Tamang), see *Prunus napaulensis*
kaule (Nepali), see *Brassica oleracea* var. *botrytis, Dodecadenia grandiflora*
kaule (Newari), see *Brassica oleracea* var. *botrytis*
kaule jhar (Majhi), see *Sida cordata*
kauli (Danuwar, Magar, Tamang), see *Brassica oleracea* var. *botrytis*
kauli (Nepali), see *Symplocos ramosissima*
kauli katahar (Majhi), see *Ananas comosus*
kaulun thunga (Tamang), see *Thunbergia coccinea, T. grandiflora*
kaune banso (Nepali), see *Sacciolepis indica*
kauni (Mooshar), see *Setaria italica*
kause phul (Nepali), see *Cotoneaster affinis*
kauwa kaphal (Nepali), see *Potentilla kleiniana*
kauwa ko kera (Nepali), see *Luisia zeylanica*
kauwa latti (Danuwar), see *Thunbergia grandiflora*
kawai (Nepali), see *Solanum nigrum*
kayensi (Nepali), see *Acacia intsia*
ke (Limbu), see *Phaseolus aconitifolius, Pisum sativum*
ke (Tibetan), see *Tsuga dumosa*
kebara (Gurung), see *Cuscuta reflexa*
kebu (Nepali), see *Strobilanthes pentastemonoides*
kegucha ghyan (Newari), see *Ageratum conyzoides*
keje (Gurung), see *Rheum moorcroftianum*
kekru (Chepang), see *Acacia pennata*
kel (Tamang), see *Abies spectabilis*
kelai (Bhojpuri), see *Phaseolus aconitifolius*
kelai (Magar), see *Rumex nepalensis*
kelang (Tamang), see *Hypericum cordifolium, H. uralum*
kella (Gurung), see *Betula utilis*
kemba girbu (Sherpa), see *Artemisia indica*
keme (Gurung), see *Oreocnide frutescens*
kemna (Danuwar, Gurung), see *Cleistocalyx operculatus*
kera (Bhojpuri, Danuwar, Mooshar, Nepali, Newari, Tharu), see *Musa paradisiaca*
kerau (Chepang, Danuwar, Nepali, Tamang, Tharu), see *Pisum sativum*
kerba (Tamang), see *Berberis aristata*
kernapa (Sherpa), see *Berberis chitria*
kerpa (Tamang), see *Berberis aristata, B. asiatica, Ilex dipyrena*
kerpa (Tibetan), see *Berberis chitria*
kerpa ko therma (Sherpa), see *Berberis chitria*
kerpal (Tamang), see *Mahonia napaulensis*
kersingi (Nepali), see *Millettia pinnata*
kesa (Gurung), see *Rheum moorcroftianum*
kesari (Nepali), see *Mahonia acanthifolia, Maytenus rufa*
kesh lahara (Nepali), see *Cardiospermum halicacabum*
ketuki (Nepali), see *Agave cantala, Yucca gloriosa*
keura (Nepali), see *Pandanus nepalensis*
kewari (Nepali), see *Gloriosa superba*
keyagu (Newari), see *Pisum sativum*
khabal (Sherpa), see *Saussurea gossypiphora*
khagan (Tamang), see *Phyllanthus parvifolius*
khaghyun (Gurung), see *Rheum australe*
khahatya (Raute), see *Ficus hirta*
khaibasi (Newari), see *Melia azedarach*
khaicho (Newari), see *Crateva unilocularis*
khaira (Danuwar), see *Acacia catechu*
khaisi (Rai), see *Juglans regia* var. *kamaonia*
khaiya (Gurung), see *Choerospondias axillaris*
khajare (Gurung, Tamang), see *Ficus semicordata*
khajima (Raute), see *Solanum nigrum*
khajur (Mooshar), see *Phoenix humilis*
khajuri (Gurung), see *Lycopodium clavatum*
khajuri (Nepali), see *Phoenix humilis*
khakatik (Lepcha), see *Momordica charantia*
khakchan (Rai), see *Zanthoxylum armatum*
khaki weed (English), see *Alternanthera sessilis*

khaksalap (Khaling), see *Holarrhena pubescens*
khaksan (Rai), see *Azadirachta indica*
khaksi (Nepali), see *Trema cannabina, T. orientalis*
khaksi pate (Nepali), see *Streblus asper*
khakunma (Rai), see *Buddleja asiatica*
khakwaphun (Rai), see *Trigonella foenum-graecum*
khale (Tamang), see *Prunus persica*
khali kaphal (Nepali), see *Ardisia solanacea*
khallu (Nepali), see *Spondias pinnata*
khalti (Nepali), see *Bistorta vivipara*
khalung (Tamang), see *Sapium insigne*
khalyu (Tibetan), see *Androsace strigillosa*
khamakhe (Limbu), see *Solanum tuberosum*
khamapu (Sherpa), see *Rhododendron campanulatum*
khamar (Nepali), see *Ribes himalense*
khamari (Nepali), see *Gmelina arborea*
khamari (Tamang), see *Thespesia lampas*
kham-bu (Tibetan), see *Prunus armeniaca, P. persica*
khamse (Limbu), see *Arachis hypogaea*
khan (Tibetan), see *Hedera nepalensis*
khanghara (Mooshar), see *Xanthium strumarium*
khan-kra (Tibetan), see *Artemisia sieversiana*
khansi (Gurung), see *Castanopsis indica*
khanyu (Nepali), see *Ficus semicordata*
kharane (Chepang, Magar), see *Viburnum cylindricum*
kharane (Nepali), see *Lindera pulcherrima, Symplocos ramosissima*
kharane jhar (Nepali), see *Stellaria vestita*
kharaute (Nepali), see *Rosa sericea*
khar banjh (Nepali), see *Quercus lanata*
kharbuja (Nepali), see *Cucumis melo* var. *melo*
kharbusya (Tamang), see *Myrica esculenta*
kharchauti (Magar), see *Boehmeria platyphylla*
kharchoti (Nepali), see *Grewia disperma*
khareto (Chepang, Nepali), see *Phyllanthus parvifolius*
khargaja (Majhi), see *Phyllanthus parvifolius*
khari (Nepali), see *Celtis australis, C. tetrandra, Grewia disperma*
khari (Tharu), see *Celtis tetrandra*
khari jhar (Chepang), see *Rungia parviflora*
khari ko sing (Chepang), see *Celtis tetrandra*
kharirwa (Sunwar), see *Celtis tetrandra*
kharising (Limbu), see *Celtis tetrandra*
kharkande (Majhi), see *Trianthema portulacastrum*
kharkandf (Nepali), see *Trianthema portulacastrum*
kharkane (Chepang, Sherpa), see *Boerhavia diffusa*
kharne (Gurung), see *Ficus semicordata*
kharo (Chepang), see *Capillipedium assimile*
kharo (Nepali), see *Galinsoga parviflora*
kharsata (Gurung), see *Dichroa febrifuga*
kharseni nowa (Tamang), see *Rungia parviflora*
kharseti (Nepali), see *Boehmeria platyphylla*
kharso (Nepali), see *Nyctanthes arbor-tritis*
kharsu (Nepali), see *Quercus semecarpifolia*
kharu (Nepali), see *Capillipedium assimile*
kharuki (Nepali), see *Pogonatherum crinitum*
kharusi (Nepali), see *Capillipedium assimile*
khas (Nepali), see *Vetiveria zizanioides*
khasarant (Nepali), see *Quercus leucotrichophora*
khasaruja (Raute), see *Gonostegia hirta*
khashyo (Gurung), see *Dioscorea bulbifera*
khasi (Danuwar), see *Hydrilla verticillata*
khasin (Newari), see *Castanopsis indica*
khasre (Gurung), see *Ficus hispida*
khasre buti (Nepali), see *Mazus surculosus*
khasre lahara (Chepang), see *Natsiatum herpeticum*
khasre lahara (Nepali), see *Cochlianthus gracilis*
khasreti (Tharu), see *Boehmeria platyphylla*
khasreto (Nepali), see *Ficus hispida*

khasro jhar (Nepali), see *Galium asperifolium*
khasuriya (Tharu), see *Elephantopus scaber*
khate jhar (Gurung), see *Portulaca oleracea*
khatire (Nepali), see *Cipadessa baccifera*
khatrya (Chepang), see *Cipadessa baccifera*
khauda (Raute), see *Solanum erianthum*
khawai (Gurung), see *Prunus napaulensis*
khayal (Tamang), see *Phyllanthus reticulatus*
khayar (Chepang, Magar, Majhi, Nepali, Sunwar, Tharu), see
    Acacia catechu
khayar (Tamang), see *Acacia catechu, Osyris wightiana*
khaya sima (Newari), see *Acacia catechu*
khayer (Lepcha), see *Acacia catechu*
khayusing (Limbu), see *Juglans regia* var. *kamaonia*
khe (Limbu), see *Dioscorea bulbifera*
kheglema (Limbu), see *Erythrina arborescens*
khejik (Limbu), see *Juglans regia* var. *kamaonia*
khel (Tibetan), see *Betula utilis*
khemona (Tibetan), see *Maesa chisia*
khenjagan sagnga (Tibetan), see *Cotoneaster microphyllus*
khesari (Nepali), see *Lathyrus sativus*
khete sag (Nepali), see *Plantago erosa*
khidang (Tamang), see *Spermadictyon suaveolens*
khije (Tibetan), see *Gentiana robusta*
khikkithuk (Lepcha), see *Asparagus racemosus*
khiknodi (Limbu), see *Trigonella foenum-graecum*
khiksing (Limbu), see *Azadirachta indica*
khilkanda (Nepali), see *Prinsepia utilis*
khir (Gurung), see *Cynoglossum zeylanicum*
khirangalo (Nepali), see *Polygonatum verticillatum*
khiraule (Nepali), see *Lilium nepalense*
khirlung (Nepali), see *Polygonatum verticillatum*
khirra (Magar, Majhi), see *Sapium insigne*
khirro (Nepali), see *Holarrhena pubescens, Sapium insigne*
khirsi (Chepang), see *Holarrhena pubescens*
khisakimba (Sherpa), see *Anemone obtusiloba*
kho (Raute), see *Ficus semicordata*
khocha (Raute), see *Centella asiatica*
khocha simi (Newari), see *Lablab purpureus*
khochchhinse (Limbu), see *Castanopsis indica*
khokala (Danuwar), see *Hygrophila auriculata*
khoksa (Danuwar), see *Ficus hirta*
khokse (Limbu), see *Ficus semicordata*
kholaksi (Rai), see *Semecarpus anacardium*
kholcha ghyan (Newari), see *Centella asiatica*
khole (Sherpa), see *Symplocos pyrifolia*
khole dhyak (Gurung), see *Pogostemon glaber*
khole jhar (Nepali), see *Lecanthus peduncularis*
khole sag (Nepali), see *Barbarea intermedia, Lecanthus peduncularis,*
    Veronica baccabunga
kholme (Nepali), see *Symplocos dryophila, S. pyrifolia*
kholo (Gurung), see *Prunus persica*
khombrekpa (Limbu), see *Prunus persica*
khondro (Tibetan), see *Dipsacus inermis*
khondro langdu (Tamang), see *Clematis buchananiana*
khong (Limbu), see *Allium wallichii*
khonri (Limbu), see *Acacia catechu*
khonsi (Newari), see *Juglans regia* var. *kamaonia*
khore (Nepali), see *Trema cannabina*
khorlinga (Nepali), see *Rhododendron falconeri*
khorpani (Newari), see *Prunus armeniaca*
khor puju (Tamang), see *Caragana brevispina*
khorsane jhar (Nepali), see *Oxalis corniculata*
khorsani (Gurung), see *Capsicum annuum*
khorsani chhi (Gurung), see *Macaranga pustulata*
khorseng (Chepang), see *Rungia parviflora*
khosang (Rai), see *Glycine max*

khosorya (Tamang), see *Nyctanthes arbor-tritis*
khosre (Tamang), see *Trema cannabina*
khra-ma (Tibetan), see *Fagopyrum tataricum, Panicum miliaceum*
khre (Tibetan), see *Setaria italica*
khrumich (Sunwar), see *Rubus ellipticus*
khrun (Gurung), see *Elaeagnus infundibularis*
khu (Magar), see *Celtis tetrandra*
khubasalanwa (Rai), see *Pisum sativum*
khudu (Tamang), see *Colquhounia coccinea*
khujhi (Tharu), see *Saccharum officinarum*
khukie chanp (Nepali), see *Magnolia globosa*
khukshi (Rai), see *Momordica charantia*
khuksi (Rai), see *Ficus semicordata*
khum (Magar), see *Saccharum officinarum*
khumbu (Chepang), see *Careya arborea*
khungliba (Limbu), see *Fraxinus floribunda*
khunkhune (Nepali), see *Microstegium ciliatum*
khunkhune jhar (Nepali), see *Evolvulus alsinoides*
khurcheni mran (Tamang), see *Oxalis corniculata*
khur dan (Gurung), see *Semecarpus anacardium*
khurhur (Danuwar, Tharu), see *Ficus semicordata*
khuri (Limbu), see *Acacia catechu*
khur-mang-mang (Tibetan), see *Taraxacum officinale*
khurmure (Chepang), see *Tridax procumbens*
khurpani (Nepali), see *Prunus armeniaca*
khursan (Gurung), see *Oxalis corniculata*
khursani (Danuwar, Magar, Majhi), see *Capsicum annuum*
khursani (Nepali), see *Agapetes serpens, Capsicum annuum*
khursani ajawan (Nepali), see *Hyoscyamus niger* var. *agrestis*
khursani jhar (Gurung), see *Solanum nigrum, Spilanthes paniculata*
khursani jhar (Nepali), see *Justicia procumbens* var. *simplex,*
    Persicaria barbata
khursani lahara (Nepali), see *Clematis buchananiana*
khursani lahara (Tamang), see *Clematis barbellata*
khursani pate (Nepali), see *Sarcococca hookeriana*
khursene (Nepali), see *Solanum nigrum*
khurseno (Gurung), see *Persicaria capitata*
khursya (Chepang), see *Capsicum annuum*
khyuru (Tamang), see *Sapium insigne*
ki (Gurung), see *Eragrostis pilosa*
kim (Magar), see *Osyris wightiana*
kimbu (Magar), see *Morus serrata*
kimbutan (Lepcha), see *Agapetes serpens*
kimu (Nepali), see *Morus australis, M. macroura, M. serrata*
kingra (Tamang), see *Zingiber officinale*
kino, Bengal (English), see *Butea monosperma*
kire jhar (Nepali), see *Boenninghausenia albiflora*
kirkito (Nepali), see *Lindera pulcherrima*
kirpu (Tibetan), see *Hippophae tibetana*
kisi (Gurung), see *Dioscorea bulbifera*
kising (Tamang), see *Tsuga dumosa*
kisi nhyakan (Newari), see *Boehmeria platyphylla, Girardinia*
    diversifolia
ki-sin men toq (Tibetan), see *Campanula pallida*
kituki (Magar), see *Agave cantala*
kiya (Nepali), see *Didymocarpus villosus*
kiyon (Chepang), see *Imperata cylindrica*
klibharok (Chepang), see *Spermadictyon suaveolens*
klowache (Tamang), see *Engelhardia spicata*
knotgrass (English), see *Paspalum distichum*
knotweed (English), see *Persicaria barbata*
knowang (Rai), see *Sterculia villosa*
kobasi (Newari), see *Myrica esculenta*
kobe (Gurung), see *Berberis aristata*
kobhi (Bhojpuri), see *Brassica oleracea* var. *botrytis*
kobi (Mooshar), see *Brassica oleracea* var. *botrytis*
kobi (Tamang), see *Asparagus racemosus*

koche (Nepali), see *Thelypteris multilineata*
koda kuro (Nepali), see *Cynoglossum zeylanicum*
kodari phul (Nepali), see *Cassia floribunda, C. occidentalis*
kodaz (Satar), see *Morus australis*
kode banso (Nepali), see *Paspalum scrobiculatum*
kode khabde (Nepali), see *Meliosma dilleniifolia*
kodo (Nepali, Tharu), see *Eleusine coracana*
kodo ghans (Nepali), see *Eleusine indica*
kodum (Lepcha), see *Neolamarckia cadamba*
kohabar (Tharu), see *Pogostemon benghalensis*
kohlrabi (English), see *Brassica oleracea* var. *caulorapa*
koibet (Tamang), see *Asparagus racemosus*
koilar (Danuwar), see *Bauhinia variegata, Melastoma malabathricum*
koilar (Tharu), see *Bauhinia variegata*
koile ghuriyo (Nepali), see *Cryptolepis buchananii*
koirali (Majhi), see *Bauhinia variegata*
koiralo (Nepali), see *Bauhinia variegata*
koire kuro (Nepali), see *Fumaria indica*
koirum (Nepali), see *Fumaria indica*
kojate (Tibetan), see *Taraxacum officinale*
kokaina (Tharu), see *Phyla nodiflora*
kokko (English), see *Albizia lebbeck*
kokoli (Nepali), see *Roscoea purpurea*
koko pasi (Newari), see *Ziziphus incurva*
kokor mran (Tamang), see *Tridax procumbens*
koksi (Chepang), see *Ficus semicordata*
kolagi (Sunwar), see *Glycine max*
koli (Majhi), see *Ziziphus oenoplia*
kolpot (Lepcha), see *Juglans regia* var. *kamaonia*
koltechhe (Tamang), see *Desmodium confertum*
kolte mhendo (Tamang), see *Stellera chamaejasme*
kolte mran (Tamang), see *Cajanus scarabaeoides*
komal siule (Nepali), see *Trichilia connaroides*
kom jhar (Chepang), see *Peristrophe speciosa*
komme (Gurung), see *Berberis aristata*
komo (Gurung), see *Mahonia napaulensis*
konabu (Newari), see *Bauhinia variegata*
kondro (Gurung), see *Dioscorea deltoidea*
konghi (Lepcha), see *Semecarpus anacardium*
konhara (Tharu), see *Cucurbita maxima*
konrayo (Nepali), see *Cirsium verutum*
kontap (Tamang), see *Bauhinia purpurea*
kontyong (Chepang), see *Isodon coetsa*
konyo (Tibetan), see *Carum carvi*
kopi (Sherpa), see *Asparagus racemosus*
kopi (Sunwar), see *Brassica oleracea* var. *botrytis*
kopibur (Lepcha), see *Brassica oleracea* var. *botrytis*
kopile jhar (Nepali), see *Blumea lacera*
kopyanchhi (Gurung), see *Boenninghausenia albiflora*
korahiya (Danuwar), see *Holarrhena pubescens*
korlingo (Nepali), see *Rhododendron fulgens, R. hodgsonii*
korosi (Chepang), see *Wendlandia coriacea*
korosi (Khaling), see *Phyllanthus emblica*
kose (Raute), see *Crotalaria albida*
kosh-ta-ki (Tibetan), see *Luffa acutangula*
kosing (Tamang), see *Ficus semicordata*
kosyang (Tamang), see *Buddleja paniculata*
kotanchhin (Tibetan), see *Dipsacus inermis*
kotasi (Sherpa), see *Juglans regia* var. *kamaonia*
koter (Tamang), see *Colebrookea oppositifolia*
koyapaito (Gurung), see *Glycine max*
kraikraing (Tamang), see *Gonostegia hirta*
krakryon (Gurung), see *Vitis lanata*
kramtha (Rai), see *Garuga pinnata*
krapodo (Tamang), see *Dipsacus inermis*
kremiye (Tibetan), see *Thalictrum foliolosum*
kremsai (Chepang), see *Solena heterophylla*

krepsin (Tamang), see *Osyris wightiana*
krichinte (Gurung), see *Solanum anguivi*
krimtata (Gurung), see *Oroxylum indicum*
krosying (Tamang), see *Rhus succedanea*
krupkrupchhi (Tamang), see *Hedera nepalensis*
kryakata (Chepang), see *Solena heterophylla*
kubhinde lahara (Nepali), see *Porana paniculata*
kubhindo (Chepang, Nepali, Tamang), see *Benincasa hispida*
kubi ghanino (Nepali), see *Smilax aspera*
kubiraina (Nepali), see *Smilax lanceifolia*
kuchakuchiye (Tharu), see *Xanthium strumarium*
kuchimran (Tamang), see *Echinochloa crus-galli*
kudu mran (Tamang), see *Scutellaria repens*
kugute jhar (Nepali), see *Hypericum japonicum*
kugute jhar (Nepali), see *Oxalis corniculata*
kukat (Chepang), see *Ricinus communis*
kukur ainselu (Nepali), see *Potentilla indica*
kukurak gentha (Tharu), see *Dioscorea deltoidea*
kukurdaino (Nepali), see *Smilax ferox, S. menispermoides, S. ovalifolia, S. perfoliata*
kukurpaile (Nepali), see *Houttuynia cordata*
kukur paile (Nepali), see *Hydrocotyle nepalensis*
kukur tarul (Nepali), see *Dioscorea bulbifera*
kul (Chepang), see *Maoutia puya*
kum (Nepali), see *Didymocarpus pedicellatus*
kumbh (Tharu), see *Semecarpus anacardium*
kumbhi (Danuwar), see *Careya arborea*
kumbhi (Nepali), see *Careya arborea, Monochoria vaginalis*
kumdha (Danuwar), see *Benincasa hispida*
kumhara (Mooshar), see *Benincasa hispida*
kum kum dhup (Gurung, Nepali), see *Didymocarpus albicalyx*
kumquat (English), see *Fortunella japonica*
kunba (Gurung), see *Citrus aurantifolia*
kundri (Nepali), see *Coccinia grandis*
kuner (Sherpa), see *Thalictrum elegans*
kungjyi (Lepcha), see *Ficus benghalensis*
kunhabu (Newari), see *Bauhinia variegata*
kunhang (Lepcha), see *Brassica napus*
kunhu (Newari), see *Aloe vera*
kunya dhap (Tamang), see *Oxalis corniculata*
kupate jhar (Nepali), see *Epilobium sikkimense*
kuphin (Chepang), see *Holmskioldia sanguinea*
kuphre (Nepali), see *Homalium napaulense*
kupindo (Sunwar), see *Benincasa hispida*
kura (Nepali), see *Holarrhena pubescens*
kuraki (Tamang), see *Picrorhiza scrophulariiflora*
kurangamhendo (Tamang), see *Persicaria hydropiper*
kurasign (Tamang), see *Colquhounia coccinea*
kurchi (Nepali), see *Holarrhena pubescens*
kurela (Tharu), see *Asparagus racemosus*
kureni (Magar), see *Clematis gouriana*
kurepat (Nepali), see *Triumfetta rhomboides*
kurgan (Magar), see *Bauhinia malabarica*
kuril (Nepali, Newari), see *Asparagus racemosus*
kurilo (Danuwar), see *Asparagus racemosus*
kurilo (Nepali), see *Asparagus filicinus*
kurkur (Nepali), see *Phyla nodiflora*
kurkure (Nepali), see *Rungia parviflora*
kurkure ghans (Nepali), see *Galium asperifolium*
kurkure jhar (Nepali), see *Equisetum diffusum, Hoya lanceolata, Polygala tartarinowii, Tridax procumbens*
kurkure kankro (Nepali), see *Herpetospermum pedunculosum*
kurkure no (Gurung), see *Equisetum diffusum*
kurkur paile (Nepali), see *Prinsepia utilis*
kurkur thotane (Nepali), see *Persicaria chinensis*
kurli (Gurung), see *Callicarpa macrophylla*

kurna (Tamang), see *Indigofera dosua*

kuro (Nepali), see *Achyranthes aspera, Bidens pilosa* var. *minor, Cyathula tomentosa, Heliotropium indicum, Sida acuta, Siegesbeckia orientalis, Urena lobata*

kuro jhar (Nepali), see *Desmodium laxiflorum*

kursimal (Nepali), see *Schefflera venulosa*

kursinglo (Sunwar), see *Rhus javanica*

kurugan (Magar), see *Bauhinia variegata*

kurung (Nepali), see *Smilax menispermoides*

kurya (Nepali), see *Arctium lappa*

kusa lapte ma (Newari), see *Bauhinia vahlii*

kush (Danuwar, Mooshar, Nepali, Newari, Sunwar, Tamang, Tharu), see *Desmostachya bipinnata*

ku-sha (Tibetan), see *Desmostachya bipinnata*

kush-man-da-k (Tibetan), see *Benincasa hispida*

kusi ma (Newari), see *Celtis tetrandra*

kusum (Nepali), see *Schleichera oleosa*

kusung tong (Tamang), see *Celtis tetrandra*

kutaki (Gurung, Nepali), see *Picrorhiza scrophulariiflora*

kut banso (Nepali), see *Setaria glauca*

kuteli kosa (Nepali), see *Vicia angustifolia*

kuthurke (Nepali), see *Dryopteris cochleata, D. sparsa, Osmunda claytoniana*

kutmero (Nepali), see *Litsea monopetala*

kutumb (Tamang), see *Lindera neesiana*

kutung (Gurung), see *Lindera neesiana*

kuturge (Gurung), see *Tectaria macrodonta*

kuturke (Gurung), see *Litsea monopetala*

kuwase (Limbu), see *Areca catechu*

kwa (Tamang), see *Triticum aestivum*

kwartang gugai (Tamang), see *Cissampelos pareira*

kwnar (Magar), see *Cassia occidentalis*

kyakalan (Tamang), see *Hypericum cordifolium*

kyakar binda (Tamang), see *Solanum aculeatissimum*

kyakar polo (Tamang), see *Castanopsis indica*

kyakpa (Sherpa), see *Cotoneaster microphyllus*

kyamun (Nepali), see *Cleistocalyx operculatus*

kyamuna (Magar, Sunwar, Tamang), see *Cleistocalyx operculatus*

kyasar (Nepali), see *Meconopsis grandis*

kyasim (Tamang), see *Schima wallichii*

kyaurino (Gurung), see *Chlorophytum nepalense*

kyo (Sunwar), see *Avena sativa*

kyobo (Limbu), see *Fagopyrum esculentum*

kyonsin (Gurung), see *Luculia gratissima*

kyosin (Gurung), see *Schima wallichii*

kyuba (Gurung), see *Oxalis corniculata*

kyubo (Gurung), see *Justicia procumbens* var. *simplex*

kyubrisi (Gurung), see *Persicaria nepalensis*

kyubro (Gurung), see *Begonia picta*

kyudabi (Gurung), see *Nephrolepis cordifolia*

kyumbamran (Tamang), see *Persicaria capitata*

kyumru (Gurung), see *Begonia picta*

kyumsa (Tibetan), see *Berberis asiatica*

kyun (Gurung), see *Phyllanthus emblica*

kyungba (Tamang), see *Physalis peruviana*

kyungwa (Tamang), see *Mangifera indica*

kyunpa-rim (Tamang), see *Rheum australe*

kyunpro (Gurung), see *Oxalis corniculata*

kyu phun (Gurung), see *Nephrolepis cordifolia*

kyurba (Tibetan), see *Oxyria digyna*

kyurchumba (Tamang), see *Persicaria nepalensis*

kyu tini (Gurung), see *Clematis grewiiflora*

labak (Lepcha), see *Raphanus sativus*

labasi (Nepali), see *Choerospondias axillaris*

labgyur (Sunwar), see *Prunus persica*

labonk (Limbu), see *Raphanus sativus*

labu (Gurung, Tamang), see *Raphanus sativus*

labu (Sunwar), see *Brassica rapa*

labujana (Tamang), see *Mirabilis jalapa*

laburnum, Indian (English), see *Cassia fistula*

lac tree (English), see *Schleichera oleosa*

lady of the night (English), see *Cestrum nocturnum*

lady's finger (English), see *Abelmoschus esculentus*

laghu patra (Nepali), see *Podophyllum hexandrum*

lahaitu (Gurung), see *Asparagus racemosus*

lahapangyu (Tamang), see *Persicaria chinensis*

lahare bakal pate (Nepali), see *Photinia integrifolia*

lahare bedule (Nepali), see *Trachelospermum lucidum*

lahare chimal (Nepali), see *Rhododendron dalhousiae, R. lindleyi*

lahare chuchcho (Nepali), see *Coix lachryma-jobi*

lahare chunetro (Nepali), see *Stachyurus himalaicus*

lahare jai (Nepali), see *Jasminum humile*

lahare jhyu (Nepali), see *Lycopodium clavatum*

lahare kuro (Nepali), see *Galium elegans*

lahare pan (Nepali), see *Piper longum*

lahare phul (Nepali), see *Hemiphragma heterophyllum*

lahare pipal (Nepali), see *Populus ciliata*

laharepriya ghans (Nepali), see *Globba racemosa*

lahare sag (Nepali), see *Ipomoea muricata*

lahare sajan (Nepali), see *Desmodium multiflorum*

lahare unyu (Nepali), see *Microsorum hymenodes*

lahar goi (Chepang), see *Ipomoea batatas*

lahari (Chepang), see *Cajanus cajan*

laharjoka (Danuwar), see *Equisetum diffusum, Sida cordata*

lahasun (Bhojpuri), see *Allium sativum*

lahasune (Nepali), see *Leea crispa, L. macrophylla*

lahi (Tharu), see *Brassica napus*

lahure mhendo (Tamang), see *Tithonia diversifolia*

lahure sag (Nepali), see *Rorippa nasturtium-aquaticum*

laimran (Tamang), see *Boenninghausenia albiflora*

lain (Newari), see *Raphanus sativus*

laincha (Newari), see *Lawsonia inermis*

lai tuto (Nepali), see *Coix lachryma-jobi*

lajabati (Nepali), see *Biophytum sensitivum*

lajamani jhar (Nepali), see *Mimosa pudica*

lajanti jhar (Nepali), see *Mimosa pudica*

lajauni (Danuwar, Mooshar), see *Mimosa pudica*

lajjawati (Nepali), see *Mimosa pudica*

lajuwa (Rai), see *Mimosa pudica*

lajyati (Nepali), see *Mimosa pudica*

lakhan (Chepang), see *Raphanus sativus*

laknda (Tamang), see *Colquhounia coccinea*

lakphesungm (Limbu), see *Centella asiatica*

la-la-phud (Tibetan), see *Trachyspermum ammi*

lalati jhar (Nepali), see *Mimosa pudica*

lal baghandi (Mooshar), see *Jatropha gossypifolia*

lal chimal (Nepali), see *Rhododendron barbatum*

lal geri (Lepcha), see *Abrus precatorius*

lal geri (Nepali), see *Abrus precatorius, Lobelia nummularia*

lali (Nepali), see *Persea odoratissima*

lali ghans (Nepali), see *Pilea symmeria*

laliguras (Nepali), see *Rhododendron arboreum*

lalimse (Limbu), see *Punica granatum*

lalisar (Magar), see *Rhododendron arboreum*

lalise (Limbu), see *Myrica esculenta*

lalmapha (Sunwar), see *Euphorbia pulcherrima*

lalpha (Danuwar, Tharu), see *Euphorbia pulcherrima*

lalpate mhendo (Tamang), see *Euphorbia pulcherrima*

lalpatta (Bhojpuri), see *Euphorbia pulcherrima*

lalpatya (Newari), see *Euphorbia pulcherrima*

lalpote (Magar), see *Euphorbia pulcherrima*

lalupate (Nepali), see *Euphorbia pulcherrima*

lamb's quarter (English), see *Chenopodium album*

lambu (Lepcha), see *Psidium guajava*

lamhendo (Tamang), see *Buddleja asiatica*
lampate (Nepali), see *Actinodaphne angustifolia, Aesculus indica, Duabanga grandiflora, Wendlandia coriacea*
lampate pangro (Magar), see *Acer acuminatum*
lanagi (Tharu), see *Citrus medica*
landu bramji (Tamang), see *Tetrastigma serrulatum*
langad (Tamang), see *Holmskioldia sanguinea*
langai (Tamang), see *Cucumis sativus*
langasani (Tamang), see *Mirabilis jalapa*
langdu (Tamang), see *Clematis buchananiana*
langduma (Nepali), see *Boehmeria platyphylla*
langkok (Magar), see *Citrus medica*
langtang kabo (Tibetan), see *Scopolia stramonifolia*
lang-thang-rtsi (Tibetan), see *Hyoscyamus niger* var. *agrestis*
lang-thang-tse (Tibetan), see *Hyoscyamus niger* var. *agrestis*
langure (Tamang), see *Fraxinus floribunda*
lankaphul (Nepali), see *Mirabilis jalapa*
lankasoni (Nepali), see *Mirabilis jalapa*
lanke chanke (Gurung), see *Clematis buchananiana*
lankuri (Nepali), see *Fraxinus floribunda*
la-phug (Tibetan), see *Raphanus sativus*
lapkyu (Sunwar), see *Prunus domestica*
lapsi (Bhojpuri, Chepang, Danuwar, Sunwar, Tharu), see *Choerospondias axillaris*
lara (Limbu), see *Ficus benghalensis*
larch, east Himalayan (English), see *Larix griffithiana*
lari phul (Nepali), see *Barleria cristata*
lasi (Newari), see *Nephrolepis cordifolia*
lasun (Danuwar, Mooshar, Nepali, Sunwar, Tharu), see *Allium sativum*
lasune (Nepali), see *Blyxa aubertii*
lasun pate (Nepali), see *Pleione praecox*
la swan (Newari), see *Taxus baccata* subsp. *wallichiana*
latam (Bhojpuri, Mooshar), see *Psidium guajava*
latamran (Tamang), see *Phaseolus aconitifolius*
latapate (Nepali), see *Peperomia pellucida*
latapate chhe (Tamang), see *Drymaria diandra*
latapatiya (Danuwar), see *Desmodium confertum*
lata pucha (Tamang), see *Hibiscus rosa-sinensis*
late angeri (Nepali), see *Osbeckia nepalensis*
lathai (Gurung), see *Cucumis sativus*
lathi bans (Nepali), see *Dendrocalamus strictus*
lati karam (Nepali), see *Hymenodictyon excelsum*
lati kath (Nepali), see *Glochidion velutinum*
latikoseli (Nepali), see *Cynanchum auriculatum, Vincetoxicum hirundinaria* subsp. *glaucum*
lati mauwa (Magar), see *Engelhardia spicata*
lato ghans (Nepali), see *Spilanthes paniculata*
lato kath (Nepali), see *Cornus oblonga*
lato lodho (Nepali), see *Ehretia macrophylla*
lattam (Rai), see *Psidium guajava*
latte (Nepali), see *Amaranthus viridis*
latte jhar (Nepali), see *Cyathocline purpurea, Polygonum plebejum*
lau (Sherpa), see *Raphanus sativus*
lauka (Magar), see *Dioscorea pentaphylla, Lagenaria siceraria*
lauka (Nepali, Newari, Sunwar, Tamang, Tharu), see *Lagenaria siceraria*
lauki (Bhojpuri), see *Lagenaria siceraria*
laurel, Indian (English), see *Terminalia alata*
lava (Newari), see *Allium sativum*
laxmi swan (Newari), see *Sesbania sesban*
laya polang (Tamang), see *Rubus fockeanus*
leabane (English), see *Artemisia indica*
leadwort, Ceylon (English), see *Plumbago zeylanica*
lebbeck tree (English), see *Albizia lebbeck*
ledap (Tamang), see *Ophioglossum nudicaule*
ledem (Chepang), see *Elatostema sessile, Pilea glaberrima*

lede sag (Nepali), see *Pilea racemosa*
lekbu (Rai), see *Saurauia napaulensis*
lekh aaru (Nepali), see *Prunus cornuta*
lekh ainselu (Nepali), see *Rubus pentagonus*
lekh bhogate (Nepali), see *Toricellia tiliifolia*
lekh chotra (Nepali), see *Ilex dipyrena*
lekh chutro (Nepali), see *Berberis chitria, B. erythroclada*
lekh katus (Nepali), see *Corylus ferox*
lekho (Magar), see *Ficus subincisa*
lekh pangro (Nepali), see *Aesculus indica*
lekh sisnu (Nepali), see *Girardinia diversifolia*
leksi (Chepang), see *Erythrina stricta*
lelbadri (Majhi), see *Boerhavia diffusa*
lel-mo-ses (Tibetan), see *Achyranthes bidentata*
lembasi (Rai), see *Pyrus communis*
lemkansi (Rai), see *Trichosanthes anguina*
lemlang (Tamang), see *Melastoma malabathricum, Osbeckia stellata, Oxyspora paniculata*
lemlong (Tamang), see *Osbeckia nepalensis*
lemon (English), see *Citrus limon*
lemongrass, Jammu (English), see *Cymbopogon pendulus*
lemsyu (Gurung), see *Centella asiatica*
lendro (Chepang), see *Corchorus aestuans*
lenja (Nepali), see *Elsholtzia eriostachya*
lenrakut (Tharu), see *Arundo donax*
lens seed (English), see *Lens culinaris*
lentil (English), see *Lens culinaris*
lenza (Sherpa), see *Elsholtzia flava*
lepe (Gurung), see *Cinnamomum tamala*
lepte (Tamang), see *Cinnamomum tamala*
les (Chepang), see *Arundinella nepalensis*
lese ghans (Chepang), see *Neyraudia reynaudiana*
lesya kuro (Nepali), see *Stellaria sikkimensis*
leto (Nepali), see *Osbeckia stellata*
lha bawari (Tamang), see *Isodon lophanthoides*
lha-ming-khrag (Tibetan), see *Allium sativum*
lhan (Gurung), see *Dicentra scandens*
lhapcha (Tibetan), see *Saussurea roylei*
lhapi karpo (Sherpa), see *Inula cappa*
lhapti karku (Tibetan), see *Inula cappa*
lhasilam (Tamang), see *Elsholtzia blanda*
lhasmin (Tamang), see *Lactuca graciliflora*
lhma (Gurung), see *Oryza sativa*
lhoro (Nepali), see *Celastrus paniculatus*
lhospan (Sunwar), see *Artemisia indica*
lhothampot (Lepcha), see *Myrica esculenta*
lhuchhi pu ma (Newari), see *Diplokenma butyracea*
lhumran (Tamang), see *Geranium refractum*
libogta (Tamang), see *Colebrookea oppositifolia*
lichi (Nepali, Newari), see *Litchi chinensis*
lidis (Chepang), see *Ricinus communis*
likhe banso (Nepali), see *Brachiaria ramosa*
lilac, Persian (English), see *Melia azedarach*
lily, blackberry (English), see *Belamcanda chinensis*
lily, climbing (English), see *Gloriosa superba*
lily, glory (English), see *Gloriosa superba*
lily, leopard (English), see *Belamcanda chinensis*
lime (English), see *Citrus aurantifolia*
limtelasing (Limbu), see *Buddleja asiatica*
link weed (English), see *Phyla nodiflora*
linseed (English), see *Linum usitatissimum*
lipe (Nepali), see *Pouzolzia sanguinea*
lipe jhar (Nepali), see *Elatostema integrifolium*
lipot (Lepcha), see *Pyrus malus*
lipot (Limbu), see *Pyrus communis*
lisai (Chepang), see *Terminalia chebula*
lise kuro (Nepali), see *Oreocnide frutescens, Urena lobata*

li-shi (Tibetan), see *Syzygium cumini*
lisi (Chepang), see *Terminalia bellirica*
liso (Gurung), see *Coelogyne flavida*
liso (Nepali), see *Dendrophthoe falcata, Ilex dipyrena, Scurrula parasitica*
litchi (English), see *Litchi chinensis*
lo (Sherpa), see *Girardinia diversifolia*
loa (Satar), see *Ficus racemosa*
lob (Gurung), see *Dactylorhiza hatagirea*
lode (Gurung), see *Amaranthus spinosus*
lodro (Tamang), see *Crassocephalum crepidioides*
logoto (Magar), see *Daphne bholua*
lohasiya (Danuwar), see *Eupatorium odoratum*
lolobabung (Rai), see *Nephrolepis cordifolia*
lomai (Gurung), see *Melissa axillaris*
longe sag (Chepang), see *Amaranthus viridis*
loofah (English), see *Luffa acutangula*
lopahirarip (Lepcha), see *Euphorbia pulcherrima*
loquat (English), see *Eriobotrya japonica*
loriya (Nepali), see *Trevesia palmata*
lotus (English), see *Nelumbo nucifera*
lovage (English), see *Trachyspermum ammi*
love apple (English), see *Paris polyphylla*
love-in-a-puff (English), see *Cardiospermum halicacabum*
luchi (Mooshar), see *Litchi chinensis*
lude (Satar), see *Amaranthus spinosus, A. viridis*
luffa (English), see *Luffa cylindrica*
lug-chhung (Tibetan), see *Eclipta prostrata*
lugro mhumpo (Tibetan), see *Prunella vulgaris*
luinche phul (Nepali), see *Polygala arillata*
luinth (Nepali), see *Taxus baccata* subsp. *wallichiana*
lukbhung (Rai), see *Michelia champaca*
lul lule (Nepali), see *Wikstroemia canescens*
luman (Tamang), see *Geniosporum coloratum, Lindenbergia grandiflora*
lumasin (Tamang), see *Brassaiopsis hainla*
lumeng (Tamang), see *Hydrocotyle nepalensis*
lumsign (Tamang), see *Brassaiopsis polyacantha*
luncha (Rai), see *Triticum aestivum*
lunde (Magar), see *Amaranthus spinosus*
lunde (Nepali), see *Amaranthus viridis*
lunde kanda (Nepali), see *Amaranthus spinosus*
lungedha (Gurung), see *Amaranthus spinosus*
lungememen (Tamang), see *Ajuga bracteosa*
lunge pucha (Gurung), see *Bidens pilosa* var. *minor*
lungri (Gurung), see *Cissampelos pareira*
luplak (Limbu), see *Acorus calamus*
lupro (Limbu), see *Psidium guajava*
lupse phu (Sunwar), see *Grevillea robusta*
lute jhar (Nepali), see *Galium hirtiflorum*
lute sottar (Nepali), see *Dennstaedtia appendiculata*
lutiri (Tamang), see *Pogostemon benghalensis*
luto jhar (Nepali), see *Lygodium japonicum*
lwange jhar (Majhi), see *Bidens pilosa* var. *minor*
lwang jhar (Nepali), see *Ludwigia perennis*
lyandru (Chepang), see *Oreocnide frutescens*
lyangsai (Chepang), see *Rubus ellipticus*
mabra (Tamang), see *Dichroa febrifuga*
mach (Gurung), see *Musa paradisiaca*
machaino (Nepali), see *Coriaria napalensis*
machha phul (Nepali), see *Asclepias curassavica*
machhe (Tamang), see *Arundinaria maling*
machhedham (Chepang), see *Sida rhombifolia*
machheno (Gurung), see *Coriaria napalensis*
machhino (Nepali), see *Coriaria napalensis*
machino (Nepali), see *Gaultheria fragrantissima*
madan (Magar), see *Rhus parviflora*

madane (Nepali), see *Asclepias curassavica, Duabanga grandiflora, Inula cappa*
madar (Tharu), see *Calotropis gigantea*
madder, Indian (English), see *Rubia manjith*
madham (Chepang), see *Catunaregam spinosa*
madhan (Danuwar), see *Bauhinia vahlii*
madhane phal (Nepali), see *Averrhoa carambola*
ma dhap (Tamang), see *Polygonatum verticillatum*
madhishe aril (Majhi), see *Ricinus communis*
madhuban (Chepang), see *Eupatorium adenophorum*
madhuban (Tamang), see *Eupatorium odoratum*
madhuwa (Bhojpuri), see *Benincasa hispida*
madilo (Nepali), see *Anemone vitifolia, Elaeagnus infundibularis, Ischaemum rugosum* var. *segetum*
madini (Gurung), see *Combretum wallichii*
madise khirro (Nepali), see *Holarrhena pubescens*
madise syuri (Nepali), see *Acacia pennata*
Madras thorn (English), see *Pithecellobium dulce*
maduwa (Bhojpuri, Danuwar), see *Eleusine coracana*
magamanda (Tamang), see *Aechmanthera gossypina*
magarkanche (Nepali), see *Begonia picta*
magar kanche (Nepali), see *Begonia rubella*
magarkanchuli (Magar), see *Begonia picta*
magar muja (Tamang), see *Scindapsus officinalis*
maguey (English), see *Agave cantala*
mahada (Rai), see *Rhus javanica*
mahadeorat (Chepang), see *Hedyotis scandens*
maharangi (Nepali), see *Maharanga bicolor, M. emodi*
mahasun (Danuwar), see *Croton roxburghii*
mahelo (Nepali), see *Viburnum mullaha*
mahison (Mooshar), see *Croton roxburghii*
mahuli (Danuwar), see *Bauhinia malabarica*
mahur (Danuwar), see *Euphorbia royleana*
mahuwa (Bhojpuri, Chepang, Danuwar, Mooshar, Nepali, Tharu), see *Madhuca longifolia*
mahuwa airag (Tamang), see *Madhuca longifolia*
maidal (Majhi), see *Catunaregam spinosa*
maidalo (Tamang), see *Catunaregam spinosa*
maidenhair, black (English), see *Adiantum capillus-veneris*
maimanthara (Tamang), see *Phyllanthus parvifolius*
main (Danuwar, Magar, Tharu), see *Catunaregam spinosa*
mainabing (Tamang), see *Kalanchoe spathulata*
maindalkanda (Nepali), see *Catunaregam spinosa*
maingdarju (Tamang), see *Catunaregam spinosa*
mainphal (Nepali), see *Catunaregam spinosa*
mairalu (Nepali), see *Catunaregam spinosa*
mairang (Chepang), see *Mimosa rubicaulis* subsp. *himalayana*
maisai (Chepang), see *Musa paradisiaca*
maisi (Chepang), see *Glochidion velutinum*
maisi chaur (Chepang), see *Eleusine indica*
maisindur (Gurung), see *Lycopodium clavatum*
maisoti phul (Gurung), see *Persicaria capitata*
mai tato (Nepali), see *Oroxylum indicum*
maitula jhar (Nepali), see *Euphorbia heterophylla*
maize (English), see *Zea mays*
majaino (Nepali), see *Malva verticillata*
majaito (Nepali), see *Micromeria biflora*
majari (Nepali), see *Campanula pallida*
majena (Magar), see *Coriaria napalensis*
majithe jhar (Nepali), see *Hedyotis diffusa, Kohautia gracilis*
majithi (Chepang), see *Galium asperifolium*
majitho (Nepali), see *Rubia manjith*
makai (Bhojpuri, Chepang, Danuwar, Gurung, Majhi, Mooshar, Nepali, Tamang, Tharu), see *Zea mays*
makai mhendo (Tamang), see *Commelina benghalensis*
makaina (Magar), see *Zea mays*
makalawa (Rai), see *Sapindus mukorossi*

makalimse (Limbu), see *Syzygium cumini*
makaman (Tamang), see *Euphorbia hirta*
maka ya gala (Newari), see *Annona squamata*
makhamali phul (Nepali), see *Gomphrena globosa*
makhamar (Gurung), see *Boenninghausenia albiflora*
makha marne jhar (Nepali), see *Drosera peltata*
makhan (Nepali), see *Hygrophila auriculata*
makhan (Tharu), see *Amaranthus spinosus*
maki (Limbu), see *Zea mays*
makkhang (Limbu), see *Allium cepa*
maklo (Chepang), see *Bauhinia vahlii*
mako (Tamang), see *Ficus auriculata*
makuri (Nepali), see *Tetrastigma serrulatum*
mala bans (Nepali), see *Bambusa nutans* subsp. *cupulata*
Malabar nut (English), see *Justicia adhatoda*
Malabar plum (English), see *Syzygium cumini*
malaburu (Magar), see *Callicarpa macrophylla*
malagiri (Nepali), see *Cinnamomum glaucescens, Lobelia nummularia, Viburnum mullaha*
malang (Tamang), see *Gaultheria nummularioides*
malati (Nepali), see *Mirabilis jalapa*
malayo (Chepang), see *Viburnum mullaha*
malemau (Chepang), see *Girardinia diversifolia*
male ponga (Tibetan), see *Dicranostigma lactucoides*
maler (Nepali), see *Viburnum mullaha*
malewa (Nepali), see *Viburnum mullaha*
malhan (Mooshar), see *Bauhinia vahlii*
malinge nigalo (Nepali), see *Himalayacalamus brevinodus*
malingo (Nepali), see *Arundinaria maling*
mali phul (Nepali), see *Hypericum cordifolium*
malkanda (Gurung), see *Catunaregam spinosa*
malkauna (Nepali), see *Celastrus paniculatus*
mallato (Nepali), see *Macaranga pustulata*
mallow, Chinese (English), see *Malva verticillata*
mallow, country (English), see *Abutilon indicum*
mallow, large (English), see *Malva verticillata*
mallow, musk (English), see *Abelmoschus moschatus*
mallow, wild (English), see *Melochia corchorifolia*
malta (Newari), see *Capsicum annuum*
malta swan (Newari), see *Hibiscus rosa-sinensis*
mal tata (Nepali), see *Oroxylum indicum*
malu (Gurung, Nepali), see *Bauhinia vahlii*
malyo (Nepali), see *Viburnum mullaha*
mama bhuzu (Tamang), see *Maytenus rufa*
mamabramji (Tamang), see *Vernonia cinerea*
mamapolang (Tamang), see *Rubus acuminatus*
ma-ma-sgog-lchags (Tibetan), see *Setaria glauca*
mambolan (Chepang, Tamang), see *Alternanthera sessilis*
mambu wala (Tamang), see *Scutellaria discolor*
mam derga (Tamang), see *Scindapsus officinalis*
mamhendo (Tamang), see *Hypericum cordifolium*
mamira (Nepali), see *Parnassia nubicola, Thalictrum foliolosum*
mamjari (Tamang), see *Osyris wightiana*
mampolo (Tamang), see *Boehmeria platyphylla*
mam pranet (Tamang), see *Viburnum cylindricum*
mamui (Gurung), see *Lindenbergia indica*
man (Chepang), see *Scoparia dulcis, Sterculia villosa*
manancha (Tibetan), see *Selinum tenuifolium*
manange jhar (Nepali), see *Laggera alata*
manchhi (Chepang), see *Sterculia villosa*
man-da-ra-ba (Tibetan), see *Datura metel*
mandarin's hat (English), see *Holmskioldia sanguinea*
mandre chotro (Nepali), see *Mahonia napaulensis*
mane (Nepali), see *Osyris wightiana*
mangai (Magar), see *Dioscorea pentaphylla*
mangdhap (Tamang), see *Bidens pilosa* var. *minor*
mangdhong (Tamang), see *Gynura nepalensis*

mangdok pena (Limbu), see *Eleusine coracana*
mangen (Nepali), see *Panax pseudoginseng*
manget (Tamang), see *Geniosporum coloratum*
manglong (Lepcha), see *Arundo donax*
mango (English), see *Mangifera indica*
mangret (Lepcha), see *Syzygium cumini*
mangsai (Chepang), see *Citrus medica*
mangtar sipuju (Tamang), see *Randia tetrasperma*
manjhi (Nepali), see *Lagerstroemia parviflora*
mankapi (Tamang), see *Anemone vitifolia*
mankero (Tamang), see *Crotalaria prostrata*
manmuk (Rai), see *Allium sativum*
mansi ghans (Nepali), see *Aerva sanguinolenta*
manthani mran (Tamang), see *Ageratum conyzoides*
ma-nu-pa-tra (Tibetan), see *Cissampelos pareira*
mapalang (Tibetan), see *Rubus ellipticus*
maphro polang (Tamang), see *Rubus reticulatus*
maple, Campbell's (English), see *Acer campbellii*
maple, Himalayan (English), see *Acer oblongum*
mara (Rai), see *Rhus javanica*
maramcho (Majhi), see *Eleusine coracana*
maran (Chepang), see *Flacourtia jangomas*
marang puju (Tamang), see *Mimosa rubicaulis* subsp. *himalayana*
marati (Magar), see *Spilanthes paniculata*
maraute jhar (Nepali), see *Potentilla kleiniana*
maraute jhar (Tharu), see *Tridax procumbens*
marcha (Nepali), see *Senecio diversifolius*
marcha (Tamang), see *Capsicum annuum*
marche jhar (Nepali), see *Vernonia cinerea*
marchi (Limbu), see *Capsicum annuum*
mardi jahr (Nepali), see *Ranunculus diffusus*
maretho (Nepali), see *Spilanthes paniculata*
margosa tree (English), see *Azadirachta indica*
marhathi (Chepang), see *Tridax procumbens*
mariche ghans (Nepali), see *Bupleurum hamiltonii*
marigold, African (English), see *Tagetes erecta*
marigold, marsh (English), see *Caltha palustris*
marijuana (English), see *Cannabis sativa*
marila (Nepali), see *Sterculia villosa*
maritidha (Gurung), see *Mirabilis jalapa*
marjoram, sweet (English), see *Origanum majorana*
marjoram, wild (English), see *Origanum vulgare*
marking nut tree (English), see *Semecarpus anacardium*
maro mulo (Nepali), see *Delphinium vestitum*
marpchi (Tamang), see *Elsholtzia fruticosa*
marpesi (Newari), see *Berberis aristata*
marphulang (Gurung), see *Rubus hypargyrus*
maru (Rai), see *Abrus precatorius*
maru (Tibetan), see *Leptodermis lanceolata*
maru geda (Tamang), see *Lobelia nummularia*
maruk (Limbu), see *Cuminum cyminum*
maruk (Limbu), see *Trachyspermum ammi*
ma-ru-tse (Tibetan), see *Butea monosperma, Cucumis melo* var. *melo*
maruwa (Mooshar), see *Eleusine coracana*
maruwa (Rai), see *Amaranthus spinosus*
maruwa (Raute), see *Fumaria indica*
maruwa pani (Nepali), see *Incarvillea arguta*
maruwa phul (Nepali), see *Origanum majorana*
marvel of Peru (English), see *Mirabilis jalapa*
mas (Nepali), see *Vigna mungo*
masari (Tharu), see *Lens culinaris*
masen (Gurung), see *Capillipedium assimile*
maseno sag (Danuwar), see *Polygonum plebejum*
masgedi (Nepali), see *Callicarpa arborea*
mas gera (Nepali), see *Cipadessa baccifera*
masiduchong (Rai), see *Phaseolus aureus*
masine kuro (Nepali), see *Cynoglossum glochidiatum*

masini (Chepang), see *Coriaria napalensis*
masino bhatamase (Nepali), see *Desmodium concinnum*
masino chapate (Nepali), see *Isodon lophanthoides*
masino dudhi (Nepali), see *Euphorbia parviflora*
masino jai (Nepali), see *Jasminum humile*
masino kanda (Nepali), see *Lantana camara*
masino kane (Nepali), see *Murdannia nudiflora*
masino kharuto (Gurung), see *Pogonatherum crinitum*
masino kimu (Nepali), see *Ribes alpestre*
masino kuro (Nepali), see *Cynoglossum zeylanicum, Triumfetta pilosa*
masino ratanaulo (Nepali), see *Impatiens puberula*
masino thotne (Nepali), see *Persicaria microcephala*
masino tori jhar (Nepali), see *Descurainia sophia*
mas lahare (Nepali), see *Gonostegia hirta*
mas lahari (Nepali), see *Cajanus scarabaeoides*
masleri (Nepali), see *Berberis aristata*
mast tree (English), see *Polyalthia longifolia*
masu ko sag (Nepali), see *Capsella bursa-pastoris*
masur (Bhojpuri), see *Lens culinaris*
masur (Sherpa), see *Rhododendron anthopogon*
masuro (Magar, Nepali), see *Lens culinaris*
masyan (Newari), see *Phaseolus aconitifolius*
masyang (Danuwar, Nepali, Sunwar), see *Phaseolus aconitifolius*
masyangri (Chepang), see *Reissantia arborea*
masyaunro (Gurung), see *Phaseolus aconitifolius*
masyene (Gurung), see *Coriaria napalensis*
matar (Bhojpuri, Danuwar, Mooshar, Nepali), see *Pisum sativum*
mataro gano (Nepali), see *Stephania glandulifera*
mata syaula (Tamang), see *Desmodium confertum*
mate (Nepali), see *Amaranthus viridis*
matiya sag (Tharu), see *Amaranthus viridis*
matrush (English), see *Fimbristylis dichotoma*
matuwa jhar (Chepang), see *Crotalaria albida*
mauchherchi (Chepang), see *Holarrhena pubescens*
mauphul (Nepali), see *Impatiens racemosa*
maura mulo (Nepali), see *Delphinium vestitum*
mauro (Nepali), see *Pteris aspericaulis, P. quadriaurita*
mauro malo (Nepali), see *Boenninghausenia albiflora, Delphinium himalayai*
mauro mulo (Nepali), see *Anemone vitifolia*
mausami (Nepali), see *Citrus sinensis*
mausuni (Chepang), see *Jasminum multiflorum*
mauwa (Gurung), see *Ficus semicordata*
mauwa (Nepali), see *Engelhardia spicata, Glochidion velutinum*
mauwa (Newari), see *Madhuca longifolia*
mawapot (Lepcha), see *Madhuca longifolia*
mawarmul (Nepali), see *Delphinium vestitum*
may (Newari), see *Vigna mungo*
maya (Nepali), see *Ardisia solanacea, Eriobotrya dubia, E. japonica*
mayakot (Nepali), see *Sambucus adnata*
mayal (Nepali), see *Pyrus pashia*
mayaso (Raute), see *Amaranthus spinosus*
mdak (Tibetan), see *Datura stramonium*
mebulang (Tamang), see *Rubus paniculatus*
mechchhen (Tamang), see *Leucosceptrum canum*
mechhedami (Chepang), see *Sida acuta*
medha giri (Nepali), see *Bacopa monnieri*
medlar, Japanese (English), see *Eriobotrya japonica*
mehandi (Bhojpuri, Danuwar, Mooshar, Nepali, Tharu), see *Lawsonia inermis*
mel (Magar), see *Pyrus pashia*
melanchi (Gurung, Majhi), see *Rubus ellipticus*
melan mili (Gurung), see *Cuscuta reflexa*
melilot, white (English), see *Melilotus alba*
melingo (Tamang), see *Prinsepia utilis*
melkar (Tamang), see *Caesalpinia bonduc*
melon (English), see *Cucumis melo* var. *melo*

melon, snap (English), see *Cucumis melo* var. *momordica*
melonm (Tamang), see *Prinsepia utilis*
melpang (Tamang), see *Arctium lappa*
meman (Tamang), see *Sanicula elata*
mendochampa (Sherpa), see *Oroxylum indicum*
menje (Tamang), see *Osyris wightiana*
me polang (Tamang), see *Rubus reticulatus*
merere (Tamang), see *Boenninghausenia albiflora*
mesi (Tamang), see *Sida cordata*
metang (Chepang), see *Pinus roxburghii*
mete (Magar), see *Euphorbia royleana*
methi (Bhojpuri, Chepang, Danuwar, Gurung, Magar, Mooshar, Nepali, Sunwar, Tharu), see *Trigonella foenum-graecum*
methighans (Nepali), see *Cassia tora*
methi ghans (Nepali), see *Salomonia cantoniensis*
methi jhar (Chepang), see *Reinwardtia indica*
methi jhar (Majhi), see *Chenopodium album, Cleome viscosa*
methi jhar (Nepali), see *Melilotus alba, M. indica*
mewa (Danuwar, Gurung, Magar, Majhi, Nepali, Newari, Sunwar, Tamang, Tharu), see *Carica papaya*
mewalang (Tamang), see *Rubus rugosus*
mha (Tamang), see *Drepanostachyum falcatum*
mhain (Gurung), see *Madhuca longifolia*
mhaira (Gurung), see *Mimosa pudica*
mhajari (Nepali), see *Disporum cantoniense*
mhanjari (Nepali), see *Stellaria monosperma*
mharu (Sherpa), see *Pyracantha crenulata*
mhelcha (Nepali), see *Sorbus lanata*
mhemjusai (Chepang), see *Oxyspora paniculata*
mhendo (Tamang), see *Aster barbellatus*
mhenko (Gurung), see *Viburnum erubescens*
mhenpalan (Gurung), see *Rubus macilentus*
mhibo (Gurung), see *Citrus limon*
mhoplan (Gurung), see *Rubus paniculatus*
mhroghya senkha (Gurung), see *Cheilanthes albomarginata*
mhyakure (Nepali), see *Bistorta milletii*
mhyuni (Nepali), see *Caryopteris bicolor*
mibalang (Magar), see *Sapium insigne*
mibhajharek (Magar), see *Lagerstroemia parviflora*
micha (Newari), see *Trigonella foenum-graecum*
michhano (Chepang), see *Spermadictyon suaveolens*
midho (Nepali), see *Quercus floribunda*
midimba (Limbu), see *Zanthoxylum armatum*
miduchhi (Gurung), see *Equisetum diffusum*
migina (Nepali), see *Stachys melissaefolia*
mignonette tree (English), see *Lawsonia inermis*
mijuki (Chepang), see *Rubia manjith*
miku langu (Tamang), see *Stephania glandulifera*
millet (English), see *Eleusine coracana*
millet, African (English), see *Eleusine coracana*
millet, broomcorn (English), see *Panicum miliaceum*
millet, cattail (English), see *Setaria glauca*
millet, common (English), see *Panicum miliaceum*
millet, finger (English), see *Eleusine coracana*
millet, foxtail (English), see *Setaria italica*
millet, hog (English), see *Panicum miliaceum*
millet, Italian (English), see *Setaria italica*
millet, kodo (English), see *Paspalum scrobiculatum*
millet, proso (English), see *Panicum miliaceum*
mimosa tree (English), see *Albizia julibrissin*
min (Gurung, Tamang), see *Boenninghausenia albiflora*
min (Magar), see *Guizotia abyssinica, Sesamum orientale*
minje (Tibetan), see *Pedicularis longiflora* var. *tubiformis*
mint, woolly (English), see *Colebrookea oppositifolia*
miplayutamon (Lepcha), see *Aloe vera*
mirch (Bhojpuri), see *Capsicum annuum*
mircha (Tharu), see *Capsicum annuum*

mirchai (Mooshar), see *Capsicum annuum*
mirge jhar (Nepali), see *Craniotome furcata*
miriri (Tamang), see *Hypericum podocarpoides*
miriye jhar (Nepali), see *Desmodium microphyllum*
mirkey laharo (Nepali), see *Ceropegia pubescens*
mirman (Tamang), see *Phyllanthus parvifolius*
mirmire jhar (Nepali), see *Scoparia dulcis*
mirmire unyu (Nepali), see *Davallia pulchra*
mirmiri (Nepali), see *Persicaria barbata*
miro (Nepali), see *Scutellaria scandens*
mirre (Nepali), see *Isodon coetsa*
mishri jhar (Nepali), see *Micromeria biflora*
mistletoe (English), see *Viscum album*
mi teptep (Tamang), see *Flemingia macrophylla*
mithiksida (Limbu), see *Aloe vera*
mithu (Gurung), see *Equisetum diffusum*
mi-tong-kar-la (Tibetan), see *Oryza sativa*
mlamran (Tamang), see *Leea macrophylla*
mlda (Gurung), see *Oryza sativa*
mobasung (Limbu), see *Cannabis sativa*
mocha (Magar), see *Musa paradisiaca, Pisum sativum*
mochhe (Tamang), see *Glycine max*
mode (Tamang), see *Glycine max*
modes (Tamang), see *Desmodium confertum*
moemran (Tamang), see *Mazus pumilus*
moharain (Tharu), see *Bauhinia vahlii*
mohini (Chepang), see *Eupatorium adenophorum*
mohini (Tamang), see *Caryopteris foetida*
mohini jhar (Nepali), see *Senecio wallichii*
mohwa tree (English), see *Madhuca longifolia*
moiso jhar (Nepali), see *Pouzolzia zeylanica*
moje (Tamang), see *Musa paradisiaca*
mokare (Nepali), see *Spatholobus parviflorus*
mokhi ghan (Nepali), see *Scrophularia urticifolia*
molangsai (Chepang), see *Rubus reticulatus*
mole maran (Tamang), see *Maytenus rufa*
molo (Nepali), see *Viburnum mullaha*
mom puju (Tamang), see *Prinsepia utilis*
mong (Lepcha), see *Eleusine coracana*
mongan (Nepali), see *Crotalaria tetragona*
mongoose plant (English), see *Ophiorrhiza fasciculata*
mongu (Gurung), see *Ficus semicordata*
monjini (Gurung), see *Colebrookea oppositifolia*
monkey jack (English), see *Artocarpus lakoocha*
monkey pod (English), see *Pithecellobium dulce*
monkey puzzle (English), see *Araucaria bidwillii*
mon-sran (Tibetan), see *Vicia faba*
moputachhe (Gurung), see *Trevesia palmata*
moramal (Nepali), see *Anemone rivularis*
morche sag (Danuwar), see *Amaranthus viridis*
moro (Chepang), see *Acacia pennata*
mosane (Nepali), see *Clerodendrum viscosum*
mosi jhar (Nepali), see *Geniosporum coloratum*
mosor (Sunwar), see *Lens culinaris*
moss, club (English), see *Lycopodium clavatum*
motha (Danuwar, Mooshar), see *Cyperus rotundus*
mothe (Nepali), see *Cyperus distans, C. rotundus, Fimbristylis schoenoides*
mother-of-thyme (English), see *Thymus linearis*
motherwort, common (English), see *Leonurus cardiaca*
mothi (Tamang), see *Trigonella foenum-graecum*
motho (Gurung), see *Eleusine indica*
moti ban (Chepang), see *Cyperus rotundus*
moti jhar (Danuwar), see *Mukia maderaspatana*
moti phul (Nepali), see *Sambucus adnata*
moti swan (Newari), see *Sambucus adnata*
mountain splitter (English), see *Vitis lanata*

mra (Gurung), see *Thysanolaena maxima*
mran (Tamang), see *Galium elegans*
mrancha (Tamang), see *Colquhounia coccinea*
mranche (Tamang), see *Flemingia strobilifera*
mratar (Tamang), see *Galinsoga parviflora*
mrigaraj (Nepali), see *Heliotropium strigosum* subsp. *brevifolium*
mrigasinghi (Nepali), see *Helicteres isora*
mro kucha (Gurung), see *Thysanolaena maxima*
mu (Newari), see *Phaseolus aureus*
muchhe (Limbu), see *Artocarpus lakoocha*
mudulo (Nepali), see *Delphinium scabriflorum*
mugi (Magar), see *Phaseolus aureus*
mugi (Sunwar), see *Musa paradisiaca, Phaseolus aureus*
mugu (Tamang), see *Ficus hispida*
mugwort (English), see *Artemisia indica*
mujero (Nepali), see *Impatiens sulcata*
mujyaro (Nepali), see *Impatiens scabrida*
mukrim (Rai), see *Euphorbia royleana*
mukuwa (Rai), see *Camellia sinensis*
mula (Magar, Nepali, Sunwar), see *Raphanus sativus*
mula jhar (Nepali), see *Potentilla peduncularis*
mula pate (Chepang), see *Elephantopus scaber*
mula pate (Nepali), see *Elephantopus scaber, Emilia sonchifolia, Launaea secunda*
mulapate (Nepali), see *Potentilla fulgens*
mula patr (Nepali), see *Dipsacus inermis*
mulberry (English), see *Morus macroura*
mulberry, Himalayan (English), see *Morus serrata*
mulberry, white (English), see *Morus macroura*
muli buti (Nepali), see *Ixeris polycephala*
mullein (English), see *Verbascum thapsus*
mumphali (Tharu), see *Arachis hypogaea*
mung (Bhojpuri, English, Nepali), see *Phaseolus aureus*
mung (Tharu), see *Phaseolus aconitifolius, P. aureus*
munga (Danuwar, Satar), see *Moringa oleifera*
munge pati (Nepali), see *Caryopteris bicolor*
mungi (Danuwar, Tamang), see *Phaseolus aureus*
mungkalha (Lepcha), see *Phaseolus aureus*
munmun (Nepali), see *Vicia hirsuta*
muntala (Nepali), see *Fortunella japonica*
mupi (Sunwar), see *Cucurbita maxima*
murai (Bhojpuri, Danuwar, Mooshar, Tharu), see *Raphanus sativus*
muran (Magar), see *Fagopyrum dibotrys*
murba (Magar), see *Bupleurum hamiltonii*
murjhanga (Tharu), see *Piper longum*
murmure (Nepali), see *Herpetospermum pedunculosum*
muruk (Magar), see *Rhus javanica*
musa kane (Nepali), see *Cerastium glomeratum*
musaledi (Nepali), see *Vernonia cinerea*
musaleri (Nepali), see *Rungia parviflora*
musaleri (Tharu), see *Curculigo orchioides*
musali (Nepali), see *Curculigo orchioides*
musalindi (Gurung), see *Vernonia cinerea*
musar (Mooshar), see *Lens culinaris*
musa thotane (Gurung), see *Persicaria chinensis*
muse chutro (Nepali), see *Berberis asiatica*
muse deli (Nepali), see *Glochidion velutinum*
muse jhar (Nepali), see *Pogonatherum crinitum*
muse lari (Nepali), see *Berchemia edgeworthii*
muse sakeno (Nepali), see *Osyris wightiana*
musi (Chepang), see *Albizia lucidior*
musli, black (English), see *Curculigo orchioides*
mustard (English), see *Brassica napus*
mustard, black (English), see *Brassica nigra*
mustard, Indian (English), see *Brassica juncea* var. *cuneifolia*
mustard, leaf (English), see *Brassica juncea* var. *cuneifolia*
mustard, wild (English), see *Cleome viscosa*

musu (Newari), see *Lens culinaris*
musure katus (Nepali), see *Castanopsis tribuloides*
musuri masye (Tamang), see *Lens culinaris*
musuro (Chepang, Danuwar), see *Lens culinaris*
mu swan (Newari), see *Origanum majorana*
musya (Newari), see *Glycine max*
musya belo (Raute), see *Cissampelos pareira*
mututchya (Rai), see *Lens culinaris*
myrobalans, belleric (English), see *Terminalia bellirica*
myrobalans, chebulic (English), see *Terminalia chebula*
myrobalans, emblica (English), see *Phyllanthus emblica*
myrtle, box (English), see *Myrica esculenta*
myrtle, crepe (English), see *Lagerstroemia indica, L. parviflora*
myuchuk (Chepang), see *Flemingia macrophylla*
myunsi (Gurung), see *Alnus nepalensis*
nabhya (Gurung), see *Phyllanthus parvifolius*
nacha mhendo (Tamang), see *Hypericum japonicum*
nachanni (Sherpa), see *Chenopodium album*
nachrim (Rai), see *Oxalis corniculata*
nadar (Nepali), see *Panax pseudoginseng, Smilax ovalifolia*
nagabhya (Tamang), see *Potentilla peduncularis*
nagakor (Nepali), see *Ranunculus scleratus*
nagamichu (Tamang), see *Drosera peltata*
nagami chu (Tamang), see *Drymaria diandra*
nagan (Tamang), see *Crotalaria cytisoides*
nagara (Tamang), see *Ichnocarpus frutescens*
nagarmothe (Nepali), see *Mariscus sumatrensis*
nagasalamran (Tamang), see *Centella asiatica*
nagbeli (Nepali), see *Lycopodium clavatum*
nagbo (Tibetan), see *Valeriana jatamansii*
nagikhre (Tamang), see *Smilax menispermoides*
nagikhre (Tamang), see *Smilax ovalifolia*
nagilangai (Tamang), see *Mukia maderaspatana*
nagkeshar (Nepali), see *Mesua ferrea*
nagnse (Limbu), see *Pyrus malus*
nagpadong (Tamang), see *Boenninghausenia albiflora*
nagpasi (Tamang), see *Homalium napaulense*
nagphani kanda (Nepali), see *Opuntia monacantha*
nagret (Tamang), see *Smilax aspera*
nahi (Chepang), see *Phoenix humilis*
nai (Nepali), see *Taxillus vestitus*
nai (Tamang), see *Ilex dipyrena, Pyrus pashia, Scurrula elata, Scurrula parasitica*
naikhre (Gurung), see *Smilax aspera*
naiki chedang (Tamang), see *Viburnum erubescens*
naikya (Newari), see *Cocos nucifera*
naipolo (Gurung), see *Girardinia diversifolia*
naitak (Chepang), see *Crotalaria cytisoides, Desmodium confertum*
najachhe (Tamang), see *Reinwardtia indica*
najhil (Nepali), see *Sorbus hedlundii*
najo (Gurung), see *Pimpinella achilleifolia*
nakabhyak (Tamang), see *Drynaria propinqua*
nakachchu (Tamang), see *Lindenbergia grandiflora*
nakachikini (Mooshar), see *Centipeda minima*
nakachyu (Tamang), see *Reinwardtia indica*
nakadansing (Tamang), see *Antidesma acidum*
nakajali (Gurung), see *Mirabilis jalapa*
nakali ashok (Nepali), see *Polyalthia longifolia*
nakapolwa (Tharu), see *Ranunculus scleratus*
nakasurka (Danuwar), see *Chrysopogon aciculatus*
nakchhi (Tamang), see *Reinwardtia indica*
nakchhi sursomba (Tamang), see *Scutellaria repens*
nake jhar (Nepali), see *Hypericum japonicum*
nakhachu kungwa (Tamang), see *Oxalis corniculata*
nakhar simbi (Nepali), see *Lotus corniculatus*
nakhru kyamba (Tamang), see *Begonia picta*
nakhrupan gyan (Tamang), see *Oxalis corniculata*

nakhunbun (Rai), see *Justicia adhatoda*
naki jhar (Chepang), see *Launaea aspleniifolia*
nakikre (Tamang), see *Smilax aspera*
nakli jatamansi (Nepali), see *Valeriana hardwickii*
nakori (Tamang), see *Ranunculus diffusus*
nakre (Tamang), see *Smilax ovalifolia*
nakulal (Nepali), see *Symplocos paniculata*
nakuri phul (Nepali), see *Ranunculus scleratus*
nalam (Nepali), see *Sorbus lanata*
nalimran (Tamang), see *Hedyotis scandens*
nal sal (Tamang), see *Scutellaria scandens*
nalsura (Nepali), see *Ehretia acuminata*
nalu (Nepali), see *Hibiscus mutabilis*
nalu kuro (Nepali), see *Urena lobata*
namachyormuk (Lepcha), see *Oxalis corniculata*
nambora (Limbu), see *Citrus margarita*
nambu (Tamang), see *Agrimonia pilosa*
namche (Chepang), see *Perilla frutescens*
namche jhar (Magar), see *Ageratum conyzoides*
name (Magar), see *Dioscorea deltoidea*
namkimro (Gurung), see *Begonia picta*
namle jhar (Nepali), see *Crassocephalum crepidioides*
namli (Sherpa), see *Berberis asiatica*
nam nam (Tamang), see *Brassica juncea* var. *cuneifolia, B. napus*
namnasing (Limbu), see *Cinnamomum camphora*
nampani (Chepang), see *Pogostemon benghalensis*
namse jhar (Chepang), see *Hyptis suaveolens*
namsing (Tamang), see *Viburnum erubescens*
namun (Tamang), see *Myrica esculenta*
nana (Tamang), see *Chenopodium album*
nandur (Gurung), see *Fragaria daltoniana*
nang (Danuwar), see *Scoparia dulcis*
nangasari (Nepali), see *Ixeris polycephala*
nange arthunge (Gurung), see *Bidens pilosa* var. *minor*
nangreu (Nepali), see *Ligularia amplexicaulis*
nangsewamen (Tamang), see *Thalictrum foliolosum*
nani bakyo ro (Chepang), see *Lindenbergia grandiflora*
nanicha (Tibetan), see *Selinum candollii*
nani jhar (Nepali), see *Mimosa pudica*
nani kanda (Nepali), see *Mimosa pudica*
nani kaphal (Nepali), see *Lonicera angustifolia*
nanimaiso (Gurung), see *Mussaenda macrophylla*
nanimaso (Gurung), see *Mussaenda roxburghii*
nani palo (Nepali, Tamang), see *Maoutia puya*
nanyungma (Sherpa), see *Rubus ellipticus*
naorochi (Khaling), see *Nardostachys grandiflora*
napre (Gurung), see *Nephrolepis cordifolia*
napta (Gurung), see *Anaphalis contorta*
na-ram (Tibetan), see *Bistorta vivipara*
narapati (Nepali), see *Skimmia laureola*
narapolo (Nepali), see *Ranunculus diffusus*
narau (Gurung), see *Eleusine coracana*
narayan pati (Nepali), see *Buddleja paniculata*
nar-dhap (Tamang), see *Maianthemum purpureum*
nare (Gurung), see *Eleusine coracana*
narga (Nepali), see *Viburnum erubescens*
narimurago (Tamang), see *Smithia ciliata*
narisal (Nepali), see *Mesua ferrea*
nariwal (Chepang, Danuwar, Magar, Tamang), see *Cocos nucifera*
nariyal (Nepali), see *Cocos nucifera*
nariyalse (Limbu), see *Cocos nucifera*
nariyar (Bhojpuri), see *Cocos nucifera*
narkat (Bhojpuri, Danuwar, Gurung, Sunwar, Tamang), see *Arundo donax*
narkat (Nepali), see *Arundo donax, Phragmites karka*
narkhapang (Tamang), see *Cynodon dactylon*
narko (Gurung), see *Viburnum erubescens*

narko (Nepali), see *Viburnum mullaha*
narsin (Chepang), see *Grewia disperma*
narsin (Chepang), see *Grewia subinaequalis*
narwal (Sunwar), see *Cocos nucifera*
naryol (Lepcha), see *Cocos nucifera*
nash (Gurung), see *Schima wallichii*
na-sha (Tibetan), see *Moringa oleifera*
nashar (Tamang), see *Anemone rivularis, Clematis buchananiana, C. graveolens*
nash jhar (Nepali), see *Eclipta prostrata, Hemiphragma heterophyllum*
nashpati (Bhojpuri, Chepang, Danuwar, Gurung, Magar, Nepali, Sunwar, Tamang), see *Pyrus communis*
nas mran (Tamang), see *Cyathocline purpurea*
naswan (Newari), see *Nardostachys grandiflora, Valeriana jatamansii*
natirakwa (Limbu), see *Trichosanthes anguina*
nator chhe (Tamang), see *Euphorbia heterophylla*
naula (Tamang), see *Galinsoga parviflora*
naulo jhar (Nepali), see *Galinsoga quadriradiata*
naurusa (Gurung), see *Leucosceptrum canum*
nawa ghyan (Newari), see *Clerodendrum philippinum, Galinsoga parviflora, G. quadriradiata, Mentha spicata*
nawali (Tamang), see *Potentilla fulgens*
nawamle (Gurung), see *Oxalis corniculata*
nawar kyun (Gurung), see *Oxalis corniculata*
nayongma (Rai), see *Ficus religiosa*
nayukre (Gurung), see *Smilax aspera*
nebu (Mooshar, Newari), see *Citrus limon*
nedhap (Tamang), see *Taraxacum officinale*
nedhar (Tamang), see *Ficus neriifolia* var. *nemoralis*
needle wood (English), see *Schima wallichii*
neem tree (English), see *Azadirachta indica*
negnmaitam (Gurung), see *Plumbago zeylanica*
neki po (Tibetan), see *Impatiens scabrida*
nelam (Tamang), see *Ficus neriifolia* var. *nemoralis*
nelau (Chepang), see *Urtica dioica*
nemung (Sherpa), see *Colebrookea oppositifolia*
nene (Tibetan), see *Polygonum plebejum*
nene dhombu (Sherpa), see *Elsholtzia flava*
Nepalese paper plant (English), see *Daphne bholua*
Nepalese white thorn (English), see *Pyracantha crenulata*
nepali bikh (Nepali), see *Campanula pallida*
nesinka jhar (Chepang), see *Adiantum capillus-veneris*
neta dha (Gurung), see *Taraxacum officinale*
nettle, Himalayan (English), see *Girardinia diversifolia*
nettle, stinging (English), see *Urtica dioica*
nettle tree (English), see *Celtis australis*
neware pati (Nepali), see *Wendlandia exserta*
newaro (Nepali), see *Ficus auriculata*
ngangri sag (Chepang), see *Emilia sonchifolia*
nhajhel (Sherpa), see *Sorbus cuspidata*
nhajyangaman (Tamang), see *Heracleum nepalense*
nhakapai (Sherpa), see *Valeriana jatamansii*
nhangali (Tamang), see *Oroxylum indicum*
nhansi (Gurung), see *Quercus lamellosa*
nhekha (Sherpa), see *Ribes glaciale*
nhyakan (Newari), see *Urtica dioica*
nhyalang (Sherpa), see *Rubus nepalensis*
nhyalang (Tibetan), see *Rubus ellipticus*
nhyapan kathi (Newari), see *Arundo donax*
nhynalang dhambu (Sherpa), see *Fragaria nubicola*
nibha (Nepali), see *Himalayacalamus hookerianus*
nibnuwa (Sunwar), see *Citrus limon*
nibo (Bhojpuri), see *Citrus limon*
nibuwa (Chepang, Nepali, Tamang), see *Citrus limon*
nicha sag (Danuwar), see *Pouzolzia zeylanica*
nichhi (Tamang), see *Ilex dipyrena*
nidaune jhar (Nepali), see *Mimosa pudica*

nigale gava (Nepali), see *Murdannia japonica, M. scapiflora*
nigalo (Nepali), see *Drepanostachyum falcatum*
nigalo bans (Nepali), see *Drepanostachyum intermedium*
Niger seed (English), see *Guizotia abyssinica*
nightshade, black (English), see *Solanum nigrum*
nightshade, Malabar (English), see *Basella alba*
nigi miyo (Tamang), see *Desmodium concinnum*
nigro (Majhi), see *Arthromeris wallichiana*
ni-gro-dha (Tibetan), see *Ficus benghalensis*
niketene (Tamang), see *Cyathula tomentosa*
niki bhenta (Tamang), see *Solanum aculeatissimum*
nikipolo (Tamang), see *Boehmeria platyphylla*
nikyu (Tibetan), see *Geranium wallichianum*
nila jhar (Nepali), see *Aeginetia indica*
nilamani (Nepali), see *Barleria cristata*
nil kanda (Nepali), see *Duranta repens*
nilo bihi (Nepali), see *Solanum anguivi*
nilo bikh (Nepali), see *Aconitum ferox*
nilo butte ghans (Nepali), see *Scutellaria barbata*
nilo chimal (Nepali), see *Rhododendron campanulatum*
nilo gandhe (Nepali), see *Ageratum houstonianum*
nilo ghortapre (Nepali), see *Lobelia nummularia*
nilo ghusure (Nepali), see *Caryopteris bicolor*
nilo jaluke (Nepali), see *Monochoria hastata*
nilo jhar (Nepali), see *Orobanche aegyptiaca*
nilo tike (Nepali), see *Wahlenbergia marginata*
nil pate (Nepali), see *Ajuga bracteosa, Scutellaria discolor*
nim (Bhojpuri, Chepang, Danuwar, Gurung, Magar, Mooshar, Nepali, Newari, Sunwar, Tamang, Tharu), see *Azadirachta indica*
nimale (Magar), see *Capsella bursa-pastoris*
nimane jhar (Nepali), see *Hedyotis lineata, H. scandens*
nimaro (Nepali), see *Ficus auriculata*
nimawa (Tharu), see *Citrus limon*
nimbu (Bhojpuri), see *Citrus aurantifolia*
nime pa (Gurung), see *Reinwardtia indica*
nim kath (Nepali), see *Picrasma quassioides*
nim-pa (Tibetan), see *Azadirachta indica, Cajanus cajan*
nimphuli (Tamang), see *Desmodium triflorum*
nimso (Chepang), see *Sesamum orientale*
nimte (Nepali), see *Jatropha curcas*
ninaura (Magar), see *Solanum nigrum*
ninde (Nepali), see *Macropanax dispermus*
ningbung (Limbu), see *Datura metel*
ningebung (Limbu), see *Brassica napus*
nini (Nepali), see *Schima wallichii*
niniya (Raute), see *Glochidion velutinum*
niphar (Chepang), see *Reinwardtia indica*
niphin (Chepang), see *Reinwardtia indica*
nipitmuk (Lepcha), see *Flemingia macrophylla*
nir (Chepang), see *Bidens pilosa* var. *minor*
nirabisi (Nepali), see *Delphinium himalayai, Parnassia nubicola*
nirbisi (Nepali), see *Cyananthus lobatus*
nirguri (Chepang), see *Jatropha curcas*
nirmasi (Nepali), see *Parnassia nubicola*
nir syaul (Nepali), see *Ilex excelsa*
nite (Nepali), see *Oreocnide frutescens*
nobo (Tamang), see *Gaultheria nummularioides*
nodi (Limbu), see *Lepidium sativum*
no dubo (Gurung), see *Cynodon dactylon*
noh (Tamang), see *Allium sativum*
nokhrek (Chepang), see *Osyris wightiana*
noryak (Chepang), see *Colebrookea oppositifolia*
nota (Gurung), see *Allium wallichii*
nowa (Tamang), see *Scrophularia urticifolia*
nuki phoko (Gurung), see *Impatiens racemosa*
numpa mhendo (Tamang), see *Hypericum cordifolium*

nun (Gurung), see *Brassica napus*
nundhik (Nepali), see *Osyris wightiana, Phyllanthus reticulatus*
nundhiki (Nepali), see *Portulaca oleracea, Securinega virosa*
nune (Nepali), see *Aechmanthera gossypina, Osyris wightiana*
nuniya sag (Mooshar), see *Portulaca oleracea*
nurigba (Limbu), see *Imperata cylindrica*
nwakyumro (Gurung), see *Oxalis corniculata*
nyacha swan (Newari), see *Asclepias curassavica*
nyage (Nepali), see *Viburnum erubescens*
nyakar (Tamang), see *Colquhounia coccinea*
nyalo (Sherpa), see *Persicaria mollis*
nyamnyung (Tamang), see *Plantago erosa*
nyamsisi (Tibetan), see *Silene stracheyi*
nyauli (Nepali), see *Mollugo pentaphylla*
nyung-kar (Tibetan), see *Brassica rapa*
nyung-ma (Tibetan), see *Brassica rapa*
oak, bull (English), see *Quercus lamellosa*
oak, Ceylon (English), see *Schleichera oleosa*
oak, kharshu (English), see *Quercus semecarpifolia*
oak, Patana (English), see *Careya arborea*
oak, silver (English), see *Grevillea robusta*
oat (English), see *Avena sativa*
oat, wild (English), see *Avena fatua*
ochong (Lepcha), see *Allium cepa*
odal (Majhi, Nepali), see *Sterculia villosa*
odal jal (Gurung), see *Dicentra scandens*
odarbau (Tharu), see *Uraria lagopodioides*
odhale (Magar), see *Hypericum cordifolium*
ogre (Nepali), see *Gaultheria fragrantissima*
okhal (Tamang), see *Satyrium nepalense*
okhar (Bhojpuri, Chepang, Danuwar, Magar, Nepali, Tharu), see *Juglans regia* var. *kamaonia*
okhre ghans (Nepali), see *Corydalis chaerophylla*
okra (English), see *Abelmoschus esculentus*
oksa (Sherpa), see *Allium wallichii*
ol (Nepali, Satar), see *Amorphophallus campanulatus*
olachi (Gurung), see *Daphniphyllum himalense*
olat (Gurung), see *Euphorbia pulcherrima*
oleander (English), see *Nerium indicum*
oleaster, bastard (English), see *Elaeagnus infundibularis*
olive, fragrant (English), see *Osmanthus fragrans* var. *longifolia*
olive, sweet (English), see *Osmanthus fragrans* var. *longifolia*
olum tree, black (English), see *Syzygium cumini*
olvi (Gurung), see *Rumex nepalensis*
ona (Gurung), see *Saurauia napaulensis*
onai (Chepang), see *Ziziphus mauritiana*
ondo (Gurung), see *Saurauia napaulensis*
ondong (Limbu), see *Mentha spicata*
ongbu lakpa (Sherpa), see *Gymnadenia orchidis*
ongu lakpa (Sherpa), see *Dactylorhiza hatagirea*
onili (Gurung), see *Ligustrum compactum*
onion (English), see *Allium cepa*
onse (Gurung), see *Cucurbita maxima*
onsila (Gurung), see *Cautleya spicata*
orange, sweet (English), see *Citrus sinensis*
orchid, marsh (English), see *Dactylorhiza hatagirea*
orchid, silver (English), see *Coelogyne ochracea*
orchid tree (English), see *Bauhinia variegata*
osaru (Chepang), see *Vernonia cinerea*
ote ghans (Nepali), see *Oplismenus burmannii*
pabale (Tamang), see *Astilbe rivularis*
pabg (Tamang), see *Pogonatherum paniceum*
pacha (Gurung), see *Artemisia indica*
pachhai (Newari), see *Brassica juncea* var. *cuneifolia*
pachyar (Tamang), see *Girardinia diversifolia*
pachyebi (Lepcha), see *Brassica juncea* var. *cuneifolia*
padake (Gurung), see *Pieris formosa*

padake (Magar), see *Albizia lucidior*
padake (Nepali), see *Albizia lucidior, Impatiens balsamina*
padake ghans (Nepali), see *Carpesium nepalense*
padakine (Nepali), see *Gaultheria fragrantissima*
padambet (Gurung), see *Bergenia ciliata*
padamchal (Nepali), see *Rheum australe*
padang (Nepali), see *Himalayacalamus hookerianus*
padari (Nepali), see *Stereospermum chelonoides*
paddy plant (English), see *Oryza sativa*
padena (Sunwar), see *Mentha spicata*
pador (Tharu), see *Trichosanthes dioica*
pagalya jhar (Nepali), see *Osbeckia stellata*
paglya jhar (Gurung), see *Osbeckia stellata*
paha phal (Nepali), see *Maesa macrophylla*
pahare pipal (Nepali), see *Ficus rumphii*
paharo ko kan (Nepali), see *Didymocarpus cinereus*
pahasingh (Chepang), see *Macaranga pustulata*
pahele (Nepali), see *Litsea sericea*
paheli (Nepali), see *Litsea doshia*
pahenli (Nepali), see *Corydalis chaerophylla*
pahenli (Nepali), see *Dodecadenia grandiflora*
pahenlo ainselu (Nepali), see *Potentilla indica*
pahenlo jhurjhuri (Nepali), see *Pentanema indicum*
pahenlo junge (Nepali), see *Clematis buchananiana*
pahenlo nundhiki (Nepali), see *Randia tetrasperma*
pahenlo singulto (Nepali), see *Schisandra grandiflora*
pahinlo singulto (Nepali), see *Schisandra propinqua*
paileti (Nepali), see *Securinega virosa*
paingi (Gurung), see *Ficus auriculata*
painjugn (Tamang), see *Persicaria mollis*
painkyum (Tamang), see *Persicaria mollis*
painnati (Tamang), see *Cipadessa baccifera*
paira jhar (Chepang), see *Tridax procumbens*
pairalo (Chepang), see *Clerodendrum viscosum*
paire golbhera (Nepali), see *Solanum nigrum*
pairethi (Majhi), see *Cipadessa baccifera*
paireti (Nepali), see *Cipadessa baccifera*
paitei (Nepali), see *Phyllanthus parvifolius*
paite jhar (Nepali), see *Portulaca oleracea*
paiyun (Nepali), see *Betula alnoides, Prunus cerasoides*
pajan (Sherpa), see *Eurya acuminata*
pajeni (Gurung), see *Thalictrum foliolosum*
pajothor (Gurung), see *Asparagus racemosus*
pakasing (Magar), see *Lyonia ovalifolia*
pakchar (Tibetan), see *Caragana sukiensis*
pakchho (Chepang), see *Portulaca oleracea*
pakha chhal (Tamang), see *Pilea glaberrima*
pakhale unyu (Nepali), see *Adiantum capillus-veneris*
pakhanbed (Gurung, Nepali), see *Bergenia ciliata*
pakhanbhetta (Nepali), see *Didymocarpus aromaticus*
pakha phul (Nepali), see *Calanthe masuca*
pakhuri (Gurung), see *Ficus glaberrima*
pakhuri (Nepali), see *Ficus glaberrima, F. sarmentosa*
pala (Newari), see *Spinacia oleracea*
palan (Gurung), see *Rubus ellipticus*
palang (Gurung), see *Rubus reticulatus*
palans (Danuwar, Nepali, Sunwar, Tamang, Tharu), see *Butea monosperma*
palanti kanta (Mooshar), see *Argemone mexicana*
palcha khari (Nepali), see *Grewia disperma*
paldungne (Tamang), see *Elsholtzia flava*
pale (Sunwar), see *Girardinia diversifolia*
palha (Gurung), see *Rubus paniculatus*
palija swan (Newari), see *Nyctanthes arbor-tritis*
palimara (Nepali), see *Alstonia scholaris*
palm, catechu (English), see *Areca catechu*
palm, date (English), see *Phoenix humilis*

palphung (Limbu), see *Lawsonia inermis*
palsai (Magar), see *Rhododendron arboreum*
pal swan (Newari), see *Nelumbo nucifera*
palu (Newari), see *Zingiber officinale*
palunget (Tamang), see *Elsholtzia flava*
palungo sag (Nepali), see *Spinacia oleracea*
palwi (Newari), see *Butea monosperma*
pam (Lepcha), see *Saccharum officinarum*
pama (Tibetan), see *Potentilla fruticosa*
pamle (Nepali), see *Chamabainia cuspidata*
pamo (Nepali), see *Juniperus indica*
pam pam ghyan (Newari), see *Oxalis corniculata*
pampurya (Nepali), see *Eriophorum comosum*
pamsali ban (Chepang), see *Tridax procumbens*
pana (Tamang), see *Pyrus pashia*
pana mhendo (Tamang), see *Deutzia staminea*
panchaphal (Nepali), see *Dillenia indica*
panchaunle (Gurung, Nepali), see *Dactylorhiza hatagirea*
panch aunle (Nepali), see *Gymnadenia orchidis*
pancherpolo (Tamang), see *Girardinia diversifolia*
pandam (Lepcha), see *Buddleja asiatica*
pandang (Raute), see *Desmodium oojeinense*
pandare (Magar), see *Eleusine coracana*
panduba (Tharu), see *Paspalum distichum*
paneli (Nepali), see *Flacourtia jangomas*
pang (Tamang), see *Aletris pauciflora, Capillipedium assimile, Digitaria ciliaris, Pennisetum flaccidum*
panga (Tamang), see *Drosera peltata*
panga lhapti (Tamang), see *Butea buteiformis*
pangali jhar (Chepang), see *Rungia parviflora*
pangbu (Sherpa), see *Nardostachys grandiflora*
pange (Magar), see *Prunus cerasoides*
pangen mbu (Tibetan), see *Gentiana capitata*
pangmhe (Nepali), see *Sorbus lanata*
pangnam (Tamang), see *Elsholtzia blanda*
pangprapa (Tamang), see *Gerbera maxima*
pangra (Nepali), see *Aesculus indica*
pangsen daima (Tamang), see *Lycopodium clavatum*
pangsingpu (Sherpa), see *Gaultheria nummularioides*
pani amala (Magar, Nepali), see *Nephrolepis cordifolia*
pani bet (Nepali), see *Calamus tenuis*
pani dubo (Nepali), see *Paspalum distichum*
pani jhar (Nepali), see *Scutellaria scandens*
pani lahara (Nepali), see *Tetrastigma serrulatum*
panimarich (Nepali), see *Sphenoclea zeylanica*
pani mothe (Nepali), see *Fimbristylis dichotoma, Schoenoplectus juncoides*
pani nyuro (Nepali), see *Diplazium esculentum*
paniphalz (Satar), see *Trapa bispinosa*
pani sag (Nepali), see *Rorippa nasturtium-aquaticum*
pani saj (Nepali), see *Duabanga grandiflora, Terminalia myriocarpa*
pani saro (Nepali), see *Cautleya spicata, Globba racemosa, Nephrolepis cordifolia*
panjyun (Tamang), see *Persicaria mollis*
pankha phul (Nepali), see *Hedychium gardnerianum, H. spicatum*
panle (Majhi), see *Osyris wightiana*
panma (Danuwar), see *Eichhornia crassipes*
panpate (Nepali), see *Potentilla fulgens*
pan polang (Tamang), see *Rubus fockeanus*
panta (Gurung), see *Anemone vitifolia*
panthan (Chepang), see *Vernonia cinerea*
pantom (Lepcha), see *Leea macrophylla*
panwar (Nepali), see *Cassia occidentalis*
panze (Tibetan), see *Pterocephalus hookeri*
papa lhapti (Tibetan), see *Butea buteiformis*
papaw (English), see *Carica papaya*
papaya (English), see *Carica papaya*

paper bush, Nepalese (English), see *Edgeworthia gardneri*
paper plant, Nepalese (English), see *Daphne bholua*
paphar (Danuwar), see *Fagopyrum esculentum*
papita (Bhojpuri), see *Carica papaya*
paradise flower (English), see *Caesalpinia pulcherrima*
paramhendo (Tamang), see *Rhododendron arboreum*
paramsing (Limbu), see *Ficus benghalensis*
paranda (Limbu), see *Solanum melongena*
para phul (Nepali), see *Coelogyne ochracea*
parari ghans (Nepali), see *Ichnocarpus frutescens*
paras (Chepang), see *Mallotus philippensis*
parasika yabani (Sherpa), see *Hyoscyamus niger* var. *agrestis*
parasol flower (English), see *Holmskioldia sanguinea*
parbar (Danuwar), see *Trichosanthes dioica*
parbata phul (Nepali), see *Scutellaria discolor*
paredhayaro (Nepali), see *Wendlandia pendula*
parenu (Nepali), see *Parthenocissus semicordata*
parijat (Nepali), see *Nyctanthes arbor-tritis*
paror (Mooshar), see *Trichosanthes dioica*
parpare (Nepali), see *Loxogramme involuta*
par-pa-ta (Tibetan), see *Capsella bursa-pastoris, Zanthoxylum acanthopodium*
parsidha (Danuwar), see *Euphorbia royleana*
pa-ru-ru (Tibetan), see *Azadirachta indica*
parwal (Bhojpuri, Lepcha, Nepali, Newari, Sunwar, Tamang), see *Trichosanthes dioica*
pas (Chepang), see *Dioscorea bulbifera*
pasa kath (Nepali), see *Salix denticulata*
pasare bethe (Nepali), see *Chenopodium ambrosoides*
pasi (Newari), see *Pyrus communis*
pasij (Mooshar), see *Euphorbia royleana*
pasing (Tamang), see *Homalium napaulense*
paski taha (Gurung), see *Brassica juncea* var. *cuneifolia*
paswan (Newari), see *Rumex nepalensis*
pat (Nepali), see *Edgeworthia gardneri*
pat (Tamang), see *Rhododendron arboreum*
pata (Gurung), see *Brassaiopsis hainla*
patak (Magar), see *Rhododendron arboreum*
pataka (Tibetan), see *Astragalus leucocephalus*
patake (Nepali), see *Litsea doshia*
patale katus (Nepali), see *Castanopsis hystrix*
patapate khar (Nepali), see *Chrysopogon gryllus*
patape (Tamang), see *Sarcococca coriacea*
patare (Nepali), see *Spermadictyon suaveolens*
patechurdham (Rai), see *Euphorbia royleana*
pate ghiraunla (Nepali), see *Luffa acutangula*
patek (Chepang), see *Artemisia indica*
patendo (Gurung), see *Viola pilosa*
pate phul (Nepali), see *Murdannia scapiflora*
pate salla (Nepali), see *Taxus baccata* subsp. *wallichiana*
patgasar (Magar), see *Rhododendron arboreum*
patha (Nepali), see *Cissampelos pareira*
pathu (Newari), see *Persicaria mollis*
pati (Magar, Tharu), see *Artemisia indica*
pati (Nepali), see *Wikstroemia canescens*
patidhuk (Sherpa), see *Anemone rivularis*
patina (Nepali), see *Mentha spicata*
patlange (Magar), see *Clerodendrum japonicum*
patoi (Nepali), see *Corchorus aestuans*
patol (English), see *Trichosanthes dioica*
pa-to-la (Tibetan), see *Trichosanthes dioica*
patpate (Nepali), see *Gaultheria fragrantissima, Physalis divaricata*
patre (Gurung), see *Dichroa febrifuga*
patu (Lepcha), see *Dendrocalamus hookeri*
patu korlingo (Nepali), see *Rhododendron grande*
patuwa (Nepali), see *Hibiscus sabdariffa*
patuwa jhar (Nepali), see *Melochia corchorifolia*

paughyan (Newari), see *Oxalis corniculata*
paundhi (Tharu), see *Borreria alata*
paunro (Nepali), see *Ribes himalense*
pawari (Nepali), see *Dodecadenia grandiflora*
payem (Gurung), see *Prunus cerasoides*
pea (English), see *Pisum sativum*
pea, garden (English), see *Pisum sativum*
pea, grass (English), see *Lathyrus aphaca, L. sativus*
pea, rosary (English), see *Abrus precatorius*
pea, smooth-leaved heart (English), see *Cardiospermum halicacabum*
pea, wild (English), see *Lathyrus aphaca*
peach (English), see *Prunus persica*
peach, wild (English), see *Prunus cornuta*
peacock flower (English), see *Caesalpinia pulcherrima, Delonix regia*
peanut (English), see *Arachis hypogaea*
pear (English), see *Pyrus communis*
pear, Nepalese wild (English), see *Pyrus pashia*
pear, prickly (English), see *Opuntia monacantha*
pear, sacred garlic (English), see *Crateva unilocularis*
pebamran (Tamang), see *Mimosa pudica*
peda (Gurung), see *Oreocnide frutescens*
pedano (Gurung), see *Pouzolzia zeylanica*
peepal tree (English), see *Ficus religiosa*
peli (Gurung), see *Bauhinia vahlii*
pelka (Tamang), see *Ficus rumphii*
pelma (Sherpa), see *Cotoneaster microphyllus*
pelnti (Gurung), see *Hydrocotyle nepalensis*
pemariy (Lepcha), see *Nelumbo nucifera*
pempakcha (Rai), see *Fagopyrum esculentum*
pendi (Limbu), see *Ficus religiosa*
pendro no (Gurung), see *Sida rhombifolia*
pennywort, Indian (English), see *Centella asiatica*
penpe (Nepali), see *Actinodaphne angustifolia*
penyale (Nepali), see *Thalictrum foliolosum*
peony (English), see *Paeonia emodi*
peony, Himalayan (English), see *Paeonia emodi*
peperano (Gurung), see *Drymaria diandra*
pepkar (Tamang), see *Quercus lanata*
pepper, long (English), see *Piper longum*
pepper, Nepal (English), see *Zanthoxylum armatum*
pepper, red (English), see *Capsicum annuum*
pepper, water (English), see *Persicaria hydropiper*
perilla, purple (English), see *Perilla frutescens*
periwinkle (English), see *Catharanthus roseus*
persimmon, Japanese (English), see *Diospyros kaki*
phabare ghans (Nepali), see *Polygala tartarinowii*
phaising (Tamang), see *Stranvaesia nussia*
phakan (Newari), see *Colocasia esculenta*
phaki (Tibetan), see *Heracleum nepalense, Pleurospermum hookeri*
phakurikabi (Lepcha), see *Amaranthus spinosus*
phalako (Chepang), see *Oroxylum indicum*
phalame (Nepali), see *Myrsine semiserrata, Rhamnus virgatus*
phalam kath (Nepali), see *Myrsine capitellata*
phalant (Nepali), see *Quercus lamellosa, Q. lanata*
phalat (Nepali), see *Quercus glauca*
phaleto (Nepali), see *Erythrina arborescens, E. stricta*
phalewa (Danuwar), see *Caesulia axillaris*
phalkichhe (Tamang), see *Thalictrum foliolosum*
phalsa (English), see *Grewia subinaequalis*
phandil (Majhi), see *Syzygium cumini*
phanir (Nepali), see *Syzygium cumini*
phanrid (Chepang), see *Syzygium cumini, S. jambos*
phaphar (Bhojpuri, Chepang, Magar, Nepali, Tamang), see *Fagopyrum esculentum*
phaphre jhar (Nepali), see *Persicaria perfoliata*
phar (Tibetan), see *Juniperus squamata*

pharaka (Chepang), see *Oroxylum indicum*
pharsa (Nepali), see *Grewia sapida, G. subinaequalis*
pharsi (Chepang, Danuwar, Mooshar, Nepali, Rai, Tamang), see *Cucurbita maxima*
pharso (Nepali), see *Grewia sclerophylla*
phasi (Newari), see *Cucurbita maxima*
phatakya (Nepali), see *Impatiens scabrida*
phawar (Tamang), see *Buddleja paniculata*
phawar singo (Tamang), see *Buddleja asiatica*
phechchi (Sunwar), see *Myrica esculenta*
pheisign (Tamang), see *Euonymus tingens*
phekwasi (Rai), see *Momordica charantia*
pheli (Tamang), see *Neillia thyrsiflora*
phelwa bhakundo (Danuwar), see *Persicaria lapathifolia* var. *lanata*
phenars (Limbu), see *Artocarpus heterophyllus*
phengse (Limbu), see *Carica papaya*
phenla chimal (Nepali), see *Rhododendron triflorum*
phese (Tamang), see *Boehmeria platyphylla*
phi (Gurung), see *Fagopyrum esculentum*
phili (Tamang), see *Lagerstroemia parviflora*
phinnarukkwa (Limbu), see *Choerospondias axillaris*
phintusi (Rai), see *Choerospondias axillaris*
phirchi (Gurung), see *Hippophae tibetana*
phirke (Nepali), see *Reissantia arborea*
phirphire (Magar), see *Sterculia villosa*
phirphire (Nepali), see *Acer campbellii, A. oblongum*
phir phire (Nepali), see *Alangium chinense*
phirphire (Nepali), see *Sarcococca hookeriana*
phirphire (Tamang), see *Hedyotis scandens*
phirumuk (Lepcha), see *Centella asiatica*
phiti bhi (Nepali), see *Sarcococca hookeriana*
phodi mran (Tamang), see *Galinsoga quadriradiata*
phoke jhar (Majhi), see *Leucas cephalotes*
phok phok (Tamang), see *Viburnum grandiflorum*
phokro no (Chepang), see *Apluda mutica*
phoksarpa (Tamang), see *Anemone vitifolia*
phoksing (Magar), see *Shorea robusta*
phole mhendo (Tamang), see *Tagetes erecta*
phommi (Rai), see *Dalbergia sisso*
phongo (Tamang), see *Herpetospermum pedunculosum*
phongretel (Chepang), see *Physalis divaricata*
phonsi (Newari), see *Artocarpus heterophyllus*
phor (Danuwar), see *Dioscorea bulbifera*
phorgel gil (Tibetan), see *Cissampelos pareira*
phoro (Sunwar), see *Juglans regia* var. *kamaonia*
phorsa (Nepali), see *Grewia optiva*
phosre (Gurung, Nepali), see *Potentilla fulgens*
phosyang (Tamang), see *Leucosceptrum canum*
phrekphrek (Tamang), see *Achyranthes bidentata*
phulchiso (Nepali), see *Rauvolfia serpentina*
phule jhar (Nepali), see *Lactuca graciliflora, Vernonia squarrosa*
phul gobi (Tharu), see *Brassica oleracea* var. *botrytis*
phuli jhar (Gurung), see *Vernonia cinerea*
phuli jhar (Nepali), see *Justicia procumbens* var. *simplex, Phyla nodiflora, Taraxacum officinale, Vernonia cinerea*
phulikorne jhar (Nepali), see *Elephantopus scaber*
phulimhendo (Tamang), see *Persicaria capitata*
phuli no (Nepali), see *Tridax procumbens*
phulki (Mooshar), see *Imperata cylindrica*
phulpat (Nepali), see *Colquhounia coccinea*
phul pati (Nepali), see *Osbeckia stellata*
phultis (Nepali), see *Buddleja paniculata*
phultiso (Nepali), see *Colquhounia coccinea*
phultit (Magar), see *Buddleja asiatica*
phultusm (Nepali), see *Callicarpa arborea*
phurke (Magar), see *Thysanolaena maxima*
phurke jhar (Danuwar), see *Elephantopus scaber*

phurke jhar (Nepali), see *Vernonia cinerea*

phurke khar (Nepali), see *Arundinella hookeri, A. nepalensis, Eragrostis nigra*

phurke pati (Nepali), see *Wikstroemia canescens*

phursedo (Nepali), see *Buddleja paniculata*

phurse kanda (Nepali), see *Rubus acuminatus*

phusre bans (Nepali), see *Bambusa nepalensis*

phusre ghans (Nepali), see *Indigofera dosua, I. pulchella*

phusre kanda (Nepali), see *Rubus paniculatus*

phusre kath (Nepali), see *Hydrangea heteromalla*

phusre nyuro (Nepali), see *Polystichum squarrosum*

phusure (Tamang), see *Potentilla fulgens*

phusuro (Nepali), see *Lindera pulcherrima*

phut (Nepali), see *Cucumis melo* var. *momordica*

phutra (Limbu), see *Benincasa hispida*

phys (Tamang), see *Thysanolaena maxima*

physic nut (English), see *Jatropha curcas*

physic nut bush, red (English), see *Jatropha gossypifolia*

pibi (Tamang), see *Sarcococca coriacea*

pibil (Tamang), see *Lindera pulcherrima*

pichar (Tamang), see *Berberis aristata*

pichikine jhyal (Gurung), see *Dicentra scandens*

pichyar (Tamang), see *Berberis aristata*

pickerel weed (English), see *Monochoria hastata*

pidalu (Danuwar), see *Colocasia esculenta*

pidhamari (Nepali), see *Torenia cordifolia*

pigeon berry (English), see *Duranta repens*

pigeon pea (English), see *Cajanus cajan*

pigweed (English), see *Amaranthus viridis, Chenopodium album*

pile (Nepali), see *Corydalis chaerophylla*

pile jhar (Nepali), see *Megacodon stylophorus*

pimnendo (Gurung), see *Solanum nigrum*

pimpernel (English), see *Anagallis arvensis*

pinase (Nepali), see *Lygodium japonicum*

pinase jhar (Nepali), see *Lysimachia alternifolia, Micromeria biflora*

pinda (Raute), see *Remusatia vivipara*

pindalu (Nepali), see *Colocasia esculenta*

pine, blue (English), see *Pinus wallichiana*

pine, chir (English), see *Pinus roxburghii*

pine, Himalayan long-leaved (English), see *Pinus roxburghii*

pineapple (English), see *Ananas comosus*

pingman (Tamang), see *Aechmanthera gossypina*

ping mhendo (Tamang), see *Justicia procumbens* var. *simplex*

ping tak tak (Sherpa), see *Lindera pulcherrima*

pingur (Tamang), see *Gonostegia hirta*

pipal (Bhojpuri, Chepang, Gurung, Magar, Nepali, Sunwar), see *Ficus religiosa*

pipal (Tamang), see *Ficus religiosa, Piper wallichii*

pipala (Nepali), see *Piper mullesua*

pipal geda (Tamang), see *Maytenus rufa*

pipal pate (Nepali), see *Hedera nepalensis*

pipa pa (Tamang), see *Maytenus rufa*

pipar (Danuwar, Mooshar), see *Ficus religiosa*

pipara (Tharu), see *Ficus religiosa*

piparmint (Nepali), see *Clinopodium piperitum*

pipi (Newari), see *Piper longum*

pipi (Tibetan), see *Lindera pulcherrima*

pipicha ghyan (Newari), see *Rungia parviflora*

pi-pi-ling (Tibetan), see *Piper longum*

pipindo (Gurung), see *Drymaria diandra*

pipiri (Nepali), see *Lindera pulcherrima, Symplocos pyrifolia*

pipla (Nepali), see *Piper longum*

pipli (Gurung), see *Butea buteiformis*

pipli (Nepali), see *Exbucklandia populnea, Gnetum montanum, Piper nepalense*

pipola (Rai), see *Ficus religiosa*

pirar (Nepali), see *Catunaregam uliginosa*

pire (Chepang), see *Spilanthes paniculata*

pire (Nepali), see *Cymbopogon pendulus, Galinsoga parviflora, Galium asperifolium, Persicaria pubescens*

pire jhar (Nepali), see *Persicaria capitata, P. tenella* var. *kawagoeana*

pire khai (Nepali), see *Persicaria hydropiper*

pire unyu (Nepali), see *Pteris aspericaulis*

pirimsing (Limbu), see *Ficus religiosa*

piringo (Nepali), see *Hedyotis corymbosa*

pirise (Lepcha), see *Pyrus communis*

piriya (Tharu), see *Persicaria barbata*

pirpite (Gurung), see *Millettia extensa*

pitamari (Nepali), see *Anagallis arvensis*

pitambar phul (Nepali), see *Oenothera rosea*

pitanga (English), see *Syzygium cumini*

pithari (Danuwar), see *Trewia nudiflora*

pitho (Mooshar), see *Trewia nudiflora*

pithochor (Nepali), see *Viburnum cylindricum*

pitimgan (Magar), see *Solanum nigrum*

pitle (Nepali), see *Persicaria capitata*

pitlemsi (Rai), see *Cleistocalyx operculatus, Syzygium cumini*

pitmare jhar (Nepali), see *Lindernia nummularifolia*

pitpir (Nepali), see *Lathyrus aphaca*

pitsir tserma (Tibetan), see *Morina longifolia*

pitta kangri (Nepali), see *Herpetospermum pedunculosum*

pittamari (Nepali), see *Verbena officinalis*

pitumse (Rai), see *Syzygium cumini*

pitunja (Danuwar), see *Coix lachryma-jobi*

piwa (Tamang), see *Galinsoga parviflora*

piwi (Tamang), see *Lindera pulcherrima*

plangasi (Chepang), see *Duabanga grandiflora*

plantain, greater (English), see *Plantago erosa*

pleta (Gurung), see *Boehmeria platyphylla, Oreocnide frutescens*

pli (Gurung), see *Engelhardia spicata*

plum, jambolan (English), see *Syzygium cumini*

plum, Java (English), see *Syzygium cumini*

plum, Malabar (English), see *Syzygium cumini*

plum, Nepalese (English), see *Choerospondias axillaris*

plum, puneala (English), see *Flacourtia jangomas*

plum, queen's (English), see *Prunus domestica*

plum, sapodilla (English), see *Manilkara zapota*

plume ro ro (Gurung), see *Butea buteiformis*

plum tree, hog (English), see *Spondias pinnata*

pode ghans (Nepali), see *Poa annua*

podo (Tamang), see *Viburnum cylindricum*

poi (Tamang), see *Nardostachys grandiflora*

poi sag (Nepali), see *Basella alba*

poinciana, royal (English), see *Delonix regia*

poinsettia (English), see *Euphorbia pulcherrima*

pojagan (Magar), see *Capsella bursa-pastoris*

poke jhar (Nepali), see *Ludwigia adscendens*

poker weed (English), see *Phytolacca acinosa*

pokrono (Gurung), see *Boehmeria ternifolia*

polancha (Newari), see *Luffa cylindrica, Trichosanthes anguina*

polang (Tamang), see *Rubus ellipticus*

polo (Gurung), see *Urtica dioica*

polo (Tamang), see *Geranium wallichianum, Urtica dioica*

polokamji (Gurung), see *Dichroa febrifuga*

poltata (Sunwar), see *Oroxylum indicum*

polung (Tamang), see *Lantana camara*

poma (Lepcha), see *Toona ciliata*

pomegranate (English), see *Punica granatum*

pomla (Gurung), see *Boehmeria platyphylla*

pondo (Gurung), see *Boehmeria platyphylla*

pongaju (Tamang), see *Rheum acuminatum*

pongam (English), see *Millettia pinnata*

ponge jhar (Magar), see *Ageratum conyzoides*

pongmuk (Lepcha), see *Cynodon dactylon*

ponki (Nepali), see *Pedicularis siphonantha*
poplar, Himalayan (English), see *Populus ciliata*
poppy, blue (English), see *Meconopsis grandis*
poppy, Mexican (English), see *Argemone mexicana*
poppy, prickly (English), see *Argemone mexicana*
porali (Chepang), see *Luffa cylindrica*
porol (Tamang), see *Luffa cylindrica*
pororo (Tamang), see *Asparagus racemosus*
porota (Gurung), see *Rhododendron arboreum*
po-son-cha (Tibetan), see *Sesbania grandiflora*
po-son-chha (Tibetan), see *Catunaregam spinosa*
pota (Gurung), see *Rhododendron arboreum*
pota (Tamang), see *Brassaiopsis hainla*
potale (Rai), see *Girardinia diversifolia*
potato (English), see *Solanum tuberosum*
potato, air (English), see *Dioscorea bulbifera*
potato, sweet (English), see *Ipomoea batatas*
pote (Nepali), see *Pieris formosa*
pote pote (Tamang), see *Colebrookea oppositifolia*
pothi sahasrabuti (Nepali), see *Plantago erosa*
poti (Gurung), see *Valeriana jatamansii*
poti (Majhi), see *Abutilon indicum*
poyepa (Limbu), see *Ficus auriculata*
pra (Tamang), see *Pieris formosa*
praba (Sherpa), see *Pieris formosa*
praba (Tamang), see *Anemone rivularis, A. vitifolia*
prabading (Tamang), see *Satyrium nepalense*
prabobho (Tamang), see *Viburnum cylindricum*
pragyum (Tamang), see *Begonia picta*
prake (Nepali), see *Pieris formosa*
prak prak (Tibetan), see *Ilex dipyrena*
pramaimran (Tamang), see *Vernonia cinerea*
pramalaman (Tamang), see *Vernonia cinerea*
prami (Gurung), see *Entada phaseoloides*
pramji (Tamang), see *Senecio diversifolius*
prat (Chepang), see *Capillipedium assimile*
prava (Nepali), see *Gaultheria fragrantissima*
prayesi (Chepang), see *Lyonia ovalifolia*
pregemgyalting (Sherpa), see *Smilax aspera*
pregyap (Tamang), see *Fagopyrum tataricum*
presi (Chepang), see *Osbeckia nepalensis*
prickly ash bark (English), see *Zanthoxylum armatum*
prickly pear (English), see *Opuntia monacantha*
primrose-willow, alligator (English), see *Ludwigia adscendens*
primrose-willow, Mexican (English), see *Ludwigia octovalvis*
printa (Gurung), see *Polygonatum cirrhifolium*
privet (English), see *Ligustrum compactum*
privet, Egyptian (English), see *Lawsonia inermis*
priya ghans (Nepali), see *Persicaria nepalensis*
pri-yung-ku (Tibetan), see *Callicarpa macrophylla*
prome (Gurung), see *Entada phaseoloides*
prongsai (Chepang), see *Capillipedium assimile*
prumo (Gurung, Tamang), see *Zanthoxylum armatum*
pruna (Tibetan), see *Cornus oblonga*
puchhi (Chepang), see *Litsea monopetala*
puchu (Gurung), see *Ilex dipyrena*
puchu (Sherpa), see *Caragana brevispina*
puchu (Tibetan), see *Berberis aristata, B. ulcina*
puchu balcha (Tibetan), see *Berberis chitria*
pudachhe (Tamang), see *Brassaiopsis hainla*
pudding pipe tree (English), see *Cassia fistula*
pudichhi (Gurung), see *Brassaiopsis hainla*
pudina (Bhojpuri, Mooshar, Nepali), see *Mentha spicata*
pujutoro (Gurung), see *Asparagus racemosus*
pukpa (Gurung), see *Vernonia cinerea*
puksur (Nepali), see *Aeginetia indica*
pukya (Chepang), see *Arundinella nepalensis*

pulia (Nepali), see *Kydia calycina*
pulikhaja (Magar), see *Callicarpa macrophylla*
pulu (Gurung), see *Urtica dioica*
pulung (Tamang), see *Rubus ellipticus*
pulunge jhar (Nepali), see *Bistorta vaccinifolia*
pummelo (English), see *Citrus margarita*
pumpkin, ash (English), see *Benincasa hispida*
pumpkin, red (English), see *Cucurbita maxima*
pumpkin, white (English), see *Benincasa hispida*
puna (Tharu), see *Lilium nepalense*
punarnava (Nepali), see *Boerhavia diffusa*
pundlukwa (Rai), see *Raphanus sativus*
pungi (Tamang), see *Oreocnide frutescens*
pungi (Tamang), see *Pouzolzia sanguinea*
pungnamu (Rai), see *Cinnamomum camphora*
punkiya (Tamang), see *Lindenbergia grandiflora*
pun pun gosaro (Tamang), see *Desmodium confertum*
puntaluk (Rai), see *Brassica rapa*
purbo (Lepcha), see *Alstonia scholaris*
pureni (Nepali), see *Ampelocissus divaricata, A. latifolia, A. sikkimensis, Cissus adnata, Vitis lanata, V. parvifolia*
purging nut (English), see *Jatropha curcas*
puri (Gurung), see *Prunus napaulensis*
puri makhan (Gurung), see *Arisaema tortuosum*
purkhe kath (Nepali), see *Viburnum erubescens*
purni (Gurung), see *Vitis lanata*
puroa (Lepcha), see *Mallotus philippensis*
purpurya (Nepali), see *Ephedra gerardiana*
purslane (English), see *Portulaca oleracea*
purslane, horse (English), see *Trianthema portulacastrum*
pustu (Gurung), see *Asparagus racemosus*
putaleso (Nepali), see *Maoutia puya*
putali (Magar), see *Boerhavia diffusa*
putali jhar (Nepali), see *Smilax rigida*
putalil kath (Nepali), see *Reissantia arborea*
putali phul (Nepali), see *Acer oblongum*
putho (Nepali), see *Brassaiopsis hainla*
puvanma (Rai), see *Bauhinia variegata*
puwa (Gurung), see *Girardinia diversifolia*
puwa (Nepali), see *Maoutia puya*
puwangma (Nepali), see *Bauhinia variegata*
puwanle (Nepali), see *Ilex excelsa*
pwatyacha (Newari), see *Brassica rapa*
pyaj (Bhojpuri, Chepang, Danuwar, Gurung, Magar, Mooshar, Nepali, Newari, Sunwar, Tamang, Tharu), see *Allium cepa*
pyanle phul (Nepali), see *Tridax procumbens*
pyar (Nepali), see *Buchanania latifolia*
pyari (Danuwar), see *Buchanania latifolia*
pyaunli (Gurung), see *Hypericum cordifolium*
pyaunli (Nepali), see *Hypericum cordifolium, Reinwardtia indica, Sauropus quadrangularis*
pyena (Gurung), see *Quercus semecarpifolia*
pyongla (Tamang), see *Mallotus philippensis*
pyuling (Chepang), see *Lindenbergia grandiflora*
quinine, Chinese (English), see *Dichroa febrifuga*
rabagachhi (Tamang), see *Glochidion velutinum*
rabarep (Tamang), see *Tridax procumbens*
rabhasepot (Lepcha), see *Artocarpus heterophyllus*
rachana (Nepali), see *Daphniphyllum himalense*
radal (Tamang), see *Cajanus cajan*
radi (Gurung), see *Sarcococca coriacea*
radish (English), see *Raphanus sativus*
radu (Nepali), see *Rhododendron wightii*
ragatageri (Nepali), see *Geranium ocellatum*
ragate jhar (Nepali), see *Phalaris minor*
ragate mothe (Nepali), see *Pycreus sanguinolentus*
raglo (Sunwar), see *Colocasia esculenta*

rahar (Majhi, Nepali), see *Cajanus cajan*
rai (Bhojpuri), see *Brassica juncea* var. *cuneifolia*
rainj (Nepali), see *Quercus leucotrichophora*
rains (Nepali), see *Cotoneaster acuminatus*
rai sag (Mooshar, Tharu), see *Brassica juncea* var. *cuneifolia*
raja bubu (Tamang), see *Impatiens bicornuta*
raja bu bu (Tamang), see *Impatiens falcifer*
rajali (Tamang), see *Disporum cantoniense*
rajama (Nepali), see *Phaseolus vulgaris*
rajani giri (Gurung), see *Jatropha curcas*
raj beli (Nepali), see *Clerodendrum philippinum*
rajbrik (Raute), see *Cassia fistula*
rajbriksha (Magar, Majhi, Nepali, Rai), see *Cassia fistula*
rajeli (Nepali), see *Excoecaria acerifolia*
raj kali (Nepali), see *Clerodendrum philippinum*
raju kanda (Nepali), see *Ziziphus incurva*
rakalamul (Nepali), see *Geranium wallichianum*
rakalop (Lepcha), see *Acorus calamus*
rakaskung (Lepcha), see *Melia azedarach*
rakhokwa (Rai), see *Acacia catechu*
raksasing (Limbu), see *Melia azedarach*
raksenjen tongbo (Tamang), see *Daphniphyllum himalense*
raksi (Chepang), see *Shorea robusta*
raksya banko (Nepali), see *Arisaema consanguineum*
rakta chandan (Nepali), see *Daphniphyllum himalense*
raktamul (Nepali), see *Geranium nepalense*
rakung (Lepcha), see *Bauhinia variegata*
ramalakan (Tamang), see *Phyllanthus parvifolius*
ramapa (Magar), see *Acacia rugata*
rambrero (Nepali), see *Trewia nudiflora*
rambu (Tibetan), see *Bistorta milletii*
ramhagam (Tamang), see *Phyllanthus parvifolius*
ramlagan (Tamang), see *Crotalaria cytisoides*
ra-mnye (Tibetan), see *Polygonatum cirrhifolium*
ramothe (Tamang), see *Flemingia macrophylla*
ram-pa (Tibetan), see *Ranunculus scleratus*
ramphal (Nepali), see *Dillenia indica*
ramritha (Nepali), see *Trewia nudiflora*
ramsikia (Nepali), see *Polygonatum cirrhifolium*
ramsinghe (Nepali), see *Garuga pinnata*
ramsyang (Sherpa), see *Alnus nepalensis*
ramtoria (Nepali), see *Abelmoschus esculentus*
ramtoriya (Newari), see *Abelmoschus esculentus*
ramtulsi (Nepali), see *Origanum vulgare*
ranabas (Nepali), see *Leea crispa*
ranabhyang (Tamang), see *Inula cappa*
ranbhera (Sunwar), see *Lycopersicon esculentum*
ranbo (Chepang), see *Bridelia retusa*
randaur sar (Gurung), see *Buddleja asiatica*
rangalo (Chepang), see *Amaranthus spinosus*
rangan (Chepang), see *Amaranthus spinosus, A. viridis*
rangati (Chepang), see *Sapium insigne*
rangchu (Chepang), see *Mimosa rubicaulis* subsp. *himalayana*
ranghya (Chepang), see *Amaranthus viridis*
rangiya (Chepang), see *Isodon coetsa*
Rangoon creeper (English), see *Quisqualis indica*
rangso (Chepang), see *Acacia rugata*
rani bhalayo (Nepali), see *Rhus succedanea*
rani bhenta (Chepang), see *Lycopersicon esculentum*
rani chanp (Nepali), see *Michelia doltsopa*
rani dhayaro (Nepali), see *Wendlandia pendula*
rani ghyeb (Magar), see *Boehmeria platyphylla*
rani khirro (Nepali), see *Wrightia arborea*
ranipha (Nepali), see *Trewia nudiflora*
rani salla (Nepali), see *Cupressus torulosa, Pinus roxburghii*
rani sinka (Nepali), see *Cheilanthes albomarginata, C. anceps, C. dalhousiae, Tectaria macrodonta*

ranki (Nepali), see *Eragrostis japonica*
rankwa (Magar), see *Eleusine coracana*
ransag (Nepali), see *Clematis acuminata*
raone (Nepali), see *Cheilanthes albomarginata*
rape, Indian (English), see *Brassica napus*
rape seed (English), see *Brassica napus*
rapha langi (Tamang), see *Desmodium confertum*
raphalki (Tamang), see *Desmodium confertum*
rapre ghans (Nepali), see *Persicaria campanulata*
rasangan (Tamang), see *Pogostemon amarantoides*
rasgari (Nepali), see *Roscoea purpurea*
raspberry (English), see *Rubus rugosus*
raspberry, golden evergreen (English), see *Rubus ellipticus*
raspberry, Himalayan wild (English), see *Rubus fockeanus*
raspberry, Himalayan yellow (English), see *Rubus ellipticus*
raspberry, wild (English), see *Rubus calycinus*
rasula (Nepali), see *Acacia rugata*
ratamur (Tharu), see *Adiantum philippense*
ratanaulo (Nepali), see *Persicaria nepalensis*
ratanaulo (Rai), see *Boerhavia diffusa*
ratan daure (Magar), see *Persicaria nepalensis*
ratango (Nepali), see *Euphorbia hirta*
ratan jot (Nepali), see *Anemone obtusiloba*
ratanjot (Tharu), see *Jatropha curcas*
ratapate (Nepali), see *Orthosiphon incurvus, Scutellaria discolor*
rate jhar (Nepali), see *Viola pilosa*
rathi (Gurung), see *Osbeckia nutans*
rati (Chepang, Newari), see *Abrus precatorius*
rati geri (Magar, Nepali), see *Abrus precatorius*
ratnaulo (Nepali), see *Persicaria capitata, P. chinensis, P. hydropiper*
rato ainselu (Nepali), see *Potentilla indica, Rubus acuminatus, R. pentagonus*
rato angeri (Nepali), see *Enkianthus deflexus*
rato bakhre ghans (Nepali), see *Desmodium elegans*
rato charpate (Nepali), see *Anisomeles indica*
rato chulsi (Nepali), see *Osbeckia stellata*
rato geri (Danuwar, Majhi), see *Abrus precatorius*
rato geri (Nepali), see *Hemiphragma heterophyllum*
rato latte (Nepali), see *Chenopodium ambrosoides*
rato mirmire (Nepali), see *Indigofera pulchella*
ratomutne (Nepali), see *Litsea monopetala*
ratopate (Gurung), see *Scutellaria discolor*
rato pire (Nepali), see *Persicaria viscosa*
rato raunne (Nepali), see *Galinsoga parviflora*
rato saro (Nepali), see *Hedychium ellipticum*
rato unyu (Nepali), see *Polystichum squarrosum*
ratyun (Magar), see *Jatropha curcas*
rauka (Magar), see *Swertia chirayita*
raunde (Chepang), see *Ageratum conyzoides*
raunja (Chepang), see *Ageratum conyzoides*
raunle (Gurung), see *Fraxinus floribunda*
raunne (Nepali), see *Ageratum conyzoides, Dennstaedtia appendiculata, Persicaria nepalensis*
rauru (Chepang), see *Clerodendrum indicum*
rawagan (Tamang), see *Phyllanthus parvifolius*
rawagen (Tamang), see *Neillia thyrsiflora*
rayo (Danuwar, Nepali), see *Brassica juncea* var. *cuneifolia*
rayol dhap (Tamang), see *Brassica juncea* var. *cuneifolia*
rda-rdu-ra (Tibetan), see *Datura stramonium*
rdo-rta (Tibetan), see *Camellia sinensis*
reb (Sunwar), see *Dioscorea deltoidea, Solanum tuberosum*
re chhema (Sherpa), see *Clintonia udensis*
reckname (Chepang), see *Crassocephalum crepidioides*
reed, Danubian (English), see *Arundo donax*
reed, giant (English), see *Arundo donax*
reed, great (English), see *Arundo donax*
reed, Italian (English), see *Arundo donax*

refesing (Tibetan), see *Ephedra gerardiana*

regmi (Danuwar), see *Solanum surattense*

rejom srok (Chepang), see *Ampelocissus divaricata*

re-lchag (Tibetan), see *Stellera chamaejasme*

remalime jhar (Nepali), see *Dichrocephala integrifolia*

rerimse (Limbu), see *Citrus aurantium*

reyar (Tharu), see *Ricinus communis*

rgun-brum (Tibetan), see *Vitis vinifera*

rgya-spos (Tibetan), see *Thymus linearis*

rhamatyak (Magar), see *Lycopersicon esculentum*

rhanisekya (Sherpa), see *Polygonatum cirrhifolium*

rhatulo (Nepali), see *Euphorbia hirta*

rhea, wild (English), see *Debregeasia longifolia*

rheuka (Tibetan), see *Anemone rivularis*

rhideme (Tamang), see *Dioscorea deltoidea*

rhododendron, giant blood (English), see *Rhododendron barbatum*

rhododendron, Indian (English), see *Melastoma malabathricum*

rhubarb (English), see *Rheum australe*

rhyuli (Nepali), see *Rosa sericea*

ri bhenta (Tamang), see *Solanum aculeatissimum*

ribirip (Lepcha), see *Mentha spicata*

rice (English), see *Oryza sativa*

ridang (Chepang), see *Inula cappa*

rikabe (Tamang), see *Anemone vitifolia*

rikhiya (Danuwar), see *Phyllanthus emblica*

rikhiya (Mooshar), see *Phyllanthus emblica*

riki (Sherpa), see *Solanum tuberosum*

rimchi (Chepang), see *Litsea doshia*

rimsi (Chepang), see *Bauhinia variegata*

rinchhai (Chepang), see *Lablab purpureus*

ringamala (Tamang), see *Butea buteiformis*

ringworm plant (English), see *Cassia tora*

riniya (Mooshar), see *Dendrophthoe falcata*

riphikung (Lepcha), see *Butea monosperma*

riphuli (Tamang), see *Dipsacus inermis*

ririno (Gurung), see *Galinsoga parviflora*

ri-sgog (Tibetan), see *Allium cepa*

rishin pojo (Gurung), see *Pyracantha crenulata*

ritha (Bhojpuri, Chepang, Danuwar, Nepali, Tamang, Tharu), see *Sapindus mukorossi*

ritori (Chepang), see *Cleome viscosa*

riwa (Sunwar), see *Justicia adhatoda*

riyakat (Lepcha), see *Jasminum humile*

rockfoil (English), see *Bergenia ciliata*

rohini (Nepali, Tharu), see *Mallotus philippensis*

rohinya (Raute), see *Mallotus philippensis*

roina (Nepali), see *Mallotus philippensis*

roiro (Chepang), see *Indigofera hebepetala, I. pulchella*

rokawala (Tamang), see *Osyris wightiana*

rongle (Sherpa), see *Lyonia ovalifolia*

ropsi (Chepang), see *Bridelia retusa*

rose, Chinese (English), see *Hibiscus rosa-sinensis*

rose, Himalayan (English), see *Rosa sericea*

roselle (English), see *Hibiscus sabdariffa*

rosewood (English), see *Dalbergia latifolia*

rtag-ngu (Tibetan), see *Drosera peltata*

rtsa-ba-brgya (Tibetan), see *Asparagus racemosus*

rtsod (Tibetan), see *Rubia manjith*

rubi ko sag (Nepali), see *Megacarpaea polyandra*

rudila (Magar), see *Elsholtzia blanda*

rudilo (Nepali), see *Pogostemon benghalensis, P. glaber*

rudrachhe (Tamang), see *Elaeocarpus sphaericus*

rudraghanti (Nepali), see *Leucas cephalotes*

rudraksha (Nepali), see *Elaeocarpus sphaericus*

rue, white (English), see *Boenninghausenia albiflora*

ruglim (Lepcha), see *Celastrus paniculatus*

rukh ainselu (Nepali), see *Rubus paniculatus*

rukh dhayaro (Nepali), see *Lagerstroemia parviflora*

rukh ghari (Nepali), see *Randia tetrasperma*

rukh kamal (Nepali), see *Magnolia grandiflora*

rukh pangra (Nepali), see *Entada phaseoloides*

rukpa (Sherpa), see *Maianthemum purpureum*

rumsing (Tamang), see *Leptodermis lanceolata*

runsi (Chepang), see *Persea bombycina*

ru-rta (Tibetan), see *Costus speciosus*

rus (Tharu), see *Justicia adhatoda*

rusi (Chepang), see *Rhus javanica*

ryak dhyak (Chepang), see *Colebrookea oppositifolia*

ryapu (Gurung), see *Rhododendron barbatum, R. cinnabarinum*

ryop jhar (Chepang), see *Tridax procumbens*

ryumsi (Chepang), see *Debregeasia salicifolia*

sa (Tamang), see *Guizotia abyssinica*

sabalo (Nepali), see *Caragana brevispina*

sabhulung (Tamang), see *Solanum aculeatissimum*

sabonla (Gurung), see *Boehmeria platyphylla*

sabonla (Gurung), see *Boehmeria ternifolia*

sa-bras (Tibetan), see *Nelumbo nucifera*

sabromo (Tamang), see *Myriactis nepalensis*

sabune jhar (Nepali), see *Anagallis arvensis*

sada (Satar), see *Streblus asper*

sadan (Nepali), see *Desmodium elegans*

sadhab (Tamang), see *Drymaria cordata*

sadiwal (Tamang), see *Symplocos pyrifolia*

sadum (Nepali), see *Millettia pinnata*

saffron (English), see *Adina cordifolia*

sage (English), see *Salvia officinalis*

sage, sweet (English), see *Acorus calamus*

sage, wild (English), see *Lantana camara*

sage, yellow (English), see *Lantana camara*

sage bush, English (English), see *Lantana camara*

sage bush, red (English), see *Lantana camara*

saghakar (Lepcha), see *Capsicum annuum*

sagino (Nepali), see *Indigofera atropurpurea*

sahad (Satar), see *Dillenia pentagyna*

sahadeya (Tharu), see *Vernonia cinerea*

sahasrabuti (Nepali), see *Blumea hieraciifolia*

sahasra buti (Nepali), see *Elephantopus scaber*

sahora (Danuwar, Mooshar), see *Streblus asper*

sain sag (Nepali), see *Polygonum plebejum*

sain su sing (Chepang), see *Cornus oblonga*

saipatin (Gurung), see *Thalictrum javanicum*

saiphing (Chepang), see *Arundinaria nepalensis, Drepanostachyum falcatum*

saisya (Magar), see *Hedychium spicatum*

saj (Nepali), see *Terminalia alata, T. myriocarpa*

sajin (Gurung), see *Jatropha curcas*

sajyon (Nepali), see *Jatropha curcas, Moringa oleifera*

sakarkhand (Nepali), see *Ipomoea batatas*

sakar time (Tamang), see *Ipomoea batatas*

sa katahar (Tamang), see *Ananas comosus*

sakhab bung (Rai), see *Grevillea robusta*

sakhino (Nepali), see *Campylotropis speciosa, Indigofera heterantha, I. pulchella*

sakhino jhar (Nepali), see *Desmodium heterocarpon*

sakhuwa (Bhojpuri, Mooshar), see *Shorea robusta*

saki (Gurung), see *Pouzolzia zeylanica*

saki (Newari), see *Colocasia esculenta*

sakkali jhare jaro (Nepali), see *Potentilla leuconota*

sakki (Rai), see *Dioscorea deltoidea*

sakkisak (Rai), see *Dioscorea bulbifera*

sal (Gurung, Nepali, Sunwar), see *Shorea robusta*

salah (Chepang), see *Eupatorium odoratum*

salaha jhar (Nepali), see *Conyza japonica*

salahako jhar (Nepali), see *Crassocephalum crepidioides*

salakha (Newari), see *Centella asiatica*
salame (Gurung), see *Imperata cylindrica*
salan (Rai), see *Shorea robusta*
salcha (Nepali), see *Sopubia trifida*
salep (English), see *Dactylorhiza hatagirea*
salidha (Gurung), see *Coelogyne ochracea*
salikal (Nepali), see *Trachelospermum lucidum*
salima (Tamang), see *Chrysopogon gryllus*
salimran (Tamang), see *Portulaca oleracea*
salin (Gurung), see *Taxus baccata* subsp. *wallichiana*
salla dhup (Nepali), see *Pinus roxburghii*
salle jhar (Nepali), see *Scoparia dulcis*
salotapot (Lepcha), see *Choerospondias axillaris*
salsale (Nepali), see *Fagopyrum dibotrys*
sal tree (English), see *Shorea robusta*
saluma (Nepali), see *Rhododendron lepidotum*
salyang (Lepcha), see *Glycine max*
salyang sai (Chepang), see *Geranium nepalense*
salyangsai (Chepang), see *Potentilla monanthes*
sama (Nepali), see *Echinochloa colona, E. crus-galli, Setaria italica*
samabri (Lepcha), see *Citrus aurantifolia, C. limon*
saman (Tamang), see *Boenninghausenia albiflora*
samaya (Nepali, Tharu), see *Valeriana jatamansii*
sambhakhu (Limbu), see *Allium hypsistum*
samden (Tamang), see *Galinsoga parviflora*
sami (Nepali), see *Ficus benjamina*
sampicha (Rai), see *Eleusine coracana*
sampur (Chepang), see *Spilanthes paniculata*
samtola (Bhojpuri, Mooshar), see *Citrus aurantium*
samylapot (Lepcha), see *Terminalia bellirica*
samyok (Limbu), see *Cynodon dactylon*
samyulop (Lepcha), see *Citrus margarita*
san (Nepali), see *Crotalaria juncea*
sanbolo (Tamang), see *Boehmeria ternifolia*
sandan (Nepali), see *Desmodium oojeinense*
sandhap (Tamang), see *Stellaria media*
sandpaper (English), see *Trema cannabina*
sand thorn (English), see *Hippophae tibetana*
sang jhar (Chepang), see *Ageratum conyzoides*
sang kaba (Sherpa), see *Ephedra gerardiana*
sang khamba (Tibetan), see *Dendranthema nubigenum*
sangle jhar (Nepali), see *Flemingia strobilifera, Tadehaji triquetrum*
sangmen (Tamang), see *Euphorbia stracheyi*
sangna (Tamang), see *Eleusine coracana*
sangsa chhe (Tamang), see *Capillipedium assimile*
sangsornyom (Lepcha), see *Cinnamomum tamala*
sanhali sag (Nepali), see *Stellaria monosperma*
sani (Nepali), see *Cassia occidentalis*
sanit (Gurung), see *Coelogyne ochracea*
sankalo (Nepali), see *Habenaria furcifera*
sankhu (Danuwar), see *Shorea robusta*
sano (Gurung), see *Centipeda minima*
sano angeri (Nepali), see *Osbeckia nepalensis, O. nutans*
sano banmara (Majhi), see *Eupatorium adenophorum*
sano bhatte (Nepali), see *Tadehaji triquetrum, Uraria lagopodioides*
sano bhattu (Majhi), see *Leucas mollissima*
sano bini (Satar), see *Solanum nigrum*
sano boksi baja (Nepali), see *Crotalaria prostrata*
sano charimeli (Nepali), see *Desmodium microphyllum*
sano chheke (Nepali), see *Crotalaria prostrata*
sano chilya (Nepali), see *Sida acuta, S. rhombifolia*
sano dedri (Nepali), see *Casearia graveolens*
sano dhable (Magar), see *Plantago erosa*
sano dhayaro (Nepali, Rai), see *Woodfordia fruticosa*
sano gangleto (Nepali), see *Elatostema platyphyllum*
sano ghortapre (Gurung), see *Hydrocotyle sibthorpioides*
sano ghortapre (Nepali), see *Hydrocotyle nepalensis*

sano ghuru (Chepang), see *Diplocyclos palmatus*
sano jhingane (Nepali), see *Eurya acuminata*
sano kakchukya (Magar), see *Clematis buchananiana*
sano karbir (Nepali), see *Thevetia peruviana*
sano khirro (Nepali), see *Holarrhena pubescens*
sano kukurdino (Nepali), see *Disporum cantoniense*
sano lodo (Nepali), see *Symplocos paniculata*
sano majitho (Nepali), see *Galium asperifolium*
sano nundhiki (Nepali), see *Breynia retusa, Securinega virosa*
sano pahenli (Nepali), see *Dicentra scandens*
sano phultis (Nepali), see *Buddleja asiatica*
sanorip (Lepcha), see *Datura metel*
sano saro (Nepali), see *Cautleya spicata, Ranunculus diffusus*
sanotapre (Nepali), see *Cassia tora*
sano tapre (Nepali), see *Hydrocotyle sibthorpioides*
sano tusare (Nepali), see *Colquhounia coccinea*
sano unyu (Nepali), see *Odontosoria chinensis*
sanse (Gurung), see *Elsholtzia stachyodes*
sansi dhauli (Majhi), see *Wendlandia pendula*
santalasi (Newari), see *Citrus aurantium*
santarkya (Tibetan), see *Dendranthema nubigenum*
santong (Lepcha), see *Carica papaya*
sanu chimal (Nepali), see *Rhododendron cinnabarinum*
sanu gulpha (Nepali), see *Rubus biflorus*
sanu kapase (Nepali), see *Abroma angusta*
sapala (Gurung), see *Potentilla indica*
sapalan (Gurung), see *Boehmeria ternifolia*
sapatu (Nepali), see *Manilkara zapota*
saphire berry (English), see *Symplocos paniculata*
saplang (Tamang), see *Hypericum cordifolium, Potentilla monanthes*
saplung (Tamang), see *Neillia thyrsiflora*
saplunme (Gurung), see *Solanum aculeatissimum*
saprumo (Tamang), see *Spilanthes paniculata*
sapsibob (Rai), see *Phaseolus aconitifolius*
sapu (English), see *Michelia champaca*
sapukawasi (Rai), see *Pyrus malus*
sapulung (Tamang), see *Potentilla indica*
saranchi sag (Danuwar, Mooshar), see *Alternanthera sessilis*
sarane (Nepali), see *Ficus benjamina*
sarasi (Chepang), see *Quercus lanata*
sarauth (Tharu), see *Chrysopogon aciculatus*
sarbhen mhendo (Tamang), see *Isodon lophanthoides*
sarchyat (Nepali), see *Grewia disperma*
sarendra (Chepang), see *Clerodendrum viscosum*
saringro (Chepang), see *Clerodendrum viscosum*
saripha (Mooshar, Nepali), see *Annona squamata*
saritamba ghugi (Tamang), see *Desmodium microphyllum*
saritambo ghugi (Tamang), see *Desmodium multiflorum*
saro (Nepali), see *Hedychium ellipticum*
sarongse (Limbu), see *Citrus aurantifolia*
sarpagandha (Nepali), see *Rauvolfia serpentina*
sarpa ko kaphal (Nepali), see *Potentilla indica*
sarpa maka (Nepali), see *Arisaema tortuosum*
sarsi (Tamang), see *Thysanolaena maxima*
sarson (Nepali), see *Brassica campestris* var. *sarson*
sarson, yellow (English), see *Brassica campestris* var. *sarson*
saru (Chepang), see *Spilanthes paniculata*
sas (Tamang), see *Terminalia alata*
sasa lingling (Tamang), see *Cassia tora*
sat (Magar), see *Grevillea robusta*
satawari (Mooshar, Nepali), see *Asparagus racemosus*
satibayar (Nepali), see *Rhus parviflora*
satibro (Tamang), see *Rhus parviflora*
satiman (Gurung), see *Jatropha curcas*
sati muja (Chepang), see *Siegesbeckia orientalis*
satisal (Nepali), see *Dalbergia latifolia*
satu (Tibetan), see *Urtica dioica*

satuwa (Gurung, Nepali), see *Paris polyphylla*
satuwa ghans (Nepali), see *Agrostemma sarmentosum*
satyanashi (Nepali), see *Argemone mexicana*
saun (Nepali), see *Phalaris minor*
sauna (Tharu), see *Oroxylum indicum*
saune tatal (Nepali), see *Oroxylum indicum*
saunf (Tamang), see *Foeniculum vulgare*
saunr (Raute), see *Celastrus stylosus*
saur (Nepali), see *Betula alnoides*
saurah (Nepali), see *Euonymus hamiltonianus*
sawan (Tharu), see *Setaria italica*
sayapatri (Nepali), see *Tagetes erecta*
sayuba (Rai), see *Buddleja asiatica*
screw tree, East Indian (English), see *Helicteres isora*
seb (Bhojpuri, Mooshar, Tharu), see *Pyrus malus*
se-ba (Tibetan), see *Rosa sericea*
sebaro (Nepali), see *Potentilla fruticosa, Rhododendron lepidotum*
se-bru (Tibetan), see *Punica granatum*
sechik (Chepang), see *Pteris vittaria*
segemete (Chepang), see *Crotalaria prostrata*
segesai (Chepang), see *Crotalaria alata*
sekkren (Sunwar), see *Zanthoxylum armatum*
sekra (Satar), see *Ziziphus rugosa*
selang (Nepali), see *Clematis buchananiana*
selkainchi (Gurung), see *Dichroa febrifuga*
sellosang (Limbu), see *Thysanolaena maxima*
sema (Tamang), see *Rosa sericea*
semal (Tamang), see *Pimpinella achilleifolia*
semali (Tharu), see *Vitex negundo*
semara (Tharu), see *Bombax ceiba*
semchare ghans (Nepali), see *Persicaria barbata*
semmar (Chepang), see *Zingiber officinale*
sen ge zil pa (Tibetan), see *Potentilla fulgens*
senghas (Chepang), see *Pogostemon benghalensis*
senna, coffee (English), see *Cassia occidentalis*
senna, sickle (English), see *Cassia tora*
senna, tea (English), see *Cassia mimosoides*
sensitive plant (English), see *Mimosa pudica*
sensosin (Limbu), see *Dalbergia sisso*
serangomen (Tamang), see *Boenninghausenia albiflora*
serangomen (Tharu), see *Achyranthes aspera*
serga (Nepali), see *Lindera pulcherrima*
se-rgod-ras (Tibetan), see *Ribes himalense*
seritakma (Limbu), see *Euphorbia royleana*
serman (Tamang), see *Elsholtzia blanda*
serpentine (English), see *Rauvolfia serpentina*
ser-po (Tibetan), see *Curcuma domestica*
serpyllum (English), see *Thymus linearis*
sesame (English), see *Sesamum orientale*
setabaduwa (Gurung), see *Daphne bholua*
setabaduws (Nepali), see *Daphne bholua*
setaberu (Nepali), see *Daphne bholua*
seta kanta arak (Satar), see *Cleome gynandra*
seta kata arak (Satar), see *Cleome gynandra*
setapodo (Satar), see *Ficus hispida*
setchhi (Gurung), see *Citrus margarita*
sete (Chepang), see *Dryopteris cochleata*
sete (Tamang), see *Acorus calamus*
setero (Tamang), see *Micromeria biflora*
seti bihi (Nepali), see *Solanum torvum*
seti birauli (Nepali), see *Symplocos pyrifolia*
seti kath (Nepali), see *Ardisia solanacea, Myrsine capitellata, Symplocos pyrifolia*
seti mauwa (Nepali), see *Engelhardia spicata*
seto behuli (Nepali), see *Trifolium repens*
seto bikh (Nepali), see *Anemone elongata, A. rivularis*
seto chande (Nepali), see *Celosia argentea*

seto chanp (Nepali), see *Michelia kisopa*
seto chuletro (Nepali), see *Brassaiopsis hainla*
seto chulsi (Nepali), see *Osbeckia nepalensis*
seto dhaturo (Nepali), see *Datura stramonium*
seto guphala (Nepali), see *Holboellia latifolia*
seto gurans (Nepali), see *Rhododendron falconeri, R. grande*
seto jara (Nepali), see *Maianthemum fuscum*
seto kaulo (Nepali), see *Persea gammieana*
seto khareto (Nepali), see *Spiraea bella*
seto khasru (Nepali), see *Ilex dipyrena*
seto kuro (Nepali), see *Plumbago zeylanica*
seto lodho (Nepali), see *Ehretia macrophylla*
seto lodo (Nepali), see *Ehretia acuminata*
seto lunde (Nepali), see *Amaranthus viridis*
seto phuli (Nepali), see *Lepidagathis incurva*
seto pire (Nepali), see *Persicaria glabra, P. posumbu*
seto ranki (Nepali), see *Dichanthium annulatum*
seto raunne (Nepali), see *Ageratum conyzoides*
seto saro (Nepali), see *Hedychium spicatum*
seto sinki (Nepali), see *Adiantum caudatum, Onychium siliculosum*
seto siris (Nepali), see *Albizia julibrissin, A. procera*
seto tapre (Nepali), see *Hydrocotyle himalaica*
seto tauke (Nepali), see *Geniosporum coloratum*
se-tres (Tibetan), see *Tinospora sinensis*
setu phul (Tamang), see *Crotalaria sessiliflora*
seunwahar (Tharu), see *Euphorbia royleana*
seuri (Tharu), see *Euphorbia royleana*
sga (Tibetan), see *Zingiber officinale*
shaddock (English), see *Citrus margarita*
shalgam (Bhojpuri, Nepali), see *Brassica rapa*
shallot (English), see *Allium ascalonicum*
shamphu jhar (Nepali), see *Ranunculus scleratus*
shampu phul (Nepali), see *Fumaria indica*
shanikhar (Nepali), see *Asclepias curassavica*
shanirwar (Nepali), see *Osbeckia stellata*
sharipha (Danuwar), see *Annona squamata*
sharma guru (Nepali), see *Swertia multicaulis*
shaving brush (English), see *Emilia sonchifolia*
sheep bur (English), see *Xanthium strumarium*
sheep's ear (English), see *Inula cappa*
shepherd's purse (English), see *Capsella bursa-pastoris*
shepherd's weather grass (English), see *Anagallis arvensis*
sherpa gangdhap (Tamang), see *Plantago erosa*
shhyura (Gurung), see *Sarcococca coriacea*
shikari jhar (Gurung), see *Clematis buchananiana*
shikari lahara (Nepali), see *Periploca calophylla*
shila jhar (Nepali), see *Agrimonia pilosa*
shing-a-rka-pa-rna (Tibetan), see *Calotropis gigantea*
shing-log-a-mra (Tibetan), see *Diospyros kaki*
shing-shug-pa (Tibetan), see *Prunus cerasoides*
shing-tog (Tibetan), see *Mangifera indica*
shinnakpa (Sherpa), see *Meconopsis grandis*
shivalingi (Nepali), see *Diplocyclos palmatus*
shoe flower (English), see *Hibiscus rosa-sinensis*
sho-mang (Tibetan), see *Rumex nepalensis*
sho-mang-ri-sho (Tibetan), see *Rumex acetosa*
sho-ma-rtsa-ba (Tibetan), see *Rumex nepalensis*
shringraj (Nepali), see *Abroma angusta*
shrok (Chepang), see *Hibiscus sabdariffa*
shu-mo-za (Tibetan), see *Daucus carota*
shwingmuk (Lepcha), see *Cannabis sativa*
si (Limbu), see *Triticum aestivum*
Siam weed (English), see *Eupatorium odoratum*
sichanphun (Rai), see *Lepidium sativum*
siddhe (Majhi), see *Lagerstroemia parviflora*
sidha (Danuwar), see *Euphorbia royleana*
sidha (Raute), see *Terminalia bellirica*

sigi (Tamang), see *Taxus baccata* subsp. *wallichiana*
sijakaulisapha (Sunwar), see *Cinnamomum tamala*
sikakai (Nepali), see *Acacia pennata, A. rugata*
sikari lahara (Nepali), see *Cuscuta reflexa*
sikari sag (Nepali), see *Maianthemum purpureum*
sikat (Mooshar), see *Phyllanthus reticulatus*
sikrebha (Tamang), see *Crotalaria sessiliflora*
siksike (Nepali), see *Piptanthus nepalensis*
sikula (Chepang), see *Geniosporum coloratum*
sikya (Limbu), see *Urtica dioica*
silam (Danuwar, Nepali), see *Perilla frutescens*
silam (Majhi), see *Hyptis suaveolens*
silame (Magar), see *Hyptis suaveolens*
silame ghans (Majhi), see *Synedrella nodiflora*
silangi (Nepali), see *Taxus baccata* subsp. *wallichiana*
sililin (Tamang), see *Mallotus philippensis*
silin poloncha (Newari), see *Luffa acutangula*
silk cotton tree (English), see *Bombax ceiba*
silk weed (English), see *Asclepias curassavica*
silparo (Nepali), see *Bergenia ciliata*
silpu (Nepali), see *Bergenia ciliata*
silsile (Nepali), see *Crotalaria cytisoides*
siltimur (Nepali), see *Lindera neesiana*
siltimuri (Gurung), see *Lindera neesiana*
siltung (Magar), see *Phaseolus aconitifolius*
silu (Sherpa), see *Rhododendron setosum*
sima (Magar), see *Asclepias curassavica*
sima (Tibetan), see *Cannabis sativa*
simal (Danuwar, Magar, Majhi, Nepali, Tamang), see *Bombax ceiba*
simali (Nepali, Rai), see *Vitex negundo*
simal jel (Gurung), see *Parthenocissus semicordata*
simaltun (Gurung), see *Bombax ceiba*
siman (Tamang), see *Caryopteris bicolor*
simar (Mooshar), see *Bombax ceiba*
simaudya (Tamang), see *Ligularia fischeri*
simdhungri (Nepali), see *Equisetum diffusum*
sime jhar (Nepali), see *Equisetum debile, E. diffusum*
sim ghans (Nepali), see *Neanotis gracilis, Utricularia aurea*
simi (Nepali), see *Lablab purpureus*
simjha (Magar), see *Euphorbia royleana*
sim jhar (Nepali), see *Rotala rotundifolia*
simkane ghans (Nepali), see *Floscopa scandens*
simli (Tharu), see *Vitex negundo*
simpate (Nepali), see *Bergenia ciliata*
simri (Nepali), see *Euphorbia milii*
simrik jhar (Nepali), see *Selaginella involvens*
sim sag (Nepali), see *Cardamine impatiens, Rorippa nasturtium-aquaticum*
simtaro (Nepali), see *Buddleja paniculata*
simthi (Chepang), see *Hyptis suaveolens*
sinajya swan (Newari), see *Lagerstroemia indica*
sinamani ghyan (Newari), see *Sida rhombifolia*
sina swan (Newari), see *Buddleja asiatica*
sinbasi (Newari), see *Bombax ceiba*
sindare (Gurung), see *Mallotus philippensis*
sindhal (Chepang), see *Lagerstroemia parviflora*
sindri (Tamang), see *Mallotus philippensis*
sindur (Majhi), see *Lycopodium clavatum*
sindure (Nepali), see *Bixa orellana*
sinduri (Magar), see *Mallotus philippensis*
sindurpang (Tamang), see *Carex filicina*
sindurya (Chepang), see *Mallotus philippensis*
singalangdu (Tamang), see *Reinwardtia indica*
singarala dong (Tamang), see *Castanopsis indica*
singarne lahara (Nepali), see *Thunbergia coccinea*
singhane (Nepali), see *Himalayacalamus falconeri*

singhara (Nepali), see *Trapa bispinosa*
singhara nut (English), see *Trapa bispinosa*
singhata lahara (Nepali), see *Schisandra grandiflora*
sin gi gser bye (Tibetan), see *Verbascum thapsus*
sing jhar (Chepang), see *Eupatorium odoratum*
sing katahar (Tamang), see *Artocarpus heterophyllus*
singmar (Tamang), see *Diplokenma butyracea*
singo (Tamang), see *Buddleja paniculata*
singring (Tamang), see *Castanopsis indica*
sing singe (Nepali), see *Crotalaria alata*
singure (Nepali), see *Mallotus philippensis*
sinka jhar (Nepali), see *Micromeria biflora*
sinkauli on (Chepang), see *Chrysopogon gryllus*
sinke kuro (Nepali), see *Bidens pilosa* var. *minor*
sinyal (Tamang), see *Vitex negundo*
siongwan (Chepang), see *Teucrium quadrifarium*
siplegan (Nepali), see *Crateva unilocularis*
siplekan (Nepali), see *Crateva unilocularis*
sipolan (Tamang), see *Rubus paniculatus*
sira (Chepang), see *Nicotiana tabacum*
siran (Nepali), see *Albizia chinensis*
siraula (Chepang, Nepali), see *Celosia argentea*
siringe (Nepali), see *Osmanthus fragrans* var. *longifolia*
siris (Chepang), see *Albizia lebbeck*
siris (Nepali), see *Albizia chinensis, A. julibrissin, A. lebbeck, Delonix regia*
siris, black (English), see *Albizia lebbeck*
siris, Burmese (English), see *Albizia lucidior*
siris, pink (English), see *Albizia julibrissin*
siris, silk (English), see *Albizia julibrissin*
sirongon (Tamang), see *Crotalaria alata*
siru (Nepali), see *Imperata cylindrica*
siru (Sherpa), see *Rhododendron setosum*
sis (Chepang), see *Lagerstroemia parviflora*
sisau (Chepang, Danuwar, Gurung, Magar, Nepali, Newari, Sunwar, Tamang), see *Dalbergia sisso*
sisava (Tharu), see *Dalbergia sisso*
sisi (Nepali), see *Lindera pulcherrima, Shorea robusta*
sisna (Tharu), see *Urtica dioica*
sisne jhar (Nepali), see *Tiarella polyphylla*
sisnu (Bhojpuri, Danuwar, Nepali), see *Urtica dioica*
siso (Mooshar, Tharu), see *Dalbergia sisso*
sisso tree (English), see *Dalbergia sisso*
sita bayar (Nepali), see *Ziziphus oenoplia*
sitaindu (Satar), see *Trema orientalis*
sitaji phul (Nepali), see *Lantana camara*
sita phal (Nepali), see *Annona reticulata*
sitini (Sherpa), see *Anemone obtusiloba*
sitli (Gurung), see *Grewia optiva*
situ (Newari), see *Cynodon dactylon*
siuri (Gurung), see *Pinus roxburghii*
siwanli (Chepang), see *Vitex negundo*
siya (Tibetan), see *Rosa macrophylla*
siyunri (Majhi), see *Ipomoea nil*
skull cup (English), see *Scutellaria discolor*
skyer-pai-me-tong (Tibetan), see *Berberis asiatica*
sky flower (English), see *Duranta repens*
skyu-ru-ra (Tibetan), see *Phyllanthus emblica*
sla (Tibetan), see *Betula utilis*
slankrilop (Lepcha), see *Colocasia esculenta*
sli pate (Majhi), see *Hypericum cordifolium*
slitanghape (Tamang), see *Scrophularia urticifolia*
smag sing (Tibetan), see *Melia azedarach*
sman-sga (Tibetan), see *Zingiber officinale*
smartweed (English), see *Persicaria hydropiper*
smartweed, vegetable (English), see *Persicaria mollis*
smilax, Italian (English), see *Smilax aspera*

snake weed (English), see *Euphorbia hirta*
snapdragon tree (English), see *Gmelina arborea*
sneeze weed (English), see *Dichrocephala integrifolia*
soap berry, Chinese (English), see *Sapindus mukorossi*
soap nut tree (English), see *Sapindus mukorossi*
so-chhas (Tibetan), see *Bombax ceiba*
sodemode (Nepali), see *Vernonia cinerea*
sog-ka-pa (Tibetan), see *Capsella bursa-pastoris*
sohijan (Mooshar), see *Moringa oleifera*
soikari (Limbu), see *Phaseolus aureus*
soippa (Limbu), see *Citrus limon, C. medica*
sok (Sherpa), see *Rhododendron campanulatum*
sokod (Satar), see *Syzygium cumini*
sokro (Chepang), see *Ampelocissus divaricata*
sokrok (Chepang), see *Crotalaria sessiliflora*
sola plant (English), see *Aeschynomene asper*
Solomon's seal (English), see *Polygonatum cirrhifolium*
Solomon's seal, false (English), see *Maianthemum purpureum*
soma (Nepali), see *Rumex nepalensis*
so-ma ra-dza (Tibetan), see *Cannabis sativa*
sombrero flower (English), see *Holmskioldia sanguinea*
somjaja (Tamang), see *Abelmoschus manihot*
somlata (Nepali), see *Ephedra gerardiana*
somphaphun (Rai), see *Foeniculum vulgare*
sonf (Nepali, Tharu), see *Foeniculum vulgare*
sonp (Danuwar, Newari, Sunwar), see *Foeniculum vulgare*
sonpat (Bhojpuri), see *Oroxylum indicum*
sonph (Nepali), see *Pimpinella aniseum*
sonsodhogbe (Tamang), see *Daphne bholua*
sontata (Tharu), see *Oroxylum indicum*
soo (Limbu), see *Saccharum officinarum*
sopa (Lepcha, Limbu), see *Foeniculum vulgare*
sop sop (Tibetan), see *Elsholtzia flava*
soranto (Majhi), see *Urena lobata*
sorchyagne (Tamang), see *Geniosporum coloratum*
sorka (Tibetan), see *Gnaphalium hypoleucum*
sorongrong (Tamang), see *Trema cannabina*
sorong tetala (Limbu), see *Cinnamomum tamala*
soror (Tamang), see *Ficus subincisa*
sorrel, creeping (English), see *Oxalis corniculata*
sorrel, dock (English), see *Rumex acetosa*
sorrel, garden (English), see *Rumex acetosa*
sorrel, Jamaica (English), see *Hibiscus sabdariffa*
sorrel, red (English), see *Hibiscus sabdariffa*
sorrel, sheep (English), see *Rumex nepalensis*
sorrel, sheep's (English), see *Rumex acetosa*
sosin (Limbu), see *Shorea robusta*
soso (Satar), see *Semecarpus anacardium*
sotalang (Limbu), see *Saccharum officinarum*
sotero (Sherpa), see *Boehmeria platyphylla*
soybean (English), see *Glycine max*
soyemba (Limbu), see *Michelia champaca*
spang-spos (Tibetan), see *Nardostachys grandiflora*
Spanish dagger plant (English), see *Yucca gloriosa*
spearmint (English), see *Mentha spicata*
spiderwort (English), see *Leucas cephalotes*
spikenard (English), see *Nardostachys grandiflora*
spikenard, West Indian (English), see *Hyptis suaveolens*
spinach (English), see *Spinacia oleracea*
spinach, Ceylon (English), see *Basella alba*
spinach, water (English), see *Ipomoea aquatica*
spindle tree (English), see *Euonymus hamiltonianus*
spittle weed (English), see *Caesulia axillaris*
sponge, vegetable (English), see *Luffa acutangula, L. cylindrica*
spos-dkar (Tibetan), see *Shorea robusta*
sprain bush (English), see *Phyla nodiflora*
spri-nag (Tibetan), see *Sesamum orientale*

spruce (English), see *Picea smithiana*
spurge, cactus (English), see *Euphorbia royleana*
spurge, garden (English), see *Euphorbia hirta*
spurge, pill-bearing (English), see *Euphorbia hirta*
spurge weed (English), see *Euphorbia parviflora*
squash, bitter (English), see *Momordica charantia*
squash, winter (English), see *Cucurbita maxima*
squirrel's tail (English), see *Colebrookea oppositifolia*
sripadi (Nepali), see *Acorus calamus*
srisin (Limbu), see *Euphorbia royleana*
Stanley's washtub (English), see *Amorphophallus campanulatus*
sta-nu (Tibetan), see *Drosera peltata*
star bu (Tibetan), see *Hippophae tibetana*
star-bu (Tibetan), see *Prunus domestica*
star-ga (Tibetan), see *Juglans regia* var. *kamaonia*
stickwort (English), see *Agrimonia pilosa*
stink weed (English), see *Datura stramonium*
strawberry, Indian (English), see *Fragaria nubicola*
strawberry, mock (English), see *Potentilla indica*
strawberry tree (English), see *Cornus capitata*
sugandha kokila (Nepali), see *Cinnamomum glaucescens*
sugandhawal (Nepali), see *Valeriana jatamansii*
suga phul (Nepali), see *Piptanthus nepalensis*
sugarcane (English), see *Saccharum officinarum*
sui bhanme (Newari), see *Cleome viscosa*
sukhar (Tibetan), see *Anaphalis contorta*
su-kshme-la (Tibetan), see *Amomum subulatum*
sukul jhar (Nepali), see *Polygonum plebejum*
sulpha phul (Nepali), see *Cuphea procumbens*
sulsing (Tamang), see *Quercus lanata, Q. leucotrichophora*
sulsule (Nepali), see *Tadehaji triquetrum*
sumac (English), see *Rhus parviflora*
sumac, Nepalese (English), see *Rhus javanica*
sumali (Nepali), see *Callicarpa macrophylla*
sumari (Lepcha), see *Lepidium sativum*
sumjiriphung (Limbu), see *Nelumbo nucifera*
sun (Tamang), see *Oryza sativa*
sunaule unyu (Nepali), see *Cheilanthes albomarginata*
sunauli unyu (Nepali), see *Cheilanthes rufa*
sun berry (English), see *Physalis divaricata*
sunchakasi (Newari), see *Citrus margarita*
sundal (Nepali), see *Aechmanthera gossypina*
sundew (English), see *Drosera peltata*
sunflower (English), see *Helianthus annuus*
sungabha (Nepali), see *Dendrobium densiflorum*
sunggingba (Limbu), see *Rubia manjith*
sungkhingba (Limbu), see *Swertia chirayita*
sungrukung (Lepcha), see *Zanthoxylum armatum*
sungur (Nepali), see *Cirsium wallichii*
sungure aunle (Nepali), see *Paeonia emodi*
sungure kanda (Nepali), see *Argemone mexicana*
sungure kanto (Majhi), see *Argemone mexicana*
sungure katus (Nepali), see *Lithocarpus pachyphylla*
sunhanduwa (Rai), see *Citrus limon*
sunpate (Nepali), see *Phyllanthus parvifolius*
sunpati (Nepali), see *Rhododendron anthopogon, R. lepidotum*
sunpekawa (Rai), see *Citrus medica*
sun phul (Gurung), see *Ranunculus diffusus*
sunphul (Gurung), see *Ranunculus scleratus*
sun phul (Nepali), see *Dendranthema nubigenum*
sunphunari (Danuwar), *Mallotus philippensis*
sun pwaeki phul (Gurung), see *Dendranthema nubigenum*
suntala (Danuwar, Gurung, Magar, Nepali), see *Citrus aurantium*
suntalo (Tamang), see *Citrus aurantium*
sun taule (Nepali), see *Deutzia staminea*
suntiki (Nepali), see *Argyreia hookeri*
suntola (Sunwar, Tharu), see *Citrus aurantium*

supare jhar (Nepali), see *Sphaeranthus indicus*
supari (Danuwar, Gurung, Magar, Nepali, Sunwar, Tamang,
    Tharu), see *Areca catechu*
supari jhar (Danuwar), see *Sphaeranthus indicus*
supari phul (Nepali), see *Gomphrena globosa*
supchun (Newari), see *Rhus javanica*
superb glory (English), see *Gloriosa superba*
sup jhar (Nepali), see *Oenanthe thomsonii*
supri (Lepcha), see *Areca catechu*
surate (Tamang), see *Osbeckia nepalensis*
surati (Tamang), see *Luculia gratissima*
surchendro (Tamang), see *Isodon coetsa*
surchenti (Tamang), see *Scutellaria discolor*
surtenden (Tamang), see *Elsholtzia blanda*
surti (Nepali, Newari), see *Nicotiana tabacum*
surtilang (Chepang), see *Clematis buchananiana*
suryamukhi phul (Nepali), see *Helianthus annuus*
swallow wort (English), see *Calotropis gigantea*
swallow wort, curassavian (English), see *Asclepias curassavica*
swami (Nepali), see *Ficus benjamina*
swanle jhar (Nepali), see *Capsella bursa-pastoris*
swata (Nepali), see *Flemingia strobilifera*
sweet flag (English), see *Acorus calamus*
sweetsop (English), see *Annona squamata*
syabal (Tamang), see *Aeschynanthus parviflorus, Coelogyne cristata*
syabe lamda (Tamang), see *Pholidota griffithii*
syagham (Chepang), see *Eleusine indica*
syak (Sherpa), see *Urtica dioica*
syakte (Tamang), see *Woodfordia fruticosa*
syalamba (Tamang), see *Pholidota imbricata, Pilea anisophylla*
syal daino (Nepali), see *Smilax aspera*
syal fusro (Nepali), see *Grewia optiva*
syal kainj (Gurung), see *Reinwardtia indica*
syal phosro (Gurung), see *Grewia optiva*
syal puchhare Tamang: dalasin (Nepali), see *Grewia disperma*
syamolhapti (Tibetan), see *Rumex nepalensis*
syang (Tamang), see *Thespesia lampas*
syang mhendo (Tamang), see *Gynura nepalensis*
syang syange (Nepali), see *Cassia occidentalis*
syanguli ma (Newari), see *Castanopsis indica*
syankamale (Chepang), see *Clerodendrum indicum*
syano bhatyaula (Nepali), see *Flemingia strobilifera*
syans (Chepang), see *Boehmeria rugulosa*
syapu (Gurung), see *Rhododendron campanulatum*
syaruj (Chepang), see *Wendlandia coriacea*
syau (Danuwar, Magar, Nepali, Newari, Sunwar, Tamang), see *Pyrus malus*
syaudhap (Tamang), see *Capsella bursa-pastoris, Rorippa nasturtium-aquaticum*
syawal nowa (Tamang), see *Hypericum japonicum*
syebal (Tamang), see *Lycopodium clavatum*
syede (Tamang), see *Acorus calamus*
syker-pa (Tibetan), see *Berberis aristata*
syodal (Tamang), see *Sida rhombifolia*
syogatong (Chepang), see *Leucosceptrum canum*
syolbakhaia (Sunwar), see *Amaranthus spinosus*
syoma (Sherpa), see *Rumex nepalensis*
syom sing (Tamang), see *Boehmeria rugulosa*
syong (Tamang), see *Plantago erosa*
syosing (Tamang), see *Camellia kissi*
syo syo (Nepali), see *Daphne bholua*
syo tolo (Tamang), see *Oreocnide frutescens*
syu (Gurung), see *Oxalis corniculata*
syu (Sherpa), see *Daphne bholua*
syudane (Gurung), see *Gonostegia hirta*
syugan (Tamang), see *Symplocos pyrifolia*
syugen (Tamang), see *Symplocos ramosissima*

syugu dhangabu (Tibetan), see *Daphne bholua*
syugu mhendo (Gurung), see *Daphne bholua*
syukapa (Sherpa), see *Juniperus indica*
syukpa (Sherpa), see *Juniperus recurva*
syukpa (Tamang), see *Juniperus indica*
syumju tikta (Tibetan), see *Swertia pedicellata*
syundi (Danuwar), see *Euphorbia royleana*
syuri (Chepang, Gurung, Nepali), see *Euphorbia royleana*
syusodesing (Tibetan), see *Rumex nepalensis*
syu syu (Gurung), see *Daphne bholua*
syutelo (Tamang), see *Pouzolzia sanguinea*
syuthani (Majhi), see *Ipomoea batatas*
ta (Gurung), see *Cheilanthes albomarginata*
ta (Sherpa), see *Triticum aestivum*
tabang (Tamang), see *Cynodon dactylon*
tabra (Tamang), see *Crassocephalum crepidioides*
tachhi (Newari), see *Avena sativa*
tadumpa (Sherpa), see *Quercus semecarpifolia*
tagling sibaman (Tamang), see *Boenninghausenia albiflora*
tag ma sin me (Tibetan), see *Rhododendron arboreum*
tagntagngent (Tamang), see *Geniosporum coloratum*
tagu bhula (Tharu), see *Chlorophytum nepalense*
tailung (Tamang), see *Trichilia connaroides*
tajalhapte (Tamang), see *Clerodendrum philippinum*
tajhawai (Tamang), see *Centella asiatica*
takabyit (Lepcha), see *Pisum sativum*
takaswan (Newari), see *Rhododendron arboreum*
takatoiy (Danuwar), see *Coix lachryma-jobi*
takbopot (Lepcha), see *Prunus persica*
takoi (Sherpa), see *Ribes glaciale*
takolkrim (Lepcha), see *Asparagus racemosus*
takpa (Sherpa), see *Betula utilis*
takpa (Tamang), see *Betula alnoides*
takpa (Tibetan), see *Prunus cerasoides*
takralakung (Lepcha), see *Shorea robusta*
takro (Chepang), see *Rhododendron arboreum*
takrukse (Limbu), see *Momordica charantia*
taksai (Chepang), see *Mangifera indica*
tak tak (Sherpa), see *Fritillaria cirrhosa*
taktriya (Danuwar), see *Coix lachryma-jobi*
talang tolo (Chepang), see *Leucas cephalotes*
talche jhar (Nepali), see *Equisetum diffusum*
taleno (Gurung), see *Euphorbia hirta*
talgoji (Nepali), see *Equisetum diffusum*
talispatra (Nepali), see *Abies spectabilis*
talis patra (Nepali), see *Larix griffithiana*
tallow, Japan (English), see *Rhus succedanea*
tal makhana (Nepali), see *Hygrophila auriculata*
talmuja (Chepang), see *Triumfetta rhomboides*
talsi (Gurung), see *Ficus semicordata*
talu (Nepali), see *Typhonium diversifolium*
tama bans (Nepali), see *Bambusa nepalensis, Dendrocalamus hamiltonii*
tamahun (Gurung), see *Nicotiana tabacum*
tamajise (Limbu), see *Terminalia bellirica*
tamarind (English), see *Tamarindus indica*
tamarind, Manila (English), see *Pithecellobium dulce*
tamatar (Danuwar), see *Lycopersicon esculentum*
tamausu (Gurung), see *Nicotiana tabacum*
tambaku (Nepali), see *Nicotiana tabacum*
tambrat (Chepang), see *Boerhavia diffusa*
tambur (Tibetan), see *Bistorta macrophylla*
tamda (Tamang), see *Lycopodium clavatum, Pteris aspericaulis, Rhamnus triqueter*
tamjha (Tamang), see *Botrychium lanuginosum*
tampait (Limbu), see *Trichosanthes dioica*
tampo (Gurung), see *Nicotiana tabacum*

tana (Gurung), see *Elsholtzia blanda, Selaginella involvens*
tana (Tamang), see *Botrychium multifidum*
tanbalaksun (Rai), see *Lawsonia inermis*
tandi chatum arak (Satar), see *Oxalis corniculata*
tanfu (Nepali), see *Ribes glaciale, R. takare*
tang (Chepang), see *Maytenus rufa, Piper wallichii*
tanga (Tamang), see *Cissampelos pareira*
tangajang (Gurung), see *Malva verticillata*
tangar (Gurung), see *Pisum sativum*
tangar (Tamang), see *Hemiphragma heterophyllum, Pisum sativum*
tangat (Lepcha), see *Cucurbita maxima*
tanghrilchyor (Lepcha), see *Rhus javanica*
tangjong tangat (Lepcha), see *Benincasa hispida*
tanglabank (Limbu), see *Brassica rapa*
tanglai (Tamang), see *Fagopyrum dibotrys*
tanglingbho (Tamang), see *Fagopyrum dibotrys*
tangnam (Tamang), see *Perilla frutescens*
tangru (Tamang), see *Betula utilis*
tangsar kato (Tamang), see *Solena heterophylla*
tangu (Sherpa, Tibetan), see *Rhododendron arboreum*
tangu nhapu (Tibetan), see *Bupleurum falcatum*
tani ta (Gurung), see *Gentiana robusta*
tankan (Chepang), see *Pilea glaberrima*
tanki (Gurung), see *Bauhinia purpurea*
tanki (Nepali), see *Bauhinia malabarica, B. purpurea*
tanki gan (Magar), see *Bauhinia purpurea*
tanki sun (Tamang), see *Coix lachryma-jobi*
tano (Tibetan), see *Origanum vulgare*
tantari (Chepang, Danuwar), see *Dillenia pentagyna*
tantari (Nepali), see *Dillenia pentagyna, Millettia fruticosa, Trichilia connaroides*
tantari (Tharu), see *Trichilia connaroides*
tapa (Tibetan), see *Cynoglossum zeylanicum*
taphwa swan (Newari), see *Tagetes erecta*
tapke (Gurung), see *Drymaria diandra*
taprangmi (Tamang), see *Hemiphragma heterophyllum*
tapre (Chepang, Majhi), see *Cassia tora*
tapre (Magar, Rai), see *Cassia occidentalis, Cassia tora*
tapre (Nepali), see *Cassia floribunda, C. tora*
tapre jhar (Magar), see *Centella asiatica*
tapri siris (Nepali), see *Albizia lucidior*
taptap (Gurung), see *Anaphalis contorta*
taptap (Tamang), see *Anaphalis triplinervis, Gnaphalium affine*
tap tap (Tamang), see *Potentilla fulgens*
taptap mhendo (Tamang), see *Anaphalis busua*
tara (Gurung), see *Vitex negundo*
tarabuja (Nepali), see *Citrullus lanatus*
tarapasara (Danuwar), see *Elephantopus scaber*
tarbare (Nepali), see *Belamcanda chinensis*
tarch (Tibetan), see *Cannabis sativa*
tare mendo (Tamang), see *Oroxylum indicum*
tare phul (Nepali), see *Aster falconeri*
tar ghans (Nepali), see *Paspalum distichum*
tarika (Nepali), see *Pandanus nepalensis*
tariya (Chepang), see *Hedychium spicatum*
tarkheta (Gurung), see *Mussaenda macrophylla*
tarma (Tamang), see *Stellaria vestita*
tar mhendo (Tamang), see *Buddleja asiatica*
taro (English), see *Colocasia esculenta*
taro (Nepali), see *Hippophae tibetana*
tarobongmat (Lepcha), see *Desmostachya bipinnata*
tarpanga (Tamang), see *Cymbopogon pendulus*
tarpucho (Gurung), see *Rubus reticulatus*
tarpujo (Gurung), see *Rumex acetosa*
taru bans (Nepali), see *Bambusa nutans* subsp. *cupulata, B. tulda, Dendrocalamus strictus*
tarul (Majhi, Tharu), see *Dioscorea bulbifera*

tarul (Newari), see *Dioscorea deltoidea*
tarwar sima (Newari), see *Oroxylum indicum*
tarwar simi (Nepali), see *Canavalia cathartica*
tashing (Sherpa), see *Abies spectabilis*
tasi (Newari), see *Citrus medica*
tassel flower (English), see *Emilia sonchifolia*
tasyu (Tibetan), see *Senecio wallichii*
tat (Tamang), see *Sterculia villosa*
tatal (Magar), see *Oroxylum indicum*
tatalasi (Chepang), see *Oroxylum indicum*
tate (Nepali), see *Albizia lebbeck*
tate amilo (Nepali), see *Tamarindus indica*
tate koiralo (Magar), see *Bauhinia purpurea*
tatelo (Nepali), see *Oroxylum indicum*
tatibari (Nepali), see *Dalbergia stipulacea*
tau (Sherpa), see *Fagopyrum esculentum*
tauchhi (Gurung), see *Ficus neriifolia* var. *nemoralis*
tauke ghans (Nepali), see *Cyathocline purpurea*
tauke jahar (Majhi), see *Leucas cephalotes*
tauke jhar (Nepali), see *Leucas cephalotes*
tauke phul (Nepali), see *Eriocaulon nepalense, Gentiana pedicellata*
taulamuja (Chepang), see *Xanthium strumarium*
tauning (Tamang), see *Osbeckia nepalensis*
taunne (Nepali), see *Galinsoga parviflora*
taurmuja (Chepang), see *Urena lobata*
tausi (Chepang), see *Phyllanthus emblica*
tautha (Gurung), see *Fagopyrum dibotrys*
tawang (Tamang), see *Alternanthera sessilis*
tawar buju (Tamang), see *Rosa brunonii*
tayabha (Tamang), see *Colocasia esculenta*
tayana (Tibetan), see *Pyrus pashia*
tayan ki puswan (Newari), see *Daphne bholua*
tayo (Gurung), see *Colocasia esculenta*
tea (English), see *Camellia sinensis*
tea, bush (English), see *Hyptis suaveolens*
tea, Mexican (English), see *Chenopodium ambrosoides*
tea, wild (English), see *Camellia kissi*
teaggo (Limbu), see *Bombax ceiba*
teak, bastard (English), see *Butea monosperma*
teak, yellow (English), see *Adina cordifolia*
tea plant, Canary Islands (English), see *Sida rhombifolia*
teasel, Nepalese (English), see *Dipsacus inermis*
tebu (Newari), see *Zanthoxylum armatum*
tebu (Tamang), see *Phyllanthus emblica*
tebya (Tamang), see *Persicaria microcephala*
te-dza-ni (Tibetan), see *Zanthoxylum acanthopodium*
tejpat (Danuwar, Nepali, Newari), see *Cinnamomum tamala*
tejpatta (Bhojpuri), see *Cinnamomum tamala*
tekui (Tharu), see *Mitragyna parvifolia*
telaile (Nepali), see *Siegesbeckia orientalis*
teli phul (Nepali), see *Eichhornia crassipes*
telparo (Nepali), see *Sarcococca coriacea*
temal (Nepali), see *Pieris formosa*
tembephutra (Limbu), see *Lagenaria siceraria*
teme (Sherpa), see *Dioscorea bulbifera*
teme (Tamang), see *Solanum tuberosum*
temen (Gurung), see *Dioscorea pentaphylla*
temign (Tamang), see *Elaeagnus infundibularis*
temme (Tamang), see *Dioscorea deltoidea*
temple tree (English), see *Plumeria rubra*
tenai (Tamang), see *Cyathula tomentosa*
tene (Gurung), see *Xanthium strumarium*
tengar (Tamang), see *Eurya acuminata, E. cerasifolia*
tengili (Tamang), see *Hedera nepalensis*
tenkar (Tamang), see *Eurya cerasifolia*
teno (Tamang), see *Thymus linearis*
tento (Gurung), see *Swertia chirayita*

tentur (Gurung), see *Dioscorea deltoidea*

tepsing (Tamang), see *Camellia kissi*

teptha (Gurung), see *Vernonia cinerea*

terkane (Rai), see *Zanthoxylum armatum*

tesang (Gurung), see *Alnus nepalensis*

tetara (Danuwar), see *Tamarindus indica*

tetlase (Limbu), see *Musa paradisiaca*

tetor (Danuwar), see *Tamarindus indica*

thabthabe (Nepali), see *Symplocos ramosissima*

thadho balu (Gurung), see *Sida rhombifolia*

thadho unyu (Nepali), see *Pteris geminata*

thadhu (Gurung), see *Catunaregam spinosa, Randia tetrasperma*

thagal (Nepali), see *Arundo donax*

thagar (Tamang), see *Elephantopus scaber*

thagne noba (Tamang), see *Elsholtzia strobilifera*

thagsi (Majhi), see *Trema cannabina*

thainyar (Nepali), see *Lyonia ovalifolia*

thakaili kanda (Nepali), see *Morina longifolia*

thakal (Nepali), see *Argemone mexicana, Cirsium wallichii, Phoenix humilis*

thakal kanda (Nepali), see *Cirsium verutum*

thakaule (Nepali), see *Combretum roxburghii*

thaklange (Chepang), see *Agrimonia pilosa*

thaksin (Tibetan), see *Rhus javanica*

thal kar rdo rje (Tibetan), see *Cassia tora*

thamni (Nepali), see *Satyrium nepalense*

thamsingdong (Tamang), see *Pinus roxburghii*

thangabima (Tamang), see *Siegesbeckia orientalis*

thangapava (Tamang), see *Clerodendrum philippinum*

thangara (Chepang), see *Sida acuta*

thangawinowa (Tamang), see *Ageratum conyzoides*

thangbua (Tamang), see *Lantana camara*

thange (Limbu), see *Linum usitatissimum*

thang mran (Tamang), see *Ageratum conyzoides*

thang-phrom (Tibetan), see *Phytolacca acinosa*

thangra (Tamang), see *Castanopsis indica*

thangsai (Chepang), see *Rubus ellipticus*

thang-shing (Tibetan), see *Cedrus deodara*

thangsing (Tamang), see *Conyza stricta*

thankaja (Gurung), see *Solena heterophylla*

thapru (Lepcha), see *Dillenia indica*

thapsang (Tamang), see *Lycopodium clavatum*

tharme (Tamang), see *Cotoneaster microphyllus*

tharuni (Nepali), see *Ranunculus scleratus*

thatur (Tamang), see *Ricinus communis*

thaune (Nepali), see *Lyonia ovalifolia*

thechar (Nepali), see *Ipomoea carnea* subsp. *fistulosa*

thegor (Tamang), see *Clematis buchananiana*

theki kath (Nepali), see *Erythrina arborescens*

theki phal (Nepali), see *Actinidia callosa*

theki phul (Nepali), see *Schisandra grandiflora*

themasin (Tamang), see *Viburnum erubescens*

themni (Nepali), see *Roscoea purpurea*

thenjo (Gurung), see *Dioscorea deltoidea*

thenr langadu (Tamang), see *Clematis buchananiana*

therma (Sherpa), see *Ilex dipyrena*

theule (Nepali), see *Geniosporum coloratum*

thikuri (Danuwar), see *Tridax procumbens*

thingo (Nepali), see *Abies spectabilis*

thingre salla (Nepali), see *Abies spectabilis, Taxus baccata* subsp. *wallichiana, Tsuga dumosa*

thinke (Magar), see *Reissantia arborea*

thinke (Nepali), see *Maesa chisia, M. montana*

thinke dar (Nepali), see *Quercus semecarpifolia*

thir gava (Nepali), see *Cymbidium devonianum*

thirjo (Nepali), see *Aeschynanthus parviflorus*

thistle, Canada (English), see *Cirsium arvense, C. wallichii*

thistle, globe (English), see *Sphaeranthus indicus*

thistle, sow (English), see *Sonchus oleraceus*

thokpheklaphun (Limbu), see *Rhododendron arboreum*

thompa (Rai), see *Mentha spicata*

thomsing (Sherpa), see *Albizia chinensis*

thongachhe (Tamang), see *Equisetum diffusum*

thongsa (Tamang), see *Elsholtzia strobilifera*

thonra (Gurung), see *Oxyria digyna*

thorn apple, Jamaica (English), see *Datura stramonium*

thorny bur (English), see *Arctium lappa*

thoro angeri (Nepali), see *Osbeckia nepalensis*

thotane (Nepali), see *Persicaria mollis*

thotane kanda (Nepali), see *Cirsium verutum*

thotne (Gurung), see *Ficus hispida*

thudi nigalo (Nepali), see *Himalayacalamus falconeri*

thukaha (Danuwar), see *Caesulia axillaris*

thuke phul (Nepali), see *Myriactis nepalensis*

thuk jhar (Nepali), see *Caesulia axillaris*

thulo aare (Nepali), see *Prunus cornuta*

thulo ainselu (Nepali), see *Rubus treutleri*

thulo anyar (Nepali), see *Melastoma malabathricum*

thulo aushadhi (Nepali), see *Astilbe rivularis*

thulo banmara (Majhi), see *Eupatorium odoratum*

thulo bhalayo (Nepali), see *Rhus wallichii*

thulo bihi (Nepali), see *Solanum anguivi, S. torvum*

thulo boksibaja (Nepali), see *Crotalaria alata*

thulo chari amilo (Nepali), see *Oxalis latifolia*

thulo chheke (Nepali), see *Crotalaria alata*

thulo chulesi (Nepali), see *Melastoma malabathricum, Osbeckia stellata*

thulo dedri (Nepali), see *Casearia elliptica*

thulo elainchi (Nepali), see *Amomum subulatum*

thulo guyenlo (Nepali), see *Callicarpa arborea*

thulo jhigane (Nepali), see *Eurya cerasifolia*

thulo lodho (Nepali), see *Ehretia macrophylla*

thulo lunden (Nepali), see *Solanum aculeatissimum*

thulo makure lahara (Nepali), see *Tetrastigma serrulatum*

thulo mayal (Gurung), see *Rhus wallichii*

thulo mirre (Nepali), see *Hyptis suaveolens*

thulo mothe (Nepali), see *Schoenoplectus mucronatus*

thulo nigalo (Nepali), see *Bambusa multiplex*

thulo nyuro (Nepali), see *Cycas pectinata, Polystichum squarrosum*

thulo pirya (Nepali), see *Persicaria barbata*

thulo piryu (Nepali), see *Siegesbeckia orientalis*

thulo sisno (Nepali), see *Girardinia diversifolia*

thulo sugandha kokila (Nepali), see *Cinnamomum glaucescens*

thulo tapre (Nepali), see *Cassia occidentalis*

thuman mhendo (Tamang), see *Oroxylum indicum*

thumro (Limbu), see *Pyrus pashia*

thunke jhar (Nepali), see *Tridax procumbens*

thunma (Nepali), see *Habenaria intermedia*

thur (Nepali), see *Rhynchostylis retusa*

thurgaujo (Nepali), see *Coelogyne flavida*

thur gava (Nepali), see *Coelogyne flaccida*

thurjo (Nepali), see *Vanda teres*

thurmang (Tamang), see *Rhamnus virgatus*

thushasansi (Rai), see *Terminalia bellirica*

thusi pangri (Nepali), see *Acer pectinatum*

thyaule (Nepali), see *Caryopteris bicolor*

thyme (English), see *Thymus linearis*

thyme, lemon-scented (English), see *Micromeria biflora*

tibe nori (Gurung), see *Hedyotis scandens*

tibro (Tamang), see *Rhus javanica*

tibru (Gurung), see *Elaeagnus infundibularis*

tibu (Gurung), see *Persicaria mollis, Rhus javanica*

tichangs (Chepang), see *Callicarpa macrophylla*

tida (Gurung, Magar, Tibetan), see *Hypericum elodeoides*

tigaji (Gurung), see *Inula cappa*

tigari (Tamang), see *Berberis asiatica*

tiger's claw (English), see *Gloriosa superba, Martynia annua*

tig-ta (Tibetan), see *Swertia chirayita*

tihare phul (Nepali), see *Inula cappa*

tihure (Magar), see *Lawsonia inermis*

tikapara (Chepang), see *Euphorbia hirta*

ti kaphal (Nepali), see *Viola pilosa*

tike ghortapre (Nepali), see *Hydrocotyle sibthorpioides*

tikhe bhanjh (Nepali), see *Quercus leucotrichophora*

tikromsi (Chepang), see *Boehmeria platyphylla*

til (Gurung), see *Elatostema platyphyllum, E. sessile, Lecanthus peduncularis*

til (Majhi), see *Sesamum orientale*

til (Nepali), see *Desmodium multiflorum, Sesamum orientale*

ti-la-dkar (Tibetan), see *Sesamum orientale*

tilari (Tamang), see *Buchanania latifolia*

tilbi (Tamang), see *Sida rhombifolia*

tili (Danuwar), see *Lecanthus peduncularis*

tili bans (Nepali), see *Dendrocalamus hookeri*

tili koshyo (Tamang), see *Lobelia nummularia*

tilikosyo (Tamang), see *Centella asiatica, Hydrocotyle nepalensis, Viola pilosa*

tili kosyo (Tamang), see *Hydrocotyle sibthorpioides*

tilime (Tamang), see *Cynoglossum zeylanicum*

tilio (Tamang), see *Elatostema sessile*

tilipalang (Tamang), see *Potentilla kleiniana*

tilke jhar (Nepali), see *Eragrostis unioloides*

tilkocha (Satar), see *Coccinia grandis*

tilkor (Danuwar, Mooshar), see *Coccinia grandis*

tilkot (Majhi), see *Coccinia grandis*

tilkuti (Majhi), see *Coccinia grandis*

tilo (Tamang), see *Lecanthus peduncularis*

tilyal (Nepali), see *Acer acuminatum*

timbur (Lepcha), see *Zanthoxylum armatum*

timchu (Nepali), see *Arisaema flavum*

timda (Tamang), see *Halenia elliptica, Swertia chirayita*

time (Gurung), see *Dioscorea deltoidea*

timi (Gurung), see *Dioscorea pentaphylla*

timila (Nepali), see *Ficus auriculata*

timju polan (Tamang), see *Rubus paniculatus*

timlagan (Tibetan), see *Gonostegia hirta*

timpuno (Tamang), see *Pholidota griffithii*

timpur (Chepang), see *Zanthoxylum armatum*

timu (Sherpa), see *Elaeagnus infundibularis*

timu gra (Tamang), see *Rubus paniculatus*

timur (Bhojpuri, Danuwar, Magar, Majhi, Tharu), see *Zanthoxylum armatum*

timur (Nepali), see *Zanthoxylum acanthopodium, Z. armatum*

timyuno (Tamang), see *Pholidota imbricata, P. anisophylla*

tin aankhle (Nepali), see *Centella asiatica*

tinai (Tamang), see *Agrimonia pilosa, Urena lobata*

tine (Gurung), see *Achyranthes aspera, Cyathula tomentosa, Cynoglossum zeylanicum*

tine (Tamang), see *Cynoglossum zeylanicum*

tinet (Chepang), see *Scurrula parasitica*

tinet (Tamang), see *Bidens pilosa* var. *minor, Cyathula tomentosa, Rubia manjith*

tingenodi (Limbu), see *Amaranthus spinosus*

tingsi (Chepang), see *Clerodendrum japonicum, Semecarpus anacardium*

tingwase (Limbu), see *Rubus ellipticus*

tinkose (Raute), see *Cassia tora*

tinno (Gurung), see *Galinsoga parviflora*

tinoei (Nepali), see *Galium elegans*

tinpate (Nepali), see *Arisaema utile*

tinru (Tamang), see *Rubia manjith*

tintinchung (Tamang), see *Oxalis corniculata*

tipla (Tamang), see *Elatostema platyphyllum*

tiple (Tamang), see *Pilea anisophylla, Strobilanthes colorata*

tipremsi (Chepang), see *Debregeasia salicifolia*

tipromsi (Chepang), see *Debregeasia longifolia*

tipru (Tamang), see *Rhus javanica*

tiribo (Chepang), see *Reinwardtia indica*

tirinkhe (Nepali), see *Mimosa rubicaulis* subsp. *himalayana*

tirino (Gurung), see *Ageratum conyzoides*

tirip mran (Tamang), see *Drymaria diandra*

tirit noba (Tamang), see *Crassocephalum crepidioides*

tirkene (Danuwar), see *Zanthoxylum armatum*

tirketa (Chepang), see *Solena heterophylla*

tiro (Tamang), see *Galium asperifolium*

tiro lahara (Nepali), see *Rubia manjith*

tiru (Gurung), see *Galium asperifolium*

tischa (Tibetan), see *Prinsepia utilis*

tisi (Mooshar, Newari), see *Linum usitatissimum*

tisinam (Lepcha), see *Linum usitatissimum*

tisy (Gurung), see *Berberis aristata*

tisya (Tibetan), see *Prinsepia utilis*

tita pati (Chepang), see *Artemisia indica*

titari (Majhi, Nepali, Rai), see *Tamarindus indica*

tite (Nepali), see *Clerodendrum viscosum, Cornus oblonga, Hedyotis scandens, Homalium napaulense, Orthosiphon incurvus, Phlogacanthus thyrsiformis, Swertia nervosa, Thlaspi arvensis, Veronica anagallis-aquatica*

tite (Tamang), see *Halenia elliptica*

tite hawi (Nepali), see *Eupatorium odoratum*

tite nigalo (Nepali), see *Drepanostachyum falcatum, D. intermedium, Himalayacalamus fimbriatus*

titepati (Danuwar), see *Artemisia indica*

titepati (Nepali), see *Artemisia caruifolia, A. dubia, A. indica*

tite phaphar (Nepali), see *Fagopyrum tataricum*

tite pidalu (Nepali), see *Lilium wallichianum*

tithe (Nepali), see *Drepanostachyum falcatum*

titi (Gurung), see *Phyllanthus emblica*

titis paun (Newari), see *Tamarindus indica*

tito (Nepali), see *Swertia chirayita*

titya (Raute), see *Clerodendrum viscosum*

tiure (Gurung), see *Lawsonia inermis*

tiuri (Tamang), see *Lawsonia inermis*

tiware ta (Gurung), see *Inula cappa*

tiya (Tamang), see *Colocasia esculenta*

toad's stool (English), see *Phyla nodiflora*

tobacco (English), see *Nicotiana tabacum*

tobre (Nepali), see *Centella asiatica*

tog damr po (Tibetan), see *Rhododendron arboreum*

toir phule (Magar), see *Emilia sonchifolia*

toi sing (Tamang), see *Castanopsis tribuloides*

tokale (Chepang), see *Crotalaria cytisoides*

tokariya (Lepcha), see *Rhododendron arboreum*

tokse (Rai), see *Rhododendron arboreum*

tomatar (Nepali), see *Cyphomandra betacea*

tomato (English), see *Lycopersicon esculentum*

tomato, tree (English), see *Cyphomandra betacea*

tompanamma (Rai), see *Ocimum tenuiflorum*

tonda (Gurung), see *Fagopyrum esculentum*

tondari (Gurung), see *Cuscuta reflexa*

tongjyer (Lepcha), see *Ficus religiosa*

toon tree (English), see *Toona ciliata*

toothache plant (English), see *Spilanthes paniculata*

toplign degni (Tamang), see *Tectaria macrodonta*

topre jhar (Gurung), see *Centella asiatica*

toragy (Gurung), see *Luffa cylindrica*

torbo (Tamang), see *Leucosceptrum canum*

toreban (Chepang), see *Inula cappa*

tore nyuro (Nepali), see *Thelypteris ciliata*

tori (Bhojpuri, Chepang, Danuwar, Magar, Mooshar, Nepali, Sunwar), see *Brassica napus*

tori ghans (Nepali), see *Capsella bursa-pastoris, Rorippa indica*

tori jhar (Nepali), see *Cleome gynandra, C. viscosa*

tori phul (Nepali), see *Emilia sonchifolia*

tori sag (Nepali), see *Capsella bursa-pastoris*

torola (Chepang), see *Cissampelos pareira*

toro lahara (Chepang), see *Stephania glandulifera*

toryang (Limbu), see *Luffa cylindrica*

tosel (Sunwar), see *Rhododendron arboreum*

tota (Gurung), see *Fagopyrum dibotrys*

totala (Danuwar), see *Oroxylum indicum*

tote (Nepali), see *Ficus hispida*

tote jhar (Nepali), see *Persicaria barbata*

totola (Lepcha), see *Oroxylum indicum*

toyoring (Tamang, Tibetan), see *Delphinium scabriflorum*

trakchh (Chepang), see *Reissantia arborea*

tree of sorrow (English), see *Nyctanthes arbor-tritis*

trishubha mran (Tamang), see *Euphorbia hirta*

trumbar (Lepcha), see *Mussaenda frondosa*

trumpet flower, Indian (English), see *Oroxylum indicum*

tsam-pa-ka (Tibetan), see *Michelia champaca*

tshar-bong (Tibetan), see *Artemisia sieversiana*

tshos-shing (Tibetan), see *Butea monosperma*

tsi-tra-ka (Tibetan), see *Capsicum annuum*

tsuputu (Gurung), see *Solena heterophylla*

tu (Newari), see *Brassica napus, Saccharum officinarum*

tube flower (English), see *Clerodendrum indicum*

tugasage (Chepang), see *Spermadictyon suaveolens*

tug-mo-nyung (Tibetan), see *Holarrhena pubescens*

tui amala (Tamang), see *Nephrolepis cordifolia*

tuisingri (Gurung), see *Periploca calophylla*

tuki jhar (Nepali), see *Cardamine violacea*

tuki phul (Nepali), see *Taraxacum officinale*

tukla (Lepcha), see *Mallotus philippensis*

tuklom (Sherpa), see *Arisaema jacquemontii*

tuktam (Rai), see *Terminalia bellirica*

tukuna (Nepali), see *Malaxis cylindrostachya*

tulsi (Bhojpuri, Danuwar, Gurung, Lepcha, Nepali, Newari, Sunwar, Tamang, Tharu), see *Ocimum tenuiflorum*

tumdusyu (Gurung), see *Oxalis corniculata*

tumsai (Chepang), see *Terminalia bellirica*

tumsun (Rai), see *Lycopersicon esculentum*

tunga (Tamang), see *Zingiber officinale*

tungbhrambra (Tamang), see *Persicaria hydropiper*

tungdhap (Tamang), see *Persicaria capitata, P. nepalensis*

tunglhap (Tamang), see *Persicaria microcephala*

tunglhapchhi (Tamang), see *Persicaria nepalensis*

tungro (Gurung), see *Persicaria nepalensis*

tuni (Gurung), see *Toona ciliata*

tuni (Nepali), see *Toona ciliata, T. serrata*

tun kaphal (Gurung), see *Melastoma malabathricum*

tupchi (Chepang), see *Terminalia bellirica, T. chebula*

tuphi (Newari), see *Thysanolaena maxima*

tur (Gurung), see *Brassica napus*

Turk's turban (English), see *Clerodendrum indicum, C. viscosum*

turmeric (English), see *Curcuma domestica*

turnip (English), see *Brassica rapa*

tursiro (Chepang), see *Mentha spicata*

tusa (Nepali), see *Drepanostachyum falcatum*

tusare (Nepali), see *Debregeasia longifolia, D. salicifolia*

tushi (Gurung), see *Maesa chisia*

tusi (Newari), see *Cucumis sativus*

tuwa (Nepali), see *Arisaema nepenthoides*

tuyu kenbu swan (Newari), see *Coelogyne corymbosa*

twang twang (Tamang), see *Viburnum cylindricum*

twari (Nepali), see *Abroma angusta*

twasilwa (Tamang), see *Adiantum caudatum*

tyaguno (Nepali), see *Dioscorea pentaphylla*

tyamno (Nepali), see *Thelypteris subpubescens*

tyamotar (Nepali), see *Cyphomandra betacea*

tyapta (Gurung), see *Eupatorium chinense*

tyauda (Gurung), see *Cautleya spicata*

tyubi (Gurung), see *Nephrolepis cordifolia*

tyure (Nepali), see *Impatiens scabrida, Lawsonia inermis*

tyuri (Sunwar), see *Lawsonia inermis*

ubherndo (Tamang), see *Reinwardtia indica*

uchung (Lepcha), see *Coriandrum sativum*

udho munto jhar (Nepali), see *Crassocephalum crepidioides*

udumuntu (Chepang), see *Crassocephalum crepidioides*

uduwa (Rai), see *Saccharum officinarum*

uinkh (Mooshar), see *Saccharum officinarum*

ukhaji swan (Newari), see *Catharanthus roseus*

ukhin dukhin jhyau (Nepali), see *Jurinea dolomiaea*

ukhu (Danuwar, Nepali, Tamang), see *Saccharum officinarum*

ukuche jhar (Nepali), see *Rungia parviflora*

ukuse jhar (Majhi), see *Lygodium japonicum*

ullu khar (Nepali), see *Thunbergia coccinea*

ulphi (Gurung), see *Elephantopus scaber, Rumex nepalensis*

ulta chirchiri (Danuwar), see *Achyranthes aspera*

ultakur (Tharu), see *Achyranthes aspera*

ulte kanda (Nepali), see *Caesalpinia decapetala*

ulte kuro (Nepali), see *Achyranthes aspera*

ultc puju (Gurung), see *Achyranthes aspera*

ultokuruva (Rai), see *Achyranthes aspera*

u-lu-zan-pa (Tibetan), see *Solanum nigrum*

umen (Tamang), see *Craniotome furcata*

umpur (Chepang), see *Zanthoxylum armatum*

unigar (Nepali), see *Pteris vittaria*

unkh (Bhojpuri), see *Saccharum officinarum*

unsi (Gurung), see *Coriaria napalensis*

unsye (Gurung), see *Benincasa hispida*

upa tikta (Tibetan), see *Gentianella paludosa*

upiyan jhar (Nepali), see *Boenninghausenia albiflora*

up tikta (Tibetan), see *Gentiana pedicellata*

urakya (Gurung), see *Curcuma domestica*

urauli phul (Nepali), see *Hypericum cordifolium*

urgen langdu (Tamang), see *Lycopodium clavatum*

urhur (Mooshar), see *Hibiscus rosa-sinensis*

urman (Tamang), see *Agrimonia pilosa*

ur mhendo (Tamang), see *Hypericum japonicum*

urn fruit (English), see *Callicarpa macrophylla*

urpolang (Tamang), see *Rubus ellipticus*

ursing (Tamang), see *Borreria alata*

uruse jhar (Nepali), see *Boenninghausenia albiflora*

using (Tamang), see *Litsea doshia*

u-su (Tibetan), see *Coriandrum sativum*

usyu (Gurung), see *Saccharum officinarum*

usyup (Tamang), see *Saccharum officinarum*

utajara (Danuwar), see *Pogostemon benghalensis*

utis (Nepali), see *Alnus nepalensis, A. nitida*

utrasum bead tree (English), see *Elaeocarpus sphaericus*

uttim noba (Tamang), see *Scutellaria discolor*

vadrachhya (Nepali), see *Elaeocarpus lanceifolius*

valerian (English), see *Valeriana hardwickii, V. jatamansii*

varnish tree, wild (English), see *Rhus succedanea*

vegetable sponge (English), see *Luffa acutangula, L. cylindrica*

velvet leaf (English), see *Cissampelos pareira*

Venus hair (English), see *Adiantum capillus-veneris*

vervain (English), see *Verbena officinalis*

vetch (English), see *Vicia hirsuta*

vetch, chickling (English), see *Lathyrus sativus*

vetch, clover (English), see *Vicia angustifolia*

vetchling, yellow (English), see *Lathyrus aphaca*
vetiver (English), see *Vetiveria zizanioides*
wa (Newari), see *Oryza sativa*
waba degni (Tamang), see *Dryopteris cochleata*
wa binyauli (Tamang), see *Cornus oblonga*
wachekalasi (Rai), see *Lagenaria siceraria*
wachitbob (Rai), see *Luffa cylindrica*
wadsoma (Limbu), see *Alnus nepalensis*
wagrans (Chepang), see *Ficus rumphii*
wahi (Rai), see *Castanopsis tribuloides*
wakarang (Chepang), see *Securinega virosa*
wakasi (Rai), see *Ficus neriifolia* var. *nemoralis*
wakholausi (Rai), see *Prunus domestica*
waklonwaphrun (Rai), see *Areca catechu*
waksi (Chepang), see *Engelhardia spicata*
wakuma (Rai), see *Alnus nepalensis*
wala (Tamang), see *Plumeria rubra*
wala mran (Tamang), see *Scutellaria discolor*
wallun (Rai), see *Alstonia scholaris*
walnut (English), see *Juglans regia* var. *kamaonia*
wangal (Nepali), see *Scopolia stramonifolia*
wangal sima (Newari), see *Ficus religiosa*
warekpa (Limbu), see *Zanthoxylum armatum*
wari (Rai), see *Quercus lanata*
warkopuchu (Tamang), see *Mimosa rubicaulis* subsp. *himalayana*
warpadi (Tamang), see *Edgeworthia gardneri*
warpati (Tamang), see *Wikstroemia canescens*
washing (Raute), see *Justicia adhatoda*
wasing (Magar, Tamang), see *Engelhardia spicata*
wasipsip (Tamang), see *Phyllanthus parvifolius*
water chestnut (English), see *Trapa bispinosa*
water couch (English), see *Paspalum distichum*
watercress (English), see *Rorippa nasturtium-aquaticum*
water hyacinth (English), see *Eichhornia crassipes*
watermelon (English), see *Citrullus lanatus*
wathatwa (Rai), see *Allium wallichii*
wattle, Australian (English), see *Acacia nilotica*
wattle plant (English), see *Acacia pennata*
wauncha ghyan (Newari), see *Oxalis corniculata*
wax tree, Japanese (English), see *Rhus succedanea*
way bread (English), see *Plantago erosa*
wheat (English), see *Triticum aestivum*
white man's foot (English), see *Plantago erosa*
wild husk (English), see *Physalis divaricata*
wintergreen, fragrant (English), see *Gaultheria fragrantissima*
wodar (Nepali), see *Osyris wightiana*
wongchagalin (Tamang), see *Cirsium wallichii*
wormseed (English), see *Chenopodium ambrosoides*
ya (Limbu), see *Oryza sativa*
yabasim (Limbu), see *Oroxylum indicum*
yachenodi (Limbu), see *Brassica juncea* var. *cuneifolia*
yadlihammuma (Rai), see *Desmostachya bipinnata*
yagon (Gurung), see *Ophiorrhiza fasciculata*

yakham (Rai), see *Piper longum*
yakkhe (Limbu), see *Colocasia esculenta*
yakla (Limbu), see *Colocasia esculenta*
yakoba (Limbu), see *Cucurbita maxima*
yakpanpa (Limbu), see *Madhuca longifolia*
yakpoma (Limbu), see *Engelhardia spicata*
yaksi (Rai), see *Colocasia esculenta*
yaksitan (Rai), see *Colocasia esculenta*
yam (Chepang), see *Oryza sativa*
yam (Danuwar), see *Mangifera indica*
yam (English), see *Dioscorea deltoidea*
yam, elephant foot (English), see *Amorphophallus campanulatus*
yam, potato (English), see *Dioscorea bulbifera*
yam, wild (English), see *Dioscorea pentaphylla*
yam jhar (Chepang), see *Pennisetum polystachion*
yang (Tibetan), see *Allium wallichii*
yangsingba (Limbu), see *Schima wallichii*
yangsung (Rai), see *Schima wallichii*
yanyan (Gurung), see *Ricinus communis*
yarling jhar (Nepali), see *Dicentra scandens*
yasaibagwa (Rai), see *Brassica juncea* var. *cuneifolia*
yasign (Tibetan), see *Geranium wallichianum*
yasik (Chepang), see *Anemone vitifolia*
yatsing (Tamang), see *Hypericum uralum*
yela (Newari), see *Amomum subulatum*
yelpos (Lepcha), see *Diplokenma butyracea*
yerma (Sherpa), see *Zanthoxylum armatum*
yew, common (English), see *Taxus baccata* subsp. *wallichiana*
yew, English (English), see *Taxus baccata* subsp. *wallichiana*
yo (Chepang), see *Diplokenma butyracea*
yobabacha (Rai), see *Zea mays*
yog-mo (Tibetan), see *Artemisia sieversiana*
yo lhapte (Tamang), see *Smilax ovalifolia*
yolpa kuta (Gurung), see *Tectaria macrodonta*
yom goidung (Chepang), see *Disporum cantoniense*
yongjigwa (Limbu), see *Maesa chisia*
yophul (Chepang), see *Equisetum diffusum*
yophuli (Chepang), see *Equisetum debile*
yormang (Sherpa), see *Prinsepia utilis*
yukisap (Chepang), see *Cipadessa baccifera*
yuklamwasun (Rai), see *Centella asiatica*
yuk maisai (Chepang), see *Scindapsus officinalis*
yu muja (Chepang), see *Cynoglossum zeylanicum*
yungs-ba (Tibetan), see *Curcuma domestica*
yungs-dkar (Tibetan), see *Brassica juncea* var. *cuneifolia*
yungs-nag (Tibetan), see *Brassica nigra*
yuyam (Rai), see *Syzygium cumini*
za-chhag (Tibetan), see *Urtica dioica*
zar-ma (Tibetan), see *Sesamum orientale*
ze-ra-dkar-po (Tibetan), see *Foeniculum vulgare*
zhu-mkhan (Tibetan), see *Eriobotrya japonica*
zulo (Tibetan), see *Anemone vitifolia*
zwa (Tibetan), see *Urtica dioica*

Index of Scientific Names

Accepted names are in **boldface**. A list of genera in each family may be found under the name of the plant family.

Berchemia axilliflora, see *B. edgeworthii*
Berchemia edgeworthii, 109–110
Berchemia flavescens, 110
Berchemia lineata, see *B. edgeworthii*
Berchemia nana, see *B. edgeworthii*
Bergenia ciliata, 25, 110
Bergera koenigii, see *Murraya koenigii*
Bernieria nepalensis, see *Gerbera maxima*
Betula acuminata, see *B. alnoides*
Betula alnoides, 110–111; Plate 8
　　var. *acuminata*, see *B. alnoides*
Betula bhojpattra, see *B. utilis*
Betula cylindrostachya, see *B. alnoides*
Betula utilis, 22, 55, 111
Betulaceae, see *Alnus, Betula, Corylus*
Bidens pilosa var. **minor**, 111
Bidens sundaica var. *minor*, see *B. pilosa* var. *minor*
Bignonia chelonoides, see *Stereospermum chelonoides*
Bignonia indica, see *Oroxylum indicum*
Bignonia suaveolens, see *Stereospermum chelonoides*
Bignoniaceae, see *Incarvillea, Jacaranda, Oroxylum, Stereospermum*
Biophytum sensitivum, 111–112
Bischofia javanica, 112
Bistorta amplexicaulis, 60, 112
Bistorta macrophylla, 60, 112
Bistorta milletii, 112
Bistorta sphaerostachya, see *B. macrophylla*
Bistorta vaccinifolia, 113
Bistorta vivipara, 113
Bixa orellana, 113
Bixaceae, see *Bixa*
Blackwellia napaulensis, see *Homalium napaulense*
Blechnaceae, see *Woodwardia*
Bletia masuca, see *Calanthe masuca*
Blumea alata, see *Laggera alata*
Blumea cinerascens, see *B. lacera*
Blumea flava, see *Blumeopsis flava*
Blumea hieraciifolia, 113
Blumea lacera, 50, 114
Blumea macrostachya, see *B. hieraciifolia*
Blumea sericans, see *B. hieraciifolia*
Blumea subcapitata, see *B. lacera*
Blumeopsis falcata, see *B. flava*
Blumeopsis flava, 50, 60, 114
Blyxa aubertii, 114, 115
Blyxa griffithii, see *B. aubertii*
Blyxa oryzetorum, see *B. aubertii*
Boehmeria frondosa, see *Oreocnide frutescens*
Boehmeria frutescens, see *Oreocnide frutescens*
Boehmeria fruticosa, see *Oreocnide frutescens*
Boehmeria hypoleuca, see *Debregeasia salicifolia*
Boehmeria macrophylla, 54, 55, 114
Boehmeria macrostachya, see *B. platyphylla*
Boehmeria nana, see *Pouzolzia zeylanica*
Boehmeria nervosa, see *B. rugulosa*
Boehmeria penduliflora, see *B. macrophylla*
Boehmeria platyphylla, 55, 115
　　var. *scabrella*, see *B. platyphylla*
Boehmeria polystachya, 55, 115
Boehmeria puya, see *Maoutia puya*
Boehmeria rotundifolia, see *B. platyphylla*
Boehmeria rugulosa, 35, 55, 56, 115
Boehmeria salicifolia, see *Debregeasia salicifolia*
Boehmeria sanguinea, see *Pouzolzia sanguinea*
Boehmeria scabrella, see *B. platyphylla*
Boehmeria squamigera, see *Chamabainia cuspidata*
Boehmeria ternifolia, 116

Boehmeria viminea, see *Pouzolzia sanguinea*
Boenninghausenia albiflora, 116
Boerhavia diffusa, 59, 116–117
Boerhavia repens, see *B. diffusa*
Bombacaceae, see *Bombax*
Bombax ceiba, 25, 35, 54, 117
Bombax malabaricum, see *B. ceiba*
Boraginaceae, see *Cordia, Cynoglossum, Ehretia, Heliotropium, Maharanga, Trichodesma*
Borago indica, see *Trichodesma indicum*
Borreria alata, 117–118
Borreria articularis, 118
Borreria hispida, see *B. articularis*
Borreria latifolia, see *B. alata*
Boschniakia himalaica, 118
Botrychium lanuginosum, 118
Botrychium multifidum, 118, 119
Brachiaria ramosa, 118–119
Brachycorythis obcordata, 25, 119
Bradleia ovata, see *Glochidion velutinum*
Bramia indica, see *Bacopa monnieri*
Bramia monnieri, see *Bacopa monnieri*
Brassaiopsis hainla, 61, 119, 120
Brassaiopsis palmata, see *B. polyacantha*
Brassaiopsis polyacantha, 119–120
Brassica, 60
Brassica campestris var. **sarson**, 48, 55, 120
Brassica juncea var. **cuneifolia**, 47, 48, 120
Brassica napus, 32, 40, 46, 47, 48, 55, 57, 120
Brassica nigra, 48, 121
Brassica oleracea
　　var. **botrytis**, 48, 121; Plate 23
　　var. **capitata**, 48, 121
　　var. **caulorapa**, 48, 121
　　var. **gemmifera**, 121
Brassica rapa, 47, 48, 121
Brassica rugosa var. *cuneifolia*, see *B. juncea* var. *cuneifolia*
Brassicaceae, see Cruciferae
Brathys laxa, see *Hypericum japonicum*
Brathys nepalensis, see *Hypericum japonicum*
Breea arvensis, see *Cirsium arvense*
Breynia patens, see *B. retusa*
Breynia retusa, 121
Bridelia retusa, 45, 122
Briza bipinnata, see *Desmostachya bipinnata*
Bromelia ananas, see *Ananas comosus*
Bromelia comosa, see *Ananas comosus*
Bromeliaceae, see *Ananas*
Bromus tectorum, 122
Bryonia grandis, see *Coccinia grandis*
Bryonia hastata, see *Solena heterophylla*
Bryonia lacinosa, see *Diplocyclos palmatus*
Bryonia nepalensis, see *Solena heterophylla*
Bryonia palmata, see *Diplocyclos palmatus*
Bryonia pedunculosa, see *Herpetospermum pedunculosum*
Bryonia scabrella, see *Mukia maderaspatana*
Bryonia umbellata, see *Solena heterophylla*
Bryonopsis lacinosa, see *Diplocyclos palmatus*
Buchanania latifolia, 122
Bucklandia populifolia, see *Exbucklandia populnea*
Bucklandia populnea, see *Exbucklandia populnea*
Buddleja asiatica, 58, 123
Buddleja neemda, see *Buddleja asiatica*
Buddleja paniculata, 58, 123
Buddleja subserrata, see *B. asiatica*
Buddlejaceae, see *Buddleja*
Bulbostylis densa, 123

Eugenia formosa, 225
Eugenia jambolana, see *Syzygium cumini*
Eugenia jambos, see *Syzygium jambos*
Eugenia operculata, see *Cleistocalyx operculatus*
Eulaliopsis binata, 55, 225–226
Euodia fraxinifolia, 226
Euonymus atropurpureus, see *E. hamiltonianus*
Euonymus hamiltonianus, 226; Plate 46
Euonymus tingens, 227
Eupatorium adenophorum, 227
Eupatorium chinense, 50, 227
Eupatorium clematideum, see *E. chinense*
Eupatorium glandulosum, see *E. adenophorum*
Eupatorium longicaule, see *E. chinense*
Eupatorium odoratum, 227
Eupatorium reevesii, see *E. chinense*
Eupatorium squamosum, see *E. chinense*
Eupatorium viscosum, see *E. chinense*
Eupatorium wallichii, see *E. chinense*
Euphorbia geniculata, see *E. heterophylla*
Euphorbia heterophylla, 227–228
Euphorbia hirta, 228
Euphorbia hypericifolia, see *E. parviflora*
Euphorbia indica, see *E. parviflora*
Euphorbia involucrata, see *E. wallichii*
Euphorbia milii, 228
Euphorbia parviflora, 57, 228
Euphorbia pentagona, see *E. royleana*
Euphorbia pilulifera, see *E. hirta*
Euphorbia prostrata, 228
Euphorbia pulcherrima, 60, 62, 228
Euphorbia royleana, 57, 61, 228–229
Euphorbia splendens, see *E. milii*
Euphorbia stracheyi, 229
Euphorbia tenuis, see *E. parviflora*
Euphorbia wallichii, 229
Euphorbiaceae, see *Antidesma, Bischofia, Breynia, Bridelia, Chrozophora, Croton, Euphorbia, Excoecaria, Glochidion, Jatropha, Macaranga, Mallotus, Ostodes, Phyllanthus, Ricinus, Sapium, Sauropus, Securinega, Trewia*
Euphrasia himalayica, 229
Eurya acuminata, 230
Eurya acuminata Wallich, see *E. cerasifolia*
Eurya cerasifolia, 230
Eurya japonica, see *E. acuminata*
Eurya symplocina, see *E. cerasifolia*
Eurya wallichiana, see *E. cerasifolia*
Evolvulus alsinoides, 230
Evolvulus nummularius, 230
Exallage ulmifolia, see *Hedyotis lineata*
Exbucklandia populnea, 230–231
Excoecaria acerifolia, 231
Excoecaria himalayensis, see *E. acerifolia*
Fabaceae, see Leguminosae
Fagaceae, see *Castanopsis, Lithocarpus, Quercus*
Fagara oxyphylla, see *Zanthoxylum oxyphyllum*
Fagopyrum cymosum, see *F. dibotrys*
Fagopyrum dibotrys, 231
Fagopyrum esculentum, 36, 46, 232
Fagopyrum sagittatum, see *F. esculentum*
Fagopyrum tataricum, 232
Falconeria insignis, see *Sapium insigne*
Falconeria wallichiana, see *Sapium insigne*
Fargesia collaris, see *Himalayacalamus falconeri*
Fatioa napaulensis, see *Lagerstroemia parviflora*
Fedia grandiflora, see *Nardostachys grandiflora*
Ficus angustifolia, see *F. glaberrima*

Ficus auriculata, 45, 232
Ficus auriculata Trimen, see *F. hispida*
Ficus benghalensis, 28, 58, 59, 232
Ficus benjamina, 232
Ficus carica, 232–233
Ficus caricoides, see *F. palmata*
Ficus caudata, see *F. subincisa*
Ficus chincha, see *F. subincisa*
Ficus clavata, see *F. subincisa*
Ficus conglomerata, see *F. semicordata*
Ficus cordifolia, see *F. rumphii*
Ficus cunea, see *F. semicordata*
Ficus daemonum, see *F. hispida*
Ficus foveolata, see *F. sarmentosa*
Ficus fruticosa, see *F. hederacea*
Ficus glaberrima, 233
Ficus glomerata, see *F. racemosa*
Ficus hederacea, 233
Ficus hirsuta, see *F. hirta*
Ficus hirta, 233
Ficus hispida, 45, 233
Ficus indica, see *F. benghalensis*
Ficus infestoria, see *F. lacor*
Ficus lacor, 59, 233–234
Ficus luducca, see *F. sarmentosa*
Ficus neriifolia var. **nemoralis**, 61, 234
Ficus palmata, 234
Ficus prominens, see *F. hispida*
Ficus racemosa, 234
Ficus religiosa, 27, 58, 59, 234
Ficus roxburghii, see *F. auriculata*
Ficus rumphii, 234
Ficus sarmentosa, 45, 235
Ficus scandens, see *F. hederacea*
Ficus semicordata, 45, 235; Plate 13
Ficus subincisa, 235
Ficus triloba, see *F. hirta*
Ficus virgata, see *F. palmata*
Fimbristylis comata, see *F. squarrosa*
Fimbristylis dichotoma, 235
Fimbristylis littoralis, see *F. miliacea*
Fimbristylis miliacea, 235
Fimbristylis monostachya, see *F. ovata*
Fimbristylis ovata, 235
Fimbristylis schoenoides, 236
Fimbristylis squarrosa, 236
Flacourtia cataphracta, see *F. jangomas*
Flacourtia jangomas, 236
Flacourtiaceae, see *Casearia, Flacourtia, Gynocardia, Homalium, Xylosma*
Flemingia bracteata, see *F. strobilifera*
Flemingia chappar, 236
Flemingia congesta, see *F. macrophylla*
Flemingia fruticulosa, see *F. strobilifera*
Flemingia grandiflora, see *Thunbergia grandiflora*
Flemingia macrophylla, 236–237
Flemingia semialata, see *F. macrophylla*
Flemingia strobilifera, 237
Floscopa hamiltonii, see *F. scandens*
Floscopa scandens, 237
Fluggea microcarpa, see *Securinega virosa*
Foeniculum vulgare, 237–238
Fortunella japonica, 238
Fragaria daltoniana, 238
Fragaria indica, see *Potentilla indica*
Fragaria nubicola, 238
Fragaria sikkimensis, see *F. daltoniana*

Myrsine acuminata, see *M. semiserrata*
Myrsine capitellata, 329
Myrsine excelsa, see *M. capitellata*
Myrsine semiserrata, 329
Myrsine sessilis, see *M. semiserrata*
Myrsine subspinosa, see *M. semiserrata*
Myrtaceae, see *Callistemon, Cleistocalyx, Eugenia, Psidium, Syzygium*
Myrtus chinensis, see *Symplocos paniculata*
Myrtus cumini, see *Syzygium cumini*
Nama javana, see *Hydrolea zeylanica*
Narcissus, 62
Nardostachys gracilis, see *N. grandiflora*
Nardostachys grandiflora, 25, 26, 28, 52, 330
Nardostachys jatamansi, see *Nardostachys grandiflora*
Nasturtium heterophyllum, see *Rorippa indica*
Nasturtium indicum, see *Rorippa indica*
Nasturtium montanum, see *Rorippa indica*
Nasturtium officinale, see *Rorippa nasturtium-aquaticum*
Natsiatum herpeticum, 50, 330
Nauclea cadamba, see *Neolamarckia cadamba*
Nauclea parvifolia, see *Mitragyna parvifolia*
Nauclela cordifolia, see *Adina cordifolia*
Neanotis gracilis, 330–331
Neillia thyrsiflora, 331
Neillia virgata, see *N. thyrsiflora*
Nelumbium speciosum, see *Nelumbo nucifera*
Nelumbo nucifera, 331
Nelumbonaceae, see *Nelumbo*
Neohymenopogon parasiticus, 57, 331–332
Neolamarckia cadamba, 332
Neolitsea cuipala, 332
Neolitsea lanuginosa, see *N. cuipala*
Nepeta indica, see *Anisomeles indica*
Nepeta leucophylla, 333
Nepeta versicolor, see *Craniotome furcata*
Nephrolepis cordifolia, 47, 333
Nerium antidysentericum, see *Holarrhena pubescens*
Nerium coronarium, see *Tabernaemontana divaricata*
Nerium divaricatum, see *Tabernaemontana divaricata*
Nerium indicum, 333–334
Nerium odoratum, see *N. indicum*
Nerium odorum, see *N. indicum*
Nerium reticulatum, see *Cryptolepis buchananii*
Nerium tomentosum, see *Wrightia arborea*
Neyraudia reynaudiana, 334
Nicandra anomala, see *Scopolia stramonifolia*
Nicandra physalodes, 334
Nicotiana tabacum, 47, 334–335
Niphobolus mollis, see *Pyrrosia mollis*
Norysca cordifolia, see *Hypericum cordifolium*
Norysca hookeriana var. *leschenaultii*, see *Hypericum choisianum*
Norysca urala, see *Hypericum uralum*
Notelaea posua, see *Osmanthus fragrans* var. *longifolia*
Nyctaginaceae, see *Boerhavia, Mirabilis*
Nyctanthes arbor-tritis, 41, 56, 57, 335
Nyctanthes multiflora, see *Jasminum multiflorum*
Nyctanthes pubescens, see *Jasminum multiflorum*
Nymphaea nelumbo, see *Nelumbo nucifera*
Ocimum basilicum, 52, 335
    var. *thyrsiflorum*, see *O. basilicum*
Ocimum benghalensis, see *Pogostemon benghalensis*
Ocimum caryophyllatum, see *O. basilicum*
Ocimum frutescens, see *Perilla frutescens*
Ocimum molle, see *Plectranthus mollis*
Ocimum sanctum, see *O. tenuiflorum*
Ocimum tenuiflorum, 62, 335–336
Ocimum thyrsiflorum, see *O. basilicum*

Ocotea sericea, see *Persea bombycina*
Odontosoria chinensis, 336
Oenanthe thomsonii, 336
Oenothera octovalvis, see *Ludwigia octovalvis*
Oenothera rosea, 336–337
Oldenlandia brachypoda, see *Hedyotis diffusa*
Oldenlandia corymbosa, see *Hedyotis corymbosa*
Oldenlandia diffusa, see *Hedyotis diffusa*
Oldenlandia gracilis, see *Kohautia gracilis*
Oldenlandia scandens, see *Hedyotis scandens*
Olea acuminata, see *Osmanthus fragrans* var. *longifolia*
Olea compacta, see *Ligustrum compactum*
Olea fragrans
    var. *acuminata*, see *Osmanthus fragrans* var. *longifolia*
    var. *longifolia*, see *Osmanthus fragrans* var. *longifolia*
Olea robustum, see *Ligustrum confusum*
Oleaceae, see *Fraxinus, Jasminum, Ligustrum, Nyctanthes, Osmanthus*
Oleandra wallichii, 337
Onagraceae, see *Epilobium, Ludwigia, Oenothera*
Onosma bicolor, see *Maharanga bicolor*
Onosma emodi, see *Maharanga emodi*
Onosma vestitum, see *Maharanga emodi*
Onychium siliculosum, 337
Ophelia angustifolia, see *Swertia angustifolia*
Ophelia chirayta, see *Swertia chirayita*
Ophelia nervosa, see *Swertia nervosa*
Ophelia racemosa, see *Swertia racemosa*
Ophioglossaceae, see *Botrychium, Helminthostachys, Ophioglossum*
Ophioglossum nudicaule, 60, 61, 337
Ophioglossum reticulatum, 61, 338
Ophiorrhiza bracteolata, see *O. fasciculata*
Ophiorrhiza fasciculata, 338
Ophiorrhiza mungo, see *O. fasciculata*
Ophioxylon serpentinum, see *Rauvolfia serpentina*
Oplismenus burmannii, 338
Opuntia monacantha, 338
Opuntia vulgaris, see *O. monacantha*
Orchidaceae, see *Brachycorythis, Calanthe, Coelogyne, Cymbidium, Cypripedium, Dactylorhiza, Dendrobium, Epipactis, Gymnadenia, Habenaria, Luisia, Malaxis, Pholidota, Platanthera, Pleione, Rhynchostylis, Satyrium, Thunia, Vanda*
Orchis cylindrostachya, see *Gymnadenia orchidis*
Orchis habenarioides, see *Gymnadenia orchidis*
Orchis hatagirea, see *Dactylorhiza hatagirea*
Orchis latifolia, see *Dactylorhiza hatagirea*
    var. *indica*, see *Dactylorhiza hatagirea*
Orchis obcordata, see *Brachycorythis obcordata*
Oreocnide frutescens, 55, 61, 339
Oreocnide fruticosa, see *O. frutescens*
Oreocome filicifolia, see *Selinum tenuifolium*
Oreoseris nivea, see *Gerbera nivea*
Origanum laxiflora, see *O. vulgare*
Origanum majorana, 339
Origanum normale, see *O. vulgare*
Origanum vulgare, 339–340
Origanum wallichianum, see *O. majorana*
Ornithidium imbricatum, see *Pholidota imbricata*
Ornus urophylla, see *Fraxinus floribunda*
Orobanchaceae, see *Aeginetia, Boschniakia, Orobanche*
Orobanche aeginetia, see *Aeginetia indica*
Orobanche aegyptiaca, 340
Orobanche indica, see *O. aegyptiaca*
Oroxylum indicum, 60, 340, 341
Orthosiphon incurvus, 340, 341
Oryza sativa, 32, 37, 40, 46, 49, 55, 340, 341; Plates 9, 47
Osbeckia chulesis, see *O. nepalensis*
Osbeckia crinita, see *O. sikkimensis*

Osbeckia nepalensis, 340–341
Osbeckia nutans, 341–342
Osbeckia sikkimensis, 342
Osbeckia speciosa, see *O. nepalensis*
Osbeckia stellata, 342
  var. *crinita*, see *O. sikkimensis*
Osmanthus acuminatus, see *O. fragrans* var. *longifolia*
Osmanthus fragrans var. *longifolia*, 342
Osmunda claytoniana, 342
Osmundaceae, see *Osmunda*
Ostodes paniculata, 343
Osyris arborea, see *O. wightiana*
Osyris nepalensis, see *O. wightiana*
Osyris wightiana, 343
Otosema extensa, see *Millettia extensa*
Otosema fruticosa, see *Millettia fruticosa*
Otosema macrophylla, see *Millettia extensa*
Ougeinia dalbergioides, see *Desmodium oojeinense*
Oxalidaceae, see *Averrhoa, Biophytum, Oxalis*
Oxalis corniculata, 344
Oxalis latifolia, 344
Oxalis pusilla, see *O. corniculata*
Oxalis repens, see *O. corniculata*
Oxalis sensitiva, see *Biophytum sensitivum*
Oxyria digyna, 344, 345
Oxyria elatior, see *O. digyna*
Oxyspora paniculata, 61, 344, 345
Oxyspora vagans, see *O. paniculata*
Padus cornuta, see *Prunus cornuta*
Paederia foetida, 345
Paederota amherstiana, see *Wulfenia amherstiana*
Paeonia emodi, 25, 345–346
Paeonia officinalis, see *P. emodi*
Paeoniaceae, see *Paeonia*
Palmae, see *Areca, Calamus, Cocos, Phoenix*
Panax assamicus, see *Macropanax undulatus*
Panax palmatum, see *Brassaiopsis polyacantha*
Panax pseudoginseng, 346
Panax schin-seng var. *nepalensis*, see *P. pseudoginseng*
Panax serratum, see *Macropanax dispermus*
Panax sikkimensis, see *Macropanax undulatus*
Pandanaceae, see *Pandanus*
Pandanus, 22
Pandanus diodon, see *P. nepalensis*
Pandanus furcatus, see *P. nepalensis*
  var. *indica*, see *P. nepalensis*
Pandanus nepalensis, 346
Panicum adscendens, see *Digitaria ciliaris*
Panicum barbatum, see *Pennisetum polystachion*
Panicum burmannii, see *Oplismenus burmannii*
Panicum ciliare, see *Digitaria ciliaris*
Panicum colonum, see *Echinochloa colona*
Panicum crus-galli, see *Echinochloa crus-galli*
Panicum dactylon, see *Cynodon dactylon*
Panicum glaucum, see *Setaria glauca*
Panicum hispidulum, see *Echinochloa crus-galli*
Panicum indicum, see *Sacciolepis indica*
Panicum italicum, see *Setaria italica*
Panicum miliaceum, 346, 347
Panicum pallidefuscum, see *Setaria pallidefusca*
Panicum polystachion, see *Pennisetum polystachion*
Panicum ramosum, see *Brachiaria ramosa*
Panicum setosum, see *Pennisetum polystachion*
Panicum supervacuum, see *Brachiaria ramosa*
Papaveraceae, see *Argemone, Dicranostigma, Meconopsis*
Paratropia venulosa, see *Schefflera venulosa*
Pardanthus chinensis, see *Belamcanda chinensis*

Parietaria indica, see *Pouzolzia zeylanica*
Parietaria zeylanica, see *Pouzolzia zeylanica*
Paris daisua, see *P. polyphylla*
Paris polyphylla, 25, 346–347
Parnassia nubicola, 347
Parnassiaceae, see *Parnassia*
Parochetus communis, 347–348
Parochetus major, see *P. communis*
Parochetus oxalidifolia, see *P. communis*
Parthenocissus himalayana, 348
Parthenocissus semicordata, 348
Paspalum commersonii, see *P. scrobiculatum*
Paspalum conjugatum, 348
Paspalum distichum, 348–349
Paspalum longifolium, see *P. scrobiculatum*
Paspalum orbiculare, see *P. scrobiculatum*
Paspalum scrobiculatum, 349
Passiflora edulis, 349
Passifloraceae, see *Passiflora*
Patrinia jatamansi, see *Nardostachys grandiflora*
Pavetta tomentosa, 349–350
Pavia indica, see *Aesculus indica*
Pedaliaceae, see *Martynia, Sesamum*
Pedicularis hookeriana, see *P. siphonantha*
Pedicularis longiflora var. *tubiformis*, 350
Pedicularis siphonantha, 350
Pedicularis tubiflora, see *P. longiflora* var. *tubiformis*
Pedicularis tubiformis, see *P. longiflora* var. *tubiformis*
Pennisetum flaccidum, 350
Pennisetum glaucum, see *Setaria glauca*
Pennisetum polystachion, 350
Pentanema indicum, 351
Pentaptera tomentosa, see *Terminalia alata*
Pentapterygium serpens, see *Agapetes serpens*
Peperomia exigua, see *P. pellucida*
Peperomia pellucida, 351
Peplis indica, see *Rotala indica*
Perdicium semiflosculare, see *Gerbera maxima*
Pergularia pallida, see *Telosma pallida*
Perilla elata, see *Elsholtzia blanda*
Perilla frutescens, 351
Perilla fruticosa, see *Elsholtzia fruticosa*
Perilla leptostachya, see *Elsholtzia stachyodes*
Perilla ocimoides, see *P. frutescens*
Perilla polystachya, see *Elsholtzia ciliata*
Periploca arborea, see *Wrightia arborea*
Periploca calophylla, 351–352
Peristrophe speciosa, 352
Peristylus orchidis, see *Gymnadenia orchidis*
Perotis polystachya, see *Pogonatherum paniceum*
Persea, 22
Persea bombycina, 352, 353
Persea gamblei, 352
Persea gammieana, 352–353
Persea odoratissima, 353
Persicaria barbata, 58, 353
Persicaria campanulata, 353
Persicaria capitata, 353–354
Persicaria chinensis, 354
Persicaria glabra, 354
Persicaria hydropiper, 58, 354
Persicaria lapathifolia var. *lanata*, 57, 354
Persicaria microcephala, 354
Persicaria minor subsp. *micrantha*, see *P. tenella* var. *kawagoeana*
Persicaria mollis, 354–355
Persicaria nepalensis, 57, 355
Persicaria perfoliata, 355

Persicaria posumbu, 355
Persicaria pubescens, 58, 355
Persicaria runcinata, 355
Persicaria tenella var. **kawagoeana**, 355–356
Persicaria vaccinifolia, see *Bistorta vaccinifolia*
Persicaria viscosa, 356
Persicaria vivipara, see *Bistorta vivipara*
Peucedanum wallichianum, see *Selinum candollii*
Phaius albus, see *Thunia alba*
Phalangium nepalense, see *Chlorophytum nepalense*
Phalaris minor, 356
Phalaris nepalensis, see *P. minor*
Phanera vahlii, see *Bauhinia vahlii*
Pharbitis nil, see *Ipomoea nil*
Phaseolus aconitifolius, 356
Phaseolus aureus, 356
Phaseolus max, see *Glycine max*
Phaseolus mungo, see *Vigna mungo*
Phaseolus vulgaris, 356, 357
Phelipaea aegyptiaca, see *Orobanche aegyptiaca*
Phelipaea indica, see *Orobanche aegyptiaca*
Philagonia fraxinifolia, see *Euodia fraxinifolia*
Phlogacanthus thyrsiflorus, see *P. thyrsiformis*
Phlogacanthus thyrsiformis, 356–357
Phlomis cephalotes, see *Leucas cephalotes*
Phlomis linifolia, see *Leucas indica*
Phlomis plukenetii, see *Leucas plukenetii*
Phoenix humilis, 357
Pholidota auriculata var. *griffithii*, see *P. griffithii*
Pholidota griffithii, 357–358
Pholidota imbricata, 358
Photinia dubia, see *Eriobotrya dubia*
Photinia eugenifolia, see *P. integrifolia*
Photinia integrifolia, 358
Photinia notoniana, see *P. integrifolia*
Phragmites karka, 358
Phragmites maxima, see *P. karka*
Phyla nodiflora, 359
Phyllanthus acidus, 359
Phyllanthus amarus, 359
Phyllanthus distichus, see *P. acidus*
Phyllanthus emblica, 359–360; Plate 17
Phyllanthus glauca, see *Securinega virosa*
Phyllanthus griseus, see *Securinega virosa*
Phyllanthus juniperinus, see *P. parvifolius*
Phyllanthus microcarpa, see *P. reticulatus*
Phyllanthus nepalensis, see *Glochidion velutinum*
Phyllanthus niruri, see *P. amarus*
Phyllanthus parvifolius, 360
Phyllanthus patens, see *Breynia retusa*
Phyllanthus quadrangularis, see *Sauropus quadrangularis*
Phyllanthus reticulatus, 360
Phyllanthus retusus, see *Breynia retusa*
Phyllanthus simplex, see *P. virgatus*
Phyllanthus taxifolius, see *P. emblica*
Phyllanthus urinaria, 360
Phyllanthus virgatus, 360
Phyllanthus virosus, see *Securinega virosa*
Phyllodium pulchellum, 360–361
Phyllomphax obcordata, see *Brachycorythis obcordata*
Phymatodes hastata, see *Crypsinus hastatus*
Physalis divaricata, 361
Physalis edulis, see *P. peruviana*
Physalis minima, see *P. divaricata*
Physalis peruviana, 361
Physalis pubescens, see *P. peruviana*
Physalis stramonifolia, see *Scopolia stramonifolia*

Phytolacca acinosa, 361–362
Phytolacca latbenia, see *P. acinosa*
Phytolaccaceae, see *Phytolacca*
Picea smithiana, 22, 362
Picrasma quassioides, 362
Picris hieracioides
    var. *indica*, see *P. hieracioides* subsp. *kaimaensis*
    subsp. **kaimaensis**, 362–363
Picrorhiza kurrooa, see *P. scrophulariiflora*
Picrorhiza scrophulariiflora, 25, 52, 363
Pieris formosa, 363
Pieris lanceolata, see *Lyonia ovalifolia*
Pilea anisophylla, 363
Pilea cordifolia, see *P. umbrosa*
Pilea glaberrima, 364
Pilea goglado, see *P. glaberrima*
Pilea producta, see *P. umbrosa*
Pilea racemosa, 364
Pilea smilacifolia, see *P. glaberrima*
Pilea subalpina, see *P. racemosa*
Pilea symmeria, 364
Pilea umbrosa, 364
Pilea wightii, see *P. symmeria*
Piliostigma malabaricum, see *Bauhinia malabarica*
Pimpinella achilleifolia, 364, 365
Pimpinella aniseum, 364
Pinaceae, see *Abies, Cedrus, Larix, Picea, Pinus, Tsuga*
Pinus, 22
Pinus brunoniana, see *Tsuga dumosa*
Pinus chylla, see *P. wallichiana*
Pinus deodara, see *Cedrus deodara*
Pinus dicksonii, see *P. wallichiana*
Pinus dumosa, see *Tsuga dumosa*
Pinus excelsa, see *P. wallichiana*
Pinus griffithiana, see *Larix griffithiana*
Pinus griffithii (Hooker fil. & Thomson) Parlatore, see *Larix griffithiana*
Pinus griffithii M'Clelland, see *P. wallichiana*
Pinus longifolia, see *P. roxburghii*
Pinus nepalensis, see *P. wallichiana*
Pinus roxburghii, 35, 52, 59, 365; Plate 18
Pinus smithiana, see *Picea smithiana*
Pinus spectabilis, see *Abies spectabilis*
Pinus tinctoria, see *Abies spectabilis*
Pinus wallichiana, 22, 365
Pinus webbiana, see *Abies spectabilis*
Piper aurantiacum, see *P. wallichii*
Piper brachystachyum, see *P. mullesua*
Piper exiguum, see *Peperomia pellucida*
Piper guigual, see *P. mullesua*
Piper longum, 365–366
Piper mullesua, 366
Piper nepalense, 366
Piper peepuloides, 366
Piper pellucidum, see *Peperomia pellucida*
Piper wallichii, 366
Piperaceae, see *Peperomia, Piper*
Piptanthus bicolor, see *P. nepalensis*
Piptanthus bombycinus, see *P. nepalensis*
Piptanthus concolor, see *P. nepalensis*
Piptanthus forrestii, see *P. nepalensis*
Piptanthus leiocarpus, see *P. nepalensis*
Piptanthus nepalensis, 366, 367
Pircunia latbenia, see *Phytolacca acinosa*
Pistacia oleosa, see *Schleichera oleosa*
Pisum sativum, 366–367
Pithecellobium dulce, 367

Serratula arvensis, see Cirsium arvense
Sesamum indicum, see Sesamum orientale
Sesamum orientale, 40, 424–425
Sesban aegyptiacus, see Sesbania sesban
Sesbania aegyptiacus, see S. sesban
Sesbania grandiflora, 425
Sesbania sesban, 42, 61, 425
Setaria glauca, 425–426
Setaria italica, 426
Setaria pallidefusca, 426
Shorea robusta, 21, 22, 24, 25, 28, 55, 56, 426; Plate 3
Shuteria involucrata, 426–427
Sicyos pentandra, see Natsiatum herpeticum
Sida acuta, 427
Sida carpinifolia, see S. acuta
Sida compressa, see S. rhombifolia
Sida cordata, 427
Sida humilis, see S. cordata
Sida indica, see Abutilon indicum
Sida multicaulis, see S. cordata
Sida nervosa, see S. cordata
Sida populifera, see Abutilon indicum
Sida rhombifolia, 427–428
Sida veronicifolia, see S. cordata
Sideritis ciliata, see Elsholtzia ciliata
Siegesbeckia brachiata, see S. orientalis
Siegesbeckia glutinosa, see S. orientalis
Siegesbeckia orientalis, 428
Silene stracheyi, 57, 428
Simaba quassioides, see Picrasma quassioides
Simaroubaceae, see Picrasma
Sinapis cuneifolia, see Brassica juncea var. cuneifolia
Sinapis nigra, see Brassica nigra
Sinarundinaria falcata, see Drepanostachyum falcatum
Sinarundinaria hookeriana, see Himalayacalamus hookerianus
Sinarundinaria intermedia, see Drepanostachyum intermedium
Sinarundinaria maling, 53, 428
Siphonanthus indica, see Clerodendrum indicum
Sison ammi, see Trachyspermum ammi
Sisymbrium indicum, see Rorippa indica
Sisymbrium nasturtium-aquaticum, see Rorippa nasturtium-aquaticum
Sisymbrium sophia, see Descurainia sophia
Siversia elata, see Geum elatum
Skimmia laureola, 428–429
Smilacaceae, see Smilax
Smilacina alpina, see Clintonia udensis
Smilacina divaricata, see Maianthemum fuscum
Smilacina finitima, see Maianthemum fuscum
Smilacina fusca, see Maianthemum fuscum
Smilacina pallida, see Maianthemum purpureum
Smilacina purpurea, see Maianthemum purpureum
Smilax aspera, 57, 429
Smilax capitata, see S. aspera
Smilax columnifera, see S. ovalifolia
Smilax elegans A. de Candolle, and Wallich ex Kunth, see S. glaucophylla
Smilax elegans Wallich ex Hooker fil., see S. menispermoides
Smilax ferox, 429
Smilax fulgens, see S. aspera
Smilax glaucophylla, 429
Smilax lanceifolia, 429
Smilax laurifola, see S. perfoliata
Smilax longibracteolata, see S. glaucophylla
Smilax macrophylla, see S. ovalifolia
Smilax maculata, see S. aspera
Smilax menispermoides, 429–430
Smilax ovalifolia, 430

Smilax parvifolia, see S. glaucophylla
Smilax perfoliata, 430
Smilax prolifera Roxburgh, see S. perfoliata
Smilax prolifera Wallich, see S. ovalifolia
Smilax retusa, see S. ovalifolia
Smilax rigida, 430
Smithia ciliata, 430
Smithia sensitiva, 430
Soja max, see Glycine max
Solanaceae, see Capsicum, Cestrum, Cyphomandra, Datura, Hyoscyamus, Lycopersicon, Nicandra, Nicotiana, Physalis, Scopolia, Solanum
Solanum aculeatissimum, 57, 431
Solanum anguivi, 57, 431
Solanum diffusum, see S. surattense
Solanum erianthum, 431
Solanum indicum, see S. anguivi
Solanum insanum, see S. melongena
Solanum jacquinii, see S. surattense
Solanum lycopersicum, see Lycopersicon esculentum
Solanum melongena, 431
Solanum nigrum, 431–432
Solanum pseudocapsicum, 432
Solanum pubescens, see S. erianthum
Solanum stramonifolium, see S. torvum
Solanum surattense, 432
Solanum torvum, 50, 432
Solanum tuberosum, 32, 36, 37, 46, 432
Solanum verbascifolium, see S. erianthum
Solanum xanthocarpum, see S. surattense
Solena heterophylla, 433
Sonchus arvensis, see S. wightianus
Sonchus asper, 433
Sonchus ferox, see S. asper
Sonchus oleraceus, 433
    var. asper, see S. asper
Sonchus wightianus, 434
Sonerila squarrosa, see Agrostemma sarmentosum
Sonneratiaceae, see Duabanga
Sophora moorcroftiana var. **nepalensis**, 434
Sopubia trifida, 434
Sorbaria tomentosa, 434–435
Sorbus crenata, see S. cuspidata
Sorbus cuspidata, 435
Sorbus foliolosa, see S. ursina
Sorbus hedlundii, 435
Sorbus lanata, 435
Sorbus microphylla, 435–436
Sorbus ursina, 436
Spatholobus parviflorus, 436
Spatholobus roxburghii, see S. parviflorus
Spergula arvensis, 436
Spermacoce alata, see Borreria alata
Spermacoce articularis, see Borreria articularis
Spermacoce exserta, see Knoxia corymbosa
Spermacoce hispida, see Borreria articularis
Spermacoce latifolia, see Borreria alata
Spermacoce teres, see Knoxia corymbosa
Spermadictyon azureum, see S. suaveolens
Spermadictyon suaveolens, 436–437
Sphaeranthus hirtus, see S. indicus
Sphaeranthus indicus, 437
Sphaeranthus mollis, see S. indicus
Sphaerocarya edulis, see Pyrularia edulis
Sphaerostema grandiflora, see Schisandra grandiflora
Sphaerostema propinqua, see Schisandra propinqua
Sphenoclea pongatium, see S. zeylanica